WHERE *to* SKI AND *SnoWboard* 2009

The 1,000 Best Winter Sports Resorts in the World

Edited by
Chris Gill
and
Dave Watts

NortonWood

Contents

That's the start of it – turn the page for the heart of it . . .

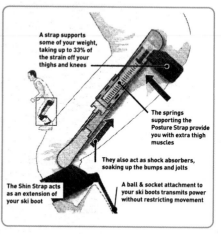

Contents 2

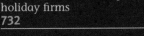

Resort chapters

8

It's simply the best

Dave Watts

Where to Ski and Snowboard is the best guide to winter sports resorts that you can buy. Here's why:

- With every new edition we aim to take a step forward. This year, we have **new chapters** on areas in Austria, Switzerland and Canada, further improvements to our two-page annotated piste maps, and more information on minor resorts in our resort directory at the back of the book. And we've used our first-hand experience of skiing trips to help design a ground-breaking insurance policy, launched on page 36.

- By making the most of technology we are able to publish at the right time while going to press very late by conventional book publishing standards – so we can include the late-breaking news that makes the book **up to date for the season ahead**. We were still feeding in news from French resorts in late July. The earliest editions of this book went to press in June; this year, it's 1 August, only a month ahead of publication day.

Chris Gill

- We work hard to make our information **reader-friendly**, with clearly structured text, comparative ratings and no-nonsense verdicts for the main aspects of each resort.

- We don't hesitate to express **critical views**. We learned our craft at Consumers' Association, where Chris became editor of *Holiday Which?* magazine and Dave became editor of *Which?* itself – so a consumerist attitude comes naturally to us.

- Our resort chapters give an **unrivalled level of detail** – including scale plans of each major resort, so that you get a clear idea of size – and all the facts you need.

- The book benefits enormously from the **hundreds of reports** that readers send in on the resorts they visit. (Every year, the 100 best reports are rewarded by a free copy of the book, and many of our best regular reporters get a free week's lift pass; prove your worth by sending us useful reports, and you could ski for free.)

- We use **colour printing** fully – we include not only piste maps for every major resort but also scores of photographs, carefully chosen so that you can see for yourself what the resorts are like.

Our ability to keep on investing in *Where to Ski and Snowboard* is largely due to the support of our advertisers – many of whom have been with us since the first edition in 1994. We are grateful for that support, and hope readers will in turn support our advertisers. It also helps if you tell them that you saw their ads in these pages: we know from book trade statistics that we outsell rival books by a huge margin, but advertisers can't be reminded too often.

We are absolutely committed to helping you, our readers, to make an informed choice; and we're confident that you'll find this edition the best yet. Enjoy your skiing and riding this season.

Chris Gill and Dave Watts
Norton St Philip, 1 August 2008

GET YOUR MONEY BACK
when you book a holiday

You can reclaim the price of Where to Ski and Snowboard when you book a winter sports holiday for the 2008/09 or 2009/10 seasons. All you have to do is book the holiday through the specialist ski travel agency Ski Solutions.

Ski Solutions is Britain's original and leading ski travel agency. You can buy whatever kind of holiday you want through them.

Ski Solutions sells the package holidays offered by all the bonded tour operators in Britain (apart from the very few who are direct-sell only). And if that isn't enough choice, they can tailor-make a holiday, based on any form of travel and any kind of accommodation. No one is better placed to find you what you want than Ski Solutions.

Making a claim

Claiming your refund could not be easier. When you make your definite booking, tell Ski Solutions that you want to take up this offer and claim the refund. They will deduct the price of the book from your bill.

Phone Ski Solutions on
020 7471 7700

Get next year's edition free
by reporting on your holiday

There are too many resorts for us to visit them all every year, and too many hotels, bars and mountain restaurants for us to see. So we are very keen to encourage more readers to send in reports on their holiday experiences. As usual, we'll be giving 100 copies of the next edition to the writers of the best reports.

There are five main kinds of feedback we need:

- what you particularly **liked and disliked** about the resort
- what aspects of the resort came as a **surprise** to you
- your other suggestions for **changes to our evaluation** of the resort – changes we should make to the ratings, verdicts, descriptions etc
- your experience of **queues** and other weaknesses in the lift system, and the **ski school** and associated child care arrangements (please take care to name the school)
- your feedback on **individual facilities** in the resort – the hotels, bars, restaurants (including mountain restaurants), nightspots, equipment shops, sports facilities etc.

We now store reports in a central database where our editors can easily access them, which means that we much prefer to receive them by email. Please send to:

reports@wtss.co.uk

It's vital that you give us the date of your trip so that we can interpret your report sensibly. And include your phone number and postal address, in case email fails to reach you.

If you prefer, you can file short reports on our website:

www.wtss.co.uk

You can see other readers' reports there, too. Eventually, we plan to develop a system where reports can be filed on individual facilities in each resort – ski schools, restaurants etc.

Consistently helpful reporters are invited to become 'resort observers', which means that when possible we'll arrange free lift passes in your holiday resorts, in exchange for detailed reports on those resorts.

The editors have their say

A VINTAGE SEASON
Let's start off on an upbeat note. What a great season 2007/08 was for snow; the Alps and the Rockies wallowed in the stuff. Dave clocked up 49 days on the slopes (it's tough researching all the resorts in this book for your benefit) and needed goggles on 46 of them because it was snowing. He was lucky to be in the right places at the right time, hitting Whistler in December, the Alps in January, March and April and North America during the Alps' dry February spell, where the snow in Utah and Canada just never stopped falling. Let's hope next season is just as good. For a round-up of last season's snow and a look at the snowiest resorts in the Alps in general, see page 38.

PISTE MAP NONSENSE
Why do resorts take backward steps? Last season the excellent booklet-style piste map covering all the ski areas in the Portes du Soleil was scrapped. Instead, each resort now has its own local area map with a Portes du Soleil overview map on the back that is totally inadequate for finding your way around in other areas. As a result, you may want to pick up detailed maps in each resort for a clearer view of local lifts and pistes. Of the maps we have seen, the Avoriaz one is by far the best, as its local area map clearly covers most (but not all) of the main circuit. The others don't: madness. We can only assume it's a misconceived cost-cutting idea.

BEWARE OF TREE WELLS
Never heard of them? Well if you ski in North America or in trees in Europe, you should be aware of them. We have two warnings about them in this edition – one in our 'Heli-skiing' chapter and the other in the Steamboat chapter. Last season, two people died in separate incidents in Steamboat after falling into tree wells beside the piste

while skiing blue intermediate trails. Tree wells are unstable hollows (they can be two metres deep or more) that form around the bases of trees when low branches prevent snow from filling in and creating snowpack around the trunk – very dangerous if you fall in (especially head first) as you can get stuck and suffocate. So if you are tree-skiing, always ski with a partner and look out for each other; if you are piste skiing on your own, stay away from the edge of the run if tree wells have formed. As it happens, there are other reasons for avoiding the edges of wooded runs, too. Read the following item ...

Ski amade

Live action in Austria's

SCHLADMING-DACHSTEIN
Tel. +43 (0) 3687/23310
info@schladming-dachstein.at

FLACHAU, WAGRAIN, ST.JOHANN/ALPENDORF, ZAUCHENSEE,
FLACHAUWINKL, KLEINARL, RADSTADT, ALTENMARKT, FILZMOOS,
Tel. +43 (0) 6457/2929, info@salzburgersportwelt.com

Not only **huge,**
but also **hugely**
attractive

greatest **ski paradise!**

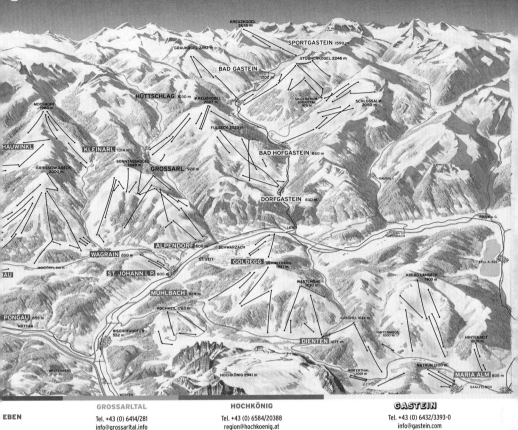

KREUZKOGEL 2686 m

SPORTGASTEIN 1590 m

GRAUKOGEL 2492 m

STÜBNERKOGEL 2246 m

BAD GASTEIN

HÜTTSCHLAG 1030 m

KREUZKOGEL 2027 m

SKIZENTRUM ANGERTAL 1075 m

SCHLOSSALM 2050 m

MOOSKOPF 1960 m

FULSECK 2033 m

HAUWINKL

KLEINARL 1014 m

SONNTAGSKOGEL 1849 m

GRIESSENKARECK 2000 m

GROSSARL 920 m

BAD HOFGASTEIN 860 m

RAURIS

DORFGASTEIN 830 m

LEND

TAXENBACH

ALPENDORF 800 m

SCHWARZACH

WAGRAIN 850 m

ST. VEIT

GOLDEGG

SCHNEEBERG 1921 m

ZELL A. SEE

MOADÖRFL 941 m

ST. JOHANN I. P. 600 m

ABERG LANGECK 1900 m

AU

MUHLBACH 920 m

WASTLHÖHE 1730 m

HOCHKEIL 1783 m

GABÜHEL 1634 m

PONGAU 855 m

HINTERMOOS 1000 m

HÜTTAU

BISCHOFSHOFEN 552 m

DIENTEN 1071 m

HINTERREIT 1000 m

NATRUN 1200 m

WERFENWENG

HOCHKÖNIG 2941 m

HINTERTHAL 1001 m

MARIA ALM 805 m

WERFEN

SAALFELDEN

EBEN

GROSSARLTAL	**HOCHKÖNIG**	**GASTEIN**
Tel. +43 (0) 6414/281	Tel. +43 (0) 6584/20388	Tel. +43 (0) 6432/3393-0
info@grossarltal.info	region@hochkoenig.at	info@gastein.com

Hugely attractive for ...

... everyone who can't get enough of endless slopes, inviting ski chalets, **value-for-money packages** and the unique feeling of live action. Each of the five ski regions in the alliance is fantastic in itself – together they provide the added value so typical of Ski amadé. And with only one ticket you can join in the live action! In no other alpine region will you find such a wide range of facilities within such a small area. And access is so easy – there are **plenty of budget flights into Salzburg,** and **transfer is only an hour** – so you'll get to spend more time on the slopes. Information on package deals, snow reports and live cams at:

Austrias´s Ski Paradise

1 Lift pass for:

- **860 km of runs** (280 km blue, 483 km red and 97 km black)

- **270 lifts**

- **Pistes up to 2,700 m**

- **120 piste grooming machines**

- at least **80 % of pistes** equipped with **snow-making-machines**

www.skiamade.com

HELMETS: THE PICTURE GETS CLEARER

It's now pretty clear that using a helmet when skiing or boarding reduces the risk of injury to a worthwhile degree, but that helmets can't help with really serious accidents.

One recent American study of fatal accidents concludes that the adoption of helmets has had no observable effect on death rates. It's partly because fatal incidents typically involve multiple injuries, so if head injury doesn't get you, something else will (eg neck injury). And it's partly because helmets have a limited effect on extreme deceleration: they are unlikely to help if your head hits a fixed object like a tree or a rock at high speed. If your head hits soft snow, you're likely to survive, with or without a helmet. If your head hits icy snow, that seems to be the situation where a helmet is most likely to be a life-saver. Ironically, therefore, helmets potentially have bigger benefits for skiers on icy pistes in the Alps than for skiers on the forest runs of the Rockies, where 60% of deaths result from collisions with trees – typically at the edge of groomed, wide, blue trails, and typically involving skilled young adult males. So one of the main lessons is that whooping it up in the good snow at the edge of a woodland cruising run isn't actually such a good idea. If the tree wells don't get you, the trees may.

Readers have clearly got the message that helmets are worthwhile. When we ran a poll about helmet use on our site at www.wtss.co.uk we got more votes than in any other poll last season. All very unscientific, of course, but: almost half of those who took part now use a helmet; of the rest, about half (ie a quarter of the total) intend to start using one. The minority who neither use nor intend to use a helmet were about equally split into those who reckon the risk of head injury is exaggerated and those who reckon helmets are intolerably uncomfortable.

GET YOUR MOJO WORKING

The Ski-Mojo is a new gadget that claims to help you save energy, adopt the perfect skiing posture and take up to a third of the strain off your thighs and knees. It is like wearing a pair of bionic legs; the photo shows how it's fitted – it is normally worn discreetly under your trousers, but here is shown worn outside for our photo.

When editor Watts first saw the Ski-Mojo at the 2007 Metro Ski Show, he was highly sceptical. But after trying it for several days last

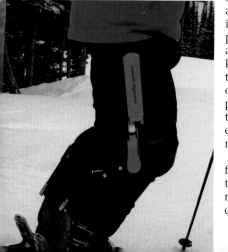

season, he's convinced there's a place for it. When activated, by flicking a switch on each leg, you immediately feel the support that it gives. It pushes you naturally into a good skiing position, and takes substantial pressure off your legs and knees as you ski. It eliminated some slight knee twinges that Watts normally gets. And after a bit of getting used to it, it helped in moguls and powder too. Former Olympic skier Martin Bell tried it too and agreed that it made groomed runs easier and less effort, but found that the springs made aggressive carving more difficult.

So if your legs get tired quickly or you suffer from minor knee or back problems, take a look at the Ski-Mojo. It's a tad awkward to put on, so you need to allow a few minutes in the morning. It costs £289. See www.skiallday.co.uk.

KÄRNTEN

Carinthia — Austria's sunny south.

EDITORIAL TRAINING REGIMES

Neither of your editors has traditionally taken pre-ski training super-seriously, but with middle age approaching we've been changing our tune a bit. Editor Watts now works out at the gym, as they say in California and Suffolk. After almost ruining a 10-day trip to Canada in early 2007 by overcooking things on day one, editor Gill was forced to accept the need for preparation, but has adopted a different and much more pleasant approach; walking up and down hills. Before the first trip of last season, Gill embarked on a week-long campaign of daily ascents of a local hill, starting with once up and down, and working up to three circuits. Result? An entirely ache-free first trip, and indeed season.

Meanwhile, Mr 'Six-Pack' Watts is itching to try the Skier's Edge training machine, which improves your ski technique as well as your fitness. Sounds just the thing for him.

TOO MANY BEDS, AND MORE ON THE WAY

The press officer of a French mega-resort (which had better remain nameless) was enthusiastically leading us around new apartment developments. Having had a hectic day on pistes already too crowded for comfort or even safety, we started to wonder if there was no limit to the number of visitor beds they would build.

When asked how the resort went about relating development plans to the capacity of the pistes, our host's response came as a bit of a shock. 'Oh,' she replied cheerfully, 'we don't look at piste capacity. The only things that limit the development of more apartments are the roads and the water supply. Obviously, it wouldn't be right to build more places if the roads couldn't take the traffic and the reservoirs couldn't supply the taps.'

Obviously. Equally obviously, if this is actually how the resorts of the Alps go about 'planning' development, the already serious crowding on the pistes of Alpine resorts will simply get worse.

STILL ON COLLISION COURSE

Last year we warned of the increased danger of collisions caused by crowded pistes and/or skiers and boarders going too fast and out of control. This was prompted by three separate reporters all mentioning collision incidents in the Three Valleys alone. This

year, you have sent us more complaints. One reader suffered two cracked ribs when he was hit on the first day of his holiday in Les Arcs 'by a French skier going at full speed who did a jump from a lip at a piste intersection and hit me while about two feet off the ground'. They ended up 30 metres apart with skis all over the piste and our reader's toe binding shattered and impossible to find. The reader asks what suggestions we can give to lift companies to make people involved in an accident immediately identifiable – eg having to wear an armband with a legible 'registration number' that would tally with an ID record held by the lift company. We're not sure that would go down well, but what other suggestions do you have? Please visit the Safety forum on our website www.wtss.co.uk if you have any ideas, or have other collisions to report.

Kim Sullivan of Direct Travel Insurance says that on French pistes alone there were 14,400 collisions in the 2006/07 season. This is a serious problem that needs urgent attention. Maybe now that Nicolas Sarkozy is president of France, something might happen there. He said during a visit to Chamonix when he was interior minister that he favours 'zero tolerance' against risky skiers: 'We cannot allow people to behave like hooligans on the slopes.'

PISTE CLASSIFICATION, AGAIN

Sorry about this. It seems like every year (maybe it actually is every year) we have a little rant in these pages about the colour classification of pistes in the Alps. This often has more to do with the resort's desire to attract all segments of the market than any desire to deliver safe and satisfactory holidays.

We came upon a classic example last winter. Grande Rochette, the gondola-served peak above the main resort village of La Plagne, has runs back to the village that appear to suit everyone – black, red and blue. Just what a mixed-ability group would like to see. Don't be fooled: the blue Mira, although a splendid cruise for much of its length, starts with a long pitch of genuine red gradient, heavily mogulled at times. It may or may not be easier than the red alternative. Blue-run skiers should be able to ski a blue run in the confidence that they will not be reduced to tears by what lies ahead. American resorts (see above left) manage to classify runs reliably. Why can't European ones?

AIRLINE EXTRAS GETTING OUT OF HAND

The EU has at last insisted on airlines quoting prices that include taxes and airport charges. But the so-called budget airlines like Ryanair and Easyjet are now piling on lots of other charges, which escalate the cost of flying off to the slopes. As we go to press (late July 2008), Ryanair is charging £12 each way for checking in one bag as hold luggage (£8 for the bag and £4 for using the airport check-in desk, which you have to do because you can check in online only if you have nothing but hand baggage), £16 each way for each extra bag. And you are still limited to 15kg of baggage, however many bags you pay for, with any excess costing £12 per kg. Skis/board cost £25 each way.

So even with only one bag and a pair of skis the extras come to a minimum of £74. Plus another £8 if you pay by credit or debit card except Visa Electron. And that's booking everything online. If you wait until you get to the airport, the charge is £16 for each bag (plus the £4 check-in fee) and £32 for skis. So that's a minimum of

no wonder people keep coming back

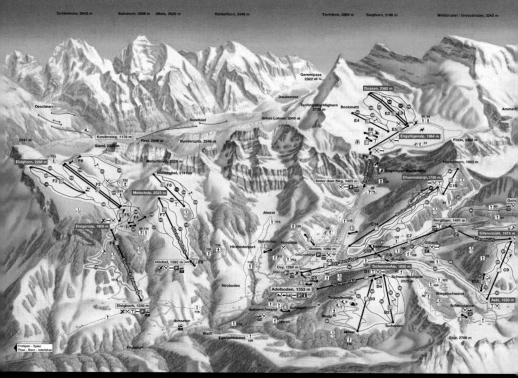

- 185 km pistes
- 56 lift facilities
- 36 ski huts and après-ski bars
- Host of the FIS Ski World Cup
  10/11.01.2009
- Family-friendly
- Snow secure from December
  to April with ski mountains
  up to 8000 ft. in height

- First accredited Alpine Wellness
  Holiday destination in Switzerland
- 1 hour drive from Berne airport
- Direct flights to Berne airport
  from Birmingham, London City,
  London Gatwick, London Stansted,
  Manchester, Southampton
  (subject to schedule changes)

Further information: **www.adelboden.ch**

– hang on, let's find a calculator – £104. And when you book online you have to remember to opt out of the £8 priority boarding and £9.49 insurance fees, or you get lumbered with paying for them too. We looked at booking a March Ryanair return flight from Stansted to Turin and the initial price came up at £78.85 including taxes and charges. By the time we got to the end of the process we were looking at a cost of £178.34 including all the extras.

SMOKE AND MIRRORS

Smoking has recently become much better controlled in France and Switzerland (it is absolutely controlled in Italy), but in Austria the smoke in public places seems to be getting denser. Maybe it actually is: we guess that some German smokers who would have headed for the Dolomites in the past now park their Mercs on the north side of the Brenner pass instead, adding to the fug in Austria. Certainly editor Watts, after spending five nights in a smoke-filled hotel in Saalbach last season, had a cough and asthma attack that lasted weeks. The official position, we are told from Vienna, is that there is at present no legal control of smoking at all, but legislation is being considered. Until new laws arrive (which just could be for next season) the only control is that larger restaurants and bars are encouraged to adopt a voluntary scheme to provide no-smoking areas. In practice, smoking rules. They need to get this sorted, or it will start to affect the holiday trade.

PHOTO FINISH

Many thanks to the readers who sent in photographs for possible publication. As last year, the contributor of the best photo wins a day's sailing on a fab yacht in the Solent, worth £145 (the day, not the yacht). We had lots of contenders this year, but in the end the judges' vote went to Alexandros Panayiotou for his picture in the Avoriaz chapter. Photos for the next edition should be sent to photos@wtss.co.uk; there will again be a suitable prize for the best.

OUR ANNUAL AWARDS

This year's winners are:

Best European Resort Development 2008 – SkiWelt, Austria

The new gondola from Brixen to a point high above Westendorf not only makes that small resort a genuine part of the SkiWelt circus at last; it is also another step along the road to the proper linking of the SkiWelt and Kitzbühel slopes.

Best North American Resort Development 2008 – Whistler, western Canada

The Peak to Peak gondola due to link Blackcomb mountain to Whistler mountain at altitude will make travel between the two sectors an everyday thing. Until now, you had to ski down to the bottom to switch mountains.

Best service for expert skiers – Deer Valley, Utah

In North America, free mountain tours are standard practice, but normally they stick to green and blue trails. Deer Valley in Utah runs these, of course, but it also runs half-day Black Diamond tours of steep and ungroomed terrain. We've taken three of these tours, and each one has been great. Other resorts, please follow suit.

WTSS online

What you'll find at www.wtss.co.uk

by **Chris Gill**

We used to think producing a printed guide to ski resorts was hard work. Now, we're not so sure – compared with developing and maintaining a website, it's a doddle. We've made quite a lot of progress with our site since my last bulletin, but we're certainly finding that improving the site takes more management time than we had expected, and there's still a long way to go.

Our own reliance on the internet has become pretty much complete. We now store readers' reports in our central online database, where they are accessible to editor Watts in Suffolk as well as editor Gill in Somerset (so please, if you can, send reports on resorts as emails now, not on paper). And as I write this, our assistant editors are sitting in their various home offices, checking final proofs of completed pages via our printer's online system.

The idea of our site is to complement the book rather than duplicate it or compete with it. Don't assume because you've got the book that you've got all the information that's available. If you haven't visited the site, I hope what follows will whet your appetite.

GET HELP WITH YOUR RESORT SHORTLIST ...

A key feature of the site is the 'expert system' that you can use to get your own personal resort shortlist. You select the three most important factors in making your holiday choice, from a list of 13. These factors correspond to the ratings at the start of each major resort chapter in the book. You can limit the results to resorts in a particular country, or more generally to Europe or North America. Press the Go button, and the system works out a score for each major resort and delivers a list in rank order. It's very quick, and to read more about a particular resort you just click on the name.

... OR USE ONE WE PREPARED EARLIER

The 20 or so resort shortlists that we print in the book are a great help to many people – check out page 103 – and we've replicated them on the site (in the Features section) so that you can check out each resort on the list that you're interested in, just by clicking on its name. Then, equipped with your short shortlist, you can settle down with the book and study them in detail.

www.wtss.co.uk – the resort shortlist-builder interface ↓

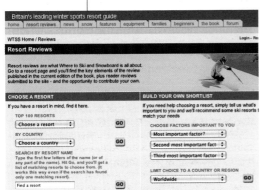

ADDRESSES BECOME LINKS

We've removed from the book lots of web and email addresses (mainly from the listings of tour operators etc in the reference section, at the back). You'll find these presented on the site as hotlinks, which not only makes them easier to use but also means we can keep them up to date. We give links to resort tourist offices and, if all goes to plan, you'll also find links to ski schools, hotels and so on.

ALL THE NEWS THAT'S FIT TO NOT PRINT

There's a constant flow of news from resorts and the travel trade, and site editor Wendy King posts interesting stuff every week (or more often if necessary) to the news section of the site. It has a searchable archive, too, so if you think you heard something about a great new hotel in Zermatt, all you have to do is key in 'Zermatt hotel' and off you go.

KEEP IN TOUCH

If you are on our email list, you'll be aware that we also now send out excellent email newsletters trailing news stories on the site, and giving links to other items of current interest – lively exchanges on the forum, for example. Sometimes we're able to carry special discount offers on holidays or equipment. The newsletter is free, and signing up to receive it couldn't be easier: there's a button on the home page of the website – click on that, enter your email address and hit the submit button.

SNOW BUSINESS

Very much a work in progress, this. Last season, site editor Wendy posted weekly summaries of snow conditions in the main skiing regions, and we got a good response to that, so we'll revive it when the time comes. (Something to look forward to, Wendy!) But we're in no doubt that we need more detailed, resort-specific information on the site, too, and snow forecast information if possible. Watch this space – well, that space, really.

ACCUMULATED WISDOM

We've started to build up a couple of specialised sections on the site to help (at present) beginners and families, by bringing together stuff that has appeared in past editions of the book – stuff that would otherwise simply disappear from view. In Families, for example, you can benefit from the ten most important lessons I learned in the course of almost 20 years of family skiing trips. When we've built up these sections sufficiently, of course, we'll turn them into books ...

FURTHER AND BETTER PARTICULARS

Although we delay as long as we can the point at which we send the book to the printers, we can't sensibly go much beyond the beginning of August, and at this point we're still lacking some useful information for the coming season – schedules and fares for rail services for example. We also find we're always running out of space to accommodate all the detail that we could provide – in the Family holidays chapter, for example, we don't have room to list the 44 UK tour operators who have their own child care facilities. So we'll be adding pages to the site with this kind of stuff.

TALK TO ONE ANOTHER

Our forum, where you can post your own observations, questions, rants or whatever, and read those of other site visitors, is now pretty active, with hundreds of registered 'members'. It's divided into subject areas ranging from beginners to North American travel. As I write, on 1 August, we've got people posting on topics ranging from taking a two-year-old skiing to planning a trip for 24 skiers wanting a 4-star chalet in a snow-sure resort. Well, how about ...

What's new?

New lifts and other major developments in top resorts

In this chapter we summarise major developments in ski resorts last season and those planned for 2008/09. Each major resort chapter has a 'News' panel near the start; you'll find many more news items in those panels. To keep up to date with resort developments, go to our website at www.wtss.co.uk and sign up for our email newsletters; you'll also find a flow of news on the opening page of the site.

ANDORRA

FASTER LIFTS FOR ARINSAL
A six-pack is due to replace the slow chair from Cota in the valley for 2008/09. Last season, a six-pack replaced the Cubil quad at Pal.

AUSTRIA

BETTER ACCESS AT ALPBACH
A mid-station is planned for the Inneralpbach gondola, to improve access to lower slopes and allow you to ride down if snow is poor.

NEW GONDOLA AND RUNS FOR BAD GASTEIN
For 2008/09 a two-stage, eight-person gondola is planned from Angertal up to Stubnerkogel. There will be two new pistes.

JUMBO GONDOLA TO OPEN AT HINTERTUX
For 2008/09 a 24-person gondola is due to replace the smaller of the two access gondolas up to Sommerbergalm.

HOCHKÖNIG REPLACES T-BARS
For 2008/09 an eight-seat gondola is due to replace successive T-bars to Sunnhütte.

GONDOLAS GALORE AROUND INNSBRUCK
Last season two new eight-seat gondolas opened – in Götzens and Oberperfuss; another is planned at Kühtai for 2008/09.

KITZBÜHEL REMOVES BOTTLENECK
Last season an eight-seat chair replaced the old double at Ehrenbachgraben, removing the last major bottleneck.

MAYRHOFEN IMPROVES AHORN, ZELL ADDS NEW LIFTS
The Ahorn gained an eight-seat chairlift last season, with snowmaking planned on the valley run for 2008/09.
At Zell im Zillertal an eight-person gondola is planned for 2008/09.

PEAK IMPROVEMENTS AT OBERGURGL
Two new eight-seat gondolas opened last season, one above Hochgurgl, the other up to a smart new restaurant at Hohe Mut.

SAALBACH-HINTERGLEMM INSTALLS EIGHT-PACK
An eight-seat chair is due to replace the Asitz quad on the return from Leogang.

CHONDOLA TO LINK SCHLADMING MOUNTAINS
For 2008/09 a chondola is planned to improve the link between Planai and Hochwurzen. New pistes are being formed.

SIX-PACK FOR SÖLL
For 2008/09 a six-pack is planned to replace the Silleralm triple chair above Hochsöll. Access to Westendorf will no longer involve buses, thanks to a new gondola from Brixen.

STUBAI GLACIER UPGRADES
The base station was revamped and a new T-bar and piste built.

WESTENDORF GETS BETTER CONNECTED
Westendorf is due to be linked properly to the SkiWelt by a new gondola from Brixen for 2008/09 – removing the need for a bus.

NEW QUAD AND RUN FOR WILDSCHÖNAU
For 2008/09 in Niederau, a fast quad is due to replace the slow chair from the village. A new run is due on Schatzberg, above Auffach.

ZELL AM SEE LIFTS RELIEVE PRESSURE
Last season an eight-seat gondola and a six-pack above it improved access from Schmittental up to Schmittenhöhe.

ZUGSPITZ ARENA CHONDOLA
The lift up from Bichlbach to Hochalm above Berwang has been replaced by the Tirol's first chondola.

FRANCE

LES ARCS BOTTLENECK REMOVED
A six-pack has replaced the old Plan Bois chair between Vallandry and Arc 1800.

NEW TERRAIN PARK AND SIX-PACK AT AVORIAZ
Avoriaz got its fourth terrain park last season, with natural and wooden features. A six-pack to Hauts Forts replaced a triple.

NEW CHAMONIX GONDOLA WILL CUT QUEUES
A 10-person gondola with double the capacity will replace the old access lift to Le Brévent for 2008/09 and cut queues coming down as well as going up.

CHONDOLA AND QUAD FOR LA CLUSAZ
Last season a chondola (a mix of eight-seat gondolas and six-person chairs) and a quad chair above it replaced old lifts at Etale.

FLAINE DEVELOPMENTS
For 2008/09 phase one of Intrawest's Montsoleil development is due to open. If all goes well, Montsoleil will be linked to Flaine by new green runs and a chairlift to and from Flaine Forêt. A six-pack was installed towards Platières last season.

SIX-PACK FOR MEGEVE
Last season a six-pack replaced an old chair above Combloux.

IMPROVED LINKS AT LES MENUIRES
A six-pack has replaced the slow Allamands chair, above the gondola from the resort to Roc des 3 Marches.

MERIBEL REMOVES CHAIRS, INCREASES CAPACITY
For 2008/09 capacity on the Pas du Lac gondola is due to be increased and the Grand Rosière and Ramees chairlifts dismantled.

MONTGENEVRE BUILDING TWO CHONDOLAS
For 2008/09 two chondolas are planned: one replacing the gondola to Gondrans; the other linking Gondrans and Chalvet.

PARADISKI SUPER LIFT TO REOPEN
The Vanoise Express cable car is due to reopen in December 2008, following repairs.

QUAD FOR PUY-ST-VINCENT
A fast quad has now replaced the Lauzes top draglifts at 2000m.

RISOUL/VARS UPGRADES LIFT
At Vars, a six-pack is due to replace the old double chair at Peynier.

Serre-Chevalier's smart new spa and hotel

For 2008/09 a big thermal spa in Le Monêtier and the resort's first 4-star hotel, the Best Western Premier in Chantemerle, will open.

Sybelles speeds up

In La Toussuire, a fast six-pack replaced a draglift last season.

Better access from Tignes to Val d'Isere

For 2008/09 a six-pack will replace the Tufs chairlift from Val Claret to Tovière. Last season the Brévières chairlift to Les Boisses was upgraded to a fixed-grip quad.

Val d'Isere upgrades old triple chair

For 2008/09, a six-pack is due to replace the triple Marmottes chair up to Bellevarde from above La Daille.

Quad for Valmorel

A fixed-grip quad has replaced the Buffle chair at St François.

Italy

Bormio closes one lift, opens another

Last season the Bormio-Ciuk gondola closed permanently, and an eight-seat gondola replaced an old double chair at Valdidentro.

Snowmaking for Cervinia's longest run

For 2008/09 there are plans to install snowmaking on the run down to Valtournenche, which should mean this will open more often.

Cortina d'Ampezzo's new connection

For 2008/09 a new chair and piste will connect Cinque Torre to Col Gallina (and so to the cable car from Passo Falzarego to Lagazuoi).

Courmayeur to replace beginner lift

For 2008/09 the draglift serving the high-altitude Tzaly beginner slope will be replaced.

Livigno invests in gondolas

An eight-seat gondola replaced the Tagliede double chair, below Costaccia last season. A second stage to the top is due for 2008/09.

Madonna di Campiglio cable car replaced

An eight-seat gondola from the centre of town has replaced the tiny cable car to the top of the Cinque Laghi. An eight-seat gondola and new runs were built at Daolasa between Folgarida and Marilleva.

Monterosa awaits replacement

The ancient Punta Indren cable car in Alagna has finally been taken out of service. Lots of fabulous off-piste will be available only by ski touring or heli-lifts until its replacement is built from Passo Salati.

New quad and runs in La Thuile

For 2008/09 a short fast quad is due to be built from near the base area. The chair will serve three new pistes with snowmaking.

Lifts in Trentino

In Canazei, a gondola has replaced the old Toè chair at Belvedere. In Calvalese, a fast quad has replaced a draglift.

Switzerland

Faster from Adelboden to Lenk

Last season a fast quad replaced the triple chair from Geils to Lavey, on the way to Lenk.

Champery chooses an eight-pack

For 2008/09 a fast eight-person chair is due to replace a quad and a drag from Les Crosets towards Champéry.

free

Le Boqueteau (1969) - **Jean Dubuffet**
Monumental sculpture located in Flaine Forum.

Big BANGFX - MCI Group   Primes Prescot Lebeau

style

FLAINE LE GRAND MASSIF

Engelberg revamps Brunni lift
For 2008/09 the cable car to Brunni is being upgraded. Last season a table-service mountain restaurant opened at Stand.

Klosters doubles up
A two-seat chair has replaced the Zügenhüttli draglift on Madrisa.

Laax rocks
For 2008/09 the new Rocksresort lodgings complex is due to open.

St Moritz increases terrain and lifts
For 2008/09 a new fast quad is expected on Corvatsch, and the top cable car from Murtèl to Corvatsch will be replaced. A new quad and new runs will link Diavolezza and Lagalb properly. Last season a fast quad replaced a drag on Corviglia.

Verbier: new gondola at La Tzoumaz; another planned
An eight-person gondola replaced the old one from La Tzoumaz on Savoleyres last season. There are plans to replace the one on the Verbier side, for 2009/10.

Zermatt removes cable cars
For 2008/09 a new beginner area and linking lift are planned just above Sunnegga. Last season the old Gornergrat-Hohtälli and Hohtälli-Stockhorn cable cars were removed, a new red piste was created from just below Hohtälli to Gifthittli, and a T-bar was added from above Triftji to Stockhorn. A fast two-way quad replaced the double chair at Findeln.

United States

California
Heavenly adds fast quad and glades
A new trail and glades are planned for 2008/09. A fast quad replaced a slow chair on the Nevada side last season.

Mammoth's new high-speed cloud
Last season a six-pack replaced the old Cloud 9 lift.

Squaw Valley's season starter
For 2008/09 a mid-station will be built on the Exhibition lift to allow early season skiing on the bottom half of the mountain.

Colorado
Breckenridge to open Peak 7
The new Peak 7 base and gondola mid-station will open for 2008/09.

Keystone upgrades gondola
The River Run gondola is being replaced by an eight-seat version, starting closer to the village.

Fast quad at Snowmass
A fast quad will replace the Sheer Bliss double chair for 2008/09.

Steamboat begins base area renewal
Demolition of part of the base area began in summer 2008. For 2007/08, a six-pack replaced three chairs in the beginner area.

Telluride opens new terrain and quad chair
For 2008/09 a new quad will serve 50 acres of expert terrain in Revelation Bowl.

UTAH

DREAMY NEW QUAD FOR THE CANYONS
A new fixed-grip quad is planned from the base of the Tombstone lift towards the Dream area, mainly to access housing.

PARK CITY EASES QUEUES WITH NEW FAST QUAD
For 2008/09 a second fast chair is due to start from the base, relieving pressure on the existing Pay Day lift.

REST OF THE WEST

JACKSON HOLE'S NEW TRAM TO OPEN
The new Tram (a cable car) that will access Rendezvous from the village is due to open in December 2008. The temporary double chairlift on Rendezvous will remain for one season as backup.

NEW ENGLAND

KILLINGTON'S FAST QUAD
A fast quad is due to replace the Skye Peak fixed-grip quad out of Bear Mountain base for 2008/09.

STOWE'S SMART NEW LODGES
The Stowe Mountain Lodge hotel complex and Spruce Camp day lodge (skier services building) are due to open at Spruce Peak.

CANADA

WESTERN CANADA

WHISTLER MOUNTAINS LINKED AT LAST
Whistler's two mountains will at last be connected at mid-mountain by the Peak to Peak gondola for 2008/09.

EASTERN CANADA

TREMBLANT INSTALLS GONDOLA
For 2008/09 an eight-seat gondola is due to link Versant Soleil with the village.

FINLAND

YLLÄS EXPANSION
Major expansion has included a new gondola and run at Sport Resort Ylläs, and a fast quad and 11 more runs at Ylläs-Ski.

LEVI'S NEW LIFTS
A new eight-seat gondola and a six-pack were opened last season.

NORWAY

HEMSEDAL KIDS GET MORE
The children's area continues to grow and now includes seven runs and eight lifts. Even more features are due for 2008/09.

SWEDEN

VEMDALEN'S SIX-PACK
A new six-pack will open at Klövsjö for 2008/09.

BULGARIA

BANSKO'S QUAD
For 2007/08 a fast quad replaced the draglift below the mid-station.

Top-notch insurance

A new policy designed by skiers, for skiers (and boarders)

by **Dave Watts**

Insurance is one of those things that we all hate dealing with. It's a necessity, but it's a drag. To choose a policy can take hours of sifting and noting key points. To thoroughly check out a policy definitely does take hours of wading through small print. I know – it used to be my job: I used to be the editor of *Which?* Magazine and its specialist financial offshoot, *Money Which?*

There's no way we can relieve you of this chore – it's up to you to establish that a policy meets your needs – but we do think we have come up with the best possible starting point. We've persuaded the insurers behind our favourite policy – Direct Travel Insurance – to develop an even better one called the Black Diamond policy, and to offer our readers a hefty discount on the premiums.

For years we have considered that Direct Travel Insurance has offered some of the best insurance policies on the market for skiers and boarders. Both of your editors have relied on their cover for several seasons, and we were helping Direct Travel to improve its cover (and, equally importantly, the definitions and explanations of its cover) even before we started working with them on the new Black Diamond policy.

Particular areas where we believe the policy sets the standard are in cover for: skiing and riding off-piste; informal 'fun' races; supposedly dangerous alternative activities such as parapenting; and theft of skis and boards that have been left outside mountain restaurants. Many policies, we believe, are much too restrictive in the way they cover these risks. Check out your current policy – you may be in for an unpleasant surprise.

We've been working with Direct Travel on this new policy for over a year. We fully expect to find ways of fine-tuning it in future, too. Late in the process of finalising the current policy, we came up with another issue. If you or your kids use terrain/snow parks, you may be surprised to hear that many policies sold in the UK do not cover that activity, on the grounds that the jumping that goes on in parks constitutes acrobatics. Clearly, competitive freestyle activity is a special thing, but for most people using terrain parks is no more dangerous than descending black runs. At our suggestion, Direct Travel has been able to include recreational use of parks.

We have also been influential in getting various cover limits raised to what we consider more realistic levels – things such as theft or loss of ski equipment (whether owned or rented), compensation for baggage that doesn't arrive at the airport when you do, and avalanche danger closing ski runs or access roads.

With our help, we believe Direct Travel Insurance has now produced a policy that is exceptional in terms of the cover it offers and in terms of value for money – particularly with the benefit of the special 10% discount offered exclusively to readers of *Where to Ski and Snowboard* and users of our website. The key features of the Black Diamond policy are set out on the facing page.

Obviously, the policy is now 'frozen' for the season ahead. But if you find it lacking in some respect, let us know, and we'll see what we can do to get it improved still further for the following season.

❖Black Diamond
Travel insurance designed by skiers

Exceptional winter sports cover including:
- ❖ recreational racing, including end-of-week ski school races
- ❖ off-piste skiing and boarding, including ski touring
- ❖ heli-skiing and cat-skiing
- ❖ recreational use of snow/terrain parks
- ❖ theft of skis from mountain restaurants
- ❖ other ski resort activities such as kite boarding, parapenting, tobogganing, tubing, zorbing
- ❖ physiotherapy back in the UK after an accident

Exceptional benefit limits including:
- ❖ medical expenses up to £10 million
- ❖ personal liability up to £3 million
- ❖ winter sports equipment up to £1,500
- ❖ delayed baggage up to £600
- ❖ piste closure up to £500

10% discount for all readers of Where to Ski and Snowboard

Discounted premiums for year-round cover
- ❖ Individual   Europe   £77.96   worldwide   £111.38
- ❖ Couple/family   Europe   £114.19   worldwide   £163.13

Based on adults aged 19–65 inclusive. European cover is available for the over-65s for an additional premium. A couple must live together but need not be married. A family covers a couple plus dependent children under 19 (23 if in full-time further education, with an additional student premium for worldwide annual cover only). Lower premiums also available for single-parent families. Single-trip policies also available. Piste closure applies if fewer than 20% of the slopes are open. Prices are valid at time of going to press, but can change.

For further details call 0845 094 9483 or go to

directtravel
insurance   **www.direct-travel.co.uk/wtss**

Let it snow

The resorts in the Alps that get the most snow

Fraser Wilkin

North America has long been obsessed with snowfall figures, and resort statistics are widely available for public consumption (as you'll see from the 'Snow reliability' sections of our resort coverage there). Not so this side of the pond, where resort authorities are less forthcoming, and reliable data is harder to obtain. We set snow-sleuth Fraser Wilkin the task of tracking down the snowiest resorts in Europe.

The table shows winter snowfall averages (at or close to village level) in some well-known Alpine resorts. It's no surprise that Lech and Zürs are near the head of the table; we have long sung their praises for powder hounds. Lech's 7.3m a season is impressive enough, but Zürs (just up the road and sharing the same ski area) gets almost half as much again with a staggering 10.4m. That's way more than Colorado's snowiest resort, Winter Park – which gets a mere 5.5m at resort level – but a fair bit less than the powder capitals of the world – Utah's Snowbird (13.3m) and Alta (11.7m).

We've always recommended Obertauern for reliable snow, too. But the resort isn't big on the UK market; it deserves a closer look considering it gets nearly 9m of snow a year and, at 1740m/5,710ft, is a high resort by Austrian standards. But the other resort in the top flight probably comes as a surprise. Avoriaz beats well-known snow-reliable names such as Tignes, Val d'Isère, Val Thorens and Cervinia. With a winter average just shy of 8m a season, Avoriaz is the snowiest resort in France. The reason the place doesn't have a reputation for amazing snow is that at 1800m/5,910ft it is by far the highest resort in the Portes du Soleil ski area that it shares with several others. The top of the ski area is only 2300m/7,550ft, most of the skiing is below Avoriaz's height, and it goes as low as 950m/3,120ft. If it's lots of powder you want, don't bother. But if it's snow in the streets you are after, then Avoriaz is hard to beat.

Down at the bottom of our Alpine league table are a hotch-potch of resorts. We've long criticised places such as Megève, Söll and Kitzbühel as being low and unreliable for snow. And Selva is saved only by the superb snowmaking and piste grooming throughout the Sella Ronda. But Chamonix, Zermatt and St Moritz? Remember that the snow statistics are taken at resort level and Chamonix town is low – a mere 1035m/3,400ft. But its slopes go up to almost 4000m/13,000ft, and in the cult sector for powder, the Grands Montets, most of the slopes are above 2000m/6,560ft, where you get serious snowfalls. Zermatt and St Moritz? As we've always said, these resorts have relatively dry climates. But they are high, and

EUROPEAN SNOWFALL LEAGUE TABLE	
Over 8m	Zürs, Obertauern
7-8m	Avoriaz, Lech
6-7m	Les Arcs (2000), Tignes, Val Thorens, Cervinia
5-6m	Val d'Isère, La Plagne, Alpe-d'Huez
4-5m	Obergurgl, St Anton, Méribel (Mottaret), Isola 2000
3-4m	Megève, Zermatt, Chamonix, St Moritz
2-3m	Selva, Kitzbühel, Söll

BRITAIN'S BEST SELLING SNOWSPORTS MAGAZINE

Published monthly from October to March, *DMS&S* has everything you need for an action packed winter season:

- Resort reviews
- Gear tests
- Technique tips
- Holiday offers
- Amazing pics
- Plus loads more

FREE DAY PACK WORTH £25*

... TO THE METRO SKI & SNOWBOARD SHOW

SUBSCRIBE NOW!

Subscribe to the UK's best selling snowsports magazine *Daily Mail Ski & Snowboard* and receive a 15-litre Salomon day pack, worth £25, free.

Subscribe today for £47.40 and enjoy two season's worth of the latest news and info – 12 issues – delivered straight to your door. Europe £88, rest of world £98.

Visit www.subscription.co.uk/dmski/sk08 or call 01858 438831 and quote SK08

* Offer applies to Direct Debit payments only, and is subject to availability

precipitation here normally falls as snow, the slopes go up to over 3000m/10,000ft, snowmaking is extensive, and grooming is good – a recipe for reliable, sunny on-piste cruising.

LESS WELL-KNOWN NAMES DO WELL, TOO

In this edition we have a chapter on the Bregenzerwald region for the first time. Never heard of it? Not surprising because it is tucked away between Germany and Switzerland at the westernmost end of Austria, skirted by all the major road and rail links and ignored by UK tour operators. But one of its biggest resorts, Warth-Schröcken, gets an average of a whopping 10.7m of snow a season, more than anywhere else in the Alps. We shouldn't be too surprised at this because it is only a few kilometres up the valley from Lech and Zürs; you can ski there and back off-piste, but the road is closed in winter because of too much snow. Nearby Damüls has its own ski area and has won an award as the most snow-sure village in the world. And where is the snowiest place in Switzerland? Little old Braunwald, whose nearest big resorts are Engelberg, Andermatt and Laax, and which averages over 9m of snow a year.

THE 2007/08 SEASON: A GOOD VINTAGE FOR SNOW

Following the meagre snowfalls of 2006/07 and media talk of global warming and the end of skiing in the Alps, it was a great relief to see early snowfalls blanketing the slopes last season. Schladming was the first non-glacial resort to fire up its lifts – on 26 October, a full month ahead of schedule. But it was November when things really kicked off, with a series of potent storms slamming into the northern side of the Alps. The heaviest snow fell across eastern Switzerland and northern Austria, where records tumbled and many resorts declared it their best start to a season for 30 years. There were fewer extremes further west, but most resorts still reported excellent early conditions. Further heavy snow fell in December and January, before warmer, drier air engulfed much of Europe in February. But, with such healthy bases, few resorts were adversely affected. The storms returned in March, and further snow in April ensured a strong finish to the season, especially at altitude.

Despite a slow start, North America had a superb season – one of the best overall since records began. The only exceptions were in parts of the south-west (California, Nevada), but even here snowfall averages were only a little below par, and there was still some great skiing to be had. Colorado certainly had a winter to remember, with Aspen, the pick of the big names, clocking a cool 11m, some 80% above average. Most Utah resorts also impressed (16.5m for super-snowy Alta), as did the northern Rockies (15.3m for the top of Jackson Hole – a new record). Most Canadian resorts had a solid rather than spectacular season, though Fernie, close to the US border, did manage over 12m, some 30% above average.

Pick the right lift pass

The choice is wider than ever

by **Wendy King**

Once upon a time, choosing a lift pass for a week's holiday was simple. In most resorts, there was only the one weekly pass, with a discounted variant for kids and the option of a pass covering a broader linked area (the Three Valleys, for example). Now, there are passes covering a few hours' skiing a day, passes for non-consecutive days, and increasing numbers of regional passes following in the footsteps of the Dolomiti Superski pass, the grandaddy of them all. Could one of these non-standard passes be the one for you?

SMART PASSES

The key to many of the latest lift pass deals is electronic passes containing 'chips', which these days are normally hands-free. These passes allow the lift companies to track which lifts you ride when, and effectively to maintain an 'account' associated with your pass. You can often buy or recharge these smart passes online, and make a small saving, even if the pass is the one-resort one-week kind. But their real value becomes clear when they offer the facility to debit your account according to usage. All of this will seem familiar to anyone with an Oyster card for use on London's tubes and buses. In some cases, though, the lift company charges your credit or debit card retrospectively.

Smart passes are potentially of most value to people making multiple visits to an area, so they are most often offered by regions or resort conglomerates.

CONGLOMERATE PASSES

The ski company pass that is likely to catch the limelight this season is the Holiski pass from Compagnie des Alpes, which runs the lifts in a very high proportion of the top resorts in France. This is a smart pass that charges your credit card according to usage, and covers about nine ski areas (it depends how you count them – see margin box). There are several CdA lift companies not covered, but one offers its own single-area equivalent – the Carte Club pass, covering Verbier and the 4 Valleys.

Vail Resorts' Epic Pass is a phenomenal bargain for anyone who can exploit it. Valid for the whole season, it gives unlimited use of the lifts at Breckenridge, Vail, Beaver Creek and Keystone in Colorado and Heavenly in California, all for $579. The catch? You have to buy by 15 November 2008.

REGIONAL PASSES

Regional passes can cover huge numbers of resorts, which may be within striking distance from a single base or may make an interesting tour from place to place. The advantages over buying separate passes are obvious: lower cost, and no repeated queueing.

Austria has some splendid options, particularly in and around Salzburger Land, to the east of the Tirol.

Ski Amadé Covers 270 lifts and is described in the introduction to Austrian resorts, later in the book.

Salzburg Super Ski Card Covers all of that territory plus a further 300 lifts. We enjoyed an excellent short tour with this pass

HOLISKI PASS

The Holiski pass from Compagnie des Alpes covers Val d'Isère, Tignes, Les Arcs (including Peisey-Vallandry), La Plagne, Méribel, Les Menuires, Flaine and neighbours, and Serre-Chevalier. There's an annual subscription of 32 euros, and discounts on the daily rate for the days you ski start at 15%.

last season, skiing Zell-Königsleiten (Zillertalarena), Saalbach, Zell am See, Kaprun and Kitzbühel.

Kitzbüheler Alpen Covers Kitzbühel plus the SkiWelt and several smaller resorts, such as Alpbach and Wildschönau.

Innsbruck Super Ski Pass Covers eight resorts around the city, plus the Stubai glacier and a day each in the Arlberg and Kitzbühel. Five days cost 213 euros last season.

Regional passes are not so common in the rest of the Alps, but there are some worth knowing about.

Switzerland: Valais SkiCard Covers over 40 resorts in the region (including the Franco-Swiss Portes du Soleil area, as well as major resorts such as Verbier and Zermatt). The pass is prepaid and activated at the first lift you use; it is then valid for two years.

Italy: Dolomiti Superski The original and still one of the most impressive: it covers 450 lifts and 1220km of pistes in 12 areas.

France: Mont Blanc Skipass Covers everything from Megève to the Grands Montets, including Courmayeur in Italy, reached through the Mont Blanc tunnel.

PASSES FOR PART-TIMERS

If you're a fair-weather skier or boarder, some resorts offer alternatives to buying passes by the day when the sun comes out. Non-consecutive passes are the norm in North America, where you will often buy a pass valid for six days in eight, for example. In Europe this isn't so common, but some resorts have similar schemes – Megève, Flaine and Davos for example.

The classic solution for late risers is the half-day lift pass valid from 12.30 or thereabouts, but a few resorts offer 'any four hours', or similar, which allows you to choose when you start/finish – La Plagne and Valloire for example. St Anton offers a graduated price scheme on day passes, whereby you receive a refund on unused time – particularly good if you fancy a short ski on departure day.

WHAT ABOUT BEGINNERS?

The most common arrangement is that beginners buy points cards – each lift has a fare expressed in points, and you prepay for a number of points, which get deducted each time you ride. Quite a few French resorts – such as Valmorel, Val d'Isère and Flaine – have several free lifts. A common deal in North America is to purchase a beginner package: lessons and ski pass together.

The thing beginners really need to be alert to is that there are some resorts where there is no alternative to buying a full lift pass, which is a big expense. Usually, these are resorts where the nursery slopes are at mid-mountain rather than village level: Ischgl, Mayrhofen and Châtel, for example.

AGE HAS ITS ADVANTAGES

It's usual for children under a certain age to get a serious discount, and for really young children to ski for free – see our 'Family holidays' chapter. Many resorts offer some sort of deal to the older skier, too. That typically means a discount of 10-15% in the Alps. But discounts range from none at all in a few European resorts (such as St Moritz and Saalbach) to half-price tickets in some American resorts (such as Park City and Jackson Hole). The best deals for the oldest skiers are in France, where most of the major resorts offer free passes to those over 72 or 75. For more detailed information on deals for senior citizens, go to www.wtss.co.uk.

Canadian heli-skiing

Fresh tracks, deserted slopes, no lift queues ... bliss!

by **Dave Watts**

HELI-ESSENTIALS

Safety: this is paramount. You'll get a thorough safety briefing and training in using avalanche transceivers, probes and shovels.

Guide: NEVER ski in front of or below your guide unless they instruct you to. It may be dangerous to do so. And obey all their instructions.

Tree wells: hollows that form around the bases of trees. It is very dangerous if you fall in (especially head first) as you can get stuck and suffocate. So always ski with a partner in the trees and look out for each other.

Tree mushrooms: large lumps of snow that form on the tops of trees and can be very heavy. Very dangerous if they fall off onto your head.

Fitness: essential if you are to make the most of a heli-skiing trip. You will be skiing deep virgin snow all day (pretty tiring if you aren't used to it) with little rest between runs.

Warm-up: arrive at a nearby resort a few days early, so you get over jet lag and find your ski legs before you heli-ski.

Fat skis: do use the specially designed fat skis that the operator normally supplies free; they make it much easier.

JOHN SCHWIRTLICH/ CERTAIN IMAGES PHOTOGRAPHY

With heli-skiing you can expect fresh tracks every run ➜

The ultimate off-piste adventure is to enjoy run after run of virgin powder snow. And that can be achieved by using the ultimate ski lift – a helicopter – in Canada's snowy wilderness of British Columbia. There are lots of heli-operators there – you stay in their lodges and are whisked up from your doorstep each day. In the last few years I've been with three of them, and this feature compares what they offer. You don't have to be an expert to enjoy heli-skiing; big fat skis help you to float through the powder and make the ultimate adventure something all good, fit intermediate skiers or riders can experience.

Western Canada is the world capital of heli-skiing. Multi-day heli-skiing packages normally include meals and accommodation in a lodge run by the heli-skiing operation just for its clients and with facilities such as a sauna, a hot tub and a massage therapist. You have dinner every night with your skiing group and guide. This creates a great atmosphere of camaraderie. The norm is to go for seven nights, Saturday to Saturday, skiing Sunday to Friday and maybe Saturday morning. But shorter trips of, say three to five days, are on offer (with some companies only early or late in the season).

Briefly this is what to expect: you are picked up by a chopper from the door of the lodge, whisked into a snowy wilderness and dropped at the top of an isolated peak, with virgin snow wherever you look. Then you and your group follow your guide, making your own fresh tracks, for maybe 700m/2,300ft vertical, find the helicopter waiting for you in another isolated spot and get whisked to the top of another run of virgin powder. Typically, you might get 10 to 15 runs in a day and between 4,000m/13,000ft and 10,000m/ 33,000ft vertical. If it's sunny, you're likely to be above the treeline and among the glaciers. If it's snowing, you're likely to be among the trees for better visibility. It's rare for the weather to be so bad that you can't fly or ski at all. Lunch is a picnic flown up to you on the mountain. Prices vary between companies and over the season, but expect to pay from around £4,000 for a week. A guaranteed minimum vertical (typically 30,500m/ 100,000ft for a week) is included in the price; some companies charge extra for every 1,000m/ 3,280ft vertical extra that you ski, others don't. You get a rebate if you are not able to do the guaranteed vertical (eg because of poor weather), and you don't have to ski extra vertical if you choose not to.

Here's a brief summary of the three companies I've been with:

Mike Wiegele (www.wiegele.com) emigrated to Canada from his native Austria in 1959, started his heli-ski business in 1970 and still runs it personally and skis and guides guests as often as he can. Wiegele has the largest single heli-skiing area in the world, covering 1,750 square miles and over 1,000 peaks and runs. He says he based his operation in Blue River (between the Monashee and Cariboo mountain ranges) because the area gets huge amounts of snow and very little wind, a recipe for perfect powder. And when I was there it hardly stopped snowing all week and the powder was as perfect as you could wish for. They operate two sizes of helicopter. With the Deluxe package you are in a group of 10 skiers with a lead guide at the front and a 'tail-gunner' guide at the back to help anyone in difficulties – unusual and an excellent idea. There are three groups (rather than four, which is the norm) per helicopter (this means less waiting for choppers and more skiing). With the Elite package you are in a small helicopter with just four skiers per group plus a guide; up to three groups per helicopter. I tried and enjoyed both. The price includes unlimited vertical. Accommodation is in 22 small log cabins scattered around the grounds, with up to six bedrooms in each. Breakfast and dinner are in an impressive base lodge built of log and stone with a dining room, bar, fitness and stretching facilities, hot tub, sauna and massage rooms. Starters at dinner are buffet style with an incredible selection (oysters, scallops, sushi etc).

CMH (www.canadianmountainholidays.com; call 020 7736 8191 for their UK agent) is the other big player in the Canadian heli-ski market. It started in 1965 and is now owned by Intrawest (of Whistler fame). Instead of Wiegele's one big lodge and huge ski area, CMH has 12 smaller lodges and areas, most taking just 44 guests who ski and fly in four groups of 11 with one guide for each group; four groups per helicopter. Six of the lodges are in the middle of the wilderness, and you and your luggage are flown to them by helicopter at the start of your week and out again at the end. This gives a great feeling of isolation and camaraderie. Any extra that you ski over the guaranteed vertical is charged at around £45 per 1,000m/3,280ft.

Great Canadian (www.canadianheli-skiing.com) is a much smaller-scale operation, personally run by owner Greg Porter, with groups of four skiers and a guide, up to three groups per helicopter and a maximum of 24 guests in the lodge. The price includes unlimited vertical. The feeling here is even more intimate than at CMH, partly because the lodge holds roughly half the number of guests and partly because you all ski in groups of four. And you get fabulous views each time you fly (in a bigger chopper you often sit facing other guests rather than next to a window).

Jobs in the mountains

Is it time to do that season on snow you hanker for?

by **Wendy King**

Working a season is a dream many winter sports fans share: endless days on the snow, new friends, fun and partying – with a little work thrown in to pay for it. The reality isn't quite like that, but there is no denying it can be a very rewarding experience.

Every winter, seasonal workers take up jobs in European and North American ski resorts; most will love it and possibly return for more. But success often depends on careful planning and realistic expectations. We hope this short article will help.

CHOOSING A JOB
The traditional winter job has always been for chalet hosts or tour operator resort representatives, but these days there are lots of other possibilities. Businesses often have administration and reception roles; most need maintenance people or bar staff too. Some employers need cover during peak weeks, such as school holidays, or when vacancies arise due to staff drop-out, illness or injury. School specialists such as PGL and TOPS have part-time placements for reps and instructors. Earnings vary widely, depending on the level of responsibility; expect £50 to £250 per week, plus season pass, accommodation and insurance.

WHERE TO FIND THEM
Major French resorts are the obvious starting point for chalet work. But Swiss, Austrian and North American resorts are generally better suited to hotel, leisure or rep work. In North America one company usually runs the whole resort infrastructure – lifts, ski school, kindergarten, ski shops – so it can be simpler to look for casual work, especially if you plan to head out independently.

WHEN TO APPLY
Recruitment generally takes place between July and October, with a second intake in November. You'll normally head out to the resort in December. But you could wait until mid-season to take advantage of drop-out vacancies.

HOW TO GO
You need to decide whether you want a 'packaged' job with a tour operator or to look for work independently. For first-timers a tour operator package has clear attractions. Heading out independently means you have to find both accommodation and employment in the resort, and sort out such things as your lift pass and insurance. You could apply to the tour operators directly. Major companies generally have the most vacancies to fill, but smaller outfits can offer a more individual and personal approach.

KEEPING INFORMED

Web-based agencies are a great source of information. They can notify you of suitable vacancies and put your CV out to potential employers. BUNAC (British Universities North America Club) is an excellent starting point if you fancy the States or Canada, although its scope is considerably wider than that. Recruitment fairs or workshops, such as those arranged by Natives, are worth a look. They generally cover what you'll need to know and you can put your questions to the experts.

WHAT ABOUT QUALIFICATIONS AND TRAINING?

Previous experience and/or relevant qualifications will almost certainly be required in some form. Some posts necessitate a formal qualification: an NNEB certificate to work with children, for example. Instructors must also be certified. Foreign language skills are helpful, but essential only for resort reps. Of course, being able to communicate effectively will make settling into resort life easier and help you to establish a better rapport with the locals. If you are hoping to improve your language skills, make sure you go to a resort where English doesn't dominate. Companies often provide pre-season training, perhaps in hygiene or customer service, or you can sign up for one of the proper courses offered, such as cookery classes or ski technician training.

DOES THE DREAM MATCH REALITY?

Reports suggest 30-40% of workers do more than one season. But seasonal work is tough, often juggling late nights and early starts. Key factors in survival seem to be development of a sensible routine and maintaining the correct attitude. Go expecting a full-on party and not much work, and you are likely to be disappointed. Go with an open mind, a strong work ethic and the determination to enjoy the experience, and you are likely to end the season planning the next. For more feedback from those who know, take a look at the Natives website.

TOP TEN TIPS FOR THE PERFECT SEASON

• *Consider the options: what type of work you would enjoy most given the skills you possess.*

• *Think about where you would like to be based: resorts vary enormously in character and size – remember you'll be spending the whole season there. But...*

• *Don't limit your choices too much; it's much harder to find something suitable if you do.*

• *Ask around: while you are on holiday, chat to your local host or rep for advice. They might be able to put you in touch with their employer.*

• *Go to a jobs fair or workshop: such as those arranged by Natives. They generally cover what you'll need to know and you can put your questions to the experts.*

• *Join an agency: web-based agencies are a great source of information. They can notify you of suitable vacancies and put your CV out to potential employers.*

• *Apply early, to get the pick of jobs and resorts. Or head out mid-season to take advantage of drop-out vacancies.*

• *Make a plan: should things go wrong, it's worth having some savings – especially if travelling independently.*

• *Acquire more skills: look out for one of the basic courses offered, such as cookery classes or ski technician training.*

• *Be realistic: seasonal work is tougher than most people expect.*

Gap year courses

How to qualify as a ski or snowboard instructor

by **Rebecca Miles**

Growing numbers of 18-year-olds, career-breakers and even early retirees are going on gap year instructor courses. Many want to become instructors. But many simply want to spend 10 weeks on the slopes and feel they've had a good time and achieved something, as well as improving their skiing or snowboarding by the end of it.

It used to take years to qualify as an instructor, slowly working your way through the different levels. But now there are lots of gap year course providers offering you the chance to get the first stage in the bag in a season. And each year, around 1,000 Brits do just that, taking instructor exams with the British (BASI), Canadian (CSIA) or New Zealand (NZSI) governing bodies, the three most popular for UK gappers. Course directors estimate that between 25% and 50% of their pupils go on to work in the snowsports industry – the rest return to their job, make a career change or go to university. Tom Saxlund, a director of New Generation, says, 'Our gappers really like skiing, want to improve and want to devote more time to doing it.' Matt Cooke, New Gen's marketing manager, adds, 'We really welcome those who want to make a career of it – we have a number of people who've trained with us and then gone on to teach with us, which is great for New Gen.'

On most courses, around two-thirds of pupils will be either pre- or immediately post-university; the other third will be made up of late-20s to 60-somethings – taking sabbaticals, giving themselves an early retirement present, or taking the opportunity to change their career, thanks to, say, a redundancy payment. On a gap course run by BASI in Nendaz, Switzerland, for example, there was a 50-year-old doctor taking a sabbatical and a 61-year-old early retiree, alongside four 18-year-olds. One of the 18-year-olds on New Gen's course in Courchevel in 2006/07 is now making a career out of instructing. Lara Crisp, having not particularly enjoyed school, found it 'a relief to be around like-minded people', and says she'd 'never learnt as much nor enjoyed learning as much' as when she was training. Since successfully completing the course, she has gone on to pass the next BASI level and her speed test first time, which is extremely rare. Once she's fully qualified, she'll work for New Generation. Richard Eason, aged 42 and from Cornwall, completed the New Gen course last season and plans to continue working through the qualifications. He says, 'The way New Gen runs the gap course is great as the

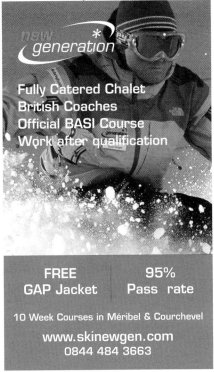
47

structured programme of coaching and instructor shadowing gives you the confidence to actually teach people.'

There is no maximum age for joining a course, but youngsters have to wait until they are over 16. And some providers also offer much shorter courses (eg four weeks), which typically include three weeks of intensive training and the week-long BASI Alpine Instructor level 1 course and exam (see below).

WHAT DO YOU DO AFTERWARDS?

How easy is it to work as an instructor after having done a gap year course? The snowsports instruction industry is a political minefield and, despite valiant efforts by BASI and others to make it possible for Brits to work in, say, France, it's just not that easy.

Thirty-seven countries are members of the International Ski Instructors Association (ISIA), a political body that recognises national qualifications and sets minimum standards that must be met for its members to be accredited. The theory is that if you have an ISIA qualification, then you can teach in any of the ISIA member countries. In practice, this isn't possible because some countries specify further qualifications to reach the top level within their governing body. So, for example, to be a fully qualified ski instructor in France, you do need to pass the notorious speed test.

BASI has a four-level system starting at instructor (two levels) and progressing to ski teacher ISIA and then international ski teacher diploma. If you pass at the end of a 10-week course, you qualify as a BASI Alpine Instructor level 2 (formerly BASI 3). This entitles you to teach in the UK, Canada, USA, Germany, Austria, Italy, Andorra, Spain, eastern Europe, Australia and New Zealand. For some countries you will need a work visa, but in New Zealand, for example, it is fairly easy for a Brit to get a temporary working visa. The 10-week course includes the BASI Alpine Instructor level 1 (formerly BASI trainee): this is done over the first week, includes first aid and child protection modules, and concludes with an exam. With a level 1 qualification, you can teach on UK dry slopes.

The Canadian system has four levels, 1 being the lowest, 4 the highest. On a gap year course, you could expect to pass level 1 and some people reach level 2. With level 1, you would be able to teach beginners, with level 2, up to blue runs. With a level 1 you can teach in Canada, USA, New Zealand, Australia and South America. To teach in most European countries, you would need to be level 4.

New Zealand also has four stages. On a typical gap year course, you would work towards the first two: the certificate in ski or snowboard instruction (CSI), which allows you to teach advanced beginners, and stage 1, which allows you to teach advanced intermediates. A CSI certificate entitles you to teach in New Zealand; stage 1 broadens your choice to include USA, Canada, Australia, Japan, Andorra, Switzerland, Austria and Italy.

HOW MUCH DOES IT COST?

The average 10-week gap year course costs around £6,700, which includes tuition (the norm is five days a week), accommodation (the norm is with five or six evening meals a week, but it may be self-catering) and a season lift pass. Lunches aren't usually included, and spending money of around £100 a week is recommended. It's worth checking that all your exam fees and necessary modules are included. Courses typically run from January to March.

New gear for 2009

The latest kit means more fun for less effort

Vastly increased versatility and customisation of skis and boots to your needs and preferences are the big trends for next season. That, plus skis continuing to get wider and wider, reverse camber technology being introduced on both skis and snowboards, and women-specific skis becoming more and more popular. And clothing is getting brighter again – with even a return to the neon fashion of the 1980s.

Salomon has introduced the revolutionary new Custom Shell ski boot for 2008/09 – pictured here. Until now customised fit has focused on the liner of your boot. But now you can customise the shell too. The boot is warmed up in an oven in the shop, you then step in to it and the plastic outer shell as well as the liner are moulded to the individual shape of your foot, especially the widest part of the forefoot where most people have the greatest problems. The boot is then allowed to cool down and you have a perfect fit. All in 20 minutes. Andy Cuthill, head equipment buyer for Snow + Rock, says: 'This will make a performance boot suitable for everyone. Up till now, people have often substituted comfort for more performance, but now you can have the best of both worlds. It is the biggest revolution in ski boots since the plastic boot took over from the leather boot.' Last season, Atomic made the big news in the boot market with its revolutionary new Hawx range of boots – pictured here. Until then, your forefoot was locked in the ski boot, but the Hawx boot allows it to flex in combination with the plastic shell underfoot, leading to more comfort and performance. This is made possible by a new 'elastic i-flex zone', which absorbs vibrations; the visible signs of that are the distinctive 'gills' at the side of the forefoot area of the boots. I now have a pair of these, and they are great: you can really feel the flex as you turn. Fischer has new Progressor boots that use Somatec technology; a key feature of this is that the anatomical last of the boot takes account of the fact that most of us naturally stand and walk with our feet pointing slightly outwards, in a V position – Somatec allows for this, so you get better performance.

Ski boots are your most important purchase. So set aside enough time for a boot fitter to find the right pair for you and fit them properly. Almost all boots today have heat-mouldable liners to mirror your foot for comfort as well as performance. Always use footbeds in your boots, especially custom-built footbeds made to the particular shape of your feet. These will support and distribute pressure evenly under the whole foot, improving comfort and control and reducing muscle cramps and foot fatigue.

Salomon Falcon
Custom Shell Pro
Atomic Hawx 110 ↑

SNOW + ROCK TIP

TOP SKI BOOTS:
FOR EXPERTS
Salomon Falcon CS Pro
FOR RED RUN SKIERS
Nordica Speedmachine 8
FOR EXPERT WOMEN
Salomon Instinct CS
FOR RED RUN WOMEN
Atomic Hawx 80

49

WINTER 09
CLOTHING, EQUIPMENT, ACCESSORIES

SNOW + ROCK

WWW.SNOWANDROCK.COM

by **Dave Watts**

↑ The Marker Griffon binding is designed specifically to get the best out of the new wider skis

SKIS ARE GETTING WIDER AND WIDER

Last March I went on a week-long test of all the new skis for 2008/09, organised by the Snowsports Industries of Great Britain (a trade body of ski distributors and retailers). Out of 633 skis from 21 different manufacturers, there was hardly a poor ski to be seen.

Skis are continuing to become wider and much more versatile, and the lines between on-piste, freeride and big mountain skis are becoming more blurred. One of my favourite skis on test was the Volkl Grizzly Wide Ride. Even though this was 89mm wide at the waist it was entered in the on-piste category; only a few years ago anything much over 70mm wide was regarded as a freeride ski. But the Grizzly works superbly well on- and off-piste, carving on the groomed runs, floating through the powder and powering through the crud off-piste. A key part of this is its 'Power Switch' system (see 'New trends' opposite). Snow + Rock are featuring this ski in both their on-piste and freeride categories (something they have never done before). Other skis that came out well in the on-piste category were the Rossignol Zenith Z10 Mutix (75mm at the waist), Head Supershape Chip (71mm) and K2 Apache Crossfire (a mere 70mm).

Of the skis entered in the freeride category, the Scott Punisher (89mm at the waist) stood out as my favourite; it's another hugely versatile ski that worked well on- as well as off-piste. Other skis that did well in the freeride category include two Salomons – the Lord (87mm and see opposite) and the X-Wing Tornado Ti Smartrack (75mm) – and the K2 Apache Xplorer (84mm).

The Big Mountain skis are really getting wide these days but many still work well on piste too. Snow + Rock picks out as its likely versatile best sellers Volkl Mantra (96mm), K2 Apache Coomba (102mm) and Obsethed (105mm), Scott Crusade (92mm) and, for women, the Volkl Aura (94mm). To ensure you get the most out of the new wider skis in terms of control and power transmission, Marker has introduced a range of wider bindings. Last year Marker offered the Duke (for touring as well as downhill) and Jester models, which went up to DIN 16. This year, it also has

cheaper versions of these that you can set at up to DIN 12 (quite enough for most of us) – the Baron and the Griffon.

For an intermediate looking to buy their first pair of skis, the Salomon Aeromax Ti stood out in the test as easy to ski and turn yet performing well when skied hard too. At only £275 including bindings they're a bargain. An even better bargain is Snow + Rock's special first-time buyer's package of Head Xenon X4 skis including bindings, Head Edge 8 boots, plus ski bag and poles – all for £279.

NEW TRENDS: FLEX ADJUSTMENT AND REVERSE CAMBER

Two years ago Rossignol were the first to introduce a way of adjusting the flex of your ski. With its 'Mutix' system, you get different sets of arms that you attach to the ski both in front and behind the bindings and interchange at will. One set is designed to make the skis softer and better for short turns and the other to make the ski stiffer for long turns and skiing hardpack. Last year, Volkl introduced its 'Power Switch' system, operated by a dial, which you can twist to activate two carbon rods that run along the length of the ski 'loading or unloading them with power to control the ski's characteristics and energy'. There are now three settings: 'cruise', 'dynamic' and 'power'. It's fitted on the Grizzly as well as the Racetiger GS and Tigershark skis. I tried it on the Grizzly and really noticed the difference between 'cruise' and 'power'.

This season, some of the manufacturers are introducing 'reverse camber' or 'rocker' technology on some of their Big Mountain and freeride skis. Basically, this means that the tips of the skis are lifted up from the snow. The idea is that they float more easily in powder and crud and make landing jumps easier. Examples include the Rossi Bandit DC (dual camber) skis – these have a cable that you can operate to put the ski into reverse camber or normal camber depending on the terrain/snow you are skiing. Salomon has non-adjustable reverse camber on the tips of some of its skis, such as the Czar, the Lord and the Lady. The Lord certainly came out well in the test, and Snow + Rock expect it to be a big seller this winter.

Another interesting new development is Atomic's 'double deck' technology. In very simplistic terms, these skis have a large 'soft' deck, which forms the base, and a smaller 'hard' deck over the central section of the ski, attached by rubber bungs. On the test, we found that the Varioflex model worked well. Atomic claims that when it is skied hard, the ski stiffens and the rubber damps down vibrations. When skied more gently, the ski is softer and this makes for a smooth ride.

WOMEN'S SKIS: A RAPIDLY GROWING MARKET

Nearly every manufacturer now produces a range of skis designed specifically for women (from novice to expert), taking account of their different physical make-up to men. In general, women tend to be lighter and less powerful; so manufacturers give their women's skis a different construction, and design the flex and shape specifically for women. All this makes for skis that are easier to turn.

In the ski test, almost a quarter of the skis were made specifically for women. And our women testers found that, compared with the unisex equivalent, nearly all the skis they tried worked very well for them. These included the K2 T:Nine, Volkl Attiva, Salomon Origins, Dynastar Exclusive, Nordica Olympia, Fischer Vision, Atomic Balanze and Rossignol's Attraxion and Bandit Women ranges. There are even special women's twin-tip skis, such as the Atomic She Devil, K2 MissDemeanor, Rossignol Scratch Girl FS and Salomon Temptress.

CLOTHING IS GETTING BRIGHTER – MORE PROTECTION TOO

Bright and neon coloured clothing is making a comeback for 2009, for both men and women. Sweet women's clothing is new for Snow + Rock this season, and the range includes bright pink and purple outfits. Kjus clothing flew off the shelves last year and is expected to again – Claire Collins of Snow + Rock said, 'It's the highest quality clothing finished to exacting standards set by legendary Olympic skier Lasse Kjus.' Putting green and brown together is popular this season for men's clothing (eg from Quiksilver and Zimtstern) and there are lots of purples and plums for women. There's going to be patterned clothing in 2009 too – brands such as Salomon, Quiksilver, Burton, Bonfire, O'Neil and Zimtstern are big in patterns.

↑ Bright coloured jackets are making a comeback for 2009. Pictured here: Kjus Luna Sweet Starbreaker

Dainese, the protective clothing specialist, has a range of outer clothing where you can, for example, zip a waistcoat/back protector into the jacket and knee protectors into the pants. And d3o (pronounced dee-three-oh) is a revolutionary new substance that can be built into clothing to give protection; it is normally soft and flexible, but upon impact the molecules react instantly to deliver outstanding shock absorption and protection.

SNOW + ROCK TIP

ULTIMATE SNOWBOARD SET-UPS:

FREERIDE

Burton Supermodel X

Burton CO2 EST binding

Burton Ion boots

ALL MOUNTAIN

Nitro Blacklight

Ride NRC binding

Vans Fargo boots

FREESTYLE SET UP

Ride DH2 DFC

Ride Delta binding

DC Balance boots

WOMEN'S ALL MOUNTAIN

Burton Troop

Salomon Relay Ring binding

Salomon W F22 boots

From left to right Three eco-friendly boards: Arbor Element, Salomon Sick Stick, K2 Zero Three new boards: Burton Custom ICS, DC HKD, Nitro Blacklight (new FX Smart Base shown) ↓

It is, for example, used in some Schoffel jackets and in some Ignite beanies that will therefore give your head added protection. Helmets themselves have become very popular, and the trends are for a sleeker look, better ventilation and bright colours. Giro and Sweet are brands that are at the cutting edge of developments.

SNOWBOARD GEAR

As with skis, more brands are introducing reverse camber into the construction of snowboards. Leading the charge is Lib Tech with its 'Banana Technology'. Reverse camber gives a more catch-free ride, makes powder riding easier even with a centred stance (so no more dreaded leg burn), and also makes freestyle riding easier. It really does benefit everything you'll do on a snowboard, be it in pipe, park, powder or pistes. To complement this, proven Magne traction technology is incorporated: instead of just two contact points in the snow, you are given seven, which means you have more control between your feet, where you need it most. Other companies to now include reverse camber or rocker technology are K2 and Ride, and next season more will surely follow suit.

More companies are also starting to develop snowboards that have less negative impact on the environment. Arbor is in the forefront of this. It started making eco-friendly boards more than ten years ago, using more sustainable materials. Salomon has a project called GIFT (Green Initiative For Tomorrow), which includes an all-new board called the Sick Stick that uses more bamboo to enhance board performance, and less resin. K2's new Zero board uses far less harmful material in the construction process than it used to, and Lib Tech is also making an effort, looking for more sustainable and eco-sound materials, such as top sheets produced from castor beans, and having the highest strength to weight ratio in the industry.

Nitro has developed a new base technology for its boards that really sets them apart, and ahead of other companies in terms of

New gear for 2009

53

speed. The FX Smart Base has been designed to adapt to changing snow conditions, so if the temperature drops or rises, the base alters density to maintain maximum speed. It therefore runs faster than a conventional base and is also tougher, making it incredibly scratch resistant. It is faster un-waxed than any other base on the market, yet when it is waxed, it holds the wax better than any other base known to man. Watch out for this on the Misfit, and the Blacklight. And be prepared to leave your mates in the dust.

Burton continues to develop its EST bindings in conjunction with its ICS boards. This really is a step forward in terms of design and ease of use. Not only do EST bindings allow you to fine tune your bindings like no other, they are also far quicker, and easier to adjust. Look out for the new Custom ICS board and Cartel EST bindings, as these are a match made in heaven. The combination gives you more board feel, control and cushioning. Union bindings are in their fourth year of production and are now established as some of the finest bindings on the market; they are virtually indestructible. As Union only produces bindings, it can really focus on making the best fitting, highest performance and most durable bindings in the business. Look out for the Cadet DLX and the Force bindings.

One of the most exciting developments at the moment is DC's much anticipated snowboard line. DC has been making innovations in snowboard boot technology for 10 years with its exclusive pump system in boots such as the Allegiance. Now, DC has unveiled a really tight, superb line of snowboards that look amazing, and ride incredibly well. All have super durable and ultra quick Sintered 7000 grade bases.

Burton has incorporated a feature that enables you to fit thermic heat packs onto some of its boots. The packs heat up to a toasty 104°F, so if you suffer from cold feet then your worries are over. They last for 14 hours on a single charge, and the level of heat can be controlled. The thermics are sold separately from the boots.

↑ Patterned clothing such as this Salomon Exposure jacket is big for 2009

The Schoffel Protect jacket has d3o built in to protect you in the event of a fall or collision

WHY BUY IN THE UK

Prices in the UK are competitive with Europe, and the range of choice available in the UK is far better. Shops in the mountains often tend to stock mainly local brands (eg French brands in France, Austrian or German in Austria). What's more, if you do find the product cheaper elsewhere in Europe, Snow + Rock offers a price pledge on all its products to give you the confidence to buy in the UK. It also offers a number of other exclusive guarantees to give you peace of mind about purchasing in England, such as a comfort guarantee on ski boots and a ski suitability and breakage guarantee.

Smart apartments

The transformation of French self-catering holidays

by **Dave Watts**

Apartment holidays used to be the budget option for most people – shoehorn six people into a studio advertised for six and you'd have a cheap but not very comfortable time. Now things have changed, especially in France, traditional home of the cramped apartment: smart, reasonably spacious apartments are now widely available. Most have dishwashers and many share a pool, sauna, steam room and gym to add to the pampering. Some even have comfortable furniture to relax in too. Sure, the budget option still exists, but now you can have a comfortable apartment holiday with all the other advantages that it brings (see below). We've looked for smart apartments to recommend throughout the Alps and included them in the resort chapters. And on page 57 is a table summarising some of what's on offer.

ERNA LOW

Many of the smart new apartment buildings have plush reception areas and good leisure facilities ↓ ↘

I've been taking my annual ski holiday with my wife and a couple of friends in apartments ever since 1992. That's because we value the freedom an apartment gives you. You don't have to stick to meal times (and meals) dictated by the hotel or chalet staff; you can slob around in whatever clothes you want; you can go out and come back in whenever you choose. And, crucially, you are free to have a big lunch up the mountain without worrying about having to eat a huge meal – which your chalet staff or hotel will have prepared for you – in the evening; if you lack the appetite for a full meal in the evening, you can buy snacks such as oysters, smoked salmon, pâté and local cheeses along with a good bottle of wine or two from the supermarket. If you are hungry, you can go out to a restaurant to eat. Staying in an apartment doesn't mean having to cook big meals – not for us anyway.

When we started this apartment lark, we couldn't find the sort of thing we were looking for in tour operators' brochures – all the apartments were of the cram-'em-in-and-make-it-cheap variety. So we ended up booking independently, through agents in resorts and direct with apartment owners. But it was hard work doing the research – especially as it was before the internet took off.

55

Now, at least in France – the country that used to have the smallest, most sordid apartments – a few tour operators (notably those advertising in this chapter) offer some really smart and spacious places. The French smart apartment concept was kick-started by apartments built by or opened in the Montagnettes and MGM names. Now they've been joined by other brands, such as Lagrange Prestige and Intrawest. Many properties constructed by MGM are now operated by other companies, such as CGH.

What can you expect in one of the places we feature in our table? First, you get more space than in your average French apartment – but not as much as you'd get as standard in North America. (Note that we haven't put any Canadian or US apartments in our table because, in our experience, they are nearly all smart.) You still need to check the space is enough to meet your expectations – I reckon an apartment for four adults needs to be at least 50m^2. And check whether the number it's advertised for involves anyone sleeping in the living room, in bunk beds, on a mezzanine or in a cabin (which can mean an alcove or an area separated by a curtain or sliding door but maybe with no window). You might also be disappointed by the amount of hanging and storage space, especially for wet ski gear and storing suitcases. Second, you get a modern design with smartish furniture (but we're sometimes disappointed by the lack of really comfy sofas and easy chairs you can sink into and relax – often because sofas double up as beds and are more comfortable to sleep in than sit on). Third, many new smart apartments now include leisure facilities such as a pool, sauna, steam room and gym (but check if there is a charge for using these). Fourth, a lot of them also have smart reception areas

with comfy furniture and log fires. Personally, we think this is a bit of a waste of space; we'd prefer more space and more comfortable furniture in the living rooms. Fifth, many new apartments come with dishwashers; but separate kitchens are rare – most new places that we've seen have small open-plan kitchen areas forming part of the living room.

You'll gather from the above that these places aren't perfect. We'd prefer to stay in a smart North American condo with loads of space, comfortable furniture and a private hot tub on our own balcony. But they are a vast improvement on what was on offer ten years ago. And if you quiz the tour operator you are booking through and tell them what you want, they will point you towards the best places for you – those advertising in this chapter don't pretend everything is perfect and don't want dissatisfied clients.

SMART APARTMENTS MENTIONED IN THE CHAPTERS	
Alpe-d'Huez	**Oz-en-Oisans:** Chalet des Neiges
Les Arcs	Arc 1950, Chalet des Neiges, Chalet Altitude, Alpages de Chantal **Peisey-Vallandry:** L'Orée des Cimes
Chamonix	Balcons du Savoy, Ginabelle **Vallorcine:** L'Ours Bleu **Les Houches:** Le Hameau de Pierre Blanche
Champéry	The Lodge
Courchevel	Chalets les Montagnettes, Chalets du Forum
Les Deux-Alpes	Alpina Lodge, Cortina, Goleon, Val Ecrin
Flaine	Montsoleil **Les Carroz:** Les Fermes du Soleil
Megève	Chateau & Residence Megève
Les Menuires	Residence Montalys, Chalets les Montagnettes, Les Alpages, Chalets du Soleil, Les Chalets de l'Adonis, Les Clarines
Méribel	Les Fermes de Méribel
Morzine	L'Aiglon
Laax	Rocksresort
La Plagne	Chalets les Montagnettes, Les Hauts Bois, Pelvoux, Les Granges du Soleil, Chalets Edelweiss **Montalbert:** Chalets de Montalbert, Les Granges **Les Coches:** Les Chalets de Wengen **Champagny-en-Vanoise:** Les Alpages de Champagny
Puy-St-Vincent	Gentianes
La Rosière	Cîmes Blanche, Balcons
Samoëns	Fermes de Samoëns, Chalet la Ferme des Fontany
Serre-Chevalier	Hameau du Rocher Blanc, Best Western Premier
Ste-Foy-Tarentaise	Les Fermes de Ste-Foy
St-Martin	Les Chalets du Gypse
Les Sybelles	**La Toussuire:** Les Hauts de Comborcière
Tignes	L'Ecrin des Neiges, Residence Village Montana, Ferme du Val Claret, Nevada **Les Brévières:** Le Belvedere
Val d'Isère	Chalets du Jardin Alpin, Chalets du Laisinant
Val Thorens	Too many to list – see resort chapter, pages 421-2

Smart apartments

57

Interactive resort shortlist builder at **www.wtss.co.uk**

Luxury chalets

The ultimate ski holiday?

by **Chris Gill** | This annual review of the top of the chalet market – places that rival good hotels for comfort and cuisine – grows in scope every year. The catered chalet concept (explained for the benefit of newcomers in the panel below) goes from strength to strength, with ever-expanding programmes from the established operators and ever-increasing numbers of competitors. And every year we find more suitable chalets in more resorts. But there is no immediate threat to the ruling trio of Méribel and Val d'Isère in France, and Verbier in Switzerland.

As the choice gets wider, it makes choosing harder work of course. Some helpful sites have been set up by agents, allowing you to sift out chalets that might suit you from the hundreds on the market; some advertise in this chapter, and elsewhere in the book.

The greatest concentration of smart chalets is found in **Méribel**. Long-time local specialist Meriski exemplifies the transformation of the chalet business over the last two decades. In the 1980s it was a run-of-the-mill operation, but then it successfully repositioned itself upmarket. The company has changed hands a couple of times recently, but it still has a wide range of impressive chalets, most of them quite small, including two new ones with hot tubs.

Purple Ski has impressive places with all the trimmings in every part of the resort, including the lovely Iamato in Village and the piste-side Kouneli, beautifully revamped in 2007. Ski Olympic took a big step into the luxury market last year with the acquisition of the 24-bed Parc Alpin, formerly run as a boutique hotel. Alpine Action has six smart-looking chalets, most with saunas and hot tubs; best is the well-positioned 14-bed chalet de Launey. Several of Ski Total's properties here deserve to be considered. Descent's portfolio includes the famously grand chalet Brames, with a two-storey living room and a glorious view up the valley towards Mont Vallon. VIP has seven impressive chalets, including Indiana Lodge – right on the slopes, with great views over the resort. Flexiski now has the 10-bed Leonardo, down near Dick's Tea Bar. A degree of

THE EVOLUTION OF THE CHALET HOLIDAY

The catered chalet holiday is a uniquely British idea. Tour operators install their own cooks and housekeepers in private chalets that they take over for the season. They package accommodation in these chalets with travel from the UK, normally offering half board. Dinner is a no-choice affair at a communal table, including wine unlimited in quantity but often severely limited in quality. You can either book a whole chalet (the smallest typically sleep six or eight) or book space in a larger chalet that you share with whoever else turns up.

In its early days, in the 1960s and 1970s, the catered chalet business didn't do luxury. Taking a chalet holiday meant roughing it in creaky old buildings, putting up with spartan furniture and paper-thin walls, and with six or more people sharing a bathroom. And the chalet girl – always a girl, back then – was often straight out of college or finishing school, and more intent on having a fun season on the slopes than preparing gourmet meals.

It was only in the late 1980s that one or two companies realised that people would pay a lot more for comfortable and stylish accommodation, good food and wine, and a little bit of personal service – just enough to make the customer feel the staff are there to do something other than have a good time. The new formula worked, probably better than anyone would have expected.

luxury can be combined with economy by staying down the hill in Les Allues (on the gondola from Brides-les-Bains). Ski Blanc has six properties here, including the 16-bed Vieille Scierie, with hot tub.

Courchevel is well established as the smartest resort in France, and now has a growing number of smart chalets on the UK package market. The resort is at the heart of the Supertravel programme; it has 10 desirable properties here – some apartments but some proper chalets including the firm's 'flagship' Montana. Kaluma has two swanky properties. Descent has the 'intensely private' 10-bed Hermine in the exclusive Hameau du Cospillot enclave. Scott Dunn Ski's properties include one of its two 'flagship' chalets, Aurea – complete with dinky swimming pool. Ski Total's portfolio includes some smart, modern places up in the Jardin Alpin area. In 1650, Le Ski's range continues to slide upmarket with six new properties last year, all with hot tub.

La Tania, not far away on the road towards Méribel, has developed quite a range of comfortable chalet properties, including the best of the Ski Amis range, the 14-bed Balkiss. Ski Power and Le Ski have some neat-looking properties with en suite bedrooms and the usual trimmings here.

Val d'Isère is the great rival to Méribel in the French chalet business. The local specialist, YSE, doesn't operate at the very top of the market, but the company's ancient Mountain Lodges are old favourites, offering no picture windows but atmospheric and comfortable living rooms, with stone walls and ample leather sofas. The newly built Chalet des Pistes is their top 'real' chalet, part of a small cluster in a great on-slope location at La Daille.

Scott Dunn's impressive portfolio here is dominated by the

12-bed Eagle's Nest – an extraordinary place, with an indoor jet-stream pool. Le Chardon Mountain Lodges has an enclave of four modern chalets at the southern extremity of the resort. Descent's extensive portfolio now includes the chalet du Crêt, a renovated farmhouse well known to many Brits in its previous, brief incarnation as a restaurant. Not far away are two very attractive places recently added to the top end of the Le Ski programme, sharing a hot tub – La Bouclia and La Pierre de Complia. VIP has some very smart places, including 12 spacious, stylish chalet apartments in its flagship Aspen Lodge on the main street – a novel concept in chalets, with a reception desk, lounge area and coffee bar. Their 200-year-old Farmhouse, by the church, is something else – a beautifully converted, er, farmhouse. Ski Total has several properties, including smart ones out in Le Legettaz.

By comparison, luxury places in **Tignes** are thin on the ground. Ski Total has some of the best properties here, including some striking modern places with pool and outdoor hot tub. Neilson has some smart places, notably chalet Les Andes, with use of a pool.

The other great French mega-area, Paradiski, offers lots of chalets in **La Plagne** and growing numbers at **Peisey-Vallandry**, on the Les Arcs side of the cable car link from La Plagne. Few deserve a mention here; start with the Ski Amis and Ski Beat brochures.

La Rosière is a new entrant into this chapter, represented by Mountain Heaven's smart-looking Penthouse, with grand top-floor living space and outdoor hot tub.

Selected luxury chalet

Luxury chalets

Weekly news updates and resort links at www.wtss.co.uk

The small-but-growing resort of **Ste-Foy** contains some very comfortable places offered by Gite de Sainte Foy and Première Neige. The swanky chalet Yellowstone is now in the Descent stable.

Chamonix isn't known for luxury chalets, but Flexiski has a bit of a gem in the wood-built eight-bed chalet Bornian. Locally based Collineige has some very individual properties.

Morzine is known mainly for cheap-and-cheerful properties, but Snowline has several interesting possibilities, including an impressive cluster of 'town house' properties right in the centre and the newly renovated, contemporary-style Alaska Lodge. Up at **Les Gets**, seductively converted farmhouses are not hard to find. Descent has the Ferme de Moudon, as seen on Channel 4's programme *Grand Designs Abroad*. There is the Ferme de Montagne – a beautifully renovated old chalet with eight rooms, with wood and stone everywhere, with hotel-style services.

In Switzerland, **Verbier** is the chalet capital, and Ski Verbier the dominant supplier to the UK market. Its portfolio includes several glorious properties, topped by the swanky Septième Ciel – high on the Savoleyres side of the resort – plus the recently built Attelas, Sorojasa and Cheyenne. Ski Verbier also has more modest places including several apartments for smaller parties. Descent's new chalet Pierre Avoi is furnished in cool, modern style.

Zermatt, curiously, has never been a great chalet resort. Scott Dunn has long been the main source, but its offerings are all in apartments. Descent has a real chalet undergoing a revamp for next season; its chalet Zen has excellent facilities and position. VIP now has a newly converted house in a central location as well as two apartment-based chalets. Ski Total's handful of properties here includes the Génépy, stylishly created within a lovely old wooden building, and two smart new little chalets with Matterhorn views.

Elsewhere in Switzerland, Descent has some fabulous places in **Klosters** and now in **Davos** too. Possibly even more remarkable is the company's palatial Chesa Albertini in hotel-dominated **St Moritz** – 'more a mansion than a chalet', as they say, and with 1000m² of floor space they are not exaggerating.

In Austria, luxury chalets are now easy to find in **St Anton**, where Kaluma's almost central Montfort made a welcome debut last season – stylish and comfortable. Scott Dunn added four swanky units last year, in a single building in the Stadle area – all in modern style, with some notably spacious bedrooms. Flexiski's absolutely central Amalien Haus got a makeover in 2006, with slick new bathrooms. Descent has the dramatically modern chalet Katharina. Supertravel has the minimalist Chiara, and this year the newly renovated Narnia. Ski Total has a good range of properties here.

Luxury chalets

Interactive resort shortlist builder at **www.wtss.co.uk**

Luxury hotels

For the perfect indulgent break – and more

by **Chris Gill** | **It's only recently that catered chalets and apartments have started to deliver anything approaching luxury. Hotels, on the other hand, have always done luxury. And they have the great attraction that you don't have to stay for a week – you can indulge yourself for a day or two without breaking the bank (though you may find it difficult to get short-stay bookings in high season).**

For many of us, of course, hotels are also the ultimate form of luxury. They may not offer the privacy of your own chalet or apartment, but in other respects – service, food, facilities – the best of the breed take some beating.

No one who has an appetite for luxurious ski hotels (and an inclination towards letting a tour operator make the arrangements) should fail to get hold of a copy of the Inghams Ski Luxury brochure, containing scores of difficult-to-resist places in North America and the Alps (plus a handful elsewhere – Andorra and Norway, for example). Of course, it's not a definitive or comprehensive guide – Inghams wouldn't pretend it is – but it contains many excellent spots.

If you like to be guided by star ratings when comparing hotels – and there is no doubt the system offers a useful short cut, whatever its imperfections – remember that the French don't do five stars, but top off their range with the '4-star luxe' category.

Speaking of which, the opening of a 4-star luxe hotel in Serre-Chevalier points up how the Best Western brand is moving seriously upmarket with its Premier sub-brand. The stylishly revamped Morgane, currently a Best Western Premier, is among the best hotels in Chamonix, and the new place in Serre-Che will be the best in town by a mile. For those used to thinking of Best Western hotels as, well, undistinguished, it takes some getting used to.

PERSONAL FAVOURITES

For me luxury all too often goes hand in hand with formality – which results in places that instead of being deeply welcoming are actually a bit impersonal. Happily, there are places that avoid this trap. Some of the best are in Italy.

One of my favourites is the Rosa Alpina, in San Cassiano, just off the Sella Ronda circuit in the Dolomites – a great combination of relaxed ambience, well-furnished rooms and superb food (it now has two Michelin stars for its serious restaurant). Not far away is the similarly welcoming Fanes. At the other

(western) end of the Italian mountains, in the Monterosa area, the Breithorn is a beautifully furnished, welcoming place – all wooden beams and panelling – with a choice of excellent restaurants. UK operator Ski 2 can fix a holiday in all these places.

There are some resorts where luxury hotels are virtually the norm. Switzerland, in many eyes the spiritual home of the luxury hotel, boasts astonishing concentrations of 4-star and 5-star places in some resorts. For me, you can keep the glitz of St Moritz. I'll settle for the Alpina in Klosters, or the peaceful Chalet d'Adrien in Verbier. Of course, you can't ignore Zermatt; but I'm not wowed by its hotels, with the exception of the impeccable Riffelalp, isolated halfway up the mountain (with evening trains to the village).

In Austria, luxury generally comes with a softening rustic edge. Lech and neighbouring Zürs are the leaders. They offer an exceptional six 5-star places – the Almhof Schneider, Arlberg and Post in Lech, and the Lorunser, Thurnher's Alpenhof and Zürserhof in Zürs (recommended by Mr Editor Watts). There is a particularly handsome range of 4-star options, both in the main village and up at Oberlech – check out our Lech chapter (which covers Zürs). Over the hill, there are a couple of places I like in St Christoph – the exceptionally welcoming Maiensee and the historic Hospiz. Last season the Hospiz passed with flying colours my acid test of class in Alpine hotels – do they let you wander into the bar in ski boots? The answer here was yes, as it routinely is in the States but rarely is in the Alps. Other Austrian favourites include the Bär above Ellmau and the Central in Sölden – not only central but the best in town.

In France, Courchevel has lots of extremely swanky places, including some of the most expensive in the Alps. Most leave me cold, but I like the Mélézin and Bellecôte – and the Chabichou has the attraction of a famous restaurant. Megève, where the old money still goes, excels in the rustic chic that seems to elude Courchevel – places like the Chalet du Mont d'Arbois, Fer à Cheval and Ferme Hôtel Duvillard come close to perfection. In Méribel, the Grand-Coeur and Altiport vie for editorial affections. In Val d'Isère the Barmes de l'Ours is very compelling, although the more central Christiania and Blizzard have attractions. In Val Thorens my favourite is the Fitz Roy, in an excellent central position.

Not surprisingly, North America has its share of deeply comfortable lodgings. In Aspen, I'll take the Little Nell or the historic Jerome. At Deer Valley in Utah, Stein Eriksen Lodge is the place to go. Big chains sometimes deliver: the Four Seasons in Jackson Hole takes some beating. In Whistler, the Fairmont Chateau Whistler has the edge – but at Lake Louise another Chateau comes second to the perfectly relaxing Post hotel.

Luxury hotels

63

Interactive resort shortlist builder at www.wtss.co.uk

A home in the snow

Make your dream of a bolt-hole in the snow come true

by **Dave Watts**

Buying a place in a ski resort has been many people's ambition for years. The credit crunch is not hitting the Alpine property market in the way it has hit the UK and US, though fewer sales are going through than last year. So now may be a good time to buy. Despite restrictions on new building in many parts of the Alps and on foreigners buying property in parts of Switzerland and Austria, there are still plenty of attractive new developments on offer, as well as resale properties.

Simon Malster, managing director of Investors in Property, has been selling property in the Alps for over 20 years. He says, 'The Alps has not experienced the huge building boom that has occurred in some countries, and although property prices have fallen in the UK, US and places such as Spain, they have held up well in the Alps. It is notoriously difficult to get planning permission to build in the Alps and locals lobby fiercely against development. The Swiss market is particularly robust as the Swiss have always restricted sales of property to foreigners, and this has succeeded in keeping prices artificially low. Interest rates if you are borrowing in euros or Swiss francs remain low, and mortgages are easier to get than in the UK.'

Now that the moratorium on sales to foreigners has been lifted, it is easier to buy in the Valais (which includes resorts such as Saas-Fee, Verbier and Crans-Montana). But you need a permit, and the number of these is still very limited. There will probably be fewer than 100 available in 2009, and they will be released in two batches in January and May and allocated on a first come, first served basis to people who have signed a 'Declaration of intention to buy'. In Veysonnaz (linked to the Verbier ski area), for example, a Swiss developer will receive permits to sell to foreigners 6 out of 10 apartments being built there that will share a spa, sauna and hot tub and are just 150m from the slopes and a lift. Three-bedroom apartments cost from around £380,000, and a UK tour operator will give a guaranteed rental income on these for those who want it.

Austria has become a popular place to buy in the last couple of years. Foreigners are still not allowed to buy in the Tirol, but there are some attractive properties in resorts close to Salzburg. Investors in Property has apartments in Viehhofen just 3km/2 miles from Saalbach and five minutes from the nearest lift and in Bad

SPACE / ERNA LOW PROPERTY

Erna Low is selling contemporary loft-style apartments in dramatically designed extensions to a restored 19th century silk mill in Briançon (part of the Serre-Chevalier ski area) ↓

Hofgastein on the edge of the traffic-free area and 10 minutes' walk from the slopes. Prices start at around £200,000 for two bedrooms, including furniture, and fully managed rental options are available.

It is rare to find property to buy in Italian resorts. But Malster says, 'We have something quite special linked to Sestriere's ski area. The Pragelato Village is a 5-star development built for the 2006 Winter Olympics and managed by the Kempinski Hotel Group. We have apartments starting at around £350,000 for a two-bedroom duplex or £700,000 for a three-bedroom chalet.' The development is a traffic-free, gated resort and includes, shops, restaurants, a bar and a luxury spa with an indoor-outdoor pool. Buyers can ask Kempinski to rent out their apartment when they aren't using it.

But France remains the favourite place for British skiers and boarders to buy property. Joanna Yellowlees-Bound, CEO of Erna Low Property, says, 'We have some fabulous properties there at the moment. One of my favourites is La Schappe, a marvellous conversion of a former silk mill that dates back to the 1840s.' It is in Briançon (part of the Serre-Chevalier ski area), which has just been made a UNESCO World Heritage Site for its medieval walled citadel that towers above the modern part of town. The first phase of La Schappe sold out very quickly. Now the next phase is being released: contemporary loft-style apartments in two dramatically designed extensions to the old mill building. The old building will house a 4-star Ramada Resort with a luxury spa and swimming pool; there will also be a museum and a covered market. Prices are expected to range from around £115,000 to £700,000. La Schappe is right in the centre of Briançon, near the main shopping street and by a park and lake – good for summer and winter stays.

↑ Revelstoke is Canada's newest and most exciting ski resort development

REVELSTOKE MOUNTAIN RESORT/ ERNA LOW PROPERTY

Pragelato Village, linked to Sestriere's ski area, offers a rare opportunity to buy in an Italian resort ↗

INVESTORS IN PROPERTY

↙ Apartments in Veysonnaz (linked to Verbier's ski area) in Switzerland will come with permits allowing foreigners to buy

INVESTORS IN PROPERTY

Erna Low and Investors in Property are both selling apartments in Vallorcine, near Chamonix. Bertie Sanderson, marketing director of Erna Low Property, says, 'This unspoilt village has a new gondola into and a piste back from the Balme ski area above Le Tour. There's also a railway station with trains that allow you to explore all the valley's ski areas without needing to drive.' The 4-star Aiguilles Rouges apartments range in price from around £250,000 for one bedroom to £600,000 for a four-bedroom duplex, and they share a pool, sauna, steam room, hot tubs and gym. Erna Low expects to launch a development of smart apartments in Avoriaz soon, too.

Erna Low also has properties in Canada's newest and most exciting resort development of Revelstoke in British Columbia. It opened last season, and for 2008/09 will have the biggest vertical in North America and 3,000 acres of terrain. The master plan provides for over 20 lifts and 10,000 acres of terrain – bigger than Whistler. It also has heli- and snowcat skiing based at the resort. It will be completed over 15 years, include 5,000 new properties and is aimed at the summer as well as the winter market, with, for example, a Nick Faldo golf course planned. The first phase sold out in three hours last March and the second phase will have one- to three-bedroom apartments and penthouses with views over the Columbia River and Monashee mountains starting at around £225,000. There are also three- and four-bedroom townhomes starting at around £500,000 and plots you can have your own house built on.

A home in the snow

67

WHAT TO LOOK FOR WHEN BUYING A HOME IN THE SNOW

First, you need to decide whether you want somewhere just for the skiing or whether you want a place in a resort that is attractive in the summer as well. Many French resorts developed after the 1950s can be deadly dull in summer, whereas all those featured here are attractive for summer as well as winter use. Second, if you want the place primarily for skiing and snowboarding, you will want reliable snow. And with global warming likely to continue, that means going for somewhere with access to high, snow-sure slopes. Third, if you intend to use the place yourself frequently, you will probably want somewhere within a couple of hours of an easily accessible airport. Fourth, make sure you understand the legal and taxation aspects – buying and running costs, all types of taxes and any resale restrictions. It is highly advisable to get professional advice on these. Fifth, make sure you understand any arrangements that you may be offered for 'sale and leaseback' or 'guaranteed return' from renting it out – these can vary enormously and are particularly common in France where you can save VAT on the purchase price in some circumstances. Sixth, if you are intending to rent the property out yourself, don't overestimate the income you will get from it.

You also need to decide whether you want to buy a new or a resale property. Building restrictions in many areas of the Alps have severely curtailed the number of new properties. But more and more old buildings are now being converted into high-quality apartments.

Interactive resort shortlist builder at www.wtss.co.uk

Family holidays

Making them possible despite the crunch

by **Chris Gill**

If there is one thing that testifies to the general wonderfulness of skiing (or boarding) as a family holiday, it is that parents are prepared to carry the cost. It's considerable, especially if the children are old enough and resilient enough to hit the slopes. Take your kids with you to the Dordogne in August, and all you have to do is rent a slightly bigger house and spend a bit more in Super U every couple of days. Take them with you to Méribel in February, and you're looking at paying for child care if you're lucky, or at clothing, equipment, lessons and lift passes if you're not – and of course wildly expensive lunches.

But you know all that, in general terms at least. What about the detail? In particular, to what extent can your choice of resort affect what you end up paying? Well, in general you'll keep all your costs down by settling for a minor resort that doesn't think of itself as an international destination. But there is one item on the list which can cost wildly varying amounts according to exactly which resort you choose – the lift pass. So I'm starting this year's bulletin from the family front with a detailed look at that angle. Well, a fairly detailed look. Then I turn to some other aspects of family skiing holidays, prompted partly by exchanges on the forum of our increasingly wonderful website at www.wtss.co.uk. One of the dozen sections of the forum is devoted to family holidays, and that would be a good place to seek advice from other readers who may already have learned the lessons you need to learn. Give it a whirl.

LIFT PASSES

Sadly, the question 'What are the kids' lift passes going to cost me?' has no simple answer. At one extreme, it may be nothing, while at the other extreme (for a child over 14 in many French resorts) it may be the full cost of an adult pass – often around the £150 mark, with the value of the pound at its currently low level. With amounts like this at stake, the cost of the kids' passes is something that may well affect your choice of destination. What follows will alert you to the range of possibilities; you might turn next to our resort chapters, in which the main deals are summarised in the margin, at least for major resorts. But bear in mind that in general what is printed in our chapters relates to last season, not the season ahead. We plan to have up-to-date prices and age limits on our website at www.wtss.co.uk, as they become available.

One way or another, you can escape paying full fare for young children. Children may of course be eligible for special treatment as beginners – discussed in the separate chapter on lift passes – but even if they aren't, they should get special treatment on age grounds. In some resorts there are simply special passes for children, and in others there are special deals for the whole family.

LIFT PASSES 2 – CHILD PASSES

When you go to get passes for your children, be sure to take evidence of their identity and age – and your own identity. Generally, child passes are available only to those buying an adult pass at the same time.

The very youngest children generally ski for free – generally up to the age of five, six, seven or eight, occasionally to a greater age.

Family holidays

69

Interactive resort shortlist builder at www.wtss.co.uk

One minor oddity is the Arlberg region (Lech, St Anton), where they charge 10 euros – although the ticket is valid all season. At the upper end of the generosity scale, Saas-Fee and Villars in Switzerland have now raised their age limit to nine years, while most of the relatively mean resorts, typically with a limit of five years, are in France – and Chamonix offers free passes only up to the age of four.

Juniors – those who don't qualify for the free pass – usually receive on average a 25-55% discount. Again the age group varies, from a limit of 13 years up to 16 years. French resorts are again relatively mean, with small discounts and low age limits. Some of the best deals include Cervinia and the SkiWelt (Söll, Ellmau and neighbours) at half price, and a very generous reduction of around 65% in Davos, St Moritz and Fernie.

Older teenagers are less likely to receive a discount; where they do, it is usually no more than a third. Yet again, France comes out at the mean end of the spectrum – often nothing beyond the standard child discounts. Some of the best opportunities are in Switzerland and Canada.

LIFT PASSES 3 – FAMILY SPECIALS

Families can save a significant amount on standard prices, when buying as a group. Two adults and two children (under 17) buying identical six-day passes in Les Arcs will save over 100 euros on the total cost of individual equivalents. Additional children pay the normal price for their age group, which doesn't seem unreasonable. In the Three Valleys, the discount is 20% and in the Italian Dolomites you'll save 140 euros on similar deals.

THE PERFECT FAMILY HOLIDAY? THE LOW-DOWN ON CHALET HOTELS

The catered chalet holiday is as popular as ever, especially with families. Since en suite bathrooms and comfy sofas became the norm rather than the exception, the attractions of the chalet formula – more private and less formal than hotels – have increased considerably. Now, more people are discovering the merits of bigger chalet hotels.

Chalet operators have for years set the pace in child care. It was a natural extension of hiring British gels as cooks and housekeepers to hire a few as nannies, too; then all they had to do was identify a suitable room in a suitable chalet, and bingo – a crèche was born. For British parents reluctant to submit their beloved to the brutality of French nurseries, the chalet was the obvious solution.

Chalet hotels are a larger version of the same thing, with some advantages. Some are purpose-built, but usually they are based on buildings that have operated as proper hotels. Typically, bedrooms are more generous than in chalets. Facilities are often better – there is likely to be a bar, and there may be a swimming pool, spa or gym, for example. There may be a menu choice at dinner.

Two of the most long-established chalet operators dominate the family chalet hotel market, between them offering a wide range of top resorts. Mark Warner have always focused on chalet hotels, and have crèches in 9 of their 14 properties. Esprit Ski were the original family chalet specialist. Their programme is still dominated by chalets, but it now includes seven chalet hotels.

Moira Clarke, Esprit's head of marketing, says chalet hotels are proving increasing popular with Esprit guests. 'This is not only because of the better facilities but also because of the communal versus private balance. Guests can choose to be as sociable or as private as they wish, either dining with other guests or just by themselves, or with their own friends. In traditional chalets guests do have to all get along together, and this doesn't suit everyone.'

Esprit's flagship chalet hotel is the super-cool Deux Domaines at Belle-Plagne, which we had a wander around just after it opened last Christmas. It has a decent pool and spa (young children not allowed in the latter), and a good ski-in/ski-out location on the edge of the village.

Interactive resort shortlist builder at **www.wtss.co.uk**

Many resorts offer free lift passes to children in late March and April, normally as part of an accommodation package booked through the tourist office. These also include discounts on rental equipment and ski schools. It can be a great way to save money and avoid the peak February crowds.

Italy's Val Gardena has a novel way for adults with an infant under three years old to share their parental responsibilities: a transferable pass – so one partner can ski while the other minds the baby (a very un-Italian concept).

CHILD CARE YOU'RE COMFORTABLE WITH

Practically every resort – these days even Italian ones, which used to rely on Mamma or grand-Mamma to do her duty – has one or more nurseries where your kids can be looked after while you indulge yourself in carefree days on the slopes. But, to judge by the reports we get, the great majority of British parents prefer to entrust their offspring to the British nannies provided by tour operators, particularly chalet operators.

Of course, the tour operators who advertise in this chapter should be your first port of call when looking for a holiday with built-in child care. Our scrupulous editorial impartiality forces us to point out that there are alternatives; but who are they? On a whim, we asked editorial daughter Laura to earn herself a summer holiday bob or two by visiting the website of every operator we know about to see just who does and does not offer child care. She seems to have identified no fewer than 44 firms that do offer some sort of child care facilities of their own – far too many to list here. Familiar names that catch our eye, though, include Inghams, Le Ski, Meriski and Ski Power. All being well, before the autumn is too far advanced we'll get the full list up as a special page within the Families section of our website at www.wtss.co.uk, and if the backroom boys play ball we'll list operators by resort, too.

LOCATION, LOCATION AND LOCATION

Yes, the famous trio of key factors are what matters when arranging a family holiday, at least according to one participant in our website forum devoted to family holidays. He went on to explain that he meant three different kinds of location: your resort should be close to your arrival airport, and your lodgings should be close to the slopes and close to the ski school meeting point.

I posted a message at the start of last season asking people to say what their own three golden rules were for a successful family trip. I'm not going to try to summarise all the responses, but one or two things did seem to crop up fairly frequently, and among them certainly was the matter of making the journey as painless as possible. For some people, this means a short airport transfer; for others, preparation with drinks and snacks; for others, a deliberately relaxed journey by car instead of plane.

Another recurring theme is the need to remember that you're taking a holiday, and that the idea is to have fun, not just to progress to the next ski school level. Even kids who enjoy skiing will also get a lot out of other activities such as tobogganing and tubing, and the holiday will be more successful as a result. 'Our kids spent at least an hour on the toboggan run every night after dinner,' said one contributor well pleased with his choice of Oberlech for his family holiday. I remember a very successful trip of ours to Les Arcs, where we had a ground-floor flat next to the piste; we were there at Easter, which meant daylight until mid-evening, and our two plus their chums had a great time sledging right outside our patio doors. Had we planned that? No, but you could.

AFFORDABLE KIT

I've written before in these pages about places where you should avoid buying kids' clothing (in Val d'Isère). What I may not have written about before are the places where we routinely stock up on gloves that are cheap enough to lose without tears: the low-cost stores Aldi and Lidl. You can get good stuff at knock-down prices at these places, provided you get there quick when they have the stuff in stock. It doesn't hang about, so you need to find out early in the autumn when it will be arriving. An alternative that doesn't require such strategic planning is TK Maxx, where you may find viable cheap clobber more or less any time.

Family holidays

Interactive resort shortlist builder at **www.wtss.co.uk**

Corporate ski trips

A great way to motivate your staff and clients

MOMENTUM SKI

Tailored corporate ski events

Conferences, off-sites and hospitality

Ski weekends

Premier resorts in Europe

020 7371 9111
www.momentumski.com

For a whole variety of reasons most companies choose to get groups of staff or clients together out of the office occasionally. Team building, rewarding performance, bonding with clients, launching new products, problem solving and planning future strategy are examples. Getting together in another boring UK hotel can seem a bit tedious – but getting together in a splendid ski resort environment most certainly will not be. That's why more and more firms are doing just that.

The mountain environment is one that has lots of advantages for corporate events. The perceived status of ski resorts is high – whoever you invite will be in no doubt that they are being given a treat (as will their friends and business colleagues). And the clear fresh air, the sun and the snowy, dramatic mountain scenery have a huge and immediate impact on people arriving from the European lowlands and their dreary winters. There is a great sense of fun and liberation, and people are happy to relax and enjoy themselves.

HOW LONG FOR AND HOW BIG A GROUP?
Corporate trips of a few days are the norm – Thursday to Sunday, say. In principle, your group can be any size you like; but with really small groups, be aware that the social success of the trip is going to depend on how the individuals mesh. Charlie Paddock of The Corporate Ski Company says that the groups they work with

by **Dave Watts**

vary in number from 15 to several hundred but that generally the average size is between 30 and 50. Momentum Ski also organises lots of corporate trips and its MD Amin Momen says, 'We get groups of all sizes from 15 to 1500, and small groups can be just as complicated to arrange as big ones.'

WHERE TO GO AND WHAT KIND OF ACCOMMODATION?

How easy it is to settle on a resort for a corporate trip depends hugely on the nature of your project. If it's a group spread around the world that you want to get together, you could consider North American resorts as well as the Alps. But if the group is UK or European based, the Alps would be best. Because corporate trips tend to be short, you'll want to keep the travel time to the minimum. Transfer times from airports to resorts generally range from one to four hours, and you'll probably want to operate at the lower end of that range if you can. On the other hand, you may want your choice of resort to carry a message to your 'delegates'. Choosing Courchevel or St Moritz is effectively saying, 'No expense spared – nothing but the best for you.'

Charlie Paddock of The Corporate Ski Company says: 'We operate in over 40 ski resorts worldwide; however, many of our groups go to Switzerland and Austria because of the excellent flight access and wider choice of 4- and 5-star hotels, which tend to be more accommodating for short stay and weekend corporate groups. Since the Winter Olympics were held in Turin in 2006, Italy has also become more accessible to corporate groups on a budget, due to a wide range of more affordable places to stay.' And Shelley Cunningham of Ski Verbier says: 'We deal with a large number of

Combining business and pleasure does not come more enjoyable than in the mountains

- Reward & incentive travel
- Entertaining top clients
- Conferences & meetings
- Team building

Skiline.co.uk

The ski specialists to the fabulous Italian Monterosa ski area

- Ski weekends and corporate events tailored to your exact specification and budget

- Traditional slope-side hotel or a 5 star luxury hideaway chalet

- Short private transfer from airport to resort

- Friendly, helpful resort staff

- British, B.A.S.I. qualified ski instructors

- Attractive traditional resort

Visit our comprehensive website, at www.ski-2.com, call us on 01962 713330 or email us at sales@ski-2.com

ABTA
The Travel Association

Corporate ski trips

Interactive resort shortlist builder at **www.wtss.co.uk**

This season will see the 10th annual City Ski Championships held in Courmayeur in Italy's Aosta valley and organised by Momentum Ski. Among their attractions is the array of celebrities who turn up. British downhill stars of the 1980s and 90s Konrad Bartelski and Graham Bell, Olympic athlete Colin Jackson and racing driver Damon Hill are regulars. In 2008, stand-up comic Marcus Brigstocke had the audience creased up with laughter at the prize-giving dinner. He is returning in 2009, and it is hoped that former Olympic downhill champion Tommy Moe, chefs Heston Blumenthal and Ainsley Harriott and TV presenters Fiona Bruce and Claire Balding will also attend. Around 200 skiers from 40 City firms take part in the event.

The Saturday GS race is the main event. But three other races are held on the Friday: the Accenture parallel slalom, the Radar Trap (speed skiing) and a Super-G snowboard race. On both days there's a race-side buffet sponsored by GAM and a Michelob ice bar. On the Friday evening there's a Cheviot welcome drinks party and on the Saturday a Mumm champagne reception followed by a gala presentation dinner, and then ... clubbing till dawn. Sunday is free for skiing or sleeping.

The 2009 event, from 19 to 22 March, promises to be extra special to celebrate the event's 10th anniversary. Konrad Bartelski will again be running the Snow+Rock pre-race ski clinics, and Graham Bell and Matt Chilton from the BBC will be doing the commentary. For more details contact Momentum on 020 7371 9111 or City Championships on 020 7863 8813 – or see www. cityskichampionships.com.

Corporate ski trips

76

corporate groups who are looking to exploit the joys of a 100-minute transfer time from Geneva to Verbier, combined with world-class skiing and a very lively nightlife. Our two boutique hotels (15 rooms each) cater perfectly for groups that want a property exclusively to themselves, combining chalet-style accommodation with a five-star service. And our flexible booking policy allows groups to go for long weekends or midweek breaks.'

Amin Momen of Momentum Ski says, 'Where to go depends entirely on what the client wants to do: hold a conference or training session, or just have a jolly, say. Each year we take a group out for Ford, combining the trip with the Geneva Motor Show; last year they were testing Mondeos, so we organised a suitable route from Geneva to Courmayeur, returning after a couple of days via Megève, with lunch at a Michelin-starred restaurant. This season they'll be testing the 4x4 Kuga on the ice driving circuit at Flaine.'

A lot of groups include non-skiers, and Angus Kinloch of Ski Line says, 'For them we may suggest hotels with good spa facilities. And we've had a couple of big groups with a lot of non-skiers and set them up in Bad Hofgastein, an Austrian spa resort with both good skiing and excellent spa facilities. They loved it.' For a really big group Kinloch says, 'You can even take over the whole village of Brand, in Austria. They will let us book all the hotel rooms and brand the whole place however you like, put banners in the streets, even change the names of hotels and streets.' At the other extreme, for smaller groups, he says, 'Chalets can be ideal. Some companies like to take over a top-class chalet for a week and invite different groups out for three or four nights each. For us it is fiddly because it

The Royal Bank of Scotland team (plus supporters) who won the 2008 City Ski Championships men's team prize ↓

Ski Verbier
The Verbier Specialists

020 7401 1101 www.skiverbier.com

usually involves organising flights from several different airports and separate transfers if they don't arrive at the same time. But it goes down well with clients.'

Whatever you do, choose a resort with a good snow record and/ or extensive snowmaking. You don't want to invite people on a skiing break to find that there's no snow. Avoid early season for the same reason. A March trip to a high resort will mean good snow, and it should mean strong sunshine, too. Don't get hung up on size – with only a couple of days to spend on the slopes, almost any resort has plenty of terrain, especially with good local guides to help you make the most of it.

If you are getting a large group together and need good conference facilities, finding the right resort and accommodation, meeting rooms and support services can be a real headache, and it's in dealing with this sort of challenge that the services of a tour operator or event management company will really pay off. If you put them in charge of the whole event, you can make them responsible for staying within budget, including on-the-spot costs, as well as the basic accommodation and travel costs.

ORGANISING THE DAYS AND EVENINGS

This is another area where the services of a tour operator or event management company will really pay off. You'll need to make sure everyone is equipped with suitable clothing, equipment and lift passes. You'll also want to organise tuition or guiding specially for your group, activities for non-skiers, lunches in mountain restaurants and evening activities such as wine tastings or dinner up the mountain followed by a toboggan run or torchlit descent on skis. Another possibility, in good weather, is a swanky picnic, with plenty of champagne buried in the snow.

Simon Brown of Ski 2, whose corporate groups normally go to Champoluc in the Monterosa region of Italy, says: 'Most of our groups are office jollies organised for bonding purposes, and we'll lay on anything they want – maybe ski instructors for beginners and heli-skiing for the good skiers, a night out at Milan's San Siro stadium to watch the soccer, a trip to the Casino in Chamonix, an evening having dinner in an old restaurant up the mountain reached by snowcat. Anything's possible.'

Interactive resort shortlist builder at **www.wtss.co.uk**

Short breaks

Making the most of a quick snow-fix

Taking short-break ski trips can give you three refreshing days on the slopes and leave you with the feeling of having been away for ages. The growth in budget airlines and greater choice of airports to fly from and to means more of us are discovering the joys of short breaks and trying a wider range of resorts. The classic short breaks are weekends, but if you can get away midweek there are many advantages. Flights and accommodation can be cheaper and popular weekend resorts can be very quiet, especially in low season. Sunday to Wednesday or Wednesday to Saturday has worked well for us. We've also met people who rent apartments for the season and go out whenever it suits, and others who book up multiple flights well in advance.

Using a specialist tour operator or travel agent such as those advertising in this chapter makes sense if you don't want to make your own arrangements, or don't have the time. They have special deals with hotels and can organise lift passes and rental equipment. In some cases, arrival/departure dates are flexible, and you can arrange your own transport if you prefer. Some operate special weekend courses, such as guided off-piste or even heli-skiing.

To maximise your slope time, it's best to catch early or late flights. An early flight from Stansted to Turin or Salzburg, for example, can put you on the slopes of Courmayeur, Champoluc, Schladming or Bad Gastein, say, before lunch. We try to avoid travelling back on Sunday evenings as traffic can be horrendous with locals going home after the weekend. And we especially try to avoid Munich airport because the airport is the other side of the city from the Alps and the motorway can be very congested.

CHOOSING AND GETTING TO THE RESORT

Book a rental car or transfer in advance; it's often cheaper and saves time the other end. Compare online prices too: we discovered the same car hire company was cheaper booked directly than through their 'special deal' with the budget airline. And it's worth considering a different car hire company from the one your airline promotes – so you avoid queuing with everyone else from your flight. Taxis are generally very expensive. In our experience, public transport times between airports are less convenient for short trips, though there are pretty good rail connections in Switzerland.

Resorts near to your arrival airport may seem the obvious choice, but if you're going for the weekend the last thing you want is to be joined by hordes

of local visitors. A little extra transfer time may be worth it for quieter slopes. Of course, midweek and early or late season trips can be a good way to enjoy blissfully empty runs. And as you will only be there for a few days, you could try some smaller resorts that you might not consider visiting for a whole week.

From Geneva, the classic destination is Chamonix, an hour from the airport. Similarly, Megève, Flaine, Morzine, Courmayeur (Italy) and Villars (Switzerland) are close by. Allow two and a half hours for Verbier and Crans-Montana and up to three hours for Tarentaise resorts. Smaller resorts to consider include the Val d'Anniviers and Anzère (opposite and next to Crans-Montana respectively).

From Zürich, Laax, Davos and Klosters are the nearest big resorts; Engelberg and Andermatt are within easy reach. Or you could try the less well-known Arosa or (in Austria) the Montafon.

From Innsbruck, there's lots of choice, from the smaller resorts surrounding the city to St Anton and Lech (also reached from Friedrichshafen), and Mayrhofen – and even the Italian Dolomites. Less well-known resorts include those of the Zugspitz Arena.

From Salzburg, most of the eastern Austrian resorts, such as Schladming and Bad Gastein, are less than two hours away. Less well-known resorts to consider include many of those covered by the Ski Amadé lift pass (see p123).

From Turin, Sauze d'Oulx, Sestriere, Courmayeur and La Thuile and (in France) Montgenèvre and Serre-Chevalier are less than two hours by car. Or you could try less well-known Champoluc or Pila.

For the Dolomites, consider Verona or Bergamo. Beware of Treviso – foggy weather is common and can mean cancelled flights.

Unless you can book at short notice, avoid low resorts where snow may be unreliable and very high resorts where the skiing is entirely above the treeline – this rules out places such as Tignes, Val Thorens, Obergurgl and Cervinia.

WHERE TO STAY

In some resorts it can be difficult to find accommodation for short-stay bookings except in very low season. But it's normally fairly easy in resorts that have a lot of accommodation because of big summer business – Chamonix and Morzine, for example. Local tourist offices can help find B&Bs. And even purpose-built Flaine now offers accommodation for two- to four-night breaks all season. You could consider staying in Salzburg or Innsbruck and taking the daily shuttles to different resorts. If you have a car, your options are very wide: we've had enjoyable stays in Chur, Switzerland (visiting Flims, Lenzerheide and Arosa – all less than 40 minutes away), Aosta, Italy (with a gondola to Pila and short drives to Courmayeur, La Thuile, Champoluc and Cervinia) and Radstadt near Salzburg.

WHAT ABOUT PRICE?

Costs vary enormously. Airlines normally release their winter flights in July, with lower fares to early bookers. Ski 2 quoted us a price of from £389 for return transfers, three nights' B&B in a 3-star hotel in Champoluc, a three-day lift pass and lunches; you book your own flights. Momentum quoted from £398 for flights, car hire or transfers, and three nights' B&B in a 3-star hotel in Courmayeur; lift passes and lunches not included. Consider renting your equipment rather than taking your own: airlines can impose hefty fees for ski/board carriage (see our 'Flying to the snow' chapter).

Short breaks

79

Interactive resort shortlist builder at www.wtss.co.uk

Flying to the snow

Flights and transfers for independent travellers

by **Wendy King**

The choice of flights to the Alps has mushroomed in the last few years. So has the number of companies offering affordable transfers to resorts. And so, sadly, has the cost of extras to basic air fares – not just taxes but also, crucially, baggage and ski or board carriage costs.

Budget airlines now operate from many UK airports. And they fly to a wide range of airports suitable for most resorts. Our map shows the arrival airports dotted around the Alps, so you can see which are likely to work for which resorts. But you can also get to airports outside the range of our map that serve areas such as Andorra and the Pyrenees, the Sierra Nevada and Bulgaria. Note that some winter flights stop operating before the end of the season.

EasyJet has by far the biggest range of flights to the key destination of Geneva and serves more than 10 Alpine destination airports from airports around the UK.

Ryanair operates mainly from Stansted, with a few flights from Bristol, Bournemouth, East Midlands, Liverpool and Glasgow. Less well-known destinations include Klagenfurt (handy for Carinthia) and Friedrichshafen (useful for western Austria and eastern Switzerland). But as we went to press, Ryanair announced it would be cutting back on some winter flights.

Flybe serves Geneva and Chambéry from several airports, including Exeter, Southampton, Birmingham and Norwich. You can also reach Berne, Salzburg, Nice and Milan.

Bmibaby flies from Cardiff, Manchester, Birmingham and East Midlands to Geneva and from Birmingham to Nice and Bergamo.

Jet2.com goes from Manchester, Leeds/Bradford and some other places, such as Blackpool. Destination airports include Geneva, Chambéry, Salzburg, Milan and Venice.

Thomsonfly goes to Salzburg from five UK airports, to Geneva from Doncaster/Sheffield and to Grenoble from Bournemouth.

Air Southwest has flights to Grenoble from a few regional airports, including Plymouth and Newquay from December.

British Airways goes to lots of relevant airports from a variety of UK ones. And foreign national carriers using the major airports are becoming increasingly competitive too – **Air France,** for example. **Swiss International Air Lines** operates several flights a day from Birmingham and Manchester to Zürich, and from Heathrow and London City to Zürich and Geneva.

Charter flights are also sometimes sold on a seat-only basis. For example, **Inghams** have Verona Brescia (for the Dolomites), Salzburg and Geneva for 2008/09. **Snowjet** have weekend charters from Bristol, Gatwick, Stansted and Manchester to Chambéry. Charter flights can also allow you to use airports not served by scheduled airlines.

80

WHAT ABOUT BAGGAGE COSTS?

Nearly all budget airlines now charge for checking in bags. And charges for carrying skis, boards and boots have soared. These extras can add up to more than the air fare, and charges and rules vary and change frequently – so it's important to check the detail carefully. Generally, you get a cheaper rate if you book online. When we went to press, for example, Ryanair charged £8 one way for the first bag (plus £4 for using the check-in desk), £16 for each extra bag and £25 for skis or board if you book them in online. So that's a minimum of £74 return for one bag plus skis. BA and Swiss carry one bag and one pair of skis or a snowboard for free. Weight allowances for both bags and skis/board vary.

The obvious way to save money in many cases, though, is to take fewer bags. SnoKart (www.snokart.com) have come up with an ingenious solution: a modular-style, multi-purpose system of bags that can carry all your gear. You can zip individual ski, boot and main wheelie bags together to form one big bag, and may only need to pay the airline for equipment carriage (dependent on weight restrictions) or one hold bag and equipment.

GETTING TO THE RESORT

Renting a car can be cost-effective if you are only going for a couple of days or as a group – but watch for hidden extra charges. Public transport is now much easier than it used to be, and independent travel has brought with it a rapid expansion in the private transfer market too. Most Swiss airports have good rail and bus links with lots of places. It might be cheaper to get a special rail pass than a return ticket – the Swiss Travel Centre (www.stc.co.uk) can help. Austria's Salzburg and Innsbruck airports are similarly well served. Buses run to the Dolomites from Verona and to the Aosta valley from Turin. Public transport to and from French resorts is slightly trickier. Private minibus transfers are now plentiful. You can either book a seat on a shared transfer, maybe having to wait for other flights, or reserve the whole minibus. Some of the key outfits and their services are listed in the directory, at the back of the book. You will find a comprehensive list of airlines, transfers etc and their relevant links on our website: www.wtss.co.uk.

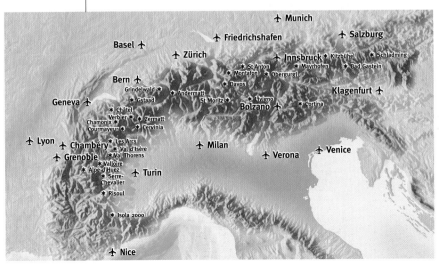

Drive to the Alps

And ski where you please

by **Chris Allan**

More and more people from Britain are doing what the French, the Germans and the Dutch have done for years, and driving to their Alpine resorts. It has various advantages, even for those going on a pretty standard week in the Alps. For many people, it's just less hassle than checking in at dawn for a flight from Gatwick, and less tedious than sitting around waiting for a delayed charter plane that's stuck in Majorca. For families (especially those going self-catering), it simplifies the job of moving half the contents of your house to the Alps. If there are four or five people in your party, the cost can be low.

If you fancy something a bit more adventurous, taking a car opens up the exciting possibility of touring around several resorts in one trip, and even making up your plans as you go, to follow the snow.

Cross-Channel ferries are faster and more pleasant than ever, with the possibility of a seriously good lunch on short crossings as an alternative to the quicker shuttle-trains through the tunnel. And the motorway networks in north-eastern France and on the approaches to the Alps have improved immensely in recent years. You can now get to most resorts easily in a day from south-east England, in some cases using motorways virtually all the way.

For us, the freedom factor is the key. If the snow is bad in your resort, if the lift queues are horrendous, or if the resort you've plumped for turns out to be a let-down, you don't have to grin and bear it – if you have a car, you can try somewhere else (provided of course that you haven't already invested in a weekly lift pass).

Another plus-point is that you can extend the standard six-day holiday – spending a full day on the slopes on the final Saturday, then driving for a few hours before stopping for the night means you won't find Sunday's journey too demanding, and you may even have time for a traditional French Sunday lunch.

AS YOU LIKE IT

If you fancy visiting several resorts, you can do it in three ways: use one resort as a base and make day trips to others; or use a strategically placed valley town as a base, and make resort visits from there; or embark on a tour, moving on every day or two. The separate chapter on lift passes describes some notable regional passes that might form the basis of a trip. The most impressive cover eastern Austria and the Italian Dolomites.

82

Take the fast run to France.

Folkestone – Calais in only 35 minutes!

- Direct motorway access
- No luggage, roof box or ski supplement
- Up to three shuttles per hour
- Fare covers 1 car, up to 9 skiers and 18 skis
- Book your ski travel early to get our best prices
  call 0870 011 36 73
  or visit eurotunnel.com/ski

GEDESS 362609

Travel from

£49

per car,
single

EURO TUNNEL

call 0870 011 36 73 or book
on-line at eurotunnel.com

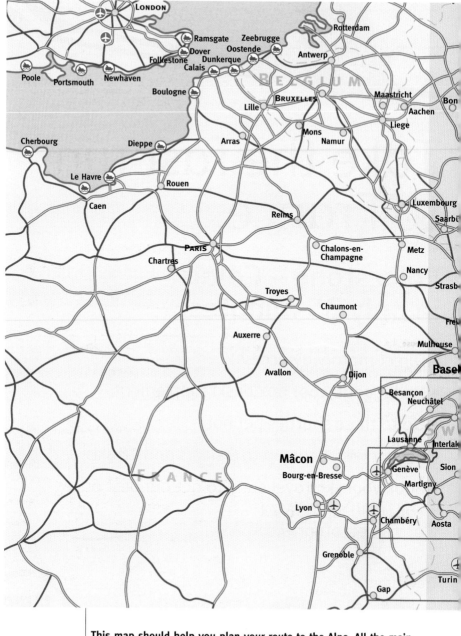

This map should help you plan your route to the Alps. All the main routes from the Channel and all the routes up into the mountains funnel through (or close to) three 'gateways', picked out on the map in larger type – Mâcon in France, Basel in Switzerland and Ulm in Germany.

Decide which gateway suits your destination, and pick a route to it from your planned arrival port at the Channel. Occasionally, using different Channel ports will lead you to use different gateways.

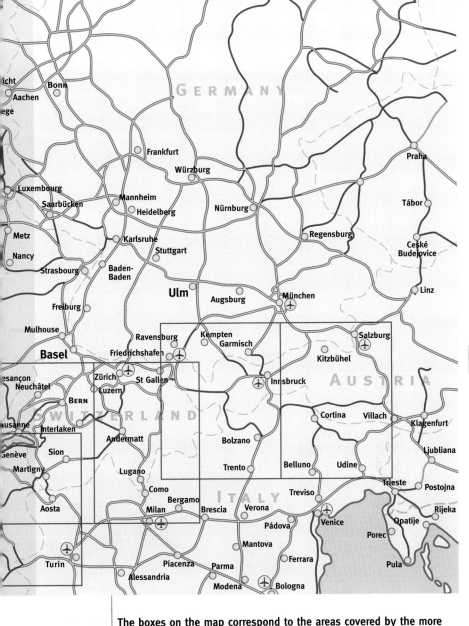

The boxes on the map correspond to the areas covered by the more detailed maps at the start of the sections of the book devoted to the four main Alpine countries:

Austria page 120
France page 240
Italy page 424
Switzerland page 486

AROUND THE ALPS IN SEVEN DAYS

The most rewarding although the least relaxing approach to exploring the Alps is to go touring, moving every day or two to a different resort and enjoying the complete freedom of going where you want, when you want. Out of high season there's no need to book accommodation before you go, so you can decide at the last minute where to go. A touring holiday doesn't mean you'll be spending more time on the road than on the piste – provided you plan your route carefully. An hour's drive after the lifts have shut is all it need take. It does eat into your après-ski time, of course.

The following chapter has some suggestions for a trip to France. Austria offers lots of possibilities. In the west, you could take in the best skiing the country has to offer, by combining the Arlberg resorts with Ischgl, and maybe Sölden. In the east, there are scores of resorts you could visit. Italy is far more suitable for tourers than day trippers, provided you're prepared to put up with some slow drives on winding passes. For example, you could start in Livigno, drive to Bormio and then to the Dolomites, visiting Madonna di Campiglio and Selva, and finish your Italian expedition in Cortina.

Eastern Switzerland also offers a very attractive touring holiday. You could start in Davos/Klosters, take in Lenzerheide and Arosa and end up in Flims. You could even include St Moritz.

There's no need to confine yourself to one country. You could imitate the famous Haute-Route by starting in Argentière in France and ending up in Switzerland's Saas-Fee, via Verbier and Zermatt.

The major thing that you have to watch out for with a touring holiday is the cost of accommodation. Checking into a resort hotel for a night or two doesn't come cheap, and can be a bit of a rip-off.

Drive to the French Alps

To make the most of them

by **Chris Gill** | **If you've read the preceding chapter, you'll have gathered that we are keen on driving to the Alps in general. But we're particularly keen on driving to the French Alps. The drive is a relatively short one, whereas many of the transfers to major French resorts from Geneva airport are relatively long. And the route from the Channel is through France rather than Germany, which for Francophiles like us means it's a pleasant prospect rather than a vaguely off-putting one.**

TRAVEL TIME

The French Alps are the number-one destination for British car-borne skiers. The journey time is surprisingly short, at least if you are starting from south-east England. From Calais, for example, you can comfortably cover the 900km/560 miles to Chamonix in about nine hours plus stops – with the exception of the final few miles, the whole journey is on motorways. And except on peak weekends the traffic is relatively light, if you steer clear of Paris.

With some exceptions in the southern Alps, all the resorts of the French Alps are within a day's driving range, provided you cross the Channel early in the day (or overnight). Weekend traffic jams used to make the journey from Albertville to the Tarentaise resorts (from the Three Valleys to Val d'Isère) a nightmare for drivers and coach passengers alike; thanks to road improvements for the 1992 Olympics these are nowhere near as serious as in the past, though the volume of traffic has built up over the last decade, and on peak-season Saturdays you can again encounter serious queues around Moûtiers. There are traffic lights placed well away from the town, to keep the queues and associated pollution away from Moûtier's tightly enclosed setting.

DAY TRIP BASES

As we explained in the previous chapter, a car opens up different kinds of holiday for the adventurous holidaymaker. Day tripping from a base resort, for example.

In the southern French Alps, Serre-Chevalier and Montgenèvre are ideal bases for day tripping. They are within easy reach of one another, and Montgenèvre is at one end of the Milky Way lift network, which includes Sauze d'Oulx and Sestriere in Italy – you can drive on to these resorts, or reach them by lift and piste. On the French side of the border, a few miles south, Puy-St-Vincent is an underrated resort that is well worth a visit for a day – as is Risoul, a little further south. The major resorts of Alpe-d'Huez and Les Deux-Alpes are also within range, as is the cult off-piste resort of La Grave. Getting to them involves crossing the high Col du Lautaret, but it's a major route and is kept open pretty reliably.

The Chamonix valley is an ideal destination for the dedicated day tripper. The Mont Blanc lift pass covers Chamonix, Les Contamines, Megève and others. Flaine and its satellites are fairly accessible – and so are Verbier in Switzerland, if the intervening passes are open, and Courmayeur in Italy, via the Mont Blanc tunnel. You could stay in a valley town such as Cluses, to escape resort prices – but Chamonix itself is not an expensive town.

Weekly news updates and resort links at **www.wtss.co.uk**

Pick the right gateway – Geneva, Chambéry or Grenoble – and you can hardly go wrong. Generally, there are no mountain passes involved. The exception is the approach to Serre-Chevalier and Montgenèvre, which involves the 2060m/6,760ft Col du Lauteret; the road is a major one and is ploughed frequently, but we have felt the need for chains here on one occasion. Crossing the French-Swiss border between Chamonix and Verbier involves two closure-prone passes – the Montets and the Forclaz. When necessary, one-way traffic runs beside the tracks through the rail tunnel beneath the passes.

7 night ski deals **from £92***per person

Escape to the slopes with sensational ski-drive deals to France, Austria or Switzerland and enjoy 7 days and nights of action and fun in the winter sun.

You can pick up some great deals and early booking offers on self-catering accommodation in some of Europe's very best ski resorts at **seafranceski.com**/snow

Terms & Conditions: Subject to availability - refer to online booking conditions. *Price based on four people and a car, includes return SeaFrance ferry travel with 7 nights self-catering accommodation. Travel from 3 January 2009.

seafranceski.com/snow

MOVING ON

A look at the map on page 88 shows that a different approach will pay dividends in the Tarentaise region of France. Practically all the resorts here – from Valmorel to Val d'Isère – are found at the end of long winding roads up from the main valley. You could visit them all from a base such as Aime, but it would be pretty hard work. If instead you stayed in a series of different resorts for a day or two each, moving on from one to the next in the early evening, you could have the trip of a lifetime. You might want to consider using the new Holiski lift pass offered by Compagnie des Alpes, described in our chapter on lift passes. This company owns the lift systems in practically all the big-name resorts of this area, with the conspicuous exceptions of Courchevel and Val Thorens.

GETTING THERE

There are three 'gateways' to the different regions of the French Alps. For the northern Alps – Chamonix valley, Portes du Soleil, Flaine and neighbours – you want to head for Geneva. If coming from Calais or another short-crossing port, you no longer have to tangle with the busy A6 from Paris via Beaune to Mâcon and Lyon. The relatively new A39 autoroute south from Dijon means you can head for Bourg-en-Bresse, well east of Mâcon.

For the central Alps – the mega-resorts of the Tarentaise, from Valmorel to Val d'Isère, and the Maurienne valley – you want to head for Chambéry. For the southern Alps – Alpe-d'Huez, Les Deux-Alpes, Serre-Chevalier – you want to head for Grenoble. And for either of these gateways first head for Mâcon and turn left at Lyon.

If you are taking a short Channel crossing, there are plenty of characterful towns for an overnight stop between the Channel and Dijon – Arras, St-Quentin, Laon, Troyes, Reims. All have plenty of choice of budget hotels, some of them in central locations where you can easily enjoy the facilities of the town, others on bleak estates on the outskirts.

From the more westerly Channel ports of Le Havre or Caen, your route to Geneva or Mâcon sounds dead simple: take the A13 to Paris then the A6 south. But you have to get through or around Paris in the process. The most direct way around the city is the notorious périphérique – a hectic, multi-lane urban motorway close to the centre, with exits every few hundred yards and traffic that is either worryingly fast-moving or jammed solid. If the périphérique is jammed, getting round it takes ages. The more reliable alternative is to take a series of motorways and dual carriageways through the south-west fringes of Greater Paris. The route is not well signed, so it's a great help to have a competent navigator.

Want to get other views?

Our website has an active forum, where readers swap experiences and views on resorts and other stuff. The WTSS editors join in, when they have time, so it's a good way to get their views.

Find out more at:

www.wtss.co.uk

Want to keep up to date?

Our website has weekly resort news throughout the year, and you can register for our monthly email newsletter – with special holiday offers, as well as resort news highlights.

Find out more at:

www.wtss.co.uk

Travelling by rail

Make tracks to the snow (green ones)

by **Wendy King** | **Whether you are wrestling with carbon footprints and soaring fuel prices, or simply want a change from overcrowded airports and congested roads, rail travel is worth considering. The options are broader than ever, and you can now get off to the flying start, as it were, offered by Eurostar services direct from London to France and Belgium.**

France is the obvious train destination, especially with journey times as low as 7.5 hours (on Eurostar direct). But don't overlook the many resorts in other countries, still accessible in a day despite several changes. We take a look at some of the special services and regular alternatives that provide the quickest routes to the Alps.

The starting point of most European rail trips is likely to be the Eurostar high-speed trains from the revamped London St Pancras station (www.eurostar.com).

DIRECT SERVICES TO THE FRENCH ALPS

There are Eurostar services direct to the Tarentaise region of the French Alps – to Moûtiers (for the Three Valleys), Aime (for La Plagne) and Bourg-St-Maurice (for Les Arcs, La Rosière, Ste-Foy, Tignes and Val d'Isère). Allow between 15 and 60 minutes for the onward bus transfers, depending on the resort.

There are overnight services that allow you eight days on the slopes, and daytime services that get you only the regular six days. There are no special sleeping arrangements on overnight services – you just doze (or not) in your seat. Overnight trains depart from London every Friday night, from 26 December until 18 April. These will get you into Bourg at 6.30am. Return services leave Bourg at 10.15pm on Saturdays. The daytime services run on Saturdays at 10.00am, getting you to Bourg by early evening. The first train out next season is on 20 December.

Standard adult returns cost from £179. For £269 you can get a Leisure Select ticket, which gets you a bigger seat pitch and meals. Seats can also be booked as part of a package holiday. There are usually discounts for the under-25s and over-60s, and you can even swap your Tesco Clubcard vouchers for the Eurostar equivalent.

INDIRECT SERVICES TO THE FRENCH ALPS

Rail Europe's Snow Train is an overnight service from Paris, timed to match Friday afternoon Eurostar arrivals – you simply change platforms at Paris Gare du Nord station. Like the overnight Eurostar service, it gets you eight days on the slopes. Unlike Eurostar, it provides couchettes (simple flat beds) to sleep on, with the traditional bar/disco carriage for those who would rather arrive knackered. Services begin 16 January 2009, until 3 April. Stops include Chambéry, Albertville, Moûtiers, Aime, Landry and Bourg-St-Maurice, giving access to more than 30 resorts in the region.

The train leaves Paris at 10.55pm, arriving in Bourg-St-Maurice at 8.30am. The return service departs early on Saturday evening, arriving in Paris on Sunday morning.

Adult fares start from £229 return in a six-berth couchette. Fares are normally released in July and you can save up to £30 if you book early.

There are also plenty of regular services to the mountains. The French rail network (SNCF) can get you to places such as Chambéry, Briançon or Grenoble for onward buses to more southerly resorts. Or you could, for example, take the overnight train from Paris Gare du Nord, arriving in St-Gervais and Chamonix next morning. Increased Eurostar services to Paris for 2008/09 should improve onward connections, but you could head for Lille instead, to avoid changing stations. SNCF has saver cards for young and older travellers – such as the Carte 12-25 that entitles you to 25% or 50% discount, depending on times/days and peak periods. They cost about 50 euros.

SERVICES TO AUSTRIA

In Austria, lots of resorts are on the rail network, but getting there requires several changes. Make an early start and you could be partying in St Anton 12 hours later if you travel via Paris and Zürich. Return tickets in 2007/08 started at £183, with Rail Europe. Services from Paris Est include nightly sleeper trains to Salzburg or Innsbruck, via Munich, arriving late morning. Lots of resorts are accessible from these two cities. Adult fares start at £265 return (from London). Check out the German rail centre (www.bahn.de/citynightline) for more details.

The Bergland Express is a special overnight sleeper service to Austria's Tirol region, stopping at several key resorts and towns, with onward connecting buses to many more. The catch is that it departs from Aachen in Germany, a short train ride from Brussels (served by Eurostar from London).

Run by the private company TTC (www.ttconline.nl), the service runs on Friday nights from 19 December to mid-March. Timetables are not yet set, but last season Bergland trains departed at 7.50pm, arriving in Austria at 8am next morning. Return journeys left Austria on Saturday evenings, arriving back Sunday morning.

Stops include: Innsbruck, Kitzbühel, St Johann in Tirol, Zell am See, Wörgl (for the SkiWelt) and Jenbach (local trains up to Mayrhofen/Zillertal). For other resorts, the company offers bus transfers – change at Schwarzach-St-Veit for Schladming and Bad Gastein, at Zell am See for Saalbach or Landeck for Ischgl. Expect to pay about £20 return.

Adult fares start at about £100 for a seat, £140 per person for a couchette and about £550 for a private sleeper compartment. Children aged 3 to 11 years old receive a discount of about £30 (one child per one adult).

SERVICES TO SWITZERLAND

New high-speed trains from Paris to Basel and Zürich have cut journey times to Switzerland. The time to Zermatt is an hour shorter than it used to be, for example. Typically

expect an overall travel time of 10-12 hours from London – with Basel, Zürich and Lausanne the three main hubs for onward journeys to the resorts.

Trains departing from Paris Est at midday for Basel or Zürich get you to many resorts by early evening. For Verbier, the train goes as far as Le Châble (with a change at Martigny), from where there is a bus (or gondola if you arrive early enough).

Return fares start at £120 for destinations via Lausanne and £165 for eastern Switzerland. It might be worth getting a Swiss Transfer ticket (from £67), which allows one return journey from the point of entry to any other station in the country, regardless of distance. You will need to buy it before you travel.

SERVICES TO ITALY

Most Italian resorts are hard work to reach, but there are exceptions. Five trains a day run from Paris to Turin and Milan, stopping at Bardonecchia (a ski resort, in case you'd forgotten) and Oulx. From Oulx, it is a 15-minute bus ride up to Sauze d'Oulx. Check out www.artesia.eu for more details.

PLANNING AND BOOKING

Unlike most air fares, rail fares are rarely subject to any hidden charges, such as baggage fees, weight excesses or extra taxes. But like air fares, the cheapest fares are often secured in advance. Rail Europe (www.raileurope.co.uk) can book most routes, up to 90 days in advance, though some local lines such as Martigny to Le Châble (for Verbier) and Bex up to Villars will have to be organised separately. Swiss Railways (www.sbb.ch/en) and its Austrian equivalent (www.oebb.at) are good sources for planning and booking journeys there. And www.seat61.com is a clear, user-friendly guide to the process.

ROUTES TO SOME ACCESSIBLE RESORTS

Resort	Route	Arrival	Fare from
Austria			
Innsbruck	Paris Est, Zürich	21:21	£207
St Anton	Paris Est, Zürich	20:10	£183
France			
Briançon*	Paris Nord	09:04	£119
Chamonix*	Paris Nord, St-Gervais	11:10	£152
Italy			
Bardonecchia	Paris Lyon	18:45	£102
Switzerland			
Andermatt	Paris Est, Basel, Göschenen	19:08	£165
Arosa	Paris Est, Zürich, Chur	20:09	£175
Grindelwald	Paris Est, Basel, Interlaken	18:39	£175
Klosters	Paris Est, Zürich, Landquart	19:25	£169
St Moritz	Paris Est, Basel, Chur	20:58	£200
Verbier	Paris Est, Lausanne, Martigny, Le Châble	20:15	£127
Villars	Paris Lyon, Lausanne, Bex	19:26	£121
Zermatt	Paris Est, Basel, Visp	19:52	£215

Evening arrivals assume you get a train from Paris departing around noon
* by overnight sleeper train

Get it right first time

Most people get to go skiing or boarding only once or twice a year, so choosing the right resort is crucially important. Chamonix, Châtel and Courchevel are all French resorts, but they are as similar as chalk and Camembert. Start to consider resorts in other countries – Alpbach in Austria, say, or Zermatt in Switzerland – and the differences become even more pronounced. For the benefit of readers with relatively narrow experience of different resorts, here is some advice on how to use our information to best effect.

Lots of factors need to be taken into account when making your choice. The weight you attach to each of them depends on your own personal preferences, and on the make-up of the group you are going on holiday with. Starting on page 103 you'll find 21 shortlists of resorts that we rate as outstanding in various key respects. And you can get your own shortlist built for you by going to our website at www.wtss.co.uk, and choosing the resort reviews page.

Minor resorts and regions not widely known in the UK are described in short chapters of two or three pages. Major resorts get more detail, and more pages. Each resort chapter is organised in the same way. This short introduction takes you through the structure and explains what you will find under each heading we use.

GETTING A FEEL FOR THE PLACE

We start each chapter with a two-line verdict, in which we aim to sum up the resort in a few words. If you like the sound of it, you might want to go next to our 'Costs' rating, in the margin. These ratings, ranging from ① ②③④⑤⑥ to ①②③④⑤⑥, reflect the total cost of a week's holiday from Britain, including a typical package of flights plus half-board accommodation, a lift pass and meals and drinks on the spot. Three coins means on the low side of average, four means on the high side. Then, in the 'Ratings' section, we rate each resort from 12 points of view – the more stars the better. (All these star ratings are brought together in one chart following this chapter, so that you can easily track down resorts that might suit you.) Still looking at the information in the margin, in most chapters we have a 'News' section; this is likely to be of most use and interest in resorts you already know from past visits.

For major resorts, the next things to look at are our lists of the main good and bad points about the resort and its slopes, picked out with ➕ and ➖. These lists are followed by a summary in **bold type**, in which we've aimed to weigh up the pros and cons, coming off the fence and giving our view of who might like the resort. These sections should give you a good idea of whether the resort is likely to suit *you*, and whether you should read our detailed analysis of it or move on to another resort.

You'll know by now, for example, whether this is a high, hideous, convenient, purpose-built resort with superb, snow-sure, challenging slopes but absolutely no nightlife; or a pretty, traditional village with gentle wooded slopes, ideal for beginners if only it had some decent snow.

THE RESORT

Resorts vary enormously in character and charm. At the extremes of the range are the handful of really hideous modern apartment-block resorts thrown up in France in the 1960s, and the captivating old traffic-free mountain villages of which Switzerland has an unfair number. But it isn't simply a question of old versus new. Some purpose-built places can have a much friendlier feel than some long-established resorts with big blocky buildings. Some places can be remarkably strung out, whereas others are surprisingly compact; our village plans are drawn to a standard scale, to help you gauge this.

The landscape can have an important impact – whether the resort is at the bottom of a shady valley or on a sunny shelf with panoramic views. Some places are working towns as well as ski resorts. Some are full of bars, discos and shops; others are peaceful backwaters. Traffic may choke the streets; or the village may be traffic-free.

In this first section of each chapter, we try to sort out the character of the place for you. Later, in the 'Staying there' section, we tell you more about the hotels, restaurants, bars and so on.

THE MOUNTAINS

The slopes Some mountains and lift networks are vast and complex, while others are much smaller and lacking variety.

Terrain parks We summarise here the specially prepared fun parks and other terrain features most resorts now arrange for freestylers.

Snow reliability This is a crucial factor for many people, and one that varies enormously. In some resorts you don't have to worry at all about a lack of snow, while others (including some very big names) are notorious for treating their paying guests to ice, mud and slush. Whether a resort is likely to have decent snow on its slopes normally depends on the height, the direction most of the slopes face (north good, south bad), its snow record and how much snowmaking it has. But bear in mind that in the Alps high resorts tend to have rocky terrain, where the runs will need more snow than those on the pasture land of lower resorts. Many resorts have increased their snowmaking capacity in recent years; in the 'Key facts' section we list the latest amount they claim to have, and comment on it in the snow reliability text.

For experts, intermediates, beginners Most (though not all) resorts have something to offer beginners, but relatively few will keep an expert happy for a week's holiday. As for intermediates, whether a resort will suit you really depends on your standard and inclinations. Places such as Cervinia and Obergurgl are ideal for those who want easy cruising runs, but have little to offer intermediates looking for more challenge. Others, such as Sölden and Val d'Isère, may intimidate the less confident intermediate who doesn't know the area well. Some areas linking several resorts, such as the Trois Vallées and Portes du Soleil, have vast amounts of terrain, so you can cover different ground each day. But some other well-known names, such as Alpbach and Courmayeur, and many North American resorts, have surprisingly small areas.

For cross-country We don't pretend that this is a guide for avid cross-country skiers. But we do try to help.

Queues Monster queues are largely a thing of the past, but it still pays to avoid the resorts with the worst queues, especially in high season. Crowding on the pistes is more of a worry in many resorts, and we mention problems of this kind under this heading. On our piste maps, we use a chair symbol to identify only fast chairs; travelling at two or three times the speed of old-fashioned chairs, these lifts offer short ride times, and shift queues quickly. Lifts not marked with a symbol are slow chairs or draglifts.

Mountain restaurants Here's a subject that divides people clearly into two opposing camps. To some, having a decent lunch in civilised surroundings – either in the sun, contemplating amazing scenery, or in a cosy hut, sheltered from the elements – makes or breaks their holiday. Others regard a prolonged midday stop as a waste of valuable skiing time, as well as valuable spending money. We are firmly in the former camp. We get very disheartened by places with miserable restaurants and miserable food (eg many resorts in America); and there are some resorts that we go to regularly partly because of the cosy huts and excellent cuisine (eg Zermatt).

Schools and guides This is an area where we rely heavily on readers' reports of their own or their friends' experiences.

Facilities for children We say what is available in each resort, including what child care is on offer from UK tour operators. But, again, to be of real help we need first-hand reports from people whose children have actually used the facilities.

STAYING THERE

How to go The basic choice is between catered chalets, hotels and self-catering accommodation. Some resorts have few hotels or few chalets. Note that we now have feature chapters on notably good hotels, as well as chalets and apartments.

Eating out The range of restaurants varies widely. Even some big resorts, such as Les Arcs, may have little choice because most of the visitors stay in their apartments. Most US resorts offer lots of choice.

Après-ski Tastes and styles vary enormously. Most resorts have pleasant places in which to have an immediate post-skiing beer or hot chocolate. Some then go dead. Others have noisy bars and discos until the early hours.

Off the slopes This is largely aimed at assessing how suitable a resort is for someone who doesn't intend to use the slopes, such as a non-skiing spouse.

Staying up the mountain/down the valley If there are interesting options for staying in isolation on the slopes above the resort village, or in valley towns below it, we pick them out in this section.

Resort ratings at a glance

AUSTRIA

	ALPBACH	BAD GASTEIN	BAD KLEIN-KIRCHHEIM	ELLMAU	HINTERTUX	HOCHKÖNIG	ISCHGL
Page	126	128	131	137	140	146	153
Fast lifts	**	**	**	**	***	**	*****
Snow	**	***	***	**	*****	***	****
Extent	*	****	**	****	***	***	****
Expert	*	***	**	*	***	**	***
Intermediate	**	****	***	****	***	****	****
Beginner	****	**	**	****	**	***	**
Convenience	**	**	***	***	**	**	**
Queues	***	***	****	****	***	****	****
Restaurants‡	***	****	***	**	**	***	****
Scenery	***	***	***	***	***	***	***
Resort charm	*****	***	**	***	***	***	***
Off-slope	***	****	***	**	*	***	***

	KITZBÜHEL	LECH	MAYRHOFEN	OBERGURGL	OBERTAUERN	SAALBACH-HINTERGLEMM	SCHLADMING
Page	160	167	176	184	189	191	198
Fast lifts	***	****	***	*****	*****	****	****
Snow	**	****	***	*****	****	**	****
Extent	***	****	***	**	**	***	***
Expert	***	****	**	**	***	**	**
Intermediate	****	****	***	***	****	****	****
Beginner	**	****	**	****	****	***	***
Convenience	**	***	*	****	****	****	***
Queues	**	****	*	*****	***	***	****
Restaurants‡	****	***	***	**	****	****	****
Scenery	***	***	***	***	***	***	***
Resort charm	****	****	***	****	**	****	***
Off-slope	*****	***	****	**	**	**	****

97

	SÖLDEN	SÖLL	ST ANTON	STUBAI VALLEY	WESTENDORF	WILD-SCHÖNAU	ZELL AM SEE
Page	202	205	212	223	225	227	231
Fast lifts	*****	**	***	***	**	**	***
Snow	*****	**	****	*****	**	**	**
Extent	***	****	****	***	****	*	**
Expert	***	*	*****	***	**	*	**
Intermediate	****	****	***	***	***	**	***
Beginner	**	***	*	**	***	***	***
Convenience	**	**	***	**	***	***	**
Queues	***	***	**	***	****	***	**
Restaurants‡	***	**	***	**	***	**	***
Scenery	***	***	***	****	***	***	***
Resort charm	**	***	****	****	****	***	***
Off-slope	**	**	**	***	**	**	****

Note: Andorra appears on the last page of the chapter ‡ Refers to mountain restaurants only

Resort ratings at a glance

Weekly news updates and resort links at www.wtss.co.uk

	ALPE-D'HUEZ	LES ARCS	AVORIAZ	CHAMONIX	CHATEL	LA CLUSAZ	LES CONTAMINES	COURCHEVEL
Page	245	255	264	268	278	283	285	287
Fast lifts	**	***	***	***	**	**	**	****
Snow	****	****	***	****	**	**	****	****
Extent	****	***	*****	***	*****	***	***	*****
Expert	****	*****	***	*****	***	***	***	****
Intermediate	****	****	****	**	****	****	*****	*****
Beginner	*****	****	****	**	***	****	**	****
Convenience	****	****	*****	*	**	***	**	****
Queues	****	***	***	**	***	***	***	****
Restaurants‡	****	***	****	**	***	****	****	****
Scenery	****	***	***	*****	****	***	****	***
Resort charm	*	*	**	****	***	****	***	**
Off-slope	****	*	*	*****	**	***	**	***

	LES DEUX-ALPES	FLAINE	LES GETS	LA GRAVE	MEGEVE	LES MENUIRES	MERIBEL	MONT-GENEVRE
Page	298	304	311	313	315	322	325	336
Fast lifts	**	**	**	***	**	***	****	**
Snow	****	****	**	***	**	****	***	****
Extent	***	****	***	*	*****	*****	*****	****
Expert	****	****	***	*****	**	****	****	**
Intermediate	**	*****	****	*	****	*****	*****	****
Beginner	***	*****	****	*	***	***	****	*****
Convenience	***	*****	***	***	**	*****	***	****
Queues	**	***	***	****	****	****	****	***
Restaurants‡	**	**	***	**	****	***	***	**
Scenery	****	****	***	****	*****	***	***	***
Resort charm	**	*	****	***	****	*	***	***
Off-slope	**	*	***	*	****	*	***	*

	MORZINE	LA PLAGNE	PUY-ST-VINCENT	RISOUL	LA ROSIERE	SAMOENS	SERRE-CHEVALIER	STE-FOY
Page	340	348	359	361	364	367	369	379
Fast lifts	**	**	***	*	**	**	**	**
Snow	**	****	***	***	***	***	***	***
Extent	*****	****	**	***	***	****	****	*
Expert	***	****	***	**	**	****	***	****
Intermediate	****	*****	***	****	***	*****	****	***
Beginner	***	****	***	****	*****	**	****	**
Convenience	**	*****	*****	****	***	*	***	***
Queues	***	***	***	****	***	****	***	*****
Restaurants‡	***	****	***	***	*	**	***	**
Scenery	***	***	****	***	***	****	***	***
Resort charm	***	*	**	**	***	****	***	***
Off-slope	***	*	*	*	*	***	***	*

	ST-MARTIN-DE-BELLEVILLE	LES SYBELLES	LA TANIA	TIGNES	VAL D'ISERE	VALMOREL	VAL THORENS	
Page	381	383	388	394	403	414	416	
Fast lifts	***	*	****	****	****	*	****	
Snow	***	***	***	*****	*****	**	*****	
Extent	*****	*****	*****	*****	*****	***	*****	
Expert	****	**	****	*****	*****	**	****	
Intermediate	*****	***	*****	*****	*****	****	*****	
Beginner	**	****	***	**	***	*****	****	
Convenience	***	***	****	****	***	*****	*****	
Queues	****	****	****	****	****	***	***	
Restaurants‡	****	**	****	***	***	**	****	
Scenery	***	***	***	***	***	***	***	
Resort charm	****	*/****	***	**	***	****	**	
Off-slope	*	**	*	*	**	**	**	

	BORMIO	CERVINIA	CORTINA D'AMPEZZO	COURMAYEUR	LIVIGNO	MADONNA DI CAMPIGLIO	MONTEROSA SKI	PASSO TONALE
Page	428	430	436	441	446	450	452	456
Fast lifts	***	****	**	***	****	****	***	****
Snow	***	*****	***	****	****	***	****	****
Extent	**	***	***	**	**	***	***	**
Expert	*	*	**	***	**	**	****	*
Intermediate	***	****	***	****	***	****	****	***
Beginner	**	*****	*****	**	****	****	**	*****
Convenience	***	***	*	*	**	***	***	***
Queues	***	***	****	***	****	****	****	****
Restaurants‡	****	***	****	****	***	***	**	**
Scenery	***	****	*****	****	***	****	****	***
Resort charm	****	**	****	****	***	***	***	*
Off-slope	****	*	*****	***	**	***	*	*

	SAUZE D'OULX	SELLA RONDA	SELVA	SESTRIERE	LA THUILE
Page	458	463	470	477	479
Fast lifts	***	***	***	***	**
Snow	**	****	****	****	****
Extent	****	*****	*****	****	***
Expert	**	**	**	***	**
Intermediate	****	*****	*****	****	****
Beginner	**	****	***	***	****
Convenience	**	***	***	***	***
Queues	***	***	***	***	****
Restaurants‡	***	****	****	**	*
Scenery	***	*****	*****	***	***
Resort charm	**	***	***	*	***
Off-slope	*	***	***	*	**

‡ Refers to mountain restaurants only

Resort ratings at a glance

99

Interactive resort shortlist builder at www.wtss.co.uk

SWITZERLAND

Resort ratings at a glance

Weekly news updates and resort links at www.wtss.co.uk

	ADELBODEN	ANDERMATT	ANZERE	AROSA	CHAMPERY	CRANS-MONTANA	DAVOS
Page	493	495	497	498	500	502	504
Fast lifts	***	**	**	***	**	***	***
Snow	***	****	**	***	**	**	****
Extent	***	*	*	**	*****	***	*****
Expert	**	****	**	**	***	**	****
Intermediate	***	**	***	***	****	****	*****
Beginner	****	*	***	****	**	***	**
Convenience	**	***	***	**	*	**	**
Queues	***	**	****	****	****	***	***
Restaurants‡	***	*	***	***	***	***	***
Scenery	****	***	****	***	****	****	****
Resort charm	****	****	***	**	****	**	**
Off-slope	****	**	***	****	***	****	*****

	ENGELBERG	GRINDEL-WALD	KLOSTERS	LAAX	MÜRREN	SAAS-FEE
Page	511	513	517	519	521	525
Fast lifts	***	****	***	****	****	****
Snow	***	**	****	***	***	*****
Extent	**	***	*****	****	*	**
Expert	****	**	****	***	***	**
Intermediate	***	****	*****	*****	***	****
Beginner	***	***	***	****	**	*****
Convenience	*	**	**	***	***	***
Queues	**	**	**	****	***	***
Restaurants‡	***	***	***	****	**	**
Scenery	****	*****	****	***	*****	****
Resort charm	**	****	****	***	*****	*****
Off-slope	****	****	****	***	***	****

	ST MORITZ	VAL D'ANNIVIERS	VERBIER	VILLARS	WENGEN	ZERMATT
Page	530	537	541	553	555	560
Fast lifts	****	**	**	***	****	*****
Snow	****	****	***	**	**	****
Extent	*****	**	*****	***	***	****
Expert	****	****	*****	**	**	*****
Intermediate	****	***	***	***	****	****
Beginner	**	***	**	****	***	*
Convenience	*	**	**	**	***	*
Queues	**	****	***	***	***	***
Restaurants‡	****	**	***	***	****	*****
Scenery	****	****	****	***	*****	*****
Resort charm	*	*****	***	****	*****	*****
Off-slope	*****	*	***	****	****	****

	CALIFORNIA			COLORADO				
	HEAVENLY	MAMMOTH	SQUAW VALLEY	ASPEN	BEAVER CREEK	BRECKEN-RIDGE	COPPER MOUNTAIN	KEYSTONE
Page	575	580	585	588	595	597	602	604
Fast lifts	***	****	***	***	*****	****	**	****
Snow	****	****	****	*****	*****	*****	*****	*****
Extent	***	***	***	****	**	**	**	**
Expert	***	****	****	*****	****	****	****	***
Intermediate	****	****	**	*****	****	****	****	****
Beginner	****	****	****	*****	*****	****	****	****
Convenience	*	**	****	**	****	***	****	**
Queues	****	****	****	****	*****	****	****	****
Restaurants‡	*	*	*	***	**	**	*	***
Scenery	****	***	***	***	***	***	***	***
Resort charm	*	**	***	****	**	***	**	**
Off-slope	**	*	*	****	***	***	*	**

						UTAH		
	SNOWMASS	STEAMBOAT	TELLURIDE	VAIL	WINTER PARK	ALTA	THE CANYONS	
Page	606	608	611	613	620	625	627	
Fast lifts	***	***	*****	*****	***	***	***	
Snow	*****	****	****	*****	*****	*****	****	
Extent	****	***	**	****	***	***	***	
Expert	*****	***	****	****	****	*****	****	
Intermediate	*****	****	***	*****	****	***	****	
Beginner	*****	*****	*****	***	*****	***	**	
Convenience	****	***	****	***	***	****	****	
Queues	****	****	*****	**	****	***	****	
Restaurants‡	***	***	*	**	***	**	***	
Scenery	****	***	****	***	***	***	***	
Resort charm	**	**	****	***	**	**	**	
Off-slope	***	**	**	***	*	*	**	

				REST OF THE WEST		NEW ENGLAND		
	DEER VALLEY	PARK CITY	SNOWBIRD	BIG SKY	JACKSON HOLE	KILLINGTON	STOWE	
Page	629	631	636	639	644	650	654	
Fast lifts	****	****	***	***	***	**	***	
Snow	****	****	*****	*****	****	***	***	
Extent	**	***	***	****	***	**	*	
Expert	***	****	*****	****	*****	***	***	
Intermediate	****	****	***	****	**	***	****	
Beginner	****	****	**	*****	***	****	****	
Convenience	****	**	*****	****	***	*	*	
Queues	****	****	***	*****	***	****	****	
Restaurants‡	****	**	*	*	*	*	**	
Scenery	***	***	***	***	***	***	***	
Resort charm	***	***	*	*	***	*	****	
Off-slope	**	***	*	**	***	*	*	

‡ Refers to mountain restaurants only

Resort ratings at a glance

101

Interactive resort shortlist builder at **www.wtss.co.uk**

Resort ratings at a glance

Weekly news updates and resort links at www.wtss.co.uk

	WESTERN CANADA BANFF	BIG WHITE	FERNIE	KICKING HORSE	LAKE LOUISE			
Page	659	666	669	674	676			
Fast lifts	****	***	**	**	***			
Snow	****	*****	*****	****	***			
Extent	****	***	***	***	****			
Expert	****	***	*****	****	****			
Intermediate	****	****	**	***	****			
Beginner	***	****	****	***	***			
Convenience	*	****	****	****	*			
Queues	****	*****	****	*****	****			
Restaurants‡	***	*	*	**	**			
Scenery	****	***	***	***	*****			
Resort charm	***	**	**	**	***			
Off-slope	*****	**	**	*	****			

	PANORAMA	SILVER STAR	SUN PEAKS	WHISTLER	EASTERN CANADA TREMBLANT			
Page	681	683	685	688	698			
Fast lifts	***	***	***	****	****			
Snow	***	****	****	****	****			
Extent	**	***	***	****	*			
Expert	****	****	***	*****	**			
Intermediate	***	***	****	*****	***			
Beginner	****	****	****	***	****			
Convenience	****	*****	****	****	****			
Queues	*****	*****	*****	**	***			
Restaurants‡	*	*	*	**	**			
Scenery	***	***	***	***	***			
Resort charm	**	***	***	***	****			
Off-slope	*	**	**	**	***			

	ANDORRA ARINSAL	PAS DE LA CASA	SOLDEU	SPAIN BAQUEIRA	NORWAY HEMSEDAL	SWEDEN ÅRE	BULGARIA BANSKO	NEW ZEALAND QUEENSTOWN
Page	111	113	115	701	707	710	713	725
Fast lifts	**	***	***	**	**	**	*****	**
Snow	****	****	****	***	****	***	***	**
Extent	*	***	***	**	*	**	*	*
Expert	*	*	*	***	**	**	**	***
Intermediate	**	***	***	****	****	****	****	***
Beginner	***	****	****	**	***	****	***	***
Convenience	***	****	***	***	**	***	**	*
Queues	***	***	***	****	****	****	***	***
Restaurants‡	*	**	**	**	*	***	***	*
Scenery	***	***	***	***	**	***	***	****
Resort charm	*	*	*	**	**	***	**	**
Off-slope	*	*	*	*	*	***	*	*****

‡ Refers to mountain restaurants only

Resort shortlists

To help you spot resorts that will suit you

To streamline the job of spotting the ideal resort for your own holiday, here are lists of the best ten or so resorts for 21 different categories. Some lists embrace European and North American resorts, but many we've confined to Europe, because the US has too many qualifying resorts (eg for beginners) or because the US does things differently, making comparisons invalid (eg for off-piste).

SOMETHING FOR EVERYONE
Resorts with everything from reassuring nursery slopes to real challenges for experts
Alpe-d'Huez, France 245
Les Arcs, France 255
Aspen, Colorado 588
Courchevel, France 287
Flaine, France 304
Mammoth, California 580
Vail, Colorado 613
Val d'Isère, France 403
Whistler, Canada 688
Winter Park, Colorado 620

INTERNATIONAL OVERSIGHTS
Resorts that deserve as much attention as the ones we go back to every year, but don't get it
Alta, Utah 625
Andermatt, Switzerland 495
Bad Gastein, Austria 128
Big Sky, Montana 639
Les Contamines, France 285
Copper Mountain, Colorado 602
Laax, Switzerland 519
Monterosa Ski, Italy 452
Risoul, France 361
Telluride, Colorado 611
Val d'Anniviers, Switzerland 537

HIGH-MILEAGE PISTE-BASHING
Extensive intermediate slopes with big lift networks
Alpe-d'Huez, France 245
Davos/Klosters, Switz 504/517
Laax, Switzerland 519
Milky Way: Sauze d'Oulx (Italy),
   Montgenèvre (France) 458/336
Paradiski, France 346
Portes du Soleil, France/Switz 358
Sella Ronda, Italy 463
Selva, Italy 470
SkiWelt/Kitzbühel, Austria
   137/160/205/225
Les Sybelles, France 383
Three Valleys, France 392
Val d'Isère/Tignes, France 403/394
Whistler, Canada 688

RELIABLE SNOW IN THE ALPS
Alpine resorts with good snow records or lots of snowmaking, and high or north-facing slopes
Bregenzerwald, Austria 134
Chamonix, France 268
Cervinia, Italy 430
Courchevel, France 287
Hintertux, Austria 140
Lech/Zürs, Austria 167
Obergurgl, Austria 184
Obertauern, Austria 189
Saas-Fee, Switzerland 525
Val d'Isère/Tignes, France 403/394
Val Thorens, France 416
Zermatt, Switzerland 560

OFF-PISTE WONDERS
Alpine resorts where, with the right guidance and equipment, you can have the time of your life
Alpe-d'Huez, France 245
Andermatt, Switzerland 495
Chamonix, France 268
Davos/Klosters, Switz 504/517
La Grave, France 313
Lech/Zürs, Austria 167
Monterosa Ski, Italy 452
St Anton, Austria 212
Val d'Isère/Tignes, France 403/394
Verbier, Switzerland 541

DRAMATIC SCENERY
Resorts where the mountains are not just high and snowy, but spectacularly scenic too
Chamonix, France 268
Cortina, Italy 436
Courmayeur, Italy 441
Heavenly, California 575
Jungfrau resorts
   (Grindelwald, Mürren, Wengen),
   Switzerland 513/521/555
Lake Louise, Canada 676
Megève, France 315
Saas-Fee, Switzerland 525
St Moritz, Switzerland 530
Selva, Italy 470
Zermatt, Switzerland 560

↑ The mountains of Chamonix, seen here from Les Houches, are among Europe's most dramatic, as well as Europe's highest.
SNOWPIX.COM / CHRIS GILL

BLACK RUNS
Resorts with steep, mogully, lift-served slopes within the safety of the piste network
Alta/Snowbird, Utah 625/636
Andermatt, Switzerland 495
Argentière/Chamonix, France 268
Aspen, Colorado 588
Beaver Creek, Colorado 595
Courchevel, France 287
Jackson Hole, Wyoming 644
Whistler, Canada 688
Winter Park, Colorado 620
Zermatt, Switzerland 560

MOTORWAY CRUISING
Long, gentle, super-smooth pistes to bolster the frail confidence of those just off the nursery slope
Les Arcs, France 255
Breckenridge, Colorado 597
Cervinia, Italy 430
Cortina, Italy 436
Courchevel, France 287
Megève, France 315
La Plagne, France 348
Snowmass, Colorado 606
La Thuile, Italy 479
Vail, Colorado 613

WEATHERPROOF SLOPES
Alpine resorts with snow-sure slopes if the sun shines, and trees in case it doesn't
Les Arcs, France 255
Courchevel, France 287
Courmayeur, Italy 441
Laax, Switzerland 519
Schladming, Austria 198
Selva, Italy 470
Serre-Chevalier, France 369
Sestriere, Italy 477
La Thuile, Italy 479

SPECIALLY FOR FAMILIES
Alpine resorts where you can easily find accommodation surrounded by snow, not by traffic and fumes
Les Arcs, France 255
Avoriaz, France 264
Flaine, France 304
Lech, Austria 167
Montchavin (La Plagne), France 348
Mürren, Switzerland 521
Puy-St-Vincent, France 359
Risoul, France 361
Saas-Fee, Switzerland 525
Les Sybelles, France 383
Valmorel, France 414
Wengen, Switzerland 555

TOP TERRAIN PARKS
Resorts with the best parks, pipes and rails for freestyle thrills
Avoriaz, France 264
Les Deux-Alpes, France 298
Laax, Switzerland 519
Lech, Austria 167
Livigno, Italy 446
Mammoth, California 580
Mayrhofen, Austria 176
Park City, Utah 631
Vail, Colorado 613
Whistler, Canada 688

CHOPAHOLICS
Resorts where you can quit the lift network and have a day riding helicopters or cats
Aspen, Colorado 588
Courmayeur, Italy 441
Fernie, Canada 669
Lech/Zürs, Austria 167
Monterosa Ski, Italy 452
Panorama, Canada 681
La Thuile, Italy 479
Verbier, Switzerland 541
Whistler, Canada 688
Zermatt, Switzerland 560

POWDER PARADISES
Resorts with the snow, the terrain and (ideally) the lack of crowds that make for powder perfection
Alta/Snowbird, Utah 625/636
Andermatt, Switzerland 495
Big Sky, Montana 639
Big White, Canada 666
Fernie, Canada 669
La Grave, France 313
Jackson Hole, Wyoming 644
Kicking Horse, Canada 674
Monterosa Ski, Italy 452
Ste-Foy, France 379

peak retreats

Beat the crowds
Traditional resorts

0844 576 0173
peakretreats.co.uk
ABTA W5537

RESORTS FOR BEGINNERS
European resorts with gentle, snow-sure nursery slopes and easy, longer runs to progress to
Alpe-d'Huez, France 245
Les Arcs, France 255
Bansko, Bulgaria 713
Cervinia, Italy 430
Courchevel, France 287
Flaine, France 304
Montgenèvre, France 336
La Plagne, France 348
Saas-Fee, Switzerland 525
Soldeu, Andorra 115

BACK-DOOR RESORTS
Cute little Alpine villages linked to big, bold ski areas, giving you the best of two different worlds
Les Brévières (Tignes), France 394
Champagny (La Plagne), France 348
Leogang (Saalbach), Austria 191
Montchavin (La Plagne), France 348
Peisey (Les Arcs), France 255
Le Pré (Les Arcs), France 255
Samoëns (Flaine), France 304
St-Martin (Three Valleys), France 381
Stuben (St Anton), Austria 212
Vaujany (Alpe-d'Huez), France 245

SNOW-SURE BUT SIMPATICO
Alpine resorts with high-rise slopes, but low-rise, traditional-style buildings
Andermatt, Switzerland 495
Arabba, Italy 464
Argentière, France 276
Les Contamines, France 285
Ischgl, Austria 153
Lech/Zürs, Austria 167
Monterosa Ski, Italy 452
Obergurgl, Austria 184
Saas-Fee, Switzerland 525
Val d'Anniviers, Switzerland 537
Zermatt, Switzerland 560

SPECIAL MOUNTAIN RESTAURANTS
Alpine resorts where mountain restaurants can really add an extra dimension to your holiday
Alpe-d'Huez, France 245
La Clusaz, France 283
Courmayeur, Italy 441
Kitzbühel, Austria 160
Megève, France 315
St Moritz, Switzerland 530
Selva, Italy 470
Söll, Austria 205
Zermatt, Switzerland 560

VILLAGE CHARM
Resorts with traditional character that enriches your holiday – from mountain villages to mining towns
Alpbach, Austria 126
Champéry, Switzerland 500
Courmayeur, Italy 441
Lech, Austria 167
Mürren, Switzerland 521
Saas-Fee, Switzerland 525
Telluride, Colorado 611
Wengen, Switzerland 555
Zermatt, Switzerland 560

MODERN CONVENIENCE
Alpine resorts where there's plenty of slope-side accommodation where you can ski from the door
Les Arcs, France 255
Avoriaz, France 264
Courchevel, France 287
Flaine, France 304
Les Menuires, France 322
Obertauern, Austria 189
La Plagne, France 348
Puy-St-Vincent, France 359
La Tania, France 388
Tignes, France 394
Valmorel, France 414
Val Thorens, France 416

LIVELY NIGHTLIFE
European resorts where you'll have no difficulty finding somewhere to boogie, and someone to do it with
Chamonix, France 268
Ischgl, Austria 153
Kitzbühel, Austria 160
Pas de la Casa, Andorra 113
Saalbach, Austria 191
St Anton, Austria 212
Sauze d'Oulx, Italy 458
Sölden, Austria 202
Val d'Isère, France 403
Verbier, Switzerland 541

OTHER AMUSEMENTS
Alpine resorts where those not interested in skiing or boarding can still find plenty to do
Bad Gastein, Austria 128
Chamonix, France 268
Cortina, Italy 436
Davos, Switzerland 504
Innsbruck, Austria 149
Kitzbühel, Austria 160
Megève, France 315
St Moritz, Switzerland 530
Zell am See, Austria 231

Resort shortlists

105

Interactive resort shortlist builder at **www.wtss.co.uk**

How to get the best out of them

FINDING A RESORT

The bulk of the book consists of the chapters listed on the facing page, devoted to individual major resorts, plus minor resorts that share the same lift system. Sometimes we devote a chapter to an area not dominated by one resort, in which case we use the area name (eg Les Sybelles, Monterosa).

Chapters are grouped by country: first, the five major European countries; then the US and Canada (where resorts are grouped by states or regions); then minor European countries; then Japan, and lastly countries in the southern hemisphere. Within each group, resorts are ordered alphabetically.

Short cuts to the resorts that might suit you are provided (on the pages preceding this one) by a table of comparative **star ratings** and a series of **shortlists** of resorts with particular merits.

At the back of the book is an **index** to the resort chapters, combined with a **directory** giving basic information on hundreds of other minor resorts. If the resort you are looking up is covered in a chapter devoted to a bigger resort, the page reference will take you to the start of that chapter, not to the exact page on which the minor resort is described.

There's further guidance on using our information in the chapter on 'Choosing your resort', on page 94 – designed to be helpful particularly to people with little or no experience of resorts, who may not appreciate how big the differences between one resort and another can be (ie like chalk and cheese).

READING A CHAPTER

The **cost** of visiting each resort is rated on a scale of one to six – ①②③④⑤⑥ to ①②③④⑤⑥ – reflecting the typical cost of a one-week trip based on a half-board package from the UK, plus a lift pass and an allowance for lunch on the mountain. We assume two people sharing a room – even in the US, where package prices may be based on four people sharing.

Star ratings summarise our view of the resort, including its suitability for different standards of skier/boarder. The more stars, the better.

We give phone numbers and internet addresses of the **tourist office** (in North America, the ski lift company) and phone numbers for recommended **hotels**. We give star ratings for hotels – either official ones or ones awarded by major tour operators. The UK tour operators offering **package holidays** in major resorts are listed in the chapter margins. For minor resorts they are listed in the directory at the back of the book.

Our **mountain maps** show the resorts' own classification of runs. On some maps we show black diamonds to mark expert terrain without defined runs. We do not distinguish single-diamond terrain from the steeper double-diamond.

We include on the map any lifts definitely planned for construction for the coming season.

We use the following symbols to identify **fast lifts**:

 fast chairlift

 gondola

 chondola – chair/gondola

 cable car

 railway/funicular

THE WORLD'S BEST WINTER SPORTS RESORTS

To find a minor resort, or if you are not sure which country you should be looking under, consult the index/directory at the back of the book, which lists all resorts alphabetically.

Our resort chapters

107

Interactive resort shortlist builder at www.wtss.co.uk

Andorra is the fourth most popular winter sports destination for Brits, attracting some 80,000 package holidaymakers – well ahead of both Switzerland and North America. With all these people basically travelling to two ski areas – Grandvalira (see the chapters on Soldeu and Pas de la Casa) and Vallnord (see the chapter on Arinsal and the description of Arcalis overleaf), it's difficult to get away from fellow Brits. It's also difficult to escape from heavy traffic and building sites.

Andorra used to be seen primarily as a cheap and cheerful holiday destination, aimed mainly at younger singles and couples looking for a good time in the duty-free bars and clubs as well as learning to ski or snowboard. But things have changed. In recent years, some more upmarket hotels have been built (though they often resemble Spanish summer package hotels, with self-service buffet meals). And lots of money has been pumped in to developing powerful lift systems and piste-grooming fleets that many well-known Alpine resorts would be proud of; this makes the slopes much more attractive to intermediates as well as beginners. Reporters tell us the cost of drinks as well as packages has edged up, and even Arinsal now seems to attract more families than youths. Andorra no longer competes with eastern Europe for the budget market; it costs more, and delivers much more.

One thing remains unchanged, happily: the ski schools have always been excellent, with lots of native English-speaking instructors, and standards in this key part of the Andorran recipe are holding up.

Despite a couple of poor seasons recently, Andorra has a relatively reliable snow record. Its situation close to both the Atlantic Ocean and the Mediterranean Sea, together with the high altitude of its resorts, mean that it usually gets substantial natural snowfalls. It has also invested heavily in snowmaking.

Package holiday prices and the cost of drinks, instruction and equipment rental are generally lower than in the Alps. Beer is reportedly no cheaper than in the UK, but large servings of spirits mean that nightlife can be lively. Some reporters find duty-free luxury goods prices not the super-bargains they had expected.

The sight of cranes – as hotels and apartments are built to keep up with demand – is still common. It is no longer true to say that the resorts resemble giant construction sites, but they all still have construction sites within them (or on the edge of them, as they expand in sprawling fashion along the roadside).

GRANDVALIRA
← Andorra is trying hard to move upmarket. Some plusher hotels have been built and it has pumped money into more fast lifts, piste grooming and snowmaking

STAYING DOWN THE VALLEY

Several valley towns can be used as alternative bases to the main resorts. **Encamp** has a powerful 18-seat gondola giving a quick way into the **Grandvalira** ski area shared by Soldeu and Pas de la Casa. It is cheap but plagued by its situation on the traffic-choked main road. **La Massana** is a more appealing town, and is linked by gondola to the Pal-Arinsal ski area. It is also more convenient for Arcalis than Arinsal or Pal (Arcalis, Pal and Arinsal are all covered by a joint **Vallnord** area lift pass). **Ordino** is slightly nearer still to Arcalis, and pleasantly rustic, but it has no direct access to slopes.

The capital, **Andorra la Vella**, is not far down the valley from Encamp and also choked by traffic and 'appalling' fumes. There are plenty of high-quality hotels and restaurants, plus bars and nightclubs and duty-free shopping. The clientele is mainly Andorran and Spanish. At Escaldes-Engordany, just outside the centre, the splendid Caldea spa has indoor and outdoor pools, fountains and waterfalls, saunas, hot tubs, Turkish baths, sunbeds, hydrotherapy, massage ... even a grapefruit bath!

OUTINGS TO ARCALIS

Arcalis is the most remote area of slopes in Andorra, tucked away at the head of a long valley, and most British visitors to Soldeu or Pas de la Casa never hear about it. But it makes a very worthwhile day trip, particularly from Arinsal and Pal. The variety of the terrain at Arcalis is greater than in most of the main resorts, the slopes are usually deserted except at weekends (when locals pour in), and the snow is usually the best you will find. It provides excellent intermediate and beginner terrain, but of all Andorra's resorts it has the most to offer experts, including lots of off-piste between the marked runs. 'A real jewel – the boarder in our group (who has visited a few Alpine resorts) was in heaven,' said a recent reporter.

There is no accommodation at the mountain, just a day lodge and a lot of car parking. Buses are not frequent.

Cheap, lively base that suits beginners best; La Massana is better if you also want to explore Arcalis (covered by the Vallnord lift pass)

COSTS

① ② ③ ④ ⑤ ⑥

RATINGS

The slopes
Fast lifts	**
Snow	****
Extent	*
Expert	*
Intermediate	**
Beginner	***
Convenience	***
Queues	***
Mountain restaurants	*

The rest
Scenery	***
Resort charm	*
Off-slope	*

NEWS

For 2007/08 a six-pack replaced the old Cubil quad at Pal, and in Arinsal the children's snow park was themed and the nursery revamped.

For 2008/09 in Arinsal, there are plans to install snow-guns on the blue Marrades piste from Comallempla back to Cota in the valley to keep it open more often. The double chair from Cota is due to be replaced by a new six-pack. More snowmaking is planned, and the aim is to have 100% snowmaking within the next few seasons.

UK PACKAGES

Airtours, Ardmore, Crystal, Directski.com, First Choice, Inghams, Neilson, Ski McNeill, Ski Wild, Skitracer, Thomson

+ Lively bars
+ Ski school geared to British needs
+ Cable car link with Pal and shared Vallnord lift pass with Arcalis (see the Andorra introduction)
+ Pretty, treelined slopes in Pal

− Very confined, bleak local slopes
− Run to village doesn't go to centre (and needs the planned snowmaking)
− Long, dour village with no focus
− Poor bus link to Arcalis

Arinsal is the most British-dominated resort in Andorra, largely because British tour operators are able to offer packages here at tempting prices. The resort attracts mainly first-time skiers and riders; reports suggest that Arinsal, like the rest of Andorra, is managing to attract more families and fewer binge drinkers.

THE RESORT

Arinsal is a long, narrow village of grey, stone-clad buildings, near the head of a steep-sided valley north of Andorra la Vella. Development in recent years has been rapid.

The gondola from the village centre is the main way to and from the slopes, and staying close to it is convenient; the alternative chairlift, 1km/0.5 miles out of town, has been largely irrelevant – though both it and the run under it are being improved (see 'News'). Or you can drive to the top of the gondola.

There is some accommodation at Pal (a bus ride from the lift base) and in the lower town of La Massana (with a gondola up to Pal's slopes). La Massana is a better place to stay if you want to visit Arcalis – it's closer and has a better bus service (from Arinsal you have to change in La Massana to reach Arcalis, though some tour ops lay on weekly excursions). Buses between Arinsal and La Massana are infrequent (and 'unreliable', says a recent reporter).

Reporters have commented on the friendliness of the locals – 'We were made to feel very welcome.'

THE MOUNTAINS

The area above Arinsal is an open, east-facing bowl. Pal, in contrast, has the most densely wooded slopes in Andorra. Most face east; those down to the link with Arinsal face north.

Slopes Arinsal's slopes consist essentially of a single, long, narrow, bowl above the upper gondola station at Comallempla, served by a network of chairs and drags, including a quad and a six-pack. Almost at the top is the cable car link to and from Pal. Pal's slopes are widely spread around the mountain, with four main lift bases, all reachable by road. The main one, La Caubella, at the opposite extreme from the Arinsal link, is the arrival point of the gondola from La Massana. The Vallnord lift pass covers Arcalis too – see the Andorra introduction. Reporters remark on the good grooming and signposting.

Terrain parks Arinsal's big freestyle area has its own lift, a huge half-pipe, a big jump, a terrain park with rails and jumps, a boardercross and a chill-out area. There is a Junior Rails Zone for beginners. Pal also has a beginners' park.

Snow reliability With most runs above 1950m/6,400ft, the north-easterly orientation and a decent amount of snowmaking, snow is relatively assured. There are plans to have 100% snowmaking on the slopes within the next few seasons.

Experts This isn't a great area for experts, but there are off-piste freeride areas marked on the map in both Arinsal and Pal – the latter offering some great tree skiing. Arcalis has more to offer.

Intermediates Arinsal offers a fair range of difficulty, but decent intermediates will want to explore the much more interesting, varied and extensive Pal and Arcalis slopes.

Beginners Around half the guests here are beginners. Arinsal and Pal both have gentle nursery slopes set apart from the main runs, but they can get very crowded at peak times. There are long easy runs to progress to, as well.

111

How to go There is a wide choice of hotel and self-catering packages.

Hotels Rooms in the hotel Arinsal (835640) are not large, but it is well run, ideally placed and has a pleasant bar. The Princesa Parc (736500) is a big, glossy 4-star place close to the gondola, with a swanky spa and a bowling alley – 'good quality food; helpful, polite staff; room was palatial'. The big 4-star St Gothard (836005) is popular, except for its position a long way down the hill from the gondola. The Xalet Verdú (737140) is a smooth little 3-star. The Micolau (835052) is a characterful stone house that is close to the centre and has simple rooms and a jolly, beamed restaurant. The valley run leads to the 3-star Crest (835866).

Self-catering There is a reasonable choice of places.

Eating out The Surf disco-pub and the Rocky Mountain do good steaks. El Cisco is a Tex-Mex place in a lovely wood and stone building. El Rusc and Micolau do good food.

Après-ski Arinsal has plenty of lively bars and discos, such as Quo Vadis ('always has the football on'), El Cau, Surf, Rocky Mountain and El Cisco. El Derby is heaving on karaoke night. If, like us, you prefer something quieter, head for the bar of the hotel Arinsal.

Off the slopes There are helicopter rides, dog sledding, snowmobiling and snowshoeing, but a recent reporter felt that family entertainment was limited in the evenings. Andorra la Vella is half an hour away by infrequent bus or inexpensive taxi.

↑ Pal's slopes are widely spread and nicely wooded

VALLNORD

KEY FACTS

Resort	1470m
	4,820ft
Slopes	1550-2560m
	5,090-8,400ft
Lifts	30
Pistes	63km
	39 miles
Green	12%
Blue	38%
Red	38%
Black	12%
Snowmaking	
	271 guns

Phone numbers
From abroad use the prefix +376

TOURIST OFFICES

Arinsal and Pal
t 737020
info@vallnordturisme.com
www.vallnord.com

Snowboarding It's a good place to learn. But over half the lifts are drags, and some of them are vicious. There are some tedious flat sections in Pal.

Cross-country There isn't any.

Queues At peak times queues can build up at Arinsal's gondola to return to the village. The cable car link with Pal can close if the wind is high.

Mountain restaurants These are mainly self-service and crowded, with snack food; a visitor says the Bella Italia at Pla de la Cot in Pal does 'tasty pizzas'. The restaurant at Comallempla is said to run a BBQ if the weather permits.

Schools and guides Over half the instructors are native English speakers. The reports we have are nearly all positive – 'one of the best'; 'first class'. But groups can be large – 'average of 15' says a recent reporter. Another visitor liked his instructor's 'laid back approach', but a friend's beginner wife was 'left on the mountain to make her own way down'.

Facilities for children There are themed ski kindergartens for four to eight year olds and nurseries for children one to four at both Pal and Arinsal.

ANDORRA

112

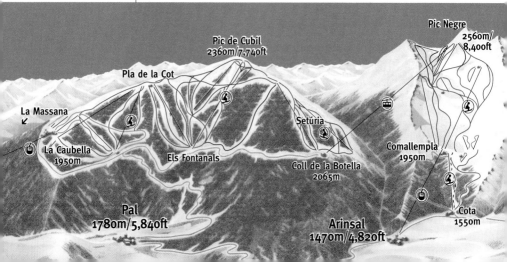

Andorra's liveliest resort – great if you like that kind of thing; we prefer to ski the extensive Grandvalira ski area from a quieter base

COSTS

①②③④⑤⑥

RATINGS

The slopes	
Fast lifts	***
Snow	****
Extent	***
Expert	*
Intermediate	***
Beginner	****
Convenience	****
Queues	***
Mountain restaurants	**
The rest	
Scenery	***
Resort charm	*
Off-slope	*

NEWS

For 2007/08 a new freeride area beside the Pic Blanc chair above Grau Roig opened. So did the Isards terrain park (for beginners and intermediates) above Abelletes. More snowmaking was installed, and more is planned for 2008/09.

KEY FACTS

Resort	2100m 6,890ft
Grandvalira (Soldeu/ El Tarter/Pas/Grau Roig)	
Slopes	1710-2560m 5,610-8,400ft
Lifts	66
Pistes	193km 120 miles
Green	16%
Blue	35%
Red	29%
Black	20%
Snowmaking	43%

UK PACKAGES

Airtours, Crystal, Directski.com, First Choice, Independent Ski Links, Inghams, Lagrange, Neilson, Ski McNeill, Skitracer, Thomson

- ➕ Grandvalira area covers Soldeu too; the joint ski area rivals major resorts in the Alps for size
- ➕ Andorra's liveliest nightlife
- ➕ Attractive hotel at Grau Roig

- ➖ Pas is an eyesore and the centre suffers from traffic (and fumes)
- ➖ Weekend crowds from France
- ➖ Very few woodland slopes – unpleasant in bad weather

The tour op brochures (and the few readers' reports we get) all say that Pas is Andorra's wildest party resort, and we don't doubt it. Having driven through it and skied down to it, we are quite happy to stay over the hill in Soldeu – or, for doorstep access to the Grandvalira slopes, at secluded Grau Roig.

THE RESORT

Sited right on the border between Andorra and France, Pas de la Casa owes its development as much to duty-free sales to the French as to skiing. It is a sizeable collection of dreary concrete-box-style apartment blocks and hotels, a product of the late 1960s and early 1970s. One reporter draws attention to 'loads of restaurants with plastic-covered faded images of burgers and chips'. Quite.

Most accommodation is conveniently placed near the lift base and slopes. The town centre boasts plenty of cheap shops and bars, as well as a sports centre. Reporters complain that the heavy traffic generates fumes, although attempts have been made to keep some areas traffic-free in the evenings, according to a reporter.

The resort attracts a lot of French and Spanish families, as well as Brits.

You can now drive to central Andorra via a toll tunnel, which avoids the Port d'Envalira pass; you exit near Grau Roig (pronounced 'Rosh'). This is a mini-resort in an attractively wooded setting that acts as the access point for day visitors arriving by road, but it also makes a good base.

THE MOUNTAINS

The Grandvalira ski area offers an extensive 193km/120 miles of pistes – comparable to big-name Alpine resorts such as Kitzbühel and Les Deux-Alpes. With the exception of a couple of attractively wooded slopes in the central valley, the slopes above Pas are all open, and vulnerable to bad weather. Soldeu is more sheltered.

Slopes The home slopes, facing north-east, descend from a high, north–south ridge; lifts go up to it at four points. Runs on the far side of the ridge converge on Grau Roig, where there is some wooded terrain at the head of the valley. And a single lift goes on further west to the bowl of Llac del Cubill and the rest of the Grandvalira ski area. On the far side of this bowl is the arrival station of the 6km/4 mile gondola up from Encamp. In the opposite direction out of Pas, a newish six-pack is the start of expansion over the French border – on the left side of our map – called Porte des Neiges. The final plan is to have three chairlifts, a gondola, 50km/31 miles of slopes, 12 runs and the largest beginner area in the Pyrenees.

Terrain parks There's a slope-style area with jumps at Grau Roig, the new Isards terrain park and a boardercross at Pas, and a rail-park over in France.

Snow reliability The combination of height and lots of snowmaking means good snow reliability and a season that often lasts until late April. But on both our visits the snow has been better in the Soldeu sector.

Experts There are few challenges on-piste – the black runs are rarely of serious steepness, and moguls are sparse. But there seem to be plenty of off-piste slopes inviting exploration – a reader recommends the bowls above Grau Roig, in particular.

Intermediates The local slopes cater for confident intermediates best, with plenty of top-to-bottom reds on the main ridge; they do rather lack variety – and can be tricky for more timid intermediates, for whom Soldeu makes a better base.

Beginners There are beginner slopes

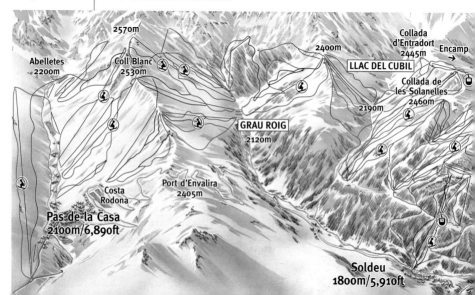

Phone numbers
From abroad use the prefix +376

Central reservations phone number
For all resort accommodation call 801074

TOURIST OFFICE
t 871900
info@grandvalira.com
www.grandvalira.com

in Pas, Grau Roig and in the French sector. The Pas area is a short but inconvenient bus ride out of town. Progression to longer runs is easier in the Grau Roig sector.
Snowboarding Boarding is popular with the young crowd the resort attracts. Drags are usually avoidable.
Cross-country There are loops totalling 13km/8 miles below Grau Roig.
Queues Queues are rarely serious during the week. But at weekends and French school holidays some can develop, especially at Grau Roig – confirmed by a recent visitor.
Mountain restaurants There are routine places at the ridge above Pas and the top of the gondola from Encamp – 'the worst I've found' says a recent reporter. In contrast, the Rifugi dels Llacs dels Pessons at the head of the Grau Roig bowl is a cosy, beamed table-service restaurant with excellent food – booking recommended.
Schools and guides The ski school has a high reputation – good English.
Facilities for children There are ski kindergartens at Pas and Grau Roig, and a non-ski one at the latter.

STAYING THERE

How to go There are lots of hotels and apartments and a few chalets.
Hotels Himàlaia-Pas (735 515) has a pool and is 'comfortable and recommendable', says a reporter. The Grau Roig hotel (755 556) is in a league of its own for comfort and seclusion. Beware of hotels catering for the 18-30 crowd.
Apartments The Frontera Blanca are simple, but at the foot of the slopes.
Eating out It's not a resort for gourmets – though one reporter had 'good charcuterie and paella at the restaurant next to the Burger King', and another 'quail and foie gras' at Husky. A local recommends Cal Padrí (Catalan food), KSB (good grills), Tagliatelle (pizza and pasta) and Chez Paulo (French cuisine). A recent reader was impressed by the 'friendly and welcoming' attitude of restaurant staff and the good-value menu options.
Après-ski Après-ski is very lively. The Milwaukee and Underground bars are popular. Billboard is 'by far the best club'; Amadeus, Habana, El Mexicano and Sabanah are other options.
Off the slopes You can go dog sledding, snowmobiling and snowshoeing; otherwise there's visiting the leisure centre, shopping, or taking a trip to Andorra la Vella for more serious shopping.

Our favourite place to stay in Andorra: a reasonably pleasant village, centrally placed in the impressive Grandvalira ski area

115

COSTS

① ② ③ ④ ⑤ ⑥

RATINGS

The slopes
Fast lifts	★★★
Snow	★★★★
Extent	★★★
Expert	★
Intermediate	★★★
Beginner	★★★★
Convenience	★★★
Queues	★★★
Mountain restaurants	★★

The rest
Scenery	★★★
Resort charm	★
Off-slope	★

NEWS

For 2007/08 the black Avet slope was improved to hold World Cup competitions. Snowmaking was increased, and more will be installed for 2008/09. A new service building is planned at the base of the gondola at Encamp – it will contain a ski school, a kids' snow garden and equipment rental shops.

+ Grandvalira area covers Pas de la Casa too; the joint ski area rivals major resorts in the Alps for size

+ Not as rowdy as it once was

+ Excellent beginner and early intermediate terrain

+ Ski school has excellent British-run section for English-speaking visitors

− Slopes can get very crowded

− Very little to interest experts

− Village is on the main road through Andorra and suffers from heavy traffic

− Some hotels are way out of town

− Not much to do off the slopes

If we were planning a holiday in Andorra, it would be in Soldeu (or the isolated hotel at Grau Roig, up the road – covered in the Pas de la Casa chapter). Despite the traffic, it is the least unattractive village, and its local slopes are the most interestingly varied (though crowded). It shares with neighbouring Pas de la Casa 193km/120 miles of pistes – an area known as Grandvalira, whose lift system includes four modern gondolas, nine six-packs and six fast quads.

THE RESORT

The village is an ever-growing ribbon of modern buildings with traditional stone cladding set on a steep hillside and lining the busy road that runs through Andorra from France to Spain. Most are hotels, apartments or bars, with the occasional shop; for serious shopping, go to Andorra la Vella.

The steep hillside leads down to the river, and the slopes are on the opposite side. A gondola or a six-pack takes you to the heart of the slopes at Espiolets, and a wide bridge across the river forms the end of the piste home, with elevators to take you up to the gondola. A lot of people leave their skis, boots and boards at the bottom or top of the gondola.

El Tarter, a few miles by road down the valley, and Canillo, a few miles further, offer alternative lifts into the slopes. Between all three resorts, hotels and apartments are being built along the main road and sold under the Soldeu banner – so check carefully where your proposed accommodation is. The Grandvalira bus service (included in the area pass) runs hourly along the valley towards Andorra la Vella – you can hop on or off at different sectors, but a recent reporter found it 'so infrequent you have to plan your journey around a particular bus (which will often be late)'.

GRANDVALIRA

A good view of the ski area, with Soldeu in the centre, El Tarter on the right and the road up to Grau Roig on the left →

KEY FACTS

| Resort | 1800m |
| | 5,910ft |

Grandvalira (Soldeu/
El Tarter/Pas/Grau
Roig)

Slopes	1710-2560m
	5,610-8,400ft
Lifts	66
Pistes	193km
	120 miles
Green	16%
Blue	35%
Red	29%
Black	20%
Snowmaking	43%

THE MOUNTAINS

The Grandvalira ski area offers an extensive 193km/120 miles of pistes – a comparable area to big-name Alpine resorts such as Kitzbühel and Les Deux-Alpes. Soldeu's main local slopes are on open mountainsides above the woods, though there are runs in the woods back to most of the lift bases.

THE SLOPES
Pleasantly varied but crowded
The gondola rises over wooded, north-facing slopes to **Espiolets**, a broad shelf that is virtually a mini-resort – the ski school is based here, and there are extensive nursery slopes. From Espiolets, a gentle run to the east takes you to an area of long, easy runs served by a six-pack. Beyond that is an extensive area of more varied slopes, served by a quad and another six-pack that links with the Pas de la Casa area. Going west from Espiolets takes you to the open bowl of **Riba Escorxada** and the arrival point of the gondola up from El Tarter. From here, another six-pack serves sunny slopes on Tosa dels Espiolets and a fourth goes to the high point of Tossal de la Llosada and the link with **El Forn** above Canillo.

TERRAIN PARKS
A good one
The terrain park situated just above Riba Escorxada is fast gaining a

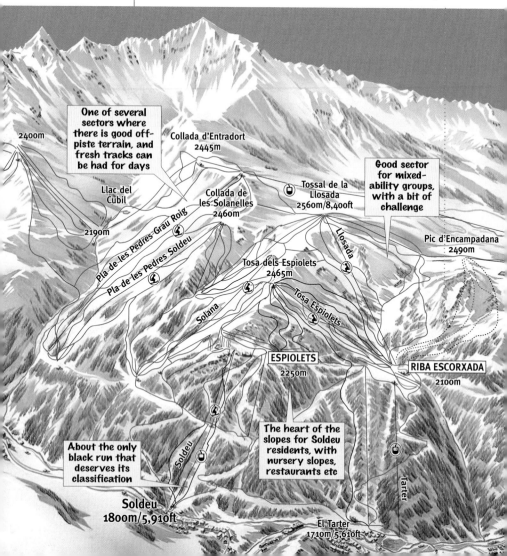

One of several sectors where there is good off-piste terrain, and fresh tracks can be had for days

Collada d'Entradort
2445m

Good sector for mixed-ability groups, with a bit of challenge

2400m

Llac del Cubil

Collada de les Solanelles
2460m

Tossal de la Llosada
2560m/8,400ft

2190m

Pla de les Pedres-Grau Roig

Pla de les Pedres Soldeu

Llosada

Pic d'Encampadana
2490m

Tosa dels Espiolets
2465m

Tosa Espiolets

Solana

ESPIOLETS
2250m

RIBA ESCORXADA
2100m

About the only black run that deserves its classification

Soldeu

The heart of the slopes for Soldeu residents, with nursery slopes, restaurants etc

Tarter

Soldeu
1800m/5,910ft

El Tarter
1710m/5,610ft

reputation throughout Europe. The triple line of kickers that ranges between 8m and 16m (26ft and 52ft) is well maintained. Last season saw the main kicker turned into a huge gap jump to a jib table that then dropped into a nice long and steep landing. It also saw the addition of a giant airbag, which is set up on the landing of a nice jump. There is a great selection of rails including a big rainbow rail and S-box and two wall rides. But fun can be had for all levels in this little freestyle oasis. For beginners there is a series of three small jumps culminating in a 5m/16ft long medium jump and a couple of fun boxes to slide on. The half-pipe is touch-and-go depending on snowfall. A draglift services the park, but there is also a speedy quad that takes you slightly higher up the hill.

SNOW RELIABILITY
Much better than people expect
Despite its name (Soldeu means Sun God) the slopes generally enjoy reliable snow. Most slopes are north-facing, with a good natural snow record (though they've recently had a couple of poor years) and there's snowmaking on 43% of the pistes. The generally excellent grooming helps maintain good snow. But a 2008 visitor was disappointed by the 'poor' piste management – 'bald patches were not marked and icy stretches were treacherous'.

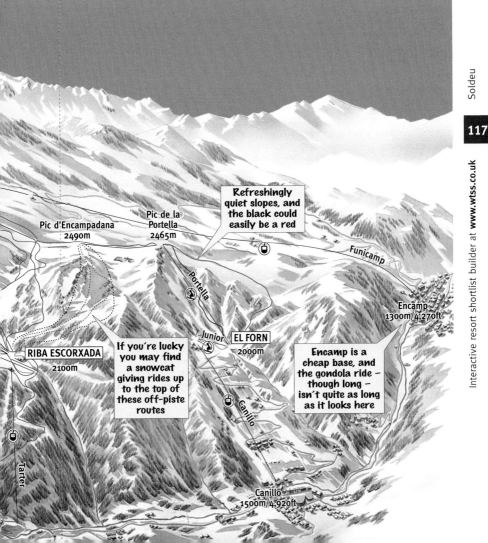

LIFT PASSES

Grandvalira

Prices in €

Age	1-day	6-day
under 12	29	141
12 to 64	41	196
over 65	18	108

Free under 6, over 70
Beginner pass in each sector for beginners' area €23 per day

Notes
Covers all lifts in Soldeu, El Tarter, Canillo, Grau Roig and Pas de la Casa; pedestrian and local day and half-day passes available

Alternative passes
The Ski Andorra pass covers all Andorran areas and allows skiing at any single one of them each day; €175 for five non-consecutive days

UK PACKAGES

Airtours, Crystal, Directski.com, First Choice, Independent Ski Links, Inghams, Neilson, Ski McNeill, Ski Wild, Skitracer, Thomson
Canillo Lagrange
El Tarter Airtours, First Choice, Inghams, Neilson

boarding

Soldeu has become the home of snowboarding in the Pyrenees. This is a perfect place for beginners to learn on wide, gentle slopes served mainly by chairs not drags. For the more advanced, Soldeu offers some good off-piste, steeper areas and the best snow park in the Pyrenees. However, true backcountry enthusiasts should head to Arcalis, which has the steepest terrain and heli-boarding. Soldeu's snowboard shop Loaded, run by British pro and Andorran resident Tyler Chorlton, is a real hub in the area, and the staff will give you plenty of pointers.

FOR EXPERTS
Hope for good off-piste
It's a limited area for experts, at least on-piste. The improved Avet black run down to Soldeu deserves its grading, but most of the other blacks would be no more than reds (or even blues) in many resorts. The blacks on Tosa dels Espiolets are indistinguishable from the neighbouring (and more direct) red and blue, for example. But there is plenty of off-piste potential – notably in the bowl above Riba Escorxada, in the Espiolets and Solanelles areas (we had a great time there in fresh powder on our last visit), and above El Forn. And the off-piste remains untouched for days because most visitors are beginners and early intermediates. When conditions permit at weekends, a snowcat takes people up to Pic d'Encampadana, from where four off-piste routes (dotted on our map) descend to Riba Escorxada.

FOR INTERMEDIATES
Explore Grandvalira
There is plenty to amuse all but the very keenest intermediates. The area east of Espiolets is splendid for building confidence, and those already confident will be able to explore the whole mountain. Riba Escorxada is a fine section for mixed-ability groups. The Canillo/El Forn sector has an easy, little-used blue run along the ridge with excellent views all the way to Pal and Arinsal and an easy black in the valley. Many of the blues and reds have short steeper sections, preceded by a 'slow' sign and netting in the middle of the piste to slow you down.

FOR BEGINNERS
One of the best
This is an excellent place to start. The Espiolets nursery area is huge, and there's a smaller area at Riba Escorxada, above El Tarter (which one reader reckons is better) – both with a moving carpet. They are relatively snow-sure, and there are numerous

easy pistes to move on to (though the crowds can be off-putting). And the ski school is top-notch. The final bend on the Esquirol run to El Tarter was named 'carnage corner' by one reporter, who recommends a return to the resort by lift for the inexperienced.

FOR CROSS-COUNTRY
Er, what cross-country?
There is no cross-country in Soldeu. There is some not far away at Grau Roig (see the Pas de la Casa chapter), but Andorra's serious cross-country resort is La Rabassa, in the south-west corner of the country – 15km/9 miles of loops at an altitude of 2000m/6,560ft.

QUEUES
Crowds more of a problem
Most of Grandvalira's key lifts are high-speed chairs or gondolas, though there are a lot of slow lifts too. But the system seems to be able to cope. A 2008 visitor recommends taking the six-pack out of Soldeu to avoid any queues for the gondola ('it's quicker and more convenient'). But allow time for the queue-prone Cubil chair back from Grau Roig. More of a problem than queues are the crowds on the blue slopes (including lots of school classes snaking along) – the reds and blacks are much quieter.

MOUNTAIN RESTAURANTS
Not a highlight
The mountain restaurants are crowded and the food generally dull (a notable exception is Rifugi dels Llacs dels Pessons – see Pas de la Casa). There is a choice of places at Espiolets, including table service at Gall de Bosc, which was recommended by a reporter. Roc de les Bruixes at El Forn claims to be 'gastronomic' and has a 'large terrace with terrific views'. Many reporters favour descending to the valley for lunch; recommendations include the Sol i Neu in Soldeu and L'Abarset at El Tarter.

SCHOOLS

Soldeu
t 890591

Classes
15hr: €108
Private lessons
€72 for 1hr for 1 person; €6 extra per additional person

CHILDREN

Nurseries run by ski school
Ages 1 to 4; 2hr €17
Snow gardens run by ski school
Ages 3 to 7; five days €144

Ski school
For ages 6 to 11; 15hr: €100

GETTING THERE

Air Toulouse 196km/121 miles (3½hr)
Rail L'Hospitalet-Près-L'Andorre (25km/16 miles); buses and taxis to Soldeu

ACTIVITIES

Indoor Thermal spas, bowling (at Pas), leisure centre (pools, hot tub, gym)
Outdoor Helicopter rides, snowmobiling, dog sledding, snowshoeing, paragliding, paintballing, archery, igloo building

Phone numbers
From abroad use the prefix +376
Central reservations phone number
Call 801074

TOURIST OFFICE

t 890500
info@grandvalira.com
www.grandvalira.com

SCHOOLS AND GUIDES
One of the best for Brits
The scale of the teaching operation here is very impressive. The ski school is effectively run as two units. One deals with English-speaking clients, is led by an Englishman and has mostly native English-speaking instructors. Some 40% of the pupils are beginners, and the school has devised a special 'team-teaching' scheme to cope with this volume. The school maintains its excellent reputation for teaching and friendliness: 'one of the reasons for returning to Soldeu', 'instructor was brilliant', 'everyone was very impressed', 'small classes of eight', 'English is first language' and 'good tuition' are typical comments.

FACILITIES FOR CHILDREN
With altitude
Children are looked after at the mid-mountain stations. There are nurseries at Espiolets, Riba Escorxada and El Forn for children from one to four years old. The Mickey Snow Club snow gardens (at Soldeu, El Canillo and El Tarter) are for three to seven year olds, and they have Disney-themed play areas on the slopes.

STAYING THERE

HOW TO GO
Be careful where you stay
A wide range of UK tour operators offer packages here, mainly in hotels but with some apartments and chalets. Location is important – many places are a bus ride from town.
Hotels The best hotels are of a far better standard than a decade ago.
*****Sport Hotel Hermitage (870550) Opened two seasons ago at the foot of the slopes; all bedrooms are suites with mountain views. A huge spa is part of the hotel.
****Sport Hotel Village (870500) Right by the Hermitage. Stylish public areas – comfortable chairs and sofas, high ceilings, beams and picture windows.
****Sport (870600) Over the road from the other two Sports. Lively, comfortable bar and a popular basement disco-bar. But dull buffet-style food.
****Piolets Park (871787) Pleasant enough, with a pool. Central.
****Hìmàlaia (878515) Refurbished, central with sauna, steam and hot tub.
Self-catering Most reporters are hotel-based, but apartments are available.

EATING OUT
Some atmospheric places
We enjoyed meals in two atmospheric old restored buildings: Borda del Rector (Andorran-run and with authentic Andorran cuisine), nearer to El Tarter than Soldeu, and British-run Fat Albert's (steaks, fish, burgers) in downtown Soldeu. L'Esquirol (Indian) and Pussycat have had good reports.

APRES-SKI
Lively
Après-ski is lively 'but not loutish' – mainly bars and rep-organised events (such as pub crawls with maybe 100 participants). The bar at Fat Albert's has videos shot on the mountain and often a live band. The Pussycat is a good late-night place, with changing party themes. The Piccadilly, under the Sport hotel, is popular. The Aspen and the nearby Avalanche attract a younger crowd. We liked the Villager. Expect noise from late-night revellers.

OFF THE SLOPES
Head downhill
There is the spa in Soldeu itself. Down in Canillo is the smart Palau de Gel (see below); in Escaldes-Engordany, there's the impressive Caldea thermal spa; and in Andorra la Vella there are some very serious shopping opportunities.

El Tarter 1710m/5,610ft
El Tarter has grown over recent years and is rather sprawling, with no real centre. Reporters recommend two 3-star hotels, del Clos (851500) ('good food but up a steep hill') and del Tarter (802080). We have had decent reviews of the big 4-star Euro Esqui (736666) halfway to Soldeu ('food adequate, rooms modern and clean'). Readers complain that the resort is 'dull at night'. The Mosquit pizzeria has been recommended.

Canillo 1500m/4,920ft
If you like the idea of deserted local slopes and don't mind riding a gondola down at the end of the day, consider Canillo, which looks an acceptably pleasant spot as you drive through it. It has the impressive Palau de Gel – an Olympic ice rink plus pool, gym, tennis and squash.

Austria's holiday recipe is quite distinctive. It doesn't suit everybody, but for many holidaymakers nothing else will do; in particular, France won't do. Austria is the land of cute little villages clustered around onion-domed churches – there are no monstrous, purpose-built, apartment-block resorts of the kind that are so common in France. It's the land of friendly wooded mountains, reassuring to beginners and timid intermediates in a way that bleak snowfields and craggy peaks will never be. It's the land of friendly, welcoming people who don't find it demeaning to speak their guests' language (if it's English, at least). And it's the land of jolly, alcohol-fuelled après-ski action – in many resorts starting in mid-afternoon with dancing in mountain restaurants and going on as long as you have the legs for it. For many visitors to Austrian resorts, the partying is as important as the skiing or riding. Of course, there are exceptions to all these norms.

In general, Austria isn't the first place you'll want to consider if reliably good snow is your top priority (though there are some wonderful exceptions to this rule, including some of the world's best glacier areas – such as those at Hintertux, at Kaprun and in the Stubai valley – and high, snow-sure ski areas such as Obergurgl, Obertauern and Ischgl). But most resorts are relatively low, and conditions are more likely to be problematic here than in higher places. However, Austrian resorts have made great strides to catch up with their rivals – most have radically increased their snowmaking capacity in the last decade. In midwinter, especially, lack of snow generally coincides with low night-time temperatures, even at low altitudes, and snowmaking comes into its own. And recent seasons have included some bumper natural snow years for much of Austria.

It's the après-ski that strikes most first-time visitors as being Austria's unique selling point. But Austrian après-ski remains very Austrian – or perhaps German. Huge quantities of beer and schnapps are drunk, German is the predominant language, and German drinking songs are common. So is loud Europop music. People pack into mountain restaurants at the end of the day – some time before the end of the day, actually – and gyrate in their ski boots on the dance floor, on the tables, on the bar, wherever there's room. There are open-air ice bars, umbrella bars and countless transparent 'igloo' bars in which to shelter from bad weather. In

Carinthia (aka Kärnten) is Austria's southernmost province, on the borders with Italy and Slovenia, and it has more hours of sunshine than most other regions of the Alps. It is now easy to reach the local Klagenfurt airport on budget airlines – for example, Ryanair's flights from Stansted several days a week.

As well as being home to several large downhill ski areas, Carinthia offers the prospect of an all-round winter holiday, with over 1000km/621 miles of cross-country trails and more than 100 frozen lakes that form natural ice rinks (and golf courses – one of the editors of this book has played ice golf on one of these, the Weissensee). There are also several spas where you can relax in natural hot springs water.

Bad Kleinkirchheim (Franz Klammer's favourite ski area) is probably the Carinthian resort best known to UK skiers and boarders, and it is covered in its own chapter later in the book. Last season, after a long fallow period, the resort hosted World Cup slalom and giant slalom races.

But Carinthia's largest ski area (with 110km/68 miles of pistes and 30 lifts, including four six-packs and four quad chairs) is the Nassfeld Ski Arena. This is Carinthia's southernmost ski area and has the longest gondola in the Alps (the 6km/4 mile, three-stage Millennium Express, which rises almost 1300m/4,270ft) and the longest floodlit piste (the last 2.2km/1.4 miles of the 7.6km/4.7 mile long Carnia piste). Most runs are red, with a few blues for beginners and a few ungroomed ski routes. There's a terrain park, a half-pipe and an area with a quarter-pipe and jumps; and the NTC Fun Sports Park offers 11 different activities, including bike boarding, tubing, snow biking and snow blading – all equipment supplied. The ski area is on the border with Italy, and you can lunch in Italian huts (some of the 25 in the area).

The Hohe Tauern region includes three separate ski areas. The Heiligenblut-Grossglockner area has 55km/34 miles of pistes between 1300m/4,270ft and over 2900m/9,510ft, served by 13 lifts. The nearby Mölltal glacier is Carinthia's only glacier and offers guaranteed good snow on over 50km/ 31 miles of pistes rising to 3120m/10,240ft, reached by a funicular, gondola and then a fast chair. There's also the nearby Ankogel-Mallnitz area of slopes with a two-stage cable-car rising to 2635m/8,650ft and two short drags serving blue, red and black runs on the upper part of the mountain.

There are several other ski areas, including Katschberg (14 lifts, 60km/37 miles of pistes, and with a new 5.5km/3.4 mile peak-to-valley run) and Gerlitzen (14 lifts, 26km/16 miles of pistes) – best suited to families, beginners and early intermediates.

All of Carinthia's ski areas are covered by the Top Ski Carinthia ski pass, which costs 175 euros for six days.

Introduction

121

Interactive resort shortlist builder at **www.wtss.co.uk**

↑ Classic Austrian skiing terrain – this is the Kitzbüheler Horn, seen from the Hahnenkamm
SNOWPIX.COM / CHRIS GILL

many resorts the bands don't stop playing until darkness falls, when the happy punters slide off in the general direction of the village to find another watering hole. After dinner the drinking and dancing starts again – for those who pause for dinner, that is.

Of course, not all resorts conform to this image. Lech and Zürs, for example, are full of rich, cool, 'beautiful' people enjoying the comfort of sophisticated 4- or 5-star hotels. And resorts such as Niederau in the Wildschönau, Westendorf and Alpbach are pretty, quiet, family resorts. But lots of big-name resorts with the best and most extensive slopes are also big party resorts – notably St Anton, Saalbach-Hinterglemm, Ischgl and Sölden.

Nightlife is not limited to drinking and dancing. There are lots of floodlit toboggan runs, and UK tour operator reps organise Tirolean, bowling, fondue, karaoke and other evenings.

One thing that all Austrian resorts have in common is reliably comfortable accommodation – whether it's in 4- or 5-star hotels with pools, saunas and spas (which the Austrians like to call 'wellness centres') or in great-value, family-run guest houses, of which Austria has thousands. Catered chalets and self-catering apartments are in general much less widely available.

The Germanic aversion to credit cards causes problems for many of our reporters. Many establishments do not accept cards – even quite upmarket hotels, as well as many ski lift companies. So check well in advance, and be prepared to pay in cash.

As smoking in bars and restaurants becomes more controlled or banned altogether in other countries, in Austria this pollution seems to be getting worse. Perhaps German smokers who used to go to the Dolomites are now going to Austria to avoid Italy's ban.

Austrian resorts are now easier to get to independently using cheap flights. The standard arrival airports are Munich, Salzburg, Innsbruck and, for western resorts, Zürich. But don't overlook less well-known airports such as Klagenfurt in Carinthia and Friedrichshafen, just over the German border and handy for resorts in western Austria such as St Anton, Lech and Ischgl.

Salzburgerland's Ski Amadé lift pass is one of the world's biggest in terms of the amount of terrain and number of lifts covered. What's more, with a car you really could aim to get around most of the resorts it covers – they are clustered close together, no high passes are involved in getting from one resort to another, and many areas are geared to people arriving by car, with out-of-town lifts and serious car parks. (They are also conveniently close to Salzburg airport – we have taken early flights and been on the slopes before lunchtime; come departure day, we have skied until the end of the day, had a leisurely drive to the airport and still had time to kill before a late flight home.)

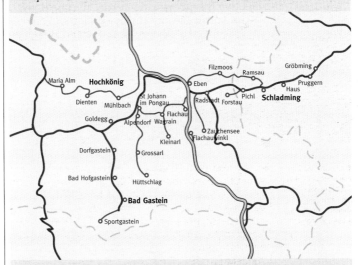

Some of the major resorts covered by the pass have their own chapters in the pages that follow. In the Schladming chapter we also cover the smaller linked resorts of Haus in Ennstal and Pichl, as well as Schladming's elevated outpost of Rohrmoos. Also close to Schladming is Ramsau in Dachstein, which has slopes at village level but also a lift up to the lip of the Dachstein glacier. In the Bad Gastein chapter we cover not only the resorts in the Gastein valley but also the next-door valley of Grossarl, which is linked over the hill to Dorfgastein.

We also have a chapter on the major area of Hochkönig's Winterreich. Though largely unknown on the British market, it has an extensive network of runs linking Mühlbach, Dienten and Maria Alm.

Another big region is the Salzburger Sportwelt. The largest linked area here is the 200km/124 mile three-valley system linking Wagrain to Flachau (home of Hermann Maier) in one direction and Alpendorf/St Johann im Pongau in the other. This area also embraces an extensive lift network linking Zauchensee, Flachauwinkl and Kleinarl, plus more modest lift systems at Filzmoos, Radstadt-Altenmarkt, Eben and Goldegg. We skied the Zauchensee and Flachauwinkl slopes for a day and enjoyed it in excellent snow (Zauchensee often has the best snow in the region because of its height and north-facing slopes).

Considering the extent of the lift networks it covers (and the generally impressive efficiency of the lifts) the Ski Amadé pass is not expensive – 189 euros in high season. This is less than you'll pay for anything vaguely similar in France or Italy. Prices on the spot are not bad either – readers report prices in the mountain restaurants (which are very numerous) lower than in areas with a bigger international reputation.

Introduction

123

Interactive resort shortlist builder at **www.wtss.co.uk**

GETTING AROUND THE AUSTRIAN ALPS

Austria presents few problems for the car-borne visitor, because practically all the resorts are valley villages, which involve neither steep approach roads nor high altitude.

The dominant feature of Austria for the ski driver is the thoroughfare of the Inn valley, which runs through the Tirol from Landeck via Innsbruck to Kufstein. The motorway along it extends, with one or two breaks, westwards to the Arlberg pass and on to Switzerland. This artery is relatively reliable except in exceptionally bad conditions – the altitude is low, and the road is a vital transport link that is kept open in virtually all conditions.

The Arlberg – which divides Tirol from Vorarlberg, but which is also the watershed between Austria and Switzerland – is one of the

few areas where driving plans are likely to be seriously affected by snow. The east–west Arlberg pass itself has a long tunnel underneath it; this isn't cheap, and you may want to take the high road when it's clear, through Stuben, St Christoph and St Anton. The Flexen pass road to Zürs and Lech (which may be closed by avalanche risk even when the Arlberg pass is open) branches off just to the west of the Arlberg summit.

At the eastern end of the Tirol, the Gerlos pass road from Zell im Zillertal over into Salzburg province can be closed. Resorts in Carinthia, such as Bad Kleinkirchheim, are usually reached by motorway, thanks to the Tauern and Katschberg tunnels. The alternative is the Radstädter Tauern pass through Obertauern, or the car-carrying rail service from Böckstein to Mallnitz.

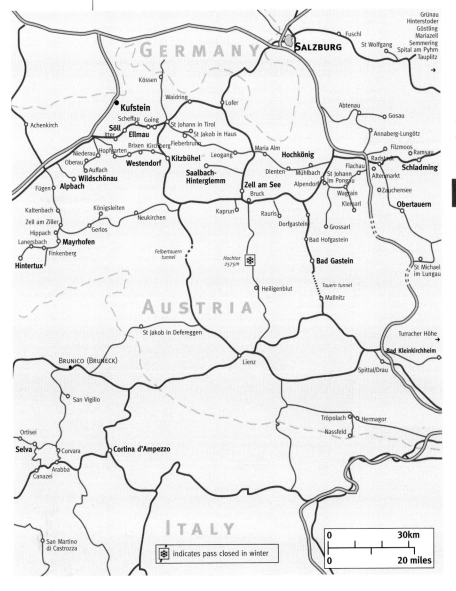

⚜ indicates pass closed in winter

| 0 | | | 30km |
| 0 | | | 20 miles |

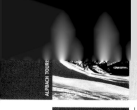

Small and beautiful: it's the pretty village rather than the extent of the slopes that have attracted generations of Brits

COSTS

①②③④⑤⑥

RATINGS

The slopes
Fast lifts	**
Snow	**
Extent	*
Expert	*
Intermediate	**
Beginner	****
Convenience	**
Queues	***
Mountain restaurants	***

The rest
Scenery	***
Charm	*****
Off-slope	***

NEWS

For 2007/08 a new reservoir was built to service the snowmaking, and the runs to the village were kept open all of last season. There is now snowmaking on 70% of the slopes.

For 2008/09 a mid-station is planned for the gondola from Inneralpbach, which will make access to the lower slopes quicker and easier and allow you to ride down if snow on the lower slopes is poor. There will be night skiing on the red run down to the base at Reith several times a week.

KEY FACTS

Resort	1000m
	3,280ft
Slopes	670-2025m
	2,200-6,640ft
Lifts	19
Pistes	52km
	32 miles
Blue	27%
Red	63%
Black	10%
Snowmaking	37km
	23 miles

126

➕ Charming, traditional, relaxed village – great for young children

➕ Handy, central nursery slopes

➕ Several other worthwhile resorts within day-trip distance

➕ Good, varied, intermediate terrain, not without challenges, but ...

➖ Slopes limited in extent and variety

➖ Main slopes are a shuttle-bus-ride away (efficient service, though)

➖ Few long easy runs for beginners to progress to

➖ Lower slopes can suffer from poor snow, despite snowmaking help

This is an old British favourite – there is even a British ski club, the Alpbach Visitors. The village is small, pretty and friendly, and inspires great loyalty in regular visitors – one who has been going since 1983 claims only junior status.

THE RESORT

Alpbach is near the head of a valley, looking south across it towards the slopes of Wiedersbergerhorn. It's an exceptionally pretty, captivating place; traditional chalets crowd around the pretty church, and the nursery slopes are only a few steps away.

The main village is the place to stay for atmosphere and après-ski, but it involves using a free shuttle-bus to and from Achenwirt, a mile away, where a gondola goes up to Hornboden – though reporters find the service 'no hassle, excellent'. The backwater hamlet of Inneralpbach is more convenient for the slopes, with its own gondola up the mountain.

The Inn valley is a few miles north, and trips east to Kitzbühel or west to Innsbruck are possible. The Hintertux and Stubaier glaciers are within reach.

THE MOUNTAINS

Alpbach's slopes, on two flanks of the Wiedersbergerhorn, are small and simple. Piste grooming is excellent.
Slopes The two gondolas take you up to open, north-facing slopes above the treeline, served by chairs and drags. The runs are mostly of 200m to 400m (660ft to 1,310ft) vertical, but you can get more down the gondolas when snow is good down to valley level. Behind Gmahkopf is a short west-facing slope. A tiny separate area at Reith is on the lift pass and, says a reporter, is 'well worth a morning's visit – well groomed and deserted'. Access is by an eight-seat gondola. Night skiing is planned for 2008/09.
Terrain parks There's a half-pipe near the top of the Achenwirt gondola.
Snow reliability Alpbach cannot claim great snow reliability, but at least most

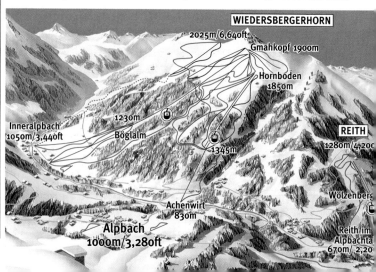

WIEDERSBERGERHORN
2025m/6,640ft
Gmahkopf 1900m
Hornboden 1850m
1230m
Inneralpbach 1050m/3,440ft
Böglalm
1345m
REITH 1280m/4,200
Achenwirt 830m
Wölzenberg
Alpbach 1000m/3,280ft
Reith im Alpbachta 670m/ 2,20

while another enjoyed 'great food and service' at the Dauerstoa Alm.

Schools and guides We've had good reports on both main schools, Alpbach and Alpbach Aktiv; the head of the Alpbach school is qualified to teach people with disabilities (and he himself has a disability).

Facilities for children Reporters find the village very child-friendly, with good ski kindergartens; babysitters can be arranged by the tourist office.

STAYING THERE

How to go Hotels and pensions dominate in UK packages.

Hotels Of the smart 4-star places, the Alpbacherhof (5237) ('superb food and excellent service'), Alphof (5371) ('excellent, with friendly and welcoming staff') and ancient Böglerhof (5227) get most votes. The Berghof (5275) has been recommended as 'an excellent 3-star; it serves wholesome meals and is only 20 metres from the nursery slopes'. The 3-star Post (5203) is 'better than a lot of 4-stars', says a recent visitor. The simpler Haus Thomas (5944), Haus Angelika (5339) and Haus Theresia (5386) have also been recommended. Pension Edelweiss (5268) is close to the nursery slopes and offers B&B and 'clean, spacious, good value apartments'.

Apartments There are quite a few to choose from, easily bookable through the tourist office website.

Eating out The popular Post and Alphof both provide 'excellent food' according to a reporter, who also favoured the 'superb' Jakober and its no-smoking room. Wiedersbergerhorn in Inneralpbach has been recommended, as has the Rossmoos Inn for its lively Tirolean evenings, 'superb' food and the toboggan run back to the resort.

Après-ski At peak times this is typically Tirolean, with lots of noisy teatime beer swilling in the bars of central hotels such as the Jakober and the Post. The latter has regular live music. A reporter preferred the Farmer's Pub to the Waschkuchl bar. Joe's Salett'l is at Inneralpbach.

Off the slopes There are pretty walks, and trips to Innsbruck and Salzburg are possible. There is also an indoor swimming pool and (at Reith) an indoor ice rink. The ski schools put on a 'ski show' on Wednesday evenings.

↑ Alpbach is a pretty place, and the nursery slopes are right by the village; the main slopes are a bus ride away
ALPBACH TOURIST OFFICE

of the Wiedersbergerhorn faces north, and 70% of the pistes are covered by snowmaking. The resort says that this allowed them to keep all the runs to the valley open all of last season.

Experts Alpbach isn't ideal, but the reds and the three blacks (often groomed) are not without challenge, and runs of 1000m/3,300ft vertical are not to be sniffed at. There are a few off-piste routes to the valley, and the schools take the top classes off-piste. A recent reporter 'skied with a guide for three hours in untracked powder'.

Intermediates There is fine intermediate terrain; the problem is that there's not much of it. This resort is for practising technique on familiar slopes, not high mileage.

Beginners Beginners love the sunny nursery slope beside the village. But the main slopes are not ideal for confidence-building as most of them are classified red and there are only a few blues.

Snowboarding There's some good freeriding terrain.

Cross-country There are 22km/14 miles of pretty cross-country trails that rise up beyond Inneralpbach.

Queues The gondola at Inneralpbach built in 2005 seems to have relieved queues for the Achenwirt gondola.

Mountain restaurants There are several mountain restaurants – each worth a visit. One reporter recommends the spit-roast chicken at the Böglalm,

Interactive resort shortlist builder at **www.wtss.co.uk**

If you fancy 'taking the cure', there are few better resorts; even if you don't, you're likely to be impressed by the slopes

COSTS

①②③④⑤⑥

RATINGS

The slopes
Fast lifts	**
Snow	***
Extent	****
Expert	***
Intermediate	****
Beginner	**
Convenience	**
Queues	***
Mountain restaurants	****

The rest
Scenery	***
Resort charm	***
Off-slope	****

➕ Extensive, varied slopes

➕ Excellent, testing long runs for confident intermediates

➕ More reliable snow than in most low-altitude Austrian resorts

➕ Lots of good, atmospheric, traditional mountain restaurants

➕ Excellent thermal spas, but ...

➖ Main resorts are spa towns, without the usual Austrian resort ambience

➖ Bad Gastein itself has a steep, confined setting and narrow streets

➖ Valley slopes are split into five areas and having a car helps

➖ Timid intermediates and beginners are better off elsewhere

The Gastein valley is starting to attract more Brits, to judge by readers' reports. Rightly so – the slopes form one of Austria's bigger, more varied and more snow-sure areas. Steeply tiered Bad Gastein itself is a difficult place to like; we much prefer rustic Dorfgastein or spacious Bad Hofgastein – described here.

THE RESORT

Bad Gastein sits near the head of the Gastein valley. It is an old spa town that has now spread widely, but still has a compact core. A bizarre mix of buildings is laid out in a cramped horseshoe, set in what is virtually a gorge. The central area is steep, and no pleasure at all to explore. Above it is a modern suburb with more of a ski resort feel – and access by gondola to the major Stubnerkogel sector of slopes. Across town, the double chair up separate Graukogel is a taxi ride from the centre. Various ski-bus routes connect the villages and lift stations. There are trains, too. The ski-bus service gets mixed reviews but a car is an advantage to help get around the different areas of slopes and visit some of the other 20+ resorts covered by the Ski Amadé lift pass (see the Austria introduction chapter).

THE MOUNTAINS

Most of the runs are on the open slopes above the treeline, though there are some woodland runs.
Slopes Stubnerkogel has runs in all directions from the peak, giving about 500m/1,640ft vertical on the open slopes above the treeline and rather more below it. There is night skiing once a week on the nursery slope. The much smaller Graukogel is unjustly neglected; its wooded runs are great in bad weather, and quiet at other times. The high slopes of Sportgastein, in contrast, are more exposed both to wind and sun. We cover the slopes above Bad Hofgastein and Dorfgastein later in the chapter. Piste marking is said to need improvement.
Terrain parks Significantly, a large new one is planned for the 2008/09 season on Stubnerkogel above Bad Gastein.
Snow reliability The area is higher than many Austrian rivals, and there is snowmaking on crucial sections. Grooming is reportedly 'adequate'.
Experts The few black runs are not severe, but many reds are long and satisfying. Graukogel has some of the most testing slopes. The other sectors have plenty of opportunity for off-piste. Sportgastein is worth the trip – the ski-route is rated 'fabulous'.
Intermediates Good for the confident, who will find long, leg-sapping runs in all the sectors in the valley. The timid are better off sticking to Schlossalm (see Bad Hofgastein, below).
Beginners Nursery slopes are scattered and none of them is ideal. The main

BAD GASTEIN TOURIST OFFICE

Driving or catching a bus to Angertal to start the day will be an even better idea next season if the new gondola is in place ↓

NEWS

For 2008/09 a new two-stage, eight-person gondola from Angertal up to Stubnerkogel is planned. Work has begun on a new black run from Schlossalm to Angertal, as well as a red run on Stubnerkogel (there may be a new blue there as well). The terrain park that was built above Bad Gastein last season will be expanded for 2008/09, and more snowmaking will be installed.

For 2007/08 a new red run was built from Schlossalm to Angertal, and a new bridge at Angertal was built to connect the fragmented beginner slopes there. At Bad Gastein, snowmaking was increased on both sides of Stubnerkogel.

KEY FACTS

| Resort | 1080m |
| | 3,540ft |

The Gastein valley and Grossarl areas	
Slopes	840-2685m
	2,760-8,810ft
Lifts	44
Pistes	201km
	125 miles
Blue	30%
Red	58%
Black	12%
Snowmaking	
	537 guns

Bad Gastein and Bad Hofgastein only	
Slopes	860-2685m
	2,820-8,810ft
Lifts	26
Pistes	121km
	75 miles

slope at Bad Gastein is too steep. And progression is tricky – the genuinely easy blue runs are often boring paths.

Snowboarding The valley hosts snowboard events, but doesn't seem to cater particularly well for holiday boarders. There's still a fairly high proportion of draglifts.

Cross-country There are 90km/56 miles of trails, but they are all low down.

Queues Recent reports vary. The new gondola at Angertal (see 'News') should solve any problems there.

Mountain restaurants Atmospheric, traditional huts abound; but they can get crowded at peak periods. The 'very inviting' Jungerstube, Ahornhütte, Bergstadl and cosy Stubneralm have been recommended.

Schools and guides Reports are generally favourable ('first-class Croatian instructor', 'patient and understanding'). A recent visitor was 'very satisfied' with his private lesson.

Facilities for children There are facilities for all-day care and there's a 'Fun Center' for kids at the top of the Stubnerkogel gondola which was a 'great success' with a reporter's small grandchildren. There's also a snow adventure park at Angertal.

STAYING THERE

How to go British tour operators sell mainly hotel-based packages.

Hotels There are lots of smart 4- and 3-star hotels with spa facilities. The Wildbad (37610) was rated 'excellent' by a recent reporter. The Alpenblick (20620) is 'comfortable and welcoming' – with a pool and spa – but well outside town – and the Mozart (2686) is 'quirky, friendly and has a brilliant chef'. The Grüner Baum (25160) is a lovely retreat, but wildly inconvenient except for langlauf (though they do have a hotel bus).

Eating out There is a fair range of restaurants. The central Wirtshaus Jägerhäusl does excellent food in a warm, traditional atmosphere (especially upstairs). The Vier Jahreszeiten, a short drive away in Böckstein, offers big portions, 'very good value and friendly service'.

Après-ski The town feels generally subdued, but there are numerous popular bars and several discos – plus a casino ('grotty but fun'). Highlights from reporters include Hirschenhütte in the Angertal, the 'cosy, friendly, wood-panelled' Hexenhäusl, the 'friendlier'

Eden and the Weinfassl for 'dancing and drinking games'. The Silver Bullet has 'excellent live bands', but 'gets packed'. Haeggbloms is popular and has 'a great atmosphere'. Places for a quiet late drink include the smart Bellini bar and the Ritz cocktail bar.

Off the slopes The thermal spa facilities are excellent and extensive ('best I've been to'). A reporter says the Healing Galleries at Sportgastein are worth a visit. And interesting excursions are possible.

Bad Hofgastein
860m/2,820ft

Bad Hofgastein is a sizeable, quiet spa village set where the valley is wide.

THE RESORT

Although sprawling, the village has a pleasant pedestrianised centre. The slopes are reached by a funicular to Kitzsteinalm starting a long walk or short shuttle-bus ride away; or you can take a longer bus ride to Angertal.

THE MOUNTAINS

Schlossalm is a broad, open bowl, with runs through patchy woods both to Bad Hofgastein and Angertal.

The slopes Schlossalm is the valley's gentlest area, with sunny open blue and red slopes. The mountain's first black run is planned above Angertal. The Kleine Scharte cable car serves a serious 750m/2,460ft vertical, with a splendid long red from Hohe Scharte to Kitzsteinalm or the valley floor.

Terrain parks There isn't one.

Snow reliability Snowmaking is now fairly extensive, but snow-cover down to the bottom is unreliable, especially on the sunny Angertal slopes.

Experts There are no real challenges on the local pistes but there is ample opportunity to go off-piste.

Intermediates All intermediates will enjoy the Schlossalm slopes – and the more confident can go further afield.

Beginners You have to catch a bus to the nursery area at Angertal.

Snowboarding Pleasantly varied terrain, but no special facilities. Draglifts are dotted around.

Cross-country Bad Hofgastein makes a fine base for cross-country when its lengthy valley-floor trails have snow.

Queues The queue-prone funicular and cable car to Schlossalm can take 'the best part of an hour to get to the top' – but there are ways round both.

130

Phone numbers
Bad Gastein
From elsewhere in
Austria add the prefix
06434 (Bad Gastein),
06432 (Bad
Hofgastein), 06433
(Dorfgastein); from
abroad use the prefix
+43 and omit the
initial '0'

TOURIST OFFICE

For all resorts in the
Gastein valley contact
t 06432 33930
info@gastein.com
www.gastein.com

Mountain restaurants Well up to the high local standards are Kleine Scharte, Hamburger Skihütte and Aeroplanstadl ('good value home cooking' and its toilets are 'in the form of a pristine mock cavern').
Schools and guides No recent reports.
Facilities for children See Bad Gastein.

STAYING THERE
How to go Mostly hotels.
Hotels Reporters have recommended the 4-star St Georg (61000; '200m to lift, spa, sauna, quite good half-board food'), Palace (67150), Salzburgerhof (62300), Germania (6232) and the Tirol (63940; 'comfortable rooms and an excellent cocktail bar'). In the village centre the Osterreichischer Hof (6216) is 'well-run' and has its own 'good' spa facilities. The 3-star Rauscher (64120) is handy for the shuttle-bus ('clean, spacious rooms and good food').
Apartments Accommodation can be organised through the tourist office.
Eating out There is a good range of restaurants. Piccola Italia is 'well worth a visit'. The Wintergarten is an intimate restaurant, the Maier one of the better informal places.
Après-ski Quiet by Austrian standards. At close of play the Aeroplanstadl and central Piccolo ice bar are popular; there are several good places for cakes, among them Café Weitmoser, a historic little castle. Later on, the

Glocknerkeller and the Gasteiner Discostadl are among the disco bars.
Off the slopes The Alpen Therme Gastein spa is 'huge', with several pools and a 'river' as well as saunas, steam baths etc. Other amenities include walking and ice skating.

Dorfgastein 830m/2,720ft

Dorfgastein is a rustic village further down the valley ('ideal for older skiers and families', says a 2008 visitor). It has its own extensive slopes, accessed by a two-stage gondola or by chairlifts starting a little way outside the village, linked with the slopes of Grossarl in the next valley. Reporters enjoy the long, varied runs, with a good mix of open and wooded terrain amid lovely scenery – ideal for beginners and intermediates. The wide, gentle blue down to Grossarl is particularly noted. And grooming is 'adequate'. The low nursery slopes can be icy though. The resort also has a terrain park. Of the mountain restaurants, the table-service Wengeralm served 'the best lunch we had all week', says a reporter. The Dorf Aktiv school is said to offer 'very good' children's classes. There are a few shops, a swimming pool and some après-ski places. A 2008 visitor found the 4-star Römerhof (7777) to be 'probably the best Austrian 4-star we've stayed at – brilliant food'.

Bad Kleinkirchheim

Large resort tucked away in Carinthia, with marvellous spa facilities and a ski area best suited to intermediates

RATINGS

The slopes	
Fast lifts	**
Snow	***
Extent	**
Expert	**
Intermediate	***
Beginner	**
Convenience	***
Queues	****
Mountain restaurants	***

The rest	
Scenery	***
Resort charm	**
Off-slope	***

➕ Mainly intermediate slopes

➕ Virtually all the slopes have snowmaking

➕ Two superb thermal spas

➕ Plenty to do off the slopes

➖ Spread-out town

➖ Still a lot of T-bars

➖ No terrain park or half-pipe

BKK, as the locals call it, is downhill race hero Franz Klammer's favourite ski area – he learned to ski here and there's a World Cup downhill run bearing his name. (What? Franz who, did you say? Oh come on! Arguably the best downhill racer ever? Innsbruck Olympics, 1976? Honestly, the young people of today ...)

Given Klammer's endorsement, it's no surprise that the resort has some serious skiing: 75% of its slopes are classified red. It perhaps is a surprise that there are few real challenges for experts. So the resort suits confident intermediates best. It's a traditional spa town (with two excellent thermal spas) but, unlike many of those, it has mainly easy-on-the-eye chalet-style buildings.

THE RESORT

BKK is tucked away on the edge of the Nock Mountain National Park in the province of Carinthia, in the far south-east of Austria, near the Italian and Slovenian borders. The nearest airports are Klagenfurt (around 50 minutes away) and Ljubljana (90 minutes). Salzburg is less than two hours away.

The old spa town has mainly chalet-style buildings with sloping roofs, rather than the more austere blocks of some spa resorts. But it is very spread out along the valley, and the most convenient place to stay is near one of the main lifts out. A ski-bus links all the main lift stations, and some buses also go to St Oswald, a smaller village at the far end of the shared ski area.

The spa facilities are excellent, with indoor and outdoor thermal pools (with temperatures of between 28° and 34°C), different types of sauna – including a tepidarium (a sauna with a lower temperature so you can sit there

The resort is popular with families ➘

KAISERBURG
2055m/6,740ft

Strohsack
1905m

MAIBRUNN
1760m/5770ft

Priedröf
1965m/6,450ft

NOCKALM

Wieser Nock
1970m/6,460ft

Brunnach
1910m/6,270ft

1280m

1370m

1025m

St Oswald

Bad Kleinkirchheim
1090m/3,580ft

Feldkirchen ↓

NEWS

For 2007/08 the new Thermal Römerbad spa opened. The 12,000 square metre centre is on three levels and offers 13 different types of sauna and steam rooms, indoor and outdoor pools, relaxation areas, a large adults-only section and children's area.

More snowmaking was installed for 2007/08, meaning that 97% of the pistes are now covered.

KEY FACTS

Resort	1090m
	3,580ft
Slopes	1100-2055m
	3,610-6,740ft
Lifts	26
Pistes	103km
	64 miles
Blue	17%
Red	75%
Black	8%
Snowmaking	97%

longer) and steam rooms, solariums, hot tubs, massage and therapy rooms. There are also water slides, waterfalls and massage jets in the pools. 'We found the spas superb,' says a reporter. 'They are a great way to unwind after skiing and mean there's plenty to do if the snow is limited, as it was for us.' The new Thermal Römerbad opened last year – see 'News'. We tried that last season and thought it was superb; we could happily have spent days there.

And for the benefit of devotees ... Franz Klammer, 1976 Olympic downhill gold medallist and winner of a record 25 World Cup Downhills, was born in Mooswald, near Bad Kleinkirchheim. His mother runs a gasthaus with his brother and sister-in-law in Fresach, about 20km/12 miles from BKK. He learned to ski at BKK, and it remains his favourite resort.

THE MOUNTAINS

BKK's shady home slopes are linked to the sunnier ones above the neighbouring village of St Oswald. Throughout, they are mainly wooded and of intermediate standard (75% are classified red).

The piste map usefully marks the mountain restaurants; it also marks 'Römer Lounges' and 'Hits am Lift' – see overleaf for what these are.

There is a speed course on the Kaiserburg run open to anyone, and it is free of charge.

The lift pass covers all the resorts in Carinthia – useful for visiting other resorts if you have a car.

Slopes BKK's main home slopes are reached by lifts from two different

parts of the village. A two-stage gondola goes up to the area's high point, Kaiserburg, at one end of the ski area, where a couple of T-bars serve the highest slopes. And a fast quad chair takes you to the other end of the same mountain face at Maibrunn. Pistes go down from both peaks to the gondola mid-station, and a chair takes you back to above Maibrunn.

From the same end of the village as the Maibrunn quad, successive old double chairs and a drag take you up the other side of the valley to the Nockalm slopes, which link in with St Oswald's slopes further along the valley. This area can also be accessed by a gondola midway between BKK and St Oswald, which can be reached by ski-bus. At St Oswald a gondola goes up to Brunnach, at the far end of the shared ski area.

Two quads link the Nockalm and St Oswald slopes, and most of the other upper lifts are drags.

Terrain parks There isn't one.

Snow reliability Being south of the Tauern mountain range, BKK can have completely different weather from the rest of Austria. So snow reliability can be better or worse, depending on the season. In general, BKK's main home slopes are north-facing and keep their snow best. The Nockalm-St Oswald slopes are more sunny. Additional snowmaking was installed for 2007/08, and they claim that virtually all the pistes (97%) are now covered.

Experts BKK has little to keep experts interested for a week. The best and most challenging black is the Franz Klammer World Cup run, which goes from Strohsack to the gondola base

RÖMER LOUNGES & HITS AM LIFT

We've seen some things marked on piste maps in our time but never 'Römer Lounge' and 'Hits am Lift' before.

A 'Römer Lounge' is an area with a red sofa designed to encourage you to take a rest and soak up the sun while admiring the panorama in a kind of sitting room complete with a TV set and Roman-style columns and mosaics on the back wall, meant to be in keeping with the new Thermal Römerbad. There's no roof, two side walls come up halfway, and the front is open to the view. There are four of these on the slopes, and we found them comfortable and relaxing with great views.

Hits am Lift? Yes, you guessed it: at the bottom of certain lifts different music (eg Austrian folk music, Rock and Roll, Italian, Evergreen) is pumped out to keep visitors amused while waiting for the lift. It works surprisingly well.

UK PACKAGES

Ardmore, BoardnLodge, Interhome, Ski Wild

Phone numbers
From elsewhere in Austria add the prefix 04240; from abroad use the prefix +43 04240

TOURIST OFFICE

t 8212
info@
badkleinkirchheim.at
www.
badkleinkirchheim.at

(the short top section is very steep and often closed). There are two short black runs below Kaiserburg and another under the Wiesernock quad. Off-piste tours that involve some hiking can be arranged (eg to Mallnock and Klomnock mountains from the top of the gondola from St Oswald and on Falkert mountain, reached by taxi from BKK and then a T-bar followed by a hike).

Intermediates Virtually all the slopes in both BKK and St Oswald are ideal for good intermediates as three-quarters of the slopes are classified red and many are long (up to 1000m/3,280ft vertical), wide and flattering. One of the most beautiful runs is the FIS K70 downhill run, classified red, which goes from top to bottom of the mountain away from all the lifts and through the trees in the lower section – on the extreme left-hand side of our piste map. It is almost 5km/3 miles long (and rarely groomed, says a local). There are two other long top-to-bottom red runs in this area too, as well as the Franz Klammer black. The Nockalm and St Oswald sectors also have long red runs, which are generally easier than those in the Kaiserburg-Maibrunn sector; so this area is better for early intermediates and families.

Beginners There are nursery slopes and draglifts for beginners at both BKK and St Oswald – the St Oswald ones are at the top of the Nochalm gondola and much warmer and sunnier in midwinter, when the low BKK ones are in the shade. One reporter said: 'I had to take my kids off the BKK nursery slope because they were freezing. But they loved the sunny slope at St Oswald.' Once off the nursery slopes, there is a long blue the length of the gondola here.

Snowboarding Although the main lifts are all gondolas or chairs, there are a lot of T-bars, which less experienced boarders may not like. And there's no terrain park or half-pipe.

Cross-country BKK takes cross-country seriously, with 54km/34 miles of tracks, some as high as 1900m/6,230ft at the top of the Nockalm.

Queues We have no reports of lift queues being much of a problem.

Mountain restaurants There are 22 mountain restaurants and huts. The most recent addition is the panoramic Nock In at the top of Brunnach above St Oswald. You might meet Franz

Klammer himself having lunch at the Kaiserburg at the top of the gondola of that name; he is always happy to have a chat and sign autographs. We also enjoyed the cosy Brentler-Hütte (excellent ham) on the way down from Nockalm to the valley and Zum Podl above St Oswald.

Schools and guides There are four schools to choose from, three based in BKK and one in St Oswald. Style Check is a twice-weekly concept, offering slope-side tips in specially marked areas from instructors to help polish your technique (five euros).

Facilities for children There's a non-skiing kindergarten for children from age two upwards at the foot of the gondola from BKK. First Steps takes children from two and a half, where they can learn to ski while playing.

STAYING THERE

How to go Several UK tour operators feature BKK.

Hotels The two 5-star hotels, the Pulverer (744) and the Thermenhotel Ronacher (282), are both near the high-speed chair and nursery slope and have excellent spa facilities. There are 21 4-stars, several 3-stars and lots of gasthofs too. BKK boasts 26 hotels with swimming pools and 50 saunas.

Apartments There are lots of self-catering apartments to rent.

Eating out There is plenty of choice, including a lot of hotel restaurants. We loved the atmospheric old Loystub'n in the hotel Pulverer (delicious venison carpaccio and pepper steak, excellent service).

Après-ski A lot of the après-ski takes place in the hotels, but there are a few interesting bars. Near the BKK gondola base are several popular places: the Almstube, Viktoria Pub, Club MC 99 and the Take Five Dancing Club.

Off the slopes There are superb spa facilities, as described in the introduction. You can buy lift tickets that include the use of the thermal swimming pools. There are also some good walks (including the Spa Boulevard route at the top of the gondola from St Oswald), a tennis centre, squash courts, an outdoor ice rink, curling, snow tubing, horse riding, sleigh rides and a 4km/2.5 mile floodlit toboggan run. Those with cars can also visit Villach (36km/22 miles away) for a shopping spree or carry on across the border into Italy.

Bregenzerwald

An unspoiled region that is hardly heard of on the British market, with a lot of relatively small ski areas covered on one big pass

Bregenzerwald is tucked away between Germany and Switzerland at the westernmost end of Austria. Skirted by all the major road and rail links, it has remained remarkably unspoiled and is still primarily a farming community famous for its cheeses (in winter the cows are safely tucked away in their sheds). But it is part of the Vorarlberg (along with more famous neighbours such as Lech and Zürs), and it has mountains rising up to over 2400m/7,870ft and almost 260km/160 miles of slopes served by 94 lifts in 22 villages.

Skiing began in Bregenzerwald in 1894 when the parish priest, Father Johann Müller – garbed in his flowing robes – careered down the slopes on two wooden planks, amazing the local farmers. Until then, if you absolutely had to get around in winter, you wore a type of snowshoe. The priest had sent away to Norway for his newfangled 'Hickoryski', and in doing so he established a trend that has transformed the region's economy.

There is now a ski lift in almost every village. But few of the many ski areas are large. They are all covered by the 3-Valley ski pass, which also covers two areas outside Bregenzerwald. The pass is valid in 34 ski areas and covers almost 340km/211 miles of slopes served by 138 lifts. There's a ski-bus service between different resorts in Bregenzerwald that is included in the pass, and there's a

special offer for families who stay for a week on certain dates in January and March 2009: children between the ages of three and six get a six-day lift pass and four days of lessons free.

Nearly all the resorts offer activities other than skiing, including walking (there are lots of cleared paths), tobogganing and cross-country skiing.

THE BIGGEST SKI AREAS

Warth and **Schröcken** share 60km/37 miles of slopes between 1500m/4,920ft and 2000m/6,560ft served by 15 lifts, including five high-speed chairs. The runs include several blacks and ski routes as well as reds and blues, and there's a terrain park, 17km/11 miles of cross-country loops and 20km/12 miles of walking trails.

Warth is only a few kilometres up the valley from Lech (see separate

Widderstein 2533m
↙ Lechtal
↙ Innsbruck
Warth 1495m
Schröcken 1260m
Damüls 1431m
Schoppernau 860m
Au 800m
Niedere 1711m
Mellau 688m
Hochhäderich 1566m
Bezau 650m
Hochälpelekopf 1463m
Schetteregg 1066m
Andelsbuch 613m
Egg 564m
Schwarzenberg 700m
Riefensberg 781m
Müselbach 585m
Bödele 1139m
Alberschwende 721m
Dornbirn 475m
Friedrichshafen
München
Stuttgart ↙
BREGENZ 400m
Feldkirch
Zürich →

chapter). The road is closed in winter, but you can ski there off-piste and the school organises weekly excursions.

The villages are small, pretty and unspoiled. There are six 4-star hotels, three 3-star hotels and one 2-star, plus inns and gasthofs. The 4-stars include the Walserberg (05583 3502) – with recently renovated rooms, several themed suites, five-course dinners, saunas, steam room and fitness room – and the Sporthotel Steffisalp (05583 3699) with rooms in four different categories, a formal restaurant, après-ski hut and umbrella bar – and a spa area with vitality pool, saunas, steam room, solarium and spa treatments.

Damüls is the biggest single ski area in Bregenzerwald, with 64km/40 miles of runs between 1430m/4,690ft and 2000m/6,560ft. Just under half of these are red runs, around 40% blue and the rest blacks and ski routes. And there's a good terrain park. Last season saw two new six-packs open, allowing expansion into the Argental valley. This is the first stage of a project to link the slopes with those of Mellau (see below), due to be complete by 2009/10. Altogether there are 12 lifts, including nine chairs (with three six-packs and a fast quad).

Damüls also has 16km/10 miles of sunny cross-country tracks and over 22km/14 miles of winter walking trails.

Although remaining a small village, it is quite spread out and has six 4-star hotels, three 3-stars plus inns and gasthofs, and most of the accommodation is ski-in/ski-out. Damüls recently won an award as the most snow-sure village in the world, we are assured.

Mellau has 20km/12 miles of mainly treelined pistes served by seven lifts including a gondola out of the village and two six-packs. They serve mainly blue and red runs (including a long red right back to the village) with one black and a ski route. There's a FIS certified slope and a terrain park. The village is at 700m/2,300ft and the top of the ski area is at 1750m/5,740ft. It has just two 4-star and one 3-star hotels and a few gasthofs.

Au and **Schoppernau** are neighbouring villages sharing the **Diedamskopf** ski area, which boasts Bregenzerwald's highest lift station at 2,060m/6,760ft. With a valley station at 820m/2,690m it has a vertical of over 1200m/3,940ft with a longest run

↑ The 3-Valley lift pass covers 34 ski areas with almost 340km/211 miles of slopes served by 138 lifts

BREGENZERWALD TOURISMUS

of over 10km/6 miles. But the lower section of this is served only by ski routes. The pistes are all above 1470m/4,820ft. Altogether there are eight lifts, including a two-stage gondola to the Panorama restaurant at the top, serving 44km/27 miles of slopes. Of these around 30% are red or black ski routes, 33% blue pistes, 20% red pistes and the rest black. The resort claims that its Sajas terrain park – with around 20 varied features including rails, boxes and kickers – is the best in Bregenzerwald, and it attracts snowboarders and freestyle skiers from across Europe. There's night skiing twice a week.

The ski school here is working on the Ski! Project, which claims to offer 'a completely new approach to skiing with a modern concept inspired by dancing lessons'. Sounds interesting – reports welcome.

At the top of the mountain, the Kids Adventure Land takes children aged three to eight years old.

Cross-country enthusiasts will find over 60km/37 miles of trails. There are 35km/22 miles of cleared walks and a natural ice rink.

The villages of Au and Schoppernau between them have eleven 4-star and five 3-star hotels plus gasthofs and plenty of dining options.

SMALLER SKI AREAS

Andelsbuch and **Bezau** share the local Niedere ski area with nine lifts serving three short blue runs, a 7km/4 mile long red, a short black and several ski routes – 20km/12 miles in total. It's a family ski area, and, given good snow, the ski routes offer more experienced

skiers a challenge too. The top height is 1715m/5,630ft. Andelsbuch has just two 3-star hotels plus a few gasthofs, and Bezau has a 4-star hotel.

Alberschwende has just 18km/11 miles of runs, served by a chairlift and seven T-bars, and is popular with beginners. There's a 10km/6 mile cross-country track and an ice rink. It has two 4-star hotels and a 3-star, plus a few gasthofs.

Riefensberg has the tiny **Hochlitten** ski area, with just 5km/3 miles of easy blue and red runs and four T-bars. It also shares the **Hochhäderich** ski area with neighbouring **Hittisau**. This has 11km/7 miles of runs (mainly blue and red but with a couple of blacks) served by four T-bars and a quad chair specially designed to be appropriate for children. It also has 12km/7 miles of cross-country tracks at altitude and 12km/7 miles of walking paths. Hittisau has a 4-star hotel and three 3-star hotels, while Riefensberg has a 2-star inn.

Egg is the biggest village in Bregenzerwald with around 3,500 inhabitants and a small ski area at **Schetteregg**, which has six lifts serving 10km/6 miles of easy blue and red runs between 1100m and 1400m (3,610ft and 4,590ft). There are also 9km/6 miles of cleared walks. There's just one 3-star hotel, and there are a couple of inns.

Schwarzenberg's local **Bödele** mountain has 30km/19 miles of runs (mainly easy blues and reds) served by 10 lifts (nine of them draglifts). There are also 6km/4 miles of cross-country tracks and 4km/2 miles of walking trails. Schwarzenberg has a 4-star and two 2-star hotels.

ALBIN NIEDERSTRASSER

Ellmau

Our favourite base on the extensive SkiWelt circuit, combining
charm with reasonable convenience – just hope the snow holds up

RATINGS

The slopes

Fast lifts	**
Snow	**
Extent	****
Expert	*
Intermediate	****
Beginner	****
Convenience	***
Queues	****
Mountain restaurants	**

The rest

Scenery	***
Resort charm	***
Off-slope	**

KEY FACTS

Resort	800m
	2,620ft

Entire SkiWelt	
Slopes	620-1890m
	2,030-6,200ft
Lifts	94
Pistes	250km
	155 miles
Blue	43%
Red	48%
Black	9%
Snowmaking	180km
	112 miles

➕ Pretty, friendly, extensive slopes – Austria's largest linked area

➕ Excellent nursery slopes

➕ Cheap by Austrian standards

➕ Quiet, charming family resort – more appealing than Söll

➕ Snowmaking is now more extensive and well used; even so ...

➖ Low altitude can mean poor snow

➖ Main lift a bus ride from village – though reachable via a draglift

➖ Upper-mountain runs are mostly short, and offer little challenge

➖ Limited range of nightlife

➖ The SkiWelt slopes can get crowded at weekends and in high season

If you like the sound of the large, undemanding SkiWelt circuit, Ellmau has a lot to recommend it as your base – quieter than Söll, but with more amenities than other neighbours such as Scheffau (covered in the Söll chapter). And Austria's largest snowmaking system makes the area less risky than it was.

THE RESORT

Ellmau sits at the north-eastern corner of the SkiWelt – an area of linked slopes that's an impressive 15km/ 9 miles across. Although sizeable, the village remains quiet, with traditional chalet-style buildings, welcoming bars and shops, and a pretty church. It has a compact centre, but accommodation is scattered – so the buses around the resort are important (and now quite well organised). There is accommodation out by the funicular to the main slopes, but we prefer to stay near the heart of the village. A guest card entitles you to various discounts, including entry to the leisure centre.

THE MOUNTAINS

The SkiWelt is the largest mountain circuit in Austria, linking seven resorts. This huge area is covered by a single piste map that has been improved recently, but is still generally poor and difficult to use in parts. Most runs are easy, and short – which means that getting around the area can take time, despite increasing numbers of fast lifts. Reporters have criticised inconsistent piste classification and 'appalling' signposting.

The SkiWelt pass also covers Westendorf, to be linked by a new gondola at Brixen for 2008/09 (see 'News') – so you no longer need to

NEWS

For 2008/09 you will be able to reach Westendorf's slopes more easily, when a new gondola opens at Brixen im Thale (see the Westendorf chapter).

At Söll: a six-pack is planned to replace the Silleralm triple chair, to improve the return to Zinsberg – above Scheffau.

LIFT PASSES

SkiWelt Wilder Kaiser-Brixental

Prices in €

Age	1-day	6-day
under 16	18	87
16 to 17	29	139
over 18	36	173

Free under 7
Senior no deals
Beginner points cards
Notes
Covers Wilder Kaiser-Brixental area from Going to Westendorf, and the ski-bus; single ascent and part-day options
Alternative passes
Kitzbüheler Alpen Skipass covers five large ski areas: Schneewinkel (St Johann), Kitzbühel, SkiWelt, Wildschönau and Alpbachtal

ON YOUR OWN?

You can team up with other skiers/boarders by turning up at 10am or 1pm at one of seven designated points in the SkiWelt; there are stickers to identify participants, and even a website forum for making prior arrangements.

take the bus; from there you can also progress to the Kirchberg-Kitzbühel slopes – see the Westendorf chapter. These, along with Waidring, Fieberbrunn and St Johann, are possible day trips covered by the Kitzbüheler Alpen Skipass.

Slopes The funicular railway on the edge of the village takes you up to Hartkaiser, from where a fine long red leads down to Blaiken (Scheffau's lift base station). Here, one of two gondolas takes you up to Brandstadl. Immediately beyond Brandstadl, the slopes become rather bitty; an array of short runs and lifts link Brandstadl to Zinsberg. From Zinsberg, long, south-facing pistes lead down to Brixen, where a new gondola will go up to Choralpe in Westendorf's area. Part-way down to Brixen you can head towards Söll, and if you go up Hohe Salve, you get access to a long, west-facing run to Hopfgarten.

Ellmau and Going share a pleasant little area of slopes on Astberg, slightly apart from the rest of the area, and well suited to the unadventurous and families. One piste leads to the funicular for access to the rest of the SkiWelt. The main Astberg chair is rather inconveniently positioned, midway between Ellmau and Going.

Terrain parks Ellmau has its own terrain park, the Kaiser-Park, with beginner and expert boxes, rails and kickers, as well as a chill-out zone.

Snow reliability With a low average height, and important links that get a lot of sun, the snowmaking that the SkiWelt has installed is essential; the Ellmau-Going sector now claims almost all its slopes are covered. Snowmaking can, of course, only be used when temperatures are low enough. The north-facing Eiberg area above Scheffau holds its snow well. Grooming is reported to be 'excellent' and reports have praised 'ace' snowmaking.

Experts There are steep plunges off the Hohe Salve summit, a ski route from Brandstadl down to Scheffau and a little mogul field between Brandstadl and Neualm, but the area isn't really suitable unless you go off-piste.

Intermediates With good snow, the SkiWelt is a paradise for those who love easy cruising. There are lots of blue runs and many of the reds deserve a blue classification. It is a big area and you get a feeling of travelling around. The main challenge is when

the snow isn't perfect – ice and slush can make even gentle lower slopes seem tricky. For timid intermediates the easy slopes of Astberg are handy.

Beginners Ellmau has an array of good nursery slopes covered by snowmaking. The main ones are at the Going end, but there are some by the road to the funicular. The Astberg chair opens up a more snow-sure plateau at altitude. The Brandstadl area has a section of short easy runs.

Snowboarding Ellmau is a good place to learn as its local slopes are easy.

Cross-country There are long, quite challenging trails (the SkiWelt area has a total of 170km/106 miles), but trails at altitude are lacking.

Queues Continued lift upgrades have greatly improved this once queue-prone area. With the exception of peak times ('10 minutes for the Aualm chair at half-term'), reporters comment on quiet and crowd-free slopes with 'few queues'. If the Hausberg chair is closed (as was the case on a 2007 reporter's two visits), you'll need to take the bus back from Hartkaiser.

Mountain restaurants The smaller places are fairly consistent in providing good-value food in pleasant surroundings. The Rübezahl above Ellmau is our favourite in the whole SkiWelt, but reportedly gets busy. The Aualm, just below Brandstadl, is recommended, especially for its cakes and glühwein. Other reporter recommendations include: the Jagerhütte (below Hartkaiser) for 'home-made strudel' and 'a drinks stop' before enjoying the 'quiet and pleasant' home-run, and the Hartkaiser for 'food quality and ambiance, and escalators to the loos'. The Bergkaiser also has 'quick service and good food'. The hut at Neualm, halfway down to Scheffau, has been praised, and the Kummereralm near the Tanzboden chair is 'excellent'. The larger self-service restaurants are functional (the Jochstuben at Eiberg is a pleasant exception) and generate queues at times.

Schools and guides The four schools (includes one at Going) have good reputations – except that classes can be very large. Top is highly rated for children's lessons – 'All our children had a great time in different classes with Top, who made sure they were in English-only speaking groups. It was a very busy week, but only our youngest was in the maximum class size of 12.'

Interactive resort shortlist builder at **www.wtss.co.uk**

↑ The craggy Wilder Kaiser makes a fine backdrop to the village
TVB WILDER KAISER

UK PACKAGES
Crystal, Crystal Finest, Inghams, Interhome, Neilson, Ski Line, Skitracer, Ski Wild

Phone numbers
From elsewhere in Austria add the prefix 05358; from abroad use the prefix +43 5358

TOURIST OFFICES

WILDER KAISER
(Ellmau, Söll, Scheffau, Going)
t 505
www.wilderkaiser. info

Ellmau
ellmau@wilderkaiser. info

Going
going@wilderkaiser. info

SkiWelt
www.skiwelt.at

Facilities for children Ellmau is an attractive resort for families, described by a regular visitor as 'so child-friendly'. Top ski school is praised (see 'Schools'). Kindergartens seem to be satisfactory and include fun ideas such as a mini train to the lifts. Kinderland has its own fun park and play areas. But we lack reports.

STAYING THERE

How to go Ellmau is essentially a hotel and pension resort, though there are apartments that can be booked locally.
Hotels The Bär (2395) is an elegant, relaxed Relais & Châteaux chalet, but pricier than most other hotels. 'It was friendly and welcoming, with a very good wellness centre,' wrote a reporter. 'Luxury without pretensions,' said another. The Hochfilzer (2501) is central, well equipped (with outdoor hot tub) and popular with reporters (as is the simpler Pension Claudia, which it owns – use of hotel facilities allowed). Kaiserblick (2230), with good spa facilities and right by the piste, is recommended by a regular visitor, who went with six families including 12 children. Another reporter rates the Kaiserhof (2022) as 'very comfortable and friendly, and with amazing food'.
Apartments There is a wide variety. The Landhof apartments continue to impress a regular visitor – 'spacious, immaculately clean, well equipped' – with pool, sauna and steam room. The supermarket on the way out of town towards Going is also rated as 'excellent'.
Eating out The jolly Gasthof Lobewein is a splendid, big, central chalet, with cheerful service in countless rooms

and excellent food. The Ellmauer Alm is also recommended (see below).
Après-ski Cafes Kaiserstüberl and Bettina are good for coffee and cakes. Memory (which has internet facilities) is the early-evening riotous party pub. Pub 66 and Ötzy have regular events such as karaoke and 'erotic dancers'. The Ellmauer Alm at the Going end of the village has fun, live entertainment and is 'always good'. Tour operator reps organise events such as bowling, sleigh rides, Tirolean folklore evenings and tubing. There's an Instructors' Ball and ski displays with 'a party atmosphere' each week, and the toboggan run from the Astberg lift is recommended.
Off the slopes The KaiserBad leisure centre is good. There are many excursions available, including ones to Salzburg and Vitipeno. Valley walks are spoiled by the busy main road. Heading up to Hartkaiser by funicular railway to relax on the terrace 'was a highlight for our non-skiers', writes a reporter.

Going 775m/2,540ft

Going is a tiny, attractively rustic village, ideal for families looking for a quiet time. It is well placed for the limited but quiet slopes of the Astberg and for the vast area of nursery slopes between here and Ellmau. Prices are low, but it's not an ideal base for covering the whole of the SkiWelt on the cheap unless you have a car for quick access to Scheffau and Söll. The Lanzenhof (2428) is a cosy central pension doing excellent traditional food in its woody dining rooms. Wellness centre includes a sauna.

Hintertux/Tux valley

Small, unspoiled, traditional villages, high snow-sure glacier slopes and lots of other areas covered by the valley lift pass

COSTS

①②③④⑤⑥

RATINGS

The slopes

Fast lifts	★★★
Snow	★★★★★
Extent	★★★
Expert	★★★
Intermediate	★★★
Beginner	★★
Convenience	★★
Queues	★★★
Mountain restaurants	★★

The rest

Scenery	★★★
Resort charm	★★★
Off-slope	★

NEWS

For 2008/09 a new 24-person gondola, Gletscherbus I, is due to replace the smaller of the two access gondolas up to Sommerbergalm.

For 2007/08 snowmaking was increased between Fernerhaus and Sommerbergalm.

140

➕ Hintertux has one of the best glaciers in the world, open summer as well as winter

➕ Lanersbach's ski area is linked to Mayrhofen and Finkenberg; and several other areas are covered by the area lift pass and free buses

➕ Some excellent off-piste opportunities

➕ A choice of quiet, unspoiled, traditional villages to stay in

➖ Not for those who want a huge choice of shops and throbbing nightlife on their doorstep

➖ Not ideal for beginners or timid intermediates, with few easy runs to valley level

➖ Glacier can be cold and bleak in midwinter, and there are lots of T-bars and slow chairs

The main attraction of Hintertux is obvious: its glacier. It is not only extensive; it arguably has the most challenging and interesting runs of any lift-served Alpine glacier. For guaranteed good snow, Hintertux is simply one of the best places to go. But the Tux valley has broader appeal: the quieter, friendlier, non-glacial slopes above Lanersbach and its nearby twin, Vorderlanersbach are linked by fast lifts with those above Mayrhofen and Finkenberg. Together, they form a fair-sized circuit. With the glacier only 15 to 20 minutes away by bus, these quiet, unspoiled, traditional villages are attractive bases – for many people, more attractive than either higher Hintertux or lower Mayrhofen (covered in its own chapter). There are other areas further down the Zillertal that are worth a day trip (see the end of the Mayrhofen chapter).

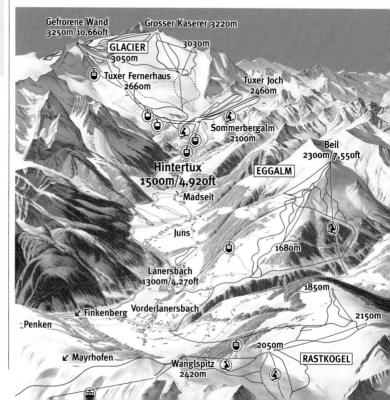

Traditional-style
buildings and fine
scenery; this is
Finkenberg →
TVB TUX-FINKENBERG

KEY FACTS

Resort	1500m
	4,920ft

Ski and Glacier World
Zillertal 3000

Slopes	630-3250m
	2,070-10,660ft
Lifts	59
Pistes	227km
	141 miles
Blue	26%
Red	58%
Black	16%
Snowmaking	121km
	75 miles

Hintertux only

Slopes	1500-3250m
	4,920-10,660ft
Lifts	21
Pistes	86km
	53 miles

For Ziller valley

Slopes	630-3250m
	2,070-10,660ft
Lifts	174
Pistes	636km
	395 miles

LIFT PASSES

Zillertaler
Superskipass

Prices in €

Age	1-day	6-day
under 15	18	88
15 to 18	29	141
over 19	36	176

Free under 6
Senior no deals
Beginner no deals
Notes
1-, 2- or 3-day passes
cover Hintertux
glacier, Eggalm,
Rastkogel and Penken
areas; 4-day and over
passes include all
Ziller valley lifts; part-
day and pedestrian
passes available

The Tux valley, an extension of Mayrhofen's Zillertal, has a variety of small villages, linked by frequent free ski-buses. A cheap (one euro) night-bus also runs until 2am. At the top of the valley, directly below the glacier, is **Hintertux**; a 15-minute bus ride down the valley, the major resorts are **Lanersbach** and **Vorderlanersbach**. Lower down still – actually in the Zillertal, and much less well served by buses – is **Finkenberg**. There is also accommodation in Juns and Madseit.

There are some good rustic restaurants and bars and a few places along the valley with discos or live music. But nightlife tends to be quieter than in many bigger Austrian resorts (Mayrhofen, for example).

All the major resort villages have gondola links into the local slopes: the Finkenberg gondola goes up to the Penken slopes shared with Mayrhofen; the Vorderlanersbach one goes to Rastkogel, which is linked with the Penken slopes; and the Lanersbach one goes to Eggalm, from which you can ski to Vorderlanersbach.

The Tux valley and Mayrhofen lifts now form what is called the Ski and Glacier World Zillertal 3000. Lift passes for four days or more also cover the other resorts in the Ziller valley (see the end of the Mayrhofen chapter).

Hintertux 1500m/4,920ft

THE RESORT
Tiny Hintertux is set at the end of the Tux valley. It is little more than a small collection of hotels and guest houses; there is another, smaller group of hotels near the lifts, which lie a 15-minute walk away from the village, across a car park that fills with day-visitors' cars and coaches, especially when snow is poor in lower resorts.

THE MOUNTAINS
Hintertux's slopes are fairly extensive and, for a glacier, surprisingly challenging. The glacier is one of the best in the world, with varied terrain that attracts national ski teams for summer training.

Slopes A series of three speedy gondolas (all with 24-person cabins) takes you up from the base to the top

ski explore excel

MAYRHOFEN HINTERTUX

0870 060 4343

of the glacier (vertical rise 1750m/ 5,740ft) in under 20 minutes. The first of these is new for 2008/09, replacing one of the two parallel access lifts up to Sommerbergalm; the increased capacity should now meet demand at peak times. The second and third stages are linked by a short slope at Tuxer Fernerhaus. A fast quad chair from Sommerbergalm serves short, easy slopes below Tuxer Joch; from the top of this sector, the excellent secluded Schwarze Pfanne ski route goes down to the base station. Between the top of the glacier and Tuxer Fernerhaus there are further chairs and draglifts to play on and links across to another 1000m/3,300ft-vertical chain of lifts below Grosser Kaserer on the west. Behind Gefrorene Wand is the area's one sunny piste, served by a triple chair. Descent to the valley involves a short ascent to Sommerbergalm on the way, achieved by a six-seater chairlift.

Terrain parks Europe's highest World Cup half-pipe is on the glacier (a popular hang-out throughout the summer), and there is a terrain park with jumps, fun boxes and rails.

Snow reliability Snow does not come more reliable than this. Even off the glacier, the other slopes are high and face north, making for very reliable snow-cover. The runs from Tuxer Fernerhaus and Tuxer Joch down to Sommerbergalm have snowmaking (improved for 2007/08), as does the Schwarze Pfanne ski route.

Experts There is more to amuse experts here than on any other glacier, with a couple of serious black runs at glacier level and steep slopes and ungroomed ski routes beneath. A lot of the off-piste is little used and one reporter said, 'We found untracked snow not far from the lifts two weeks after the last snowfall.'

Intermediates The area particularly suits good, confident intermediates. The long runs down from Gefrorene Wand and Kaserer are fun. And there is a pleasant, treelined ski route to the valley from Sommerbergalm and another from Tuxer Joch. Moderate intermediates will love the glacier.

Beginners There is a nursery slope at valley level, but the glacier isn't an ideal place to progress to.

Snowboarding There are some great off-piste opportunities, but boarders complain about the number of T-bars.

Cross-country See the Lanersbach

information later in the chapter.

Queues There used to be huge queues at Hintertux when snow was poor elsewhere. Improved lifts have largely solved this problem and the new gondola from the valley should cut queues there. But the main runs can get crowded, and then it is best to head over to the quieter Kaserer lifts and runs.

Mountain restaurants The mountain restaurants tend to get very crowded and the big self-service places lack charm. One exception is the out-of-the-way Tuxer Joch Haus – 'amazing views', says a 2008 visitor. Another is the almost-100-year-old Spannagelhaus – 'fun atmosphere'. There are great views from 'friendly' Gletscherhütte, at the top. The self-service at Sommerbergalm is reportedly 'dull but with a pleasant terrace'.

Schools and guides There are three schools, which serve all the resorts in Tux, but we lack reports on them. Tux 3000 has special guiding, touring and race-training programmes.

Facilities for children Most of the ski schools run classes for children aged four to 14 and lunch is provided. There's a children's fun area on the glacier.

STAYING THERE

How to go Most hotels are large and comfortable and have spa facilities, but there are also more modest pensions.

Hotels Close to the lifts are the 4-star Vierjahreszeiten (8525) and Neuhintertux (8580) in which a 2007 reporter found 'a good wine list' and enjoyed the 'large pool, saunas, steam baths and modern spa'. Reporters also recommend the 4-star Berghof (8585) with its 'good service and spa' and the Thermal Badhotel Kirchler (8570) for its good food and 'welcoming bar' (but it was a good 20 minute walk to the lifts, and buses were not frequent in May/June when we were there). The 4-star Alpenhof (8550) has also been praised and we have enjoyed staying in the 3-star Hintertuxerhof (8530): good food, sauna and steam room. Pensions Kössler (87490) – 3-star – and the 2-star Willeiter (87492) are in the heart of the village.

Apartments There are plenty of self-catering apartments.

Eating out Restaurants are mainly hotel-based. The Vierjahreszeiten is pleasant and informal.

im Zillertal
TUX.at
Finkenberg
850 - 3250 m

100%
SNOW GUARANTEE

picture. marcotoniolo.com

www.tux.at

225 km of ski runs · 365 days of the year snowfun on the Hintertux Glacier

Rooms, Brochures, Information: Tourismusverband Tux-Finkenberg, A-6293 Tux, Lanersbach 472,
tel. +43/(0)5287/8506, e-mail: info@tux.at · info@finkenberg.at · **www.tux.at** · **www.finkenberg.at**

resort. And prices are relatively low. Vorderlanersbach is even smaller, with a gondola up to the Rastkogel area.

THE MOUNTAINS

Slopes The slopes of Eggalm, accessed by the gondola from Lanersbach, offer a small network of pleasantly varied, intermediate pistes, usually delightfully quiet. You can descend on red or blue runs back to the village or to Vorderlanersbach, where a gondola goes up to the higher, open Rastkogel slopes; here, two fast chairlifts – one a covered eight-seater – serve some very enjoyable long red and blue runs and link with Mayrhofen's slopes. The linking run is classified red but can get very mogulled and many people opt to ride the 150-person cable car down; a short rope-tow cuts out the need to hike up to the top station. The lower half of the run back from Rastkogel to Eggalm is now a ski route, but is really quite easy and is served by snowmaking. The alternative is to ride the gondola down to Vorderlanersbach (there are no pistes to the village) and catch the bus to Lanersbach.

Terrain parks The Mayrhofen and Hintertux pipes and parks are easily accessed.

Snow reliability Snow conditions are usually good, at least in early season; by Austrian standards these are high slopes and snowmaking covers some runs on both Eggalm and Rastkogel. But Rastkogel is basically south-facing, so snow quality can suffer.

Experts There are no pistes to challenge experts, but there is a fine off-piste route starting a short walk from the top of the Eggalm slopes and finishing at the village.

Intermediates The local slopes suit intermediates best – and you have Mayrhofen's slopes to explore too.

Beginners Lanersbach has a nursery slope (as do Madseit and Juns) but there are few ideal progression slopes – most of the easy runs are on the higher lifts of the Rastkogel sector.

Snowboarding The area isn't great for novices – there are draglifts dotted around, some in key places.

Cross-country There are 14km/9 miles of cross-country trails, alongside the Tux creek, between Madseit and Vorderlanersbach, and a 6km/4 mile skating track in Juns/Madseit.

Queues We have no reports of any problems. Indeed, Eggalm can be delightfully quiet.

↑ Lanersbach is an attractive, traditional village, bypassed by valley traffic
TVB TUX-FINKENBERG

Après-ski There can be a lively après-ski scene both at mid-mountain (Sommerbergalm) and at the base; the 'very lively' Hohenhaus Tenne has several different bars, the Rindererhof has a popular tea dance, and there are a couple of local bars. The cheap (one euro) night-bus gets you to and from the other villages until 2am, but this is not the place for keen clubbers.

Off the slopes The spa facilities are excellent, including a thermal indoor pool, but there are many more options in Mayrhofen.

Lanersbach 1300m/4,270ft

Lanersbach and neighbouring Vorderlanersbach have long been attractive bases for exploring the resorts of the Zillertal and Tuxertal. Since their ski areas were linked with Mayrhofen's slopes, their attractions are greatly reinforced.

THE RESORT

Lanersbach is an attractive, spacious, traditional village, largely unspoiled by the busy road up to Hintertux that passes the main lift. The quiet centre near the pretty church is bypassed by the road, yet is within walking distance of the gondola up to Eggalm. It is a small and delightfully unspoiled village, but it has all you need in a

ACTIVITIES

Indoor Bowling, squash, saunas, fitness rooms and pools in hotels open to public

Outdoor Ice rink, curling, winter hiking trails, paragliding, tobogganing, cave excursions, snowshoe tours

Mountain restaurants There's no shortage but most, though fairly rustic, are self-service with simple food; the small Lattenalm on Eggalm is a table-service exception with a terrace that has splendid views of the Tux glacier.

Schools and guides There are three schools in the valley, but we lack recent reports on them.

Facilities for children The non-ski nursery takes children aged from one to three, and most of the schools take children from four upwards. There's a children's garden, including a carousel and a bob-run, on Eggalm.

STAYING THERE

How to go Both villages are essentially hotel-based resorts.

Hotels The better places tend to be on the main road, but readers tell us noise is no problem. The Lanersbacherof (87256) is a good 4-star with pool, sauna, steam and hot tub close to the lifts ('Comfortable if small rooms; great food'). The 3-star Pinzger (87541) and Alpengruss (87293) are cheaper alternatives. In Vorderlanersbach the 3-star Kirchlerhof (8560) is repeatedly recommended – 'welcoming, with good food, comfortable rooms'; good spa.

Apartments Quite a lot are available.

Eating out Restaurants are mainly hotel-based, busy, and geared to serving dinner early. A 2008 visitor recommends the Forelle for 'delicious trout'.

Après-ski Nightlife is generally quiet by Austrian standards, which suits us. We enjoyed the jolly Hühnerstall in Lanersbach (an old wooden building with traditional Austrian music). Gletscherspalte is a new disco.

Off the slopes Facilities are fairly good for small resorts. Some hotels have pools, hot tubs and fitness rooms open to non-residents. Innsbruck and Salzburg are possible excursions.

Finkenberg 840m/2,760ft

Finkenberg is a small, quiet village with a gondola into the Penken slopes shared with Mayrhofen.

THE RESORT

Finkenberg is no more than a collection of traditional-style hotels, bars, cafes and private homes. There is a pretty central area around the church, but most of the buildings (and hotels) are spread along the busy, steep, winding main road up to Lanersbach. Beware slippery pavements. Some hotels are within walking distance of the gondola, and many of the more distant ones run their own minibuses; there is also an inefficient village minibus service.

THE MOUNTAIN

Finkenberg shares Mayrhofen's main Penken slopes.

Slopes A two-stage gondola gives direct access to the Penken slopes – and in good conditions you can ski back to the village on a ski route (though it is often closed).

Snow reliability The local slopes are not as well-endowed with snowmaking as those on Mayrhofen's side.

Experts Not much challenge, except off-piste and the Harakiri piste.

Intermediates The whole area opens up from the top of the gondola.

Beginners There are nursery areas at the top of the gondola, on Penken, but Mayrhofen is a more suitable base.

Snowboarding No special facilities.

Cross-country Cross-country skiers have to get a bus up to Lanersbach.

Queues Few problems reported. The gondola to and from the Penken may have queues at peak times.

Mountain restaurants See the Mayrhofen chapter.

Schools and guides The Finkenberg school has a good reputation.

Facilities for children There's a non-ski nursery, and the ski nursery takes children from age four.

STAYING THERE

Hotels The Sporthotel Stock (6775), owned by the family of former downhill champion Leonard Stock, is near the gondola station, and has great spa facilities. The Eberl (62667) has been recommended ('attentive staff, excellent food – but avoid the annexe rooms'), and the Kristall (62840) is 150m/490ft from the gondola ('superb wellness spa'). All these are 4-stars.

Eating out Mainly in hotels, notably the Eberl.

Après-ski The main après-ski spots are the lively Laterndl Pub at the foot of the gondola and Finkennest ('welcoming, cosy, weird decor', but 'more civilised than the Laterndl').

Off the slopes OK for the active: curling, ice skating, swimming and good local walks.

Hochkönig

An unusual combination: small unspoiled villages and a large uncrowded ski area, virtually unknown on the British market

COSTS

① ② ③ ④ ⑤ ⑥

RATINGS

The slopes	
Fast lifts	**
Snow	***
Extent	***
Expert	**
Intermediate	****
Beginner	***
Convenience	**
Queues	****
Mountain restaurants	***

The rest	
Scenery	***
Resort charm	***
Off-slope	***

146

AUSTRIA!
Ski Chalets
www.ElevationHolidays.com
0845 6443578

+ Traditional quiet villages

+ Plenty of uncrowded terrain

+ Friendly locals

– Little for experts except ski routes and off-piste

– Buses needed in parts, and there are some slow chairs and T-bars

The picturesque Salzburgerland villages of Maria Alm, Hintermoos, Hinterthal, Dienten and Mühlbach combine to provide a sizeable ski area, best suited to intermediates and beginners. The lift system is not completely linked, so you'll have to drive or catch the ski buses to explore it all.

THE RESORT

Maria Alm, though small, is one of the two largest villages; it's a pretty place with a splendid old church boasting the highest spire in Salzburgerland. The peaks of the Selbhorn and Schonfeldspitze provide a dramatic backdrop. Hinterthal, the next real village up the valley, is even smaller – little more than a few 4-star hotels and chalets (some owned by the rich and famous) and a couple of ski shops and bars; it has some of the best mountain views in the region. Further up the road and over a pass is Dienten, a tiny, picturesque village with a handful of traditional hotels and guest houses. Mühlbach, at the eastern end of the ski area, is a similar size to Maria Alm and, unlike the other villages which are set off the main road, sprawls along it for quite a distance. The spectacular Hochkönig (which means 'High King') massif, from which the region gets its name, can be seen from many of the slopes but is not part of the ski area.

THE MOUNTAINS

There are 150km/93 miles of pistes, on a par with well-known names such as Kitzbühel and Mayrhofen.
Slopes The main slopes spread along several small mountains running east along the valley from Maria Alm to Mühlbach. Many of the runs are north-facing and have splendid views over to the high peaks opposite. Just to the west of Maria Alm is the tiny little area of Hinterreit, where the British ski team trains. Maria Alm has its own small Natrun ski area, served by what was the world's first chondola (a mix of chairs and gondola cabins). A red run leads off the back to the main local Aberg-Langeck mountain served by an eight-seat gondola; but most people catch the bus round to Aberg (you have to catch it back, too). You also need a bus from Aberg to the rest of the main ski area, starting at Hinterthal – but you can get back from Hinterthal to Aberg along a gentle track with some flat/uphill sections. From Hinterthal you can go via Dienten

SCHNEEBERG
1920m/6,300ft

Sunnhütte
1750m/5,740ft

WASTLHÖHE
1730m/5,680ft

Bischofshofen

1560m

HOCHKEIL
1785m/5,860ft

Mühlbach
855m/2,810ft

Dienten
1070m/3,510

↑ Pretty little Maria Alm is one of the two largest villages

HOCHKÖNIG TOURIST OFFICE

NEWS

A new eight-seat gondola is planned for 2008/09 to replace successive T-bars to Sunnhütte. More snow-guns are planned, and 75% of the pistes will then have snowmaking.

KEY FACTS

Resorts	800-1070m
	2,620-3,510ft
Slopes	800-1900m
	2,620-6,230ft
Lifts	36
Pistes	150km
	93 miles
Blue	35%
Red	55%
Black	10%
Snowmaking	75%

TOURIST OFFICES

region@hochkoenig.at
www.hochkoenig.at
Maria Alm
t 06584 7816
infoalm@
hochkoenig.at
Dienten
t 06461 263
info@dienten.co.at
Mühlbach
t 06467 7235
info@muehlbach.co.at

to Mühlbach (where the gondola back up is a bus ride from the village centre). The piste map is poor, covering the whole area in one view – it would benefit from more detail.

Terrain parks Of the five terrain parks the biggest and best is on Aberg.

Snow reliability Although low altitude, the region is in a snow pocket, so tends to have good conditions for its height (there was no shortage of snow on our April visit). Some 75% of the pistes have snowmaking.

Experts There are several ungroomed ski routes, the best of which is in a huge off-piste bowl behind the Aberg ridge. It is not well marked and having a guide is useful; a local says 'there are lots of ways in and it's better than Vail's back bowls'. With a guide you can explore other excellent off-piste too, such as in the trees off Aberg and on Schneeberg. There's one genuinely steep black piste on Aberg.

Intermediates The area between Hinterthal and Mühlbach is best for adventurous intermediates, with mainly challenging red runs. You really get a feeling of travelling around here. There are a few easy cruising blue runs in the centre of this area, served by fast lifts, and on Aberg.

Beginners All the villages have good nursery slopes, and the runs at the foot of the Aberg and by Hinterthal village are good progression runs.

Snowboarding Good for beginners and intermediates, but there are draglifts.

Cross-country There are over 40km/ 25 miles of prepared tracks.

Queues Not usually a problem.

Mountain restaurants There are 37, including some nice little huts. We liked Griessbachhütte (an isolated hut with very simple food and good views on Aberg's ski route); we also had good table-service Bauerngröstl at Tiergartenalm below Sunnhütte. A local also recommends the Tischlerhütte (Aberg), the Alm Bar (Hinterthal – good spare ribs) and Almhäusl (just above Dienten – sun deck and umbrella bar).

Schools and guides All four main villages have schools and many instructors speak good English. Maria Alm's school was 'great and catered for all our different levels' and 'only three in our group'.

Facilities for children The kindergartens at all the main base areas take children from age two. The ski schools take them from four. Babysitting is now available by prior arrangement. The Schneewutzel children's park has its own lifts and playground.

STAYING THERE

How to go No big tour ops come here.

Hotels There are plenty of good 3- and 4-star hotels, many with spa facilities, especially in Maria Alm. In Hinterthal Haus Salzburg (06584 23497) is a chalet-hotel run by an English couple (Carl is a ski instructor who guides his guests on the Hinterthal-Mühlbach 'safari') and the 4-star Urslauerhof (06584 8164) has just built more rooms.

Eating out The Ubergossene Alm just outside Dienten and the restaurant in the hotel Thalerhof in Maria Alm have good menus. Haus Salzburg (see 'Hotels') serves international rather than traditional Austrian food.

Après-ski Maria Alm is by far the most animated village. The Dengl Alm gets packed and has zither music, dancing and jolly bar staff in lederhosen. Almer Tenne has live music and a disco. Orgler Keller and Chili's are good for a quieter time. The Alm Bar in Hinterthal can be lively and opens till late, as does the Haus Salzburg bar. Saustall is a decent 'pub' in Mühlbach.

Off the slopes Maria Alm has curling, tobogganing, bowling, sleigh rides, swimming and nice walks.

UK PACKAGES

Maria Alm Elevation Holidays, Equity, Interhome, Rocketski **Dienten** Made to Measure **Hinterthal** Elevation Holidays **Hintermoos** Elevation Holidays

Innsbruck

Stay in a small, historic, cultured city and visit a different ski area every day, including one of Austria's best glacier areas

INNSBRUCK TOURISMUS

COSTS

① ② ③ ④ ⑤ ⑥

NEWS

In Innsbruck a new funicular now goes from the city centre to the cable car from Hungerburg to Seegrube. You should now be able to reach the Nordpark base from the city centre in about 20 minutes. In Igls, two new restaurants – one at the top of the cable car and one at the base – and a race training centre with a new draglift opened last season. In Oberperfuss, an eight-seat gondola replaced a chairlift. In Götzens, an eight-seat gondola from the village base to the top was built. For 2008/09 in Kühtai, a new eight-seat gondola, the Kaiserbahn, is planned.

Nordpark-Seegrube is Innsbruck's local hill, accessed by funicular from the city centre ↓

Innsbruck is not a ski resort in the usual sense. It is a historic university city of around 140,000 inhabitants, with a vibrant cultural life, and is a major tourist destination in summer. The city has twice hosted the Olympic Winter Games, and is surrounded by several ski areas that share a lift pass and are accessible by efficient bus services. Among them are a glacier that is one of the best in the world, the Stubaier Gletscher (see Stubai valley chapter) and one of Austria's highest, most snow-sure non-glacier areas, Kühtai (2020m/6,630ft).

The Inn valley is a broad, flat-bottomed trench here, but Innsbruck manages to fill it from side to side. It is a sizeable city, and as you would expect from its Olympic background, it has an excellent range of winter sports facilities, as well as a captivating car-free medieval core. It has smart, modern, shopping areas, trendy bars and restaurants, museums (including one devoted to the Olympics), concert halls, theatres, a zoo and other attractions that you might seek out on a summer holiday, but wouldn't expect to find when going skiing.

Winter diversions off the slopes include 117km/73 miles of cross-country trails (some at valley level but others appreciably above it), curling and skating at the Olympic centre, several toboggan runs totalling 100km/62 miles (the longest – above Birgitz – an impressive 11km/7 miles) and rides on a four-man bob at Igls.

Not the least of the attractions of staying in such a place is that you don't pay ski resort prices.

There are hotels, inns and B&Bs of every standard, with 3-star and 4-star hotels forming the nucleus. Among the more distinctive hotels are the grand 5-star Europa Tyrol (59310), the

ancient Goldener Adler (571111), 'comfortable, convenient' Schwarzer Adler (587109), Grauer Bär (5924) – all 4-stars – and the 3-star Weisses Kreuz (59479) in the central pedestrian zone, and the 4-star art nouveau Best Western Neue Post (59476).

As well as traditional Austrian restaurants there are several Italians, plus a smattering of more exotic alternatives, from Mexican to Japanese.

There is an impressive 1400m/4,590ft vertical of slopes on the south-facing slopes of **Nordpark-Seegrube**, reached by a new funicular from the city centre (see 'News') to the base of the access cable car from Hungerburg on the outskirts of the city. Although there are red runs to the valley, the snow is not reliable. You go up here expecting to ski the red runs of 370m/1,210ft vertical below Seegrube, served by a chairlift. A further stage of the cable car rises 350m/1,150ft to access the Karinne ski route, which is said to be very steep. If you ski it with a guide you can collect a T-shirt and certificate to prove it.

But for visitors, if not for residents, skiing usually means heading for the opposite side of the Inn trench. The runs on **Glungezer**, above Tulfes, are on north-facing slopes. The chairlift from the bottom serves red and blue runs and another chair up to the tree line serves a red run. This in turn leads to a drag and a chairlift serving open red runs from the top at 2305m/7,560ft – almost 1400m/4,590ft above the village.

The standard Innsbruck lift pass covers the lifts in all the resorts dealt with here, plus the slopes of Schlick 2000 above Fulpmes (see the Stubai valley chapter later in the book).

Free ski-bus services run to and from all the lift-pass-covered areas, but only at the beginning and end of

↑ Kühtai is set at over 2000m/6,560ft and is one of Austria's most snow-sure resorts

TVB INNSBRUCK

KEY FACTS

Resort	575m
	1,890ft
Slopes	800-3210m
	2,620-10,530ft
Lifts	78
Pistes	282km
	175 miles
Blue	32%
Red	49%
Black	19%
Snowmaking	200km
	124 miles

LIFT PASSES

Innsbruck Gletscher Skipass

Prices in €

Age	1-day	6-day
under 15	13	102
15 to 18	21	136
19 to 59	27	170
over 60	21	136

Free under 7
Beginner no deals
Notes
Day pass is price for Nordpark area only
Alternative passes
Day passes for individual areas; Super Ski pass also covers days in the Arlberg (St Anton) and Kitzbühel

the day. A car makes life more convenient, especially if you are staying outside downtown Innsbruck.

There are terrain parks at Seegrube, Axamer Lizum, the Stubaier Gletscher, Kühtai and Oberperfuss.

A major road runs southwards from Innsbruck over the Brenner pass to Italy – opening up the possibility of excursions to resorts in the Dolomites.

IGLS 900m/2,950ft

Igls seems almost a suburb of Innsbruck – the city trams run out to the village – but it is a small resort in its own right. Its famous downhill race course is an excellent piste.
The village of Igls is small and quiet, with not much in the way of diversions apart from the beautiful walks, an outdoor ice rink, the Olympic bob run and the tea shops. You can stay in Igls, and a few UK operators sell packages there. Most hotels are small and in the centre of the village, a bit of a walk from the cable car station. An exception is the family-run 4-star Sporthotel (377241), which occupies the prime site between the tram and the cable car stations ('excellent facilities, good food and nice bar').

The skiing on Patscherkofel is very limited and revolves around the excellent, varied, long red run that formed the men's downhill course in 1976, when Franz Klammer took ski racing (and the Olympic gold medal) by storm. There is a blue-run variation on this run, but few other pistes. A cable car rises 1050m/3,440ft from the village (and you can take it down if the lower runs are poor or shut). At the top, a chair rises a further 275m/900ft to the summit offering wonderful views over Innsbruck and ski routes back down. Two fast quads and a couple of drags serve the other slopes. There is a short beginner lift at village level, and another a short bus-ride up the hill. For 2007/08 there were new restaurants and a race

training centre (see 'News'). We have received mixed reports on the grooming of the trails.

Après-ski is quiet. The resort suits families but others might prefer to stay in Innsbruck.

AXAMER LIZUM 1580m/5,180ft

The mountain outpost of the Inn-side village of Axams is a ski station and nothing more, but it does have some good slopes and reliable snow conditions – and, as a reporter says, 'You feel as if you are in a wilderness.'
Axamer Lizum could scarcely provide a sharper contrast to Igls. It offers much more varied slopes and a network of lifts, with the base station at a much higher altitude. The slopes here hosted all the Olympic Alpine events in 1976 except the men's downhill, and this is the standard local venue for

Phone numbers
Calling long-distance
Add the prefix given below for each resort; when calling from abroad use the country code 43 and omit the initial '0'.

Innsbruck, Igls, Mutters
0512

Axamer Lizum
05234

Oberperfuss
05232

Kühtai
05239

weekends – hence the huge car park at the base.

The main slopes are blues and reds, almost entirely above the trees but otherwise nicely varied, and there is scope to 'play in gullies and bumps, as well as true off-piste', says a reporter. The vertical of the main east-facing slopes above the main lift station is 700m/2,300ft and there is the possibility (given good snow conditions) of a 1300m/ 4,260ft descent at the end of the day from Pleisen to the outskirts of Axams – an easy 6.5km/4 mile black. On the opposite side of the valley, a chairlift serves a fairly easy black slope. Beyond it are the slopes of Mutters, which re-opened three seasons ago after being closed since 2001; there are plans to link the Axamer and Mutters slopes but there is no definite timescale for this. Snowmaking covers 75% of the slopes and there is a large restaurant with panoramic views on Hoadl. There are two good nursery lifts, and two ski schools.

You can stay up here – there is a 4-star hotel, the Lizumerhof (68244) at the lift base – 'nice rooms and decent modern Austrian cuisine' – and a couple of other hotels too. But there's little in the way of après-ski apart from a couple of bars – the Alm bar is

the most atmospheric – and you have to eat in your hotel or go to Axams.

There is also accommodation not far away at lower altitude in Axams – including three 3-star hotels – and nearby villages such as Götzens (four 3-star places) and Birgitz (two 3-stars).

MUTTERS 830m/2,720ft
Almost as close to Innsbruck as Igls, Mutters is a charming rustic village at the foot of long slopes of 900m/2,950ft vertical. Its slopes were closed in 2001, but were re-opened three seasons ago with three new lifts. The gentle slopes suit beginners and families best. An eight-seat gondola from the village serves long blue and red runs and an equally long toboggan run. Above that a high-speed quad takes you to the summit at 1800m/5,910ft and serves its own red run plus another long red down to Götzens along the valley (with a new gondola back up). There's also a T-bar.

There are plans to link the slopes with those of Axamer Lizum. But there is no timescale for this at the moment.

The five hotels in Mutters are 3- and 4-stars. There is a lively après-ski scene and great off-slope facilities including tennis courts, saunas, skating and curling.

Innsbruck

151

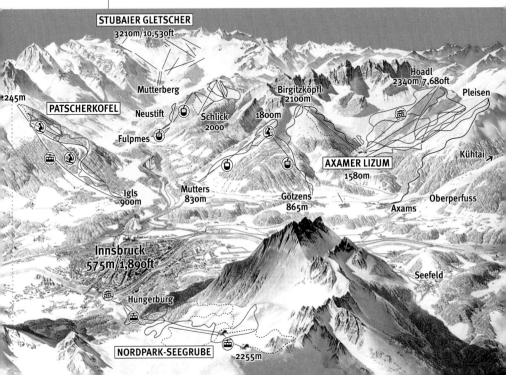

STUBAIER GLETSCHER
3210m/10,530ft

PATSCHERKOFEL
245m

Mutterberg
Neustift
Fulpmes
Schlick 2000
1800m
Birgitzköpfl 2100m
Hoadl 2340m/7,680ft
Pleisen

Igls 900m
Mutters 830m
Götzens 865m
Axams
AXAMER LIZUM 1580m
Oberperfuss
Kühtai

Innsbruck 575m/1,890ft

Seefeld

Hungerburg

NORDPARK-SEEGRUBE
2255m

TOURIST OFFICES

Innsbruck
t 53560
info@innsbruck.info
www.innsbruck.info

Igls
t 377101
igls@innsbruck.info
www.innsbruck.info/
igls

Axamer Lizum
t 68178
axams@innsbruck.info
www.innsbruck.info/
axams/

Mutters
t 548410
mutters@innsbruck.
info
www.innsbruck.info/
mutters

Oberperfuss
t 81489
oberperfuss@
innsbruck.info
www.innsbruck.info/
oberperfuss

Kühtai
t 5222
kuehtai@
innsbruck.info
www.kuehtai.info

OBERPERFUSS 815m/2,675ft
A small resort with a small ski hill,
Rangger Köpfl, now covered by the
Innsbruck area lift pass.
The hill is a very limited one, with five
lifts, including a new eight-seat
gondola for 2007/08, in a largely linear
arrangement serving 17km/11 miles of
easy-intermediate slopes – but an
impressive vertical of 1200m/3,940ft.
And over two-thirds of the pistes have
snowmaking. The village is small but
self-sufficient, with most things you
need (eg pharmacy, bakery) and a big
3-star hotel, the Krone (81465). It is
prettily rustic, and targets the family
market with the aid of a moving carpet
lift on the nursery slopes. There is
night skiing and tobogganing on
Tuesdays and Fridays.

KÜHTAI 2020m/6,630ft
A collection of comfortable hotels
spread along a high road pass
25km/16 miles west of Innsbruck –
higher and cheaper than equally
snow-sure Obergurgl or Obertauern.
Glaciers apart, Kühtai's altitude means
it is one of Austria's most snow-sure
resorts. That is its main attraction,
given the limited nature of the village.

A new eight-seat gondola, three
fast quad chairs and several draglifts
serve 37km/23 miles of mainly red
cruisers of up to 500m/1,640ft vertical
on either side of the road, plus some
token blue and black runs (which may
be easier than the reds because they
get less traffic). There is a good
nursery slope, but no easy blues to
graduate to. There's also a terrain park
with kickers and rails. And on
Wednesdays and Saturdays there's
night skiing. The resort attracts
families during school holidays and
day trippers on fine weekends –
especially if lower resorts are short of
snow – but it is otherwise crowd- and
queue-free. There are three mountain
restaurants and three ski schools.

The village is quiet in the evening,
but for its size has 'a reasonable
selection of bars and restaurants', says
a report – practically all in hotels. The
4-star hotels include the Jagdschloss
(5201) – an old hunting lodge ('a gem
of a hotel, great food, wonderful
ambience'). Other visitors have
recommended the 4-star Mooshaus
(5207) – 'convenient, excellent service
and food' – and the 3-star Elisabeth
(5240) – 'very friendly, excellent food'.
The Alpin Resort (7155510) has smart
apartments from 1 to 4 bedrooms plus
a fitness centre. Reporters say that
English is not spoken everywhere.

There are several free post buses
from Innsbruck morning and afternoon,
but the journey takes over an hour.

STUBAIER GLETSCHER
The Stubaier Gletscher is one of the
best glacier ski areas in the world; it
is open in summer as well as in winter
and is covered in more detail in the
Stubai valley chapter later in the book.
The glacier is accessed by two
alternative two-stage gondolas from
the huge car park at Mutterberg. A
third gondola from Eisgrat at 2900m/
9,500ft takes you right to the top of
the slopes at over 3200m/10,500ft.

On the glacier a variety of chairs
and draglifts (including three six-
person chairs) allow fabulous high
altitude cruising on blue and red runs,
which normally have excellent snow on
slopes between 3200m and 2300m
(10,500ft and 7,550ft). A lovely 10km/
6 mile ungroomed ski route through a
deserted bowl takes you down to the
valley – or, if you start at the top, a
descent of about 14km/9 miles and
1450m/4,760ft vertical is possible.

Ischgl

Ischgl is unique: high, snow-sure slopes, a superb lift system, and a traditional-style Tirolean village with extraordinary après-ski

RATINGS

The slopes

Fast lifts	★★★★★
Snow	★★★★
Extent	★★★★
Expert	★★★
Intermediate	★★★★
Beginner	★★
Convenience	★★★
Queues	★★★★
Mountain restaurants	★★★★

The rest

Scenery	★★★
Resort charm	★★★
Off-slope	★★★

NEWS

For 2007/08 the Fimbabahn gondola was upgraded with eight-seat cabins and heated seats. The base and mid-stations were rebuilt for easier access.

A new restaurant, Salaas, opened on the Swiss side between Greitspitz and Alp Trida Eck. And snowmaking was improved in the same area.

The terrain park was redesigned.

➕ Towny Tirolean village, with lots of upmarket hotels

➕ High slopes with reliable snow

➕ Broad area of slopes crossing the Swiss border to Samnaun, with some great long runs

➕ Superb modern lift system

➕ Après-ski that could be described as lively and uninhibited, or ...

➖ Après-ski that could be described as excessively dependent on alcohol, and weirdly dependent on displays of near-naked women

➖ Not ideal for beginners or timid intermediates, for various reasons

➖ Few seriously steep runs

➖ Very little wooded terrain to give shelter in bad weather

Ischgl is gradually finding a place on the UK package holiday market, and on the radar of British independent travellers. About time, too – we've been droning on about it for years. The lift system is particularly impressive, topping our fast lifts league table. Unless cost is an obstacle, or you insist on lots of woodland runs with unreliable snow, put it on your Austrian shortlist.

And the après-ski? Well, it's easy to avoid the pole dancing and lap dancing if that's not your scene, so it shouldn't cause anyone to stay away – except on principle. But it is part of a more general vulgarity about Ischgl that is less easy to pin down, and less easy to escape. You might prefer to stay in Samnaun.

THE RESORT

Ischgl is a compact village tucked away south of St Anton in the long, narrow Paznaun valley, on the Swiss border; the ski area is shared with Swiss Samnaun. The wooded flanks of the valley rise steeply from the village, which gets almost no sun in January.

The buildings are predominantly traditional chalet style, with one or two modern exceptions, but this is no rustic backwater – the narrow streets give it a towny air, and the style is swanky and brash rather than tasteful. There's a selection of lively bars and an excellent sports centre; shops are mainly confined to winter sports. The narrow main street plus a couple of side streets are mostly traffic-free – the valley road up to Galtür bypasses

the village – and at the west end of the pedestrian zone is the main gondola to the mid-mountain focus of Idalp. On the eastern fringe of the village, over a low hill but reachable via an underground moving walkway, is another gondola to Idalp, and a third to Pardatschgrat, higher up.

The best location, overall, is on or near the main pedestrian street. Beware of accommodation across the bypass road, a long way from the lifts.

A regional pass is available covering Galtür further up the valley and Kappl and See down the valley, all described at the end of this chapter. All are worth a visit and would make cheaper bases. There are frequent ski-buses to all of them. A car makes trips to St Anton viable. It's a very long taxi ride from Samnaun, should you get stuck there.

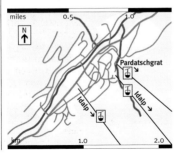

THE MOUNTAINS

Ischgl is a fair-sized, relatively high, snow-sure area. Practically all the slopes are above the treeline, the main exception being the steep lower slopes above the village and a couple of short runs low in the Fimbatal.

The piste map is 'good', but signposting can be a bit confusing, says a 2008 reporter.

LIFT PASSES

VIP Skipass

Prices in €

Age	1-day	6-day
under 17	24	112
17 to 59	42	187
over 60	37	159

Free under 8

Beginner no deals

Notes

Covers all lifts in Ischgl and Samnaun and local buses; half-day pass available; 2-day-plus pass available only to those staying in Ischgl or Mathon on presenting a guest card

Alternative passes

Regional pass covers Ischgl, Samnaun, Galtür, Kappl and See

THE SLOPES
Cross-border cruising

The sunny **Idalp** plateau, reached by the 24-person Silvrettabahn and newly upgraded eight-seat Fimbabahn, is the hub of the slopes. It can be very crowded, especially at ski school meeting time, lunchtime and the end of the day. Pardatschgrat, reached by the third gondola, is about 300m/980ft higher, and offers testing runs of 1260m/4,130ft vertical to the village. From Idalp, lifts radiate to a wide variety of mainly north-west- and west-facing runs. The red runs back down to Ischgl provoke regular complaints. Neither is easy, conditions can be tricky, and beer-lubricated crowds don't help. Quite a few people ride the gondolas down; you can leave your skis and boots at Idalp if you wish. The wide, quiet piste down the pretty Velilltal is much more pleasant, but

doesn't entirely avoid the steep bottom part of run 1A to the Pardatschgratbahn, which should probably be a black.

A short piste brings you from Idalp to the lifts serving the **Höllenkar** bowl, leading up to the area's south-western extremity and high point at Palinkopf. Runs of 900m/2,950ft vertical from here lead down to the **Fimbatal**. On the Swiss side, the hub of activity is **Alp Trida**, surrounded by south- and east-facing runs with great views. From here a scenic red run goes down to Compatsch, where a short walk takes you to buses to Ravaisch – for the cable car back – and Samnaun. From Palinkopf there is a long, beautiful red run down an unspoiled valley to Samnaun-Dorf – not difficult, but excessively sunny in parts and prone to closure by avalanche risk. There is a long flat stretch at the end.

Lovely long run, with a jolly restaurant at the end, on the outskirts of Samnaun – so a great way to end the morning or the day

Palir
28

Greitspitz
2870m/9,420ft

Samnaun Dorf
1840m/6,040ft

Salaas

Greitspitz

Viderjoch II

Idjo

Alp Trida
Sattel
2490m

Idjoch
2760m

Ravaisch Pendelbahn

Luftseilbahn

Viderjoch I

Flimjoch

Sattel

Laret

Flimsattel

Velillscharte
2555m

Velill

Compatsch

Alp Trida
2265m

Marmotte

ALP TRIDA

Visnitz

Not a slow lift in sight in this sector – or in most other sectors, actually

Muller

Grivalea

Grivalea
2700m

2640m

TERRAIN PARKS
One of Europe's best

The huge SnowArt park situated above Idalp, served by the Idjochbahn, is in itself enough to draw freestylers to Ischgl. It is now 1600m/5,250ft long and is always well-shaped and maintained. The park is split into public/beginner, intermediate and king-size lines. New rails and boxes were added last season, as well as several good intermediate and entry-level kickers. The big pro-line consists of several 15-17m/50-56ft kickers and three corner jumps in a row. The main weakness is that there are no fluid lines allowing you to hit several obstacles in a row. There is another small park on the Swiss side. 'Style on Art' weeks are held every January – where rails and wall rides get a makeover by local and national street artists.

SNOW RELIABILITY
Very good

All the slopes, except the runs back to the resort, are above 1800m/5,910ft, and many of those on the Ischgl side are north-west-facing. So snow conditions are generally reliable; we've always had good snow here, and we are not alone. There is snowmaking on a good proportion of the slopes, including the descents to Ischgl and Samnaun – increased again recently. Piste grooming is good.

FOR EXPERTS
Not much on-piste challenge

Ischgl can't compare with St Anton for exciting slopes, and some of the runs marked black on the piste map would be red elsewhere. But by general Tirolean standards Ischgl serves experts quite well.

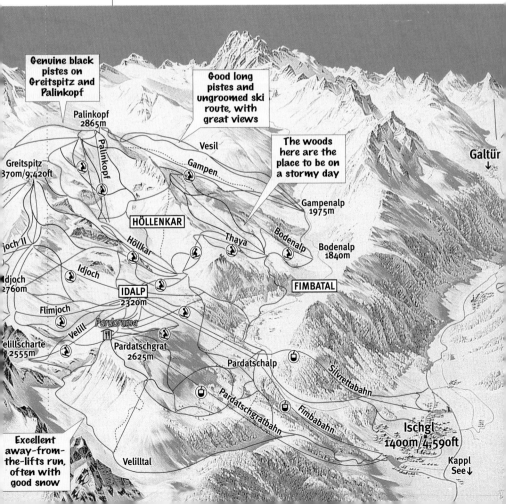

Genuine black pistes on Greitspitz and Palinkopf

Good long pistes and ungroomed ski route, with great views

The woods here are the place to be on a stormy day

Galtür

Palinkopf 2865m

Vesil

Greitspitz 2870m/9,420ft

Palinkopf

Gampen

Gampenalp 1975m

HÖLLENKAR

Höllkar

Thaya

Bodenalp

Bodenalp 1840m

joch II

Idjoch

Idjoch 2760m

IDALP 2320m

FIMBATAL

Flimjoch

Pardorama

Velill

elillscharte 2555m

Pardatschgrat 2625m

Pardatschalp

Silvrettabahn

Pardatschgratbahn

Fimbabahn

Ischgl 1400m/4,590ft

Excellent away-from-the-lifts run, often with good snow

Velilltal

Kappl See↓

to and around Alp Trida on the Swiss side – but these can get crowded. Timid intermediates should avoid the steep runs back to town.

FOR BEGINNERS
Up the mountain
Beginners must buy a full lift pass and go up the mountain to Idalp, where there are good, sunny, snow-sure nursery slopes served by drags and a fast chair. The blue runs on the east side of the bowl offer pleasant progression for fast learners. Over at Alp Trida there are further easy expanses – you can return by lift.

FOR CROSS-COUNTRY
Plenty in the valley
There are 48km/30 miles of track in the valley between Ischgl, Galtür and Wirl. This tends to be shady, especially in early season, and is away from the main slopes, which makes meeting downhillers for lunch inconvenient.

QUEUES
OK once you're up the mountain
Ischgl tops our fast lift league table – 62% of its lifts are fast ones. The upgrade of the Fimbabahn gondola last season has helped relieve pressure on the other two gondolas, which have nearby car/coach parks and can build serious queues. Up the mountain, more of a problem is crowds on the runs, especially at Idalp and the easier runs on the Swiss side. We've found lots of people skiing too fast and too close to others.

MOUNTAIN RESTAURANTS
New and improved
Mountain restaurants have tended to offer quite good quality, but inadequate capacity. But things have improved recently, with new places opening on both sides of the border. **Editors' choice** The Marmotte (+41 81 868 5221) at Alp Trida on the Swiss side wins no prizes for interior design but serves reliably good food in calm and comfortable surroundings. On the

None of the black runs is particularly steep, but all are genuine blacks and in combination with testing reds offer excellent, challenging descents. Head first for Palinkopf and Pardatschgrat – piste 4 is a favourite – but don't neglect Greitspitz. The wooded lower slopes of the Fimbatal are delightful in a storm. There are off-piste opportunities around the pistes all over the place; there is plenty of serious off-piste to be found with a guide; and powder doesn't get tracked out quickly. There are also ski routes. Ski route 39 from Palinkopf is recommended to leave you 'suitably exhausted' after a testing 1000m/3,280ft descent.

FOR INTERMEDIATES
Something for everyone
Most of the slopes are wide, forgiving and ideal for intermediates.

At the tough end of the spectrum our favourite runs are those from Palinkopf down to Gampenalp at the edge of the ski area, with great views of virgin slopes. There are also interesting and challenging black runs down the Höllspitz chair, and on Greitspitz. The reds from Pardatschgrat and Velillscharte down the beautiful Velilltal and the red from Greitspitz into Switzerland are great for quiet, high-speed cruising.

For easier motorway cruising, there is lots of choice, including those down

boarding
Ischgl has long been a popular spot for snowboarders, with its long, wide, well-groomed slopes served by snowboard-friendly gondolas and high-speed chairlifts. Although the off-piste terrain is less steep than in some other resorts, its above-the-treeline, easily accessible nature and good snow record makes for great riding for most ability levels. Ischgl is home to one of Austria's best terrain parks. Silvretta Sports and Intersport Mathoy are recommended snowboard shops.

Sunny Kappl is worth a visit, or indeed an alternative base for a family holiday →
TVB KAPPL

GETTING THERE

Air Innsbruck 100km/62 miles (1½hr); Zürich 300km/186 miles (3hr); Munich 300km/186 miles (3hr)

Rail Landeck (30km/19 miles); frequent buses from station

SCHOOLS

Ischgl
t 5257/5404

Classes
5 days (3hr) €160
Private lessons
€103 for 90 min; each additional person €20

CHILDREN

Kindergarten
t 5257/5404
Run by ski school at Idalp: non-skiing children 10am to 4pm, €36 per day incl. lunch; ski-kindergarten for ages 3 to 5 €49 per 4hr day; lunch available

Ski school
Takes children from the age of 5 (5 full days €158)

Austrian side, in the past we've had fabulous spicy prawns and ox fillet at the glass-sided Pardorama complex (606800) at the top of Pardatschgrat. **Worth knowing about** At Idalp the newish Alpenhaus has a choice of table- or self-service, and gets top marks from a reporter for its 'stunning' interior design, with a mention too for the barbecued steak. The Paznauner Thaya, above Bodenalp, has table- and self-service sections, and often has live bands or throbbing disco music. Some reporters prefer the quieter Bodenalpe, down in Fimbatal: 'service with a smile' and 'huge portions'. From Gampenalp you can be towed 5km/3 miles by snowmobile to the remote Heidelberger hütte – the way back is quite hard work, though.

On the Swiss side the new Salaas is a spacious, sunny, glass-sided place just above Alp Trida Eck, with self-service and 'limited' table service – but it disappointed a 2008 visitor. the woody Alp Bella is good value and a consistent favourite – 'fabulous rösti and delicious desserts'. The Skihaus Alp Trida and the Panorama Sattel are mentioned, not least for the views.

SCHOOLS AND GUIDES
Best for late risers
The school meets up at Idalp and starts very late (11.00). In the past we've had rave reviews, but reporters said class sizes were large at around 12 people and their instructor spoke limited English. The school also organises off-piste tours.

FACILITIES FOR CHILDREN
High-altitude options
The child care facilities are all up at Idalp – there's an enclosed learning zone and adventure garden with cartoon characters.

STAYING THERE

HOW TO GO
Increasing choice of packages
Several British tour operators now feature Ischgl.
Hotels There is a good selection from luxurious and expensive to simple B&Bs, and no shortage of recommendations from readers.
*****Trofana Royal** (600) One of Austria's most luxurious hotels, with prices to match. A celebrity chef runs the kitchen. Sumptuous spa facilities.
****Madlein** (5226) Convenient, 'hip', modern hotel. Pool, sauna, steam room. Nightclub and disco.
****Elisabeth** (5411) Right by the Pardatschgrat gondola, with lively après-ski. Pool, sauna and steam room.
****Solaria** (5205) Near the Madlein and just as luxurious, with a 'friendly family atmosphere' and 'helpful staff'.
****Brigitte** (5646) Central, but quiet location. Pool. Highly recommended.
****Piz Tasna** (5277) Up hill behind church: 'Quiet location, friendly, lovely views over village.'
****Goldener Adler** (5217) Central, smart, modern hotel, with 'outstanding food'. Sauna and whirlpool.
****Olympia** (5432) Family-run hotel with reportedly good-sized rooms. Bar and restaurant. Sauna and solarium.
****Jägerhof** (5206) 'Jewel of a hotel.' Friendly, good food, large rooms. Sauna.
****Post** (5232) 'Excellent central position; very nice staff,' says a 2008 visitor. Wellness centre.
****Christine** (5346) Probably the best B&B in town. 'Huge rooms, nice views, good position near the lifts.'
****Dorfschmiede** (5769) Small, central B&B with 'friendly service'.
****Lamtana** (56095) Near the

↑ It's a densely developed village and a steep-sided valley
ISCHGL TOURIST OFFICE

UK PACKAGES

Alpine Answers, Crystal, Crystal Finest, Directski.com, Independent Ski Links, Inghams, Interhome, Kuoni, Made to Measure, Momentum, Ski Expectations, Ski Independence, Ski Safari, Ski Solutions, Ski Wild, Skitracer, Snow Finders **Galtür** Crystal, Directski.com, Inghams, Lagrange, Neilson, Ski Independence, Ski McNeill

ACTIVITIES

Indoor Silvretta Centre (bowling, billiards, swimming pool, tennis, sauna, solarium, massage), museums, concerts

Outdoor Ice rink, curling, sleigh rides, hiking tours, 7km/ 4 miles floodlit toboggan run

---

Silvrettabahn. 'Very good buffet breakfast; spacious, modern rooms', says a 2008 reporter. Wellness area. ***Alpengluehn** (5294) Convenient, recently refurbished and good value. Recommended by a 2008 visitor. **Apartments** Some attractive apartments are available. Recommendations include the Golfais by the Pardatschgrat gondola and the apartments in the hotel Solaria (with use of its spa).

EATING OUT
Plenty of choice

Most of our reporters eat in their hotels. For lighter meals try the Nona, the Schatzi or the Trofana Alm ('good ribs'), which is as much a bar as a restaurant, and for fondue or ribs the Kitzloch, with its galleries over the dance floor. The Allegra and Salz & Pfeffer 'pasta and pizza' have been recommended. The Grillalm and Salnerhof are popular, 'traditional Austrian fare, huge portions'. A reporter pronounces the Nudelhimmel (hotel Solaria) his favourite – local dishes at reasonable prices. The Nevada is also recommended: 'Excellent venison and duck – all well presented and moderately priced.'

APRES-SKI
Very lively

Ischgl is one of the liveliest resorts in the Alps, from early afternoon on. Lots of people are still in ski boots late in the evening. Mountain restaurants such as Paznauner Thaya slide into après mode directly after lunch. When you manage to get back to the village, the obvious ports of call are Trofana Alm near the Silvrettabahn or the Schatzi bar of the hotel Elisabeth by the Pardatschgratbahn – with indoor and outdoor bars and scantily clad

---

dancing girls. Niki's Stadl across the road is the place for a Tirolean knees-up, with DJs and 'a riot of après-ski classics'. The Kitzloch 'rocks', with dancing on the tables in ski boots. The Kuhstahl under the Sporthotel Silvretta and Feuer & Eis over the road are packed all evening. The Romantic Hütte is 'an upmarket hut decorated with the bottles of champagne previous partygoers have drunk'. The bar at the hotel Sonne, the Höllboden and the Golden Eagle are 'good for live bands'. The Allegra livens up after dinner. There's lap dancing at the huge Trofana Arena and the Coyote Ugly at the hotel Madlein. There's a branch of the famous Pacha nightclubs, also in Ibiza and London (a bit 'tacky', says a visitor). The Living Room (hotel Grillalm) is allegedly 'more hands-on' than table dancing. And the club under the hotel Post has an ancient Roman theme.

OFF THE SLOPES
No sun but a nice pool

The village gets little sun in the middle of winter, and the resort is best suited to those keen to hit the slopes. But there's no shortage of off-slope activities. There are 24km/15 miles of well-marked and maintained walks (many at altitude), a 7km/4 mile floodlit toboggan run and a splendid sports centre. And you can browse upmarket shops, which sell Versace and Bogner. It's easy to get around the valley by bus and the Smuggler's Pass for pedestrians enables them to use specially selected lifts.

Samnaun 1840m/6,040ft

Small, quiet duty-free Samnaun is in a corner of Switzerland more easily reached from Austria. It is virtually Brit-free. There are four small components, roughly 1km/0.5 mile apart: Samnaun-Dorf, prettily set at the head of the valley is the main focus, with some swanky hotels and duty-free shops; Ravaisch, where the cable car goes up; tiny Plan; and the hamlets of Laret and Compatsch, at the end of the main run down from the slopes. We've stayed happily on the edge of Dorf in the Waldpark B&B (8618310), and have eaten well at the Pasta in the hotel Montana (8619000). Reporters recommend the hotel Post (8619200) ('good food but pricey') and the Stammerspitze Cafe there. The

Castello hotel (8618060) and spa is newish in Dorf. There's a smart AlpenQuell spa-pool-fitness centre.

The Schmuggler Alm at the bottom of the long run from Palinkopf is a popular après-ski spot and does 'a good lunch'. A reporter also recommends a 'delicious amaretto hot chocolate' at the Almraus (hotel Cresta), at Compatsch.

Kappl 1260m/4,135ft

Kappl, a 15-minute bus ride down the valley from Ischgl, is worth a visit – we've had a great half-day there. Both the village and the slopes are family-oriented, and delightfully quiet compared with Ischgl. The village, with a couple of dozen hotels and guest-houses, sits on a shelf 100m/330ft above the valley floor. The Sunny Mountain area at the top of the access gondola has a big kindergarten and outside play area. There's a long floodlit toboggan run from here back to the village.

There are 40km/25 miles of sunny, largely south-facing pistes going up to 2640m/8,660ft. The slopes – served by an access gondola from the roadside and fast quads above it – offer plenty of variety, with several tough reds, including the Lattenabfahrt down a deserted valley from the top – 8km/5 miles long, 985m/3,230ft vertical, more if you go on to the valley floor. Most of the slopes are open, but the run down the gondola offers some shelter for bad-weather days. Snowmaking covers all except the highest slopes.

See 1050m/3,440ft

See, a 10-minute bus ride further down the valley from Kappl, has 33km/ 21 miles of predominantly easy, largely north-facing slopes. It is worth a visit from Ischgl to get away from the crowds, if you don't mind the limited extent of the slopes.

We found great powder here on our recent April visit – excellent for making your first turns off-piste. There's a good nursery slope at the top of the access gondola, and easy runs to progress to. Piste 10 is a beautiful red run round the back of the mountain, away from all lifts, with spectacular views – a pleasant ski to start with and then a road you cruise along admiring the views. Bambini

World offers child care. There's a popular toboggan run.

See is worth considering as a base for families – it's quieter and cheaper than Ischgl; but the village is not especially attractive and is rather spoiled by the main road through it. Accommodation is largely in 3-star hotels and guest houses strung along the road.

Galtür 1585m/5,200ft

Galtür is a charming, peaceful, traditional village clustered around a pretty little church, amid impressive mountain scenery at the head of the valley (and so unspoiled by through-traffic). Rebuilt and fortified after the devastating avalanche of 1999, the village is now home to the impressive Alpinarium, an avalanche-protection structure featuring an exhibition centre, climbing wall, internet and archive room – 'definitely worth a visit', says a reporter, despite the fact that it's all in German.

Sunnier, cheaper and much quieter than Ischgl, Galtür is a good base for families and mixed-ability groups – and the free buses to Ischgl are regular and quick. There are good 3- and 4-star hotels, including the Almhof (8253), Flüchthorn (8202), Alpenrose (8201) and Ballunspitze (8214).

Galtür's own slopes rise to 2295m/7,530ft above a lift base at Wirl, a short bus ride from the village. The ski area has been re-branded Silvapark, with six 'sectors' to help guests make the most of the mountain. The slopes are not very challenging and can be bleak in poor weather; but the black runs are ideal for intermediates and there are fine nursery slopes. The area on the far right of the piste map, served by a slow double chair and a T-bar, has some good off-piste in a bowl and among well-spaced trees. There's a terrain park beside the Zeinislift drag. The school has a high reputation and offers small classes. Kinderland has its own tow, carousel and moving carpet. Galtür has 45km/28 miles of cross-country loops, some quite testing. The cosy, wooden Wieberhimml mountain hut has waitresses in traditional costume.

Off-slope facilities are limited, but there's a sports centre with pool, tennis and squash. Night skiing and sledding are available on Wednesdays.

Phone numbers
Calling long-distance
Add the prefix given below for each resort; when calling from abroad use the country code +43 and omit the initial '0'

Ischgl
05444

Galtür
05443

Samnaun
(Switzerland)
From elsewhere in Switzerland add the prefix 081; from abroad use the prefix +41 81

TOURIST OFFICES
Ischgl
t 05099 0100
info@ischgl.com
www.ischgl.com

Samnaun
(Switzerland)
t 868 5858
info@samnaun.ch
www.samnaun.ch

Kappl
t 05099 0300
kappl@kappl-see.com
www.kappl.at

See
t 05099 0400
see@kappl-see.com
www.kappl-see.com

Galtür
t 05099 0200
info@galtuer.com
www.galtuer.com

Interactive resort shortlist builder at www.wtss.co.uk

Kitzbühel

The extensive slopes are mostly pretty tame; the medieval town at the base, though, is something special – cute and lively

COSTS

① ② ③ ④ ⑤ ⑥

RATINGS

The slopes
Fast lifts	★★★
Snow	★★
Extent	★★★
Expert	★★★
Intermediate	★★★★
Beginner	★★
Convenience	★★
Queues	★★
Mountain restaurants	★★★★

The rest
Scenery	★★★
Resort charm	★★★★
Off-slope	★★★★★

NEWS

For 2007/08 an eight-seat chair with heated seats replaced the old double chair at Ehrenbachgraben to Steinbergkogel, removing the last major bottleneck on the mountain.

Snowmaking was increased around the new lift and between the Jochberg and Resterhöhe sectors.

Another ski school – Element3 – has started up.

A couple of new bars and restaurants have opened in the resort, and work continues to update various hotels – the Schloss Lebenberg will reopen following refurbishment, and a new retail area and cafe are also due to open for 2008/09.

160

- ➕ Large, attractive, varied slopes offering a sensation of travel
- ➕ Beautiful medieval town centre
- ➕ Vibrant nightlife
- ➕ Lots to do off-the-slopes, both for the sporty and not-so-sporty
- ➕ Plenty of cheap and cheerful accommodation
- ➕ Excellent mountain restaurants
- ➕ A gondola now accesses the high Resterhöhe slopes, for the best snow in the area, but ...

- ➖ Snow in the lower sectors close to Kitzbühel is often poor, especially on runs to the valley (though there's now quite a bit of snowmaking)
- ➖ Surprisingly little challenging terrain – though plenty of off-piste
- ➖ Disappointing nursery area
- ➖ Some crowded pistes

Kitzbühel is one of the big names of the ski world, largely thanks to its Hahnenkamm downhill race course – the most spectacular on the World Cup circuit. And there is a lot to like about the resort – particularly the beautiful, traffic-free centre, complete with cobbled streets and lovely medieval buildings. Some of these contain elegant, upscale hotels. But there is a huge amount of inexpensive accommodation which attracts low-budget visitors, many of whom are young and out to party in the resort's famous après-ski haunts.

The low altitude of the slopes is a real problem. In countless visits over a 20-year period we've encountered good snow down to the village precisely once. Our advice is to book late, when you know the conditions are good.

THE RESORT

Set at a junction of broad, pretty valleys, Kitzbühel is a large, animated town. The beautiful walled medieval centre – with quaint church, cobbled streets and attractively painted buildings – is traffic-free and a compelling place to stay. Many visitors love the sophisticated, towny ambience and swanky shops and cafes. But the resort spreads widely, and busy roads surround the old town,

reducing the charm factor somewhat. Visitors used to peaceful little Austrian villages are likely to be surprised by its urban feel.

A gondola from the edge of the town goes up to the Hahnenkamm, start of the main area of slopes. Across town, close to the railway station but some way from the centre, another gondola accesses the much smaller Kitzbüheler Horn sector. The size of Kitz makes choice of location important. Many visitors prefer to be

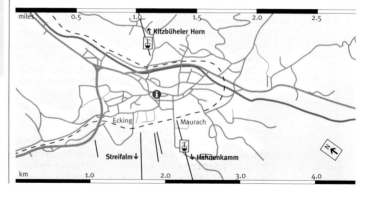

Lifts and runs radiate
in all directions from
Ehrenbachhöhe →

KEY FACTS

Resort	760m	
	2,490ft	
Slopes	800-2000m	
	2,620-6,560ft	
Lifts	55	
Pistes	168km	
	104 miles	
Blue	40%	
Red	46%	
Black	14%	
Snowmaking	91km	
	57 miles	

close to the Hahnenkamm gondola. Beginners should bear in mind that the Hahnenkamm nursery slopes are often lacking in snow, and then novices are taken up the Horn. Reporters continue to say the buses around town get overcrowded and some suggest taking taxis if you don't want to walk. But the post bus service is said to be 'cheap and efficient'.

A car is useful for visiting other resorts covered by the Kitzbüheler Alpen Skipass – though one of those, Westendorf, is now linked by the Ki-West gondola from near Aschau.

THE MOUNTAINS

Kitzbühel's extensive slopes – shared with Kirchberg and other, smaller villages – offer a very attractive mixture of entirely open runs higher up and patchy forest lower down. Most face north-east or north-west.

The piste map is praised as 'very clear and easy to use'.

THE SLOPES
Big but bitty
The slopes can be divided into several identifiable areas, most linked.

The **Hahnenkamm** gondola takes you to the bowl of Ehrenbachgraben, a major lift bottleneck in the past but now transformed by installation of not only a six-pack to Ehrenbachhöhe, the arrival point of lifts from Kirchberg, but also a new eight-pack to the high-point of Steinbergkogel. Suddenly, this is a place you might want to do laps.

Beyond is the slightly lower peak of

Pengelstein, whence several long west-facing runs go down to Skirast, where there is a gondola back up, or Aschau. Ski buses from these points will take you to the Westendorf lifts or to Kirchberg. It reportedly takes up to an hour to reach the Westendorf slopes, including the bus connection (quicker direct by bus from town).

Pengelstein is also the start of the impressive 30-person cross-valley 3S gondola to **Wurzhöhe** above Jochberg. This peak-to-peak link has great views (downwards if you hit the cabin with the partial glass floor).

Further lifts then take you to the **Resterhöhe** sector above Pass Thurn – well worth the excursion, for better snow and fewer crowds. There is a long, scenic, sunny red run to Breitmoos, mid-station of the gondola up from the valley to the south of Pass Thurn. Runs are otherwise short, but mostly served by fast chairs.

The **Kitzbüheler Horn** gondola second stage leads to the sunny Trattalm bowl, with an alternative cable car taking you up to the summit of the Horn, from where a fine, solitary piste leads down into the Raintal on the east side – popular with boarders apparently. There's a blue piste and two ski routes back towards town.

There's floodlit skiing on Thursday and Friday on **Gaisberg**, a small area of slopes at Kirchberg, across the resort from the main ski area.

The separate **Bichlalm** area, which used to offer lift-served off-piste, has reopened for guided snowcat skiing. A new lift is planned, but not imminent.

Kitzbühel

161

Interactive resort shortlist builder at **www.wtss.co.uk**

TERRAIN PARKS
Take the Hornbahn

The park is on the Kitzbüheler Horn,
under the Alpenhaus ski lift and has a
variety of intermediate tabletop jumps,
rails, boxes and a boardercross course.
The park is relatively cramped and can
get crowded during peak season.
There are plenty of good kicker spots
easily spotted on the nearby
ungroomed terrain. The park in
Westendorf is far bigger and better –
worth the trip for park aficionados.

SNOW RELIABILITY
More snowmaking now

The problem is that Kitzbühel's slopes
have one of the lowest average
heights in the Alps. To make matters
worse, the Horn is also sunny. Even in
an exceptionally good snow year some
reporters complain of worn patches,
ice and slush on the lower slopes. In a
normal year, the lower slopes can be
very tricky or bare at times (though
the snow at the top is often OK). The
expansion of snowmaking has

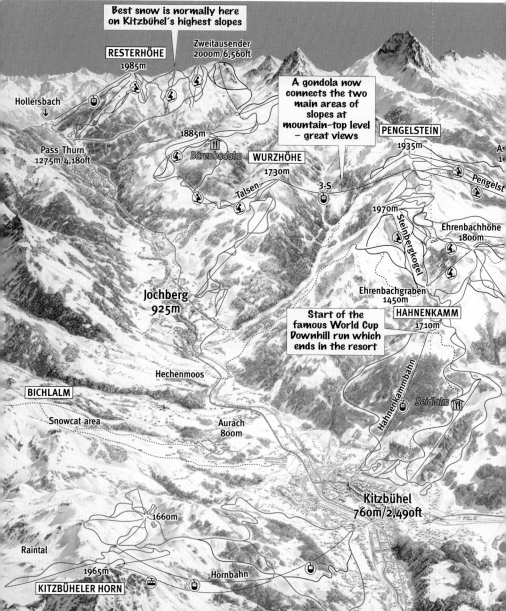

**Best snow is normally here
on Kitzbühel's highest slopes**

RESTERHÖHE
1985m

Zweitausender
2000m/6,560ft

Hollersbach
↓

Pass Thurn
1275m/4,180ft

1885m

Bärenbadalm

**A gondola now
connects the two
main areas of
slopes at
mountain-top level
– great views**

PENGELSTEIN
1935m

WURZHÖHE
1730m

Talsen

3-S

Pengelst

1970m

Steinbergkogel

Ehrenbachhöhe
1800m

Jochberg
925m

Ehrenbachgraben
1450m

**Start of the
famous World Cup
Downhill run which
ends in the resort**

HAHNENKAMM
1710m

Hechenmoos

BICHLALM

Snowcat area

Aurach
800m

Hahnenkammbahn

Seidlalm

Kitzbühel
760m/2,490ft

1660m

Raintal

1965m

Hornbahn

KITZBÜHELER HORN

THE HAHNENKAMM DOWNHILL

Kitzbühel's Hahnenkamm Downhill race, held in mid-January each year, is the toughest as well as one of the most famous on the World Cup circuit. On the race weekend the town is packed and there is a real carnival atmosphere, with bands, people in traditional costumes and huge (and loud) cowbells everywhere. The race itself starts with a steep icy section before you hit the famous Mausfalle and Steilhang, where even Franz Klammer used to get worried. The course starts near the top of the Hahnenkamm gondola and drops 860m/2,820ft to finish amid the noise and celebrations right on the edge of town. The course is normally closed from the start of the season until after the race, but after the race weekend ordinary mortals can now try most of the course, if the snow is good enough – it's an unpisted ski route mostly. We found it steep and tricky in parts, even when going slowly – it must be terrifying at race speeds of 80mph or more.

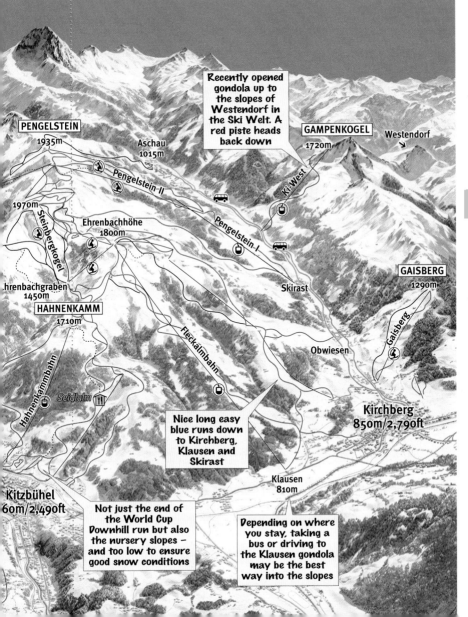

PENGELSTEIN
1935m

Aschau
1015m

Pengelstein-II

Recently opened gondola up to the slopes of Westendorf in the Ski Welt. A red piste heads back down

GAMPENKOGEL
1720m

Westendorf

Ki-West

1970m

Steinbergkogel

Ehrenbachhöhe
1800m

Pengelstein-I

hrenbachgraben
1450m

Skirast

GAISBERG
1290m

HAHNENKAMM
1710m

Gaisberg

Fleckalmbahn

Obwiesen

Hahnenkammbahn

Seidlalm

Kirchberg
850m/2,790ft

Nice long easy blue runs down to Kirchberg, Klausen and Skirast

Kitzbühel
60m/2,490ft

Not just the end of the World Cup Downhill run but also the nursery slopes – and too low to ensure good snow conditions

Klausen
810m

Depending on where you stay, taking a bus or driving to the Klausen gondola may be the best way into the slopes

Kitzbühel

Interactive resort shortlist builder at **www.wtss.co.uk**

The Hahnenkamm
race course – here
being used for a
slalom – ends right in
the town ➜

BILDARCHIV KITZBÜHEL TOURISMUS

LIFT PASSES

Kitzbühel

Prices in €

Age	1-day	6-day
under 16	20	90
16 to 18	31	144
over 19	39	180

Free under 7
Senior 60+: day pass
€20 on Tue only; 80+:
season pass €15
Beginner seven free
lifts (three in
Kitzbühel)

Notes
Covers all lifts in
Kitzbühel, Kirchberg,
Jochberg, Pass Thurn,
Mittersill/Hollersbach;
50% reduction on
pool entry with
passes for 2 days or
more; single ascent,
hourly and pedestrian
tickets; family
reductions

Alternative passes
Kitzbüheler Alpen
Skipass covers five
large ski areas –
Kitzbühel,
Schneewinkel (St
Johann), Ski Welt,
Alpbach and
Wildschönau;
Salzburg Super Ski
Card covers 21 ski
areas in the Salzburg
province

improved matters when it's cold enough to make snow – runs down to Kitzbühel, Kirchberg, Klausen and Jochberg are covered. But many slopes still remain unprotected. If snow is poor, head for Resterhöhe.

FOR EXPERTS
Plan to go off-piste
Steep slopes – pistes and off-piste terrain – are mostly concentrated around the bowl of Ehrenbachgraben, now equipped with two fast chairs. Direttissima is seriously steep, but sometimes groomed – fabulous. The other blacks dotted around are easier. There are plenty of long, challenging reds. When conditions allow, there is plenty of gentler off-piste potential to be found – some of it safely close to pistes, some requiring a guide.

FOR INTERMEDIATES
Lots of alternatives
The Hahnenkamm area is prime terrain. Good intermediates will want to do the World Cup downhill run, of course (see the feature panel). And the long blues of around 1000m/3,300ft vertical to Klausen and to Skirast from are also satisfying. The black to Aschau is not difficult, and a lovely way to end the day (check bus times first). The east-facing Raintal run on the Horn is excellent.

The Wurzhöhe runs are good for mixed abilities, and the short, high runs at Resterhöhe are ideal if you are

more timid. There are easy reds down to Pass Thurn and Jochberg. Much of the Horn is good cruising.

FOR BEGINNERS
Not ideal
The Hahnenkamm nursery slopes are no more than adequate, and prone to poor snow conditions. The Horn has a high, sunny, nursery-like section, and quick learners will soon be cruising home from there on the long Hagstein piste. There are some easy runs to progress to if the snow is OK. But there are many more conveniently arranged places to start.

FOR CROSS-COUNTRY
Plentiful but low
There are around 40km/25 miles of trails scattered around, but all are at valley level and prone to lack of snow.

QUEUES
Major improvements
Queues to get out of the town have almost been forgotten, and the chair upgrades at Ehrenbachgraben – a six-pack and a new eight-pack – have solved the main problem on the mountain. The slow Maierl chairs out of Kirchberg are still tiresome. But we have had reports of bearable queues at half-term, and queue-free weeks at other times. Both the Horn and the Hahnenkamm can have crowded pistes – though the gondola to Wurzhöhe has helped to spread the traffic.

boarding

Kitzbühel has never been known as a snowboarders' hub, but it's growing in popularity, according to a 2007 reporter. In order to attract a more freestyle-orientated clientele, a decent terrain park has been built, as well as a boardercross and speed course. There are some good off-piste runs and fun natural obstacles on the Hahnenkamm and around Pengelstein. All major lifts are gondolas and chairlifts – the area suits beginners and intermediates well.

There is no non-ski nursery, but babysitters and nannies can be hired

Ski school
From age 3 (6 days
€170 – Rote Teufel)

Air Salzburg 80km/50 miles (1½hr); Munich 160km/99 miles (2hr); Innsbruck 95km/59 miles (1½hr)

Rail Mainline station in resort. Post bus every 15min from station

Airtours, Alpine Answers, Alpine Weekends, Crystal, Crystal Finest, Directski.com, Elegant Resorts, First Choice, Independent Ski Links, Inghams, Interactive Resorts, Interhome, Kuoni, Made to Measure, Momentum, Neilson, Ski Freshtracks, Ski Line, Ski McNeill, Ski Solutions, Ski Wild, Skitracer, Snowscape, Thomson
Kirchberg Airtours, Directski.com, First Choice, Interhome, Neilson, Ski McNeill, Snowscape, Thomson

Rote Teufel (Red Devil)
t 62500

Element3
t 72301

Classes
(Rote Teufel prices)
6 days (2hr am and pm) €170

Private lessons
€150 for 2hr

MOUNTAIN RESTAURANTS
A highlight

There are many attractive restaurants – 'one of the reasons we keep going back', says one of our Kitz regulars. **Editors' choice** The Seidlalm (63135), right by the lower part of the downhill course, is relatively quiet and delightfully rustic; regularly praised by reporters too. Next time, though, we'll try the newly built Bärenbadalm (0664 8557994), halfway to Resterhöhe – reportedly 'a super hut, with comfy sofas, a roaring fire and fantastic ribs'. **Worth knowing about** In the Hahnenkamm sector we had a jolly meal at Berghaus Tyrol, below Ehrenbachhöhe. The Hockeckhütte has 'excellent food and atmosphere'. Melkalm 'is worth the effort of finding'. The Hochbrunn and the Schutzhütte Steinbergkogel are recommended. The expensive Hochkitzbühel at the top of the gondola has good food, but service has been criticised. A 2007 visitor enjoyed the 'bright and modern' Ehrenbachgraben. On Pengelstein, the Usterweis on the way to Skirast is a nice woody place with a limited menu but satisfying food. The Kasereckhütte on the ski route to Jochberg is 'brilliant'. At Wurzhöhe, Jägerwurzhütte is mentioned, as is Trattenbachalm; Hanglalm has 'great Kaiserschmarrn', and Panoramaalm great views. On the Horn, Hornköpfl-Hütte's good food and sunny terraces get praised. Alpenhaus 'does excellent self-service meals for great prices' but can get crowded; the quieter Gipfelhaus has 'super views'.

SCHOOLS AND GUIDES
Good recent reviews

The Kitzbühel Rote Teufel (Red Devils) have absorbed several other local schools (including the Total school). Reports are favourable. A recent visitor 'learned more than ever before' in his week with them. Another reporter 'progressed very quickly with an excellent instructor'. The other schools emphasise their small scale. Element3 was new in 2007 – an adventure company now offering ski/snowboard classes. Reports please.

FACILITIES FOR CHILDREN
Not an ideal choice

Provided your children can take classes, you can deposit them at any of the schools. Rote Teufel takes kids from three years old – 'no complaints', says a 2007 reporter.

HOW TO GO
Mainly hotels and pensions

Kitz is essentially a hotel resort, though a few tour operators run chalets and chalet hotels here. Crystal's chalet hotel Hofer is an excellent spot, with simple but satisfactory rooms and a smart bar, in a quiet location close to the centre and near a ski-bus stop.
Hotels There is an enormous choice, especially 4-star and 3-star hotels.
*****Tennerhof (63181) Luxurious former farmhouse, with renowned restaurant. Beautiful panelled rooms.
*****Weisses Rössl (71900) Smartly traditional, exclusive 5-star aparthotel. Extensive spa facilities.
****Golfhotel Rasmushof (652520) Right on the slopes by the finish area of the Hahnenkamm race, close to centre of town. 'Excellent service from friendly staff. Book a room overlooking the slopes (a golf course in summer).'
****Schloss Lebenberg (69010) Modernised 'castle' with smart pool; inconvenient location but free shuttle-bus. Free nursery for kids aged 3-plus. Being refurbished for 2008/09.
****Goldener Greif (64311) Elegant, historic inn; vaulted lobby-sitting area, panelled bar, casino.
****Jägerwirt (6981) Modern chalet. Not ideally placed, but has been recommended.
****Schwarzer Adler (6911) Traditional hotel, near centre, highly praised by a reporter. Refurbished for 2007/08. New pool.
****Best Western Kaiserhof (75503) Next to the Hahnenkamm gondola. 'Great spa, indoor pool and excellent food – can't fault it,' says a 2007 reporter.
****Schweizerhof (62735) Comfortable chalet right by Hahnenkamm gondola.
***Strasshofer (62285) Central location. 'Friendly, good with children, quiet rooms at back.' 'Excellent value and location.'
**Mühlbergerhof (62835) Small, friendly pension in good position.
Apartments Many of the best (and best-positioned) are attached to hotels.

EATING OUT
Something for everyone

There is a wide range of restaurants to suit all pockets, including pizzerias and fast-food outlets (even

ACTIVITIES

Indoor Aquarena Centre (pools, slides, sauna, solarium, mud baths, aerated baths, underwater massage) – discounted entry with lift pass; tennis, fitness centre, beauty centre, indoor riding school, climbing wall, bowling, museums, casino, cinema

Outdoor Ice rink (curling and skating), snowshoeing, tobogganing, ballooning, helicopter flights, paragliding, wildlife park, 65km/40 miles of cleared walking paths

Phone numbers
Kitzbühel
From elsewhere in Austria add the prefix 05356; from abroad use the prefix +43 5356
Kirchberg
From elsewhere in Austria add the prefix 05357; from abroad use the prefix +43 5357

TOURIST OFFICES

Kitzbühel
t 777
info@kitzbuehel.com
www.kitzbuehel.com
Kirchberg
t 2000
kirchberg@kitzbuehel-alpen.com
www.kirchberg.at

McDonald's). The Neuwirt in the Schwarzer Adler hotel is regarded as the best in town and wins awards in food guides; the Schwedenkapelle is also highly rated. Chizzo does fine-dining in one of the oldest buildings in Kitzbühel; recommended by a 2008 visitor. Good, cheaper places include the traditional Huberbräu-Stüberl, Eggerwirt and, a little out of town with great views, Hagstein. Goldene Gams has both traditional and modern dining rooms, plus a wide menu. Barrique does 'great pizza', as does Gallo – a newish Italian. On Fridays and Saturdays you can dine at the top of the Hahnenkamm gondola (Hochkitzbühel). For something different take a taxi to Rosi's Sonnbergstub'n. Choose the speciality lamb or duck and expect to be serenaded by Rosi herself.

APRES-SKI
A main attraction
Nightlife is one of Kitz's great selling points. There's something for all tastes, from throbbing bars full of teenagers to quiet places, nice cafes and smart spots for fur-coat flaunting.

Immediately after the slopes close, the town is jolly without being much livelier than many other Tirolean resorts. The Streifalm bar at the foot of the slopes is popular, with 'white pine and slate, open fire, widescreen TV and Europop music', as is the Sportcafe Hölzl. Cafes Praxmair, Kortschak, Langer and Rupprechter are among the most atmospheric tea-time places for cakes and pastries. The new Lounge Cafe at the gondola station is smoke-free. The lively Stamperl is 'classy and fun'. The Seidlalm has weekly Tirolean evenings (free). Later Lichtl's (with thousands of lights hanging from the ceiling) has karaoke. Seppi's Pub shows sport on TV and does bar-meals. The Londoner Pub is a famous drinking place, well summarised by visitors as: 'Very crowded, very noisy and great fun', but the bar staff are reportedly 'rude and sulky'. The Fonda has been recommended for the 'younger generation'. The Python, Highways and Take Five are the main discos.

OFF THE SLOPES
Plenty to do
The lift pass gives a reduction for the pools in the impressive Aquarena leisure centre. The new Sports Park

(with ice rink, ice hockey etc) is recommended. There's a museum, and concerts are organised. The railway makes excursions easy (eg Salzburg).

Kirchberg 850m/2,790ft

THE RESORT
Kirchberg is a large, spread-out, lively village that makes a perfectly sensible alternative base – particularly if you are thinking of spending a lot of time exploring Resterhöhe There are three ways into the slopes, all a bus ride from the village.

THE MOUNTAIN
Slopes The Fleckalmbahn from Klausen to Ehrenbachhöhe is the main way into the slopes shared with Kitzbühel. The alternative Maierl chairlifts are excruciatingly slow. The gondola from Skirast is a better alternative, accessing a choice of fast chairs to Pengelstein which links to the gondola to Wurzhöhe. The separate small Gaisberg ski area is on the other side of the valley.
Terrain parks Head for Kitzbühel.
Snow reliability Kirchberg suffers from the same unreliable snow as Kitzbühel.
Experts Few challenging slopes.
Intermediates The main slopes back are easy cruises when snow is good.
Beginners There's a beginner lift and area at the foot of the Gaisberg slopes.
Snowboarding Kitzbühel has the edge, with the terrain park on the Horn.
Cross-country There are lots of trails – but they can suffer from lack of snow.
Queues There are some bottlenecks.
Mountain restaurants There are some good local huts.
Schools and guides We lack recent reports on the four schools.
Facilities for children There are non-ski and ski kindergartens.

STAYING THERE
How to go There's a wide choice of chalet-style hotels and pensions.
Hotels The 4-star Klausen (2128), close to the main gondola, and the Sporthotel Tyrol (2787), a bit out of the centre, have been recommended.
Apartments There are some available.
Eating out Mostly in hotels, but there's a pizzeria and a steak house too.
Après-ski There's a toboggan run on Gaisberg. Nightlife is very lively.
Off the slopes Some hotels have swimming pools and saunas.

Lech

If you can afford it, simply one of the best: a captivating blend of reliable snow, village charm and deeply comfortable hotels

COSTS

① ② ③ ④ ⑤ ⑥

RATINGS

The slopes	
Fast lifts	****
Snow	****
Extent	****
Expert	****
Intermediate	****
Beginner	****
Convenience	***
Queues	****
Mountain restaurants	***
The rest	
Scenery	***
Resort charm	****
Off-slope	***

NEWS

For 2008/09 a new 5-star hotel is planned in Lech.

For 2007/08 snowmaking was increased above Oberlech and Zürs. And a 300m/980ft long tunnel opened at Oberlech (see 'The resort').

+ Picturesque traditional village

+ Sunny and usually uncrowded slopes with excellent snow record and extensive snowmaking

+ Sizeable area of mainly intermediate pistes, plus good, extensive off-piste

+ Easy access by bus to the slopes of St Anton and other Arlberg resorts

+ Some very smart hotels, including ski-in/ski-out options at Oberlech

+ Lots of lovely heated chairlifts

+ Lively après-ski scene, but ...

− Few non-hotel bars or restaurants

− Surprising shortage, for a smart resort, of seductive shopping

− Local traffic intrudes on main street of Lech (and really spoils Zürs)

− Very few challenging pistes

− Nearly all slopes are above the treeline, and unpleasant in bad weather

− Blue runs back to Lech are rather steep for nervous novices

− Generally expensive

− Still a few slow, old chairlifts

Lech and its higher, linked neighbour Zürs are the most fashionable resorts in Austria, each able to point to a string of rich and celebrated regular visitors, and to pull in Porsche-borne Germans on an unmatched scale. But, like all such 'exclusive' resorts, they aren't actually exclusive in any real sense. A holiday here doesn't have to cost a lot more than in countless other international resorts in the Alps. We don't feel out of place here, and neither would you.

The real point about these resorts is that they offer a rare and attractive combination of impressive snowfall, traditional Alpine atmosphere and excellent hotels offering a truly personal service from their family owners. And they attract people who want to get out on the hill – they have few of the flash shopping opportunities of St Moritz or Cortina, for example.

THE RESORT

Lech is an old farming village set in a high valley that spent long periods of winter cut off from the outside world until the Flexen Pass road through Zürs was constructed at the end of the 19th century. (Even now, the road can be closed for days on end after an exceptional snowfall; a road tunnel is planned, but is not imminent.)

The village is attractive, with upmarket hotels built in traditional chalet style, a gurgling river plus bridges, adequately impressive scenery and a high incidence of snow on the streets. But don't expect a rustic

backwater: away from the central area the place is fairly ordinary, and the appeal is dimmed by traffic on the main street – although the pavements have been widened and parking is controlled, it can still get very busy, especially at weekends.

British visitors are outnumbered 10:1 by Germans and 3:1 by Austrians.

The heart of the village is a short stretch of the main street beside the river; most of the main hotels are clustered here, along with the one serious emporium, Strolz. Right on this street is the base station of the Rüfikopf cable car, departure point for exploration of the Zürs slopes. A short walk away, across the river, are the Schlegelkopf chairlifts, leading up into Lech's main area of slopes. Chalets, apartments and pensions are dotted around the valley, and the village spreads along the main street for 2km/1.5 miles. Some of the cheaper accommodation is quite a walk from the lifts. There's also an 'excellent' supermarket.

Practically all the slopes are treeless, the main exception being the lower runs just above Lech. Most are quite sunny – very few are north-facing.

The toughest runs are classed as unpatrolled 'ski routes' or 'high-alpine touring runs', which are not protected against avalanche and should be skied only with a guide. We have no problem with the latter category – in other resorts, these off-piste runs would simply not appear on the piste map at all. But the ski route concept is used too widely, reducing the resort's responsibility for runs that are a key part of the area, and that should be patrolled pistes. Ski routes form the only ways down to Zug; the only way to complete the Lech-Zürs-Lech circuit; and most of the identified runs from Kriegerhorn. To add to the confusion, some of these routes may be groomed (or part-groomed) after a heavy snowfall; and in practice most people ski them as if they were pistes. The St Anton chapter has more on this ludicrous state of affairs.

The piste map, which attempts to cover the whole of the Arlberg region in one view, was redesigned a few years ago, but is still unclear or misleading in places – particularly around Oberlech. Piste marking is generally adequate, but there is a confusing, loopy system that in places gives the same number to several pistes. Piste classification understates difficulty in places, though not to the degree found in St Anton.

THE SLOPES
One-way traffic
The main slopes centre on **Oberlech**, 250m/82oft above Lech (just below the treeline), and can be reached from the village by chairlifts as well as the cable car. The wide, open pistes above Oberlech are perfect for intermediates, and there is also lots of off-piste. Zuger Hochlicht, the high point of this

---

AUSTRIA

168

www.wtss.co.uk

Weekly news updates and resort links at www.wtss.co.uk

↑ The lovely away-from-the-lifts red run from Muggengrat to Zürs – a perennial favourite of ours
SNOWPIX.COM / CHRIS GILL

KEY FACTS

Resort	1450m
	4,760ft

Arlberg region	
Slopes	1305-2650m
	4,280-8,690ft
Lifts	85
Pistes	276km
	172 miles
Blue	39%
Red	50%
Black	11%
Snowmaking	59%

For Lech-Zürs only	
Slopes	1450-2450m
	4,760-8,040ft
Lifts	33
Pistes	117km
	73 miles

Not far from the centre is the cable car up to Oberlech: a small, traffic-free collection of 4-star hotels set on the mountainside, with an underground tunnel system under the central piste, linking the hotels and lift station – used routinely to move baggage, and by guests in bad weather. The system was completed for 2007/08, with a tunnel to the hotel Sonnenburg. The cable car works until 1am, allowing access to the mother resort's nightlife.

Zug is a hamlet 3km/2 miles from Lech, with a lift into the Lech slopes. The limited accommodation here is mostly B&B, with one pricey 4-star hotel. It's not ideal for sampling Lech's nightlife, but there is an evening bus service (see 'Après-ski')

Lech is linked by lifts and runs to higher Zürs, described at the end of this chapter. There is a free, regular but often very crowded ski-bus service between the two resorts. And a reporter complains of long walks from the lifts to the bus stop. Buses (also crowded) run to St Anton, St Christoph and Stuben, too, all covered by the Arlberg pass. The post bus offers a less crowded option, but is not free.

The Sonnenkopf area at Klösterle, reached by ski-bus from Stuben, is also covered – 'worth a trip' for its combination of gondola rides and quiet, wide, woodland runs ('perfect for intermediates') – not least in bad weather, say reporters.

Lech's upper-crust image has not stood in the way of its snowboarding development. The jewel in the Arlberg crown has some of the best backcountry riding in Austria, and abundant snowfalls mean it is a popular destination for freeriders. Lech is also a regular stop on the Snowpark tour – a prestigious event on the freestyle calendar. A blend of impeccable piste grooming, modern chairlifts and few draglifts makes for nice learning conditions; but be careful on the west-facing slopes at Zürs, which have many flat/uphill sections.

LIFT PASSES

Arlberg Ski Pass

Prices in €

Age	1-day	6-day
under 16	25	119
16 to 19	38	173
20 to 64	42	199
over 65	38	173

Free no one, but season pass only €10 if under 8 or over 75

Senior min. age for senior women is 60

Beginner points ticket

Notes
Covers all St Anton, St Christoph, Lech, Zürs and Stuben lifts, and linking bus between Rauz and Zürs; also covers Sonnenkopf (10 lifts) at Klösterle, 7km/4 miles west of Stuben (bus link from Stuben); single ascent, half-day and pedestrian options

---

sector, gives stunning views.

The **Rüfikopf** cable car takes Lech residents to the west-facing slopes of Zürs. This mountainside, with its high point at **Trittkopf**, is a mix of quite challenging intermediate slopes and flat/uphill bits. On the other side of Zürs the east-facing mountainside is of a more uniform gradient. Chairs go up to **Seekopf** with intermediate runs back down. There's a chair from Zürsersee up to **Muggengrat** (the highest point of the Zürs area). This has a good blue run back under it and accesses the long, scenic, lift-free and quiet Muggengrat Täli; it starts with a choice between a catwalk and a mogul field, but develops into a fine, varied red with lots of nearby off-piste options on the way down to Zürs; at the bottom you can take lifts up the other side or walk through the village. Another chair from Zürsersee – slow and vulnerable to closure by wind – goes up to Madloch-Joch and the long, scenic ski route back to the fringes of Lech, completing a clockwise circuit. You can peel off part-way down and head for Zug and the slow chairlift up to the Kriegerhorn above Oberlech, instead.

TERRAIN PARKS
In Lech only

Just above the Schlegelkopf and visible from town lies what has become one of the best snow-parks in Austria. There are two main kicker lines, separated into medium and pro categories, which will suit good riders as well as seasoned pros. The kickers are outstanding, and are followed by two kinked boxes and a wall ride. The rails are also set in lines so you can hit several in a row. A fun box, 8m/26ft down rail, rainbow and a C-box, lie next to an easy rail and kicker line for beginners. There is a also a designated area made up of little banks and jumps, great for getting used to air time. Check www.mellowparks.com for the latest news.

SNOW RELIABILITY
One of Austria's best

Lech and Zürs both get a lot of snow. Lech gets an average of almost 8m/26ft of snow between December and March, almost twice as much as St Anton and three times as much as Kitzbühel; but Zürs gets 50% more than Lech. The altitude is high by Austrian resort standards, and there is

Lech

Interactive resort shortlist builder at www.wtss.co.uk

excellent snowmaking, helping to counter the sunny exposure of Lech and much of Zürs. This was increased for 2007/08, including coverage of the nursery slopes at Zürs.

This combination, together with excellent grooming, means that the Lech-Zürs area normally has good coverage until late April.

FOR EXPERTS
Off-piste is main attraction

There is only one (very short) black piste on the map, and there is no denying that for the competent skier who prefers to stick to patrolled runs the area is very limited. But the two

types of off-piste route explained earlier offer lots to enjoy. Experts will get a lot more out of the area if they have a guide, as there is plenty of excellent off-piste other than the marked ski routes, much of it accessed by long traverses – and the ski routes get heavily skied, not surprisingly. By comparison with St Anton, fresh powder lasts well here.

Many of the best runs start from the top of the fast Steinmähder chair, which finishes just below Zuger Hochlicht. Some routes involve a short climb to access bowls of untracked powder. From the Kriegerhorn there are shorter off-piste runs down

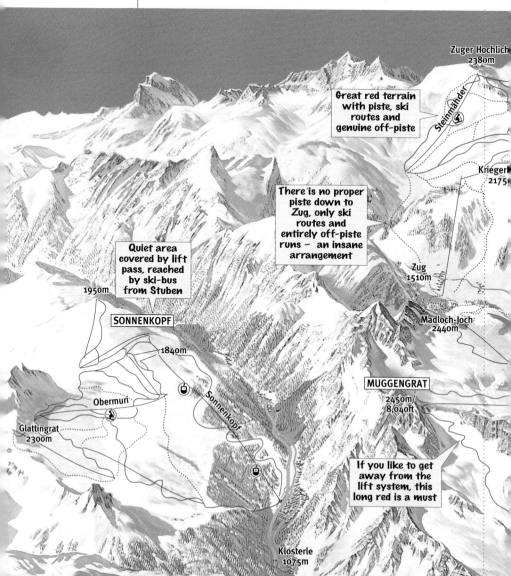

Zuger Hochlich
2380m

Great red terrain
with piste, ski
routes and
genuine off-piste

Krieger
2175

There is no proper
piste down to
Zug, only ski
routes and
entirely off-piste
runs – an insane
arrangement

Zug
1510m

Quiet area
covered by lift
pass, reached
by ski-bus
from Stuben

1950m

SONNENKOPF

Madloch-Joch
2440m

1840m

MUGGENGRAT

2450m/
8,040ft

Obermuri

Glattingrat
2300m

If you like to get
away from the
lift system, this
long red is a must

Klosterle
1075m

towards Lech and a very scenic long ski route down to Zug (followed by a slow chair and a rope tow to pull you along a flat area). Most runs, however, are south- or west-facing and can suffer from sun. At the end of the season, when the snow is deep and settled, the off-piste off the shoulder of the Wöstertäli from the top of the Rüfikopf cable car down to Lech can be superb. And a reporter enjoyed great April powder at Zuger Hochlicht. There are also good runs from the Trittkopf cable car in the Zürs sector, including a tricky one down to Stuben.

The steeper red runs (notably on Zuger Hochlicht and both sides of Zürs) are well worth a try, and you'll want to visit St Anton during your stay, where there are more challenging pistes as well as more off-piste.

Heli-lifts are available to a couple of remote spots, at least on weekdays.

FOR INTERMEDIATES
Flattering variety for all
The pistes in the Oberlech area are nearly all immaculately groomed blue runs, the upper ones above the trees, the lower ones in wide swathes cut through them. It is ideal territory for cruisers not wanting surprises.

Strong intermediates will want to do the circuit to Zürs and back.

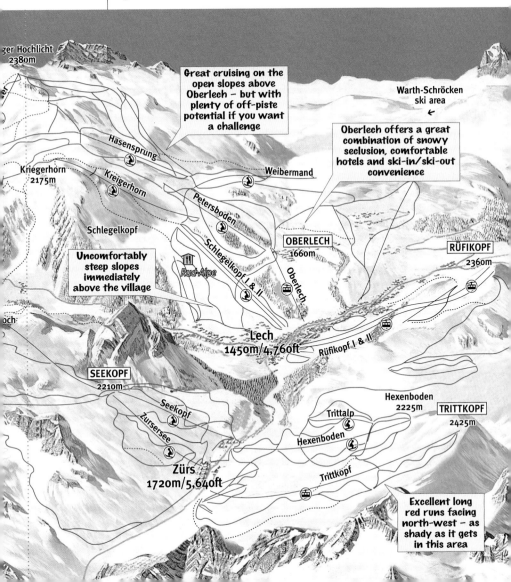

ger Hochlicht
2380m

Great cruising on the open slopes above Oberlech – but with plenty of off-piste potential if you want a challenge

Warth-Schröcken ski area

Häsensprung

Oberlech offers a great combination of snowy seclusion, comfortable hotels and ski-in/ski-out convenience

Kriegerhorn
2175m

Kriegerhorn

Weibermand

Petersboden

Schlegelkopf

OBERLECH
1660m

RÜFIKOPF
2360m

Schlegelkopf I & II

Oberlech

Uncomfortably steep slopes immediately above the village

Rud-Alpe

Lech
1450m/4,760ft

Rüfikopf I & II

SEEKOPF
2210m

Seekopf

Hexenboden
2225m

TRITTKOPF
2425m

Trittalp

Zürssee

Hexenboden

Zürs
1720m/5,640ft

Trittkopf

Excellent long red runs facing north-west – as shady as it gets in this area

SCHOOLS

Lech
t 2355

Oberlech
t 2007

Zürs
t 2611

**Omeshorn Alpincenter
Lech**
t 39880

Classes
(Lech prices)
6 days (2hr am and
2hr pm) €180

Private lessons
€216 for 1 day; each
additional person €16

CHILDREN

Mini-clubs run 9am to
4pm, Sun to Fri, and
children must be
toilet-trained

Miniclub Lech
t 21610
From age 3

Little Zürs
t 2245252
From age 3

Kinderland Oberlech
t 2007
From age 2½; free for
children staying in
Oberlech

Babysitting list
Held by tourist office

Ski school
From 4½ to 14:
6 days €166

Whether it's wise for less confident intermediates to tackle the beautiful red ski route from Madloch depends, simply, on the conditions. It is not steep, and parts may be groomed despite its non-piste status, but parts can be heavily mogulled and congested, and lots of people find the run a struggle.

It's worth noting that the final blue-run descents to Lech (as opposed to Oberlech) are uncomfortably steep for nervous novices.

More adventurous intermediates will want to spend time on the fast Steinmähder chair on Zuger Hochlicht – a choice of satisfying pistes and ski routes, and from there take the scenic red run all the way to Zug (the latter part on a ski route rather than a piste). Lech is an excellent place to try skiing deep snow for the first time.

Zürs has many more interesting red runs, on both sides of the village. We like the north-west-facing reds from Trittkopf and the excellent Muggengrat Täli (see 'The Slopes').

FOR BEGINNERS
Easy slopes in all areas
The main nursery slopes are in Oberlech, but there is also a nice dedicated area in Lech. There are good, easy runs to progress to, both above and below Oberlech.

FOR CROSS-COUNTRY
Picturesque valley trail
A 19km/12 mile trail starts from the centre of Lech and leads through the beautiful but shady valley, along the Lech river to Zug and back. A reporter recommends the Älpele for lunch en route. In Zürs there is a 4km/2.5 mile track to the Flexen Pass and back.

QUEUES
Still a few bottlenecks
The resort proudly boasts that it limits numbers on the slopes to 14,000 for a more enjoyable experience. Most reporters also stress how much quieter Lech's slopes are than St Anton's. There have been significant lift improvements and feedback is generally positive, but there are still one or two bottlenecks – the Schlegelkopf fast quad out of Lech gets very busy first thing ('20 minutes at Easter') and the crucial ('slow and cold') Madloch double chair at the top of the Zürs area generates peak-time queues on the Lech-Zürs-Lech circuit –

'up to 30 minutes', says a March 2008 visitor. Some readers mention the Rüfikopf cable car to Zürs as generating queues, particularly at peak times. Reporters have also praised the care taken by attendants to help children on to lifts.

MOUNTAIN RESTAURANTS
On the up
The lunch scene is dominated by the many big places in Oberlech and the hotels in Zürs, and more remote restaurants are not a traditional highlight; things have improved somewhat in recent years (though overcrowding is still a problem). **Editors' choice** Rud-Alpe (41825), on the lower slopes above Lech, just counts as a mountain restaurant – a welcoming rustic place, lovingly rebuilt using timbers from other old huts. We got only a quick drink on the terrace, but happily we have reports of 'very good food' and 'friendly staff'. There's a daily changing set menu, as well as more standard stuff. **Worth knowing about** The smartly revamped Balmalp (aka Palmenalp), above Zug, has a non-smoking area among its various spaces (unusual for Austria) and is very popular with reporters – 'an absolute beauty', 'stunning views', 'quick service', 'huge portions of pasta and pizza', 'trendy music'. Kriegeralpe is rustic and charming, with 'jolly music and delicious food'. Above Zürs, Seekopf now offers table service, and does 'quality food at decent prices'.

At Oberlech there are several big sunny terraces set prettily around the piste. Quite often you'll find a live band playing outside one. Reader recommendations include the Ilga Stuble, the lovely old Alter Goldener Berg, the Mohnenfluh, and the Petersboden hotel's round tent. The Burgwald is also highly rated: 'lovely food and really friendly service'.

A reporter praises the restaurants down in Zug, especially the Klösterle – 'lovely restored farmhouse'.

SCHOOLS AND GUIDES
Excellent in parts
The ski schools of Lech, Oberlech and Zürs all have good reputations and the instructors speak good English. Group lessons are divided into no fewer than 10 ability levels. A regular visitor writes: 'I've used the same instructor for three seasons; probably the best I

Air Zürich 200km/
124 miles (2½hr);
Innsbruck 120km/
75 miles (1½hr).
Friedrichshafen
130km/81 miles
(1½hr)

Rail Langen (17km/
10 miles); regular
buses from station,
buses connect with
international trains

have ever had – friendly, helpful, knowledgeable.' 'Very highly praised,' says another. A few years ago the mountain guides office started the Omeshorn Alpincenter school. In peak periods, you should book instructors and guides well in advance, as many are booked every year by regular visitors.

FACILITIES FOR CHILDREN
Oberlech's fine, but expensive
Oberlech makes an excellent choice for families who can afford it, particularly as its hotels are so convenient for the slopes. Reporters have praised the family-friendly approach and attention paid to children using the lifts: 'Mountain staff were really polite and helpful.' Goldener Berg has an in-house kindergarten. Children of visitors staying in Oberlech have free access to the kindergarten there, Kinderland. The Oberlech school is normally well-regarded (small groups, good English spoken), but a 2008 parent found the kindergarten 'a bit disorganised' for his four-year-old. Private lessons were more successful – 'my older children improved immediately.'

STAYING THERE

HOW TO GO
Surprising variety
Hotels and guest houses dominate, though there are alternatives.
Chalets There are a couple run by British operators, including two chalet hotels by Ski Total, one with pool.
Hotels There are three 5-stars (another is planned for 2008/09), over 30 4-stars and countless modest places.
LECH
*****Arlberg (21340) Elegantly rustic central chalet. Pool. 'Probably the best in Lech.'
*****Post (22060) Lovely old Relais & Châteaux place on the main street; pool, sauna. 'Outstanding'; 'Superb service and food.'
****Angela (2407) Perfect for keen skiers: in a piste-side location up the hill from the Schlegelkopf chairlift.
****Brunnenhof (2349) Highly recommended by a reporter.
****Elisabeth (2330) 'Very friendly, family-run, much better food than usual,' says a 2007 reporter.
****Gottharn (35600) – 'Warm service, spacious room, great breakfast spread, large spa with pool – a real find.'

Lech

173

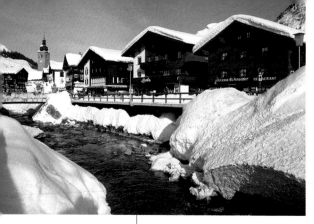

↑ Lech is at its most charming in the centre, where the main street runs beside the river
LECH ZÜRS TOURISMUS

****Haldenhof** (24440) Friendly and well run, with antiques and fine paintings. 'Highly recommended.'

****Kristiania** (25610) 'Outstanding decor, ambience and service – feels very homely,' says a reporter.

****Krone** (2551) One of the originals, by the river. 'Food, service faultless', but 'small rooms and some noise', 'superb' wellness centre with pool.

****Monzabon** (2104) 'Characterful, with friendly staff.' Pool and an indoor ice rink.

****Schwarzwand** (2469) Perfectly positioned for beginners, by the separate nursery slope. Sauna, steam room, solarium.

****Sursilva** (29700) Good value, small place. Sauna. 'Good food; beautifully cooked and presented.' Recommended by two 2008 visitors.

****Tannbergerhof** (2202) Splendidly atmospheric inn on the main street, with outdoor bar and popular disco (tea time as well as later). Pool.

***Pension Angerhof** (2418) Beautiful ancient pension, with wood panels and quaint little windows.

OBERLECH
****Burg Vital** (3140) 'Excellent – no criticism,' said a reporter.

****Burg** (22910) Sister hotel of Burg Vital – same facilities and with famous outdoor umbrella bar.

****Montana** (2460) Welcoming chalet run by the family of Patrick Ortlieb. 'Best hotel food ever, friendly and efficient service,' says a repeat visitor. Pool, smart wellness centre.

****Sonnenburg** (2147) Family-run chalet with a relaxed, traditional atmosphere. Good children's facilities. Pool, impressive wellness centre.

****Pension Sabine** (2718) 'Comfortable and charming with spa facilities', 'excellent food, very friendly and welcoming'.

Apartments There are lots available to independent bookers.

EATING OUT
Mainly hotel-based
There are over 50 restaurants in Lech, but nearly all of them are in hotels. Reporter recommendations include the Krone and the Post (which serves modern Austrian food). The Madlochblick is very cosy, with a typically Austrian restaurant, and Rudi's Stamperl is 'top-notch and reasonably priced'. Hûs Nr 8 is one of the best non-hotel restaurants for traditional Austrian food. Schneggarei is a 'smart' place that does good pizza. The Fux does 'modern/Asian food, utterly un-Austrian', and the Lecher Stube (hotel Gotthard) is 'very good value'. The Olympia has been suggested for cakes and coffee stops.

In Oberlech, hotel Montana is consistently praised and a 2007 visitor had 'the perfect' Wiener schnitzel in the hotel Sonnenburg.

In Zug, the Rote Wand is excellent for traditional Austrian food, but is 'frighteningly expensive'. Reporters recommend the 'simple and charming' Alphorn and the Gasthof Älpele (3km/ 2 miles from the road, up the valley on the XC loops, reached by covered wagons attached to snowcats).

APRES-SKI
Good but expensive
At Oberlech, the umbrella bar of the Burg hotel is popular immediately after the slopes close, as is the champagne bar in hotel Montana.

Down in Lech the outdoor bars of hotels Krone (in a lovely, sunny setting by the river) and Tannbergerhof (where there's an afternoon as well as a late-night disco) are popular. Later on, discos in the hotels Almhof-Schneider and Krone liven up too. The latter's K-Club has a selection of rare whiskies. The Ilga is a good place for a drink, as is S'Pfefferkörndl. Two 'smart' choices are Schneggarei's for funky house music early and late and the modern Fux jazz bar/restaurant, which has live music and a huge wine list. Archiv is good for cocktails and attracts a younger crowd.

Zug makes a good night out: you can take a sleigh ride for a meal at the Rote Wand, Klösterle or Auerhahn, and have drinks at the 'highly recommended' Vinothek wine bar at the s'Achtele restaurant.

After 7.30pm the free resort bus becomes a pay-for bus called James, which runs until 3am.

OFF THE SLOPES
At ease

Many visitors to Lech don't indulge in sports, and the main street often presents a parade of fur-clad strollers. The range of shopping is surprisingly limited – Strolz's plush emporium (including a champagne bar) right in the centre is the main attraction.

It's easy for pedestrians to get to Oberlech or Zug for lunch. The village outdoor bars make ideal posing positions. There are various sporting activities and 29km/18 miles of walking paths ('superb, very well marked') – the one along the river to Zug is 'outstandingly' beautiful, and recommended by several readers.

There is a floodlit sledging run from Oberlech to town: 'loved by kids and not to be missed', say reporters.

Zürs 1720m/5,640ft

Some 10 minutes' drive towards St Anton from Lech, Zürs is almost on the Flexen Pass, with good snow virtually guaranteed. Austria's first recognisable ski lift was built here in 1937. Along with snow, Zürs offers some excellent hotels, and once inside them, all is well with the world. But the village as a whole doesn't have much appeal – it has nothing resembling a centre, few shops – and intrusive traffic to/from Lech on the central through-road.

The village is a fraction of the size of Lech, but still has three 5-star hotels. We stayed at the 5-star Zürserhof (25130) and found it excellent – great service, food and spa facilities. Thurnher's Alpenhof (2191) has a palatial spa, a piano bar, and its own ski instructor on tap. There are nine 4-stars. The Hirlanda (2262) offers 'excellent food and service'.

If you want to eat out in the evening, it will probably be in another hotel. The Kaminstüble (hotel Schweizerhaus) and Toni's Einkehr have been recommended. Nightlife is quiet. Vernissage (22710), is said to be the best nightspot. There's a disco in the Edelweiss hotel (26620) and a piano bar in the Alpenhof (21910).

Many of the local Zürs instructors are booked up for private lessons for the entire season by regular clients.

175

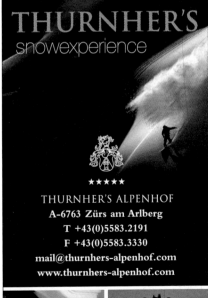

Lech

Lech

Large, lively resort with relatively reliable snow on local slopes and access to other good areas nearby, including a glacier

➕ Good for confident intermediates

➕ Snow more reliable than usual in the Tirol, plus the snow guarantee of the Hintertux glacier nearby

➕ Several worthwhile nearby areas on the same pass and reached by free bus or train

➕ Lively après-ski – though it's easily avoided if you prefer peace

➕ Excellent children's amenities

➖ Often long queues for the gondola to Penken – the main slopes

➖ Slopes can be crowded

➖ Many lodgings a bus ride from lifts

➖ Runs mostly short, though linked Lanersbach slopes are longer

➖ Few steep pistes – though they do include Austria's steepest

➖ No pistes to the valley from Penken

Mayrhofen has long been a British favourite. Like so many popular Tirolean resorts, it manages to meet the needs of young people bent on partying and families looking for a quieter time. What makes it different from the Tirolean norm is its relatively high, relatively snow-sure slopes.

If it's the skiing that mainly attracts you, be sure to check out the Hintertux chapter, which also covers quieter villages between Mayrhofen and Hintertux that offer quicker access to the slopes they share with Mayrhofen. And don't forget that the valley lift pass is valid in lots of other places that are well worth exploring – it covers 167 lifts and 640km/400 miles of pistes.

THE RESORT

Mayrhofen is a fairly large resort sitting in the flat-bottomed, steep-sided Zillertal. Most shops, bars and restaurants are on the one long main street, with hotels and pensions spread over a wider area. The valley road bypasses the village, but it is not traffic-free. As the village has grown, architecture has been kept traditional.

Despite a reputation for lively après-ski, Mayrhofen is not dominated by lager louts. They exist, but tend to gather in a few easily avoided bars. The central hotels are mainly slightly upmarket, and overall the resort feels pleasantly civilised.

The main lift to the major Penken sector of slopes is set towards one end of the main street, and the newish cable car to the much smaller Ahorn sector starts 200m/660ft further along the road. The free bus service can be crowded, and it finishes early (5pm), so location is important. The original centre, around the market, tourist office and bus/railway stations, is now on the edge of things. The most convenient area is on the main street, close to the Penken gondola station.

Free buses and trains linking the Zillertal resorts mean you can easily

have an enjoyably varied week visiting different areas on the Ziller valley lift pass including the excellent glacier up at Hintertux (which has its own chapter). At the end of this chapter we

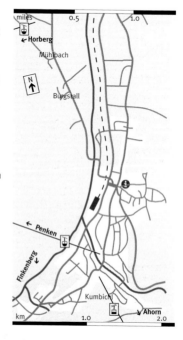

KEY FACTS

Resort	630m
	2,070ft

Ski and Glacier World Zillertal 3000

Slopes	630-3250m
	2,070-10,660ft
Lifts	59
Pistes	227km
	141 miles
Blue	26%
Red	58%
Black	16%
Snowmaking	121km
	75 miles

Mayrhofen-Lanersbach only (ie excluding Hintertux glacier)

Slopes	630-2500m
	2,070-8,200ft
Lifts	48
Pistes	157km
	98 miles

For Ziller valley

Slopes	630-3250m
	2,070-10,660ft
Lifts	174
Pistes	636km
	395 miles

LIFT PASSES

Zillertaler Superskipass

Prices in €

Age	1-day	6-day
under 15	18	88
15 to 18	29	141
over 19	36	176

Free under 6
Senior no deals
Beginner no deals

Notes
1-, 2- or 3-day passes cover Mayrhofen areas only; 4-day and over passes include all Ziller valley lifts; part-day and pedestrian passes available

PETER GILLETT

The link between Zell and Gerlos involves some high and exposed lifts and runs
➔

boarding

Mayrhofen has long been popular with snowboarders. There is a large British contingent who make this their winter home because of the extensive off-piste available. But beginners may have a hard time getting around, as the terrain tends to be relatively steep, the nursery slopes are inconvenient, and the area still has quite a few draglifts. Intermediates and upwards, however, will relish the abundance of good red runs and easily accessible off-piste. The terrain park is one of the best in Europe. Snowbombing, a music festival and snowboard contest, is held in April as well as the 5-star TTR event, Ästhetiker Wängl Tängl.

cover the Zillertal Arena area, which starts at Zell im Zillertal, a short drive down the valley. The other major Zillertal area is Hochzillertal/Hochfugen above Kaltenbach, dealt with in the Directory at the back of the book.

THE MOUNTAINS

Practically all Mayrhofen's slopes are above the treeline, and many are challenging reds.

THE SLOPES
Rather inconvenient
The larger of Mayrhofen's two areas of slopes is **Penken-Horberg**, accessed by the main gondola from one end of town. It is also accessible via gondolas at Hippach and Finkenberg, both a bus ride away. You cannot get back to Mayrhofen on snow – you can catch the main gondola down or, if snow cover is good enough (it rarely is), you can descend to either Finkenberg or Hippach on unpisted ski routes. The buses back from Finkenberg run at only hourly intervals.

A big cable car links the Penken area with the **Rastkogel** slopes above Vorderlanersbach, which is in turn linked to **Eggalm** above Lanersbach – see the Hintertux chapter. These links

are a great asset, and the run to Eggalm has been more reliable since snowmaking was installed. Getting back from Rastkogel on skis means braving a red run that can be heavily mogulled, but you can avoid it by taking a rope-tow up to the top station of the linking cable car and riding that down.

The smaller, gentler **Ahorn** area is good for beginners. It tends to be neglected, but has some impressive lifts – access is now by a 160-person cable car; the main lift at altitude is a new eight-seat chairlift. There is a lovely, long red run (over 1300m/4,260ft vertical) to the valley.

TERRAIN PARKS
Comprehensive
One of the finest parks in the Alps (now sponsored by Vans Shoes – www.vans-penken-park.com, and bigger than ever) is built beneath the Sun-Jet chairlift on Penken – but it can get crowded. There's an easy beginner line (also with a great mini wall ride), an intermediate line and a pro line of tabletops ranging in length between 3m/10ft and 19m/62ft, as well as a big hip jump. Every year there are more combinations of kinked, curved and flat boxes and rails for all levels. But

SCHOOLS

Die Roten Profis
(Manfred Gager)
t 6380

Total (Max Rahm)
t 63939

Mount Everest
(Peter Habeler)
t 62829

Mayrhofen 3000
(Michael Thanner)
t 64015

Classes
(Roten Profis prices)
6 days (2½hr am or
pm) €110

Private lessons
1 day: €118 for 1
person

AUSTRIA

178

this great park can be intimidating, as it is home to a lot of local and international pros. The half-pipe was improved for the 2007/08 season; but pipe jocks should head to the 360m/1,180ft long super-pipe in Hintertux.

SNOW RELIABILITY
Good by Tirolean standards
Although the lifts go no higher than 2500m/8,200ft, the area is better than most Tirolean resorts for snow because the slopes are mostly above 1500m/ 4,920ft. Snowmaking covers the whole Ahorn area, nearly all the main slopes on Penken-Horberg and some on Rastkogel and Eggalm. More is expected for 2008/09. At Hintertux is probably the best glacier in the world.

FOR EXPERTS
Commit Harakiri
Austria's steepest piste, called Harakiri and under the Knorren chair, has a gradient of 78% or 38°. It is certainly steep for a European piste; when we tried it, the run was mogul-free but rock hard except near the edges; not surprisingly, it was delightfully deserted. A reporter described it as 'one hell of a ride'. It does offer a worthwhile challenge for the brave but is quite short. The black run under the

Schneekar chair on Horberg is a good, fast cruise when groomed, but there are few other steepish pistes. The long unpisted trail to Hippach is quite challenging but rarely has good snow because of its low altitude. There is, however, some decent off-piste to be found, such as from the top of the Horbergjoch at the top of Rastkogel – we had a great time there in fresh powder – and under the cable car linking to Lanersbach. You can also try the other resorts covered by the valley lift pass – see the end of this chapter.

FOR INTERMEDIATES
On the tough side
Most of Mayrhofen's slopes are on the steep side of the usual intermediate range – great for confident or competent intermediates. And the Lanersbach expansion has made the area much more interesting for avid piste-bashers, with some good long runs on Rastkogel and delightfully quiet runs on Eggalm. But many of the runs in the main Penken area are quite short. And (except on Ahorn) there are few really gentle blue runs, making the area less than ideal for nervous intermediates or near-beginners. The overcrowding on many runs can add to the intimidation factor.

If you're willing to travel, each of

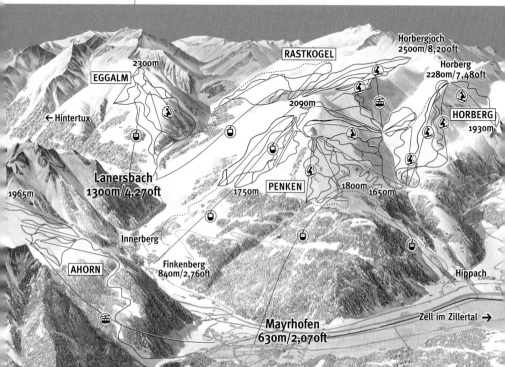

CHILDREN

Wuppy's Kinderland
t 63612
Ages 3mnth to 7yr;
9am to 5pm, Mon-Fri

Die Roten Profis
t 6380
From age 3;
10am-4pm

Total
t 63939
Ages 2 to 4, 9.30-3.30

Ski school
All run classes for children aged 4 or 5 to 14. Lunch can be provided (6 days including lunch €130)

GETTING THERE

Air Salzburg 175km/109 miles (3hr); Munich 190km/118 miles (2½hr); Innsbruck 75km/47 miles (1hr)

Rail Local line through to resort; regular buses from station

UK PACKAGES

Crystal, Crystal Finest, Directski.com, Equity, First Choice, Independent Ski Links, Inghams, Interhome, Kuoni, Neilson, Rocketski, Ski Expectations, Ski Line, Ski McNeill, Ski Wild, Skitracer, Skiworld, Snowcoach, Thomson **Gerlos** Interhome **Kaltenbach** Lagrange **Zell im Zillertal** Crystal,

ACTIVITIES

Indoor Adventure pool, two hotel pools open to the public, massage, sauna, squash, fitness centre, indoor tennis centre, climbing wall

Outdoor Ice rink, curling, 45km/28 miles of paths, snowshoeing, paragliding, snow biking, tobogganing

---

the main mountains covered by the Ziller valley pass is large and varied enough for an interesting day out.

FOR BEGINNERS
Overrated: big drawbacks
Despite its reputation for teaching, Mayrhofen is not ideal for beginners. The Ahorn nursery slopes are excellent – high, extensive and sunny – and an Easter 2008 reporter found them 'very quiet' too. But intermediate mates will want to be on Penken. The Penken nursery area is less satisfactory and there are very few easy blues to progress to.

FOR CROSS-COUNTRY
Go to Lanersbach
There is a fine 20km/12 mile trail along the valley to Zell im Zillertal, plus small loops close to the village. But snow down here is not reliable. Higher Vorderlanersbach has a much more snow-sure trail.

QUEUES
Still a real problem
The Penken gondola is very oversubscribed at peak times. Reports of queues of 45 or 60 minutes at the morning peak are still common. An alternative is to take the bus to one of the other gondolas (those at Lanersbach and Vorderlanersbach are quieter than those at Finkenberg and Hippach). There can be queues for some lifts once you get up the mountain and to get down at the end of the day, too. No queues have been reported for the Ahorn cable car, and a reader recommends using it to do the 1300m/4,26oft vertical 'lovely swooping' red run down while waiting for the Penken queue to subside.

MOUNTAIN RESTAURANTS
Plenty of them
Most of Penken's many mountain restaurants are attractive and serve good-value food, but they can get crowded. The Schneekar restaurant at the top of the Horberg section has been highly recommended ('table-service, traditional food, open fire, wooden beams, leather sofa, sometimes with a jazz pianist', say reporters). The Almstüberl at the mid-station of the Finkenberg gondola 'was usually quiet when others were packed'. Schiestl's Sunnalm and Kressbrunnalm have also been recommended.

SCHOOLS AND GUIDES
Excellent reputation
Mayrhofen's ski schools have good reputations, and a high proportion of guests take lessons. We have received many positive reports over the years, but a few negative ones too – including, strangely, reports of a shortage of English-speaking instructors. More reports welcome.

FACILITIES FOR CHILDREN
Good but inconvenient
Mayrhofen majors on child care and the facilities are excellent. But children have to be bussed around and ferried up and down the mountain.

STAYING THERE

HOW TO GO
Plenty of mainstream packages
There is a wide choice of hotel holidays available from UK tour operators, but few catered chalets.
Hotels Most of the hotels packaged by UK tour operators are centrally located, a walk from the Penken gondola. You can stay at the White Lounge ice-hotel too (see 'Après-ski').
*****Elisabeth** (6767) The only 5-star. 'Superb, excellent food and service.'
****Manni's** (633010) Well placed, smartly done out; pool.
****Kramerwirt** (6700) Lovely hotel, oozing character. 'Friendly and helpful staff, good rooms.'
****Strass** (6705) By the gondola. Lively bars, disco, fitness centre, pool; but very big and with a downmarket feel and rooms that lack style.
****Neuhaus** (6703) 'First-class facilities,' says a reporter; good food, but rooms above the bar are not ideal.
****Rose** (62229) Well placed, near centre. Good food.
****Neue Post** (62131) Convenient, family-run, on the main street – 'nice big rooms'.
Apartments A 2008 visitor recommends the newish Sonnenhof apartments (62520), near the gondola. 'Lovely.'

EATING OUT
Wide choice
Mayrhofen has a wide range of restaurants, from local specialities to Chinese. Manni's has been rated as 'expensive' for wine but does good pizzas. Wirthaus zum Griena is a 'wonderful old wooden building with traditional cuisine'. We had good lamb and pepper steak at Tiroler Stuben.

Interactive resort shortlist builder at **www.wtss.co.uk**

is a mixed one. The slopes suit intermediates best. You can really get a sense of travelling around: the trip takes you over several peaks and ridges, and overall the area stretches a distance of 17km/11 miles from west to east beyond Königsleiten.Our attempt to explore it last season was spoilt by thick fog, but a more fortunate reporter said: 'Starting from Zell im Zillertal, a return trip is a full day's skiing. We did the tour over two days to fit in all the other runs.' Most runs are fairly short, the longest being down to Gerlos (4km/2.5 miles).

Zell im Zillertal, the main town in the area, is a real working town rather than just a resort – it is a sprawling place, and has the oldest working brewery in the Tirol. There are some good hotels, including the 4-star Zapfenhof (2349) on the outskirts (with pool) and the Brau (2313) in the centre. Both have sauna, steam room and hot tub. The town is a bus ride from the two gondolas into the ski area. You have to ride these down as well as up – there is no piste. Après-ski centres around a few bars near the base of the gondola.

Gerlos has the advantage of being centrally situated in the ski area, allowing you to explore in either direction each day – but you would need to, because the local slopes are rather limited, despite a 1000m vertical. It is a bustling resort that straddles the road up to the Gerlos pass and is a bus ride from the gondola that takes you into the slopes. The home slope benefits from top-to-bottom snowmaking; there's a good local terrain park and half-pipe, and a new coaster-style toboggan run. Après-ski is lively and there are several good local hotels, including the 4-star Gaspingerhof (52160) with a very smart spa offering treatments as well as a gym, indoor-outdoor pool, saunas and steam room.

Königsleiten is an unusual resort – very spread-out, in a scenic wooded setting above a dam; mostly small chalets, but half a dozen hotels including the 4-star Königsleiten (82160). It has more extensive slopes than Gerlos, on either side of the Gerlospass road, but less vertical. On the north side, the runs are mostly genuine reds, radiating from the peak of Königsleitenspitze (2315m/7,595ft). The lower southern sector has a row of quad chairs serving easier slopes.

APRES-SKI
Lively but not rowdy

Après-ski is a great selling point. At close of play, the umbrella bar at the top of the Penken gondola, the Ice Bar at the hotel Strass and Nicki's Schirmbar in the Brücke hotel get packed out. Some of the other bars in the Strass are rocking places later on, including the Speak Easy Arena, with live music and dancing until 4am. Reporters have preferred the Apropos ('great music') and Brücke's Schlüssel Alm ('still the best all-round late-night venue'). Mo's American theme bar and Scotland Yard remain popular with Brits, but you might judge the latter to be 'dated, dirty and smoky'. The Neue Post bar and the Passage are good for a quiet drink. You can also party (or stay overnight) at the White Lounge ice-hotel at the top of the Ahorn gondola.

OFF THE SLOPES
Good for all

Innsbruck is easily reached by train. There are also good walks and sports amenities, including the swimming pool complex – with saunas, solariums and lots of other fun features. Pedestrians have no trouble getting up the mountain to meet friends for lunch.

Zillertal Arena

The Zillertal Arena was created in 2000 by linking the slopes of Zell im Zillertal, a short drive down the valley from Mayrhofen, to those above the villages of Gerlos and Königsleiten. They now share 51 lifts and 160km/ 99 miles of pistes (as much as the Mayrhofen-Lanersbach area). The slopes reach as high as 2400m/ 7,870ft, and most of them are above the 1500m/4,900ft mark, but they also get a lot of sun, so the snow message

Montafon

Extensive slopes in several areas covered by a single lift pass – and attractive places to stay, well off the beaten package path

COSTS

①②③④⑤⑥

NEWS

For 2007/08 several marked snowshoe trails and a 6km/ 4 mile floodlit cross-country loop opened at Silvretta Nova.

There's a new walkers' lift pass. And day passes bought in either Silvretta Nova or Hochjoch are now valid for both areas.

The ski schools have introduced telemark classes.

MONTAFON TOURISMUS

The towns and villages are quite pleasant places ↓

The 40km/25 mile long **Montafon** valley contains no fewer than 11 resorts and five main lift systems. Packages from the UK are few, but for the independent traveller the valley is well worth a look – especially the **Silvretta Nova** area (linking Gaschurn and St Gallenkirch) and high, tiny, isolated Gargellen.

The Montafon is neglected by the UK travel trade. Its location in Vorarlberg, west of the Arlberg pass, makes it a bit remote from the standard Austrian charter airport of Salzburg, although it's easily reached from Zürich and Friedrichshafen. And the valley is said to lack the large hotels that big operators apparently need. But it is being discovered by more independent travellers from the UK, and resort literature is available in English.

The valley runs south-east from the medieval city of Bludenz – parallel with the nearby Swiss border. The first sizeable community you come to is Vandans, linked to its Golm ski area by gondola. Next are Schruns, at the foot of Hochjoch, and Tschagguns, across the valley at the foot of Grabs. Further on are St Gallenkirch and Gaschurn, at opposite ends of the biggest area, Silvretta Nova. Up a side valley near St Gallenkirch is Gargellen, close to the Swiss border – a tiny village, but not unknown in Britain.

The valley road goes on up to Partenen. You can take a cable car from Partenen to Trominier, and then a minibus (covered by the area pass) on up to Bielerhöhe and the Silvrettasee dam, at the foot of glaciers and Piz Buin (of sunscreen fame) – the highest peak in the Vorarlberg. Bielerhöhe is a great launch pad for ski tours, and there are high, snow-sure cross-

country trails totalling 22km/13 miles on and around the lake. From here you can ski down to Galtür, near Ischgl. Some ski schools organise trips, with the return to Bielerhöhe by snowcat; you end the day with a long run back down to Partenen.

There are more ordinary cross-country trails along the valley, and an 11km/7 mile woodland trail at Kristberg, above Silbertal – up a side valley east of Schruns. One trail in Silvretta Nova is floodlit each evening. Trails total over 100km/62 miles.

The shared valley lift pass covers the post bus service and the Bludenz-Schruns trains, as well as the 62 lifts. But a reader who explored the valley last season rates a car essential.

The top heights hereabouts are no match for the nearby Arlberg resorts; but there is plenty of skiing above the mid-mountain lift stations at around 1500m/4,920ft, and most of the slopes are not excessively sunny, so snow reliability (aided by snowmaking on quite a big scale) is reasonable. Practically all of the slopes are above the trees, so exposed in bad weather. Nearly all the pistes are accurately classified blue or red, but there is plentiful off-piste (and quite a few 'ski routes') to amuse experts. There are terrain parks in most sectors, including the NovaPark at Silvretta Nova. Reports suggest few lift queues.

There are 10 ski schools in the valley, operating in each of the different ski areas ('excellent', says a reporter about the Hochjoch school). And the eight ski kindergartens take kids from age two.

Tobogganing is popular, and there are several runs on the different mountains, the Silvretta Nova's 6km/ 4 mile floodlit run down to St Gallenkirch being the most impressive.

For those with a car, there is accommodation in various smaller villages in addition to those dealt with below. Reporters suggest the Zum Guten Tropfen (8322) and Partenerhof

181

Piz Buin 3310m
Bielerhöhe
Partenen 1050m
1480m
2010m
1720m
SILVRETTA NOVA
Gaschurn 1000m/3,280ft
Gortipohl 950m
2275m/7,460ft
2100m
1850m
St Gallenkirch 900m/2,950ft
2150m
SCHAFBERG
Gargellen 1425m/4,680ft
Kreuzjoch 2395m/7,860ft
2300m
1850m
HOCHJOCH
1335m
Hochegga 1600m
GRABS
Grüneck 2085m
GOL
1520m
1000m
Tschagguns
Vanc 655m/25
Schruns 700m/2,300ft
Silbertal 890m
Kristberg

Weekly news updates and resort links at www.wtss.co.uk

182

KEY FACTS

Resorts	655-1425m
	2,150-4,680ft
Slopes	680-2395m
	2,230-7,860ft
Lifts	62
Pistes	222km
	138 miles
Blue	50%
Red	36%
Black	14%
Snowmaking	97km
	60 miles

TOURIST OFFICE

Montafon
t 722530
info@montafon.at
www.montafon.at

The tourist office is in Schruns, so from elsewhere in Austria add the prefix 05556, from abroad use the prefix +43 5556

UK PACKAGES

Gargellen Interhome
Schruns Interhome
Gaschurn Made to Measure

(8319) in Partenen, and the Adler (67118) in St Anton im Montafon.

GARGELLEN 1425m/4,680ft
Gargellen is a real backwater – a tiny, friendly village tucked up a side valley, with a small but varied piste network on Schafberg that is blissfully quiet.

The eight-person gondola from the village up to the Schafberg slopes seems rather out of place in this tiny collection of hotels and guest houses, huddled in a steep-sided, narrow valley. The runs it takes you to are gentle, with not much to choose between the blues and reds; but there is lots of off-piste terrain, including five ski routes. A special feature is the day tour around the Madrisa – a small-scale off-piste adventure taking you over to Klosters in Switzerland. It involves a 300m/980ft climb (which can take 40 minutes, observes a reporter), but is otherwise easy.

The altitude of the village (the highest in the Montafon) and north-east facing slopes make for reasonable snow reliability. And there is snowmaking on one of the several pistes to the valley, which include a couple of excellent, scenic away-from-the-lifts runs at the extremities of the area. With care you can ski to the door of some hotels, including the highly rated hotel Madrisa (6331) – 'Superb

staff, excellent facilities. The hotel made the holiday,' enthuses a visitor. Behind the hotel is a rather steep nursery slope. There are four pleasant mountain restaurants: the Schafberghüsli at the top of the gondola and two rustic huts at the tree line – the Obwaldhütte and the Kesslhütte. The Obwaldhütte 'features photos from the owner's recent encounter with a bear' and holds a weekly après-ski party after the lifts close, followed by a torchlit descent. The Barga pizzeria at the foot of the Vergalden drag can also be reached by walkers.

SCHRUNS 700m/2,300ft
Schruns is the most rounded resort in the valley – a towny little place, with the shops in its car-free centre catering for locals and for summer tourists.

A cable car and gondola go up from points outside the village into the Hochjoch slopes. Above the trees is a fair-sized area of easy blue runs, with the occasional red alternative, served by slow chairs and drags and the fast eight-seat Seebliga chair. A 2008 reporter enjoyed 'excellent' guided off-piste there. There are restaurants at strategic points – the Wormser Hütte is a climbing refuge with 'stunning' views, the Grasjoch Hütte is 'pleasant' and the Kapell has 'good choices'.

↑ Practically all the slopes are above the trees, and exposed to the weather
MONTAFON TOURISMUS

Phone numbers
From elsewhere in Austria, add the prefix 05557 (Gargellen), 05556 (Schruns), 05558 (Gaschurn); from abroad, use the prefix +43 and omit the initial '0'

Parents can leave their kids under supervision at the huge NTC Dreamland children's facility at the top of the cable car, by the skier services building. The blue run from Kreuzjoch back to Schruns is exceptional: about 12km/7 miles long and over 1600m/5,250ft vertical. Snow-guns cover the lower half of this, plus the Seebliga area.

Easily accessible across the valley are the limited slopes of Grabs, above the formless village of Tschagguns, and the more extensive area of Golm, where a gondola goes from Vandans up to a handful of chairs and drags serving easy slopes above the trees, and offering a vertical descent of over 1400m/4,590ft. A six-pack goes to the top of the area, linked via a ski tunnel to a quad on the Aussergolm slopes on the back of the hill. This serves the Diabolo black run, reputedly the steepest in the Montafon. Snow-guns cover most of the upper slopes, and the run to the valley.

As you are reminded frequently, Ernest Hemingway ensconced himself in Schruns in 1925/26, and his favourite drinking table in the hotel Taube (72384) can be admired. The Löwen (7141) and the Alpenhof Messmer (726640) ('great meals') are elegant, well-equipped 4-stars with big pools, the former a hub of the 'quite lively' après-ski scene.

GASCHURN / ST GALLENKIRCH
1000m/3,280ft / 900m/2,950ft
Silvretta Nova is the biggest lift and piste network in the valley. As a result, German cars fill to overflowing the huge car parks at the valley lift stations. Gaschurn is an attractive place to stay.
The two main resorts here are quite different. Whereas St Gallenkirch is strung along the main road and spoiled by traffic, Gaschurn is a pleasant village, bypassed by the valley traffic, with the wood-shingled Posthotel Rössle (8333) in the centre.

The lift network covers two parallel ridges running north-south, with most of the runs on their east- and west-facing flanks. The slopes are accessed from three points along the valley. A gondola from Gaschurn (prone to peak-season queues) takes you up to the east ridge, while another gondola from St Gallenkirch goes up to Valisera on the west ridge. A chairlift to Garfrescha from a roadside station at Gortipohl, between the resorts, serves its own slopes and gives access to central valley. Snowmaking covers almost half the area, including runs down to two valley stations.

This is generally the most challenging area in the valley, with as many red as blue runs, and some nominal blacks. Most of the slopes are above the treeline, typically offering a modest 300m/980ft vertical. The Rinderhütte six-pack serves more red pistes from the top of the area. There is lots of off-piste potential, including steep (and quite dangerous) slopes down into the central valley. The map now shows seven 'ski routes'.

The NovaPark terrain park features a half-pipe and boardercross course.

There are lots of mountain restaurants, many impressive in different ways. At the top of the east ridge, the state-of-the-art Nova Stoba can seat over 1,500 people in various rooms catering for different markets, including splendid panelled rooms with table service. The big terrace bar gets seriously boisterous in the afternoons. At the top of the other ridge is the splendidly woody Valisera Hüsli ('great food'). The Zur Brez'n and the Lammhütta on run 1a down to Gaschurn are also worth trying.

In the evening, the Heuboda disco bar and Fischer's Fritz (at Gortipohl) are 'lively'. And the Brunellawirt has live music at 6pm on Saturdays.

Obergurgl

A combination of high altitude and traditional Alpine atmosphere keeps the regulars going back, despite the drawbacks

NEWS

Two new eight-seat gondolas opened last season.

A two-stage gondola replaced the successive slow old chairs from the resort to Hohe Mut – a huge improvement. And the small Hohe Mut hut at the top was replaced by a larger and smarter Hohe Mut Alm with great views. The ski route from Hohe Mut was replaced by a new red run, leading across to the top of the fast Steinmann chair, while a black piste starting part-way down the new gondola became a ski route.

The second new gondola replaced the old Schermerspitz double chair above Hochgurgl.

➕ Glaciers apart, one of the Alps' most reliable resorts for snow – especially good for a late-season holiday

➕ Excellent area for beginners, timid intermediates and families

➕ Mainly queue- and crowd-free

➕ Traditional-style village with very little traffic

➕ Jolly teatime après-ski

➖ Limited area of slopes, with no tough pistes and no terrain park or half-pipe

➖ Exposed setting, with very few sheltered slopes for bad weather

➖ Few off-slope leisure amenities except in hotels

➖ Village is spread out and disjointed

➖ For a small Austrian resort, hotels are rather expensive

A loyal band of visitors go back every year to Obergurgl or its higher satellite Hochgurgl, booking a year in advance in recognition of the limited supply of beds. We understand the appeal of high, snow-sure, uncrowded, easy-intermediate slopes. But if we're going to a bleak, remote resort where there is not much to do but ski or board, we'd rather go somewhere with more skiing or boarding to do. Of course, most such places aren't in Austria – and perhaps that is the key to Obergurgl's appeal. It's snow-sure, and it's in Austria.

THE RESORT

Obergurgl is based on a traditional old village, set in a remote spot, the dead end of a long road up past Sölden. It is the highest parish in Austria and is usually under a blanket of snow from November until May. The surrounding slopes are bleak.

Obergurgl has no through traffic and few day visitors. The village centre is mainly traffic-free, and entirely so at night. Village atmosphere is relaxed during the day, jolly immediately after the slopes close, but rather subdued later at night; there are nightspots, but most people stay in their hotels.

Despite its small size, this is a village of widely separated parts; moving between them means long walks, an 'excellent, prompt' shuttle-bus, or taxis charging a flat rate. At the northern entrance to the resort is a cluster of hotels near the Festkogl gondola, which takes you to all the local slopes. The road then passes another group of hotels set on a little hill to the east, around the ice rink (beware steep, sometimes treacherous walks here). The village proper starts with an attractive little square with church, fountain, and the focal village hotel (Edelweiss und Gurgl). Just above are the Rosskar chairlift and new Gaisberg gondola stations. There is an underground car park in the centre.

Hochgurgl, a mid-mountain gondola-ride away, is little more than a handful of hotels at the foot of its own slopes. It looks like it might be a convenient resort dedicated to skiing from the door, but in practice it isn't: from nearly all the hotels you have to negotiate roads and/or stairs to get to or from the snow. Hochgurgl is even quieter than Obergurgl at night.

In the valley is Untergurgl – linked by gondola to Hochgurgl and by regular ski-buses to Obergurgl, and worth considering as a budget base. For a day out, it's a short bus or car trip to Sölden, and a long car trip to Kühtai (a high area near Innsbruck). Much closer is the tiny touring launch pad of Vent.

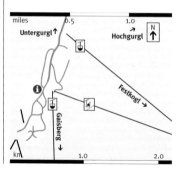

↑ The Top Mountain Star restaurant at Wurmkogl has stunning views
ÖTZTAL TOURISMUS / BERNDT RITSCHEL, G MANGOLD

KEY FACTS

Resort	1930m
	6,330ft
Slopes	1795-3080m
	5,890-10,100ft
Lifts	23
Pistes	110km
	68 miles
Blue	32%
Red	50%
Black	18%
Snowmaking	90%

THE MOUNTAINS

The gondola between Obergurgl and Hochgurgl means that the two can be thought of as forming a single area (though the gondola closes absurdly early at 4pm). Even so, the slopes are quite limited and most of them are very exposed – with few woodland runs to head to in poor conditions. Wind and white-outs can shut the lifts and, especially in early season, severe cold can curtail enthusiasm.

The lift pass is quite expensive for the relatively small area, but the low cost upgrade to cover a day in Sölden is still available (note that this must be requested at the time of purchasing the full pass). Piste grooming is very good. Signposting and piste edge marking is continually criticised: 'amazingly awful', 'non-existent in places – we found ourselves inadvertently off-piste on two occasions', 'one of our group plunged 15 metres off the edge of a blue run in a white-out and took 30 minutes climbing back up'.

THE SLOPES
Limited cruising
Obergurgl is the smaller of the two linked areas. It is in two sections, with a link at altitude in only one direction. The gondola from the village entrance and the Rosskar fast quad chair go to the higher **Festkogl** section. This is served by two drags and a chair up to 3035m/9,960ft. From here you can head down to the gondola base or over to the **Gaisberg** sector, now also reached from the village via a gondola, which goes on to the sector high point at Hohe Mut. A blue run links across from the mid-station of the gondola to slopes served by a slow quad and a six-pack, and a red run links across from the top.

There are two ski routes called 'varientenabfahrt'. The term is not explained but we believe it means ungroomed, largely unmarked, possibly unpatrolled; take care. There are 8km/5 miles of night skiing on Tuesdays ('excellent'). The slopes of **Hochgurgl** consist of high, gentle bowls, with fast lifts – chairs and two gondolas – serving the main slopes above the village, but drags serving the more testing outlying slopes. From the top stations there are spectacular views to the Dolomites. A single run leads down through the woods from Hochgurgl to Untergurgl.

TERRAIN PARKS
There isn't one
There used to be a terrain park and pipes at Festkogl; these were scrapped a few years ago and there are no current plans to revive them.

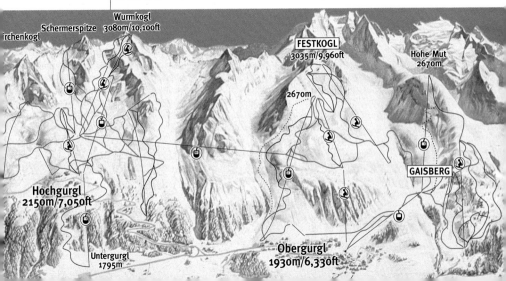

Wurmkogl
Schermerspitze 3080m/10,100ft
irchenkogl

FESTKOGL
3035m/9,960ft

Hohe Mut
2670m

2670m

GAISBERG

Hochgurgl
2150m/7,050ft

Untergurgl
1795m

Obergurgl
1930m/6,330ft

SNOW RELIABILITY
Excellent
Obergurgl has high slopes and is arguably the most snow-sure of Europe's non-glacier resorts – even without its snowmaking, which covers 90% of pistes. It has a long season by Austrian standards.

FOR EXPERTS
Not generally recommendable
There are few challenges on-piste – most of the blacks could easily be red, and where they deserve the classification it's only for short stretches (for example, at the very top of Wurmkogl). The ski routes can offer a challenge, and there is a lot of easy off-piste to be found with a guide – the top school groups often go off-piste when conditions are right. This is a well-known area for ski touring, and we have reports of very challenging expeditions on the glaciers at the head of the valley.

FOR INTERMEDIATES
Good but limited
There is some perfect intermediate terrain here, made even better by the normally flattering snow conditions. The problem is, there's not much of it. Keen piste-bashers will quickly tire of skiing the same runs and be itching to catch the bus to Sölden, down the valley – you can upgrade a week's lift pass at the time of purchase to include a day on Sölden's slopes.

Hochgurgl has the bigger area of easy runs, and these make good cruising. For more challenging intermediate runs, head to the Vorderer Wurmkogllift, on the right as you look at the mountain. Less confident intermediates may find the woodland piste down from Hochgurgl to the bus stop at Untergurgl tricky.

The Obergurgl area has more red than blue runs but most offer no great challenge to a confident intermediate. There is some easy cruising around mid-mountain on the Festkogl. The blue run from the top of the Festkogl gondola down to the village, via the Gaisberg sector, is one of the longest cruises in the area. And there's another long enjoyable run down the length of the gondola, with a scenic off-piste variant in the adjoining valley.

On Gaisberg, there are very easy runs in front of the Nederhütte and back towards the village. We have a report that the new red run from Hohe Mut tends to be icy and wind-blown.

FOR BEGINNERS
Fine for first-timers
The inconveniently situated Mahdstuhl nursery slope above Obergurgl is adequate for complete beginners. One reporter reckons there is 'less near-beginner terrain than you might expect', but there doesn't seem to us to be a shortage. The gentle Gaisberg run – under the new gondola out of the village – is ideal to move on to as soon as a modicum of control has been achieved. The easy slopes that are served by the Bruggenboden chair are also suitable.

The Hochgurgl nursery slopes are an awkward walk from the hotels, but otherwise satisfactory. And there are good blue slopes to move on to.

The quality of the snow and piste preparation make learning here easier than in most lower Austrian resorts.

CROSS-COUNTRY
Limited but snow-sure
Three small loops, one each at Obergurgl, Untergurgl and Hochgurgl, give just 12km/7 miles of trail. All are relatively snow-sure and pleasantly situated. Lessons are available.

QUEUES
Few problems
Major lift queues are rare.

MOUNTAIN RESTAURANTS
Unremarkable choice
Perhaps because the villages are so easily accessible for lunch, mountain huts are not a highlight, though a 2007 reporter praises 'reasonably priced food and lots of atmosphere'. **Editors' choice** The jolly Nederhütte

boarding
Beginners can access most of the slopes without having to ride draglifts but two of the most interesting areas in Hochgurgl are accessible only by long drags (which some of a 2008 reporter's group had trouble with). There's some good off-piste potential for more advanced riders but the lack of any terrain features or park is a major drawback for most.

SCHOOLS

Obergurgl
t 6305
Hochgurgl
t 626599

Classes
(Obergurgl prices)
6 days (2hr am and pm) €198
Private lessons
From €116 for 2hr; €8 for additional person

CHILDREN

Alpina and Hochfirst hotels
Kindergartens in these hotels
Bobo Mini-club
t 6305
From age 3; can include some skiing

Ski schools
From age 4 (6 days €192)

GETTING THERE

Air Innsbruck 90km/56 miles (2hr); Salzburg 288km/179 miles (3hr); Munich 240km/149 miles (4hr)

Rail Train to Ötz; regular buses from station, transfer 1½hr

(6425) at Gaisberg is one of the best, with 'outstanding' gröstl, 'good' käsespätzle, 'exceptional service' and several identified vegetarian dishes. **Worth knowing about** David's Skihütte is 'very friendly', cheerful and good value. We look forward to trying the new Hohe Mut Alm which has fabulous glacial views and at Hochgurgl, the 'stunning' glass-walled Top Mountain Star panoramic restaurant Wurmkogl, recently opened by the Top Hotel.

SCHOOLS AND GUIDES
Positive reports
We continue to receive positive reports of the Obergurgl school and guides, with good English spoken, a maximum of nine per group and excellent lessons and organisation. Reporters find the instructors 'friendly, supportive and professional', and classes 'a very positive and pleasant experience' with 'excellent' English spoken. Demand for private instruction appears to be increasing and it is advisable to book ahead during all peak periods.

FACILITIES FOR CHILDREN
Check out your hotel
Children's ski classes start at four years and children from age three can join Bobo's ski-kindergarten. There's lunchtime supervision for ski school and kindergarten children alike. Many hotels offer child care of one sort or another, and the Alpina has been particularly recommended.

STAYING THERE

HOW TO GO
Plenty of good hotels
Most tour operators feature hotels and pensions. Demand exceeds supply, and for once it is true that you should book early to avoid disappointment. Inghams has an especially wide

selection of hotels here and Neilson a good selection too. Family specialist Esprit has a couple of large chalets and also features a couple of hotels; all its guests have access to its usual comprehensive child care facilities.
Hotels Accommodation is of high quality: most hotels are 4-stars, and none is less than a 3-star. A cheaper option is to stay down the valley in Untergurgl, where the 4-star Jadghof (6431) has been recommended. Some hotels don't accept credit cards.
OBERGURGL
****Edelweiss und Gurgl** (6223) The focal hotel – biggest, oldest, one of the most appealing; on the central square, near the main lifts. Pool and outdoor whirlpool. 'Good marks for food, service, comfort and location.'
****Alpina de Luxe** (6000) Big, smart, excellent children's facilities. Pool.
****Bergwelt** (6274) Recommended as 'very smart'. Beauty and spa facilities, including outdoor pool.
****Hochfirst** (63250) 'Superb' spa facilities, comfortable, 'very good food', four or five minutes from gondola. Ski-bus stop outside. Casino.
****Crystal** (6454) Near the Festkogl lift. If you don't mind the ocean-liner appearance, it's one of the best.
****Gamper** (6545) 'Excellent,' says a reporter. 'Good food, friendly staff.' Far end of town, past the square.
****Gotthard-Zeit** (6292) 'Elegant', spacious, comfortable, good food. Spa facilities. Small pool. Convenient for skiing, but a 'steep walk from the village' if you venture out.
****Jenewein** (6203) 'Convenient with attractive spa facilities.'
****Josl** (6205) Modern, convenient – next to the gondola. Recently refurbished. Sauna and steam room. Recommended by a 2007 visitor.
***Wiesental** (6263) Comfortable, well situated, good value. Terrace popular for lunch and après-ski. 'Good food,

Interactive resort shortlist builder at **www.wtss.co.uk**

↑Hochgurgl isn't as convenient as it looks; from most hotels it's a walk to and from the slopes

UK PACKAGES

Airtours, Alpine Answers, Crystal, Crystal Finest, Directski.com, Esprit, First Choice, Independent Ski Links, Inghams, Interactive Resorts, Made to Measure, Momentum, Neilson, Ski Expectations, Ski Freshtracks, Ski Independence, Ski McNeill, Ski Solutions, Ski Total, Skitracer, Snow Finders, Thomson Hochgurgl Crystal Finest, Inghams, Neilson, Ski Expectations, Thomson

ACTIVITIES

Indoor Pools, saunas, whirlpools, steam baths and massage in hotels; bowling, library

Outdoor Natural ice rink, curling, snowshoeing, winter hiking paths

Phone numbers
From elsewhere in Austria add the prefix 05256; from abroad use the prefix +43 5256

TOURIST OFFICE

t 05720 0100
info@obergurgl.com
www.obergurgl.com

very friendly staff.'
***Granat-Schlössl** (6363) Amusing pseudo-castle, surprisingly affordable.
***Pension Gurgl** (6533) Friendly B&B near Festkogl lift; pizzeria; same owners as Edelweiss und Gurgl.
***Haus Schönblick** (6251) B&B with downhill walk to main lifts. 'Big rooms, hearty breakfast, friendly.'
HOCHGURGL
*****Top Hotel Hochgurgl** (6265) Relais & Chateaux – the only 5-star in the area. Luxurious, with pool.
****Angerer Alm** (62410) 'Staff really friendly and helpful.' Pool.
****Riml** (6261) Ski-in/ski-out location. Large rooms. 'Excellent' pool, spa. A 2007 visitor was 'very impressed'.
***Sporthotel Ideal** (6290) Well situated for access to the slopes. Pool and new spa facilities.
***Laurin** (6227) Well-equipped, traditional rooms, excellent food.
Apartments The Lohmann is modern and well placed for the slopes, less so for the village centre below. The 3-star Pirchhütt has apartments close to the Festkogl gondola, and the Wiesental hotel has more central ones.

EATING OUT
Wide choice, limited range
Hotel à la carte dining rooms dominate almost completely. Remember, credit cards are not widely accepted. A reporter recommends the independent and rustic Krumpn's Stadl (where staff dress in traditional clothing). The Hexenkuchl in the Jenewein receives favourable reports, serving 'good quality Austrian food'. The Romantika at the hotel Madeleine and the Belmonte are popular pizzerias. Hotels Alpina, Hochfirst ('food excellent, good wine selection') and Gotthard-Zeit have been recommended. The Angerer Alm does 'good meals in relaxing surroundings'. The two restaurants in the Edelweiss und Gurgl are reportedly

'superb', and food at the Josl 'excellent'. The 5-star Top Hotel Hochgurgl was recommended for a 'delicious' treat. Some evenings you can eat on the hill, at Nederhütte (a fondue and live music evening, which 'rocks') and David's Skihütte – both popular snowmobile destinations.

APRES-SKI
Lively early, quiet later
Obergurgl is more animated than you might expect, at least in the early evening. Nederhütte at Gaisberg is the place to be when the lifts close ('get there at 2pm if you want a table inside'). It has live music most days and 'even 70-year-olds were dancing on the tables', says a 2008 reporter. You ski home afterwards though (or ride down on a snowmobile). All the bars at the base of the Rosskar and Gaisberg lifts are also popular at close of play – the Pic-Nic is said to be lively and friendly. The Hexenkuchl at the Jenewein is also popular and a reporter enjoyed the 'excellent' and 'popular sun terrace' at the Wiesental.
Later on, the crowded Krumpn's Stadl barn is the liveliest place in town with live music on alternate nights. The Josl Keller is popular with all ages and gets busy with 'a western-style saloon downstairs and a posh wine bar upstairs'. The Jenewein and Edelweiss und Gurgl ('terrible live music but good service and comfy sofas') hotels have atmospheric bars. The Lodge is a 'smart' bar at the Hotel Bellevue. The Austria-keller disco attracts a wide age range – 6 to 60. There's a casino at the hotel Hochfirst. Reporters enjoy the Tuesday night ski school display/mountain party/night ski on Festkogl ('great night out').
Hochgurgl is very quiet at night except for Toni's Almhütte bar with live music in the Sporthotel Olymp. There's also the African Bar disco.

OFF THE SLOPES
Very limited
There isn't much to do during the day – few shops, limited public facilities. Innsbruck is over two hours away by post bus. Sölden (20 minutes away) has a leisure centre and shopping facilities. Pedestrians can ride gondolas to restaurants for lunch, or walk to the Gaisberg area; there are 12km/7 miles of hiking paths. The health suite at the Hochfirst is said to be open to non-residents.

Obertauern

High, snow-sure, French-style purpose-built resort on a small scale but with acceptable architecture and Austrian après-ski

RATINGS

The slopes	
Fast lifts	*****
Snow	****
Extent	**
Expert	***
Intermediate	****
Beginner	****
Convenience	****
Queues	****
Mountain restaurants	****

The rest	
Scenery	***
Resort charm	**
Off-slope	**

KEY FACTS

Resort	1740m
	5,710ft
Slopes	1630-2315m
	5,350-7,600ft
Lifts	26
Pistes	95km
	59 miles
Blue	59%
Red	37%
Black	4%
Snowmaking	86km
	53 miles

WENDY-JANE KING

Snow-sure Obertauern is modern, not unattractive and set at the top of the Tauern pass ↓

➕ Excellent snow record

➕ Efficient modern lifts

➕ Slopes for all abilities

➕ Good mountain restaurants

➕ Lively but not intrusive après-ski

➕ Compact resort core, but...

➖ Village lacks traditional charm and spreads along the pass a long way

➖ Peaks are not high, so slopes are of limited vertical and extent is too small for keen piste-bashers

➖ Lifts and snow can suffer from exposure to high winds

Obertauern's attractions are unique. If you're looking for a change from the slush and ice of lower Austrian resorts, moving up in the world by 1000m/ 3,300ft or so could be just the ticket – French-style snow without losing that inimitable Austrian après-ski jollity.

THE RESORT

In the land of picture-postcard resorts grown out of rustic villages, Obertauern is different – a mainly modern development at the top of the Tauern pass road. Built in (high-rise) chalet style, it's not unattractive – though it's a linear affair, lacking a central focus of shops and bars. Although the core is compact, accommodation is spread widely along the road, with lifts going up either side of the road at various points.

THE MOUNTAINS

The slopes and lifts form a circuit around the village that can be travelled either way in a couple of hours. Visitors used to big areas will soon start to feel they have seen it all. Runs are short and vertical is limited – most major lifts are in the 200m to 400m (660ft to 1,310ft) range. The piste map and signposting are both poor. Although the pistes are now numbered on both the map and the mountain, 'the colours don't always agree', says a 2008 visitor. Edge markers rarely reflect the piste classification – appalling.

Slopes Most pistes are on the sunny slopes to the north of the road and village: a wide basin of mostly gentle runs, some combining steepish pitches with long schusses. The slopes on the other side of the road – Gamsleitenspitze – are quieter and have some of the steeper runs. There is floodlit skiing twice a week.

Terrain parks The small Longplay Park is above the Almrausche hut, on the far left on our piste map.

Snow reliability The resort has exceptional snow reliability because of its altitude. But lifts can be closed by wind (which may blow snow away too). Snowmaking is said to be good, but grooming needs improvement.

Experts There are genuinely steep black pistes from the top Gamsleiten chair, but it is prone to closure. The icy race course under the Schaidberg-bahn is also a challenge. And try the black run from Seekarspitze and the ski route from Hundskogel (flat to start, steep moguls later). Reporters recommend joining an off-piste guided group to explore the area.

Intermediates Most of the circuit is of intermediate difficulty. Stay low for easier pistes, or try the tougher runs higher up; you can't do the whole circuit without skiing reds.

Beginners The nursery slopes are very good, but they are spread around and may involve long walks to and from accommodation. The Schaidberg chair

NEWS

For 2007/08 numbers were introduced onto the piste map to correspond with those on the mountain.

The Snowgolf World Championship will be held here from 29 to 31 January 2009.

UK PACKAGES

Alpine Answers, Crystal Finest, Inghams, Ski Wild, Snowscape, Thomson

Phone numbers
From elsewhere in Austria add the prefix 06456; from abroad use the prefix +43 6456

TOURIST OFFICE

t 7252
info@obertauern.com
www.obertauern.com

leads to a high-altitude beginners' slope and there is an easy run down.

Snowboarding Draglifts are optional except for beginners. Blue Tomato is a specialist school.

Cross-country There are 17km/11 miles of trails in the heart of the resort.

Queues The lift system is impressively efficient and lifties reportedly fill the chairs. Crowded pistes can be more of a problem than queues. But the Grünwaldkopfbahn quad still generates long queues in the mornings – huge when we visited. The Sonnenlift double chair can have problems at ski school time and the slow Hundskogel double is a bottleneck.

Mountain restaurants Mountain restaurants are numerous and good, but crowded. Treff 2000 ('excellent, good value dishes'), the 'cosy' Mankeialm, the Sonnhof ('best gröstl of the week', 'fast table-service'), Flubachalm ('traditional Austrian dishes'), Heu-Stadl ('superb goulash') and Almrausch ('fine selection of main courses') have been recommended. All the places at Kringsalm are praised, but a reporter rates the Almstube in the Seekarhaus as 'the best on the mountain – excellent fillet steak, succulent beef'. The Achenrainhütte by the Gamsleitenbahn has a 'jolly atmosphere' and the Hochalm gets 'very animated' – that is, busy.

Schools and guides Of the six schools, we have good reports on Frau Holle, Willi Grillitsch, Krallinger and Koch.

Facilities for children Most of the schools take children.

STAYING THERE

How to go A handful of tour operators offer packages here.

Hotels Practically all accommodation is in hotels (mostly 3-star and 4-star) and guest houses. The following have been recommended: Steiner (7306) 'Smart and comfortable'; Frau Holle (7662) 'Comfortable rooms and great breakfast'; Kohlmayr (7272) 'Excellent ambiance'; Enzian (72070) 'Very good facilities'; Schütz (72040) Pool and spa; D'Glöcknerin (7805) 'Lovely bar and spa facilities'; Marietta (72620) 'Couldn't fault it; the Beatles stayed here when filming *Help*'; Apparthotel Hubertus (20084) 'spacious and comfortable rooms'; Youth Hostel Schaidberg (7214) 'cheap and clean'.

Eating out The choices are mostly hotels and the busy après-ski bars at the foot of the lifts. The Almrausch, north of the town, is 'fantastic'.

Après-ski It's lively and varied. The Latsch'n Alm, with terrace and dancing, is good at tea time, as is the Lürzer Alm – 'full of character, lively, one of the best'. The Gruber Stadl is 'built to charm' and equally popular. The Tauernkönig hotel has 'a cosy outdoor après area hidden away off the 8a home run'. Monkey's Heaven and the People bar have dancing. The Taverne, Römerbar and the 'quaint' Nanu Irish bar have been recommended too.

Off the slopes There's an excellent, large sports centre – no pool, though. There are marked walks up to Kringsalm. Salzburg is an easy trip.

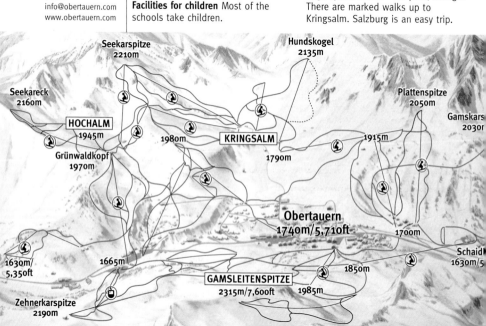

SAALBACH-HINTERGLEMM TOURIST OFFICE

Saalbach-Hinterglemm

Lively, noisy, traditional-style villages and extensive, varied, prettily wooded slopes; pity they are mostly so sunny

COSTS

① ② ③ ④ ⑤ ⑥

RATINGS

The slopes

Fast lifts	****
Snow	**
Extent	***
Expert	**
Intermediate	****
Beginner	***
Convenience	****
Queues	***
Mountain restaurants	****

The rest

Scenery	***
Resort charm	****
Off-slope	**

KEY FACTS

Resort	1000m
	3,280ft
Slopes	930-2095m
	3,050-6,870ft
Lifts	55
Pistes	200km
	124 miles
Blue	45%
Red	48%
Black	7%
Snowmaking	
on all main slopes	

➕ Large, well-linked, intermediate circuit, good for mixed groups

➕ Impressive lift system

➕ Saalbach is a big but pleasant, affluent village, lively at night

➕ Village main streets are largely traffic-free

➕ Lifts and pistes are conveniently close to centres of both villages

➕ Atmospheric mountain restaurants

➕ Large snowmaking installation

➕ Sunny slopes, but ...

➖ Most slopes are low as well as sunny, and the snow suffers

➖ Limited steep terrain

➖ Nursery slopes in Saalbach are not ideal – sunny, and crowded in parts

➖ Saalbach spreads along the valley – some lodgings are far from central

➖ Hinterglemm sprawls along a long street with no clearly defined centre

➖ Both are noisy from 4pm and Saalbach can get rowdy at night

An Austrian tour last season confirmed that the 'Skicircus' is in most respects the best of the major ski areas east of Innsbruck – it has more challenging intermediate terrain and better mountain restaurants than the SkiWelt (Söll, Ellmau etc), slicker lifts than Kitzbühel, and has the edge on both in terms of village altitude and ski convenience, provided you pick your spot.

The snowmaking is now good enough to make a midwinter holiday a fairly safe bet, but there is a limit to what snowmaking can achieve on low, sunny slopes as spring approaches. Like the other areas we mention, this is really a place to book at short notice, when conditions are good.

191

THE RESORT

Saalbach and Hinterglemm are separate villages, their centres 4km/ 2.5 miles apart, which have expanded along the floor of their dead-end valley. They haven't quite merged, but some years back adopted a single marketing identity. This doesn't mean

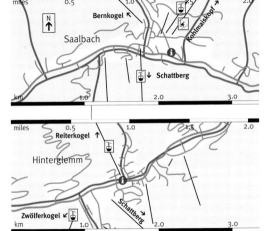

they offer a single kind of holiday.

Saalbach is an attractive, typically Austrian village, with traditional-style (although mostly modern) buildings huddled together around a classic onion-domed church. But it is more convenient than most Austrian villages, with lifts into three sectors of the slopes starting close to the traffic-free village centre; the result is near to an ideal blend of Austrian charm with French convenience.

Saalbach has a justified reputation as a party town – but those doing the partying seem to be a strangely mixed bunch. Big-spending BMW and Mercedes drivers, staying in the smart, expensive hotels that line the main street, share the bars with teenagers (including British school kids) spending more on alcohol than on their cheap and cheerful pensions strung along the valley road.

Hinterglemm also has lifts and runs close to the centre, and offers quick access to some of the most interesting slopes – and, importantly, to most of the north-facing runs. It is a more diffuse collection of hotels and holiday homes, where prices are lower and

NEWS

For 2008/09 an eight-pack with heated seats and covers is due to replace the Asitz quad up to Kl. Asitz on the return from Leogang.

Snowmaking now covers 90% of the slopes and is due to be improved again for 2008/09.

You can now 'programme' your lift pass to record your distance and altitude on the slopes. At the end of the day you receive a printout showing the results.

less cash is flashed. The main street, lined with bars and hotels, has been relieved of through traffic, though it is not quite traffic-free.

Both villages get very noisy from mid-afternoon till the early hours, with music blasting out of bars the norm. Saalbach in particular can get very rowdy, with drunken revellers still in their ski boots long after dark. Some of our reporters form part of the festivities, but others find the noise a problem ('quite rowdy if your hotel is on the main street', 'persistent noise from the bars', 'request a rear-facing room').

In both villages, the amount of walking depends heavily on where you stay. There is a good valley bus service, but it isn't perfect: it finishes early, gets very busy at peak times and doesn't get you back to hotels in central Hinterglemm, or to hotels set away from the main road – and a reporter even complains of poorly marked stops too, which resulted in him 'wandering about lost'. Taxis are plentiful and not expensive. The Nightliner bus runs intermittently from 7.30pm to 2am between Saalbach and Hinterglemm.

Several resorts in Salzburg province are reachable by road – including Bad Hofgastein, Kaprun and Zell am See, the last a short bus ride away.

THE MOUNTAINS

The slopes form a 'circus' almost entirely composed of broad slopes between swathes of forest.

THE SLOPES
User-friendly circuit
Travelling anticlockwise, you can make a complete circuit of the valley on skis, crossing from one side to the other at Vorderglemm and Lengau – if you wish you can stick to blues almost the whole way. Going clockwise, you have to truncate the circuit – there is no lift on the south side at Vorderglemm – and there is more red-run skiing to do (and a black if you want to do the full circuit).

The lift system is very impressive, with mainly gondolas and fast chairs.

On the south-facing side, five sectors can be identified, each served by a lift from the valley – from west to east, **Hochalm, Reiterkogel, Bernkogel, Kohlmaiskopf** and **Wildenkarkogel.** The links across these south-facing slopes work well: when traversing the whole hillside you need to descend to the valley floor only once – at Saalbach, where the main street separates Bernkogel from Kohlmaiskopf. The Wildenkarkogel sector connects via Seidl-Alm to the slopes of **Leogang**; a small, high, open area served by three fast lifts (including a new eight-pack) leads to a long, north-facing slope down to the base of an eight-seat gondola near Hütten, 3km/2 miles from Leogang village.

Back in the main valley, the north-facing slopes are different in character: two widely separated and steeper mountains, one split into twin peaks. An eight-seat gondola rises from Saalbach to **Schattberg Ost,** where the high, open, sunny slopes are served by a fast quad. The slightly higher peak of **Schattberg West** is reached by gondola from Hinterglemm. And a gondola now makes the link from Schattberg Ost to Schattberg West. The second north-facing hill is **Zwölferkogel,** served by a two-stage eight-seat gondola from Hinterglemm. A six-pack and draglift serve open slopes on the sunny side of the peak, and a second gondola from the valley provides a link from the south-facing Hochalm slopes. The Hinterglemm nursery slopes are well used, and floodlit every evening.

TERRAIN PARKS
Excellent
There's a floodlit terrain park with half-pipe near the nursery slopes just above Hinterglemm ('loved' by one reporter's teenagers), and another below Kl. Asitz on the way to Leogang. Below Seidl-Alm there's a boardercross course. Several dedicated 'carving' and 'mogul' zones are dotted around the area.

boarding

Saalbach is great for boarding. Slopes are extensive, lifts are mainly chairs and gondolas (though there are some connecting drags), and there are pistes to appeal to beginners, intermediates and experts alike – with few flats to negotiate. For experienced boarders, there's plenty of off-piste terrain between the lifts.

↑ Looks to us like mid-morning, early in the season: Saalbach is still in the shade, Hinterglemm just getting a bit of sun

TVB SAALBACH-HINTERGLEMM

LIFT PASSES

Skicircus Saalbach Hinterglemm Leogang

Prices in €

Age	1-day	6-day
under 16	19	93
16 to 18	31	149
over 19	39	186

Free under 6
Senior no deals
Beginner points card
Notes
Covers Saalbach, Hinterglemm and Leogang, and the ski-bus; also Reiterkogel toboggan run at night; part-day passes available; supplement for swimming pool
Alternative passes
Salzburg Super Ski Card covers all lifts and pistes in Salzburgerland including Zell am See, Kaprun, Schladming and Bad Gastein

SNOW RELIABILITY
A tale of two sides
Most slopes are low (below 1900m/ 6,235ft) and the south-facing slopes are in the majority; they can suffer when the sun comes out (when we were there in early March 2007, the south-facing side just had strips of machine-made snow amid green and brown fields). The north-facing slopes keep their snow better but can get icy. The long north-facing run down to Leogang often has the best snow in the area. Piste maintenance is good and snowmaking now covers 90% of the area, including many top-to-bottom runs; but the low altitude is a problem that won't go away.

FOR EXPERTS
Little steep stuff
There are a few challenging slopes on the north-facing side. The long (4km/2.5 mile) Nordabfahrt run beneath the Schattberg Ost gondola is a genuine black – a fine fast bash first thing in the morning if it has been groomed and not icy. The Zwölferkogel Nordabfahrt at Hinterglemm is less consistent, but its classification is justified by a few short, steeper pitches. The World Cup downhill run from Zwölferkogel is interesting, as is the 5km/3 mile Schattberg West– Hinterglemm red (and its scenic 'ski route' variant). Off-piste guides are available, but snow conditions and forest tend to limit the potential. Given decent snow, however, you can have a good time (a lucky 2007 reporter 'had two days of powder and saw no more than 20 other skiers off-piste – excellent').

FOR INTERMEDIATES
Paradise for most
The sunny side of the area is ideal for both the mileage-hungry piste-basher and the more leisurely cruiser, although more than one early-intermediate reporter has judged the majority of the blues quite testing. For those looking for more of a challenge, the long red runs to the valley ranged along the north side are good fun. The otherwise delightful blue run from Bernkogel to Saalbach gets really crowded at times.

The north-facing area has some more challenging runs, with excellent relentless reds from both Schattberg West and Zwölferkogel, and a section of relatively high, open slopes around Zwölferkogel – good for mixed-ability groups wishing to ski together, a happy reporter points out. None of the black runs is beyond an adventurous intermediate. The long, pretty run to Vorderglemm gets you right away from lifts – but it gets a bit steep and tricky towards the end, and probably should be red not blue.

Our favourite intermediate run is the long, off-the-main-circuit cruise (on relatively good snow) to Leogang.

FOR BEGINNERS
Head for Hinterglemm
Saalbach's two sunny nursery slopes are right next to the village centre. But the upper one gets a lot of through-traffic. Alternatives are trips to the short, easy runs at Bernkogel and Schattberg.

Hinterglemm's spacious nursery area is separate from the main slopes and preferred by reporters. It faces

Several hotels have nurseries

Ski schools
Some take children in mini-clubs from about age 3 and can provide lunchtime care; from about age 4, children can join ski school (€205 for 6 days, including lunch – Fürstauer prices)

north, so lacks sun in midwinter but is more reliable for snow later on.

There are lots of easy blue runs to move on to, especially on the south-facing side of the valley, but it pays to take advice on which are easiest.

FOR CROSS-COUNTRY
Go to Zell am See
Some 10km/6 miles of trails run beside the road along the valley floor from Saalbach to Vorderglemm, between Hinterglemm and the valley end at Lindlingalm, and there is a high trail on the Reiterkogel. In mid-winter the valley trails get very little sun, and are not very exciting. The area beyond nearby Zell am See offers more scope.

QUEUES
A problem in high season
In high season, the lifts from Saalbach up the south-facing slopes can have waits of up to 15 minutes at peak times, at the end as well as the start of the day. A mid-February visitor found 30-minute queues for the Schönleiten gondola up from Vorderglemm. High-season queues can also arise for the chair to Hasenauer Köpfl. Recent March visitors have found few queues, but one reader did complain about the slow and unreliable Bernkogel chairlift out of Saalbach – 'the poor link in an otherwise impressive system'. One reader found crowded lower slopes.

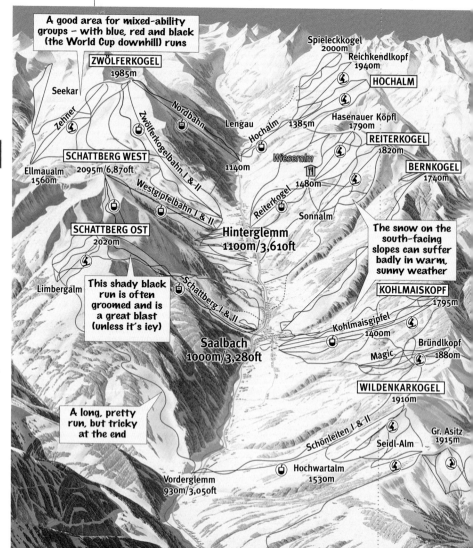

A good area for mixed-ability groups – with blue, red and black (the World Cup downhill) runs

ZWÖLFERKOGEL 1985m

Seekar

Zehner

Nordbahn

Zwölferkogelbahn I & II

Lengau

Hochalm 1385m

Spieleckkogel 2000m

Reichkendlkopf 1940m

HOCHALM

Hasenauer Köpfl 1790m

REITERKOGEL 1820m

SCHATTBERG WEST 2095m/6,87oft

Ellmaualm 1560m

Westgipfelbahn I & II

1140m

Wieseralm

1480m

BERNKOGEL 1740m

SCHATTBERG OST 2020m

Reiterkogel

Sonnalm

Hinterglemm 1100m/3,610ft

The snow on the south-facing slopes can suffer badly in warm, sunny weather

Limbergalm

This shady black run is often groomed and is a great blast (unless it's icy)

Schattberg I & II

KOHLMAISKOPF 1795m

Kohlmaisgipfel 1400m

Saalbach 1000m/3,28oft

Magic

Bründlkopf 1880m

WILDENKARKOGEL 1910m

A long, pretty run, but tricky at the end

Schönleiten I & II

Seidl-Alm

Gr. Asitz 1915m

Vorderglemm 930m/3,05oft

Hochwartalm 1530m

SCHOOLS

Saalbach

Fürstauer
t 8444

Snow Academy
t 668256

Hinterholzer
t 7607

Zink
t 0664 162 3655

Snowboard
t 20047

easySki
t 0699 111 80010

Hinterglemm

Hinterglemmer
t 634640

Activ
t 0676 517 1325

Classes
(Fürstauer prices)
5 days (4hr) from
€145

Private lessons
From €135 for 3hr,
for 1 or 2 people;
extra person €15

MOUNTAIN RESTAURANTS
Excellent quality and quantity

The area is liberally scattered with around 40 attractive huts, most serving good food. Many have warm, rustic interiors and a lively ambience.

Editors' choice The Wieseralm (6939), at the heart of the Hinterglemm south-facing slopes, is a welcoming woody chalet doing table service of satisfying dishes; fine views from the terrace.

Worth knowing about On the south-facing slopes, the Panoramaalm on Kohlmaiskopf serves particularly good food as does the Walleggalm on Hochalm – 'brilliant atmosphere', says a 2008 visitor. The 'cosy' Thurneralm close to Bründlkopf serves 'delicious BBQ ribs and glüwein' and is good for a beer on the terrace. At the base of the Bernkogel chair, the Bäckstättstall has 'warm and wonderful hospitality'. The Bärnalm near the top of the Bernkogel chair does 'good food, good value'; the Westernstadl lower down has a 'cowboy-themed interior'. The Grabenhütte, tucked away from the main piste, has been praised and the rustic Alte Schmiede at the top of the Leogang gondola is 'still one of the very best with great pizza'. Across in the Hinterglemm direction, the Rosswaldhütte has 'excellent rösti'.

On the north-facing slopes, the Simalalm at the base of the Limbergalm quad chair is 'great for the sun and the views', the Bergstadl – halfway down the red run from Schattberg West – has stunning views, good food and is 'very good value'.

Ellmaualm, at the bottom of the Zehner lift has been praised and the Breitfussalm, down from Zwölferkogel, 'stood out' for a 2007 visitor.

SCHOOLS AND GUIDES
Plenty of choice

With eight schools there's plenty of choice. We've had good reports on the Snow Academy recently – in 2007 a beginner had a week of group morning and afternoon lessons which 'brought him on a treat'. A boarder had 'worthwhile' lessons with Hinterglemmer. One member of a 2008 reader's group enjoyed two 'excellent' days with the Fürstauer school.

FACILITIES FOR CHILDREN
Hinterglemm tries harder

Saalbach doesn't go out of its way to sell itself to families, although it does have a ski kindergarten. Hinterglemm has some good hotel-based nursery facilities – the one at the Theresia is reportedly excellent.

STAYING THERE

HOW TO GO
Cheerful doesn't mean cheap

Chalets We are aware of a few 'club hotels', but Saalbach isn't really a chalet resort.

Hotels There are a large number of hotels in both villages, mainly 3-star and above. Be aware that some central hotels are affected by disco noise and front rooms by all-night street noise.

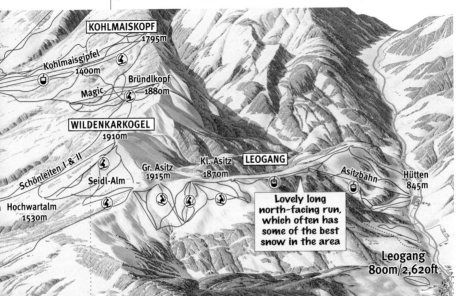

KOHLMAISKOPF
1795m

Kohlmaisgipfel
1400m

Magic

Bründlkopf
1880m

WILDENKARKOGEL
1910m

Schönleiten I & II

Gr. Asitz
1915m

Seidl-Alm

Kl. Asitz
1870m

LEOGANG

Asitzbahn

Hütten
845m

Hochwartalm
1530m

Lovely long
north-facing run,
which often has
some of the best
snow in the area

Leogang
800m/2,620ft

↑ The excellent blue run from Bernkogel brings you right to the heart of the village; but like many blues here, it is steep enough to dismay some novices

GETTING THERE

Air Salzburg 90km/ 56 miles (2hr); Munich 218km/135 miles (3½hr)

Rail Zell am See 19km/12 miles (40min); hourly buses

SAALBACH
****Alpenhotel** (6666) Luxurious, with open-fire lounge, disco, small pool. Various bars, restaurants, Arena club.
****Berger's Sporthotel** (6577) Lively, with a daily tea dance, disco and lap-dancing club. Small pool.
****Gartenhotel Eva** (7144) 'Small, good quality with sophisticated, simple, low calorie food,' said a reporter.
****Kendler** (62250) Position second to none, right next to the Bernkogel chair. Classy, expensive, good food.
****Kristiana** (6253) Near enough to lifts but away from night-time noise. 'Excellent food.' Sauna, steam bath.
****Panther** (6227) 'Excellent, practically ski-in/ski-out, good food.'
****Saalbacher Hof** (71110) Retains a friendly feel despite its large size; 'excellent wellness centre'; 'well above average food'.

****Haider** (6228) Best-positioned of the 3-stars, right next to the main lifts.
****Peter** (6236) 'Excellent value for main street location. Food OK.'
HINTERGLEMM
*****Egger** (63220) 'I'll stay here next time, on the slopes,' says a reader.
*****Theresia** (74140) Hinterglemm's top hotel, and one of the best for families. Out towards Saalbach, but nursery slopes nearby. Pool. 'Superb food and friendly staff.' 'Their spa worked wonders for tired muscles.'
*****Wolf** (63460) Small but well-equipped 4-star in excellent position. 'Superb food and gala dinners.' Pool and 'excellent spa facilities'.
****Sonnblick** (6408) Convenient 3-star in a quiet location. 'Friendly service', 'excellent buffet breakfast and tasty choice at dinner', says a visitor.
Haus Ameshofer (8119) 'Great value ski-in/ski-out B&B.' At Reiterkogel lift.
Apartments There's a big choice for independent travellers.

EATING OUT
Wide choice of hotel restaurants
This is essentially a half-board resort, with strikingly few restaurants other than those in hotels. A very welcome newcomer in Saalbach is the Kohlmais Stub'n at the foot of the Kohlmaiskopf slopes – excellent steaks, good friendly service, warm woody ambience. The hotel Peter's restaurant, at the top of Saalbach's main street, is atmospheric and serves excellent meat dishes cooked on hot stones. The Alpenhotel's Trattoria is a good place for a casual meal. The Auwirt hotel on the outskirts of Saalbach has a good à la carte restaurant. Berger Hochalm part way up the toboggan track has great views and serves 'the best pasta ever and excellent pizzas'.

APRES-SKI
It rocks from early on
Après-ski is very lively from mid-afternoon until the early hours, and can get positively wild. Most places are packed by 4pm. On the hill, just above Saalbach, the rustic Hinterhagalm has live bands and rock music; when it closes around 6pm, the crowds slide down to the already packed Bauer's Schi-alm – an old cow shed and 'one of the liveliest and most atmospheric après-ski bars in Austria'. The Bäckstättstall is recommended for tea dancing and is 'the place to start', according to one

Airtours, Alpine
Answers, BoardnLodge,
Chalet Group, Crystal,
Crystal Finest,
Directski.com, Equity,
Erna Low, First Choice,
Inghams, Interactive
Resorts, Interhome,
Neilson, Rocketski, Ski
Expectations, Ski
Independence, Ski
McNeill, Ski Miquel, Ski
Wild, Skitracer,
Snowscape, Thomson
Leogang Inntravel

Indoor Swimming
pools, sauna,
massage, solarium,
tennis

Outdoor Ice rink,
curling, tobogganing,
sleigh rides,
snowshoeing,
snowmobiling, quad
bikes, ice karts,
40km/25 miles of
cleared paths,
archery, paragliding

Phone numbers
From elsewhere in
Austria add the prefix
06541 (Saalbach),
06583 (Leogang);
from abroad use the
prefix +43 and omit
the initial '0'

Saalbach
t 680068
contact@saalbach.com
www.saalbach.com

Leogang
t 8234
info@saalfelden-
leogang.at
www.leogang-
saalfelden.at

2007 visitor. The Berger's Sporthotel main bar also has dancing when the lifts close; its separate Prosecco bar is reportedly the quieter, relaxed alternative. The tiny Zum Turm (next door to the church) is a medieval jail that also offers 'unusual bar games'. The Neuhaus Taverne has live music and attracts a mature clientele. Alibi's plays 'great tunes'. Jack-in has wi-fi and big screen TVs so attracts the sports fans. Bobby's Pub is cheap, often full of British school kids, has bowling and serves Guinness. King's, Arena and Castello's are clubs that liven up later on and have lap dancing adjuncts. For a civilised drink, a reader recommends the bar of the central Alpenhotel.

In Hinterglemm there are a number of ice bars, popular at close of play, including the central Gute Stube of hotel Dorfschmiede, with loud music blasting out and people spilling into the street. A wider age group enjoys the live music later on at the smart, friendly Tanzhimmel – an open, glass-fronted bar with a dance floor. The Hexenhäusl gets packed. Several readers have enjoyed the lively and rustic goat-themed Goasstall. Bla Bla is small and smart, with reasonable prices. The Almbar has good music and some dancing.

Tour operator reps organise tobogganing, sleigh rides and bowling.

OFF THE SLOPES
Surprisingly little to do
Saalbach is not very entertaining if you're not into winter sports. There are few shops other than supermarkets and ski shops. There are some cleared paths and a walkers' lift pass (60 euros) gives access to two lifts per day – which also meant a 2007 reporter's mixed group of skiers and non-skiers could easily meet for lunch. Hinterglemm's toboggan run is said to be great fun and great value. There are excursions to Salzburg.

STAYING UP THE MOUNTAIN
It's quiet
It is possible to stay up the mountain in several hotels and gasthofs – a good way of avoiding village noise and rowdiness. A 2007 reporter recommends the 3-star Sonnhof (6295) near the top of the Hochalmbahn: 'Large rooms, good value and instant access to the slopes for first tracks daily.'

Leogang 800m/2,620ft

A much less expensive alternative to Saalbach-Hinterglemm.

THE RESORT
Leogang is quiet, attractive and rather scattered. It's best to stay in the hamlet of Hütten, near the gondola into the main ski area.

THE MOUNTAIN
The village is linked to the eastern end of the main ski circuit.
Slopes A gondola from Hütten takes you into the ski area. The local slopes tend to be delightfully quiet.
Snow reliability The local slopes have some of the best snow in the region, being north- and east-facing, with snowmaking on the run home.
Experts Not much challenge locally.
Intermediates Great long blue/red run cruise home from the top of the gondola. Plus the circuit to explore.
Beginners Good nursery slopes by the village, and short runs to progress to.
Snowboarding The whole area is great for boarding and there's a terrain park.
Cross-country The best in the area. There are 20km/12 miles of trails, plus a panoramic high-altitude trail.
Queues No local problems.
Mountain restaurants A couple of good local huts. One visitor recommends the Forsthofalm – 'the nicest I have ever been in'.
Schools and guides Leogang Altenberger school has a good reputation: 'Excellent service and lessons; highly recommended.'
Facilities for children There is a non-ski nursery, and children can start school at four years old.

STAYING THERE
Hotels The luxury Krallerhof (8246) has its own nursery lift, which can be used to get across to the main lift station. The 4-star Salzburger Hof (7310) is well placed, a two-minute walk from the gondola; sauna and steam.
Apartments There are quiet apartments available.
Eating out Restaurants are hotel-based. The upscale Krallerhof has excellent food and the much cheaper Gasthof Hüttwirt has a high reputation.
Après-ski The rustic old chalet Kraller Alm is very much the focal tea-time and evening rendezvous.
Off the slopes Excursions to Salzburg are possible.

Saalbach-Hinterglemm

197

Interactive resort shortlist builder at www.wtss.co.uk

Schladming

Old valley town with pleasant main square and extensive intermediate slopes on four linked mountains

COSTS

① ② ③ ④ ⑤ ⑥

RATINGS

The slopes
Fast lifts	****
Snow	****
Extent	***
Expert	**
Intermediate	****
Beginner	***
Convenience	***
Queues	****
Mountain restaurants	****

The rest
Scenery	***
Resort charm	***
Off-slope	****

➕ Extensive intermediate slopes in four main sectors

➕ Very sheltered slopes, among trees

➕ Lots of good mountain restaurants

➕ Appealing town with friendly people

➕ Extensive snowmaking, good grooming and shady slopes mean good piste conditions, but ...

➖ The mainly north-facing runs can be cold in early season

➖ Slopes lack variety

➖ Very little to entertain experts

➖ Nursery slopes are inconvenient if you stay in the village centre

➖ Runs to valley level are not easy

➖ Limited but improving nightlife

With its four distinct mountains all linked by lifts (and to varying degrees by pistes), Schladming offers the keen intermediate a real sense of travelling around on the snow. But you may find one slope rather like another.

The resort does not offer one of Austria's wildest après-ski scenes, but most of our reporters don't mind that – they find its solid, valley-town ambience a pleasant change from the Austrian norm.

NEWS

For 2008/09 the link at Planai West between Planai and Hochwurzen will be further improved by a chondola up to the middle of the Hochwurzen slopes. (Two years ago, the chairlifts on the Planai side were replaced by a gondola.) New pistes are being formed.

For 2007/08 the Hohenhaus Tenne entertainment and après-ski centre opened at the Planai base station. Snowmaking was increased.

KEY FACTS

Resort	745m
	2,440ft

Schladming Ramsau/ Dachstein area	
Slopes	745-2015m
	2,440-6,610ft
Lifts	91
Pistes	175km
	109 miles
Blue	29%
Red	61%
Black	10%
Snowmaking	99%

THE RESORT

The old town of Schladming has a long skiing tradition and has hosted World Cup races for many years.

The town has a pleasant, traffic-free main square, prettily lit at night, around which you'll find most of the shops, restaurants and bars (and some appealing hotels). The busy main road bypasses the town. Much of the accommodation is close to the centre; the sports centre and tennis halls are five minutes' walk away.

Schladming sits at the foot of Planai, one of the resort's four linked mountains. A gondola a few minutes' walk from the centre goes most of the way up this hill. From the western suburbs of Schladming, chairlifts and a new chondola for 2008/09 serve the next peak to the west, Hochwurzen. The chairlifts access Rohrmoos, a quiet, scattered village set on an elevated slope that forms a giant nursery area – an excellent base for beginners. From Hochwurzen you can progress to Reiteralm.

To the east of Schladming is the small, attractively rustic village of Haus, where a cable car and gondola go up to the highest of the four linked mountains, Hauser Kaibling.

There are timetabled buses linking the villages and lift bases, but they are not as frequent as reporters wish. A night bus runs until 1am (4 euros).

There are several other separate mountains nearby and covered by the local lift pass – Fageralm, Galsterbergalm, Ramsau, the Dachstein glacier and Stoderzinken. The Ski Alliance Amadé lift pass also covers many other resorts. A car is useful for getting the most out of it: trips are feasible to Bad Gastein, Wagrain/ Flachau, Kleinarl and Hochkönig. The station is served by direct trains from Salzburg, so Schladming makes an excellent short break destination.

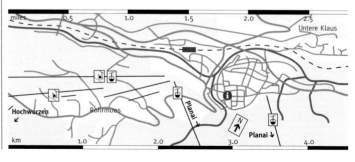

LIFT PASSES

Ski Alliance Amadé
Ski Pass

Prices in €

Age	1-day	6-day
under 17	20	95
17 to 19	33	153
over 20	39	182

Free under 6
Senior no deals
Beginner no deals

Notes
Day-pass price is for Schladming Ramsau Dachstein only; part-day tickets available; 2-day-plus passes cover the 865km/ 538 miles of pistes and 270 lifts in five regions: Dachstein Tauern; Gastein; Salzburger Sportwelt; Grossarl; Hochkönig Winterreich

Alternative pass
Salzburg Super Ski Card: all lifts in Salzburgerland including Zell am See, Kaprun and Saalbach-Hinterglemm

THE MOUNTAINS

Most pistes are on the wooded north-facing slopes above the main valley, with some going into the side valleys higher up; there are a few open slopes above the trees.

Piste maps (you can get separate ones for each mountain) are generally clear and easy to use. At the Skiline terminals at the Planai base you can get a printout showing lifts you used, height gained and distance covered in the day – a neat free souvenir.

THE SLOPES
Four linked sectors – and more
Each of the sectors is quite a serious mountain, with a variety of lifts and runs to play on. **Planai** and **Hauser Kaibling** are linked at altitude via the high, wooded bowl between them. But the links to **Hochwurzen** and **Reiteralm** are at valley level (and the first involves riding a gondola both ways). The new lifts between Planai and Hochwurzen should make access to Reiteralm less time-consuming.

Several lower runs go across roads that aren't well signposted – care is needed, particularly with children. There are handy ski lockers to rent at the Planai base station.

TERRAIN PARKS
Head for Hochwurzen
The Playground terrain park on Hochwurzen, by the Gipfelbahn, has rails, boxes, straight and pro jumps – floodlit until 10pm. Reiteralm has a half-pipe, and there's another park on the Dachstein glacier.

SNOW RELIABILITY
Excellent in cold weather
The northerly orientation of the slopes and good maintenance help keep the pistes in better shape than in some neighbouring resorts. The serious snowmaking operation makes it a particularly good choice for early holidays; coverage is comprehensive, and the system is put to good use. More snowmaking was added last season. Reporters regularly complain of poor conditions on the lower slopes, notably on the steep bottom part of the World Cup downhill run back to town. Piste grooming has been excellent on our recent visits.

FOR EXPERTS
Strictly intermediate stuff
Schladming's status as a World Cup downhill venue doesn't make it macho. The steep black finish to the Men's Downhill course and the moderate mogul runs at the top of Planai and Hauser Kaibling are the only really challenging slopes. Hauser Kaibling's off-piste is good, but limited. The area around run 5 on Reiteralm has been recommended.

FOR INTERMEDIATES
Red runs rule
The area is ideal for intermediate cruising. The majority of runs are red but it's often difficult to distinguish them from some of the blues. One notable exception is the final very red section of the run below Rohrmoos, which makes it awkward for near-beginners to get to the Planai link.

The open sections at the top of

Schladming

199

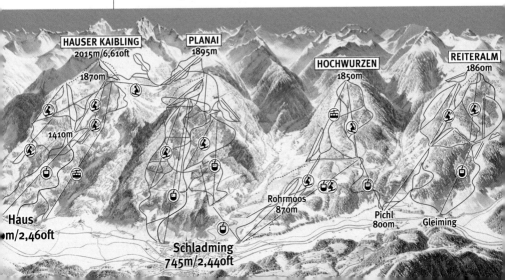

HAUSER KAIBLING 2015m/6,610ft 1870m 1410m

PLANAI 1895m

HOCHWURZEN 1850m

REITERALM 1860m

Rohrmoos 870m

Pichl 800m Gleiming

Haus ●m/2,460ft

Schladming 745m/2,440ft

SCHOOLS

Tritscher
t 2264711

Hopl (Hochwurzen-Planai)
t 23582

Blue Tomato (snowboard)
t 2422333

Classes
(Tritscher prices)
5 days €154

Private lessons
Half day €96; each additional person €20

CHILDREN

Mini club
t 22647
For ages 3 and 4

Nannies
Details at tourist office

Ski school
From age 4 (€204 for 5 days including lunch – Tritscher price)

Planai and Hauser Kaibling have some more challenging slopes. And the two World Cup pistes, and the red that runs parallel to the Haus downhill course to the village, are ideal for fast intermediates in good snow conditions but can get very icy and tricky.

Hauser Kaibling has a lovely meandering blue running from top to bottom, and Reiteralm has some gentle blues with good snow. Runs are well groomed, so intermediates will find the slopes generally flattering.

FOR BEGINNERS
Good slopes but poorly sited
The ski schools generally take beginners to the extensive but low-altitude Rohrmoos nursery area – fine if you are based there, a discouraging bus ride away if you are not. Another novice area near the top of Planai is more convenient for residents of central Schladming and has better snow, but the runs are less gentle.

FOR CROSS-COUNTRY
Extensive network of trails
Given sufficient snow-cover, there are 400km/250 miles of trails in the region, and the World Championships have been held at nearby Ramsau. There are local loops along the main valley floor and between Planai and Hochwurzen.

QUEUES
Avoid peaks at Planai
Generally reporters have found few problems. The Planai gondola can have morning queues at peak-season and weekends and a New Year visitor experienced 'serious' waits for lifts on Hochwurzen. Crowded pistes are also criticised there. But the gondola into the Planai slopes from the base of Hochwurzen is an excellent development and the new chondola

---

from there should greatly relieve pressure in the other direction. The quiet, outlying Fageralm area is a recommended option on exceptionally busy days.

MOUNTAIN RESTAURANTS
A real highlight
There are plenty of attractive rustic restaurants in all sectors, and most get enthusiastic reports from readers ('too many – we couldn't decide which to try', 'fabulous').

On Planai: the 'quiet' Schladminger Hütte, at the top of the gondola is recommended ('good pasta', 'friendly and efficient service'). Onkel Willy's Hütte does 'great pasta' and often has live music. Schafalm offers 'excellent service, incredible food' but it gets crowded. We enjoyed good home-cooked food at the pleasant Weitmoosalm – tucked away in the gentle Larchkogel area on Planai. The Holzhackerstub'n on the lower part of the World Cup run has 'high-quality freshly made food'.

On Hochwurzen the 'cosy' Hochwurzenalm is praised. On Reiteralm 'you absolutely must visit' the Gasslhöh-Hütte for the 'awesome' spare ribs. On Hauser Kaibling the tiny Kulmhoferhütte has a real mountain hut atmosphere, with fur-lined walls. Higher up, the hut off the Almlift feels wonderfully isolated, with great views and soup. The Knapplhof is full of ski-racing mementos and Harry's Lärchenpavillion is highly recommended ('fantastic soup').

SCHOOLS AND GUIDES
Generally okay reports
We have generally had good reports: 'In five visits I have never had a bad instructor or a wasted lesson,' says a 2007 visitor. 'Excellent' is the verdict on private lessons with the Hopl school and another reader had a 'nice instructor who tried his best' despite poor January conditions. But the Tritscher school has been rated 'poor' for both adults' and children's classes.

FACILITIES FOR CHILDREN
Rohrmoos is the place
The extensive gentle slopes of Rohrmoos are ideal for building up youngsters' confidence. There are Kinderlands on Planai and Hochwurzen. The Top school at Pichl has been praised for 'excellent' children's classes.

boarding

Schladming is popular with boarders. Most lifts on the spread-out mountains are gondolas or chairs, with some short drags around. The area is ideal for beginners and intermediates, except when the lower slopes are icy, though there are few exciting challenges for expert boarders bar the off-piste tree runs. The Blue Tomato snowboard shop runs the 'impressive' specialist snowboard school.

GETTING THERE

Air Salzburg 90km/ 56 miles (1½hr)

Rail Main line station in resort

UK PACKAGES

Alpine Answers, Crystal, Crystal Finest, Equity, Interhome, Rocketski, Skitracer, Snowscape

ACTIVITIES

Indoor Swimming pool, fitness club, tennis, sauna

Outdoor Ice skating, curling, tobogganing, snowshoeing, sleigh rides, 50km/ 31 miles of cleared paths

Phone numbers
From elsewhere in Austria add the prefix 03687 (Schladming), 03686 (Haus); from abroad use the prefix +43 and omit the initial '0'

TOURIST OFFICES

Schladming
t 22777
urlaub@schladming.at
www.schladming.at
www.skiamade.com

Haus
t 22340
info@haus.at
www.haus.at

STAYING THERE

HOW TO GO
Packages mean hotels
Packaged accommodation is in hotels and pensions, but there are plenty of apartments for independent travellers.
Hotels Most of the accommodation is in modestly priced pensions but there are also a few more upmarket hotels.
****Sporthotel Royer** (200) Big and comfortable, a few minutes' walk from the main Planai lift. Pool, sauna.
****Stadttor** (24525) 'Quiet, spacious and comfortable, with excellent food.' The Hogmanay gala dinner was 'a jolly event', says a 2007 visitor.
****Almdorf-Reiteralm** (72444) Ski-in/ ski-out village at Hochalm, above Pichl. Individual chalets and a hotel; restaurant, shop and spa facilities. Accessed by mountain road.
***Kirchenwirt** (22435) Just off the main square. 'Wonderful food', 'great value for money', 'very atmospheric', but a little weird'.
***Neue Post** (22105) Large rooms, friendly, good food, central.
***Zum Kaiserweg** (22038) Family run. Very near the Planai West gondola. 'Quiet location and good rooms', but 'lacks charm', says a 2008 visitor.
***Rohrmooser Schlössl** (61237) Just downhill from the Planai West gondola. 'Really friendly', with 'excellent food and views'.
Apartments Haus Girik (22663) is close to the town gondola. Schütter (23230) at Planai West is 'excellent, spacious and comfortable'.

EATING OUT
Some good places
Recommendations include the Kirchenwirt hotel ('fine home cooking'), Giovanni's (pizza), Charly's Treff, Talbachschenke ('good grills and atmosphere'), the Alte Post and Neue Post hotel ('good but expensive'). Mäk's is a new pizza and pasta place at the Hohenhaus Tenne (see 'Après-Ski'). Maria's Mexican has 'fabulous food and service'. Biochi specialises in organic and vegan food. We liked the Lasser Cafe and the Stadttor for coffee and cakes, and the Schwalbenbräu.

APRES-SKI
A lively new place to try
Some of the mountain restaurants are lively at the end of the afternoon. The Schladminger Hütte at the top of the gondola has live music at après-ski time on Wednesdays and the gondola stays open to bring you down.
But in town, the focus is the new Hohenhaus Tenne by the Planai gondola station. This smart woody building has a fabulous main bar, dance floor and regular live music – great when the lifts close. Later on there's a disco and various other bars to entertain. Charly's Treff (with umbrella bar) opposite the Planai gondola also gets busy. A 2007 reporter preferred the Tauernalm on Hochwurzen. Many of the central bars stay open until dawn, but they lack the 'buzz' of other Austrian resorts. The Neiderl and Szenario are 'small and friendly'. The Neue Post is 'lively without being raucous'. Hanglbar has 'good music and a nice, friendly atmosphere'. The Sonderbar is a disco with three bars.

OFF THE SLOPES
Good for all but walkers
Non-skiers are fairly well catered for. There's a floodlit 7km/4 mile toboggan run at Hochwurzen, 'excellent' pool and an ice rink. Some mountain restaurants are accessible to pedestrians. The town shops and museum are worth a look. Trips to Salzburg or Radstadt are easy.

Haus 750m/2,460ft

Haus is a real village with a life of its own and its own ski schools and kindergartens. The user-friendly nursery slopes are between the village and the gondola. There's a railway station, so excursions are easy, but off-slope activities and nightlife are very limited. Hotel prices are generally lower here.

FRANK HEUER

*A valley town dominated by traffic and throbbing après-ski/
nightlife – but with excellent slopes reaching glacial heights*

202

COSTS
①②③④⑤⑥

RATINGS

The slopes
Fast lifts	*****
Snow	*****
Extent	***
Expert	***
Intermediate	****
Beginner	**
Convenience	**
Queues	***
Mountain restaurants	***

The rest
Scenery	***
Resort charm	**
Off-slope	**

NEWS

For 2007/08 more snowmaking was added to cover all slopes on Giggijoch, links to Rotkogl and the lower section of the Rettenbach glacier.

➕ Excellent snow reliability, with access to two high glaciers

➕ Fairly extensive network of slopes suited to adventurous intermediates

➕ Impressive lift system

➕ Very lively après-ski/nightlife, but ...

➖ It's a bit raunchy, and can be rowdy

➖ Busy road through sprawling village

➖ Some central hotels are distant from the two main access lifts

➖ Inconvenient beginners' slopes

➖ English not universally spoken

Sölden deserves a close look from intermediates keen on Austrian après-ski – as long as you are prepared to deploy your German occasionally (British visitors are still few, although several tour ops go there). The resort has invested massively in lifts to link its extensive glaciers to the lower slopes, and there are some seriously long runs to be done.

THE RESORT

Despite its traditional Tirolean-style buildings and wooded valley setting, Sölden is no beauty: it is a large, traffic-filled place that sprawls along both sides of a busy main road and across the valley floor. The resort attracts a young, lively crowd – mostly Dutch and German – bent on partying. Ads for strip clubs are prominent.

Gondolas from opposite ends of town go up to Sölden's home slopes – the peak of Gaislachkogl and the lift

junction of Giggijoch. A free shuttle-bus serves both lift stations, which a 2008 reporter found efficient and frequent. High above the town is the satellite resort of Hochsölden – a group of 4-star hotels, and little else.

THE MOUNTAINS

Practically all the slopes you spend your days on are above the trees, though there are red runs through trees to the village. A low-cost pass for a day in nearby Obergurgl (hourly

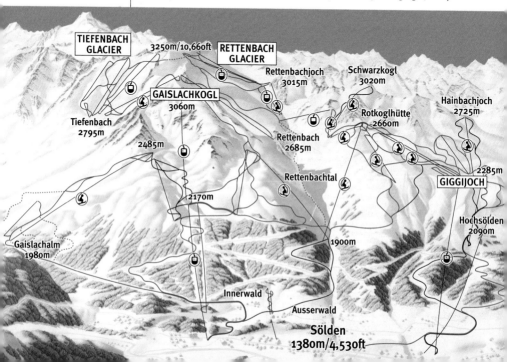

TIEFENBACH GLACIER 3250m/10,66oft RETTENBACH GLACIER

Rettenbachjoch 3015m

Schwarzkogl 3020m

GAISLACHKOGL 306om

Tiefenbach 2795m

2485m

Rettenbach 2685m

Rettenbachtal

Rotkoglhütte 266om

Hainbachjoch 2725m

2170m

2285m
GIGGIJOCH

Gaislachalm 1980m

1900m

Hochsölden 2090m

Innerwald

Ausserwald

Sölden
1380m/4,53oft

KEY FACTS

Resort	1380m
	4,530ft
Slopes	1370-3250m
	4,490-10,660ft
Lifts	34
Pistes	146km
	91 miles
Blue	35%
Red	43%
Black	22%
Snowmaking	60%

Giggijoch – even if
there's no band,
there's a party in the
afternoon ↓

buses) is available (when purchasing a full pass in the resort).

Slopes The two similar-sized home sectors are linked by chairlifts (one a six-pack) out of the Rettenbachtal that separates them. Fast lifts from the Giggijoch sector lead to the Rettenbach glacier, and on to Tiefenbach. Our repeated attempts to get to the glaciers have been thwarted by the weather; reporters repeatedly judge the link a 'long, slow trek'.

Reporters have complained of poor piste marking, notably around the Gaislachkogl.

Terrain parks There is a park above Giggijoch, with half-pipe, beginner and pro kickers, waves, rails, boxes and a chill-out zone. There are two separate race courses – one timed.

Snow reliability The slopes are high and mainly north-east- or south-east-facing; and there are two extensive glaciers. Snowmaking now covers 60% of the area, including all slopes on Giggijoch. Grooming is generally good.

Experts None of the black pistes dotted around Sölden's map is serious, and some are silly; but you won't lack vertical – Hainbachjoch to the valley is 1400m/4,590ft. There are quite a few

non-trivial reds. And there are extensive off-piste possibilities with a guide. At the top of the valley is one of the Alps' premier touring areas.

Intermediates Most of Sölden's main slopes are genuine red runs ideal for keen intermediates, and there are serious verticals to be done – almost 1700m/5,580ft from Gaislachkogl to the village. There are several easy blacks. The long, quiet red to Gaislachalm is relatively easy, and ideal for high-speed cruising. Giggijoch offers gentler gradients, but the blues here get extremely crowded. Less confident intermediates should beware the tricky red runs to town from Giggijoch and from Rettenbachtal – restored to red classification after a year as a black.

Beginners The beginners' slopes are situated inconveniently, just above the village at Innerwald. They are prone to poor snow and not ideal as the busier home runs converge there. Near-beginners can use the blues at Giggijoch. Stay away from Hochsölden.

Snowboarding Sölden is not ideal for beginners but there's great freeriding for experienced boarders. And all draglifts can be avoided.

↑ The town sprawls along and across the valley

TVB SÖLDEN-ÖTZTAL ARENA / ALBIN NIEDERSTRASSER

UK PACKAGES

Crystal, Crystal Finest, Independent Ski Links, Interhome, Kuoni, Neilson, Ski Wild, Snow Finders

Phone numbers
From elsewhere in Austria add the prefix 05254; from abroad use the prefix +43 5254

TOURIST OFFICE

t (0)57 200
info@soelden.com
www.soelden.com

Cross-country There are a couple of uninspiring loops by the river, plus small areas at Zwieselstein and Vent.

Queues Expect big queues at the Einzeiger and Seekogl chairs on the way to and from the glacier – taking the Rettenbachtal ski route home allows you to avoid Seekogl. A 2008 visitor experienced morning queues for the six-pack up from the Rettenbachtal. Another reader suggests taking the single Hochsölden chair ('no one seemed to use it') to avoid '20-minute' queues for the Giggijoch gondola.

Mountain restaurants The self-service places around Giggijoch can get very crowded. To escape the crowds try the Hühnersteign at Gaislachalm ('excellent chicken'), or the big, modern Schwarzkogl on run 24. Gampealm, towards the end of piste 11, is a fine panoramic spot. Eugens Obstlerhütte below Hochsölden is a favourite – 'cosy, efficient; good food'.

Schools and guides The four schools all restrict class sizes. The Sölden school has 'patient' instructors, though spoken English can be limited.

Facilities for children The Sölden school is praised. There are kindergartens at both schools. Yellow Power takes children from three years. There are special family lift pass deals.

STAYING THERE

How to go There are few UK packages.
Hotels The warmly welcoming Central (22600) is not only central but also the biggest and best in town – the

only 5-star; beautiful pool. We were very happy in the Stefan (2237), right next to the Giggijoch gondola; good food. Reporters recommend Gasthof Grauer Bär (2564) – 'large rooms, excellent food', the Bergland (2240) and the Grüner-Hof B&B (2477) above town on run 7. The 'lavishly beautiful' Valentin (2267) at Gaislachkogl is also mentioned.

Eating out We usually end up in the Tavola in the hotel Rosengarten, because it doesn't take reservations, and haven't been disappointed. Recommendations from readers: Dominic, Cafe Hubertus, Nudeltopf and Corso for pizza; and s'Pfandl, above the town at Ausserwald, for traditional Tirolean food.

Après-ski Sölden's après-ski is justly famous. It starts up the mountain, notably at Giggijoch, and progresses (possibly via the 'crowded' Philipp's Eisbar at Innerwald) to packed bars in and around the main street, and later to countless places with live bands and throbbing discos, often with table dancing and/or striptease. Readers also mention: Snow Rock Cafe ('best atmosphere'), Otzi's, BlaBla, Fire and Ice and Alibi's ('smartest bar, good live music'). Try Grizzley's for a quieter time. The Rodelhütte has 'go-go' girls. There are nightly toboggan evenings – starting at Gaislachalm.

Off the slopes There's a sports centre, a swimming pool and an ice rink. Ice climbing and sleigh rides can be arranged. Trips to Innsbruck are possible. Aqua Dome is a thermal spa centre at Längenfeld.

Söll

The ski area is big, but the attractive village is surprisingly small and intimate; shame it is not set right by the lifts

COSTS

① ② ③ ④ ⑤ ⑥

RATINGS

The slopes

Fast lifts	**
Snow	**
Extent	****
Expert	*
Intermediate	****
Beginner	***
Convenience	**
Queues	***
Mountain restaurants	**

The rest

Scenery	***
Resort charm	***
Off-slope	**

NEWS

For 2008/09 a six-pack is planned to replace the Silleralm triple chair above Hochsöll, improving the return to Zinsberg.

Access to the slopes of Westendorf will no longer involve buses, thanks to a new gondola at Brixen.

For 2007/08 three more pistes (3km/ 2 miles) were floodlit for night skiing at Hochsöll, and snowmaking was added to the toboggan run.

➕ Part of the SkiWelt, Austria's largest linked ski and snowboard area

➕ Local slopes are north-facing, so they keep their snow relatively well

➕ Plenty of cheap and cheerful pensions for those on a budget

➕ Pretty village with lively après-ski

➕ Snowmaking is now more extensive and well used; even so ...

➖ Low altitude can mean poor snow

➖ Long walk or inadequate bus service from the village to the lifts

➖ Little to amuse experts or to challenge good intermediates

➖ Not ideal for beginners, either

➖ The SkiWelt slopes can get crowded at weekends and in high season – especially above Söll

➖ Mostly short runs in the local sector

Söll has long been popular with British beginners and intermediates, attracting both singles looking for a fun week and families looking for a quiet time.

The resort is in fact far from ideal for beginners but, when the snow is good, Söll can be a great place for intermediates – cruising the attractive, friendly pistes of Austria's largest linked area. You get the use of Austria's largest snowmaking operation too, so the lack of altitude is less of a problem than it once was – but of course snowmaking is not a complete solution.

Many visitors are surprised by the small size of the village and the long trek out to the slopes. We'd prefer to stay near the lifts, and trek into the village in the evening. Bear in mind, also, that at this end of the SkiWelt, around the area high point of Hohe Salve, there are alternative bases that might suit you better – Itter, Hopfgarten and Brixen, dealt with at the end of this chapter.

205

THE RESORT

Söll is a pleasant, friendly village, bypassed by the main valley road; although its chalets spread quite widely, the core is compact – you can explore it thoroughly in a few minutes. New buildings are traditional in design and there's a huge church near the centre, its graveyard lit by candles. There aren't many shops.

The slopes are well outside the village, on the other side of a busy road crossed by a pedestrian tunnel. You can leave your equipment at the bottom of the gondola for a small charge. There is some accommodation out near the lifts, but most is in or around the village centre. A location on the edge nearest the lifts means you might be able to walk to the slopes. From the centre, it's a 15-minute walk or a crowded ski-bus, heavily criticised by reporters ('totally inadequate', '40 minutes queuing' were recent comments). A base on the far side of the village may mean that you can board the bus before it gets too crowded. But the bus does not serve every corner of the community.

KEY FACTS

Resort	700m
	2,300ft

Entire SkiWelt	
Slopes	620-1890m
	2,030-6,200ft
Lifts	94
Pistes	250km
	155 miles
Blue	43%
Red	48%
Black	9%
Snowmaking	180km
	112 miles

THE MOUNTAINS

The SkiWelt is the largest piste network in Austria, linking eight resorts. It will easily keep an early or average intermediate amused for a week. The piste map is hopelessly over-ambitious in trying to show the whole area in a single view; it has been improved recently, but is still generally poor, difficult to use in parts and generates lots of criticism from reporters. Signposting is also 'appalling'. Most runs are easy, and short – which means that getting around the area can take time, despite increasing numbers of fast lifts.

The SkiWelt pass also covers Westendorf, linked by a new gondola from Brixen for 2008/09; from there you can also progress to the Kitzbühel slopes – see the Westendorf chapter. These, along with Waidring,

Fieberbrunn and St Johann, are possible day trips covered by the Kitzbüheler Alpen Skipass.

THE SLOPES
Short run network

A gondola takes all but complete beginners up to the mid-mountain shelf of Hochsöll, where there are a couple of short lifts and connections in several directions.

These include an eight-seat gondola to the high point of Hohe Salve. From here there are stunning views and runs down to Kälbersalve, Rigi and Hopfgarten. Rigi can also be reached by chairs and runs without going to Hohe Salve – to which it is itself linked by chairs. Rigi is also the start of runs down to Itter. From Kälbersalve you can head down south-facing runs to Brixen or up to Zinsberg and Eiberg and towards Ellmau.

boarding

Söll is a good place to try out boarding: slopes are gentle and there are plenty of gondolas and chairs. For competent boarders it's more limited – the slopes of the SkiWelt are tame. A reporter recommends the Scheffau school.

TERRAIN PARKS
You have to travel

There are no parks directly above Söll, but there's a park at Ellmau and a long-standing and popular park at Westendorf. Obviously, getting to them is a non-trivial affair.

SNOW RELIABILITY
Erratic – but has artificial help

Leaving aside generally poor seasons, the SkiWelt has had some good seasons of late, with several reporters experiencing good fresh powder for much of their holidays. But it is not always like that, and with a low

average height, and important links that get a lot of sun, the snow can suffer badly in warm weather and from precipitation falling as rain. So the snowmaking that the SkiWelt has installed is essential. At 180km/112 miles and covering over 70% of the area's pistes, it is Austria's biggest snowmaking installation. Reporters are regularly impressed by its use and efforts to maintain the pistes in times of drought. We were there one January before any major snowfalls, and snowmaking was keeping the links open well. It did not, however, stop slush and ice forming.

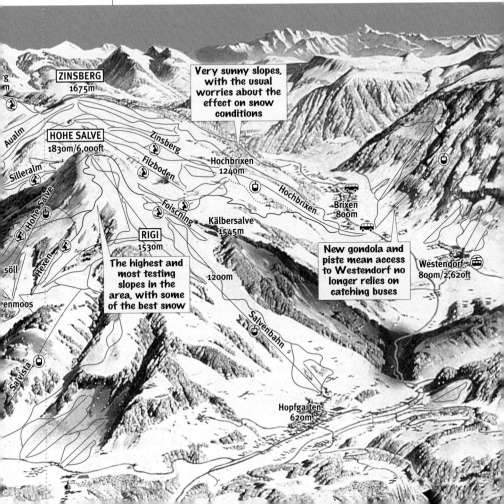

LIFT PASSES

SkiWelt Wilder Kaiser-Brixental

Prices in €

Age	1-day	6-day
under 16	18	87
16 to 17	29	139
over 18	36	173

Free under 7

Senior no deals

Beginner points cards

Notes
Covers Wilder Kaiser-Brixental area from Going to Westendorf, and the ski-bus; single ascent and part-day options

Alternative passes
Kitzbüheler Alpen Skipass covers five large ski areas: Schneewinkel (St Johann), Kitzbühel, SkiWelt, Wildschönau and Alpbachtal

The village of Söll with Brandstadl in the background; the nursery slopes are on the extreme right ↓

FOR EXPERTS
Not a lot
The two black runs from Hohe Salve towards Hochsöll and Kälbersalve and the black run alongside the Brixen gondola are the only challenging pistes. There are further blacks in Scheffau and Ellmau, but the main challenges are off-piste – from Brandstadl down to Söll, for example.

FOR INTERMEDIATES
Mainly easy runs
When blessed with good snow – not something to bank on – the SkiWelt is a paradise for early intermediates and those who love easy cruising. It is a big area and you really get a feeling of travelling around. There are lots of blue runs and many of the reds could be blue. In general the most difficult slopes are those from the mid-stations to the valleys – to Blaiken, Brixen and Söll, for example.

FOR BEGINNERS
Not ideal
The big area of nursery slopes between the main road and the gondola station is fine when snow is good – gentle, spacious, uncrowded and free from good skiers whizzing past. But it can get icy or slushy. In poor snow the Hochsöll area may be used. Progression to longer runs is likely to be awkward – there aren't many blue runs in this part of the SkiWelt. One is the narrow blue from Hochsöll, on which fast learners can get home when the run is not too icy.

FOR CROSS-COUNTRY
Neighbouring villages are better
Söll has 30km/19 miles of local trails but they are less interesting than the 15km/9 miles between Hopfgarten and Kelchsau or the ones around and beyond Ellmau. There is a total of 170km/106 miles in the SkiWelt area. Lack of snow-cover can be a problem.

QUEUES
Some high-season waits
Lift upgrades have greatly improved this once queue-prone area. But the nursery drag up to the gondola at Söll remains a serious obstacle, particularly at ski-school time in the mornings, and there are several bottlenecks at slow chairs around the mountain (including in the Rigi area). The new Silleralm chair for 2008/09 should improve the return to Ellmau and Brixen from Söll. When snow is poor, the links between Zinsberg and Eiberg get crowded.

MOUNTAIN RESTAURANTS
Good, but crowded
There are quite a few jolly little chalets scattered about, but we have had a few complaints of insufficient seating and long queues. There are three places at Hochsöll; the one called Hochsöll itself is reportedly 'excellent', but the atmospheric converted cow shed Stöckalm gets readers' vote: 'highly recommended' for 'superb spit-roasted chicken' – as elsewhere, you have to eat early or late to avoid the queues. The highly rated Hohe Salve (top of the gondola) offers a large revolving terrace and 'stunning views' – accessible to non-skiers via a moving carpet. The Stoagrub'nhütte above Hopfgarten serves 'generous and reasonably priced spaghetti'. Above Brixen the Filzalm isn't shown on the map, but is a good place for a quick drink on the way back from the circuit. Check out our Ellmau chapter for more recommendations in that sector of the SkiWelt.

SCHOOLS AND GUIDES
A good reputation
The Söll-Hochsöll school has a fairly good reputation. A 2007 reporter and her family enjoyed 'very good' lessons; the children 'were confidently doing red runs by the end of the week', but groups were large ('up to 12'). Another visitor 'improved immensely due to excellent instruction'.

The distinctive peak of Hohe Salve, seen from Kitzbühel's Hahnenkamm ➔

SNOWPIX.COM / CHRIS GILL

CHILDREN

Mini-club
t 0664 4412 2773
9am–4.30; ages
6mnth to 4yr

Monti's Kinder-welt (bambinis)
t 5454
10am–4pm; for ages 3 to 5

Ski school
Takes children from 5 to 14 for 4hr daily (5 days €138)

GETTING THERE

Air Salzburg 94km/58 miles (2hr); Innsbruck 73km/45 miles (1½hr)

Rail Wörgl (13km/8 miles) or Kufstein (15km/9 miles); bus to resort

SCHOOLS

Söll-Hochsöll
t 5454

Classes
5 4-hr days: €138
Private lessons
€55 for 1hr; each additional person €20

FACILITIES FOR CHILDREN
Fast becoming a family resort

Söll has fairly wide-ranging facilities – the focus is the Söll-Hochsöll school's Kinder-welt at the gondola mid-station, which takes children from age 3 to 14 years and has a well-equipped snow garden. The Mini-club caters for children aged four and under. There's a special kids-only drag and slope on the opposite side of the village to the main lifts. Reports welcome.

STAYING THERE

HOW TO GO
Mostly cheap, cheerful gasthofs

The major mainstream tour operators offer packages here.

Hotels There is a wide choice of simple gasthofs, pensions and B&Bs, and an adequate amount of better-quality hotel accommodation – mainly 3-star.

****Greil (5289) Attractive, but out of the centre and far from the lifts.

****Postwirt (5081) Attractive, central and traditional, with built-in stube.

****Alpenpanorama (5309) Far from lifts but with own bus stop; wonderful views; pleasant rooms.

***Bergland (5454) Well placed between the village and lifts. Recently refurbished.

***Tulpe (5223) Next to the lifts.

***Feldwebel (5224) Central.

***Hexenalm (5544) Next to the lifts.

***Gasthof Tenne (5282) B&B gasthof between centre and main road.

Chalets There are few catered chalets, but there are a couple of big 'club hotels' run by British tour operators.

Apartments The central Aparthotel Schindlhaus has nice accommodation. Some of the best apartments in town are attached to the Bergland hotel, but

a 2007 reporter recommends the 'ideally located' Alpin apartments ('fabulous', 'outstanding in terms of cleanliness and space').

EATING OUT
A fair choice

Some of the best restaurants are in hotels. The Greil and Postwirt ('extensive and delicious New Year buffet') are good. The Schindlhaus is said to be the best, at least if you enjoy 'rich meat' dishes. Giovanni does excellent, large pizzas, while other places worth a visit include the Dorfstub'n ('varied menu, extremely good steaks') and the Venezia.

APRES-SKI
Still some very loud bars

Söll is not as raucous as it used to be, but it's still very lively and a lot of places have live music. The Salvenstadl (Cow Shed) bar is regularly recommended by reporters ('nice atmosphere', 'the best live music'). The Whisky-Mühle is a large disco that can get a little rowdy, especially after the bars close. Buffalo's is popular and the hotel Austria bar has 'cool music and pool tables'. Rossini is a 'lovely, modern bar', recommended for cocktails and live music.

OFF THE SLOPES
Not bad for a small village

You could spend a happy day in the wonderfully equipped Panoramabad: taking a sauna, swimming, lounging about. There's tobogganing from the top of the gondola. The large baroque church would be the pride of many tourist towns. There are numerous coach excursions, including trips to Salzburg, Innsbruck and even Vipiteno over in Italy.

Söll

209

Interactive resort shortlist builder at **www.wtss.co.uk**

ACTIVITIES

Indoor Swimming, sauna, solarium, massage, bowling, squash

Outdoor Natural ice rink (skating, curling), sleigh rides, 3km/ 2 miles of floodlit ski and toboggan runs, walks, paragliding

UK PACKAGES

Airtours, Crystal, Directski.com, First Choice, Independent Ski Links, Inghams, Interactive Resorts, Neilson, Ski Hillwood, Ski Line, Ski McNeill, Ski Wild, Skitracer, Thomson
Scheffau Crystal, Esprit, Neilson, Ski Line, Ski Wild, Thomson
Hopfgarten Contiki, First Choice, Lagrange

Brixen 800m/2,620ft

It may not be pretty, but with its new gondola Brixen will now make a very efficient base for exploration of the SkiWelt circuit, on one side, and the slopes of Westendorf (and thus Kitzbühel) on the other.

THE RESORT
Brixen im Thale is a very scattered roadside village at the south-east edge of the main SkiWelt area. The main hotels are near the railway station, a bus ride from the lifts. Through-traffic intrudes, and the village is in any case not particularly cute, but for keen skiers it is worth considering.

THE MOUNTAIN
Brixen is on the south side of the main SkiWelt circuit, and on the north side of the Westendorf slopes.
Slopes One gondola takes you to Hochbrixen, where lifts diverge for Hohe Salve and Söll, or Astberg and Ellmau. There's a small area of north-facing runs, including nursery slopes, on the other side of the village, and a new gondola up to Choralpe on Westendorf's slopes.
Terrain parks None locally but there's a good park nearby at Westendorf.
Snow reliability A chain of snow-guns on the main south-facing piste helps to preserve the snow as long as possible and the area as a whole now has effective snowmaking.
Experts The black run alongside the Brixen gondola is one of the few challenging pistes in the area.
Intermediates When snow is good, Brixen has some of the best slopes in the SkiWelt – including some challenging ones.
Beginners The nursery slopes are secluded and shady, but meeting up with friends for lunch is a hassle – the area is a bus ride from the village.
Snowboarding See Söll.
Cross-country In addition to valley-floor trails, a 3km/2 mile loop up the mountain at Hochbrixen provides fine views and fairly reliable snow.
Queues Lift upgrades have improved the once queue-prone area.
Mountain restaurants The Filzalm above Brixen has been recommended.
Schools and guides The ski schools run the usual group classes, and mini-groups for up to six people.
Facilities for children There is an all-day ski kindergarten.

STAYING THERE
How to go There are plenty of hotels and pensions.
Hotels The Alpenhof (88320) and Sporthotel (8191) are 4-stars with pool.
Eating out Mainly hotel-based, but the restaurant opposite the gondola has been recommended.
Après-ski Après-ski is quiet, but livelier Westendorf is a short taxi ride away.
Off the slopes Activities include tennis, hotel-based spa facilities and days out to Salzburg, Innsbruck and Kitzbühel.

Scheffau 745m/2,440ft

This is one of the most attractive of the SkiWelt villages.

THE RESORT
Scheffau is a rustic little place complete with pretty white church. It is spacious yet not sprawling, and has a definite centre 1km/0.5 miles off the busy main road (away from the slopes), which increases its charm at the cost of convenience – you can ski to the SkiWelt lifts at Blaiken (where there are several hotels) but you need a bus to get back.

THE MOUNTAIN
Scheffau is well placed for the best (and most central and snow-sure) section of pistes in the SkiWelt.
Slopes Two gondolas (including an eight-seater) give rapid access directly to Brandstadl from Blaiken.
Snow reliability Eiberg is the place to go when snow is poor.
Experts The pistes above Blaiken are some of the longest and steepest in the SkiWelt.
Intermediates This is as good a base as any in the area.
Beginners The nursery slope is in the village, nowhere near other slopes, making Scheffau a poor choice for mixed-ability parties; but a reporter rates the easy blues at Brandstadl as 'excellent for beginner snowboarders'.
Cross-country See Söll and Ellmau.
Queues The two gondolas shift weekend queues well at Blaiken.
Mountain restaurants See Söll, Ellmau.
Schools and guides The school is well regarded, but groups can be large. A reporter's private snowboarding lesson was 'the best I've ever had'.
Facilities for children Both the ski kindergarten and non-ski nursery have good reputations. The children's ski area and school 'Kinder-Kaiserland' is

also reported to be 'very good'. And excellent progress was made by a four-year-old at Ski Esprit's nursery.

STAYING THERE
How to go Major operators offer packages here.
Hotels The best hotels – both with pool, sauna and steam room – are the 4-star Kaiser (8000) and 3-star Alpin (8556) – 'excellent food, lots of choice, spacious rooms'. Pool ('a bit cold') and sauna. The Zum Wilden Kaiser (8118) has 'a sauna and good fish dishes'. The central Gasthof Weberbauer (8115) is said to be 'good value' and 'efficient'. At the Blaiken gondolas, the Blaiken (8126) and Waldhof (8122) are good-value gasthofs.
Eating out There aren't many village restaurants. Donatello has been recommended for pizza.
Après-ski 'Non-existent,' says one happy reporter, but there are a couple of bars. The Sternbar is nearest to the gondolas and lively after the lifts close. The usual rep-organised events such as bowling and tobogganing are available.
Off the slopes Walking apart, there is little to do. Tour operators organise trips to Innsbruck and Salzburg.

Hopfgarten 620m/2,030ft

Hopfgarten is an unspoiled, friendly, traditional resort off the main road.

THE RESORT
The village is a good size: small enough to be intimate, large enough to have plenty of off-slope amenities. Most hotels are within five minutes' walk of the lift to Rigi.

THE MOUNTAIN
Hopfgarten is at the western extremity of the SkiWelt.
Slopes Hopfgarten offers queue-free access to Rigi and Hohe Salve – the high point of the main SkiWelt circuit.
Terrain parks None locally but it's a short bus ride to Westendorf.
Snow reliability The resort's great weakness is the poor snow quality on the south-west-facing home slope – especially vulnerable in late season.
Experts Experts should venture off-piste for excitement.
Intermediates When snow is good, the runs down to Hopfgarten and the nearby villages of Brixen and Itter are some of the best in the SkiWelt.

Beginners There is a beginners' slope in the village, but it is sunny as well as low; lack of snow-cover means paying for a lift pass to higher slopes. There are few easy longer runs to progress to in this part of the SkiWelt.
Snowboarding The SkiWelt is best suited to freeriding the extensive intermediate slopes.
Cross-country Hopfgarten is one of the best cross-country bases in the area. There are fine trails to Kelchsau (11km/7 miles) and Niederau (15km/9 miles), and the Itter-Bocking loop (15km/9 miles) starts nearby. Westendorf's trails are close. But all of these trails are at valley level.
Queues We've had no reports of queues to leave the village since the eight-seat gondola was installed.
Mountain restaurants See Söll.
Schools and guides Partly because Hopfgarten seems to attract large numbers of Australians, English is widely spoken in the two schools.
Facilities for children Hopfgarten is a family resort, with a nursery and ski kindergarten.

STAYING THERE
How to go Cheap and cheerful gasthofs, pensions and little private B&Bs are the norm here.
Hotels The comfortable hotels Hopfgarten (3920) and Sporthotel Fuchs (2420) are both well placed for the main lift.
Eating out Most of the restaurants are hotel-based, but there are exceptions, including a Chinese and a pizzeria.
Après-ski Après-ski is generally quiet, though a lively holiday can usually be ensured if you go with Aussie-dominated Contiki Travel.
Off the slopes Off-slope amenities include swimming, riding, bowling, skating, tobogganing and paragliding. The railway makes trips to Salzburg, Innsbruck and Kitzbühel possible.

Itter 700m/2,300ft

Itter is a tiny village half-way around the mountain between Söll and Hopfgarten, with a gondola just outside the village up to Hochsöll above Söll, and so into the SkiWelt.
There's a hotel and half a dozen gasthofs and B&Bs. The school has a rental shop, and there are nursery slopes close to hand – but there are few easy longer runs to progress to in this part of the SkiWelt.

Phone numbers
From elsewhere in Austria add the prefix 05358 (Wilder Kaiser, Scheffau), 05333 (Söll), 05332 (Hohe Salve), 05335 (Hopfgarten, Itter), 05334 (Brixen); from abroad use the prefix +43 and omit the initial '0'

TOURIST OFFICES

WILDER KAISER
(Söll, Scheffau, Going, Ellmau)
t 505
www.wilderkaiser.
info

Söll
t 5216
soell@
wilderkaiser.info

Scheffau
t 7373
scheffau@
wilderkaiser.info

HOHE SALVE
(Hopfgarten, Itter)
www.hohe-salve.com

Hopfgarten
t 2322
hopfgarten@hohe-salve.com

Itter
t 2670
itter@hohe-salve.com

BRIXEN
t 8433
brixen@kitzbuehel-alpen.com
www.kitzbuehel-alpen.com

SKIWELT
www.skiwelt.at

St Anton

If what you seek is dumps, bumps, boozing and bopping, there's nowhere quite like it – and with a neat Tirolean town as a bonus

COSTS

① ② ③ ④ ⑤ ⑥

RATINGS

The slopes
Fast lifts ★★★
Snow ★★★★
Extent ★★★★
Expert ★★★★★
Intermediate ★★★
Beginner ★
Convenience ★★★
Queues ★★
Mountain
  restaurants ★★★
The rest
Scenery ★★★
Resort charm ★★★★
Off-slope ★★

NEWS

For 2008/09 the Kandahar Haus ski museum is being fully revamped.

Snowmaking will be increased at Rendl and Schindlergrat, extending cover to 95% of St Anton's slopes.

The resort continues to add new hotels: the 4-star Arlmont is planned for 2008/09 and the upmarket Banyan opened near the Fang lift last season.

For 2007/08 snowmaking was increased.

212

- ✚ Varied terrain for experts and adventurous intermediates – and a lot of it, once you include Lech-Zürs, a bus ride away
- ✚ Heavy snowfalls, backed up by a fair amount of snowmaking
- ✚ Despite expansion, the resort retains solid traditional charm – and the animated village centre is mainly car-free
- ✚ Very lively après-ski, from mid-afternoon onward
- ✚ Improved lift system has cut queues from the base areas, but …

- ▬ Still some queues up the mountain
- ▬ Slopes really don't suit beginners or timid intermediates
- ▬ Pistes can get very crowded – some of them dangerously so
- ▬ Most of the tough stuff is off-piste – including many popular runs
- ▬ Main slopes get a lot of sun, quickly affecting snow conditions
- ▬ Resort spreads widely, with long treks from some lodgings to key lifts and bars
- ▬ Can get rowdy, with noisy drunks in the centre in the early hours

St Anton is one of those resorts that quickens the pulse of competent skiers and riders – one of the resorts your editors aim to get to every winter, rather than delegating the job. We're drawn by the splendid bowls below the Valluga, and the ambience of the village. Other fans – notably the cream of the world's ski-bums – might put equal stress on the 3pm-to-3am après-ski. (We, of course, ski until 5pm and rarely manage more than a quiet nightcap after dinner.)

But it doesn't suit everyone, as our list of ▬ points makes clear. If you are thinking of trying an Austrian change from a major French resort, or of taking a step up from Kitzbühel or Söll, take full account of this list, especially if you get thrown by blues that should be red, and reds that might be black.

We were delighted last year to give our award for Best European Resort Development to St Anton for its impressive new Galzig gondola. We look forward to presenting a similar award when the resort eventually deals with the dangerously busy piste down the Steissbachtal by constructing a new piste from Galzig to share the traffic. There is already a red ski route; let's get the diggers in, and carve out a blue piste. Please?

THE RESORT

St Anton is at the foot of the road up to the Arlberg pass, at the eastern end of a lift network that spreads across to St Christoph and over the pass to Stuben. These two tiny villages are described at the end of the chapter.

The resort is a long, sprawling mixture of traditional and modern buildings crammed into a narrow valley. It used to be sandwiched between the busy bypass road and the mainline railway; but since the railway was moved in 2000, a little area of parkland has taken its place.

Although it is crowded and commercialised, St Anton is full of

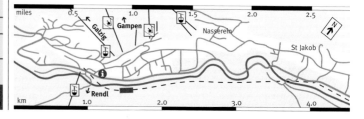

↑ The western suburbs, catching the sun here, are quite a walk from the centre

JILL COOK

character, its traffic-free main street lined by traditional-style buildings. It is an attractively bustling place, day and night. Its shops offer little in the way of entertainment, but meet everyday needs well – self-catering reporters have observed that it has a 'wonderful Spar', for example.

The hub of the resort is around the base stations of the lifts to Gampen (a fast quad chair) and to Galzig (the fancy jumbo gondola that won our Best European Resort Development award last year). The main street is only a short walk from these lifts, and for most purposes a location on or close to this main street is ideal.

The resort spreads down the valley, thinning out before broadening again to form the suburb of Nasserein. This backwater has an eight-person gondola up to Gampen, and makes an appealing base for a quiet time. The nightlife action is a short bus ride or 15-minute walk away ('quite a hike'). Staying between the centre and Nasserein is fairly convenient too as the Fang chairlift gives access to the Nasserein gondola.

On the other side of the main road a gondola goes up to the Rendl area. This is linked one-way by rope tows and a moving carpet from the end of St Anton's main street – but the return

St Anton

Interactive resort shortlist builder at **www.wtss.co.uk**

still involves a bus ride or short walk.

St Anton spreads up the hill to the west, towards the Arlberg pass – first to Oberdorf, then Gastig, 10 minutes' walk from the centre. Further up the hill are the suburbs of Stadle, Dengert and Moos – a long way out, but the latter two next to the slopes.

Regular free ski-buses go to Stuben, Zürs and Lech (the latter two described in the Lech chapter) and the less well-known but worthwhile Sonnenkopf area above Klösterle. Changes may be involved. These buses can get crowded early and late in the day and often provoke complaints from reporters. The post bus offers a less-crowded alternative, but is not free. Minibus-style taxis can be economic if shared.

Serfaus, Ischgl and Sölden are also feasible outings by car.

THE MOUNTAINS

The main slopes are essentially open: only the lower Gampen runs and the run from Rendl to the valley offer much shelter from bad weather.

St Anton vies with Val d'Isère for the title of 'resort with most underclassified slopes'. During our visit last season we paid particular attention to this; we didn't ski every blue, but all those we skied would have been better classified as red; there are also plenty of reds that could be black – but paradoxically, none of the blacks is seriously steep.

Many of the most popular steep runs marked on the piste map are classified as 'ski routes'. These have markers and are protected from avalanches, but they are essentially ungroomed and, more importantly, are

Albonagrat 2400m

Underused area of worthwhile runs, though you have to put up with slow lifts (cold ones on the front side)

ALBONA

1840m

Rauz is the hub of the ski-bus services – you can ski to here and catch a bus to Lech

Rauz 1620m

Stuben 1405m

Flexen Pass

Lech / Zurs ↓

Excellent long red/blue down towards Stuben – over 1000m/ 3,280ft vertical

Valfagehr

Arlenmähder

St Christoph

St Christoph 1800m/5,910ft

Hospiz Alm

GALZIG 218

Resort	1305m
	4,280ft
Arlberg region	
Slopes	1305-2650m
	4,280-8,690ft
Lifts	85
Pistes	276km
	172 miles
Blue	39%
Red	50%
Black	11%
Snowmaking	59%
St Anton, St	
Christoph and Stuben	
Slopes	1305-2650m
	4,280-8,690ft
Lifts	40
Pistes	120km
	75 miles

not patrolled. Clearly these routes should not be tackled alone; in practice though, they are treated like pistes and should be classified thus.

On Rendl there is a lift serving no pistes but only a single ski route, which more or less follows the line of the lift. Why is it not a patrolled piste?

The piste map also shows (at Stuben and Lech) lots of 'high-alpine touring runs', which are not marked on the ground at all and not protected against avalanche.

The Arlberg lift companies seem determined to present all their widely spread terrain in a single view. The map has been considerably improved on previous efforts – but smaller, separate maps would be better.

Piste marking is adequate. The local cable TV shows the state of the pistes and queues – very useful.

THE SLOPES
Large linked area
St Anton's slopes fall into three main sectors, two of them linked.

The major sector is that beneath the local high-spot, the **Valluga**, accessed by the jumbo gondola to Galzig, then a cable car. The tiny top stage of the cable car to the Valluga itself is mainly for sightseeing – you can take skis or a board up only if you have a guide to lead you down the tricky off-piste run to Zürs. The slightly lower station of Valluga Grat gives access to St Anton's famous high, sunny bowls, and to the long, beautiful red/blue run to Alpe Rauz, at the western end of St Anton's own slopes. From here there's a six-pack, the Valfagehr, to return, or you can go on to explore the rather neglected slopes of Stuben.

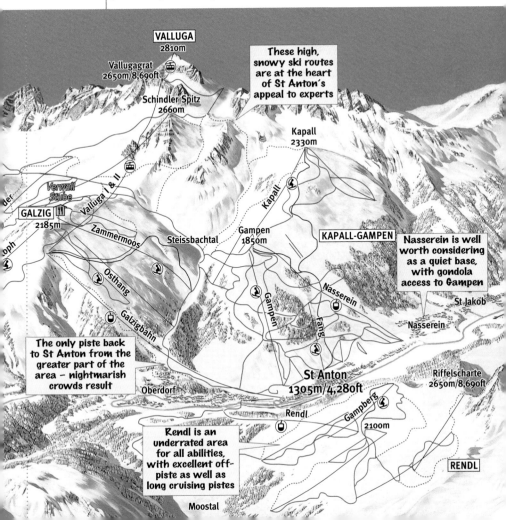

VALLUGA
2810m

Vallugagrat
2650m/8,690ft

Schindler Spitz
2660m

These high, snowy ski routes are at the heart of St Anton's appeal to experts

Kapall
2330m

Verwall Stube

GALZIG
2185m

Valluga I & II

Zammermoos

Steissbachtal

Kapall

Gampen
1850m

KAPALL-GAMPEN

Nasserein is well worth considering as a quiet base, with gondola access to Gampen

St Jakob

Osthang

Nasserein

Nasserein

Galzigbahn

Gampen

Fang

The only piste back to St Anton from the greater part of the area – nightmarish crowds result

Oberdorf

St Anton
1305m/4,28oft

Rendl

Riffelscharte
2650m/8,69oft

Gampberg

2100m

Rendl is an underrated area for all abilities, with excellent off-piste as well as long cruising pistes

RENDL

Moostal

The off-piste runs in the huge bowl beneath the summit of the Valluga, reached by either the Schindlergrat chair or the Valluga I cable car, are justifiably world-famous. In good snow, this whole area is an off-piste delight for experts.

Except immediately after a fresh snowfall, you can see tracks going all over the mountain. There are two main ski routes marked on the piste map – both long, steep descents that quickly get mogulled. The Schindlerkar is the first you come to and it divides into two – the Schindlerkar gully being the steeper option. For the second, wider and somewhat easier Mattun run, you traverse further at the top. Both these feed down into the Steissbachtal where there are lifts back up to Galzig and Gampen.

There are, of course, more adventurous ways down than the identified ski routes. The Schweinströge starts off in the same direction as the red run to Rauz, but you traverse the shoulder of the Schindler Spitze and descend a narrow gully. Perhaps the ultimate challenge is to ski off the back of the Valluga – a great adventure, according to readers who have done it. For more information see our off-piste panel later in the chapter.

These high runs can also be accessed by riding the Schindlergrat triple chair, though some involve a half-hour hike – even so, this can be quicker than waiting for the cable car, as an energetic reporter has proved.

Other runs from **Galzig** go south-west to St Christoph and east into the Steissbachtal. Beyond this valley, with lift and piste links in both directions, is the **Kapall-Gampen** sector, reachable by chairlift from central St Anton or gondola from Nasserein. From Gampen at mid-mountain, pistes lead back to St Anton and Nasserein. Or you can ride a six-pack on up to Kapall to ski the treeless upper mountain.

A handful of lifts (including a fast six-pack to Gampberg) serve the west-facing runs at the top of **Rendl**, with a single north-facing piste returning to the gondola bottom station.

The slopes above **Stuben** are described at the end of the chapter.

TERRAIN PARKS
Head for Rendl
The 200m/66oft-long park on Rendl, just below the top of the gondola, doesn't touch the park over in Lech for maintenance or size – but it will easily keep beginners and intermediates entertained. Due to its narrow nature the park has only a single kicker line, in the form of various-sized tabletops and a corner jump. Around the jumps are four to six rails. There's a large A-frame and flat slidebox, a small rainbow and an A-frame rail.

SNOW RELIABILITY
Generally very good cover
If the weather is coming from the west or north-west (as it often is), the Arlberg gets it first, and as a result St

Anton and its neighbours get heavy falls of snow. They often have much better conditions than other resorts of a similar height, and we've had great fresh powder here as late as mid-April. But many of the slopes face south or south-east, causing icy or heavy conditions at times. It's vital to time descents of the steeper runs off the Valluga to get decent conditions, or you can find yourself in trouble.

The lower runs are well equipped with snowmaking, which generally ensures the home runs remain open. But reporters regularly complain of poor and limited piste grooming; many blue runs are steep enough to develop moguls when snow is soft.

FOR EXPERTS
One of the world's great areas
St Anton vies with Chamonix, Val d'Isère and a handful of other resorts for the affections of experts. There are countless opportunities for going off-piste, and guidance is very desirable. Read the feature panels on the Valluga runs and off-piste routes.

Lower down, there are challenging runs in many directions from both Galzig and Kapall-Gampen. These lower runs can be doubly tricky if the snow has been hit by the sun.

Don't overlook the Rendl area, which has plenty of open space served by the top lifts, and several quite challenging itineraries. This is a great area for a mixed group and is generally quieter than the main sector.

One of our reporters particularly liked the quieter Sonnenkopf area, down-valley from Stuben, for its excellent off-piste route to Langen. See also the Stuben section.

Each of the main sectors has its

toughest piste classified as black; a couple deserve their classification, but most don't – the Fang race course from Gampen used to be red, in fact. The distinction between reds and blacks is in general a fine one.

FOR INTERMEDIATES
Some real challenges
St Anton is well suited to good, adventurous intermediates. As well as lots of testing pistes, they will be able to try the Mattun ski route and the easier of the Schindlerkar routes from Valluga Grat (see Valluga Runs feature panel). The run from Schindler Spitze to Rauz is very long (over 1000m/3,300ft vertical), varied and ideal for good (and fit) intermediates. Alternatively, turn off from this part-way down and take the Steissbachtal to the lifts back to Galzig or Gampen. The Kapall-Gampen section is also interesting, with sporty bumps among trees on the lower half. Good intermediates may enjoy the men's downhill run from the top to town.

Timid intermediates will find St Anton less to their taste. There are few easy cruising pistes; most blues would be red elsewhere and get bumpy,

especially just after a snowfall. The most obvious cruisers are the short blues on Galzig and the Steissbachtal (aka 'Happy Valley'). These are reasonably gentle but get extremely crowded (see 'Queues'). The blue from Kapall to Gampen is wide and cruisy.

In the underrated Rendl area a variety of trails suitable for good and moderate intermediates criss-cross, including the long and genuinely blue Salzböden. The long treeline run to the valley (over 1000m/3,280ft vertical from the top) is the best run in the area when visibility is poor, but it has some quite awkward sections and can get very busy at the end of the day – early intermediates beware.

FOR BEGINNERS
Far from ideal
The best bet for beginners is to start at Nasserein, where the nursery slope is less steep than the one close to the main lifts. There are further slopes up at Gampen, and a short, gentle blue run at Rendl, served by an easy draglift. But there are no easy, uncrowded runs for beginners to progress to. A mixed party including novices would be better off staying in

boarding

Many consider St Anton as the Mecca of Austrian freeriding. Countless steep gullies and backcountry powder fields with challenging terrain form a big draw for advanced riders. The Arlberg Snowboard academy has a great reputation for showing all levels where best to apply their respective skills – whether you are a beginner on the wide-open pistes, or a more advanced rider wanting guidance through the trees or steeps and deep off-piste. Rendl is an excellent mountain for freeriders and freestylers alike.

Lech or Zürs; those who want to explore St Anton can get on the bus.

FOR CROSS-COUNTRY
Limited interest
St Anton is not a great cross-country resort, but trails total around 40km/ 25 miles and snow conditions are usually good. There are a couple of uninspiring trails near town, another at St Jakob 3km/2 miles away, and a pretty trail through trees along the Verwalltal to the foot of the Albona area. There is also a tiny loop at St Christoph. A couple of recent visitors enjoyed private lessons with the Arlberg Ski School.

QUEUES
Much improved, but ...
Queues are not the problem they once were, thanks to recent lift upgrades. The replacement of the cable car to Galzig by the gondola has reduced queueing significantly. A March 2008 visitor confirms: 'we hardly had to queue all week; I was impressed'.
  But there are still problems up the mountain, notably the Valluga I cable car from Galzig. In peak season, especially when powder beckons, queues here can run into hours. And the Zammermoos chair out of the Steissbachtal still generates queues (sadly, its singles line seems to be little-used). A reporter found it as quick to ski down to the Galzig gondola as to wait in the long queues at the weekend. The Nasserein gondola is 'very efficient' and a visitor over New Year found no queues there.
  At Rendl, the gondola gets busy when poor weather closes the lifts in the main area but one reporter was surprised to find that queues there were very 'orderly and polite'.
  Perhaps more of a worry than the lift queues are the crowded pistes. Clearly the worst (at least when the top Valluga runs are open) is the Steissbachtal and the home run below it, which can be uncomfortably

crowded even in January and a nightmare on a peak weekend. So acute is this problem at times that several reporters have preferred to catch a bus home from Rauz or St Christoph. Another alternative is the ski route under the gondola, but it can be quite testing. When heavy snow closes the top runs on the Valluga, the crowds shift to Rendl, where the home run again gets unpleasantly busy.

MOUNTAIN RESTAURANTS
Lots of options
Editors' choice The Verwallstube at Galzig (2352501) is in a class of its own – an expensive table-service place with all the trimmings. We had a seriously good lunch here last season, but wouldn't want to do it every day. There is a no-smoking room, but of course smokers get the big windows with the fab views. It may not be a proper mountain restaurant, but we often lunch in St Christoph at the atmospheric, buzzing Hospiz Alm (3625), famed for its slide down to the toilets as well as its satisfying table-service food and amazing wine cellar. Service gets stretched at times, but most reports are positive.
Worth knowing about The Arlberg Taja is a 'jolly and welcoming' alternative to the Hospiz Alm in St Christoph. Reader recommendations on Galzig include the Ulmer Hütte near the top of the Arlenmähder chair, and the big, smart self-service restaurant at Galzig itself. Lower down, the Sennhütte offers 'excellent choices'. The Rodelalm on Gampen is regularly praised: 'a real hut with good food at low prices and a lovely fire'; 'a Tirolean treat'. Just above the village, the Mooserwirt is better known for après-ski than food, but serves typical Austrian food; the Heustadl is popular with 'good choices and efficient service'; the Krazy Kanguruh does burgers, pizzas and snacks; and Taps Bar next door is a 'firm favourite' – 'half of St Anton was sunbathing there' at the end of last

The Arlberg region is an off-piste skier's dream – renowned for its consistently high snowfall record, incredible deep powder and enormous diversity of terrain. We invited Piste to Powder Mountain Guides to give us an introduction to the possibilities. Remember you should never explore far off-piste without a guide.

Piste to Powder Mountain Guides
St. Anton – Austria

Piste to Powder Mountain Guides

All day guiding 9am to 5pm. Choose from four skill levels. All safety equipment provided.

t 01661 824318
00 43 664 174 6282
info@pistetopowder.com
www.pistetopowder.com

Runs from Rendl

After initial practice close to the pistes, the natural progression is to go beyond the furthest lift to access the wide rolling bowls of powder of Rossfall.

More serious routes from Rendl take you well away from all lifts. The North Face, accessed from the Gampberg six-seat chair, offers challenging terrain to the intermediate/confident off-piste skier. The Riffel chairlifts access the imposing Hinter Rendl – a gigantic high-mountain bowl offering a huge descent down to St Anton, often in deep powder. A variant involves a climb to Rendl Scharte and a demanding descent with sections of 35° down the remote Malfontal to the village of Pettneu and a taxi back to St Anton.

Runs from Albona, above Stuben

Stuben's outstanding terrain, reached from the Albonagrat chair, is suited to the more experienced off-piste skier, as the descents are long. The open treelines of the Langen forest, where the powder is regularly knee to waist deep, form some of the world's finest tree skiing. A 30-minute climb from Albonagrat, with skis on shoulder, opens up further outstanding terrain from Maroikopfe – either west, down undulating open slopes to Langen, or east, down steep 40° slopes to Verwalltal, where this glorious run ends with a glass of wine at an old hunting lodge.

Runs from the Valluga

The legendary runs from the summit cable car of the Valluga must be on the tick list of all keen and experienced off-piste skiers – the North Face, Bridge Couloir or East Couloir. Your pulse will race as you trace a steep ski line between cliff bands in the breathtaking scenery of the Pazieltal, leading down to Zürs. Here, at the top of the Madloch chairlift and after a short hidden climb, you will be roped down into the steep Valhalla Couloir, accessing 1200m/3,940ft vertical of open slopes ending in the hamlet of Zug, close to Lech.

St Anton

219

season. The Griabli has also been praised: 'great and rarely busy at lunch time'. Over on Rendl, the self-service Rendl restaurant has an 'excellent salad bar and immaculate toilets', but gets very busy. A better plan is to head down the valley run to the 'welcoming' Bifang-Alm, for regional specialities and excellent service.

piste outfit run by British guide Graham Austick. 'Absolutely corking day with a great guide.' 'Wonderful week; exactly the right balance of instruction and guiding.' 'Graham was excellent – tips for improving our powder skiing, untracked powder every day.' If you have particular ambitions, make sure your group is all of the required standard, though.

Kindergartens (run by ski schools)
t 3411 / 3563
From age 30mnth; must be toilet trained

Ski schools
Both Austrian schools take children aged from 5 (6 days including lunch €301)

SCHOOLS AND GUIDES
Mixed reports
The St Anton school and the Arlberg school are under the same ownership but continue to operate separately. Past reports on the Arlberg school are mixed: one reporter commented, 'Not enough attention was paid to putting equal standards together and groups were big.' But other reporters are very happy: an adult beginner made 'good progress' with five days of group lessons. One reader joined a top-level guided group and was impressed with the 'superb value'.

We have had good reports in 2008 on Piste to Powder, a specialist off-

FACILITIES FOR CHILDREN
Nasserein 'ideal'
The youth centre attached to the Arlberg school is excellent, and the special slopes both for toddlers (at the bottom) and bigger children (at Gampen) are well done. Children's instruction is reportedly 'very good' too. At Nasserein there is a moving carpet lift on the baby slope, and a reporter rates this an 'absolutely ideal' place to stay with young kids. There's also a good children's area by the Gampen fast quad. Family specialists Esprit Ski and Mark Warner both have their own child care facilities in chalets or chalet hotels in the Nasserein area.

Interactive resort shortlist builder at www.wtss.co.uk

UK PACKAGES

Albus, Alpine Answers, Alpine Weekends, Chalet World Ski, Crystal, Crystal Finest, Descent International, Directski.com, Elegant Resorts, Erna Low, Esprit, First Choice, Flexiski, Friendship Travel, Independent Ski Links, Inghams, Interactive Resorts, Kaluma, Kuoni, Made to Measure, Mark Warner, Momentum, Neilson, Oxford Ski Co, Powder White, Scott Dunn, Ski Activity, Ski Expectations, Ski Freshtracks, Ski Independence, Ski Line, Ski McNeill, Ski Safari, Ski Solutions, Ski Total, Skitracer, Ski-Val, Ski Wild, Skiworld, Snow Finders, Snoworks, Snowscape, Solo's, St Anton Ski Company, Supertravel, Thomson, White Roc

Stuben Alpine Answers

St Christoph Alpine Answers, Crystal Finest, Elegant Resorts, Flexiski, Jeffersons, Made to Measure, Neilson, Powder Byrne, Scott Dunn, Thomson

STAYING THERE

HOW TO GO
Austria's main chalet resort

There's a wide range of places to stay, from quality hotels to cheap and cheerful pensions and apartments.

Chalets Plenty of catered chalets are offered by UK operators, and they now include some seriously smart ones. Scott Dunn operates four luxury chalets in the Stadle area, with outdoor hot tubs – and very good bedrooms, in our experience – and a very swanky new place at the opposite end of the resort. Last season Kaluma added the smooth 10-bedroom Villa Montfort, close to the centre. Flexiski's Amalien Haus has a great position on the main street, and was recently refurbished. Ski Total has several chalets here, and Albus is a St Anton specialist with chalets in Nasserein. Family specialist Esprit has three chalets in Nasserein. Mark Warner has a central chalet-hotel, child-free except during school holidays, as well as its child-friendly one in Nasserein. Inghams has some chalets, too.

Hotels There are two 5-star hotels and lots of 4- and 3-stars and B&Bs.

*****Raffl's St Antoner Hof (2910) Best in town, but its position on the bypass is less than ideal. Pool.

****Alte Post (2553) Atmospheric central place with lively après-ski bar.

****Banyan (30361) New up-market B&B with 39 rooms and a fitness centre with pool.

****Brunnenhof (2293) 'Romantic and cosy with fantastic five course dinners.' In St Jakob, beyond Nasserein – hotel minibus to lifts.

****Post (2213) Comfortable if uninspiring at the centre of affairs, close to both lifts and nightlife.

****Schwarzer Adler (22440) Centuries-old inn on main street. Varying bedrooms. 'Lovely pool.'

****Sporthotel (3111) Central position, varied bedrooms, good food. Pool.

****Galzig (42770) Smart, central place near the gondola. Recommended in 2008 by a regular visitor.

****Kertess (2005) in Oberdorf. 'Very comfortable, good food, friendly staff and a large pool.'

***Goldenes Kreuz (22110) A comfortable B&B hotel halfway to Nasserein, ideal for cruising home.

***Grischuna (2304) Welcoming and family-run in peaceful position up the hill west of town; close to the slopes.

***Rendlhof (3100) in Nasserein: 'friendly'.

***Nassereinerhof (3366) Close to the Nasserein gondola. Family-run with sauna, steam room. Recommended.

Pepi's skihotel (2830) Stylish B&B recommended by a 2008 reporter.

Almjur (2728) Convenient B&B near the Museum. 'Good breakfasts.'

Pension Alpenheim (3389) 'Basic but good breakfast, ski-in/ski-out to Nasserein lifts.'

Apartments There are plenty available, but package deals are few and far between. Reporters like the Bachmann apartments ('spacious and comfortable') and the H Strolz ('well equipped'), both in Nasserein, and Haus Rali at the western end of St Anton ('very friendly, family-owned, a bargain for New Year').

EATING OUT
Some excellent spots

There's a lot of half board in St Anton, so the restaurant scene is not huge. Our standard port of call for a drink or two and a relaxed meal is the cool Hazienda – a basement place in the main street, with a wide-ranging menu (steaks, seafood, pasta); you can eat at the bar. For more of a blow-out, it's up the hill to village museum's restaurant – excellent sophisticated food and wine served in elegant

panelled rooms. Or to the very different Ben.venuto in the Arlberg-well.com building – stark decor, eclectic menu, excellent food and service. Places such as the Trödlerstube serve big portions of traditional Austrian food. Readers have also recommended Scotty's and Pomodoro for pizzas, the Sporthotel Steakhouse and the Dolce Vita. The Funky Chicken is popular for 'good food at reasonable prices', including 'top-notch curry'. The cosy Sonnbichl has been mentioned. In Nasserein, the Tenne is noted for game dishes and Robi's Rodel-Stall at the end of the toboggan run has a cosy log fire.

APRES-SKI
Throbbing till late
St Anton's bars rock from mid-afternoon until the early hours. Après-ski starts in a collection of bars on the slopes above the village. The Krazy Kanguruh is probably the most famous but the Mooserwirt is the favourite with many reporters – 'still great and a must-visit'. It fills up with revellers as soon as the lunch trade finishes – reputedly dispensing more beer than any other bar in Austria. Waiters plough into the crowds, laden with trays of beers for sale. The Heustadl is 'the best place to boogie Tirolean-style, and shouldn't be missed'. The Sennhütte also has 'a fantastic atmosphere'. All this is followed by a slide down the piste in the dark. The bars in town are in full swing by 4pm, too. Most are lively, with loud music; sophisticates looking for a quieter time are less well provided for. The Anton bar is 'a great place to watch the world go by' and has comfy sheepskin on the chairs outside. The Hazienda and the Piccadilly (live bands, singing and late-night dancing) are popular choices – a 2008 visitor was entertained by 'a very talented German singer/guitarist'; 'the place rocked'. Underground on the Piste has 'a great party atmosphere, super staff and live music'. Reporters have also recommended Scotty's (in Mark Warner's chalet hotel Rosanna), Bar Cuba ('a good party'), Jacksy's ('good for a quiet drink'), Kandahar ('best for watching sport') and Funky Chicken. The St Antoner Hof is suggested for pre-dinner 'canapés and champagne'. In Nasserein, the Fang House and 'jolly' Sonnegg are recommended.

The Mooserwirt goes into après mode as soon as the lunch tables are cleared →

ACTIVITIES

Indoor Swimming pool (also hotel pools open to the public, with sauna and massage), fitness centre, tennis, squash, museum, library

Outdoor Cleared walking paths, natural ice rink (skating, curling), sleigh rides, snowshoeing, tobogganing, paragliding

Phone numbers
From elsewhere in Austria add the prefix 05446 (St Anton and St Christoph), 05582 (Stuben); from abroad use the prefix +43 and omit the initial '0'

TOURIST OFFICES

St Anton
t 22690
info@stantonam
arlberg.com
www.
stantonamarlberg.com

St Christoph
www.tiscover.com/
st.christoph

Stuben
t 399
info@stuben.at
www.stuben.com

OFF THE SLOPES
Some improvement

St Anton is a resort for keen skiers and riders. But the fitness, swimming and skating facilities of Arlberg-well. com are impressive and highly recommended by reporters. The village is lively during the day, but has few diverting shops. Getting by bus to the other Arlberg resorts is easy, as is visiting Innsbruck by train. Some of the better mountain huts are accessible by lift or bus. A reporter suggests using the winter walking trails to visit Pettneu and another enjoyed the walk to Verwall. The ski museum is getting a revamp for 2008/09.

STAYING DOWN THE VALLEY
Nice and quiet

Beyond Nasserein is St Jakob. It can be reached on snow, but is dependent on the free shuttle-bus in the morning.

Stuben 1405m/4,610ft

Stuben (in Vorarlberg) is linked by lifts and pistes over the Arlberg pass to St Anton (in Tirol). There are infrequent buses from the village to Lech/Zürs, and more frequent ones from Rauz, the roadside lift station for St Anton.

Dating back to the 13th century, Stuben is a small, unspoiled village, with an old church, a few unobtrusive hotels, a school, two or three bars, a couple of banks and a few little shops. Heavy snowfalls add to the charm.

The Albona above Stuben makes a refreshingly quiet change from the busy slopes of St Anton. It has north-facing slopes that hold powder well and some wonderful, deserted off-piste descents, including beautiful long runs down to Langen and to St Anton ('lovely sense of travel and isolation'). A regular visitor recommends the small Rasthaus

Verwall for lunch at the end of the latter. Staying within the lift network, the Albonagratstube gets a good review and the Berghaus is repeatedly recommended, not least for 'excellent rösti and pizza'. The slow village chair can be a cold ride but blankets are available. A 2008 reporter recommends the school ('good English spoken'). A quicker and warmer way to get to St Anton in the morning, if you have a car, is to drive up the road to Rauz. Stuben has sunny nursery slopes separate from the main slopes, but lack of easy runs to progress to makes it unsuitable for beginners. A covered moving carpet between Stuben and St Anton, at Rauz, omits the need to ride the awkward draglift.

Evenings are quiet, but several places have a pleasant atmosphere. The charming old Post (761) ('very good lunch') and Albona (712) are very comfortable and owned by the same family. The Hubertushof (5582) is 'a real little gem' – 'gourmet food, kids' menu and great wellness centre'.

St Christoph 1800m/5,910ft

St Christoph is small collection of smart and expensive hotels, restaurants and bars just down from the summit of the Arlberg pass. There are decent beginner slopes served by draglifts and a fast quad chairlift to the heart of St Anton's slopes at Galzig, but the blue back down is not an easy run to progress to. St Christoph is quiet at night. You can't miss the huge 5-star Arlberg-Hospiz (2611), with luxurious health and spa facilities – also recommended for 'very good food and an incredible wine list'. A more affordable but still excellent place is the 4-star Maiensee (21610), right on the slopes by the chair up to Galzig, with health and spa facilities and treatments.

Stubai valley

A choice of pretty little villages with their own wooded slopes, and one of the best glaciers in the world at the head of the valley

RATINGS

The slopes
Fast lifts	★★★
Snow	★★★★★
Extent	★★★
Expert	★★★
Intermediate	★★★
Beginner	★★
Convenience	★★
Queues	★★★
Mountain restaurants	★★

The rest
Scenery	★★★★
Resort charm	★★★★
Off-slope	★★★

NEWS

For 2007/08, at the glacier, a new T-bar and ski run were built, and the Mutterberg base station was rebuilt with Austria's largest ski and boot storage facility. A new run with snowmaking was created to the bottom of Schlick 2000, and a new après-ski bar there called Schlussliacht opened. There are plans to replace some T-bars with chairlifts on the glacier, and they hope to make the Stubai-Superski pass covering all four ski areas available as a day pass as well as in multi-day form.

KEY FACTS

Resort	935-1000m
	3,070-3,280ft
Slopes	935-3210m
	3,070-10,530ft
Lifts	44
Pistes	147km
	91 miles
Blue	40%
Red	31%
Black	29%
Snowmaking	some

+ High, snow-sure glacier slopes plus lower bad-weather options

+ Quiet, pretty Tirolean villages

– Beginners are better off sticking to the lower slopes

– Not much to challenge experts

Think Austrian glaciers, and the Stubaier Gletscher should feature near the top of your list. It is the country's largest glacier ski area, and among the world's best. For a winter holiday you need non-glacial slopes as well, for the bad-weather days – and the Stubai valley has plenty at Schlick 2000 (above Fulpmes), Elfer (above the village of Neustift) and Serles (above Mieders).

The Stubai valley lies a short drive south of Innsbruck. It is a long valley (about 30km/19 miles) with countless hamlets dotted along it – and a handful of bigger villages, three of which have their own wooded ski slopes and lift systems and are described in this chapter. Altogether the valley offers a sizeable area of mostly intermediate terrain, all of which is covered by the Stubai-Superski lift pass (which also covers the shuttle-bus). All the villages have impressive toboggan runs.

The Stubaier Gletscher offers an extensive area of runs between 3200m/10,500ft and 2300m/7,550ft accessed by two alternative two-stage gondolas from the huge car park at Mutterberg to the two mid-mountain stations of Eisgrat and Gamsgarten. A third gondola from Eisgrat takes you right to the top of the slopes.

The glacier area is broken up by rocky peaks giving more sense of variety than is normal on a glacier. Chairs (including three six-packs) and draglifts serve fabulous blue and red cruising runs, all of which normally have excellent snow, naturally. There is also a lovely 10km/6 mile ungroomed ski route (Wilde Grub'n) down to the valley – a run of 1450m/4,760ft vertical from the top of the glacier. And some good off-piste can be found with a guide.

There aren't the challenges here that there are on the Hintertux glacier. But there are some good long runs, two blacks (one is a pretty steep mogul field) and five more ski routes. For intermediates it is splendid territory, with lots of fabulous cruising. Novices are better off learning lower down, but there is a short beginner slope at Gamsgarten.

The area is popular with snowboarders. There are lots of natural hits and kickers across the mountain, and a new terrain park was built two seasons ago with rails, boxes, kickers and a boardercross. There's also a 4.5km/3 mile cross-country loop.

Queues are no longer a serious problem. But on a busy weekend there can be short delays at the gondola mid-station – and at the Eisjoch six-pack, too.

There are two huge self-service places at Eisgrat and Gamsgarten (where 'the large terrace is very popular' and the Zur Goldenen Gams has table service). At Jochdohle, Austria's highest restaurant gives stunning views but can get crowded. The Dresdnerhütte near the gondola mid-station is 'charming' and 'a nice alternative to the impersonal cafeterias', say reporters.

There is a ski school at the glacier. Club Micky Maus is a comprehensive child care facility at Gamsgarten. Children under ten get a free lift pass when with an adult.

Après-ski starts up the mountain in the lively snow bar at Gamsgarten.

NEUSTIFT 1000m/3,280ft
The major village closest to the glacier, 20km/12 miles away, and served by regular buses. It's an attractive, traditional Tirolean village, with limited local slopes at Elfer.
The slopes at Elfer consist of a narrow chain of runs and lifts from Elferhütte at 2080m/6,820ft down to the village. The pistes are all red and there's not much to entice experts, but it is a quiet place for intermediates to practise. This area is north-east-facing; there is a sunny nursery slope at

↑ The Stubaier Gletscher is one of the best glacier ski areas in the world
TVB STUBAITAL

UK PACKAGES
Neustift *Crystal, Crystal Finest, Interactive Resorts, Interhome, Jeffersons, Made to Measure*
Fulpmes *Crystal, Lagrange*

Phone numbers
From elsewhere in Austria add the prefix 05226; from abroad use the prefix +43 5226

TOURIST OFFICE
t 05018 810
info@stubai.at
www.stubai.at

village level, on the other side. There are some 45km/28 miles of cross-country trails.

There are lots of 3- and 4-star hotels. The 4-star Tirolerhof (3278) is excellent – comfortable and relaxed with good food. It has a hire shop, and the owner is a qualified instructor and guide. Three 4-stars have been recommended – the central Sonnhof (2224); the Gasteigerhof in Gasteig (2746) is good for families with a pool and a children's fun area; and the Almhof-Danler (2626) has sauna, steam and hot tub.

Nightlife is focused on the Dorf and Bierfassl bars and Hully Gully and Rumpl discos. Most restaurants are hotel-based. Past recommendations include Bellafonte's pizzas and the atmospheric Hoferwirt.

Neustift has quite a lot to offer off the slopes: a good leisure centre with two pools, saunas and a bowling alley.

FULPMES 935m/3,070ft
Fulpmes (with its satellite village of Telfes) sits at the foot of Schlick 2000, the most extensive of the lower ski areas. The pretty village is said to be the sunniest in the Stubaital. It attracts few British visitors.

The ski area at Schlick 2000 sits in a sheltered bowl beneath the Sennjoch. A two-stage gondola takes you to Kreuzjoch (2135m/7,000ft), from where a series of draglifts and a quad serve a few short, mainly north-east-facing blue and red runs and a ski route. The runs suit intermediates best, are 'rarely crowded' and have some 'genuinely testing' sections. A long blue with snowmaking winds its way down the valley from the Sennjoch at 2225m/7,300ft. The main beginner area is beside the gondola mid-station at Froneben. There's also a children's area, Ronny's Kinderland, with moving carpets and fun features. Schlick 2000 is a good area for snowboarders, with a freeride zone on the Sennjoch and a terrain park lower down, at Schlickeralm. There are two schools.

There's a good choice of 3- and 4-star hotels, most with pools and spa facilities. The 4-star Stubaierhof (62266) is central, with a pool and a children's play room. A recent reporter praises the food at Café Dorfkrug.

The nearest leisure centre is in Neustift, but Fulpmes has ice skating, tobogganing and sleigh rides.

MIEDERS 980m/3,220ft
Mieders is near the entrance to the Stubai valley, 15 minutes' drive from Innsbruck. It's an unspoiled village with its own tiny area of slopes.
The slopes of Serles are limited to a couple of blues and a short red, but there are four ski routes. A gondola takes you to Kopponeck at 1680m/5,510ft, where a couple of T-bars serve the upper runs. There are a couple of mountain restaurants and 29km/18 miles of cross-country tracks above 1600m/5,250ft. The village has a small selection of hotels and guest houses.

STUBAIER GLETSCHER
3210m/10,530ft
1720m
ELFER
2080m
SCHLICK 2000
Sennjoch
2225m
Neustift
1000m/3,280ft
Schlickalm
Schlickalm
SERLES
1680m
Fulpmes
935m
Froneben
Telfes
Mieders
980m

Westendorf

This cute little village has access to a vast amount of terrain and should start attracting a lot more keen intermediates

COSTS

①②③④⑤⑥

RATINGS

The slopes
Fast lifts	**
Snow	**
Extent	****
Expert	**
Intermediate	***
Beginner	***
Convenience	***
Queues	****
Mountain restaurants	***

The rest
Scenery	***
Resort charm	****
Off-slope	**

SNOWPIX.COM / CHRIS GILL
The long run down to Kitzbühel gets the morning sun ↓

➕ Charming traditional village, with jolly if rather limited après-ski

➕ Now a proper part of the extensive SkiWelt circuit, also with access to Kitzbühel's slopes

➕ Slopes highest in the SkiWelt area

➕ Good local beginners' slopes, but ...

➖ Local slopes are mainly of genuine red gradient, with easier runs for novices to progress to confined to the lower mountain

➖ Access to Kitzbühel depends on a valley bus ride

The burghers of cute little Westendorf must think all their Christmases have arrived. Three years after the resort was effectively linked to Kitzbühel, this season it is due to get gondola and piste links with the SkiWelt – the mega area between Söll and Brixen with which it has long shared a lift pass. If you overlook a short bus ride on the Kitzbühel side, you could say Westendorf is now at the heart of one of the biggest lift-linked ski areas in the Alps.

THE RESORT

Westendorf is a small village with a charming main street and attractive onion-domed church (it was once declared 'Europe's most beautiful village' in a floral competition). The centre is close to the nursery slopes but a five-minute walk from the main gondola outside the village.

THE MOUNTAINS

The local slopes are separated by valleys from the main SkiWelt circuit to the north and from the Kitzbühel slopes to the east. From this season, a new gondola at Brixen and a piste down from Choralpe will provide a direct connection to the SkiWelt. Getting to Kitzbühel (covered by the regional Kitzbüheler Alpen pass) will still involve a bus ride.

Slopes A gondola takes you into the slopes. At mid-mountain, you can take a chair to Choralpe, for the new run to Brixen, or take the second stage of the gondola to Talkaser, then progress to the further peaks of Fleiding and Gampenkogel. The latter is the start of the long run (about 800m/2,625ft vertical) down to the valley for the bus to Skirast and the Kitzbühel lifts. All four of the peaks have other short runs to be done, mostly facing east or west. One main north-west-facing red run goes back to the resort (with blue options on the lower half). A couple of quiet, pretty runs from Fleiding go down past the lifts to hamlets served by buses – Schrandlhof and Burghof.

The piste map is the general SkiWelt one, which doesn't deal well with these slopes.

There's weekly floodlit skiing.

Terrain parks There's an excellent terrain park with something for all levels – jumps, boxes, rails and a half-pipe (www.boardplay.com).

Snow reliability Westendorf's snow reliability is a bit better than some

NEWS

Westendorf is due to be linked properly to the SkiWelt by a new gondola from Brixen up to Choralpe for 2008/09; the valley station will be linked by a bridge to the Hochbrixen gondola that accesses the main SkiWelt slopes

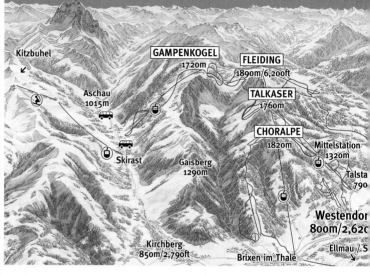

KEY FACTS

Resort	800m
	2,620ft

Westendorf only	
Slopes	800-1890m
	2,620-6,200ft
Lifts	14
Pistes	45km
	28 miles
Blue	49%
Red	40%
Black	11%
Snowmaking	40km
	25 miles

For SkiWelt	
Slopes	620-1890m
	2,030-6,200ft
Lifts	94
Pistes	250km
	155 miles
Blue	43%
Red	48%
Black	9%
Snowmaking	180km
	112 miles

UK PACKAGES

Inghams, Thomson

Phone numbers
From elsewhere in Austria add the prefix 05334; from abroad use the prefix +43 5334

TOURIST OFFICES

Westendorf
t 6230
westendorf@
kitzbuehel-alpen.com
www.kitzbuehel-alpen.
com

SkiWelt
www.skiwelt.at

other SkiWelt resorts and nearly all of its pistes now have snowmaking. Grooming is excellent, says one visitor.
Experts The slopes are among the most testing in the SkiWelt area, and we guess it's possible to have a lot of fun off-piste with a guide.
Intermediates Nearly all the local terrain is genuinely red in gradient, though some former reds have been reclassified blue. The rest of the SkiWelt area has lots of easier intermediate runs. And it's fairly easy to access Kitzbühel-Kirchberg.
Beginners Extensive village nursery slopes are Westendorf's pride and joy. There are a couple of genuine blues to progress to, but they are on the lower mountain where snow isn't so good.
Snowboarding There are some tedious catwalks at altitude locally, but lots of long, gentle runs in main SkiWelt area.
Cross-country There is a total of 170km/106 miles in the SkiWelt area but snow-cover is erratic.
Queues Given good conditions, queues are rare, and far less of a problem than in the main SkiWelt area. If poor weather closes the upper lifts, queues can become long.
Mountain restaurants Alpenrosenhütte is woody and warm, with good food. The quiet, pleasant Brechhornhaus and the Choralpe are popular. The Gassnerwirt – on the run to the bus-stop at Burghof.
Schools and guides We lack recent reports, but private lessons with the Top school have been praised and the Westendorf school has received reviews for 'excellent' instruction and good spoken English.

Facilities for children Westendorf sells itself as a family resort. The nursery and the ski kindergarten open all day.

STAYING THERE

How to go A couple of mainstream operators offer packages here.
Hotels There are central 4-star hotels: the Jakobwirt (6245) and the 'excellent' Schermer (6268) – and a dozen 3-star ones. The 3-star Post (6202) is good value, central and 'traditional and charming'. Among more modest guest houses, Haus Wetti (6348) is popular, and away from the church bells, Pension Ingeborg (6577) has been recommended – next to the gondola.
Apartments The Schermerhof apartments are of good quality.
Eating out Most of the best places are in hotels – the Schermer and Jakobwirt are good. The Wastlhof and Klingler have also been recommended, as has Berggasthof Stimlach (a taxi ride out).
Après-ski Nightlife is quite lively, but it's a small place with limited options. The Liftstüberl, at the bottom of the gondola, is packed at the end of the day. The Moskito Cafe Bar has a new funky design, but still does live music and theme nights. The Village Pub is very popular, with 'good Irish craic' and Guinness. In's Moment has been recommended for live music. The Karat is a smart lounge bar.
Off the slopes There are excursions by rail or bus to Innsbruck and Salzburg. Walks and sleigh rides are very pretty. In February, the Jump and Freeze night is recommended viewing – 'all good fun' in a party atmosphere.

Wildschönau

Wildschönau is the dramatic-sounding name for a valley with a group of family-friendly resorts, each with small areas of slopes

COSTS

①②③④⑤⑥

RATINGS

The slopes

Fast lifts	**
Snow	**
Extent	*
Expert	*
Intermediate	**
Beginner	***
Convenience	***
Queues	***
Mountain restaurants	**

The rest

Scenery	***
Resort charm	***
Off-slope	**

KEY FACTS

Resort	830m
	2,720ft
Slopes	830-1905m
	2,720-6,250ft
Lifts	26
Pistes	70km
	43 miles
Blue	21%
Red	62%
Black	17%
Snowmaking	30km
	19 miles

Oberau has nursery slopes and a short black run ↓

- 🞥 Traditional, family-friendly villages
- 🞥 Good nursery slopes at Niederau and Oberau
- 🞥 Jolly après-ski scene

- 🗖 Three separate ski areas, linked by ski-buses
- 🗖 Each area has limited slopes
- 🗖 Natural snow reliability not the best (but extensive snowmaking)

Niederau, Oberau and Auffach are contrasting villages with contrasting small areas of slopes on a shared lift pass. The area best suits families and those looking for a friendly, relaxing holiday rather than hitting the slopes non-stop.

THE RESORT

Niederau has long been a favourite resort with British beginner and early intermediate skiers. It is the main resort in the Wildschönau and is quite spread out, with a cluster of restaurants and shops around the gondola station forming the nearest thing to a focal point. But few hotels are more than five minutes' walk from a main lift.

Auffach, 7km/4 miles away, is a smaller, quieter, attractive old village and has the area's highest and most extensive slopes.

On a low col between the two is **Oberau** – almost as big as Niederau and the valley's administrative and cultural centre.

The villages are unspoiled, with traditional chalet-style buildings. Roads are quiet, except on Saturdays, and the valley setting is lovely.

THE MOUNTAINS

Niederau's slopes are spread over a wooded mountainside that rises to only 1600m/5,250ft. The slopes at Auffach continue above the treeline.
Slopes The main lifts from Niederau are an eight-person gondola to Markbachjoch and, new for 2008/09, a fast quad a few minutes' walk away. Above the quad is a steep drag to the high point of Lanerköpfl. Beginner runs at the bottom of the mountain are served by several short draglifts. The whole area is very small – you can ski most of it in an hour or two. There's a sizeable 'Race 'n' Boarder Arena'; races are run here, but you can also take race-training lessons.

A reliable free bus goes to Auffach. Its sunny, east-facing area, consisting almost entirely of red runs, goes up to Schatzberg, with a vertical of 1000m/3,28oft. The main lift up is a two-stage gondola and two six-packs serve the

top runs on open slopes – an impressive set-up. Again the area is very small – the top chairs serve verticals of under 300m/980ft.

The Kitzbüheler Alpen Skipass covers resorts in the Schneewinkel, Kitzbühel ski region, SkiWelt and Alpbachtal as well.

Terrain parks There's a 90m/300ft half-pipe and a terrain park with a quarter-pipe, jumps, wave and fun-box served by a draglift on Schatzberg.

Snow reliability The low altitude means that natural snow reliability is relatively poor. But almost 40% of the pistes have snowmaking, including the main runs down at both Niederau and Auffach from top to bottom, and more is planned for 2008/09. And Auffach has most of its runs above mid-mountain, making for more reliable snow there than at Niederau. Grooming is good.

Experts The several black pistes are short and not severe. We skied the main black piste from the bottom of the draglift below Lanerköpfl to Niederau when it was well groomed and thought it great for fast carving, but of almost blue gradient for much of its length. There are a couple of ungroomed, unpatrolled ski routes at Niederau, which were bumpy and had patchy snow when we skied them. There are proper off-piste routes to be found, too – including the Gern route, which is marked on the piste map, from the top of Schatzberg down a

deserted valley to the road a little way from Auffach.

Intermediates Niederau's red runs generally merit their status but there's no blue run from top to bottom. The main black piste mentioned above is enjoyable, but the blue to reach it is just a path. Auffach has more intermediate terrain, with several short reds at the top (and a new run promised for this season), and the long main piste from the top to the village is attractive. But all this does not add up to very much – keen intermediate piste-bashers will be able to ski it all in a day. The slopes are best suited to confident but leisurely intermediates who are happy to take it easy and have a relaxing holiday.

Beginners There are excellent nursery slopes at the top and bottom of Niederau's main slopes, but the low ones don't get much sun in midwinter. Auffach has nursery slopes near the gondola mid-station. Oberau has its own nursery slopes, with a short black run above them, but there is a lack of really easy longer runs to progress to.

Snowboarding It's best for intermediates here. The number of draglifts may deter novices.

Cross-country There are 50km/31 miles of trails along the valley, which are good when snow is abundant.

Queues One reporter said: 'Very little queueing.' Another complained of queues for the Niederau gondola. We saw long queues for the beginner

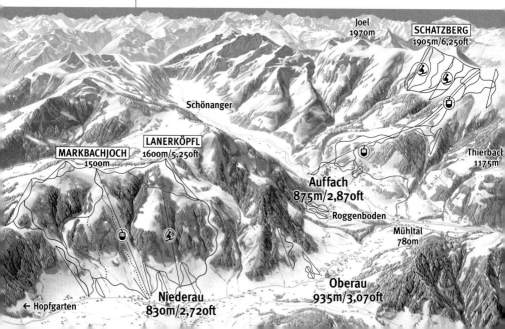

Joel
1970m

SCHATZBERG
1905m/6,250ft

Schönanger

LANERKÖPFL
1600m/5,250ft

MARKBACHJOCH
1500m

Thierbach
1175m

Auffach
875m/2,870ft

Roggenboden

Mühltal
780m

← Hopfgarten

Niederau
830m/2,720ft

Oberau
935m/3,070ft

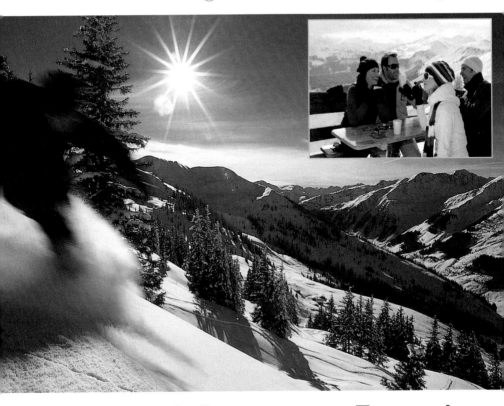

↑ Niederau and its small ski area best suits families and those looking for a relaxing time
TVB WILDSCHÖNAU

UK PACKAGES

Niederau *Airtours, Directski.com, First Choice, Inghams, Neilson, Ski McNeill, Thomson* **Oberau** *First Choice, Inghams, Interhome, Neilson*

Phone numbers
From elsewhere in Austria add the prefix 05339; from abroad use the prefix +43 5339

TOURIST OFFICE

t 8255
info@wildschoenau.com
www.wildschoenau.com

draglifts; these should have eased after a new beginner lift was built a couple of years ago. And pressure on the gondola should be eased by the new fast quad built for this season (see 'News').

Mountain restaurants These are good but can get very busy. Many people lunch in the villages.

Schools and guides The ski schools have good reputations both for English and for teaching beginners, and a reporter raved about his beginner lessons. But note that classes can be large.

Facilities for children The kindergarten and nursery take kids from age two.

STAYING THERE

How to go There are a number of attractive hotels and guest houses in the three main villages – many with pools. Several major British tour operators run packages to Niederau and Oberau.

Hotels In Niederau the 4-star Sonnschein (8353) and the Austria (8188) are central recommendations. Pension Diane (8562) is close to the main lift and 'a really good place and good value', says a recent visitor. (The owner is a local by birth, but spent 13 years working in Birmingham.) The Vicky, run by Thomson, has 'friendly staff, excellent food, brilliant nursery', says a reporter. The 3-star Kellerwirt (8116) in Oberau dates from 1745 and was highly recommended by a recent reporter ('comfort, character, excellent food'). But bear in mind that you are distant from both major areas of slopes if based here.

Eating out The restaurants at the hotels Alpenland and Wastlhof in Niederau have been recommended.

Après-ski Niederau has a nice balance of après-ski – neither too noisy for families nor too quiet for the young and lively. The Heustadl bar is very popular at the end of the day. The Cave bar/disco ('great spot, very friendly and lively') is popular later on. The Almbar has become O'Malleys Irish Pub and has live music every night. The Drift-Inn at hotel Vicky has also been recommended. Cafe Treff is an internet cafe.

The other villages are quieter, once the tea-time jollity is over for the night – though Oberau claims a pub with disco music.

Off the slopes There are excellent sleigh rides, horse-riding trips and 40km/25 miles of organised walks as well as the Slow Train Wildschönau – on wheels not rails – which offers varied excursions. There are a couple of local museums. Several of the Niederau hotel swimming pools are open to the public. There's a long toboggan run at Auffach, from the mid-station of the gondola down to the bottom – a distance of 5km/3miles – and there's a guided trip on Sundays from Schatzberg to Thierbach. (Off-piste tobogganing, eh? The mind boggles.) Floodlit tobogganing is also organised twice-weekly at Oberau. Excursions to Innsbruck are possible.

Zell am See

A real one-off, this: a charming lakeside town, with varied local slopes and a very worthwhile glacier option nearby at Kaprun

COSTS

① ② ③ ④ ⑤ ⑥

RATINGS

The slopes

Fast lifts	★★★
Snow	★★
Extent	★★
Expert	★★
Intermediate	★★★
Beginner	★★★
Convenience	★★
Queues	★★
Mountain restaurants	★★★

The rest

Scenery	★★★
Resort charm	★★★
Off-slope	★★★★

NEWS

For 2008/09 more snowmaking is due at Zell am See.

For 2007/08 an eight-seat gondola, TrassXpress, opened at Schmittental, relieving pressure on the nearby cable cars. And a six-pack with covers replaced the Breiteck triple chair that meets the top of the new gondola – just below the summit of Schmittenhöhe.

On Kaprun's glacier, a six-pack with covers replaced an old T-bar above the Alpincenter, serving another 4km/2.5 miles of new blue pistes. And the children's adventure park gained a moving carpet.

➕ Pretty, treelined slopes with great views down to the lake

➕ Lively, but not rowdy, nightlife

➕ Charming old town centre with beautiful lakeside setting

➕ Lots to do off the slopes

➕ Huge range of cross-country trails

➕ Kaprun glacier nearby

➕ Varied terrain including a couple of genuine black runs

➖ Sunny, low slopes often have poor conditions, despite snowmaking

➖ Very limited area, especially when lower slopes are in poor shape

➖ Many hotels are distant from the lifts, and buses can be crowded

➖ Less suitable for beginners than most small Austrian resorts

➖ The Kaprun glacier gets lengthy queues when it is most needed

Zell am See is not a rustic village like most of its Austrian rivals, but a lakeside summer resort town with a charming old centre. Its prominence on the UK market probably has more to do with abundant hotel accommodation than with the merits of its ski area; although varied and in places challenging, it is very limited in extent, especially when snow low down is poor.

Kaprun and its Kitzsteinhorn glacier are nearby; it makes a great day out – unless snow is generally in short supply, when queues grow and grow.

THE RESORT

Zell am See is a long-established, year-round resort town set between a large lake and the mountain. Its charming, traffic-free medieval centre occupies a flat promontory.

A gondola at the edge of town goes up the southern arm of the horseshoe-shaped mountain. You can also stay at Schmittental, in the centre of the horseshoe (2km/1 mile west of Zell) where there are two cable cars and a newish gondola. Another alternative is to stay 3km/2 miles south of Zell in Schüttdorf, where there is another gondola and large car park. But it is a characterless and lifeless dormitory with little else going for it. Cross-country skiers and families wishing to use the Areitalm nursery stand to gain most from staying in Schüttdorf – and perhaps those with a car planning multiple outings to Kaprun.

Kaprun's snow-sure glacier slopes are only a few minutes by crowded buses; getting on in Schüttdorf can be a particular problem. The slopes can be crowded too; one 2007 reporter 'gave up and went back to Zell'.

Saalbach is easily reached by bus, Hochkönig less so. Rauris is worth a look. Bad Hofgastein is not far, and you can get into the Kitzbühel slopes from Hollersbach, near Mittersill.

THE MOUNTAINS

Zell's horseshoe-shaped mountain is open at the top, mostly densely wooded lower down.

THE SLOPES
Varied but limited

Gondolas from Zell and Schüttdorf go up along the southern arm of the horseshoe to Schmittenhöhe, meeting the gondola from Schmittental. The several lifts on the back of the hill and on the sunny slopes of the northern arm are accessed via Schmittenhöhe or by riding another cable car from Schmittental to Sonnalm.

Black runs descend from various points to Schmittental; intermediate runs go down the southern arm to Zell and Schüttdorf.

KEY FACTS

Resort	755m
	2,480ft

Zell and Kaprun

Slopes	755-3030m
	2,480-9,940ft
Lifts	55
Pistes	136km
	85 miles
Blue	42%
Red	35%
Black	23%
Snowmaking	94km
	58 miles

Zell (Schmittenhöhe) only

Slopes	755-2000m
	2,480-6,560ft
Lifts	27
Pistes	77km
	48 miles

Kaprun only

Slopes	785-3030m
	2,580-9,940ft
Lifts	28
Pistes	59km
	37 miles

LIFT PASSES

Kaprun–Zell am See

Prices in €

Age	1-day	6-day
under 16	19	92
16 to 18	31	147
over 19	39	184
Free	under 6	
Senior	no deals	
Beginner	limited pass	

Notes
Covers Zell and Kaprun; one-day price is for Schmittenhöhe (Zell) only

Alternative passes
Kitzsteinhorn only and Maiskogel only; Salzburg Super Ski Card covers a huge area round Salzburg province and is available for three days or more

TERRAIN PARKS
Head for the City
There's a half-pipe and the Jumping City terrain park on Schmittenhöhe.

SNOW RELIABILITY
Good snowmaking, but sunny
Zell am See's slopes can be badly affected by the sun. Over 70% of pistes are now covered by snow-guns, including all the runs to the valley and mostly top-to-bottom. More is planned for 2008/09. But holidays can still be marred by slush, ice and bare patches. The Kaprun glacier is snow-sure, but oversubscribed when snow is short in the region. Grooming is good.

FOR EXPERTS
Several blacks, but still limited
Zell has more black runs than most resorts this size, but they are not seriously steep and are usually groomed. The winding, shady runs down to Schmittental are great fun if the snow is good, quite challenging if it's hard. Off-piste opportunities are limited, but there is a nice 'glade' area on the back of the hill, under the Gipfelbahn chairlift.

FOR INTERMEDIATES
Bits and pieces for most grades
Good intermediates have a couple of fine, long runs, but this is not a place for high mileage. The blacks are within a confident intermediate's capability unless icy. The red home run to Schüttdorf is great when conditions are good, but a struggle for many at the end of a warm day. The wide Sonnkogel runs are relatively quiet – great for carving. The timid can cruise the southern ridge blues.

Kaprun's high, snow-sure glacier runs are also ideal for intermediates.

FOR BEGINNERS
Two low nursery areas
There are small nursery slopes (which can be crowded) at Schmittental and at Schüttdorf, both covered by snow-guns. There are short, easy runs at Schmittenhöhe, Areitalm and Breiteckalm (some used by complete beginners when snow conditions are poor, but it means buying a lift pass).

FOR CROSS-COUNTRY
Excellent if snow allows
The valley floor has extensive areas and at altitude there are short loops, above Zell and on the Kitzsteinhorn,

making a total of 30km/19 miles, with 18km/11 miles on the Kaprun golf course. There are specialist centres at Schüttdorf and at Kaprun.

QUEUES
Valley problems easing
Despite lots of fast lifts, queues to get out of the valley in the morning have always been a problem – we've had reports of a 40-minute wait for the gondola out of Schüttdorf and lengthy waits for the Zell and Schmittental lifts. But recent investment seems to be easing the situation. The new gondola from Schmittental has relieved pressure there, and once you are on the mountain, there aren't many problems. When snow is poor there are few daytime queues at Zell – many people are away queueing at Kaprun. Reporters regularly complain about the buses back from Kaprun – 'chaotic – a heaving mass, all scrambling and fighting to get on'.

MOUNTAIN RESTAURANTS
Plenty of little refuges
There are plenty of cosy, atmospheric huts dotted around the Zell slopes, helpfully named on the piste map. Among the best are Glocknerhaus, Kettingalm, Areitalm ('gets busy'), Breiteckalm and Blaickner's Sonnalm. Pinzgauer Hütte, in the woods behind Schmittenhöhe, is regularly

SCHOOLS

Zell am See
t 56020

Sport Alpin
t 0664 453 1417

Snowboard Academy
t 0664 253 0381

Classes
(Zell prices)
5 days (2hr am and pm) €154

Private lessons
€56 for 1 hr; €10 for each additional person

GUIDES

Ski Safari
t 0664 336 1487

CHILDREN

Kinderskiwelt Areit
t 56020
From age 2; with ski lessons for over 3s

Babysitter list
At the tourist office

Ski schools
From age 4 (5 days €154 – Zell price)

boarding

Zell is well suited to boarders and most lifts are chairs, gondolas or cable cars. You'll also find plenty of life in the evenings. The Kaprun glacier has powder in its wide, open bowl. But it also has a fair proportion of draglifts (though they are gradually being replaced) – a day of this and the 'small walk' to enter the main terrain park exhausted some reporters. Snowboard Academy is a specialist school.

recommended by reporters ('superb'); snowmobiles will tow you back to the lifts ('great fun'). The Schmiedhofalm has 'great views' and serves regional specialities ('best Tirolean pancake we've had'). The Berghotel at Schmittenhöhe is good, but expensive. Its bar with loud music is lively in the afternoons (see 'Après-ski'). The Panorama-Pfiff gets crowded, but 'has wonderful views'. The Ebenbergalm just above the town has 'excellent home cooked food'.

SCHOOLS AND GUIDES
A wide choice
There is a choice of schools. We get few reports, but one speaks of 'excellent' lessons with a 'delightful instructor' at the main Zell school. Groups are said to be quite large.

FACILITIES FOR CHILDREN
Schüttdorf's the place
We have no recent reports on the child care provisions, but staying in

Schüttdorf has the advantage of direct gondola access to the Areitalm snow-kindergarten. There's a children's adventure-park on the mountain.

STAYING THERE

HOW TO GO
Choose charm or convenience
Lots of hotels, pensions and apartments.
Hotels A broad range of hotels (more 4- than 3-stars) and guest houses.
*****Salzburgerhof (7650) Best in town; pool. It's nearer the lake than the gondola, but has a courtesy bus.
****Feinschmeck (725490) Fine traditional hotel in good position in the pedestrian core of Zell.
****Freiberg (72643) 'Fantastic' lakeside setting. 'Great views, excellent food, service and spa,' says a 2008 visitor. Minibus to the lifts.
****Lebzelter (7760) In pedestrian area. 'Friendly and welcoming; good sports bar.'

233

****Schloss Prielau** (72911) 'Superb' converted castle on the outskirts of town, but with a shuttle-bus service. Highly rated by a 2008 visitor. ****Tirolerhof** (7720) In the old town. Pool, hot tub, steam room. 'Very comfortable; friendly, efficient staff.' ****Zum Hirschen** (7740) Comfortable. Easy walk to Zell gondola. Sauna, steam room, splash pool, popular bar. ***Margarete** (72660) B&B at Schmittental, by the cable cars. ***Villa Klothilde** (72660) 'Family run, friendly, clean and comfortable.' On the slopes two minutes' walk from town.

Apartments Lots of options. Lederer is close to the Ebenberg lift. More central are Diana and Seilergasse.

EATING OUT
Plenty of choice
Zell has more non-hotel places than is usual in a small Austrian resort. Giuseppe's is an Italian with excellent food. Kupferkessel and Traubenstüberl both do wholesome regional dishes. Mayer's (beside the Schloss Prielau hotel) is 'amazing but pricey'. There are Chinese restaurants in Zell and Schüttdorf. Car drivers can try the excellent Erlhof at Thumersbach.

APRES-SKI
Plenty for all tastes
Après-ski is lively and varied, with cafes, bars and discos aplenty. When it's sunny, the ice bar outside the Berghotel, up at Schmittenhöhe, really buzzes, with live music and dancing. The Pinzgauer Diele club rocks – 'younger crowd but fun'. Villa Crazy Daisy has three lively bars. Greens XL has a live band and 60s and 70s music. The Mem bar is new at Giuseppe's. Two 2008 visitors enjoyed the 'trendy' Insider bar. The B17 Hangar bar ('cracking cocktails and a party buzz') and Our's Lounge ('relaxed vibe with big sofas') are both popular. The 'excellent' Viva disco allows no under 18s. Or try the smart Hirschenkeller, the 'classy' Ginhouse, the cave-like Lebzelter Keller and the Sportstüberl, with nostalgic ski photos on the walls.

OFF THE SLOPES
Lots of choices
There is plenty to do in this year-round resort. The train trip to Salzburg is a must, Kitzbühel is also well worth a visit and Innsbruck is within reach.

You can often walk across the frozen lake to Thumersbach, plus there are good sports facilities, a motor museum, sleigh rides, Alpine flights and you can watch ice hockey. There are marked paths at Schmittenhöhe.

STAYING UP THE MOUNTAIN
Several options
As well as the Berghotel (72489) at the Schmittenhöhe cable car, the Breiteckalm (73419), Blaikner's Sonnalm (73262) and Pinzgauer Hütte (53472) restaurants have rooms.

Kaprun 785m/2,580ft

Apart from providing Zell's snow guarantee, Kaprun is a worthwhile destination in its own right.

THE RESORT
Kaprun is a pleasant and quite lively village, bypassed by the road up to the glacier. It sprawls over a considerable area, so it's worth staying centrally to get the best out of it.

THE MOUNTAIN
There is a small area of easy intermediate slopes on the outskirts of the village at **Maiskogel**, served by five lifts, including a cable car, a six-pack and fast quad. There is also a separate nursery area. But most people will want to spend most of their time on the slopes of the nearby **Kitzsteinhorn** glacier or on Zell am See's slopes. Buses to and from both are often crowded at peak times – it's worth timing your trips carefully. The lift pass covers only one ascent of the Kitzsteinhorn access gondola per day.
Slopes A 15-person, two-stage gondola goes up to the Alpincenter and main slopes. The first stage runs parallel to an older eight-seat gondola and the second stage parallel to a fast quad chair. The main slopes are in a big bowl above the Alpincenter, served by a cable car, lots of T-bars and four chairs (including a six-pack). The area above the top of the Alpincenter is open in summer and is particularly good for an early pre-Christmas or late post-Easter break.
Terrain parks There are three on the Kitzsteinhorn. The main one, Gletscher Park, is open all year round.
Snow reliability Snow is nearly always good because of the glacier. And there's snowmaking too.
Queues Queues have always been a

Phone numbers
From elsewhere in Austria add the prefix 06542 (Zell), 06547 (Kaprun), 06544 (Rauris); from abroad use the prefix +43 and omit the initial '0'

TOURIST OFFICE

Zell am See/Kaprun
t 770
welcome@zellamsee-kaprun.com
www.zellamsee-kaprun.com

Rauris
t 20022
info@raurisertal.at
www.raurisertal.at

A quiet (January) day on the Kitzsteinhorn; in the distance, the wooded mountain is Zell's Schmitten; the Zeller See is under the valley fog ↓

problem here, in spring at least. Some reports tell of 10- to 15-minute waits for most of the lifts; though one lucky visitor reports few queues on his March 2008 visit. High winds may shut the top lifts, increasing crowds lower down the slopes.

Mountain restaurants There are some decent ones. The Gletschermühle near the Alpincenter has 'awesome views' and a 'good selection'. The Krefelder Hütte below it is a genuine mountain refuge. The Häusalm near the gondola mid-station has also been recommended. Bella Vista at the top of the mountain has good views and is 'reasonably priced'.

Experts There's little to challenge experts on-piste – the blacks are not steep, and groomed when we last visited – but some good off-piste possibilities.

Intermediates Pistes are mainly gentle blues and reds, and make for great easy cruising. From Alpincenter there is an entertaining red run down to the gondola mid-station, away from the lifts. There's a good unpisted ski route.

Beginners There are two nursery slopes in the village and some gentle blues on the glacier to progress to.

Snowboarding Intermediates and better will love the wide open powder bowl. Beginners may find there are too many T-bars for their liking.

Cross-country The 18km/11 miles of trails on the Kaprun golf course are good, but at altitude there is just one short loop – at the top of the glacier.

Schools and guides There are several.

Facilities for children All the schools offer children's classes and there's a kindergarten in the village.

STAYING THERE

How to go There are some catered chalets and chalet hotels. The new Dorfkrug apartments are recommended ('cosy, traditional').

Hotels The 4-star Orgler (8205) and Tauernhof (8235), and 'spacious' 3-star Mitteregger (8207) are probably the best bets.

Eating out Good restaurants include the Dorfstadl, Hilberger's Beisl and Schlemmerstube.

Après-ski Nightlife is quiet, but the Baum bar is lively. The Kitsch & Bitter has 'great live music and cocktails'.

Off the slopes There's a sports centre with outdoor rapids. A visitor enjoyed the 'rustic' bowling at the Sportsbar.

TIROLER ZUGSPITZ ARENA

Zugspitz Arena

Half a dozen family-friendly little resorts sharing a lift pass and (to a degree) spectacular views of the Zugspitze

COSTS

① ② ③ ④ ⑤ ⑥

NEWS

For 2007/08 the lift up from Bichlbach to Hochalm above Berwang was replaced by the Tirol's first hybrid chair/gondola (chondola), mixing six-seat chairs with eight-seat bubbles.

KEY FACTS

Resorts	990-1340m	
	3,250-4,400ft	
Slopes	990-2960m	
	3,250-9,710ft	
Lifts		50
Pistes		147km
		91 miles
Blue		55%
Red		40%
Black		5%
Snowmaking		75km
		47 miles

236

Zugspitz Arena is the name adopted by a group of small villages in the Tirol just to the west of the mighty Wetterstein massif, which forms the border with Germany. They appeal particularly to families, who will be happy with limited and mainly gentle ski areas. As you can see from the pictures in the chapter, there is the bonus of spectacular scenery.

Three of the Zugspitz Arena villages – Ehrwald, Lermoos and Biberwier – sit around the edge of a little plain, the Lermooser Moos, from which the Wetterstein massif rises dramatically 2000m/6,560ft to the peak of the Zugspitze. There is skiing on the Zugspitze itself, on glacier slopes on the German side of the border but accessible via a spectacular cable car from the Austrian side, and each of the villages has its local slopes too. The other villages operating under the Zugspitz Arena banner – Berwang and Bichlbach – are a few miles to the west of the Moos.

The Zugspitz Arena lift pass covers 50 lifts and 147km/91 miles of pistes. There is also a more extensive pass – the Happy Ski Card – which also covers Seefeld and Garmisch (on the German side of the Zugspitze). Garmisch has its own lifts up to the Zugspitze (including a cog railway), and worthwhile slopes lower down on the shady side of the Wetterstein.

There are also over 100km/62 miles of cross-country trails in the Zugspitz Arena area, with the potential to string together some long days. And 60km/37 miles of cleared footpaths.

EHRWALD 1000m/3,280ft
Ehrwald is a pleasant village set right under the towering western wall of the Wetterstein massif, with easy access to three small ski areas.
There are two separate ski areas starting at valley level – Wetterstein and Ehrwalder Alm. Ehrwald is also the nearest village to the cable car up to the Zugspitze slopes.

The gentle **Wetterstein** slopes directly above the village are accessed by draglifts from the village fringes, linking to the main Wetterstein triple chairlift, slightly further out. The runs total only 10km/6 miles, with a top height of 1530m/5,020ft and a longest run of under 500m/1,640ft vertical. There's a 120m/390ft half-pipe.

Although it's a tiny area, there are three restaurants, all with some après-ski as well as lunchtime animation.

The **Ehrwalder Alm** slopes on the sunny side of the Wetterstein massif are accessed by an eight-seat gondola starting just outside the village. Ehrwalder Alm is at the heart of a modest area served by two six-packs, an old double chair and some short draglifts. There's a blue run back down the gondola. Start from the top of the

Zugspitze
2960m/9,710ft

Sonnenspitze
2410m/7,910ft

ZUGSPITZPLATT

MARIENBERG

Eibsee-Seilbahn

Issentalkopf
1900m

EHRWALDER ALM

GRUBIGSTEIN

BERWANGERTAL

Biberwier
990m/3,250ft

Berwang
1340m/4,400ft

WETTERSTEIN

Tiroler
Zugspitzbahn

Obermoos
1225m/4,020ft

Ehrwald
1000m/3,280ft

Lermoos
1005m/3,300ft

Bichlbach
1080m/3,540ft

Heiterwang
995m/3,260ft

area and you get a run of 7km/4 miles (and over 800m/2,620ft vertical) to the base station. The runs total 26km/16 miles, mostly blue. Half the area has snowmaking, including the valley run.

The terrain park in the centre of the slopes has easy, medium and pro lines of rails, boxes and kickers.

A couple of miles outside the village in the opposite direction, a spectacular cable car climbs an impressive 1725m/5,660ft up to the peak of the **Zugspitze**; then another cable car takes you down to the slopes of the Zugspitzplatt, where there are half a dozen drags and one six-seater chairlift. None of these lifts rises more than 350m/1,150ft vertical, and the blue and red slopes they serve are gentle. The longest approaches 3km/2 miles in length. There's a self-service rustic restaurant with a big terrace and 'umbrella' bar, and another hut for drinks and snacks.

The Zugspitze is the highest mountain in Germany, and a major tourist attraction, with a museum at the peak as well as a restaurant.

There are two ski schools, Ehrwald Total and Intersport Tiroler.

Accommodation in the village is dominated by 4-star hotels, but there are plenty of cheaper alternatives.

You can stay right at the base of the Zugspitze cable car. The 4-star Ferienanlage Tiroler Zugspitze (2309) offers spacious family apartments as well as hotel rooms. It has an extensive spa with swimming pool.

Twice a week the 3.6km/2 mile home run from Ehrwalder Alm is floodlit for evening tobogganing, and the restaurants at the top and halfway down are kept open.

The Zugspitz Arena FamilienBad is a big, bright leisure centre with multiple pools, gym and massage.

LERMOOS 1005m/3,300ft

Directly across the Moos from the Zugspitze, Lermoos and its slopes – arguably the best in the Zugspitz Arena area – offer great views of the dramatic Zugspitze.

Lermoos has lifts on the north-east-facing slopes of Grubigstein, a mainly wooded peak rising about 1000m above the village. The top height of 2060m/6,760ft, shady orientation and snowmaking on about two-thirds of the slopes means that (apart from the glacial Zugspitze) this is the most

TIROLER ZUGSPITZ ARENA

Lermoos has the best slope network in the area, on Grubigstein
↓

Zugspitz Arena

Interactive resort shortlist builder at **www.wtss.co.uk**

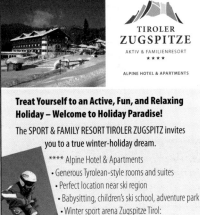

↑ Ehrwald sits right under the hugely impressive Zugspitze
TIROLER ZUGSPITZ ARENA

UK PACKAGES
Berwang First Choice
Lermoos Interhome

Phone numbers
From elsewhere in Austria add the prefix 05673; from abroad use the prefix +43 5673

TOURIST OFFICE
Zugspitze
t 20000
info@zugspitzarena.com
www.zugspitzarena.com

snow-sure of the local areas. The slopes total 33km/21 miles, about half blue; there are three short blacks, and the rest are red. You can descend the whole mountain, top to bottom, on red or blue runs.

Lermoos is a slightly more compact, towny place than Ehrwald, more tightly focused on the main street running through it. (This was an important thoroughfare until Fernpass traffic was banished to a tunnel in the 1980s.)

There are several 3-star hotels, but notably two 'superior' 4-star hotels, which are quite different in style but equally impressive. The hotel Post (22810) is an ancient inn, greatly expanded over the years and entirely revamped a couple of years back. It now offers 60 suites, and the facilities include a swanky 2,000m² spa. The terrace has the perfect view across the Moos to the Zugspitze. In the nearby Post Schlössl – a listed historical monument dating from the 16th century – there are 17 apartments of various sizes and styles. The Leading Family Hotel & Resort Alpenrose (2424) is an amazing place for families – it is indeed a resort in itself, with a 1000m² indoor play area among countless facilities.

At Grubigalm (1710m/5,610ft) there's a fun park (called NTC) with tubing, snow scooters and various other diversions. A 3km/2 mile toboggan run goes from Brettalm (1330m/4,360ft) to the valley. There's skating and curling on a natural open-air rink.

BIBERWIER 990m/3,250ft
The third of the villages around the Moos, Biberwier is set in the valley leading up to the Fernpass, with its own small area of slopes.
The mainly shady Marienberg slopes total 14km/9 miles, more or less equally split into blue and red, with over a third protected by snowmaking. A six-pack serves a long blue slope at the bottom; a double chair up to 1675m/5,500ft serves red runs above that; and on the back of the hill a drag serves a sunny slope from the top height of 1880m/6,170ft. Back at the base, the beginner lifts include an exceptionally long magic carpet. There's a half-pipe, and an NTC fun park as at Lermoos. At altitude there are a couple of pleasant restaurants, and an umbrella bar next to the nursery slopes.

Like Lermoos, the village benefits from the tunnel keeping Fernpass traffic out of the centre. The best base is the solid old gasthof Goldenen-Löwen (2293). There's a curling rink.

BICHLBACH 1080m/3,540ft
Bichlbach is a quiet valley village with fast lift access to the slopes of higher Berwang (described next).
On the fringes of Bichlbach, the Tirol's first hybrid chair/gondola lift goes up to Hochalm (1610m/5,280ft), for access to Berwang. You can ski to it from the top of the village nursery slope. There's a short, easy toboggan run, and a natural open-air ice rink.

TOURIST OFFICES

Berwang
t 20000 400
info@berwang.at
www.berwang.at

Biberwier
t 20000
biberwier@
zugspitzarena.com
www.tiscover.at/
biberwier

Bichlbach
t 20000 500
bichlbach@
zugspitzarena.com
www.bichlbach.at

Ehrwald
t 20000 208
ehrwald@
zugspitzarena.com
www.ehrwald.com

Heiterwang
t 20000 700
heiterwang@
zugspitzarena.com

Lermoos
t 20000 300
info@lermoos.at
www.lermoos.at

BERWANG 1335m/4,380ft
Berwang is a quiet village tucked away in a slightly elevated valley, about 350m/1,150ft higher than the other villages in the region. It claims the most skiing, but most of the runs are short as well as easy.

The slopes total 40km/25 miles, making this the most extensive network in the area on paper, but some of the blue runs are more like cross-country than downhill pistes, and the few reds and occasional black don't offer a genuine challenge.

The compact village has lifts rising on two sides, and slopes running down the very gentle valley. On the sunny side, the Sonnalmbahn quad chair goes up to Hochalm where it meets the chondola up from Bichlbach; the shady runs to Bichlbach are about the best in the local area, giving over 500m/1,640ft vertical to the lift base station. All the runs from Hochalm have snowmaking. Across the village, drags go up the shady side. Runs down the valley dropping only about 50m/164ft in 1.5km/1 mile bring you to further lifts, including the Panoramabahn double chairlift to the area high-point at 1740m/5,710ft. From here there are runs of 450m/1,480ft vertical to Rinnen, and ski routes to Brand. There are plenty of restaurants on the slopes.

The cross-country loops up here (totalling 25km/16 miles) are separate from those down in the main valley, and to our untutored eye look a bit more challenging.

There are three 4-star hotels, four 3-stars and lots of guest houses. The 4-star Kaiserhof (8285) is a giant family-oriented chalet-style place with pools and spa. There's a 1.5km/1 mile toboggan run dropping 120m/390ft from Jägerhaus to Berwang, open most evenings; and skating and curling on a natural open-air rink. There are lots of local footpaths.

HEITERWANG 995m/3,260ft
Another valley-level base for access to the Berwang slopes.

Heiterwang is a little way down the valley from Bichlbach, a short drive or bus ride from the chondola up to the Berwang slopes. It's near a sizeable lake and is a major cross-country centre (venue for the 2006 Austrian championships). There are a couple of short local downhill slopes, too.

France

Over one-third of British skiers and snowboarders choose France for their holidays each year, almost double the number who go to Austria, the next most popular country. It's not difficult to see what attracts us to France. The country has the biggest lift and piste networks in the world; for those who like to cover as many miles in a day as possible, these are unrivalled. Most of these big areas are also at high altitude, ensuring high-quality snow for a long season. And French mountains offer a mixture of some of the toughest, wildest slopes in the Alps and some of the longest, gentlest and most convenient beginner runs.

French resort villages can't be quite so uniformly recommended; but, equally, they don't all conform to the standard image of soulless, purpose-built service stations, thrown up without concern for appearance during the boom of the 1960s and 1970s. Many resorts are based on more traditional villages, or have such places on the fringes of their slopes. Another advantage of smaller villages and less well-known resorts is that they tend to be cheaper. Some of the big-name resorts can now be very expensive – none more so than Courchevel 1850, where you can pay quite silly prices for hotel rooms, food and drink. In the light of the strong euro, prices in Alpine countries have risen in terms of pounds. One advantage that France has is that lots of British tour operators run chalets there. Staying in a chalet means you don't have to worry about extras like drinks and wine with dinner.

Towards the front of the book there is a special chapter on driving to the French Alps – still very popular, especially with people going self-catering, despite the growth of the budget airlines. The French Alps are easy to get to by car, and luxurious apartments are becoming more common as property developers see the market opportunities.

ANY STYLE OF RESORT YOU LIKE

← France has quite a few 1960s purpose-built resorts, but there are prettier bases too; and places like Les Menuires (pictured here) are trying hard to smarten up their appearance

The main drawback to France, hinted at above, is the monstrous architecture of some of the purpose-built resorts. But not all French resorts are hideous. Certainly, France has its fair share of Alpine eyesores, chief among them central Les Menuires, central La Plagne, Flaine, Tignes, Isola 2000 and Les Arcs. But all these places have learned from past mistakes, and newer developments there are being built in a much more attractive, traditional chalet style. In Les Menuires, they have even knocked down a couple of the original hideous buildings (as we advised them to do ten editions ago) and replaced them with tasteful wood and stone structures.

Château d'Oex · Gstaad · Adelboden
Lenk
THONON · Leysin · Leukerbad
La Chapelle-d'Abondance · Les Diablerets · Crans-Montana
GENEVA · Villars · Anzère · SIERRE · VISP
Châtel · Morgins
Morzine · Avoriaz · Champéry · Nendaz · SION
Les Gets · SWITZERLAND
Praz-de-Lys · Morillon · Verbier
Samoëns · MARTIGNY · Saas Fee
Les Carroz · Zermatt
Flaine · Le Tour
Le Chinaillon · Le Grand-Bornand · Argentière
ANNECY · Chamonix · Cervinia
La Clusaz · Combloux · Les Houches · Mt Blanc
Praz · Le Bettex · St-Gervais · tunnel · Valtournenche
-sur- · St Nicolas · Gressoney-la-Trinité
Notre-Dame-de- · Megève · MONT · Champoluc
Bellecombe · Les Contamines · BLANC · Courmayeur
Les Saisies · AOSTA
ALBERTVILLE · Arèches · La Thuile
La Rosière
CHAMBÉRY · Bourg-St-Maurice · Villaroger
AIME · Les Arcs · Ste-Foy
Combelouvière · Montchavin · Vallandry
MOÛTIERS · Les Coches · Peisey
Valmorel · Brides-les- · La Plagne · Tignes
Bains · Champagny · Val d'Isère
St-François- · La Tania
Longchamp · Courchevel · Pralognan · Bonneval
St-Martin- · Méribel
de-Belleville · Les Menuires
St-Colomban · Val Cenis
Les · ST-JEAN-DE- · Val Thorens
Sept- · Les Sybelles · La Toussuire · MAURIENNE
Laux · St-Sorlin-d'Arves · Le Corbier · La Norma
GRENOBLE · St-Jean- · Les Karellis · MODANE
Villard-de-Lans · d'Arves · Valloire · Valmeinier · Valfréjus
Chamrousse · Vaujany · Fréjus tunnel
Villard- · Oz · Alpe-d'Huez
Reculas · Auris · La Grave · Bardonecchia
BOURG- · Col du Lautaret
D'OISANS · Les Deux-Alpes · Sauze d'Oulx
Cesana Torinese · Sestriere · TURIN
Serre-Chevalier · Claviere
Briançon · Montgenèvre
Puy-St-Vincent
Superdévoluy
Orcières-Merlette
GAP · Risoul · Vars
Les Orres

0 · 30km
0 · 20 miles

✳ indicates pass closed in winter

Off the map:
Pra-Loup
La Foux-d'Allos
Auron
Isola 2000

Getting around the French Alps

Pick the right gateway – Geneva, Chambéry or Grenoble – and you can
hardly go wrong. The approach to Serre-Chevalier and Montgenèvre involves
the 2060m/6,76oft Col du Lauteret; but the road is a major one and kept
clear of snow or reopened quickly after a fall (or you can fly to Turin and
avoid that pass). Crossing the French-Swiss border between Chamonix and
Verbier involves two closure-prone passes – the Montets and the Forclaz.
When necessary, one-way traffic runs beside the tracks through the rail
tunnel beneath the passes.

The later generation of purpose-built resorts, such as Valmorel, La Rosière, La Tania and Arc 1950 have been built in much more sympathetic style. The big advantages of the high, purpose-built resorts are the reliability and quality of the snow, and the amazing slope-side convenience of most of the accommodation.

If you prefer, there are genuinely old mountain villages to stay in, linked directly to the big lift networks. These are not usually as convenient for the slopes, but they give you a feel of being in France rather than in a winter-holiday factory. Examples include Montchavin or Champagny for La Plagne, Vaujany for Alpe-d'Huez, St-Martin-de-Belleville, Les Allues or Brides-les-Bains for the Trois Vallées, and Les Carroz, Morillon or Samoëns for Flaine. There are also old villages with their own slopes that have developed as resorts while retaining at least some of their rustic ambience – such as Serre-Chevalier and La Clusaz.

Megève deserves a special mention – an exceptionally charming little town combining rustic style with sophistication; shame about the traffic. It has now been overtaken by Courchevel 1850 as the most expensive resort in France, largely because of Courchevel's popularity not just with the Paris jet set but also with rich Russians.

And France has Alpine centres with a long mountaineering and skiing history. Chief among these is Chamonix, which sits in the shadow of Mont Blanc, Europe's highest peak, and is the centre of the most radical off-piste terrain in the Alps. Chamonix is a big, bustling town, where winter sports go on alongside tourism in general. By contrast, simple La Grave is at the foot of mountains that are almost as impressive – the highest within France.

PLAT DU JOUR

France has advantages over most rival destinations in the gastronomic stakes. Although many of its mountain restaurants serve fast food, most also do at least a plat du jour that is in a different league from what you'll find in Austria or the US. It is generally possible to find somewhere to get a half-decent lunch and have it served at your table, rather than having to queue repeatedly for every element of your meal. In the evening, most resorts have restaurants serving good traditional French food as well as regional specialities. And the wine is decent and affordable.

Many French resorts (though not all) have suffered from a lack of nightlife, but things have changed in recent years. In resorts dominated by apartments with few international visitors, there may still be very little going on after dinner, but places such as Méribel and Val d'Isère are now distinctly lively in the evening.

IMPROVING APARTMENTS

One of the most welcome developments on the French resort scene in recent years has been the availability of genuinely comfortable and stylish apartments, in contrast to the cramped and, frankly, primitive places that have dominated the market since the 1960s. Our luxury apartments chapter is largely about this new generation of French apartments, which have opened up self-catering holidays to people who previously would not have contemplated them.

PERFECT PISTES

France is unusual among European countries in using four grades of piste (instead of the usual three). The very easiest runs are classified green; except in Val d'Isère, they are reliably gentle. This is a genuinely helpful system, which ought to be used internationally.

AVOID THE CROWDS

French school holidays mean crowded slopes, so they are worth avoiding if possible. The country is divided into three zones, with three fortnight holidays staggered between 7 February and 8 March 2009 – with two zones overlapping between 14 February and 1 March – so expect that period to be particularly busy.

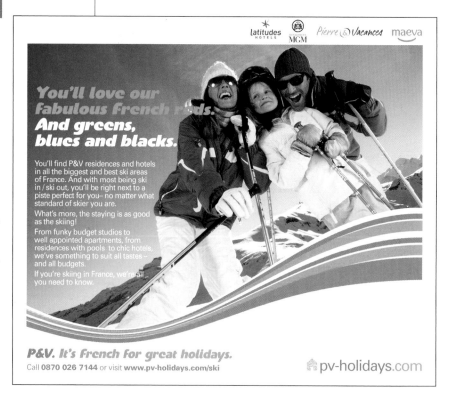

Alpe-d'Huez

Impressive and sunny slopes above a hotchpotch of a purpose-built village, but with attractive alternative bases where we prefer to stay

COSTS

① ② ③ ④ ⑤ ⑥

RATINGS

The slopes
Fast lifts	**
Snow	****
Extent	****
Expert	****
Intermediate	****
Beginner	*****
Convenience	****
Queues	****
Mountain restaurants	****

The rest
Scenery	****
Resort charm	*
Off-slope	****

NEWS

For 2007/08 more snowmaking was added and another 75 guns are planned for 2008/09. Hands-free lift passes were introduced throughout the Grandes Rousses area. In Vaujany, a moving carpet was installed in the kids' snow garden.

➕ Extensive, high, sunny slopes, split interestingly into different sectors

➕ Huge snowmaking installation

➕ Vast, gentle, sunny nursery slopes

➕ Efficient lift system, mostly

➕ Some good mountain restaurants

➕ Livelier than many French resorts

➕ Pleasant alternative bases in outlying villages and satellites

➖ Some main intermediate runs get badly overcrowded in high season

➖ Many of the tough runs are very high, and closed in bad weather

➖ Practically no woodland runs to retreat to in bad weather

➖ Lots of south-facing runs that can be icy early and slushy later

➖ Sprawling resort with no central focus and very little charm

There are few places to rival Alpe-d'Huez and its Massif des Grandes Rousses for extent and variety of terrain – in good wintery conditions it's one of our favourites. But as the season progresses the effects of the strong southern sun become more and more of a problem. The village of Alpe-d'Huez has few fans, but if you don't like the sound of it, you always have the alternative of staying in rustic Vaujany, in Villard-Reculas, or in the modern ski stations of Oz-en-Oisans or Auris-en-Oisans. All are described at the end of this chapter.

THE RESORT

Alpe-d'Huez is a large, modern resort on a high, open, sunny mountainside east of Grenoble. Although developed for skiing, it has grown in a seemingly unplanned, sprawling fashion.

The resort spreads down a gentle slope in a triangular shape from the main lift station at the top corner. Access roads enter the village at the two lower corners, west and east. The nearest thing to a central focus is the main Avenue des Jeux in the middle, where you'll find an indoor-outdoor swimming pool, ice skating and some of the shops, bars and restaurants. The buildings come in all shapes, sizes and designs. Many look overdue for

renovation, although some wood cladding and smartening-up can now be seen. Towards the bottom of the triangle is the original core of the resort, with a couple of streets that have a slightly more traditional feel.

Two satellite 'quarters' are a bit of a trek from the centre but with their own lifts, bars and restaurants. Les Bergers is at the eastern entrance to the resort; a chalet suburb is expanding this quarter uphill – convenient for skiing but even more remote from the village centre. L'Eclose is to the south of the main village.

There is also accommodation down the hill in the old village of Huez, linked by lift to the resort.

Reporters have remarked on the warm welcome from the locals, compared with other French resorts.

The 'reliable' bus service around the resort is free with the lift pass, and during the day there's a bucket-lift (with a piste beneath it) running through the resort to the main lifts. This is handy but slow, and some people don't like jumping on and off.

Outings by road are feasible to other resorts covered on a week's lift pass, including Serre-Chevalier and Les Deux-Alpes. A helicopter does day trips to Les Deux-Alpes (only 63 euros), and a bus goes every Wednesday and Thursday, but you need to book.

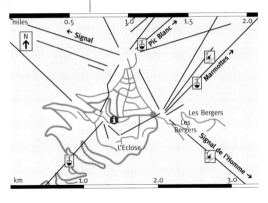

KEY FACTS

Resort	1860m
	6,100ft
Slopes	1120-3320m
	3,670-10,890ft
Lifts	86
Pistes	249km
	155 miles
Green	19%
Blue	21%
Red	32%
Black	28%
Snowmaking	
	860 guns

LIFT PASSES

Visalp

Prices in €

Age	1-day	6-day
under 13	26	142
13 to 59	38	199
over 60	26	142

Free under 5, over 72
Beginner day pass
€12

Notes
Covers all lifts in Alpe-d'Huez, Auris, Oz, Vaujany and Villard-Reculas; half-day passes; discounts for families and regular visitors; 2-day-plus passes cover sports centre, ice rink, swimming pools, concerts, two museums and shuttle service; 6-day-plus passes allow one day's skiing at one of Serre-Chevalier, Puy-St-Vincent and the Milky Way in Italy, and two days in Les Deux-Alpes

Alternative passes
Auris only, Oz-Vaujany only, Villard-Reculas only

THE MOUNTAINS

Alpe-d'Huez is a big-league resort, ranking alongside giants such as Val d'Isère or La Plagne for the extent and variety of its slopes. Practically all the slopes are above the treeline, and so there may be little to do when a storm socks in. Because of the weather no lifts above 2100m/6,890ft were working on our two-day visit in 2008.

Reporters find the piste grading unreliable. You may find some reds rather tame, others 'steeply mogulled halfway down'. 'Even the greens around the DMC gondola seemed on the tough side,' said a 2008 reporter.

THE SLOPES
Several well-linked areas
The slopes divide into four sectors, with good connections between them, though one reporter complained of having to pole or walk between lifts.

The biggest sector is directly above the village, on the slopes of **Pic Blanc**. The huge Grandes Rousses gondola, otherwise known as the DMC (a reference to its clever technology), goes up in two stages from the top of the village. Above it, a cable car goes up to 3320m/10,890ft on Pic Blanc itself – the top of the small Sarenne glacier and start of the longest piste in the Alps (see the feature panel). The glacier is also reached via the Marmottes gondola, which also serves lower runs from Clocher de Macle.

The Sarenne gorge separates the main resort area from **Signal de l'Homme**. It is crossed by a down-and-up fast chairlift from the Bergers part of the village. From the top you can take excellent north-facing slopes towards the gorge, or head south to Auris or west to tiny Chatelard.

On the other side of town from Signal de l'Homme is the small **Signal** sector, reached by draglifts next to the main gondola or by a couple of chairs lower down. Runs go down the other side of the hill to the old village of Villard-Reculas. One blue run back to Alpe-d'Huez is floodlit twice a week.

The generally quieter **Vaujany-Oz** sector consists largely of north-west-facing slopes, accessible from Alpe-d'Huez via red runs. At the heart of this sector is Alpette, the mid-station of the cable car from Vaujany. From here a disastrously sunny blue/red goes down to Oz, a much more reliable blue goes north to the Vaujany home slopes around Montfrais, and a shady black plunges down to L'Enversin, just below Vaujany. Using different black, red and blue pistes and ending up at L'Enversin gives an on-piste descent of 2200m/7,220ft from Pic Blanc – not the biggest vertical in the Alps, but not far short. The links back to Alpe-d'Huez are by the top cable car from Alpette, or a gondola from Oz.

TERRAIN PARKS
A choice
There are two parks: one for novices near the bottom of the slopes, with various jumps and rollers ('excellent, the jumps were beautifully graded'); and a 1.5km/1 mile advanced park near the Babars drag, with half-pipe, jumps, hips, big air and a boardercross course ('good; fast and aggressive'). Teenagers can sign up for freestyle classes with ESF. There's also a beginners' park above Vaujany.

SNOW RELIABILITY
Affected by the sun
Alpe-d'Huez is unique among major purpose-built resorts in the Alps in having mainly south- or south-west-facing slopes. The strong southern sun means that late-season conditions may

There are vast amounts of off-piste terrain in Alpe-d'Huez, from fairly tame to seriously adventurous. Here we pick out just a few of the many runs to be explored – always with guidance, of course.

There are lots of off-piste variants on both sides of the Sarenne run that are good for making your first turns off-piste. The Combe du Loup, a beautiful south-facing bowl with views over the Meije, has a black-run gradient at the top, and you end up on long, gentle slopes leading back to the Sarenne gorge. La Chapelle Saint Giraud, which starts at Signal de l'Homme, includes a series of small confidence-boosting bowls, interspersed with gentle rolling terrain.

For more experienced and adventurous off-piste skiers, the Grand Sablat is a classic that runs through a magnificently wild setting on the eastern face of the Massif des Grandes Rousses. This descent of 2000m/6,560ft vertical includes glacial terrain and some steep couloirs. You can either ski down to the village of Clavans, where you can take a pre-booked helicopter or taxi back, or traverse above Clavans back to the Sarenne gorge. In the Signal sector, there are various classic routes down towards the village of Huez or to Villard-Reculas.

The north-facing Vaujany sector is particularly interesting for experienced off-piste enthusiasts. Route finding can be very tricky, and huge cliffs and rock bands mean this is not a place to get lost. From the top of Pic Blanc, a 40-minute hike takes you to Col de la Pyramide at 3250m/10,660ft, the starting point for the classic itinerary La Pyramide with a vertical of over 2000m/6,560ft. Once at the bottom of the long and wide Pyramide snowfield, you can link into the Vaujany pistes.

alternate between slush and ice on most runs, with some lower runs closed altogether. There are shady slopes above Vaujany and at Signal de l'Homme. The glacier area is small.

In midwinter the runs are relatively snow-sure, thanks to extensive snowmaking on the main runs above Alpe-d'Huez, Vaujany and Oz. But reports suggest that neither the grooming nor the snowmaking is as enthusiastic as we would wish.

FOR EXPERTS
Plenty of blacks and off-piste
There are long and challenging pistes as well as some serious off-piste routes (see feature box).

The slope beneath the Pic Blanc cable car, usually an impressive mogul field, is reached by a 300m/980ft tunnel from the back side of the mountain. Despite improvements to the tunnel exit, the start of the actual slope is often awkward. The slope is of ordinary black steepness, but can be very hard in the mornings because it gets a lot of sun. Get advice.

The long Sarenne run on the back of the Pic Blanc is described in a special feature panel. Thanks to snowmaking, we've been able to ski the black Fare piste to L'Enversin on each of our last two visits – a highly enjoyable and varied long run, away from the lifts but not steep (really of red gradient with some blue sections, we thought). The Marmottes II gondola serves genuine black runs from Clocher de Macle; Balcons is steep and quiet, often with good snow; Clocher de Macle is easier but busier; don't miss the beautiful, long, lonely Combe Charbonnière. The Lièvre Blanc chairlift serves further testing slopes – Balme, looping away from the lifts, is a black, and one or two reds would be classified black in many resorts.

A great view of the village with Les Bergers to the right, Signal mountain on the left and the huge area of easy slopes coming back down to town ↓

FOR INTERMEDIATES
Fine selection of runs

Good intermediates have a fine selection of runs all over the area. In good snow conditions the variety of runs is difficult to beat. Every section has some challenging red runs to test the adventurous intermediate. The Canyon run is one of the most challenging. There are lovely long runs down to Oz – the Champclotury blue from the mid-station of the gondola above Oz is a lovely, gentle run and usually quiet – and to Vaujany, with space for some serious carving. The Villard-Reculas and Signal de l'Homme sectors also have long challenging

reds. Those at Signal de L'Homme are quieter, which keeps their snow better.

The Chamois red from the top of the gondola down to the mid-station is quite narrow, and miserable when busy and icy and/or heavily mogulled. Fearless intermediates should enjoy the super-long Sarenne black run. For less ambitious intermediates, there are usually blue alternatives, except on the upper part of the mountain. The main Couloir blue from the top of the big gondola is a lovely run, well served by snowmaking, but it does get scarily crowded at times.

There are some great cruising runs above Vaujany; but the red runs

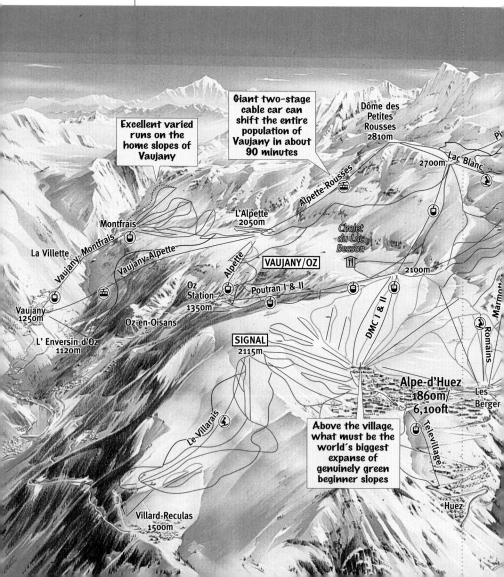

THE LONGEST PISTE IN THE ALPS – AND IT'S BLACK?

It's no surprise that most ski runs that are seriously steep are also seriously short. The really long runs in the Alps tend to be classified blue, or red at the most. The Parsenn runs above Klosters, for example – typically 12km to 15km (7 to 9 miles) long – are manageable in your first week on skis.

So you could be forgiven for being sceptical about the 'black' Sarenne run from the Pic Blanc: even with an impressive vertical of 2000m/6,560ft, a run 16km/10 miles in length means an average gradient of only 11% – typical of a blue run. But the Sarenne is a run of two halves. The bottom half is virtually flat (boarders beware), but the top half is a genuine black if you take the direct route – a demanding and highly satisfying run (with stunning views) that any keen, competent skier will enjoy. The steep mogul field near the top can be avoided by taking an easier option (or by using the Marmottes III gondola); and the whole run can be tackled by an adventurous intermediate. It gets a lot of sun, so pick your time with care – there's nothing worse than a sunny run with no sun. You can ski the Sarenne by 'moonlight' occasionally during the season. Take the last lift up, have a gourmet dinner, then ski back down with guides. The cost is 50 euros per person.

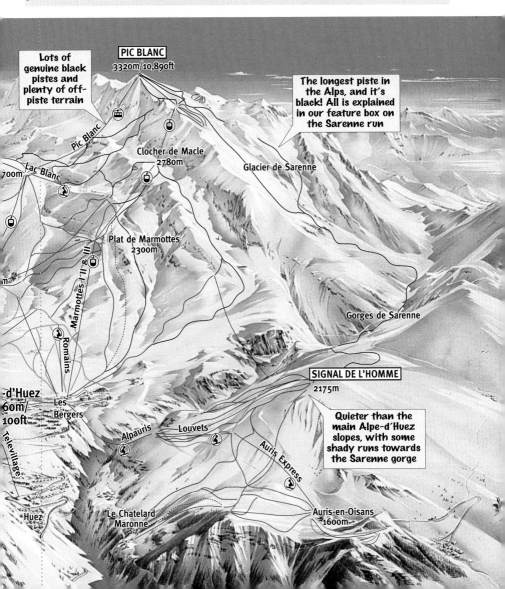

boarding

The resort suits experienced boarders well – the extent and variety of the mountains mean that there's a lot of good freeriding to be had; the off-piste is vast and varied and well worth checking out with a guide. There are quite a few flat areas to beware of though. The nursery slopes are excellent for learning but accessed mainly by draglifts (which can be avoided once a modicum of control has been achieved). Planète Surf is the main snowboard shop.

SCHOOLS

ESF
t 0476 803169
International
t 0476 804277
Masterclass
t 0476 809383
Stance
t 0680 755572

Classes (ESF prices)
6 days (3hr am and
2½hr pm) €191
Private lessons
€38 for 1hr, for 1 or 2 people

GUIDES

Mountain guide office
t 0476 804255

CHILDREN

Les Crapouilloux
t 0476 113923
From age 4; 9.30-5.30
Les Intrépides
t 0476 112161
Ages 6mnth to 3yr;
8am-6.30
Les Eterlous (ESF)
t 0476 806785
Ages 2½ to 5
Tonton Mayonnaise
(International school)
Ages 2½ to 3½;
10am-12 noon

Ski schools
Take children from 4
to 16 (ESF 6 days
€180)

between Vaujany and Alpe-d'Huez can be too much for early intermediates. You can travel via Oz on gondolas, if you are that keen to get around.

Early intermediates will also enjoy the gentle slopes leading back to Alpe-d'Huez from the main mountain, and the Signal sector.

FOR BEGINNERS
Good facilities

The large network of green runs immediately above the village is as good a nursery area as you will find anywhere. The six-pack installed at Les Bergers a few seasons ago has made that part much easier for novices. Sadly, these slopes get very crowded and carry a lot of fast through-traffic. A large area embracing half a dozen runs has been declared a low-speed zone, but the restriction is not policed and so achieves very little. All in all, with a special lift pass covering 11 lifts, Alpe-d'Huez makes a good choice.

FOR CROSS-COUNTRY
High-level and convenient

There are 50km/31 miles of trails, with three loops of varying degrees of difficulty, all at around 2000m/6,560ft and consequently relatively snow-sure.

QUEUES
Generally few problems

Even in French holiday periods, the modern lift system ensures there are few long hold-ups. The village bucket-lift is said to generate lengthy queues first thing. Queues can build up for the gondolas out of the village, but the DMC shifts its queue quickly and the bottom section can be avoided by taking alternative lifts.

Although they may not cause queues, there are lots of old draglifts scattered around.

Over much of the area a greater problem than lift queues is that the main pistes can be unbearably crowded. We and many reporters rate the Chamois and Couloir runs from the top of the DMC among the most

crowded we've seen. The reds to Vaujany and Oz are also too busy for comfort – 'carnage all the way', said one reporter of the Oz run.

MOUNTAIN RESTAURANTS
Some excellent rustic huts

Mountain restaurants are generally good – even self-service places are welcoming, and there are more rustic places with table service than is usual in high French resorts. But the restaurants in the more obvious positions get over-busy.

Editors' choice Compared with some of the places on the main pistes, the cosy little Chalet du Lac Besson (0476 806537) is an oasis of calm – tucked away on the cross-country loops north of the DMC gondola mid-station (and now with an official access piste, the Boulevard des Lacs). Food and service are excellent. It's repeatedly endorsed by enthusiastic reporters – 'fabulous place', 'worth every cent'.

Worth knowing about There are a couple of good spots low down – not mountain restaurants as such, but very popular targets nonetheless. The pretty Forêt de Maronne hotel at Chatelard, below Signal de l'Homme, is 'a delightfully quiet suntrap', enthuses a reporter, and has a good choice of traditional French and international cuisine: 'The chicken satay kept us raving about the place all week.' The Bergerie at Villard-Reculas has good views and is 'highly recommended'.

The Combe Haute, at the foot of the Chalvet chair in the gorge towards the end of the Sarenne run, is welcoming but gets very busy ('excellent profiteroles'). The Signal is quieter and has 'postcard views'. The 'cosy' Perce Neige, just below the Oz-Poutran gondola, 'made a great lunch' for a recent visitor. The Plage des Neiges at the top of the nursery slopes is one of the best places available to beginners. The Cabane du Poutat, halfway down from Plat de Marmottes, does good food but is

↑ The Avenue des Jeux is just to the right of the ice rink here; and the lift that goes up through the village is to the left (along with a piste down)

OT ALPE-D'HUEZ / FRANCOIS MAIRE

GETTING THERE
Air Lyon 150km/ 93 miles (3hr); Geneva 220km/137 miles (4hr); Grenoble, 99km/62 miles (1½hr)
Rail Grenoble (63km/ 39 miles); daily buses from station

Phone numbers
From abroad use the prefix +33 and omit the initial '0' of the phone number

TOURIST OFFICE
Alpe-d'Huez
t 0476 114444
info@alpedhuez.com
www.alpedhuez.com

inadequately staffed – go early.

The restaurants in the Oz and Vaujany sectors tend to be cheaper, but no less satisfactory. At Montfrais, the Airelles is a rustic hut, built into the rock, with a roaring log fire, atmospheric music and excellent, good-value food (the plat du jour is consistently recommended: 'best ever', 'top-notch duck à l'orange'). The Auberge de l'Alpette also gets enthusiastic reviews emphasising that it is 'really good value'. The P'Oz is also worth a visit.

SCHOOLS AND GUIDES
Plenty of choice
Stance was a new school for 2007/08. It's run by two experienced instructors and specialises in teaching British clients. We've received rave reviews: 'absolutely terrific', 'my technique moved forward several notches in the two hours', 'very impressed'. Past reports of Masterclass, an independent school run by British instructor Stuart Adamson, have been favourable ('solid instruction', 'constructive, individual attention without overloading on technical detail') – but a 2008 reporter said, 'It was very friendly but we did not progress much as we were not really pressed.' However, the same reporter said of the ESF: 'We learned much more, they pushed us harder and were determined for us to progress.' But we have past reports of a child being found 'sobbing' after being 'shouted at' by an ESF instructor, while another child was found 'curled in a ball crying, totally ignored'. 'Don't even think about going to the ESF,' said another reporter. Groups can be big: one reporter counted an astonishing 25 in one class. The International school got generally good reviews for private lessons from a 2008 reporter's party:

the two snowboarders 'were given all kinds of things to practise and learn', and the three skiers thought their lessons 'great', 'quite good' and 'alright'. The Bureau des Guides has a good reputation.

FACILITIES FOR CHILDREN
Positive reports
Les Crapouilloux day care centre (for children aged four plus) is reported to be 'very well organised'. The children's garden and nursery at Vaujany have been recommended.

STAYING THERE

HOW TO GO
Something of everything
Chalets UK tour operators run a few chalets and chalet hotels, many in the area above Les Bergers; Ski à la Carte has a place here and another in the old part of the village.
Hotels There are more hotels than is usual in a high French resort, and there's a clear downmarket bias, with more 1-stars than 2- or 3-stars, and only two 4-stars.
****Royal Ours Blanc (0479 650765) Central, but public areas lack atmosphere. Fitness centre.
****Au Chamois d'Or (0476 803132) Good facilities, modern rooms, one of the best restaurants in town and well placed for the main gondola.
***Grandes Rousses (0476 803311) A visitor says, 'Great atmosphere, charming Madame, goodish food and a good guitarist.' Close to the lifts.
***Alpages (0476 110799) Recently renovated B&B. Modern rooms with lots of wood. Small bar. Close to lifts.
***Pic Blanc (0476 114242) Across car park from Les Bergers lifts. Comfortable; we stayed in 2008 in a big ('superior') room.
**Gentianes (0476 803576) Close to the Sarenne gondola in Les Bergers; a range of rooms, the best comfortable.
**Ancolie (0476 111313) Good-value chalet down the hill in Huez.
Apartments There is an enormous choice available. The Pierre et Vacances apartments near the Marmottes gondola in Les Bergers offer good facilities, but as usual in France they are too small if fully occupied. The Maison de l'Alpe close to the DMC has been recommended for its ideal location and good facilities. Privately owned Chalet Gothix is 'comfortable and spacious'.

ACTIVITIES

Indoor Sports centre (tennis, gym, squash, aerobics, swimming, shooting range, climbing wall), sauna, cinemas, concerts, theatre, library, museum

Outdoor Ice rink, curling, cleared walking paths, snowshoeing, microlight flights, sightseeing flights, ice cave, off-road vehicle tours, hang-gliding, paragliding, ice driving school

SMART LODGINGS

Check out our feature chapters at the front of the book.

EATING OUT
Good value

Alpe-d'Huez has dozens of restaurants, some of high quality; many offer good value by resort standards. Last season we had a fabulous meal (four types of foie gras, carré d'agneau, mango tatin) at Au P'tit Creux, which also gets rave reviews from reporters. The Crémaillère is recommended by a frequent visitor. The Pomme de Pin is repeatedly approved of. A 2008 visitor liked the 'good selection of steaks' at Lounge 21. Of the pizzerias, the Origan serves 'fabulous pizza and pasta', and we enjoyed a calzone there in 2008; Pinocchio 'gets very busy early', says a reporter, who also liked the 'enormous helpings' at Smithy's Tavern (Tex-Mex). The 'spruced up' Edelweiss is recommended for its 'excellent value set menus and grills'. The Nabab (Moroccan) is recommended for 'tender slow-cooked lamb' in a room 'decorated like a Turkish harem'. A recent reporter was very impressed by the helpful staff at both the Fondue en Folie and the Crêperie des Jeux.

APRES-SKI
Plenty going on

There's a wide range of bars, some of which get fairly lively later on. There are several British-run bars in chalet hotels, mostly pretty basic and appealing mainly to a young crowd. The small but 'lively' Sphere bar is popular after the lifts close. O'Sharkey's (with 'comfortable leather sofas') and the Pacific (sister bar to the one in Val d'Isère) are also popular. Smithy's has 'plenty of atmosphere' but can get pretty rowdy late on. The live bands at the Grotte du Yéti make for 'some great nights', but a reporter said it had 'all the atmosphere of a youth club'.

The Etalon, Underground ('fun') and Free Ride cafes ('relaxed, cheery atmosphere with great sports videos') have been recommended. The Zoo is great for a relaxed drink. The Sporting is 'a great bar with class bands' but has 'the highest prices in town'; this and the Igloo club ('head there if you're on your 29th vodka!') liven up in peak season.

OFF THE SLOPES
Good by high-resort standards

There is a wide range of facilities, including an indoor pool, a big indoor-outdoor pool (boxer-style cozzies not allowed), an Olympic-size ice rink and a splendid sports centre – all covered by the lift pass. There's also an ice driving school and a toboggan run. You can try airboarding and snow biking on Fridays, beside the Poutran lift. Visits to the Ice Cave are highly recommended by reporters. Shops are numerous but limited in range. The helicopter excursion to Les Deux-Alpes is amusing. There are well-marked walkers' trails (map available), and there's a pedestrian lift pass. The better mountain restaurants are widely spread though – and some are too remote for pedestrians.

Selected chalets in Alpe-d'Huez

Airtours, Alpine Answers, Chalet Group, Chalet World Ski, Club Med, Crystal, Directski.com, Equity, Erna Low, Esprit, First Choice, Independent Ski Links, Inghams, Interactive Resorts, Interhome, La Source, Lagrange, Made to Measure, Neilson, Rocketski, Ski à la Carte, Ski Activity, Ski Collection, Ski Expectations, Ski France, Skifrance4less, Ski Freshtracks, Skiholidayextras.com, Ski Independence, Ski Leisure Direction, Ski Line, Ski McNeill, Ski Miquel, Ski Solutions, Ski Supreme, Skitracer, Skiworld, Thomson
Villard-Reculas La Source
Oz-en-Oisans AmeriCan Ski, Erna Low, Independent Ski Links, Lagrange, Peak Retreats, Ski Activity, Ski France, Skiholidayextras.com, Ski Independence
Auris-en-Oisans Lagrange
Vaujany AmeriCan Ski, Erna Low, Peak Retreats, Ski France, Skiholidayextras.com, Ski Independence, Ski Leisure Direction, Ski Peak

Villard-Reculas

1500m/4,920ft

Villard-Reculas is a secluded village just over the hill (Signal) from Alpe-d'Huez, complete with an old church and set on a small shelf wedged between an expanse of open snowfields above and tree-filled hillsides below. A fast quad up to Signal has increased the village's popularity as a base. Its visitor beds are mainly in self-catering apartments and chalets, booked either through the tourist office or La Source – an English-run agency that also runs a comfortable catered chalet in a carefully converted stone barn. There is one 2-star hotel, the Beaux Monts (0476 804314). There is a store 'almost like a trading post' and a couple of bars and restaurants.

The local slopes have something for everyone, including a nursery slope at village level. And there's an ESF.

But a reporter warns that the place is 'dull at night' and also that beginners 'will be stuck here because the runs that link to the rest of the skiing are undergraded'. In his party two near-beginners were 'very put off'.

Oz-en-Oisans Station

1350m/4,430ft

The purpose-built ski station above the old village of the same name is a 'thriving small resort', says a reporter who has an apartment there. It has been built in an attractive style, with much use of wood and stone, and has a ski school, sports shops, nursery

slopes, bars, restaurants, supermarket, skating rink, large underground car park and now two mid-range hotels. The pool in the hotel Les Cristaux is open to all. But another reporter complains that there is still no nightlife. Two gondolas whisk you out of the resort – one goes to Alpette above Vaujany and the other goes in two stages to the mid-station of the DMC above Alpe-d'Huez. The main run home is liberally endowed with snow-guns, but it needs to be. One clear advantage of staying here is that the slopes above Oz are about the best in the area when heavy snow is falling – and those based elsewhere may not be able to reach them.

The smart Chalet des Neiges apartments are in chalet-style buildings with pool, sauna, restaurant. Available through Peak Retreats.

Auris-en-Oisans 1600

1600m/5,250ft

Auris-en-Oisans 1600 is another tiny, purpose-built ski station – a series of wood-clad, chalet-style apartment blocks with a few shops, bars and restaurants set just above the treeline. It's a compact family resort, with a ski school, a nursery and a ski kindergarten. Beneath it is the original old village of Auris, complete with attractive traditional buildings, a church and all but one of the resort's hotels. Staying here with a car you can drive up to the lift base or make excursions to other resorts.

Unsurprisingly, evenings are quiet, with a handful of bar-restaurants to

253

Alpe-d'Huez

*Interactive resort shortlist builder at **www.wtss.co.uk***

Selected chalet in Villard-Reculas

Phone numbers
From abroad use the prefix +33 and omit the initial '0' of the phone number

Weekly news updates and resort links at www.wtss.co.uk

choose from. The Beau Site (0476 800639), which looks like an apartment block, is the only hotel in the upper village. A couple of miles down the hill, the traditional Auberge de la Forêt (0476 800601) gives you a feel of 'real' rural France.

Access to the slopes of Alpe-d'Huez is no problem (but returning to Auris may prove difficult for novices – the top of Signal de L'Homme is a bit steep). There are plenty of local slopes to explore, for which there is a special lift pass. Most runs are intermediate, though Auris is also the best of the local hamlets for beginners.

Vaujany 1250m/4,100ft

Vaujany is a quiet, growing village (the number of visitor beds is due to double from 2,000 in 2007 to 4,000 by the end of 2009), perched on a sunny hillside opposite its own sector of the domain. Hydroelectric riches have financed huge continuing investment in lifts and other infrastructure. A giant 160-person cable car whisks you into the heart of the Alpe-d'Huez lift system, and a two-stage gondola takes you to the local slopes at Montfrais via a mid-station below the tiny, rustic hamlet of La Villette. Accommodation is mainly in apartments, and Peak Retreats has a good selection available.

As you enter the village, you come to a couple of small, simple hotels. The Rissiou is exceptionally well run by British tour operator Ski Peak: delicious food and ever-helpful staff. Ski Peak also runs comfortable,

tastefully decorated catered chalets in Vaujany and La Villette; a minibus service for guests is available.

You then come to a recently built complex around a small pedestrian square, Place Centre Village, with spacious, mid-range apartments built in traditional style. There's a good ski shop, a restaurant, food shops, a cafe/bar and a cavernous underground car park – and an escalator down to the nearby cable car and gondola stations. An elevator takes you further down the hill to the superb sports centre.

An impressive enclosed escalator goes up the hillside past chalets and farm buildings to the top of the village, where sizeable apartment buildings are grouped around the Galerie Marchande – a small car-free zone with a small supermarket, a food shop, a couple of bars and a couple of restaurants. Since most of the visitor beds are up here, it is naturally the focus of evening activity.

There are no slopes leading directly to the village. But there is a 'pulse' gondola up from L'Enversin where the Fare black run finishes (a great run and not steep – see 'For experts' earlier in chapter), or you can take a blue to the mid-station of the Montfrais gondola and ride down. Beginner children are taken to a gentle roped-off area at the top of the gondola and adult beginners to the nursery slope at the cable car mid-station. There's a good self-service restaurant with sunny terrace right by the children's learning area. The ski school (adults' and children's) and the nursery have been praised.

Les Arcs

Three first-generation purpose-built resorts plus a cute modern alternative – with an exceptional variety and extent of slopes

COSTS

① ② ③ ④ ⑤ ⑥

RATINGS

The slopes

Fast lifts	★★★
Snow	★★★★
Extent	★★★
Expert	★★★★★
Intermediate	★★★★
Beginner	★★★★
Convenience	★★★★
Queues	★★★
Mountain restaurants	★★★

The rest

Scenery	★★★
Resort charm	★
Off-slope	★

NEWS

The Vanoise Express cable car linking Les Arcs and La Plagne, which was closed last season, is due to reopen after repairs in December 2008.

For 2007/08 a six-pack, the Derby, replaced the old Plan Bois chairlift between Vallandry and Arc 1800. Eight runs were identified as ungroomed 'natural' pistes.

At Arc 1950 the final buildings, Manoir Savoir and Chalet des Lys, opened last year. The new spa facility should be ready for 2008/09.

➕ A wide variety of pistes and easily accessed off-piste terrain; great for mixed-ability groups

➕ Exceptional amounts of genuinely challenging skiing above Arc 2000

➕ Some excellent woodland runs

➕ Mainly traffic-free villages with easy slope access from most lodgings

➕ Some quiet alternative bases

➕ Fast cable car link to La Plagne

➕ Very easy rail access from UK

➕ Arc 1950 offers a rare blend of convenience and ambience, but ...

➖ Original village centres lack charm, and aren't always so convenient

➖ Few off-slope diversions

➖ Still a lot of slow old chairlifts

➖ Fairly quiet nightlife, though bars/restaurant choice improving

➖ No green runs for novices to progress to – normally a feature of French resorts

➖ Lots of flat linking runs to annoy snowboarders

➖ Accommodation in high villages is nearly all in apartments

We've always liked Les Arcs' slopes: they offer impressive variety, including some of the longest descents in the Alps, and plenty of steep stuff. And the link with La Plagne puts these resorts in the same league as the Three Valleys (though its closure for repairs last season doesn't seem to have prompted many complaints from reporters – Les Arcs has more than enough terrain to keep most mixed-ability groups happy).

The main villages have always put us off – fairly functional, but drab. But the new Arc 1950 mini-village is something else: a resort that's even more conveniently arranged than the others, and a lot more pleasant to inhabit.

THE RESORT

Les Arcs is made up of four modern resort units, linked by road, high above the railway terminus town of Bourg-St-Maurice. The four villages are all purpose-built and apartment-dominated, and offer doorstep access to the snow with no traffic hazards.

Reporters repeatedly comment on the friendliness of the locals.

Arc 1600 was the first Arc. For rail travellers it is the obvious choice, with a funicular railway up from Bourg-St-Maurice. 1600 is set in the trees and has a friendly, small-scale atmosphere; and it enjoys good views along the valley and towards Mont Blanc. The central area is particularly good for families: uncrowded, compact, and set on even ground. But it is very quiet in the evening. Above the village, chairlifts fan out over the lower slopes.

Much the largest of the villages is Arc 1800. It has three sections, though the boundaries are indistinct. Charvet and Villards are small shopping centres, mostly open-air but still managing to seem claustrophobic.

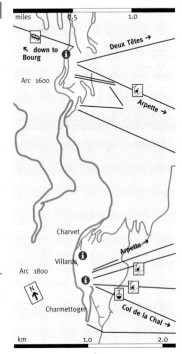

KEY FACTS

Resort	1600-2120m
	5,250-6,960ft
Slopes	1200-3225m
	3,940-10,580ft
Lifts	54
Pistes	200km
	124 miles
Green	1%
Blue	51%
Red	30%
Black	18%
Snowmaking	12km
	7 miles

Paradiski area	
Slopes	1200-3250m
	3,940-10,660ft
Lifts	144
Pistes	425km
	264 miles
Green	5%
Blue	56%
Red	27%
Black	12%

FRANCE

256

OT LES ARCS / S LEONTIF

The wooded setting
and broad views
make up for the block
buildings ↓

Both are dominated by huge apartment blocks. More easy on the eye is Charmettoger, with smaller, wood-clad buildings nestling among trees. There are also apartments up the hillside in Le Chantel. The lifts depart from Villards – including a big gondola to the top of Arc 2000.

Arc 2000 is just a few hotels, apartment blocks and the Club Med, huddled together in a bleak spot, with little to commend it but immediate access to the highest, toughest skiing. Some more upmarket apartments have been built; there is only a handful of restaurants and shops.

Just below Arc 2000 and linked to it by a short gondola, the new mini-village of Arc 1950 is the best-designed of the villages in every way – see feature panel later in this chapter.

There are lifts all around Arc 1950 and 2000, including the Varet gondola up towards the Aiguille Rouge.

At the southern end of the area is Peisey-Vallandry; the cable car link with La Plagne begins here. At the northern end of the ski area is the rustic hamlet of Villaroger. These are described at the end of the chapter.

THE MOUNTAINS

Les Arcs' terrain is notably varied; it has plenty of runs for experts and intermediates and a good mixture of high, snow-sure slopes and low-level woodland runs ideal for bad weather.

A cable car from Plan-Peisey links to La Plagne, covered by the Paradiski passes. Even from Arc 1950 you can be at the cable car in 20 minutes, ready for a long day at La Plagne.

Day trips by car to Val d'Isère-Tignes are possible. La Rosière and Ste-Foy-Tarentaise are also nearby.

Signposting and the piste map are generally very clear.

THE SLOPES
Well planned and varied

Arc 1600 and Arc 1800 share a west-facing mountainside laced with runs down to one or other village. At the southern end is an area of woodland runs down to Peisey-Vallandry.

From various points on the ridge above 1600 and 1800 you can head down into the wide Arc 2000 bowl. Across this bowl, lifts take you to the highest runs of the area, from the Aiguille Rouge and the Grand Col. As well as a variety of steep north-west-facing runs back to Arc 2000, the Aiguille Rouge is the start of an epic run (over 2000m/6,560ft vertical and 7km/4 miles long) down to Villaroger.

Last season the resort identified eight of the toughest runs as 'natural' pistes. It just means they are ungroomed. Strangely, as well as seven serious blacks the group includes the red Malgovert.

On the lower half of the Aiguille Rouge is a speed-skiing run, which is sometimes open to the public; the fee includes helmet, goggles and skis.

There's floodlit skiing twice weekly.

TERRAIN PARKS
State of the art

The Apocalypse Parc is above Arc 1600 and served by the Clair Blanc chairlift. For years, this has been one of the most advanced parks in the Alps – on a par with Avoriaz. Snow-guns have now been installed due to recent poor snowfall, which means there will always be something built. Three kicker lines are in place for beginners, intermediates and advanced riders. This is coupled with a nice rail and box line, and a big wall ride – varied and fun for all ('the kids loved it'). On the far side of the park is a 500m/1,640ft long boardercross course. There are often queues at peak times. There is also a good-sized half-pipe at Arc 2000 that is floodlit until late, plus a boardercross below Col de la Chal. There's also a small park above Peisey-Vallandry.

SNOW RELIABILITY
Good – plenty of high runs

A high percentage of the runs are above 2000m/6,560ft and when necessary you can stay high by using lifts that start around that altitude. Most of the slopes face roughly west, which is not ideal. Those from the Col de la Chal and the long runs down to

boarding

Les Arcs has always been a hot spot for snowboarders. Regis Rolland, founder of A-Snowboards (renamed APO), has for years been exploiting the potential of some of the most varied board-friendly terrain in Europe and has played a huge part in popularising the sport here. Les Arcs offers incredible off-piste terrain, mainly in the back bowls of Arcs 2000. Gullies, trees, natural jibs and hits, steep terrain – this place has it all (enthusiastically endorsed by a 2008 visitor). The good mix of terrain also means that there are plenty of wide-open rolling slopes for beginners, especially in Vallandry or just above Arc 1800. Be careful of the long traverses on near-flat cat-tracks and some of the blues at Arc 2000. Fast chairlifts and gondolas service much of the area, which is an added bonus. For freestyle junkies, there is a good terrain park at 1600.

LIFT PASSES

Massif Les Arcs / Peisey-Vallandry

Prices in €

Age	1-day	6-day
under 14	32	149
14 to 64	42	223
over 65	32	149
Free under 6, over 72		
Beginner six free lifts		

Notes
Covers Les Arcs lifts; half-day pass and one-day Paradiski extension possible; free access to ice rink (1800) and pool (1600)

Paradiski Découverte

Prices in €

Age	6-day
under 14	159
14 to 64	211
over 65	159
Free under 6, over 72	
Beginner no deals	

Notes
Covers all lifts in Les Arcs areas with one day in Paradiski

Paradiski

Prices in €

Age	1-day	6-day
under 14	35	178
14 to 64	46	237
over 65	35	178
Free under 6; over 72 €8		
Beginner no deals		

Notes
Covers all lifts in Les Arcs area and La Plagne area and a day in Val d'Isère-Tignes or Three Valleys

Villaroger are north-facing, and the blacks on the Aiguille Rouge face near enough north to keep their snow well, even in spring. The limited snowmaking is being gradually extended, including full coverage for the terrain park at 1600. Grooming gets mixed reviews, but it was good on our recent visit.

FOR EXPERTS
Challenges on- and off-piste
Les Arcs has a lot to offer experts – at least when the high lifts are open (the Aiguille Rouge cable car, in particular, is often shut in bad weather).

There are a number of truly black pistes above Arc 2000, and a couple in other areas. After a narrow shelf near the top (which can be awkward), the Aiguille Rouge-Villaroger run is superb, with remarkably varying terrain throughout its vertical drop of over 2000m/6,560ft. There is also a great deal of off-piste potential. There are steep pitches on the front face of the Aiguille Rouge and secluded runs on the back side, towards Villaroger. A short climb to the Grand Col from the chairlift of the same name gives access to several routes, including a quite serious couloir and an easier option. From Col de la Chal there is an easy route down to Pont Bodin near Nancroix. The wooded slopes above 1600 are another attractive possibility and there are open slopes beside the pistes all over the place.

FOR INTERMEDIATES
Plenty for all abilities
One strength of the area is that most main routes have easy and more difficult alternatives, making it good for mixed-ability groups. An exception is the solitary Comborcière black from Les Deux Têtes down to Pré-St-Esprit, which has no nearby alternatives. This

long mogul-field justifies its rating and can be great fun for strong intermediates. Malgovert, from the same point towards Arc 1600, is now classified a 'natural' piste and is tricky – it is narrow, as well as mogulled.

The woodland runs at either end of the domain, above Peisey-Vallandry and Villaroger, and the bumpy Cachette red down to 1600, are also challenging. We especially like the Peisey-Vallandry area: its well groomed, treelined runs have a very friendly feel and are remarkably uncrowded much of the time, allowing great fast cruising – readers agree; notably for the isolated Combe run (though it is often closed and snow conditions can be challenging). Good intermediates can enjoy the Aiguille Rouge-Villaroger run. The lower half of the mountainside above 1600/1800 is great for mixed-ability groups, with a choice of routes through the trees. The red runs down from Arpette and Col des Frettes towards 1800 are quite steep but usually well groomed (except Clair Blanc). Cautious intermediates have plenty of blue cruising terrain. Many of the runs around 2000 are rather bland and prone to overcrowding. Edelweiss is more interesting, with a short red alternative, and takes you to Arc 1950 from Col des Frettes. The blues above 1800 are attractive but also crowded. A favourite blue of ours is Renard, high above Vallandry, usually with excellent snow.

And, of course, you have the whole of La Plagne's slopes to explore if you get bored locally.

FOR BEGINNERS
1800 or Peisey-Vallandry best
There are 'ski tranquille' nursery-slope zones above each of the three main Arcs, and at mid-mountain above

Peisey-Vallandry; though we and readers haven't found them always tranquil. Three of their serving lifts (at 1600, 1800 and 2000) are free to use at the weekends – which a reporter found 'good for a warm-up on arrival day'; others require a lift pass or points card. There are also a few enclosed learning areas with draglifts, used by the schools. In all sectors there are long, easy blue runs to move on to.

FOR CROSS-COUNTRY
Very boring locally
Short trails, mostly on roads, is all you can expect, but the pretty Nancroix valley's 40km/25 miles of pleasant trails are easily accessible by free bus.

QUEUES
Not without problems
The lift system generally works well, but it has its flaws. A bigger issue than queues is the time spent on slow chairlifts, some of them very long, and

cold (one reader claims to have suffered frostbite in his glutei). One prime example – the Plan Bois above Vallandry – was replaced last year.

The main bottleneck is at Arc 2000, particularly in warm weather: the Arcabulle fast chair above the resort then gets serious queues, and the alternative Bois de l'Ours then suffers too. The Varet gondola to the shoulder of the Aiguille Rouge is always busy, but shifts its queue quickly because it has lifties filling the cabins – excellent. The cable car to the top builds 'shocking' queues; go at lunchtime, or late in the day to avoid them.

At 1800 the Transarc gondola is a bottleneck, especially late in the day

At 1600 the Cachette chair gets queues when crowds arrive on the funicular from the valley. Higher up, the Clair Blanc serving the Apocalypse terrain park gets busy at peak times.

At Plan Peisey, a reporter complains of morning queues for the chair when ski school classes start. The new

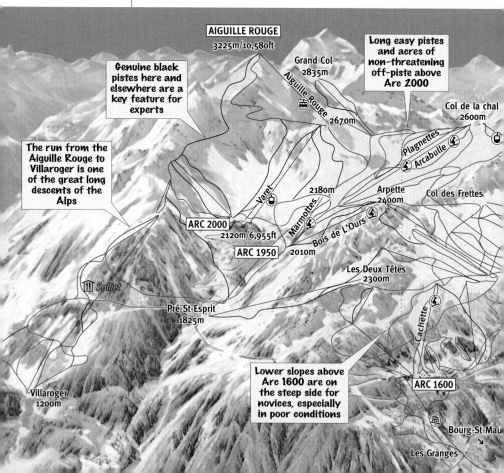

Derby six-pack above Vallandry is not queue free, though naturally less of a problem than the Plan Bois chair it replaced. At peak periods crowded pistes can be a problem, too.

MOUNTAIN RESTAURANTS
Not much choice high-up

The proper mountain restaurants are mainly unremarkable.

Editors' choice New owners last season have given the Solliet (0612 533627) above Villaroger a big boost, creating a warm ambience in this charming, woody chalet and delivering excellent food. There's table- or self-service and great views from the terrace.

Worth knowing about Our former choice, the Chalets de l'Arc, just above Arc 2000, is a welcoming, rustic place built in wood and stone. We've used it regularly for years, and enjoyed excellent food; and we have multiple reports of 'fabulous' lunches ('divine pork and blueberry sauce'). Notably good home-baked bread. But we and

readers have had poor service of late. More reports, please.

Below Arc 2000, the 500-year-old Belliou la Fumée at Pré-St-Esprit is set beside a car park; but it is charmingly rustic, and we've had good meals here. The Arpette, above 1800, serves a 'delicious croziflette'. The little Blanche Murée, near the Transarc mid-station, is good for a simple table-service lunch in the sun ('good salads and wine'). The Cordée above Plan-Peisey is 'excellent, with good tasty food'. There are places to eat in the villages, of course. The Ferme ('very good, but crowded') and Aiguille Rouge ('nice omelettes') down at Villaroger are two old favourite targets.

SCHOOL AND GUIDES
Several, including a Brit school

The ESF here is renowned for being the first in Europe to teach ski évolutif, where you start by learning parallel turns on short skis, gradually moving on to longer skis. Progress can

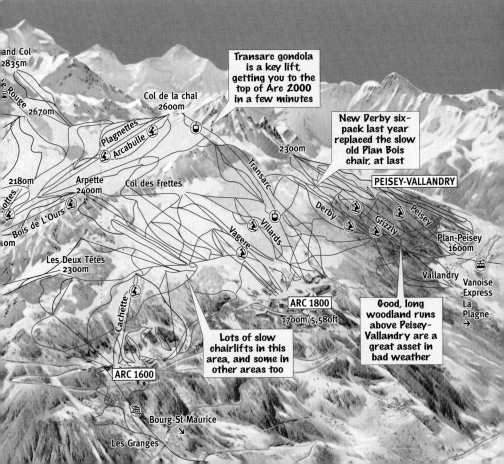

and Col
2835m

le Rouge 2670m

Plagnettes

Arcabulle

Transarc gondola is a key lift, getting you to the top of Arc 2000 in a few minutes

Col de la chal
2600m

New Derby six-pack last year replaced the slow old Plan Bois chair, at last

2300m

2180m

Arpette
2400m

Col des Frettes

Transarc

PEISEY-VALLANDRY

lottes

Bois de L'Ours

om

Villards

Vagere

Derby

Grizzly

Peisey

Plan-Peisey
1600m

Les Deux Têtes
2300m

Vallandry

Vanoise-Express
La Plagne
→

Cachette

ARC 1800

1700m/5,580ft

Good, long woodland runs above Peisey-Vallandry are a great asset in bad weather

Lots of slow chairlifts in this area, and some in other areas too

ARC 1600

Bourg-St-Maurice
↘

Les Granges

GETTING THERE

Air Geneva 156km/ 97 miles (3½hr); Lyon 200km/124 miles (3½hr); Chambéry 127km/79 miles (2½hr)

Rail Bourg-St-Maurice; frequent buses and direct funicular to resort

SMART LODGINGS

Check out our feature chapters at the front of the book.

be spectacular, but classes can be large ('beginners in a group of 24 – appalling'). And one reader's son 'progressed quickly', despite being 'the only British child in a class of French'. The 2000 branch gets glowing comments though from this year's reporters: 'our daughters had an excellent instructor who really moved them on', 'top guy; lots of fun'. Kids' classes were 'very highly praised by a 14-year-old boy and 10-year-old girl'. British school New Generation has a 'small but strong' team in Vallandry and are consistently praised, as in other resorts: 'their teaching methods are tailored to the individual – you set your own objectives'; 'brilliant'; 'absolutely first rate'; 'I cannot praise them highly enough'; 'worth every penny'. The International school (aka Arc Aventures) has impressed reporters. One reporter recommends the private lessons of Snow Escape, also in Vallandry. The Spirit school in 1950 gets good reviews all round, for small classes, 'friendly' English-speaking instructors and flexible private lessons ('grandma successfully learnt to ski'). Off-piste discovery days are also recommended.

FACILITIES FOR CHILDREN
Good reports
Spirit 1950 reportedly provides good care and facilities for smaller children, returning them well fed and rested. We have received good reports on the Pommes de Pin facilities in Arc 1800. The Cariboos Club at Arc 1950 now takes children from nine months to five years. Comments on children's ski classes have been favourable, too: 'Classes were crowded but teaching/ child care was good.' There is a children's area at 1800, complete with moving carpet lifts, a sledging track and a climbing wall. There are also a couple of discovery pistes, at 1800 and 1600, for children to find out about flora and fauna of the Alps.

STAYING THERE

HOW TO GO
New chalets and apartments
Most resort beds are in apartments. There is a long-established Club Med presence in Arc 2000 and there's a smarter 'village' at Peisey-Vallandry.
Chalets There are lots of catered chalets in the Peisey-Vallandry area, and Villaroger has a couple (see end of this chapter), but there are few in the high villages. Family specialist Esprit has chalet apartments in Arc 2000, sharing a pool.
Hotels The choice of hotels in Les Arcs is gradually widening.
***Grand Paradiso** (1800) (0479 076500) Locally judged to be worth four stars rather than its actual three.
***Golf** (1800) (0479 414343) An expensive but good 3-star, with 'friendly and comfortable' jazz bar, a sauna, gym, kindergarten, covered parking. New spa and heated pool. Accepts weekend bookings.
***Cachette** (1600) (0479 077050) Recommended, but expect lots of kids – 1600's child care facilities are here.
Aiguille Rouge (2000) (0479 075707) 'Stylish' lounge bar. Free ski guiding.
Mélèzes (2000) (0479 075050) 'Fantastic value for a mixed family group. Good food, great choices for vegetarians.' Spa.
Beguin (1600) (0479 070292) 'Fantastic hotel, patient and friendly staff, superb food.'
Apartments The various apartment developments at Arc 1950 vary in style and space, but the general level of comfort is very high by French

CHILDREN

Arc 1600:
Garderie La Cachette
t 0479 077050
8.30 to 6pm; ages
4mnth to 11yr

Arc 1800
t 0479 042431
Ages 1 to 6

Arc 1950: Le Cariboo
t 0479 070557
8.30 to 6.30; from
age 9mnth

Arc 2000: Les
Marmottons
t 0479 076425
Ages 18mnth to 6yr

Ski school
Generally take
children from age 3:
6 days (2hr am or
pm) €139 (ESF prices)

Phone numbers
From abroad use the
prefix +33 and omit
the initial '0' of the
phone number

standards. In Arc 2000 the Chalet des
Neiges and Chalet Altitude offer
'luxury' apartments. The Alpages de
Chantel above Arc 1800 is typical of
MGM apartments – attractive and
comfortable, with pools, saunas and
gyms. It is very convenient for skiing,
but a bit isolated. You'll find most of
the better apartment developments in
the brochures of Erna Low, Ski
Collection and Ski Independence.

The Ruitor apartments, set among
trees between Charmettoger and
Villards (in Arc 1800), are reported to
be 'excellent in all respects'. The
Aiguille Grive apartments are
reportedly spacious and convenient.

EATING OUT
Good choice in Arc 1800
In Arc 1600 and 2000 there are very
few restaurants, but they include some
excellent ones. Chalet de L'Arcelle in
1600 is repeatedly recommended
('worth a Michelin star'). Malouine
('excellent pierrade') and 'friendly' Chez
Fernand ('beware the prune brandy')
are praised. In 2000 Chez Eux gets the

thumbs-up for 'excellent' Savoyard
meals. 1800 has a choice of about 15
restaurants; an ad-based (so not
comprehensive) guide is given away
locally. Readers have been satisfied by
Equipage and 'great service' at the
Triangle. Casa Mia is an excellent all-
rounder with exceptionally friendly
service ('good food but expensive
wine'). The Laurus is a 'good
alternative' – 'superb goat-cheese
tartiflette'. The Mountain Café does
much more than the Tex-Mex it
advertises, and copes well with big
family parties. Chez les Filles is worth
a visit for 'exceptional views' and
'good food'. Tantra has a traditional
menu. At 1950, there is a good choice,
but many places get oversubscribed.
We had an excellent gourmet meal
(though the purple whipped potato
was unusual) at the new Table des
Lys, as did a reporter. Los Chicanos
does fine Mexican, tasty desserts and
very good service even when full. The
Bolée serves a wide range of sweet/
savoury crêpes. Hemingway's
('excellent value three-course dinner'),

Les Arcs

261

Interactive resort shortlist builder at www.wtss.co.uk

WHERE NORTH AMERICA MEETS EUROPE: ARC 1950

*Arc 1950, just below Arc 2000, is a fully functioning mini-resort with powerful
attractions. It is high and relatively snow-sure; absolutely traffic-free (cars have
to go in the underground multi-storey pay-garage); very conveniently laid out,
offering ski-in/ski-out lodgings; comfortable, with apartments of a standard
higher than the French norm; and it is built in a traditional, easy-on-the-eye
style. Although entirely new – built over the last five years by Canadian
company Intrawest, developer of Whistler – it feels thoroughly established.*

*All the accommodation is in apartments, furnished to a high standard. The
living rooms are spacious, at least by French standards, but some incorporate
tiny kitchens – and the bedrooms are mostly compact. The outdoor hot tubs and
pools, saunas and steam rooms are added attractions – as are the 'animations'
planned every evening, such as fireworks and live music.*

*You can eat out in a different place each night, there is a reasonable choice of
après-ski bars, a tiny but well stocked supermarket, a bakery, a gift shop, a
crêperie, ski and board equipment shops. There is a free gondola up to Arc
2000, perched higher up the steep hillside, but we didn't use it.*

Action Outdoors, Airtours, Alpine Answers, Chalet Group, Chalet World Ski, Club Med, Crystal, Crystal Finest, Directski.com, Erna Low, Esprit, First Choice, Hucksters, Independent Ski Links, Inghams, Interactive Resorts, Interhome, Kuoni, Lagrange, Neilson, Optimum, Rocketski, Ski Activity, Ski Adventures, Ski Amis, Ski Beat, Ski Collection, Ski Expectations, Ski France, Skifrance4less, Ski Freshtracks, Ski High Days, Skiholiday extras.com, Ski Independence, Ski Leisure Direction, Ski Line, Ski McNeill, Ski Olympic, Ski Supreme, Ski Total, Skitracer, Skiworld, Thomson, UCPA, Vanilla Ski **Peisey-Vallandry** Chalet Group, Club Med, Erna Low, Esprit, Independent Ski Links, Lagrange, Peak Retreats, Ski Beat, Ski Collection, Ski France, Ski Hiver, Ski Independence, Ski Leisure Direction, Skiholidayextras.com, Ski Line, Ski Olympic **Bourg-St-Maurice** Chill Chalet, Erna Low, Interhome, Peak Retreats, Ski Collection, Ski Freshtracks

Valentino's ('good pizza') and East (Asian dishes) are popular. A 2008 reporter praised Meli's snack bar as 'great for the kids'.

APRES-SKI
Arc 1800 is the place to be

1800 is the liveliest centre. The JO bar is open until the early hours and has a friendly atmosphere with live music. The Tantra has a lounge bar – reports please. Reporter recommendations include the friendly Red Hot Saloon for bar games and 'surprisingly good' live music, the Jungle Café for cocktails, the Jazz Bar in the Hotel Golf ('civilised place for an aperitif') and Chez Boubou at Charvet. The Etranger (formerly the Gabotte) in Place Miravaldi is a 'cosy upstairs bar'. The Arpette mountain restaurant has also been recommended – especially the 'fun, up-beat torchlit descent'.

In 1600 the Bar des Montagnes opposite (and belonging to) the hotel Cachette has games machines, pool and live bands, and can be quite lively even in low season, and the Beguin is suggested. The Abreuvoir has 'good live bands'.

In 2000 the Red Rock has 'lots of seasonaires, but lots of atmosphere'. The Tavern is also popular. The Whistler's Dream, in the Chalet des Neiges, could be worth a try. At 1950, Chalet de Luigi has a bar and nightclub, Hemingway's a bar and the Belles Pintes 'great Guinness'. The new O'Chaud is 'the best' – stays open late, with live music or a DJ.

OFF THE SLOPES
Very poor

Les Arcs is not the place for an off-the-slopes holiday. There is very little to do, though several of the newer apartment blocks have pools; new spa facilities at Arc 1950 are due for 2008/09. There's bowling at 1800 and skating at 1800 and 2000. The cinemas have English films weekly. You can visit the Beaufort dairy and go shopping in Bourg-St-Maurice and there are a few walks – nice ones up the Nancroix valley. There's also an ice grotto at the top of the Transarc, which pedestrians can reach.

Peisey-Vallandry

WENDY-JANE KING

The Bois de L'Ours is one of the pistes now branded 'natural' ➔

1600m/5,250ft

Plan-Peisey and Vallandry are small, still-developing ski stations above the old village of Peisey, which has a bucket-lift up to Plan-Peisey. They market themselves as Peisey-Vallandry, and the cluster of villages hereabouts is known collectively as Peisey-Nancroix. Clear as mud, eh?

The cable car to La Plagne leaves from Plan-Peisey, which has one hotel, a few shops, bars and restaurants but no real focus other than the lift station. A fast six-seat chair takes you into the slopes. The hotel Vanoise (0479 079219) has been recommended by readers for its position, food and staff ('very welcoming, very French', with few British guests). UK operator Ski Beat has nine specially built chalets here, with 8 to 17 beds – and is highly rated by a 2008 reporter ('comfortable, very good food and excellent child care'). Family specialist Esprit has an enclave of six neat chalets, each with hot tub. For dining, reporters recommend the Cordée ('excellent, frequented by locals'), Armoise ('superb food, exceptional value menus'), the Vache ('good quality food, relaxed atmosphere') and Solan ('brasserie, cosy inside, large terrace'). The Flying Squirrel is British-run, has a popular happy hour, live music, 'gourmet-burgers', weekly quiz night and live sport on TV.

Reporters have enjoyed staying down the hill in the characterful old village of Peisey which dates back 1,000 years and has a fine baroque church. The other, mostly old, buildings include a few shops and a couple of bars and restaurants – a reader enjoyed the Ormeline. There are several chalets run by UK operators, including Ski Beat's Edelweiss.

Vallandry is a few hundred metres away from Plan-Peisey and linked by shuttle-bus. A fast quad takes you into the slopes. There are lots of chalets and a small pedestrian-only square at the foot of the slopes with a small supermarket and a ski shop.

Ski Olympic's big piste-side chalet hotel La Forêt got a rave review last year ('Outstanding food, good rooms, fabulous views, friendly and helpful staff'). Among the other developments are some notable self-catering properties. The Orée des Cimes is a comfortable, traditional-style CGH development with a pool and great views.

There are several 'great' locally owned restaurants. Recommendations from reporters include the Calèche for duck, the Dahu, the Bergerie de Raphael, the Refuge ('super pizzas') and the Ourson. There is a 'good' crêperie by the Vanoise Express. Jimmy's bar is popular but 'noisy'. Mont Blanc Bar is a Brit hang-out.

Villaroger 1200m/3,940ft

Villaroger is a charming, quiet, rustic little hamlet with three successive chairlifts (the first two quite slow) going up to a point above Arc 2000. It has a couple of small bar-restaurants and a couple of British-run chalets, including chalet Tarentaise – a lovingly renovated old farmhouse run by Optimum Ski. All bedrooms are en-suite and there's a sauna and massage room (complete with qualified masseuse). The chalet also has WiFi internet access. And the chef is said to be a bit of a star. Note that Villaroger is not suitable for beginners.

Les Granges 1200m/3,940ft

This hamlet at the mid-station of the funicular up from Bourg makes an interestingly rustic alternative to the

bigger resorts if you want a quiet time. It's reached from 1600 by two red runs and a winding blue following a minor road. There is a good (but low and sunny) free nursery slope and kids' snow garden. Non-skiers have access to forest walks. No restaurants or bars, last train from Arc 1600 at 8pm (9pm weekends); taxis are reasonable if shared. UK operator Ski Adventures has three good-looking ski-in/ski-out catered chalets at attractive prices, and will ferry guests to/from Arc 1600 and Arc 1800 for après-ski.

Bourg-St-Maurice
850m/2,790ft

Bourg-St-Maurice is a real French town, with cheaper hotels and restaurants and easy access to other resorts for day trips. The funicular starts next to the TGV station and goes straight to Arc 1600 in seven minutes – but beware, the last one down is at 8pm. Reporters recommend Hostellerie du Petit-St-Bernard (0479 070432) – 'looks run-down, but is friendly with super food', and the cheap and cheerful Savoyard (0479 070403) – 'take earplugs to sell to other guests'.

Avoriaz 1800

The 'ski to and from the door' purpose-built resort option on the French side of the big Portes du Soleil circuit

RATINGS

The slopes

Fast lifts	★★★
Snow	★★★
Extent	★★★★★
Expert	★★★
Intermediate	★★★★
Beginner	★★★★
Convenience	★★★★★
Queues	★★★
Mountain restaurants	★★★★

The rest

Scenery	★★★
Resort charm	★★
Off-slope	★

NEWS

For 2008/09 there are plans for a new beginner package called Soft Ski. This will include a lift pass, ski hire and lessons in a dedicated area on the Proclou sector near the top of the village.

For 2007/08 the triple Combe du Machon chair, serving steep black runs (and a blue back to Avoriaz) from Hauts Forts, was upgraded to a six-pack. And a new terrain park called The Stash was built in partnership with Burton Snowboards – see 'Terrain parks'.

The home of French ski holidays.

Book online now!

pv-holidays.com/ski

+ Good position on the main Portes du Soleil circuit, giving access to very extensive, quite varied runs

+ Generally has the best snow in the Portes du Soleil

+ Accommodation right on the slopes

+ Good children's facilities

+ Snowy paths entirely free of cars are an attractive formula, but ...

− Non-traditional architecture, which some find ugly

− Much of Portes du Soleil is low for a major French area, with the risk of poor snow low down

− Can get very crowded at weekends

− Little to do off the slopes

− Few hotels or chalets – mostly no-frills, cramped apartments

Of the purpose-built resorts thrown up in the 1960s, Avoriaz is one of the more sympathetically designed. It is compact, its buildings (which you love or hate) are wood-clad with sloping roofs and it is truly car-free, with cars kept completely separate from its reliably snow-covered paths and pistes. And it has the highest and most snow-sure slopes of the relatively low Portes du Soleil region. It is also dramatically set above and below cliffs (floodlit at night).

THE RESORT

Avoriaz 1800 is a purpose-built, traffic-free resort perched above a dramatic, sheer rock face. From the edge of town horse-drawn sleighs or snowcats transport people and luggage from car parks to the accommodation – or you can borrow a sledge for a small deposit and transport your own. The problem of horse mess has been cut since horses now wear 'nappies' and staff on snowmobiles scoop up what escapes! Cars are left in paid-for outdoor or underground parking – choose the latter to avoid a chaotic departure if it snows. You can book space in advance.

As our scale plan suggests, it's a compact place, with everything close to hand (turn forward to Chamonix, for a striking comparison). But the village is set on quite a slope; elevators inside the buildings (and chairlifts

outside, during the day) mean moving around is no problem except when paths are icy, but if you plan to go out much in the evening, it's worth staying near the central focus. Wherever you stay, you should be able to ski from the door.

The village is all angular, dark, wood-clad, high-rise buildings, mostly apartments. But the snow-covered paths and pistes give the place quite a friendly Alpine feel.

The evenings are not especially lively, but reporters have enjoyed 'a good ambience, both day and night', and a 'brilliant parade in half-term week, with a fire-eating display'. Family-friendly events are laid on all season. A floodlit cliff behind the resort adds to its nocturnal charm.

You can also stay in the lower hamlets of Ardent and Les Prodains.

Avoriaz is on the main lift circuit of the Portes du Soleil – for an overview, look at our separate chapter. It has links to Châtel in one direction and Champéry (Switzerland) in the other – both covered in separate chapters. It is above the valley resort of Morzine, to which it is linked by gondola (but not by piste). The slopes of Morzine and Les Gets, on the far side of Morzine, are part of the Portes du Soleil but not on the core circuit; both are covered in their own chapters.

Car trips to Flaine and Chamonix are possible.

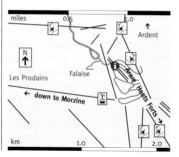

miles 0 0.5 1.0

N ↑

↑ Ardent

Les Prodains

Falaise

← down to Morzine

Ardent Hauts Forts

km 1.0 2.0

Resort	1800m
	5,910ft

Portes du Soleil	
Slopes	950-2300m
	3,120-7,550ft
Lifts	202
Pistes	650km
	404 miles
Green	13%
Blue	40%
Red	37%
Black	10%
Snowmaking	
	694 guns

Avoriaz only	
Slopes	1100-2275m
	3,610-7,460ft
Lifts	38
Pistes	150km
	93 miles

THE MOUNTAINS

The slopes closest to Avoriaz are bleak and treeless, but snow-sure. The main Portes du Soleil circuit is easily done by intermediates of all abilities. Going clockwise avoids two snags in Morgins – the excessively sunny lower slopes of Bec de Corbeau and the uphill walk to the next lift. The booklet-style piste map has given way to a map that shows most of the linked Portes du Soleil circuit (but not the Super-Châtel sector and not the whole of Morzine-Les Gets; so you may want to pick up detailed maps of those areas if you go there). The circuit breaks down at Châtel, where you catch a shuttle-bus.

THE SLOPES
360˚ choice
The village has lifts and pistes fanning out in all directions. Facing the village are the slopes of **Arare-Hauts Forts** and, when snow conditions allow, there are long, steep runs down to Les Prodains. The lifts off to the left go to the **Chavanette** sector on the Swiss border – a broad, undulating bowl. Beyond the border is the infamous Swiss Wall – a long, mogul slope with a tricky start, but not the terror it is cracked up to be unless it's icy or you're on a snowboard. It's no disgrace to ride the chair down – lots of people

do. At the bottom of the Wall is the open terrain of Planachaux, above Champéry, with links to the even bigger open area around Les Crosets and Champoussin.

Taking a lift up through the village of Avoriaz to the ridge behind it is the way to the prettily wooded **Lindarets-Brocheaux** valley, from where lifts and runs in the Linga sector lead to Châtel.

TERRAIN PARKS
Still leading the way
Avoriaz was one of the pioneers of snowboarding in France, and the first terrain park to be built in the country was here in 1993. Avoriaz is still leading the way, and there are now four permanent parks and a super-pipe. The main park is Arare, next to the Bleue du Lac piste; it has its own draglift and is a pro-park, often used for high-profile contests. Four big kickers with red and black take-offs, big rails, a C-box, wall ride and corner jump are the order of the day.

Beginners and intermediates should head to the La Chapelle park, via the Tour or Prolays chairlifts. This is littered with jumps of all sizes and fun little boxes. Trashers was new last season and is strictly for kids. It is located by La Falaise and has several mini-jumps and ride-on boxes. In 2007/08 Avoriaz in association with Burton Snowboards created a fourth park. Named 'The Stash', and situated in the Lindarets forest, it consists of wooden and natural elements, bringing all mountain riding and freestyle together in a serene environment ('I was impressed', says a 2008 visitor). It has banked corners and a host of different obstacles (check www.thestash.com).

Just above the town centre next to the Prodains lift is a good super-pipe. Avoriaz does a brilliant job of keeping the parks maintained, and as a result a lot of riders make this their winter home. Terrain park lift passes are available at around 18 euros for a day, 34 euros for two days.

SNOW RELIABILITY
High resort, low slopes
Although Avoriaz itself is high, its slopes don't go much higher – and some parts of the Portes du Soleil circuit are much lower. Considering their altitude, the north-facing slopes below Hauts Forts hold snow well and the snow in Avoriaz is usually much

↓ Champéry-Les Crosets   ↓ Champéry

Pointe de Mossettes
2275m

CHAVANETTE   2215m

ARARE-
HAUTS FORTS

Châtel

Col du
assachaux
1920m

Avoriaz 1800

LINDARETS-BROCHEAUX

Les Lindarets
1495m

Ardent
1200m

Les Prodains
1145m

Morzine
1000m/3,280ft

Avoriaz 1800

265

Interactive resort shortlist builder at **www.wtss.co.uk**

LIFT PASSES

Portes du Soleil

Prices in €

Age	1-day	6-day
under 16	26	127
16 to 59	39	189
over 60	31	151

Free under 5
Beginner 1 day €21
(Avoriaz only)

Notes
Covers lifts in all resorts; half-day pass available

Alternative passes
Avoriaz only; limited pass for boarders

SCHOOLS

ESF
t 0450 740565

International (L'Ecole de Glisse)
t 0450 740218

Alpine (AASS)
t 0450 383491

Classes
(ESF prices)
6 days (2½hr am and pm) €159

Private lessons
€38 for 1hr, for 1 or 2 people

CHILDREN

Les P'tits Loups
t 0450 740211
9am to 6pm; ages 3mnth to 5yr; 6 days €189

Annie Famose Children's Village
t 0450 740446
From age 3; 9am to 5.30; 6 days with meal €233

Ski schools
Take children from 4 to 12 (6 days €143)

Avoriaz is great for expert riders. As well as top parks (see 'Terrain parks') special ungroomed snowcross areas full of natural obstacles have been created (see 'For experts'). Check www.snowparkavoriaz.com for details. It is well worth hiring a guide here to exploit the vast quantity of good off-piste riding too. There are also plenty of wide, easy slopes, and very few draglifts left, making this a great resort for beginners and intermediates as well. Chalet Snowboard, the first chalet company to target snowboarders, has a couple of chalets at Les Prodains.

better than over the border on the south-facing Swiss slopes. But when snow was sparse on one of our visits we found the smooth, grassy, lower slopes of Les Gets much better than the rocky ones around Avoriaz, which need more snow cover. We've had reports of poor piste maintenance.

FOR EXPERTS
Several challenging runs
Tough terrain is scattered about. The challenging runs down from Hauts Forts to Prodains (including a World Cup downhill) are excellent. There is a tough red and several long, truly black runs. Two chairlifts serve the lower runs, which snow-guns help to keep open. The Swiss Wall at Chavanette will naturally be on your agenda, and Châtel is well worth a trip. The black runs off the Swiss side of Mossettes and Pointe de l'Au are worth trying, and one reporter had a 'very good day' here exploring off-piste with a guide. Four 'snowcross' runs – ungroomed but avalanche controlled and patrolled – have been introduced in the Hauts Forts, Lindarets, Chavanette and Mossettes areas. They are marked on the piste map, closed when dangerous and an excellent idea.

FOR INTERMEDIATES
Virtually the whole area
Although some sections lack variety, the Portes du Soleil is excellent for all grades of intermediates when snow is in good supply. Timid types not worried about pretty surroundings need not leave the Avoriaz sector; reporters recommend the 'wonderfully quiet' and 'scenic' blues to Prodains. Arare and Chavanette are gentle, spacious and above-the-treeline bowls. The Lindarets area is also easy, with pretty runs through the trees, but several reporters complain about long flat sections where poling is required. Champoussin has a lot of easy runs, reached without too much difficulty via Les Crosets and Pointe de l'Au. Better

intermediates have virtually the whole area at their disposal. The runs down to Pré-la-Joux and L'Essert on the way to Châtel, and those either side of Morgins, are particularly attractive – as are the long runs down to Grand-Paradis near Champéry when snow conditions allow. Brave intermediates may want to take on the Wall, but Pointe de Mossettes offers an easier route to Switzerland.

FOR BEGINNERS
Convenient and good for snow
The nursery slopes seem small in relation to the size of the resort, but are adequate because so many visitors are intermediates. The slopes are sunny, yet good for snow, and link well to longer, easy runs. The main problem can be the crowded pistes.

FOR CROSS-COUNTRY
Varied, with some blacks
There are 45km/28 miles of trails, mainly between Avoriaz and Super-Morzine, with others around Lindarets and Montriond.

QUEUES
Main problems now gone
Most of the bad queues have been eliminated by new high-speed lifts. The main long-standing problem is the queue for the cable car at Prodains. Recent visitors report few other problems. But crowds on the pistes (especially at weekends and around the village) can be bad, with care needed to avoid collisions.

MOUNTAIN RESTAURANTS
Good choice over the hill
Editors' choice The rustic chalets at Les Lindarets form one of the great concentrations of mountain huts in the Alps. The jolly Crémaillère (0450 741168) has wonderful chanterelle mushrooms and great atmosphere, but on a good day it's difficult to beat the Terrasse (0450 741617). **Worth knowing about** In Les Lindarets,

The slopes around Avoriaz often have the best snow in the Portes du Soleil →

GETTING THERE

Air Geneva 80km/ 50 miles (2hr); Lyon 200km/124 miles (3½hr)

Rail Cluses (42km/ 26 miles) or Thonon (45km/28 miles); bus and cable car to resort

UK PACKAGES

Alpine Answers, Club Med, Crystal, Directski. com, Erna Low, First Choice, Independent Ski Links, Interactive Resorts, Lagrange, Mountain Tracks, Neilson, Rude Chalets, Ski Activity, Ski Collection, Ski France, Skifrance4less, Skiholidayextras.com, Ski Independence, Ski Leisure Direction, Ski McNeill, Skitracer, Thomson, White Roc **Ardent** Family Ski Company

ACTIVITIES

Indoor Health centre 'Altiform' (sauna, gym, hot tub), squash, ice rink, cinema, bowling **Outdoor** Ice rink, dog sledding, ballooning, mountain biking on snow, ice diving, walking, sleigh rides, snowshoeing, paragliding, snowmobiling, helicopter flights

Phone numbers From abroad use the prefix +33 and omit the initial '0' of the phone number

TOURIST OFFICE

t 0450 740211 info@avoriaz.com www.avoriaz.com

a 2008 reporter recommends Marmottes ('superb beef bourguignon'). Near the top of the gondola from Morzine, the rustic Grenouille du Marais has good food and views. The table-service Abricotine does 'excellent galettes'. Refuge des Brocheaux at Les Brocheaux and Pas de Chavanette, at the top of the Swiss Wall have also been recommended.

SCHOOLS AND GUIDES
Try AASS
The ESF has a good reputation; classes can be large, but we have reports of satisfied beginners making 'very good progress' and very successful private snowboard lessons. Another visitor had 'inspirational' snowboard lessons with former pro Angelique Corez-Hubert through the International school. The Avoriaz Alpine Ski School has British instructors and has been highly recommended, especially for 'quite excellent children's lessons'. One reporter tried both ESF and AASS for private lessons; he thought the AASS's higher price wasn't justified and criticised its 'haphazard admin system'. However, his son rated the advanced snowboard lessons as 'excellent'.

FACILITIES FOR CHILDREN
'Annie Famose delivers'
The Village des Enfants, which takes children from age three and is run by ex-downhill champ Annie Famose, is a key part of the family appeal of Avoriaz. Its facilities are excellent – a chalet full of activities and special slopes with Disney characters.

STAYING THERE

HOW TO GO
Self-catering dominates
Alternatives to apartments are few.
Chalets There are several available – comfortable and attractive but mainly designed for small family groups.
Hotels There is one good hotel.
***Dromonts (0450 740811) The original core of the resort, taken over and renovated by a celebrity French chef and in the Hip Hotels guidebook. 'Bit expensive but very nice with excellent food,' said a recent reporter.
Apartments Reporters say that some apartments need refurbishing, and others are typically 'cramped and basic'. But the Falaise apart-hotel, the Balcons du Soleil, Sepia and Datcha

('very basic') residences have all been recommended. The 'Shopi supermarket is far superior to the Sherpa'.

EATING OUT
Good; booking essential
There are more than 30 restaurants but there isn't much variety and they get very busy; a 2008 visitor says 'book a table, otherwise you might have long waits'. The hotel Dromonts' Table du Marché restaurant is 'pricey but excellent'. The Bistro and Cabane have been recommended for 'good food and value', as have the Fontaines Blanches for Savoyard food, Douchka for its 'excellent Moroccan lamb shank', Intrêts for pizza, pasta and Savoyard fare, Au Briska for a cosy night out, Falaise for 'good pizza' and Changabang at the bottom end of town for cheap burgers and salads.

APRES-SKI
Lively, but not much choice
A few bars have a good atmosphere, particularly in happy hour. The Yeti is busy at 4pm. The Tavaillon attracts Brits and has Sky TV and 'good draught beers', and the Fantastique is worth a visit. For late-night dancing the Place has bands.

OFF THE SLOPES
Not much at the resort
Those not interested in the slopes are better off in Morzine – though Avoriaz does have the Altiform Fitness Centre, with saunas and hot tubs. Pedestrians are not allowed to ride the chairlifts.

Avoriaz 1800

267

Interactive resort shortlist builder at www.wtss.co.uk

Chamonix

Traditional tourist/mountaineering town with great atmosphere and towering mountains, offering stunning views and off-piste

COSTS

① ② ③ ④ ⑤ ⑥

RATINGS

The slopes
Fast lifts	★★★
Snow	★★★★
Extent	★★★
Expert	★★★★★
Intermediate	★★
Beginner	★★
Convenience	★
Queues	★★
Mountain restaurants	★★

The rest
Scenery	★★★★★
Resort charm	★★★★
Off-slope	★★★★★

NEWS

For 2008/09 the old access lift to Le Brévent is to be replaced, at last, by a 10-person gondola with double the capacity, easing queues to return to the valley as much as queues to go up. More snowmaking is planned for Flégère.

The Aiguille de Midi valley station is being redeveloped and extended to include skier services, retail and accommodation facilities.

- A lot of very tough terrain, especially off-piste
- Stunning views
- Amazing cable car to the Aiguille du Midi, for the famous Vallée Blanche (or just the views)
- Lots of different resorts and areas covered on Mont Blanc lift pass
- Town steeped in Alpine traditions
- Easy access by road, rail and air – excellent short break destination

- Several separate mountains: mixed ability groups are likely to have to split up, and the bus service gets mixed reviews
- Pistes in each area are quite limited
- Bad weather can shut the best runs
- Still some old lifts and queues in key spots
- Few good mountain restaurants
- It's a busy town, with lots of road traffic – not a relaxing place

Chamonix could not be more different from the archetypal high-altitude, purpose-built French resort. Unless you are based next to one of the half-dozen separate mountains and stick to it, you have to drive or take a bus each day. There is all sorts of terrain, but the place really makes sense as destination only for the expert and the adventurous would-be expert. Chamonix is neither convenient nor conventional.

But it is special. The Chamonix valley cuts deeply through Europe's highest mountains and glaciers. The runs it offers are everything really tough runs should be – not only steep, but high and long. If you like your snow and scenery on the wild side, give Chamonix a try. But be warned: there are those who try it and never go home – including lots of Brits.

THE RESORT

Chamonix is a long-established tourist town that spreads for miles along the valley in the shadow of Mont Blanc.

It's a bustling place with scores of hotels and restaurants, visitors all year round and a lively Saturday market. The car-free centre of town is full of atmosphere, with cobbled streets and squares, beautiful old buildings, a fast-running river, pavement cafes crowded with shoppers and tourists staring at the glaciers above. Not everything is rosy: there are lots of obtrusive apartment blocks, some of the old buildings have fallen into disrepair, and traffic clogs the streets around the centre at times.

Chamonix has shops dealing in everything from tacky souvenirs to high-tech climbing and skiing gear. If you're in the market for the latter, there's no better place to go.

On either side of the centre, just within walking distance, are base stations of the famous cable car to the Aiguille du Midi, starting point of the famous Vallée Blanche glacier run, and

a new gondola to Le Brévent. The third high-altitude area close to the town, La Flégère, is reached by cable car from the nearby village of Les Praz. The three other major ski areas are more widely spread along the valley.

At the top of the valley are villages of Le Tour, at the foot of the Balme slopes, and Argentière, at the foot of the Grands Montets – for many visitors, the core of Chamonix's appeal. These villages are described at the end of the chapter, but their slopes are taken in to the main part of the chapter. In the opposite direction, down the valley, is Les Houches. This is entirely described at the end of the chapter, because its lifts are separately owned and not covered by the basic Chamonix pass. Regular buses, free with a guest card, link all these points but can get very crowded and aren't always reliable. The evening service finishes early. Like many reporters, we rate a car essential. A car also means you can get easily to other resorts covered by the regional Skipass Mont Blanc, such as Megève and Les Contamines, and Courmayeur in Italy.

↑ The slopes of Les Houches give great views of the Mont Blanc massif

SNOWPIX.COM / CHRIS GILL

KEY FACTS

Resort	1035m
	3,400ft
Slopes	1035-3840m
	3,400-12,600ft
Lifts	48
Pistes	153km
	95 miles
Green	16%
Blue	36%
Red	32%
Black	16%
Snowmaking	
	125 guns

The obvious place to stay for the full experience is in downtown Chamonix, unless you plan to spend your time mainly on one mountain, such as the Grands Montets.

THE MOUNTAINS

Each of the different areas is worth exploring. Practically all the slopes – with the notable exception of Les Houches – are above the treeline; there are some runs through woods to the valley, but the ones to Chamonix, in particular, are often tricky or closed.

There is a valley piste map and individual area maps. Reporters repeatedly complain of poor signing and marking of runs – 'virtually non-existent', and 'several reasonably experienced members of our party went off the edge of a long cat-track at Balme in near white-out conditions'.

THE SLOPES
Very fragmented

There are several low beginner areas dotted along the Chamonix valley but there are five main areas.

The gondola for **Le Brévent** (see 'News') departs a short, steep walk or bus ride from the centre of town. There are runs on open slopes below the arrival point at 2000m/6,560ft, and a cable car above takes you to the summit. There is lift link to **La Flégère**, also accessible via an inadequate old cable car from the village of Les Praz. Both of these sunny areas give stunning views of Mont Blanc.

Up the valley at Argentière a cable car or chairlift take you up to **Les Grands Montets**. Chairs and a gondola serve excellent steep terrain above mid-mountain, but much of the best terrain is accessed by a further cable car of relatively low capacity, not covered by the basic valley pass

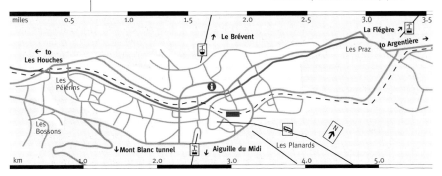

(Chamonix Le Pass). This shady area can be very cold in early season.

A little way further up the valley the secluded village of Le Tour sits at the foot of the **Balme** area of mainly easy pistes. A gondola goes up to mid-mountain, with a mix of drags and lifts above. The slopes are also accessible from Vallorcine. It is also the starting point for good off-piste runs, some of which end up in Switzerland.

Les Houches is the only major area down-valley of Chamonix. This low, wooded area is accessed by a gondola or cable car from the village. The lifts are not covered by the standard pass, and we describe the skiing separately at the end of the chapter.

TERRAIN PARKS
There is one at last

For years talk of a terrain park here was sacrilege because of the excellent natural hits and off-piste terrain. However, due to popular demand, and several winters of poor snow conditions, the Snow Bowl park has been built on the Grands Montets. The experienced HO5 crew, responsible for parks in several other resorts and headed by ex-international pro Nico Watier, has been working hard to fine tune the 800m long course that hosts over 16 obstacles including jumps, rails and a wall ride. You can check the latest details at www.ho5park.com. The fun zone is designed for beginners wanting their first taste of air time.

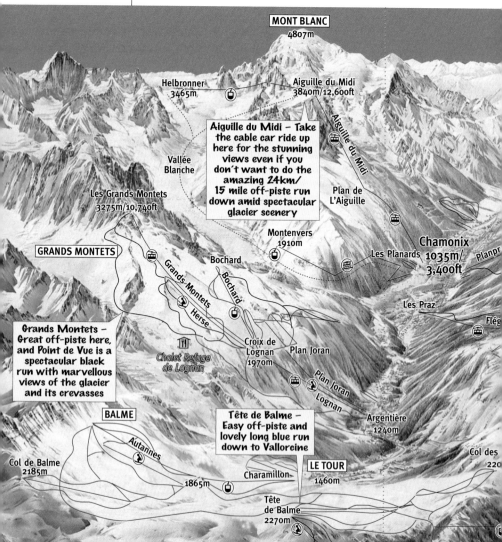

SNOW RELIABILITY
Good high up; poor low down

The top runs on the north-facing Grands Montets slopes above Argentière generally have good snow, and the season normally lasts well into May. The risk of finding the top lift shut because of bad weather is more of a worry. There's snowmaking on the busy Bochard piste and the run to the valley, which can now be kept open late in the season. Balme has a snowy location, a good late-season record and snowmaking on the run down to the valley at Le Tour. The largely south-facing slopes of Brévent and Flégère (due more snowmaking for 2008/09) suffer in warm weather, and the steep black runs to the resort are

often closed. Don't be tempted to try these unless you know they are in good condition – they can be very tricky. Some of the low beginners' areas have snowmaking. Most of our reporters have been surprised by the respectable piste grooming.

FOR EXPERTS
One of the great resorts

Chamonix is renowned for its extensive steep terrain and deep snow. To get the best out of the area you really need to have a local guide. There is also lots of excellent terrain for ski-touring on skins. See the feature panel for more on off-piste possibilities.

The Grands Montets cable car offers stunning views from the observation

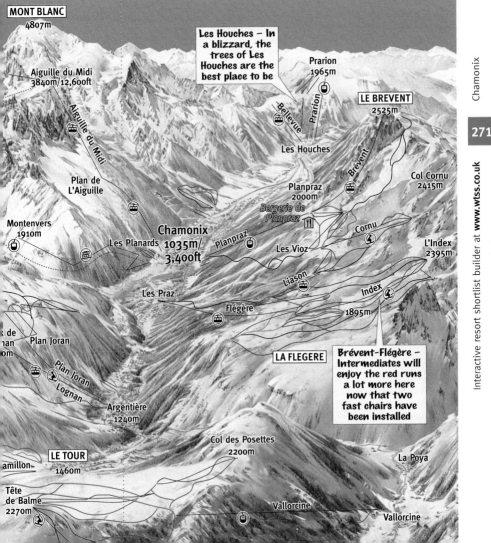

MONT BLANC
4807m

Aiguille du Midi
3840m/12,600ft

Aiguille du Midi

Les Houches – In a blizzard, the trees of Les Houches are the best place to be

Prarion
1965m

Prarion

Bellevue

LE BREVENT
2525m

Brévent

Les Houches

Plan de L'Aiguille

Planpraz
2000m

Bergerie de Planpraz

Col Cornu
2415m

Montenvers
1910m

Chamonix 1035m/ 3,400ft

Les Planards

Planpraz

Les Vioz

Cornu

L'Index
2395m

Les Praz

Liason

Index
1895m

Flégère

LA FLEGERE

Brévent-Flégère – Intermediates will enjoy the red runs a lot more here now that two fast chairs have been installed

Plan Joran

Plan Joran

Lognan

Argentière
1240m

Col des Posettes
2200m

La Poya

LE TOUR
1460m

amillon

Tête de Balme
2270m

Vallorcine

Vallorcine

boarding

The undisputed king of freeride resorts, Chamonix is a haven for advanced snowboarders who relish the steep and wild terrain. This means, however, that in peak season it gets crowded and fresh snow gets tracked out very quickly. The rough and rugged nature of the slopes means it is not best suited to beginners, but rather to more experienced adventurous riders, willing to try true all-mountain riding. If you do the Vallée Blanche, be warned: the usual route is flat in places. Check out former British champ Neil McNab's excellent extreme backcountry camps at www.mcnabsnowboarding.com. Most areas are equipped mainly with cable cars, gondolas and chairs. However, there are quite a few difficult drags at Balme that cause inexperienced boarders problems – though you can avoid these if you can hack the cat tracks to take you to other lifts, says a reporter. There is a terrain park on Grands Montets and a new one at Les Houches.

LIFT PASSES

Chamonix Le Pass

Prices in €

Age	1-day	6-day
under 16	30	148
16 to 59	37	185
over 60	30	148

Free under 4; over 70
Beginner no deals

Notes
Covers Brévent, Flégère, Balme, Grands Montets except top cable car plus four small beginner areas; family reductions

Alternative passes
Mont Blanc Unlimited pass covers all the above plus Les Houches, top cable car at les Grands Montets, Aiguille du Midi cable car, the Helbronner gondola, the Montenvers-Mer de Glace railway, the Tramway du Mont-Blanc and a day in Courmayeur in Italy; Skipass Mont Blanc covers all the lifts in the 13 resorts of the Mont Blanc area

platform above the top station – if you've got the legs and lungs to climb the 121 steep metal steps. (But beware: it's 200 more slippery steel steps down from the cable car before you hit the snow.) The ungroomed black pistes from here – Point de Vue and Pylones – are long and exhilarating. The former sails right by some dramatic sections of glacier, with marvellous views of the crevasses.

The Bochard gondola serves a challenging red back to Lognan and a black to either Plan Joran or the chairlift below. Shortly after you have made a start down the black, you can head off-piste down the Combe de la Pendant bowl ('excellent, so much space, always great snow').

At Le Brévent there's more to test experts than the piste map suggests – there are a number of variations on the runs down from the summit. Some are very steep and prone to ice. The runs in Combe de la Charlanon are quiet and include one red piste and excellent off-piste if the snow is good.

At La Flégère there are further challenging slopes – in the Combe Lachenal, crossed by the linking cable car, say – and a tough run back to the village when the snow permits. The short draglift above L'Index opens up a couple of good steep runs (a red and a black) plus a good area of off-piste.

Balme boasts little tough terrain on-piste but there are off-piste routes from the high points to Le Tour, towards Vallorcine or into Switzerland.

FOR INTERMEDIATES
It's worth trying it all
For less confident intermediates, the Balme area above Le Tour is good for cruising and usually free from crowds (a 2007 reporter enjoyed 'untracked powder here well into the afternoon').

There are excellent shady, steeper runs, wooded lower down, on the north side of Tête de Balme, served by a fast quad. A blue run goes on down to Vallorcine but it is prone to closure.

Don't be put off the other, apparently macho areas, all of which actually provide a good mix of genuine blue and red runs as well as the seriously steep unpisted terrain that attracts the experts. Even the Grands Montets has an excellent area of blue runs at mid-mountain, served by several chairs (all slow, sadly). The step up to the red terrain higher up is quite pronounced, however.

If the snow and weather are good, confident intermediates can join a guided group and do the Vallée Blanche (see feature panel).

A day trip to Courmayeur makes an interesting change of scene, especially when the weather is bad (it can be sunny there when Chamonix's high lifts are closed by blizzards or high winds).

FOR BEGINNERS
Head for Le Tour
There are nursery slopes either side of Chamonix itself, but they are limited, low and (in the case of Les Planards) dark and cold in mid-winter. They are separated from the other sectors of slopes, so moving on to longer runs is a major upheaval. La Vormaine, at Le Tour, is a much better bet: extensive, relatively high, sunny, and connected to the slopes of the Balme sector, where there are easy long runs to progress to.

FOR CROSS-COUNTRY
A decent network of trails
Most of the 43km/27 miles of prepared trails lie at valley level in and between Chamonix and Argentière. All the trails are shady and cold in midwinter, and

SCHOOLS

ESF
t 0450 532257

Evolution 2
t 0450 559022

All Mountain Performance
t 0450 532833

Summits
t 0450 535014

Classes
6 half days: €178

Private lessons
€39 for 1hr, for 1 or 2 people

GUIDES

Compagnie des Guides
t 0450 530088

Chamonix Experience
t 0450 540936

GETTING THERE

Air Geneva 86km/
53 miles (1½hr); Lyon 226km/140 miles (3hr)

Rail Station in resort, on the St Gervais-Le Fayet/Vallorcine line.

Direct TGV link from Paris on Friday evenings and at weekends

they fade fast in the spring sun. Catch the bus rather than ski between the Chamonix and Argentière areas, suggests a 2007 reporter, as the link is by 'steep and difficult trails'.

QUEUES
Ancient lifts, serious queues

The news of the overdue replacement of the Brévent gondola for 2008/09 is very welcome, and will doubtless bring about a huge improvement at both ends of the day (it's normal to have to ride down). But this is only one of the valley's problem lifts. The ancient and inadequate Flégère cable car can generate queues of an hour or more – and there are often queues to come down again. The lifts out of Argentière build queues, and the chairlift appears to be on its last legs – it no longer operates from the main station, but starts a short way up the slope. At mid-mountain, the top cable car is a famous bottleneck. You can book slots in advance (at the ticket office or online) and it's 'best to do this the day before as places tend to sell out early', says a reporter. You can instead join the 'stand by' queue, which we've found to be an effective alternative. At Les Houches the two access lifts are widely separated, and it's worth going for the modern gondola rather than the inadequate Bellevue cable car. Both lifts build queues in poor

weather when woody Les Houches gets crowded. Expect queues on the hill, too – all the chairs here are slow.

Crowded pistes are also reported to be a problem in places – most notably at Lognan on Grands Montets.

MOUNTAIN RESTAURANTS
Mainly dull

Editors' choice On Le Brévent the Bergerie de Planpraz (0450 530542) is the most attractive option: a wood and stone building with self- and table-service and good food; but it gets very busy. On the Grands Montets the tiny, rustic Chalet-Refuge de Lognan (06 8856 0354), off the Variante Hôtel run to the valley, has marvellous views and simple but satisfying food.

Worth knowing about On Le Brévent the little Panoramic at the top enjoys amazing views over to Mont Blanc and the food is fine. There's a self-service place at La Flégère with a large terrace and excellent views. On the Grands Montets the Plan Joran has table- and self-service ('excellent pizzas'), but gets busy. There's also an indoor picnic area and 'good sunny terrace'. Tucked away in the woods to skier's right of the home run, the Crémerie du Glacier is a cosy spot for a croute. At Balme at the top of the gondola from Le Tour, there's an adequate self-service, Chalet de Charamillon, and

THE BEST OFF-PISTE SKIING IN THE WORLD?

Chamonix is renowned as an extreme sports Mecca, with arguably some of the best off-piste skiing in the world. And while thrill seekers and off-piste specialists are spoiled for choice, there is plenty for those looking for their first powder experience, too.

Les Houches and *Balme*, at opposite ends of the Chamonix Valley, are ideal for a first taste off the beaten track. The forested slopes of Les Houches are easy to navigate on bad-weather days, with gentle blue runs bringing you back to the valley. Balme's open slopes are perfect for a foray into deep snow in between the pistes, with firmer ground just a few reassuring metres away.

Snowboarders flock to *La Flégère* after a snowfall, its array of boulders and drop-offs turning it into a massive terrain park. The open bowl of Combe Lachenal is easily accessed from the top of the Index lift, and the south-facing slopes of this ski area provide excellent spring skiing.

From the top of *Les Grands Montets* (3275m/10,740ft) skiing is mostly off-piste and on glacial terrain. The vast north-facing slope of the main face offers countless ways down, satisfyingly steep without being at all intimidating, with snow conditions that are often among the best in the valley. Off the back, there are several rewarding ways down to the Glacier d'Argentière. In the opposite direction you have access to the steep Pas de Chèvre run. Skiing under the colossal granite spire of Le Dru, with views of the Vallée Blanche, is an unforgettable experience. The Couloir du Dru and the Rectiligne are also on this face, reserved for the adventurous – with some slopes of 40/45°.

These are just some of the off-piste options in the Chamonix valley, but the possibilities are endless. Together with ski-touring itineraries like the Haute Route (Chamonix to Zermatt), and heli-skiing on the Italian side of Mont Blanc and in neighbouring Switzerland, the wealth of off-piste on offer could keep you skiing for a lifetime. The Vallée Blanche is covered in a feature panel later in this chapter.

also a picnic area. The charming Chalet-Refuge du Col de Balme – a short hike beyond the lifts – used to be famed for its grumpy reception, but we're told visitors are now 'welcomed rather than treated as a nuisance'. Reports are welcome on the inviting little chalet recently opened at the foot of the Aiguillette draglift.

SCHOOLS AND GUIDES
The place to try something new
The schools here are particularly strong in specialist fields – off-piste, glacier and couloir skiing, ski touring, snowboarding and cross-country. English-speaking instructors and mountain guides are plentiful, and specialist Chamonix tour operators can arrange them in advance for guests. At the Maison de la Montagne is the main ESF office and the HQ of the Compagnie des Guides, which has taken visitors to the mountains for 150 years. Both offer ready-made week-long 'tours' taking clients to a different mountain or resort each day. We have a good report of the ESF Ski Fun Tour, where they ski a different Mont Blanc region resort each day, transport included: 'Fantastic – we cannot speak highly enough of the guides.' Reporters have also praised the ESF instructors provided by Club Med ('a

witty, friendly instructor who spoke excellent English'; but 'some class sizes were large – up to 14'). Competition is provided by a number of smaller, independent guiding and teaching outfits. Evolution 2 has been recommended. Mark Gear, who runs All Mountain Performance, has been highly praised by a recent reporter. Chamonix Experience offers a full range of options, from classic itineraries and Italian heli-skiing to hidden off-piste routes and avalanche courses.

FACILITIES FOR CHILDREN
Couple of choices
The ESF's Panda Club is used by quite a few British visitors and reports have been enthusiastic. The Argentière base can be inconvenient for meeting up with children for the afternoons. Specialist family tour operator Esprit Ski has a nursery in its Sapinière chalet hotel, which is situated near the Savoy nursery slope.

THE VALLEE BLANCHE

This is a trip you do for the stunning scenery. The views of the ice, the crevasses and seracs – and the spectacular rock spires beyond – are simply mind-blowing. The standard run, although exceptionally long, is not steep – mostly effortless gliding down gentle slopes with only the occasional steeper, choppy section to deal with. In the right conditions, it is well within the capability of a confident, fit intermediate (but the usual route is rather flat for snowboarders). If snow is sparse, as it can be in early season especially, the run can be very tricky – there can be patches of sheet ice, exposed stones and rocks, and narrow snow bridges over gaping crevasses. And if fresh snow is abundant, different challenges may arise. Go in a guided group – dangerous crevasses lurk to swallow those not in the know – and check conditions before signing up. The trip is popular – on a busy day 2,500 people do it; book in advance at the Maison de la Montagne or other ski school offices. To miss the crowds go very early on a weekday, or in the afternoon if you are a good skier and can get down quickly.

The Aiguille du Midi cable car takes you to 3840m/12,600ft. Across the bridge from the top station on the Piton Nord is the Piton Central; a stair-climb higher the 3842 cafeteria (claimed to be Europe's highest restaurant) – the view of Mont Blanc from here should not be missed, and it gives you the opportunity to adjust to the dizzying altitude. Be prepared for extreme cold up here, too. A tunnel delivers you to the infamous ridge-walk down to the start of the run. Except at the start of the season, the walk is well prepared, with regular steps cut in the snow, a wall of snow between you and the drop to Chamonix, and fixed guide-ropes for you to hang on to. If you are prepared with a backpack capable of carrying your skis, and crampons to give your heels some grip, it's no problem. Without those accessories, it can be tiring and worrying. Many parties rope up to their guides.

There are variants on the classic route, of varying difficulty and danger. Lack of snow often rules out the full 24km/15 mile run down to Chamonix; a steep stairway and slow gondola link the glacier to the station at Montenvers, for the half-hour mountain railway ride down to the town.

**Panda Club
(Argentière)**
t 0450 540476
From age 3

Piou Piou
0450 532257
Run by ESF; ages
from 3

Babysitter list
Available from the
tourist office

Ski schools
Take children aged 3
to 12 (6 half days
from €107 – ESF
price)

IAN STRATFORD

At the Aiguille du
Midi, you are
2800m/9,190ft above
the town – truly
amazing ↓

HOW TO GO
Any way you like
There is all sorts of accommodation,
and lots of it.
Chalets Many are run by small
specialist operators. Quality tends to
be high and value for money good.
Hotels A wide choice, many modestly
priced, the majority with no more than
30 rooms or so. Bookings for short
stay are no problem – the peak
season is summer. Club Med has three
linked buildings near the centre;
reporters rate it 'amazing value'.
★★★★Hameau Albert 1er (0450 530509)
Smart, 100-year-old chalet-style hotel
with 'truly excellent' food (two Michelin
stars) but expensive rooms (especially
in the farmhouse annexe). Pool.
★★★★Auberge du Bois Prin (0450
533351) A small modern chalet with a
big reputation; great views; bit of a
hike into town (closer to Le Brévent).
★★★★Mont-Blanc (0450 530564) Grand
19th-century place in a central
location, with gastro restaurant.
★★★★Jeu de Paume (Lavancher) (0450
540376) Alpine satellite of a chic
Parisian hotel: a beautifully furnished

modern chalet halfway to Argentière:
'Tasteful ... friendly staff ... lovely.'
★★★★Grand Hotel des Alpes (0450
553780) Elegant, central; with pool,
sauna, hot tub. Friendly Italian staff.
★★★★Morgane (0450 535715)
Completely revamped last year in cool
modern style; seriously good
restaurant; convenient location
between centre and Aiguille de Midi
cable car; pool, sauna.
★★★Alpina (0450 534777) Much the
biggest in town: modernist-functional
place just north of centre.
★★★Croix-Blanche (0450 530011)
Central, dates from 1793. Reportedly
traditional, simply-furnished rooms.
★★★Gourmets et Italy (0450 530138)
Spot-on central mid-price B&B hotel.
★★★Labrador (Les Praz) (0450 559009)
Scandinavian-style chalet close to the
Flégère lift. Good restaurant.
★★★Prieuré (0450 532072) Mega-chalet
on northern ring-road – handy for
drivers, quite close to centre.
★★★Vallée Blanche (0450 530450)
Smart, low-priced 3-star B&B hotel,
handy for centre and Aiguille du Midi.
★★★Gustavia (0450 530031) Good,
central position. 'Spacious, clean and
modern rooms.'

***Hermitage** (0450 531387) Central, very close to sports centre and cross-country tracks. Said to be 'modern and Savoyard-style smart'.

***Savoyarde** (0450 530077) Handy for the Brévent lifts. Recommended by a reporter.

****Richemond** (0450 530885) Traditional, with good public areas. Gets mixed reviews from reporters.

****Arve** (0450 530231) Central, by the river; small rooms. Praised for good service and modest prices.

****Faucigny** (0450 530117) Cottage-style; in centre.

Clubhouse (0450 909656) Boutique hotel with a wide choice of rooms. 'Excellent roast dinners.'

Le Vert (0450 531358) Good value with en suite rooms for one to six people. 'Good bar, pool table and Sunday roast.'

Apartments Many properties in UK package brochures are in convenient but cramped blocks in Chamonix Sud. The Balcons du Savoy and Ginabelle are a cut above the rest: spacious, pool, gym, steam room etc.

EATING OUT
Plenty of quality places
The top hotels all have excellent restaurants and there are many other good places. One or two local guides give useful information about a selection of places.

The Impossible is a favourite with us and with readers – a rustic chalet a bit out of the centre with a varied menu ('Superb, one of the best meals we've had in the Alps,' said a 2007 reporter). We always enjoy the intimate Atmosphère, by the river, despite its two-sitting system ('excellent', 'cosy, trendy, friendly efficient service' say reporters). The National, next door, has also been suggested. The Panier des Quatre Saisons is another favourite – better than its shopping-gallery setting would suggest. Alan Peru is an excellent Asian-fusion place that makes a great change from the French norm.

Other reader recommendations include Maison Carrier in the Albert 1er hotel ('Bustling, rustic with great value traditional food'), Monchu (Savoyard specialities), Chaudron ('outstanding', 'excellent service') Bergerie ('traditional' and 'fantastic'), Casa Valerio for pasta and pizza, Pitz ('decent, not too expensive meal'), and Tigre Tigre ('English-run curry house').

Munchies is Swedish-owned and does fusion food ('small, friendly, good atmosphere'). New places include: the Sahara cafe (Asian) and Petite Kitchen (traditional French).

APRES-SKI
Lots of bars and music
Many of the bars around the pedestrianised centre of Chamonix get crowded at sundown – none more so than the Choucas video bar. During the evening, The Pub ('friendly staff and good British/Irish beer') and Bar'd Up are busy. The Chambre Neuf at the Gustavia hotel has live music and dancing ('crowded, noisy, but great fun'). The Micro Brasserie is 'very good', with live bands and DJs. No Escape is a 'funky, upmarket' lounge bar/restaurant. Along with Privilege, it's aimed 'at a more discerning clientele who like their après-ski at a less frantic pace'. Elevation 1904 is also 'quieter'. The Brit-run Dérapage is 'small but cosy'.

There's a lively variety of nightclubs and discos. The Choucas (again) and Garage ('lap dancing') are popular. The Cantina sometimes has live music. Bar Terrasse has 'live rock' every night and serves 'a good snack menu till 10pm'. The Soul Food cafe on the rue du Moulin has 'bags of atmosphere'.

OFF THE SLOPES
An excellent choice
There's more off-slope activity here than in many resorts. Excursion possibilities include Annecy, Geneva, Martigny, Courmayeur and Turin. The Alpine Museum is 'very interesting but all in French', the library has a selection of English language books and there's a good sports centre, ice skating and pool. A special lift pass is available for pedestrians (cost 40 euros per week in 2007/08).

Argentière 1240m/4,070ft

The old village is in a lovely setting towards the head of the valley – the Glacier d'Argentière pokes down towards it and the Aiguille du Midi and Mont Blanc still dominate the scene down the valley. There's a fair bit of modern development, but it still has a rustic appeal.

A number of the hotels are simple, inexpensive and handy for the village centre – but it's a fair hike (uphill on the way back) or a bus ride to and

ACTIVITIES

Indoor Sports complex (swimming pool, sauna, steam room, tennis, squash, ice rink, fitness room, climbing wall), Alpine museum, library, cinemas, bowling

Outdoor Ice rink, snowshoeing, walking paths, horse sleigh rides, tobogganing, dog sledding, paragliding, paintballing

UK PACKAGES

Argentière Action Outdoors, Alpine Answers, AmeriCan Ski, BoardnLodge, Chamonix Backcountry, Collineige, Crystal, Erna Low, Independent Ski Links, Interactive Resorts, Interhome, Lagrange, Peak Retreats, Ski France, Ski Freshtracks, Ski holidayextras.com, Ski Independence, Ski Leisure Direction, Ski Weekend, TheWhite Chalet.com, White Roc **Les Houches** Alpine Answers, Alpine Ski and Golf Company, AmeriCan Ski, Barrelli, Bigfoot, Erna Low, Holiday in Alps, Inghams, Lagrange, Peak Retreats, Ski Expectations, Ski France, Skiholiday extras.com, Ski Leisure Direction, Skiweekends. com **Les Praz** Bigfoot

Phone numbers From abroad use the prefix +33 and omit the initial '0' of the phone number

TOURIST OFFICES

Chamonix t 0450 530024 info@chamonix.com www.chamonix.com

Argentière t 0450 540214 argentiere.info @chamonix.com

Les Houches t 0450 555062 info@leshouches. com www.leshouches.com

from the slopes. The 3-star Grands-Montets (0450 540666) is handy for the slopes but a hike to the village. It's a large chalet-style building and 'offers the comfort and service of a 4-star' says a visitor; 'luxurious rooms and a superb pool' says another. The family-run 3-star Montana (0450 541499) provides 'lovely rooms, excellent food', the 2-star Couronne (0450 540002) is basic but 'a great value, old-fashioned French hotel', the 2-star Dahu (0450 540155) is 'excellent value'.

Restaurants and bars are informal and inexpensive. The Dahu is recommended by a 2007 reporter for 'great food, good value set menus', has a 'lovely terrace' and is 'busy with locals and residents'. The Stone serves 'authentic pizzas and a few pasta dishes' and 'is the place for a game of darts or table football'. The Office is always packed with Brits and Scandinavians and has live bands and 'terrific cooked breakfasts'. The Savoy bar is another traditional favourite – 'lively, friendly, well priced'. The 'friendly' Rencard plays reggae music and 'is a great place to relax with fine pizzas, omelettes and beer'. The Rusticana is 'laid back' with 'friendly staff, good selection of beers and decent food', says a 2007 visitor.

Le Tour 1455m/4,770ft

Le Tour is a charming, unspoiled hamlet at the head of the Chamonix valley, handy for Argentière. A gondola from here serves the Domaine de Balme slopes, an area of mainly easy runs that it shares with Vallorcine in the next valley. The valley's best nursery slopes are next to the village, at La Vormaine.

Vallorcine 1255m/4,120ft

Vallorcine is a small, but developing, traditional mountain village over the Col des Montets, near the Swiss border and 16km/10 miles from Chamonix. The village shares with Le Tour the main valley's Balme area.

A gondola and chairlift take you to Tête de Balme. A gentle blue run leads back to the village, but it is prone to closure. There's a separate small area of local slopes at La Poya.

Accommodation is mainly apartment-based. The 4-star L'Ours Bleu, with pool and spa facilities, is due to open near the gondola for

2008/09. There's a limited choice of restaurants and bars. The Buvette at the station is recommended for drinks whilst waiting for the train back to Chamonix (it takes 20 minutes).

Les Houches 1010m/3,310ft

Les Houches is 6km/4 miles down the valley from Chamonix. The wooded slopes – popular when bad weather closes other areas – are the biggest single area of pistes in the valley. But the lifts are owned separately, and are not covered by the standard Chamonix pass – you need the Mont Blanc Unlimited or the resort's own pass.

Les Houches is a pleasant village, sitting in the shade of the looming Mont Blanc massif. There is an old core with a pretty church, but modern developments in chalet style have spread widely along the road at the foot of the slopes, with the result that some of them are quite a way from the lifts. These are widely separated – a queue-prone cable car and a recently renovated gondola, going to opposite ends of the slopes. Up the mountain, all the lifts are drags or slow chairs – even the most recent additions. There are some awkward links in the network, and signing is poor.

There are some gentle runs at the top of the main lifts (including newly-improved nursery slopes), and long, worthwhile runs back towards the village – blue, red and black. The last is Chamonix's World Cup Downhill race course: an excellent intermediate run, scarcely deserving its black status.

Beyond the summit ridge is a very gentle area with cross-country loops and then some pleasant, sunny woodland runs on the back of the mountain with views across to the slopes of Megève.

In good weather the slopes are quiet, and the views superb from the several attractive restaurants, which are cheaper than others in the valley. Recommendations include the Terrain, Vieilles Luges and the Ferme des Agapes ('excellent'). Snow-cover on the lower slopes is not reliable, but there is a fair amount of snowmaking.

The village is quiet, but there are some pleasant bars and restaurants. Reporters have recommended the 3-star du Bois (0450 545035). There are some good apartments available, including the MGM Hameau de Pierre Blanche ones with pool, sauna etc.

OT CHÂTEL / JEAN-FRANÇOIS VUARAND

Châtel

A distinctively French base in an ideal position for exploring the huge Portes du Soleil circuit which spans the French-Swiss border

RATINGS

The slopes

Fast lifts	**
Snow	**
Extent	*****
Expert	***
Intermediate	****
Beginner	***
Convenience	**
Queues	***
Mountain restaurants	***

The rest

Scenery	****
Resort charm	***
Off-slope	**

NEWS

For 2007/08 a new terrain park aimed at intermediates and experts, the Happy Park, was built by the Cornebois chairlift. Two toboggan runs for children have been built at Pré-la-Joux.

In La Chapelle-d'Abondance a six-pack, the Crêt Béni, replaced an old double chair.

278

- ➕ Very extensive, pretty, intermediate terrain – the Portes du Soleil
- ➕ Wide range of cheap and cheerful, good-value accommodation
- ➕ Pleasant, lively, French-dominated old village, still quite rustic in parts
- ➕ Local slopes are among the best in the Portes du Soleil and relatively queue-free
- ➕ Easily reached – one of the shortest drives from the Channel, and close to Geneva

- ➖ Traffic congestion can be a problem at weekends and in peak season
- ➖ Both the resort and the slopes are low for a French resort, with the resulting risk of rain and poor snow – though snowmaking is now extensive
- ➖ Some main lifts are a bus ride from the village centre
- ➖ Best nursery slopes are reached by bus or gondola

Châtel offers an attractive blend of qualities much like that of Morzine – another established valley village in the Portes du Soleil. Morzine is a bit more polished, Châtel (with a claimed 40 working farms) more rustic. But its key advantage is that it is part of the main Portes du Soleil circuit. There is a gap in the circuit at Châtel, filled by buses; but this is more of an irritant to those passing through than for Châtel residents, for many of whom the excellent local bus services are part of the daily routine. At weekends it's worth trying the slopes of nearby La Chapelle-d'Abondance, which are pleasantly uncrowded.

THE RESORT

Châtel lies near the head of the wooded Dranse valley, at the north-eastern limit of the French-Swiss Portes du Soleil ski circuit.

It is a much expanded but still attractive old village. Modern unpretentious chalet-style hotels and apartments rub shoulders with old farms where cattle still live in winter.

Although there is a definite centre, the village sprawls along the road in from lake Geneva and the diverging roads out – up the hillside towards Morgins and along the valley towards the Linga and Pré-la-Joux lifts.

Lots of visitors take cars and the centre can get clogged with traffic – especially at weekends. Street parking is difficult but there is underground (paid-for) parking and day car parks at Linga and Pré-la-Joux (where the parking can still get very full in peak season despite the provision of new spaces). Other main French Portes du Soleil resorts are easy to reach by piste, but not by road.

The free resort bus service is approved of by most reporters. A central location gives the advantage of getting on the ski-bus to the outlying

lifts before it gets very crowded, and simplifies après-ski outings – the night bus finishes at 9.30pm. But there is accommodation near the Linga lift if first tracks are the priority.

A few kilometres down the valley is the rustic village of La Chapelle-d'Abondance (for more information see the end of this chapter).

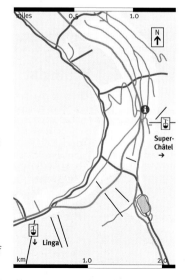

KEY FACTS

Resort	1200m
	3,940ft

Portes du Soleil	
Slopes	950-2300m
	3,120-7,550ft
Lifts	202
Pistes	650km
	404 miles
Green	13%
Blue	40%
Red	37%
Black	10%
Snowmaking	
	694 guns

Châtel only	
Slopes	1100-2205m
	3,610-7,230ft
Lifts	45
Pistes	83km
	52 miles
Green	23%
Blue	34%
Red	33%
Black	10%
Snowmaking	
	97 guns

THE MOUNTAINS

Châtel sits between two sectors of the main Portes du Soleil circuit, each offering a mix of open and wooded slopes, and linked by an 'excellent, practically continuous though sometimes crowded' free bus service. The circuit is easily done by intermediates of all abilities and there are sectors within it that you are likely to want to spend time exploring without doing the whole circuit more than once or twice during a week. The booklet-style piste map has been abandoned in favour of a map for each resort with a Portes du Soleil map on the back (a backward step which means you may want to pick up detailed maps in each resort for a clearer view of local lifts and pistes).

THE SLOPES
Two sectors to choose between
Directly above the village is **Super-Châtel** – an area of easy, open and lightly wooded slopes, accessed by a gondola or two-stage chair; the lifts in this sector are rather antiquated. From here you can embark on a clockwise Portes du Soleil circuit by heading to the Swiss resort of Morgins, travelling via Champoussin and Champéry to cross back into France above Avoriaz. Or you can head north for the slopes straddling a different bit of the Swiss border, above **Torgon** (which has great views over Lake Geneva). You can also access these slopes by chairlifts from Petit Châtel, down the valley.

An anticlockwise circuit starts outside the village with a lift into the

Linga sector – a gondola from Villapeyron or a choice of fast chairs from Pré-la-Joux. The fastest way to Avoriaz is via Pré-la-Joux. There is night-skiing on the Stade de Slalom run on Linga every Thursday.

TERRAIN PARKS
A choice of three
For 2007/08 a new park for intermediates and experts – Happy Park – was built in the Cornebois sector. The existing Smooth Park at Super-Châtel was redesigned to suit beginner and intermediate freestylers including a half-pipe and boardercross. La Chapelle-d'Abondance also has a 360m/1,180ft long park with half-pipe. A special park-only pass is available.

SNOW RELIABILITY
The main drawback
The main drawback of the Portes du Soleil is that it is low, so snow quality can suffer when it's warm. Châtel is at only 1200m/3,940ft and some runs home can be tricky or shut. But a lot of snowmaking has been installed at Super-Châtel and on runs down to resort level. Linga and Pré-la-Joux are mainly north-facing and generally have the best local snow. The pistes to Morgins and Lindarets get full sun.

FOR EXPERTS
Some challenges
The best steep runs – on- and off-piste – are in the Linga and Pré-la-Joux area. Beneath the Linga gondola and chair there's a pleasant mix of open and wooded ground, which follows the fall line fairly directly. And there's a mogul-

↑ Châtel has some of the best red runs on the Portes du Soleil circuit
OT CHATEL / JF VUARAND

field between Cornebois and Plaine Dranse, which has been described as 'steeper and narrower than the infamous Swiss Wall in Avoriaz'. An area under the Cornebois chair has been turned into the Happy Park (see 'Terrain parks'). Two pistes from the Rochassons ridge are steep and kept well groomed. On the way to Torgon from Super-Châtel, the Barbossine black run is long, steep and quite narrow and tricky at the top. There's good off-piste to be explored with a guide: on our 2007 visit we did a great run from Tête du Linga over into the next (deserted) valley of La Leiche.

FOR INTERMEDIATES
Some great local terrain
When conditions are right the Portes du Soleil is an intermediates' paradise. Good intermediates need not go far from Châtel to find amusement; Linga and Plaine Dranse have some of the best red runs on the circuit. The moderately skilled can do the PdS circuit without problem, and will particularly enjoy runs around Les Lindarets and Morgins. Even timid types can do the circuit, provided they take one or two short-cuts and ride chairs down trickier bits. But some blues are said to be difficult: the 'narrow, steep and icy' route to

Morgins provoked a complaint from a recent reporter, who witnessed skiers 'in tears' on its top section. The chair from Les Lindarets to Pointe de Mossettes leads to a red run into Switzerland, which is a lot easier than the 'Swiss Wall' from Chavanette and speeds up a journey round the circuit.

Visits to the Hauts Forts runs above Avoriaz are worthwhile. And note that the runs back to Plaine Dranse are real reds, and the Rochassons piste especially can get extremely busy at the end of the day.

Don't overlook the Torgon sector, which has some excellent slopes including challenging ones. There are great views over Lake Geneva too.

FOR BEGINNERS
Three possible options
There are good beginners' areas at Pré-la-Joux (a bus ride away) and at Super-Châtel (a gondola ride). And there are nursery slopes at village level if there is snow there. Reporters have praised the Super-Châtel slopes and lifts, which 'allow the beginner to progress' and 'safely practise' on gentle gradients away from the main runs. Getting up to them is a bit of an effort, though. The home run to the village from Super-Châtel is not recommended – it is narrow, busy and steep at the end, which, coupled with often poor and icy conditions, makes it very tricky for beginners and timid intermediates. The Pré-la-Joux slopes are said to have 'less variety of slopes and quite a steep draglift'.

FOR CROSS-COUNTRY
Pretty, if low, trails
There are 15 pretty trails (20km/12 miles) along the river and through the woods on the lower slopes of Linga, but snow-cover can be a problem. When combined with La Chapelle-d'Abondance's trails, the total is 60km/37 miles. The tourist office produces good maps with suggested routes and trail times.

QUEUES
Bottlenecks have been eased
Queues have been eased throughout the Portes du Soleil circuit in recent years by the introduction of several fast chairlifts. But queues form for the gondola to Super-Châtel when school parties gather and you can face queues to get back down again if the slope back is shut by poor snow. The

SCHOOLS

ESF
t 0450 732264
International
t 0450 733192
Henri Gonon
t 0450 732304
Francis Sports
t 0450 813251
Snow Ride (Ecole de Glisse)
t 0608 337651

Classes
(ESF prices)
6 half-days (2½hr am or pm) €116
Private lessons
€35 for 1hr, for 1 or 2 people

CHILDREN

Mouflets Garderie
t 0450 813819
Ages 3mnth to 6yr;
8am to 7pm; half-day
€25
Le Village des Marmottons
t 0450 733379
Ages 3 to 6; 6 days
€352 (with lunch)
Le Jardin des Pitchounes
t 0450 813251
Ages 3 and 4

Ski schools
Generally take children from age 4 or 5 (International 6 half-days €145)

ACTIVITIES

Indoor Cinemas, library, drawing lessons

Outdoor Ice rink, walks, horse riding, paragliding, cheese factory visits, ice diving, skijoring, snowshoeing (special route map for Châtel and Morgins), ice fishing

GETTING THERE

Air Geneva 75km/
47 miles (1½hr)

Rail Thonon les Bains
(40km/25 miles)

boarding

Avoriaz is the hard-core destination in the Portes du Soleil. Châtel is not a bad place to learn or to go to as a budget option. But many lifts in the Super-Châtel sector are drags and reporters warn they can be a 'painful experience'. The Linga area has good, varied slopes and off-piste possibilities as well as more boarder-friendly chairlifts.

slow chair above here has queues too, as it can't cope if the gondola is coming up full. Reporters have also found lengthy queues at the Tour de Don and Chermeu draglifts at certain times of day, causing difficulties for skiers rushing back to Super-Châtel to pick up children from ski school.

MOUNTAIN RESTAURANTS
Some quite good local huts
Atmospheric chalets can be found, notably in a cluster at Plaine Dranse – the Bois Prin, Tan ô Marmottes, Vieux Chalet ('fabulous meal, low ceilinged, laden with teddies, run by a mad woman'), Chaux des Rosées and Chez Denis have been recommended. In the Linga area the Ferme des Pistes, 'a cosy alpine barn, complete with stable-door', is said to do 'simply the best tarte aux pommes'. The Perdrix Blanche at Pré-la-Joux scarcely counts as a mountain restaurant, but is an attractive (if expensive and crowded) spot for lunch. At Super-Châtel the Portes du Soleil at the foot of the Coqs drags is much better than the big place at the top of the gondola. The Escale Blanche is worth a visit. The 'reasonable-priced' Panoramique at Torgon has 'views to die for'. Don't forget to check out the chapters on other Portes du Soleil resorts – particularly Avoriaz.

SCHOOLS AND GUIDES
Plenty of choice
There are five ski and snowboard schools in Châtel. The International school has been recommended by reporters, including recent visitors who had a private lesson that was 'one of our best ever' and a 2008 visitor's grandson who had 'so much more fun' than at the ESF. But the ESF has also been praised, with comments such as 'very helpful and customer-focused'.

FACILITIES FOR CHILDREN
Good reports
The Marmottons nursery has good facilities, including toboggans, painting, music and videos, and

children are reportedly happy there. Francis Sports ski school has its own nursery area with a drag lift and chalet at Linga: 'Very organised, convenient and reasonably priced.'

STAYING THERE

HOW TO GO
A wide choice, including chalets
Although this is emphatically a French resort, packages from Britain are no problem to track down. A recent reporter praised the personal service he received from a Ski Addiction weekend visit: 'Met me at train station, waited at hotel then took me to hire shop, guided me round slopes, nothing was too much trouble.'
Chalets A fair number of UK operators have places here, including some Châtel specialists.
Hotels Practically all the hotels are 2-stars, mostly friendly chalets, wooden or at least partly wood-clad.
***Macchi** (0450 732412) Smart, modern chalet, with spacious, comfortable rooms and good restaurant; small pool, sauna, jacuzzi; most central of the 3-stars.
***Fleur de Neige** (0450 732010) Welcoming chalet on edge of centre; Grive Gourmande restaurant is one of the best in town.
Belalp (0450 732439) Simple chalet with small rooms, but offering 'very good food'.
Choucas (0450 732257) Recently refurbished. 'Friendly owner.'
Kandahar (0450 733060) One for peace lovers: a Logis by the river, a walkable distance from the centre.
Lion d'Or (0450 813440) In centre, 'basic rooms, good atmosphere'.
Rhododendrons (0450 732404) 'Great service, friendly, comfortable.'
Tremplin (0450 732306) 'Excellent, good value. Owner cooks well but speaks no English'.
Apartments Many of the better places are available through agencies specialising in Châtel or in self-drive holidays. The Gelinotte (out of town but near the Linga lifts and children's

↑ The village is quite rustic but also quite spread out

OT CHATEL / J-F VUARAND

every night (the caramel vodka has been recommended). The Avalanche is a very popular English-style pub with a 'good atmosphere and live music'. The Godille – close to the Super-Châtel gondola and crowded when everyone descends at close of play – has a more French feel. The 'small and cosy' Isba is the locals' choice, and shows extreme-sports videos. The bowling alley, the Vieille Grange du Père Crincheux, also has a good bar.

OFF THE SLOPES
Less than ideal

Those with a car can easily visit places such as Geneva, Thonon and Evian. There are some pleasant walks, you can visit the cheese factory or the two cinemas, or join in daily events organised by the tourist office.

The Portes du Soleil as a whole is less than ideal for non-skiers who like to meet their more active friends for lunch: they are likely to be at some distant resort at lunch time and very few lifts are accessible to pedestrians.

village) and the Erines (five minutes from the centre; can also be provided catered) look good. The Avenières is right by the Linga gondola. Châtel's supermarkets are reported to be small and over-crowded. There is a large supermarket out in the direction of Chapelle-d'Abondance.

EATING OUT
Fair selection

There is an adequate number and range of restaurants. The Macchi and Fleur de Neige hotels both have expensive gastronomic restaurants (we enjoyed excellent foie gras and venison at the Macchi). We've also enjoyed the Table d'Antoine restaurant (good crayfish and charming patronne) of the hotel Chalet d'Alizée.

The rustic Vieux Four does ambitious dishes alongside Savoyard specialities and is approved by readers ('good value and the best food we had all week' said a recent reporter). The Pierrier ('friendly, food good but not exceptional') and the Fiacre ('superb pizza and moules') are more modest, everyday restaurants. The Refuge du Mille Pâtes does 'bargain' set menus. L'Escalier has an interestingly different menu – eg filet steak marinaded in Jack Daniels.

Out of town, the Ripaille, almost opposite the Linga gondola, is popular with locals and praised by reporters, especially for its fish and the 'fantastic local Gamay wines'. The hotel Cornettes in La Chapelle-d'Abondance is worth a trip – see below.

APRES-SKI
All down to bars

The Tunnel bar is very popular with the British and has a DJ or live music

La Chapelle-d'Abondance
1010m/3,310ft

This unspoiled, rustic farming community, complete with old church and friendly locals, is 5km/3 miles along a beautiful valley from Châtel. 'A car and a bit of French are virtually essential,' says a reporter. It has its own quiet little north-facing area of easy wooded runs and a gondola a bus ride away links it to slopes between Torgon in Switzerland and Super-Châtel and hence the Portes du Soleil circuit.

Nightlife is virtually non-existent – just a few quiet bars, a cinema and torchlit descents on Tuesdays. However, we hear that a new and popular microbrewery, the Fer Rouge, has opened, with live music.

The hotel Cornettes (0450 735024) is an amazing 2-star that has been run by the Trincaz family since 1894, with renovated rooms and 4-star facilities, including an indoor pool, a sauna, a steam room and hot tubs. It has an atmospheric bar and an excellent restaurant (we had a brilliant dégustation of foie gras) with extremely good-value menus. Look out for the showcases displaying puppets and dolls and for eccentric touches, such as ancient doors that unexpectedly open automatically.

FRANCE

282

Weekly news updates and resort links at www.wtss.co.uk

UK PACKAGES
Ardmore, Chalet Group, Connick, Equity, Interactive Resorts, Interhome, Lagrange, Rocketski, Ski Addiction, Skialot, Ski France, Skiholiday extras.com, Ski Independence, Ski Leisure Direction, Ski Line, Ski Rosie, Skitracer, Snow Finders, Snowfocus, Susie Ward
La Chapelle-d'Abondance Ski Addiction, Ski La Cote

Phone numbers
From abroad use the prefix +33 and omit the initial '0' of the phone number

TOURIST OFFICES
Châtel
t 0450 732244
touristoffice@chatel.com
www.chatel.com
La Chapelle-d'Abondance
t 0450 735141
ot.lachapelle@valdabondance.com
www.lachapelle74.com

La Clusaz

Attractive, scenic, distinctively French all-rounder; we like it a lot –
but we'd like it a lot more if it was 500 metres higher

NEWS

For 2007/08 in the Etale area a new chondola (a mix of eight-seat gondolas and six-person chairs) and a quad chair above it replaced the old cable car and chair. The Joux run on Etale and the green Envers back to La Clusaz (which has been improved) now have snowmaking.

La Croix-Fry is no longer included in the lift pass.

KEY FACTS

La Clusaz only		
Resort	1100m	
	3,610ft	
Slopes	1100-2470m	
	3,610-8,100ft	
Lifts		45
Pistes		128km
		80 miles
Green		28%
Blue		35%
Red		28%
Black		9%
Snowmaking		
		151 guns

➕ Traditional village in scenic setting

➕ Extensive, interesting slopes

➕ Very French atmosphere

➕ Very short transfer from Geneva

➕ Good, rustic mountain restaurants

➖ Snow conditions unreliable because of low altitude, but increased snowmaking has helped

➖ Lots of slow old chairlifts

➖ Crowded at weekends

Few other major French resorts are based around what is still, essentially, a genuine mountain village that exudes rustic charm and Gallic atmosphere. Combine that with more than 200km/124 miles of largely intermediate slopes (if you add in nearby Le Grand-Bornand), above and below the treeline, and there's a good basis for an enjoyable, relaxed week. Snowmaking is continually increased, but of course it makes no difference if the temperatures are too high.

THE RESORT

The village is built beside a fast-flowing stream at the junction of a number of narrow wooded valleys. It has had to grow in a rather rambling way, with roads running in a confusing mixture of directions. But, unlike so many French resorts, La Clusaz has retained the charm of a genuine and friendly mountain village, and the new buildings have been built in chalet style and blend in well. You can hire a locker next to the slopes to leave kit.

As it is close to Geneva and Annecy, La Clusaz is good for short transfers, but it does get crowded, and there can be weekend traffic jams.

THE MOUNTAINS

Like the village, the slopes are rather sprawling. There are five main areas.
Slopes Several points in La Clusaz have lifts giving access to the predominantly west- and north-west-facing slopes of L'Aiguille. From here you can reach the slightly higher and shadier slopes of the La Balme area, and a gondola returns you to Côte 2000 on L'Aiguille. La Balme is a splendid, varied area with good lifts. Going the other way from L'Aiguille leads you to L'Etale via the Transval cable car, which shuttles people between the two areas. Since last season, L'Etale has been served by two new lifts – see 'News'. From L'Etale you can make your way over to Merdassier and the Manigod area; or from the bottom of L'Etale, you can take a piste to the village and the

gondola up to the Beauregard sector, which, as the name implies, has splendid views and catches a lot of sunshine. From the top you can link via an easy piste and a two-way chair with La Croix Fry (no longer covered by the lift pass). Free buses link La Clusaz to Le Grand-Bornand's 100km/62 miles or so of largely intermediate pistes (covered by the area lift pass). There is night skiing once a week.
Terrain parks The park – on the L'Aiguille – has jumps, tables, rails, a boardercross and a super-pipe.
Snow reliability Most of the ski area is low by French standards (below 2000m/6,560ft) so the snow can deteriorate if it's warm. The best snow is on the north-west-facing slopes at La Balme (the highest area, reaching 2470m/8,100ft). There is a lot of snowmaking on the lower mountain, and the home runs can depend on it. A 2008 visitor found the run from L'Aiguille to L'Etale closed in January.
Experts The piste map doesn't seem to have a lot to offer experts, but most sectors present off-piste variants, and there are more serious adventures to undertake. The best terrain is at La Balme – the black Vraille run, which leads to the speed-skiing slope, is seriously steep. On the opposite side of the sector, the entirely off-piste Combe de Bellachat can be reached.

The Noire run down the face of Beauregard can be tricky in poor snow and is often closed. The Tétras on L'Etale is steep only at the top; the Mur Edgar bumps run on L'Aiguille is steep but short. L'Aiguille has a good off-piste run down the neglected

UK PACKAGES

Alpine Answers, Aravis
Alpine Retreat, Chalet
Group, Classic Ski,
Crystal, Interhome,
Karibuni, Lagrange,
Last Resort, Ski France,
Skiholidayextras.com,
Skitopia, Skitracer, Ski
Weekend, Snowlife

Phone numbers
From abroad use the
prefix +33 and omit
the initial '0' of the
phone number

TOURIST OFFICE

t 0450 326500
infos@laclusaz.com
www.laclusaz.com

Combe de Borderan and the long
Lapiaz black piste runs down the
Combe de Fernuy from Côte 2000.

Intermediates Early intermediates will
delight in the gentle slopes at the top
of Beauregard (plus the blue Guy
Périllat run, with lovely views, back
down to the bottom) and the slopes
at Manigod. L'Etale and L'Aiguille have
more challenging but wide blue runs.
More adventurous intermediates will
prefer the steeper slopes of La Balme.

Beginners There are nursery slopes at
village level, and better ones up on
Beauregard and at Crêt du Merle.
Beauregard has lovely gentle blue runs
to progress to; those from Crêt du
Merle are steeper, but there is a green.

Snowboarding There are some good
nursery slopes, served by chairlifts,
and cruising runs to progress to. La
Balme is great for good freeriders.

Cross-country The region has much
better cross-country facilities than
many resorts, with around 70km/
43 miles of loops of varying difficulty.

Queues These aren't usually a
problem, except on peak weekends.

Mountain restaurants A highlight: there
are lots of them, and most are rustic
and charming, serving good food at
reasonable prices. Readers repeatedly
recommend the Télémark ('fine food')
above the chairlift to L'Etale. The 'good
value' Chez Arthur at Crêt du Merle has
table- and self-service. The Relais de
L'Aiguille at Crêt du Loup, Bercail
('good but very crowded'), La Vieille
Ferme at Merdassier ('excellent menu
du jour') and U'Freddy at the base of

the chondola ('Savoyard specialities')
have been recommended.

Schools and guides A 2008 visitor
hired an ESF instructor as a guide:
'Serge was very friendly and we had a
great day skiing in all five areas.'

Facilities for children We have no
recent reports on the kindergarten.

STAYING THERE

How to go La Clusaz is offered mostly
by smaller operators.

Hotels Small, friendly 2- and 3-star
family hotels are the mainstay here;
luxury is not an option. Reporters
recommend the 3-star Alp'Hotel (0450
024006) – 'brilliant place' – and
Carlina (0450 024348) – 'excellent
food and a good wine list' – and the
2-star ski in/ski out Les Sapins (0450
633333) – 'good food, superb views'.

Apartments There's quite a good
choice, but some are out of town.

Eating out There's a wide choice of
restaurants, some a short drive away.
The St Joseph at the Alp'Hotel is
regarded as the best in the village.
Recent reporters recommend L'Ecuelle
('fantastic food, great ambience') and
Scierie ('lovely alpine feel').

Après-ski The 'olde-worlde' Caves du
Paccaly has live music, the 'quaint' Le
Salto Sky TV and draught Guinness,
and L'Ecluse nightclub an 'excellent
atmosphere'. The Bar au Vin and La
Grolle were 2008 recommendations.

Off the slopes There's tobogganing, an
excellent aquatic centre, an ice rink
and good walks.

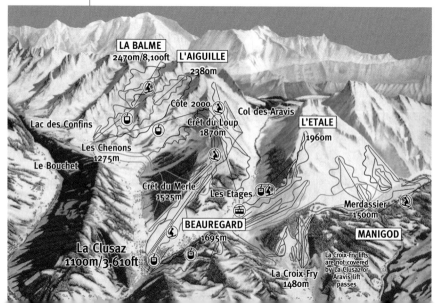

Les Contamines

A traditional French village with its own area of reliably snowy slopes and easy road access to nearby big-name resorts

285

COSTS

① ② ③ ④ ⑤ ⑥

RATINGS

The slopes

Fast lifts	**
Snow	****
Extent	***
Expert	***
Intermediate	****
Beginner	**
Convenience	**
Queues	***
Mountain restaurants	****

The rest

Scenery	****
Resort charm	***
Off-slope	**

NEWS

Snowmaking is being increased, with more planned for 2008/09. And a gourmet restaurant/ wine bar, O-à-la-Bouche, opened in early 2007.

+ Largely unspoiled French village
+ Fair-sized intermediate area
+ Good snow record for its height
+ Lift pass covers nearby resorts

– Lifts a bus ride from main village
– Can be some lengthy queues
– Lack of smart lodgings
– Quiet nightlife

Only a few miles from the fur coats of Megève and the ice axes of Chamonix, Les Contamines is quite a contrast to both, with pretty wooden chalets, an impressive old church, a weekly market in the village square and prices more typical of rural France than of international resorts. Its position at the shoulder of Mont Blanc gives it an enviable snow record.

THE RESORT

The core of the village is compact, but the resort as a whole spreads widely, with chalets scattered over a 3km/2 mile stretch of the valley, and the main access lift is 1km/0.5 miles from the centre. There's expanding development by the lift at Le Lay but you can stay in the village centre, a shuttle-bus ride away. Bizarrely, the local pass does not cover the buses (eight euros per week). The weekly Mont Blanc pass does cover them, plus the lifts of Chamonix and Megève (among other resorts). A car is useful.

THE MOUNTAINS

Most of the slopes are above the treeline and there are some magnificent views, though the runs down from Signal are bordered by trees (as is the run from La Ruelle down to Belleville).
Slopes From Le Lay a two-stage

gondola climbs up to the slopes at Signal. Another gondola leads to the Etape mid-station from a car park a little further up the valley, with a fast quad above it. Above these, a sizeable network of open, largely north-east-facing pistes fans out, with lifts approaching 2500m/8,200ft in two places. You can drop over the ridge at Col du Joly to south-west-facing runs down to La Ruelle, with a single red run going on down to Belleville. From Belleville, a 16-person gondola runs back up to La Ruelle, followed by a fast chair to Col du Joly.
Terrain parks They call these X Zones. There are two in the main ski area (on Aiguille Croche) and a third zone in the tiny Loyers area by the village, which has a 120m/390ft super-pipe.
Snow reliability Many of the shady runs on the Contamines side are above 1700m/5,580ft, and the resort has a justifiable reputation for good snow late into the season, said to be the result of proximity to Mont Blanc.

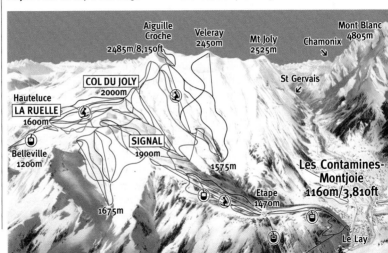

Aiguille Croche 2485m/8,150ft · Veleray 2450m · Mt Joly 2525m · Chamonix · Mont Blanc 4805m
COL DU JOLY 2000m · St Gervais
Hauteluce · LA RUELLE 1600m · SIGNAL 1900m
Belleville 1200m · 1575m
1675m · Etape 1470m
Les Contamines-Montjoie 1160m/3,810ft
Le Lay

KEY FACTS

Resort	1160m
	3,810ft

Les Contamines-Montjoie/Hauteluce	
Slopes	1160-2485m
	3,810-8,150ft
Lifts	24
Pistes	120km
	75 miles
Green	19%
Blue	21%
Red	36%
Black	24%
Snowmaking	
	258 guns

UK PACKAGES

Action Outdoors, Alpine Answers, Chalet Kiana, Classic Ski, Interhome, Lagrange, Ski Expectations, Ski France, Skiholiday extras.com, Ski Line, Skitracer, UCPA

Phone numbers
From abroad use the prefix +33 and omit the initial '0' of the phone number

TOURIST OFFICE

t 0450 470158
info@lescontamines.com
www.lescontamines.com

OT LES CONTAMINES-MONTJOIE

The village is traditional and pleasant, though not chocolate-box cute ↓

Snowmaking now covers runs from Col du Joly down to the valley and some runs towards La Ruelle/Belleville. More is planned for 2008/09. We have several reports of snow being better here when poor elsewhere; and a regular visitor tells of the combination of natural and man-made snow and careful piste management giving 'good conditions from December to April'.

Experts The steep western section has black runs, which are enjoyable but not terribly challenging. But there is substantial and varied off-piste terrain within the lift system and outside it – including a 'seriously steep and challenging' descent to Megève.

Intermediates Virtually all the runs are ideal for good intermediates, with a mix of fairly similar blues and reds. Some of the best go from the gondola's top station to its mid-station, and others are served by the Roselette and Bûche Croisée lifts. Given good snow, the south-facing runs down to La Ruelle are a delight. And the black runs are enjoyable for good intermediates. Timid intermediates might find sections of many blue runs too steep for comfort.

Beginners In good snow, the village nursery area is adequate for beginners. There are other areas at the mid-station and the top of the gondola. And there's a long green run from Col du Joly to La Ruelle. Novices should take the gondola down to the village at the end of the day – the narrow red runs can be icy.

Snowboarding There are quite a few draglifts, including four marked on the piste map as difficult, so inexperienced boarders beware. But there is excellent off-piste boarding on offer.

Cross-country There are 26km/16 miles of trails of varying difficulty. One of

the loops is floodlit once a week.

Queues There can be 15- to 20-minute peak-period queues for the gondolas, especially if people are bussed in from other resorts which have less snow. The fast quad from Etape helps to relieve pressure on the Signal gondola. More irritating on our 2007 visit was a long wait for the old Grevettaz draglift when it kept breaking down.

Mountain restaurants There are quite a few lovely woody huts – not all of which are marked on the piste map. Ferme de la Ruelle is a jolly barn, and the Grange just above it does a 'great-value plat du jour'. Roselette ('classic Savoyard cooking') and Bûche Croisée (also known as R'mize à Louis) are two cosy chalets consistently recommended by reporters, and Chez Gaston has great views. Signal is not rustic, but does 'tasty, reasonably priced food'.

Schools and guides In the past we have had mixed reports on the ESF. But 2007 beginners found it 'fun, friendly and progressive'. There's an alternative International school, and mountain guides. One visitor enjoyed the 'challenging off-piste' found for him by Miage Aventure. Excursions are offered, including the Vallée Blanche.

Facilities for children The kindergarten next to the central nursery slopes takes children from age one. Children can join ski school from age four.

STAYING THERE

How to go There are some catered chalets and nine modest hotels.

Hotels The 'comfortable' 3-star Chemenaz (0450 470244) at Le Lay has been praised. The Ferme de Bon Papa is a lovingly restored old farmhouse offering B&B.

Eating out Recommendations include the Husky, Op Traken and, for Savoie specialities, the Savoisien and Auberge du Chalézan. The O-à-la-Bouche has stylish gourmet dining (including the Marmot fondue restaurant).

Après-ski Après-ski is quiet, but there are several bars. The Saxo and the Ty Breiz with live music are rated the liveliest venues and O-à-la-Bouche has a smart wine bar. There's a varied programme of weekly events, including floodlit skiing twice-weekly.

Off the slopes There are good walks, a toboggan run, snowmobiling, dog sledding, snowshoeing and a natural ice rink, but the village is limited.

Courchevel

Arguably the best of the half-dozen resorts that make up the famous Three Valleys – with a choice of four different villages

COSTS

① ② ③ ④ ⑤ ⑥

RATINGS

The slopes

Fast lifts	★★★★
Snow	★★★★
Extent	★★★★★
Expert	★★★★
Intermediate	★★★★★
Beginner	★★★★
Convenience	★★★★
Queues	★★★★
Mountain restaurants	★★★★

The rest

Scenery	★★★
Resort charm	★★
Off-slope	★★★

NEWS

For 2008/09 there will be a new run from the Pralong chair to the start of the Suisses chair and there is to be snowmaking in the Combe de la Saulire, Bouc Blanc and Arolles areas. More lifts are to be fitted with the child safety 'Magnestick' system that was introduced in 2007/08 (see 'Facilities for children'). Work on a new swimming pool complex has begun in 1550 with completion expected for 2009/10.

+ Extensive, varied local terrain to suit everyone from beginners to experts – plus the rest of the Three Valleys easily accessible

+ Lots of slope-side accommodation

+ Impressive lift system, piste maintenance and snowmaking

+ Wooded setting is pretty, and useful in bad weather

+ Choice of four very different villages

+ Some great restaurants, and good après-ski by French standards

– Some pistes get unpleasantly crowded (but they can be avoided)

– Rather soulless villages, with intrusive traffic in places

– 1850 has some of the priciest hotels, bars and mountain restaurants in the Alps, and it's getting worse

– Losing its French feel as more foreign visitors discover its attractions

– Little to do away from the slopes, especially during the day

Courchevel is the most extensive and varied sector of the famous Three Valleys, the biggest linked ski area in the world; it has slopes to satisfy everyone, from broad green motorways to narrow black couloirs. And in the course of countless visits over many years, we've established beyond doubt that the snow over here is reliably better than in chief rival Méribel, over the hill. Although links via Méribel-Mottaret to Val Thorens (at the head of the third valley) are good, a high proportion of visitors stray over the ridge rarely, or not at all. If we're heading for the 3V, more often than not we'll head for Courchevel.

But it's not one destination: the four villages making up the resort vary widely. It's high, swanky 1850 that catches the headlines, with its airstrip, ritzy hotels, grand chalets and Michelin-starred restaurants. Actually, even 1850 has plenty of affordable accommodation and restaurants, but the other villages – 1650, 1550 and 1300 – have none of 1850's pretensions. All have lots of apartments, plus an ever-expanding body of chalets attracting British visitors – particularly 1650, which continues to move gradually upmarket (gaining a swanky 4-star hotel last season alongside a smart new 3-star a couple of seasons back).

Courchevel 1850 in the foreground and 1650 in the background are minutes apart by road, but have distinct sectors of slopes →

KEY FACTS

Resort	1260-1850m
	4,130-6,070ft

The Three Valleys	
Slopes	1260-3230m
	4,130-10,600ft
Lifts	180
Pistes	600km
	373 miles
Green	15%
Blue	38%
Red	37%
Black	10%
Snowmaking	33%

Courchevel/ La Tania only	
Slopes	1260-2740m
	4,130-8,990ft
Lifts	62
Pistes	150km
	93 miles
Green	22%
Blue	37%
Red	33%
Black	8%
Snowmaking	31%

THE RESORT

Courchevel is made up of four varied villages, generally known by numbers very loosely related to their altitudes. A road winds up from 1300 (Le Praz) past 1550, through 1650 to 1850. On the slopes, things work a bit differently: runs go down from 1850 to 1550 and 1300, but the slopes of 1650 form a distinct sector.

1850 is the largest village, and the focal point of the area, with most of the smart nightlife and shops. Two gondolas go over its lower slopes towards the links with Méribel and the rest of the Three Valleys. Although the approach is dreary and the centre not much better, parts are conspicuously upmarket, with some very smooth hotels on the slopes just above the village centre, and among the trees of the Jardin Alpin (a suburb served by its own gondola). There's a spreading area of smart private chalets.

You can pay through the nose to eat, drink and sleep here, but more affordable places are not impossible to find. Pressure on the restaurants is highest when big-spending Russians are in town – in early January and the second week in March – but we are no longer getting reports from readers unable to get a table.

1650 by comparison is an ordinary resort, dominated by large apartment

blocks beside the main through-road up to 1850. But there's also a pleasant village centre, several lively bars and plenty of quietly situated chalets. Its local slopes (whose main access is a gondola) are also relatively peaceful. 1550 is a quiet dormitory, a gondola or chair ride below 1850. It has the advantage of having essentially the same position within the ski area as 1850, with cheaper accommodation and restaurants. But it's a long trip to 1850 by road if you want to go there in the evening.

1300 (Le Praz) is an old village set amid woodland. It remains a pleasant spot despite expansion triggered by the 1992 Olympics – the Olympic ski jump is a prominent legacy. Ancient gondolas go up to 1850 and towards Col de la Loze, for Méribel. It is a low-key place where pre-skiing children can have fun in the snow. But novice skiers face rides down from ski school as well as up to it.

Efficient free buses run between and within the villages. Champagny is an easy road outing, for access to the extensive slopes of La Plagne.

THE MOUNTAINS

Although there are plenty of trees around the villages, most of the slopes are essentially open, with the notable exception of the runs down to 1550 and to 1300, and the valley between 1850 and 1650. These are great areas for experts when the weather closes in. Many reporters recommend buying only a Courchevel pass and then one-day extensions for the Three Valleys as necessary.

THE SLOPES
Huge variety to suit everyone
A network of lifts and pistes spreads out from 1850, which is very much the focal point of the area. The main axis is the **Verdons** gondola, leading to a second gondola to La Vizelle and a nearly parallel cable car up to La Saulire. These high points of the **Saulire-Creux** sector give access to a wide range of terrain above Courchevel (including a number of couloirs), to Méribel and all points to Val Thorens. Next to the Verdons gondola is the Jardin Alpin gondola, which leads to runs back to 1850, and serves the higher hotels until 8pm. It also gives access via the valley of Prameruel to the Chanrossa slopes above 1650.

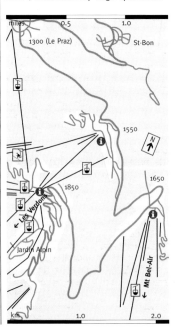

LIFT PASSES

Three Valleys

Prices in €

Age	1-day	6-day
under 13	33	165
13 to 64	44	220
over 65	38	187

Free under 5, over 75
Beginner limited pass €12

Notes
Covers Courchevel, La Tania, Méribel, Les Menuires and St-Martin; family reductions; pedestrian and half-day passes

Alternative passes
Courchevel/La Tania only with one-day Three Valleys extension; Courchevel 1650 only

To the right looking up from 1850 the Chenus gondola goes towards the **Loze-Praz** sector, a second link with Méribel. Runs go back to 1850, and through the woods to La Tania (see separate chapter) and 1300.

There are various ways up from 1650 to the minor high-points of Bel Air and Signal, and on into the **Chanrossa** sector. From here you can link across via the valley of Prameruel to Saulire-Creux, or head for the far end of the sector, where there is another link to Saulire-Creux via the col of Chanrossa.

TERRAIN PARKS
Something for everyone

Courchevel has undergone a bit of a change. The four freestyle areas it used to have have now shrunk to two, both in the 1850 sector. Along the Loze piste you'll find a decent boardercross. The main terrain park at Plantrey, just below 1850 on the way to 1300, has become a rail park only. It is accessible via the Ecureuil chairlift or the Epicea drag. You'll find good boxes and rails along with a wall ride and rainbow box. Two shapers are on constant duty keeping the park in great shape and offering help if you need it.

SNOW RELIABILITY
Very good

The combination of Courchevel's orientation (its slopes are north- or north-east-facing), its height, an abundance of snowmaking and excellent piste maintenance usually guarantees good snow down to at least the 1850 and 1650 villages. A 2007 reporter comments: 'In a difficult year for snow in the Alps, the skiing was excellent and the pistes well-groomed.' On countless visits we have found that the snow is usually much better than in neighbouring Méribel, where the slopes get more sun – and one side gets the afternoon sun, in particular. The runs to 1300 are still prone to closure in warm weather. Daily maps are available, showing which runs have been groomed overnight (normal in America but very rare in Europe).

FOR EXPERTS
Some black gems

There is plenty to interest experts, even without considering the rest of the Three Valleys.

The most obvious expert runs are the couloirs you can see on the right near the top of the Saulire cable car. The three main ways down were once designated black pistes (some of the steepest in Europe), but now only the Grand Couloir remains a piste – it's the widest and easiest of the three, but you have to pick your way along the narrow, bumpy, precipitous access ridge to reach it.

There is a lot of steep terrain, on- and off-piste, on the shady slopes of La Vizelle, both towards Verdons and towards the link with 1650. Some of the reds on La Vizelle verge on black and the black M piste is surprisingly little used. If you love moguls, try the black Suisses and Chanrossa runs – and the off-piste moguls under the Chanrossa chair. For a change of scene and a test of stamina, a couple of long (700m/2,300ft vertical), genuinely steep blacks cut through the trees down to 1300.

In good snow conditions you can ski all the way down (around 2000m/ 6,560ft vertical) from La Saulire to Bozel, way below 1300, over meadows and through trees on the final section, and catch a bus back.

There is plenty of off-piste terrain to try with a guide – see the feature panel later in the chapter.

Le Ski
the chalet specialists

COURCHEVEL
VAL D'ISÈRE AND LA TANIA

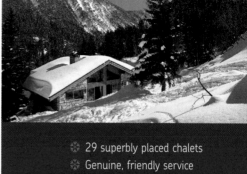

- ❄ 29 superbly placed chalets
- ❄ Genuine, friendly service
- ❄ Delicious food and wine
- ❄ Sunday flights to Chambéry

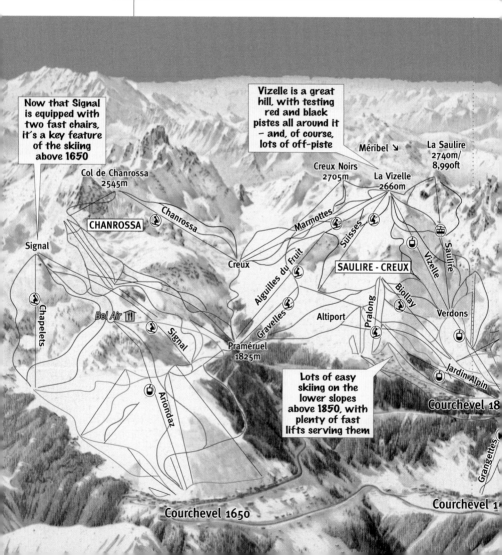

Now that Signal is equipped with two fast chairs, it's a key feature of the skiing above 1650

Vizelle is a great hill, with testing red and black pistes all around it – and, of course, lots of off-piste

Lots of easy skiing on the lower slopes above 1850, with plenty of fast lifts serving them

Méribel ↘

La Saulire
2740m/
8,990ft

Col de Chanrossa
2545m

Creux Noirs
2705m

La Vizelle
2660m

Chanrossa

CHANROSSA

Marmottes

Süisses

Saulire

Signal

Creux

Aiguilles du Fruit

SAULIRE - CREUX

Vizelle

Chapelets

Bel Air

Signal

Gravelles

Altiport

Pralong

Biollay

Verdons

Ariondaz

Praméruel
1825m

Jardin Alpin

Courchevel 18

Grangettes

Courchevel 1650

Courchevel 1

ulire
om/
90ft

Saulire

rdons

Coqs

Chenus

Jardin Alpin

rchevel 1850

Grangettes

Touvets

urchevel 1550

↙ Méribel

Col de la Loze
2275m

Chenus
2245m

LOZE - PRAZ

Dou des Lanches

Plantrey

Praz-Juget
Bouc Blanc

Forêt

Praz

La Tania

Courchevel 1300 (Le Praz)
126om/4,13oft

La Tania
135om/4,43oft

> **Excellent, testing runs in the woods, which really come into their own in bad weather**

> **A new green run built a couple of seasons ago has made La Tania a much better place for beginners than it was**

Les Écoles du Ski Français

De Courchevel

1550	1650	1850
www.esf-courchevel.com	www.esfcourchevel1650.com	www.esf-courchevel.com
+33(0)4 79 08 21 07	+33(0)4 79 08 26 08	+33(0)4 79 08 07 72

FOR INTERMEDIATES
Paradise for all levels

The Three Valleys is the greatest intermediate playground in the world, but all grades of intermediates will love Courchevel's local slopes too.

Early intermediates will enjoy the gentle Pyramides and Grandes Bosses blues above 1650, and the Biollay and Pralong blues above 1850. Those of average ability can handle most of the red runs without difficulty. Our favourite is the long, sweeping Combe de la Saulire from top to bottom of the cable car first thing in the morning, when it's well groomed and free of crowds; but it's a different story at the end of the day – cut up snow and very crowded. Creux, behind La Vizelle, is another splendid, long red that gets bumpy and unpleasantly crowded later on. Marmottes from the top of Vizelle is quieter and more challenging.

The Loze-Praz sector has excellent blues and reds down towards 1850 and 1550 and through the trees towards La Tania – long, rolling cruises. Over at 1650, the Chapelets and Rochers reds right at the edge of the whole Three Valleys ski area are great fun for fast cruising, although the newish six-pack serving them means they are now more heavily used than they once were.

FOR BEGINNERS
Great graduation runs

There are excellent nursery slopes above both 1650 and 1850. At the former, lessons are likely to begin on the short drags close to the village, but quick learners will soon be able to go up the gondola. The best nursery area at 1850 is at Pralong, above the village, near the airstrip. A reporter points out that getting to it from the village isn't easy, unless you go by road, which absolute beginners would. A blue path links this area with chairs to 1650, so adventurous novices can soon move further afield. The Bellecôte green run down into 1850 is an excellent, long, gentle slope – but it is used by other skiers returning to the village and does get unpleasantly crowded. It is served by the Jardin Alpin gondola, and a drag that is one of eight free beginner lifts. 1550 and 1300 have small nursery areas, but most people go up to 1850 for its more reliable snow.

Courchevel's image is of upmarket luxury and pampered piste skiing. But it is one of the world's best resorts for off-piste too. Manu Gaidet is a Courchevel mountain guide and a ski instructor with the Courchevel ESF. He is also one of the world's top freeriders and won the Freeride World Championship three years running. We asked him to pick out a few of the best runs.

These suggested routes are limited to the Courchevel valley. There is great off-piste in the rest of the Three Valleys, too. And you can heli-ski in Italy and Switzerland (it is banned in France). But never venture off-piste without a qualified ski instructor or mountain guide and safety equipment.

For a first experience off-piste, the Tour du Rocher de l'Ombre is great. Access is easy from the left of the Combe de la Saulire piste and you are never far from the piste. It is very quiet, the slope is very broad and easy and you get a real sense of adventure as you plan your way between the rocks. And the view of the Croix des Verdons is impressive. Keep to the left for the best snow.

Les Avals is one of my favourite routes. The easiest way to get to it is to take the Roc Merlet piste from the top of the Chanrossa chairlift. Leave the piste on the right as soon as you can, then climb up and cross the ridge. Once you've arrived at a group of rocks (in the form of towers) descend the south side. This run is not technically difficult and is particularly beautiful in spring conditions. Another possibility from the Chanrossa chair is to traverse towards the Aiguille du Fruit. Almost anywhere along this very wide slope, you can choose your spot to start skiing down to rejoin the end of the Chanrossa black piste at the bottom. A technically more difficult run, for experienced off-piste skiers only, is Plan Mugnier. This starts with a 20-minute walk from the top of the Chanrossa chair but you are normally rewarded by very good snow because the slope you ski down faces north. Le Curé is in the Saulire area: this narrow gully starts under a towering rock and offers a steady 35° slope; it is only for expert skiers who don't mind climbing to the Doigt du Curé starting point.

The Courchevel **ESF** is the largest ski school in Europe with over 700 instructors. They can help you find the best off-piste and explore it safely. For phone numbers see the schools list. The websites of the three different branches (1550, 1650, 1850) can be accessed through www.courchevel.com.

Courchevel

293

Interactive resort shortlist builder at **www.wtss.co.uk**

FOR CROSS-COUNTRY
Long wooded trails
Courchevel has a total of 66km/ 41 miles of trails, the most in the Three Valleys. 1300 is the most suitable village, with trails through the woods towards 1550, 1850 and Méribel. Given enough snow, there are also loops around the village.

QUEUES
Not a problem
Even at New Year and in mid-February, when 1850 in particular positively teems with people, queues are minimal, thanks to the excellent lift system. However, there can be a build-up at 1850 for the gondolas and chairs as the ski school gets going. The Biollay chair is very popular with the ski school (which gets priority) and can be worth avoiding. Queues for the huge Saulire cable car are rare. A visitor to 1650 says that the main gondola 'had a bit of a backlog at the start of each day, and around lunch time. Other lifts had virtually no queues at all, and the well-trained lifties were quick to organise efficient filling of chairs when necessary.'

MOUNTAIN RESTAURANTS
Good but can be very expensive
Mountain restaurants are plentiful and pleasant, but it is sensible to check the prices, which are generally high and can be sky-high.
Editors' choice The Bel Air (0479 080093), at the top of the gondola above 1650, stands out in an area where it's easy to pay a lot for indifferent meals. It has good-value simple food, friendly and efficient table service, and a splendid tiered terrace. Our readers agree: 'superb food', 'stunning views' and 'excellent service' are some of the 2008 comments we've received. Our other favourite in the area is the Bouc Blanc (0479 088026) just over in La Tania (see that chapter).
Worth knowing about The Chenus at the top of the gondola of that name has 'fabulous views' and is recommended for its 'quality of food combined with reasonable prices'. The Soucoupe, near here too, also has good food and views; we tried the cosy, atmospheric table-service section upstairs in 2007 and found the steaks OK, but the prices for both food and

Despite being an upmarket resort, Courchevel has always been popular with snowboarders. There are miles of well-groomed pistes, and the lifts are in general very modern and quick, with few drags. As it is very expensive, Courchevel best suits intermediates and advanced riders who can fully take advantage of this resort's resources. The big snowboard hangout in 1850 is Prends ta luge et tire toi, a combined shop/bar/internet cafe.

SCHOOLS

ESF in 1850
t 0479 080772

ESF in 1650
t 0479 082608

ESF in 1550
t 0479 082107

ESF Centre Pralong
t 0479 011581

Supreme
t 0479 082787
(UK: 01479 810800)

New Generation
t 0479 010318
www.skinewgen.com

Magic Snowsports Academy
t 0479 081199

Oxygène
t 0479 551745

Classes
(ESF 1850 prices)
6 days (2½hr am and pm): €288

Private lessons
€70 for 1½hr

GUIDES

Guides de Courchevel
t 0623 924612

wine were a bit steep. The Bergerie on the Bellecôte piste has 'a lot of atmosphere but the prices are quite steep', and a reporter found that the food at the Arc en Ciel (top of the Verdons gondola) 'lived up to our fond memories of it'. The Panoramic at the top of Saulire 'is very traditional, but not cheap'.

There are one or two other places you should know about, if only to avoid. Cap Horn, near the airstrip, is said to be the leading lunchtime rip-off spot. A 2007 reporter found it 'overpriced and snobbish', and a 2008 reporter comments, 'We expected to be fleeced – and we were not disappointed! A simple one-course lunch, with drinks, came to £27 each. Charming service, though.' Chalet de Pierres, on the Verdons piste close to 1850, is more to our taste but not far behind in price.

SCHOOLS AND GUIDES
Plenty of choice
Courchevel's branches of the ESF add up to the largest ski school in Europe, with over 700 instructors. Reports vary: 'we had a private lesson every day with ESF 1650 – the instructor was fantastic, joking around, and he taught us a great deal'; 'in 1850 my daughter's boyfriend had an English instructor and a great time learning quickly, but my wife had a non-English speaking grumpy old man and stayed on the nursery slopes all week'. A 2008 reporter had an 'excellent' private lesson with an ESF instructor.

New Generation is a school run by top British instructors. We continue to receive rave reviews about this outfit: 'really great lesson – we both got a lot out of it', 'the highlight of the trip', 'head and shoulders above any other ski school I've come across'.

Supreme in 1850 is also British-run, and a 2007 reporter who had one of their French instructors for a private lesson reckoned 'it was one of the best lessons I have ever had'.

In 2007/08 Ski Academy, an

independent group of French instructors, joined forces with Magic in Motion and is now known as Magic Snowsports Academy. Reports would be welcome.

The Bureau des Guides runs all-day off-piste excursions. There's also an area at the foot of Les Suisses piste with at least weekly transceiver practice and avalanche rescue sessions with dogs and pisteurs (free).

FACILITIES FOR CHILDREN
Lots of chalet-based options
A 2008 visitor whose young children went to the ESF Club des Piou-Piou at 1650 found it 'very well run and a good introduction to skiing for children'. The ESF at 1850 offers a Kids 'Up' programme for English-speaking children between 6 and 12 years with a maximum of eight children per group. Several tour operators run their own nurseries in their chalets – using British nannies – and the tourist office holds a list of nursery nurses who are available for hire. The lift company is expanding the use of 'Magnestick' – its magnetic system to hold children securely on chairlifts.

STAYING THERE

HOW TO GO
Value chalets and apartments
Huge numbers of British tour operators go to Courchevel.
Chalets There are plenty of catered chalets available – specialist travel agents list dozens of them. And the resort literature lists a score or more of swanky places to rent.

In 1850 several operators offer notably comfortable chalets, and a few genuinely luxurious ones. Kaluma, Descent, Scott Dunn and Supertravel would be the first to look at.

Ski Total, Mark Warner and Skiworld all have central chalet hotels in 1850.

Le Ski has 14 chalets from comfortable to classy in 1650, including six new ones introduced in 2007/08 (all with hot tub, sauna or steam room). Ski Olympic has the central Les Avals chalet hotel in 1650 (complete with Rocky's bar) plus a couple of large chalets. Finlays has six chalets in 1550, and a couple up in 1850. Ski Power runs the hotel Chanrossa, close to the centre of 1550, as a chalet hotel, with its own public bar. Family specialist Esprit Ski has several chalets and chalet apartments down in 1300.

Hotels There are more than 40 hotels in Courchevel than at 1850 or 1650 – including more 4-stars than anywhere else in France except Paris (18 at the last count, with 12 in the top '4-star luxe' category). 1650's first 4-star, the Manali, opened in December 2007.

Courchevel 1850
****+Airelles (0479 003838) 'Super flash and over the top.' Extended in 2007/08 with 11 new suites and a new spa.
****+Saint Roch (0479 080266) Newly renovated for the 2007/08 season.
****+Annapurna (0479 080460) Facing south on the Pralong slope. Gault-Millau recommended.
****+St Joseph (0479 081616) Like a plush country house 'with 14 fab rooms and two stunning apartments'.

****+Mélézin (0479 080133) Superbly stylish and luxurious – and in an ideal position beside the Bellecôte slope.
****+Carlina (0479 080030) Luxury piste-side pad, next to Mélézin.
****+Palace des Neiges (0479 009800) Used to be Byblos, now under new ownership. Spacious public rooms, good pool, sauna, steam complex.
****Bellecôte (0479 081019) Our favourite among the more swanky places – it offers some Alpine atmosphere as well as sheer luxury.
****Chabichou (0479 080055) Distinctive white building, right on the slopes; family-run, friendly and rustic with very good food plus the option of a restaurant with 2 Michelin stars.
****Sivolière (0479 080833) Recently renovated, pleasantly set among pines.
***Rond Point (0479 080433) Family atmosphere, central position.
***Croisette (0479 080900) Next to main lifts above the Jump bar. 'Simple and clean, staff very helpful.'
***New Solarium (0479 080201) Recently renovated, near first stop on Jardin Alpin gondola, 'sensible prices and very friendly service'.

GETTING THERE

Air Geneva 149km/ 93 miles (3½hr); Lyon 187km/116 miles (3½hr); Chambéry 110km/68 miles (1½hr); direct flights to Courchevel altiport from London on request only (contact tourist office for details)

Rail Moûtiers (24km/ 15 miles); transfer by bus or taxi

ACTIVITIES

Indoor Ice rink, bowling, exhibitions, concerts, cinemas, language and computer courses, cookery courses, library; in hotels: health and fitness centres (swimming pools, saunas, steam room, hot tub, water therapy, weight training, massage)

Outdoor Hang-gliding, helicopter flights, paragliding, flying lessons, dog sledding, ice driving, go-karts on ice, snowshoeing, snowmobile rides, climbing, ice karting, ballooning, walking on cleared paths, tobogganing

SNOWPIX.COM / CHRIS GILL

Broad, open slopes above 1850 –this is looking directly down the Pralong chair, with the Biollay chair coming up from skier's left to meet it →

***Ducs de Savoie (0479 080300) 'Comfortable, friendly' hotel in the Jardin Alpin area, says a regular visitor.
**Courcheneige (0479 080259) On Bellecôte piste. 'A real find: lovely staff, good food.' Quiet.
**Potinière (0479 080016) 'Small, friendly' hotel with 'simple rooms', says a 2008 reporter.
COURCHEVEL 1650
*****+Manali (0479 080707) New for 2007/08 and the first 4* luxe in 1650; right by the piste just above the gondola; spa and pool (open to the public).
***Golf (0479 009292) Rather impersonal but in a superb position on the snow next to the gondola.
***Seizena (0479 082636) Stylish and central (over road from the gondola).
1300 (LE PRAZ)
***Peupliers (0479 084147) Smartly renovated and expanded, good restaurant – but prices now 'approach 1850 levels', we hear.
Apartments Leaving aside the swanky private chalets you can rent through local agents, the best bets are the Montagnettes at the top end of 1650 – a choice of apartments and semi-detached chalets – and the Chalets du Forum in the heart of 1850.

EATING OUT
Pick your price
There are a lot of good, very expensive restaurants in Courchevel, and some that are more affordable. A non-comprehensive pocket guide is distributed locally.

In 1850, among the best and priciest, with two Michelin stars, are the Chabichou (a recent visitor recommends the three course set menu lunch – 'absolutely fantastic'), and the Bateau Ivre. And a 'wine restaurant' – Il Vino – opened in 2007/08, focusing on matching wine to food. Reporters praise the Chapelle for

lamb cooked on an open fire, and a 2008 reporter had a 'nice meal but a little pricey' at the Anerie. Also mentioned by readers are the Tremplin ('exemplary lamb', expensive but 'worth every penny') and the good-value Italian Cendrée. The Saulire (aka Chez Jacques) is a reliable spot that we have enjoyed, endorsed by a 2008 reporter: 'civilized, slightly smart, good food but at surprisingly reasonable prices'. Another recommends the Mangeoire's 'good simple food at acceptable prices, considering there is live music every night'. The hotel Tovets is reported to be 'very good value'. A local recommends the Grand Café (underneath the hotel St Joseph) for good Asian cuisine. Visitors have enjoyed both the Tex-Mex and the pizza at Kalico: 'very good, tasty and reasonable'.

In 1650 the smart hotel Seizena has built a good reputation for 'inventive, reasonably priced' food; the new hotel Manali is 'good but pricey'. The cosy Eterlou was praised by a 2008 visitor for its 'excellent array of local dishes, with plenty of local speciality meat and cheese dishes'. The Petit Savoyard is recommended for its 'excellent' pizzas. We've had several reports of the Ours Blanc, at the bottom of the slopes: 'good burgers', 'good value food', 'service is cheerful though sometimes overwhelmed'. A reporter also recommends the Table de Marie, at the back of the same building for 'a more traditional Savoyard meal'.

In 1300, Bistrot du Praz is expensive but excellent. The Ya-ca is small and 'very French'. We've had excellent meals at the hotel Peupliers (good pepper steak).

APRES-SKI
1850 has most variety
If you want lots of nightlife, it's got to be 1850. There are some exclusive

nightclubs, such as the Caves, with top Paris cabaret acts and sky-high prices. The popular Kalico (open from 9am to 4am) has live bands and DJs. The Bergerie has themed evenings – food, music, entertainment – but prices are high.

The 'reasonably priced' Jump at the foot of the main slope seems to be the place to be as the lifts close. Others have had 'a great time' in the Milk Pub: 'sensibly full and good atmosphere'. The 'lively public bar of the Potinière hotel is also popular. The Petit Drink, specialising in wine and tapas, at the entrance to 1850 next to the new MGM apartments is affordable, and popular with locals.

Piggys attracts 'fur coats carrying pampered dogs'. Mangeoire has 'an excellent piano bar (with high prices) and is extremely lively from about 11pm'.

Cinemas in 1850 and 1650 show English-speaking films.

The Bubble is the hub of activity in 1650, with satellite TV, internet access, 'reasonable' bar prices, 'good' local beers, live music, quiz nights and 'very friendly' atmosphere. One reporter says, 'It was our bar of choice all week.' It has a largely British clientele.

One 2007 reader's favourite was the Signal bar. A 2008 visitor enjoyed Rocky's and thought it 'not prohibitively over-priced', but warned that the nearby Schuss bar charged 'extortionate' prices. The Funky Fox (formerly the Lounge Bar) has pool, games and live music or DJs and the local disco – the Club (formerly the Taverne) – stays open till 4am.

In 1550 the Chanrossa bar is British-dominated, with occasional live music, and the Taverne is recommended as 'friendly, cosy and cheerful'. In 1300 the Escorch'vel bar is 'a good, lively place'.

OFF THE SLOPES
1850 isn't bad
There are a fair number of shops in 1850, plus markets at most levels. Snowshoeing among the trees is growing in popularity. A pedestrian lift pass for the gondolas and buses in Courchevel and Méribel makes it easy for non-slope users to meet up the mountain for lunch. A 2008 visitor recommends the toboggan run from 1850 to 1550 ('great fun … very fast'). And you can take joyrides from the altiport. A non-skiers' guide is distributed by the tourist office.

Les Deux-Alpes

Sprawling resort with a high, narrow ski area that will disappoint many intermediates; popular for summer skiing and boarding

COSTS

① ② ③ ④ ⑤ ⑥

RATINGS

The slopes
Fast lifts	**
Snow	****
Extent	***
Expert	****
Intermediate	**
Beginner	***
Convenience	***
Queues	**
Mountain restaurants	**

The rest
Scenery	****
Resort charm	**
Off-slope	**

NEWS

For 2007/08 a hands-free lift pass was introduced. The Super Diable black has been reclassified red with a blue alternative to the steepest section. The Tanking Center has become the Acqua Center with pool, steam room, sauna, hot tub and massage.

298

➕ High, snow-sure, varied slopes, including an extensive glacier area

➕ Lots of good off-piste terrain

➕ Stunning views of the Ecrins peaks

➕ Lively resort with varied nightlife

➕ Wide choice of affordable hotels

➖ Piste network modest by big resort standards and congested in places

➖ Home runs are either steep and icy or dangerously overcrowded – so people queue for a lift down

➖ Virtually no woodland runs

➖ Spread-out resort

We have a love-hate relationship with Les Deux-Alpes. We quite like the buzz of the village and we understand the appeal of its vibrant nightlife. We love the high-Alpine feel of its main mountain, and the good snow to be found on the north-facing slopes at mid-mountain. But we're unimpressed by the limited extent of the pistes and we hate the congestion that results in peak season when most of the town's 35,000 visitors are crammed on to them.

THE RESORT

Les Deux-Alpes is a narrow village sitting on a high, remote col. Access is from the Grenoble-Briançon road to the north. The village is a long, sprawling collection of apartments, hotels, bars and shops, most lining the busy main street and the parallel street that completes the one-way traffic system. It has a lively ambience.

The village has grown haphazardly over the years, and there is a wide range of building styles, from old chalets through 1960s blocks to more sympathetic recent developments. It looks better as you leave than as you arrive, because all the balconies face the southern end of the resort.

Lifts are spread fairly evenly along the village and there is no clear

centre. But three sectors can be identified. As you enter the village from the north, roads go off on the left to wind up the hill to Les 2 Alpes 1800 – inconvenient for shopping and nightlife, though not necessarily for skiing. Carry on and you come to the geographical centre of the resort, with the major gondola stations, popular outdoor ice rink and lots of shops and restaurants. At the end of the resort is Alpe de Venosc, with many of the nightspots and hotels, the most character, the fewest cars, the best shops and the Diable gondola. The free shuttle-bus service saves some long walks.

The six-day pass covers two days in Alpe-d'Huez and one in Serre-Chevalier (an hour away over the Col du Lautaret) and a day in several other resorts. Helicopter trips to Alpe-d'Huez are good value at £50 return – a 'must', says a reporter. More economical is the shuttle-bus service on Wednesdays and Thursdays.

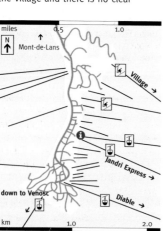

THE MOUNTAINS

For a big resort, Les Deux-Alpes has a disappointingly small piste area, despite improvements over the years. A recent reporter confirms our view: 'A real lack of mileage; we skied pretty much everything in a day.' The piste map is inadequate, especially for the area around Toura and Crêtes. A few blue runs have short steep sections and some runs are different colours on the map and on the mountain.

KEY FACTS

Resort	1650m
	5,410ft
Slopes	1300-3570m
	4,270-11,710ft
Lifts	51
Pistes	225km
	140 miles
Green	20%
Blue	40%
Red	21%
Black	19%
Snowmaking	
	214 guns

LIFT PASSES

Super ski pass

Prices in €

Age	1-day	6-day
under 13	29	136
13 to 64	36	172
over 65	29	136

Free under 5, over 72
Beginner four free draglifts

Notes
Covers all lifts in Les Deux-Alpes; half-day and pedestrian passes; family rates; 6-day pass includes entry to swimming pool and ice rink and access to La Grave and two days in Alpe-d'Huez and one day in Serre-Chevalier, Puy-St-Vincent and the Milky Way

Alternative passes
Ski Sympa covers 21 lifts

THE SLOPES
Long, narrow and fragmented

The western **Pied Moutet** side of Les Deux-Alpes is served by lifts from various parts of town and is relatively low (the top is 2100m/6,890ft) and the snow has never been good enough to try it on our visits. As well as the short runs back to town, which get the morning sun, there's a north-facing red run down through the trees to the village of Bons. The only other tree-lined run in Les Deux-Alpes goes down to another low village, Mont-de-Lans.

On the broad, gentle slope east of the resort are about a dozen beginner lifts, and above it a steep slope running up to the ridge of **Les Crêtes**. To get back to the village you have a choice of one winding green run, often very crowded, or four short black runs. These are usually mogulled (two are ungroomed), and often icy at the end of the day. Many visitors ride down.

The ridge has lifts and gentle runs along it, and behind it lies the deep, steep Combe de Thuit. Lifts span the combe to the mid-mountain station at **Toura** at the heart of the slopes. We seem to spend a lot of time on three key fast lifts. Above Toura, the Glaciers chair takes you up 600m/1,970ft for blue and red runs back down. Below it, the Bellecombes chair serves a range of good, high slopes. And off to the north, the Fée chair serves its own (relatively quiet) sector. The chairs going up to La Toura serve short runs and various terrain features. The middle section of the mountain, around Toura, is very narrow, and prone to crowding (you can avoid the narrow section below Toura by going down to La Fée and taking the gentle piste to the Truite and Voûte chairs).

The top **Glacier du Mont de Lans** section has fine, easy runs with great views, served by an underground funicular and draglifts. You can go

from the top all the way down to Mont-de-Lans – a descent of 2270m/7,450ft vertical that we believe is the world's biggest on-piste vertical. A walk (or snowcat tow) takes you to the slopes of La Grave (covered by the lift pass). There are more slopes off to the north, served by chairs.

TERRAIN PARKS
A real highlight

The heavyweight terrain park is located on the Toura run in the winter, then shifts up to the glacier in the summer and reopens mid-June (www.2alpes-snowpark.com). Easily one of the top parks in Europe, this has something for everyone (including beginners). All sizes of kickers, hips, rails and boxes will keep all levels challenged throughout the day. The highlights of this 800m/2,620ft-long park are an impeccable super-pipe in

Interactive resort shortlist builder at **www.wtss.co.uk**

boarding

Les Deux-Alpes has become a snowboard Mecca over the past few years. Its cheap and cheerful atmosphere counts for a lot – while the limited pisted slopes aren't as off-putting to boarders as to skiers. The kick-off to the French winter season begins here with a huge Mondial du Snowboard event (31 October-2 November in 2008). In town there are good trampoline facilities and a huge airbag to get a feeling of what air-time is all about. Although the focus is on the terrain park, the freeriding is not to be underestimated, with plenty of steep challenging terrain. Beginners will find the narrow, flat crowded areas mid-mountain and the routes down to the village intimidating. Most of the lifts on the higher slopes are chairs, and there are the specialist Primitive and Bliss snowboard schools.

SCHOOLS

ESF
t 0476 792121

International
St-Christophe
t 0476 790421

European
t 0476 797455

Primitive Snowboard
(Salomon)
t 0607 907135

Ski Privilege
t 0476 792344

Easiski
t 0682 795734

Bliss
t 0476 795676

Damien Albert
t 0476 795038

Classes
(ESF prices)
6 half days (2¼hr am
or pm) €142.50

Private lessons
€36 for 1hr

GUIDES

Bureau des guides
t 0476 113629

the winter and two of them in the glacier park for the summer. There are two boardercross courses and a freecross area. DJs regularly play music, and a BBQ area and snow-skate park complete the mix.

SNOW RELIABILITY
Excellent on higher slopes
The snow on the higher slopes is normally very good, even in a poor winter. Above 2200m/7,220ft most of the runs are north-facing, and the top glacier section guarantees good snow. More of a concern is bad weather shutting the lifts, or extremely low temperatures at the top. But the runs just above the village from Les Crêtes face west, so they get a lot of afternoon sun and can be slushy or icy. Snowmaking has been improved on the lower slopes – but a January visitor skiing on rocky pistes saw it used 'not once'. We have never found the snow on the relatively low Pied Moutet sector good enough to ski.

FOR EXPERTS
Off-piste is the main attraction
The area offers wonderful off-piste sport – see opposite. We loved the long, deserted Chalence run which is easier than it looks from the bottom. There are also serious routes that end

well outside the lift network, with verticals of over 2000m/6,560ft. Reporters consistently recommend the renowned descent to St-Christophe (you get a taxi back); one said, 'Though the resort's slopes were hard-packed, this run had superb powder.'

A free weekly Free Respect event promotes off-piste safety (see 'Schools and guides').

The Super Diable chairlift, from the top of the Diable gondola, serves a steep red piste. The Bellecombes and Fée chairs serve challenging pistes and ski routes – marked and patrolled, but not protected; don't miss the Grand Couloir and its off-piste variant (which often has better snow). If the conditions are right, an outing to the serious slopes of La Grave is a must.

FOR INTERMEDIATES
Limited cruising
Les Deux-Alpes can disappoint keen intermediates because of the limited extent of the pistes. Avid piste-bashers will cover the pistes in a couple of days, especially if the snow in the Pied Moutet sector is not good enough to be enjoyable. A lot of the runs are either rather tough – some of the blues could be reds – or boringly bland. The runs higher up generally have good snow, and there is some

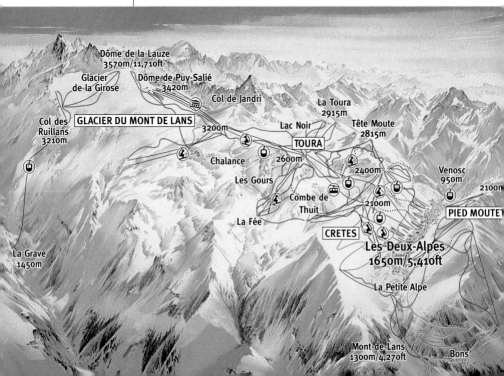

The off-piste routes in Les Deux-Alpes are numerous and varied in difficulty, the easiest permitting skiers even of an intermediate level to enjoy their first 'freeride experience'. We've asked Jeremy Edwards of the European Ski and Snowboard School to share some of his favourites.

For something slightly technical, both sides off the Bellecombes piste – 2800m-2300m (9,190ft-7,550ft) – offer a wide range of varying terrain; it's important to take care here – there are several small cliff faces. For those keen to tackle couloirs – steep, narrow slopes between rocks – this descent offers small ones that are ideal for your first attempts; they can be avoided, though.

Traversing across the top of the black Grand Couloir piste leads to the North Rachas area, with off-piste faces that offer cold snow conditions all winter. The first large valley leads to three couloirs – one fairly broad and easy, the others much narrower and steeper, and certainly not for the timid. Traversing further leads to a much wider descent that avoids the three couloirs.

The **European Ski and Snowboard School** does classes and guiding in small groups. Its instructors are of several nationalities, but all speak excellent English.
t 00 33 476 797455
europeanskischool@
worldonline.fr
www.europeanskischool.
co.uk

For tree skiing it's best to head for the Vallée Blanche area, reached via the lifts on Pied Moutet. The north-east face, towards the chairlift at Bons, offers great routes over generally deserted wooded terrain with excellent cold snow conditions.

Strong skiers will enjoy the famous Chalance run, which starts just below the glacier and descends 1000m/3,280ft vertical to the Gours run; there are several variations, mixing wide open slopes and rocky pitches. These faces are at times subject to quite a high avalanche risk because of wind slab.

Traversing above the north face of the Chalance leads to the couloir Pylone Electrique – a steep, narrow 200m/660ft-long couloir with the reward below it of an excellent wide powder field of moderate gradient. A rest on the Thuit chairlift is a must after this adrenalin-charged descent.

These routes and many more play a large part in the off-piste freeride courses offered by the European Ski and Snowboard School.

Les Deux-Alpes

301

EUROPEAN SKI & SNOWBOARD SCHOOL

British orientated ski and snowboard school

Summer and winter

Quality instruction all in English

British instructors

Ski group courses

Adults or children Maximum 8 per group in 3-hour sessions over 5/6 days at all levels. Video analysis, progress reports, medals. Certificates for children.

Natural born skiers Whole mountain philosophy. Maximum 4 per group in 2-hour sessions over 5 days. Higher levels. Lift queue priority.

Free ride for experienced skiers. Discover Les Deux Alpes off-piste. 3 or 6 days, half or full days.

Private tuition on a 2-hourly basis, all levels. Ski, Snowboard, Telemark, Snowblades.

La Grave Guided trips to this off-piste Mecca.

Race camps Summer and winter.

Snowboard courses First go, Improving, Snow park, Free ride. Maximum 4 per group in 2-hour sessions over 3 or 6 days. Lift queue priority.

Interactive resort shortlist builder at **www.wtss.co.uk**

European Ski and Snowboard School, 95 Avenue de la Muzelle, 38860 Les Deux Alpes, France.
Email europeanskischool@worldonline.fr www.europeanskischool.co.uk Tel/fax 0033 476 797455

CHILDREN

Crèche 2 Alpes 1800
t 0476 790262
Ages 6mnth to 2yr;
8.30-5.30
Bonhomme de Neige
t 0476 790677
Ages 2 to 6; 8.30-5.15
(also activity centre
for ages 6 to 17)
Jardins des Neiges
t 0476 792121
Ages 4 to 6; 9.15-12
noon, 2.30-5pm; 6
mornings €135

Ski schools
Classes for ages 6 to
12 (6 mornings €119
with ESF)

UK PACKAGES

Airtours, Alpine
Answers, AmeriCan Ski,
Chalet Group, Chalet
World Ski, Club Med,
Crystal, Equity, Erna
Low, First Choice,
Independent Ski Links,
Inghams, Interactive
Resorts, Interhome,
Lagrange, Made to
Measure, Mark Warner,
McNab Snowsports,
Neilson, Peak Retreats,
Rocketski, Ski Activity,
Ski France, Skifrance
4less, Skiholidayextras.
com, Ski Independence,
Ski Leisure Direction,
Ski Line, Ski Solutions,
Ski Supreme, Skitracer,
Skiworld, Snoworks,
Solo's, Thomson, UCPA

SMART LODGINGS

Check out our feature
chapters at the front
of the book.

great fast cruising, especially from the glacier to Toura and on the mainly north-facing pistes served by the chairlifts off to the sides. You can often pick gentle or steeper terrain in these bowls as you wish. The chairlifts at the glacier serve great carving pistes. Many visitors do day trips to Alpe-d'Huez (by helicopter).

Less confident intermediates will love the quality of the snow and the gentleness of most of the runs on the upper mountain. Their problem might lie in finding the pistes too crowded.

FOR BEGINNERS
Good slopes
The nursery slopes beside the village are spacious and gentle. The run along the ridge above them is excellent, too. The glacier also has a fine array of very easy slopes.

FOR CROSS-COUNTRY
Needs very low-altitude snow
There are small, widely dispersed areas. Given good snow, Venosc, reached by a gondola down, has the only worthwhile picturesque ones. Total trail distance is 20km/12 miles.

QUEUES
Can be a problem
Les Deux-Alpes has some impressive lifts, but the village is large, and queues at the morning peak can be 'diabolically' long for the Jandri Express and Diable gondolas (you can avoid these by taking an alternative route by fast chairs). The top lifts are prone to closure if it's windy, putting pressure on the lower lifts. We have repeated reports of queues for the gondolas back to the village when snow is poor low down.

MOUNTAIN RESTAURANTS
A few good places
There are mountain restaurants at all the major lift junctions, but they are generally unremarkable.
Editors' choice Diable au Coeur (0476 799950) at the top of the Diable gondola has excellent food (we had delicious confit de canard in 2008) and service. On the terrace, get as far as you can from the noisy adjacent chairlift machinery. The bigger but similarly excellent Chalet la Toura (0476 792096), in the middle of the domain, reopened for 2007/08 after being devastated by fire.
Worth knowing about The table-service

half of the Panoramic at Toura is recommended for its 'mouth-watering cuisine' – but 'it gets very crowded'. There is a small table-service restaurant attached to the big self-service Les Glaciers at 3200m/10,500ft.

SCHOOLS AND GUIDES
We are all Europeans now
A recent reporter 'highly recommends' Easiski who were 'very helpful and friendly'. We have a positive report on the tuition and organisation of the European school, composed of instructors of various nationalities, all speaking good English. Class sizes are small – as few as four pupils if you go for their advanced classes. Bliss is a snowboard school, featuring two-hour beginner courses. There's a free Free Respect off-piste awareness course (held Monday evening and Tuesday daytime) run by guides and patrollers who provide transceivers, shovels, probes etc and teach you to use them.

FACILITIES FOR CHILDREN
Fine facilities
The village nursery takes kids from six months to two years, the kindergarten from three to six years, and there are chalet-based alternatives run by UK tour operators. There are also four free T-bars for children at the village level and a kids' freestyle area.

STAYING THERE

HOW TO GO
Wide range of packages
Les Deux-Alpes has plenty of that rarity in high-altitude French resorts, reasonably priced hotels.
Chalets Several UK tour operators run catered chalets; some use apartments, but Neilson has some proper little chalets, including the recently built Chartreuse. Mark Warner runs an excellent chalet hotel, the Bérangère – in a slope-side position on the road up to Les 2 Alpes 1800.
Hotels There are about 30 hotels, of which the majority are 2-star or below.
****Farandole** (0476 805045) The one 4-star. At the Venosc end of the resort.
***Mariande** (0476 805060) Highly recommended, especially for its 'excellent' five-course dinners. At the Venosc end of the resort.
***Chalet Mounier** (0476 805690) Smartly modernised. Good reputation for food. Swimming pool and fitness room. At the Venosc end of the resort.

↑ The resort sprawls a long way along the dead-end access road

OT LES DEUX-ALPES

GETTING THERE

Air Lyon 160km/ 99 miles (3½hr); Grenoble 120km/ 75 miles (2½hr); Chambéry 126km/ 78 miles (3hr); Geneva 230km/ 143 miles (4½hr)

Rail Grenoble (70km/43 miles); four daily buses from station

ACTIVITIES

Indoor Swimming pool, hot tub, sauna, sports centres (Club Forme, Acqua Center), cinemas, games rooms, bowling, museum, library

Outdoor Ice rink, snowmobiles, paragliding, quad bikes, snowshoeing, ice climbing, helicopter rides, Kanata (Inuit) village visit

Phone numbers
From abroad use the prefix +33 and omit the initial '0' of the phone number

TOURIST OFFICE

t 0476 792200
info@les2alpes.com
www.les2alpes.com

***Souleil'or** (0476 792469) Looks like a lift station, but pleasant and comfortable. Rooms and food reported to be 'fantastic'. Central.
Lutins (0476 792152) Central, 'basic, dated décor but very convenient, clean and friendly'.
Côte Brune (0476 805489) Slope-side, near Jandri Express. Large, basic, modern rooms.
Apartments Erna Low and Peak Retreats both have several apartments and the latter has self-catered chalets too (including two with pools and saunas down in Venosc). Cortina apartments at the south end are spacious, with sauna, steam room and hot tubs. Alpina Lodge is central and right by the slopes. Goleon and Val Ecrin were new for 2007/08, at the entrance to the resort, and are smart, with sauna and steam room.

EATING OUT
Plenty of choice
Chalet Mounier's P'tit Polyte restaurant has a high reputation. Petite Marmite has good food and atmosphere at reasonable prices. Bel'Auberge does classic French and is 'quite superb'. The Patate, Cloche and Crêpe à Gogo ('great food') and Etable ('best pizza ever') are reader recommendations. You can get a relatively cheap meal at Bleuets bar, the Vetrata or the Spaghetteria. One regular visitor says that Smokey Joe Tex-Mex is the best value in the resort.

The resort has contrived ways of dining at altitude – snowmobile to the glacier and back, eating on the way, or at full moon ski or board back to town after dinner (with ski patrollers).

APRES-SKI
Unsophisticated fun
Les Deux-Alpes is one of the liveliest of French resorts, with plenty of bars, several of which stay open until the early hours. Smithy's Tavern is a 'massive party venue' that pulls in a young crowd and serves 'amazing fajitas'. Pub le Windsor is a smaller, quieter place popular with locals. Smokey Joe's is a popular central sports bar and the Secret has live music, big-screen TV, and a wide choice of beers. Other places mentioned by reporters include Bar Brésilien and Bleuets. The main bar at 1800 is O'Brian's; the Tribeca has 'a lovely ambience for grown-ups'. The Avalanche is the main nightclub, at the Venosc end of town; up at 1800, the Opéra is recommended by locals.

OFF THE SLOPES
Limited options
The pretty valley village of Venosc is worth a visit by gondola, and you can take a scenic helicopter flight to Alpe-d'Huez. There are lots of walks and the Acqua Center has a pool, sauna, steam room and hot tub. Several mountain restaurants are accessible to pedestrians. The White Cruise in a snowcat takes you across the glacier and provides wonderful views. You can visit an exhibition on avalanches (which includes a simulator showing you what it's like to be caught in one).

STAYING DOWN THE VALLEY
Worth considering
Close to the foot of the final ascent to Les Deux-Alpes are two little Logis de France hotels, near-ideal for anyone thinking of visiting Alpe-d'Huez, La Grave and Serre-Chevalier – the cheerful Cassini (0476 800410) at Le Freney and the even more appealing Panoramique (0476 800625) at Mizoën – approved of by a recent reporter for 'hearty food, informative Dutch hosts' and the 'wondrous' panorama.

An alternative is to stay in one of the hamlets close to the bottom of the gondola up from Venosc.

Les Deux-Alpes

Interactive resort shortlist builder at **www.wtss.co.uk**

Flaine

Uncompromisingly modern, high-altitude resort sharing a big, broad area of varied slopes with more rustic alternatives

COSTS

① ② ③ ④ ⑤ ⑥

RATINGS

The slopes
Fast lifts	**
Snow	****
Extent	****
Expert	****
Intermediate	*****
Beginner	*****
Convenience	*****
Queues	***
Mountain restaurants	**

The rest
Scenery	****
Resort charm	*
Off-slope	*

NEWS

For 2008/09 the first phase of Intrawest's major development at Flaine Montsoleil, Terrasses d'Eos, is due to open. If all goes well, Montsoleil will be linked to Flaine by new green runs to and from Flaine Forêt, with a new chairlift giving access to these runs from Forêt.

At Les Carroz, a new skier services facility is planned at the gondola base station.

For 2007/08 a long six-pack, Tête des Verds, was installed from the bottom of the resort towards Platières. Work to improve some pistes included widening the main Tourmaline blue run at Grand Vans. And the 3-star Pleiades apartments opened in Flaine Forêt.

304

➕ Big, varied area, with plenty of terrain to suit everyone

➕ Reliable snow in the main bowl

➕ Compact, convenient, mainly car-free village, plus traditional villages on the lower fringes of the area

➕ Excellent facilities for children

➕ Scenic setting, and glorious views

➕ Very close to Geneva but ...

➖ Weekends can be busy as a result

➖ Lots of slow old chairlifts

➖ Austere modern buildings

➖ In bad weather, main Flaine bowl offers little to do, and links to outer sectors of the area may be closed

➖ Nightlife not a highlight

➖ Little to do off the slopes (in Flaine)

Flaine is best known as a convenient resort catering particularly well for families, but it has a much broader appeal than that. The Grand Massif is almost a match for Val d'Isère/Tignes in terms of extent, at least.

Flaine's family orientation is underlined by the domination of self-catering accommodation. But you open up more accommodation options by considering the outlying villages – Les Carroz, Samoëns and Morillon (the last two now covered in the separate Samoëns chapter). Not only are they more attractive, rounded places to stay in, but also they offer some sheltered woodland slopes for bad-weather days.

THE RESORT

The concrete Bauhaus-style blocks that form the core of Flaine were conceived in the sixties as 'an example of the application of the principle of shadow and light'. They look particularly shocking from the approach road – a mass of blocks nestling at the bottom of the impressive snowy bowl. From the slopes they are less obtrusive, blending into the rocky grey hillside. For us, the outdoor sculptures by Picasso, Vasarely and Dubuffet do little to improve Flaine's austere ambience.

In contrast, the Hameau-de-Flaine is built in a much more attractive chalet style – but is inconveniently situated 1km/0.5 miles from the slopes and main village, and has only one shop/ bar/restaurant. In the same direction is Intrawest's new Montsoleil mini-resort – again designed in a more visually pleasing way (opening this year).

In Flaine proper, everything is close by: supermarket, sports rental shops, ski schools, main lifts out etc.

There are two parts to the main resort. The lower part, Forum, is centred on a snow-covered square with buildings on three sides, open fourth side blending with the slopes. Flaine Forêt, up the hillside and linked by lift, has its own bars and shops, and most of the apartments.

There are children all over the place; they are catered for with play areas, and the resort is supposed to be traffic-free. In fact, roads penetrate the village and you don't have to go far to encounter traffic; but the Forum, leading to the pistes, is pretty safe.

The bus service to/from Hameau is 'excellent' but runs only to Forêt, not Forum – except Saturdays, when we're told it runs only to Forum 'leaving you a 10-minute walk to the nearest lift'. A car gives you the option of visiting the Portes du Soleil, Chamonix, Megève or Courmayeur in Italy.

THE MOUNTAINS

The Grand Massif is an impressive area; but the greater part of the domain lies outside the main Flaine bowl and the links can be closed by

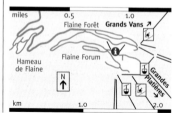

KEY FACTS

Resort	1600m
	5,250ft
Grand Massif (Flaine, Les Carroz, Morillon, Samoëns, Sixt)	
Slopes	700-2480m
	2,300-8,140ft
Lifts	78
Pistes	265km
	165 miles
Green	11%
Blue	42%
Red	36%
Black	11%
Snowmaking	
	218 guns

For Flaine only	
Slopes	1600-2480m
	5,250-8,140ft
Lifts	28
Pistes	140km
	87 miles
Green	13%
Blue	37%
Red	42%
Black	8%

excessive wind or snow.

Signing seems to have improved, but the piste map is rubbish – hopelessly ambitious in trying to cover such a big and complex area in a single view. In the middle of the area are several distinct bowls that are simply not detectable on the map.

THE SLOPES
A big white playground

The day begins for most people at the **Grandes Platières** jumbo gondola, which speeds you in a single stage up the north face of the Flaine bowl to the high-point of the Grand Massif, and a magnificent view of Mont Blanc. A new six-pack offers an alternative, going part-way up.

Most of the runs are reds (though there are some blues curling away to skier's right, and one direct black). There are essentially four or five main ways down the barren, treeless, rolling terrain back to Flaine, or to chairs in

the middle of the wilderness.

On the far right, the Cascades blue run leads away from the lift system behind the Tête Pelouse down to the outskirts of Sixt, dropping over 1700m/5,580ft vertical in its exceptional 14km/9 mile length. The gentle/flat top half is hard work, so we're not greatly concerned that the run isn't reliably open; readers seem more impressed than we are. At the end you can get buses (often crowded) to the lifts at Samoëns. Or spend some time exploring the slopes of Sixt – very quiet, with a non-trivial vertical.

On the other side of the Tête Pelouse, a broad catwalk leads to the experts-only **Gers** bowl. At the bottom, a flat trail links with the lower (more interesting) half of the Cascades run.

Back at Platières, an alternative is to head left down the long red Méphisto to the **Aujon** area – again mostly red runs but with some blues further down. The lower slopes here are used as slalom courses. This sector is also reachable by gondola or draglifts from below the resort.

The eight-seat Grands Vans chair, reached from Forum by means of a slow bucket-lift – reportedly not open all day – gives access to the extensive slopes of Samoëns, Morillon and Les Carroz. You come first to the wide Vernant bowl, equipped with three fast chairlifts. Beyond here are the slopes of **Les Carroz**, **Morillon** and **Samoëns**.

TERRAIN PARKS
Cater for kids to experts

The main terrain park (called the JamPark Pro – standing for Jib and Air Maniacs) is in Flaine's Aujon area. It has a quarter-pipe, tables, rails, a boardercross course and chill-out zone. Watch out for the 'downright dangerous' Aujon draglift, though, which is still as much of a challenge as the park. There's a tiny kids' park in Samoëns, a boardercross course in Les Carroz and another kids' park, JamPark Kids, with a boardercross on the Morillon side.

bOArding

Flaine suits boarders quite well – there's lots of varied terrain and plenty of off-piste with interesting nooks and crannies, including woods outside the main bowl. The key lifts are now chairs or gondolas (but beware the absurdly vicious Aujon draglift, which serves the terrain park). There's a big terrain park in Flaine and a couple of smaller kids' areas. Black Side is the local specialist shop, with a new cafe and bar in the central Forum.

SNOW RELIABILITY
Usually keeps its whiteness

The main part of Flaine's slopes lie on the wide north- and north-west-facing flank of the Grandes Platières, and keep snow well. There is snowmaking on the greater part of the Aujon sector and on the nursery slopes. The runs towards Samoëns 1600 and Morillon 1100 are north-facing too, and some lower parts have snowmaking, but below these mid-stations the runs can be tricky or closed. The Les Carroz runs are south-west-facing and low, and can suffer from strong afternoon sun as a result, but a few runs have snowmaking.

Piste grooming is repeatedly commended by readers.

FOR EXPERTS
Great fun with guidance

Flaine has some seriously challenging terrain, despite its family orientation. But much of it is off-piste and, although some of it looks like it can safely be explored without guidance, this impression is mistaken. The Flaine bowl is riddled with rock crevasses and potholes, and should be treated with the same caution that you would use on a glacier. We are told that these hazards cause deaths most years.

All the black pistes on the map deserve their classification. The Diamant Noir, down the line of the main gondola, is tricky because of moguls, narrowness and other people,

The long, lift-free Cascades run to Sixt, which excites some readers but not us

LES GRANDES PLATIERES
2480m/8,140ft

Tête Pelouse

Tête des Linda

Grandes Platières

Têtes des Verds

Aup de Veran

Tête de Véret
2315m

GERS
1715m

Les Grands Vans
2205m

Grands Vans

Vernant

Flaine
1600m/5,250ft

Tête des Saix
2120m

Le Lac

Vernant

Les Mollie

Sixt

1900m

Lots of slow chairlifts above Samoëns 1600

150

SAMOENS
1600m

Sairon

Esserts

Samoëns Village
720m/2,360ft

Grand Massif

Saix

Good runs down the old gondola from Vercland, none down the newer one from close to Samoëns

Vercland

MORILLON
1100m

Morillon

Morillon
700m

LIFT PASSES

Grand Massif

Prices in €

Age	1-day	6-day
under 12	28	135
12 to 15	30	147
16 to 59	38	187
over 60	30	147

Free under 5, over 75
Beginner four free lifts

Notes
Covers all lifts in Flaine, Les Carroz, Morillon, Samoëns and Sixt

Alternative passes
Flaine area only

---

rather than great steepness; the first pitch is the steepest, with spectators applauding from the chairlift.

To skier's left of the Diamant Noir are several short but steep off-piste routes through the crags.

The Lindars Nord chair serves a shorter slope that often has the best snow in the area, and some seriously steep gradients. Mind the chair doesn't whack you as you exit.

The Gers draglift, outside the main bowl, serves great expert terrain. The Styx piste is a proper black, but nearby off-piste slopes reach 45°. The main Gers bowl is a great north-facing horseshoe of about 550m/1,800ft vertical, powder or moguls top to bottom, all off-piste, ranging from

steep to very steep. There are more adventurous ways in from the Grands Vans and Tête de Véret lifts.

There are further serious pistes on the top lifts above Samoëns 1600.

There are some scenic off-piste routes from which you can be retrieved by helicopter – such as the Combe des Foges, next to Gers.

FOR INTERMEDIATES
Something for everyone

Flaine is ideal for confident intermediates, with a great variety of pistes (and usually the bonus of good snow conditions, at least above Flaine itself). As a reporter puts it, 'There may not be many challenging runs, but there are very few dull ones.' The

S GRANDES PLATIERES
2480m/8,140ft
Pelouse
Tête des Lindars
Grandes Platières
Têtes des Verds
Aup de Véran
AUJON
2035m
de Véret
315m
Grands ans 05m
Grands Vans
Vernant
Flaine
1600m/5,250ft
des Saix 2120m
Le Lac
Vernant
Les Molliets

Excellent woodland runs immediately above Les Carroz, served by a gondola – great on a bad day

1900m
Kédeuze
LES CARROZ
1140m/3,740ft
SAMOENS
om
1500m
Sairon
Esserts
MORILLON
1100m
Morillon

Good cruising above Morillon

Morillon
700m

SCHOOLS

ESF
t 0450 908100

International
t 0450 908441

Moniteurs indépendants
t 0450 937978

Flaine Super Ski
t 0681 061906

Flaine Ski Clinic
t 0699 862538

Freecimes
t 0664 118329

François Simond
t 0450 908097

Bruno Uyttenhove
t 0610 183082

Le Hameau Master Class
t 0450 908716

Classes (ESF prices)
6 days (3hr per day)
€132

Private lessons
€38 for 1hr, for 1 or 2 people

diabolically named reds that dominate the Flaine bowl tend to gain their status from short steep sections rather than overall difficulty. The relatively direct Faust is great carving territory, at least in January when it isn't cluttered. There are gentler cruises from the top of the mountain – Cristal, taking you to the Perdrix chair, or Serpentine, all the way home. The blues at Aujon are excellent for confidence building, but the drag serving them is not.

The connections with the slopes outside the main bowl are classified blue but several blue-run reporters have found them tricky because of narrowness, crowds or poor snow. Once the connection has been made, however, all intermediates will enjoy the long tree-lined runs down to Les Carroz, as long as the snow is good. The Morillon slopes are also excellent intermediate terrain – the long green Marvel run to Morillon 1100 is an easy cruise with excellent signs along the way explaining the local wildlife.

Crowds on the lower slopes returning to Flaine have been a source of complaint, but the problem has been relieved to some degree by the red Aventurine piste, allowing better skiers to go left well above the village.

FOR BEGINNERS
Fairly good
There are excellent nursery slopes right by the village, served by free lifts which make a pass unnecessary until you are ready to go higher up the mountain. The area is roped off, but it is still used as a short cut back to the village by other skiers. A new beginner area, with two long green runs, is

planned for 2008/09 to be served eventually by a quad (see 'News'). There are some gentle blues to progress to over on skier's right, beneath Tête Pelouse. Progress to the 'interesting and gentle blues' in the Aujon sector is not easy due to several steep draglifts. If you have a really nervous intermediate to deal with, it's worth driving or bussing down the access road to a couple of 'fine' and quiet greens at Vernant.

CROSS-COUNTRY
Very fragmented
The Grand Massif claims 64km/40 miles of cross-country tracks but only about 17km/11 miles of that is around Flaine itself. The majority is on the valley floor and dependent on low snow. There are extensive tracks between Morillon and Les Carroz, with some tough uphill sections.

QUEUES
A few problems
Many of the trouble spots have now been eliminated and several reporters have had queue-free weeks, even in high season. But there can be problems when the resorts are full and at weekends (the area is very close to Geneva). Towards the end of the day expect delays at the Vernant chair to get back to the Flaine bowl (an alternative is to descend to one of the lift-bases along the access road, and catch a bus) and at Les Molliets – 'horrendous' at times, partly thanks to frequent failure of the machinery or its power supply. The Aup de Veran gondola is still 'inadequate' despite recent cabin upgrades. But the new six-pack that goes part way up the

CHILDREN

Les P'tits Loups
t 0450 908782
Ages 6mnth to 3yr

Rabbit Club
t 0450 908100
Ages 3 to 11; 9am-
5pm; 6 days with
lunch €243

La Souris Verte
t 0450 908441
Ages from 3

**MMV Hotels Flaine
and Aujon**
t 0492 126212
Ages 18mnth to 14yr

Ski school
For ages 3 to 11:
€110 for 6 days, 3hr
per day (ESF prices);
English-speaking
specialist private
tuition for children:
Catherine Pouppeville
(0699 862538)

GETTING THERE

Air Geneva 90km/
56 miles (1½hr)

Rail Cluses (30km/
19 miles); regular bus
service

SMART LODGINGS

Check out our feature
chapters at the front
of the book.

ACTIVITIES

Indoor Swimming
pool, sauna, solarium,
gymnasium, massage,
bowling, cinema,
climbing wall, cultural
centre with art gallery
and library

Outdoor Ice rink,
snowshoeing, dog
sledding, paragliding,
helicopter rides, quad
bikes, ice driving

same slopes should now ease queues there and for the Grand Platières gondola.

Queues elsewhere can build up at weekends and when the lifts out of the Flaine bowl are shut due to high winds or when the weather is warm and the lower resorts outside the bowl have poor snow. (When this happens, the queues to go down can be worse than those to go up.)

MOUNTAIN RESTAURANTS
Back to base, or quit the bowl
In the Flaine bowl, there are few restaurants above the resort's upper outskirts. Reports suggest most are overcrowded – notably the Grandes Platières self-service, which gets mixed reviews from reporters. The rustic Blanchot, at the bottom of the Serpentine run has a restaurant and a snack bar – both recommended. At Forum level, across the piste from the gondola, is the welcoming Michet ('definitely worth a visit'), with very good Savoyard food and table service, and the 'rustic' Eloge. Up the slope a bit, the Cascade is self-service but with a good terrace. Epicéa is 'high quality', but we've received a report of 'poor service'.

Up at Forêt level, the recently refurbished Bissac has a good atmosphere and 'good fare'.

Outside the Flaine bowl, we love the remote Gîte du Lac de Gers (book in advance and ring for a snowcat to tow you up from the Cascades run) – simple food but splendid isolation. The cosy and rustic Igloo above Morillon is 'friendly, with good food and service'. We had an excellent plat du jour there. The self-service Telemark in this sector gets mixed reviews. The woody Chalet les Molliets is repeatedly praised – 'top food', 'excellent plats du jour'. Cupress above Les Carroz has 'friendly table service'.

SCHOOLS AND GUIDES
Getting better
We've received good reports for ESF in Flaine and Les Carroz: 'We advanced more than in any other resort we have been to.' However, one reader found that classes were 'far too big – twenty in a couple of cases'. A beginner boarder enjoyed an 'excellent' week with the International school last season. The competition-oriented Super Ski has 'small classes, good instruction'.

FACILITIES FOR CHILDREN
Parents' paradise?
Flaine prides itself on being a family resort, and the number of English-speaking children around is a bonus. There are some free children's lift passes available in low season weeks. The International school offers classes for three to five year olds. The P'tits Loups nursery takes children from six months. Crystal's 'well-organised and popular' hotel Le Totem has good child care facilities for residents only.

STAYING THERE

HOW TO GO
Plenty of apartments
Accommodation is overwhelmingly in self-catering apartments.
Chalets There are few catered chalet options, but they include a couple of Scandinavian-style huts in Hameau. The 'excellent food, friendly staff, good rooms' and child care facilities of Crystal's Totem club hotel continue to impress reporters.
Hotels The other hotels now seem to be called 'club' hotels, marketed by big French agencies – but also bookable through UK operator Erna Low. B&B is available at the Cascade restaurant, above the village.
Apartments The best apartments are out at Hameau – 'fabulous', says one visitor. In Flaine Forêt, the Forêt and Grand Massif apartment buildings are attractively woody. The new Pleiades are 'very smart and spacious'. The Montsoleil apartments open this year, and should be excellent.

EATING OUT
Enough choice for a week
The choice is adequate, no more. Reporters have enjoyed the small Chez Pierrot pizzeria for 'lovely local specialities', the Perdrix Noire (seafood and grills) for 'friendly and pleasant service' and the family-friendly Chez Daniel – which also serves a good range of Savoyard specialities. The 'lively' Brasserie les Cîmes has 'very good food, good prices, very friendly service'. The Sucré Salé is an arty place serving pitta and pastry specials. A couple of places close to the village and described under 'Mountain restaurants' are open in the evening – the Michet and the Bissac. The Ancolie in Hameau is said to be worth the trip for its 'great food' and 'beautiful wooden chalet interior'.

Hôtel Le Bois de la Char

Your stay right on the pistes

Les Carroz-d'Arâches
40 minutes from Geneva Airport
10 minutes from highway A40

Tel: 00 33 (0) 4 50 90 06 18
E-mail: contact@hotel-boisdelachar.com
Website: www.hotel-boisdelachar.com

Photo credit: PHOTOTEM – Claude Monvoisin

UK PACKAGES

Action Outdoors, Alpine Answers, Altitude, Classic Ski, Crystal, Crystal Finest, Erna Low, First Choice, Independent Ski Links, Inghams, Lagrange, Neilson, Ski Collection, Ski France, Skifrance 4less, Ski Freshtracks, Skiholidayextras.com, Ski Independence, Ski Leisure Direction, Skitracer, Ski Weekend, Thomson

Les Carroz 360 Sun and Ski, Alps Accommodation, Altitude, AmeriCan Ski, Crystal Finest, Erna Low, Holiday in Alps, Lagrange, Peak Retreats, Ski Activity, Ski France, Skiholiday extras.com, Ski Independence, Ski Leisure Direction, Skiology.co.uk

Sixt AmeriCan Ski, Chalet Group, Lagrange, Peak Retreats

Phone numbers
From abroad use the prefix +33 and omit the initial '0' of the phone number

TOURIST OFFICES

Flaine
t 0450 908001
welcome@flaine.com
www.flaine.com

Les Carroz
t 0450 900004
carroz@lescarroz.com
www.lescarroz.com

APRES-SKI
Signs of life

You can eat and drink into the early hours here if you move around a bit – but you don't have much choice of venue. The White pub has a big screen TV, rock music and punters trying to get pints in before the end of happy hour – but 'not a pleasant atmosphere', says a 2007 visitor. The Flying Dutchman is lively early on, with karaoke and themed evenings, but 'tends to wind down around 11pm'. The bar at the bowling alley is popular with families, and also stays open late – 'the only place still serving food until 3am'. The Diamant Noir has live music and pool. There's one nightclub, but drinks are reportedly 'very expensive' and the music 'not up to much'.

OFF THE SLOPES
Curse of the purpose-built

Flaine is not recommended for people who don't want to hit the slopes. But there is a great ice driving circuit where you can take a spin (literally) in your car or theirs. Snowmobiling and dog sledding are popular, and there's a cinema, gymnasium and swimming pool. Shopping is limited; save your souvenir shopping for the one evening a week when there is a free hands-on display of large wooden games, enjoyed by visitors of all ages.

Want help making a shortlist?
Our website will build one for you, putting your priorities together with our resort ratings. Go to:
www.wtss.co.uk

Les Carroz 1140m/3,740ft

This is a sprawling, sunny, traditional, family resort where life revolves around the village square with its pavement cafes and restaurants. It is a sizeable place – much bigger than Flaine, in fact – that has the lived-in feel of a real French village, with more après-ski animation than Flaine. But a thorough report tells us that things are much quieter later on: the Marlow pub is popular at close of play but soon becomes quiet; Pointe Noire, next door, is cheaper and more animated; Carpe Diem is devoid of customers until the other places close. The Servages d'Armelle is praised for its 'truly outstanding dinner'.

The Bois de la Char (0450 900618) is still 'well managed, perfectly situated, excellent value'. The hotel Arbaron (0450 900267) has been commended for food and views.

Les Fermes du Soleil is an MGM development of five chalet-style buildings, with comfortable apartments and a good pool, hot tub and sauna – 'first class', says a 2008 reporter.

The gondola starts a steep 300m/98oft walk up from the centre – the nursery drag is a help or you can catch the free ski-bus. It serves some excellent slopes in the woods above the village, so this is a great place on a bad-weather day. It's a good place for novices: a 2008 visitor had good beginner lessons with ESF and there's a wide green to progress to.

The ski school's torchlit descent is 'not to be missed' – ending with vin chaud and live jazz in the square.

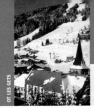

Les Gets

Friendly village with a very French feel to it and two local areas of slopes; but it's not a good base for the main Portes du Soleil circuit

RATINGS

The slopes

Fast lifts	**
Snow	**
Extent	***
Expert	***
Intermediate	****
Beginner	****
Convenience	***
Queues	***
Mountain restaurants	***

The rest

Scenery	***
Resort charm	****
Off-slope	***

Extent rating
This relates only to the Les Gets/Morzine slopes, not the whole Portes du Soleil.

Piste map
The whole local area is covered by the map in the Morzine chapter.

NEWS

There is now a boardercross and a new beginners' rope tow, both near the top of Chavannes.

OT LES GETS / NICOLAS JOLY

Given good snow the local slopes, shared with Morzine, are ideal intermediate terrain ↓

- ➕ Good-sized, varied local piste area shared with Morzine – plus excellent, neglected Mont Chéry
- ➕ Attractive chalet-style village, with through-traffic kept on fringes
- ➕ Relatively short drive from the UK
- ➕ Few queues locally
- ➕ Part of the vast Portes du Soleil ski pass region, but ...

- ➖ It's quite a long way to the main Portes du Soleil circuit at Avoriaz
- ➖ Modest altitude means there is always a risk of poor snow, though increased snowmaking has helped
- ➖ Few challenging pistes
- ➖ Too many slow, old chairs
- ➖ Weekend crowds

Les Gets is an attractive, small, family-friendly resort with a very French feel to it, partly because of local shops lining the main street selling delicious-looking food and wine. The area of slopes that it shares with Morzine offers the most extensive local slopes in the Portes du Soleil, and in some respects Les Gets is the better base for them. But if you intend to visit the main Portes du Soleil circuit a lot, it makes sense to stay closer to it.

THE RESORT

Les Gets is an attractive, sunny village of traditional chalet-style buildings, on the low pass leading to Morzine. The main road bypasses the attractive village centre, which is now part way through a programme aimed at making it even more pedestrian-friendly. It has two 'well-stocked' supermarkets, plenty of attractive food and other shops and restaurants lining the main street. There's also a popular outdoor ice rink, which adds to the charm. It's a good resort for families.

Although the village has a scattered appearance, most facilities are close to the main lift station – and the free 'petit train' road-train shuttle is a cute way of travelling around. There are also free conventional buses around the village and to Morzine. The village is fairly quiet in the evenings but gets busier and livelier at weekends.

THE MOUNTAINS

Les Gets is not an ideal base for the Portes du Soleil, but its local slopes are extensive. The local pass saves a fair bit on a Portes du Soleil pass, and makes a lot of sense for many visitors.
Slopes The main local slopes – accessed by a gondola and fast chair-lift from the nursery slopes beside the village – are shared with Morzine, and are mainly described in that chapter. On the opposite side of Les Gets is Mont Chéry, accessed by a gondola and parallel chair. The slopes include some of the most challenging in the area, and are usually very quiet. Both sectors offer wooded and open slopes.
Snow reliability The nursery slopes benefit from a slightly higher elevation than Morzine, but otherwise our general reservations about the lack of altitude apply. A lot more snow-guns have improved runs to the resort when

KEY FACTS

Resort	1170m
	3,840ft

Portes du Soleil	
Slopes	950-2300m
	3,120-7,550ft
Lifts	202
Pistes	650km
	404 miles
Green	13%
Blue	40%
Red	37%
Black	10%
Snowmaking	
	694 guns

Morzine-Les Gets only	
Slopes	1000-2010m
	3,280-6,590ft
Lifts	50
Pistes	110km
	68 miles

Phone numbers
From abroad use the prefix +33 and omit the initial '0' of the phone number

TOURIST OFFICE

t 0450 758080
lesgets@lesgets.com
www.lesgets.com

peak retreats

Beat the crowds
Traditional resorts

0844 576 0173
peakretreats.co.uk
ABTA W5537

FRANCE

312

Weekly news updates and resort links at www.wtss.co.uk

it's cold enough to make snow. The front slopes of Mont Chéry face south-east – bad news at this altitude; but grooming is good, and the other two flanks are shadier. On a visit when snow was sparse, we found the Les Gets pistes much better than in the higher Three Valleys resorts and Avoriaz (largely because the grassy slopes need less snow-cover) and better than in neighbouring Morzine.

Terrain parks There's a park on the upper slopes of Mont Chéry with airbag, hips, handrails, tables and a wall; plus a Jib park with a table and handrail. And there's a boardercross near the top of Chavannes.

Experts Black runs on the flank and back of Mont Chéry are quite steep and often bumped. In good snow there's plenty to do off-piste, including some excellent wooded areas.

Intermediates High-mileage piste-bashers might prefer direct access to the main Portes du Soleil circuit, but the local slopes have a lot to offer, with excellent reds on Mont Chéry.

Beginners The village nursery slopes are convenient, and there are better, more snow-sure ones at Chavannes, with lots of easy runs to progress to.

Snowboarding The local slopes are good for beginners and intermediates.

Cross-country There are 18km/11 miles of good, varied loops on Mont Chéry and Les Chavannes.

Queues See the Morzine chapter. Mont Chéry is crowd-free. But there are a lot of slow, old chairs.

Mountain restaurants See Morzine.

Schools and guides A 2008 reporter says the instructors at Ecole de Ski 360 'spoke very good English' and her six-year-old daughter was 'cruising down the main slopes on day two'. The 'good but pricey' British Alpine Ski & Snowboard School is here, too.

Facilities for children This is a good resort for families. As well as comprehensive resort facilities, family-specialist tour operators Esprit Ski, Ski Famille and Ski Hillwood all operate here. And the British-run Snowkidz nursery takes babies as well as infant

UK PACKAGES

Alpine Answers, AmeriCan Ski, Chalet Group, Descent International, Esprit, Ferme de Montagne, First Choice, Independent Ski Links, Interactive Resorts, Lagrange, Oxford Ski Co, Peak Retreats, Reach4theAlps, Ski Activity, Ski Expectations, Ski Famille, Ski France, Ski Hillwood, Skiholidayextras. com, Ski Independence, Ski Total, Skitracer, Snow Finders

skiers, and is reported to be 'superb – absolutely faultless'. A 2008 reporter hired a nanny from Cheeky Monkeys (in Morzine) and raved about her.

STAYING THERE

How to go Several tour operators have catered chalets.

Hotels We've stayed at the Ferme de Montagne (0450 753679) and loved it (see the Luxury Chalets chapter – but it's as much a small hotel as a chalet). It is a beautifully renovated farmhouse with eight luxury bedrooms, gourmet food, ski guiding, sauna, outdoor hot tub, massage therapist; right on the edge of town at La Turche. 'High standards of service, comfort and food,' said a recent reporter. The Crychar (0450 758050), 100m/330ft from central Les Gets at the foot of the slopes, is one of the best 3-star hotels ('first rate, ideal location, great restaurant'). The 2-star Alpen'Sports (0450 758055) is a friendly, family-run hotel ('excellent food and good value for money' but 'soundproofing and room size not good'). We've had good reports of the Nagano (0450 797146), the Marmotte (0450 758033) – 'great maître d'; large, warm pool' – and the Alpages (0450 758088) – 'friendly; good heated outdoor pool' – all 3-star.

Apartments The central Sabaudia apartments have a pool and hot tub. Tour operator Peak Retreats offers several self-catered chalets (some luxurious) as well as apartments.

Eating out The Ferme de Montagne has wonderful food, beautifully presented in a splendid renovated wooden dining room. The Tyrol and the Schuss are good for pizza, the rustic Vieux Chêne for Savoyard specialities. The Flambeau, Tanière and Tourbillon have been recommended.

Après-ski Après-ski is quiet, especially on weekdays. The Irish Pub, Canadian Bar above it, Copeaux and the Bush (Scottish owned and with Sky Sports) are recommended by reporters. The Igloo is a popular disco.

Off the slopes There's a well-equipped fitness centre with a pool, an outdoor ice rink and bowling. The Mechanical Music Museum is strongly recommended by a reporter. There's a cinema; husky sleigh rides, snowshoeing and parapenting are possible. There is a good selection of shops, and visits to Geneva, Lausanne and Montreux are feasible.

La Grave

A world apart: an unspoiled mountain village beneath high, untamed off-piste slopes, some of them extreme and hazardous

COSTS

① ② ③ ④ ⑤ ⑥

RATINGS

The slopes

Fast lifts	★★★
Snow	★★★
Extent	★
Expert	★★★★★
Intermediate	★
Beginner	★
Convenience	★★★
Queues	★★★★
Mountain restaurants	★★

The rest

Scenery	★★★★
Resort charm	★★★
Off-slope	★

NEWS

La Grave does not change much, and that is half the charm of the place.

➕ Legendary off-piste mountain

➕ Usually crowd-free

➕ Usually good snow conditions

➕ Link to Les Deux-Alpes

➕ Easy access by car to other nearby resorts

➖ Village spoiled by through-traffic

➖ Poor weather means lift closures – on average, two days per week

➖ Suitable for experts only, despite some easy slopes at altitude

➖ Nothing to do off the slopes

La Grave enjoys legendary status among experts. It's a quiet old village with around 500 visitor beds and just one serious lift – a small stop-start gondola serving a high, wild and almost entirely off-piste mountainside. The result: an exciting, usually crowd-free area. Strictly, you ought to have a guide, but in good weather many people go it alone.

THE RESORT

La Grave is a small, unspoiled mountaineering village set on a steep hillside facing the impressive glaciers of majestic La Meije. It's rather drab, and the busy road through to Briançon doesn't help. But it has a rustic feel, some welcoming hotels, friendly inhabitants and prices that are low by resort standards. The single serious lift starts just below the centre. Storms close the slopes on average two days a week – so a car is useful for access to nearby resorts.

THE MOUNTAIN

A slow two-stage 'pulse' gondola (with an extra station at a pylon halfway up the lower stage) ascends into the slopes and finishes at 3200m/10,500ft. Above that, a short walk and a draglift give access to a second drag serving twin blue runs on a glacier slope of about 350m/1,150ft vertical – from here (after another walk) you can ski to Les Deux-Alpes. But the reason that people come here is to explore the legendary slopes back towards La Grave. These slopes offer no defined, patrolled, avalanche-protected pistes – but there are two marked itinéraires (with several variations now indicated on the 'piste' map) of 1400m/4,590ft vertical down to the pylon lift station at 1800m/5,910ft, or all the way down to the valley – a vertical of 2150m/7,050ft.

Slopes The Chancel route is mostly of red-run gradient; the Vallons de la Meije is more challenging but not too steep. People do take these routes without a guide or avalanche protection equipment, but we couldn't possibly recommend it.

There are many more demanding runs away from the itinéraires, including couloirs that range from the

OT LA GRAVE-LA-MEIJE

← It's spectacular, rugged terrain

313

KEY FACTS

Resort	1450m
	4,760ft
Slopes	1450-3550m
	4,760-11,650ft
Lifts	4
Pistes	5km
	3 miles
Green/Blue	100%

The figures relate only to pistes; practically all the skiing – at least 90% – is off-piste

Snowmaking	none

UK PACKAGES

Alpine Answers, AmeriCan Ski, Interhome, Lagrange, Mountain Tracks, Peak Retreats, Ski Freshtracks, Ski Weekend

Phone numbers
From abroad use the prefix +33 and omit the initial '0' of the phone number

TOURIST OFFICE

t 0476 799005
ot@lagrave-lameije.com
www.lagrave-lameije.com

straightforward to the seriously hazardous, and long descents from the glacier to the valley road below the village, with return by taxi, bus, or strategically parked car. The dangers are considerable (people die here every year), and good guidance is essential. You can also descend a 'spectacular valley' southwards to St-Christophe, returning by bus and the lifts of Les Deux-Alpes.

Terrain parks There aren't any.

Snow reliability The chances of powder snow on the high, north-facing slopes are good, but if conditions are tricky, there are no pistes to fall back on apart from the three short blue runs at the top of the gondola.

Experts La Grave's uncrowded off-piste slopes have earned it cult status among hard-core skiers. Only experts should contemplate a stay here – and then only if prepared to deal with bad weather by sitting tight or struggling over the Col du Lautaret to the woods of Serre-Chevalier.

Intermediates The itinéraires get tracked into a piste-like state, and adventurous intermediates could tackle the Chancel. But the three blue runs at the top of the gondola won't keep anyone occupied for long. The valley stations of Villar d'Arène and Lautaret, around 3km/2 miles and 8km/5 miles to the east respectively, and Chazelet, 3km/2 miles to the

north-west, offer very limited slopes with a handful of intermediate and beginner runs (two newish ones at Villar d'Arène).

Beginners Novices tricked into coming here can go up the valley to the beginner slopes at Le Chazelet, which has two guns for snowmaking.

Snowboarding There are no special facilities for boarders, but advanced freeriders will be in their element on the open off-piste powder.

Cross-country There is a total of 20km/12 miles of loops in the area.

Queues Normally, there are queues only at weekends. March is reportedly the busiest month, when queues can be serious. If snow conditions back to the valley are poor, queues can build up for the gondola down from the mid- and lower stations.

Mountain restaurants Surprisingly, there are three decent mountain restaurants; the jury is out on which is the best, but reporters like both the refuge on the Chancel itinéraire ('best omelette in the world') and the Haut-Dessus at the top ('great pizzas').

Schools and guides There are claimed to be 30 or so guides, offering a wide range of services through their bureau. 'Excellent,' say recent reporters. See also 'Hotels' below.

Facilities for children Babysitting can be arranged through the tourist office.

STAYING THERE

How to go There are very few options.
Hotels The Edelweiss (0476 799093) is strongly recommended for its 'excellent' restaurant with 'phenomenal wine list', comfortable rooms and cosy bar. The Skiers Lodge (Hotel des Alpes; 0476 110318) – which offers all-inclusive week-long packages including guiding – is in the centre of the village. A recent visitor had an 'excellent' week, advising that 'you need to get really fit beforehand'.
Apartments Bookable through the tourist office.
Eating out Most people eat in their hotels, though there are alternatives.
Après-ski The central Café des Glaciers, and the bar of hotel Castillan are the standard teatime venues. The bars of both the Edelweiss and the Skiers Lodge have live music. The Vieux Guide gets crowded later.
Off the slopes Anyone not using the slopes will find La Grave much too small and quiet.

La Meije 3980m
Dome de la Lauze
St-Christophe
Les 2 Alpes
3550m/11,650ft
Glacier de la Girose
Glacier du Rateau
Les Ruillans 3200m
Glacier de la Meije
Brèche Pacave
Refuge Chancel
Peyrou d'Amont 2400m
Chalvachère
P1 1800m
Cascades de glace de la Grave
La Lauzette
La Grave 1450m/4,760ft

Megève

One of the traditional old winter holiday towns; best for those who enjoy relaxed cruising among splendid scenery

COSTS

① ② ③ ④ ⑤ ⑥

RATINGS

The slopes
Fast lifts	**
Snow	**
Extent	*****
Expert	**
Intermediate	****
Beginner	***
Convenience	**
Queues	****
Mountain restaurants	****

The rest
Scenery	*****
Resort charm	****
Off-slope	****

NEWS

For 2008/09 a luxury hotel and restaurant are planned at Rochebrune.

For 2007/08 a six-pack replaced the old Pertuis chair above Combloux, towards Christomet. The Chable chair below it was removed. Snowmaking was increased in the same sector.

An underground car park was built beside the Mont d'Arbois gondola.

Two new ski schools (including a branch of Evolution 2) and several restaurants have also opened up.

- ➕ Extensive easy slopes
- ➕ Scenic setting, with splendid views
- ➕ Charming old village centre
- ➕ Some very smart hotels and shops
- ➕ Both gourmet and simple mountain lunches in attractive surroundings
- ➕ Excellent cross-country trails
- ➕ Great for weekends
- ➕ Great when it snows – woodland runs with no one on them
- ➕ Plenty to do off the slopes

- ➖ With most of the slopes below 2000m/6,560ft there's a risk of poor snow – although the grassy terrain does not need a thick covering, and snowmaking has improved a lot
- ➖ Lots of slow, old lifts remain – an irritant to mileage-hungry skiers
- ➖ Three separate mountains, only two linked (and by lift but not by piste)
- ➖ Not many challenging pistes – though there is good off-piste
- ➖ Very muted après-ski scene

Megève is the essence of rustic chic. It has a medieval heart but it was, in a way, the original purpose-built French ski resort – developed in the 1920s as an alternative to St Moritz. Although Courchevel took over as France's swankiest resort ages ago, Megève's smart hotels still attract 'beautiful people' with fur coats and fat wallets. Happily, you don't need either to enjoy the place. And it is enjoyable – the list of plus points above is as long as they come.

The risk of poor snow still makes us wary of low resorts like this. But it is true that a few inches of snow is enough to give skiable cover on the grassy slopes, and when there's fresh snow falling this is a great place to be.

The resort's managers can't do much about the altitude. What they could do, though, is buy some more modern lifts: the area still ranks close to the bottom of our fast lifts league table. Of course, clocking up piste mileage is not the top priority for Megève's main clientele

THE RESORT

Megève is in a lovely sunny setting and has a beautifully preserved, traditional, partly medieval centre, which is pedestrianised and comes complete with open-air ice rink, horse-drawn sleighs, cobbled streets and a fine church. Lots of smart clothing, jewellery, antique, gift and food shops add to the chic atmosphere.
The main Albertville-Chamonix road bypasses the centre, and there are expensive underground car parks. But the resort's clientele arrives mainly by car and the resulting traffic jams and fumes are a major problem. It's worst at weekends, but can be serious every afternoon in high season.
Visitors are mainly well-heeled French couples and families, who come here for an all-round winter holiday. What they don't come for is après-ski action. The tea-time atmosphere is muted, and later on the nightlife is smart rather than lively.

The Chamois gondola, within walking distance of central Megève, gives direct access to one of the three mountains, Rochebrune. This sector can also be reached by a cable car from the southern edge of town. The main lifts for the bigger Mont d'Arbois sector start from an elevated suburb

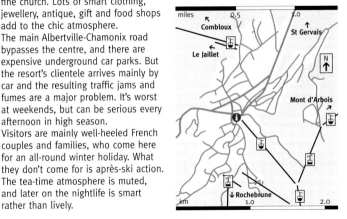

Grand views from Le Jaillet across to Mont d'Arbois and Mont Blanc beyond →

SNOWPIX.COM / CHRIS GILL

KEY FACTS

Megève		
Resort	1100m	
	3,610ft	
Slopes	850-2355m	
	2,790-7,730ft	
Lifts	88	
Pistes	325km	
	202 miles	
Green	17%	
Blue	30%	
Red	40%	
Black	13%	
Snowmaking		
	227 guns	

of the resort – though there is also a cable car link from Rochebrune. The third sector, Le Jaillet, starts out on the north-west fringes of the town. Staying close to one of the main lifts makes a lot of sense. Some accommodation is a long walk from the lifts, and the free bus services are a source of complaints, although a first-time visitor armed with a timetable from the tourist office tells us he found it reliable. There are several alternative bases (which offer some good-value lodging) on the fringes of the area. St-Gervais and Le Bettex above it have gondola access (St-Gervais is described at the end of this chapter). But beware slow access lifts from otherwise attractive spots such as St-Nicolas and Combloux. The most recently linked village, La Giettaz, is out on a limb but offers interesting local terrain. The Evasion Mont Blanc lift pass also covers Les Contamines. As we go to press, it's not clear whether this year Megève will be offering the Mont Blanc weekly pass, also covering the Chamonix valley. A car is handy for visiting these resorts.

THE MOUNTAINS

The three different mountains provide predominantly easy intermediate cruising, much of it prettily set in the woods and with some spectacular views. The wooded slopes make it a great resort in poor weather. Some reporters say piste classification is inconsistent. Signposting is poor. Given the lack of fast lifts, it's not surprising that the piste map doesn't mark them, but it is regrettable.

THE SLOPES
Pretty but low
The biggest, highest and most varied sector is **Mont d'Arbois**, accessible not only from the town but also by a gondola from La Princesse, way out to the north-east of town, with extensive free car parking. It offers some wooded slopes but is mainly open.

The slopes above the resort are sunny, but there are north-east-facing slopes to Le Bettex and on down to St-Gervais. A two-stage gondola returns you to the top. You can work your way over to Mont Joux and up to the small Mont Joly area – Megève's highest slopes. And from there you can go to the backwater village of St-Nicolas-de-Véroce (there's a splendid red run along the ridge with wonderful views of Mont Blanc); the return to Mont Joux is now faster with a six-pack in place.

From the Mont d'Arbois lift base, the Rocharbois cable car goes across the valley to **Rochebrune**. Alpette is the starting point for Megève's historic downhill course, now revived as an off-piste route, and narrow enough to be quite tricky. A network of gentle, wooded, north-east-facing slopes, served by drags and mainly slow chair lifts, leads across to the high point of Côte 2000, which often has the best snow in Megève.

The third area is **Le Jaillet**, accessed by gondola from just outside the north-west edge of town, or from Combloux, linked by a series of long, gentle treelined runs – served by a new six-pack at the top. In the other direction is the high point of Le Christomet, which is linked to the

LIFT PASSES

Evasion Mont Blanc

Prices in €

Age	1-day	6-day
under 15	28	133
15 to 59	35	166
over 60	32	150

Free under 5, over 80
Beginner no deals

Notes
Covers lifts at Les Contamines as well as those of the Megève pass (see list below); family reductions

Alternative passes
Megève pass (covers Megève, La Giettaz, Combloux, St-Gervais and St-Nicolas); Jaillet-Combloux-Giettaz only pass; pedestrian pass

UK PACKAGES

Alpine Answers, AmeriCan Ski, Classic Ski, Erna Low, Flexiski, Interhome, Lagrange, Made to Measure, Momentum, Oxford Ski Co, Peak Retreats, Simon Butler Skiing, Ski Collection, Ski Expectations, Ski France, Skiholiday extras.com, Ski Independence, Ski Leisure Direction, Ski Solutions, Skitracer, Ski Weekend, Snow Finders, Stanford Skiing, White Roc
St Gervais AmeriCan Ski, Chalet Group, Erna Low, Holiday in Alps, Interhome, Lagrange, Mountain Tracks, Peak Retreats, Ski France, Skifrance4less, Skiholidayextras.com, Ski Leisure Direction, Snowcoach
Combloux Erna Low, Lagrange, Peak Retreats

boarding

Boarding doesn't really fit with Megève's traditional, rather staid, upmarket image. But freeriders will find lots of untracked off-piste powder for days after new snowfalls. It's a good place to try snowboarding for the first time, with plenty of fairly wide, quiet, gentle runs and a lot of chairlifts and gondolas; though there are a fair number of draglifts, they are generally avoidable. There are no specialist schools, but all the ski schools offer boarding lessons. There's a terrain park on Mont Joux and smaller ones above Combloux and La Giettaz.

slopes of Le Torraz, above **La Giettaz**, a tiny resort halfway to La Clusaz. The slopes of Le Torraz are worth visiting, not least for the spectacular views from the summit – the link used to be hard going (plenty of skating and poling), but now has a short draglift to pull you across the flat section.

TERRAIN PARKS
Three, surprisingly
You wouldn't have thought there was much call for terrain parks from Megève's clientele. But there is a 320m/1,050ft slope on Mont Joux with a half-pipe, quarter-pipe, pyramid and, apparently, some moguls. A sound system at the bottom helps to motivate the faint-hearted. There's a small park, Snowtap, on the upper slopes above Combloux and another above La Giettaz.

SNOW RELIABILITY
The area's main weakness
The problem is that the slopes are low, with very few runs above 2000m/6,560ft, and partly sunny – the Megève side of Mont d'Arbois gets the afternoon sun. So in a poor snow year, or in a warm spell, snow on the lower slopes can suffer badly. Fortunately, the grassy slopes don't need much depth of snow. A 2008 visitor found conditions much better at Combloux when patchy elsewhere. And the resort has an extensive snowmaking network (50 new snow-guns joined the fleet this year) but that can't work in warm weather. Piste grooming is of a high standard.

FOR EXPERTS
Off-piste is the main attraction
One of Megève's great advantages for expert skiers is that there is not much competition for the powder – you can often make first tracks on challenging slopes many days after a fresh dump.
The Mont Joly and Mont Joux sections offer the steepest slopes. The top chair here serves a genuinely

black run, with some serious off-piste off the back of the hill, and the slightly lower Epaule chair has some steep runs back down and also accesses some good off-piste, as well as pistes, down to St-Nicolas. The steep area beneath the second stage of the Princesse gondola can be a play area of powder runs among the trees. Cote 2000 has a small section of steep runs, including good off-piste.
The terrain under the Christomet chair can be a good spot to practise off-piste technique, given decent snow.

FOR INTERMEDIATES
Superb if the snow is good
Good intermediates will enjoy the whole area – there is so much choice it's difficult to single out any particular sectors. Keen skiers are likely to want to focus on the fast lifts, and happily several of these serve excellent terrain – the Princesse and Bettex gondolas on Mont d'Arbois, the Fontaine and Alpette chairs on Rochebrune and the Christomet chair in the Le Jaillet sector. But don't confine yourself to those – there are lots of other interesting areas, including the shady north-east-facing slopes on the back of Mont d'Arbois and Mont Joux and the front of Rochebrune, and the genuinely red/black slopes of La Giettaz. The slopes above Combloux are well worth exploring, particularly the quiet, sheltered reds/blacks served by the Jouty chairlift. It's also a great area for the less confident. A number of comfortable runs lead down to Le Bettex and La Princesse from Mont d'Arbois, while nearby Mont Joux accesses long, problem-free runs to St-Nicolas. Alpette and Cote 2000 are also suitable.
Even the timid can get a great deal of mileage in. All main access lifts have easy routes down to them (there is a blue down the Princesse gondola and a 5km/3 miles long blue from Le Christomet to La Giettaz). There are some particularly good, long, gentle

cruises between Mont Joux and Megève via Mont d'Arbois. But in all sectors you'll find long, easy blue runs to build your confidence.

FOR BEGINNERS
Good choice of nursery areas
There are beginner slopes at valley level, and more snow-sure ones at altitude on each of the main mountains. There are also plenty of very easy longer green runs to progress to.

FOR CROSS-COUNTRY
An excellent area
There are 43km/27 miles of varied trails spread throughout the area. Some are at altitude (1300m-1550m/ 4,270ft-5,090ft), making lunchtime meetings with Alpine skiers simple.

QUEUES
Few weekday problems
Megève is relatively queue-free during the week, except at peak holiday time. But school holidays and sunny Sunday crowds can mean some delays. The Lanchettes drag between Cote 2000 and the rest of the Rochebrune slopes gets busy ('ridiculously long waits') – as does the cable car linking the two mountains. Crowded pistes at Mont Joux and Mont d'Arbois can also be a problem. But out of peak season, slow lifts and breakdowns (eg of the gondola from St Gervais) provoke more complaints than queues or crowds. And on a snowy day (especially in January), the slopes can be delightfully quiet as the pampered clientele stay in bed, leaving the fresh snow to you and us.

CHILDREN

Meg'Accueil
t 0450 587784
Ages 18mnth to 12yr
Club des Piou-Piou
t 0450 589765
Ages 3 and 4

Ski schools
From age 3 or 4 (ESF
prices: 5 mornings
€105 for ages 3 and
4, €125 for ages 5 to
12)

MOUNTAIN RESTAURANTS
Something for all budgets

Megève has some chic, expensive, gourmet mountain huts but plenty of cheaper options too. Booking ahead is advisable for table-service places.

Editors' choice On Mont d'Arbois, the Ravière (0450 931571), tucked away in the woods near the La Croix chair, is a tiny rustic hut that does a set three-course meal and where booking is essential. On Rochebrune, Alpette (0450 210369), on top of the ridge, has excellent all-round views outside, a good atmosphere inside, friendly people and good food.

Worth knowing about The Mont d'Arbois area is very well endowed with restaurants. There are two suave places popular with poseurs with small dogs and fur coats – the Club House

and the Idéal 1850. The Mont d'Arbois self-service has a varied menu. Chalet des Princesses is 'beautifully located' halfway down the Princesse gondola. The Igloo, 'quiet but expensive', with wonderful views of Mont Blanc, has both self- and table-service sections. At the base of the Mont Joux lift, Chez Marie du Rosay has been recommended. Prices are lower on the back side of the hill. The hut at the bottom of the Mont Rosset chair is worth a visit, say reporters. Above St-Nicolas are several little chalets offering great charm and good food and views at modest prices.

On Rochebrune, at the foot of the Cote 2000 slopes is the popular Auberge de la Cote 2000, a former farm ('We went in for a drink and staggered out three hours and five

SCHOOLS

ESF
t 0450 210097

International
t 0450 587888

Freeride
t 0450 212745

Summits
t 0450 933521

Agence de Ski
t 0450 891273

Evolution 2
t 0450 583541

Classes (ESF prices)
5 mornings (2½hr)
€142

Private lessons
€39 for 1hr

GUIDES

Compagnie des Guides
t 0450 215511

courses later,' writes a reporter); Radaz, up the slope a little, enjoys better views but can get busy. Other recommendations include the 'cosy' Chalet Forestier and the Super Megève. On Le Jaillet the Auberge du Christomet is highly rated for its plats du jour. It is also accessible to walkers, and gets booked out. We hear the Face au Mont Blanc at the top of the gondola does a great fixed-price buffet and one visitor found the Auberge de Bonjournal on the link to La Giettaz was 'well placed, well priced and excellent'. The places down at Le Plan, the lift station for La Giettaz, are said to offer 'great value'.

SCHOOLS AND GUIDES
Two new options
The International school has been more popular with readers than the ESF, but we have several reports of successful private lessons with the ESF. The popular Evolution 2 school has a branch here now and Agence de Ski is also new – both offer private classes. Expeditions to the Vallée Blanche (in Chamonix) and to heli-skiing (in Italy) can be arranged, and mountain guides are available (we had a great morning powder skiing in the trees with Alex Périnet: 0685 428339).

FACILITIES FOR CHILDREN
Language problems
The kindergartens offer a wide range of activities. But lack of English-speaking staff could be a drawback. The slopes are family-friendly and the schools rated by reporters. There are snow gardens in the main sectors.

HOW TO GO
Few packages
Relatively few British tour operators go to Megève, but there is an impressive range of accommodation.
Chalets A few UK tour operators offer catered chalets. For a cheap and very cheerful base, you won't do better than Stanford's Sylvana – a creaky, unpretentious old hotel, reachable on skis, run along chalet lines.
Hotels Megève offers a range of exceptionally stylish and welcoming hotels, and more modest places, too.
****Mont Blanc (0450 212002) Megève's traditional leading hotel – elegant, fashionable, central.
****Chalet du Mont d'Arbois (0450 212503) Prettily decorated Relais & Châteaux hotel secluded near the Mont d'Arbois gondola.
****Chalet St Georges (0450 930715) Central, very close to the gondola. Only 24 rooms, so intimate for a 4-star. 'Two very good restaurants.'
****Fer à Cheval (0450 213039) Rustic-chic at its best, with a warmly welcoming wood-and-stone interior and excellent food. Close to the centre. New spa and pool for 2007/08. 'A memorable stay,' writes a reporter.
***Prairie (0450 214855) Central, 'reasonably priced' B&B. Close to the Chamois lift.
***Coin du Feu (0450 210494) 'Very well managed' chalet midway between Rochebrune and Chamois lifts.
***Coeur de Megève (0450 212530) Central, very close to the gondola. Restaurant has been highly rated.

SMART LODGINGS
Check out our feature chapters at the front of the book.

GETTING THERE
Air Geneva 70km/ 43 miles (1hr); Lyon 180km/112 miles (2½hr)

Rail Sallanches (12km/7 miles); regular buses from station

ACTIVITIES
Indoor Sports centre (tennis, ice rink, climbing wall, swimming pool, sauna, solarium, gym), beauty treatments, health and fitness centres, bowling, museum, library, cinemas, casino, language courses, concerts and exhibition, bridge, painting on wood

Outdoor Cleared paths, snowshoeing, ice rink, sleigh rides, dog sledding, ice climbing, paintballing, adventure park, sightseeing flights, hot air ballooning, paragliding, paintballing

Phone numbers
From abroad use the prefix +33 and omit the initial '0' of the phone number

TOURIST OFFICES
Megève
t 0450 212728
megeve@megeve.com
www.megeve.com

St-Gervais
t 0450 477608
welcome@st-gervais.net
www.st-gervais.net

***Ferme Duvillard** (0450 211462) Smartly restored farmhouse, perfectly positioned for the slopes, at the foot of the Mont d'Arbois gondola.
**Sévigné (0450 212309) Ten minutes from the centre, but 'very quaint', says a reporter.
Apartments Chateau & Residence Megève, set on the Mont d'Arbois road overlooking the village, is a completely renovated chalet; indoor/outdoor pool, steam, sauna, restaurant.

EATING OUT
Very French
Lots of upmarket restaurants – many recommended in the gastro guides. Flocons de Sel (two Michelin stars) and the restaurants in all the best hotels are excellent but very pricey. The fashionable Cintra, also expensive, is 'great for fresh seafood'.
    The Brasserie Centrale 'serves almost anything you ask for', says an impressed reporter. The Prieuré has been highly rated for atmosphere, food and good value, while the Bistrot does 'good' salads and pizzas. The Delicium is also popular. The Crystobald and Bouddha Moor (Asian) are new places – the latter good news for the reporters who wish there was more variety in the resort.

APRES-SKI
Strolling and jazz
Megève is a pleasant place to stroll around after the lifts close, but exciting it isn't. If there are atmospheric bars for a post-piste beer, they have eluded us. And those looking for loud disco-bars later may be disappointed. We liked the Club de Jazz (aka the 5 Rues) – a very popular, if rather expensive, jazz club-cum-cocktail bar, that gets some big-name musicians and opens from tea-time to late. But one reporter reckons 'it's cold, impersonal, and the pure jazz

seems to have given way to more rock and roll.' The Cocoon is popular with Brits, and the Wake-Up attracts seasonaires. The casino is more slot machines than blackjack tables. Palo Alto has two discos.

OFF THE SLOPES
Lots to do
There is a 'fantastic' sports centre with pool, an outdoor ice rink, cinemas and a weekly market. Trips to Annecy and Chamonix are possible. Walks are excellent, with 50km/30 miles of marked paths classified for difficulty on a special map. Meeting friends on the slopes for lunch is easy.

STAYING UP THE MOUNTAIN
Several possibilities
As well as mid-mountain Le Bettex, there are hotels on Mont d'Arbois.

St-Gervais 850m/2,790ft

St-Gervais is a handsome 19th-century spa town set in a narrow river gorge, on the far side of Mont d'Arbois, with access to the slopes via a 20-person gondola from just outside the town. It's an urban but pleasant place, with interesting food shops and cosy bars, thermal baths and an Olympic skating rink. Prices are noticeably lower than in Megève. Buses are reported to be regular and convenient. Two hotels convenient for the gondola are the Liberty Mont Blanc (0450 934521), a pleasantly traditional 2-star, and the 'quite charming' 3-star Carlina (0450 934110), with a small pool and sauna. The 2-star Val d'Este (0450 936591) and its restaurant (the Serac) have been praised.
    On the opposite side of St-Gervais is a rack-and-pinion railway, which in 1904 was intended to go to the top of Mont Blanc but actually takes you to the slopes of Les Houches.

Les Menuires

The bargain base for the Three Valleys – with increasing amounts of stylish accommodation as well as the original dreary blocks

COSTS

① ② ③ ④ ⑤ ⑥

RATINGS

The slopes
Fast lifts	***
Snow	****
Extent	*****
Expert	****
Intermediate	*****
Beginner	***
Convenience	*****
Queues	****
Mountain restaurants	***

The rest
Scenery	***
Resort charm	*
Off-slope	*

Ski Olympic

Chalet Holiday
Specialists
Fully Catered
Flights or Coach
Top Resorts

01302 328820
www.skiolympic.co.uk

322

+ Great local slopes on La Masse, and quick links with Val Thorens

+ Lots of slope-side accommodation

+ New, outlying parts of the resort are much more attractive than the core

– Big, dreary blocks and gloomy indoor shopping malls in centre

– Main intermediate and beginner slopes get a lot of sun

– Some lower slopes get crowded

Les Menuires is in a great position – you can get quickly from it to all parts of the Three Valleys. And its local slopes on La Masse are some of the best for good skiers: challenging, usually with good snow, and rarely used by visitors from the other valleys. There is no denying the ugliness of the original buildings of La Croisette – the main resort centre. Happily, there are now attractive satellites built in chalet style, in wood and stone – though the mother resort is still the place to stock up on jambon cru and tarte aux abricots.

THE RESORT

The original buildings that surround the main lift base, La Croisette, are among the worst examples of the thoughtless building of the 1960s/70s. But the resort is trying hard to smarten up. In outposts such as Reberty and Hameau des Marmottes, the latest additions are in stone-and-wood chalet style. These outposts have their own shops and bars – Les Bruyères is now a more-or-less self-contained resort. They have also demolished a couple of the original buildings (as we advised them to ten editions ago) and are rebuilding in a more attractive style.

THE MOUNTAINS

Les Menuires is set at about the treeline, with almost all open slopes.
Slopes The major part of the network spreads across the broad, west-facing mountainside between Les Menuires and St-Martin, with links to the Méribel valley at four points and to Val Thorens. A gondola and a fast chair go up from La Croisette, and a gondola from Les Bruyères (also accessible from much of Reberty). Lifts – a chair and gondola – to a steeper mountain, La Masse, start below the village.
Terrain parks There's a terrain park with slides, tables, pyramids and a boardercross above Reberty.

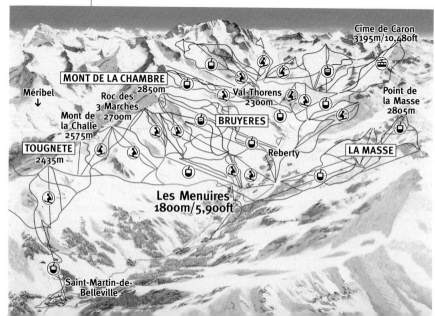

For 2008/09 more snowmaking will be installed on the Pelozet piste to improve connections with St-Martin. A new chalet-style MGM apartment complex, Les Clarines, is due to open in December 2008.

For 2007/08 a new six-pack with covers above the gondola from the resort to Roc des 3 Marches replaced the slow Allamands chair. Snowmaking was installed on the Bettex piste.

Snow reliability La Masse's height and orientation ensure good snow for a long season. The west-facing slopes have lots of snowmaking but the snow lower down is often icy or slushy. The lift company is continuing to expand the snowmaking facilities.

Experts The upper slopes of La Masse are virtually all of stiff red/soft black steepness – great fast cruises when groomed. There is also a huge amount of off-piste, including Vallon du Lou – a broad, sweeping route towards Val Thorens, and the ESF organises groups for exploring it (praised by a reporter).

Intermediates With good snow, you may be content with the local slopes, which are virtually all blue and red. In poor snow you can head up to Val Thorens on blue runs. Don't miss La Masse – the blacks are not super-steep – but beware the steep Masse draglift.

Beginners There are wide and gentle slopes and a special lift pass for beginners, but the snow quality on the nursery slopes is a worry and the progression slopes can be crowded.

Snowboarding There are few drags but some flattish sections of piste.

Cross-country The 28km/17 miles of prepared trails are along the valley between St-Martin and Les Menuires.

Queues Not usually a problem, though a 2008 reporter had problems with the Bruyères gondola and the Mont de la Chambre chair. Acute overcrowding on the slopes down to the resort centre is more of a problem.

Mountain restaurants Visitors praise the Grand Lac, at the base of the Granges chair ('good food, atmosphere, value and service'). Just above Les Menuires is the Etoile: 'still one of the better places, friendly

Les Menuires

323

Interactive resort shortlist builder at **www.wtss.co.uk**

La Sapinière is one of several chalet-style developments; behind is la Croisette →

OT LES MENUIRES / P JACQUES / FOC

KEY FACTS

Resort	1800m
	5,910ft

Three Valleys	
Slopes	1260-3230m
	4,130-10,600ft
Lifts	180
Pistes	600km
	373 miles
Green	15%
Blue	38%
Red	37%
Black	10%
Snowmaking	33%

Les Menuires / St-Martin only	
Slopes	1400-2850m
	4,590-9,350ft
Lifts	36
Pistes	160km
	99 miles
Green	8%
Blue	42%
Red	40%
Black	10%
Snowmaking	45%

UK PACKAGES

Chalet Group, Club Med, Crystal, Directski.com, Erna Low, Family Ski Company, First Choice, Independent Ski Links, Interhome, Lagrange, Neilson, Silver Ski, Ski Amis, Ski Collection, Ski France, Skiholidayextras.com, Ski Independence, Ski Leisure Direction, Ski McNeill, Ski Olympic, Ski Supreme, Skitopia, Skitracer

Phone numbers
From abroad use the prefix +33 and omit the initial '0' of the phone number

TOURIST OFFICE

t 0479 007300
lesmenuires@
lesmenuires.com
www.lesmenuires.com

service, good food; prices are not low but reasonable for what you get'. At higher altitude the Alpage, on the 4 Vents piste, offers 'excellent food in generous portions' and 'very efficient self-service'. Two 2008 visitors recommend the Sonnailles, on the Boulevard Cumin run: 'great little restaurant', 'tasty, cheap meals', 'love the views, the sun, the quiet'. Many people head down to the villages for lunch; you retain some sense of being on the mountain at the Ferme, beside the piste at Reberty; the Kaya hotel terrace near here serves excellent food; and a regular visitor comments that the Ruade in the Preyerand area as 'one of the cheapest places for a salad and for children's meals'. The Cocon des Neiges in the new chalet hotel Isatis in Les Bruyères opens its terrace at lunchtime.

Schools and guides A 2008 reporter had disappointing group lessons with the ESF in Bruyères – very large group, mainly French, changes of instructor. A 2008 reporter used SnowBow and says: 'We had one of the scariest instructors I have met but, boy, did she teach us technique.'

Facilities for children Family Ski Company has its own nursery in Reberty – and sends a minder with kids going to ski school.

STAYING THERE

How to go Some big UK tour operators offer holidays here, and some chalet operators have a presence in Reberty. There is a Club Med above Reberty.

Chalets The cluster known as Reberty Village has been virtually taken over by UK chalet operators – particularly Family Ski and Ski Olympic. Ski Amis has groups of chalets at Les Bruyères and below Les Menuires in Le Bettaix.

Hotels The two best are on the slopes at Reberty: the Kaya (0479 414200) is

the resort's only 4-star – attractively smart and modern. The top 3-star is the Ours Blanc (0479 006166). A new 'chalet hotel', Isatis (0479 004545), opened in Les Bruyères in 2008 – basically, chalet-style apartments with an attached restaurant.

Apartments In contrast to the blocks of the main resort, there are lots of new developments in chalet style on the slopes. At La Sapinière are the excellent Montalys and Chalets les Montagnettes. Further up in Reberty 2000 is Les Alpages, an MGM development; and further up still the Chalets du Soleil; down the slope in Balcons des Bruyères is Les Chalets de l'Adonis; all these have pools. The new MGM complex, Les Clarines, is due to open in December 2008 – three chalet-style buildings, with a swimming pool and spa.

Eating out Reporter recommendations include: the Trattoria, the Refuge ('reasonably priced menus'), the Marmite de Géant ('excellent food, good value'). Chalet-boy night off is no problem in Reberty: the Ferme, on the spot, is 'consistently good – good food, good atmosphere, good value, good service' and the smart restaurant in the hotel Kaya is a gourmet option. A new restaurant, the Myrtilles, is to open in La Croisette for 2008/09.

Après-ski There is no shortage of bars in La Croisette, but many are in the dreadful shopping gallery. The Marmottes in Les Bruyères is 'lively and welcoming', and 2008 reporters recommend the 'friendly and welcoming' Medz'ery at Preyerand, both early and late in the evening. A visitor says, 'It's known locally as the gay bar, but we "straight" fifty-somethings had a very good evening there – excellent entertainment.' There are discos.

Off the slopes This is a resort for keen skiers and boarders.

FRANCE

324

Weekly news updates and resort links at www.wtss.co.uk

Méribel

The enduring British favourite: a comfortable, upmarket chalet-style resort in the centre of the wonderful Three Valleys

COSTS

① ② ③ ④ ⑤ ⑥

RATINGS

The slopes

Fast lifts	****
Snow	***
Extent	*****
Expert	****
Intermediate	*****
Beginner	****
Convenience	***
Queues	****
Mountain restaurants	***

The rest

Scenery	***
Resort charm	***
Off-slope	***

NEWS

For 2008/09 capacity on the Pas du Lac gondola is due to be increased and the Grand Rosière and Ramees chairlifts dismantled. There are plans to improve the beginner area at Rond-Point.

The Olympic Centre will have new fitness facilities.

For 2007/08 a six-pack with covers replaced the upper Tougnète gondola. The draglift beside it was removed. More snow-guns were installed and two beginner areas created above Mottaret.

+ In the centre of the biggest linked lift network in the world – ideal for intermediates, great for experts, too

+ Pleasant chalet-style architecture – much less brutal than other purpose-built resorts

+ Impressive lift system

+ Excellent piste maintenance and snowmaking; nevertheless ...

– Not the best snow in the 3V, especially on the west-facing side

– Pistes can get very crowded

– Sprawling main village, with lots of accommodation far from the slopes

– Expensive

– Full of Brits (record number of UK tour operators)

– Méribel-Mottaret and Méribel-Village satellites are rather lifeless

A loyal band of regular visitors just love Méribel, and you can see why. For keen piste-bashers who like to rack up the miles but dislike tacky purpose-built resorts, it's difficult to beat. The Three Valleys can keep anyone amused for a fortnight – and Méribel-Mottaret, in particular, has quick access to every part. Unlike other purpose-built resorts, Méribel has always insisted on chalet-style architecture. What more could you ask? Well, our – points are mostly non-trivial, and other 3V resorts have the edge in some respects. For better snow opt for Courchevel or Val Thorens. For a smaller village, St-Martin or La Tania. For lower prices, Les Menuires. For a lower concentration of Brits, go virtually anywhere. But the other resorts have their drawbacks, too.

THE RESORT

Méribel occupies the central valley of the Three Valleys system and consists of two main resort villages.

The original resort is built on a single steepish west-facing hillside with the home piste running down beside it to the main lift stations at the valley bottom. All the buildings are wood-clad, low-rise and chalet-style, making it one of the most tastefully designed of French purpose-built resorts. A road winds up from the village centre to the Rond Point des Pistes, and goes on through woods to the outpost of the altiport (a snow-covered airstrip).

The resort was founded by a Brit, Peter Lindsay, in 1938, and has retained a strong British presence and influence ever since. It spreads widely, and although some accommodation is right on the piste, much depends on use of buses (or tour operator minibuses). There are collections of shops and restaurants at a couple of points on the road through the resort – Altitude 1600 and Plateau de Morel. The lodgings at Altiport enjoy splendid isolation in the woods.

The satellite resort of Méribel-Mottaret, a mile or two up the valley, is centrally placed in the Three Valleys ski area, offering swift access to Courchevel, Val Thorens and Les

KEY FACTS

Resort	1400-1700m
	4,590-5,580ft

Three Valleys	
Slopes	1260-3230m
	4,130-10,600ft
Lifts	180
Pistes	600km
	373 miles
Green	15%
Blue	38%
Red	37%
Black	10%
Snowmaking	
	33%

Méribel only	
Slopes	1400-2950m
	4,590-9,680ft
Lifts	53
Pistes	150km
	93 miles
Green	11%
Blue	47%
Red	30%
Black	12%
Snowmaking	42%

Menuires. The resort has spread up both steep sides of the valley. Both sides are served by lifts for pedestrians – but the gondola up the east-facing slope stops at 7.30pm and it's a long, tiring walk up.

Mottaret looks modern, despite wood cladding on its apartment blocks. Even so, it's more attractive than many other resorts built for slope-side convenience. It has far fewer shops and bars and much less après-ski than Méribel. Some visitors feel it lacks atmosphere.

The hamlet of Méribel-Village, on the road from Méribel to Courchevel, has a chairlift up to Altiport with a blue run back and has developed into a pleasant mini-resort. There are some luxury chalets and apartments here but little else apart from a bread shop, small supermarket, fitness centre, bar, pizzeria and a couple of restaurants.

There are some alternative bases lower down the mountain (and price scale) – see the end of this chapter.

Local buses are free but readers complain that they are inadequate. Many UK tour operators run their own minibus services to and from the lifts. A car is mainly of use for outings to other resorts.

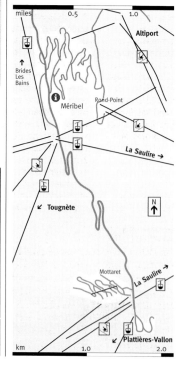

THE MOUNTAINS

Most of the slopes are above the treeline, but there are some sheltered runs for bad-weather days. Piste classification is not always reliable – a problem compounded by exposure of many slopes to a lot of sun. Daily maps are available showing which runs were groomed overnight. Signposting could be better, according to one reporter.

THE SLOPES
Highly efficient lift system

The Méribel valley runs roughly north-south, and in late season you soon get into the habit of skiing one side in the morning and the other after lunch.

On the morning-sun side, a gondola and then a new six-pack go from Méribel to **Tougnète**, from where you can get down to Les Menuires or St-Martin-de-Belleville. Several runs back to Méribel from here have now been reclassified from red to black and vice versa. You can also head for **Mottaret** from here. From there, a fast chair then a drag take you to another entry point for the Les Menuires runs in the next valley.

On the afternoon-sun side, gondolas leave both Méribel and Mottaret for **Saulire**. From here you can head back down towards either village or over the ridge towards Courchevel 1850.

South of Mottaret are some of the best slopes in the valley, in the **Plattières-Vallon** sector. The Plattières gondola ends at another entry point to Les Menuires. To the east of this is the big stand-up gondola to the top of Mont du Vallon (wonderful views from the top). A fast quad from near this area goes up to Mont de la Chambre, giving direct access to Val Thorens.

TERRAIN PARKS
There's a choice

There are two parks in the area. The main Moonpark is accessed by the Arpasson draglift (www.moonpark.net), but has grown and now spills over onto the Grive slope. It includes a triple kicker line for all levels with smooth take-offs; and the rails here are quite advanced, as is the big spine jump. There is a new step-up to step-down obstacle, and S-box. The Magic ski school gives free lessons in the Moonpark between 2pm and 5pm. A new beginner area was also built last

The drags on Mont de la Challe serve some of the shadiest slopes in the valley →
OT MERIBEL

season, including some mini jumps, boxes and even a small boardercross.

SNOW RELIABILITY
Not the best in the Three Valleys
Méribel's slopes aren't the highest in the Three Valleys, and they mainly face east or west; the latter (the runs down from Courchevel) get the full force of the afternoon sun. So snow conditions are often better elsewhere. And grooming seems to be rather better in neighbouring Courchevel.

Snowmaking has been increased and the lower runs have substantial cover. Lack of snow is rarely a problem, but ice at the start of the day or slush at the end can be. The north-west-facing slopes above Altiport generally have decent snow.

At the southern end of the valley, towards Les Menuires and Val Thorens, a lot of runs are north-facing and keep their snow well, as do the runs on Mont du Vallon.

FOR EXPERTS
Exciting choices
The size of the Three Valleys means experts are well catered for. In the

Méribel valley, Mont du Vallon has lots to interest. The long, steep Combe Vallon run here is classified red; it's a wonderful, long, fast cruise when groomed (which it normally is), but presents plenty of challenge when mogulled. And there's a beautiful off-piste run in the next valley to main pistes, leading back to the bottom of the gondola.

A good mogul run is down the side of the double Roc de Tougne draglift which leads up to Mont de la Challe. And there are steep, unrelenting runs from Tougnète back to Méribel – the upper Ecureuil piste is now a black ('deservedly so', says a reporter) and Combe Tougnète has been reclassified red. At the north end of the valley the Face run was built for the women's downhill in the 1992 Olympics. Served by a fast quad, it's a splendid cruise when freshly groomed (with good views over the village), and you can terrify yourself just by imagining what it must be like to go straight down.

Nothing on the Saulire side is as steep or as demanding as on the other side of the valley. The Mauduit red run is quite challenging, though –

Méribel

327

www.wtss.co.uk

Interactive resort shortlist builder at

boarding

Méribel is a favourite for British snowboarders. The terrain is good and varied, with a lot more tree runs than in neighbouring Val Thorens. There is some very good steep freeriding that stays relatively untracked on Mont du Vallon. And there's a real wealth of red runs here for intermediates and mellow blues and greens for beginners. Most lifts are chairs or gondolas but beware some of the flat sections on the main routes to and from Val Thorens – avoid the Ours blue run down to Mottaret from Mont du Vallon, which is very hard work. Specialist shops include Board Brains (in Méribel) and Quiksilver Gotcha Surf (in Mottaret).

it used to be classified black.

Throughout the area there are good off-piste opportunities – see the feature panel later in this chapter.

FOR INTERMEDIATES
Paradise found

Méribel and the rest of the Three Valleys is a paradise for intermediate skiers and riders; there are few other resorts where a keen piste-basher can cover so many miles so easily. Virtually every slope in the region has a good intermediate run down it, and to describe them all would take a book in itself.

For less adventurous intermediates, the run from the second station of the Plattières gondola above Mottaret back to the first station is ideal, and used a lot by the ski school. It is a gentle, north-facing, cruising run and is generally in good condition. But below that the run can get tricky, bumpy and very crowded later in the day. The red run into Mottaret on the other side of the valley, which used to be a blue, also gets dangerously icy and crowded. Nothing has been done yet to tackle these two problems, which spoil an otherwise ideal intermediate area.

Even early intermediates should find the runs over into the other valleys well within their capabilities, opening up further vast amounts of intermediate runs. In Courchevel or Val Thorens you also get the bonus of better snow.

Virtually all the pistes on both

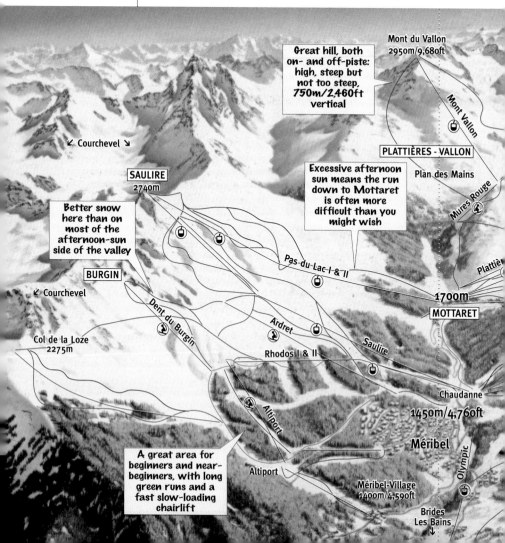

Mont du Vallon
2950m/9,680ft

Great hill, both
on- and off-piste:
high, steep but
not too steep,
750m/2,460ft
vertical

↙ Courchevel ↘

PLATTIÈRES - VALLON

Mont Vallon

SAULIRE
2740m

Excessive afternoon
sun means the run
down to Mottaret
is often more
difficult than you
might wish

Plan des Mains

Mures Rouge

Better snow
here than on
most of the
afternoon-sun
side of the valley

BURGIN

Pas-du-Lac-I & II

Plattiè

↙ Courchevel

Dent du Burgin

1700m

MOTTARET

Col de la Loze
2275m

Ardret

Saulire

Rhodos I & II

Chaudanne

1450m/4,760ft

Altiport

Méribel

Olympic

A great area for
beginners and near-
beginners, with long
green runs and a
fast slow-loading
chairlift

Altiport

Méribel-Village
1400m/4,590ft

Brides
Les Bains
↓

sides of the Méribel valley will suit more advanced intermediates. Few of the reds are easy.

FOR BEGINNERS
Strengths and weaknesses

Méribel has an excellent slope for beginners (where one of the editors of this book learned to ski many years ago). But it's out of the resort up at Altiport, which is a bit of a nuisance. There is a small nursery slope at Rond-Point, at the top of the village, which is mainly used by the children's ski school and there are two new enclosed beginner areas ('zen zones') at Plattières, above Mottaret.

The Altiport area is accessible from the village by the Morel chairlift, or by free bus. Once you have found your

feet, a free draglift takes you halfway up a long, gentle, wide, treelined green run – ideal except that it can get crowded and have good skiers speeding through. Next, a longer drag takes you to the top of this run, then a chair a bit higher, then another chair higher still, on to an excellent blue usually blessed with good snow.

FOR CROSS-COUNTRY
Scenic routes

There are about 33km/21 miles in total. The main area is in the forest near Altiport and great for trying cross-country for the first time. There's also a loop around Lake Tueda, in the nature reserve at Mottaret, and for the more experienced an itinéraire from Altiport to Courchevel.

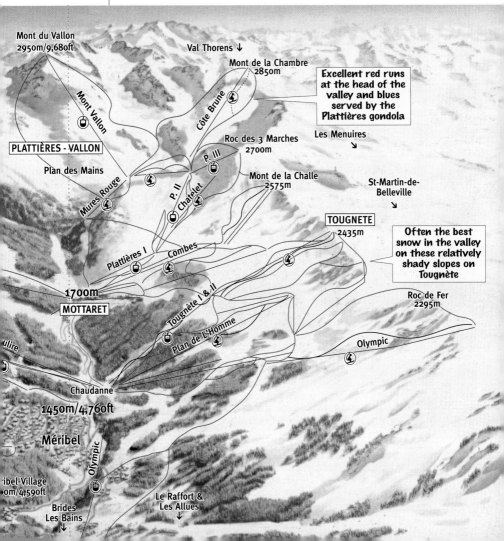

SCHOOLS

ESF Méribel
t 0479 086031

ESF Méribel-Mottaret
t 0479 004949

Euro Ski Adventure
t 0479 007433

Magic Snowsports
t 0479 085336

New Generation
t 0479 010318
www.skinewgen.com

Parallel Lines
t 01702 589580

Snow Systems
t 0479 004022

Snow D'Light
t 0664 816010

Classes
(ESF prices)
5 half-days (2½hr per
day): €143

Private lessons
From €97 for 2hr

GUIDES

Mountain guide office
t 0479 003038

QUEUES
3V traffic a persistent problem
Huge lift investment over the years has paid off in making the area virtually queue-free most of the time, despite the vast numbers of people. Generally, if you do find a queue, there is an alternative quieter route you can take. The real problems result from the tidal flows of people between the three valleys in the morning (when the tide coincides with the start of ski school) and in the late afternoon. Whether improvements to the Pas du Lac gondola will help much remains to be seen – especially since the alternative way up to Saulire from here is due to be removed. Some reporters complain that the lift staff don't fill up the gondolas and chairs at busy times ('very frustrating'). The queue for the Plattières gondola at Mottaret has been eased by the fast Combes and Chatelet chairs giving a viable alternative route. A new six-pack has replaced the upper Tougnète gondola, but this means that you have to queue twice to go all the way up from the village. You can still find big queues at the Côte Brune chair to Mont de la Chambre and the Plan des Mains chair (used by everyone returning from Val Thorens to avoid the ridiculously flat 'blue' Ours valley run).

MOUNTAIN RESTAURANTS
Less than wonderful
Few places are worth singling out so there's no 'Editors' choice' here – and there aren't enough places to meet the demand, so many get very crowded (you might want to take lunch early or late). The three-part Plan des Mains near Mont Vallon gondola failed to impress a 2007 reporter who experienced very slow service in the sandwich bar. We continue to get good reports on the 'small and cosy' Arpasson at the mid-mountain station

of the Tougnète gondola ('a variety of good-value choices'). The 'delightfully quaint' Crêtes, near the top of Tougnète, generally gets good reviews, but a 2008 reporter found 'average food and poor service'. Lower down, at the bottom of the Roc de Tougne drags, the Togniat has 'good' table- and self-service choices. The Chardonnet, at the mid-station of the Mottaret-Saulire gondola, has table service and excellent food, but is expensive. The Rhododendrons, at the top of the Altiport drag, remains a popular spot for its large terrace and 'good food' – but is 'disorganised', according to one visitor. The Rond Point, just below the mid-point of the Rhodos gondola, is popular but some visitors have preferred the views, food and service from the Darbollées, a bit lower down. The expensive Altiport hotel scarcely counts as a mountain restaurant, but has a great outdoor buffet in good weather, and lovely tarts. And the new Coeur de Cristal, low down beside the Adray chair, is also recommended for 'very nice, well presented food and sweet display worthy of a 5-star hotel'. Two self-service places notable for their views are the Pierres Plates, at the top of Saulire, and the Sittelle above the first section of the Plattières gondola.

SCHOOLS AND GUIDES
No shortage of instructors
The ESF is by far the biggest school, with over 450 instructors. It has a special international section with instructors speaking good English. Past reports have been mixed. It offers useful options, such as off-piste groups, heli-skiing on the Italian border and Three Valleys tours.

Snow Systems is enthusiastically praised by 2008 reporters for private instruction and personal service – 'a really excellent company', says one.

Méribel has a lot of very good off-piste to discover, as well as the pistes that the Three Valleys is famous for. We asked Pierre-François Papet, head of Méribel's Snow Systems ski school, to pick out some of the best off-piste runs for skiers with at least some off-piste experience. Don't tackle them without guidance.

Some of the best snow is to be found on the north-facing run accessed from the 3 Vallées 2 chairlift at Val Thorens. Ducking the rope at the top takes you into varied terrain mixing couloirs and gentle slopes, with exposures from north-east to north-west. Eventually you join the red Lac de la Chambre piste.

The run from near Roc de Fer to Le Raffort, a mid-station on the gondola from Brides-les-Bains, is an adventure with exceptional views. You ride the Olympic chairlift, go along the ridge, then ski a gentle bowl to finish among the trees.

The wide, west-facing slope above Altiport is enjoyable when the snow is fresh – varied terrain, from average to steep, some open some wooded, reached from the Tétras black run.

There are lots of runs suitable for more accomplished off-piste skiers. One is a descent known as The Cairn from the Mouflon piste at the top of the Plattières gondola; it starts in a fairly steep couloir and becomes wider, with a consistent pitch, until you reach the Sittelle piste.

The Roc de Tougne draglift accesses some challenging runs. To the right of the Lagopéde red piste is an area we call the Spot – a rather technical and steep descent to the Sittelle piste. Alternatively, a 15-minute hike brings you to the Couloir du Serail, leading to the Mouflon red piste – one of my favourites because of the vertical, the constant pitch and the quality of snow.

The Col du Fruit is a classic, far away from the lifts and resorts. You ride the Creux Noirs chairlift in Courchevel, then walk along the ridge for 15 minutes before descending through the national park to Lac de Tueda and the cross-country tracks … 800m/2,620ft of flat ground from the Mottaret lifts.

Mont Vallon offers a big choice of routes and exposures – quite steep at the top but with easier slopes from the middle. The challenging northern couloir starts at the top of the Campagnol run.

Snow Systems is a ski school that operates from both Méribel and Mottaret. As well as group and private on- and off-piste lessons, they run children's lessons, snowboard lessons and instructor training.

t 0479 004022
www.snow-systems.com

Méribel

331

Interactive resort shortlist builder at **www.wtss.co.uk**

GETTING THERE

Air Geneva 135km/
84 miles (3½hr); Lyon
185km/115 miles
(3½hr); Chambéry
95km/59 miles (1½hr)

Rail Moûtiers
(18km/11 miles);
regular buses to
Méribel

OT MERIBEL / J M GOUEDARD
Méribel is Chalet
Central, but not all
chalets have such
rural settings as
these ↘

'We had complete confidence in our
instructor; all three of us learned a
lot.' Others comment: 'They managed
to teach us while making it great fun';
'my wife had no confidence, but by
the last day was skiing from the top to
the bottom of the mountain'; 'a
fantastic and enjoyable time'. New
Generation, a British school which
operates in Courchevel and Méribel,
continues to receive excellent reports.
One reader said, 'I cannot recommend
them highly enough, they were patient
and kept groups small.' Another
reporter 'progressed quickly in a group
of only three; the instructor explained
and demonstrated techniques clearly'.
Magic Snowsports Academy, the
second largest school, also offers heli-
skiing, couloir and extreme sessions
as well as normal lessons. A 2008
reporter has used them twice and
rates them 'superb – significant
progress while having a fantastic time'.

FACILITIES FOR CHILDREN
Tour operators rule
We guess readers needing child care
use the facilities of chalet operators
who run their own nurseries – we
rarely get reports on resort facilities.

HOW TO GO
Huge choice but few bargains
Package holidays are easy to find,
both with big tour operators and
smaller Méribel specialists.
Chalets Méribel has more chalets
dedicated to the British market than
any other resort, and over 50
operators offering them – many, as
you may have noticed, advertising
their properties in these pages. The
specialist agents list scores. What
really distinguishes Méribel is the
range of recently built luxury chalets.
Some are perfectly positioned for the
slopes, but many rely on minibuses to
compensate for their inconvenient
locations. Many have saunas, hot tubs
or both.

Méribel specialists include Meriski,
with 12 small, smart chalets including
two new ones with outdoor hot tubs;
Purple Ski, with places in different
parts of the resort, including the lovely
Iamato in Village; and Ski Blanc who
are based in Les Allues (see 'Staying
down the valley'). At the top of the
market, Ski Olympic has the Parc Alpin
(now fully refurbished) at 1600 with 12

CHILDREN

Les Saturnins
t 0479 086690
Ages 18mnth to 3yr

Kids Etc
t 0479 007139
From 3mnth to 7yr

Les Piou Piou
t 0479 086031 (Mér)
t 0479 004949 (Mot)
Ages 3 to 5; 9am-5pm

Childminder list
Available from the
tourist office

Ski school
The ESF runs classes
for ages 5 to 13: 6
half-days (2½hr) from
€116

ACTIVITIES

Indoor Parc
Olympique (ice rink,
swimming pool,
climbing wall, karting
on ice), fitness
centres in hotels,
bowling, library,
cinemas, museum,
heritage tours

Outdoor Flying
lessons and
excursions,
snowmobiles,
snowshoeing, cleared
paths, paragliding

SMART LODGINGS

Check out our feature
chapters at the front
of the book.

luxurious rooms (all with plasma
screen TVs), dinky pool and sauna.
Alpine Action has six smart-looking
chalets, most with saunas and hot
tubs. VIP, Descent, Flexiski and Scott
Dunn have upmarket properties here.
Total has lots of chalets here and Ski
Beat and Neilson have several.

Of the few chalet hotels, Mark
Warner's Tarentaise (with a sauna and
hot tub) has a great position, right on
the piste at Mottaret. Family specialist
Esprit's Alba is also in a good slope-
side position, up at Rond Point.

Hotels Méribel has some excellent
hotels, but they're not cheap.

****Grand Coeur (0479 086003) Our
favourite almost-affordable hotel in
Méribel. Just above the village centre.
Welcoming, mature building with plush
lounge. Magnificent food. Huge hot
tub, sauna etc.

****Mont-Vallon (0479 004400) The
best hotel at Mottaret; good food, and
excellently situated for the Three
Valleys' pistes. Pool, sauna, squash,
fitness room etc.

***Altiport (0479 005232) Smart and
luxurious hotel, isolated at the foot of
the Altiport lifts. Convenient for
Courchevel, not for Val Thorens.

***Arolles (0479 004040) Right on the
slopes at Mottaret. Highly rated by a
reporter. Pool and sauna.

***Eterlou (0479 088900) One of three
sister hotels near main lifts that share
a health club. 'Great hotel, fantastic
location.'

**Adray Télébar (0479 086026)
Welcoming piste-side chalet with
pretty, rustic rooms, good food and
popular sun terrace.

Roc (0479 003618) A good-value B&B
hotel, in the centre, with a bar-
restaurant and crêperie below.

Apartments Les Fermes de Méribel (in
Méribel-Village) is a classic tasteful
MGM development of six large chalets
with the usual impressive pool.

EATING OUT
Fair choice

There is a reasonable selection of
restaurants, from ambitious French
cuisine to pizza and pasta. For the
best food in town, in plush
surroundings, there are top hotels –
try Grand Coeur, Allodis and Kouisena
('traditional food at justifiably high
prices'). A 2008 reporter recommends
the Lodge de Village in Méribel-Village,
which also has a 'lively' bar (see
'Après-ski'). Readers have also enjoyed
Chez Kiki for steaks; the 'relaxed'
Taverne; Enfants Terribles near the
Morel chairlift (also with live music)
and the Refuge for crêpes. The
Tremplin serves 'good pizzas'. The
Grange, the Cactus Café, the 'tiny' Bibi
Phoque ('good crêpes') and the Cava

Interactive resort shortlist builder at www.wtss.co.uk

Selected chalets in Méribel

UK PACKAGES

Airtours, Alpine Action, Alpine Answers, Belvedere Chalets, Chalet Group, Chalet World Ski, Club Med, Cooltip Mountain Holidays, Crystal, Crystal Finest, Descent International, Directski. com, Elegant Resorts, Erna Low, Esprit, First Choice, Flexiski, Friendship Travel, Independent Ski Links, Inghams, Inspired to Ski, Interactive Resorts, Interhome, Kaluma, Lagrange, Made to Measure, Mark Warner, Meriski, Momentum, Mountain Tracks, Neilson, Oxford Ski Co, Powder White, Purple Ski, Scott Dunn, Silver Ski, Ski Activity, Ski Amis, Ski Basics, Ski Beat, Ski Blanc, Ski Collection, Ski Cuisine, Ski Expectations, Ski France, Skifrance4less, Ski Hame, Skiholiday extras.com, Ski Independence, Ski Leisure Direction, Ski Line, Ski McNeill, Ski Olympic, Ski Solutions, Ski Total, Skitracer, Ski Weekend, Skiworld, Snow Finders, Snowline, Snoworks, Solo's, Supertravel, Thomson, VIP, White Roc
Mottaret Airtours, Alpine Answers, Crystal, First Choice, Neilson, Ski France, Skiholidayextras.com, Ski Independence, Ski Line, Skiworld
Brides-les-Bains AmeriCan Ski, Crystal, Directski.com, Erna Low, First Choice, Lagrange, Peak Retreats, Ramblers, Ski France, Skiholiday extras.com Ski Leisure Direction, Ski McNeill, Ski Weekends
Les Allues Chalet Group

Phone numbers
From abroad use the prefix +33 and omit the initial '0' of the phone number

TOURIST OFFICE

t 0479 086001
info@meribel.net
www.meribel.net

have all been recommended for 'quick service and good value' food.

Alternatives include the Galette, the Fromagerie and Cro-Magnon up the hill in Morel – all popular for raclette and fondue. The Blanchot just below Altiport offers the choice of two dining areas, one dedicated to dishes of the region. Scott's does good American-style food.

At Les Allues, the Tsaretta will pay for a taxi to ferry you to the creations of the Australian chef. The Chaumière is a pleasant, rustic place with 'good value inclusive menus'. The Chemina is another recommendation as is the Martagon at Le Raffort between Méribel and Les Allues.

APRES-SKI
Méribel rocks – loudly

Méribel's après-ski revolves around British-run places. Dick's Tea Bar is well established but is remote from the slopes. At close of play it's the piste-side Rond Point that's packed ('very good on Wednesdays') – happy hour starts around 4pm – and has live music and 'almost infamous toffee vodka'. The terrace of Jack's, near the main lift stations, remains popular.

The ring of bars around the main square do good business at tea time. The Taverne (sister to Dick's Tea Bar) gets packed. Just across the square is the Pub, with videos, pool and sometimes a band – also 'good later on'. In Méribel-Village, the Lodge de Village is suggested and has 'occasional live music'.

If you don't fancy the loud pubs, there are a couple of alternatives. Try the Poste for 'more of a French option' or the Barometer, which has lots of leather seating. Late dancing kicks off at Scott's (next to the Pub) and, of course, at Dick's Tea Bar where you can party 'until the early hours'.

In Mottaret the bars at the foot of the pistes get packed at tea time – Rastro has been a regular favourite and it also has a lively disco later on. Down Town is popular too, though reporters say that Zig-Zag has lower prices. Both villages have a cinema.

✤
Want to get the next edition free?
Send us a useful report on your holiday, and win one of 100 free copies. Find out more at:
www.wtss.co.uk

OFF THE SLOPES
Plenty to do

The Olympic Centre has the ice rink where the Olympic events were held in 1992 and where you can watch regular ice hockey matches. It also has a good public swimming pool, a climbing wall and a new spa. A fitness area is expected to open for 2008/09. You can take joyrides in the little planes that operate from the altiport. There are pleasant, marked walks in the altiport area and a signposted trail through some of the hamlets down to Les Allues (you can return from there or Le Raffort in the Olympic gondola). The pedestrian's lift pass covers all the gondolas, cable cars and buses in the Méribel and Courchevel valleys, and makes it very easy for pedestrians to meet friends for lunch.

A non-skier's guide to Courchevel, Méribel and La Tania is distributed free by the tourist office.

STAYING DOWN THE VALLEY
Quieter, cheaper choices

For the 1992 Olympics the competitors were accommodated in Brides-les-Bains (600m/1,970ft), an old spa town way down in the valley, and a gondola was built linking it to Méribel. It offers a quieter, cheaper alternative to the higher resorts and has some simple hotels, adequate shops and 'plenty of good-value restaurants and friendly bars used by locals', says a reporter. Ski Weekends runs a chalet hotel here. There is a casino, but evenings are distinctly quiet. The long gondola ride to and from Méribel (about 25 minutes) is tedious, can be cold, stops 'ridiculously early' at 5pm and arrives at a point that's a bit of a trek from the main lifts up the mountain. But in good conditions you can ski off-piste to one or other of the mid-stations at the end of the day (or in exceptional conditions down to Brides itself). Given a car, Brides makes a good base for visiting other resorts.

Some UK tour operators have places in the old village of Les Allues, close to a mid-station on the gondola from Brides-les-Bains. Ski Blanc has six good-looking chalets here, including four with a hot tub. Next door to one of them is an independent British-run playgroup. There are a couple of bars – and a good-value, well-renovated hotel, the Croix Jean-Claude (0479 086105); rooms are small, though.

Montgenèvre

The snowiest part of the Milky Way circuit reaching across to Sauze d'Oulx in Italy – now with through-traffic buried in a tunnel

COSTS

① ② ③ ④ ⑤ ⑥

RATINGS

The slopes

Fast lifts	**
Snow	****
Extent	****
Expert	**
Intermediate	****
Beginner	*****
Convenience	****
Queues	***
Mountain restaurants	**

The rest

Scenery	***
Resort charm	***
Off-slope	*

NEWS

For 2008/09 the Chalmettes gondola up the Gondrans sector is due to be replaced by a chondola (a mixture of gondola cabins and chairs on the same lift). Also, another chondola, Serre Thibauld, is planned to link the Gondrans to the Chalvet sector, so cutting out an uphill walk. The long blue from Col de l'Alpet to La Bergerie on the Chalvet side is due to have snowmaking.

For 2007/08, a tunnel allowing you to ski from the Chalvet to the Gondrans sector was opened near the Charmettes chondola. A luxury hotel, Le Chalet Blanc, opened, as did a new building containing the tourist office, ski schools, kindergarten, meeting place and medical centre. Two toboggan runs opened – one for children, the other for adults.

336

+ Good snow record, and local slopes largely north-facing – often the best snow in the Milky Way area

+ Plenty of intermediate cruising and good, convenient nursery slopes

+ A lot of accommodation close to the slopes, and some right on them

+ Great potential for car drivers to explore other nearby resorts

− Poor base for exploring the Italian Milky Way resorts unless you have the use of a car

− Lots of slow lifts and mainly short runs in local area

− Local mountain restaurants poor

− Little to challenge experts on-piste

− Limited and unsophisticated restaurants and après-ski places

Montgenèvre is set on a minor pass between France and Italy, at one end of the big cross-border Milky Way network. On snow, it's a time-consuming trek from here to Sestriere and Sauze d'Oulx at the far end (you may have to ride some slow lifts down as well as up). But you can get to these worthwhile resorts much more quickly by car, which also facilitates day trips in the opposite direction to other excellent French resorts such as Serre-Chevalier. Thanks to the setting on a high pass, the local slopes shared with Claviere (in Italy, but very close) often have the best snow in the region.

The village is pleasant, and must be much more so now that traffic between France and Italy has been consigned to a 400m/1,310ft tunnel.

THE RESORT

Montgenèvre is a narrow roadside village set on a high pass only 2km/1 mile from the Italian border – this is an area where the euro has really simplified things. Cheap and cheerful cafes, bars and restaurants line the road running along the bottom of the nursery slopes, now happily free of through-traffic, giving an animated atmosphere sometimes missing from French resorts. And tucked away off the main road is a quite pleasant old village, complete with quaint church and friendly natives. The place gets a lot of weather – sometimes wind but also snow, which adds to the charm factor when the sun comes out.

The slopes are convenient, despite the road; most of the accommodation is less than five minutes from a lift. Some of the newer accommodation is

uphill, away from the slopes – but there is a free shuttle-bus. The main lifts are gondolas from opposite ends of the village.

On the village side of the col are the south-facing slopes of Le Chalvet. The more extensive north-facing slopes of Les Gondrans are across the main road, with nursery slopes at the bottom. Both sectors have piste links with Claviere, gateway to the other Italian resorts of the Milky Way – Sansicario, Sestriere and Sauze d'Oulx.

The best way to get to other resorts is by car. Serre-Chevalier and Puy-St-Vincent, with lift pass sharing arrangements, are easily reached, and well worth an outing each. Different lift pass options cater for most needs.

THE MOUNTAINS

Montgenèvre's local slopes are best suited to leisurely intermediates, with lots of easy cruising on blues and greens, both above and in the woods.

Run classification on the local area and Milky Way piste maps have differed in the past, which can be confusing – however, none of the blacks is much more than a tough red.

[map: miles 0.5 1.0 / N / Le Chalvet / i / km 1.0 2.0]

THE SLOPES
Nicely varied

The major north-facing **Les Gondrans** sector offers easy intermediate slopes above the mid-mountain chondola (see below) station, with more of a mix of runs lower down. It has a high-altitude link via Collet Vert (and a stiff red run) into the slopes above Claviere (**L'Aigle**). This whole area around the border is attractively broken up by rocky outcrops and woods and the scenery is quite spectacular.

The runs of the sunny sector across the road – **Le Chalvet** – are mainly on open slopes above its mid-mountain gondola station. This sector is connected to the main area by a red piste and bridge across the road, plus a new tunnel you can ski through near the new Chalmettes chondola (a mix of gondolas and chairs). The link the other way has been an uphill walk till now – but another new chondola is planned for 2008/09. When conditions permit, a long blue run from this sector goes down to Claviere, for access to Italy.

TERRAIN PARKS
High and remote

There's a terrain park with a half-pipe and boardercross near the Prarial chair and a freeride zone higher up on the Gondrans sector, next to the Observatoire chair.

SNOW RELIABILITY
Excellent locally

Montgenèvre has a generally excellent snow record, receiving dumps from westerly storms funnelling up the valley. The high north-facing slopes naturally keep their snow better than the south-facing area. Snowmaking covers several higher pistes as well as most lower slopes – 'intensive and very effective', says a 2008 reporter.

FOR EXPERTS
Limited, except for off-piste

There are very few challenging pistes locally. Many of the runs are overclassified. There is, however, ample off-piste terrain. The remote north-east-facing bowl beyond the Col de l'Alpet on the Chalvet side is superb in good snow and has black and red pistes, too. The open section between La Montanina and Sagnalonga on the Italian side is another good powder area. A 2008 visitor was taken on long, two hour off-piste runs off the back of Les Anges by ESF instructors. Those with a car should visit Sestriere for more challenging on-piste runs. Heli-skiing can be arranged on the Italian side.

FOR INTERMEDIATES
Plenty of cruising terrain

The overclassified blacks are just right for adventurous intermediates, though none holds the interest for very long. The pleasantly narrow tree-lined runs to Claviere from Pian del Sole, the steepest of the routes down in the Chalvet sector and the runs off the back of Col de l'Alpet are all fine in small doses. Average intermediates will enjoy the red runs, though most are short. On the major sector, both

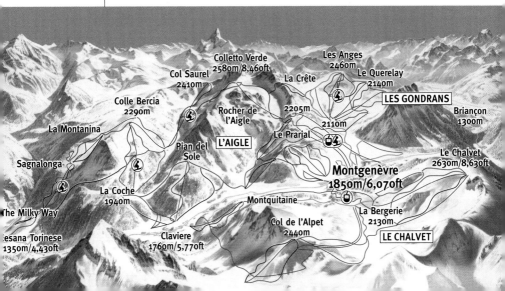

Montgenèvre has plenty of easy-cruising terrain →

OT MONTGENEVRE

FRANCE

338

Weekly news updates and resort links at www.wtss.co.uk

LIFT PASSES

Montgenèvre + Monts de la Lune

Prices in €

Age	1-day	6-day
under 12	25	119
12 to 59	30	149
over 60	25	119

Free under 6, over 75
Beginner no deals

Notes
Covers Montgenèvre and Claviere; 6-day and over pass allows one day in the Milky Way

Alternative passes
Montgenèvre only and Voie Lactée (Milky Way) area passes

SCHOOLS

ESF
t 0492 219046
A-Peak
t 0492 244997

Classes (ESF prices)
6 half days (2½hr)
€100
Private lessons
€33 for 1hr

CHILDREN

Les Sourires
t 0492 215250
Ages 6mnth to 6yr
Piou Piou (ESF)
t 0492 219046
Ages 3 to 5; 6 days
€230

Ski school
For ages 5 to 12
(6 half days €98)

the runs from Colletto Verde – one into Italy and one back into France – can be great fun. Getting to Cesana via the lovely sweeping run starting at Colle Bercia, and heading home from Pian del Sole, are both easier than the classifications suggest, and can be tackled by less adventurous intermediates, who also have a wealth of cruising terrain high up at the top of the Les Anges sector. The runs down to the village are easy cruises.

FOR BEGINNERS
Good for novices and improvers
There is a fine selection of convenient nursery slopes with reliable snow at the foot of the north-facing area. Progression to longer runs could not be easier, with a very easy blue starting at Les Anges, leading on to a green and finishing at the roadside.

FOR CROSS-COUNTRY
Having a car widens horizons
Montgenèvre is the best of the Milky Way resorts for cross-country enthusiasts, but it's useful to have a car. The two local trails, totalling 17km/11 miles, offer quite a bit of variety, but a further 60km/37 miles of track starts in Les Alberts, 8km/5 miles away in the Clarée valley.

QUEUES
Mixed reports
Most reporters say that queues are a problem only at weekends or when snow in Italy is bad, so people come

here instead. But serious queues for the main lifts out of the village can occur first thing in high season (a 2008 reporter mentioned 20- and 30-minute waits). Another 2008 reporter (only there for a day) said, 'We never walked straight on to a lift; there were always waits of up to five minutes but never more.' Links with Italy are gradually improving with the replacement of old lifts.

MOUNTAIN RESTAURANTS
Head for Italy
Most of the local options are large self-service places, but recent reporters enjoyed the Bergerie in the Chalvet sector ('very friendly', 'good food', 'marvellous views'). In the Claviere sector there is a choice of atmospheric little mountain huts; the two places at La Coche are 'good and reasonably priced'. There are plenty of places for lunch in the village.

SCHOOLS AND GUIDES
Encouraging reports
A recent reporter found the ESF 'well organised, with English-speaking instructors friendly and helpful'. They found that some 'prompting' was needed to get children in the right groups, but praised the friendliness and the 'secure area with indoor and outdoor facilities' for younger children. A 2008 visitor joined the top ESF class, and although it was merged with another class because of low numbers, 'all capabilities were catered

boarding

There's plenty to attract boarders to Montgenèvre. There are good local beginner slopes and long runs on varied terrain for intermediates. The only real drawback is that a fair number of the lifts are drags and there are some flat sections (especially getting to and from Sestriere). There are some excellent off-piste areas with a few natural hits for more advanced boarders and a dedicated freeride area at Les Gondrans (now shown on the piste map). Snow Box is a specialist shop.

UK PACKAGES

Airtours, AmeriCan Ski, Crystal, Crystal Finest, Equity, Erna Low, Independent Ski Links, Lagrange, Neilson, Peak Retreats, Rocketski, Ski Etoile, Ski France, Skiholiday extras.com, Ski Leisure Direction, Skitopia, Skitracer **Claviere** Crystal, Crystal Finest, Equity, First Choice, Rocketski

GETTING THERE

Air Turin 98km/ 61 miles (2hr); Grenoble 145km/ 90 miles (3hr); Lyon 253km/157 miles (4½hr)

Rail Briançon (12km/ 7 miles) or Oulx (15km/9 miles); buses available from both five times a day

ACTIVITIES

Indoor Cinema, exhibition hall

Outdoor Natural ice rink, snowshoeing, snowmobiling, walking, airboarding, tobogganing

Phone numbers
From abroad use the prefix +33 and omit the initial '0' of the phone number

TOURIST OFFICE

Montgenèvre
t 0492 215252
info@montgenevre.com
www.montgenevre.com

Claviere
t 0122 878856
claviere@montagnedoc.it
www.claviere.it

---

for' and 'instruction was good'. His beginner wife joined A-Peak and thought they were 'very good'.

FACILITIES FOR CHILDREN
Hugely improved
With the intrusive main road traffic removed, Montgenèvre would now seem a fine family resort. Reports on the school's children's classes have been complimentary about both class size and spoken English.

STAYING THERE

HOW TO GO
Limited choice
UK tour operators concentrate on cheap and cheerful catered chalets, though some apartments are also available and a few operators also package hotels.
Hotels There is a handful of places.
Chalet Blanc (0492 442702) Opened last season. Upmarket. Spa.
***Valérie** (0492 219002) Central, rustic. 'Quiet and nicely French.'
***Napoléon** (0492 219204) On the roadside.
*Chalet des Sports** (0492 219017) Among the cheapest in the Alps.
Apartments Résidences La Ferme d'Augustin are simple, ski-to-door apartments on the fringes of the main north-facing slopes.

EATING OUT
Cheap and cheerful
There are a dozen places to choose from. The 'pick of the bunch' is reportedly the Estable – 'a great find, full of locals'. We also have good reports of the Refuge ('excellent and extensive menu') and Le Napoléon ('fantastic Italian food'). The 'magnificent calzone pizzas' at the 'no-frills' Italian-run Capitaine are said to be 'perfect for hungry people on a budget'. A trip to Claviere is worthwhile – reporters have testified to the excellence of the restaurants.

APRES-SKI
Mainly bars, but fun
The range is limited. A 2008 visitor found the outside bar at the Napoléon hotel best. The Graal is a friendly, unsophisticated place with big TVs; the Ca del Sol bar is a cosy place with open fire. The Chaberton, with pool tables, is also recommended, although a recent visitor found it 'pretty quiet'. The Blue Night disco is popular; it

---

'supplies half-decent music and not too over-priced drinks till very, very late', attracting a mixed crowd. The Refuge, the Crepouse and the Jamy are the focal cafe-bars at tea time.

OFF THE SLOPES
Very limited
There is a weekly market and you can walk the cross-country routes, but the main diversion is a bus trip to the beautiful old town of Briançon.

STAYING UP THE MOUNTAIN
It's possible
The Sporthotel Sagnalonga is halfway down the piste to Cesana (on the Italian side of the border) and reached by chairlift or snowmobile. We've had mixed reports on it. Even during February holiday weeks you get the immaculately groomed local slopes to yourself until skiers based elsewhere arrive, mid-morning. It's quiet in the evenings, but livens up considerably when Italian weekenders arrive to party. It's in some UK package programmes.

Claviere 1760m/5,770ft

Claviere is a small, traditional village, barely a mile to the east of Montgenèvre and just over the border in Italy. It's no great beauty, and the main road to Montgenèvre and Briançon that divides it in two has an obvious impact, but visitors seem to like its quiet, relaxed ambience, and are ready to go again.

The slopes of Montgenèvre are as easily reached as those on the Italian side of the border.

Claviere's nursery slope is small and steep but usually uncrowded and snow-reliable. We have had mixed reports of its ski school – from 'lovely instructors, brilliant with the kids' to 'only average' and 'big classes'.

Morzine

A large, lively, year-round resort with its own attractive slopes and linked by lift to the main Portes du Soleil circuit

+ Larger local piste area (shared with Les Gets) than other resorts in the vast Portes du Soleil area

+ Good nightlife by French standards

+ Quite attractive old town

+ Few queues locally

+ Lots of tree-lined runs

− Just off the Portes du Soleil circuit

− Bus-ride or long walk to lifts from much of the accommodation

− Low altitude means there is an enduring risk of rain and poor snow

− Few tough pistes for experts

− Weekend crowds

Morzine is a long-established year-round resort, popular for its easy road access, traditional atmosphere and gentle wooded slopes; bad weather rarely causes problems (except that it rains here not infrequently). For keen piste-bashers wanting to ski the Portes du Soleil circuit regularly, the main drawback is having to take a bus and cable car or several lifts to get to the main circuit.

Such problems can be avoided by taking a car or using a tour operator who will drive you around. The little-used Ardent gondola, a short drive from Morzine, is a particularly neat option, giving the alternative of a shorter circuit that misses out Avoriaz, where the worst crowds tend to be found.

THE RESORT

Morzine is a traditional mountain town sprawling along both sides of a river gorge. In winter, under a blanket of snow, its chalet-style buildings look charming, and in spring the village quickly takes on a spruce appearance. Morzine is a family resort, and village ambience tends to be fairly subdued – but there is plenty of après-ski action.

The centre is close to the river, around the tourist office. Restaurants and bars line the street up to the lifts to Le Pléney, where a busy one-way street runs along the foot of the slopes. Accommodation is widely scattered, and a 'brilliant' multi-route bus service (including two electric buses) links all parts of the town to outlying lifts, including those for Avoriaz. There's a bus to Les Gets too.

As the extensive network of bus routes and a growing number of hotel mini-buses imply, Morzine is a town where getting from A to B can be tricky. The best plan is to stay in the centre of town or near one of the gondolas. Our view that the resort suits car drivers is widely shared. But the roads are busy and the one-way system takes some getting used to.

THE MOUNTAINS

The local slopes suit intermediates well, with excellent areas for beginners and near-beginners too.

THE SLOPES
No need to go far afield

Morzine is not an ideal base for the Portes du Soleil main circuit but it has an extensive local area of slopes shared with Les Gets (covered in a separate chapter).

A gondola rises from the edge of central Morzine to **Le Pléney**. (The parallel cable car is for the hotel up there and ski school kids only, unless

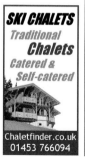

NEWS

For 2007/08 the new Aiglon apartments opened with the L'Eau Noire spa inside. A new nursery for young children and two new bars opened.

LIFT PASSES

Portes du Soleil

Prices in €

Age	1-day	6-day
under 16	26	127
16 to 59	39	189
over 60	31	151

Free under 5

Beginner no deals

Notes
Covers lifts in all resorts; half-day pass available

Alternative passes
Morzine-Les Gets only

the gondola breaks down.) Numerous routes return to the valley, including a run down to Les Fys – a quiet junction of chairs which access **Nyon** and, in the opposite direction, the ridge separating Morzine from the Les Gets slopes. The Nyon sector has two peaks – Pointe de Nyon and Chamossière – accessible from Nyon and Le Grand Pré respectively (by slow chairs only). Nyon can also be accessed by cable car, situated a bus ride from Morzine. Beyond Chamossière are two more ridges – Le Ranfoilly and La Rosta. In the valley between these two, no fewer than five chairlifts have their base stations clustered together.

Beyond Les Gets, **Mont Chéry** is notably quiet, and well worth a visit.

Across town from the Le Pléney sector – a handy 'petit train' shuttle service runs between the two – is a gondola leading (via another couple of lifts and runs) to Avoriaz and the main Portes du Soleil circuit. You take the gondola down at the end of the day to get back to Morzine (there's no piste back). Alternatives are a bus ride or short drive to either Les Prodains, from where you can get a (queue-prone) cable car to Avoriaz or a chairlift into the **Hauts Forts** slopes above it, or to Ardent, where a gondola accesses Les Lindarets for lifts towards Châtel, Avoriaz or

Champéry. The tree-lined slopes at Les Lindarets are good in poor visibility and the area at the top of the gondola is a good place for mixed-ability groups to meet up. Car trips to Flaine and Chamonix are feasible. The signposting and grooming are good.

TERRAIN PARKS
Mont Chéry, or head for Avoriaz
Nothing locally, except a boardercross on the Les Gets slopes. Try one of the four terrain parks in Avoriaz (see Avoriaz chapter) or head to Mont Chéry (see Les Gets chapter).

SNOW RELIABILITY
Poor
Morzine has a very low average height, and it can rain here when it is snowing higher up (almost every year some reporters mention days of rain). But because you ski on grassy pastures you need relatively little depth of snow for satisfactory coverage. There is some snowmaking, most noticeably on runs linking Nyon and Le Pléney, and on the home runs.

FOR EXPERTS
A few possibilities
The runs down from Pointe de Nyon and Chamossière are quite challenging, as are the black runs down the back of Mont Chéry and the excellent Hauts Forts blacks at Avoriaz. There is plenty of off-piste scope – see feature panel.

FOR INTERMEDIATES
Something for everyone
Good intermediates will enjoy the challenging red and black down from Chamossière. Mont Chéry, on the other side of Les Gets, has some fine steepish runs which are usually very quiet, as everyone heads from Les Gets towards Morzine. Those looking for something less steep have a great choice. Le Pléney has a compact network of pistes that are ideal for

boarding

Morzine is very popular with boarding seasonaires because of the extensive slopes, the splendid terrain parks in Avoriaz and the lower prices here. Chalet Snowboard, one of the first chalet companies to target snowboarders, has chalets here. And check out Rude Chalets, another rider-friendly operation (www.rudechalets.com). Former British champ Becci Malthouse runs the British Alpine Ski & Snowboard School. Specialist boarding shops include The Park and Misty Fly. The slopes in Morzine are great for all abilities of rider, with very few draglifts and flat areas. Plenty of treelined runs make for scenic and interesting snowboarding and the more adventurous should hire a guide to explore off-piste.

Phone numbers
From abroad use the prefix +33 and omit the initial '0' of the phone number

groups with mixed abilities: there are blue and red options from every lift. One of the easiest cruises on Le Pléney is a great away-from-it-all, snow-gun-covered blue from the top to the valley lift station. Heading from Le Ranfoilly to Le Grand Pré on the blue is also a nice cruise. And the slopes down to Les Gets from Le Pléney are easy when conditions are right (the slopes face south). The Ranfoilly and Rosta sectors have easy blacks and cruisey reds served by fast chairs. And, of course, there is the whole of the extensive Portes du Soleil circuit to explore by going up the opposite side of the valley.

FOR BEGINNERS
Good for novices and improvers
The wide village nursery slopes are convenient, and benefit from snow-

guns, though crowds are reported to be a problem. Some of the best progression runs are over at Nyon, and the slopes around Super-Morzine are also recommended. Adventurous novices also have the option of easy pistes around Le Pléney. Near-beginners can get over to Les Gets via Le Pléney, and return via Le Ranfoilly.

FOR CROSS-COUNTRY
Good variety
There are 95km/59 miles of varied cross-country trails, not all at valley level. The best section is in the pretty Vallée de la Manche beside the Nyon mountain up to the Lac de Mines d'Or, where there is a good restaurant. The Pléney-Chavannes loop is pleasant and relatively snow-sure.

Good, challenging runs both on-and off-piste

POINTE DE NYON
2010m/6,590ft

Chamossière
2000m

Le Ranfoilly
1850m

Ranfoilly

La

Chez
Nannon

Charniaz

Nauchets

Grains

Pointe
de Nyon

Des Têtes

Nyon
1420m

Le Grand Pré

Les Chavannes
1485m

Belvédère

Les Fys

1510m **LE PLENEY**

Les Ge
1170m/3,

The gondola is a link to Avoriaz from the centre of town. But you have to catch it down too – there's no piste back

Pléney

← Avoriaz

Super Morzine

Morzine
1000m/3,280ft

Lovely easy blue run away from all the lifts

CHILDREN

L'Outa nursery
t 0450 792600
Ages 3mnth to 6yr; 6
days €169; meals
€5.50

Club des Piou-Piou
t 0450 791313
From age 3; with ESF
instruction and lunch

Cheeky Monkeys
t 0450 750548
Ages from 3mnth

Jack Frosts
t 01579 384993
Ages 3mnth to 13yr

Ski school
ESF takes children
from age 5: 6 half
days €111

QUEUES
Resort-level problems

There can be long waits at peak
periods for both the gondolas out of
the resort – towards Avoriaz and to Le
Pléney – and for the cable car from
Les Prodains to Avoriaz. But there are
chairlift alternatives to the last two of
these. The Nyon cable car and
Belvédère chairlift (Le Pléney) are
weekend bottlenecks. There can be
queues for lift passes too: 'Try buying
from the tourist office,' advises a
recent reporter.

Once you are up the mountain,
queues are not usually a problem in
the local area.

MOUNTAIN RESTAURANTS
Some excellent huts

Editors' choice We have had several
very enjoyable Savoyard lunches at

the rustic Chez Nannon (0450 792115),
near the top of the Troncs chair
between Nyon and Chamossière – cosy
inside and a nice terrace. And we look
forward to trying the Pointe du Nyon
(0450 791174), which reporters rave
about ('we swapped our boots for
slippers'; 'the food was good quality';
'extremely well run with carpeted steps
down to pristine toilets').

Worth knowing about The nice little
Atray des Neiges at the foot of the
d'Atray chair is good. The tiny Lhottys
hut has had mixed reviews ('amazing
fresh seafood', 'mediocre spaghetti
Bolognese'). The Vaffieu at the top of
the Folliets chair has had several
recommendations ('liked the food,
service, location and atmosphere' and
'good food, large portions'), as has the
Chasse Montagne opposite the same
chair ('fantastic views'). The Nabor at

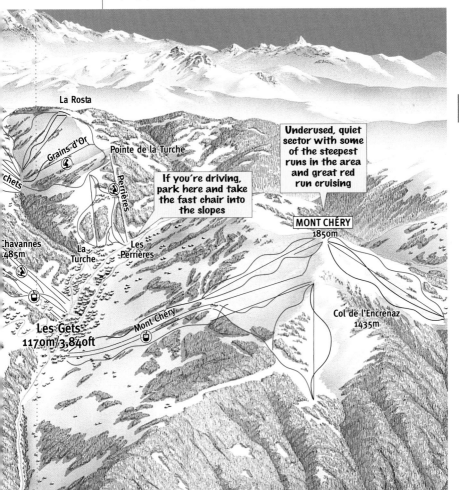

La Rosta

Grains-d'Or

Pointe de la Turche

chets

Perrières

**If you're driving,
park here and take
the fast chair into
the slopes**

**Underused, quiet
sector with some
of the steepest
runs in the area
and great red
run cruising**

havannes
485m

La
Turche

Les
Perrières

MONT CHÉRY
1850m

Les Gets
1170m/3,840ft

Mont Chéry

Col de l'Encrenaz
1435m

FRANCE

344

Weekly news updates and resort links at www.wtss.co.uk

SCHOOLS

ESF
t 0450 791313

Easy 2 Ride (E2SA) – International
t 0450 790516

Snow School
t 0486 688840

BASS
t 0450 747859
(0871 780 1500 UK)

Mint Snowboard
t 0680 776609

Classes
(ESF prices)
6 half days (2½hr am or pm) €120

Private lessons
€35 for 1hr for 1 to 3 people

GUIDES

Mountain Office
t 0450 747223

Pléney has 'the best soup I've ever tasted'. The Mouflon at the top of Rosta has 'good food but bad toilets'. The Tanière in Les Gets, at the bottom of the Chavannes chair, has been recommended for its 'varied food and lower prices'. Also on Chavannes the Yeti is praised for 'serving the most amazing coffee'. On Mont Chéry, the Grand Ourse is praised by a 2008 reporter for 'excellent food, comforting log fire and very good service', and two recent visitors recommend the Chanterelle on the back of the mountain ('lasagne to die for') and the rustic Ancrenaz Bar. One reporter complained that many small huts were overcrowded even midweek in January.

SCHOOLS AND GUIDES
Good reports
The British Alpine Ski & Snowboard School (BASS) is pricey but gets good reports: 'Wonderful for children –

↑ The area is great for intermediates with lots of easy cruising
STUART MCWILLIAM

brilliant instructors but book early,' said a recent reporter. 'Absolutely first class,' said another. The beginners in another's group had private lessons with 'great instructors' from the ESF (which is half the price). And others had a private lesson with 'an excellent instructor' at E2SA (International).

FACILITIES FOR CHILDREN
Lots of possibilities
The facilities of the Outa nursery are quite impressive, but we've received reports of poor English and low staff ratios. There is a big children's area, the Zone Enfant, in the Chavannes area. An ESF child care centre, Club des Piou-Piou looks after children between the ages of 3 and 14 after skiing ('Our younger children were

---

OFF-PISTE RUNS IN THE PORTES DU SOLEIL AREA

The Portes du Soleil offers a lot of great lift-served off-piste. Here is a small selection. Like all serious off-piste runs, these should only be done with a guide.

Morzine – Nyon/Chamossière area
From the Chamossière chairlift, heading north brings you to two runs – one on the same north-west slope as the pistes, the other via a col down the north-east slope to the Nyon cable car in the Vallée de La Manche – a wild area, with a great view of Mont Blanc at first.

Avoriaz area – two suggestions
From the Fornet chairlift on the Swiss border, you head west to descend a beautiful, unspoiled bowl leading down to the village of L'Erigné. In powder snow you descend the west-facing slopes of the bowl; when there is spring snow, you traverse right to descend the south-facing slopes. Medium-pitch slopes, for skiers and snowboarders.

From the top of the Machon chairlift you traverse west, beneath the peaks of Les Hauts Forts, across Les Crozats de la Chaux – a steep, north-facing slope. You then turn north to descend through the forest to the cable car station at Les Prodains. Testing terrain, for very good skiers. And beware that the traverse can be dangerous following a snowfall.

Châtel area
From the top of the Linga chair, head north-west to cross the ridge on your right at a col and then head down the La Leiche slope to the draglift of the same name. It's a north-facing slope, starting in a white wilderness, taking you through trees back to civilisation. Steep slopes – for good skiers only.

GETTING THERE

Air Geneva 75km/ 47 miles (1½hr); Lyon 195km/121 miles (3½hr)

Rail Cluses or Thonon (30km/19 miles); regular bus connections to resort

ACTIVITIES

Indoor Ice rink, fitness centre, sauna, hot tub, climbing wall, library, cinemas

Outdoor Snowshoeing, helicopter flights, snowmobiles, ice diving, ballooning, tobogganing, paintballing, paragliding, cheese factory visits

SMART LODGINGS

Check out our feature chapters at the front of the book.

UK PACKAGES

Alpine Answers, Alpine Weekends, AmeriCan Ski, Chalet Chocolat, Chalet Company, Chalet Entre Deux Eaux, Chalet Group, Chalet Gueret, Chalet Snowboard, Challenge Activ, Classic Ski, Crystal, Directski.com, Erna Low, First Choice, Haig, Independent Ski Links, Inghams, Inspired to Ski, Interactive Resorts, Lagrange, Momentum, Mountain Tracks, Oxford Ski Co, Peak Retreats, Reach4the Alps, Ride&Slide, Rude Chalets, Ski Activity, Ski Chamois, Ski Expectations, Ski France, Ski Independence, Ski Line, Ski McNeill, Ski Morzine, Ski Weekend, Skiholidayextras.com, Skitracer, Snow Finders, Snowline, Sugar Mountain, Thomson, Trail Alpine, White Roc

TOURIST OFFICE

t 0450 747272
info@
morzine-avoriaz.com
www.morzine-avoriaz.
com

quite happy, the older ones a little bored,' says a recent visitor). Recent reporters had mixed experiences with Cheeky Monkeys. One found the nanny to be 'brilliant', another suffered due to a shortage of nannies through illness and wouldn't recommend them. Jack Frosts has been highly praised. Tour operator Crystal has the fine Family Club Hotel Viking right on the slopes at Le Pléney ('impressive for families' said a recent reporter).

STAYING THERE

HOW TO GO
Good-value hotels and chalets
The tour operator market concentrates on hotels and chalets.

Chalets There's a wide choice, but position varies enormously and you need to check this carefully before booking. Reporters have recommended the independently run Farmhouse (0450 790826): 'excellent service, good ski guide'; 'gourmet dinner with fine wines and invaluable minibus service to the lifts'. A 2008 snowboarder reporter praises Ride&Slide's chalets again ('our third time and we can't fault them; new outdoor hot tub this year') and one of our assistant editors had a 'fun, laid-back week' with Rude Chalets. Snowline has some central places (most with hot tub and/or sauna).

Hotels The handful of 3-star hotels includes some quite smart ones; and there are dozens of 2-stars and 1-stars.
***Airelles** (0450 747121) Central 3-star close to Pléney lifts and bus routes. Good pool.
***Champs Fleuris** (0450 791444) Comfy 3-star next to Pléney lifts. Pool.
***Dahu** (0450 759292) 3-star linked to centre by footbridge over river; good restaurant; pool. Shuttle to lifts.
***Tremplin** (0450 791231) Next to lifts; 'friendly, good food, small rooms'.
***Viking** (0450 791169) is now run by Crystal. On the slopes at top of gondola. Specialises in families. Pool.
***Bergerie** (0450 791369) Rustic B&B chalet, in centre. Friendly staff. Outdoor pool, sauna, massage.
Côtes (0450 790996) Simple 2-star on the edge of town. Pool.
Equipe (0450 791143) One of the best 2-stars; next to the Pléney lift.
Soly (0450 790945) 'Great value, loads of car parking, fabulous and generous portions of food.'
Apartments The smart Aiglon

development was new for 2007/08 with pool, sauna, steam room, hot tub and is featured by tour operators Erna Low and Peak Retreats.

EATING OUT
A reasonable choice
The best restaurant in town is probably L'Atelier in hotel Samoyède, which offers traditional and modern cuisine – we enjoyed lobster ravioli, truffle risotto and scallops. The hotel Airelles has a fine restaurant and the hotel Dahu also has good food. The Chamade looks the part (elegant table settings) but reports are mixed. The Grange does 'excellent food, but at a price'. Locals rate the Chalet Philibert highly. The unpretentious Etale is popular with visitors ('excellent friendly service' and 'big, busy, nice ambience, huge portions'). The Pique Feu does Savoyard food at 'reasonable prices'. The Tyrolien has 'tartiflette to die for' and 'good steaks'. Clin d'Oeil has been praised. The hotel Rhodos has a 'child-friendly restaurant'. The 'traditional' Kinkerne is 'friendly and does excellent salads'.

APRES-SKI
One of the livelier French resorts
On Tuesday evenings there's a 'ski retrospective' on the slopes at Le Pléney, and on Thursdays there's a torchlit descent and floodlit skiing.
   Nightlife is good by French resort standards. Bar Robinson is basic but always busy as the slopes empty. The Dixie has sport on TV, MTV, a cellar bar and some live music. Between the slopes and the centre, and all in the same building are: the Cavern, which is popular with resort staff; the Coyote for arcade games and DJ; the Boudha Café, with Asian decor. At the nearby Crépu dancing on the tables in ski boots to deafening music seems compulsory. L'Opéra and Laury's are late-night haunts.

OFF THE SLOPES
Quite good; excursions possible
There are two cinemas, an excellent ice rink and lots of pretty walks, and a visit to the cheese factory is recommended by a 2008 visitor. Some hotels have pools open to non-residents. 'Morzine is a shoppers' paradise,' says a recent visitor. Buses run to Thonon for more shopping, and car owners can drive to Geneva, Annecy or Montreux.

Paradiski

Les Arcs and La Plagne are pretty impressive resorts in their own right; the ability to explore both is just the icing on the cake

KEY FACTS

Paradiski area	
Slopes	1200-3250m
	3,940-10,660ft
Lifts	144
Pistes	425km
	264 miles
Green	5%
Blue	56%
Red	27%
Black	12%

December 2003 saw the opening of the world's largest cable car – a double-decker holding 200 people – which swoops low across a wooded valley to link the resorts of Les Arcs and La Plagne. The result was Paradiski – one of the biggest joint ski areas in the world. When it opened, we were a bit sceptical about its value, particularly in view of the sheer physical dimensions of the La Plagne area. But we're now quite used to staying in Arc 1950 and having lunch above Champagny, or staying in Belle-Plagne and having lunch above Arc 2000.

We hope heads have rolled as a result of last season's emergency closure of the lift following discovery of flaws in the cables. All being well, it will be open again in time for the 2008/09 season.

The cable car, called the Vanoise Express, spans the 2km/1 mile-wide valley between Plan-Peisey (in the Les Arcs area) and a point 300m/980ft above Montchavin (in La Plagne).

The linking of these two major resorts is good news for the great British piste-basher who likes to cover as much ground as possible. For those who like a bit of a challenge, getting from your home base to both far-flung outposts of the Paradiski area – Villaroger in Les Arcs and Champagny-en-Vanoise in La Plagne – would make quite a full day.

The link is also good for experts. Those based in either resort can more easily tackle the north face of La Plagne's Bellecôte, finishing the run in Nancroix. Those based in La Plagne who are finding the piste skiing a bit tame can easily get across to Les Arcs' Aiguille Rouge.

If you want to make the most of the link it's sensible to stay near one of the cable car stations. But once you start to study the piste maps you realise that it's easily accessible from many other bases.

On the Les Arcs side, **Plan-Peisey** and nearby **Vallandry** are in pole position. They are basically small, low-rise, modern developments, but built in a much more sympathetic style than the original Les Arcs resorts. They are quiet places to stay, but are expanding rapidly and a few UK operators have chalets there. You can also stay in the unspoiled old village of **Peisey**, 300m/980ft below and linked by bucket-lift to Plan-Peisey.

It's easy to get to the cable car station at Plan-Peisey from the main resort parts of Les Arcs. One lift and a blue run is all it takes to get there from **Arc 1800**, which is the most attractive of the main resort units. From quieter **Arc 1600**, along the mountainside from 1800, it takes two lifts. **Arc 2000** and the stylish **Arc 1950** development seem further away, over the ridge that separates them from 1600 and 1800; but all it takes is one fast chair to the ridge and one long blue run down the other side. Beyond and below the bowl of Arc 2000, Villaroger-Le Pré is not an ideal starting point.

346

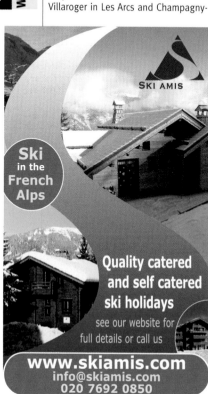

LIFT PASSES

Paradiski
Covers lifts in whole
Paradiski area.
6-day pass €237
(over 65 and under
14 €178).

Paradiski Découverte
Covers lifts in Les
Arcs area or La Plagne
area plus one day
Paradiski extension.
6-day pass €211
(over 65 and under
14 €159)

On the La Plagne side, the obvious place to stay is **Montchavin**, which is below the Vanoise Express station. Montchavin is a well-restored traditional old village with modern additions built in traditional style. **Les Coches**, across the mountain from the station, is most easily reached with the help of a lift. It is entirely modern, but built in a traditional style. From either, one lift brings you to the Vanoise Express cable car.

The other parts of La Plagne are some way from the cable car. But one long lift is all it takes to get from monolithic **Plagne-Bellecôte** up to L'Arpette, from which point it's a single long blue descent. The most attractive of the resort villages, **Belle-Plagne**, is only a short run above Plagne-Bellecôte. From the villages further across the bowl – **Plagne-Villages**, **Plagne-Soleil**, dreary **Plagne-Centre**, futuristic **Aime-la-Plagne** – you have to ride a lift to get to Plagne-Bellecôte. From **Plagne 1800**, below the bowl, add another lift. From the villages beyond the bowl – rustic, sunny

Champagny-en-Vanoise and expanding **Montalbert** – it's going to be pretty hard work, but it's certainly possible.

RIDING THE VANOISE EXPRESS
The cable car ride from one resort to the other takes less than four minutes.

The system is designed to be able to operate in high winds, so the risk of getting stranded miles from home is low. It can shift 2,000 people an hour, and end of the day crowds don't seem to be a problem.

The lift company offers a six-day pass covering the whole Paradiski region, which is perhaps most likely to appeal to people based in the villages close to the lift, who might divide their time between the two ski areas as the mood takes them – one day here, the next day.

But it also offers a pass (Paradiski Découverte) which includes just one day's use of the Vanoise Express and the lifts in the other resort.

Alternatively, you can buy one-day extensions to a Les Arcs or La Plagne six-day lift pass.

Paradiski

347

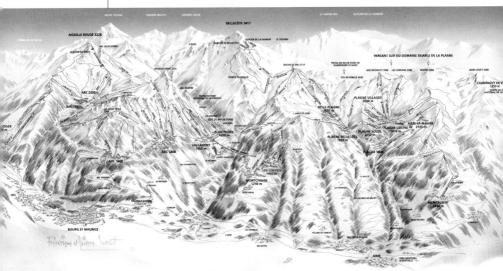

La Plagne

Villages from the rustic to the futuristic, spread over a vast area of intermediate terrain – mainly high and snow-sure

NEWS

The cable car linking La Plagne to Les Arcs, which was closed for 2007/08, is due to reopen in December 2008.

For 2008/09 at Les Coches a bucket-lift is planned to connect with the nursery area. Snowmaking is due to be increased throughout the area and several new residences opened.

For 2007/08 Les Coches gained a nursery area, several pistes were widened and more hotels and residences opened.

➕ Extensive and varied intermediate slopes, plus plentiful, excellent off-piste terrain

➕ Good nursery slopes

➕ High and fairly snow-sure – and with some wide views

➕ Choice of convenient purpose-built resorts at altitude and attractive, traditional-style villages lower down

➕ Wooded runs of lower satellite resorts are useful in poor weather

➕ Cable car link to Les Arcs from one of those satellite villages

➖ Challenging pistes are few, and confined to a couple of sectors, of which one is not reliably open

➖ Pistes get very crowded in places

➖ Still lots of slow old chairlifts

➖ Lower villages can have poor snow – sunny Champagny especially

➖ Unattractive architecture in some of the higher resort units

➖ Hardly any green runs – though some blues are very easy

➖ Upscale accommodation still rare, though things are improving

With 225km/140 miles of its own slopes, of which 85% are blue or red, La Plagne is an intermediate's paradise, even without the link to Les Arcs (which was out of action for repairs last season). It's also a splendid resort for going off-piste, with vast areas of easily accessed slopes within the piste network and some long descents that are much less heavily skied than the classic off-piste runs of more macho resorts like Val d'Isère. But for many visitors the limited on-piste challenge can be a disappointment.

The choice of bases here is unparalleled, from the monolithic blocks of bleak Aime-la-Plagne to the chalets and orchards of Montchavin. La Plagne remains the least fashionable of French mega-resorts, but there are now some genuinely good hotels, chalets and apartments, and they are increasing every year.

THE RESORT

La Plagne consists of no fewer than ten separate 'villages', each a self-sufficient mini-resort.

Six of the villages are purpose-built at altitude in the main bowl, on or above the treeline. Even these vary a lot in character. The first to be built, in the 1960s, was Plagne-Centre – still the focal point for shops and après-ski. Typical of its time, it has ugly blocks and dreary indoor 'malls' that house a reasonable selection of shops,

bars and restaurants. Recent developments are more traditional and more pleasing to the eye.

Lifts radiate from Centre to all sides of the bowl, the major one being the big twin-cable gondola to Grande Rochette. A cable car goes to the even more obtrusive 'village' of Aime-la-Plagne – a group of monolithic blocks. Below these two, and a bit of a backwater, is Plagne 1800, where the buildings are small-scale and chalet-style. Access to the main bowl from here is by lifts to Aime-la-Plagne.

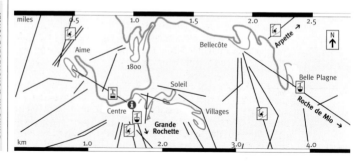

Interactive resort shortlist builder at **www.wtss.co.uk**

↑ Broad, open slopes above chalet-style Belle-Plagne; it's a pity you have to descend to Plagne-Bellecôte for access to the main lifts

SNOWPIX.COM / CHRIS GILL

KEY FACTS

Resort	1800-2100m
	5,900-6,890ft

La Plagne only	
Slopes	1250-3250m
	4,100-10,660ft
Lifts	106
Pistes	225km
	140 miles
Green	7%
Blue	60%
Red	22%
Black	11%
Snowmaking	
	309 guns

Paradiski area	
Slopes	1200-3250m
	3,940-10,660ft
Lifts	144
Pistes	425km
	264 miles
Green	5%
Blue	56%
Red	27%
Black	12%

A little way above Plagne-Centre is Plagne-Soleil, with modern chalets and apartments, and a growing mini-resort centre. This area is officially attached to Plagne-Villages, which is a rather strung-out collection of small-scale apartments and chalets in traditional style, handy for the slopes; the few restaurants and shops are mostly around the station for a lift link with Plagne-Centre.

The two other core resort units are a bus ride away, on the other side of a low hill. Belle-Plagne is another slope-side development in chalet style, now quite large, and spread over a quite steep hillside that provokes complaints from readers who find its multiple levels exhausting to get around in the evening. Down the hill, the huge apartment buildings of Plagne-Bellecôte form a wall at the foot of the slopes leading down to it.

Outside the main bowl, at the northern edge of the area, are Montchavin and Les Coches. At the southern edge is rustic Champagny. Beyond Aime-la-Plagne, at the western edge, is growing Montalbert. These are described later in the chapter.

A free bus system between the core villages within the bowl runs until after midnight. Lifts between some resort units run until 1am.

A cable car from Montchavin links to Les Arcs via Peisey-Vallandry – great if you are based reasonably close.

Day trips by car to Val d'Isère-Tignes or the Three Valleys resorts are possible.

THE MOUNTAINS

The majority of the slopes in the main bowl are above the treeline, though there are trees scattered around most of the resort centres. The slopes outside the bowl are open at the top but descend into woodland.

Some runs are more difficult than their classification suggests, while others are easier – note our warning in 'For intermediates'. Piste names and classification seem to alter on a regular basis, too. Signposting and the piste map are good. There are a lot of slow old lifts still around.

THE SLOPES
Multi-centred; can be confusing
La Plagne boasts 225km/140 miles of pistes over a wide area that can be broken down into seven distinct but interlinked sectors. From Plagne-Centre you can take a lift up to **Le Biolley**, from where you can head back to Centre, to Aime-la-Plagne or progress to **Montalbert**, from where you ride several successive lifts back up. But the main lift out of Plagne-Centre leads up to **La Grande Rochette**. From here there are good sweeping runs back down and an easier one over to Plagne-Bellecôte, or you can drop over the back into the mainly south-facing **Champagny** sector, for excellent long runs and great views over to Courchevel.

From Plagne-Bellecôte and Belle-Plagne, you can head up to **Roche de Mio**, and have the choice of a gondola, or two successive fast chairs (the first of which also accesses Champagny). From Roche de Mio, runs spread out in all directions – towards La Plagne, Champagny or **Montchavin/ Les Coches**. This sector can also be reached by taking an eight-seat chair from Plagne-Bellecôte to L'Arpette.

From Roche de Mio you can also take a gondola down then up to the **Bellecôte glacier**. It is prone to closure by high winds or poor weather. The top chair is normally shut in winter – but if open, it offers excellent snow and stunning views. You can descend 2000m/6,560ft vertical to Montchavin, with a not-difficult off-piste stretch in the middle of the run.

The piste map marks half a dozen draglifts as 'difficult', and reporters say some are very much so.

Plagne-Centre has night skiing on the slalom slope.

LIFT PASSES

La Plagne

Prices in €

Age	1-day	6-day
under 14	31	149
14 to 64	41	198
over 65	31	149
Free under 6, over 72		
Beginner 12 free lifts		

Notes
Covers all lifts in La Plagne areas; individual village-area and half-day passes; Paradiski extension

Paradiski Découverte

Prices in €

Age	6-day
under 14	159
14 to 64	211
over 65	159
Free under 6, over 72	
Beginner no deals	

Notes
Covers all lifts in La Plagne areas with one day in Paradiski

Paradiski

Prices in €

Age	1-day	6-day
under 14	35	178
14 to 64	46	237
over 65	35	178
Free under 6; over 72 €8		
Beginner no deals		

Notes
Covers all lifts in Les Arcs area and La Plagne area and a day in either Val d'Isère-Tignes or Three Valleys

TERRAIN PARKS
Lots of choices

Belle-Plagne, Montchavin/Les Coches and Champagny all have decent parks and there's another one at Montalbert. The Snowpark above Plagne-Centre, serviced by the Colorado chairlift, is one of the better parks in France. There are three lines: the expert line has three big kickers, several standard rails and an S-rail; the intermediate line features only boxes and rails, though still good fun for advanced riders. The easy line has three small rollers and several ride-on rails and boxes for first timers. A park-only pass costs 20 euros a day. Plagne-Bellecôte is now home to two half-pipes; go to Belle-Plagne to ride the boardercross.

SNOW RELIABILITY
Generally good except low down

Most of La Plagne's runs are snow-sure, being at altitudes between 2000m and 2700m (6,560ft and 8,860ft) on the largely north-facing open slopes above the purpose-built centres. The lift company is nearing the end of a five-year plan to increase snowmaking on the main runs to all the villages – more is planned for 2008/09. The two sunny runs to Champagny are often closed. Grooming could be better.

FOR EXPERTS
A few good blacks; good off-piste

There is challenging piste skiing in two widely separated sectors. There are two beautiful, long, steep and bumpy black runs from Bellecôte to a lift below Col de la Chiaupe – almost 1000m/3,280ft vertical. But don't count on them: in countless visits over the years, we have found these open only once. The other pistes from the glacier, to the gondola station, are more reliable and certainly worthwhile; Chiaupe has been reclassified black, which it merits for a short stretch.

The other tough sector is Biolley. The long Emile Allais red run (previously black) down to La Roche, on the road up from the valley, is little used, north-facing and very enjoyable in good snow. On the back of the hill, the Coqs and Morbleu blacks are seriously steep, Palsembleu less so. From the very top of this sector, Etroits (as its name suggests) owes its black status to a quite short pitch that is both steep and narrow, but is otherwise harmless.

But experts will get the best out of La Plagne if they hire a guide and explore the vast off-piste potential – which takes longer to get tracked out than in more 'macho' resorts. The two sectors discussed above have some excellent off-piste terrain. More serious undertakings include numerous runs from Bellecôte to Les Bauches (a drop of over 1400m/4,590ft). For the more experienced, the north face of Bellecôte presents a splendid challenge with usually excellent snow at the top. You can descend to Peisey-Nancroix (a drop of 2000m/6,500ft) and then catch a taxi or free bus to the Vanoise Express cable car. Another beautiful and out-of-the-way run starts with a climb and goes over the Cul du Nant glacier to Champagny-le-Haut.

FOR INTERMEDIATES
Great variety

Virtually the whole of La Plagne's area is a paradise for intermediates, with blue and red runs wherever you look.

For early intermediates there are plenty of gentle blue motorway pistes in the main La Plagne bowl, and a long, interesting run from Roche de Mio back to Belle Plagne, the Tunnel (going through, er, a tunnel). The blue runs either side of Arpette, on the Montchavin side of the main bowl, are glorious cruises – but beware, the blues further down towards Montchavin are quite challenging. The easiest way to and from Champagny is from the Roche de Mio-Col de Forcle area. Warning: the Mira piste from Grande Rochette back towards Plagne Centre is the steepest blue run we have ever encountered – it should without question be red; lower down it turns into an excellent cruise. Verdons, nearby, is a great cruise too.

Better intermediates have lots of delightful long red runs to try. There are challenging red mogul pitches down from Roche de Mio to Les Bauches (a drop of 900m/2,950ft) – the first half is a fabulous varied run with lots of off-piste diversions possible; the second half, Les Crozats, has reverted to black status after a period as a red, and can be tricky if snow is less than ideal. The Sources red to Belle Plagne is a good run, too.

The Champagny sector has a couple of tough reds – Kamikaze and Hara-Kiri – leading from Grande Rochette. And the long blue cruise Bozelet has one surprisingly steep section. The

Plagne-Centre

▲ **GRANDE ROCHETTE**

Verdons 2500m
2500m
Col de Forcle
2270m

Belle-Plagne 2500m
Plagne-Bellecôte ↓

ROCHE DE MIO
2700m

Col de la-Chiaupe
2550m

Bellecôte
3417m

Les Borseliers

Chalet
Verdons Sud

Rossa

Champagny-le-Haut

Le Planay

Champagny-en-Vanoise
1250m

La Plagne

351

Interactive resort shortlist builder at **www.wtss.co.uk**

long Mont de la Guerre red, with 1250m/4,100ft vertical from Les Verdons to Champagny, is a fine away-from-all-lifts run with a decent red-gradient stretch half-way down, but long flattish tracks at the start and finish. There are further excellent red slopes in the other outlying areas – including the winding, treelined Les Coches, above ... Les Coches.

FOR BEGINNERS
Excellent facilities
La Plagne is a good place to learn, with generally good snow and above-average facilities for beginners, especially children. Each of the main centres has nursery slopes on its doorstep. There's a free draglift in

each resort as well. But there are no long green runs to progress to. Although a lot of the blue slopes are easy, you can't count on that; some, as we note above, are very testing. The Plan Bois area above Les Coches has good gentle slopes, served by a six-pack; there is also a new nursery area on the other side of Les Coches – soon to be accessed by a bucket-lift (see 'News'). But the blue runs back into Plagne 1800 and Montchavin are difficult for novices.

CROSS-COUNTRY
Open and wooded trails
There are 80km/50 miles of prepared cross-country trails scattered around. The most beautiful of these are the

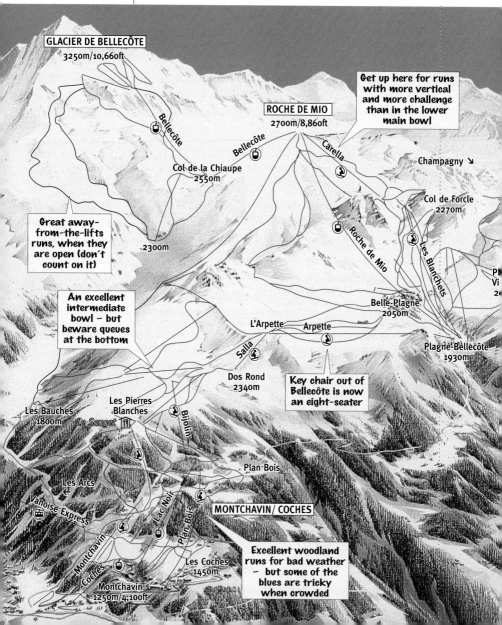

GLACIER DE BELLECÔTE
3250m/10,66oft

ROCHE DE MIO
2700m/8,86oft

Get up here for runs
with more vertical
and more challenge
than in the lower
main bowl

Bellecôte

Bellecôte

Carella

Champagny ↘

Col de la Chiaupe
2555m

Col de Forcle
2270m

Roche de Mio

Les Blanchets

Great away-
from-the-lifts
runs, when they
are open (don't
count on it)

2300m

An excellent
intermediate
bowl – but
beware queues
at the bottom

L'Arpette

Arpette

Belle-Plagne
2050m

P
Vi
2

Plagne-Bellecôte
1930m

Salla

Dos Rond
2340m

Key chair out of
Bellecôte is now
an eight-seater

Les Pierres
Blanches

Bijolin

Les Bauches
1800m

Le Sauget

Plan Bois

Les Arcs

Vanoise Express

Lac Noir

Plan Bois

MONTCHAVIN / COCHES

Montchavin

Excellent woodland
runs for bad weather
– but some of the
blues are tricky
when crowded

Coches

Les Coches
1450m

Montchavin
1250m/4,100ft

boarding

With such a huge amount of terrain, there is something for everyone in La Plagne. Expert freeriders, however, are advised to hire a guide as there is so much hidden terrain to be had off the mainly motorway-style pistes. When light gets flat hit the lower tree runs, as the open nature of the higher slopes will be a nightmare. Although this is a great place for beginners, with huge wide-open rolling pistes, be careful as there is also a lot of flat land, especially above Belle-Plagne, in the middle of the Tunnel run and the blue run linking Montchavin with Les Bauches. Make sure to get enough speed, or to avoid such areas, or you'll be doing a lot of walking. Most draglifts have been replaced, and others can be avoided; the more difficult ones are marked on the resort piste map.

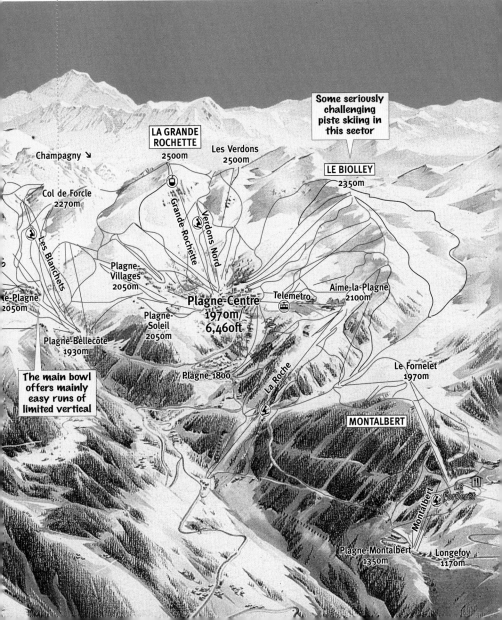

Some seriously challenging piste skiing in this sector

Champagny

LA GRANDE ROCHETTE
2500m

Les Verdons
2500m

LE BIOLLEY
2350m

Col de Forcle
2270m

Les Blanchets

Grande-Rochette

Verdons Nord

Plagne-Villages
2050m

Plagne-Soleil
2050m

Telemetro

Aime-la-Plagne
2100m

-Plagne
2050m

Plagne-Centre
1970m/
6,460ft

Plagne-Bellecôte
1930m

La Roche

Plagne 1800

Le Fornelet
1970m

The main bowl offers mainly easy runs of limited vertical

MONTALBERT

Le Forperet

Montalbert

Plagne-Montalbert
1350m

Longefoy
1170m

UK PACKAGES

Action Outdoors, Airtours, Alpine Answers, Chalet Group, Chalet World Ski, Club Med, Crystal, Crystal Finest, Equity, Erna Low, Esprit, Finlays, First Choice, Independent Ski Links, Inghams, Interactive Resorts, Interhome, Kuoni, Lagrange, Mark Warner, Mountain Heaven, Neilson, Oxford Ski Co, Richmond Holidays, Rocketski, Silver Ski, Ski Activity, Ski Amis, Ski Beat, Skibug, Ski Collection, Ski Expectations, Ski France, Skifrance4less, Ski Freshtracks, Ski holidayextras.com, Ski Independence, Ski Leisure Direction, Ski Line, Ski Olympic, Ski Soleil, Ski Solutions, Ski Supreme, Skitracer, Skiworld, SnowCrazy, Snowline, Thomson **Montchavin** *Chill Chalet, Lagrange, Peak Retreats, Ski Leisure Direction, Ski Soleil* **Les Coches** *Erna Low, Family Ski Company, Finlays, Independent Ski Links, Interactive Resorts, Lagrange, Mountainsun, Peak Retreats, Ski Activity, Ski France, Skiholiday extras.com, Ski Independence, Ski Leisure Direction, Ski Line* **Montalbert** *Interhome, Lagrange, Ski Amis* **Champagny** *Barrelli, Chill Chalet, Erna Low, Independent Ski Links, Lagrange, Peak Retreats, Ski France, Skiholidayextras.com, Ski Independence, Ski Leisure Direction*

22km/14 miles of winding track set out in the sunny valley around Champagny-le-Haut. The north-facing areas have more wooded trails that link the various centres. A car will help you make the most of it all.

QUEUES
Main problems being sorted

La Plagne's lift and piste network has some fundamental flaws – to get from one sector to another you often have to descend to Plagne-Centre or, particularly, to Plagne-Bellecôte. 'You knew you were in for a 20/30 minute wait,' says one high-season reporter. The Roche de Mio gondola here is a persistent cause of complaint, but the chairs towards Centre and Montchavin are not queue-free. What's needed is some lifts from Belle-Plagne, to relieve Bellecôte. There are other queue-prone lifts that you can't avoid, once you've descended to them – at Les Bauches for example, and in the Champagny sector (especially Verdons Sud, warns one reader). The gondola to the glacier is queue-prone when snow is poor lower down.

Crowds on the pistes are now as much of a problem as lift queues. Plagne-Bellecôte and Belle-Plagne are the main areas affected, and Roche de Mio – 'quite dangerous'. The slopes outside the main bowl are quieter.

MOUNTAIN RESTAURANTS
An enormous choice

Mountain restaurants are an attraction of the area: numerous and varied – and crowded only in peak periods.

Editors' choice Chalet des Verdons Sud (0621 543924) above Champagny offers excellent, appetising food and service on a big terrace with a fine view, or in the warmly woody interior. The Rossa (0479 082803), at the top of the Champagny gondola, has friendly staff, and good, basic cooking. A great rustic place in which to hole up in poor weather is Le Sauget (0479 078351), above Montchavin. Above Montalbert, Le Forperet (0479 555127) is an old farm with 'superb tartiflette', 'great frites', 'excellent salads' and modest prices.

Worth knowing about Plein Soleil at Plan Bois is a bit cramped inside but does excellent food. Recommendations include the 'terrific' Roc des Blanchets, and the Borseliers ('great atmosphere and food'); the cosy Au Bon Vieux Temps, just below Aime-la-Plagne; the

Inversans ('good quality food', 'great views and roaring log fire'); the 'cosy' Ferme de Cesar above Montchavin ('varied menu, large terrace'); Chalet des Colosses above Plagne-Bellecôte; the 'very French' Chalet du Friolin at Les Bauches; and the Bergerie, with 'fantastic fireplace', above Plagne-Villages.

Many people have lunch in one of the resorts – particularly Champagny or Montchavin/Les Coches

SCHOOLS AND GUIDES
Better alternatives to ESF

Each centre has its own ESF school. High-season classes can be much too large (up to 20) and good English cannot be relied upon. Reports for group lessons are generally poor: one youngster 'was repeatedly told off for falling over'; 'glorified guiding', says another visitor. But feedback on private lessons is more positive, the schools in Les Coches and Montalbert have come in for praise, and one visitor had an excellent day with an ESF guide.

The alternatives to the ESF are preferable. The Oxygène school in Plagne-Centre continues to impress: 'Excellent. My three-year-old son got on fine.' 'Superb private lessons.' 'Good English, great instruction.' We have had glowing reports on the El Pro school in Belle-Plagne, but a 2008 visitor who booked with them warns that her son's classes were actually with ESF – the school claimed that 'they were not allowed to do group classes outside the school holidays'. We have also had good reports on Evolution 2 (based in Montchavin): 'One of the most positive experiences I've had in a while, and good value.' Reflex is based in 1800 and private lessons get good reviews: 'The best for several years; pitched at the right level to test and enjoy.' 'Very helpful.' Antenne Handicap offers private lessons for skiers with any kind of disability.

FACILITIES FOR CHILDREN
Good choice

Children are well catered for with facilities in each of the villages. The nursery at Belle-Plagne is 'excellent, with good English spoken'. The one in Les Coches is not apparently (see 'Les Coches'). Be wary of ESF classes. Several UK chalet operators run child care services.

Air Geneva 149km/
93 miles (3½hr); Lyon
196km/122 miles
(3½hr); Chambéry
92km/57 miles (2½hr)

Rail Aime (18km/
11 miles) and Bourg-
St-Maurice (35km/
22 miles) (Eurostar
service available);
frequent buses from
stations

OT LA PLAGNE

The northern slopes
give good views of
Mont Blanc ↓

STAYING THERE

HOW TO GO
Plenty of packages
The resort is apartment-dominated,
but alternatives are increasing. There
are two Club Meds.
Chalets There's a large number
available – the majority are fairly
simple, small, and located in 1800. Ski
Beat has no fewer than 16 chalets
here, ranging from 6 beds to 18.
Skibug has two neat-looking places.
Family specialist Esprit has the
exceptionally cool chalet hotel Deux
Domaines, in an excellent position at
Belle-Plagne, with good pool and spa.
Mark Warner and Ski Olympic have
chalet hotels in Centre (Graciosa is
highly praised in 2008: 'great team,
service and food'.) See also our
descriptions of lower villages.
Hotels There are very few, most of
2-star or 3-star grading.
***Araucaria (0479 092020) Very
modern 3-star at Plagne-Centre.
***Balcons (0479 557655) 3-star at
Belle-Plagne. Pool.
***Carlina (0479 097846) Welcoming,
well-run 3-star beside the piste below
Belle-Plagne. Pool and spa.

***Terra Nova (0479 557900) Big,
120-room 3-star in Plagne-Centre.
Apartments There is a huge amount of
apartment accommodation, including
new places of a high standard
available through UK operators such
as Erna Low and Peak Retreats.
Chalets les Montagnettes in Belle-
Plagne are spacious with good views.
The MGM/CGH Les Hauts Bois in Aime-
la-Plagne is highly recommended
('excellent, with a decent pool'). The
4-star Pelvoux is newish in Plagne-
Centre. MGM/CGH have opened Les
Granges du Soleil at Plagne-Soleil, and
will add more apartments to it for
2008/09. And Lagrange is due to add
a luxury 4-star residence, Chalet
Edelweiss, in Plagne 1800 for 2008/09.

EATING OUT
A surprising amount of choice
There is a good range of casual
restaurants including pizzerias and
traditional Savoyard places.
Reader recommendations in Plagne-
Centre include the Métairie, the Vega
('pricey but friendly'), the Maison
('worth a trip, great steaks'), and the
Refuge ('great meal in charming, rustic
atmosphere'). Scotty's is 'good for

La Plagne

355

Interactive resort shortlist builder at **www.wtss.co.uk**

CHILDREN

Les P'tits Bonnets
(Plagne-Centre)
t 0479 090083
Ages from 10wk
Marie Christine
(Plagne-Centre)
t 0479 091181
Ages 2 to 6
ESF nurseries (ages from 18 mnth or 2yr):
Aime 0479 090475
Belle 0479 090668
Bellecôte 0479 090133
1800 0479 090133
Snow gardens run by ESF: ages from 3 to 5

Ski schools
Children's classes are available to 12 or 16 depending on the village: 6 days from €204 (ESF prices)

SMART LODGINGS

Check out our feature chapters at the front of the book.

ribs'. The Legend cafe is a trendy new place with a terrace.

In Plagne-Villages, the Casa de l'Ours is good for pizzas and steaks, the Grizzli is 'superb' for Savoyard food and 'worth visiting for the chocolate cake alone'.

In Plagne 1800, the Mère-Grand has 'good food, but a short menu', the Loup Blanc ('fine steaks and local specialities'), Petit Chaperon Rouge ('great atmosphere, excellent home cooking and reasonable prices') and Mama Mia's have been praised.

At Aime-la-Plagne, Au Bon Vieux Temps on the slopes is open in the evening. The Cave, buried deep in the main block, has 'exceptional' food. The smart Arlequin is 'family-friendly' and does a 'rather special rack of lamb'.

In Plagne-Bellecôte, the Ferme and Chalet des Colosses ('gets busy') have been recommended. In Belle-Plagne, recommendations include Pappagone pizzeria, the Chalet Maître Kanter ('good value'), the Cloche, the 'friendly' Face Nord and the Matafan ('homely feel and great pierrade').

APRES-SKI
Bars, bars, bars

Though fairly quiet during low season, La Plagne has plenty of bars, catering particularly for the younger crowd.

In Belle-Plagne, the Tête Inn and the Cheyenne are the main bars. The Maître Kanter has been recommended. The No BI'm Café, with a massive TV and occasional live music, is the liveliest bar in Plagne-Centre. Plagne 1800 is fairly quiet at night – though the Mine (complete with old train and mining artefacts) is an exception: 'good beer and live music'. Mama Mia's is 'fun and eccentric'. The Petit Chaperon Rouge has 'lots of neon and plasma screens'. Plagne-Bellecôte is limited at night, with only one real bar – Show Time Café, which is popular for karaoke. But there is bowling, and tubing. Aime-la-Plagne is also quiet.

The Luna (Plagne-Centre), the Jet (Plagne-Bellecôte) and the Saloon (Belle-Plagne) are the main discos. There are cinemas at Aime, Bellecôte and Plagne-Centre.

OFF THE SLOPES
OK for the active

As well as the sports and fitness facilities, winter walks along marked trails are pleasant: 'There are enough walks to keep you busy for six days,' says one reporter. It's also easy to get up the mountain on the gondolas, which both have restaurants at the top. There's an ice grotto on the glacier (special pass available). The Olympic bobsleigh run is a popular evening activity (see feature box). Excursions are limited.

Selected chalets in La Plagne

ACTIVITIES

Indoor Sauna and solarium in most centres, squash (1800), fitness centres (Belle-Plagne, 1800, Centre, Bellecôte), library (Centre), climbing wall, bowling

Outdoor Heated swimming pool, bobsleigh, marked walks, tobogganing, paragliding, helicopter rides, snowmobiles, ice climbing, ice rink, ice karting, paintballing, snow quad bikes, snowshoeing, dog sledding

Phone numbers
From abroad use the prefix +33 and omit the initial '0' of the phone number

TOURIST OFFICES

La Plagne
t 0479 097979
bienvenue@
la-plagne.com
www.la-plagne.com
Montchavin-Les Coches
t 0479 078282
info@montchavin-
lescoches.com
www.montchavin-
lescoches.com
Montalbert
t 0479 077733
maison.montalbert@
la-plagne.com
Champagny
t 0479 550655
info@champagny.com
www.champagny.com

Montchavin 1250m/4,100ft

Montchavin is based on an old farming hamlet and has an attractive traffic-free centre. There are adequate shops, a kindergarten and a ski school. The local slopes have quite a bit to offer – pretty, sheltered runs, well endowed with snowmaking, with nursery slopes at village level. The blue home runs can be quite tricky. Après-ski is quiet, but the village doesn't lack atmosphere and has a couple of nice bars, a nightclub, cinema and night skiing. The Bellecôte hotel (0479 078330) is convenient for the slopes.

Les Coches 1450m/4,760ft

Les Coches is a little way above Montchavin, across the hillside, and shares the same slopes. It is a sympathetically designed, quiet, modern mini-resort with a traffic-free centre. There are nursery slopes up at Plan Bois – reached by a six-pack, and now at village level. It has its own school and kindergarten. But we've received a scathing report on the nursery from a 2008 visitor.

The Last One pub is a 'great place for a beer', with a big screen TV and live bands. Poze (for pizza), the Lauzes, the Savoy'art ('stunning interior'), and Taverne du Monchu are recommended for eating out. There's a shuttle to the cinema in Montchavin. Finlays has six chalets here, mostly with en suite bathrooms.

Montalbert 1350m/4,430ft

Montalbert is a traditional but much expanded village – now with a proper little front de neige. The lift out of the village is a fast one, but your progress to the main bowl depends on two further slow ones, and at that point you are still a couple of lifts from

Roche de Mio or the Les Arcs link. The local slopes are easy and wooded – a useful insurance against bad weather. There are 'heaps of restaurants for such a small place' and the Tourmente pub is 'great'. The Aigle Rouge (0479 555105) is a simple hotel. Ski Amis has an all-en-suite chalet with all the trimmings here. Mountain Heaven has apartments in three modern developments; the Chalets de Montalbert and Les Granges are reportedly 'simply furnished but pleasantly spacious'.

Champagny 1250m/4,100ft

Champagny is a charming village in a pretty, wooded, sunny setting, with its modern expansion done sensitively. It is at the opposite end of the slopes from the link to Les Arcs but the tricky red runs to the village will be a bigger drawback for many potential visitors. Even in good snow, they are rather steep and narrow for nervous intermediates – and the snow is often far from good, despite artificial help. The village is well placed for an outing by taxi or car to Courchevel.

There are several hotels, of which the two best are both Logis de France. The Glières (0479 550552) is a rustic old hotel with varied rooms, a friendly welcome and good food. The Ancolie (0479 550500) is smarter, with modern facilities (recommended by a reporter). The Club Alpina (0479 550459) is 'consistently good for both food and rooms', says a regular visitor, and is close to the lift.

The Alpages de Champagny is an impressive-looking chalet-style development, with a pool and sauna.

The village is quiet in the evenings, but the restaurant Poya is 'superb for atmosphere, friendliness and food' and so is the Rochelle, near the church – 'lovely food, by far the best value'.

TRY THE OLYMPIC BOBSLEIGH RUN – YOU CAN NOW DO IT SOLO

If the thrills of a day on the slopes aren't enough, you can round it off by having a go on the bobsleigh run built for the 1992 Winter Olympics. The floodlit 1.5km/1 mile run has 19 bends, generating forces as high as 3g.

You can go in a driverless bob-raft (34 euros) reaching 80kph/50mph, which most people find quite exciting enough. Then there's the faster solo mono-bob (95 euros); we found this a great thrill – we had to close our eyes on the sharper bends. Fastest of all is the 'taxi-bob' (100 euros), where three of you are wedged in a real four-man bob behind the driver – advertised speed 110kph/68mph. Be sure your physical state is up to the ride; there are minimum age limits. The run is open on certain days only – book ahead. Additional insurance is available. A 2008 visitor loved the ride, but found the staff rude and impatient: 'They rushed us through, despite the fact that we were early.'

SNOWPIX.COM / CHRIS GILL

Portes du Soleil

Low altitude, largely intermediate circuit of slopes straddling the French-Swiss border, with a variety of contrasting resorts

PISTE MAP MADNESS

Last season the excellent booklet-style piste map covering all the ski areas in the Portes du Soleil was scrapped. Instead, each resort now has its own local area map with a Portes du Soleil overview map on the back that is totally inadequate for finding your way around in other areas. This means you may want to pick up detailed maps in each resort for a clearer view of local lifts and pistes. Of the maps we have seen, Avoriaz's is by far the best, as its local area map clearly covers most (but not all) of the main circuit. But the others don't: madness. We can only assume it's a misconceived cost-cutting idea.

The Portes du Soleil vies with the Trois Vallées for the title 'World's Largest Ski Area', but its slopes are very different from those of Méribel, Courchevel, Val Thorens and neighbours. The Portes du Soleil's slopes are spread out over a large area, and not all are linked – but most are part of an extensive circuit straddling the French-Swiss border. You can travel the circuit in either direction, with a short bus ride needed at Châtel. There are smaller areas to explore slightly off the main circuit. The runs are great for keen intermediates who like to travel long distances and through different resorts. There are few of the tightly packed networks of runs that encourage you to stay put in one area – though there are exceptions in one or two places. The area also has some nice rustic mountain restaurants, serving good food in pleasant, sunny settings.

The lifts throughout the area have been improved in recent years, with several new high-speed chairlifts eliminating some bad bottlenecks – though there are still plenty of drags and slow chairs. But the slopes are low by French standards, with top heights in the range 2000m to 2300m (6,560ft to 7,550ft), and good snow is far from assured (though snowmaking has been expanded in recent years). When the snow is good you can have a great time racing all over the circuit. But the slopes can get very crowded, especially at weekends and in the Avoriaz area.

We have separate chapters on the major Portes du Soleil resorts. On the French side, purpose-built **Avoriaz** and

the traditional old mountain village of **Châtel** are on the main circuit. (On a spur off the main circuit at Châtel – and covered briefly in that chapter – are the slopes above **Torgon** in Switzerland and **La Chapelle d'Abondance** in France.) **Morzine** and **Les Gets** are another two traditional old French mountain villages but are set off the main circuit and share their own area of local slopes.

On the Swiss side, **Champéry** is a classic, charming Swiss village – but again just off the main circuit. In the Champéry chapter we also cover briefly the other main Swiss resorts: **Morgins** (another old village) and **Champoussin** and **Les Crosets** (both purpose-built).

Puy-St-Vincent

Underrated small modern resort with limited but varied slopes – good for young families who haven't been spoilt by mega-resorts

SNOWPIX.COM / CHRIS GILL

COSTS

① ② ③ ④ ⑤ ⑥

RATINGS

The slopes
Fast lifts	★★★
Snow	★★★
Extent	★★
Expert	★★★
Intermediate	★★★
Beginner	★★★
Convenience	★★★★★
Queues	★★★
Mountain restaurants	★★★

The rest
Scenery	★★★★
Resort charm	★★
Off-slope	★

NEWS

A new nursery at the children's snow garden in Station 1400 opened for 2007/08.

A fast quad has now replaced the Lauzes top draglifts at 2000m/6,560ft. But the planned chairlift at La Balme looks unlikely to happen for a few years.

OT PUY-ST-VINCENT

Although the village is limited, there are quite a few outdoors activities ↓

+ Mostly convenient, friendly, not too hideous purpose-built resort
+ Splendid scenery
+ Fairly reliable snow
+ Some great cross-country routes
+ Good variety of pleasantly uncrowded slopes with challenges for all abilities, but ...

− Slopes very limited in extent
− Upper village has only apartment-based accommodation
− Queues in French holidays
− Still lots of draglifts
− Limited après-ski/restaurants
− Limited village diversions

Puy-St-Vincent's ski area may be limited, but when we visited we found ourselves liking it more than we expected. It offers a decent vertical and a lot of variety, including a bit of steep stuff. Provided you pick your spot with care, it makes an attractive choice for a family not hungry for piste miles.

THE RESORT

Puy-St-Vincent proper is an old mountain village, but you're not likely to be staying there. The modern resort of Puy is basically a two-part affair – the minor part, Station 1400, is just along the mountainside from Puy-St-Vincent proper at 1400m/4,590ft; the major part, Station 1600, is a few hairpins further up (yes, at 1600m/5,250ft), consisting of long, low apartment blocks. Spreading up the hillside from here are newer developments in a more traditional style – sometimes referred to as Station 1800.

Some of the accommodation is slope-side, but not all – take care when picking your spot if this matters. We and our reporters have found PSV friendly ('even the lift operators'), and it is understandably popular with families.

THE MOUNTAINS

Within its small area, PSV packs in a lot of variety, with runs from green to black that justify their classification. It doesn't get crowded, which adds considerably to the attraction.

Slopes There are gentle slopes between the two villages, but most of the runs are above 1600. A fast quad goes up to the treeline at around 2000m/6,560ft. Entertaining red runs go back down, and a green takes a less direct route. The main higher lift is a long chair to 2700m/8,860ft, serving excellent open slopes of red and genuine black steepness. Drags and a fast quad – which replaced the Lauze double draglifts in 2006/07 – either side serve further open runs here, and access splendid cruising runs that curl around the edges of the area into the woods – one linking to a blue, La Balme, all the way down to 1400. 1400 has a six-pack up into the main slopes. The six-day Galaxie pass covers a series of major resorts

359

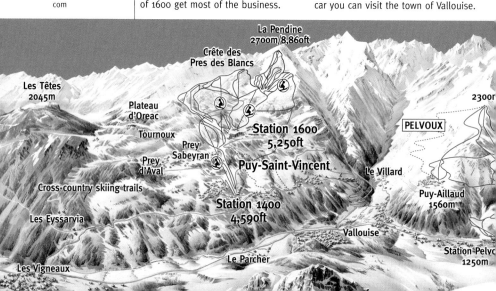
KEY FACTS

Resort	1400-1600m
	4,590-5,250ft
Slopes	1250-2700m
	4,100-8,860ft
Lifts	12
Pistes	75km
	47 miles
Green	18%
Blue	41%
Red	35%
Black	6%
Snowmaking	10km
	6 miles

UK PACKAGES

*Erna Low, Interhome,
Lagrange, Ski
Collection, Ski France,
Skiholidayextras.com,
Skitracer, Snowbizz*

SMART LODGINGS

**Check out our feature
chapters at the front
of the book.**

Phone numbers
From abroad use the
prefix +33 and omit
the initial '0' of the
phone number

TOURIST OFFICE

t 0492 230531
infos@
paysdesecrins.com
www.paysdesecrins.
com

beyond Briançon. More to the point, it
also covers a day's skiing above the
valley hamlet of Pelvoux, 10 minutes'
drive away. This area has quiet, very
rewarding blue, red and black runs,
and a vertical of over 1000m/3,280ft.

Terrain parks There is a floodlit terrain
park with half-pipe at 1600 and a
boardercross course higher up.

Snow reliability The slopes face north-
east and are reasonably reliable for
snow. Snowmaking now covers much
of the slopes at 1600 and on runs to
1400. Grooming is OK.

Experts The black runs are short but
genuinely black, and are 'totally
ungroomed, with serious moguls'.
There are off-piste routes to be tackled
with guidance.

Intermediates Size apart, it's a good
area for those who like a challenge –
but there aren't many very easy runs.

Beginners Beginners should be happy
on either of the nursery slopes, and
on the long green from 2000m/6,560ft.

Snowboarding There are slopes to suit
all levels, but still some draglifts.

Cross-country There are 30km/19 miles
of cross-country trails, including some
splendid routes between 1400m and
1700m (4,590ft and 5,580ft), ranging
from green to black difficulty.

Queues In a family resort like this,
there are bound to be some problems
in French holiday times – but with fast
chairs at the lower levels and a newish
fast quad high up, these should be
minimal.

Mountain restaurants There is a
modern but pleasantly woody place at
mid-mountain, but the sunny terraces
of 1600 get most of the business.

Schools and guides You have a choice
of French and International ski school.
British tour operator Snowbizz has
merged its school with the
International school; together they
claim to form the largest English-
speaking children's school in the
French Alps. A 2007 reporter found
them 'excellent, with a very high
standard'.

Facilities for children There are
nurseries taking children from 18
months in 1400 and 1600, and both
schools run ski kindergartens. 'A great
resort for my five-year-old daughter to
start her skiing career,' sums up a
2007 reporter.

STAYING THERE

How to go A number of UK operators
now offer accommodation here; most
of it is in self-catering apartments at
the foot of the slopes.

Hotels There are three cheap hotels in
1400, but none in 1600.

Apartments The Gentianes apartments
at 1800 are 'good-sized, very
reasonably priced', with the use of an
indoor pool. They are handy for the
slopes but not for shops.

Eating out The Petit Chamois is
'friendly, with a good children's menu'.

Après-ski Après-ski amounts to a few
bar-restaurants in each village.

Off the slopes Village diversions are
very limited, but there are outdoor
pursuits – 30km/19 miles of paths.
parapenting, tobogganing, dog sled
rides and outdoor skating. The cinema
shows English-speaking films. With a
car you can visit the town of Vallouise.

Risoul

Modern, family-friendly resort with a range of accommodation in an attractive setting – and a big area of slopes shared with Vars

361

COSTS

① ② ③ ④ ⑤ ⑥

RATINGS

The slopes

Fast lifts	*
Snow	***
Extent	***
Expert	**
Intermediate	****
Beginner	****
Convenience	****
Queues	****
Mountain restaurants	***

The rest

Scenery	***
Resort charm	**
Off-slope	*

NEWS

At Vars, investment has concentrated on the sunny Peynier sector, which got extra snow-guns in 2007/08. There are plans for a six-pack to replace the old double chair here for 2008/09.

The 4-star Hameau des Rennes apartments are due to open at Les Claux in December 2008.

➕ One of the more attractive and convenient purpose-built resorts

➕ Fair-sized, scenic, uncrowded area of slopes shared with Vars

➕ High resort, reasonably snow-sure

➕ Good resort for beginners, early intermediates and families

➕ Plenty of good-value places to eat

➖ Still some long draglifts, though most are avoidable

➖ Not too much to challenge expert skiers and boarders

➖ Little to do off the slopes

Slowly but surely the international market is waking up to the merits of the southern French Alps. Were they nearer Geneva, Risoul and its linked neighbour Vars would be as well known as Les Arcs and Flaine – the village of Risoul is more attractive than either and Vars is quietly developing. Brush up your school French before you go, especially for Vars.

THE RESORT

Risoul, purpose-built in the late 1970s, is a quiet, apartment-based resort, popular with families. Set among the trees, it is made up of wood-clad buildings – mostly bulky, but with some concessions to traditional style. It has a busy little main street that, surprisingly, is very far from traffic-free. But the village meets the mountain in classic French purpose-built style, with sunny restaurant terraces facing the slopes. Reporters have commented on the friendliness of the natives. The village does not offer many resort amenities. The resort isn't as difficult to reach now that flights to Grenoble are available.

THE MOUNTAINS

Together with neighbouring Vars, the area amounts to one of the biggest domains in the southern French Alps – marketed as the Forêt Blanche.
Slopes The slopes, mainly north-facing, spread over several minor peaks and bowls, and connect with the sunnier slopes of neighbouring Vars via the Pointe de Razis and the lower Col des Saluces. The upper slopes are open, but those back to Risoul are prettily wooded, and good for bad-weather days. Despite several recent lift upgrades, there are still too many long and steep draglifts. Piste markings and classifications are unreliable.

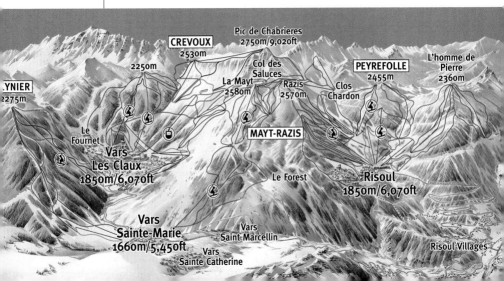

↑ Risoul has a classic French purpose-built front de neige

SNOWPIX.COM / CHRIS GILL

KEY FACTS

Resort	1850m
	6,070ft

The entire Forêt Blanche ski area

Slopes	1660-2750m
	5,450-9,020ft
Lifts	51
Pistes	180km
	112 miles
Green	16%
Blue	38%
Red	36%
Black	10%
Snowmaking	35km
	22 miles

The self-service Tetras is just 'OK'. Snack Attack, near the Forêt Blanche apartments, and the Refuge de Valbel have been suggested.

Schools and guides We've had a good report on the ESF. 'The instructors were excellent for both adults and kids – patient, with good English. Classes no bigger than eight.' There is also the Internationale school.

Facilities for children Risoul is very much a family resort. It provides an all-day nursery for children over six months. Both ski schools operate ski kindergartens, slightly above the village, reached by a child-friendly lift.

Terrain parks There are three good terrain parks, one at resort level. There are two half-pipes, boardercross course and various rails and jumps.

Snow reliability Risoul's slopes are all above 1850m/6,070ft and mostly north-facing, so despite its southerly position snow reliability is reasonably good. Snowmaking is fairly extensive. Visitors recommend going over to the east-facing Vars slopes for the morning sun, and returning to Risoul in the afternoon. Grooming is adequate.

Experts The pistes in general do not offer much to interest experts. However, Risoul's main top stations access a couple of steepish descents. And there are some good off-piste opportunities if you take a guide.

Intermediates The whole area is best suited to intermediates, with some good reds and blues in both sectors. Almost all Risoul's runs return to the village, making it difficult to get lost.

Beginners Risoul's local area includes good, convenient, nursery slopes with a free lift, and a lot of easy longer pistes to move on to: 'pretty much perfect', says a 2007 visitor.

Snowboarding There is a lot of good freeriding to be done throughout the area, although beginners might not like the large proportion of draglifts. There are weekly competitions.

Cross-country There are 45km/28 miles of cross-country trails in the whole domain. A trail through the Peyrol forest links the two resorts together.

Queues Outside French school holidays, the slopes are impressively quiet. There may be a wait to get back from Vars at the end of the day.

Mountain restaurants Most people return to the village terraces, but the mountain restaurants are improving.

How to go Most visitors stay in self-catering apartments, but there are a few hotels and more chalets are becoming available from UK operators.

Hotels The 'value for money' Chardon Bleu (0492 460727) is right on the slopes. You can also stay overnight at the Tetras mountain refuge (0492 460983) at 2000m/6,560ft.

Apartments The Constellation Forêt Blanche apartments, although small, have been praised for convenience and quality. Bételgeuse and Pégase opened a few years ago.

Eating out There's plenty of choice, from pizza to good French food, and it's mostly good value – the Ecureuil and the Chalet are both 'excellent'.

Après-ski The centre is livelier than most people expect and après-ski goes on through the night. There are half a dozen 'extremely friendly' bars and three clubs to move between. The best bars are, apparently, the 'trendy' Caribbean-themed Babao and the Chalet or Eterlou for a quieter drink.

Off the slopes There is little to do; excursions to Briançon are possible.

Vars 1850m/6,070ft

THE RESORT

Vars includes several small, old villages on or near the road running southwards towards the Col de Vars, chief among them Vars-Ste-Marie. But for winter visitors it mainly consists of purpose-built Vars-les-Claux, higher up the road. The resort has convenience and reasonable prices in common with Risoul, but is bigger and has far more amenities; less English is spoken though. There are a lot of block-like apartments, but Vars-les-Claux is not a

Phone numbers
From abroad use the prefix +33 and omit the initial '0' of the phone number

complete eyesore, thanks to a wooded setting and several new chalet-style developments. There are two centres: the original, geographical one – base of the main gondola – has most of the shops and accommodation; Point Show is a group of bars and shops, 10 minutes' walk away.

Lower Vars-Ste-Marie makes a more attractive base now that fast chairs take you to the top of La Mayt and are planned for Peynier. But it's 'dead' in the evenings.

THE MOUNTAINS

There are slopes on both sides of the village, linked by pistes and by chairlift at the lower end of Les Claux. Lifts also run up from both sides of Ste-Marie, lower down the mountain.
Slopes The wooded, west-facing Peynier area is the smaller sector, and reaches only 2275m/7,460ft – though there are good long descents down to Les Claux and Ste-Marie. A new six-pack planned here for 2008/09 should greatly improve access. The main slopes are in an east-facing bowl with direct links to the Risoul slopes at the top, Col du Vallon (via a tunnel) and at the Col des Saluces. There's also a speed-skiing course. Beneath it are easy runs, open at the top but descending into trees. A six-pack has improved the connection towards Crevoux, above Les Claux.
Terrain parks There's a terrain park at Crevoux, with rails and jumps for all.
Snow reliability The main slopes get the morning sun, and are centred at around 2000m/6,560ft, so snow reliability is not as good as in Risoul, but snowmaking is widespread – with more added at Peynier this year.
Experts There is little of challenge for experts, though the Crête de Chabrières top section accesses some off-piste, an unpisted route and a tricky couloir at Col de Crevoux. The Olympic red run from the top of La Mayt down to Ste-Marie is a respectable 920m/3,020ft vertical.
Intermediates Most of the area is fine for intermediates, with a good mixture of comfortable reds and easy blues.
Beginners There is a nursery area close to central Vars ('fantastic'), with lots of 'graduation' runs throughout the area. Quick learners will be able to get over to Risoul by the end of the week.
Snowboarding There is good freeriding to be done throughout the area,

although beginners might find the number of draglifts a problem.
Cross-country There are 25km/16 miles of trails in Vars itself. Some start at the edge of town, but those above Ste-Marie are more extensive.
Queues Queues are rare outside the French holidays, and even then Vars is not as busy as most family resorts.
Mountain restaurants There are several in both sectors, but a lot of people head back to the villages for lunch. The Cassette, at the bottom of the Mayt chair, has 'delighted' visitors.
Schools and guides Two recent beginners enjoyed 'good' classes with ESF, but a lack of English speaking may be a problem.
Facilities for children The ski school runs a nursery for children from two years old. There is a ski kindergarten.

STAYING THERE

How to go There are a few small hotels, but Les Claux is dominated by apartments. The 4-star Hameau des Rennes chalet-style residence is new.
Hotels The Caribou (0492 465043) is the smartest of the hotels and has a pool. The Ecureuil (0492 465072) is an attractive, modern B&B chalet. At Ste-Marie there are two typically attractive members of the Logis de France 'chain' – the 3-cheminée Alpage (0492 465052) and the simpler but 'highly satisfactory' Vallon (0492 465472).
Eating out The range of restaurants is impressive, with good-value pizzerias, crêperies and fondue places. Reporters liked Taverne du Torrent and Chez Plumot. Chaudron is new at Ste-Marie.
Après-ski Après-ski is animated at tea time, less so after dinner – except at weekends when the discos warm up.
Off the slopes The amenities are rather disappointing: 35km/22 miles of walking paths, a cinema and an ice rink – and that's it.

Risoul

363

Interactive resort shortlist builder at **www.wtss.co.uk**

La Rosière

The sunniest slopes in the Tarentaise, but also about the snowiest; the link to La Thuile in Italy adds an extra dimension

RATINGS

The slopes

Fast lifts	**
Snow	***
Extent	***
Expert	**
Intermediate	***
Beginner	*****
Convenience	***
Queues	***
Mountain restaurants	*

The rest

Scenery	***
Resort charm	***
Off-slope	*

364

+ Attractive, friendly, purpose-built resort with glorious views

+ Fair-sized area of slopes shared with La Thuile in Italy

+ Sunny home slopes

+ Heli-skiing over the border in Italy

+ Good nursery slope

+ Big dumps of snow when storms sock in from the west, but ...

− Wind can close link with Italy, which involves a tough red and long drag

− Snow affected by sun in late season

− Lots of slow old lifts

− Few on-piste challenges for experts

− One run is much like another – though La Thuile is more varied

− Limited après-ski

− Few off-slope diversions

La Rosière is much smaller and quieter than the nearby mega-resorts such as Val d'Isère-Tignes, Les Arcs and La Plagne; and all our recent reporters stress the friendliness of the locals. The ski area is remarkably sunny, but gets a lot of snow; and the link with the north-facing slopes of La Thuile in Italy adds variety. All in all, the resort best suits families and groups of skiers with mixed abilities looking for a relaxed time.

THE RESORT

La Rosière has been built in attractive, traditional chalet style beside the road that zigzags its way up from Bourg-St-Maurice towards the Petit-St-Bernard pass to Italy (closed to traffic in winter – the Italian side becomes a piste). It's a quiet place with a few shops and friendly locals; don't expect lively nightlife. The most convenient accommodation is in the main village near the lifts, or in the rapidly developing alternative base of Les Eucherts, a short bus ride – or 'great woodland walk' – to the east and served by its own fast chair.

THE MOUNTAINS

La Rosière and La Thuile in Italy share a big area of slopes called Espace San Bernardo. La Rosière's sunny home slopes are south-facing with great views over the valley to Les Arcs and La Plagne. The link with Italy's slopes is prone to closure because of high winds or heavy snow and early intermediates may find it tricky.

Slopes Two fast chairs, one in La Rosière and one at Les Eucherts, take you into the heart of the slopes, from where a series of lifts, spread across the mountain, takes you up to Col de la Traversette. From there, you can get over the ridge and to the lifts which link with Italy at Belvédère.

Terrain parks There's a terrain park served by the Poletta draglift, just above the village centre and a boardercross course by the Fort chair below Col de la Traversette.

Snow reliability The slopes get a lot of snow from storms pushing up the valley, but in late season the sunny orientation takes its toll.

Experts There's little to keep experts amused. The steepest terrain is on the lowest slopes, down the Marcassin black run below Les Eucherts and down the Ecudets black to the west of Le Gollet. There's also a freeride area just above the latter and some enjoyable off-piste between the pistes. And there's excellent heli-skiing from

La Thuile
Belvedere 2610m/8,560ft
Col du Petit Saint Bernard 2190m
Le Roc Noir 2330m
COL DE LA TRAVERSETTE 2385m
Le Gollet
1175m
La Rosière 1850m/6,070ft
Les Eucherts
1500m

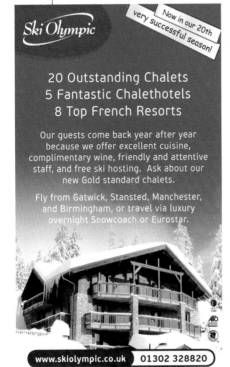

↑ The village and its slopes, seen from the road up to Arc 2000

NEWS

For 2007/08 a sports and shopping complex including an ice rink and bowling alley opened at Les Eucherts and the footpath between there and the village was landscaped. For 2008/09 74 more snow-guns are planned.

just over the Italian border (you ski or board back into France, arriving just a few miles from La Rosière – see the La Thuile chapter).

Intermediates There's a fair amount to explore if you take into account La Thuile. The main part of La Rosière's area is a broad open mountainside offering straightforward red and blue pistes. More interesting is the Fontaine Froide red, dropping 750m/2,460ft vertical through woods to the Ecudets chair, far below the village at the western end – 'an absolute jewel' says a 2008 visitor. The red beyond Col de la Traversette has good snow and views, but is narrow at the top.

Beginners There are good nursery slopes and short lifts near the main village and near Les Eucherts.

Snowboarding Most of the lifts are chairs, making the place good for learner and early intermediate boarders. And the sunny slopes are good for gentle freeriding when the snow is soft.

Cross-country There are 14km/9 miles of trails near the altiport.

Queues Not usually a problem.

Mountain restaurants Most people have lunch in the village. Mountain recommendations include the self-service Plan du Repos for its 'friendly staff, huge pasta portions and lovely salads', the San Bernardo (on the border) and the Vieux Chalet (at the bottom of the Ecudets chair) for snacks ('very friendly service').

Schools and guides Evolution 2 is praised for its 'small groups' and 'friendly instructors', who are good with children. And we have good reports of the ESF – 'dedicated English-only classes and a great place to learn off-piste with a guide'. Former technical director at the ESF, Brit Simon Atkinson has opened the Elite ski school – but we lack reports.

Facilities for children Club des Galopins has a 'very good' snow garden, and British tour operators Esprit, Crystal and Ski Beat (see 'Chalets') all have their own child care facilities here.

STAYING THERE

How to go A number of British tour operators now offer packages here.

Hotels There are a few 2-star hotels in the village, and more in the valley.

Chalets There is an increasing number of companies with chalets here. Ski Olympic has operated here for years and has a chalet hotel and four chalets (including two with access to a

Interactive resort shortlist builder at www.wtss.co.uk

pool, sauna, steam and hot tub). Ski Beat has six places purpose-built for themselves in Les Eucherts, with child care facilities and two shared saunas. Mountain Heaven has a splendid-looking penthouse there too with a huge top-floor living room, six en-suite rooms and an outdoor hot tub. And Skiworld has three smart new chalets there. Family-specialist Esprit Ski has several chalets and its usual comprehensive child care facilities.

Apartments The best places are newly built at Les Eucherts. Cîmes Blanches is smart with a pool, hot tub, sauna and steam room. The Balcons units can accommodate larger groups. Both are available through Ski Collection and the former through Erna Low too.

Eating out A useful pocket guide to restaurants is distributed locally. The Génépi serves 'fabulous French cuisine', says a recent visitor. The Turia is a rustic, smart establishment in the centre. The Marmottes is said to serve 'good salads'. We've had mixed reports on the food and service at the 'charming' Ancolie. The Relais du Petit

St Bernard is popular.

Après-ski Après-ski is limited to a couple of bars in the village. 'Good live band and relaxed, no-smoking lounge upstairs at Le Petit Danois,' says a recent reporter.

Off the slopes There are scenic flights and walks and a cinema. And you can try paragliding, dog sledding and snowshoeing. Mountain restaurants are inaccessible on foot.

Staying up the mountain The Hotel San Bernardo (0165 841444), on the border and reachable only on skis, provided a memorable two-night stay for an adventurous reporter – 'simple, comfortable and peaceful', with a 'spectacular collection of grappas'.

SNOWPIX.COM / CHRIS GILL

Samoëns

Characterful but inconvenient base for the extensive and varied Grand Massif, shared with Flaine, Morillon and Les Carroz

➕ Lovely historic village, with traffic-free centre and weekly market

➕ Lift into big, varied area shared with Flaine and Les Carroz

➕ Glorious views from top heights

➕ Very close to Geneva, but ...

➖ Weekends can be busy as a result

➖ Main access lift is way outside the village – yet has no return piste

➖ Slow lifts above mid-mountain

➖ Not the best base for beginners

➖ Surprisingly intrusive traffic

The impressive Grand Massif area is chiefly associated in Britain with high, purpose-built, apartment-dominated Flaine; but the network can also be accessed from much more attractive traditional villages – Les Carroz, Morillon and Samoëns. And the cutest of these, if not the most convenient, is Samoëns.

THE RESORT

Samoëns is a 'Monument Historique' – once a thriving centre for stonemasons, with their work much in evidence. There is a small traffic-free centre of narrow streets lined by appealing food shops, and nearby a pretty square (sadly not traffic-free) with a stone fountain, an ancient linden tree, a fine church and other medieval buildings. Also nearby is a nominally car-free area of modern development. The village as a whole retains the feel of 'real' rural France. There is a good weekly market.

So it's a lovely spot, but it has flaws. We get continued flack, from people with an interest in the resort, about our view that it is an inconvenient base. Well, the situation is simple. You have a choice of two gondolas, both a drive or bus ride from the village: an old one that you can ski back to if conditions permit (and you can hack a proper red), and a newer one with its base station in a ridiculous spot halfway between the slopes and the village, which you can't reach on skis. So it's a gondola ride and a bus ride at the end of the day. Not a problem, but not convenient.

THE MOUNTAINS

Most of the skiing directly above Samoëns is on open slopes beneath the peak of Tête des Saix, from which point there are links to the next-door Morillon sector and the slightly more distant sectors of Les Carroz and Flaine (both of these are covered in the Flaine chapter).

Slopes The two gondolas from the valley arrive at separate points on the 'hilly plateau' of Samoëns 1600. This mini-resort is also reachable by road. Tête des Saix is reached by parallel chairlifts in two stages. These slow lifts are a real drawback: a couple of six-packs are urgently needed. From the Tête you can descend to Morillon or Les Carroz; one more (fast) chair is needed for access to the Flaine bowl.
Terrain parks There is now only a tiny kids' park. The main park is in Flaine.
Snow reliability The slopes above Samoëns face due north, so above 1600 snow is fairly reliable. There is snowmaking around 1600.
Experts The upper pistes on Tête des Saix are among the most testing in the Grand Massif, and there is lots of good off-piste in the valleys and bowls between Samoëns and Flaine.
Intermediates If you can put up with the slow lifts mentioned above, Samoëns makes a perfectly satisfactory base for all but the most timid intermediates, who might be better off in Morillon. From Tête des Saix you have a choice of good long

Phone numbers
From abroad use the prefix +33 and omit the initial '0' of the phone number

runs in various directions. In good snow the valley runs to Vercland are highly enjoyable – the black is little steeper than the red, and used less.
Beginners Beginners buy a special pass and go up to 1600, where they will find gentle, snow-sure slopes – excellent when not crowded – but no long green runs to progress to. Morillon is a better bet; and the nursery slopes at Sixt are 'very good'.
Snowboarding Beware draglifts on the nursery slopes.
Cross-country There are trails on the flat valley floor around Samoëns, and more challenging ones up the valley beyond Sixt and up at Col de Joux Plane (1700m/5,580ft).
Queues We've had reports of queues at 1600 for access to Tête des Saix.
Mountain restaurants There are places to eat at Samoëns 1600, but the most captivating places are above Morillon and Les Carroz – see Flaine chapter.
Schools and guides We lack recent reports, but one reader had a 'poor' lesson with the ESF and a 'much better one' from 360 International. Another visitor found the ESF's private boarding instruction 'very good'.
Facilities for children The kindergarten takes kids from three years old, and ski lessons are available. The Zig Zag school offers multi-activity courses.

STAYING THERE

How to go A few specialist UK operators now go to Samoëns.
Hotels We and readers have enjoyed the Neige et Roc (0450 344072), a walk from the centre – 'friendly staff, excellent food, big spa area'. Avoid the annexe, though. The central Glaciers

(0450 344006) is recommended.
Chalets Samoëns doesn't seem to figure in the programmes of major operators, but we have glowing reports of owner-run chalets Marie Stuart and Moccand and an impressively orchestrated set of endorsements for chalet Bezière ('wonderful hospitality', 'great food', 'nothing too much trouble').
Apartments Self-catering is mostly in small-scale developments, and quite a lot of it in individual chalets. Appealing places available through UK firms include the Fermes de Samoëns (with pool), and Ferme de Fontany.
Eating out The Table de Fifine is a short drive from the centre, but a fine spot for a proper dinner – beautiful wooden interior and 'good quality, imaginative menu'. The Muscade et Basilic is 'excellent, with an extensive wine list' and the Bois de Lune has 'great food'. The Louisiane has 'great' pizzas but when busy the staff will rudely turn you away.
Après-ski There are several bars – including an Irish pub, Covey's, which a 2007 reporter's teenager daughters rated 'the only place worth a visit'.
Off the slopes Samoëns offers quite a range of activities. Snowmobiling up at Samoëns 1600 is wilder than is usual in the Alps. A reader recommends the snowshoeing. There is an outdoor, covered ice rink, hosting regular hockey matches, and a new sports and cultural centre.

Serre-Chevalier

Villages that are an odd mixture of ancient and modern sit beneath an extensive and varied mountain – with lots of woodland runs

COSTS

①②③ ④ ⑤ ⑥

RATINGS

The slopes
Fast lifts	**
Snow	***
Extent	****
Expert	***
Intermediate	****
Beginner	****
Convenience	***
Queues	***
Mountain restaurants	***

The rest
Scenery	***
Resort charm	***
Off-slope	***

KEY FACTS

Resort	1200-1500m
	3,940-4,920ft
Slopes	1200-2735m
	3,940-8,970ft
Lifts	68
Pistes	250km
	155 miles
Green	22%
Blue	28%
Red	37%
Black	13%
Snowmaking	
	over 30% of pistes

- ➕ Big, varied mountain
- ➕ Lots of good woodland runs
- ➕ One of the few big French areas based on old villages with character
- ➕ Good-value and atmospheric old hotels, restaurants and chalets
- ➕ New upscale hotel in Chantemerle

- ➖ Crowds/queues in French holidays
- ➖ Still too many slow, old lifts – including some vicious drags
- ➖ Busy road runs through the villages
- ➖ A lot of indiscriminate new building took place in the 1960s and 70s
- ➖ Limited nightlife

Serre-Chevalier is one of the few French resorts offering the ambience you might look for on a summer holiday – a sort of Provence in the snow, with lots of small, family-run hotels and restaurants in old stone buildings (though the immediate impression is of insensitive development along the main road).

The excellent, varied slopes are split into different segments, so you get a sensation of travel. What really sets the area apart from the French norm is the quantity of sheltered woodland runs – though there are open bowls, too.

Great strides are being made in bringing the lift system up to date, and upmarket accommodation is starting to appear. Who knows? Maybe Serre-Chevalier is at last going to make an impact on the international market.

THE RESORT

The resort is made up of a string of 13 villages set on a valley floor running roughly north-west to south-east, below the north-east-facing slopes of the mountain range that gives the resort its name. From the north-west – coming over the Col du Lautaret from Grenoble – the three main villages are Le Monêtier (or Serre-Che 1500), Villeneuve (1400) and Chantemerle (1350), spread over a distance of 8km/5 miles. Finally, at the extreme south-eastern end of the mountain, is Briançon (1200) – not a village but a town (the highest in France). Some of the nine smaller villages give their names to the communes: Villeneuve is in the commune of La Salle les Alpes, for example. Confusing.

Serre-Chevalier is not a smart resort, in any sense. Although each of its parts is based on a simple old village, there is a lot of more modern development, which ranges from brash to brutal, and even the older parts are roughly rustic rather than chocolate-box pretty. (A ban on corrugated iron roofs would help.) Because the resort is so spread out, the impact of cars and buses is difficult to escape, even if you're able to manage without them yourself. But when blanketed by snow the older villages and hamlets do have an unpretentious charm, and we find the place as a whole easy to like. Every year reporters stress how friendly and welcoming the locals are – hardly the norm in France.

There are few luxury hotels or notably swanky restaurants, though a new 4-star, Best Western Premier hotel in Chantemerle, is due to open this year (see feature panel). On the other hand, there are more hotels in the modestly priced Logis de France 'club' here than in any other ski resort. This

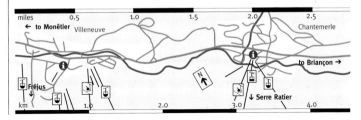

accommodation is across the main
road – 'quite a long walk from the
lifts', says a weary visitor.

At the top of the valley, **Le Monêtier**
has one main access lift – a fast quad
chair to mid-mountain, reached from
the village by bus or a 10-minute walk
(downhill in the morning, uphill at the
end of the day and tricky when ice is
around, though you can leave your
boots at the lift base). Le Monêtier is
the smallest, quietest and most
unspoiled of the main villages, with a
Provençal feel to its narrow streets
and little squares, and new building
which is mostly in sympathetic style.
Sadly, the road to Grenoble, which
skirts the other villages, bisects Le
Monêtier; pedestrians stroll about
hoping the cars will avoid them.

Briançon has a gondola from the
town to mid-mountain and on almost
to the top. The area around the lift
station has a wide selection of modern
shops, bars, restaurants, hotels, and a
casino, but no character. In contrast,
the 17th-century fortified upper quarter
is a delight, with narrow cobbled
streets and traditional restaurants,
auberges and patisseries; it has just
been made a UNESCO World Heritage
Site. Great views from the top, too.

Ski-buses, covered on the free
guest card and all lift passes, circulate
around each village and link all the
villages and lift bases along the valley.
But they finish quite early, to the
annoyance of some reporters (the local
navettes stop soon after the lifts
close, and the valley buses at
approximately 7pm), and a couple of
reporters have found the service
inadequate; taxis aren't cheap.

A six-day area pass (or rather your
receipt) covers a day in each of Les
Deux-Alpes, Alpe-d'Huez, Puy-St-
Vincent and the Milky Way. All of these
outings are possible by bus, but are
easier by car. The road from Grenoble
and Lyon goes over the Col du
Lautaret, which may require chains
and is very occasionally closed.

is a family resort, which fills up (even
more than most others) with French
children in the February/March school
holidays. Be warned (see introduction
to France chapter for 2009 dates).

The heart of the resort is
Villeneuve, which has two gondolas
and a fast quad chair going up to
widely separated points at mid-
mountain. The central area of new
development near the lifts is brutal
and charmless. But not far away is the
peaceful hamlet of Le Bez, which has a
third gondola, and across the valley is
the old village of Villeneuve, its quiet
main street lined by cosy bars, hotels
and restaurants.

Chantemerle, not far down the
valley, gives access to opposite ends
of the mid-mountain plateau of Serre
Ratier via a gondola and a cable car,
both with second stages above.
Chantemerle has some tasteless
modern buildings in the centre and
along the main road. The old sector is
a couple of minutes' walk from the
lifts, with a lovely church and most of
the small hotels, restaurants, bars and
nightlife. However, a lot of

THE MOUNTAINS

Trees cover almost two-thirds of the
mountain, providing some of France's
best bad-weather terrain (we once had
a great day here when all the upper
lifts were closed by high winds). The
Serre-Chevalier massif is not notably
dramatic, but from the peaks there are
fine views of the Ecrins massif.

boarding

For 2008/09 a smart new thermal spa with pools, saunas etc will open in Le Monêtier. And the resort's first 4-star hotel, the Best Western Premier, will open in Chantemerle, with 51 rooms and suites (see feature panel).

For 2007/08 a six-pack replaced two draglifts at Serre-Ratier above Chantemerle. Snowmaking was further extended and over 30% of the pistes are now covered. A new fenced-off beginners' ski area opened at the top of the Aravet gondola in Villeneuve. New piste signage was installed and the piste map was altered to tie in with it.

The term 'natural playground' could have quite easily been coined in Serre-Chevalier. The slopes are littered with natural obstacles that seem made for confident snowboarders. Try the Cucumelle slope and the areas around the Rocher Blanc lift at Prorel for such terrain. For beginners and intermediates the many draglifts can be a problem, as can the flat areas – one reporter's group stayed mostly in the Chantemerle sector, simply because they could cover a lot of ground using major chairlifts. Generation Snow in Chantemerle is a school that offers all sorts of courses from beginners' lessons to advanced freestyle courses.

A piste map now ties in with new piste signposting. Piste classification is unreliable – many reds, in particular, could be classified blue, but there are occasional stiff blues, too.

THE SLOPES
Interestingly varied and pretty
Serre-Chevalier's 250km/155 miles of pistes are spread across four main sectors above the four main villages. The sector above **Villeneuve** is the most extensive, reaching back a good way into the mountains and spreading over four or five identifiable bowls. The main mid-station is Fréjus. This sector is linked to the slightly smaller **Chantemerle** sector. The link from Chantemerle to **Briançon** is over a high, exposed col via a six-pack. The link between Villeneuve and **Le Monêtier** is liable to closure by high winds or avalanche danger. Travelling from here towards Villeneuve is a slow business – and it involves a red run, so timid intermediates may prefer to use the bus.

TERRAIN PARKS
Fully featured
Legendary French ripper Guillaume Chastagnol and the Serre Che Brigade have been building the freestyle infrastructure here for several years, trying to improve the terrain park. The park is situated on the Forêt chairlift, above Villeneuve. It incorporates 20 different features for all levels, including ramps, step-ups, rails and kickers. Improvements in the 2007/08 season included new beginner ride-on rails and a tree trunk jib on the expert line. A lot of work went into shaping the earth over the summer for better jumps, come the snowfall. A new boardercross course has been shaped at Grand Alpe, above Chantemerle – 'good, fast and flowing' says a 2008 visitor. There's also a half-pipe at the bottom of the Aravet gondola in Villeneuve.

SNOW RELIABILITY
Good – especially upper slopes
Most slopes face north or north-east and so hold snow well, especially high up (there are lots of lifts starting above 2000m/6,560ft). The weather pattern is different from that of the northern Alps and even that of Les Deux-Alpes or Alpe-d'Huez, only a few miles to the west. Serre-Che can get good snow when there is a shortage elsewhere, and vice versa.

Snowmaking covers over 30% of the pistes, including long runs down to each village. Piste grooming is generally excellent.

FOR EXPERTS
Deep, not notably steep
There is plenty to amuse experts – except those wanting extreme steeps.

The broad black runs down to Villeneuve and Chantemerle are only just black in steepness, but they are fine runs with their gradient sustained over an impressive vertical of around 800m/2,620ft. One or the other may be closed for days on end for racing or training. The rather neglected Tabuc run, sweeping around the mountain away from the lifts to Le Monêtier, has a couple of genuinely steep pitches but is mainly a cruise; it makes a fine end to the day. For moguls, look higher up the mountain to the steeper slopes served by the two top lifts above Le Monêtier and the three above Villeneuve. The runs beside these lifts – on and off-piste – form a great playground in good snow; the slope under the Yret chair is steep and shady. The more roundabout Isolée black is a reader's favourite – 'scenic and challenging' after a rather scary ridge start.

There are huge amounts of off-piste terrain throughout the area – both high-up and in the trees above Villeneuve and Chantemerle. Last season we enjoyed the La Voie Jackson run above Le Monêtier, which includes

Grand Serre-Che

Age	1-day	6-day
Prices in €		
under 12	29	140
12 to 64	38	181
over 65	29	140

Free under 6, over 75
Beginner limited pass in each area: eg Villeneuve €14

Notes
Covers all lifts in Briançon, Chantemerle, Villeneuve and Le Monêtier; 6 days or more passes give one day in each of Les Deux-Alpes, Alpe-d'Huez, Puy-St-Vincent and Voie Lactée (Milky Way); reductions for families

Alternative passes
Individual areas of Serre-Chevalier

a short climb between rocks to a deserted open bowl. There are plenty of more serious off-piste expeditions, including: Tête de Grand Pré to Villeneuve (a climb from Cucumelle); off the back of L'Eychauda to Puy-St-André (isolated, beautiful, taxi ride home); L'Yret to Le Monêtier via Vallon de la Montagnolle; Tabuc (steep at the start, very beautiful). The experts' Mecca of La Grave is nearby.

FOR INTERMEDIATES
Ski wherever you like

Serre-Chevalier's slopes ideally suit intermediates, who can buzz around without worrying about nasty surprises on the way. On the trail map red runs far outnumber blues – but most reds are at the easy end of the scale and the grooming is usually good, so even nervous intermediates shouldn't have problems with them. The broad, open bowls above Grande Alpe and Fréjus offer lots of options.

There's plenty for more adventurous intermediates, though. Many runs are wide enough for a fast pace. Cucumelle on the edge of the Villeneuve sector is a beautiful long red, away from the lifts. The red runs off the little-used Aiguillette chair in the Chantemerle sector are worth seeking out – quiet, enjoyable fast cruises. Other favourites include Aya and Clos Galliard at Le Monêtier, and the wonderful long run from the top to the bottom of the gondola at Briançon (with great views of the town).

If the reds are starting to seem a bit tame, there is plenty more to progress to. Unless ice towards the bottom is a problem, the (often well-groomed) blacks on the lower mountain should be first on the agenda, and the bumpier ones higher up can be tackled if snow is good.

FOR BEGINNERS
All four areas OK

All four sectors have nursery areas (at Chantemerle the area is small, and you

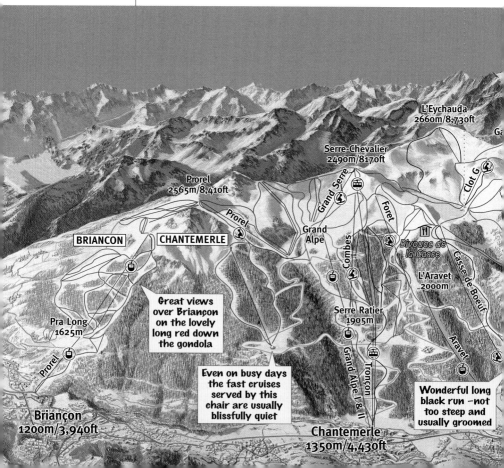

L'Eychauda
2660m/8,730ft

Serre-Chevalier
2490m/8170ft

Prorel
2565m/8,410ft

Clot G

Grand Serre

Foret

Prorel

BRIANCON

CHANTEMERLE

Grand Alpe

Combes

Bivouac de la Casse

L'Aravet
2000m

Prorel

Pra Long
1625m

Great views over Briançon on the lovely long red down the gondola

Serre Ratier
1905m

Casse de Boeuf

Aravet

Prorel

Even on busy days the fast cruises served by this chair are usually blissfully quiet

Tronçon

Grand Alpe I & II

Wonderful long black run – not too steep and usually groomed

Briançon
1200m/3,940ft

Chantemerle
1350m/4,430ft

SCHOOLS

ESF In all centres
t 0492 241741
Génération Snow
(Chantemerle)
t 0492 242151
Evasion (Chantemerle)
t 0492 240241
Buissonnière
(Villeneuve)
t 0492 247866
EurekaSki
t 0679 462484
Axesse (Villeneuve)
t 0662 765354
Altitude (Villeneuve)
t 0608 025182
Internationale
(Le Monêtier)
t 0683 670642

Classes (ESF prices)
6 half days from €108
Private lessons
From €37 for 1hr

generally go up to Serre Ratier or Grand Alpe – both rated as good by a beginner reporter) and there are some easy high runs to progress to. Villeneuve has excellent green runs above Fréjus.

Both Chantemerle and Villeneuve have green paths down from mid-mountain that are narrow, and not enjoyable when the runs become hard and others are speeding past. Le Monêtier's easy runs are at resort level, next to excellent nursery slopes, which beginners have recommended for 'better snow and fewer people'. But progression to long runs here isn't so easy, and the link to Villeneuve involves the red Cucumelle run.

FOR CROSS-COUNTRY
Excellent if the snow is good
There are 35km/22 miles of tracks along the valley floor, mainly following the gurgling river between Le Monêtier and Villeneuve and going on up towards the Col du Lautaret.

QUEUES
Investment at last
A range of big lifts means there are few problems getting out of the valley. But the many old, slow lifts at altitude still cause queues, as well as slowing down the whole process of exploration. New six-packs have helped, but more are needed. Bottlenecks include the slow and unreliable Balme chair on the way to Le Monêtier, the Fréjus chair above the Pontillas gondola and the Crètes draglift it links with.

More than most resorts, Serre-Chevalier seems to fill up with French families in the February holidays, producing serious mid-mountain queues, especially in the central sectors. The lower slopes above Chantemerle, in particular, can get hideously crowded – head for the Aiguillette chair in these circumstances (see 'For intermediates').

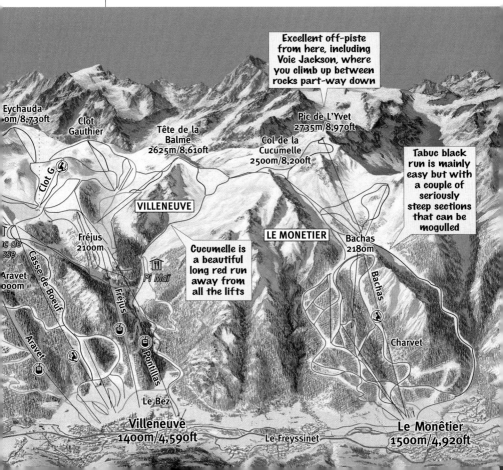

Excellent off-piste from here, including Voie Jackson, where you climb up between rocks part-way down

Eychauda om/8,73oft

Clot Gauthier

Tête de la Balme 2625m/8,61oft

Pic de L'Yvet 2735m/8,97oft

Col de la Cucumelle 2500m/8,200ft

Tabuc black run is mainly easy but with a couple of seriously steep sections that can be mogulled

Clot G

VILLENEUVE

LE MONETIER

Bachas 2180m

c de sse

Fréjus 2100m

Casse de Boeuf

Pi Maï

Cucumelle is a beautiful long red run away from all the lifts

Bachas

Aravet ooom

Fréjus

Charvet

Aravet

Pontillas

Le Bez

Villeneuve 1400m/4,59oft

Le Freyssinet

Le Monêtier 1500m/4,92oft

MOUNTAIN RESTAURANTS
Some good places

Mountain restaurants are quite well distributed (and, usefully, marked clearly on the piste map).

Editors' choice Just above the Casse du Boeuf quad, the Bivouac de la Casse (0492 248772) is an attractive chalet with both self- and table-service (inside and out). We were mightily impressed by both the food and service – even our rejection of a wine was handled superbly. Several 2008 reporters found the 'food excellent'. Pi Maï (0492 248363) in the hamlet of Fréjus (so not easy to get to) is a fine retreat on a bad day, with excellent food such as 'steaks cooked over a log fire' but expensive.

Worth knowing about The Echaillon, just below the Bivouac, is a lofty chalet with open fire and a table-service section doing 'good-value mountain dishes'. The Fermière, just below the Fréjus chair top station, is 'basic but good value', with lengthy queues for food at times and the 'worst toilets ever'. The Bercail, at the top of the Aravet lift, is a 'good relaxed place'. In the Chantemerle sector, the busy Soleil pleases reporters – 'sun trap', 'excellent food for good prices'. The Relais de Ratier is said to be 'cheaper than elsewhere' and the food is praised. We had a good lunch at the chalet hotel Serre Ratier. The Grand Alpe is spacious, and also 'a bit cheaper than some others'.

In the Briançon sector, the 'attractive' Pra Long chalet at the gondola mid-station has good views, and food in both table- and self-service sections is 'excellent'. The little Chalet de Serre Blanc, just down from the top of Prorel, has great views and has 'good hot chocolate'.

Above Le Monêtier the choice is between the self-service Bachas at mid-mountain ('good value – prices don't seem to have changed in three years') and the cosy, friendly Peyra Juana ('surprisingly good wholesome food') much lower down. Both get packed on bad-weather days.

SCHOOLS AND GUIDES
Nearly all good

EurekaSki, British-run by BASI Alpine Trainer Gavin Crosby, gets consistently good reports every year. A 2008 visitor says, 'My 14-year-old nephew in his second week made a huge amount of

CHILDREN

Les Schtroumpfs
t 0492 247095
Ages 6mnth upwards;
9am-5pm

Les Poussins
t 0492 240343
Ages 8mnth upwards;
8.45-5pm

Les Eterlous
t 0492 244575
Ages 18mnth to 6yr
(6mnth to 6yr out of
school holidays);
9am-5pm

Ski school
Snow gardens for
ages 3 to 5; from age
7 children can join ski
school classes (ESF 6
half-days €95)

progress. My beginner parents (aged 68 and 70) were challenged without being scared.' Another couple 'learnt a lot' in their first ventures off-piste. Classes with a maximum size of six (for adults and children) range from beginner to off-piste adventure. Gavin also offers 'Explore Serre-Chevalier' days, which take in as much terrain as possible with instructional tips and lift priority, for £40 per person per day.

We have received a number of reports on the Ecole de Ski Buissonnière over the years – most of them full of praise ('I learnt 10 times more because of the personal service,' says a 2008 reporter), but in the past we have had a distressing report of early-intermediate boarders being put with a couple of experts. Two absolute beginners in a 2008 visitor's group were 'satisfied' with their snowboard lessons with Generation Snow.

We lack recent reports of group classes with the ESF. 'Children's classes seemed to have two instructors,' observed one February reporter. But another saw 'tiny kids in groups of 12 to 13 with one instructor'. Private lessons have been praised for 'good, supportive instructors, with a sense of

humour'. The Internationale school 'gave the impression of being rather more professional than the ESF', and one reporter saw 'small groups of five to six children maximum'.

We have had great mornings skiing off-piste with Bertrand Collet of Axesse school (which specialises in off-piste and advanced techniques) and the ESF. And we had a great day touring the area (in bad visibility) with Gavin Crosby of Eureka.

FACILITIES FOR CHILDREN
Facilities at each village
The Ecole de Ski Buissonnière has been praised in the past, and Les Schtroumpfs in Villeneuve was 'brilliant, and the baby loved it'.

STAYING THERE

HOW TO GO
A good choice of packages
There's a wide choice of packages from UK tour operators.
Chalets Several operators offer chalets. Hannibals' Marmottes is a well renovated old farmhouse in old Chantemerle, all en suite. Chez Bear (0492 211170) is a wonderful

GETTING THERE

Air Turin 108km/
67 miles (1½hr);
Grenoble 92km/
57 miles (2hr); Lyon
208km/129 miles
(3hr)

Rail Briançon (6km/
4 miles); regular
buses from station

ACTIVITIES

Indoor Swimming
pools, sauna, fitness
centres, thermal
baths, cinemas,
libraries

Outdoor Ice rinks,
paragliding, cleared
paths, snowshoeing,
snowmobiling, ice
driving, ice climbing,
sleigh rides,
snowkites, skijoring,
horse riding

SMART LODGINGS

Check out our feature
chapters at the front
of the book.

conversion of an 18th-century
farmhouse into a luxury chalet for 10 –
remotely set above Briançon, but the
owners will ferry you around. Ski-In
has a newly renovated self-catered
chalet in Villeneuve.

Hotels One of the features of this
string of little villages is the range of
attractive family-run hotels – many of
them members of Logis de France.

LE MONETIER

***Auberge de Choucas** (0492
244273) Smart but small wood-clad
rooms. 'Excellent, seven-course
dinners in stone-vaulted restaurant.'
We enjoyed staying there in 2008.
****Europe** (0492 244003) Simple well-
run Logis in heart of old village, with
pleasant bar and 'very good' food.
****Alliey** (0492 244002) 'Excellent
rooms with an indoor/outdoor spa.'
Good restaurant.
***Rif Blanc** (0492 244135) Good value,
family-run, friendly, refurbished hotel.
Popular bar.

VILLENEUVE

***Christiania** (0492 247633) Civilised,
family-run hotel on main road,
crammed with ornaments.
***Cimotel** (0492 247822) Modern and
charmless, with good-sized rooms and
'excellent' food.
****Vieille Ferme** (0492 247644) Stylish
conversion on the edge of the village.
***Chatelas** (0492 247474) Prettily
decorated simple chalet by river in old
part of town.

CHANTEMERLE

****Best Western Premier** (0820
204305) Upscale, 300m/980ft from the
lifts, indoor/outdoor pool (see feature
panel).
***Plein Sud** (0492 241701) Modern;
pool, sauna; 'superbly run by a Brit'.
****Grand** (0492 241516) Right by the
lifts; 85 varied rooms.
****Boule de Neige** (0492 240016) In
the old centre. 'Good food,
comfortable and friendly.'
***Ricelle** (0492 240019) Charming, but
across the valley from the slopes in
Villard-Laté. Good food.
Apartments The Hameau du Rocher
Blanc, by the slopes in Chantemerle
(pool, gym, sauna, steam), is a cut
above what was on offer before. A new
4-star Résidence Arts et Vie with 40
apartments and 10 chalets is due in Le
Monêtier for 2008/09. The hotel Alliey
in Le Monêtier has apartments too.
Ski-In has a newly renovated self-
catered chalet and apartment, both in
Villeneuve.

EATING OUT
Unpretentious and traditional

In Le Monêtier, there are several good
hotel-based options. At the upper end,
the Maison Alliey (hotel Alliey) has a
good reputation and we had an
excellent dinner at the Auberge du
Choucas last season. The Europe has
reliable cooking at more modest
prices. The Boîte à Fromages has been
recommended and Brasera is a 'good'
pizzeria. The Kawa and the Belote are
recommended for 'cosy atmosphere,
good staff and excellent value'.

In Villeneuve the Swedish-run
Vieille Ferme is a 'great, stylish eating
place'. The Frog is 'better than its
name suggests'. The Marotte, a tiny
stone building with classic French
cuisine in the old part of Villeneuve,
'offers a wide choice of very good
food at very reasonable prices'. The
Refuge specialises in fondue and
raclette. And there are good crêperies

LUXURY COMES TO SERRE-CHEVALIER

*This season Serre-Chevalier will see its first 4-star hotel open, the Best Western Premier in
Chantemerle, just 300m/980ft from the lifts. All 51 rooms and suites have a fully fitted kitchen,
flat-screen TV with international channels, and balcony. Facilities include a bar, restaurant, indoor/
outdoor pool, sauna, business centre, underground parking, washing and drying facilities, and Wi-Fi
internet access throughout. There is also a ski room with lockers and boot dryers. With more than
4,000 hotels, Best Western is the world's largest hotel marketing chain. Each hotel is individually
owned and run and has to meet certain standards to be able to join the Best Western group. Best
Western Premier hotels have to meet even higher standards and offer extra facilities.*

↑ Serre Ratier above Chantemerle has a good choice of places for lunch
SNOWPIX.COM / CHRIS GILL

UK PACKAGES

Action Outdoors, Alpine Answers, Alpsholiday, AmeriCan Ski, Chalet Group, Club Med, Crystal, Equity, Erna Low, First Choice, Hannibals, Independent Ski Links, Interactive Resorts, Interhome, Lagrange, Neilson, Peak Retreats, Rocketski, Ski Activity, Ski Expectations, Ski France, Skifrance4less, Skiholidayextras.com, Ski-in.co.uk, Ski Independence, Ski Leisure Direction, Ski Miquel, Skitopia, Skitracer, Snow Finders, Thomson
Briançon BoardnLodge, Ski Leisure Direction

Phone numbers
From abroad use the prefix +33 and omit the initial '0' of the phone number

TOURIST OFFICE

t 0492 249898
contact@
ot-serrechevalier.fr
www.serre-chevalier.
com

– try the Manouille. Over in Le Bez, the Bidule is said to have 'first-class food and service, at good value' and is recommended by locals. The Ours Blanc and Passé Simple ('terrific pizzeria') have been recommended.

In Chantemerle, we had delicious warm foie gras in cider vinegar and jugged wild boar at the unpretentious Loup Blanc last season. Arbre à Pain ('cheap and cheerful', 'excellent tartiflette'), Petit Chalet ('charming and friendly'), Bistro, Cabassa and Batchi have been recommended by reporters.

In Briançon, the Club, Origan, Esperance ('great pizzas') and Péché Gourmand ('excellent value') meet with approval.

APRES-SKI
Quiet streets and few bars
Nightlife seems to revolve around bars, scattered through the various villages, and several reporters complain that the resort is too quiet.

In Le Monêtier the British-run Alpen has a happy hour, free nibbles and welcoming staff; the bar at the hotel Rif Blanc is popular, and the Que Tal warms up later on. In Villeneuve, Loco Loco in the old village was reportedly 'the place to go, with funky music and a French atmosphere'; but another visitor took a dim view, reporting 'tedious music and high prices'. The Frog has 'good local beer', and the Grotte du Yeti has live music and is for 'serious fun seekers' and does 'great vin chaud'. In Chantemerle the Kitz shows sporting events on TV and 'does good pizzas'. The other Chantemerle bars to look out for are

the Taverne de la Bière, the Xtreme bar and the Triptyque (described as 'popular and trendy').

In Briançon, the Auberge Mont Prorel, right by the gondola base, had live music and was full of Brits and Danes rounding off their day when we paid a teatime visit.

OFF THE SLOPES
Try the hot baths
The old town of Briançon is well worth a visit. There is a leisure complex with pools, sauna, hot tub and steam room. Briançon also has an ice hockey team – their games make 'a good night out', says one reporter. In Le Monêtier the thermal bath has been redeveloped into a large spa complex, Les Grands Bains, with indoor and outdoor pools, saunas, steam rooms and a waterfall (some areas only for the over-18s), which opened in summer 2008. The hotel Alliey has a pool and spa. There is a public swimming pool and health spa near the hotel Sporting in Villeneuve. Each of the main villages has a cinema. Chantemerle, Villeneuve and Briançon have ice rinks, and there is good walking on 'well-prepared trails'. You can also learn to drive a piste grooming machine.

STAYING UP THE MOUNTAIN
Worth considering
Pi Maï (0492 248363) above Villeneuve and the chalet hotel Serre Ratier (0492 205288) above Chantemerle have rooms (see also 'Mountain restaurants').

Ste-Foy-Tarentaise

Tasteful, modern mini-resort appealing to families and experts – and to motorists as a base for expeditions to nearby mega-resorts

COSTS

① ② ③ ④ ⑤ ⑥

RATINGS

The slopes

Fast lifts	**
Snow	***
Extent	*
Expert	****
Intermediate	***
Beginner	**
Convenience	***
Queues	*****
Mountain restaurants	**

The rest

Scenery	***
Resort charm	***
Off-slope	*

NEWS

The fast Marquise six-pack was installed for 2006/07, on the upper slopes to the east of the resort's main area, along with a new blue run. A new red run is planned here in the future.

For 2007/08 snowmaking was increased at resort level – more is planned higher up the mountain in the next couple of seasons.

+ Safe untracked powder within the lift system, and epic runs outside it

+ Cheap lift pass and good quality and good-value lodging

+ Quiet, good for families, but ...

– Too quiet for many other visitors

– Very limited piste network

– Mainly slow chairlifts

– Lack of good long green runs on the higher slopes

Ste-Foy is a small, attractive, unpretentious resort built in the last few years, at the foot of what started life as a cult off-piste mountain. It remains excellent for experts but is now very attractive for families too. But the extent of the pistes is tiny and keen piste-bashers will want to travel to big resorts nearby.

THE RESORT

Ste-Foy itself is a village straddling the busy road up from Bourg-St-Maurice to Val d'Isère. Its slopes start at Ste-Foy-Station (sometimes called Bonconseil), set 4km/2.5 miles off the main road up to Val d'Isère. Ste-Foy-Station is a complete resort in miniature, with a limited choice of bars and restaurants, a small supermarket and a newsagent; these are surrounded by a growing cluster of chalets and chalet-style apartment blocks, all in the traditional Savoyard style of wood and stone.

You can also stay down the hill in Ste-Foy village or other local hamlets; there are free but infrequent buses. With a car you can make the most of some excellent nearby restaurants and explore other nearby resorts – Val d'Isère, Tignes, Les Arcs, La Plagne and La Rosière. You can have a day at each for around 22 euros a time with a Ste-Foy five-day pass.

THE MOUNTAIN

There is an attractive mix of wooded slopes above the village and open slopes higher up.

Slopes The slow quad from the village takes you up to a tiny mid-mountain station at Plan Bois. A second goes on to the treeline, and a third to Col de l'Aiguille accesses almost 600m/1,970ft of vertical above the treeline. The two black runs from this chair form the basis of two special off-piste zones; the piste map shows these but does not explain them – we're told they are avalanche controlled. Slightly further down the hill is another such zone, less steep. The two lower chairs serve a few pleasant runs through trees and back to the base station. A six-pack opened to the east of the main area a couple of seasons ago, along with a new blue run. A new red run is also planned, probably for 2009/10. Most reporters have been amazed by the off-piste terrain the few lifts access: 'The map gives no indication of the variety of options,' said one. But don't expect miles of groomed pistes.

Terrain parks There isn't one. But in the lower off-piste zone mentioned above you are encouraged to build your own features.

Snow reliability The slopes face north or west. Snow reliability is good on the former but can suffer on the latter, especially as there is snowmaking only on the run down to the resort.

Experts Experts can have great fun on and between Ste-Foy's black and red runs, exploring lots of easily accessible off-piste and trees, including the special zones mentioned above. The lack of crowds means you can still make fresh tracks days after a storm.

379

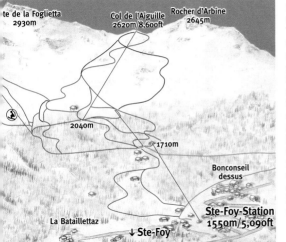

te de la Foglietta
2930m

Col de l'Aiguille
2620m/8,600ft

Rocher d'Arbine
2645m

2040m

1710m

Bonconseil dessus

Ste-Foy-Station
1550m/5,090ft

La Bataillettaz

↓ Ste-Foy

The main attraction of Ste-Foy's slopes for experts and adventurous intermediates is the extensive off-piste →

KEY FACTS

Resort	1550m
	5,090ft
Slopes	1550-2620m
	5,090-8,600ft
Lifts	5
Pistes	35km
	22 miles
Green	6%
Blue	24%
Red	47%
Black	23%
Snowmaking	Minimal

peak retreats

Beat the crowds
Traditional resorts

0844 576 0173
peakretreats.co.uk
ABTA W5537

UK PACKAGES

Phone numbers
From abroad use the prefix +33 and omit the initial '0' of the phone number

TOURIST OFFICE

t 0479 069519
info@saintefoy.net
www.saintefoy.net

There's more serious off-piste on offer too, for which you need a guide. There are wonderful runs from the top of the lifts down through deserted old villages, either to the road up to Val d'Isère or back to the base, and a splendid route which takes you through trees and over a stream down to the tiny village of Le Crot. The new six-pack has made the lower part of this more accessible; previously it involved a hike up to the Pointe de la Foglietta (which still gives a longer run). The ESF runs group off-piste trips, with transport back to base from the village of Le Miroir, where the route ends. There's also a Bureau des Guides, which can arrange heli-skiing in Italy, including a route which also brings you back to Le Miroir.

Intermediates Intermediates can enjoy 900m/2,950ft vertical of uncrowded reds and blues on the upper slopes, and worthwhile descents to the village when conditions are good. The red from the Col de l'Aiguille is a superb test for confident intermediates, who would also be up to the off-piste routes, especially the Monal route back to base. Anyone not wanting to try off-piste will tire of the limited runs in a day or two and be itching to get to Val d'Isère or Les Arcs.

Beginners Not the best place, but there have been improvements at the base, including a children's area near the ski school, and a moving carpet lift on the small nursery slope. After that you can progress to a long green run off the first chair and then gentle blues higher up.

Snowboarding Great freeriding terrain, with lots of trees and powder between the pistes to play in, plus a dedicated freestyle area for building kickers.

Cross-country No prepared trails.

Queues Except in peak season and on fresh powder days, despite all the new building and slow lifts, reporters have still failed to find queues at Ste-Foy.

Mountain restaurants There are two rustic restaurants at Plan Bois; they are tiny and get over busy. Les Brevettes ('friendly and lively', 'good omelettes') has the edge over Chez Léon. Many people head back to the base, where the Maison à Colonnes gets consistently good reports.

Schools and guides We've had good reports of the ESF, especially for children (from age four). K Spirit opened here last season.

Facilities for children Les P'tits Trappeurs takes children from age three to 11. UK tour operator Première Neige also runs a nursery.

STAYING THERE

How to go Plenty of small tour operators can organise accommodation here.

Hotels Auberge sur la Montagne (0479 069583), just above the turn-off at La Thuile, Ferme du Baptieu (0479 069752) and the smartly refurbished Monal (0479 069007) in Ste-Foy village have good reputations.

Chalets and apartments Première Neige has lots of chalets and apartments here, with catered and self-catered options. Peak Retreats offers Les Fermes de Ste-Foy, with pool, hot tub, sauna, steam, fitness.

Eating out In Ste-Foy-Station the central Bergerie is traditionally styled in wood and stone and does excellent food. The Maison à Colonnes is 'simple and good', especially for traditional Savoyard dishes. Chez Alison offers simple fare. In the village of Le Miroir, Chez Mérie is excellent (for lunch as well as dinner). So is the Auberge sur la Montagne. A regular reporter says the hotel Monal in Ste-Foy village has 'the best restaurant this Francophile has ever eaten in'.

Après-ski Pretty quiet. Reporters enjoyed the Iceberg piano bar. The Pitchouli is the place to go for a drink later on. The bar of the hotel Monal can get busy, too, and tastings are held in the new wine bar there.

Off the slopes There's not a lot to do off the slopes, but paragliding, dog sledding and snowshoeing are available. The excellent pool and spa at the Balcons de Ste-Foy apartments are open to non-residents for a fee.

SNOWPIX.COM / CHRIS GILL

St-Martin-de-Belleville

Explore the Three Valleys from a traditional old village – and so avoid the Méribel crowds who descend on it for lunch

381

COSTS

① ② ③ ④ ⑤ ⑥

RATINGS

The slopes
Fast lifts	★★★
Snow	★★★
Extent	★★★★★
Expert	★★★★
Intermediate	★★★★★
Beginner	★★
Convenience	★★★
Queues	★★★★
Mountain restaurants	★★★★

The rest
Scenery	★★★
Resort charm	★★★★
Off-slope	★

KEY FACTS

Resort	1400m
	4,590ft

Three Valleys	
Slopes	1260-3230m
	4,130-10,600ft
Lifts	180
Pistes	600km
	373 miles
Green	15%
Blue	38%
Red	37%
Black	10%
Snowmaking	
	33%

Les Menuires / St-Martin only	
Slopes	1400-2850m
	4,590-9,350ft
Lifts	36
Pistes	160km
	99 miles
Green	8%
Blue	42%
Red	40%
Black	10%
Snowmaking	45%

NEWS

For 2008/09 snowmaking will be installed on the Gros Tougne piste.

For 2007/08 the Bouitte in St-Marcel was awarded its second Michelin star.

+ Attractively developed traditional village with pretty church

+ Easy access to the whole of the extensive Three Valleys network

+ Long, easy intermediate runs on rolling local slopes

+ Extensive snowmaking keeps runs open in poor conditions, but ...

– Snow at resort level suffers from altitude, and sun in the afternoon

– No green runs for beginners to progress to

– The climb up from the lower part of the village can be taxing

– Limited après-ski

– Few off-slope diversions

St-Martin is a lived-in, unspoiled village with an old church (prettily lit at night), small square and buildings of wood and stone, a few miles down the valley from Les Menuires. As a quiet, inexpensive, attractive base for exploration of the Three Valleys as a whole, it's unbeatable.

THE RESORT

In 1950 St-Martin didn't even have running water or electricity. It remained a backwater until the 1980s, when chairlifts were built linking it to the slopes of Méribel and Les Menuires. The old village, set on a steep slope, has been developed, of course, but the new buildings fit in well, and it remains small – you can walk around it in a few minutes. The main feature remains the lovely old 16th-century church – prettily floodlit at night. There are some good local shops and few 'touristy' ones.

THE MOUNTAINS

The whole of the Three Valleys can easily be explored from here. The piste map for Les Menuires covers this area.
Slopes A gondola followed by a fast quad take you to a ridge from which you can access Méribel on one side and Les Menuires on the other.
Terrain parks There isn't a terrain park in the St-Martin sector, but you can get to those above Les Menuires and Méribel relatively easily.
Snow reliability The local slopes face west and get the full force of the afternoon sun, and the village is quite low. There is snowmaking from top to bottom of the main run to the village, and reporters agree that it is effective at keeping the run open. You can ride the gondola down if snow is poor.
Experts Locally there are large areas of gentle and often deserted off-piste. A reader recommends the descent from

Roc de Fer to the village of Béranger. Head to La Masse for steep slopes.
Intermediates The local slopes are pleasant blues and reds, mainly of interest to intermediates. One of our favourite runs in the Three Valleys is the long, rolling, wide Jerusalem red. The Verdet blue from the top of the Méribel lifts is a wonderful easy cruise with great views and is usually very quiet – though reporters say it is often closed for no apparent reason.
Beginners St-Martin is far from ideal – there's a small nursery slope but no long green runs to progress to. Note that the lift pass included in the beginners' package covers only the two lifts above St-Martin.
Snowboarding There is some great local off-piste freeriding available.
Cross-country There are 28km/17 miles of trails in the Belleville valley.
Queues St-Martin's popularity as a lunch destination often leads to serious queues in the afternoon for the chair to Tougnète, and a 2008 visitor says that there now seem to be queues for it all day.
Mountain restaurants There are three atmospheric old places on the run down to the village: Chardon Bleu ('friendly staff, lovely food'), Corbeleys at mid-mountain ('one of our favourites') and the Loy, lower down ('great food and atmosphere – never disappoints', 'the best steak and chips'). The Grand Lac at the bottom of the Granges chair is a favourite of a 2007 reporter.
Schools and guides Reports on ESF lessons are generally positive: a 2008

Weekly news updates and resort links at **www.wtss.co.uk**

UK PACKAGES

Alpine Club, Chalet Group, Crystal, Erna Low, First Choice, Independent Ski Links, Kaluma, Mountain Action, Oxford Ski Co, Peak Retreats, Ski Activity, Ski France, Skiholidayextras.com, Ski Independence, Ski l'Alpage, Ski Leisure Direction, Skitracer

SMART LODGINGS

Check out our feature chapters at the front of the book.

Phone numbers
From abroad use the prefix +33 and omit the initial '0' of the phone number

TOURIST OFFICE

t 0479 002000
stmartin@st-martin-belleville.com
www.st-martin-belleville.com

reporter found the group lessons 'very helpful', and friends who had several private lessons found them 'excellent'. **Facilities for children** The Piou Piou club at the ESF takes children from age two-and-a-half to five years. A list of babysitters is available.

STAYING THERE

How to go For a small village there's a good variety of accommodation.
Hotels The Alp Hôtel (0479 089282) is at the foot of the slope by the main lift; readers using the restaurant approve, but we lack reports on staying there. A recent visitor was 'made to feel very welcome' by the owners of the 'charming' Saint-Martin (0479 008800), right on the slope, and the Edelweiss (0479 089667) is in the village itself. All are 3-stars. The Bouitte restaurant (0479 089677) in St-Marcel (see 'Eating out') has three lovely rooms – spacious, woody and furnished with antiques – and two suites plus a spa that is open to the public.
Chalets The owners of Les Chalets de St Martin have finally retired after operating here since the first lift was built. The Brit-run Alpine Club – which isn't really a club – has two chalets with good food and service. Ferme de Belleville is a nicely renovated 400-year-old farmhouse in the heart of the old village; Maison de Belleville, overlooking the village, is newly built, spacious, light and airy. They run a minibus to and from the gondola.
Apartments The stylish CGH/MGM Chalets du Gypse is well placed beside the piste, with a smart pool.

Eating out For such a small village there is a good variety of restaurants. Readers still enjoy the Montagnard: 'great atmosphere', 'good food' are examples of this year's comments. The popular Voûte is 'the best all-rounder' with 'an extensive menu and reasonable prices'. Next door is the Petit Creux, for 'enormous and very fine pizzas, steaks and kebabs at good prices'. The Ferme de la Choumette, slightly out of the village, is a working farm – 'a little gem' doing 'very good food', says a 2008 reporter.

The Etoile des Neiges is a smart, traditionally French restaurant, recommended by a 2007 reporter.

We have had superb meals at the Bouitte up the road in St-Marcel, which got its second Michelin star in 2008. As a 2008 regular visitor says: 'It continues to be exceptional.' Two readers recommend the Ferme du Dahu in Villarbon 2km/1 mile down the valley (the owners will ferry you at no charge): 'extremely atmospheric', 'one of the best meals in years', 'grossly underpriced'.
Après-ski The Pourquoi Pas? is well patronised by British visitors; it has live music and is cosy with a roaring log fire and comfortable sofas. Brewski's has nightly entertainment and stays open till 2am. The Dahlia, at the bottom of the gondola, is 'popular for après-ski drinks'.
Off the slopes If you don't use the slopes, there are better places to base yourself. However, there are dog sledding and snowshoe trips, and there are also pleasant walks, a sports hall, a new museum and musical events in the church.

Les Sybelles

Chalk-and-cheese resorts linked rather tenuously by slow lifts to form an area that's one of the biggest in the Alps

➕ Extensive area of largely easy intermediate slopes and gentle, uncrowded off-piste

➕ Inexpensive by French standards

➕ Unusual mixture of stark, purpose-built resorts and old villages

➖ Lift network still painfully slow to get around, despite improvements

➖ Few pistes steep enough to interest adventurous intermediates

➖ Après-ski limited and quiet

➖ Mainly simple accommodation

➖ Few off-slope diversions

Les Sybelles is not a resort but a lift network linking a handful of little-known resorts in the Maurienne massif in the French Alps. When formed in 2003, Les Sybelles' 310km/193 miles of pistes put it straight into the big league, alongside such giants as Val d'Isère-Tignes.

Our first visit to the newly launched Les Sybelles gave us a bit of a shock; we had forgotten just how slow progress can be on a mountain with 70 slow lifts and just one fast one. Matters have since improved – there are now seven fast chairs. But Les Sybelles still languishes at the bottom of our fast-lift league table, with only one fast lift in ten. And installation of fast lifts out of the big resorts without similar improvements at altitude seems to create queue problems in peak season for the draglifts that form the links. So we still say: more six-packs, please.

The resorts are sharply contrasting in character. La Toussuire and Le Corbier are most politely described as modern, functional and downmarket, while St-Sorlin-d'Arves and St-Jean-d'Arves are largely unspoiled, traditional villages that are expanding tastefully and have attracted some major UK tour operators.

The links between the resorts are high – mostly over 2000m/6,560ft – so they are relatively snow-sure – though some slopes get a lot of sun and can suffer in late season. They are easily negotiated by adventurous intermediates, consisting of easy reds and tough blues (one or two of which might be better classified red). But getting from one resort to another can be slow going, because of slow lifts.

LE CORBIER 1550m/5,090ft

Le Corbier is centrally placed in the ski area, with direct links to St-Jean-d'Arves in one direction and La Toussuire in the other, as well as a high link to St-Sorlin.

THE RESORT

Designed in the 1960s, Le Corbier is a no-compromise functional resort. Most of its accommodation is in eight inner-city-style tower blocks – one as high as 19 storeys – with subterranean shops beneath. To our eye, it looks like a blot on the landscape. But it does accommodate its 9,000 visitors

efficiently in the minimum space, and in functional terms it is hard to criticise – it is compact, family-friendly and traffic-free with all ski-in/ski-out accommodation. The apartment blocks line the foot of the slopes, and in the other direction the resort's balcony setting gives good views over the valley. And newer buildings are now in traditional style. It sells itself firmly as a family resort and runs a French Family Championship with teams made up of mother, father and one child.

THE MOUNTAIN

Le Corbier's local ski area has 90km/ 56 miles of gentle pistes. Although the altitudes are modest – the top height is 2265m/7,430ft – there are hardly any trees.

Slopes The Sybelles Express, a six-seat fast chair, rises over 700m/2,300ft vertical to Pte du Corbier, from where pistes and lifts go along the ridge to the hub of Les Sybelles at Pte de L'Ouillon. Runs spread across a wide, north-east-facing mountainside return to the resort, and there are links at

KEY FACTS

Slopes	1100-2620m
	3,610-8,600ft
Lifts	83
Pistes	310km
	193 miles
Green	21%
Blue	39%
Red	35%
Black	5%
Snowmaking	
	233 guns

the extremities to La Toussuire and St-Jean-d'Arves.

Terrain park There's a park on the lower slopes just above the resort.

Snow reliability The mix of reasonable altitude and lack of crowds cutting up the pistes means the snow tends to stay in fairly good condition high up. There is snowmaking on all the main pistes back to the resort. The low connection from La Toussuire is a problem spot.

Experts The area lacks challenges – the one short black piste scarcely deserves a red classification. There are off-piste options in the valley between Le Corbier and La Toussuire.

Intermediates Le Corbier's gentle slopes are ideal cruising terrain, though the runs aren't very long and they rather lack variety.

Beginners There is an extensive nursery area with a moving carpet right in front of the resort, with gentle progression runs directly above.

Snowboarding The wide, open terrain is ideal for riders, as long as they don't want anything too challenging.

Cross-country There are narrow loops across the mountainside either side of the resort, one of which leads to La Toussuire and back. It's all a bit bleak.

Queues We have no reports of problems, but see introduction.

Mountain restaurants La Picoraille table-service restaurant, next to Le Yeti, has 'large portions at reasonable prices'. Le Charmun, at the foot of the Vadrouille area has been recommended for 'delicious crozets with wild mushrooms and lardons' and Chalet 2000 near the top has also been praised.

Schools One past reporter judged the ESF 'disdainful, uncaring, very disorganised; bad tuition'.

Facilities for children The Nursery takes children from six months. A reporter praised the ski kindergarten (for age three up): 'Nice, well-equipped ski-park; good instructors.' Its location up on the pistes means a bit of a hike.

STAYING THERE

How to go There are several UK operators selling packages here.

Chalets Equity Ski runs its own chalet hotel, described by one reporter as 'clean, comfortable and very good value' and approved by others, too.

Hotels None in resort.

Apartments Nearly all the accommodation here is in apartments. There's a central reservations system.

Eating out The Grillon, 3km/2 miles away in the Villarembert, makes a pleasant, rustic change from Le Corbier's tower blocks - and serves traditional French food.

Après ski Very quiet. The Equity Ski chalet-hotel bar is popular. Roches

Blanches restaurant in the centre includes a cosy bar area with an open fire. For dancing, the Président gets busy only at peak holiday periods. **Off the slopes** There's a natural ice rink and a fitness centre. The outdoor pool is open, and there's dog sledding, snowmobiling and snowshoeing.

LA TOUSSUIRE 1700m/5,580ft

La Toussuire, along with Le Corbier, is one of the central resorts of the new network – the two have been linked at low altitude since 1986. It makes a convenient base with good local intermediate slopes and three fast lifts which give reasonably quick access to the hub of Les Sybelles at Pte de L'Ouillon.

THE RESORT
La Toussuire has grown up over many years but is predominantly modern, with a car-free and snow-covered main street lined by dreary-looking buildings dating from the 1960s and 1970s and plagued when we were there by piped music from loudspeakers. The resort has now spread widely from here, with wooden chalets as well as older hotels and small apartment blocks scattered across the mountainside.

THE MOUNTAIN
The local slopes amount to 45km/ 28 miles of pistes and were judged by a 2008 reporter to be the best in the area for variety and snow conditions. All the slopes are above the treeline. **Slopes** The resort sits in the pit of a wide bowl. Drags and chairlifts (including three six-packs) rise just over 500m/1,640ft vertical to the high point of Tête de Ballard and the link to L'Ouillon. At one end of the bowl is the low-level link to Le Corbier and at the other the start of a long red run of

900m/2,950ft vertical to the hamlet of Les Bottières.
Terrain park There's a boardercross course in the centre of the bowl.
Snow reliability With every run above 1800m/5,910ft snow-cover is fairly assured, but some of the slopes are rather exposed to the sun – particularly the low-level connection to Le Corbier.
Experts There are few challenges here, and not much space left between the pistes. The main interest is the ungroomed black Vallée Perdue run, which descends the valley separating La Toussuire from Le Corbier, away from the lifts. But it gets a lot of sun, and snow conditions can suffer. The link lifts towards L'Ouillon open up off-piste routes down this valley.
Intermediates This is ideal terrain for cruisers who don't mind mainly short runs. The longer run that goes down to Les Bottières is one of the most appealing in the whole area –but you face a long drag ride back, too.
Beginners There are nice, gentle nursery slopes immediately above the centre of the village, and good, easy progression slopes.
Snowboarding There are quite a few draglifts in the area.
Cross-country A narrow loop goes to Le Corbier, but it is in bleak surroundings and close to the road. There are also loops on the lower slopes of Le Grand Truc. There's 15km/9 miles in total.
Queues We have no reports of problems, but see introduction.
Mountain restaurants Reporters like the Foehn at Le Marolay for its 'stunning views' and interesting interior of old photos and carvings, and the Cigales, near the foot of the bowl. The refuge on the Bouyans blue run down to St-Colomban has a 'fantastic setting' and 'great vin chaud'. The Carlines self-service at Tête de Bellard has a 'huge' sun terrace and does 'nice local sausages', according to a 2008 visitor. The Chamois, with its ski racing memorabilia, is also recommended.
Schools A lack of English-speaking tuition can be a problem, as confirmed by a visitor with children. However, he also 'had a fantastic time in the ESF advanced adult class with a great bilingual teacher'.
Facilities for children The nursery accepts children from three to six. Language may be a problem.

↑ St-Sorlin spreads along a sunny low shelf, with a piste running along its length

SNOWPIX.COM / CHRIS GILL

UK PACKAGES

Le Corbier *Equity, Erna Low, Interhome, Lagrange, Rocketski, Ski Collection, Ski France, Ski Independence, Ski Leisure Direction, Skiholidayextras.com* **La Toussuire** *Erna Low, Interhome, Lagrange, Ski Collection, Ski France, Ski Leisure Direction, Skiholiday extras.com* **St-Sorlin-d'Arves** *AmeriCan Ski, Crystal, Erna Low, Lagrange, Peak Retreats, Ski France, Ski Independence, Ski Leisure Direction, Skiholidayextras.com, Thomson* **St-Jean-d'Arves** *Peak Retreats, Ski France, Ski Independence, Ski Leisure Direction, Skiholidayextras.com, Thomson*

STAYING THERE
How to go A few UK tour operators serve the resort.
Hotels There are several small 3-star and 2-star places. The 3-star Ruade (0479 830179) and Soldanelles (0479 567529) both have pools and saunas.
Apartments The Hauts de Comborcière is new with pool, sauna, steam, hot tub. Chalet Goélia has been recommended. The Ecrins chalets are large 3-star apartments. Most others are cheap and not so cheerful.
Eating out The options are mostly inexpensive pizzerias and bar-restaurants.
Après-ski Fairly dire. There are a few bars, including the Tonneau. The Alpen Rock nightclub can get busy at peak French holiday time.
Off the slopes There's a reasonable amount to do, including snowshoeing, snowmobiling, dog sledding, skating on a 'very seedy' rink on the roof of a building in the main street, and hang-gliding.

ST-SORLIN-D'ARVES 1600m/5,250ft
St-Sorlin's major advantages are that it is based on a traditional village and that it has the most interesting slopes in the area for good intermediates – the slopes on Les Perrons, reached by two fast quads.

THE RESORT
St-Sorlin-d'Arves is a real, medium-sized village with a year-round life outside skiing. It's a picturesque collection of well-preserved traditional farmhouses, with a baroque church and long-established shops – fromagerie, boulangerie, crafts etc – alongside more modern resort development. Its setting on a narrow shelf gives fine views but doesn't allow much room for expansion, so the village has grown in a ribbon-like fashion along the main road – not ideal for strolling around. There is a frequent bus service, but some visitors have complained that it is 'crowded and disorganised'.

THE MOUNTAIN
St-Sorlin's local slopes form the biggest single sector of the linked network, with 120km/75 miles of piste. Although very much an intermediate mountain, it does offer much more variety, including some steeper options, than the rest of the area.
Slopes There are two distinct sections. The lower, gentler left side on La Balme, reached by a choice of slow chairs from the village, is crammed with lots of short, easy runs. The higher, right side on Les Perrons, reached by two successive fast six-packs, has long, sweeping, generally steeper pistes. The Vallons run off the back of Les Perrons (which forms the first part of the link to L'Ouillon and onwards to the other resorts) and the runs from Petit Perron have added a lot of interest to the local skiing.
Terrain park There is one on La Balme, accessed by a chairlift.
Snow reliability Not bad. Les Perrons slopes are the highest in the area and the main runs back to the village are covered by snowmaking. Grooming seems to be erratic, with some slopes not pisted.
Experts There isn't much on-piste challenge, but Les Perrons has the best off-piste in the whole area; the slopes beneath the Petit Perron chair offer more interest.
Intermediates The long top-to-bottom reds on both sides of Les Perrons are the best pistes in the whole area and quite challenging, as is the Perrons red run to the village – expect major moguls unless recently groomed. There is only one run on the back of Les Perrons and a couple on the front, but they have the whole mountainside to themselves, giving a great away-from-it-all feel. La Balme has shorter, more leisurely runs. Timid intermediates may find the rather narrow Combe Balme blue to the village tricky and crowded at the end of the day.
Beginners The nursery slope is right by the village, and there are plenty of slopes to progress to on La Balme.
Snowboarding The terrain suits beginners and intermediates but there

Phone numbers
From abroad use the
prefix +33 and omit
the initial '0' of the
phone number

TOURIST OFFICES

t 0479 598800
info@les-sybelles.com
www.les-sybelles.com

La Toussuire
t 0479 830606
info@la-toussuire.com
www.la-toussuire.com

Le Corbier
t 0479 830404
info@le-corbier.com
www.le-corbier.com

St-Sorlin-d'Arves
t 0479 597177
info@saintsorlin
darves.com
www.saintsorlin
darves.com

St-Jean-d'Arves
t 0479 597330
info@saintjeandarves.
com
www.saintjeandarves.
com

**St-Colomban-des-
Villards**
t 0479 562453
villards@wanadoo.fr
www.saint-colomban.
com

Les Bottières
t 0479 832709
info@bottieres-jarrier.
com
www.bottieres-jarrier.
com

are a lot of draglifts. Freeriders will
enjoy the quiet off-piste slopes.
Cross-country There's a narrow 16km/
10 mile loop along a side valley past
the foot of La Balme's Alpine area,
with good views of the Aiguilles
d'Arves.
Queues There may be queues out of
the village first thing and when
moving between sectors.
Mountain restaurants We enjoyed
lunch and stunning views of the
Aiguilles d'Arves from the sunny
terrace of the rustic Bergerie at La
Balme – endorsed by a reporter.
Schools ESF children's classes have
been criticised: 'Almost no feedback
from their teacher, classes a bit too
big and poor English.'
Facilities for children The Petits
Diables nursery accepts children from
three months; a 2007 reporter said, 'It
was poor; good English spoken but
made no effort to be welcoming. We
left after two days.' The ski
kindergarten accepts kids from three-
and-a-half years. Language can be a
problem.

STAYING THERE
How to go Some major UK tour
operators now offer holidays here.
Hotels Only two (both 2-star and both
attractive chalets): the Beausoleil
(0479 597142) and Balme (0479
597021).
Apartments There are scores of small
properties (and the Grignotte bakery
sells 'the best bread ever', says one
reporter).
Eating out The choice is limited to
cheap and cheerful pizzerias and
raclette/fondue places. The Table de
Marie, Gargoulette, Petit Ferme ('hearty
portions of lasagne') and the place
above the Avalanche cafe have been
recommended. A 2008 visitor enjoyed
the 'quiet' Regal Savoyard ('best
choice, best prices').
Après-ski St-Sorlin-d'Arves is even
quieter than the other major resorts,
but there is now the lively Yeti bar and
D'sybell nightclub. The Avalanche
reportedly attracts more of a 'student-
age' group and the Godille is
frequented by locals.
Off the slopes There is not much to
do. Dog sledding and snowshoeing are
options, but it's fairly tame territory.

ST-JEAN-D'ARVES 1550m/5,090ft
St-Jean-d'Arves is a small, yet quite
scattered community. Reporters

generally find it very friendly. The
original old village, with the usual
ancient church, is set across the valley
from the slopes, which are at the mid-
mountain hamlet of La Chal. Here,
where a tasteful development of
chalet-style buildings is still
expanding, there are nursery slopes,
small terrain park and the lift link to
and piste back from Le Corbier.

St-Jean/La Chal is not a good base
for anyone wanting to exploit the
larger area – and that will include
most energetic beginners as well as
intermediates. The chairlift towards Le
Corbier is painfully slow – 'enough to
make you cry', say reporters. The
return slopes are excessively sunny –
bare and rocky when we visited; there
is snowmaking, but a cure is unlikely.
Usually it will be better to take the
shuttle-bus to St-Sorlin to use its fast
lifts.

Off-slope diversions are few – dog
sledding, snowshoeing, tobogganing
and cheese farm visits. Après-ski is
basic, with a few bars, an Irish pub,
night-tobogganing with music, and a
cinema. The Marmottes and the
Fontaine du Roi apartments are joined
by the Hameau de St Jean this year, as
about the best self-catering options in
the area.

ST-COLOMBAN-DES-VILLARDS
1100m/3,610ft
St-Colomban-des-Villards is a tiny old
village in the next valley to La
Toussuire, only a few miles up from
the Maurienne valley.

There is a chain of drags and
chairlifts on north- and east-facing
slopes to the south of the village, with
a high point at Mt Cuinat, and a link
to L'Ouillon, at the hub of Les
Sybelles. The run down is reportedly
'interesting and attractive', but the
return lifts take an hour. A battery of
snow-guns keeps the home slope
open. The Auberge du Coin at Ormet
has 'lovely views', table- and self-
service choices.

LES BOTTIERES 1300m/4,270ft
Down the mountain from La Toussuire,
this tiny hamlet offers little
infrastructure and extremely indirect
access to the main network – it takes
three long lifts to get over to La
Toussuire, before setting off for
L'Ouillon. The restaurant at the bottom
of the Marmottes draglift has 'good
food and excellent service'.

La Tania

A very attractive budget base for the vast slopes of Courchevel and Méribel – and not bad looking, for a purpose-built resort

COSTS

① ② ③ ④ ⑤ ⑥

RATINGS

The slopes
Fast lifts	★★★★
Snow	★★★
Extent	★★★★★
Expert	★★★★
Intermediate	★★★★★
Beginner	★★★
Convenience	★★★★
Queues	★★★★
Mountain restaurants	★★★★

The rest
Scenery	★★★
Resort charm	★★★
Off-slope	★

NEWS

For 2007/08 the Lac Bleu and Bouc Blanc pistes were remodelled, and the signposting in the Loze sector was improved. The apartments in the Britannia have been renovated.

➕ Part of the Three Valleys – the world's biggest linked ski area

➕ Quick access to the slopes of Courchevel and Méribel

➕ Long, rolling intermediate runs through woods back to the village

➕ Good green run to the village means it's now more attractive for beginners and timid intermediates

➕ Greatly improved snowmaking

➕ Attractive, small, traffic-free village

➖ Small development: little choice of après-ski, no doctor, no pharmacy

➖ Main nursery slope is part of the blue run to the village, and gets a lot of through-traffic

➖ Some accommodation is a hike from the centre and the gondola

➖ Access to the highest and most rewarding slopes of the Three Valleys takes time

La Tania has carved out its own niche as a good-value, quiet, family-friendly base from which to explore the slopes of its swanky neighbours, Courchevel and Méribel. Trips to the furthest corners of the immense Three Valleys are certainly possible, but they take a little more time than from better-placed starting points.

It is a second-generation purpose-built resort, and at 1350m/4,430ft about the lowest you'll find; its wood-clad buildings sit comfortably in a pretty woodland setting – quite a contrast to classic French ski stations such as Les Menuires.

THE RESORT

La Tania is set just off the minor road linking Le Praz (Courchevel 1300) to Méribel. It has grown into a quiet, attractive, car-free collection of mainly ski-in/ski-out chalets and apartments set among the trees, most with good views. There are few shops other than food and sports shops, and you can walk around the village in a couple of minutes. It does have a few bars and restaurants, but as one reporter puts it, 'it doesn't exactly have a huge nightlife'.

A gondola leads up into the slopes, and there are two wonderful sweeping intermediate runs back down. The nursery slope is on your doorstep, and visitors say that La Tania is very child friendly. The steepness of the longer runs above the village used to be a key weakness, but the Plan Fontaine green run from Praz-Juget to the village – opened in 2005/06 – gives novices a long easy slope to progress to. Getting back from Courchevel still involves tackling a blue though.

Free buses go to Courchevel. For those with a car, Méribel is probably a bigger draw – and a lot nearer than Courchevel 1850.

THE MOUNTAINS

The slopes immediately above La Tania and nearby Le Praz are wooded, and about the best place in the whole Three Valleys in bad weather. Above mid-mountain, the slopes are open.

The slopes of Courchevel and Méribel are both only two lifts away from La Tania – but if you want speedy access to La Saulire, or Mont Vallon, or the slopes of Val Thorens, this is not the ideal starting point.

Slopes The gondola out of the village goes to Praz-Juget. From here draglifts go on up to Chenus or to Loze and the slopes above Courchevel 1850, and a fast quad goes to the link with Méribel via Col de la Loze. From all these points, varied, interesting intermediate runs take you back into the La Tania sector.

Terrain parks There is no local terrain park or half-pipe, but you can get to Courchevel's parks easily.

Snow reliability Good snow-cover down to Praz-Juget is usual all season. Snowmaking covers the whole of the blue run back to the village; if, despite this, the run is icy in the afternoon, you have the option of riding the gondola down.

Experts There are no particularly testing runs directly above La Tania, but the Jean Blanc and Jockeys blacks from Loze to Le Praz are genuine challenges, and there is good off-piste terrain beneath the Col de la Loze ridge, with more close by above Courchevel.

Intermediates There are two lovely, long, undulating intermediate runs back through the trees to La Tania – though there's little difference in gradient between the blue and the red, and timid intermediates may want to use the Plan Fontaine green. On the higher slopes you have a choice of three or four pistes. Both the red Lanches and the black Dou des Lanches are excellent and challenging.

Beginners There is a good beginner area and lift right in the village, and children are well catered for. But there's a lot of through traffic on the main slope. The green run from Praz-Juget – opened in 2005/06 – is an excellent run to progress to once you are off the nursery slope.

Snowboarding It's easy to get around on gondolas/chairs, avoiding drags.

Cross-country There are 36km/22 miles of trails with links through the woods to Méribel and Courchevel – which has an extensive 66km/41 miles of trails.

Queues A queue can build up for the village gondola but it is quick-moving, and one of the attractions of La Tania in general is the lack of crowds. However, a visitor in March 2008 reported that the lifts out of the village were late opening every day of his holiday, sometimes by as much as 45 minutes.

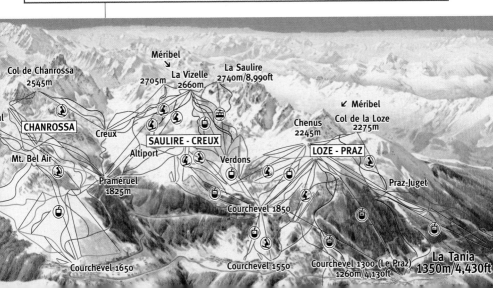

Weekly news updates and resort links at www.wtss.co.uk

KEY FACTS

Resort	1350m
	4,430ft

The Three Valleys

Slopes	1260-3230m
	4,130-10,600ft
Lifts	180
Pistes	600km
	373 miles
Green	15%
Blue	38%
Red	37%
Black	10%
Snowmaking	33 %

Courchevel/
La Tania only

Slopes	1260-2740m
	4,130-8,990ft
Lifts	62
Pistes	150km
	93 miles
Green	22%
Blue	37%
Red	33%
Black	8%
Snowmaking	31%

Mountain restaurants Bouc Blanc (0479 088026), near the top of the gondola out of La Tania, is our favourite: it has friendly table service in a wood-clad dining room, good food (reliable plat du jour) and a big terrace – we've had several very satisfactory lunches there. Reporters in 2008 agree with us about the excellence of the food, but we also have reports of 'disastrously slow' service. Roc Tania, higher up at Col de la Loze, is tiny, but very pretty inside.

Schools and guides Our most recent reports of the ESF have been positive. Magic in Motion has now joined forces with Ski Academy to become Magic Snowsports Academy: a third-season skier in 2007 'really enjoyed' lessons with them.

Facilities for children UK tour operators Le Ski and Ski Beat both operate nurseries. The Maison des Enfants kindergarten for non-skiing children no longer operates; the tourist office assures us there will be an alternative; the Jardin des Neiges takes skiing children from the age of four. A list of babysitters (for children over six months old) is available from the tourist office.

STAYING THERE

How to go Over 30 British tour operators go here – an amazingly high number for such a small place.

Hotels The Montana (0479 088008) is a slope-side 3-star next to the gondola with a sauna and fitness club. The Télémark (0479 089349) – which is set in the forest – is recommended by a reader: 'Compact but very comfortable; friendly staff and good value.'

Chalets There are dozens of catered chalets here – online agent Ski Line lists over 40 from UK tour operators. Major Courchevel operator Le Ski has four chalets here, including one new in 2007/08; three are particularly child-friendly – offering family rooms – and two operate nurseries. Ski Amis has three chalets – one aimed at families, one budget and one premium (with sauna) – plus some self-catering places. Ski Power aims to deliver food

---

Selected chalets in La Tania

SKI AMIS *www.skiamis.com*   **T 0207 692 0850 F 0207 692 0851**

↑ CHALET CHRISTINE

La Tania
3 quality catered chalets close to the piste and lifts

Chalet Balkiss
• premium catered service
• sleeps up to 14 people
• sauna and hot-tub

Chalet Christine
• sleeps up to 28 people
• child prices available

Chalet Tangara
• sleeps up to 12-15 people
• sauna facility
• great value for money

CHALET BALKISS ↑

and particularly wine of above average standard in its five chalets, one of which has spa-baths in its en suite bathrooms, as well as a hot tub. Alpine Action now has five smart chalets near the centre, four with outdoor hot tubs, one with spa-baths in the bathrooms. Ski Beat has five chalets, one split into two units; most offer skiing from the door if not to the door. A reader approves their chalet Beriozka this year.

Apartments There are lots of apartments – and most are more spacious and better equipped than usual in France. There is a deli and a bakery, as well as a small supermarket.

Eating out The Ferme de la Tania offers good Savoyard fare, and the Farçon has a Michelin star: a recent reporter says, 'We had an excellent lunch, and it did not cost a fortune.' The Chanterelles is reported to be 'excellent', and a 2007 reporter recommends the Marmottons for 'good food and reasonable prices'. A 2008

visitor rated the restaurant of the Télémark hotel 'completely fantastic: exemplary pork ... chips worthy of Heston Blumenthal'.

Après-ski The Ski Lodge has long been the focal après-ski place and has live bands – a 2008 visitor comments: 'It is always good, but it can get quite busy.' The hotel Télémark is reported to be 'welcoming and reasonably priced, with charming staff', and the Taïga has been recommended in the past. The hotel Montana bar is also worth trying for a quiet drink, and the locals' bar – the Arbatt – is popular as the slopes close. We hear the new Chrome bar has already built up a following – regular live music.

Off the slopes Unless you have a car, La Tania is not the best place for someone not intending to hit the slopes – it is too small and limited. However, snowmobile trips, snowshoeing, tobogganing and paragliding are possibilities, and the hotel Montana has a fitness club with a swimming pool.

La Tania

391

Chalets and small-scale apartment blocks are set in the forest →

The Three Valleys

With the swankiest resort in the Alps at one end, and the highest at the other: the biggest lift-linked ski area in the world

Despite competing claims, notably from the Portes du Soleil, in practical terms the Three Valleys cannot be beaten for sheer quantity of lift-served terrain. There is nowhere like it for a keen skier or boarder who wants to cover as much mileage as possible while rarely taking the same run repeatedly. It has a lot to offer everyone, from beginner to expert. And its resorts offer a wide range of alternatives – not only the widely known attractions of the big-name mega-resorts but also the low-key appeal of the smaller villages.

What's more, the area undersells itself. It should actually be known as the Four Valleys, because several years ago it expanded south into the Maurienne. But when you've spent millions on building a brand name why change? Three Valleys or four – whatever, the place is huge.

The runs of the Three Valleys and their resorts are dealt with in six chapters. The four major resorts are Courchevel, Méribel, Les Menuires and Val Thorens, but we also give chapters to St-Martin-de-Belleville, a village down the valley from Les Menuires, and La Tania, a modern development between Courchevel and Méribel.

None of the resorts is cheap. **Les Menuires** has some budget accommodation but its original buildings are hard on the eye. New developments have been built in a much more acceptable style and two of the original buildings have been demolished and are being rebuilt in a much more sympathetic style – something we suggested ten editions ago. Across the valley are some of the best (and quietest) challenging pistes in the Three Valleys on the north-facing La Masse. Down the valley from Les Menuires is **St-Martin-de-Belleville**, a charming traditional village that has been

expanded sympathetically. It has good-value accommodation and lift links towards Les Menuires and Méribel.

Up rather than down the Belleville valley from Les Menuires, at 2300m/7,550ft, **Val Thorens** is the highest resort in the Alps, and at 3230m/10,600ft the top of its slopes is the high point of the Three Valleys. The snow in this area is almost always good, and it includes two glaciers where good snow is guaranteed. But the setting is bleak and the lifts are vulnerable to closure in bad weather. The purpose-built resort is very convenient. Visually it is not comparable to Les Menuires, thanks to the smaller-scale buildings and more thorough use of wood cladding.

Méribel is a multi-part resort. The highest component, **Méribel-Mottaret,** is the best placed of all the resorts for getting to any part of the Three Valleys system in the shortest possible time. It's now quite a spread-out place, with some of the accommodation a long way up the hillsides – great for access to the slopes, less so for access to nightlife. **Méribel** itself is 200m/660ft lower and has long been a British favourite, especially for chalet holidays. It is the most attractive of the main Three Valleys resorts, built in chalet style beside a long winding road up the hillside. Parts of the resort are very convenient for the slopes and the village centre; parts are very far from either. The growing hamlet of **Méribel-Village** has its own chairlift into the system but is very isolated and quiet. You can also stay below Méribel in the valley town of **Brides-les-Bains,** or in hamlets along the route of the gondola to Méribel.

Courchevel has four parts. 1850 is the most fashionable resort in France, and can be the most expensive resort in the Alps (though it doesn't have to cost a fortune to stay there). The less expensive parts – 1300 (Le Praz), 1550 and 1650 – don't have the same choice of nightlife and restaurants. Many people rate the slopes around Courchevel the best in the Three Valleys, with runs to suit all standards.

La Tania was built for the 1992 Olympics, just off the small road linking Le Praz to Méribel. It has now grown into an attractive, car-free collection of chalets and chalet-style apartments set among the trees, and is popular with families. It has a good nursery slope and good intermediate runs in the woods above.

Tignes

Stark apartment blocks and a bleak, treeless setting are the prices you pay for the high, snow-sure slopes and varied terrain

COSTS

① ② ③ ④ ⑤ ⑥

RATINGS

The slopes

Fast lifts	****
Snow	*****
Extent	*****
Expert	*****
Intermediate	*****
Beginner	**
Convenience	****
Queues	****
Mountain restaurants	***

The rest

Scenery	***
Resort charm	**
Off-slope	*

NEWS

For 2008/09 the Tufs chairlift from Val Claret to Tovière will be replaced by a new six-pack. Also in Val Claret a new MGM 4-star hotel will open, the Nevada. It's the second phase to an apartment development that opened in 2006.

For 2007/08 the Brévières chairlift up to Les Boisses was upgraded to a fixed-grip quad.

394

➕ Good snow guaranteed for a long season – about the best Alpine bet

➕ One of the best areas in the world for lift-served off-piste runs

➕ Huge amount of varied terrain, with swift access to Val d'Isère

➕ Lots of accommodation close to the slopes

➕ Efforts to make the resort villages more welcoming are paying off

➖ Resort architecture not to everyone's taste (including ours)

➖ Bleak, treeless setting – many lifts prone to closure by storms

➖ Still a few long, slow chairlifts – though progress is being made

➖ You need an area pass to find long green runs

➖ Limited, but improving, après-ski

The appeal of Tignes is simple: good snow, spread over a wide area of varied terrain, shared with Val d'Isère. The altitude of Tignes is crucial: a forecast of 'rain up to 2000m' means 'fresh snow down to village level in Tignes'.

We prefer to stay in Val, which is a more human place. But in many ways Tignes makes the better base: appreciably higher, more convenient, surrounded by intermediate terrain, with quick access to the Grande Motte glacier. And the case gets stronger as results flow from Tignes' campaign to reinvent itself in a more cuddly form. The place is a lot less hostile to the visitor than it once was.

In the last few seasons the resort has also, at last, got around to installing some fast chairs on the western side of the Tignes bowl. But there are still a few key links that need upgrading.

THE RESORT

Tignes was created before the French discovered the benefits of making purpose-built resorts look acceptable. But things are improving, and the villages are gradually acquiring a more traditional look and feel.

Tignes-le-Lac is the hub of the resort. Some of the smaller buildings in the central part, Le Rosset, are being successfully revamped in chalet style. But the place as a whole is dreary, and the blocks overlooking the lake from the quarter called Le Bec-Rouge will remain monstrous until the day they are demolished. It's at the point where these two sub-resorts meet – a snowy pedestrian area, with valley traffic now passing through a tunnel beneath – that the lifts are concentrated: a powerful gondola towards Tovière and Val d'Isère and a fast six-pack up the western slopes. Some attractive new buildings are being added both in the centre and on the fringes, in a suburb built on the lower slopes known as Les Almes. A nursery slope separates Le Rosset from the fourth component part, the group of apartment blocks called Le Lavachet, below which there are good fast lifts up both sides of the valley.

Val Claret (2km/1 mile up the valley, beyond the lake) was also mainly developed after Le Rosset, and is a bit more stylish. The main part of the village, Centre, is an uncompromisingly 1960s-style development on a shelf above the valley floor. Below this, fast

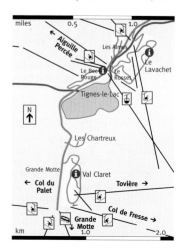

KEY FACTS

Resort	2100m
	6,890ft

Espace Killy	
Slopes	1550-3455m
	5,090-11,340ft
Lifts	89
Pistes	300km
	186 miles
Green	15%
Blue	40%
Red	28%
Black	17%
Snowmaking	
	378 guns

Tignes only	
Slopes	1550-3455m
	5,090-11,340ft
Lifts	43
Pistes	150km
	93 miles

chairs head up in three directions: to the western slopes, towards Val d'Isère and to the Grande Motte. An underground funicular also accesses the Grande Motte.

Beside the road along the valley to the lifts is a ribbon of development in traditional style, named Grande Motte (after the peak). The two levels of Val Claret are linked by a couple of (unreliable) indoor elevators and stairs and by hazardous paths.

Below the main resort villages are two smaller places. Tignes-les-Boisses, quietly set in the trees beside the road up, consists of a barracks and a couple of simple hotels. Tignes-les-Brévières is a renovated old village at the lowest point of the slopes – a favourite lunch spot, and a friendly place to stay.

Location isn't crucial, as a regular free bus service connects all the villages until midnight – though in the daytime the route runs along the bottom of Val Claret, leaving residents of Val Claret Centre with a climb.

THE MOUNTAINS

The area's great weakness is that it can become unusable in bad weather. There are no woodland runs except immediately above Tignes-les-Boisses and Tignes-les-Brévières. Heavy snow produces widespread avalanche risk and wind closes the higher chairs.

Piste classification here is more reliable than in Val d'Isère and signposting is 'very clear'. But we've had complaints that lift and piste opening information is unreliable.

THE SLOPES
High, snow-sure and varied

Tignes' biggest asset is the **Grande Motte** – and the runs from, as well as on, the glacier. The underground funicular from Val Claret whizzes you up to over 3000m/9,840ft in seven minutes. There are blue, red and black runs to play on up here, as well as beautiful long runs back to the resort.

The main lifts towards Val d'Isère are efficient: a high-capacity gondola from Le Lac to **Tovière**, and a fast chair with covers from Val Claret to **Col de Fresse**. You can head back to Tignes from either: the return from Tovière to Tignes-le-Lac is via a steep black run but there are easier blue runs to Val Claret.

Going up the opposite side of the valley takes you to a quieter area of predominantly east-facing slopes split into two main sectors, linked in both directions – **Col du Palet** and **l'Aiguille Percée**. This whole mountainside has at last been given some of the fast lifts it has needed for years – there are five so far.

The Col des Ves chairlift, at the south end of the Col du Palet sector, serves Le SPOT (see 'For experts') freeride and freestyle learning area. You can descend from l'Aiguille Percée to Tignes-les-Brévières on blue, red or black runs. There's an efficient gondola back, but the chairs above it are old and slow ('a quicker route back is the

bus'). A new fixed-grip quad replaced the existing chairlift between Tignes-les-Brévières and Tignes-les-Boisses for 2007/08, but a fast lift or two above it would be more useful.

TERRAIN PARKS
New but not improved

Tignes was one of the first French resorts to build a terrain park. This means that the local shaping crew are not short of experience and know how to build a good park – although a

2007 visitor found it 'disappointing for a resort of its size'. Whether they can be bothered to keep it maintained is another story. The park is in Val Claret by the Palais ski lift and is long, has several small-to-medium-sized jumps including a gap jump, a hip and several medium-sized rails. Head to Val d'Isère for better obstacles. Tignes, however has a 120m/390ft long half-pipe which is well shaped and a good size for those not comfortable with a super-pipe. It is right at the bottom of

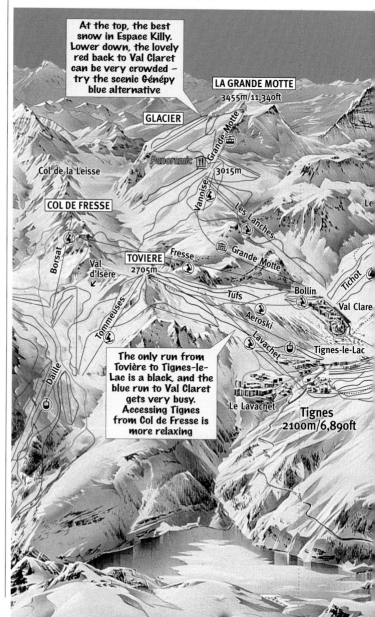

At the top, the best snow in Espace Killy. Lower down, the lovely red back to Val Claret can be very crowded – try the scenic Génépy blue alternative

LA GRANDE MOTTE
3455m/11,340ft

GLACIER

Panoramic

Col de la Leisse

3015m

Grande Motte

Vannise

COL DE FRESSE

Les Lanches

Borsat

TOVIERE
2705m

Fresse

Grande Motte

Val d'Isère

Tichot

Tufs

Bollin

Val Clare

Tommeuses

Aeroski

Lavachet

Tignes-le-Lac

Daille

The only run from Tovière to Tignes-le-Lac is a black, and the blue run to Val Claret gets very busy. Accessing Tignes from Col de Fresse is more relaxing

Le Lavachet

Tignes
2100m/6,890ft

the mountain, which means if you have the energy to hike, you can ride it for free. In the summer the park doubles in size and moves up to the Grande Motte for freestyle camps. There's also a boardercross as part of Le SPOT (see 'For experts') and a children's park in Le Lac.

SNOW RELIABILITY
Difficult to beat

Tignes has all-year-round runs (barring brief closures in spring or autumn) on its Grande Motte glacier. And the resort height of 2100m/6,89oft generally means good snow-cover right back to base for most of the long winter season – November to May. The west-facing runs down from Col de Fresse and Tovière to Val Claret suffer from the afternoon sun, although they now have serious snowmaking. Some of the lower east-facing and south-east-facing slopes on the other side of the valley can suffer late in the season, too. Grooming is 'excellent'.

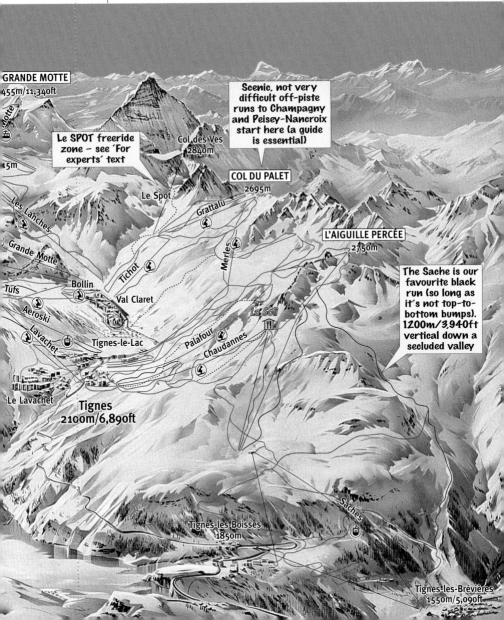

GRANDE MOTTE
3455m/11,340ft

Scenic, not very difficult off-piste runs to Champagny and Peisey-Nancroix start here (a guide is essential)

Le SPOT freeride zone – see 'For experts' text

Col des Ves
2840m

COL DU PALET
2695m

Les Lanches

Le Spot

Grattalu

Merles

L'AIGUILLE PERCÉE
2750m

Grande Motte

Tichot

The Sache is our favourite black run (so long as it's not top-to-bottom bumps). 1200m/3,940ft vertical down a secluded valley

Tufs

Bollin

Val Claret

Aeroski

La Soli

Lavachet

Palafour

Chaudannes

Tignes-le-Lac

Le Lavachet

Tignes
2100m/6,89oft

Saches

Tignes-les-Boisses
1850m

Tignes-les-Brévières
1550m/5,090ft

Tignes has always been a popular destination for snowboarders. Lots of easily accessible off-piste and the fact that it's cheaper than Val d'Isère are the main attractions, and quite a few top UK snowboarders make this their winter home. For those who buy the Espace Killy lift ticket, the backside of Col de Fresse in Val d'Isère is a natural playground. There are a few flat areas (avoid Génépy and Myrtilles), but the lift system relies more on chairs and gondolas than drags (though a long drag serves the boardercross area). There are long, wide pistes to blast down, such as Grattalu, Carline and Piste H, with acres of powder between them to play in. There are four specialist snowboard schools (Kebra, Snocool, Surf Feeling and Alliance) and a snowboarder chalet (www.dragonlodge.com). Go to Snowpark-shop in Tignes-le-Lac for all your freestyle needs.

FOR EXPERTS
An excellent choice

Tignes has converted six of its black runs into 'naturides', which means they are never groomed (a neat way of saving money!) but they are marked, patrolled and avalanche protected. Many of them are not especially steep (eg the Ves run – promoted from red status and renamed after the local freeride hero Guerlain Chicherit). Perhaps the most serious challenge is the long black run from Tovière to Tignes-le-Lac, with steep, usually heavily mogulled sections (the top part, Pâquerettes, is now a naturide, but the bottom part, Trolles, is a normal black). Parts of this run get a lot of afternoon sun. Our favourite black run (still a 'normal' black) is the Sache, from l'Aiguille Percée down a secluded valley to Tignes-les-Brévières. It can become very heavily mogulled, especially at the bottom – you can avoid this section by taking the red (used to be blue) Arcosses piste option part-way down.

But it is the off-piste possibilities that make Tignes such a draw for experts. Go with one of the off-piste groups that the schools organise and you'll have a great time. See the feature box for a few of the options.

The whole western side of the Tignes ski area has lots of off-piste possibilities. The terrain served by the slow, old Col des Ves double chair has been designated Le SPOT (Skiing the Powder of Tignes) area and has various ungroomed off-piste zones: Hardride for experts, Softride for the less experienced, and Backcountry freestyle with jumps. It is explained at length on the back of the piste map. At Chalet Freeride here you can learn to use an avalanche transceiver, practise searching for avalanche victims, read avalanche bulletins and

study maps and photos of the terrain.

And the bizarre French form of heli-skiing is available: mountaintop drops are forbidden, but from Tovière you can ski down towards the Lac du Chevril to be retrieved by chopper.

FOR INTERMEDIATES
One of the best

For keen intermediate piste-bashers the Espace Killy is one of the top three or four areas in the world.

Tignes' local slopes are ideal intermediate terrain. The red and blue runs on the Grande Motte glacier nearly always have superb snow. The glacier run from the top of the cable car is classified red, but is wide and mostly easy on usually fabulous snow. The Leisse run down to the chairlift is classified black and can get very mogulled but has good snow. The long red run all the way back to town is a delightful long cruise – though often crowded. The roundabout blue alternative (Génépy) is much gentler and quieter.

From Tovière, the blue 'H' run to Val Claret is an enjoyable cruise and generally well groomed. But again, it can get very crowded. There is lots to do on the other side of the valley and the runs down from l'Aiguille Percée to Tignes-les-Boisses and Tignes-les-Brévières are also scenic and fun. There are red and blue options as well as the beautiful Sache black run – adventurous intermediates shouldn't miss it. The runs down from l'Aiguille Percée to Le Lac are gentle, wide blues – now accessed by a fast chair.

FOR BEGINNERS
Good nursery slopes, but ...

The nursery slopes of Tignes-le-Lac and Le Lavachet (which meet at the top) are excellent – convenient, snow-sure, gentle, free of through-traffic and

SCHOOLS

ESF
t 0479 063028

Evolution 2
t 0479 064378

Snocool
t 0479 400858

Kebra
t 0479 064337

333
t 0479 062088

Surf Feeling
t 0479 065363

Alliance
t 0677 577 860
0844 484 9390 (UK)

Classes (ESF prices)
6 half days: €135

Private lessons
From €38 for 1hr

GUIDES

Mountain Guides
t 0614 629024

Tetra
t 0479 419707

served by a slow chair and a drag. The ones at Val Claret are less appealing: an unpleasantly steep slope within the village served by a drag, and a less convenient slope served by the fast Bollin chair. All of these lifts are free.

Although there are some fairly easy blues on the west side of Tignes, for long green runs you have to go over to the Val d'Isère sector. You need an Espace Killy pass to use them, and to get back to Tignes you have a choice between the blue run from Col de Fresse (which has a tricky start) or riding the gondola down from Tovière. And in poor weather, the high Tignes valley is an intimidatingly bleak place – enough to make any wavering beginner retreat to a bar with a book.

FOR CROSS-COUNTRY
Interesting variety
The Espace Killy has 40km/25 miles of cross-country trails. There are tracks on the frozen Lac de Tignes, along the valley between Val Claret and Tignes-le-Lac, at Les Boisses and Les Brévières and up on the Grande Motte.

QUEUES
Very few
The queues here depend on snow conditions. If snow low down is poor, the Grande Motte funicular generates

queues; the fast chairs in parallel with it are often quicker, despite the longer ride time. These lifts jointly shift a lot of people, with the result that the run down to Val Claret can be unpleasantly crowded. The worst queues now are for the cable car on the glacier – half-hour waits are common.

Of course, if higher lifts are closed by heavy snow or high winds, the lifts on the lower slopes have big queues. Otherwise there are usually few problems; crowded pistes are more of an issue.

MOUNTAIN RESTAURANTS
A couple of good places
The mountain restaurants are not a highlight – a regular hazard of high, purpose-built resorts, where it's easy to go back to the village for lunch. **Editors' choice** Lo Soli (0479 069863) at the top of the Chaudannes chair is a clear favourite. The terrace shares with the adjacent self-service Alpage a superb view of the Grande Motte; a reporter endorses our opinion: 'excellent food, ambience and service; excellent gâteau d'agneau, Caesar salad and melt-in-the-mouth pot-au-feu'. The table-service bit of the Panoramic (0479 064721) at the top of the funicular competes; one regular reporter gives it the edge: 'a veritable

A MECCA FOR OFF-PISTE SKIERS

Tignes is renowned for offering some of the best lift-served off-piste skiing in the world. There is a tremendous choice, with runs to suit all levels, from intermediate skiers to fearless freeriders and off-piste experts. Here's just a small selection. Don't go without a guide.

*For a first experience of off-piste, **Lognan** is ideal. These slopes – down the mountainside between the pistes to Le Lac and the pistes to Val Claret – are broad and not very difficult.*

*One of our favourite routes is the **Tour de Pramecou**. After a few minutes' walking at the bottom of the Grande Motte glacier, you pass around a big rock called Pramecou. There is then a multitude of possibilities, varying in difficulty – so routes can be found for skiers of different abilities.*

***Petite Balme** is a run for good skiers only – access is easy but leads to quite challenging north-facing slopes in real high-mountain terrain, far from the pistes.*

*To ski **Oreilles de Mickey** (Mickey's Ears) you start from Tovière and walk north along the ridge to the peak of Lavachet, where you get a great view of Tignes. The descent involves three long couloirs, narrow and pretty steep, which bring you back to Le Lavachet.*

*The best place to find good snow is the **Chardonnet** couloirs – they never get the sun. The route involves a 20-minute walk from the top of the Merle Blanc chairlift.*

*The **Vallons de la Sache** is one of the most famous routes – a descent of 1200m/3,940ft vertical down a breathtaking valley in the heart of the National Park, overlooked by the magnificent Sache glacier. Starting from l'Aiguille Percée you enter a different world, high up in the mountains, far away from the ski lifts. You arrive down in Les Brévières, below the Tignes dam.*

*One of the big adventures is to go away from the Tignes ski area and all signs of civilisation, starting from the Col du Palet. From there you can head for **Champagny** (linked to La Plagne's area) or **Peisey-Nancroix** (linked to Les Arcs' area) – both very beautiful runs, and not too difficult.*

CHILDREN

Les Marmottons
t 0479 065167
Ages 3 to 8

Ski schools
Evolution 2 takes children from age 5 and ESF takes children from age 4 (6 days €197)

GETTING THERE

Air Geneva 165km/103 miles (3½hr); Lyon 240km/ 149 miles (3½hr); Chambéry 130km/ 81 miles (2½hr)

Rail Bourg-St-Maurice (30km/19 miles); regular buses or taxi from station

joy – excellent rack of lamb, tiramisu'. **Worth knowing about** The atmospheric chalet at the top of Tovière is 'fairly basic' but does 'very good portions'. A reporter found the 'service just OK'. At the top of the Tichot chair from Val Claret, the Palet 'serves good food at good prices'. The big Panoramic self-service restaurant at the top of the funicular gets crowded, but has great views from its huge terrace and 'good portions at reasonable prices'.

There are lots of easily accessible places for lunch in the resorts. One ski-to-the-door favourite of ours in Le Lac is the hotel Montana, on the left as you descend from l'Aiguille Percée. In Val Claret the Fish Tank is 'very good value'. The Taverne des Neiges has 'good food and service'. In Le Lac, the Arbina offers 'consistent high quality'.

At the extremity of the lift system, Les Brévières makes an obvious lunch stop. A short walk round the corner into the village brings you to places much cheaper than the two by the piste. Sachette, for example, is crowded with artefacts from mountain life and offers 'lots of good cheese dishes' including 'superb tartiflette'. The Etoile des Neiges 'serves great, typical Savoyard food'.

SCHOOLS AND GUIDES
Plenty of choice
There are over half-a-dozen schools, including four specialist snowboard schools, plus various independent instructors. A 2008 reporter recommends Ali Ross Skiing Clinics (pre-booking required) – 'a great character who achieved results'. Reporters advise that at busy times pre-booking is 'essential' for normal schools as well. ESF gets mixed reviews: one 2008 reporter tells of an instructor losing a pupil, who then had to find and fund his own way home

from Val d'Isère, and all of those in this reporter's group who tried the ESF had 'bad experiences'. But one child from 2007 was 'admirably looked after' and the instructor showed 'great professionalism and understanding'.

Reports on Evolution 2 are generally positive for adult tuition. Members of a 2007 reporter's group were pleased with their progress and one took private lessons with an 'encouraging and very patient instructor'. The off-piste 'Tarentaise Tour' has also been praised ('a superb long day, with an enthusiastic guide'). But one visitor was 'very unhappy' with the children's lessons: 'The children changed level every class. At the end of one lesson, the class arrived back without our child – when asked where she was, the instructor said he simply didn't know. She returned later with another group.' The same reporter moved his children to the 333 school where 'the difference was dramatic – I would highly recommend them'.

BASS has 'excellent, small group clinics', and we have a glowing report of a British-run snowboarding outfit, Alliance: 'They teach with passion and enthusiasm; by far the best week's instruction I have received.'

FACILITIES FOR CHILDREN
Mixed reports
We have had good reports on the Marmottons kindergartens – 'brilliant' said a father of a four year old in 2007 – and the Spritelets ski classes arranged by Esprit Ski and Evolution 2: 'She loved her class and could snowplough by the end of the week.' But we received a poor report for Evolution 2 last year (see 'Schools').

STAYING THERE

HOW TO GO
Improving range of options
All three main styles of accommodation are available through tour operators. More luxury options are appearing.
Chalets The choice of catered chalets is increasing. Ski Total and Neilson both have several smart chalets, including some with pool, hot tub and sauna. Total's Chalet Arctik is not only hip but also 'excellent, comfortable', with pool and sauna. Family specialist Esprit has a chalet hotel and several chalets here. Ski Olympic's chalet hotel

SNOWPIX.COM / CHRIS GILL

Tignes-le-Lac as seen from the black run down from Tovière ↓

Rosset and chalet Madeleine have been recommended by reporters; their other chalets look good too. Skiworld has several good-looking chalets, mostly with sauna, steam room or hot tub; their chalet hotel has a pool too. Mark Warner has two chalet hotels, one with an outdoor pool. Snowstar's Chalet Chardon is an exceptionally spacious apartment.

Hotels The few hotels are small and concentrated in Le Lac.

***Campanules (0479 063436) Smartly rustic chalet in upper Le Lac, with good restaurant. One reporter was impressed enough to suggest that it deserved a 4-star rating.

***Village Montana (0479 400144) Stylishly woody, on the east-facing slopes above Le Lac, with a 4-star suites section. Outdoor pool, sauna, steam, hot tub.

***Lévanna (0479 063294) Central in Le Lac – comfortable, with a 'generous hot tub'; a reporter found 'friendly staff but a woeful lack of them'.

***Diva (0479 067000) Biggest in town (121 rooms). On lower level of Val Claret, a short walk from lifts. 'Very comfy rooms, excellent meals.' Recommended again in 2008. Sauna.

**Arbina (0479 063478) Well-run place close to the lifts in Le Lac, with lunchtime terrace, crowded après-ski bar and one of the best restaurants.

**Marais (0479 064006) Prettily furnished, simple hotel in Les Boisses.

Génépy (0479 065711) Simple Dutch-run chalet in Les Brévières.

Apartments There are lots of apartments in all price ranges. Erna Low and Ski Collection have some good-looking options and Ski Amis does self-catered places here too. The growing number of smart places include the Ecrin des Neiges in lower Val Claret and Residence Village Montana above Le Lac. MGM has recently opened the Ferme du Val Claret at the foot of the Grande Motte funicular and the Nevada in Val Claret. In Les Brévières, the Belvedere has very smart large apartments and chalets with three to six bedrooms. All the above have access to pool, sauna etc, but at extra cost in some cases.

The Chalet Club in Val Claret is a collection of simple studios, but it has a free indoor pool, sauna and in-house restaurant and bar. The supermarket at Le Lac is reported to be 'comprehensive but very expensive'.

Tignes

UK PACKAGES

Action Outdoors, Alpine Answers, Chalet Group, Chalet World Ski, Club Med, Crystal, Crystal Finest, Directski.com, Erna Low, Esprit, First Choice, Friendship Travel, Independent Ski Links, Inghams, Inspired to Ski, Interactive Resorts, Interhome, Kuoni, Lagrange, Mark Warner, Mountain Tracks, Mountainsun, Neilson, Peak Retreats, Ski Activity, Ski Amis, Ski Collection, Ski Expectations, Ski France, Ski Freshtracks, Skiholidayextras.com, Ski Independence, Ski Leisure Direction, Ski Line, Ski McNeill, Ski Olympic, Ski Solutions, Ski Supreme, Ski Total, Skitracer, Skiworld, Snoworks, Snowstar, Solo's, Thomson, UCPA

Phone numbers
From abroad use the prefix +33 and omit the initial '0' of the phone number

TOURIST OFFICE

t 0479 400440
information@tignes.
net
www.tignes.net

EATING OUT
Good places scattered about

The options in Le Lavachet are rather limited, though a recent reporter enjoyed the Grenier with its 'excellent cold meats and tartiflette' and another the 'novel experience' of eating with over-wintering farm animals on display through a viewing window at the 'atmospheric' Ferme des 3 Capucines. And we have very positive reports of the British-run Brasero: 'This restaurant is establishing a good reputation in Tignes; the food was quite simply excellent. We were made to feel very welcome.' Finding anywhere with some atmosphere is difficult in Le Lac, though the food in some of the better hotels is good. The Campanules has 'exemplary service', but the food 'wasn't as memorable as on other occasions', says a regular visitor. The Arbina continues to provide 'outstanding food, very good value and first-class service'. The Escale Blanche is almost as popular. Two visitors recommend the 'delicious food' at the 'quirky' Clin d'Oeil. Bagus Cafe's 'eclectic cuisine' is also praised. One visitor particularly highlights the Monday champagne nights at the Alpaka Lodge – 'a relaxed restaurant with duck breast the star attraction'. A 2007 visitor enjoyed 'traditional food' at the Eterlou.

In Val Claret the Caveau is recommended for a special treat – 'superbly presented food and good service in an intimate cellar setting'. The Petit Savoyard 'is friendly with efficient service'. The buffet at the Indochine has been strongly recommended by several reporters. Pepe 2000 has 'reasonable prices and helpful staff', but a reporter says the Pignatta 'slightly trumps it' and is enjoyable at lunchtime too – one reporter's group 'savoured really tasty meals'. The Auberge des 3 Oursons

was recommended for 'massive portions, friendly service'.

The Cordée in Les Boisses offers unpretentious surroundings, good traditional French food, modest prices.

APRES-SKI
Hidden away

Reporters agree that there is plenty going on if you know where to find it. Val Claret has some early-evening atmosphere, and happy hours are popular. Reporters differ on the merits of the Crowded House and Fish Tank (both popular with Brits). Grizzly's is 'cosy and atmospheric, but you pay for the ambience'. The 'whisky lounge' in the Couloir is a 'great place to relax'.

Le Lac is a natural focus for immediate après-ski drinks. The 'lively' Loop, with pool table, has a 'two for one' happy hour from 4 to 6pm. The bar of the hotel Arbina is our kind of spot – adequately cosy, friendly service. It's a great place to sit outside and people-watch. The Alpaka Cocktail Bar is 'hard to leave', 'a real gem later on'. Embuscade is said to be 'the only proper French bar' while TC's bar is 'very friendly, with good music'. Jack's is a popular late haunt.

OFF THE SLOPES
Forget it

Despite the range of alternative activities, Tignes is a resort for those who want to use the slopes, where anyone who doesn't is liable to feel like a fish out of water. Some activities do get booked up quickly as well – a reporter said it was impossible to find a free dog sledding slot in April. The ice skating on the lake includes a 500m/1,640ft circuit as well as a conventional rink. There's ice driving at Les Brévières. The Lagon leisure centre, with various pools, slides, wellness and fitness facilities, meets with readers' approval.

Val d'Isère

One of the great high mega-resorts, particularly (though not only) for experts – with a very attractive town at the base

COSTS

① ② ③ ④ ⑤ ⑥

RATINGS

The slopes

Fast lifts	****
Snow	*****
Extent	*****
Expert	*****
Intermediate	*****
Beginner	***
Convenience	***
Queues	****
Mountain restaurants	***

The rest

Scenery	***
Resort charm	***
Off-slope	**

NEWS

For 2008/09, a six-pack is due to replace the triple Marmottes chair up to Bellevarde from above La Daille. And a new bar/restaurant/nightclub (the Doudoune Club) and a new 4-star hotel (Avenue Lodge) are due to open. The 4-star Savoie hotel reopened last year after complete renovation and with a spa open to the public.

The World Alpine Skiing Championships are being held here from 3 to 15 February 2009.

+ Huge area shared with Tignes, with lots of runs for all abilities

+ One of the great resorts for lift-served off-piste runs

+ Once the snow has fallen, high altitude of slopes keeps it good

+ Wide choice of schools, especially for off-piste lessons and guiding

+ For a high Alpine resort, the town is attractive, very lively at night, and offers a good range of restaurants

+ Wide range of package holidays – including very swanky chalets

– Some green and blue runs are too challenging, and all runs back to the village are tricky

– You're quite likely to need the bus at the start and end of the day

– Most lifts and slopes are liable to close when the weather is bad

– Nursery slopes not ideal

– Main off-piste slopes get tracked out very quickly

– At times seems more British than French – especially in low season

– Increasingly pricey

Val d'Isère is one of the world's best resorts for experts – attracted by the extent of lift-served off-piste – and for confident, mileage-hungry intermediates. You don't have to be particularly adventurous to enjoy the resort; but it would be much better for novices if the piste classifications were more reliable.

The many drawbacks listed above are mainly not serious complaints, whereas most of the plus-points weigh heavily in the balance. For a combination of seriously impressive skiing and captivating village ambience, there aren't many places we'd rather go – especially if we're looking for a luxurious chalet.

THE RESORT

Val d'Isère spreads along a remote valley, which is a dead end in winter. The road in from Bourg-St-Maurice brings you dramatically through a rocky defile to the satellite mini-resort of La Daille – a convenient but hideous slope-side apartment complex and the base of lifts into the major Bellevarde sector of the slopes. The outskirts of Val proper are dreary, but as you approach the centre the improvements put in place over the last 15 years become more evident: wood- and stone-cladding, culminating in the tasteful pedestrian-only Val Village complex. Many first-time visitors find the resort much more pleasant than they expect a high French resort to be.

Turn right at the centre and you drive under the nursery slopes and two of Val's big lifts up the mountains to a lot of new development in the suburbs of Le Joseray, Le Châtelard and Le Legettaz. Continue up the main valley instead, and you come to Le Laisinant, a peaceful little outpost with a fast lift out of the valley, and then to

Le Fornet, the fourth major lift station. There is a lot of traffic around, but the resort has worked hard to get cars under control and has made the centre more pedestrian-friendly. The location of your accommodation isn't crucial, unless you want to ski from the door or be close to a nursery slope. The main lift stations are linked by efficient free shuttle-buses; in peak periods you never have to wait more

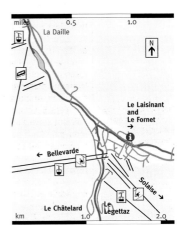

↑ That's Val d'Isère in the valley; above it you can see the tremendous scope for off-piste in high open bowls
OT VAL D'ISERE / AGENCE NUTS

than a few minutes. But in the evening frequency plummets and dedicated après-skiers will want to be within walking distance of the centre.

The developments up the side valley beyond the main lift station – Le Châtelard and La Legettaz – are mainly attractive, and some offer ski-in/ski-out convenience. La Daille and Le Fornet have their (quite different) attractions for those less concerned about nightlife. A car is of no great value around the resort.

THE MOUNTAIN

Although there are wooded slopes above the village on all sectors, in practice most of the runs here are on open slopes above the treeline, and a lot of lifts can close in bad weather. Piste grooming is better than it used to be, but we still get complaints about poor signing (especially at piste junctions) and the piste classification. Many blue and some green runs are simply too steep, narrow and even bumpy; we are pleased to see that some pistes have recently been reclassified but more need to be.

If you plan a return visit, keep your lift pass – you may get a 'loyal customer' reduction.

The local radio carries weather reports in English as well as in French.

THE SLOPES
Vast and varied

Val d'Isère's slopes divide into three main sectors, two reachable from the village. **Bellevarde** is the mountain that is home to Val d'Isère's two famous downhill courses: the OK piste that is used for the World Cup every December and the Face piste that was used for the 1992 Winter Olympics and will be used for the World Championships. You can reach Bellevarde quickly by underground funicular from La Daille or the powerful Olympique gondola from near the centre of town. From the top you can descend to the valley, play on a variety of drags and chairs at altitude or take a choice of lifts to the slopes of Tignes (see separate chapter).

Solaise is the other mountain accessible directly from the village. The Solaise fast quad takes you a few metres higher than the parallel cable car. Once up, a short drag or rope tow takes you over a plateau and down to a variety of chairs that serve this very sunny area of predominantly gentle pistes. From near the top of this area you can catch the fast Leissières chair (which climbs over a ridge and down the other side) to the third main area, in the valley running up to the **Col de l'Iseran**. This area can also be reached by the fast chair from Le Laisinant or by cable car from Le Fornet. At the top here is the **Glacier de Pissaillas**.

TERRAIN PARKS
Beginners and experts welcome

Above the La Daille gondola and served by the Mont Blanc chairlift lies the very good DC terrain park (www. valdiserevalpark.com). Maintenance can be a bit hit or miss, but on a good day this park has a bit of everything. There are four kicker lines, with jumps ranging from 3m/10ft in the blue line to 20m/66ft in the pro line. With more and more earth work being done during the summer to pre-shape jumps, there are now up to five jumps in a row on some of the lines, so prepare your legs. The large hip is now a main attraction of the park. A plethora of rails including flat downs, a C-box, rainbow, and a range of boxes form a nice contour around a somewhat cramped park. A half-pipe is on the cards for 2008/09, or head over to the Tignes pipe.

SNOW RELIABILITY
Only early season issues

In years when lower resorts have suffered, Val d'Isère has rarely been short of snow. Once a big dump of snow has fallen, the resort's height means you can almost always get back to the village. But even more important is that in each sector there are lots of lifts and runs above mid-mountain, between about 2300m and 2900m (7,550ft and 9,510ft). Many of the slopes face roughly north. And there is access to glaciers at Pissaillas or over in Tignes, although both take a while to get to. Snowmaking continues to be extended.

FOR EXPERTS
One of the world's best

Val d'Isère is one of the top resorts in the world for experts. The main attraction is the huge range of beautiful off-piste possibilities – see the feature panel.

There may be better resorts for really steep pistes – there are certainly lots in North America – but there is plenty of on-piste action to amuse most experts, despite the small number of blacks on the piste map. Many reds and blues are steep enough to get mogulled.

On Bellevarde the famous Face run is the main attraction – often mogulled from top to bottom, but not worryingly steep. Epaule is the sector's other black run – where the moguls are hit by long exposure to sun and can be slushy or rock hard (it is prone to closure for these reasons too). There are several challenging ways down from Solaise to the village: all steep, though none fearsomely so (Piste S is now classified a 'Naturide' – which means it is never groomed).

THE BEST LIFT-SERVED OFF-PISTE IN THE WORLD?

Few resorts can rival the extent of lift-served off-piste skiing in Val d'Isère. Here is a selection of what's on offer. But don't try any of it without a guide and essential safety equipment.

Some runs are ideal for adventurous intermediates looking to try off-piste for the first time. The **Tour du Charvet** goes through glorious scenery from the top of the Grand Pré chairlift on the back of Bellevarde. For most of the way it is very gentle, with only a few steeper pitches. It ends up at the bottom of the Manchet chair up to the Solaise area. The **Pays Désert** is an easy run with superb views on the Pissaillas glacier, high above Le Fornet and reached by traversing away from the pistes above cliffs from the top of the lift system. You end up at the Pays Désert T-bar.

For more experienced off-piste skiers, **Col Pers** is one of our favourite runs. Again, it starts a traverse from the Pissaillas glacier. You go over a pass into a big, fairly gentle bowl with glorious views and endless ways down. If there is enough snow, you drop down into the Gorges de Malpasset and ski over the frozen Isère river back to the Fornet cable car. If not, you can take a higher route.

Cugnai is a wide, secluded bowl reached from the chair of the same name at the top of the Solaise sector. A steep (37 degree) slope at the far end descends beneath a sheer black rock wall and then narrows into a gulley to the valley floor, leading to the Manchet chair.

Banane is reached via the Face de Bellevarde piste and is a long and impressive run (37 to 40 degrees) with spectacular views over the Manchet valley. For a real challenge intrepid experts should try the **Couloir des Pisteurs**, which requires a 20-minute climb from the Tour de Charvet. The view from the top is simply stunning. A very narrow steep couloir (44 degrees) bounded by rock faces brings you out on to a wide open slope above Le Grand Pré, right opposite Bellevarde.

Then there's the whole of Tignes' extensive off-piste to explore of course.

KEY FACTS	
Resort	1850m
	6,070ft
Entire Espace Killy area	
Slopes	1550-3455m
	5,090-11,340ft
Lifts	89
Pistes	300km
	186 miles
Green	15%
Blue	40%
Red	28%
Black	17%
Snowmaking	
	378 guns
Val d'Isère only	
Slopes	1785-3300m
	5,860-10,830ft
Lifts	46
Pistes	150km
	93 miles

FRANCE

406

Weekly news updates and resort links at www.wtss.co.uk

LIFT PASSES		
Espace Killy		
Prices in €		
Age	**1-day**	**6-day**
under 14	34	162
14 to 64	42	203
over 65	34	162
Free under 5, over 75		
Beginner free lifts on nursery slopes		

Notes
Covers Tignes and Val d'Isère; half-day and pedestrian passes; family discounts; 5-day plus passes valid for one day in the Three Valleys, one day in Paradiski (La Plagne-Les Arcs), and reduced price in La Rosière and Ste-Foy

Alternative pass
Val d'Isère only

Le Ski
the chalet specialists

GLACIER DE PISSAILLAS

Col Pers – one of our favourite off-piste runs, from the glacier down to Le Fornet

3300m/10,830ft

Worth getting out here for the snow and the views

2950m

COL DE L'ISERAN
2765m

2900m

Cascade

Leissières

Cugnai

Pyramides

Vallon de l'Iseran

Glacier

Madeleine

2325m

Laisinant

SOLAISE
2560m

Edelweiss

Fornet

Le Cha

Good shady red run served by the Laisinant fast chair

Le Fornet
1930m

No easy way back to the village from Solaise

Solaise

Le Laisinant

Val d'Isère
1850m/6,070ft

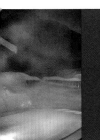

Good area of varied intermediate runs at altitude, with a couple of fast chairs

2900m

Excellent runs down to the Manchet chair – though affected by sun later in the season

Lots of long, high easy runs – but also lots of slow old chairlifts

The blue from here is the easiest and least crowded intermediate route to Tignes

Glacier de la Grande Motte

Cusnai

Madeleine

Manchet

Le Manchet
1940m

Grand Pre

COL DE FRESSE
2770m

Borsat

Tignes

Fresse

TOVIERE
2705m

BELLEVARDE
2705m

Marmottes

Tommeuses

Loyes

L'Olympique

Le Châtelard

Fruitière

Solaise

Bellevarde

Funival

Daille

The world's trickiest green run – narrow in parts and crowded and mogulled at the end of the day

l d'Isère
m/6,07oft

The 1992 Winter Olympic men's downhill course is now a genuine black run and often mogulled from top to bottom

La Daille
1785m

Weekly news updates and resort links at **www.wtss.co.uk**

boarding

Val d'Isère's more upmarket profile attracts a different kind of holiday boarder from Tignes; the resort is, perhaps, seen as Tignes' less hardcore cousin. But the terrain here is phenomenal and still draws a fair few boarders. The easier slopes are suitable for beginners, and there are now very few draglifts. But there are quite a few flat areas where you'll end up scooting or walking. There is a very good terrain park, and specialist snowboard shops such as Misty Fly and Quiksilver Boardriders. Check your email and have a coffee at the snowboarder-run Powder Monkey cafe.

Wayne Watson of off-piste school Alpine Expérience puts a daily diary of off-piste snow conditions and runs on the web at www.alpineexperience.com.

FOR INTERMEDIATES
Quantity and quality
Val d'Isère has just as much to offer intermediates as experts. There's enough here to keep you interested for several visits – though pistes can be crowded in high-season, and the less experienced should be aware that many runs are under-classified.

In the Solaise sector is a network of gentle blue runs, ideal for building confidence. And there are a couple of beautiful runs from here through the woods to Le Laisinant – ideal in bad weather, though prone to closure in times of avalanche danger.

Most of the runs in the Col de l'Iseran sector are even easier – ideal for early and hesitant intermediates. Those marked blue at the top of the glacier could really be classified green.

Bellevarde has a huge variety of runs ideally suited to intermediates of all levels. From Bellevarde itself there is a choice of green, blue and red runs of varying pitch. The World Cup

Downhill OK piste is a wonderful rolling cruise when groomed. The wide runs from Tovière normally offer the choice of groomed piste or moguls.

A snag for early intermediates is that runs back to the valley can be challenging. The easiest way is down to La Daille on a green run which would be classified blue or red in most resorts. It gets very crowded and moguled by the end of the day. None of the runs from Bellevarde and Solaise back to Val itself is easy. Many early intermediates ride the lifts down.

FOR BEGINNERS
OK if you know where to go
The nursery slope right by the centre of town is 95% perfect; it's just a pity that the very top is unpleasantly steep. The lifts serving it are free.

Once off the nursery slopes, you have to know where to find easy runs; many of the greens should be blue, or even red. One local instructor admits: 'We have to have green runs on the map, even if we don't have so many green slopes – otherwise beginners wouldn't come to Val d'Isère.'

A good place for your first real runs off the nursery slopes is the Madeleine

SCHOOLS

Alpine Expérience
t 0479 062881

BASS
t 0679 512405

DC
t 0479 220263

Development Centre
t 0615 553156

ESF
t 0479 060234

Evolution 2
t 0479 411672

Misty Fly Snocool
t 0479 243094

Mountain Masters
t 0479 060514

New Generation
t 0479 010318
www.skinewgen.com

Ogier
t 0479 061893

Oxygène
t 0479 419958

Progression
t 0621 939380

Ski Concept
t 0479 401919

Ski Leisure
t 0672 120140

Ski-lesson.com
t 0621 652944

Ski Mastery
t 0479 401768

Snow Fun
t 0479 061979

Top Ski
t 0479 061480

Val Gliss
t 0479 060072

Classes (ESF prices)
6 days (3hr am, 2½hr pm) €225

Private lessons
From €41 for 1hr

green run on Solaise – served by a fast six-pack. The Col de l'Iseran runs are also gentle and wide, and not overcrowded. There is good progression terrain on Bellevarde, too – though getting to it can be tricky. From all sectors, it's best to take a lift back down to the valley.

FOR CROSS-COUNTRY
Limited
There are a couple of loops in each of three areas – towards La Daille, on Solaise and out past Le Laisinant. More picturesque is the one going from Le Châtelard (on the road past the main cable car station) to the Manchet chair. But keen cross-country enthusiasts should go elsewhere.

QUEUES
Few problems
Queues to get out of the resort have been kept in check by lift upgrades and additions. At Solaise the slow Lac chair up to the Tête Solaise can generate queues but a 2008 reporter praises 'the good queueing systems with each chair filled to capacity'. Crowded pistes in high season is a more common complaint than queues these days.

MOUNTAIN RESTAURANTS
Acceptable – at long last
It's been a long, slow business, but a couple of editions ago Val eventually managed a three-star rating for mountain restaurants, which mainly consist of big self-service places at the top of major lifts. There are now more exceptions – but they are too few, so they are too busy, so high-season service can be poor.

Editors' choice The wood-and-stone Edelweiss (0610 287064), above Le Fornet, is our current favourite for the best food. We've had delicious duck and fish there and accommodating

staff have managed to serve us fantastic lamb after the kitchen had officially closed; reporters also send us rave reviews. The Fruitière (0479 060717) at the top of La Daille gondola, kitted out with stuff rescued from a dairy in the valley, crams in way too many people but handles them well. We had a good lunch here, but others have been unimpressed; more reports, please.
Worth knowing about We've always enjoyed the busy Trifollet halfway down the OK run on Bellevarde, but we're getting reports from disappointed visitors. On the lower slopes at La Daille, and reachable on snow and by pedestrians, Tufs serves good food. The Marmottes, in the middle of the Bellevarde bowl, is an efficient self-service with a big sunny terrace and good food ('big portion of Moroccan couscous and chicken'). And the Tanière (popular with locals) set between the two chairs going up Face de Bellevarde has been recommended by a reporter.

On Solaise, the small and friendly Bar de L'Ouillette, at the base of the Madeleine chairlift, does good food at reasonable prices. La Datcha at the bottom of the Glacier Express has a small table-service section ('succulent slow-cooked lamb'). The Clochetons, in the Manchet valley, has excellent food and is a good place to meet up with walkers or cross-country skiers.

The Signal at the top of the cable car from Le Fornet has self- and table-service sections and has been recommended for its 'huge bowls of filling vegetable soup with lashing of cheese and croutons'.

Of course there are lots of places in the resort villages. When at Col de l'Iseran, one idea is to descend to the rustic Arolay ('excellent for both lunch and dinner, with a lovely terrace') at Le Fornet. And the self-service Crozets

Interactive resort shortlist builder at **www.wtss.co.uk**

CHILDREN

Le Village des Enfants
t 0479 400981
Ages 3 to 13; 9am-
5.30 (Sun-Thu); 9am-
2pm (Fri)

Le Petit Poucet
t 0479 061397
Ages from 3; 9am-
5.30

Babysitter list
Contact tourist office

Ski schools
Most offer classes for
ages 5 up (ESF prices
from €219 for 6 days)

at the bottom of the slopes in Le Fornet is recommended as a good place for skiers and non-skiers to meet. The terrace of hotel Brussel's in Val d'Isère, right by the nursery slopes, has 'good food and excellent service' and the Grand Paradis, next door, is 'an enjoyable lunch venue, very well run and efficient'. The Gourmandine serves 'very good lunches and is popular with locals'. This year, reporters' main gripe has been having to pay to use the loos in many mountain restaurants, regardless of being a patron or not.

SCHOOLS AND GUIDES
A very wide choice

There is a huge choice of schools, guides and private instructors. But as they all get busy, at peak periods it's best to book in advance. Practically all the schools run off-piste groups at various levels of competence, as well as on-piste lessons. Outside the ESF, practically all the instructors and guides speak good English, and many are native English-speakers.

New Generation, a British-run school, has a branch here. Reports are very positive: 'The morning we had was one of the highlights of our holiday – lots of fun and we learned a lot too' and 'Worth every euro'. The Development Centre, based in the Precision Ski shop in the heart of the village, is a group of British instructors who offer intensive clinics for all levels of skier, and have been highly praised.

Mountain Masters is a group of British and French instructors and guides, and a reporter said: 'They knew exactly how to take me over that seventh-week plateau.' Progression is a new British-run school with a maximum group size of 6 or 8, and a 2008 reporter thought they had 'a great attitude and were very accommodating, gave plenty of individual attention and ensured great progress in the space of one lesson'.

We've heard from lots of satisfied pupils of Snow Fun ('good value and good instructors', said one) and Evolution 2. Reporters consistently praise Bernard Chesneau of Ski Mastery. Misty Fly is a specialist snowboard school. Private lessons with BASS get a rave review from a reporter, whose nervous wife 'was skiing with competence and confidence after a few hours' lessons'.

YSE
Val d'Isère

Val d'Isère Chalet Specialist
26 Chalets & Gourmet Food
Winter 2008-09
0845 122 1414
www.yseski.co.uk

GETTING THERE

Air Geneva 180km/ 112 miles (4hr); Lyon 220km/137 miles (4hr); Chambéry 130km/81 miles (3hr)

Rail Bourg-St-Maurice (30km/19 miles); regular buses from station

SNOWPIX.COM / CHRIS GILL

The off-piste Tour de Charvet run takes its name from this peak and goes round the back; Epaule and Santons pistes are on the right of this pic ↓

Alpine Expérience and Top Ski specialise in guided off-piste groups – an excellent way to get off-piste safely without the cost of hiring a guide as an individual. We have had great mornings out with both, and a 2008 reporter says of Alpine Expérience: 'We had great days with them, including our first experience of putting on skins to make some fresh tracks.' Heli-skiing trips can be arranged from over the border in Italy – heli-drops are banned in France. Henry's Avalanche Talk at Dick's Tea Bar (every Tuesday and Thursday evening) was 'very engaging and interesting', says a reporter.

FACILITIES FOR CHILDREN
Good tour op possibilities
Many people prefer to use the facilities of UK tour operators such as Mark Warner, Ski Beat or Esprit. But there's a 'children's village' for three to eight year olds, with supervised indoor and outdoor activities on the village nursery slopes. A reporter was 'very pleased' with the child care there: 'The staff speak English and are very organised, in particular about safety.'

STAYING THERE

HOW TO GO
Lots of choice
More British tour operators go to Val than anywhere else except Méribel.
Chalets This is Planet Chalet, with properties at every level of the market. Many of the most impressive are in the side valley running south from the village – some in the elevated enclave of Les Carats. YSE is a Val d'Isère specialist, with 25 varied chalets – from swanky apartments for four or six to proper big chalets. Companies with top-end properties include VIP, Scott Dunn and Descent International. Le Ski has nine chalets (all with Wi-Fi), including six splendid all-en-suite places grouped together just up from the main street (with a big outdoor hot tub) and two swanky chalets for eight nearby (which share another outdoor hot tub). Ski Total has several very smart places, including some with sauna, steam room, hot tub or pool. Ski Beat has five en-suite apartments in one grand chalet at La Daille. Finlays has 10 chalets plus a self-catered apartment. There are several chalet hotels. Mark Warner has four, including the family-friendly Cygnaski, the nightlife hot spot Moris and the central Val d'Isère with outdoor swimming pool. Total has the modern Champs Avalin at La Daille. Esprit, the

Val d'Isère

Interactive resort shortlist builder at **www.wtss.co.uk**

ACTIVITIES

Indoor Swimming pool, sports hall (badminton, gym etc), cinema, fitness and health clubs, yoga, bridge, chess

Outdoor Ice rink, walking, snowshoeing, snowmobiles, ice climbing, dog sledding, ice driving, paragliding, microlight flights, helicopter flights, igloo evenings

SMART LODGINGS

Check out our feature chapters at the front of the book.

OT VAL D'ISERE / NUTS.FR

The centre of Val looks pretty at night; and it's pleasant in the day time too ↓

family specialist, has the Ducs de Savoie and another large chalet André near the centre. Ski Olympic has the Gelinotte nestled in the pine trees overlooking the centre.

Hotels There are about 40 to choose from and they have moved distinctly up-market in the last few years; there are now eight plush 4-stars (but there are plenty of 2- and 3-stars too),

****Barmes de L'Ours (0479 413700) The best in town. Good position, close to slopes and centre. The fabulous rooms are in a different style on each floor. Three restaurants. Excellent indoor pool, and spa.

****Christiania (0479 060825) Big chalet. Chic but friendly. Pool, sauna.

****Blizzard (0479 060207) Comfortable. Convenient. Indoor-outdoor pool and sauna. Good food.

****Aigle des Neiges (0479 061888) Highly rated refurbished version of former Latitudes. Cool and central.

****Savoie (0479 000115) Completely refurbished. Central. Smart spa.

****Brussel's (0479 060539) Excellent location, right on nursery slope, with big terrace. Sauna, steam, hot tub.

****Tsanteleina (0479 061213) On the main road. 'Courteous staff, welcoming

bar area, but not outstanding food.'

***Savoyarde (0479 060155) Rustic decor. Leisure centre. Good food (except for vegetarians). Small rooms.

***Grand Paradis (0479 061173) Next to Brussel's. Good food.

***Kandahar (0479 060239) Smart, newish building above Taverne d'Alsace on main street.

***Mercure (0479 061293) 'The food and wine list are excellent.' 'Convenient and pleasant.'

***Sorbiers (0479 062377) Modern but cosy B&B, not far out. 'Clean, comfortable, good-sized rooms.'

***Samovar (0479 061351) In La Daille. Traditional, with good food. 'Very friendly and helpful staff.'

**Danival (0479 060065) B&B, piste-side location. 'Very reasonable.'

Apartments There are thousands of apartments available. Among the best are Chalets de Solaise (with outdoor pool) and Alpina Lodge close to the centre, Chalets du Jardin Alpin at the foot of Solaise and Chalets du Laisinant (at Laisinant). Erna Low, Ski Amis, Ski Independence, Val d'Isère à la Carte, Ski Collection and local agency Val d'Isère Agence (0479 067350) have good selections.

UK PACKAGES

Action Outdoors, Airtours, Alpine Answers, Alpine Weekends, Chalet World Ski, Chardon Mountain Lodges, Club Med, Crystal, Crystal Finest, Descent International, Directski. com, Elegant Resorts, Erna Low, Esprit, Finlays, First Choice, Flexiski, Friendship Travel, Independent Ski Links, Inghams, Inspired to Ski, Interactive Resorts, Interhome, Jeffersons, Kuoni, Lagrange, Le Ski, Made to Measure, Mark Warner, Momentum, Mountain Tracks, Neilson, Oxford Ski Co, Powder White, Scott Dunn, Silver Ski, Ski Activity, Ski Amis, Ski Beat, Ski Collection, Ski Expectations, Ski France, Skifrance4less, Ski Freshtracks, Ski holidayextras.com, Ski Independence, Ski Leisure Direction, Ski Line, Ski McNeill, Ski Olympic, Ski Solutions, Ski Supreme, Ski Total, Skitracer, Ski-Val, Ski Weekend, Skiworld, Snow Finders, Snowline, Snoworks, Supertravel, Thomson, UCPA, Val d'Isère A la Carte, VIP, White Roc, YSE

Phone numbers
From abroad use the prefix +33 and omit the initial '0' of the phone number

TOURIST OFFICE

t 0479 060660
info@valdisere.com
www.valdisere.com

EATING OUT
Plenty of good places

The 70-odd restaurants offer a wide variety of cuisines; there's a free *Guide des Tables* booklet covering 23, but many worthwhile places are missing.

The Grande Ourse, by the nursery slope, is one place to head for a top-of-the-range meal. Another is Les Clochetons, out in the Manchet valley (they run a free minibus service) – we enjoyed the foie gras and duck. The Table de l'Ours, in the Barmes de l'Ours hotel, has a Michelin star. The hotel Aigle des Neiges restaurants are rated highly by locals.

There are plenty of pleasant mid-priced places. We always enjoy the unchanging Taverne d'Alsace. The Perdrix Blanche went through a bad spell but has now improved again. Tufs, on the snow at La Daille, is open in the evenings (see 'Mountain restaurants'). The 'impressive' Austrian-influenced menu of the Schuss restaurant in the Grand Paradis hotel has been recommended. The Barillon de la Rosée Blanche is 'completely splendid, with great steaks and home-made ice-creams'. Bar Jacques is 'small but very welcoming with excellent food'. Chez Paolo has been praised for 'excellent' pizza and pasta; the Corniche for being 'traditional French, very enjoyable'; Casa Scara does 'good food'; the Canyon 'caters to all pockets'; but service at these last two has been criticised. The Grand Cocor has 'excellent food and choice', plus a 'very accommodating manager who'd show Champions League matches if asked'. The Belle Etoile is popular with locals for 'excellent French/Asian cuisine'. 1789 has 'great service, excellent meals and value for money', plus 'outstanding' côte de boeuf that kept a group of 30-year-old lads coming back for more.

APRES-SKI
Very lively

Nightlife is surprisingly energetic, given that most people have spent a hard day on the slopes. There are lots of bars, many with happy hours and then music and dancing later on.

The Folie Douce, at the top of the La Daille gondola, has become an Austrian-style tea-time rave, with music and dancing; you can ride the gondola down. At La Daille the bar at the Samovar hotel is 'a good spot for a beer after skiing'. In downtown Val, Bananas (cosy wooden chalet with nice terrace), Café Face ('cheap beer, friendly atmosphere'), the Moris pub (live music at tea time and later) and Saloon (underneath hotel Brussel's) fill up as the slopes close; the 'friendly' Boubou, Bar Jacques and the Perdrix Blanche are popular with locals. The Petit Danois is said to be better than Victor's bar. The Pacific Bar has sport on big-screen TVs. The basement Taverne d'Alsace is quiet and relaxing. For a civilised drink in welcoming surroundings head for the first-floor bar of the hotel Blizzard.

Later on, the famous Dick's Tea Bar is the main disco, but it gets mixed reviews. The Graal is 'usually good'. And a new nightclub, the Doudoune, is due to open for 2008/09.

OFF THE SLOPES
A reasonable amount to do

Val is primarily a resort for those keen to get on to the slopes. But there's a swimming pool, sports centre, outdoor ice rink and the range of shops is better than in most high French resorts. Lunchtime meetings present problems: the easily accessible mountain restaurants are few, and your friends may prefer lunching miles away. A reporter suggests the 'fascinating' nature walk from Le Fornet to Pont St Charles.

Val d'Isère

413

Interactive resort shortlist builder at **www.wtss.co.uk**

Valmorel

The purpose-built resort the French got mainly right: easy on the eye, as well as convenient; sadly, they didn't pick the ideal site

414

OT VALMOREL / AD GROSS

The main route out of the village is a fast quad. And the main route back is a steepish red under it, which can be quite bumpy and tricky by the end of the day ↓

- ➕ A sympathetically designed purpose-built, car-free resort
- ➕ Largely slope-side accommodation
- ➕ Extensive easy slopes linked to St-François-Longchamp give even the timid a chance to travel around
- ➕ Beginners and children particularly well catered for

- ➖ Most pistes are easy, and of limited vertical
- ➖ Fairly low, so snow can suffer
- ➖ Still lots of slow lifts and drags, with peak-season lift queues
- ➖ Steep site, and outlying parts are very separate from the main street
- ➖ Few alternatives to self-catering

Built from scratch in the mid-1970s, Valmorel was intended to look and feel like a mountain village – or perhaps a tiny mountain town; shops and restaurants line the cute, narrow, traffic-free main street. Compared with its illustrious neighbours in the Three Valleys, the mountain feels a bit second-rate; but it really competes for French family business with cheaper resorts to the south.

THE RESORT

Valmorel is the main resort in 'Le Grand Domaine' – a ski area shared with St-François and Longchamp, across the Madeleine pass. Bourg-Morel is the heart of the resort – an intimate, traffic-free street where you'll find most of the shops and restaurants. It's pleasant and usually lively, with a distinctly family feel and 'friendly locals', says a 2008 visitor. Scattered here and there on the hillside are the six 'hameaux' with most of the lodgings. Hameau-du-Mottet is convenient – it is at the top of the Télébourg (the cross-village lift) with good access to the main lifts and from the return runs. All the mega-resorts of the Tarentaise are within driving distance.

THE MOUNTAINS

Variety is not lacking, and the extent is enough to provide interesting day trips. There are still a lot of draglifts and slow chairs.

Slopes The pistes are spread over a number of minor valleys and ridges either side of the Col de la Madeleine. The most heavily used route out of the village is the fast Altispace quad chair. From the top, a network of lifts and pistes takes you to the Col de la Madeleine and beyond that to Lauzière or the slopes of Longchamp and St-François. The Pierrafort sector has its own runs back towards the village, or you can work your way round to the Beaudin and Madeleine sectors.

Terrain parks The Snowzone at the top of the Crève Coeur chair has a park with jumps, rails and tables, half-pipe and boardercross. A park-only pass is available. A second boardercross was built at the Biollène chair and there's another at St François.

Snow reliability There's snowmaking on the nursery slopes and the main runs back to base, but when we visited a couple of seasons ago it wasn't used sufficiently and slopes were bare and icy. The area is low by local standards, and quite sunny – not good news.

Experts There are a few challenging pistes; the steepest are in the Pierrafort sector; but there is good off-piste that doesn't get skied out.

Intermediates The whole area – except for the steepest black runs – is ideal,

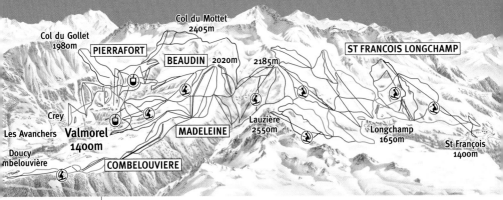

Col du Mottet 2405m
Col du Gollet 1980m
PIERRAFORT
BEAUDIN 2020m 2185m
ST FRANCOIS LONGCHAMP
Crey
Les Avanchers Valmorel
1400m
MADELEINE
Lauzière 2550m
Longchamp 1650m
St François 1400m
Doucy mbelouvière
COMBELOUVIERE

Valmorel

415

Interactive resort shortlist builder at www.wtss.co.uk

KEY FACTS

| Resort | 1400m |
| | 4,590ft |

Le Grand Domaine

Slopes	1250-2550m
	4,100-8,370ft
Lifts	49
Pistes	152km
	94 miles
Green	33%
Blue	39%
Red	19%
Black	9%
Snowmaking	
	202 guns

For Domaine de Valmorel only

Slopes	1250-2405m
	4,100-7,890ft
Lifts	38
Pistes	95km
	59 miles

UK PACKAGES

Alpine Answers, Crystal, Erna Low, Independent Ski Links, Interactive Resorts, Lagrange, Neilson, Ski France, Skiholiday extras.com, Ski Independence, Ski Leisure Direction, Ski Supreme, Skitracer
St-François Erna Low, Lagrange, Ski Independence, Ski Leisure Direction

Phone numbers
From abroad use the prefix +33 and omit the initial '0' of the phone number

TOURIST OFFICE

t 0479 098555
info@valmorel.com
www.valmorel.com

though the main home run can be quite daunting at the end of the day. We have had mixed reports about piste grooming.
Beginners There are dedicated learning areas ('Still the best we've seen, 10/10') right by the village for both adults and children. There's a free beginner lift at Le Crey.
Snowboarding There are decent intermediate runs; but new boarders will find some of the draglifts tricky.
Cross-country Trails adding up to 20km/12 miles can be reached by bus.
Queues The Altispace chair out of the resort is reportedly slow to start in the morning, and both village lifts can build big queues at peak times; depending on your location, you may be able to avoid these.
Mountain restaurants There are half a dozen or so. Banquise 2000, with a great location at Col de la Madeleine, and Prariond ('excellent, lovely terrace' and 'delicious raspberry flan') have been recommended. Also mentioned are the Altipiano for 'very good food and service' and the Alpage – 'very good location and value'. The Arbet self-service does 'good omelettes'.
Schools and guides Recent reports have been positive for both adult and children's classes. A recent reporter said that his children's private lessons were 'very good', the instructor 'punctual and good'. Teaching for first-timers is a speciality of the resort.
Facilities for children Valmorel goes out of its way to cater for children. Piou-Piou club is a comprehensive child care – 18 months to 6 years – facility run by the ski school, and children taking ski lessons can have lunch there, too. Advance booking is essential.

STAYING THERE

How to go Self-catering packages are the norm.
Hotels The Village Club du Soleil (0479 098777) is right on the slopes. The 'ideally located' 2-star Hotel du Bourg (0479 098666) is reportedly 'a bit faded but fit-for-purpose'.
Apartments The Athamante et Valeriane apartments have been praised.
Eating out The Petit Prince ('excellent, friendly service'), Marmite, Table du Berger and Ski Roc win approval from reporters.
Après-ski Immediate après-ski centres on the lively cafe-bars with terraces at the foot of the slopes; after-dark activities centre on the main street.
Off the slopes It's not a great place to hang around but there are various activities, such as snow-shoeing and horse sleigh rides. There's a fitness centre, a cinema and a toboggan run.
Staying down the valley Doucy Combelouvière is at the end of a long gentle green run below Valmorel at 1260m/4,130ft. The way back is via a chair and successive draglifts. It's a small place with a 2-star hotel and apartments. We used to have a regular reporter who stayed there and said 'it has almost as much ski convenience as Valmorel, with a pleasanter home run at the end of the day'. It's quiet in the evenings though.

✳ **Want to get the next edition free?**
Send us a useful report on your holiday, and win one of 100 free copies. Find out more at:
www.wtss.co.uk

Val Thorens

Europe's highest resort, with guaranteed good snow – and other attractions: stylish lodgings and good restaurants among them

NEWS

For 2008/09 a new apartment building, the Sabot de Venus, is to open. Some of the apartments will be run on a catered chalet basis.

For 2007/08 the Cairn and Caron gondolas (leading to the Cîme de Caron cable car) were replaced by new eight-seat gondolas. The stations were revamped too. A new blue run was created under the Cairn gondola and a new terrain park opened in the Plateau sector.

+ Extensive local slopes to suit all abilities, and good access to the rest of the vast Three Valleys

+ The highest resort in the Alps and one of the most snow-sure, with mainly north-facing slopes

+ Convenient, gentle nursery slopes

+ Not as much of an eyesore as most high, purpose-built resorts, with more and more smart lodgings

+ Compact village with direct slope access from most accommodation

– Not a tree in sight – in bad weather it can be bleak, and in seriously bad weather entirely closed

– Parts of the village are much less attractive to walk through in the evening than to ski past in the day

– Not much to do off the slopes

– Some very crowded pistes and dangerous intersections

– Still some queues – and really serious ones for the Cîme de Caron cable car

For the enthusiast looking for the best snow available, it's difficult to beat Val Thorens. That wonderful snow lies on some pretty wonderful slopes suitable for everyone from beginner to expert. And the village – always one of the better-designed high-altitude stations – gets more attractive as it continues to develop, and gain more smart accommodation and restaurants.

But we still prefer a cosier base elsewhere in the Three Valleys. That way, if a storm socks in, we can play in the woods; if the sun is scorching, we have the option of setting off for Val Thorens. The formula simply doesn't work the other way round. For a pre-Christmas or an April trip, though, it's the best base.

THE RESORT

Val Thorens is built high above the treeline on a sunny, west-facing slope at the head of its valley, surrounded by peaks, slopes and lifts. The streets are supposedly traffic-free. Most visitors' cars are banished to car parks, except on Saturday. Workers' cars still generate a fair amount of traffic, though, and Saturdays can be mayhem. A reporter recommends booking parking in advance: 'It's cheaper and you are less likely to get a far distant parking spot.'

Many buildings are designed with their 'fronts' facing the slopes, and their relatively dreary backs facing the streets. There is quite good everyday shopping, a fair choice of bars and restaurants, and a good sports centre.

It is a classic purpose-built resort, with lots of convenient slope-side accommodation (but some of the newer buildings are less convenient – see below). It's quite a complex little village; but it's compact – our scale plan is one of the smallest in these pages. At its heart is the snowy Place de Caron, where pedestrians mix with skiers and boarders. Many of the shops and restaurants are clustered here, along with the best hotels; the sports and leisure centres are nearby.

The village is basically divided in two by a little slope (with a draglift) that leads down from here to the broad main nursery slope running the length of the village. The upper half of the village is centred on the Place de Péclet. A road runs across the hillside from here to the chalet-style Plein Sud area, where many of the most attractive new apartments have been built. The highest of these can be reached and left on snow only by awkward off-piste sections ('not for the faint-hearted on ice') or by road ('frequent ski-bus, about 200m/660ft walk to piste'). The lower half of the village is more diffuse, with the Rue du Soleil winding down from the

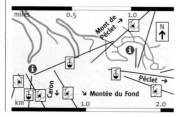

The 'fourth valley', south of the main area – slow chairs to the high-point of the Three Valleys →

KEY FACTS

Resort	2300m
	7,550ft

Three Valleys		
Slopes	1260-3230m	
	4,130-10,600ft	
Lifts		180
Pistes		600km
		373 miles
Green		15%
Blue		38%
Red		37%
Black		10%
Snowmaking		33%

Val Thorens only		
Slopes	1800-3230m	
	5,900-10,600ft	
Lifts		29
Pistes		140km
		87 miles
Green		12%
Blue		37%
Red		40%
Black		11%
Snowmaking		38%

LIFT PASSES

Three Valleys

Prices in €		
Age	**1-day**	**6-day**
under 13	33	165
13 to 64	44	220
over 65	38	187

Free under 5, over 75
Beginner Four lifts for 50% of Val Thorens day rate

Notes
Covers Courchevel, La Tania, Méribel, Val Thorens, Les Menuires and St-Martin; family reductions; pedestrian and half-day passes

Alternative pass
Val Thorens-Orelle only

dreary bus station (visitors praise the free bus service) to the big Pierre & Vacances apartments.

Seen from the slopes, the resort is not as ugly as many of its rivals. The buildings are mainly medium-rise and wood-clad; some are distinctly stylish.

THE MOUNTAINS

The main disadvantage of Val Thorens is the lack of trees. Heavy snowfalls or high wind can shut practically all the lifts and slopes, and even if they don't close, poor visibility can be a problem. Piste marking and signposting have been criticised by reporters. Piste classification is generally accurate (but see 'For intermediates', below).

THE SLOPES
High and snow-sure
The resort has a wide piste going right down the front of it, leading down to a number of different lifts. The big **Péclet** gondola, with 30-person cabins, rises 700m/2,300ft to the Péclet glacier, with a choice of red runs down. One links across to a wide area of intermediate runs served by lifts to cols either side of the **Pointe de Thorens**. You can take red or blue runs into the 'fourth valley', the Maurienne,

from one of these – the **Col de Rosaël**, now served by the Grand Fond 30-person gondola.

Above **Orelle** in the Maurienne valley two successive slow chairs go up to 3230m/10,600ft on the flanks of Pointe du Bouchet – the highest lift-served point in the Three Valleys, with stunning views. The former black run off the back of here is now off-piste because of crevasse and avalanche danger, and often poor snow.

The 150-person cable car to **Cîme de Caron** is one of the great lifts of the Alps, rising 900m/2,950ft in no time at all. It can be reached by skiing across from mid-mountain, or by coming up on the Caron gondola that starts below the village. From the top there are fabulous views and a choice of red and black pistes down the front, or a black into the Maurienne.

The relatively low **Boismint** sector is overlooked by many visitors, but is actually a very respectable hill with a total vertical of 860m/2,820ft.

Chairlifts heading north from the resort serve sunny slopes above the village and also lead to the link to the Méribel valley. Les Menuires can be reached via these lifts; the alternative Boulevard Cumin along the valley floor is nearly flat, and can be hard work.

boarding

Val Thorens has always been popular with snowboarders as it is the highest and most snow-sure of the Three Valleys resorts, as well as having a younger and more affordable feel in comparison with Courchevel and Méribel. The terrain is rather bleak; however, there are great steep runs, gullies and groomed pistes for all levels and forms of snowboarding. The lifts are mainly chairs and gondolas.

TERRAIN PARKS
More than adequate

The terrain park moved to the 'Plateau' during the 2007/08 season and has greatly improved. It is accessible via various chairlifts, and has a nice open layout (www. snowparkvalthorens.com). There are four different areas that range from beginner to pro, with all sorts of kickers, rails and box combinations. There is a half-pipe that can – depending on snow conditions – be good. There is also a bordercross course, which has some great banked turns. The whole park is well maintained, and new obstacles are often built for local competitions. The park also has a giant airbag jump, to test your aerials before you take them to the snow. Neighbouring Les Menuires has a good terrain park, above Reberty.

SNOW RELIABILITY
One of the best

Few resorts can rival Val Thorens for reliably good snow-cover, thanks to its altitude and generally north-facing slopes. Snowmaking covers a lot of the key pistes, including the crowded south- and west-facing runs on the way back from the Méribel valley and in the Orelle sector. But the terrain is rocky and needs a lot of snow for good coverage – we have found the higher runs patchy in recent early season visits when snow throughout the Alps has been slow to arrive. The resort offers a 'snow guarantee' that at

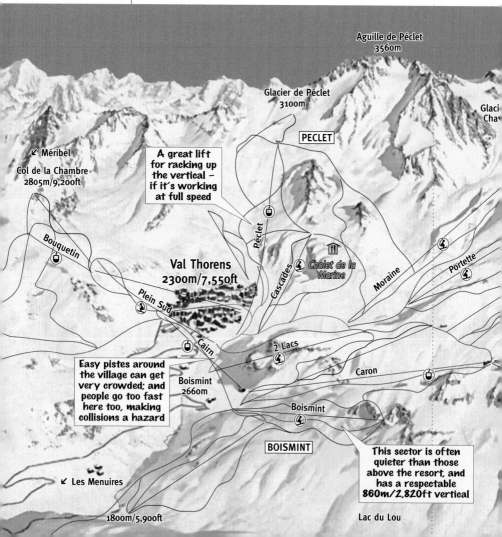

Aguille de Péclet
3556m

Glacier de Péclet
3100m

PECLET

Méribel
Col de la Chambre
2805m/9,200ft

A great lift for racking up the vertical – if it's working at full speed

Péclet

Val Thorens
2300m/7,550ft

Bouquetin

Cascades

Chalet de la Marine

Moraine

Portette

Plein Sud

Cairn

2 Lacs

Caron

Easy pistes around the village can get very crowded; and people go too fast here too, making collisions a hazard

Boismint
2660m

Boismint

BOISMINT

This sector is often quieter than those above the resort, and has a respectable 860m/2,820ft vertical

Les Menuires

1800m/5,900ft

Lac du Lou

least 70% of the area's lifts will be open, with free skiing days on a future visit if this guarantee is not met.

FOR EXPERTS
Lots to do off-piste

Val Thorens' local pistes are primarily intermediate terrain; many of the blacks could easily be classified red instead. The fast Cascades chair serves a short but steep black run that quickly gets mogulled. The pistes down from the Cîme de Caron cable car are challenging, but not seriously steep, and there's a good, sunny black run off the back into the fourth valley – the highlight of the trip for one reporter this year.

The red Chamois, Falaise and Variante runs from Col de Rosaël can get heavily mogulled and challenging. The sunny Marielle run, one of the routes from the Méribel valley, is one of the easiest blacks we've come across, but it can get crowded and be icy in the morning.

There is a huge amount of very good off-piste terrain to explore with a guide – see the special off-piste feature panel overleaf.

FOR INTERMEDIATES
Great in good weather

The scope for intermediates throughout the Three Valleys is enormous. It will take a keen intermediate only 90 minutes or so to get to Courchevel 1650 at the far end, if not distracted by the endless runs on the way.

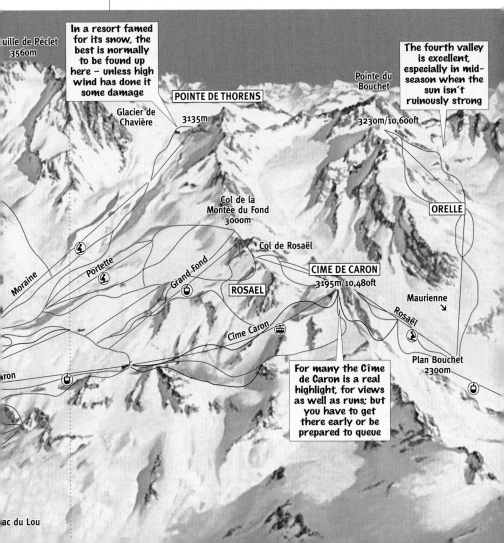

uille de Péclet
3556m

In a resort famed for its snow, the best is normally to be found up here – unless high wind has done it some damage

POINTE DE THORENS

Glacier de Chavière   3135m

Pointe du Bouchet

The fourth valley is excellent, especially in mid-season when the sun isn't ruinously strong

3230m/10,600ft

ORELLE

Col de la Montée du Fond 3000m

Col de Rosaël

CIME DE CARON
3195m/10,480ft

Maurienne

Rosaël

Moraine

Portette

Grand Fond

ROSAEL

Cîme Caron

Plan Bouchet
2300m

ron

For many the Cîme de Caron is a real highlight, for views as well as runs; but you have to get there early or be prepared to queue

ac du Lou

UK PACKAGES

Airtours, Alpine
Answers, Chalet World
Ski, Club Med, Crystal,
Crystal Finest,
Directski.com, Erna
Low, First Choice,
Flexiski, Independent
Ski Links, Inghams,
Interactive Resorts,
Interhome, Kuoni,
Lagrange, Made to
Measure, Neilson, Ski
Activity, Ski Amis, Ski
Collection, Ski
Expectations, Ski
France, Skifrance4less,
Ski Freshtracks,
Skiholidayextras.com,
Ski Independence, Ski
Leisure Direction, Ski
Line, Ski McNeill, Ski
Solutions, Ski Supreme,
Ski Total, Skitracer, Ski
Weekend, Skiworld,
Thomson

The local slopes in Val Thorens are some of the best intermediate terrain in the region. Most of the pistes are easy reds and blues (the runs on the top half of the mountain are steeper than those back into the resort) and made even more enjoyable by the excellent snow. One reporter reckons that the Hermine blue is unusually challenging for a blue.

The snow on the red Col run is normally some of the best around. The blue Moraine below it is gentle and popular with the schools. The Grand Fond gondola serves a good variety of red runs. The red and blue runs from the Péclet gondola are excellent. The Pluviomètre from the Trois Vallées chair is a glorious varied run, away from the lifts. Adventurous intermediates shouldn't miss the Cîme de Caron runs. The black run is not intimidating – it's very wide, usually has good snow, and is a wonderful fast cruise when freshly groomed (though reports suggest this is less likely than it was). Don't neglect the excellent, quiet Boismint area next door to Caron, either.

FOR BEGINNERS
Good late-season choice
The slopes at the foot of the resort are very gentle and provide convenient, snow-sure nursery slopes, now with moving walkway lifts. There are no long green runs to progress to, but the blues immediately above the village are easy. The resort's height and bleakness make it cold in midwinter, and intimidating in bad weather.

FOR CROSS-COUNTRY
Go to Les Menuires
There are no cross-country trails in Val Thorens. Your best bet is the 28km/17 mile link between Les Menuires and St-Martin-de-Belleville.

QUEUES
Persistent at the Cîme de Caron
Recent reports suggest that the longest queues are for the largest and most rewarding lifts, notably the Cîme de Caron cable car. The queues move fairly quickly, but reporters warn that visits to the Cîme de Caron really need to be timed to miss the crowds – get there very early if you can. A 2008 visitor comments: 'The queues for the Cîme de Caron seem to be worse than ever – the new gondola and interchange station have made access more comfortable, but simply bring more people to queue.'

In good weather the Rosaël chair back from the fourth valley is a serious bottleneck. And when snow is in short supply elsewhere, the pressure on the Val Thorens lifts can increase markedly.

But crowded pistes and people going too quickly, especially around the village, is a bigger problem than

FABULOUS OFF-PISTE IN VAL THORENS

Val Thorens offers a huge choice of off-piste. And because of the high altitude, the snow stays powdery longer here than in lower parts of the Three Valleys.

For those with little off-piste experience, the Pierre Lory Pass run is ideal. It is a very large and gentle slope, and you access the pass by doing an easy traverse on the Chavière glacier from the top of the Col chairlift. When you arrive at Pierre Lory Pass there are breathtaking views of the Aiguilles d'Arves in the Maurienne valley, and you will be just above the glacier du Bouchet, which you then ski down, rejoining the lift system at Plan Bouchet.

For those with more off-piste under their belt already, the Lac du Lou is a famous off-piste run of 1400m/4,590ft vertical. It is easily accessible from the Cîme de Caron. The many ways into this long, wide valley allow plenty of variety and opportunities for making first tracks; because many of the slopes face north or north-west it is not unusual to find good powder most of the ski season, even in late April. The views are stunning and you'll notice the quietness and vastness of the whole valley.

La Combe sans Nom in the fourth valley, also accessible from the Cîme de Caron cable car, usually offers superb skiing and snowboard conditions. There's a choice of south-, west- and, on the far side, some east-facing slopes, which makes for excellent spring skiing conditions.

For the more adventurous there are many options, including hiking up from the Col chairlift to a long run over the Gébroulaz glacier down to Méribel-Mottaret.

But don't even think about doing any off-piste runs without a fully qualified guide or instructor. Route finding can be difficult, there can be avalanche danger, and hidden hazards such as cliffs and crevasses lurk.

SCHOOLS

ESF
t 0479 000286

Ski Cool
t 0479 000492

Prosneige
t 0479 010700

Attitude
t 0479 065772

Classes (ESF prices)
6 half-days (2hr
45min am) €138

Private lessons
from €38 for 1hr

GUIDES

Mountain office
t 0689 292336

CHILDREN

**Nursery/mini-club
(ESF)**
t 0479 000286
Ages from 3mnth

Ski school
The schools offer
classes for children
aged 4 and over (ESF:
6 mornings from
€125)

GETTING THERE

Air Geneva 160km/
99 miles (3½hr); Lyon
193km/120 miles
(3½hr); Chambéry
112km/70 miles
(2½hr)

Rail Moûtiers
(37km/23 miles);
regular buses from
station

SMART LODGINGS

Check out our feature
chapters at the front
of the book.

queues. We noticed this on our 2007 visit and several reporters have commented on it too; one was crashed into by an out-of-control (British) intermediate while 'standing watching the children'.

MOUNTAIN RESTAURANTS
Lots of choice
For a high, modern resort, the choice of restaurants is good.
Editors' choice We've had several good lunches at the table-service section of the Chalet de la Marine (0479 000186), on the Dalles piste ('yummy dessert buffet' says a 2008 visitor). And it has a big terrace with music after 3pm – 'not bad après for France'. The self-service section below does 'fantastic quality pizzas'.
Worth knowing about The big Chalets de Thorens at the base of the Moraine chairlift gets good reports: 'fresh home-made waffles', 'friendly, chatty staff'. And the Chalet des 2 Ours on the Blanchot run in the Boismint sector gets repeated recommendations – 'one of the best we've experienced: tasty, well-portioned fare and great views', 'good food and price'. The Moutière, near the top of the chair of the same name, is one of the more reasonably priced huts. The Chalet Chinal Donat in the Maurienne valley is very popular, but a 2008 visitor was not impressed. The Caribou (formerly the Genépi), on the Genépi run, offers 'good but expensive' food; a 2008 visitor found the service 'stretched' and the toilets 'not clean'. The Chalet des 2 Lacs is 'the best piste-side restaurant', says a 2008 visitor: 'good service', 'great French onion soup'.
If you head back to the village you're sure of a good lunch at the Fitz Roy or Oxalys – both have slope-side terraces. A 2008 reporter says, 'The 48 euro set lunch at the Oxalys is superb value, but anything else will cost an arm and a leg. The service is great too.' The Chamois d'Or, next to the twin draglifts in the resort centre has also been recommended in 2008: 'really good pizza', 'nice open fire when it's cold and a nice terrace when it's warm'.

SCHOOLS AND GUIDES
A mixed bag
The ESF offers 3Vallées X-ploration groups for those who want to cover a lot of ground while receiving lessons – they're available by the day or the

week, and can include off-piste. Two 2007 boarder beginners were 'delighted' with their lessons. And a 2008 visitor was pleased to tell us that there is now an English instructor on the ESF staff. Prosneige was recommended by a 2007 visitor for 'small groups and friendly instruction'. Ski Cool class sizes are guaranteed not to exceed 10. There are several specialist guiding outfits.

FACILITIES FOR CHILDREN
Coolly efficient
We lack recent reports on the ESF nursery. The Prosneige school takes children from age five, and a 2008 reporter was 'very happy' with the standard of instruction and care provided.

STAYING THERE

HOW TO GO
Wide range of options
Accommodation is of a higher standard than in many purpose-built resorts – more comfortable as well as stylish.
Chalets There are apartments operated as catered chalets. Ski Total offers several, including some brand new for 2008/09, as well as an actual chalet sold as two units sharing a sauna.
Hotels Unusually for a high, purpose-built resort, there are plenty of hotels, and there's a Club Med, too.
****Fitz Roy (0479 000478) The sole 4-star is smart with good service and lovely rooms. Good restaurant with flexible half-board menu. Pool. Well placed.
***Val Thorens (0479 000433) Next door to Fitz Roy. 'Comfortable and friendly.'
***Sherpa (0479 000070) Highly recommended for atmosphere and food and 'wonderful, hard working staff'. Less than ideal position near

ACTIVITIES

Indoor Sports centre (spa, sauna, fitness room, hot tub, tennis, squash, swimming pool, volleyball, table tennis, badminton, football), cinema, bowling, concerts

Outdoor Paragliding, sightseeing microlight flights, snowmobiles, snowshoeing, walks, tobogganing

Phone numbers
From abroad use the prefix +33 and omit the initial '0' of the phone number

TOURIST OFFICE

t 0479 000808
valtho@valthorens.com
www.valthorens.com

the top of the resort.
***Val Chavière** (0479 000033) Friendly, convenient.
***Bel Horizon** (0479 000477) Friendly, family-run.
Apartments Val Thorens has quite a few above-average apartment developments, many offered by UK 4-star apartment specialist Ski Collection. In the Plein Sud area above the main village Balcons de Val Thorens, Chalet Altitude, Chalets du Soleil, Chalet Val 2400 have all been recommended; some have a pool. A 2008 reporter praises the Chamois d'Or apartments, just above the base of the Retour drags – 'simply furnished, extremely helpful staff'. On its own just above the village is the Chalet des Neiges, with pool. At the very bottom of the resort, the Residence Oxalys has its own wonderful restaurant (see 'Eating out') as well as a large lounge, pool and sauna. There are three Montagnettes developments in different locations. A very smart new residence, the Sabot de Venus is to open for 2008/09.

EATING OUT
Surprisingly wide range
Val Thorens has something for most tastes and pockets. The resort's excellent pocket guide contains a useful restaurant section.

Top of the range is the Michelin-starred restaurant in the Residence Oxalys ('the highest star in Europe', the resort claims). We tried it in 2007 and had a delicious and very inventive meal. Expensive, but worth it.

The Fitz Roy (where we also had a delicious meal) and Val Thorens hotels do classic French food and were the best in town before Oxalys appeared.

For something more regional, the best bets are the Vieux Chalet and the Galoubet. A recent reporter says that the Chaumière is a good, cheaper alternative. Other recommendations by readers include the Auberge des Balcons ('huge' but 'sometimes difficult to get a table'), Cabane ('authentic French feel, great food and friendly staff'), the Montana ('good-quality food, but no longer reasonably priced'), El Gringo's, the Toit du Monde and the Joyeuse Fondue. The Blanchot is a stylish wine bar with a simple but varied carte. Several pizzerias are recommended, including the Scapin ('friendly staff').

APRES-SKI
Livelier than you'd imagine
Val Thorens is more lively at night than most high-altitude ski-stations. The Red Fox up at Balcons is crowded at close of play, with karaoke. At the opposite extreme there's the Moo Bar (formerly the Sherlock) in the Temples du Soleil. The Frog and Roastbeef at the top of the village claims to be the highest pub in Europe and is a cheerful British ghetto – it changed hands last season and a 2008 visitor reports that it has been given 'a long overdue decor update' and that 'the food is a big step up'. The Saloon (formerly Friends) and the Viking pub are lively bars on the same block. The Underground nightclub in Place de Péclet has an extended happy hour but 'descends into Europop' when its disco gets going. The Malaysia cellar bar is recommended for good live bands, and gets very crowded after 11pm. Quieter bars include O'Connells and the cosy Rhum Box Café (aka Mitch's).

OFF THE SLOPES
Forget it
There's a good sports centre with big pool, saunas, steam room, hot tubs, gym etc and a leisure centre with bowling lanes and pool tables. Free weekly concerts are held in the church, there's a small cinema and twice-weekly street markets. A 2008 visitor recommends the toboggan run – 'ideal for bad visibility days'. You can get to some mountain restaurants by lift, and the 360° panorama from the top of the Cîme de Caron cable car is not to be missed. But it is not a good place to choose if you're not going to hit the slopes.

The French Pyrenees

An underrated region with decent skiing and boarding at half the price of the Alps and villages that remain distinctly French

UK PACKAGES

Bareges Borderline
La Mongie Lagrange
Cauterets Lagrange, Ski
Collection, Ski Leisure
Direction
Font-Romeu Lagrange,
Pyrenees Ski
Experience, Ski
Collection, Ski France,
Skiholidayextras.com,
Solo's
St-Lary-Soulan
Lagrange, Ski
Collection, Ski France,
Skiholidayextras.com,
Ski Leisure Direction

Phone numbers
From abroad use the
prefix +33 and omit
the initial '0' of the
phone number

TOURIST OFFICES

www.pyrenees-online.fr
Barèges
t 0562 921600
www.tourmalet.com
www.bareges.com
La Mongie
t 0562 919415
www.tourmalet.fr
www.bagneresde
bigorre-lamongie.com
Cauterets
t 0562 925050
www.cauterets.com
Font-Romeu
t 0468 306830
www.font-romeu.fr
St-Lary-Soulan
t 0562 395081
www.saintlary.com

It took us a long time to get round to visiting the resorts of the French Pyrenees – mainly because we had the idea that they were second-rate compared with the Alps. Well, it is certainly true that they can't compete in terms of size of ski area with the mega-resorts of the Three Valleys and Paradiski. But don't dismiss them: they have considerable attractions, including price – hotels cost half as much as in the Alps, and meals and drinks are cheap.

The Pyrenees are serious mountains, with dramatic, picturesque scenery. They are also attractively French. Unlike the big plastic mega-resorts, many Pyrenean bases have a rustic, rural Gallic charm.

One of the biggest ski areas – shared by **Barèges** and **La Mongie** – is called **Domaine Tourmalet**. It has 100km/62 miles of runs (69 pistes) and 42 lifts. Most are drags and slow chairs but there are three high-speed chairs. The runs are best suited to intermediates, with good treelined runs above Barèges and open bowl skiing above La Mongie. The best bet for an expert is to try off-piste with a guide – one beautiful run away from all the lifts starts with a scramble through a hole in the rocks. There is a terrain park. Rustic mountain huts are scattered around the slopes; Chez Louisette is one of the best. There are 20km/12 miles of cross-country.

Barèges is a spa village set in a narrow, steep-sided valley, which gets little sun in midwinter; the lift base is at Tournaboup, 4km/2.5 miles up the valley and served by ski-bus. It's the second oldest ski resort in France and the pioneer of skiing in the Pyrenees. Accommodation is mainly in 2-star hotels such as the Igloo, Central and Europe, which reporters recommend for good food and a friendly welcome. A recent reporter found the 300-year-old chalet Les Caillaux (www.mountainbug.com) to be of a 'very high standard', and the owners offer free ski guiding. Another stayed in nearby Luz in the Chimes hotel, describing the food as 'divine'. The rather drab buildings and one main street of Barèges grow on you, though there's little to do in the evenings other than visit the thermal spa and a restaurant. La Mongie is a modern, purpose-built resort: 'small, friendly, great restaurants but not cheap'.

Cauterets is another spa town but a complete contrast to Barèges – it's much bigger and set in a wide, sunny valley. It is a popular summer resort, and even in March we were able to sit at a pavement cafe with a drink after dinner. A gondola takes you up to the slopes 850m/2,790ft above the town – you have to ride it down as well as up. There are only 36km/22 miles of usually quiet slopes (mainly beginner and intermediate), set in a bowl that can be cold and windy. But Cauterets' jewel is its cross-country, a long drive or bus ride from town at Pont d'Espagne and served by a gondola. It is the start of the Pyrenees National Park and the old smugglers' route over the mountains between France and Spain. The 36km/22 miles of snow-sure cross-country tracks run up this beautiful deserted valley, beside a rushing stream and stunning waterfall.

Font-Romeu has 23 lifts, serving 58km/36 miles of mainly easy and intermediate pistes, and is popular with families. The slopes get a lot of sun, but it has the biggest snowmaking set-up in the Pyrenees. When weekend crowds arrive lifts and pistes can get crowded. It has 100km/62 miles of cross-country skiing. The village is a bus ride from the slopes, and hotels are m... 3-star.

The other m... ...rt is **St-Lary-Soula...** with houses... cable car... slopes, ... 62 mil... It has... The... **E**...

423

Italy

Italy has a lot going for it as a ski or snowboard holiday destination. It is the cheapest of the four major Alpine countries; the atmosphere is jolly; it has good food and wine; the scenery, especially in the Dolomites and Courmayeur, is simply stunning; the lift systems include some of the most modern and powerful in Europe; the snowmaking is state-of-the-art (and they use it well); the grooming is top-notch; and most of the slopes are ideal for beginners and intermediates.

Italian resorts vary as widely in their characteristics as they do in location – and they are spread along the full length of the Italian border, from Sauze d'Oulx to the Dolomites.

A lot of Italian runs, particularly in the north-west, seem flatteringly easy. This is partly because grooming is immaculate and partly because piste classification seems to overstate difficulty. Nowhere is this clearer than in the linked slopes of La Rosière in France and La Thuile – in Italy, despite the French-sounding name. Venturing from the Italian motorways to the French moguls is like moving from the shelter of the harbour to the open sea.

Many Italians based in the northern cities ski at weekends, and it's very noticeable that many resorts become busy only then. It's a great advantage for those of us who are there for the whole week. This pattern is especially noticeable at the chic resorts, such as Cortina, Courmayeur and Madonna, and resorts that have not yet found international fame such as the Monterosa region; it's much less pronounced in parts of the Dolomites favoured by German visitors who, like Brits, tend to go for a week.

In general, Italians don't take their skiing or boarding too seriously. A late start, long lunch and early finish are the norm – leaving the slopes delightfully quiet for the rest of us. Mountain restaurants are welcoming places almost everywhere, encouraging leisurely lunching. Pasta – even in the most modest establishment – is delicious. And eating and drinking on the mountain is still cheaper than in other Alpine resorts. But one drawback that many reporters remark upon is the primitive hole-in-the-ground toilets that are the norm in mountain restaurants (and sometimes in resorts, too). Another is the ludicrous system in many self-service places where you have to queue to pay and then queue again to acquire your food or drink.

One thing that Italian resorts do have to contend with is erratic

SNOWPIX.COM / CHRIS GILL

← Fabulous scenery is part of the deal in the Dolomites – this is Cinque Torre, near Cortina

snowfall. While the snow in the northern Alps tends to come from the west, Italy's tends to come from storms arriving from the south. So it can have great conditions when other countries are suffering; or vice versa. Italian resorts have extensive snowmaking, and our observation is that they tend to use it more effectively than other Alpine countries. We have skied in Courmayeur and in the Dolomites when little natural snow has fallen, and in each case there has been excellent cruising on man-made snow.

Italy seems to be in the grip of 'legislation fever' at present, with mixed results. Italian bars and restaurants are now smoke-free, a huge improvement. And it is now compulsory for children (under 14, we understand) to wear helmets on the slopes. But many areas have also made it illegal to go off-piste near their pistes.

DRIVING IN THE ITALIAN ALPS

There are four main geographical groupings of Italian resorts, widely separated. Getting to some of these resorts is a very long haul, and moving from one area to another can involve very long drives (though the extensive motorway network is a great help).

The handful of resorts to the west of Turin – Bardonecchia, Sauze d'Oulx, Sestriere and neighbours in the Milky Way region – are easily reached from France via the Fréjus tunnel, or via the good road over the pass that the resort of Montgenèvre sits on.

Further north, and somewhat nearer to Turin than Milan, are the resorts of the Aosta valley – Courmayeur, Cervinia, La Thuile and the Monterosa area are the best known. These (especially

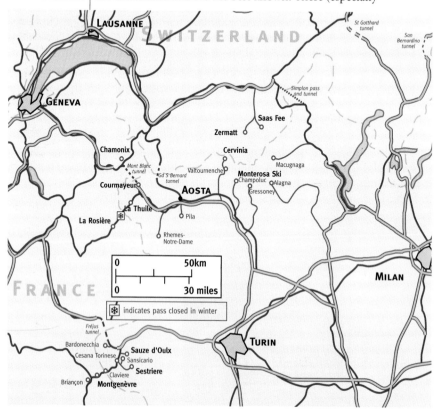

Courmayeur) are the easiest of all Italian resorts to reach from Britain (via the Mont Blanc tunnel from Chamonix in France). The Aosta valley can also be reached from Switzerland via the Grand St Bernard tunnel. The approach is high and may require chains. The road down the Aosta valley is a major thoroughfare, but the roads up to some of the other resorts are quite long, winding and (in the case of Cervinia) high.

To the east is a string of scattered resorts, most close to the Swiss border, many in isolated and remote valleys involving long drives up from the nearest Italian cities, or high-altitude drives from Switzerland. The links between Switzerland and Italy are more clearly shown on our larger-scale Switzerland map at the beginning of that section than on the map of the Italian Alps included here. The major routes are the St Gotthard tunnel between Göschenen (near Andermatt) and Airolo – the main route between Basel and Milan – and the San Bernardino tunnel reached via Chur.

Finally, further east still are the resorts of the Dolomites. Getting there from Austria is easy, over the Brenner motorway pass from Innsbruck. But getting there from Britain is a very long drive indeed – allow at least a day and a half. We wouldn't lightly choose to drive there and back for a week's skiing, except as part of a longer tour including some Austrian resorts. It's also worth bearing in mind that once you arrive in the Dolomites, getting around the intricate network of valleys linked by narrow, winding roads can be a slow business – it's often quicker to get from village to village on skis. Impatient Italian driving can make it a bit stressful, too.

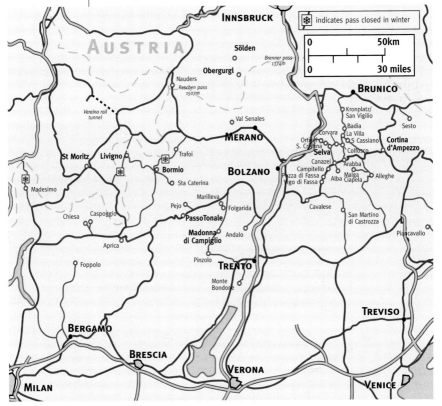

Bormio

One on its own, this: a tall, narrow mountain above a very unusual, historic town – a spa as well as a ski resort

428

COSTS

① ② ③ ④ ⑤ ⑥

RATINGS

The slopes
Fast lifts	★★★
Snow	★★★
Extent	★★
Expert	★
Intermediate	★★★
Beginner	★★
Convenience	★★★
Queues	★★★
Mountain restaurants	★★★★

The rest
Scenery	★★★
Resort charm	★★★★
Off-slope	★★★★

NEWS

The Bormio-Ciuk gondola (the smaller of the two access lifts) closed permanently in 2007. There are no current plans to replace it.

For 2007/08 an eight-seat gondola replaced the old Isolaccia double chair at Valdidentro, cutting the ride time to four minutes.

KEY FACTS

Resort	1225m
	4,020ft

Bormio, S Caterina and Valdidentro	
Slopes	1225-3010m
	4,020-9,880ft
Lifts	34
Pistes	100km
	62 miles
Blue	27%
Red	60%
Black	13%
Snowmaking	49km
	30 miles

Bormio only	
Slopes	1225-3010m
	4,020-9,880ft
Lifts	14
Pistes	50km
	31 miles

➕ Good mix of high, open pistes and woodland runs adding up to some good long descents

➕ Worthwhile neighbouring resorts

➕ Attractive ancient town centre – quite unlike any other ski resort

➕ Good mountain restaurants

➖ Slopes all of medium steepness

➖ Rather confined main mountain, with other areas some way distant

➖ No imminent replacement for gondola to Ciuk

➖ Town-centre hotels inconvenient

If you like historic Italian towns and don't insist on a traditional Alpine resort atmosphere, you'll find the town of Bormio very appealing – though you're unlikely to be staying right in the old centre. Given the limited slopes of Bormio's own mountain, plan on taking the free bus out to the Oga-Valdidentro area and perhaps on making longer outings – to Santa Caterina or Livigno.

THE RESORT

Bormio, a spa since Roman times, has a splendid 17th-century town centre, with narrow, cobbled streets and grand stone facades – very colourful during the evening promenade. It is in a remote spot, close to the Swiss border; the airport transfer approaches three hours.

The town centre is a 15-minute walk from the gondola station across the river to the south. There are reliable free shuttle-buses, but many people walk. Closer to the lifts is a suburban sprawl of hotels for skiers. Several major hotels are on Via Milano, leading out of town, which is neither convenient nor atmospheric.

THE MOUNTAINS

There's a nice mix of high, snow-sure pistes and lower wooded slopes. The main slopes are tall (vertical drop 1800m/5,900ft) and narrow. Most pistes face north-west. The Oga-Valdidentro area, a short bus ride out of Bormio, shouldn't be overlooked. The open and woodland runs are very pleasant and usually empty (and have great views). A new gondola for 2007/08 has improved access from Isolaccia.

Day trips to Santa Caterina (20 minutes by bus) and Livigno (90 minutes) are covered by the Alta Valtellina lift pass. A pass of three days or more entitles you to half-price on a one-day pass in St Moritz (three hours away).

Slopes The main access lift is an eight-seat gondola to the mid-mountain mini-resort of Bormio 2000, with a cable-car going on up to the top at over 3000m/10,000ft and a couple of fast chairs also serving the top. There are no immediate plans to replace the defunct Ciuk gondola (closed two seasons back) yet bizarrely it was still marked on the 2007/08 piste map. Both the piste map and the piste marking need substantial improvement.

Terrain parks The resort has a terrain park and super-pipe on the slopes at Bormio 2000. As well as the usual jumps and rails, there's also a separate beginner area.

Snow reliability Runs above Bormio 2000 are usually snow-sure, and snowmaking now covers most slopes, though this doesn't necessarily help in late March. The Valdidentro area is more reliable, and the high, shaded, north-facing slopes of Santa Caterina usually have good snow.

Experts There are a couple of short black runs in the main area, but the greatest interest lies in off-piste routes from Cima Bianca to both east and west of the piste area.

Intermediates The men's downhill race course starts with a steep plunge, but otherwise is just a tough red, ideal for strong intermediates. Stella Alpina, down to 2000, is also fairly steep. Many runs are less tough – ideal for most intermediates. The longest is a superb top-to-bottom cruise. The outlying mountains are also suitable for early intermediates.

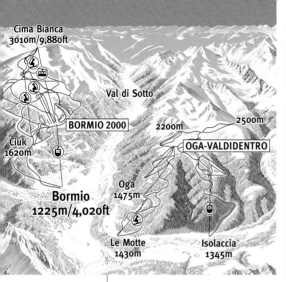

There is plenty of accommodation at the foot of the slopes ↗

ALTA VALTELLINA

Beginners The nursery slopes at Bormio 2000 offer good snow, but there are no very easy longer pistes to move on to. Novices are better off at nearby Santa Caterina.

Snowboarding The terrain-park is the main attraction. The slopes are too steep for novices, and there's little to attract experienced boarders either. Hang Five (Bormio 2000) is a specialist school.

Cross-country There are some trails either side of Bormio, towards Piatta and beneath Le Motte and Valdidentro, but cross-country skiers are better off at snow-sure Santa Caterina.

Queues There should be few problems outside of real peak weeks; perhaps surprisingly, closure of the Ciuk gondola has not triggered reports of queues elsewhere. The fast chairs to Cima Bianca relieve the pressure on the top cable car.

Mountain restaurants The mountain restaurants are generally good – 'wonderful', says a 2007 visitor. Bormio 2000 has several options, including an efficient self-service. Above Ciuk, the Rocca is a smart, woody chalet with table- or self-service and a large terrace. Past reporters have recommended the Baita de Mario as a great place for a long lunch.

Schools and guides There is a choice. The Nazionale school reportedly offers 'satisfactory lessons in English'.

Facilities for children The ski schools take children from the age of three from 10am to 4pm. The Contea di Bormio school at Bormio 2000 has its own snow garden and kindergarten.

How to go There are plenty of apartments, but hotels dominate the package market.

Hotels There are 40-plus hotels, mostly 2- and 3-star. The 4-star Palace (0342 903131) is the most luxurious. The Posta (0342 904753) is in the centre of the old town – rooms vary widely. The Baita dei Pini (0342 904346) is the best placed of the top hotels – on the river, between the lifts and centre. The Ambassador (0342 904625) is close to the gondola, and heartily recommended by a 2007 visitor.

Apartments Try the modern Cristallo apartments.

Eating out There's a wide choice. The Kuerc and Vecchia Combo are the best known and there are some excellent pizzerias. Other recommendations include the Rododendri at San Antonio and the atmospheric Al Taula.

Après-ski The action starts on the mountain at the Rocca, and at bars around the bottom lift stations. The Clem Pub, Cafe Mozart and the Aurora are popular. The Sunrise is a nightclub and restaurant, with live music.

Off the slopes Diversions include thermal baths and the Roman baths, riding and walks in the Stelvio National Park. Excellent sports centre, ice rink and 'superb' swimming pool. St Moritz and Livigno are popular excursions.

Staying up the mountain The modern Girasole 2000 (0342 904652), at Bormio 2000, is simple but comfortable; lots of evening events.

UK PACKAGES

Directski.com, Interhome

Phone numbers
From abroad use the prefix +39 (and do **not** omit the initial '0' of the phone number)

TOURIST OFFICE

t 0342 903300
infobormio@provincia.so.it
www.alta-valtellina.it

Cervinia

Mile after mile of high-altitude, easy, snow-sure cruising above a hotchpotch of a village; especially good for late-season trips

➕ Miles of long, consistently gentle runs – ideal for early intermediates and anyone wary of steep slopes or bumps

➕ High, sunny and snow-sure slopes amid impressive scenery

➕ Excellent village nursery slope

➕ Link with Zermatt in Switzerland provides even more spectacular views and good lunches

➖ Very little to interest good or aggressive intermediates and above

➖ Little to do in bad weather – almost entirely treeless, and lifts prone to closure by wind

➖ Still a few slow old lifts

➖ Steep climb to main gondola, followed by lots of steps in station

➖ Not particularly attractive village

➖ Few off-slope amenities

If there is a better resort than Cervinia for those who like gentle cruising in spring sunshine on mile after mile of easy, snow-sure, well-groomed slopes, we have yet to find it. And then there's the easiest of Zermatt's slopes just over the Swiss border, and linked by lift and piste.

But what about the rest of us? Well, to be frank, the rest of us are better off elsewhere. In particular, those who might be harbouring thoughts about bumps or powder over in Zermatt should probably think about staying there, not here. The link between the two resorts is unreliable (especially in early season) because of the risk of high winds. But recent lift improvements in Zermatt have made access to its best slopes much quicker when the link is open.

THE RESORT

Cervinia is at the head of a long valley leading off the Aosta valley on the Italian side of the Matterhorn. The old climbing village developed into a winter resort in a rather haphazard way, and it has no consistent style of architecture. It's an uncomfortable hotchpotch, neither pleasing to the eye nor as offensive as the worst of the French purpose-built resorts. The centre is pleasant, compact and traffic-free. But ugly surrounding apartment blocks and hotels make the whole place feel less friendly and welcoming than it could be.

Staying near the village centre, at the foot of the nursery slopes, has always been best for après-ski purposes. A six-pack now makes this area better for accessing the slopes too, because it cuts out the need for an awkward uphill walk to the main gondola lift.

There are also modern developments above the main village, closer to the gondola. Some hotels run their own shuttle-bus and there's an efficient public bus from the Cieloalto complex.

At weekends and public holidays, the resort can fill up with day trippers and weekenders from Milan and Turin. There are surprisingly few off-slope amenities, such as marked walks and spa facilities.

The slopes link to Valtournenche further down the valley (covered by the lift pass) and Zermatt in Switzerland (covered by a daily supplement, or a more expensive weekly pass – take your passport as random checks are made).

Day trips by car are possible to Courmayeur, La Thuile and the Monterosa Ski resorts of Champoluc and Gressoney (all covered by the Aosta valley lift pass).

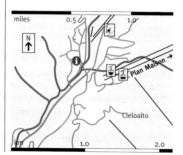

NEWS

For 2008/09 there are plans to install snowmaking at last on the run down from Salette to Valtournenche, which should enable this run to be opened much more often. Snowmaking will also be increased higher up in the Valtournenche ski area. More terrain park features are also planned.

For 2007/08 two new restaurants opened in Cervinia: the Belle Epoque and the Maison Jean Bich di Pers.

THE MOUNTAINS

Cervinia's main slopes are high, open, sunny and mostly west-facing. If the weather is bad, the top lifts often close because of high winds – and even the lower slopes may suffer poor visibility because of the lack of trees. Piste signing and information needs improvement. Old decommissioned lifts being left on the slopes give 'an atmosphere of shabby neglect', says a recent reporter.

THE SLOPES
Very easy
Cervinia has the biggest, highest, most snow-sure area of easy, well-groomed pistes we've come across. The area has Italy's highest pistes and some of its longest (a claimed 13km/8 miles from Plateau Rosa to Valtournenche, interrupted only by a newish quad part-way). Nearly all the runs are accessible to average intermediates. The high number of red runs on the piste map is misleading: most of them would be classified blue elsewhere. There is now a handy quick-folding piste map that covers both Cervinia's and Zermatt's slopes fairly clearly – although Cervinia's 2008 map was not as up to date as Zermatt's (still showing an old cable car).

The main gondola from above the village centre and a parallel cable car take you to the mid-mountain base of **Plan Maison**. We've rarely seen the cable car working, but a regular visitor assures us it does (though not necessarily at the same time as the gondola). The six-pack from the village nursery slopes followed by an old, slow chair now makes a viable alternative route to Plan Maison. From Plan Maison a further gondola goes to Laghi Cime Bianche and then a giant cable car goes up to **Plateau Rosa** and one link with Zermatt. The alternative link goes via three successive fast quads from Plan Maison up to a slightly lower point on the border. Between the fast quads and Laghi Cime Bianche, and going all the way back to the village, is a deep gorge that separates Cervinia's slopes into two main sections.

Plateau Rosa is the start of the splendid wide Ventina run. Part-way down you can branch off left down towards **Valtournenche**. The slopes here are now served by three very efficient chairlifts, above a modern gondola from Valtournenche – but the final lift back to Cervinia is still a long draglift.

There is also the very small, little-used **Cieloalto** area, served by a slow old chair to the south of the gondola at the bottom of the Ventina run. This has some of Cervinia's steeper pistes and the only trees in the area.

TERRAIN PARKS
One of Italy's best
The 'Indian' terrain park (www.indianpark.it; in Italian only) by the Fomet run is one of the best parks in Italy and is serviced by a quick quad. Run by *Snowboard Italy*'s former editor, it goes from strength to strength and 2008/09 promises further development. The park has been shaped so that riders can hit an easy line or an intermediate line. There are also expert jumps that culminate in a 20m/66ft monster. There were loads of new boxes and rails for 2007/08, including 6m/20ft and 10m/33ft tube

boarding

The wide, gentle and always groomed slopes, generally good snow and lack of many draglifts make Cervinia pretty much ideal for beginner and early intermediate boarders. But there are some long, flat parts to beware of and there's not much to interest better boarders – just as there's not much to interest better skiers. Serious boarders will enjoy the terrain park, and there's an exclusive terrain park pass that costs 27 euros a day; they could also try heli-boarding.

rails. For a half-pipe head to Zermatt, which has an equally impressive freestyle area (and a park on the glacier, open in the summer from July to September for freestyle camps; see www.big-a.it for the latest offers).

SNOW RELIABILITY
Superb
The mountain is one of the highest in Europe and, despite getting a lot of afternoon sun, can usually be relied on to have good snow conditions from early to late season. Grooming is generally very good too.

The village nursery slopes, all except the top section of the Ventina run and runs under the top chairlifts down to Plan Maison have snowmaking. It was increased above

Valtournenche last season, with more planned for 2008/09. Part of these plans is to install snowmaking from Salette down to Valtournenche at last – this long run was often closed or in poor condition in the past.

FOR EXPERTS
Forget it
This is not a resort for experts. High winds can blow the snow off what accessible off-piste there is, though a couple of 2008 reporters found 'brilliant and deserted' untracked powder – in particular, around Plan Torrette and Rocce Bianche. Good value heli-drops with guides can be arranged – from 440 euros per person (see Zermatt chapter for routes). There are a few black runs scattered here

Cervino
t 0166 949034

Breuil
t 0166 940960

Matterhorn-Cervinia
t 0166 949523

Classes
(Cervino prices)
6 days (2hr 45min per
day) €175

Private lessons
€36 for 1hr for 1
person

and there, but most of them would be classified red elsewhere. Many reporters head over to Zermatt for more challenging slopes and find it easier to reach them now that new lifts have improved the links – see the 'Zermatt connection' box overleaf.

FOR INTERMEDIATES
Miles of long, flattering runs
Virtually the whole area can be covered comfortably by average intermediates. But, as one reporter so aptly put it, 'strong, aggressive intermediates will get bored quickly'. If you like wide, easy, motorway pistes, you'll love Cervinia: it has more long, flattering runs than any other resort. The easiest slopes are on the left as you look at the mountain. From top to

bottom there are gentle blue runs, and almost as gentle reds in the beautiful scenery beneath the Matterhorn.

The area on the right as you look at the mountain is best for adventurous intermediates. The Ventina red is a particularly good fast cruise. You can use the cable car to do the top part repeatedly, or go all the way down to Cervinia (8km/5 miles and over 1400m/4,600ft vertical).

The runs down towards Valtournenche are great cruises and very popular with reporters; many of the reds are more like blue gradient. The 13km/8 mile run all the way down is very satisfying, through splendid rocky scenery (and snowmaking is at last being installed on the lower part for 2008/09).

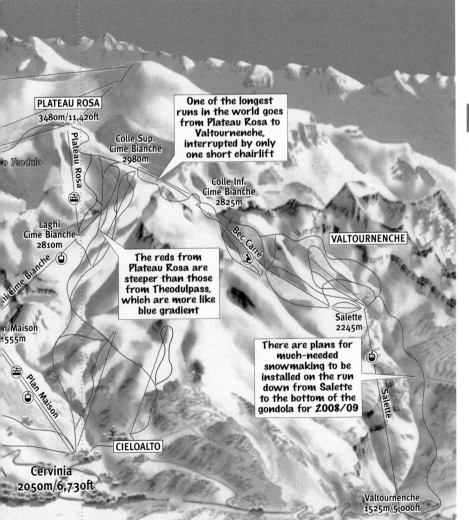

PLATEAU ROSA
3480m/11,420ft

Colle Sup.
Cime Bianche
2980m

o Teodulo

Plateau Rosa

Colle Inf.
Cime Bianche
2825m

Laghi
Cime Bianche
2810m

Bec Carré

VALTOURNENCHE

ni Cime Bianche

One of the longest runs in the world goes from Plateau Rosa to Valtournenche, interrupted by only one short chairlift

The reds from Plateau Rosa are steeper than those from Theodulpass, which are more like blue gradient

n Maison
555m

Plan Maison

Salette
2245m

There are plans for much-needed snowmaking to be installed on the run down from Salette to the bottom of the gondola for 2008/09

Salette

CIELOALTO

Cervinia
2050m/6,730ft

Valtournenche
1525m/5,000ft

Getting to Zermatt's classic terrain on the Rothorn/Stockhorn sectors is now much quicker since the Furi to Riffelberg gondola opened. Several 2008 readers comment that getting there and returning to Cervinia by mid-afternoon is now 'no problem'.

But do leave ample time for your return journey, as there can be long queues for the Klein Matterhorn cable car and for the alternative long, slow T-bars.

LIFT PASSES

Breuil-Cervinia

Prices in €

Age	1-day	6-day
under 13	17	93
13 to 64	34	185
over 65	26	139

Free under 6
Beginner limited day pass €13

Notes
Covers all lifts on the Italian side, including Valtournenche; half-day passes; daily Zermatt extension

Alternative passes
International (covers Italian side and Zermatt); Aosta Valley pass

CHILDREN

Mini-Club
t 0166 940201
Ages up to 10yr;
9am-5pm daily

Ski school
Classes for children over 5

FOR BEGINNERS
Gentle progress
Complete beginners start on the good village nursery slope, with its long moving carpet. They should graduate quickly to the fine flat area around Plan Maison and its gentle blue runs. Fast learners will be going all the way from top to bottom of the mountain by the end of the week.

FOR CROSS-COUNTRY
Hardly any
There are two short trails – 3km/2 miles and 5km/3miles – but this is not a cross-country resort.

QUEUES
A few problems
Readers do not normally find queues a big problem. We experienced few delays on our March 2008 visit – the newish chairs above Valtournenche were blissfully crowd free. An upgrade to the Cervinia-Plan Maison gondola and a fast six-pack from the nursery slopes has eased pressure out of the resort at peak times, but the Plan Maison chair above does still get busy – a 2007 reporter waited 15 minutes here. There can, of course, be queues for many lower lifts when upper lifts are shut due to wind.

MOUNTAIN RESTAURANTS
OK if you know where to go
There are some good places if you know where to go. Toilet facilities are a traditional cause of complaints from reporters, but several have now been improved. You can, of course, head over to Zermatt for lunch.
Editors' choice The table-service section (there's self-service too) of Chalet Etoile (0166 940220), on a blue run above Plan Maison. Readers love it too: 'top quality cuisine in an authentic Italian style', 'fantastic pasta, great wine list', 'lovely location'. The more basic table-service section of Rifugio Teodulo (0166 949400) at Theodulpass is another good option – we had excellent pasta there. Booking is recommended at both.
Worth knowing about Several readers recommend Bontadini at the top of the Fornet chair ('good value and superb view'). Other reporter tips include Tuktu at Plan Maison for 'good food and drink at reasonable prices', and the 'bright and cheerful' Ventina self-service. The British-run Igloo, near the top of the Bardoney chair, has a

'UK-style' toilet. Near the bottom of the Cretaz pistes, Ski D'Oro is 'well worth a visit'. The restaurants are cheaper and less crowded on the Valtournenche side. On the upper slopes there, the Motta does 'basic, but good pasta and goulaschsuppe' (and speciality hot white wine), and 2008 visitors enjoyed Lo Baracon dou Tene above Salette (Becca d'Aran chair), for 'friendly, excellent service' and 'good pasta of the day'.

SCHOOLS AND GUIDES
Generally positive reports
Cervinia has three main schools, Cervino, Breuil and Matterhorn-Cervinia. The Cervino school got more good than bad reports in 2008: 'excellent off-piste week', says one who was with Club Med (they use Cervino instructors); 'well organised, learnt a lot', says another. One reader's group had 'great' private snowboard lessons – 'by the end of the week they were zipping down the hill', but they criticise group ski lessons as 'not particularly helpful'. The Breuil school has been praised.

FACILITIES FOR CHILDREN
No recent reports
The Cervino ski school runs a ski kindergarten. And there's a babysitting and kindergarten area at Plan Maison. The Mini-Club takes children until 10 years old. But we lack recent reports on them. The slopes, with their long gentle runs, should suit families.

STAYING THERE

HOW TO GO
Plenty of hotel packages
Most of the big operators come here, offering a wide selection of hotels, though other types of accommodation are rather thin on the ground. Crystal's club hotel Petit Palais is reportedly 'excellent'. Club Med is 'comfortable, excellent food, huge pool'.
Hotels There are almost 50 hotels, mostly 2- or 3-stars. Unless they run their own minibus to the slopes, choose your location with care.
****Hermitage (0166 948998) Small, luxurious Relais et Château just out of the village on the road up to Cieloalto. Pool. Minibus to the lifts. Great views.
****Excelsior Planet (0166 949426) Comfortable, near the nursery slopes. Pool, spa and minibus to the lifts. Regularly recommended by reporters.

Cervinia's architecture isn't very inspiring; but this newish fast chair has improved access to the slopes →

AIAT MONTE CERVINO / STEFANO VENTURINO

GETTING THERE

Air Turin 118km/ 73 miles (2½hr); Geneva 220km/ 137 miles (2½hr)

Rail Châtillon (27km/17 miles); regular buses from station

UK PACKAGES

Alpine Answers, Club Med, Crystal, Crystal Finest, Elegant Resorts, First Choice, Independent Ski Links, Inghams, Interhome, Italian Safaris, Jeffersons, Kuoni, Momentum, Ski Activity, Ski Solutions, Ski Supreme, Ski Weekend, Ski4you, Skitracer, Thomson

ACTIVITIES

Indoor Hotels with swimming pools and saunas, fitness centre, squash, bowling

Outdoor Natural ice rink, paragliding, dog sledding, hiking, mountaineering, snowmobiles, snowshoeing, air boarding, snow biking, ice climbing, ice cave visit

Phone numbers
From abroad use the prefix +39 (and do **not** omit the initial '0' of the phone number)

TOURIST OFFICE

t 0166 949136
breuil-cervinia@ montecervino.it
www.montecervino.it
www.cervinia.it

****Sertorelli Sport Hotel (0166 949797) Excellent food, sauna and hot-tub. Ten minutes from lifts.
****Europa (0166 948660) Family run; near centre. Pool. 'Exceptionally friendly and helpful, very good room'.
***Astoria (0166 949062) Family run, basic, comfortable. Right by gondola.
***Furggen (0166 948928) Top of the Campetto chair, with minibus into town. 'Cosy, warm and pleasant.'
***Mignon (0166 949344) Central – 50 yards from the lifts. 'We always stay there,' says a 2008 visitor.
***Edelweiss (0166 949078) Four-minute walk from gondola, minibus to/ from lift too. 'Cosy rooms, good bar and spa,' says a 2007 reporter.
**Marmore (0166 949057) Friendly, family run, on main street – an easy walk to the lifts.
**Meynet (0166 948696) Central, family hotel. 'Super service.'
Apartments There are many apartments, but few are available via UK tour ops. The Escargot ones in Cieloalto are 'very spacious'.

EATING OUT
Plenty to choose from
Cervinia's 50 or so restaurants allow plenty of choice. The Chamois and Matterhorn are excellent, but quite expensive. The food is 'amazing' at Jour et Nuit, says a 2008 visitor. The Maison de Saussure does 'very good local specialities'. The Vieux Grenier at the hotel Grivola has 'excellent pizza and is lively'. You'll find 'good pizza and pasta' at Capanna Alpina and Al Solito Posto. Pizzeria Bar Falcone and il Rustico have been recommended for their 'reasonably priced, excellent local food and wine', as has Lino's (by the ice rink) for 'excellent pizzas and cheap beer'. An evening out at the Baita Cretaz mountain hut makes a change. Belle Epoque and Maison Jean Bich di Pers are new – reports please.

APRES-SKI
Disappoints many Brits
Plenty of Brits come here looking for action but find there isn't much to do except tour the bars. 'Take a good book,' said one reporter. The hotel Grivola's bar, next to the Vieux Grenier restaurant, is attractively woody. The Copa Pan is lively, with great music ('Really liked it, difficult to leave,' says a 2008 visitor). The Dragon Bar is popular with Brits and Scandinavians and has satellite TV and videos, but a

2008 visitor preferred the 'friendly' Yeti for 'dark ale and Grolla Friendship drinks'. The Ymeletrob, next to the Punta Maquignaz hotel, is 'cosy, has live music and great canapés'. Other recommendations include Gran Beca for traditional Italian atmosphere and Hostellerie des Guides (with mementos of the owner's Himalayan trips). Discos liven up at weekends; Bianconiglio's can be 'a bit cheesy, but it's great on Friday night', says a 2008 reporter.

OFF THE SLOPES
Little attraction
There is little to do for those who don't plan to hit the slopes. Village amenities include hotel pools, a fitness centre and a natural ice rink. The walks are disappointing. The mountain restaurants reachable by gondola or cable car are not special.

STAYING UP THE MOUNTAIN
To beat the queues
Up at Plan Maison, Lo Stambecco (0166 949053) is a 50-room 3-star hotel ideally placed for early nights and early starts.

STAYING DOWN THE VALLEY
Great home run
Valtournenche, 9km/5.5 miles down the road, is cheaper than Cervinia. The village spreads along the busy, steep, winding road up to Cervinia.
   A gondola leaves from the edge of town and fast lifts have speeded up the journey after that. The exceptionally long run back down is a nice way to end the day – and should have snowmaking for 2008/09 (see 'News'). There's a fair selection of simple hotels; some with shuttle-buses. The 3-star Bijou (0166 92109) is 'friendly', says a 2008 reporter, but the pool and leisure centre next door are 'closed in the evenings and the village is not so much quiet as dead'. The 3-star Les Rochers (0166 92119) has 'excellent food; very good value'.

Cervinia

435

Interactive resort shortlist builder at **www.wtss.co.uk**

Cortina d'Ampezzo

The scenery will take your breath away even if the slopes don't;
take your posh frock if you want to feel part of the evening scene

COSTS

① ② ③ ④ ⑤ ⑥

RATINGS

The slopes
Fast lifts	**
Snow	***
Extent	***
Expert	**
Intermediate	***
Beginner	*****
Convenience	*
Queues	****
Mountain restaurants	****

The rest
Scenery	*****
Resort charm	****
Off-slope	*****

NEWS

For 2008/09 a new link (a chair followed by a piste) will allow access from the Cinque Torre area to the Col Gallina area (and the cable car from Passo Falzarego to Lagazuoi) without taking the shuttle-bus. For 2007/08 a new fast quad replaced an old double chairlift in the small Auronzo di Cadore area (33km/ 21 miles from Cortina).

436

➕ Magnificent Dolomite scenery – a quite exceptional setting

➕ Marvellous nursery slopes and good long cruising runs

➕ Access to the vast area covered by the Dolomiti Superski pass

➕ Attractive, although rather towny, resort, with lots of upmarket shops

➕ Good off-slope facilities

➕ No crowds or queues

➖ Several separate areas spread around all sides of the resort and linked by buses

➖ Erratic snow record

➖ Expensive by Italian standards

➖ Gets very crowded in town and in restaurants during Italian holidays

➖ Very little to entertain experts

➖ Mobile phones and fur coats may drive you nuts

Cortina is one on its own. Sure, it has a quantity of well-maintained, enjoyable intermediate slopes, and in one or two sectors it has efficient lifts. But you shouldn't even think about a holiday here if matters like these are top of your agenda – if skiing or riding from dawn to dusk is your priority.

If, on the other hand, you like lazy days centred around indulgent lunches on sunny terraces, gazing at scenery that is just jaw-droppingly wonderful, this is the place. Dramatic, pink-tinged cliffs and peaks rising vertically from the top of the slopes ring the town, giving picture-postcard views wherever you look. Every time we go back, the memory has faded and our jaws drop again.

Cortina has a regular upmarket clientele from Rome and Milan, many of whom have second homes here and enjoy the strolling, shopping, people-watching and lunching as much as the slopes. A good proportion of visitors don't go near the slopes except to drive up to a 'mountain restaurant' for lunch.

As an occasional change from serious ski resorts, we love it.

THE RESORT

Although Cortina leapt to international prominence as host of the 1956 Winter Olympics, it is not a sporty place. Most people go not for any form of exertion but for the clear mountain air, the stunning views, the shopping, the cafes and the posing potential – 70% of all Italian visitors don't bother taking to the slopes. Cortina attracts the rich and famous from the big Italian cities. Fur coats and glitzy jewellery are the norm.

The resort itself is a widely spread town rather than a village, with exclusive chalets scattered around the outskirts. The centre is the traffic-free Corso Italia, full of chic designer clothes, jewellery and antique shops, art galleries and furriers – finding a ski shop can seem tricky. The cobbles and picturesque church bell tower add to the atmosphere.

People leave the slopes early, and by 5pm hardly anyone is still in ski

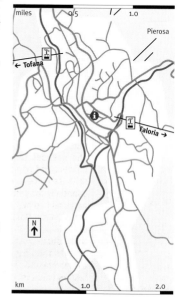

THE MOUNTAINS

There is a good mixture of slopes above and below the treeline and new lifts are slowly replacing old ones.

THE SLOPES
Inconveniently fragmented

All Cortina's smallish separate areas are a fair trek from the town centre. The largest is **Pomedes**, accessed by chair and draglifts a bus ride away. You can reach it by piste from **Tofana**, Cortina's highest area, accessed by cable car from near the ice rink.

On the opposite side of the valley is the tiny **Mietres** area. Another two-stage cable car from the east side of town leads to the **Faloria** area, from where you can head down to chairs that lead up into the limited but dramatic runs beneath **Cristallo**.

Other areas are reachable by road – in particular the road west over Passo Falzarego towards San Cassiano and the Sella Ronda area. (Taxis are an affordable means of access if shared.)

First, there's the small but spectacular Cinque Torri area, where a new chair and piste are planned for 2008/09 to link with the Col Gallina area (see below). Excellent north-facing cruising runs are accessed by a fast quad, followed by an ancient one-person chair; beyond that, a rope tow leads to a sunny, panoramic red run over the hill to Fedare – the new chair will start near the bottom here.

This new chair will link to the tiny Col Gallina area – north-facing, again – from where you can take a green back to Cinque Torri. The cable car from nearby Passo Falzarego up to Lagazuoi serves an excellent red run back down to the base station and accesses a longer red run down a beautiful 'hidden valley' to Armentarola on the fringe of the Alta Badia area. (For more on this run – one of our favourites – see the Sella Ronda chapter.)

Two other tiny out-of-town areas are San Vito di Cadore (11km/7 miles away) and Auronzo di Cadore (33km/20 miles) – each has just three or four lifts.

Reporters consistently praise the excellent grooming and quiet slopes but complain about other things – too many to list – related to signs, piste classification and marking, and the piste map. But most reporters judge that Cortina's other charms more than make up for the grumbles.

gear; the streets are packed with people parading up and down in their evening finery, shouting and gesticulating into their mobile phones. It's all pretty flat, so it's easy to get around in Gucci loafers.

Unlike most of the Dolomites, Cortina is pure Italy. The Veneto region has none of the Germanic traditions of the Südtirol. And everyone is 'friendly and welcoming', say reporters.

Surrounding the centre is a busy one-way system, reportedly less traffic-clogged than it was last time we tackled it on a weekend. The lifts to the two main areas of slopes are a fair way from the centre, and at opposite sides of town. Other lifts are bus rides away.

There's a wide range of hotels, both in the centre and scattered on the outskirts. Staying centrally is best. The local bus service is good ('very efficient and punctual'), and free to ski-pass holders. A car can be useful, especially for getting to the outlying areas and to make the most of other areas on the Dolomiti Superski pass, but a recent visitor found parking 'inadequate'. San Cassiano is a short drive to the west, with links from there to Corvara and the other Sella Ronda resorts (see the Sella Ronda chapter).

KEY FACTS

Resort	1225m
	4,020ft
Slopes	1225-2930m
	4,020-9,610ft
Lifts	51
Pistes	140km
	87 miles
Blue	33%
Red	62%
Black	5%
Snowmaking	95%

ITALY

438

boarding

*Despite its upmarket chic, Cortina is a good resort for learning to board. The
Socrepes nursery slopes are wide, gentle and served by a fast chairlift. And
progress on to other easy slopes is simple because you can get around in all areas
using just chairs and cable cars – although there are drags, they can be avoided.
Boarderline is a specialist snowboard shop that organises instruction as well as
equipment hire. There's little off-piste, but there are some nice trees and hits
under the one-person chair at Cinque Torri.*

One way to tour the area is to use special ski itineraries (maps are available at the tourist and ski pass offices). 'Skitour Olympia' takes you on the 1956 Olympic courses and the bobsleigh run. 'Skitour Romantik View' covers the Lagazuoi-Cinque Torri area.

TERRAIN PARKS
Not a bad one
There is a terrain park at Faloria that has some decent kickers and rails, and a half-pipe. It's not open to skiers.

SNOW RELIABILITY
Lots of artificial help
The snowfall record is erratic – it can be good here when it's poor on the north side of the Alps, and vice versa. But 95% of the pistes are now covered by snowmaking, so cover is good if it is cold enough to make snow. The run from Tofana to Pomedes involves a steep, narrow, south-facing section (with wonderful views over the town) that often has poor snow conditions and is often closed.

FOR EXPERTS
Limited
The run down from Tofana mentioned above is deservedly graded black; it goes through a gap in the rocks, and gives wonderful views of Cortina way down in the valley below. There are short but genuinely black runs below Pomedes and Duc d'Aosta. Cortina's other major steep run goes from the top of the Cristallo area at Forcella Staunies. A chairlift takes you to a south-facing couloir that is often shut due to avalanche danger or poor snow (tougher than it looks from below, warns a reporter).

Other than these runs there are few challenges. There are some great long red runs though, and if it snows, you'll also have very little competition for first tracks. Heli-skiing is available.

FOR INTERMEDIATES
Fragmented and not extensive
To enjoy Cortina you must like cruising in beautiful scenery, and not mind doing runs repeatedly.

The runs at the top of Tofana are short but normally have the best snow. The highest are at over 2800m/9,190ft and mainly face north. But be warned: the only way back down is by the tricky black run described above or by cable car. The reds in the linked Pomedes area offer good cruising and some challenges.

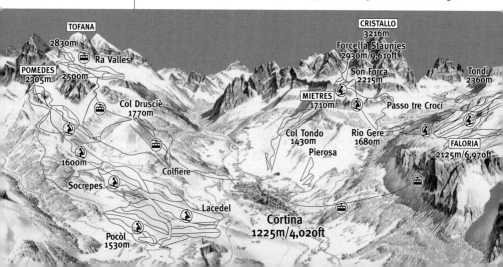

SCHOOLS

Cortina
t 0436 2911
Azzurra Cortina
t 0436 2694
Cristallo
t 0436 870073
Dolomiti
t 0436 862264
Boarderline
t 0436 878261

Classes (Cortina
prices)
6 mornings (2½hr)
€230
Private lessons
€451 for 1hr; each
additional person €16

GUIDES

Guide Alpine
t 0436 868505

GETTING THERE

Air Venice 160km/
100 miles (2hr).
Treviso 132km/
82 miles (1¾hr). Sat
and Sun transfers for
hotel guests (advance
booking required);
35-minute heli-
transfers from Venice

Rail Calalzo (35km/
22 miles) or Dobbiaco
(32km/20 miles);
frequent buses from
station

Faloria has a string of fairly short north-facing runs – we loved the Vitelli red run, round the back away from the lifts. And the Cristallo area has a long, easy red run served by a fast quad.

It is well worth making the trip to Cinque Torri for wonderful, deserted fast cruising on usually excellent north-facing snow ('bliss', says a recent reporter). And do not miss the wonderful 'hidden valley' red run from the Passo Falzarego cable car (see the Sella Ronda chapter).

FOR BEGINNERS
Wonderful nursery slopes
The Socrepes area has some of the biggest nursery slopes and best progression runs we have seen. You'll find ideal gentle terrain on the main pistes but some of the blue forest paths can be icy and intimidating.

FOR CROSS-COUNTRY
One of the best
Cortina has around 75km/47 miles of trails suitable for all standards, mainly in the Fiames area, where there's a cross-country centre and a school – and night skiing on a Wednesday. Trails include a 25km/16 mile itinerary following an old railway from Fiames to Cortina, and there is a beginner area equipped with snowmaking. Passo Tre Croci offers more challenging trails, covering 10km/6 miles. A Nordic area pass is available.

QUEUES
No problem
Most Cortina holidaymakers rise late, lunch lengthily and leave the slopes early – if they get on to them at all. That means few lift queues and generally uncrowded pistes – a

different world from the crowded Sella Ronda circuit. Queues can form for the cable car to Lagazuoi, but most reporters are generally impressed. 'The lack of queues was one of the highlights of our holiday,' said one reporter. 'No queues even on a Saturday,' said another. One visitor was delighted to find that the slopes got emptier in the afternoons, as the Italians left them, but that lifts stayed open as late as 5pm.

MOUNTAIN RESTAURANTS
Good, but get in early
Lunch is a major event for many Cortina visitors. At weekends you often need to book or turn up very early to be sure of a table. Many restaurants can be reached by road or lift, and fur coats arrive as early as 10am to sunbathe, admire the views and idle the time away on their mobile phones. Skiers are often in a minority.

Although prices are high in the swishest establishments, we've found plenty of reasonably priced places, serving generally excellent food. A recent visitor says they are all 'brilliant – never found a bad one'. In the Socrepes area, the Rifugio Col Taron is highly recommended and the Rifugio Pomedes is endorsed by a recent visitor. The Piè de Tofana and El Faral are also good.

At Cristallo the Rio Gere at the base of the quad chair is worth a visit, according to a recent reporter.

The restaurants at Cinque Torri – the Scoiattoli ('magnificent home-made pastas' and 'excellent service') and the Rifugio Averau ('marvellous pasta and great wine') – offer fantastic views. The Rifugio Fedare, over the back of Cinque Torri, is also recommended –

UK PACKAGES
Alpine Answers, Crystal, Elegant Resorts, Italian Safaris, Kuoni, Made to Measure, Momentum, Ski Freshtracks, Ski Solutions, Ski Supreme, Ski Weekend, Ski Yogi, Snow Finders, White Roc

CHILDREN
Gulliver Park
at the Pocòl ski area
t 0340 055 8399

Ski school
The schools offer all-day classes for ages 4 to 14

ACTIVITIES
Indoor Swimming pool, saunas, health spa, fitness centre, ice stadium, curling, museums, art gallery, cinema

Outdoor Olympic bobsleigh run, snow rafting down Olympic ski jump, snowshoe tours, sleigh rides, 6km/
4 miles of walking paths, tobogganing

Phone numbers
From abroad use the prefix +39 (and do **not** omit the initial '0' of the phone number)

TOURIST OFFICE
t 0436 866252
cortina@dolomiti.org
www.cortina.dolomiti.org

'great pasta with hare sauce'. Rifugio Lagazuoi, a short hike up from the top of the Passo Falzarego cable car, also has great views.

SCHOOLS AND GUIDES
Mixed reports
Of the four ski schools, we've had mixed reports of the Cortina school over the years – though we lack recent reports. The Guide Alpine offers off-piste and touring.

FACILITIES FOR CHILDREN
Better than average
By Italian standards child care facilities are outstanding, with all-day care arrangements for children of practically any age. But don't count on good spoken English. And the fragmented area can make travelling around with children difficult. A reporter commented how well the lift staff and instructors look after children.

STAYING THERE

HOW TO GO
Mainly hotels
Hotels dominate the market but there are some catered chalets.
Hotels There's a big choice, from 5-star luxury to 1-star and 2-star pensions.
*****Miramonti Majestic (0436 4201) Spectacularly grand hotel, 2km/1 mile south of town. Pool.
*****Cristallo (0436 881111) A hike from the lifts and town centre, but there's a shuttle bus. Has a pool etc.
****Poste (0436 4271) At the heart of the town. Large rooms, some with spa baths. 'We felt very well looked after,' says a recent visitor.
****Ancora (0436 3261) Elegant public rooms. On the traffic-free Corso Italia.
****Parc Victoria (0436 3246) Rustic and family-run with small rooms but good food, at the Faloria end of town. Recommended by a recent reporter.
****Corona (0436 3251) Family run, very friendly, but a 2007 reporter says, 'How it qualifies for 4 stars is a mystery.' Near Tofana lift.
****Park Faloria (0436 2959) Near ski jump, splendid pool, good food.
***Olimpia (0436 3256) Comfortable B&B hotel in centre, near Faloria lift.
***Menardi (0436 2400) Welcoming roadside inn, a long walk from centre.
***Villa Resy (0436 3303) Small and welcoming, just outside centre, with British owner.
***Alpes (0436 862021) On the edge

of town. 'Excellent food and service and friendly staff.' Hot tub.
**Montana (0436 862126) 'Excellent B&B. Amazing value and central location,' says a reporter.
Apartments There are some chalets and apartments – usually out of town – available for independent travellers.

EATING OUT
Huge choice
There's an enormous selection of restaurants, both in town and a little way out, doing mainly Italian food. The very smart and expensive El Toulà is in a beautiful old barn, just on the edge of town. Many of the best restaurants are further out: the Michelin-starred Tivoli, the Meloncino al Camineto, the Leone e Anna, the Rio Gere and the Baita Fraina. Reasonably priced central restaurants include the Cinque Torri, Croda (recommended by a recent reporter) and the Passetto for pizza and pasta.

APRES-SKI
Lively in high season
Cortina is a lively social whirl in high season, with lots of well-heeled Italians staying up very late.
The Lovat is one of several high-calorie teatime spots. There are many good wine bars: Enoteca has 700 wines and good cheese and meats; Osteria has good wines and local ham; and Villa Sandi and LP26 have been recommended. A reporter enjoyed 'delicious Prosecco and mandarin juice' at the Poste. The liveliest bar is the Clipper, with a bobsleigh by the door. Discos liven up after 11pm.

OFF THE SLOPES
A classic resort
Cortina attracts lots of people who don't use the slopes. The town is attractive and the shopping 'fabulous'; as well as high fashion 'you can get anything and everything at the Co-operativa di Cortina'. Mountain restaurants are accessible by road (a car is handy). And there's plenty more to do, such as swimming and skating. There is an observatory at Col Drusciè that has star-gazing tours. You can have a run (with driver!) down the Olympic bobsleigh run and try Adrenalin Park. There's horse jumping and polo on the snow occasionally. Excursions to Venice are easy. You can visit the First World War tunnels at Lagazuoi or the memorial at Pocòl.

Courmayeur

Stunning scenery and seductive, charming village, on the opposite side of the valley from its small area of slopes

COSTS

① ② ③ ④ ⑤ ⑥

RATINGS

The slopes
Fast lifts	★★★
Snow	★★★★
Extent	★★
Expert	★★★
Intermediate	★★★★
Beginners	★★
Convenience	★
Queues	★★★
Mountain restaurants	★★★★

The rest
Scenery	★★★★
Resort charm	★★★★
Off-slope	★★★

NEWS

For 2008/09 the draglift serving the high-altitude Tzaly beginner slope will be replaced. Snowmaking will be further increased.

The 10th City Ski Championships, in association with Momentum Ski, will be held on 19 to 22 March 2009.

➕ Charming old village, with car-free centre and stylish shops and bars

➕ Stunning views of glacial Mont Blanc massif

➕ Access to the famous Vallée Blanche glacier run to Chamonix (day trips there are possible by road, too)

➕ Heli-skiing available

➕ Comprehensive snowmaking

➕ Some very good mountain restaurants

➖ Relatively small area, with mainly short runs; high-mileage piste-bashers should stay away

➖ Lack of nursery slopes and easy runs for confidence-building

➖ No tough pistes

➖ No pistes back to the village, only to Dolonne (where you catch a bus)

➖ Like so many Italian resorts, crowded at weekends

Courmayeur is a great place for a weekend away (or a day trip to escape bad weather in Chamonix), and we always look forward to a quick visit here. (Excellent restaurants both on and off the mountain plus village bars among the most civilised in the skiing world are factors, we admit.) Whether it makes sense for a week's holiday is another matter. Its pistes are best suited to competent intermediates, who are likely to have an appetite for mileage that Courmayeur will arouse but not satisfy. Off-piste, there is more to do; experts who hire a guide (and the odd helicopter) can have a fine time. And with a car you can explore several other worthwhile resorts nearby.

THE RESORT

Courmayeur is a traditional old Italian mountaineering village that, despite the nearby Mont Blanc tunnel road, has retained much of its character. The village has a charming traffic-free centre of attractive shops, cobbled streets and well-preserved buildings. An Alpine museum and a statue of a long-dead mountain rescue hero add to the historical feel.

The centre has a great evening atmosphere, focused around the Via Roma. As the lifts close, people pile into the many bars, some of which are very civilised. Others wander in and out of the many small shops, which include a salami specialist and a good bookshop. At weekends people-watching is part of the evening scene, when the fur coats of the Milanese and Torinese take over.

The village is quite large, and the huge cable car to Plan Checrouit is on the southern edge. The gondola from Dolonne now offers an alternative way up. Both are bus-served, and while parking at the cable car is very limited, there's a big new car park at Dolonne. Drivers can also go to Entrèves, up the

valley, where there is a large car park at the cable car. Most people leave skis or boards and boots in lockers up the mountain or at the lift base.

Buses, infrequent but timetabled, go to La Palud, just beyond Entrèves,

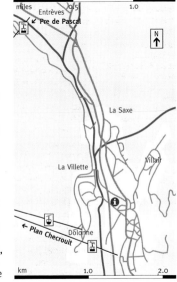

KEY FACTS

Resort	1225m
	4,020ft
Slopes	1210-2755m
	3,970-9,040ft
Lifts	16
Pistes	100km
	62 miles
Blue	27%
Red	62%
Black	11%
Snowmaking	
	252 guns

LIFT PASSES

International

Prices in €

Age	1-day	6-day
under 12		99
12 to 64	41	199
over 65		149

Free under 6

Beginner two free
nursery lifts

Notes
Covers Val Veny and
Checrouit, and the
lifts on Mont Blanc up
to Punta Helbronner;
half-day passes; some
single ascent passes;
3+ day passes allow
at least one day in
the Aosta valley,
Flaine and on most of
the Chamonix lifts

Alternative passes
Non-skier

for the Monte Bianco cable car to
Punta Helbronner (for Vallée Blanche).
Taxis are easily arranged for evening
excursions to valley restaurants.

THE MOUNTAINS

The pistes suit intermediates, but are
surprisingly limited for such a well-
known, large resort. They are varied in
character, if not gradient. Signposting
of pistes and hazards is 'poor, virtually
non-existent', but a newly improved
map for 2007/08 at least now shows
lift names and direction. There are still
a few old, slow chairs, although these
can largely be avoided. Chamonix, La
Thuile and Pila are an easy drive or
bus ride and Cervinia is reachable.

THE SLOPES
Small but interestingly varied
There are two distinct sections, both
almost entirely intermediate. The east-
facing **Checrouit** area, accessed by the
Checrouit gondola, catches morning
sun, and has open, above-the-tree-line
pistes. The 25-person, infrequently
running Youla cable car goes to the
top of Courmayeur's pistes. There is a
further tiny cable car to Cresta d'Arp.

This serves only long off-piste runs but
it is no longer compulsory to have a
guide with you to go up it.

Most people follow the sun over to
the north-west-facing slopes towards
Val Veny in the afternoon. These are
interesting, varied and tree lined, with
great views of Mont Blanc and its
glaciers. There are a few alternative
routes between the Checrouit and Val
Veny areas; it's not always easy to
figure them out, even with the new
clearer piste map. The Val Veny slopes
are also accessible by cable car from
Entrèves, a few miles outside
Courmayeur.

A little way beyond Entrèves is La
Palud, where a cable car goes up in
three stages to Punta Helbronner, at
the shoulder of **Mont Blanc**. There are
no pistes from the top, but you can do
the famous Vallée Blanche run to
Chamonix from here without the scary
ridge walk that forms the start on the
Chamonix side. There are buses back
from Chamonix through the Mont
Blanc tunnel. Or you can tackle the
tougher off-piste runs on the Italian
side of Mont Blanc. For obvious
reasons, none of these glacier runs
should be done without a guide.

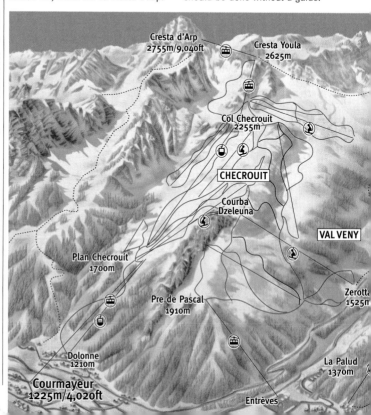

Cresta d'Arp
2755m/9,040ft

Cresta Youla
2625m

Col Checrouit
2255m

CHECROUIT

Courba
Dzeleuna

VAL VENY

Plan Checrouit
1700m

Pre de Pascal
1910m

Zerotta
1525m

Dolonne
1210m

La Palud
1370m

Courmayeur
1225m/4,020ft

Entrèves

↑ Like most of the mountain, the main slope down to Plan Checrouit is a red, and a bit testing for nervous intermediates

AIAT MONTE BIANCO

TERRAIN PARKS
Just a boardercross
Like a lot of Italian resorts, Courmayeur has no terrain park or half-pipe. For the past few seasons, there has been a boardercross run (500m/1,640ft) near the top of the Plan de la Gabba fast chair. But it was not rebuilt for 2007/08, and we have no news of 2008/09.

SNOW RELIABILITY
Good for most of the season
Courmayeur's slopes are not high – mostly between 1700m and 2250m (5,600ft and 7,400ft). Those above Val Veny face north or north-west, so keep their snow well, but the Plan Checrouit side is rather too sunny for comfort in late season. There is snowmaking on most main runs and this was increased for 2007/08 to include the red run to Dolonne, in the valley. So good coverage in early- and mid-season is virtually assured – we've been there in a January snow drought and enjoyed decent skiing entirely on man-made snow. Piste grooming is 'not taken very seriously'.

FOR EXPERTS
Off-piste is the only challenge
Courmayeur has few challenging pistes. The black runs on the Val Veny side are not severe, and few moguls form elsewhere. But if you're lucky enough to find fresh powder – as we have been several times – you can have fantastic fun among the trees.

Classic off-piste runs go from Cresta d'Arp, at the top of the lift network, in three directions – a clockwise loop via Arp Vieille to Val Veny, with close-up views of the Miage glacier; east down a deserted valley to Dolonne or Pré St Didier; or south through the Youla gorge to La Thuile.

On Mont Blanc, the Vallée Blanche is not a challenge (though there are more difficult variations), but the Toula glacier route on the Italian side from Punta Helbronner to Pavillon most certainly is, often to the point of being dangerous. There are also heli-drops available, including a wonderful 20km/12 mile run from the Ruitor glacier down into France – you ride the lifts back up from La Rosière and descend to La Thuile (a taxi ride from Courmayeur). Prices start at about £150. A day trip to Chamonix is well worth thinking about.

FOR INTERMEDIATES
Good reds, but limited extent
The whole area is suitable for most intermediates, but it is small. The avid piste-basher will ski it in a day. It also lacks long, easy runs to suit the more timid.

The open Checrouit section is pretty much go-anywhere territory, but it is basically just one wide red slope. Timid skiers should head up the fast six-seater Pra Neyron chair for access to the area's few blues. The Val Veny side of the mountain is basically steeper, with manageable blacks going close to the fall line and good reds and the occasional blue taking less direct routes. These runs link in with the pretty, wooded slopes heading down to Zerotta. The fast Zerotta chair dominates the Val Veny side, serving runs of varying difficulty over a decent vertical of 560m/1,840ft – including a long blue.

boarding
Courmayeur's pistes suit intermediates well, and most areas are easily accessible by novices as the main lifts are cable cars, chairs and gondolas. For the more adventurous, there are good off-piste routes and a boardercross run. Although it's a bit steep for absolute beginners, a 2007 reporter says, 'I'd bring beginner friends to Courmayeur with a clean conscience. And for intermediates and experts it's lots of fun – there seemed to be an above-average number of lumps and bumps to the side of the piste for playful frolics.'

SCHOOLS

Monte Bianco
t 0165 842477

Courmayeur
t 0165 848254

Classes
(Monte Bianco prices)
5 days (3hr per day)
€175

Private lessons
From €35 for 1hr;
additional person €11

GUIDES

Guides Courmayeur
t 0165 842064

AIAT MONTE BIANCO

The cute old village is lively in the evenings
↓

The Vallée Blanche, although off-piste, is easy enough for adventurous, fit intermediates to try. So is the local heli-skiing.

FOR BEGINNERS
Consistently too steep
Courmayeur is not well suited to beginners. There are several nursery slopes, none ideal. The area at Plan Checrouit gets crowded, and there are few easy runs for the near-beginner to progress to. The small area just above the Entrèves cable car top station, has decent beginner terrain, and it tends to have good snow. And there are easy blues at Dzeulena (top of the Pra Neyron chair). The Maison Vieille chair can be ridden both ways, for access to the Tzaly blue slope.

FOR CROSS-COUNTRY
Beautiful trails
There are 35km/22 miles of trails. The best are the four covering 20km/12 miles at Val Ferret, served by bus. Dolonne has a couple of short trails.

QUEUES
Weekend crowds pour in
The introduction of the Dolonne gondola a couple of seasons ago seems to have reduced the weekend and peak period queues for the Checrouit and Val Veny cable cars, offering a 'quick and efficient' way up and down the mountain. The infrequent Youla cable car may require patience – only worth it for those

heading off-piste. Overcrowded slopes on weekends, particularly down to Zerotta, can also be a problem.

MOUNTAIN RESTAURANTS
Lots – some of them very good
The area is lavishly endowed with 27 establishments ranging from rustic little huts to a large self-service place. Most huts do table service of delicious pizza, pasta and other dishes and it is best to reserve tables in advance. But there are also snack bars selling more basic fare and relying on views and sun to fill their terraces.

Several restaurants are excellent. At Plan Checrouit, Chiecco serves the best and most refined food, with friendly service: 'the owner is passionate about her food'; 'wonderful pasta and amazing meat courses – expensive but worth it'. Reporters also enjoy the 'convenient' Christiania (book a table downstairs) – 'great pizzas'; 'excellent food and service, but had to wait a long time for a table.' Further up the hill, Maison Vieille is a welcoming rustic place with traditional Italian food including good home-made pastas. There is another clutch of worthwhile places in Val Veny, all with excellent views: the jolly Grolla and Zerotta have lovely sunny terraces, though one reporter preferred the food at the nearby Petit Mont Blanc. Baita da Geremia (just below Grolla) is a simple snack bar with some hot food and occasional 'themed' days – eg sushi or a live band. Courba Dzeleuna just below the top of the Dzeleuna chair also serves snacks, but is best known for its delicious home-made myrtle grappa (but beware of the alcohol-soaked berries left in the glass).

SCHOOLS AND GUIDES
Good reports
The Monte Bianco ski school gets good reviews: 'the best instructor for ages – possibly ever'. There is a thriving guides' association ready to help you explore the area's off-piste; it has produced a helpful booklet showing the main possibilities.

FACILITIES FOR CHILDREN
Good care by Italian standards
Child care facilities are well ahead of the Italian norm. There's a children's garden and fun zone in Dolonne.

Air Geneva 105km/ 65 miles (2hr); Turin 150km/93 miles (2hr)

Rail Pré-St-Didier (5km/3 miles); regular buses from station

Indoor Swimming pool and sauna at Pré-St-Didier (5km/ 3 miles), Alpine museum, cinema, library, art gallery, sports centre with climbing wall, ice rink, curling, fitness centre, indoor golf, squash, tennis

Outdoor Walking paths in Val Ferret, snowshoeing, paragliding, hang-gliding, golf on snow, snow biking, dog sledding

Fun park Dolonne 9am-4.30

Ski schools Take children from age 5

Check out our feature chapters at the front of the book.

Phone numbers From abroad use the prefix +39 (and do **not** omit the initial '0' of the phone number)

t 0165 842060
info@aiat-monte-bianco.com
www.aiat-monte-bianco.com

STAYING THERE

HOW TO GO
Plenty of hotels
Courmayeur's long-standing popularity ensures a wide range of packages (including some excellent weekend deals), mainly in hotels. Tour op Momentum is a Courmayeur specialist and can advise about and fix pretty much whatever you want here. One or two UK operators have catered chalets.

Hotels There are nearly 50 hotels, spanning the star ratings.

****Royal e Golf** (0165 831611) Large, grand place in centre just off Via Roma. Outdoor pool, sauna, piano bar.

****Gran Baita** (0165 844040) Luxury place with antique furnishings, panoramic views. Pool. Shuttle-bus to cable car.

****Pavillon** (0165 846120) Comfortable 4-star near cable car, with a pool. Friendly staff.

****Auberge de la Maison** (0165 869811) Small, atmospheric hotel in Entrèves; owned by the same family as Maison de Filippo (see 'Eating out').

***Walser** (0165 844824) Near main road. 'Good value hotel with exemplary service.'

***Bouton d'Or** (0165 846729) Small, friendly B&B near main square. 'Very welcoming, owner ferries you to/from lifts if you wish,' says a reporter.

***Berthod** (0165 842835) Friendly, family-run hotel near centre.

***Grange** (0165 869733) Rustic stone-and-wood farmhouse in Entrèves.

***Triolet** (0165 846822) Comfortable hotel with an excellent location near the lifts.

***Maison Saint Jean** (0165 842880) Central, family-run, pool.

Edelweiss (0165 841590) Friendly, cosy, good value; close to the centre.

Scoiattolo (0165 846716) Good rooms, good food, shame it's at the opposite end of town to the cable car.

Apartments The Grand Chalet is central and has spacious apartments and hot tub, steam room and sauna.

EATING OUT
Jolly Italian evenings
There is a great choice; there's a handy promotional booklet describing many of them (in English as well as Italian). In downtown Courmayeur, we've been impressed by the traditional Italian cuisine of both Pierre

Alexis and Cadran Solaire. But the popular Terrazza is reportedly the 'best in town, with wonderful local food and great service'. The 'good value' Mont-Fréty, the Tunnel pizzeria and the Vieux Pommier (for fondue and raclette) have also been recommended. And the Aria has 'an amazing wine list'. Within taxi range, the touristy but very jolly Maison de Filippo in Entrèves is rightly famous for its fixed-price, 36-dish feast. A local recommends the restaurant in the hotel Dente del Gigante at La Palud and the Clotz in Val Ferret ('expensive but modern, refined Italian cuisine').

APRES-SKI
Stylish bar-hopping
Courmayeur has a lively evening scene – at weekends, at least – centred on stylish bars with comfy armchairs or sofas to collapse into, often serving free canapés in the early evening. Our favourites are the Roma, the back room of the Caffè della Posta and the Bar delle Guide. The Cadran Solaire is where the big money from Milan and Turin hangs out. The Privé serves great cocktails. Poppy's is popular for drinks and pizza and the American Bar has good music and a fine selection of wines. Maquis is the better of the two night clubs in Entrèves.

OFF THE SLOPES
Lots on for non-slope users
If you're not interested in hitting the snow, you'll find the village pleasant – parading up and down is a favourite pastime for the many non-skiers the resort attracts. You can go by cable car up to Punta Helbronner, by bus to Aosta, or up the main cable car to Plan Checrouit to meet friends for lunch. The huge sports centre is good (but no pool). Don't miss a visit to the thermal baths at Pre St Didier – with over 30 spa 'experiences' including saunas, waterfall and outdoor thermal pools.

STAYING UP THE MOUNTAIN
Why would you want to?
Visiting Courmayeur and not staying in the charming village seems perverse – if you're that keen to get going in the morning, this is probably the wrong resort. But at Plan Checrouit, the 1-star Christiania (0165 843572 – see 'Mountain restaurants') has simple rooms; the 3-star Baita (0165 843570) is smarter; book way in advance.

Livigno

Lowish prices and highish altitude – a tempting combination, especially when you add in a quite pleasant Alpine ambience

COSTS

① ② ③ ④ ⑤ ⑥

RATINGS

The slopes
Fast lifts	****
Snow	****
Extent	**
Experts	**
Intermediates	***
Beginners	****
Convenience	**
Queues	****
Mountain restaurants	***

The rest
Scenery	***
Resort charm	***
Off-slope	**

NEWS

For 2007/08 an eight-seat gondola replaced the Tagliede double chair at the north end of the village, below Costaccia. A second stage to the top is being built for 2008/09.

Also last season, a new terrain park opened at Polvere on Carosello 3000.

The first phase of a new thermal spa and wellness centre is due to open in December 2008.

446

- ✚ High altitude plus snowmaking means reliable snow
- ✚ Large choice of beginners' slopes
- ✚ Impressive modern lift system
- ✚ Cheap by the standards of high resorts, with the bonus of duty-free shopping (eg for new equipment)
- ✚ Lively, friendly, quite smart village with some Alpine atmosphere
- ✚ Long, snow-sure cross-country trails

- ▬ No challenging pistes
- ▬ Long and gruelling transfers – 5hr from Bergamo, less from Innsbruck
- ▬ Two widely separated slope areas
- ▬ Village is very long and straggling – with no buses later in the evening
- ▬ Few off-slope amenities
- ▬ Bleak setting, susceptible to wind
- ▬ Nightlife can disappoint

Livigno's recipe of a fair-sized mountain, high altitude and fairly low prices is uncommon, and obviously attractive. Despite its duty-free status, the hotels, bars and restaurants are not much cheaper than in other Italian resorts, but shopping is – there are countless camera and clothes shops. As a relatively snow-sure alternative to the Pyrenees or to the smallest, cheapest resorts in Austria, Livigno may make your shortlist. But don't overlook the drawbacks.

THE RESORT

Livigno is an amalgam of three villages in a wide, remote valley near the Swiss border – basically a string of hotels, bars, specialist shops and supermarkets lining a single long street. The buildings are small in scale and mainly traditional in style, giving the village a pleasant atmosphere.

The original hamlet of San Antonio is the nearest thing Livigno has to a centre, and the best all-round location. Here, the main street and those at right angles, linking it to the busy bypass road, are nominally traffic-free, but actually are just through-traffic-free. The road that skirts the centre is constantly busy, and becomes intrusive in the hamlets of Santa Maria, 1km/0.5 miles to the north, and San Rocco, a bit further away to the south (and a bit uphill).

Lifts along the length of the village access the western slopes of the valley. The main lift to the eastern slopes is directly across the flat valley floor from the centre.

Depending on where you are based, you may make heavy use of the free bus services. They are fairly frequent, but get overcrowded at peak times and stop mid-evening. A 2007 visitor comments: 'The three colour-coded bus routes are actually simple, but not easy to understand at first.

People often find themselves travelling in the wrong direction.' Taxis (including minibus taxis for groups) are an affordable alternative.

The Alta Valtellina lift pass covers Bormio and Santa Caterina, an easy drive or bus ride (free with the lift pass) if the high pass is open. A pass of three days or more entitles you to half-price on a day in St Moritz – an excursion not easily done from any other major resort.

The airport transfers are long and winding – not great for kids.

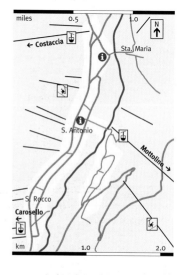

Livigno

Prices in €

Age	1-day	6-day
under 13	29	118
13 to 59	35	171
over 60	29	118

Free under 8

Beginner points card

Notes
Covers Livigno only;
half-day passes and
reduced Saturday
passes; family
reductions; for passes
of 2+ days, 50%
reduction on a one-
day St Moritz pass

Alternative passes
Alta Valtellina pass
covers Livigno,
Bormio and Santa
Caterina

boarding

Livigno offers a refreshing sense of space. There really is something for everyone here, from big, wide, open and rolling motorways to natural gullies, hits, tree runs and powder. The back of Mottolino is a perfect example. The terrain park infrastructure is very good, and has a long history of hosting world-class events. Helmets and body armour are supplied for free at the park, a nice new perk. Beginners be warned: practically all the smaller lower slopes are serviced by drags. But the resort still attracts good numbers of beginners, and Madness snowboard school (see www.madnessnow.com) gets good reports (see 'Schools').

THE MOUNTAINS

The mainly open slopes, on either side of the valley, are more extensive than in many other budget destinations.

THE SLOPES
Widely spread
There are three sectors, two of them linked high-up and low-down.

A new two-stage gondola (see 'News') at the north end of the village takes you up to **Costaccia**, where a long fast quad chairlift goes along the ridge towards the **Carosello** sector. The blue linking run back from Carosello to the top of Costaccia is flat in places and may involve energetic poling if the snow conditions and the wind are against you. Carosello is more usually accessed by the optimistically named Carosello 3000 gondola at San Rocco, which goes up, in two stages, to 2750m/9,020ft. Most runs return towards the village, but there are a couple on the back of the mountain, on the west-facing slopes of Val Federia, served by a six-pack.

The ridge of **Mottolino** is reached by an efficient gondola from Teola, a tiresome walk or a short bus-ride across the valley from San Antonio. From the top, you can descend to fast quads on either side of the ridge; you can take a slow antique chair up the ridge to Monte della Neve, but it's better to descend to faster lifts.

We don't show on our map a low-level link from the nursery drags at the bottom of Carosello to those below Costaccia; it's more of a walk than a run – not recommended for boarders. Signposting is patchy and the piste map does not identify runs. Night skiing is available on Thursdays.

TERRAIN PARKS
Serious facilities
The main Budrider's park behind Mottolino is an awesome freestyle zone for all levels of riders. It also plays host to the world rookie fest and River Jump contest – both on the Ticket to Ride calendar. It has three kicker lines for all levels and a hip. This is bordered by a big super-pipe, often used as a training ground by pros. There are advanced rails that are placed in and around the jumps as well. Beyond lies the smaller Snow-

Livigno

447

KEY FACTS

Resort	1815m
	5,950ft
Slopes	1815-2800m
	5,950-9,190ft
Lifts	32
Pistes	110km
	68 miles
Blue	25%
Red	58%
Black	17%
Snowmaking	70km
	43 miles

↑ Livigno's terrain parks are world-class
APT LIVIGNO

SCHOOLS

Livigno Inverno/Estate
t 0342 996276
Azzurra Livigno
t 0342 997683
Livigno Italy
t 0342 996767
Livigno Galli Fedele
t 0342 970300
Madness Snowboard
t 0342 997792
Top Club Mottolino
t 0342 970822

Classes
(Livigno Inverno/
Estate prices)
6 days (2hr per day)
€100
Private lessons
€37 for 1hr; each
additional person €6

CHILDREN

Kinder Club Dau di Livigno
t 0342 996276
Ages 3 and over; 6
days €185 incl. lunch
Miniclub Top Club Mottolino
t 0342 970822
M'eating Point
t 0342 970025
Spazio gioco Per i bimbi
t 0342 970711
Ages 18mnth to 3yr;
8.30-1pm

Ski school
Takes children from
age 4 (6 2hr days
€100)

park Medio with nice lines of small to intermediate kickers, good entry-level rails of varying difficulty, a mini spine and a small boardercross. New for 2008 is the Carosello 3000 park, littered with ride-on boxes and rails for beginners as well as good intermediate jumps. There is a new park with specially built, visually pleasing wooden rails and boxes.

SNOW RELIABILITY
Very good, despite no glacier
Livigno's slopes are high (you can spend most of your time around 2500m/8,200ft), and with snow-guns on the lower slopes of Mottolino and Costaccia, the season is long. Despite the generally poor snow in Europe, January 2007 reporters were 'very pleasantly surprised' by the snow.

FOR EXPERTS
Not recommended
The piste map shows a few black runs, but these are really no more than stiff red in gradient. There is off-piste to be done between the pistes.

FOR INTERMEDIATES
Flattering slopes
Good intermediates will be able to tackle all the blacks without worry. The woodland black run from Carosello past Tea da Borch is narrow in places and can get mogulled and icy in the afternoon. Moderate intermediates have virtually the whole area at their disposal. The long run beneath the Mottolino gondola is one of the best, and there is also a long, varied, under-used blue going less directly to the valley. Leisurely types have several long cruises available; the run beneath the fast chair at the top of Costaccia is a splendid slope.

FOR BEGINNERS
Excellent but scattered slopes
A vast array of nursery slopes along the sunny lower flanks of Costaccia, and other slopes around the valley, make Livigno excellent for novices – although some of the slopes at the northern end are steep enough to cause difficulties. There are lots of longer runs to progress to.

CROSS-COUNTRY
Good snow, bleak setting
Long snow-sure trails (40km/25 miles in total) follow the valley floor, making Livigno a good choice, provided you don't mind the bleak scenery. There is a specialist school, Livigno 2000, and the resort organises major races.

QUEUES
Few problems these days
Queues are generally not a problem. Delays can occur at the main gondolas at peak times, but the new Costaccia lift should have resolved any problems there – even better when the planned second stage is built. A bigger problem is that winds can close the upper lifts, causing crowds lower down.

MOUNTAIN RESTAURANTS
More than adequate
On Mottolino, the M'eating Point refuge at the top of the gondola is 'beautiful'. The self-service section gets 'very busy', but the smart table-service section is 'very good, not that much dearer and much more pleasant'. And there are more charming places lower down. The rustic restaurants at Passo d'Eira and Trepalle are quieter options – the Trela has been recommended. And the welcoming Tea is at the base of the same sector. Costaccia's Berghütte is pleasantly rustic and sunny, with good food and a great atmosphere. Carosello has a popular but acceptable self-service place and the Stuvetta table-service restaurant below. Tea da Borch, in the trees lower down, has a Tirolean-style atmosphere.

SCHOOLS AND GUIDES
Watch out for short classes
There are several schools. Reports are generally complimentary, praising good instruction and excellent English. Classes are short at only two hours, but are rated as great value for money. The Madness snowboard school offers 'relatively small' groups.

GETTING THERE

Air Bergamo 200km/124 miles (5hr); Innsbruck 185km/115 miles (5hr)

Rail Tirano (48km/ 30 miles), Zernez (Switzerland, 28km/ 17 miles); regular buses from station, weekends only

UK PACKAGES

Airtours, Directski.com, First Choice, Independent Ski Links, Inghams, Interhome, Italian Safaris, Neilson, Panorama, Ski McNeill, Skitracer

ACTIVITIES

Indoor Saunas, fitness rooms and swimming pools (in hotels), badminton, billiards, chess, bowling, basketball, cinema

Outdoor Cleared paths, ice rink, snowshoeing, horse riding, ice climbing, dog sledding, go-karts on ice, snowmobiling, paragliding, tobogganing

Phone numbers
From abroad use the prefix +39 (and do **not** omit the initial '0' of the phone number)

TOURIST OFFICE

t 0342 052200
info@livigno.eu
www.livigno.it

FACILITIES FOR CHILDREN
Not bad for Italy
The schools run children's classes. The Livigno Inverno-Estate school offers all-day care; the staff speak English.

STAYING THERE

HOW TO GO
Lots of hotels, some apartments
Livigno has an enormous range of hotels and a number of apartments. There are some attractively priced catered chalets from UK operators and the newish Park Village at Teola offers smart chalet accommodation.
Hotels There is a wide choice of 2-, 3- and 4-star places.
****Intermonti** (0342 972100) Modern with pool and other mod cons; on the Mottolino side of the valley.
****Touring** (0342 996131) 'Very comfortable and competitively priced.'
****Bivio** (0342 996137) In central Livigno; with pool.
****Camana Veglia** (0342 996310) Charming old wooden chalet. Popular restaurant, well placed in Santa Maria.
***Steinbock** (0342 970520) Nice little place, far from major lifts.
***Loredana** (0342 996330) Modern chalet on the Mottolino side.
***Montanina** (0342 996060) Central.
***Alpi** (0342 996408) In San Rocco, not far from Carosello gondola.
***Larice** (0342 996184) Stylish little B&B well placed for Costaccia lifts.
***Champagne** (0342 996437) 'In lovely condition and close to centre.'
Silvestri (0342 996255) Comfortable place in the San Rocco area.
Apartments All the big tour operators that come here offer apartments.

EATING OUT
Still value for money
Livigno's restaurants are mainly traditional, unpretentious places, many hotel-based. Hotel Concordia is

considered one of the best. Mario's impressed a 2007 visitor with its 'great food and service'. Similarly praised are the 'good value' Helvetia, the Baita and Astoria. Another 2007 visitor enjoyed the Mirage. And the Bellavista has a 'bustling bistro style', with 'simple tasty food'. Readers also praise Galli's, the Grolla, Garden and Echo. The Rusticana is a good-value pizzeria and Pesce D'Oro specialises in seafood and Italian cuisine. Grand Chalet, at the Park Chalet Village near the Mottolino lifts, and the Canoa are the most recent additions.

APRES-SKI
Lively, but disappoints some
The scene in Livigno is quieter than some people expect in a duty-free resort. Pas de la Casa it is not – to the relief of most reporters. Also, the best places are scattered about, so the village lacks evening buzz. At tea time Tea del Vidal, at the bottom of Mottolino, gets lively, as does the Stalet bar at the base of the Carosello gondola and the central umbrella bar. Nightlife gets going only after 10pm. Galli's pub, in San Antonio, is the place to party. The Kuhstall under the Bivio hotel is an excellent cellar bar with live music, as is the Helvetia, over the road. The San Rocco end is quietest, but Daphne's has a 'great party atmosphere' and Marco's is popular. Kokodi is the main disco.

OFF THE SLOPES
Look lively, or go shopping
Livigno offers a small range of outdoor alternatives to skiing and boarding – a recent visitor 'thoroughly enjoyed' the dog-sledding. Tobogganing is also popular. A new thermal spa/wellness centre is due to open for 2008/09 (see News). Walks are uninspiring. There's always duty free shopping, of course – and trips to Bormio and St Moritz.

Interactive resort shortlist builder at **www.wtss.co.uk**

Madonna di Campiglio

Chic, very Italian but rather spread-out resort with mainly easy intermediate local slopes amid stunning scenery

450

+ Pleasant, friendly town in a pretty valley with splendid views

+ Generally easy slopes, best for beginners and early intermediates

– Spread-out village and infrequent shuttle-bus service

– Quiet après-ski

Campiglio is a pleasant Dolomite town with an affluent, almost exclusively Italian, clientele – a bit like Cortina, though the scenery isn't in quite the same league. Folgarida and Marilleva (to which the slopes are linked) and Pinzolo (which may be linked by 2009/10) are quite different and worth exploring by adventurous intermediates and better. They are covered in our Trentino chapter.

THE RESORT

Campiglio is a long-established, traditional-style but largely modern town, set in a prettily wooded valley beneath the impressive Brenta Dolomites, with slopes in three linked sectors. The town spreads out along the approach roads and includes a pretty frozen lake. The centre is fairly compact: the lifts to Cinque Laghi (to the west) and to Pradalago (to the north) bracket most of the central hotels, and are about a five-minute walk apart. Five minutes outside the centre is a gondola to Monte Spinale, leading to the Grostè sector; there is another gondola to Grostè starting a short bus ride outside the town. Beyond this lift station are the main nursery slopes at Campo Carlo Magno.

Campiglio attracts an affluent Italian clientele; it has lots of smart shops. The village is busy all day, and promenading is an early evening ritual.

The free ski-bus is not frequent but some hotels run minibuses.

↑ Strolling around the traffic-free centre and window shopping are popular activities

APT MADONNA DI CAMPIGLIO

KEY FACTS

Resort	1520m
	4,990ft
Madonna, Folgarida, and Marilleva combined area	
Slopes	1300-2505m
	4,270-8,220ft
Lifts	46
Pistes	120km
	75 miles
Blue	35%
Red	50%
Black	15%
Snowmaking	77km

Phone numbers
From abroad use the prefix +39 (and do **not** omit the initial '0' of the phone number)

TOURIST OFFICE

t 0465 447501
info@campiglio.to
www.campiglio.to

THE MOUNTAINS

The Pradalago sector is linked by lift and piste to Monte Vigo, and so to the slopes of Folgarida and Marilleva.

Slopes The terrain is mainly easy intermediate, both above and below the tree line. Reporters have been very impressed with the 'immaculate' grooming and piste marking.

Terrain parks The Ursus park, at Grostè, includes boardercross, half- and quarter-pipes and, new for last season, rails, a fun box and a kicker.

Snow reliability Although many of the runs are sunny, they are at a fair altitude, and there has been hefty investment in snowmaking. As a result, snow reliability is reasonable.

Experts Experts should plan on heading off-piste. The trees under the Genziana chair are 'a good spot for untracked snow'. But the 3-Tre race course and Canalone on Cinque Laghi and the Spinale Direttissima are steep. For other steep runs head to Marilleva.

Intermediates Grostè and Pradalago have long, easy runs, and early or timid intermediates will love them. Cinque Laghi, Campiglio's racing mountain, is a bit tougher, as are the runs at Folgarida, Marilleva and Pinzolo, which confident intermediates should explore (see Trentino chapter).

Beginners The nursery slopes at Campo Carlo Magno are excellent, but do involve a bus ride. The draglift here is not covered by the main lift pass and you have to buy a separate day ticket when you get there. Progression to longer runs is easy.

Snowboarding The resort is popular with boarders and some major events have been held here.

Cross-country There are 22km/14 miles of pretty trails through the woods.

Queues Reporters did not find queuing a worry this year. The most serious bottleneck – access to Cinque Laghi

– has been transformed by the new gondola to the top.

Mountain restaurants Reporters like the table-service Cascina Zeledria ('a great lunch', said a 2008 reporter) in the trees off blue run 7 on Pradalago. On our 2006 visit we enjoyed good local sausages at Viviani, near the top of Pradalago. Malga Montagnoli in the lower part of Grostè is a charming old (self-service) refuge and Boch, higher up, has been recommended, as has Cinque Laghi ('stunning views').

Schools and guides Language can be a problem. A recent visitor found the Nazionale school 'very good'; he was the only Brit in his group but managed OK as he spoke a little Italian.

Facilities for children Very limited.

STAYING THERE

How to go There is a wide choice of hotels and some self-catering.

Hotels Of the 4-stars, we enjoyed the Zeledria (0465 441010) out at Campo Carlo Magno on our 2006 visit. Spinale (0465 441116), Bertelli (0465 441013) – 'excellent food' – and Alpen Suite (0465 440100) – 'clean, welcoming, good food' – are well positioned. The Savoia Palace (0465 441004) is 'comfortable and friendly', but the location can be noisy. Of the 3-stars, St Hubertus (0465 441144) was highly praised by a 2008 visitor ('charming B&B in centre'). Previous reader recommendations have included the central Arnica (0465 442227; 'super B&B, very friendly owners'), Milano (0465 441210), Bonapace (0465 441 019) and Crozzon (0465 442222).

Eating out There are around 20 restaurants. A 2008 reporter recommended Da Alfiero ('pricey but worth it'), La Tana dell Orso ('unusual Tirolean menu and music') and Stube Rosengarten ('good food, long pizza menu'). 'All the ones we tried were good,' says a recent reporter and Belvedere, Antico Focolare, Roi, Stube Diana and Locanda degli Artisti ('worth the expense for a special night out') have all been recommended. Some of the mountain huts also open at night.

Après-ski Après-ski is quiet. Stube di Franz-Joseph, Bar Suisse, Bacchus Enotica and Cantina del Suisse have been recommended. The Alpes is perhaps the smartest club.

Off the slopes Skating on the lake and walking are popular. There's also dog-sledding and paragliding.

Monterosa Ski

One of Europe's best kept secrets: three unspoiled villages, slopes with easy pistes and uncrowded off-piste for all standards

COSTS

①②③④⑤⑥

RATINGS

The slopes
Fast lifts	***
Snow	****
Extent	***
Expert	****
Intermediate	****
Beginner	**
Convenience	***
Queues	****
Mountain restaurants	**

The rest
Scenery	****
Resort charm	***
Off-slope	*

KEY FACTS

Slopes	1200-2970m
	3,940-9,740ft
Lifts	33
Pistes	180km
	112 miles
Blue	26%
Red	64%
Black	10%
Snowmaking	100km
	62 miles

452

- ➕ Fabulous off-piste and heli-skiing, for both intermediates and experts
- ➕ Slopes usually very quiet weekdays
- ➕ Panoramic views
- ➕ Good snow reliability and grooming
- ➕ Quiet, unspoiled villages
- ➕ Three-valley lift/piste network gives a sensation of travel, but ...

- ➖ Virtually no choice of route when touring the three valleys on-piste
- ➖ Few challenging pistes – mainly easy cruising
- ➖ High winds can close links
- ➖ Few off-slope diversions
- ➖ Limited après-ski

Monterosa Ski's three resorts – Champoluc, Gressoney and Alagna – are popular with Italian weekenders, who drive up from Milan and Turin, but they are hardly heard of on the international market. As a result, they retain a friendly, small-scale, unspoiled Italian ambience that we and a growing band of readers like a lot. Strangely, few UK tour operators feature the area. But that suits us, as it makes it more likely the area will retain its unique character.

The three-valley network of lifts and pistes is anything but small-scale: Alagna and Champoluc, at opposite ends, are no less than 17km/11 miles apart – slightly further apart than Courchevel and Val Thorens in France's more famous Three Valleys area. It's around a four-hour trip by road to get from Alagna to Champoluc if you miss the last lift. But a glance at the piste map reveals that the Italian network between the two extremes is skeletal compared with the full-bodied French one. Outside the piste network, however, is a lot of great off-piste terrain, some lift-served, which has long attracted experts.

It was only four seasons ago that Alagna became accessible by piste from the top of the Gressoney lifts. Expert skiers may be inclined to regret the fact that a splendid off-piste run was sacrificed; but that's progress. They have plenty more bowls to play in – and the black Olen piste is a cracker.

THE RESORT

There is one main village in each of the area's three long valleys. Champoluc in the western valley and Gressoney in the central one are both about an hour's drive up from the Aosta valley, to the south. Alagna is even more remote, and approached from the Italian lakes, to the east.

Champoluc is a pleasant but not notably pretty place, strung out along the valley road without much ski resort ambience – the centre is more or less devoid of bars and inviting shops. The village gondola starts from a kind of micro-resort several minutes' walk up the road. You can store boots and skis/boards there overnight. The valley road continues past several hotels towards Frachey, where there is a chairlift into the slopes.

Gressoney La Trinité is a quiet, neat little village, with cobbled streets,

wooden buildings and an old church. It is about 800m/0.5 miles from the chairlift into the local slopes, where there are a few convenient hotels. Links with the other valleys revolve around Stafal at the head of the valley, reached by bus (seven euros for a weekly pass). There is accommodation here, too. Gressoney St Jean, a bigger village, is 5km/3 miles down the valley and has its own separate slopes.

Alagna is a peaceful, rustic village with a solid church and some lovely old wooden farmhouses built in the distinctive Walser style. It bears no resemblance to a conventional ski resort. We visited on a sunny morning in March, and found the place deserted. A gondola starts from the village centre.

Trips to Cervinia, La Thuile, Courmayeur and Pila (all covered by the Aosta Valley pass) are possible by car.

For 2007/08 the ancient Punta Indren cable car in Alagna was finally taken out of service. A new cable car is planned from Passo Salati to service the same area (all off-piste), but it won't be ready until 2009/10 at the earliest. Until it is, lots of fabulous off-piste will be available only by ski touring or heli-skiing. There may also be further lifts in the area in the more distant future. More snowmaking was put in place for 2007/08 at Frachey near Champoluc and around Punta Jolanda above Gressoney La Trinité. In the Estoul area (see piste map), a new double chair has replaced two draglifts.

THE MOUNTAINS

The slopes of Monterosa Ski are relatively extensive, and very scenic. The pistes are almost all intermediate (and well groomed), and the lifts are virtually all chairs and gondolas. The terrain is undulating and runs are long, but many lifts serve only one or two pistes. Reporters visiting at various times have found the top lifts that make the connection between valleys closed by wind, severely limiting the available terrain.

Slopes Champoluc residents reach Colle Sarezza on two successive gondolas and a quad chair. From the top, a steep, narrow, bumpy run is the link with the long cruising runs below Colle Bettaforca. A lot of timid intermediates find this run very difficult – improvements are promised for 2008/09 – but it can be avoided by taking the bus to the Frachey chair.

At Stafal a cable car followed by a fast chair bring you back towards Champoluc, while two successive gondolas opposite take you to Passo Salati. From there, runs lead back down to Stafal and to Gressoney La Trinité and Orsia, both served by chairlifts. Or you can head towards Alagna via the fabulous black Olen piste (which was originally classed as a red), or take a blue that goes only as far as the mid-station of the cable car back to Passo Salati.

From Alagna a modern gondola goes to Pianalunga at mid-mountain. From here, a cable car takes you to Passo Salati (with a pause at the mid-station). The tiny, ancient cable car to Punta Indren from above Pianalunga was finally closed for the 2007/08 season. It is to be replaced with a new cable car from Passo Salati, serving only off-piste routes to Alagna and Gressoney (but see 'News' for the timing on this).

Gressoney St Jean, Antagnod (near Champoluc) and Estoul (above Brusson) have their own small areas of slopes. The St Jean slopes have one lift and a drag, but two reporters enjoyed half days there. Antagnod is used by local instructors on bad-weather days and has some good off-piste terrain.

Terrain parks Gressoney has a boardercross but there's no park. Big air jumps are sometimes built near the top of the gondola from Champoluc.

Snow reliability Generally good, thanks to altitude, extensive snowmaking and good grooming, and last winter's excellent season in Europe meant great natural snow. Reporters are generally impressed by the snowmaking – a February 2007 visitor said: 'There was limited snow-cover, but the pistes were very well groomed and the snowmaking excellent, so on-piste skiing remained good through a week of warm sunshine. All pistes and connections were open all week.'

Experts The attraction is the off-piste, with great runs from the high points of the lift system in all three valleys and some excellent heli-drops. Among the adventures we've enjoyed here was a

Monterosa Ski

453

heli-drop on Monte Rosa, skiing down to Zermatt and returning off-piste from the top of the Cervinia lifts. The lift to Punta Indren (see 'News') is important for off-piste opportunities, but a recent visitor discovered 'loads more off-piste in Champoluc after hiring a mountain guide, including an area of forest above Frachey that the locals keep to themselves. And the off-piste from the Rifugio Guglielmina at Passo Salati was very enjoyable.'

Intermediates For those who like to travel on easy, undemanding pistes, the area is excellent, with long cruising runs from the ridges down into the valleys ('wonderful, carefree carving'). Down towards Alagna, the black Olen piste (which is more like a tough red and was graded red originally) is a great blast. There isn't much on-piste challenge for more demanding intermediates, but those willing to take a guide and explore some of the gentler off-piste will have a good time.

Beginners The high nursery slopes at mid-mountain above Champoluc, served by two moving carpets, are better than the lower ones at Gressoney. But neither area has ideal gentle runs to progress to (taking the

bus to Frachey and moving on to the Del Lago run above there is the best Champoluc option).

Snowboarding There's a boardercross at Gressoney and great freeriding.

Cross-country There are long trails: 24km/15 miles around St Jean, 17km/11 miles in Champoluc; Brusson, in the Champoluc valley, has 30km/19 miles and the best trails in the area.

Queues Few problems, say reporters. Usually they occur only at weekends and peak periods. 'There were moderate queues for most of the lifts at the weekend, but the only really bad one was for the Alpe Mandria lift above Frachey, which was 15 minutes,' says a 2008 visitor. The double chair to Belvedere, on the way back from Frachey/Bettaforca to Champoluc, can have long queues at the end of the day ('We waited 15 minutes,' says a recent reporter). She also found short waits for the gondola from Champoluc at 9.30 and for the cable car back from Alagna as everyone headed back in the afternoon. Pistes can get crowded at weekends, but the off-piste is still delightfully quiet.

Mountain restaurants The mountain restaurants are generally simple, but there are plenty of them. The following have been enjoyed by reporters: the 'lively' Belvedere (one of the few mountain restaurants in the region to have a sit-down loo), the Ostafa ('great food – the portions of sausage are staggeringly large') and the Tana del Lupo above Champoluc, the modern Campo Base at the top of the Frachey lift ('serves a Tibetan meal once a week – one meal is enough for two to share') and Stadel Soutzun above Frachey ('charming, with an excellent limited menu; booking essential'). In the Gressoney valley there are recommendations for the Sitten ('excellent specials and stunning view') and Gabiet ('good gnocchi and pasta at reasonable prices'), both above Stafal, also the Bedemie and Morgenrot above Orsia, the Mandria ('excellent and friendly') and the Chamois ('small but charming') at Punta Jolanda and the Del Ponte above Gabiet ('simple, good food'). Over in the Alagna valley the Alpen Stop at Pianalunga and the Baita just below have been recommended. A diversion to the right at the top of the run from Passo Salati to Alagna brings you to the Rifugio Guglielmina ('fab place, great food and views').

↑ Most of the pistes are easy: great for intermediates who enjoy leisurely cruising
SNOWPIX.COM / CHRIS GILL

UK PACKAGES

Champoluc Alpine Answers, Crystal, Interactive Resorts, Kuoni, Momentum, Mountain Tracks, Ski 2, Ski Expectations, Ski Yogi, Skitracer, Snow Finders, White Roc
Gressoney la Trinité Alpine Answers, Crystal, Crystal Finest, Inghams, Inspired to Ski, Momentum, Mountain Tracks, Ski Freshtracks, Ski Yogi, Skitracer, Snoworks
Alagna Alpine Answers, Italian Safaris, Mountain Tracks, Ski Freshtracks, Ski Weekend, Ski-Monterosa
Gressoney St Jean Alpine Answers, Italian Safaris

Phone numbers
From abroad use the prefix +39 (and do **not** omit the initial '0' of the phone number)

TOURIST OFFICE

t 0125 303111
info@monterosa-ski.com
www.monterosa-ski.com

Schools and guides We have had mixed reports on the Italian ski schools but universally good reports on the Monterosa mountain guides ('One of the best day's skiing ever,' said a recent reporter) and the ski school run by tour op Ski 2 ('good, friendly instructors').

Facilities for children There is a special kids' ski school and snow park at Antagnod near Champoluc and a mini snow park and tubing and adventure park at Gressoney St Jean.

STAYING THERE

How to go Surprisingly few tour operators feature the area. We've had good reports of Monterosa specialists Ski 2 ('great from pick-up to drop-off').

Hotels For a small place, Champoluc has a striking range of attractive hotels. Recent reporters liked the central Relais des Glaciers (0125 308182) – a welcoming 4-star with spa and shuttle to the gondola ('food excellent' and 'helpful to guests with children'). The central, 3-star, creaky old Castor (0125 307117) is 'an absolute gem' with 'good food and magnificent puddings'; it is managed by a British guy ('great fun') who married into the family who have owned it for generations. Our favourite luxury option is the 4-star Breithorn (0125 308734), just up the road, with beautifully furnished public areas, beamed bedrooms and good spa facilities. 'It's a gem,' says one well-travelled reporter – 'superb service'. Food in the elegant dining room or more casual brasserie is excellent. A recent visitor recommends the 3-star Champoluc (0125 308088) for its 'attentive staff, clean rooms, good food'. Out beyond the lift base the 3-star California (0125 307977) is chiefly notable for the pop music themes applied to the rooms and the big saloon bar; and the 3-star Rocher (0125 308711) is 'friendly, welcoming, with good food, spa and sauna'.

At Gressoney La Trinité reporters recommend the 4-star Jolanda Sport (0125 366140), with gym, saunas, pool; it's right by the lift and 'very cosy and friendly with a good choice of food'. The 3-star Nordend (0125 366807) has 'modern, spacious rooms and a spa – and the Monterosa guides office is in the same building'. The 3-star Dufour (0125 366139) ('amazing plentiful food and welcoming staff') has been recommended as has the 3-star Lysjoch (0125 366150). The Ellex (0125 366637) at Stafal is 'comfortable with good food, a couple of minutes' walk to the lifts'. Up the mountain the Guglielmina refuge (01631 91444) at the top of Col d'Olen was praised in 2008 ('Better than some hotels I've stayed in! Good selections of drinks plus choice of food for evening meal'). In Alagna, try the 3-star Monterosa (0163 922993), 4-star Cristallo (0163 922822) or the Residence Mirella (0163 922965) ('superb breakfasts').

Eating out Both Gressoney and Champoluc have a few stand-alone restaurants; most are in hotels. In Champoluc, the Bistrot has been recommended. In Gressoney, the Walserchild pizzeria got a good review from a recent reporter, and the Capanna Carla in Stafal is 'a rustic gem serving excellent traditional fare', says a 2007 visitor. In Alagna, the Unione is 'reasonably priced; excellent food'.

Après-ski Après-ski is quiet. In Champoluc, the bar of the hotel Castor is cosy and popular with resort workers; the Golosone is a small, atmospheric, authentic Italian wine bar; the Galion opposite the gondola is busy as the lifts close; the West Road pub in the hotel California has karaoke some nights. At weekends the Gram Parsons disco beneath the California gets going. Gressoney is even quieter; there's the La Pulce bar, and 'the tour-op-organised wine tasting at Hirsch Stube was excellent'. The Da Giovanni underneath the Nordend hotel in Stafal has 'cool decor and music'. In Alagna, the An Bacher Wi wine bar does 'fantastic wine and beer and good tapas style snacks'.

Off the slopes There is an outdoor ice rink at Champoluc; otherwise there's little on offer.

Passo Tonale

Purpose-built village set on a high pass, with easy, snow-sure slopes, now linked to more challenging wooded terrain

COSTS

① ② ③ ④ ⑤ ⑥

RATINGS

The slopes
Fast lifts	****
Snow	****
Extent	**
Expert	*
Intermediate	***
Beginner	*****
Convenience	***
Queues	****
Mountain restaurants	**

The rest
Scenery	***
Resort charm	*
Off-slope	*

TRENTINO

ITALIA

456

NEWS

The resort claims there is now 100% snowmaking throughout the ski area.

KEY FACTS

Resort	1885m
	6,180ft

Passo Tonale and Ponte di Legno combined area	
Slopes	1120-3015m
	3,670-9,890ft
Lifts	30
Pistes	100km
	62 miles
Blue	21%
Red	60%
Black	19%
Snowmaking	100%

➕ Good-value, plain accommodation

➕ Sunny, easy, snow-sure slopes

➕ Good for beginners and early or timid intermediates

➕ Link to Ponte di Legno adds attractive, steeper, treelined runs

➖ Not much for experts or (except at Ponte di Legno) keen intermediates

➖ Local slopes above the treeline and unpleasant in bad weather

➖ Purpose-built village straddling the pass road lacks charm

Passo Tonale offers that rare combination of a fair-sized, uncrowded, snow-sure ski area and slope-side hotels at a bargain price. Who cares if it lacks charm? It's a great place for beginners and, now that it is linked to the slopes above Ponte di Legno, a more interesting destination for intermediates than it was.

THE RESORT

Passo Tonale sits on a wide, treeless pass; it is in Trentino but right on the border with Lombardia. The village is a compact, functional affair, developed mainly for skiing and devoid of charm, with its hotels, shops, bars and restaurants spread along both sides of the busy through-road.

THE MOUNTAINS

The home slopes are entirely above the treeline, and bad weather can mean white-outs and closures. The Tonale slopes are linked to those of Ponte di Legno, below the pass in Lombardia; these slopes are generally steeper and quieter than Passo Tonale's main area. Tonale's lift system is impressive, with seven fast chairs in the bigger of its two local areas of slopes.

Slopes Tonale's slopes are spread over two main sectors on opposite sides of the valley. The broad, south-facing area is much the larger, starts right in the village and is served by a well-laid-out mix of chairs and drags. Runs are short because of the limited vertical. The north-facing Presena area is steeper, narrower and taller. First, there is an eight-seat gondola; above that is a double chairlift; and at the top, on the Presena glacier, there are two draglifts.

Ponte di Legno is reached by a blue/red run through the trees (mostly wide and easy but with a short, much steeper section) followed by an (easy) black run that you can't avoid on the Ponte di Legno side. A gondola link takes you back.

Terrain parks There's a park with kickers, boxes and a half-pipe served by the fast Valena chair at Passo Tonale.

Snow reliability The local slopes are high and include a glacier, so they are fairly snow-sure. But the main south-facing area gets a lot of sun, and there can be slush or ice in March and April. Ponte di Legno's slopes are lower and more dependent on snowmaking. It is claimed that all the joint area's pistes are now covered by snowmaking.

Experts This isn't a resort for experts. The black piste down the gondola on the Presena sector deserves its grading but is not a serious challenge. In the right conditions there are epic off-piste runs from the glacier, including the impressive 16km/10 mile Pisgana run towards Ponte di Legno (a vertical of 1650m/5,410ft) – you should take a guide.

Intermediates The south-facing slopes offer gentle terrain ideal for cruising; many of these runs are graded red but are really no more than gentle blue gradient. We particularly enjoyed the 4.5 km/3 mile Alpino piste down a deserted valley to the village. The runs at the top of the glacier are short and easy, and we couldn't see much difference between the reds and the black marked here. Below that the run beneath the chair is no more than a cat-track, but the black beneath the gondola will be too much for timid intermediates, who should ride down. The runs at Ponte di Legno are much more serious reds and deserve their grading. You could use the regional pass and visit Marilleva (free daily buses) and Madonna (free bus on Wednesdays) down the valley.

Cima Presena
3015m/9,89oft

Corno Lacoscuro
3160m/10,36oft

2120m

1905m/6,250ft

PRESENA

Passo Paradiso
2585m

Corno d'Aola
1920m/6,300ft

Valbione Temu
1500m

Vermiglio
1260m/4,14oft

Tonale
1885m/6,180ft

Ponte di legno
1255m/4,120ft

Passo
Contrabbandieri
2575m

2180m

2210m

Maga Valbiolo
2245m

2525m

2500m

Passo Tonale

457

UK PACKAGES

Airtours, Ardmore,
Crystal, Directski.com,
Equity, First Choice,
Independent Ski Links,
Inghams, Neilson,
Rocketski, Ski McNeill,
Ski Supreme, Ski Wild,
Thomson

Phone numbers
From abroad use the
prefix +39 (and do **not**
omit the initial '0' of
the phone number)

TOURIST OFFICE

t 0364 903838
tonale@valdisole.net
www.adamelloski.com
www.valdisole.net

Beginners It's an excellent resort for
novices. The sunny lifts on gentle
slopes right by the village are ideal,
and there are plenty of easy blue runs
to choose from – good for 'giving lots
of confidence', says a reporter.
Snowboarding The gentle slopes and
ability to get around mainly on
chairlifts mean the area is good for
beginner and intermediate boarders.
Cross-country There are 44km/
27 miles of trails, with loops at Passo
Tonale, in the valley and at altitude at
Ponte di Legno.
Queues We have no reports of queues.
Mountain restaurants Readers have
generally been unimpressed with the
mountain restaurants. Many people
return to the resort for lunch. A 2008
visitor liked the 'helpful staff' at
Scorpion Bay at the top of the Valbiolo
chair and the 'rustic' Cappanna
Valbione at the top of the Valbione
chair from Ponte di Legno – 'best
experience we had'. Another liked the
Nigritella, at the top of the chair of the
same name, with its 'charming
owners'. Serodine, at the foot of the
slopes, has received mixed reviews
from 2008 visitors.
Schools and guides We've heard of
'pure chaos' at ski school meeting
times, but most reports are more
positive: 'The instructors are not all
fluent in English but we didn't find it a
problem'; 'Our instructor (Presena
school) was very patient, encouraging
and cheerful, with excellent English.'
Facilities for children There's a
kindergarten at hotel Miramonti for
ages four to 12, and the ski school
takes children from age four.

STAYING THERE

How to go Passo Tonale has long been
popular with tour operators.
Hotels There are around 30, most of
them 3-stars. Reader recommendations
include the Savoia (0364 91340) –
'basic but clean'; Adamello (0364
903886) – 'friendly, good service';
Gardenia (0364 903769) – 'food basic,
inexpensive'. The 4-star Miramonti
(0364 900501) has a pool and spa.
Apartments There are 1,400 beds in
apartments, a few on the UK market.
Eating out Mainly hotel restaurants.
Après-ski Reader recommendations
include the Magic Pub, El Bait, Nico's
Bar, Heaven and the Miramonti disco.
Off the slopes If you don't intend to
hit the slopes, forget Tonale. There's
snowmobiling, snowshoeing, etc.

Tonale's high, snow-
sure slopes include
the Presena glacier ➔

Sauze d'Oulx

'Suzy does it' still, up to a point – a lively village beneath an attractive area of slopes, but with persistent drawbacks

COSTS

① ② ③ ④ ⑤ ⑥

RATINGS

The slopes

Fast lifts	***
Snow	**
Extent	****
Expert	**
Intermediate	****
Beginner	**
Convenience	**
Queues	***
Mountain restaurants	***

The rest

Scenery	***
Resort charm	**
Off-slope	*

NEWS

For 2008/09 a new piste is planned between the Clotes and Sportinia chairlifts, providing a direct connection between the two sectors. Snowmaking is expected for the Bourget red run and another terrain park is planned to replace the main Sportinia park, which was closed last season.

For 2007/08 snowmaking was increased to cover the whole beginners' area at Sportinia.

In Sansicario, the Olympic taxi bob run opened to the public. Rides are available daily between 5pm and 8pm.

Pros

➕ Extensive and uncrowded slopes – great intermediate cruising

➕ Mix of open and tree-lined runs is good for all weather conditions

➕ Entertaining nightlife

➕ Some scope for off-piste adventures

➕ One of the cheapest major resorts – and more attractive than its reputation suggests

➕ Part of Milky Way network, but ...

Cons

➖ Full exploration of the Milky Way area really requires a car or taxis

➖ Erratic snow record – and far from comprehensive snowmaking

➖ Still lots of ancient slow lifts, including many drags

➖ Crowds at weekends

➖ Very few challenging pistes

➖ Mornings-only classes, and the best nursery slopes are at mid-mountain

➖ Steep walks around the village, and an inadequate shuttle-bus service

Sauze is cheap, cheerful and the closest decent-sized ski area to Turin, which helps to account for its enduring popularity with impecunious Brits on charter flights and with the city's residents looking for weekend homes. If you were a tabloid reader in the 1980s, you couldn't fail to notice that Sauze was over-run by British youth on the binge. But these days things are much more in balance, at weekends at least. It still has lively bars and shops festooned in English signs, but sober Brits like you and us need not stay away. When we visit, we find ourselves liking Sauze more than we expect to – as do many reporters.

But Sauze still has a problem: investment, lack of. With its acutely unreliable natural snow, it needs the kind of comprehensive snowmaking that the Sella Ronda resorts enjoy. Until it gets it, booking a trip well in advance will remain a gamble. And its programme of lift upgrading needs serious acceleration.

THE RESORT

Sauze d'Oulx sits on a sloping mountain shelf facing north-west across the Valle di Susa to the mountains bordering France.

Most of the resort is modern and undistinguished, made up of block-like hotels relieved by the occasional chalet, spreading down the steep hillside from the slopes. It rather gives the impression of falling behind the times, with none of the investment in smart, woody hotels and apartments that goes on in more dynamic resorts.

The village has an attractive old core, with narrow, twisting streets and houses roofed with huge stone slabs. There is a central car-free zone, but the rest of the village can be congested morning and evening. The roads have few pavements and can become icy.

Despite the decline in lager sales, the centre is still lively at night; the late bars are usually quite full, and the handful of discos do brisk business –

at the weekend, at least. Noise can be a problem in the early hours.

Out of the bustle of the centre, there are secluded apartment blocks in quiet, wooded areas and a number of good restaurants also tucked away.

Most of the hotels are reasonably central, but the lifts are less so: the Clotes chair is at the top of the village, up a short but steep hill, and the Sportinia chair is an irritatingly long walk beyond that. Ski-buses (not covered by the lift pass) are infrequent, inadequate and absent around lunchtime. The Via Lattea (Milky Way) lift pass covers not only Sestriere and Sansicario, easily

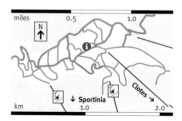

↑ Friendly, prettily wooded slopes are typical of the area – this is at Sportinia

PAUL CARTER

reached on skis, but also the more remote area of slopes around the French border, above Claviere and Montgenèvre. These resorts are much more easily reached by car, or by taxi, though it is possible by bus.

THE MOUNTAINS

Sauze's mountains provide excellent intermediate terrain. The piste classification changes from year to year, but it doesn't matter much – many runs classified red or even black should really be blue. The higher slopes are open, the lower ones pleasantly wooded.

THE SLOPES
Big and varied enough for most
Sauze's local slopes are spread across a broad wooded bowl above the resort, ranging from west- to north-facing. The main lifts are chairs, slow from the top of the village up to **Clotes** and fast from the western fringes to **Sportinia** – a sunny mid-mountain clearing in the woods, with a ring of restaurants and hotels and a small nursery area.

The high point of the system is **Monte Fraiteve**. From here you can travel west on splendid broad, long runs to **Sansicario** – and on to a two-stage gondola near **Cesana Torinese** that links with **Claviere** and then **Montgenèvre**, in France, the far end of the Milky Way (both are reached more quickly by car).

You normally get to **Sestriere** from the lower point of Col Basset, on the shoulder of M Fraiteve, but there is

also a run from M Fraiteve itself. Both runs are sunny, and not reliably open – and on the latest maps the lower parts are shown as off-piste routes. Plan on riding the gondolas down.

As in so many Italian resorts, piste marking, signposting and piste map design aren't great, but reporters are noticing gradual improvements. A 2008 visitor thought the latest map 'clearer than in previous years'.

TERRAIN PARKS
Will they, won't they?
The main park was moved from Col Basset to Sportinia a couple of seasons ago, keeping the usual array of jumps and rails – but it was not rebuilt in 2007/08. We're told a new one is due for 2008/09. There was a small park at Triplex this year, instead of the one expected at Clotes. There are also parks at Sansicario and Sestriere.

SNOW RELIABILITY
Can be poor, affecting the links
The area is notorious for erratic snowfalls, suffering droughts with worrying frequency. Another problem is that many of the slopes get a lot of afternoon sun – as explained above, the links with Sestriere are very vulnerable. Snowmaking is being increased throughout the area (including the Sportinia nursery slopes) but coverage is still far from complete. But reporters have been impressed by the efforts to keep runs open in poor conditions ('they worked miracles') and grooming is in general 'superb'.

KEY FACTS

Resort	1510m
	4,950ft

Milky Way	
Slopes	1390-2825m
	4,560-9,270ft
Lifts	82
Pistes	400km
	249 miles
Blue	24%
Red	56%
Black	20%
Snowmaking	130km
	81 miles

Sauze d'Oulx-Sestriere-Sansicario	
Slopes	1390-2825m
	4,560-9,270ft
Lifts	38
Pistes	250km
	155 miles
Snowmaking	95km
	59 miles

boarding

Sauze has good local tree-lined slopes (with space in the trees, too), high, open terrain, and links to other Milky Way resorts. But a 2008 reporter found little to interest adventurous boarders and 'far too many drags'. And there are a lot of drags – a serious drawback for novice riders, despite a fair number of chairs. There's normally a terrain park – a new one is planned for 2008/09 (see 'News').

ITALY

460

FOR EXPERTS
Head off-piste

Very few of the pistes are challenging. The best slopes are at virtually opposite ends of Sauze's local area – a short, high, north-facing run from the shoulder of M Fraiteve, and the sunny slopes below M Moncrons. There are plenty of minor off-piste opportunities within the piste network, but the highlights are long, top-to-bottom descents of up to 1300m/4,270ft vertical from M Fraiteve, ending (snow permitting) at villages dotted along the valleys. The best known of these runs is the Rio Nero, down to the road near Oulx. When snow low down is poor, some of these runs can be cut short.

FOR INTERMEDIATES
Splendid cruising terrain

The whole area is ideal for confident intermediates who want to clock up the kilometres. For the less confident, the piste map doesn't help because it picks out only the very easiest runs in blue – when actually there are many others that are manageable. The Belvedere and Moncrons sectors at the east of the area are served only by drags but offer some wonderful, uncrowded high cruising, some of it above the treeline.

The long runs down to Jouvenceaux are splendid, flattering intermediate terrain, as are those below Sportinia ('ideal for perfecting technique').

The slopes above Sansicario are also excellent (including the undemanding Olympic Ladies Downhill) – served by two fast quad chairlifts – but the link via the shoulder of M Fraiteve can be problematic – a seriously steep double draglift on the way out, and the steepest pitch in the whole area on the way back. A chairlift is needed here, to solve both problems and open up Sansicario to everyone.

At the higher levels, where the slopes are above the treeline, the terrain often allows a choice of route. Lower down are pretty runs through

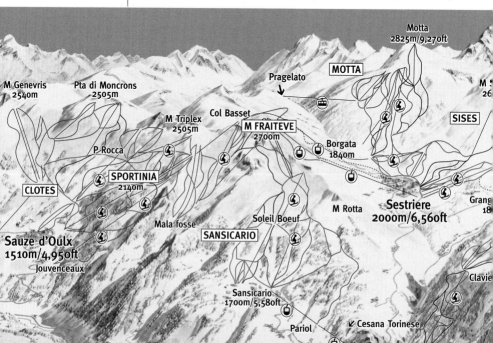

SCHOOLS

Sauze Sportinia
t 0122 850218
Sauze d'Oulx
t 0122 858084
Sauze Project
t 0122 858942

Classes
(Sauze Sportinia prices)
6 3hr days: €170
Private lessons
€35 for 1hr

GUIDES

Marco Degani
t 0335 398984

CHILDREN

Ludoteca Sauze In
t 0347 691 3531
Mon-Sat; 9am-5pm;
€60 a day

Ski school
6 half days €170
(Sportinia prices)

---

the woods, where the main complication can be route-finding. The mountainside is broken up by gullies, limiting the links between pistes that appear to be quite close together.

FOR BEGINNERS
There are better choices
There are signs that the resort is trying to improve life for novices but its village-level slopes are a bit on the steep side and the main nursery area is up the mountain, at Sportinia. Equally importantly, the mornings-only classes don't suit everyone. Once off the nursery slopes, the main problem is a psychological one – that most of the mountain is classified red, though the gradient is generally blue.

FOR CROSS-COUNTRY
Severely limited, even with snow
There is very little cross-country skiing, and it isn't reliable for snow.

QUEUES
Slow lifts the biggest problem
There can be irritating waits at Sportinia, especially when school classes set off, or just after lunch; otherwise the system has few major bottlenecks. But fast lifts are scarce – the dominance of ancient and terribly slow lifts 'a major disappointment' for some reporters. The quad that replaced the old double chair out of the village to Clotes can still generate queues. Breakdowns of elderly lifts may be a nuisance: the old one-person chair at Col Basset is an important link, and when it fails they may resort to 'dragging skiers behind snowmobiles'.

We're still receiving reports of mid-week lift closures, with a 'skeletal' service experienced by a January 2008 visitor. Some lifts are opened only at weekends when the Italian crowds arrive.

MOUNTAIN RESTAURANTS
Some pleasant possibilities
Restaurants are numerous and generally pleasant, though few are particularly special. The hotel Capricorno, at Clotes, is the place to head for a civilised table-service lunch. It is not cheap, and midweek in low season it can be amazingly quiet. The quiet Eros has been praised for 'good value meals' and Bar Clotes is 'a must' for hot chocolate stops and does 'great lasagne'. The rustic Ciao Pais, further up the hill is 'superb, ideal when the weather closes in', writes one, but 'a bit pricey', according to another. The Clot Bourget has also pleased visitors and the 'friendly' Bar Basset at Rio Nero has 'superb views'. Cicci's House, at the halfway point of the Jouvenceaux chair, serves 'good food and hot chocolate'. There are several places at Sportinia; Orso Bianco and Capanna Kind are 'popular, with a wide choice', if perhaps a little pricier than elsewhere. The Rocce Nere is repeatedly praised for 'good food and service'. The Soleil Boeuf above Sansicario, with its 'nice sun terrace', and the Marmotta on M Triplex are also worth a visit.

SCHOOLS AND GUIDES
Lessons variable
One reporter found his daughter enthusiastic about her lesson (in a group of eight, in low season), and another writes of 'patient instructors with good English spoken', though past reports have been mixed.

FACILITIES FOR CHILDREN
Tour operator alternatives
You might want to look at the nursery facilities offered by major UK tour operators in the chalets and chalet-hotels that they run here. All the schools take children from four years, and spoken English should be OK.

Interactive resort shortlist builder at **www.wtss.co.uk**

Air Turin 84km/
52 miles (1½hr)

Rail Oulx (5km/
3 miles); frequent
buses

Airtours, Crystal,
Directski.com, First
Choice, Independent
Ski Links, Inghams,
Interhome, Neilson,
Panorama, Rocketski,
Ski High Days, Ski
McNeill, Ski4you,
Thomson
Sansicario Crystal,
Thomson

Indoor Cinema, sauna,
solarium, massage

Outdoor Ice rink,
bobsleigh run,
snowmobiling

Phone numbers
From abroad use the
prefix +39 (and do **not**
omit the initial '0' of
the phone number)

Sauze d'Oulx
t 0122 858009
sauze@montagnedoc.
it
www.montagnedoc.it
www.vialattea.it

**Cesana Torinese
(Sansicario)**
t 0122 89202
cesana@montagne
doc.it

STAYING THERE

HOW TO GO
Packaged hotels dominate
All the major mainstream operators
offer hotel packages here, but there
are also a few chalets.
Hotels Simple 2-star and 3-star hotels
form the core, with a couple of 4-stars
and some more basic places.
****Torre** (0122 859812) Cylindrical
landmark 200m/650ft below the
centre. Excellent rooms, mini-buses to
lifts. Newish pool and health suite.
***Gran Baita** (0122 850183)
Comfortable place in quiet, central
backstreet, with excellent food and
good rooms, some with sunset views.
***Terrazza** (0122 850173) In a quiet
part of town, near the Clotes chair.
***Des Amis** (0122 858488) Down in
Jouvenceaux, near bus stop; simple
hotel run by Anglo-Italian couple.
Biancaneve (0122 850160) Pleasant,
with smallish rooms. Near the centre.
Hermitage (0122 850385) Neat
chalet-style hotel beside the piste.
Villa Cary (0122 850191)
Comfortable two-star, 'far better' than
its rating. 'Service and food excellent
again,' says a 2008 visitor.
*Stella Alpina** (0122 858731) Between
main lifts. Friendly Anglo-Italian family.
Recommended by a reporter.
Apartments Apartments and chalets
available, some through UK operators.

EATING OUT
Caters for all tastes and pockets
Typical Italian banquets of five or six
courses can be had in the upmarket
Godfather ('excellent food') and Cantun
restaurants. But a 2008 reporter firmly
pronounces the Falco as 'the best in
town, terrific; the owner is a proper
gent'. In the old town, the Borgo and
the Griglia are popular pizzerias. The
Lampione does good-value Chinese,
Mexican and Indian food. Paddy
McGinty's does Mexican and steaks.
The Faraglioni also gets good reviews.

APRES-SKI
Suzy does it with more dignity
Sauze's bars now impress reporters
young and old. Choice is wide, with
multiple happy hours.
   The Assietta terrace is popular for
at the end of the day, as is the Forgia.
The New Scotch bar in the hotel Stella
Alpina serves English beer and is
popular, with a 'friendly welcome,
good service'. After dinner, more

places warm up. One of the best is the
smart, atmospheric cocktail bar
Moncrons, which holds regular quiz
nights. But one reporter preferred the
Gran Trun, a converted barn in the old
part of town, complete with resident
entertainer who 'loves you to request
all the old sing-a-long songs'.
Reporters also like the 'interesting'
Village Cafè with its many metal
artefacts; you can eat here too
('excellent pizzas'). The Cotton Club
provides good service, directors'
chairs, video screen and draught cider.
The Lounge (formerly Crowded House)
is a 'modern and comfortable' bar.
Max's and Scatto Matto are both
popular for 'excellent food, service and
ski videos'. Miravallino is a 'very
Italian' cafe bar. Try the Derby for a
quiet, civilised drink in a cosy
atmosphere. The trendy Ghost Bar is
'lively, friendly and relaxed' and serves
'a wonderful array of burgers' and
Osteria dei Vagabondi claims itself the
only live music venue in Sauze. Of the
discos, Clarabella is a walk away, and
popular with Italians. Schuss runs
theme nights and drink promotions.

OFF THE SLOPES
Go elsewhere
Shopping is limited, there are no
gondolas or cable cars for pedestrians
and there are few off-slope activities,
though things are improving: you can
now have a go on the Olympic
bobsleigh run at Sansicario and there's
said to be a new sports centre. Turin
and Briançon are worth visiting.

STAYING UP THE MOUNTAIN
'You pays your money ... '
The 4-star Capricorno (0122 850273),
up at Clotes, is the most attractive and
expensive hotel in Sauze. It's a
charming little chalet beside the piste,
with only eight bedrooms.
   Not quite in the same league are
the places up at Sportinia – though
reporters have enjoyed them.

Sansicario 1700m/5,580ft

Sansicario is ideally placed for
exploration of the whole Milky Way. It
is a modern, purpose-built, self-
contained but rather soulless little
resort, mainly consisting of apartments
grouped around the small shopping
precinct. The 45-room Rio Envers
(0122 811333) is a comfortable,
expensive hotel.

Sella Ronda

Endless intermediate slopes amid spectacular Dolomite scenery,
with a choice of attractive valley villages, mainly German-speaking

COSTS

① ② ③ ④ ⑤ ⑥

RATINGS

The slopes
Fast lifts   ***
Snow   ****
Extent   *****
Expert   **
Intermediate *****
Beginner   ****
Convenience   ***
Queues   ***
Mountain
  restaurants   ****

The rest
Scenery   *****
Resort charm   ***
Off-slope   ***

NEWS

In Alta Badia: for 2007/08 snowmaking was increased to cover 90% of the slopes. The village of Pedraces changed its name to Badia, and a new quad replaced an old double on the link from there to La Villa. A new mountain restaurant, I Tamá, and a new hotel, Melodia del Bosco, opened in Badia. These improvements are presumably connected to the fact that, as from two seasons ago, a free bus to and from Badia provides a link to the Plan de Corones (Kronplatz) ski area (covered by the Dolomiti Superski lift pass).

ALAN LIPTROT
_____

Alta Badia's slopes are gentle and sunny; this photo was taken at almost 4pm in late December, and most of the runs are still in the sun ➔

+ Vast network of connected slopes – suits intermediates particularly well

+ Stunning, unique Dolomite scenery

+ Lots of mountain huts with good food

+ Excellent value for money

+ Extensive snowmaking – one of Europe's best systems, but ...

− They need it: natural snowfall is erratic in this southerly region

− Few challenges, and off-piste limited – possibly banned in places

− Mostly short runs with limited vertical

− Crowds on the Sella Ronda circuit

− Still some old draglifts

− Après-ski is not a highlight

The Sella Ronda is an amazing circular network of lifts and pistes taking you around the Gruppo Sella – a mighty limestone massif with villages scattered around it. Among the main attractions is the simply spectacular Dolomite scenery – like something Disney might have conjured up for a theme park. But the geology that provides the visual drama also dictates the nature of the slopes. Sheer limestone cliffs rise out of gentle pasture land, which is where you spend your time. Individual runs are short; verticals of more than 500m/1,640ft are rare, while runs of under 300m/980ft vertical are not. And they are predominantly easy: there's scarcely a black run to be seen and very little off-piste.

But the distances you can cover on skis are huge. In overall scale, the network rivals the famed Three Valleys in France. In addition to the main Sella Ronda circuit, major lift systems lead off it at three main points along the way – Selva, covered in the chapter after this – Corvara and Arabba. These three should obviously be on your shortlist as potential destinations. But there are other villages worth considering, notably: Santa Cristina and Ortisei, next to Selva, and covered in that chapter; San Cassiano, which shares with La Villa a friendly area of largely very easy slopes, just off the main circuit and linked to Corvara; and Canazei and Campitello, at the south-west corner of the circuit – in Trentino, and mainly covered in our separate chapter on that province.

This is one of the few areas where we unreservedly welcome continuous sunny weather; the snowmaking is fantastic and we really don't want clouds and snow to interfere with our lunches gazing at the views.

CHOOSING A BASE

It's important to pick the right resort. For good skiers, the best bases are Selva (covered in a separate chapter) and Arabba, a small village where classic Dolomite terrain gives way to longer, steeper slopes. Corvara and San Cassiano are better for novices, with abundant gentle slopes. Canazei has the most limited local slopes, but access to Arabba is speedy.

The vast number of slopes seems to require a vast selection of piste maps – 12 in all, plus variations. There are individual ones for each resort. Some cover the main circuit – others do not – and a 2008 reporter complained that it was very difficult when doing the Sella Ronda circuit to pick up detailed local maps of each area as you passed through. Reporters generally find the system confusing. To add to the confusion, the main resorts

now promote additional tours, away from the main circuit. A First World War circuit of 78-100km/ 48-62 miles is one ('A macho day out for mileage-hungry intermediates,' said a recent reporter).

The Dolomiti Superski pass covers not only the Sella Ronda resorts but dozens of others, amounting to an impressive 1220km/758 miles. We'd recommend anyone based in Corvara or San Cassiano to make a day trip to Cortina, ending the day with the famous 'hidden valley' run from Passo Falzarego – see feature panel.

ARABBA 1600m/5,250ft

Arabba, diagonally opposite Selva on the Sella Ronda circuit, is a small, quiet village appealing particularly to good skiers because of its relatively steep, shady local slopes. Off the circuit there is good skiing to be done on the Marmolada glacier.

THE SELLA RONDA CIRCUIT

The Sella Ronda is a unique circular tour around the Sella massif, easily managed in a day by even an early intermediate. The slopes you descend are almost all easy and take you through Selva, Colfosco, Corvara, Arabba and Canazei (or at least the slopes above it). You can do the circuit in either direction by following very clear coloured signs. The clockwise route is slightly quicker and offers more interesting slopes. Reporters repeatedly find the anticlockwise route less crowded though; and many prefer it because of that. Some resort piste maps incorporate a Sella Ronda map of the usual panoramic kind; map-literate people will want the proper topographical one with contour lines, from the tourist office (not lift stations).

The runs total around 23km/14 miles and the lifts around 14km/9 miles. The lifts take a total of about two hours (plus any queuing). We've done the circuit in just three and a half hours excluding diversions and hut stops; five or six hours is a realistic time in busy periods, when there are crowds both on the pistes and on the lifts. If possible, choose low season or a Saturday, and start early.

Not everyone likes it. Reporters' comments include: 'it's a bit of a slog', 'too busy and crowded', 'over-hyped, over-sold and over-regimented' and 'not a relaxing business when it's busy'. And boarders should be aware that there are quite a few flat bits.

If you set out early, you can make more of the day by taking some diversions from the circuit. Among the most entertaining runs are the long ones down from Ciampinoi to Santa Cristina and Selva, from Dantercëpies to Selva, from the top of the Boé gondola back down to Corvara, and from the top of the Arabba gondola. Take in all those in a day doing the circuit and you'll have had a good day.

Intermediates could explore the off-the-circuit area towards San Cassiano and La Villa from Corvara. Groups of different abilities can do the circuit and arrange to meet along the way at some of the many welcoming rifugios.

THE RESORT

Arabba is a small, traditional-style village; it is growing fast, and we are receiving more reports on it. Staying in the older part involves an uphill walk to reach the ski area, which provokes a few complaints from reporters. A new area of hotels and chalets has opened higher up, better placed for the lifts and slopes. There are some shops, bars and restaurants, but this is not a place for lively nightlife.

LIFT PASSES

Dolomiti Superski

Prices in €

Age	1-day	6-day
under 16	29	147
16 to 59	42	209
over 60	38	188

Free under 8

Beginner no deals

Notes

Covers 1220km/758 miles of piste and 450 lifts in the Dolomites, including all Sella Ronda resorts

THE MOUNTAIN

Arabba's local slopes cover 62km/ 39 miles and have some of the best natural snow and steepest pistes in the Dolomites. In various places around Arabba, reporters reckon the runs are at the steep end of their classification, and in one or two cases blues might be better classed as reds. Runs from the high point of Porto Vescovo are north-facing and longer than most in the region. The Marmolada glacier, beyond Arabba, is open most of the winter and is included on the main lift pass. It is a trip to do as much for its spectacular views as for skiing, though the red run from top to bottom is a notable 1490m/4,900ft vertical.

Slopes The two-stage DMC gondola and the cable car beside it rise almost 900m/2,950ft vertical to the high point at Porto Vescovo (2475m/8,120ft). From here a choice of runs return to the village or you can head off around the Sella Ronda circuit, following a busy red run to Pont de Vauz. From the mid-station of the DMC, a series of chairs take you to Passo Padon and onwards to the Marmolada glacier.

On the opposite side of the village, a fast quad gets you on the way to Burz and Passo Campolongo. You can then head directly down to Corvara and the rest of the Sella Ronda or divert right on to the quieter, gentle slopes towards San Cassiano.

Terrain park None in Arabba. There's a half-pipe at Belvedere above Canazei.

Snow reliability Arabba offers some of the most snow-sure slopes in the Sella Ronda region. Good snow is far from assured, but snowmaking is extensive and the main runs are north-facing.

Experts Arabba has the best steep slopes of all the Sella Ronda resorts. The north-facing blacks and reds from Porto Vescovo offer genuine challenges and are great fun. Off-piste is limited – see feature panel.

Intermediates The local slopes suit adventurous intermediates best. Most are quite challenging and those on the main circuit suffer from crowds.

Beginners It is not a good choice for beginners. There is a small nursery slope near the Burz chair, but access to longer easy runs is tricky.

Snowboarding Porto Vescovo offers some decent challenges. Most of the lifts are fast chairs or gondolas.

Cross-country There is one loop at village level.

Queues New lifts have vastly improved access to and from the village, and a recent reporter spent no more than five minutes in a queue locally (but did notice big queues elsewhere, especially on the Sella Ronda circuit). Another recent reporter found that an upgrade to the cable car to Porto Vescovo has eased the queue problem at the bottom but created a bottleneck at the top. And, despite the recent upgrading of the Marmolada cable cars, we are still getting reports of long waits at the bottom station – a 2008 reporter had a 40-minute wait at lunchtime (he advises going early morning before people based further away have time to get there). He also found a 15-minute queue at the Sass de la Vegla chair (the first – and unavoidable – chair on the route from Arabba to Marmolada).

Mountain restaurants There's lots of choice, from rustic huts to larger places. Most are lively with good food. The Bec de Roces and Col de Burz are both suntraps (with 'amazing Bombardinos' at the latter). Cherz above Passo di Campolongo has great views of Marmolada. The Luigi Gorze at the top of the Porto Vescovo lifts has been recommended for 'excellent food' and 'stunning views', as have the 'lively' Rifugio Plan Boé, the Fodom ('first class, good-value pizza'), at the bottom of the Lezuo Belvedere

Sella Ronda

465

Interactive resort shortlist builder at **www.wtss.co.uk**

There are relatively few major off-piste routes in this area because of the nature of the mountains – gentle pasture, surmounted by cliffs. But the routes that are available are spectacular.

The cable car from Passo Pordoi gets you up on to the Sella massif. There are fairly direct descents from here back to the pass (the very sunny Forcella) or down the Val Lasties towards Canazei. But the classic run is the Val Mesdì, a long, shady couloir on the northern side of the Gruppo Sella down to Colfosco, reached by skiing and hiking across the massif.

Marmolada, the highest peak of the Dolomites, now reached by reasonably efficient lifts from Malga Ciapela, is the other obvious launching point. It offers a range of big descents on and off the glacier.

Proguide in Arabba offers guidance on these and other routes – see www.proguide.it.

chair below Passo Pordoi, and Capanna Bill, near the Marmolada lifts, on the way back to Arabba ('good food, table service').

Schools The local Arabba school offers group and private classes. Proguide guides off-piste – see feature panel.

Facilities for children The kindergarten at the ski school takes children from two years.

STAYING THERE

How to go Several UK tour operators offer packages. New accommodation has been built at the top end of town, closer to the lifts.

Chalets There are several, including a good selection from Neilson.

Hotels Of the dozen or so hotels, several 3-stars get support from readers. The Portavescovo (0436 79139) has been described as 'excellent: wonderful food, nicely furnished rooms and a well-equipped fitness centre', but a recent reporter warns of a noisy disco every night and a chilly pool. The Malita (0436 79103) is 'comfortable with good food, at reasonable prices'. A group with experience of both reports that the Evaldo (0436 79109) is better than either – 'great food', pool and sauna. It's away from the lifts, whereas the Mesdì (0436 79119) is close to the Burz lift with 'lovely rooms, health suite and wonderful five-course dinners'. The Garnì Laura (0436 780055) B&B is also near the Burz lift and praised by a recent guest – 'the top-floor rooms have wonderful beamed ceilings and the wellness suite is pure 5-star luxury'. The B&B Garnì Royal (0436 79293) is 'a real gem' – large rooms, sauna, hot tub and Turkish bath – but is further from the lifts. The Al Forte (0436 79329) 'has good food, and is built around the old fort' and has a 'sauna and free bus'. Recent reporters praise two

4-stars: the Sporthotel (0436 79321) is 'very good value for money with good food; slightly above the lifts', and the Grifone (0436 780034) is out of town at Passo Campolongo – 'remote but food and service were superb, excellent bar and health club/pool'. A 2008 reporter likes the 'friendly' Garnì Astor (0436 79326) near the Burz lift. The 3-star family-run Olympia (0436 79135) was also recommended.

Apartments Self-catering accommodation is available.

Eating out Restaurant choice is limited. The central hotels all have busy restaurants. Reporters love Micky's Grill in the Hotel Mesdì ('best steaks in the Alps'; 'best restaurant in Arabba'). The Alpenrose hotel will send its horse-drawn sleigh to pick you up if you book a table in its Stube Ladina ('good food and surroundings'). The 7 Sass does 'delicious pizzas'. The restaurant in the Portavescovo hotel is 'great with very well cooked food at a great price'. You can go up to Rifugio Plan Boé by snowmobile on Thursdays for a 'special' three-course dinner and dancing – 'the best meal we had'.

Après-ski The après-ski is cheap but very limited. 'There are still only three bars, but at last there are signs of life,' says one regular. 'At Easter the Bar Peter had a live DJ at 4pm most days.' The Stube bar has live music on Saturday as does the Treina on Sunday. Cosy hotel bars are other options in the village. The atmospheric Rifugio Plan Boé up the mountain is good for a last drink on the pistes before heading back to the village – 'loud 70s, 80s and Europop music'. It is possible to take a taxi to nearby Corvara (6km/4 miles away) for a more animated choice.

Off the slopes Off-slope diversions are few. There's a small selection of shops, and cafes, and there's an ice rink. Snowmobile excursions are available.

CORVARA 1570m/5,150ft

Gentle slopes at the heart of the Sella Ronda circuit. There are plenty of hotels, restaurants, bars and sports facilities, making Corvara one of the better bases for families and novices.

THE RESORT

Corvara is the most animated village east of Selva and central to the Alta Badia region. The main shops and some hotels cluster around a small piazza, but the rest of the place sprawls along the valley floor.

THE MOUNTAIN

Corvara is well positioned with village lifts heading off to reasonably equidistant Selva, Arabba and San Cassiano. The local slopes are gentle and confidence-boosting.

Slopes A long gondola heads out of the village towards Boé and the clockwise Sella Ronda circuit. Two successive fast quads head in the opposite direction towards Colfosco and the anticlockwise route. The area around both lifts can get congested at peak times. A slow chair and a couple of drags take you towards the quieter area of slopes shared with San Cassiano and La Villa. A faster alternative from the other side of town is a gondola to Col Alto.

Terrain park There is a terrain park on the Ciampai run above San Cassiano.

Snow reliability As with the rest of the Sella Ronda area, natural snowfall is erratic, but snowmaking is excellent.

Experts Very few of Corvara's slopes offer any real challenges, and those that do are short. There are very few black runs – the one above Boé 'was red 28 years ago and is no harder now', a reporter points out. There's the long World Cup run at La Villa. See the feature panel for off-piste runs.

Intermediates The slopes are superb for cruising and confidence-boosting and there's a vast network of interconnected slopes to explore; don't miss the Val Stella Alpina area (see Colfosco below) and the easy runs between Corvara and San Cassiano. The red underneath the Boé cable car in Corvara is usually uncrowded and retains good snow. The adventurous can head for the steeper, wooded pistes above La Villa.

Beginners There's a nursery area and lots of easy runs to progress to.

Snowboarding Novices can make rapid progress on gentle slopes. A few awkward draglifts remain, but most can be avoided.

Cross-country The Alta Badia area offers 38km/24 miles of trails, including a 16km/10 mile valley loop on the way to Colfosco.

Queues New lifts have improved the area. But we still get reports about long waits for the Borest chair between Corvara and Colfosco (on the anticlockwise Sella Ronda circuit).

Mountain restaurants Lots of choice. A recent reporter enjoyed 'brilliant food' at the Brancia, above Col Alto.

Schools There's a local branch of the Alta Badia school – reports welcome.

Facilities for children Kinderland takes children from the age of three.

STAYING THERE

How to go There is a wide choice of accommodation, but some can be a longish walk from the lifts.

Hotels The 4-star hotel Posta Zirm (0471 836175) has a large spa facility, and is recommended by a reporter: 'very good food, ski-in/ski-out, comfortable rooms'. Also recommended are the pensione Villa Tony (0471 836193) – 'very reasonably priced half board, on the main street' – and the 4-star Col Alto (0471 831100): 'top class and cosy with beautifully prepared five-course meals and a free minibus service', says a 2008 visitor.

Eating out A reasonable choice. Most of the hotels have restaurants – the Stüa de Michil in the Perla has a Michelin star. See also San Cassiano.

Après-ski The Posta Zirm in Corvara does a ski-boot tea dance, but support may depend on tour ops organising group transport back to other villages. 'I can't recommend this bar enough,' says a 2008 visitor. The hotel Tablè is recommended by reporters for its piano bar and good cakes. Other suggestions from reporters are the smart bar in the Perla hotel and the 'trendy' cocktail bar at the Marmolada.

Off the slopes There's a covered ice rink, indoor tennis courts and an outdoor artificial climbing wall.

COLFOSCO 1645m/5,400ft

Colfosco is a smaller, quieter satellite of Corvara, 2km/1 mile away. It has a fairly compact centre with a sprawl of large hotels along the road towards Passo Gardena. It's connected to Corvara by a horizontal chairlift. In the opposite direction, a gondola goes to

UK PACKAGES

Arabba *Independent Ski Links, Inghams, Italian Safaris, Momentum, Neilson, Ski Yogi* **Corvara** *Italian Safaris, Neilson, Ski Yogi* **Colfosco** *Italian Safaris* **San Cassiano** *Alpine Answers, Italian Safaris, Mountainsun, Powder Byrne, Scott Dunn, Ski 2* **La Villa** *Italian Safaris, Powder Byrne*

AZIENDA TURISTICA ARABBA LIVINALLONGO

Arabba's shady and relatively steep slopes make it an attractive base for good skiers ↘

Passo Gardena. There are a couple of short nursery slopes and the runs back from Passo Gardena are easy, long cruises. Immediately above the village, the Val Stella Alpina (aka Edelweisstal), off the Sella Ronda circuit, offers gentle, normally quiet pistes ideal for fast cruising. The three pleasant restaurants can get very busy. A 2007 visitor recommends the slope-side hotel Sport (0471 836074) with 'spacious rooms, excellent food'.

SAN CASSIANO 1530m/5,020ft

A quiet village with some good hotels, easy slopes away from the main Sella Ronda circuit and with easy access to the famous 'hidden valley' run.

THE RESORT

San Cassiano is a pleasant little village, set in an attractive, tree-filled valley. It is bypassed by the road to Cortina and is working towards becoming car-free. It's a quiet, civilised resort, without much animation.

THE MOUNTAIN

The local slopes, shared with Corvara and La Villa, form a spur off the main Sella Ronda circuit.

Slopes The gondola, a drive from the centre (many hotels run buses), rises to Piz Sorega. From the top, fast chairs form the links with Corvara and La Villa, or you can head for Pralongia and the long runs home. Most of the area has very gentle slopes, ideal for easy cruising.

Terrain park It's at Ciampai, with boardercross, jumps, rails and humps.

Snow reliability The Dolomites have an erratic snowfall record, but snowmaking is excellent.

Experts Experts would be wise to stay elsewhere. There are a few steeper runs at La Villa, but not much else.

Intermediates Pretty much ideal if you love easy cruising on flattering, well-groomed runs. The red option back to town is a serious red though.

Beginners There are nursery slopes a short bus ride away at Armentarola and at the top of the gondola – not ideal. But there are plenty of long, easy slopes to progress to.

Snowboarding Endless carving on quiet pistes and there's a terrain park.

Cross-country There's a branch of the Dolomiti Nordicski in Armentarola. It offers tuition and equipment hire, as well as 23km/14 miles of trails.

If you like runs surrounded by spectacular scenery well away from all signs of civilisation, don't miss the easy red run from Lagazuoi, reached by cable car from Passo Falzarego. The pass is easily accessible from Armentarola, close to San Cassiano – shared taxis run an affordable shuttle service (5 euros each) to the pass from here. There's also a bus from San Cassiano, but a recent reporter says that it is 'very crowded and slow'. And buses go to the pass from Cortina.

The run is one of the most beautiful we've come across, and usually delights reporters. Views from the top of the cable car are splendid, and the run offers isolation amid sheer, pink-tinged Dolomite peaks and frozen waterfalls. 'There is a tremendous sense of solitude and isolation as you descend between those sheer pink cliffs,' says a 2008 first-time visitor. Make time to stop at the atmospheric Rifugio Scotoni near the end ('nice kaiserschmarren').

At the bottom, it's a long skate to a horse-drawn sled with ropes attached, which tows you back to Armentarola (for a couple of euros). This is more of a challenge than the run, and the risk of a pile-up if someone falls has concerned a couple of reporters. At Armentarola there is a draglift up to a run back to San Cassiano.

Phone numbers
From abroad use the prefix +39 (and do **not** omit the initial '0' of the phone number)

TOURIST OFFICES

ALTA BADIA
t 0471 836176
www.altabadia.org

Corvara
corvara@altabadia.org

Colfosco
colfosco@altabadia.org

San Cassiano
s.cassiano@altabadia.org

La Villa
lavilla@altabadia.org

ARABBA
t 0436 780019
info@arabba.it
www.arabba.it

VAL DI FASSA
www.fassa.com

Canazei
t 0462 609600
infocanazei@fassa.com

Campitello
t 0462 609620
infocampitello@fassa.com

Queues Few problems.
Mountain restaurants There are countless options. Piz Sorega gets very crowded – a reporter suggests going down to the Pic Pre, which is 'badly marked on the map and consequently quiet'. The woody Soraghes is 'friendly and popular', and the Pralongia is 'welcoming and cosy' and 'a great place for a last drink before descending' . Punta Trieste has a collection of wooden owls and serves 'excellent spaghetti'. Las Vegas is smart, modern and trendy.
Schools We have no reports.
Facilities for children The school offers the usual arrangements for children and there are several kids' parks.

STAYING THERE
How to go Tour operator Ski 2 offers a wide range of options.
Hotels The Rosa Alpina (0471 849500) is a splendid place, coupling genuine comfort, great food and a good spa with a relaxed atmosphere. Its three restaurants include the St Hubertus, which has two Michelin stars. The Fanes (0471 849470) is a smart chalet-style place with indoor-outdoor pool and a spa. You can stay up the mountain at the modern, trendy Las Vegas restaurant (0471 840138).
Eating out As well as the Rosa Alpina's St Hubertus, two restaurants have one Michelin star in the area; one, the Siriola in the hotel Ciasa Salares, is in Armentarola, just up the road; for the other see Corvara.
Après-ski It starts up the mountain with loud music at Las Vegas. A reporter recommends the Utia on the home run and skiing down after dark. Nightlife is very limited.

Off the slopes There are some lovely walks amid the stunning scenery.

LA VILLA 1435m/4,710ft
La Villa is similar to neighbouring San Cassiano in most ways – small, quiet, pretty, unspoiled. But the home pistes (served by a gondola) are challenging – a genuine red and a just-about-genuine black dropping 600m/1,970ft through woods to the village. There's a kids' snow garden at the top. Across the village, a fast chair serves a blue and a red slope and a link to Badia.

BADIA (FORMERLY PEDRACES) 1325m/4,350ft
This small roadside village has become more important to skiers since a free bus link started between here and Piccolino (20 mins) where you can take a gondola into the Plan de Corones/Kronplatz ski area – well worth a day trip and covered by the Dolomiti Superski lift pass. At the end of the village a new quad takes you to the link with La Villa (and hence the rest of the Alta Badia and Sella Ronda area). The village also has its own small ski area on the other side of the valley with a fast quad (with a red run underneath) and a slow double chair (with a blue underneath) to Santa Croce (2045m/6,710ft). A reporter recommends Ospizió di S Croce ('fabulous views, good omelette').

CANAZEI AND CAMPITELLO
Canazei is a sizeable village at the south-west corner of the Sella Ronda circuit. Campitello next door is smaller and quieter. They share a substantial ski area and are covered in the chapter on Trentino rather than here.

Sella Ronda

469

Interactive resort shortlist builder at **www.wtss.co.uk**

Selva/Val Gardena

Pleasant village amid spectacular Dolomite scenery, with the vast Sella Ronda lift network on its doorstep

➕ Part of the Sella Ronda region, with all the plus points we list in that chapter (immediately before this one): vast intermediate area, extensive snowmaking, stunning scenery, good mountain huts

➕ Attractive but strung-out village in an impressive wooded setting

➕ Excellent local slopes, with big verticals by Sella Ronda standards

➕ Mix of open and wooded slopes

➕ Excellent nursery slopes, but ...

➖ All the minus points of the Sella Ronda region too: erratic natural snowfall, few challenges for advanced skiers, mostly short runs with limited vertical, crowds on Sella Ronda circuit

➖ Progression to easy long runs involves bus or taxi rides

➖ Bus services are frequently criticised by reporters

➖ Busy road through the village

Selva (known to 'Ski Sunday' viewers as **Val Gardena** – the name of the valley) is one of the main bases to consider for a visit to the unique **Sella Ronda** region; the Sella Ronda as a whole is covered in a separate chapter, immediately before this one – so see that chapter too. Selva (and neighbouring Santa Cristina, which is now virtually a suburb of Selva) remains one of our favourite bases in the area, essentially because of the local slopes, including two race courses through woods to the village that are among the most satisfying runs in the area – not least because they offer decent verticals. Beginners and near-beginners, though, are probably better off elsewhere – in Corvara, Colfosco or San Cassiano. And places such as San Cassiano and Arabba have much more of a small village feel than sprawling Selva.

THE RESORT

Selva is a long roadside village at the head of the Val Gardena, almost merging with the next village of Santa Cristina. It suffers from traffic but has traditional-style architecture and an attractive church. The valley is famed for wood carvings, which are on display (and sale) wherever you look.

The village enjoys a lovely setting under the impressive pink-tinged walls of Sassolungo and the Gruppo Sella – a fortress-like massif about 6km/4 miles across that lies at the hub of the Sella Ronda circuit (see

separate chapter). Despite the World Cup fame of Val Gardena, Selva is neither upmarket nor brash. It's a good-value, civilised family resort – relaxed and family-friendly once you get away from the intrusive through-road.

For many years this area was part of Austria, and it retains a Tirolean charm. German is the main language, not Italian, and many visitors are German, too. Most places have two names: Selva is also known as Wolkenstein and the Gardena valley as Gröden. We do our bit for Italian unity by using the Italian place names. The

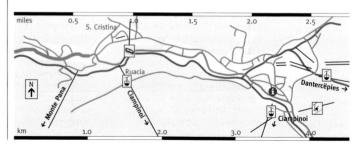

↑ The area is ideal for intermediates; but some runs can get busy
VAL GARDENA TOURIST OFFICE

KEY FACTS

Resort	1565m
	5,130ft

The linked lift network of Val Gardena, Alta Badia, Arabba, and the Canazei and Campitello slopes of Val di Fassa

Slopes	1005-2520m
	3,300-8,270ft
Lifts	211
Pistes	460km
	286 miles
Blue	38%
Red	53%
Black	9%
Snowmaking	376km
	234 miles

Val Gardena-
Alpe di Siusi only

Slopes	1005-2520m
	3,300-8,270ft
Lifts	81
Pistes	175km
	109 miles
Blue	30%
Red	60%
Black	10%
Snowmaking	150km
	93 miles

local language, Ladin, also survives – giving a third name to some places. Not surprisingly, a visitor found this confusing, 'especially on the buses'.

Ortisei, the administrative centre of Val Gardena, is described at the end of the chapter; it is not so convenient for the Sella Ronda slopes.

From the village, gondolas rise in two directions. The Ciampinoi gondola goes south from near the centre of the village to start the anticlockwise Sella Ronda route. The Dantercëpies gondola, for the clockwise Sella Ronda route, starts above the village at the top of the nursery slopes (but accessible via a central chairlift and a short run down). The most convenient position to stay is near this chair or one of the gondolas. There are local buses until early evening – five euros for a weekly card – but they generate numerous complaints from reporters about infrequency, unreliability, inadequate capacity (especially at the end of the day), poorly sited stops and lack of services to Corvara and Plan de Gralba. There's a night bus between Selva and Ortisei. Many reporters use taxis, although they are expensive unless you share. All the four-star hotels run their own free transport.

The Dolomiti Superski pass covers not only Selva and the Sella Ronda resorts but dozens of others. It's an easy road trip to Cortina – worth it for the fabulous scenery alone.

THE MOUNTAINS

Selva's own slopes cover both sides of the valley, including the quieter Seceda area above Santa Cristina and Ortisei. Practically all are ideally suited to intermediates. Most of the lifts stay open until around 5pm in high season.

The local piste map covers Selva and Alpe di Siusi (accessed from Ortisei); there are several variations, which reporters find confusing. The maps show neither names nor numbers for the runs. Piste marking and signing also provoke complaints.

THE SLOPES
High mileage piste excursions
The **Ciampinoi** gondola accesses several shady pistes, including the famous World Cup Downhill run, leading back down to Selva and Santa Cristina. In the opposite direction, runs go on to **Plan de Gralba** – and to the anticlockwise Sella Ronda circuit.

The **Dantercëpies** gondola serves lovely runs back to Selva and accesses the clockwise Sella Ronda circuit.

The sunny **Seceda** area is accessed by a gondola on the outskirts of Santa Cristina. This is also accessible by descending from Ciampinoi to ride a very efficient underground train across the valley. Runs descend to Santa Cristina or to Ortisei – a red run of about 7km/4 miles. And from Ortisei a cable car on the other side of the valley takes you to and from **Alpe di**

Selva/Val Gardena

471

Interactive resort shortlist builder at **www.wtss.co.uk**

LIFT PASSES

Dolomiti Superski

Prices in €		
Age	1-day	6-day
under 16	29	1471
16 to 59	42	209
over 60	38	188

Free under 8

Beginner no deals

Notes
Covers 1220km/758 miles of piste and 450 lifts in the Dolomites, including all Sella Ronda resorts

Alternative pass
Val Gardena only

Siusi – a gentle elevated area of quiet, easy runs, cross-country tracks and walks. This area can also be accessed via the big gondola from the village of Siusi, to the west.

TERRAIN PARKS
Facilities spread around
There are boardercross runs at Passo Sella by the Cavazes Grohmann chair and at Piz Sella by the Comici chair. And there's a half-pipe and a natural pipe at Plan de Gralba. Alpe di Siusi has a terrain park and a half-pipe by the Laurin chair.

SNOW RELIABILITY
Excellent when it's cold
The slopes are not high – there are

few above 2200m/7,220ft and most are between 1500m and 2000m (4,920ft and 6,560ft). Natural snowfalls are erratic, but Selva's slopes, like those of much of the area, are well covered by snowmaking. We have enjoyed excellent pistes here in times of severe natural snow shortage, and our reporters are impressed – 'a revelation', 'wonderful', 'stunning', 'unbelievable coverage and quality'. Problems arise only in poor snow years if it is too warm to make snow.

FOR EXPERTS
A few good runs
Experts may find the slopes too tame; there are few challenges, essentially no moguls (the blacks all get

Porta Vescovo
248om

Passo Pordoi

Marmolada
3340m

Sassolungo/
Langkofel
318om

Arabba
1600m

Gruppo del Sella
Sella Gruppe
315om

Canazei
1465m

PASSO SELLA
2245m

Corvara
157om

Sella Ronda

Sella Ronda
Sole

Sotsaslong
Comici-I

Piz Sella

2255m

Sochers

**Good, long blue runs
for beginners to
progress to – but
you have to catch a
bus from Selva to
avoid a tricky red
from Ciampinoi**

Piz Seteur

Piz Sella

PLAN DE GRALBA

Cir

DANTERCEPIES
2300m

Plan de Gralba
180om

CIAMPINOI

Dantercepies

Ciampinoi

Saslong

**Efficient
underground train
links the gondolas
for the Ciampinoi
and Seceda sectors**

**Lovely long reds;
the one on skier's
right of the
gondola used to be
the Women's
Downhill run**

Selva/Wolkenstein
1565m/5,130ft

Vallunga

Col Raiser

Col Raiser

SE

groomed) and a low likelihood of powder. There are few major off-piste routes because of the nature of the terrain; see the off-piste panel in the Sella Ronda chapter.

The Val Gardena World Cup piste, the Saslong, is one of several steepish runs between Ciampinoi and both Selva and Santa Cristina. Unlike many World Cup pistes it is kept in racing condition for Italian team practices, but it is open to the public much of the time and makes a wonderful fast cruise – it's one of our favourite runs and especially good in January, when it's not too crowded. A 2008 reporter says, 'Any skiers out of their depth are removed from the run by police.'

FOR INTERMEDIATES
Fast cruising on easy slopes
There are huge amounts of skiing to do, in several areas.

Competent intermediates will love the red and black descents from Dantercëpies and Ciampinoi to Selva.

The blue runs in the Plan de Gralba area are gentle; the red run to get there from Ciampinoi is a real obstacle – steep and crowded – but reporters find it worth the struggle. The high-altitude route back used to involve a tricky black run, but the resort claims to have made it wider and therefore easier (reports welcome). The quiet runs at Mont de Seura, above Monte Pana, are worth exploring.

The Alpe di Siusi above Ortisei is

Ideal area for early intermediates – very gentle pistes (almost flat in places), quiet and set amid superb scenery

Punta d'Oro/Goldknopf 2210m

ALPE DI SIUSI

1940m

Paradiso

Fiè/Völs 880m

Mont de Seura 2115m

Alpe di Siusi Seiser Alm 2000m

Siusi/Seis 1005m

2100m

Sochers

Castel Rotto/Kastel Ruth 1060m

Mont Seura

Saslong

1665m MONTE PANA

Alpe di Siusi

S Cristina/St Christina 1430m

Beautiful long run with a vertical drop of 1300m/4,270ft; not steep but quite narrow in places; wonderful views over the valley and through a very picturesque canyon

Ortisei/St Ulrich 1235m/4,050ft

2280m

The Saslong World Cup Downhill piste is a wonderful, fast, rolling cruise that's especially good in January when it's not too crowded

Furnes

SECEDA

Seceda 2520m

Selva attracts few boarders. There's little to challenge experts, and off-piste opportunities are limited, but the nursery slopes are good and there are lots of gentle runs to progress to. The main lifts out of the village are all gondolas or chairs. There's a terrain park at Alpe di Siusi and a couple of half-pipes.

SCHOOLS

Selva Gardena
t 0471 795156

2000
t 0471 773125

Ski Academy Peter Runggaldier (Ski Factory)
t 0471 795156

Top School Val Gardena
t 0471 794099

Classes
(Selva prices)
6 days €168
Private lessons
€35 for 1hr

GUIDES

Mountain Guides Val Gardena
t 0471 794133

CHILDREN

Selvi mini club
0471 795156
Ages 0 to 4; 9am to 4pm
Casa Bimbo
(at S Cristina)
0471 793013
From 4mnth to 7yr

Ski school
For age 4 to 12:
6 days (10am to 4pm)
€333, lunch included
(Factory school price)

ideal for confidence-building – very gentle (almost flat in places), quiet, set in superb scenery with no crowds. Runs are mostly short, the main exception being the red down to Saltria from Punta d'Oro, offering 500m/1,640ft vertical.

The Seceda sector has good red and blue runs at altitude, and splendid runs to the valley – an easy blue/red to Santa Cristina and the beautiful red Cucasattel, passing through a narrow, natural canyon to Ortisei.

FOR BEGINNERS
Great slopes, but ...

The village nursery slopes below the Dantercëpies gondola are excellent – spacious, convenient, and kept in good condition. There are lots of gentle, long runs to progress to, but Selva isn't the ideal base to access them. Plan de Gralba has easy blues, but you need to take a taxi to get there. Near-beginners would be better placed taking the bus to Ortisei and the cable car to Alpe di Siusi.

FOR CROSS-COUNTRY
Beautiful trails

There are 98km/61 miles of trails, all enjoying wonderful scenery. The 12km/7 mile trail up the Vallunga-Langental valley is particularly attractive, with neck-craning views all around. Almost half the trails have the advantage of being at altitude, running between Monte Pana and across Alpe di Siusi.

QUEUES
Now few problems

New lifts have vastly improved the area, and there are now fewer bottlenecks, especially away from the main Sella Ronda circuit. However, the Dantercëpies gondola still generates complaints from reporters ('the usual scramble' says a 2008 visitor), as does the Ciampinoi gondola.

MOUNTAIN RESTAURANTS
One of the area's highlights

There are lots of huts all over the area, and virtually all of them are lively, with helpful staff, good food, and

lots of character and modest prices. Reporters love them ('not a bad one all week' is a typical comment).

The Panorama is a small, cosy, rustic suntrap at the foot of the drag near the top of Dantercëpies. The 'attractive' Ciampac at the bottom of the Val double chair is worth a visit ('brilliant for morning coffee or lunch and for sunbathing' confirms a 2008 reporter). On the way down to Plan de Gralba from Ciampinoi, the Vallongia is tucked away on a corner of the piste. In the Plan de Gralba area the top station of the cable car does excellent pizza; the Comici is atmospheric, with a big terrace. Piz Seteur has 'superb lasagne' and is also recommended late in the day (see 'Après-ski').

In the Seceda sector there are countless options. The cosy Sangon has 'bags of atmosphere', though another reporter pronounces Baita Gamsblut her favourite: 'super rustic hut with a good menu and a warm, friendly atmosphere'. The Seceda does 'wonderful food' although the waitresses in miniskirts or leather shorts seem to have disappeared, much to one visitor's disappointment. Other recent reporters recommend Daniel's Hütte, Curona ('excellent service') and Sofie ('good vegetable soup with sausage').

On Alpe di Siusi the rustic Sanon refuge gets a good review, particularly since 'the barman came out to serenade us with his accordion'. The Ritsch Schwaige is praised for its gulaschsuppe, apple strudel, cakes and service. The table-service restaurant at the bottom of the Monte Piz lift is also highly rated – 'good value', 'huge portions'. The Williams Hütte at the top of the Florian chair has 'superb views'.

SCHOOLS AND GUIDES
Positive reports

Ski Academy Peter Runggaldier, run by 90s racing star Peter Runggaldier (and also called The Ski & Boarders Factory), gets favourable reports from readers: 'We had a two-hour private lesson and thought they were very

good.' Another praised the 'very beneficial' advanced level groups at the 2000 school. But a lady and her friend were disappointed with 2000 this year: 'We were typecast as two elderly female skiers and were placed in a low intermediate class. On day five the instructor told us we were excellent skiers and should have been in the gold class.' Private lessons with the Ski & Boarders Factory are said to be good value – but booking ahead is advised as it gets busy.

FACILITIES FOR CHILDREN
Good by Italian standards
There are comprehensive child care arrangements, but German and Italian are the main languages here and English is not routinely spoken. That said, in the past we have had reports of very enjoyable lessons and of children longing to return. Casa Bimbo at Santa Cristina provides day care for babies from four months to children of 7-8 years. Family specialist tour operator Esprit has its own child care facilities here.

Air Verona 190km/ 118 miles (3hr); Bolzano 40km/ 25 miles (45min); Treviso 130km/ 81 miles (2½hr)

Rail Chiusa (27km/ 17 miles); Bressanone (35km/22 miles); Bolzano (40km/ 25 miles); frequent buses from station

STAYING THERE

HOW TO GO
A reasonable choice
Selva features in most major tour op brochures. Inghams, Neilson and Crystal Finest all have some of the best hotels here.

Chalets There is a fair choice of catered chalets, including some good ones with en suite bathrooms. Family specialist Esprit has chalets here, as do Total and Crystal.

Hotels There are 18 4-stars in Selva, some 43 3-stars and numerous lesser hotels. Few of the best are well positioned.

****Gran Baita (0471 795210) Large, luxurious sporthotel, with lots of mod cons including indoor pool. A few minutes' walk from centre and lifts. Highly recommended in 2006 ('they couldn't do enough for us').

****Granvara (0471 795250) 'Just out of town but free hotel bus, great food and views, indoor pool and a spa. Recommended.'

****Aaritz (0471 795011) Best-placed 4-star, opposite the Ciampinoi gondola, and with an open fire.

****Tyrol (0471 774100) 'Friendly and fantastic value, indoor pool and handy for nursery slopes, but a bit of a way to the Sella Ronda.'

****Oswald (0471 771111) Near a ski bus stop and with its own free bus. 'Good rooms and fantastic food.'

***Rodella (0471 794553) 'Just outside Selva but friendly pensione, with free taxi, spa and delicious meals.'

***Linder (0471 795242) 'Cosy, comfortable, family-run with fantastic dinner menu and excellent free guiding service.' Indoor pool.

***Pralong (0471 795370) Uphill walk from the centre, but 'one of the best hotels we've visited', says a reporter.

UK PACKAGES

Selva Alpine Answers, Chalet World Ski, Crystal, Crystal Finest, Esprit, First Choice, Independent Ski Links, Inghams, Interactive Resorts, Italian Safaris, Kuoni, Momentum, Neilson, Ski Activity, Ski Total, Ski Yogi, Skitracer, Snow Finders, Thomson
Ortisei Inghams, Interhome, Italian Safaris, Neilson, Ski Expectations

ACTIVITIES

In Val Gardena:

Indoor Swimming pool, sauna, bowling, squash, ice rink, museum, library, chess, billiards, tennis, climbing wall, fitness centre

Outdoor Sleigh rides, snowshoeing, tobogganing, ice climbing, ice rink, horse riding, paragliding, extensive cleared paths, climbing

Phone numbers
From abroad use the prefix +39 (and do **not** omit the initial '0' of the phone number)

TOURIST OFFICES

VAL GARDENA
t 0471 777777
info@valgardena.it
www.valgardena.it

Selva
t 0471 777900
selva@valgardena.it

Ortisei
t 0471 777600
ortisei@valgardena.it

***Solaia** (0471 795104) Superbly positioned for lifts and slopes.
***Des Alpes** (0471 772700) Near lifts and bus stop – 'warm, friendly staff and amply portioned four-course meals', says a reporter.
***Wolkenstein** (0471 772200) In S Cristina. Reporters sing its praises this year – 'superb service and food – the place to go for lively après-ski', 'excellent food and spacious rooms'.
Villa Seceda (0471 795297) A 'friendly' B&B near the nursery slopes.
Apartments We have had excellent reports of the Villa Gardena and Isabell apartments.

EATING OUT
Plenty of good-value choices
The higher-quality restaurants are mainly hotel-based – reporters highly recommend Armin's Grill in the hotel of the same name, and the Sal Fëur in the Broi B&B. The Sun Valley Stübele does 'excellent pasta and pizza', says a recent visitor, as does Rinos. Another reader enjoyed 'wonderful goulash and dumplings' at Des Alpes. The Bellavista is also good for pasta, and Costabella is 'highly recommended' for Tirolean specialities. The Kronestube has good 'food and service'.

APRÈS-SKI
Lively for a family resort
Nightlife is reasonably lively and informal, though the village is so scattered there is little on-street atmosphere.

La Stua is an après-ski bar on the Sella Ronda route, with live music on some nights. For an early drink we are told that the Piz Seteur bar, above Plan de Gralba, is worth a little detour from the route – 'fun, loud and a bit raunchy' (you may find scantily clad girls dancing on the bar).

For a civilised early drink try the good-value ski-school bar at the base of the Dantercëpies piste. Or the Costabella – cosy, serving good glühwein. Café Mozart on the main street 'serves the best hot chocolate in the world and the cakes are mouth-wateringly delicious'.

For thigh-slapping in Selva later on, the Laurinkeller has good atmosphere though it's 'quite expensive', while the popular Luislkeller is 'very German', 'lively' and 'packed', with loud music and barmaids in Tirolean garb. A 2006 reporter also enjoyed the Goalie's Irish bar with its hockey memorabilia: 'The

music was particularly suited to 30 or 40 somethings.' The bar by the Ski Factory is said to be a 'jolly place' – and noted for its flaming cocktails.

The place to go after midnight is Dali, where a mixed British and Italian crowd dances till the small hours.

OFF THE SLOPES
Good variety
There's a sports centre, snowshoeing, lovely walks (buy a map at the tourist office for 3.50 euros) tobogganing and sleigh rides on Alpe di Siusi. One reporter enjoyed an organised bowling night ('great fun'). There is a bus to Ortisei, which is well worth a visit – see Ortisei below.

Pedestrians can reach numerous good restaurants by gondola or cable car. There are buses to Bolzano, tour operators do trips to Cortina, and Innsbruck is within reach by car.

Ortisei 1235m/4,050ft

Ortisei is an attractive, prosperous market town with a life of its own apart from tourism. It's full of lovely buildings, pretty churches and pleasant shops and has an interesting museum, a large hot-spring swimming pool and an ice rink. The local slopes aren't on the main Sella Ronda circuit. The lift to the Seceda slopes is easily reached from the centre by a 300m/980ft-long series of underground moving walkways and escalators. The Alpe di Siusi lifts are a similar distance out, and the cable car is now accessed via a long pedestrian footbridge, an improvement over the previous steep, icy, uphill walk. The nursery area, school and kindergarten are at the foot of these slopes, and there's a fair range of family accommodation on the piste side of the road. The fine public indoor pool and ice rink are also here.

There are hotels and self-catering accommodation to suit all tastes and pockets and many good restaurants, mainly specialising in local dishes. A reporter recommends the 4-star hotel Alpenheim (0471 796515): 'luxurious rooms', 'excellent food', but not central. Another says that the 5-star Adler (0471 775000), which has a very impressive spa, is 'an excellent hotel'. A 2008 visitor recommends the Tablick (0471 796051) for its 'great food, efficient staff and the ski bus to the door'. Après-ski is quite jolly, and many bars keep going till late.

Sestriere

Altitude is the main attraction of this, Europe's first purpose-built resort; some would say it's the only attraction

COSTS

① ② ③ ④ ⑤ ⑥

RATINGS

The slopes

Fast lifts	★★★
Snow	★★★★
Extent	★★★★
Expert	★★★
Intermediate	★★★★
Beginner	★★★
Convenience	★★★
Queues	★★★
Mountain restaurants	★★

The rest

Scenery	★★★
Resort charm	★
Off-slope	★

NEWS

Snowmaking is gradually being extended throughout the Via Lattea area.

KEY FACTS

Resort	2000m
	6,560ft

Milky Way	
Slopes	1390-2825m
	4,560-9,270ft
Lifts	82
Pistes	400km
	249 miles
Blue	24%
Red	56%
Black	20%
Snowmaking	120km
	75 miles

Sestriere-Sauze d'Oulx-Sansicario	
Slopes	1390-2825m
	4,560-9,270ft
Lifts	38
Pistes	250km
	155 miles
Snowmaking	95km
	59 miles

＋ Local slopes suitable for most levels, with some tougher runs than in most neighbouring resorts

＋ Part of the extensive Milky Way area, with improved links to Sansicario and Pragelato

＋ Snowmaking covers all but one or two marginal slopes, but ...

－ It needs to, given the very erratic local snowfall record

－ The village is an eyesore, despite changes for the 2006 Olympics

－ For a purpose-built resort, not conveniently arranged

－ Weekend and peak-period queues

－ Little après-ski during the week

Sestriere was built for snow – high, with north-west-facing slopes – and it has very extensive snowmaking, too. So even if you are let down by the notoriously erratic snowfalls in this corner of Italy, you should be fairly safe here – certainly safer than in Sauze d'Oulx, over the hill. All of which makes Sestriere a great weekend away for the residents of Torino. As a holiday destination for residents of Tunbridge Wells, it doesn't have such a strong case.

THE RESORT

Sestriere was the Alps' first purpose-built resort, developed by Fiat's Giovanni Agnelli in the 1930s, though now run by a local business consortium. It sits on a broad, sunny and windy col, and neither the site nor the village, with its large apartment blocks, looks very hospitable – though the buildings have benefited from recent investment for the 2006 Winter Olympics. This is not the most convenient of purpose-built resorts, either – some of the walks are non-trivial. The satellite of Borgata, 200m/66oft lower, is less convenient for nightlife and shops. The valley town of Pragelato is a viable alternative base now that it has a cable car link up to Borgata.

THE MOUNTAINS

The local skiing is on shady slopes, mainly open with some woodland, facing the village. Sestriere is at one extreme of the big Franco-Italian Milky Way area.

Slopes The local slopes, served by drags and chairs, are in two main sectors: Sises, directly in front of the village, and Motta, above Borgata; Motta is more varied and bigger, with almost twice the vertical. Across the valley, gondolas go up from Borgata for Sauze d'Oulx and from a car park west of the village for Sansicario and the rest of the Milky Way. For the return to Sestriere there are red runs down both gondolas, but they are sunny and rarely open. Signposting is poor, and the piste map is said to be 'clearer than in previous years' but still inadequate. There's night skiing twice a week.

Terrain parks There is a park by the Garnel chair at Alpette.

Snow reliability With most of the local slopes facing north-west and ranging from 1840m to 2825m (6,040ft to 9,270ft), and an 'impressive' snowmaking network, snow-cover is usually reliable, except on the runs down the gondolas mentioned above. The notoriously erratic snowfalls in the Milky Way often leave the rest of the area seriously short of snow.

Experts There is a fair amount to amuse – steep pistes served by the drags at the top of both sectors. There is some decent off-piste, given snow. Don't count on it – or on moguls, which are erased religiously.

Intermediates Both sectors also offer plenty for confident intermediates, who can explore practically all of the Milky Way areas, conditions permitting. The runs in the Motta sector offer more of a challenge.

Beginners The terrain is good for beginners, with several nursery areas and the gentlest of easy blue runs down to Borgata. But there is a lack of easy intermediate runs to progress to.

Snowboarding Sestriere has a reasonable number of chairs, but there are also lots of draglifts.

477

↑ It's not a pretty place, but it serves its purpose

PISTE MAP

Sestriere is covered on the Sauze d'Oulx map a few pages back

UK PACKAGES

Alpine Answers, Club Med, Club Pavilion, Crystal, Equity, First Choice, Independent Ski Links, Inghams, Interhome, Just Skiing, Kuoni, Momentum, Neilson, Rocketski, Ski Weekend, Ski4you, Skitracer, Thomson

Phone numbers
From abroad use the prefix +39 (and do **not** omit the initial '0' of the phone number)

TOURIST OFFICE

t 0122 755444
sestriere@
montagnedoc.it
www.montagnedoc.it
www.sestriere.it
www.vialattea.it

Cross-country There are three loops covering a total of 10km/6 miles.
Queues The lifts are mainly modern, though there are still some inadequate, 'painfully slow', old ones. The main lifts have queues at weekends and holidays; there can be lengthy delays for the Cit Roc chair up M Sises. Queues occur when poor weather closes the gondola link to Sauze, but the gondola to M Fraiteve has improved the connection with Sansicario and the Via Lattea. Reporters here, as in Sauze, complain that some lifts may be kept closed during the week, to conserve money or snow – with the result that crowded pistes can also become a problem.
Mountain restaurants The woody Raggio di Sole at Anfiteatro is 'cosy' and the Alpette has 'spectacular views'. Readers also like the Tana della Volpe at the top of the Banchetta chair, the Teit pizzeria at Borgata for 'good choices at reasonable prices' and the busy Gargote at Garnel for hot chocolates. The Capret by the lift of the same name is also mentioned. On the whole, local places are only fair; there are better ones further afield.
Schools and guides Lack of spoken English can be a problem, but a 2007 visitor comments that his instructor spoke 'great' English as well as being 'brilliant and very friendly'. Another reporter says her class included such a mixture of abilities that it was 'totally untesting' for her and 'far too difficult' for her friend.
Facilities for children There are no special facilities for children.

STAYING THERE

How to go Most accommodation is in apartments. The complex of apartments built for the 2006 Winter Olympics are an option too.
Hotels There are a dozen hotels, mostly 3-star or 4-star. You might want to stay near one of the gondolas. The Shackleton Mountain Resort (0122 750773) is a smart, modern complex with pool and wellness centre. The Savoy Edelweiss (0122 77040) ('charming, excellent staff') and the Du Col (0122 76990) are central; and just out of the village is the luxurious Principi di Piemonte (0122 7941). Grangesises offers an alternative base – it's 2km/1 mile from Sestriere and linked by bus.
Eating out There are plenty of options. The cosy Antica Spelonca in Borgata has 'an interesting menu' and the atmospheric Lu Periol does traditional pasta dishes. Last Tango and the Baita are well regarded. Previously recommended Tre Rubinetti has closed down.
Après-ski Après-ski is quiet during the week, but Il Caminetto (formerly the Prestige) is lively at weekends when Turin decamps. The Pinky is a popular bar and restaurant, with low sofas in the classic Italian casual-chic style, good pizzas and an antipasto buffet.
Off the slopes There are some smart shops and there's a fitness centre, an ice rink, a sports centre and pool. Thanks to the recent cable car link from Borgata it is possible to visit the town of Pragelato.

La Thuile

A revitalised mining town and a modern lift-base complex, combined with extensive, easy slopes and a link with France

RATINGS

The slopes

Fast lifts	**
Snow	****
Extent	***
Expert	**
Intermediate	****
Beginner	****
Convenience	***
Queues	****
Mountain restaurants	*

The rest

Scenery	***
Resort charm	***
Off-slope	**

NEWS

For 2008/09 a new fast quad is due to be built from near the base area, rising by just 180m/590ft. The chair will serve three new pistes with snowmaking – blue, red and black.

+ Fair-sized area linked to La Rosière in France

+ Free of crowds and queues

+ Excellent beginner and easy intermediate slopes

– Most of the seriously tough pistes are low down, and most of the low, woodland runs are tough

– Winds can close links with France

– Not the place for lively après-ski

La Thuile deserves to be better known internationally. The slopes best suit beginners and intermediates looking for smooth cruises, but are not devoid of interest for experts, particularly if the snow conditions are good – and expeditions to La Rosière add interest. Those who try it seem to appreciate the quiet village as much as the quiet slopes.

THE RESORT

At the foot of the lifts is the modern Planibel complex, with places to stay, a leisure centre, bars, shops and restaurants – like a French purpose-built resort, but with a distinctly Italian atmosphere. But many people find this rather soulless and prefer to stay in the old village across the river (served by a regular free bus service). Much of the old village has been restored and new buildings tastefully added. There are reasonable restaurants and bars.

The slopes link with La Rosière, over the border in France. Courmayeur is easily reached by car, and Cervinia is about an hour away.

THE MOUNTAINS

La Thuile has quite extensive slopes, with the great attraction that they are normally very uncrowded. Many runs are marked red, but deserve no more than a blue rating. A 2008 visitor found the grading 'variable' while another found the 'signposting not always as good as it should be'. The link with La Rosière adds adventure; the runs there are steeper, sunnier and bumpier – and the start of the route back is a fairly tricky red. Reporters have found that strong winds can close the high lifts, including the link.
Slopes The lifts out of the village (a gondola and a fast chair) take you to Les Suches, with shady black runs going back down directly to the village through the trees, and reds taking a more roundabout route. From here chairs take you to Chaz Dura for access to a variety of gentle bowls facing east. You can go off westwards from here to the Petit St Bernard road or across to a quad up to Belvedere, the launch pad for excursions to La Rosière. Below Belvedere are the slopes of Gran Testa, served by a fast and a slow chair and a drag.
Terrain parks None in La Thuile.
Snow reliability Most of La Thuile's slopes are north- or east-facing and above 2000m/6,560ft, so the snow generally keeps well. There's also a decent amount of snowmaking and 'grooming is immaculate'.
Experts The steep pistes down through the trees from Les Suches – the Diretta, Berthod and Muret – are serious stuff. The Fourclaz area has some genuinely black terrain and plenty of off-piste – the fast quad means you can do quick circuits in this area. A recent reporter was still making fresh tracks there three days after snowfall. The short black Maisonettes, by the Arnouvaz chair, is usually quiet.
Heli-lifts are available. The Ruitor

VEDERE
m/8,560ft

Col de
Fourclaz

Chaz Dura
2580m

OL DE LA
VERSETTE

2385m
La Rosière

Arnouvaz

Les
Suches
2200m

La Thuile
1440m/4,720ft

African decor with very friendly staff and good lasagne'. The self-service Mélèze, near the top of the gondola, serves 'tasty and generous portions'. A couple of places provide an incentive to tackle the long San Bernardo home run: the Maison de Neige is 'fabulous', and the four-course menu is 'worth every penny'; the Riondet serves 'good food at astonishing speed'.

Schools and guides In the past we've had good reports, but a 2008 reporter found them 'horrendously obstructive when trying to book in advance'.

Facilities for children There's a mini-club and snow garden for ages four to 12. Children over the age of five can join adult ski classes. A 2007 reporter with two small children complained that restaurants didn't serve food before 7pm, but we are told the Brasserie du Bathieu serves all day.

STAYING THERE

How to go The number of tour operators going there is increasing.

Hotels The 4-star Planibel (0165 884541) is large and characterless, but recommended by a few reporters for its 'ideal location' right at the foot of the slopes and 'clean and spacious' accommodation, though 'the food was not up to 4-star standard', says a 2008 visitor. It has a pool, gym, sauna and steam room too. There are also a few 3-stars and some simpler places. Reporters like the 'quiet, friendly, family-run' hotel du Glacier (0165 884137), a short walk above the lifts, and Chalet Eden (0165 885050), near the gondola ('excellent value').

Apartments A 2008 reporter was 'very pleased' with the Planibel apartments (in the same building as the hotel above); they are spacious, by the lifts and good value.

Eating out Reader recommendations include Bricole ('a very decent eatery – try the lamb'), Lune for good value steaks and salads, and Rascard ('tremendous jumbo prawns'). Chocolat is a cafe 'not to be missed'.

Après-ski Nightlife is 'even quieter' than one reporter expected. The Bricolette bar and the neighbouring Bricole 'videodiscopub' are the liveliest bars. The Fantasia disco at the Planibel warms up well after midnight.

Off the slopes There are few shops; the Planibel complex has a pool and there are marked walks. Pedestrians can ride up the gondola for lunch.

↑ There are lots of easy slopes above the treeline, many of them classed as reds but really of blue gradient
CONSORZIO OPERATORI TURISTICA LA THUILE

KEY FACTS

Resort	1440m
	4,720ft

Espace San Bernardo (La Rosière and La Thuile)

Slopes	1175-2610m
	3,850-8,560ft
Lifts	38
Pistes	150km
	93 miles
Green	9%
Blue	36%
Red	40%
Black	15%
Snowmaking	
	30km/18 miles

UK PACKAGES

Alpine Answers, Crystal, First Choice, Independent Ski Links, Inghams, Interski, Just Skiing, Neilson, Skitracer, Thomson

Phone numbers
From abroad use the prefix +39 (and do **not** omit the initial '0' of the phone number)

TOURIST OFFICE

t 0165 883049
info@lathuile.it
www.lathuile.it

glacier offers a 20km/12 mile run to Ste-Foy, a short taxi ride from La Rosière and the lifts back to La Thuile.

Intermediates La Thuile has some good intermediate runs. The bowls above Les Suches have many gentle blue and red runs, ideal for cruising. There are also long reds through the trees back to the resort. A 2007 reporter enjoyed runs around the Argillien Express for 'fast turns and empty pistes'. The red runs on the other side of the top ridge, in the Fourclaz area, down towards the Petit St Bernard road, offer more challenge. The road forms the roundabout San Bernardo red to the village, taking 11km/7 miles to drop 1100m/3,610ft; 'bleak' is one view, 'boring' probably nearer the mark; avoid in fresh snow.

Beginners There are nursery slopes at village level and up at Les Suches, and long easy blues above there, including Promenade, which is served by draglifts. You ride the gondola down.

Snowboarding These are great slopes for learning. You need ride only chairlifts and the gondola, and most of the slopes are easy. For the more experienced there are great tree runs, good freeriding and some good carving runs. But there are some frustratingly flat sections too.

Cross-country La Thuile has four loops of varying difficulty on the valley floor, adding up to 17km/11 miles of track.

Queues Short queues may form at the gondola first thing, but not at the chair. There aren't any problems once up the hill.

Mountain restaurants Maison Carrel on run 6 near the bottom of the Argillien Express chair is a good-value table-service place with floor to ceiling windows and 'excellent food'. The Clotze, at the foot of the Chalets chairlift, does 'tasty table-service food at reasonable prices'. The Off Shore, above Arnouvaz, has an 'eclectic

ITALY

480

Weekly news updates and resort links at www.wtss.co.uk

Trentino

Not a resort, but a region with a few big resorts and a lot of smaller ones that deserve to be better known on the UK market

Trentino is a fabulously scenic region that is rather neglected by the British. It has a few large resorts, two of which (Madonna di Campiglio and Passo Tonale) are covered in their own chapters, resorts linked to the Sella Ronda (such as Canazei and Campitello, covered below), and a lot of small ski areas that you may not have heard of. The following guide is not comprehensive; but it includes all the places that are likely to be of international interest, and more.

NEWS

In Folgarida and Marilleva: for 2007/08 a new eight-seat gondola was built between these two resorts from the roadside village of Daolasa, with a new red run with snowmaking underneath the top half and a new beginner area at the mid-station.

In Canazei: on the Belvedere slopes a new gondola has replaced the old Toè chair.

In Cavalese: a new quad with covers has replaced a draglift.

In San Martino di Castrozza: a new terrain park was built on the Tognole area.

In Pinzolo: a long-planned link between Pinzolo and Madonna di Campiglio may be completed for 2009/10.

WESTERN TRENTINO

Madonna di Campiglio is Trentino's biggest and best-known resort – a chic place with mainly easy slopes that attracts an affluent, almost exclusively Italian clientele. It has its own chapter. Its ski area is linked to those of much smaller Marilleva and Folgarida.

The slopes above **Marilleva** are excellent, steep, north-facing reds (with a few blues higher up the mountain), much better for adventurous intermediates than Campiglio's main Pradalago slopes. And the snow is usually the best in the area because of the largely north-facing orientation. There's also a serious black run served by a two-stage chair to Doss della Pesa (2230m/7,320ft). And there's a gondola that connects with a six-pack to Monte Vigo (2180m/7,150ft) and the links to Campiglio and Folgarida.

Marilleva itself is a modern resort consisting of several 1960s-style, ugly but functional, low-rise concrete buildings (most of them well screened by trees, thankfully) built on a mid-mountain shelf at 1400m/4,590ft and reached by road or gondola from the lower part of the resort at 900m/2,950ft, on the valley floor.

The slopes down to **Folgarida** are gentler than those above Marilleva but in general somewhat more challenging than Campiglio's main slopes.

The main part of Folgarida itself is clustered around the gondola station at 1400m/4,590ft – and purpose-built in a much more traditional style than Marilleva. It feels much more upmarket, with smart hotels, a few shops and fur-clad patrons. There's another base area at 1300m/4,270ft by another gondola station.

Midway between Marilleva and Folgarida, a new eight-seat gondola running from the village of Daolasa up to Val Mastellina was built for 2007/08 plus a new red run and a beginner area. A 2008 reporter enjoyed the new

481

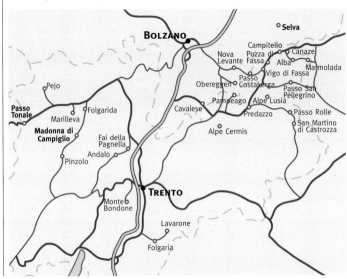

Trentino

Tread into Temptation

Trentino Marketing ; ph: S. Angelani

Promise to enjoy yourself and we promise to entice you. Sun, snow, fast pistes, slow food - stray no further for your winter thrills. The Dolomites promise you the passion of Italy on seductive slopes. Trentino - for those who can resist everything except temptation.

visittrentino.it

TRENTINO

ITALIA

run, which was 'open, wide, empty, and had fantastic snow-cover'.

A planned link between the Cinque Laghi slopes of Madonna di Campiglio and those above **Pinzolo** (780m/2,560ft), currently a 20-minute drive to the south, is taking longer than was originally hoped, but it may be complete by 2009/10. From Pinzolo, a gondola followed by a fast chair take you to the area's high point of Doss del Sabion (2100m/6,890ft), where there are great views of the Brenta massif. The area has mainly genuinely challenging red runs and an excellent groomed black (the Competition piste), and the snow keeps in condition because most of the runs are northish facing. The Cioca and Patagonia reds are lovely steep cruises (though Cioca is steep enough to be a black in parts). Usefully, the average and maximum gradients of these and other runs are marked at the top of each (something we haven't seen elsewhere). The first two chairlifts that are to be part of the link to Campiglio were in place when we visited in 2006. When the link is complete, Madonna di Campiglio, with its outlying links to Pinzolo, Marilleva and Folgarida, will be a much more attractive place for good intermediates to visit.

Pinzolo itself is not a conventional ski resort but the main town of the Val Rendena.

Passo Tonale is a short drive west of Marilleva and Folgarida – a good-value, high, snow-sure resort set on the border of Lombardia and linked to Ponte di Legno over that border. Passo Tonale has its own chapter.

Just down the Val di Sole (which means Valley of Sun) is **Pejo** (1400m/4,590ft), a spa village with a narrow but tall slope area rising to 2340m/7,680ft, served by a gondola, three chairlifts and a couple of drags.

All these areas (and the resorts described in the 'Around Trento' section below) are covered by the Superskirama Adamello-Brenta ski pass. If you have a car, it is perfectly possible to explore all these areas in a week. And a 2007 reporter recommends staying in 'a little-known gem' of a place called **Fucine**, which is not a ski resort in itself but sits in the centre of all of these resorts. He says the hotel Pangrazzi has 'fantastic food' and relaxing leisure club.

Trento is the main town of Trentino, and its local hill is **Monte Bondone**. Five roadside chairlifts serve partly wooded slopes here on Palon (2090m/6,860ft), with a longest run of 4km/2.5 miles dropping 800m/2,620ft and served by a fast quad. The whole area is covered by snowmaking. There's a terrain park – and great views to the Brenta Dolomites around Madonna.

To the south-east of Trento are the small resorts of **Folgaria** (1165m/3,820ft – not to be confused with Folgarida near Madonna) and **Lavarone**. Lavarone has a handful of lifts, but Folgaria has more than 20, serving 60km/37 miles of runs with 100% snowmaking.

To the north-west are the slopes on Paganella (2125m/6,970ft) shared by **Fai della Paganella** (1000m/3,280ft) and **Andalo** (1050m/3,440ft). Andalo is a sizeable resort and a pleasant enough place with a small local town feel. A 2008 visitor recommends the Cristallo hotel (0461 585744). We visited for half a day and enjoyed the small ski area very much. One eight-seat gondola goes up from near the centre of Andalo, and another leaves from a big car park nearby. Five of the other 16 lifts are fast chairs. The runs are mainly genuinely challenging reds and can be long (a maximum vertical of almost 1100m/3,610ft); most are northish-facing and so keep their snow in good condition. We especially enjoyed the Dosa Larici and La Rocca reds down to Santel (the nearest lift base to Fai). There's a beginner area near the Andalo base but only a few short blue runs (all at the top), so we don't recommend it for novices or timid intermediates.

Canazei and Campitello in the **Val di Fassa** are in Trentino, and the slopes above them are part of the famous Sella Ronda circuit; the Marmolada glacier is also in Trentino and is reachable on skis from Arabba on the circuit. See the Sella Ronda chapter for a description of the skiing. Here we cover the main Trentino resorts linked to the Sella Ronda.

Canazei is a sizeable, bustling, pretty, roadside village of narrow streets, rustic old buildings, traditional-style hotels and nice little

Trentino's scenery is simply stunning ➔

UK PACKAGES

Andalo Equity, Rocketski
Canazei First Choice, Independent Ski Links, Inghams, Interhome, Neilson, Ski Wild, Thomson
Campitello Crystal, First Choice, Neilson, Thomson
Cavalese Crystal, Thomson
Falcade Ardmore
Folgaria Ardmore, Equity, Ski Wild
Folgarida Ardmore, Equity, Rocketski
Marilleva Ardmore
Monte Bondone Headwater, Solo's
Pozza di Fassa Crystal

shops, set at 1465m/4,810ft beneath the Sella Ronda's most heavily wooded section of mountains. The grand 3-star hotel Dolomiti (0462 601106) in the centre is one of the original resort hotels – 'spacious room with private hot tub and superb service', says a 2008 reporter; the charming, chalet-style Diana (0462 601477) is five minutes from the centre.

There are numerous restaurants, and the après-ski is really animated. La Stua di Ladins serves local wines and the Husky (sometimes with live music) and Roxi bars are worth a visit.

Off-slope entertainment consists of beautiful walks and shopping. There's also a pool, sauna, Turkish baths and skating in neighbouring Alba.

A 12-person gondola is the only mountain access, but it shifts the queues (which can be long) quickly.

A single piste runs back to the village, but it is often closed. The local Belvedere slopes are easy, and for 2007/08 a new gondola replaced the old Toè chair. The village nursery slope is good but inconvenient.

Campitello (1445m/4,740ft) is a pleasant, unremarkable village, smaller and quieter than next-door Canazei, and still unspoiled. It's quiet during the day, having no slopes back to the village. A 2008 visitor recommends the 3-star Gran Paradis (0462 750135) – 'good food and amazing wine list'. Campitello has quite lively après-ski – the Da Giulio bar gets packed. There's an ice rink. A cable car takes you up to the slopes: in high season this can generate 'massive queues at the beginning of the day'. To get home you can take the cable car down or the piste to Canazei and catch a bus.

OTHER TRENTINO RESORTS

Still in the Val di Fassa, close to Canazei, **Alba** has its own slopes, linked to **Pozza di Fassa**. A reporter recommends the 4-star Gran Baita hotel (0462 764163) – 'excellent service'. Over the road from Pozza another small area of slopes is linked to **Vigo di Fassa**. Not far from the valley town of Moena is the lift system of **Alpe Lusia**. Off to the east are more extensive slopes at **Passo San Pellegrino**, linked with **Falcade** in Veneto. There is another lift network at **Passo Costalunga**, linked with **Nova Levante** (Welschnofen) in Alto Adige.

Continuing downstream, you are now in the Val di Fiemme. Near **Predazzo** there is a lift up to the slopes shared with **Pampeago** and **Obereggen**, across the border in Alto Adige. Finally, the town of **Cavalese** has lifts up to the Alpe Cermis slopes – a new quad with covers replaced a drag there for 2007/08.

To the south of the Val di Fassa/Val di Fiemme axis, a steep road over the high **Passo Rolle** – where there is a small network of drags and chairs serving easy slopes on either side of the road – leads down to the resort of **San Martino di Castrozza** (1470m/4,820ft). San Martino has a fabulous setting beneath a soaring wall of Dolomite cliffs and peaks – the Pale di San Martino. The village is not notably cute – there are some large, block-like buildings – but it is pleasant enough. The slopes – which are entirely intermediate in difficulty – are split into three sectors, only two of them linked (at altitude). There's a new terrain park (see 'News').

Trentino

485

Switzerland is home to some of our favourite resorts. Only three resorts in this book are awarded ✶✶✶✶✶ for both resort charm and spectacular scenery – the essentially traffic-free Swiss villages of Wengen, Mürren and Zermatt. Many other Swiss resorts are not far behind. Many resorts have impressive slopes, too – including some of the biggest, highest and toughest runs in the Alps – as well as a lot of good intermediate terrain. For fast, queue-free lift networks, Swiss resorts are not known for setting the standards – too many historic cable cars and mountain railways for that. But the real bottlenecks are steadily disappearing. And there are compensations – the world's best mountain restaurants, for one, and pretty reliable accommodation too.

People always seem to associate Switzerland with high prices. But we believe that's a myth, especially since the euro has strengthened so much against the pound. Recently, we have found most Swiss resorts cheaper or on a par with most French ones – though some Swiss resorts, such as Zermatt, Verbier and St Moritz, do tend to be pricey. What is clear is that what you get for your money in Switzerland is generally first class.

Many Swiss resorts have a special relationship with the British, who invented downhill skiing in its modern form in Wengen and Mürren by persuading the locals to run their mountain railways in winter, and so act as ski lifts, and by organising the first downhill races. An indication of the continuing strength of the British presence in these resorts is that Wengen has an English church.

While France is the home of the purpose-built resort, Switzerland is the home of the mountain village that has transformed itself from traditional farming community (or health retreat) into year-round holiday resort. Many of Switzerland's most famous mountain

486

WENGEN TOURIST OFFICE

Swiss resorts can justly claim some of the most spectacular mountain scenery. This is the Wengen-Grindelwald ski area
↓

↑ There are many charming, unspoiled Swiss resorts. This is the Val d'Anniviers

COEUR DU VALAIS

resorts are as popular in the summer as in the winter, or more so. This creates places with a more lived-in feel to them and a much more stable local community. Many villages are still dominated by a handful of families lucky or shrewd enough to get involved in the early development of the area.

This has its downside as well as advantages. The ruling families are able to stifle competition and prevent newcomers from taking a slice of their action. Alternative ski schools, competing with the traditional, nationally organised school and pushing up standards, are still less common than in other Alpine countries, for example. We are only now beginning to see this grip weakened.

Switzerland means high living as well as high prices, and the swanky grand hotels of St Moritz, Gstaad, Zermatt and Davos are beyond the dreams of most ordinary holidaymakers. (St Moritz now has an amazing five 5-star hotels.) Even in more modest places, the quality of the service is generally high. The trains run like clockwork to the advertised timetable (and often they run to the top of the mountain, doubling as ski lifts). The food is almost universally of good quality and much less stodgy than in neighbouring Austria. Even the standard rustic dish of rösti is haute cuisine compared to Austrian sausages. And in Switzerland you get what you pay for: the cheapest wine, for example, is not cheap, but it is reliable.

Perhaps surprisingly for such a traditional, rather staid skiing nation, Switzerland has gone out of its way to attract snowboarders. Davos may hit the headlines mainly when it hosts huge economic conferences, but yards from the conference hall there are dudes getting big air on the Bolgen slope's training kickers. Little-known Laax claims Europe's best terrain park.

ANZÈRE

EVOLÈNE RÉGION

NAX/MAYA-MT-NOBLE

SION

THYON RÉGION

VEYSONNAZ

+41 (0)848 848 027
www.sion-region.ch

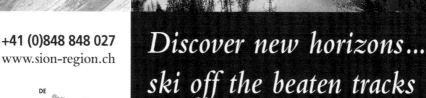

Discover new horizons...
ski off the beaten tracks

Up to 420 km with one skipass

20'000m² snowpark

Family resorts

Ski touring, heliski

GETTING AROUND THE SWISS ALPS

Access to practically all Swiss resorts is fairly straightforward when approaching from the north – just pick your motorway. But many of the high passes that are perfectly sensible ways to get around the country in summer are closed in winter, which can be inconvenient if you are moving around from one area to another.

There are very useful car-carrying trains in various places; they

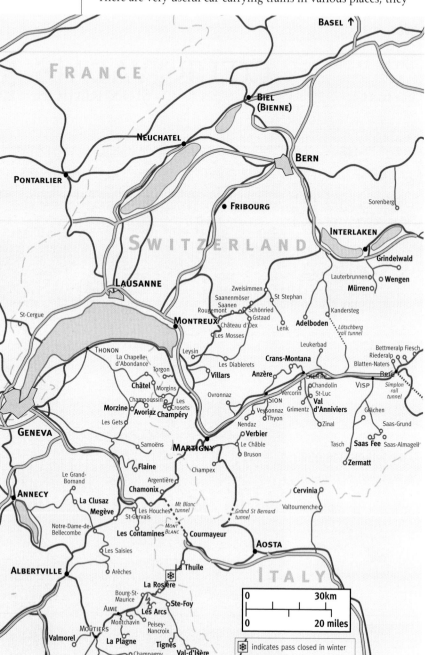

can cut out huge amounts of driving. One key link is between the Valais (Crans-Montana, Zermatt etc) and Andermatt via the Furka tunnel, and another is from Andermatt to the Grisons (Laax, Davos etc) via the Oberalp pass – closed to road traffic in winter but open to trains except after very heavy snowfalls. Another rail tunnel that's very handy is the Lötschberg, linking Kandersteg in the Bernese Oberland with Brig in the Valais. Last year a new tunnel

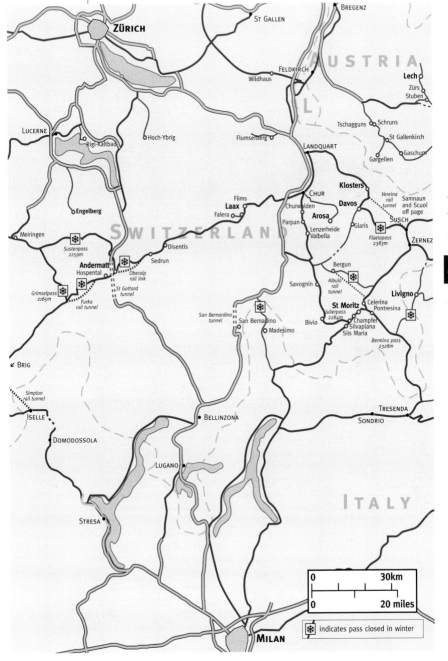

Introduction

Interactive resort shortlist builder at www.wtss.co.uk

opened in parallel – the lower, longer, faster Lötschberg Base Tunnel. But it takes only passenger and freight trains – car-carrying trains continue to use the old tunnel.

St Moritz is more awkward to get to than other resorts. The main road route is over the Julier pass. This is normally kept open, but at 2285m/7,500ft it is naturally prone to heavy snowfalls that can shut it for a time. Fallbacks are car-carrying rail tunnels under the Albula pass and the Vereina tunnel from near Klosters – a relatively new option, opened in 1999.

These car-carrying rail services are generally painless. Often you can just turn up and drive on. But carrying capacities are obviously limited. Some services (eg Oberalp) carry only a handful of cars, and booking is vital. Others (eg Furka, Lötschberg, Vereina) are much bigger operations with much greater capacity – but that's a reflection of demand, and at peak times there may be long queues – particularly for the Furka tunnel from Andermatt, which Zürich residents use to get to the big Valais resorts. There is a car-carrying rail tunnel linking Switzerland with Italy – the Simplon. But most routes to Italy are kept open by means of road tunnels. See the Italy introduction for more information.

To use Swiss motorways (and it's difficult to avoid doing so if you're driving serious distances within the country) you have to buy an annual permit to stick on your windscreen. Permits cost SF40 and are valid for 14 months – from December to the end of January. They are sold at the border, and are, for all practical purposes, compulsory.

Chocolate-box village with plenty to do off the snow – but also with extensive slopes including an area shared with Lenk

COSTS

①②③④⑤⑥

RATINGS

The slopes
Fast lifts	★★★
Snow	★★★
Extent	★★★
Expert	★★
Intermediate	★★★
Beginner	★★★★
Convenience	★★
Queues	★★★
Mountain restaurants	★★★

The rest
Scenery	★★★★
Resort charm	★★★★
Off-slope	★★★★

NEWS

For 2007/08 a fast quad replaced the triple chair from Geils to Lavey, improving the connection to Lenk.

A 500m/1,640ft-long boardercross course opened at Silleren.

It's a splendid setting; the high, shady bowl in the distance is Engstligenalp ↓

+ Traditional, pretty mountain village in a splendid setting

+ Good off-slope facilities

+ Some pleasantly uncrowded slopes linked to Lenk, but ...

– The slopes are fragmented and widely spread – access can be slow

– Few challenges on-piste – though plenty of off-piste opportunities

– Quiet, limited nightlife

Adelboden is unjustly neglected by the international market: for intermediates looking for a relaxing holiday in pretty surroundings – and perhaps spending some time doing things off the slopes – it has a lot of appeal. Surprisingly, the resort literature includes English translations.

THE RESORT

Adelboden fits the traditional image of a Swiss mountain village: old chalets with overhanging roofs line the quiet main street (cars are discouraged), and 3000m/10,000ft peaks make an impressive backdrop. The village is fairly compact, and there are 'infrequent' buses to the outlying areas (most covered on the lift pass) – the ideal location for most people is close to the main street. The Jungfrau resorts (Wengen, Mürren etc) are within day-trip range, as is Gstaad.

THE MOUNTAINS

Adelboden's slopes are split into five varied sectors, spread over a wide area. One sector stretches across to the village of Lenk, with a sixth area of slopes a bus ride across the valley. Piste marking is reportedly poor.
Slopes Village lifts access three of the sectors. A small cable car/gondola hybrid goes up to Tschentenalp, just

above the village. An even smaller one goes down to Oey (where there is a car park). From here, a proper gondola goes up to the Chuenisbärgli sector and then on (in two further stages) to more remote Silleren-Hahnenmoos. This is much the biggest sector, with long, gentle runs (and some short, sharp ones) from 2200m down to 1350m (7,220ft down to 4,430ft) – back to the village and over to Lenk.

Engstligenalp, a flat-bottomed high-altitude bowl, is reached by a cable car 4km/2.5 miles south of the resort; Elsigenalp (with another cable car) is more extensive, but remote.
Terrain parks The Gran Masta Park at Hahnenmoos has jumps, big air, rails, snack bar and chill-out zone. There's a new boardercross run at Silleren, a park at Lenk and a natural playground at Engstligenalp.
Snow reliability Despite unremarkable top heights, most slopes are above 1500m/4,920ft, so snow reliability is reasonable. Tschentenalp often has the best snow on its north-facing slopes. Snowmaking covers over half the main pistes. Grooming is reportedly good.
Experts The few genuine black pistes don't add up to much. But off-piste possibilities are good and don't get tracked out quickly; the Lavey and Luegli chairs in the Geils bowl access routes to Adelboden and Lenk. Engstligenalp has off-piste potential – and is a launching point for tours.
Intermediates All five areas deserve exploration by intermediates. At Geils there is a lot of ground to be covered. Tschentenalp has some gentler off-piste opportunities and is a 'wonderfully quiet' alternative, say reporters. Various timed runs are dotted around the area.

493

Map labels:
2290m
Elsigenalp
ELSIGEN
Elsigbach
1250m
Adelboden
1355m/4,450ft
1645m
1905m
Unter Birg CHUENISBÄRGLI
Oey Boden
1260m
1950m
1540m
TSCHENTENALP
ENGSTLIGENALP
2360m/7,730ft
Geils
1710m
Sillerenbühl
1975m
1960m
Luegli
2140m
Metschstand
2105m
Lavey
2200m
Bühlberg
1665m
SILLEREN-HAHNENMOOS
BETELBERG
Stoss
1645m
Rothenbach
1070m
Lenk
1070m/3,510ft 1135m

KEY FACTS

Resort	1355m
	4,450ft
Slopes	1070-2360m
	3,510-7,740ft
Lifts	56
Pistes	185km
	115 miles
Blue	41%
Red	52%
Black	7%
Snowmaking	64km
	40 miles

UK PACKAGES

Crystal, Interhome, Kuoni, Switzerland Travel Centre

Phone numbers
From elsewhere in Switzerland add the prefix 033; from abroad use the prefix +41 33

TOURIST OFFICE

t 673 8080
info@adelboden.ch
www.adelboden.ch

Beginners There are good nursery slopes in the village and at the foot of nearby sectors. At Geils there are glorious long, easy runs to progress to. Engstligenalp is 'superb'.
Snowboarding Two specialist schools offer lessons. There's a freeride zone at Engstligenalp. The many draglifts are gradually being replaced.
Cross-country There are extensive trails along the valley towards Engstligenalp with its high altitude, snow-sure circuit.
Queues Few problems, say our 2008 reporters. The main access gondolas get busy at peak times, but the minibus service to the main sector is an alternative. The new fast quad from Geils to Lavey has greatly improved the return to Adelboden from that sector, and from Lenk. If snow low down is poor, queues for the Engstligenalp cable car build up.
Mountain restaurants There are numerous pleasant restaurants. The Tschenten Alp is reportedly 'the best' with 'excellent meals'. The self-service Sillerenbühl is highly rated, with good children's areas and live music. The Hahnenmoospass is recommended, as is the restaurant at Aebi.
Schools and guides The main Adelboden school has received mixed reviews but we have no new reports.
Facilities for children Snowlis kindergarten takes children from three to five years. There are snow gardens at Geils, Elsigen and Engstligenalp. Several hotels offer child care.

STAYING THERE

How to go Several UK operators go there, there is locally bookable self-catering, and some 30 pensions and hotels (mainly 3- and 4-star).
Hotels The 4-star Cambrian hotel (673

8383) (formerly the Regina) has been renovated and re-opened for 2008/09. Pool and smart new spa. The central 3-star Adler Sporthotel (673 4141) is pretty, with a sports/wellness centre. The little Bären (673 2151) is a simple but captivating wooden chalet. The Waldhaus-Huldi (673 8500) is 'very welcoming'. The Beau-Site (673 2222) has a good, central location, as does the Viktoria-Eden (673 8888) – 'decent rooms; good breakfast'.
Eating out Possibilities are varied, and include a couple of mountain restaurants. The Bären is 'good value'. Guests on half board can 'dine around' at affiliated hotels twice a week.
Après-ski There are several bars and tea rooms – Cafe Hauetar is recommended. The Time Out bar has a 'good atmosphere'. The Arte Bar offers a bit of artistic flair. Scott's bar (Cambrian hotel) is smart, modern and 'absolutely the best'. The Berna-Bar nightclub is 'surprisingly good'.
Off the slopes There are plenty of activities – indoor and outdoor curling and skating, sleigh rides, toboggan runs, hiking paths, hotel pools open to the public. Some mountain huts are reachable on foot. Special lift passes are available for walkers.

Lenk 1070m/3,510ft

Lenk is a traditional village linked to Adelboden by cable car at Rothenbach, or six-pack from Bühlberg further up the mountain. Both lifts are a bus ride from the centre and 'infrequently timetabled', says a 2008 reporter. Closer to town are the gondola and fast chair serving the local Betelberg slopes (covered on the area lift pass) – a series of gentle reds and blues. There are a couple of 'delightfully quiet', wooded runs back to the valley.

Andermatt

A slow-paced, old-fashioned resort with some great steep, high terrain on- and off-piste (and the snowfall to go with it)

COSTS

① ② ③ ④ ⑤ ⑥

RATINGS

The slopes
Fast lifts	**
Snow	****
Extent	*
Expert	****
Intermediate	**
Beginner	*
Convenience	***
Queues	**
Mountain restaurants	*

The rest
Scenery	***
Resort charm	****
Off-slope	**

NEWS

Work is due to start in 2009 on a luxury development that will eventually include five new hotels and a spa/leisure complex. Plans for a new chairlift on Gemsstock have been shelved for now.

KEY FACTS

Resort	1445m
	4,740ft
Slopes	1445-2965m
	4,740-9,730ft
Lifts	25
Pistes	130km
	81 miles
Blue	23%
Red	50%
Black	27%
Snowmaking	40 km
	25 miles

UK PACKAGES

Alpine Answers, McNab Snowsports, Mountain Tracks, Ski Freshtracks, Ski Weekend, Switzerland Travel Centre

➕ Attractive, traditional village

➕ Excellent snow record

➕ Some excellent steep pistes and great off-piste terrain – plus ski-touring opportunities

➕ Easy access from Zürich

➖ Slopes split into separate, rather limited sectors

➖ Unsuitable for beginners

➖ Limited off-slope diversions

➖ Little English spoken

➖ Busy at weekends

Little old Andermatt was rather left behind in the mega-resort boom of the 1960s and 1970s. If current plans come to fruition (see 'News'), it may soon start to catch up. Meanwhile, its attractions have not faded for those who like their mountains tall, steep and covered in deep powder. It makes a tempting spot for a short midweek break – the residents of Zürich arrive at weekends.

THE RESORT

Andermatt is quite busy in summer and gets weekend winter business, but at other times seems deserted apart from residents of the local barracks. The town is quietly attractive, with wooden houses lining the main street that runs from the central river bridge to the cable car, and some grand churches. In winter, east-west links with the Grisons and the Valais rely on car-carrying trains.

THE MOUNTAINS

Andermatt's local skiing is split over two unlinked mountains, both limited in extent. Most slopes are above the trees and piste marking is slack, which is bad news in a white-out. The lift pass also covers the small Winterhorn area (above Hospental) along the valley, and Sedrun's slopes – 20 minutes away and a popular excursion. The lift pass covers linking trains.
Slopes A two-stage cable car from the edge of the village serves the open, steep, north-facing and usually empty slopes of Gemsstock. Across town is the gentler, sunny Nätschen area.
Terrain parks Gemsstock has one.
Snow reliability The area has a justified reputation for reliable snow. Nätschen gets a lot of sun. Piste grooming is generally good.
Experts It is most definitely a resort for experts. The north-facing bowl beneath the top Gemsstock cable car is a glorious, long, steep slope (about 900m/2,950ft vertical), usually with excellent snow, down which there are

countless off-piste routes, an itinerary and a piste. Outside the bowl, the Sonnenpiste is a fine open red run curling away from the lifts to the mid-station, with more off-piste opportunities. From Gurschen to the village there is a black run, not steep but often tricky. Routes outside the bowl go down the Felsental or Guspis valleys towards Hospental, or steeply into the deserted Untertal, to the east (ending in a bit of a walk). Nätschen and Winterhorn both have black pistes and off-piste opportunities, including worthwhile itinerary routes.
Intermediates Intermediates needn't be put off Gemsstock: the Sonnenpiste can be tackled and there is a pleasant red run and some short blues at mid-mountain. Nätschen's sunny mountain is well worth a visit.
Beginners Not ideal; but the lower half of Nätschen has a long, easy blue run.
Snowboarding The cable car accesses some great freeride terrain.
Cross-country There are 40km/25 miles of loops along the valley.
Queues The Gemsstock cable car can generate queues on fine weekends.
Mountain restaurants The Gadäbar (Gemsstock) is a simple, quiet hut serving 'delicious rösti and strudel'.
Schools and guides Bergschule Uri/Mountain Reality, a guiding outfit run by local big wheel Alex Clapasson, is very pricey. The Swiss ski school has cheaper options. Snowlimit is a specialist snowboard school.
Facilities for children There are slopes they can handle at Nätschen, and the Swiss school does classes. There are children's parks at Realp and Sedrun.

Phone numbers
From elsewhere in Switzerland add the prefix 041; from abroad use the prefix +41 41

TOURIST OFFICE

t 887 1454
info@andermatt.ch
www.andermatt.ch

STAYING THERE

How to go Andermatt's accommodation is in cosy 2- and 3-star hotels.
Hotels Our 2008 reporters have all been greatly impressed by the River House (887 0025), a stylish, upmarket B&B in a 250-year-old building – 'comfortable rooms; charming, helpful staff'. And see 'Eating out'. Gasthaus Sternen (887 1130) is an attractive central chalet with a cosy restaurant and bar. The lovely old 3-star Sonne (887 1226), between the centre and the lift, is welcoming and comfortable. Alpenhotel Schlüssel (888 7088) is 'good value', with spacious rooms.
Apartments Those at hotel Monopol (887 1575) are central and 'very good'.
Eating out We can't wait to try the tiny Alte Apotheke at the River House B&B – 'best food of the trip: wonderful home-made ravioli'. Gasthaus Tell and the Sonne do 'good schnitzel' and Stefano 'very good pizzas'.
Après-ski The bar at the River House is 'excellent, with live music later'; the Spycher and Piccadilly are also popular. The Curva at the hotel Monopol is 'very pleasant'. Dancing at Gotthard livens up at weekends.
Off the slopes There's a toboggan run at Nätschen. The fitness centre at the hotel Drei König is open to the public. There are maintained footpaths.

Hospental 1455m/4,780ft

Hospental is a quiet, old village below Winterhorn's north-facing slopes. From Andermatt, go by bus (SF2) to avoid a long walk up to the lifts from the train station. Two slow lifts serve several pistes, including a black, down the 1000m/3,280ft vertical. Lückli at mid-mountain does 'good food'.

Sedrun 1450m/4,760ft

Sedrun is a sizeable roadside village east of the Oberalp Pass, with the most extensive piste skiing in the area. From a tiny train station at the pass, lifts take you over two ridges to the main slopes around Milez, which go on down to Dieni on the outskirts of Sedrun. There's a good choice of red runs, a rewarding black and a 'freeride' route, plus plenty of scope for off-piste. At Milez there's a terrain park. Sedrun has several hotels and a popular spa centre.

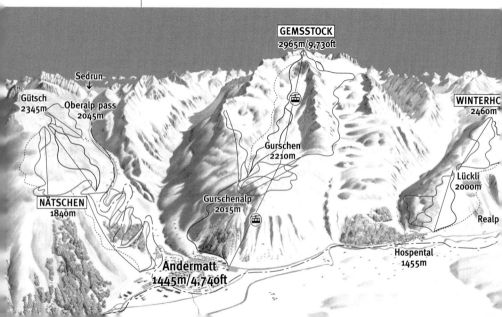

Anzère

Attractive, purpose-built resort set in a sunny position, with spectacular views and a small area of intermediate slopes

COSTS

① ② ③ ④ ⑤ ⑥

RATINGS

The slopes
Fast lifts	**
Snow	**
Extent	*
Expert	**
Intermediate	***
Beginner	***
Convenience	***
Queues	****
Mountain restaurants	***

The rest
Scenery	****
Resort charm	***
Off-slope	***

KEY FACTS

Resort	1500m
	4,920ft
Slopes	1500-2,420m
	4,920-7,940ft
Lifts	11
Pistes	40km
	25 miles
Blue	8%
Red	75%
Black	17%
Snowmaking	7km
	4 miles

UK PACKAGES

Ardmore, Interhome, Lagrange

Phone numbers
From elsewhere in Switzerland add the prefix 027 (Anzère) and 0848 (Coeur du Valais); from abroad use the prefix +41 and omit the initial '0'

TOURIST OFFICES

Anzère
t 399 2800
anzere@
coeurduvalais.ch
www.anzere.ch
Coeur du Valais/Sion
t 848 027
info@coeurduvalais.ch
www.coeurduvalais.ch

+ Attractive and family-friendly with traffic-free central square
+ Sunny intermediate slopes good for leisurely cruising

− Small area of slopes
− Little to interest experts

This small resort set on a sunny shelf with great views over the Rhône valley is little-known on the UK market. Its position and small area of local slopes makes it good for a quiet, relaxing time and for families. It will be of more interest to keen piste-bashers when the planned link to Crans-Montana happens.

THE RESORT

Anzère is an attractive, purpose-built resort dating from 1965. It is set on a sunny plateau at 1500m/4,920ft facing south with spectacular views over the Rhône valley to the 4000m/13,120ft peaks and glaciers beyond. The heart is the traffic-free Anzère village square with shops, restaurants, terraces, a children's area and an ice rink.

THE MOUNTAINS

The village sits at the western end of the ski area, which spreads eastwards to Les Rousses, from where a link to Crans-Montana is planned (but dates haven't been set for this).
Slopes From the western end of the village a gondola takes you up to Pas de Maimbre at 2360m/7,740ft. From there a series of lifts (mostly drags) serves mainly red runs leading to the high point of Le Bâte and a lovely long red run down to Les Rousses.
Terrain parks There is a park.
Snow reliability The slopes are not especially high and face south, so the snow can suffer in warm weather.
Experts There's a 5km/3 mile black run from Pas de Maimbre back to the village served top-to-bottom by snowmaking and a marked ungroomed itinerary. But not much else of interest except off-piste.
Intermediates This is primarily an intermediate resort, with 75 per cent of the runs being red. But with only 40km/25 miles of slopes, keen piste-bashers will find the extent limited.
Beginners There's a village nursery slope and short, easy blue slopes at the top of the gondola.
Snowboarding The snow soon softens in the sun – good for boarding. But there are a lot of draglifts for beginner

boarders to cope with.
Cross-country The 5km/3 mile Go cross-country trail heads off west from the village and is ideal for beginners.
Queues No problems reported.
Mountain restaurants We enjoyed the table-service section of the Pas de Maimbre at the top of the gondola. A reporter recommends Les Rousses at the end of the slope there. We were also taken to a ski school cabin for a lovely mid-morning drink and snack.
Schools and guides We have no reports on either the Swiss School or the rival Glycérine Sliding School.
Facilities for children This is very much a family resort, with a playground in the village square, a toboggan run, and a nursery open from 9am to 4pm Monday to Friday. The ski school takes children from age four.

STAYING THERE

How to go A few small operators run packages here.
Lodging There are three 3-star hotels and lots of apartments.
Eating out For a small place there's a reasonable choice – from gastronomic to pizzerias.
Après-ski As well as seven bars there are three discos. And activities are arranged – such as a vin chaud welcome evening in the village square.
Off the slopes There are 166km/100 miles of marked walks, three snowshoe trails, a parapenting school, an ice rink and a 3km/2 mile toboggan run. Down in the valley, the old town of Sion is at the heart of the Coeur du Valais region of which Anzère is part, and is worth exploring. Attractions include Europe's largest navigable underground lake and walking in the Val d'Hérens, as well as trying the local Valais wines.

Arosa

A classic all-round winter resort, where walking is as much part of the scene as skiing; choose your spot with care

COSTS

① ② ③ ④ ⑤ ⑥

RATINGS

The slopes

Fast lifts	★★★
Snow	★★★
Extent	★★
Expert	★★
Intermediate	★★★
Beginner	★★★★
Convenience	★★
Queues	★★★★
Mountain restaurants	★★★

The rest

Scenery	★★★
Resort charm	★★
Off-slope	★★★★

NEWS

For 2007/08 a mini-funicular opened at the 5-star Tschuggen Grand Hotel, taking guests on to the slopes.

Plans for an Arosa-Lenzerheide lift link are proceeding; if the communities support it, the link could be built in 2009.

KEY FACTS

Resort	1800m
	5,910ft
Slopes	1800-2655m
	5,910-8,710ft
Lifts	13
Pistes	60km
	37 miles
Blue	27%
Red	60%
Black	13%
Snowmaking	30 km
	19 miles

- ➕ Classic winter resort ambience
- ➕ Excellent cross-country loops
- ➕ Few queues
- ➕ Choice of good nursery slopes
- ➕ Relatively good snow reliability
- ➕ Prettily wooded setting, but ...

- ➖ Block-like buildings in main village
- ➖ Spread-out village lacks a heart
- ➖ Slopes too limited for mileage-hungry intermediates
- ➖ Few challenging pistes for experts – though there is good off-piste

Picture it: an isolated, snowy Swiss village, with skating on a frozen lake, horse-drawn sleighs jingling along and people strolling around in fur coats. Arosa offers exactly that. It's just a pity that many of its comfortable hotels date from an era when wood and pitched roofs were out of fashion.

THE RESORT

High and remote, Arosa is in a sheltered basin at the head of a beautiful wooded valley, in sharp contrast to the open slopes above it. It's a long, winding drive or splendid rail journey from Chur (both take just under an hour).

The main resort development is around Obersee – a pretty spot, centred as you might guess on a frozen lake, but spoilt by the surrounding block-like buildings. Lifts go up from here into the Weisshorn sector of the slopes. The rest of Arosa is scattered, much of it spreading up the steep road separating Obersee from the older, prettier Inner-Arosa, where lifts from opposite extremities go up into both sectors of the slopes. Arosa is quiet; its relaxed ambience attracts an unpretentiously well-heeled clientele of families and older people. Very few of them are British. But a 2008 visitor felt very welcome: 'everyone was helpful and friendly'.

Some accommodation is a long walk from the lifts; there are frequent free ski-buses, but they get crowded.

THE MOUNTAINS

Arosa's slopes form a wide, open bowl, facing north-east to south-east, with all the runs returning eventually to the village at the bottom. All the slopes are above the tree line, except those just above Obersee.

Slopes The slopes are spread widely over two main sectors. The major lift junction in the Weisshorn sector is Tschuggen (strangely un-named on the resort piste map), 500m/1,640ft away from the Mittelstation of the Weisshorn cable car, and reachable from both Obersee and Inner-Arosa. From Mittelstation, you can take a chair to the lower peak of Brüggerhorn. The main access to the Hörnli sector is a slow gondola from Inner-Arosa. Well-used walking paths wind across the mountainsides, and great care is needed where they cross the pistes. Piste marking is generally OK, although the long blue run from the Brüggerhorn to Obersee can present problems. Various night-skiing events are held once a week at Tschuggen.

Terrain parks There is a park with jumps, rails and a 150m/490ft long half-pipe.

Snow reliability The slopes are quite high, but the Weisshorn sector gets a lot of sun; the shadier Hörnli slopes hold their snow well. Grooming is good, and snowmaking on the home runs is often used. Snowmaking now covers 30km/19 miles of pistes.

Experts Arosa isn't an obvious target for experts, but there is plenty of gentle off-piste terrain. The Brüggerhorn is generally considered the freeride mountain, and used to be promoted as such; but it no longer features any marked ski routes.

Intermediates This is a good area for intermediates who aren't looking for high mileage or huge challenges. The runs from Hörnli are enjoyable cruises, the black including a short steeper pitch. The Weisshorn runs are generally steeper, with some rewarding reds. The long blue to Obersee from Brüggerhorn via Prätschli is a great way to end the day, with fab views of

Interactive resort shortlist builder at www.wtss.co.uk

UK PACKAGES

Alpine Answers, Crystal Finest, Interhome, Kuoni, Made to Measure, Momentum, Powder Byrne, Ski Weekend, Snow Finders, Snowy Pockets, Switzerland Travel Centre, White Roc

Phone numbers
From elsewhere in Switzerland add the prefix 081; from abroad use the prefix +41 81

TOURIST OFFICE

t 378 7020
arosa@arosa.ch
www.arosa.ch

sunlit peaks from the shady piste.

Beginners The easy slopes up at Tschuggen are excellent and usually have good snow, but they get a lot of through traffic. Inner-Arosa has a quieter, 'gentle' area for kids.

Snowboarding Bananas is the specialist school and Mountain Surf Club offers two-day freeride camps.

Cross-country Arosa's modest 26km/16 miles of loops include some of the best and most varied in the Alps.

Queues Arosa does not suffer from serious queues – even in half-term. The Weisshorn cable car may generate short delays, though they are not generally a problem.

Mountain restaurants There's a fair choice, several with indulgent sunbeds on which you can lunch while sunbathing; Carmennahütte has row upon row of them. A 2008 reporter enjoyed 'fine rösti and delicious soup' there too. Tschuggenhütte has choices for all the family. Alpenblick is 'cosy, friendly', with 'great food' and Hörnli commands a fabulous high position.

Schools and guides Swiss and ABC are the main schools. Class sizes can be large. There's a lot of demand for private lessons.

Facilities for children Arosa's appeal as a family resort has led to Disney endorsement, with 12 hotels and the Swiss Ski school forming the Alpine Club Mickey Mouse. We've had good reviews: 'excellent, friendly instructors who spoke English'. Club Mickey also includes a kindergarten, kids' restaurants and games areas.

STAYING THERE

How to go Arosa is a hotel resort, with a high proportion of 3- and 4-stars. But Snowy Pockets' catered chalet Runca is a welcome departure.

Hotels The 4-star Waldhotel National (378 5555) with direct access to the slopes is 'quite delightful'. The 4-star Sporthotel Valsana (378 6363) has been praised. The 5-star Tschuggen Grand (378 9999) has a spectacular wellness centre (designed by a famous architect) with a dozen treatment rooms, two pools and so on.

Apartments The Paradies apartments are recommended. Quiet, spacious. Pool and sauna.

Eating out Most restaurants are hotel-based, some with a very high reputation. The Kachelofa-Stübli at the Waldhotel National is excellent. The Luna does pasta and Osteria Poltera serves Swiss dishes.

Après-ski Après-ski is quite lively. The Carmenna hotel by the ice rink has a popular piano bar. The Sitting Bull is busy and cheerful. The Grischuna bar and restaurant is worth a try. The Vista is the place to go for dancing and concerts.

Off the slopes There's an indoor pool. You can get a pedestrian's lift pass, and many mountain restaurants are reachable via 60km/37 miles of cleared, marked paths shown on a special map ('my non-skiing wife very much enjoyed her hikes'). Sleigh rides are popular, and there are indoor and outdoor ice rinks. Shopping is limited.

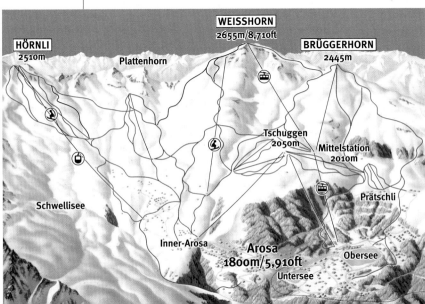

Picture-postcard village that few UK tour operators feature these days, with access to the Portes du Soleil circuit

COSTS

① ② ③ ④ ⑤ ⑥

RATINGS

The slopes

Fast lifts	**
Snow	**
Extent	*****
Expert	***
Intermediate	****
Beginner	**
Convenience	*
Queues	****
Mountain restaurants	***

The rest

Scenery	****
Resort charm	****
Off-slope	***

NEWS

For 2008/09 a fast eight-person chair is due to replace a quad and a drag from Les Crosets towards Champéry.

- ➕ Charmingly rustic mountain village
- ➕ Cable car or fast six-packs take you into the Portes du Soleil circuit
- ➕ Quiet, relaxed – yet plenty to do off the slopes

- ➖ Local slopes suffer from the sun
- ➖ No runs back to the village – and sometimes none back to the valley
- ➖ Not good for beginners
- ➖ Not many tough slopes nearby

Champéry is great for intermediate skiers looking for a quiet time in a lovely place. Access to the Portes du Soleil circuit is not bad: Avoriaz is fairly easy to get to – and there may be good snow there when Champéry is suffering.

THE RESORT

Set beneath the dramatic Dents du Midi, Champéry is a village of old wooden chalets. Friendly and relaxed, it would be ideal for families if it wasn't separated from its slopes by a steep, fragmented mountainside.

Down a steepish hill, away from the main street, are the cable car, sports centre and railway station.

THE MOUNTAINS

Once you get up to them, the local slopes are open, friendly and relaxing.

Slopes Champéry's sunny slopes are part of the big Portes du Soleil circuit, which links resorts in Switzerland and France. The village cable car or a fast six-seat chairlift from Grand Paradis, a short free bus ride from Champéry, go up to Croix de Culet, above the bowl of Planachaux. But many of the lifts on the route from Les Crosets to Morgins via Champoussin are ancient and in dire need of modernisation. If snow is good there are a couple of pistes back to Grand Paradis, with an efficient bus

service back to the village, but no pistes back to Champéry. There is night skiing on Wednesdays and Saturdays until 10pm.

Terrain parks The Superpark is a good terrain park at Les Crosets. The 25 features include gaps, kickers, rails, hips, spines and boxes. The Micropark is for beginners and schools.

Snow reliability The snow on the north-facing French side of the link with Avoriaz is usually better than on the sunnier Swiss side. The local Champéry area would benefit from more snowmaking.

Experts Few local challenges and badly placed for most of the tough Portes du Soleil runs. The Swiss Wall, on the Champéry side of Chavanette, is long and bumpy, but not terrifyingly steep. There's scope for off-piste at Chavanette and on the broad slopes of Les Crosets and Champoussin.

Intermediates Confident intermediates have the whole Portes du Soleil at their disposal. Locally, the runs home to Grand Paradis are good when the snow conditions allow. Les Crosets is a junction of several fine runs. There are

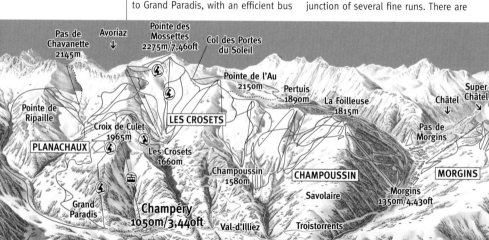

There's a decent choice of mountain restaurants with sunny terraces →

KEY FACTS

Resort	1050m	
	3,440ft	

Portes du Soleil		
Slopes	950-2300m	
	3,120-7,550ft	
Lifts	202	
Pistes	650km	
	404 miles	
Green	13%	
Blue	40%	
Red	37%	
Black	10%	
Snowmaking		
	694 guns	

Swiss side only		
Slopes	1050-2275m	
	3,440-7,460ft	
Lifts	34	
Pistes	100km	
	62 miles	

UK PACKAGES

Alpine Answers, Chalet Group, Erna Low, Ski Freedom, Ski Independence, Ski Weekend, Skitracer, White Roc

Phone numbers
From elsewhere in Switzerland add the prefix 024; from abroad use the prefix +41 24

TOURIST OFFICES

Champéry
t 479 2020
info@champery.ch
www.champery.ch

Les Crosets Champoussin
t 477 2077
info@valdilliez.ch
www.valdilliez.ch

Morgins
t 477 2361
touristoffice@morgins.ch
www.morgins.ch

slightly tougher pistes from Mossettes and Pointe de l'Au, Champoussin's leisurely cruising, and delightful tree-lined meanders to Morgins. A highlight is the quiet, beautiful, long blue from Col des Portes du Soleil to Morgins via the 'cute' restaurant at Tovassière.

Beginners Not good. The Planachaux runs, where lessons are held, are steepish and small and some of the local blue runs are verging on red.

Snowboarding Not ideal for beginners (see above) and there are several draglifts (some quite steep). Good terrain parks in Les Crosets and Avoriaz for experts though, and some good powder areas between pistes.

Cross-country It's advertised as 10km/6 miles with 4km/2 miles floodlit every night, but it's very unreliable snow.

Queues If snow is poor, expect end-of-day queues for the cable car down.

Mountain restaurants Chez Coquoz at Croix de Culet offers lovingly prepared food (try the lamb shank), and a knockout Valais wine list (we loved the Cornalin). Above Champoussin, Chez Gaby does 'marvellous rösti'. The tiny Lapisa on the way to Grand Paradis is delightfully rustic – they make cheese and smoke meat on site. Marmottes by the Rippaille draglift has 'good food and friendly service' and the Toupin near Les Crosets serves 'excellent ham and cheese on toast'.

Schools and guides The few reports that we've had on the Swiss Ski and Snowboard school are free of criticism ('professional but friendly'). The Freeride Co and Redcarpet Snowsport School provide healthy competition.

Facilities for children The tourist office has a list of childminders. The Swiss ski school takes children at age three.

STAYING THERE

How to go Limited packages available. Easy access for independent travellers.

Hotels Prices are low compared with smarter Swiss resorts. The 3-star Beau Séjour (479 5858) is friendly, family-run, with 'large rooms'. The 3-star National (479 1130) has 'excellent food, very friendly and helpful staff'. The Auberge Le Paradis (479 1167) is 'charmingly rustic but noisy'.

Apartments The Lodge has very smart, spacious apartments with good views and contemporary decor.

Eating out Mitchell's is stylish and modern and we enjoyed good Thai spring rolls, shark and reindeer there

in 2007. The Café du Centre has a 'modern Asian menu in a wonderfully restored building'. The Vieux Chalet (hotel Beau Séjour) and the bistro in the hotel National have been praised. Two of the best for local specialities are just outside the village: Cantines des Rives and Auberge Le Paradis.

Après-ski Fairly quiet. But Mitchell's is popular at tea time – big sofas and a fireplace. Below the 'rather seedy' Pub, the Crevasse disco is one of the liveliest places. The Café du Centre has a micro brewery. Try the Bar des Guides in the hotel Suisse, or the Avalanche cellar nightclub.

Off the slopes Walks are pleasant and the railway allows lots of excursions. There's the Swiss national ice sports centre with indoor pool and tennis; plus ice climbing and snowshoeing.

Les Crosets 1660m/5,450ft

A good base for a quiet time and slopes on the doorstep. The 3-star Télécabine hotel (479 0300) has 'basic rooms but extremely helpful staff and the five-course dinner is delicious'.

Champoussin 1580m/5,180ft

A good family choice – no through traffic, near the slopes, with the 3-star Royal Alpage Club hotel (pool, gym, disco, two restaurants – 476 8300).

Morgins 1350m/4,430ft

A fairly scattered, but attractive, quiet resort with a gentle nursery slope. The hotel Reine des Alpes (477 1143) is well thought of, and there are catered chalets. The ESS ski school and village kindergarten have been recommended.

Interactive resort shortlist builder at www.wtss.co.uk

Crans-Montana

Sun-soaked slopes and stunning panoramic views above a big town base – not for those who love powder though

COSTS

①②③④⑤⑥

RATINGS

The slopes

Fast lifts	★★★
Snow	★★
Extent	★★★
Expert	★★
Intermediate	★★★★
Beginner	★★★
Convenience	★★
Queues	★★★
Mountain restaurants	★★★

The rest

Scenery	★★★★
Resort charm	★★
Off-slope	★★★★

NEWS

For 2007/08 links between the main sectors were improved by a six-pack replacing the Nationale chairlift from the mid-station of the Violettes gondola to Cry d'Er. It almost doubled the capacity of the old lift. Snowmaking was also improved.

502

MOMENTUM SKI

Weekend & a la carte ski holiday specialists

100% Tailor-Made

Premier hotels & apartments

Flexible travel arrangements

020 7371 9111
www.momentumski.com

- ➕ Large, varied piste area
- ➕ Splendid setting and views
- ➕ Excellent, gentle nursery slopes
- ➕ Excellent cross-country trails
- ➕ Very sunny slopes, but ...

- ➖ Snow badly affected by sun
- ➖ Large town (rather than village), devoid of Alpine atmosphere
- ➖ Bus or car rides to lifts from much of the accommodation
- ➖ Few challenges except off-piste

When conditions are right – clear skies above fresh, deep snow – Crans-Montana takes some beating: the mountains you bounce down are charmingly scenic, the mountains you gaze at are mind-blowing, and you can forgive Crans-Montana its sprawling layout and towny feel. Sadly, conditions are more often wrong. Except in the depths of winter, the strong midday sun bakes the pistes.

THE RESORT

Set on a broad shelf facing south across the Rhône valley, Crans-Montana is really two towns, their centres a mile apart and their fringes merging. Strung along a busy road, the resort's many hotels, villas, apartments and smart shops are mainly dull blocks with little traditional Alpine character. Crans is the more upmarket part, with fancy shops; it has now had a revamp to make it more pedestrian-friendly.

The resort is reached by road or by a fast funicular railway from Sierre. It has a big summer conference trade; hotels tend to be formal, and visitors dignified. The main gondola stations are above the main road – there is a free shuttle-bus during the day but it can get crowded and is 'not dependable' says a reporter.

There are other gondola bases and places to stay at Les Barzettes and at Aminona. Anzère is nearby, and you can get to Zermatt, Saas-Fee and Verbier by road or rail.

THE MOUNTAINS

Crans-Montana has slopes with few challenges and no nasty surprises, and there is a pleasant mix of open and wooded slopes, but signing is ridiculously slack. The views over the Rhône valley to the peaks bordering Italy are breathtaking.

The slopes The slopes are spread over a broad mountainside, with lifts from four valley bases. Gondolas from Crans and Montana meet at Cry d'Er – an open bowl descending into patchy forest. There is free night skiing here on Fridays. The next sector, focused on Les Violettes, is accessed from Les Barzettes. A new six-pack from the mid-station here up to Cry d'Er opened for 2007/08. Above Les Violettes, a jumbo gondola goes up to the Plaine Morte glacier. The fourth sector is served by a gondola up from Aminona. Some of the runs down to the valley are narrow woodland paths.

Terrain parks Aminona has a good park with features for all levels and a boardercross course. There is a half-pipe at Cry d'Er.

Snow reliability The runs on the Plaine Morte glacier are limited and nearly all the other slopes get a lot of direct sun. There is snowmaking on the main runs, but we have never found good snow on the runs down to the valley. A reporter tells of bare spots just 'two days after a 19-inch dump'.

For experts There are few steep pistes and the only decent moguls are on the short slopes at La Toula. There's plenty of off-piste, particularly beneath Chetseron and La Tza.

For intermediates Pistes are mostly wide, and many of the red runs don't justify the grading. They tend to be uniform in difficulty from top to bottom, with few surprises. Avid piste-bashers enjoy the length of many runs, plus the fast lifts and good links that allow a lot of mileage. The 12km/8 mile run from Plaine Morte to Les Barzettes starts with top-of-the-world views and powder, and finishes among pretty woods. The Piste Nationale downhill course is a good fast cruise.

For beginners There are three excellent nursery areas, including the golf

↑ The views across the Rhône valley from the slopes and many of the restaurants are spectacular

CRANS-MONTANA TOURISME

KEY FACTS

Resort	1500m
	4,920ft
Slopes	1500-3000m
	4,920-9,840ft
Lifts	28
Pistes	140km
	87 miles
Blue	38%
Red	50%
Black	12%
Snowmaking	17km
	11 miles

Phone numbers
From elsewhere in Switzerland add the prefix 027; from abroad use the prefix +41 27

TOURIST OFFICE

t 485 0404
information@crans-montana.ch
www.crans-montana.ch

course fairways which are great learning slopes.

Snowboarding Despite the resort's staid image, boarding is very popular. The Avalanche Pro is a specialist shop and school. The main lifts are chairs and gondolas, and the draglifts are usually avoidable.

For cross-country The 40km/25 miles of trails include a glacier area.

Queues Investment in gondolas has helped cut queues out of the village, and a recent visitor found the slopes were deserted before 10.30. The new six-pack for 2007/08 should have improved access to Cry d'Er from the Violettes/Barzettes sector.

Mountain restaurants There are 21 mountain restaurants, usefully marked on the piste map. Above Crans, Merbé is one of the most attractive (and expensive), Chetseron has good views and Chez Erwin 'gorgeous home-made cake'. Bella-Lui, Cabane des Violettes ('good food at fairly reasonable

prices') and Petit Mont-Bonvin are worth a look.

Schools and guides The Swiss schools have attracted mainly favourable comments over the years.

Facilities for children There's a snow garden and nursery above Montana, but we lack reports.

STAYING THERE

How to go There is a wide choice of hotels and apartments.

Hotels This conference resort has over 50 mainly large, comfortable, pricey hotels. Pas de l'Ours (485 9333) is our favourite – chic and attractive. Aïda Castel (485 4111) is also well-furnished in rustic style. Art de Vivre (481 3312) has a relatively new wellness centre.

Eating out A good variety of places, from French to Lebanese. The best is the Bistrot in the Pas de l'Ours hotel. The Chalet, Plaza, Rafaele's, and Padrino have been recommended. Club de la Nouvelle Rôtisserie doubles as an Indian restaurant and wine bar.

Après-ski There are tents on the hill for late-afternoon drinks, but nightlife and evening atmosphere may disappoint. The George & Dragon in Crans is one of the liveliest bars. Reporters recommend Bar 1900 and the Grange. Recent additions include the Baiser de la Rose and Harry's Club.

Off the slopes There are swimming pools (in hotels), two ice rinks, dog sledding, snow tubing, a cinema and a casino. There are also 60km/37 miles of walking. Sierre and Sion are close.

Crans-Montana

503

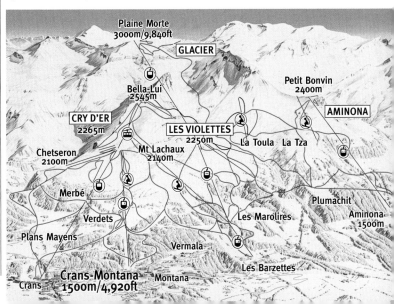

Plaine Morte
3000m/9,840ft

GLACIER

Bella-Lui
2545m

Petit Bonvin
2400m

CRY D'ER
2265m

LES VIOLETTES
2250m

La Toula   La Tza

AMINONA

Chetseron
2100m

Mt Lachaux
2140m

Merbé

Plumachit

Verdets

Les Marolires

Aminona
1500m

Plans Mayens

Vermala

Crans-Montana
1500m/4,920ft

Montana

Les Barzettes

Crans

A grey urban sprawl at the centre of a glorious Alpine playground (for skaters and langlaufers as well as downhillers)

COSTS

① ② ③ ④ ⑤ ⑥

RATINGS

The slopes
Fast lifts	***
Snow	****
Extent	*****
Expert	****
Intermediate	*****
Beginner	**
Convenience	**
Queues	***
Mountain restaurants	***

The rest
Scenery	****
Resort charm	**
Off-slope	*****

NEWS

For 2007/08 the valley run to Davos Dorf was extended to finish closer to the Parsenn bottom station. Snowmaking was increased on all five mountains.

Several hotels were revamped and a new igloo village opened on Parsenn.

504

+ Very extensive slopes

+ Some superb, long, and mostly easy pistes away from the lifts, with trains to bring you back to base

+ Lots of accessible off-piste terrain, with several marked itineraries

+ Good cross-country trails

+ Plenty to do off the slopes – from skating to shopping

− Davos is a huge, city-like place with dreary block-style buildings, plagued by traffic, lacking Alpine atmosphere and après-ski animation

− Slopes spread over five separate areas

− Lots of T-bars, and some other inadequate lifts

− The only piste back to town from the main Parsenn area is a black

One of your editors learned to ski in Davos, so it has a special place in our affections. Many return visits have confirmed the appeal of its slopes, which are both distinctive and extensive – you could say it was the original mega-resort – and have revealed its considerable off-piste potential. But the town/city (it could never be called a village) does not get any easier to like, however familiar it becomes. Davos may be the more convenient base for access to most of the mountains it shares with Klosters but, when choosing a place to stay, for us there is no contest: Klosters has the welcoming, intimate feel of a ski resort, and Davos does not.

THE RESORT

Davos is set in a high, broad, flat-bottomed valley, with its lifts and slopes either side. Arguably it was the very first place in the Alps to develop its slopes. The railway up the Parsenn was one of the first built for skiers (in 1931), and the first draglift was built on the Bolgen nursery slopes in 1934. But Davos was already a health resort; many of its massive luxury hotels were built as sanatoriums.

Sadly, that's just what they look like. There are still several specialist clinics and it is for these, along with its conferences and sporting facilities, that Davos has become well known. The place has the grey, neat, rectilinear feel of a Swiss lowland city rather than the ambience of a mountain village.

It has two main centres, Dorf and Platz, about 2km/1 mile apart. Transport is good, with buses around the town as well as the railway linking Dorf and Platz to Klosters and other villages. Easiest access to the slopes is from Dorf to the main Parsenn area, via the funicular railway; Platz is better placed for the Jakobshorn area, the big sports facilities, the smarter shopping and the evening action.

Trips are possible by car or rail to St Moritz (via the Vereina rail tunnel) and Arosa, and by road to Laax-Flims and Lenzerheide – but none of them is quick enough to have wide appeal.

Although the resort is reachable by train, the trip from Zürich airport involves two changes. The Davos Express coach transfer service is a recommended alternative. Or you can take the Graubünden Express service from Friedrichshafen airport.

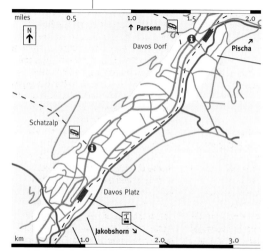

↑ Wooded slopes rise steeply from the valley floor, with gentler, open slopes higher up

KEY FACTS

Resort	1550m
	5,090ft
Slopes	810-2845m
	2,660-9,330ft
Lifts	58
Pistes	305km
	190 miles
Blue	20%
Red	44%
Black	36%
Snowmaking	50km
	30 miles

THE MOUNTAINS

Davos shares its slopes with the famously royal resort of Klosters, which gets its own chapter. They have something for everyone, though experts and nervous intermediates need to choose their territory with care. Piste classification has been questioned by a reporter, who felt that there 'did not seem to be much difference between blue and red runs'. The piste map generally looks clear, but tries to cover too much ground in a small space – at some points, it is simply misleading. Signposting is generally good, but a lack of edge marking has been criticised.

THE SLOPES
Vast and varied
You could hit a different mountain around Davos nearly every day for a week. The out-of-town areas tend to be much quieter than the ones directly accessible from the resort.

The Parsennbahn funicular from Davos Dorf ends at mid-mountain, where a choice of fast six-pack or old funicular take you on up to the major lift junction of Weissfluhjoch, at one end of the **Parsenn**. The only run back to the valley is a black that used to end on the outskirts of Dorf, but now finishes in the centre, close to the bottom station. At the other end of the wide, open Parsenn bowl is Gotschnagrat, reached by cable car from the centre of Klosters. There are exceptionally long intermediate runs down to Klosters and other villages (see feature panel).

Across the valley, **Jakobshorn** is reached by cable car or chairlift from Davos Platz; this is popular with snowboarders but good for skiers too. **Rinerhorn** and **Pischa** are reached by bus or (in the case of Rinerhorn) train.

Pischa is now a designated freeride area, with half the runs left ungroomed and just three main lifts. Several of the runs here are now unpatrolled as well as ungroomed – a very unusual arrangement for runs going down beside a lift, and one we don't like. This year a visitor tells us that one had 'dual purpose markers – so it could be operated either as a black or a ski route, by switching the poles'. Bizarre.

Beyond the main part of Klosters, a gondola goes up from Klosters Dorf to the sunny, scenic **Madrisa** area.

There are too many T-bars for the comfort of some reporters – Rinerhorn and Pischa have little else. It's time Davos invested in more chairs.

TERRAIN PARKS
Lots of choice
All four of the surrounding mountains have terrain parks; the main one is the Sunrise park on Jakobshorn – home to the O'Neill Evolution contest. It is open as early as November, weather permitting, and is by far the best in the area. There is a good variety of jumps and rails, and a large number of boxes including a nice C-box. But the park is quite narrow, and can feel cramped when busy. Two floodlit pipes are the training grounds for a host of Swiss professionals such as Michi Albin, and evening sessions until 9.30pm are popular with locals. For smaller crowds but a less well-maintained park, head to Pischa; next to the Mitteltäli lift you'll find an array of rails and kickers. There are two boardercross courses, one at Parsenn; the other on Madrisa, 200m/66oft below the top of the Schaffürggli lift. There is also a mini park for beginners next to the Trainer lift in Rinerhorn.

SNOW RELIABILITY
Good, but not the best

Davos is high by Swiss standards. Its mountains go respectably high, too – though not to glacial heights. Not many of the slopes face directly south, but Pischa does suffer from excessive sun. Snow reliability is generally good higher up. It can be poor lower down, but in 2007 (considered a poor snow year) the lower runs were reportedly functional into late March. Snow-guns cover a few of the upper runs on the Parsenn, several on the Jakobshorn, and the home runs from the Parsenn to Davos Dorf and Klosters. Piste grooming is generally good; but some runs on Parsenn are said to be 'poorly maintained' – in particular, the super-long runs to the valley.

FOR EXPERTS
Plenty to do, given snow

The appeal of this area for experts depends to a degree on the snow conditions. Although there are challenges to be found at altitude, most of the rewarding runs descend through the woods to valley level, and are not reliable for snow.

The black pistes include some distinctive, satisfying descents. The Meierhofer Tälli run to Wolfgang is a favourite – quite steep, narrow and 'exciting'. The run from Parsennhütte to Wolfgang is less challenging; it probably owes its black status due to one short 'tricky' section.

There are also some off-piste itineraries – runs that are supposedly marked but not patrolled. At one time,

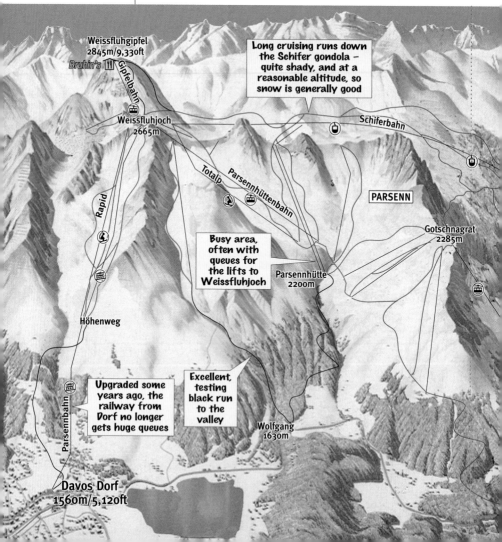

Weissfluhgipfel
2845m/9,330ft
Bruhin's
Gipfelbahn

Long cruising runs down
the Schifer gondola –
quite shady, and at a
reasonable altitude, so
snow is generally good

Weissfluhjoch
2665m

Schiferbahn

Totalp

Parsennhüttenbahn

PARSENN

Rapid

Busy area,
often with
queues for
the lifts to
Weissfluhjoch

Gotschnagrat
2285m

Parsennhütte
2200m

Höhenweg

Upgraded some
years ago, the
railway from
Dorf no longer
gets huge queues

Parsennbahn

Excellent,
testing
black run
to the
valley

Wolfgang
1630m

Davos Dorf
1560m/5,120ft

The runs from Weissfluhjoch that head north, on the back of the mountain, make this area special for many visitors. The pistes that go down to Schifer and then to Küblis, Saas and Serneus, and the one that curls around the mountain to Klosters, are a fabulous way to end the day, given good conditions. If you are based in Davos, the return journey is by train (included in the lift pass).

The runs are classified red but are not steep. The latter parts can be challenging – they are not reliably groomed, and you need to remember that you are at low altitudes by the end (1190m/3,900ft at Klosters, 810m/2,560ft at Küblis). Signposting is not always good, either.

What marks these runs out is their sheer length (10-12km/6-7 miles) and the resulting sensation of travel they offer – plus a choice of huts in the woods at Schifer and lower down on the way to Klosters (see 'Mountain restaurants'). You can descend the 1100m/ 3,610ft vertical to Schifer as often as you like and take the gondola back. Once past there, you're committed to finishing the descent.

508

SWITZERLAND

Weekly news updates and resort links at www.wtss.co.uk

LIFT PASSES

Davos/Klosters

Prices in SF

Age	1-day	6-day
under 13	23	100
13-18	46	200
over 18	65	285

Free under 6
Senior no deals
Beginner no deals

Notes
Covers all Davos and Klosters areas

Alternative passes
Individual and combined areas (eg Parsenn/Gotschna, Jakobshorn, Pischa/ Rinerhorn/ Madrisa); pedestrian single tickets

Phone numbers
From elsewhere in Switzerland add the prefix 081; from abroad use the prefix +41 81

these runs were a key attraction for adventurous skiers not wanting to pay for guidance, but over the decade to 2005 no fewer than 10 of them disappeared from the map, including the infamous Gotschnawang run down the top stage of the Klosters cable car and its less fearsome neighbours, Drostobel and Chalbersäss. Many of these abandoned runs have had piste status at some time in the past, and are not difficult to follow if you know what you are doing. Two of the most satisfying itineraries that remain are the long ones from the top of Jakobshorn, both with restaurants at the end where a good lunch can be had. The start of the run to Mühle is not obvious, which has led more than one reporter into difficulty; once found, the run is 'nowhere steeper' than a tough red'. The run to Teufi is more often closed: it goes first down a steep 200m gulley, but thereafter is 'not difficult'.

There is also excellent 'proper' off-piste terrain, for which guidance is more clearly needed. Reporters have enjoyed heading away from the pistes above Serneus and Küblis. The long descent from Madrisa to St Antönien, north of Küblis, is popular, not least for the 'spectacular views' along the way. And there are some short tours to be done. Arosa can be reached with a bit of help from a train or taxi, and from there you can go on to Lenzerheide, but you'll need a train back. From Madrisa you can make circular tours to Gargellen in Austria.

FOR INTERMEDIATES
A splendid variety of runs
For intermediates this is a great area. There are good cruising runs on all five mountains, so you would never

get bored in a week. This variety of different slopes, taken together with the wonderful long runs to the Klosters valley, makes it a compelling area with a unique character.

As well as the epic runs described in the feature panel there is a beautiful away-from-the-lifts run to the valley from the top of Madrisa back to Klosters Dorf via the Schlappin valley (it's an easy black – classified red until the mid-1990s).

The Jakobshorn has some genuine challenges, notably by the Brämabüel drag. Rinerhorn is more of a cruise. Pischa is the gentlest of the Davos mountains but now branded as freeride territory; in good snow it should be a decent spot for first attempts at skiing ungroomed stuff.

FOR BEGINNERS
Platz is the more convenient
The Bolgen nursery slope beneath the Jakobshorn is adequately spacious and gentle, and a bearable walk from the centre of Platz. But Dorf-based beginners face more of a trek out to Bünda – unless staying at the hotel of the same name. There is no shortage of easy runs to progress to, spread around all the sectors. The Parsenn sector probably has the edge, with long, easy intermediate runs in the main Parsenn bowl, as well as in the valleys down from Weissfluhjoch.

FOR CROSS-COUNTRY
Long, scenic valley trails
Davos is a popular spot for langlauf. It has a total of 75km/47 miles of trails running along the main valley and reaching well up into the side valleys of Sertigtal, Dischmatal and Flüelatal. There is a cross-country ski centre and special ski school on the outskirts.

SCHOOLS

Swiss Davos
t 416 2454

Top Secret
t 413 4043

Inandout Sports
t 413 0888

Fullmoons
t 420 1477

Pat. Skilehrer Rageth
t 416 3901

Schneeportlehrer Sieber
t 416 1246

Classes
(Swiss prices)
6 4hr days SF310

Private lessons
Half day SF200

CHILDREN

Kinderland Pischa
t 416 1313
Ages from 3; 11am to 4pm

Bobo Club
t 416 2454
Ages 4 to 10;
10am-noon, 2pm-4pm

Babysitter list
At tourist office

Ski school
Takes ages 5 to 14 (6 days SF310)

GETTING THERE

Air Zürich 160km/ 99 miles (2hr by car, 3hr by rail or bus)

Rail Stations in Davos Dorf and Platz

UK PACKAGES

Alpine Answers, Alpine Weekends, Crystal, Crystal Finest, Descent International, Flexiski, Headwater, Independent Ski Links, Inghams, Interhome, Kuoni, Made to Measure, Momentum, Oxford Ski Co, Ski Freshtracks, Ski Independence, Ski Safari, Ski Solutions, Ski Weekend, Skitracer, Switzerland Travel Centre, White Roc

QUEUES
Few problems mid-week

Davos has improved its key lifts and now generates relatively few complaints, at least midweek ('none longer than three minutes', says a March visitor). But there are still long queues at peak times. The weekend hot spots are the cable car out of Klosters and the Totalp chair on the mountain at Parsenn. Crowded pistes have raised concern – in the Parsenn sector around Weissfluhjoch especially. In contrast, the Jakobshorn is said to be quiet.

MOUNTAIN RESTAURANTS
Stay high or go low

The main high-altitude restaurants are dreary self-service affairs – but there are exceptions. Overall, reports are mixed – slow service a regular comment.

Editors' choice The best is the highest of all: Bruhin's at Weissfluhgipfel (417 6644) – a great place for a hang-the-cost blow-out, with table service of excellent rustic as well as gourmet dishes, and some knockout desserts. **Worth knowing about** The Gruobenalp at Gotschnagrat is 'well-liked' with 'friendly table service'. There are other compelling places lower down in the Parsenn sector. Readers enjoy the Höhenweg at the Parsennbahn mid-station for 'excellent pizzas' and 'quick service, even when busy'. There are several rustic 'schwendis' in the woods on the way down to the Klosters valley: the cosy Chesetta gets good reviews, with its 'super sun terrace'. These are fun places to end up as

darkness falls – some sell wax torches for your final descent.

On Jakobshorn the Jatzhütte near the terrain park is wild – with changing scenery such as mock palm trees, parrots and pirates. One 2007 visitor enjoyed the 'small and cosy' Chalet Güggel on Jakobshorn: 'fast service and tasty portion of cured meat with asparagus'. On Pischa, the Mäderbeiz at Flüelamäder is a friendly and spacious woody hut, cheering on a cold day. On Rinerhorn, the Hubelhütte is the best bet.

There are several handy valley restaurants; the Kulm at Wolfgang is rated 'one of the best' and the Gotschnastübli at Serneus has 'brilliant food and service'; the Alpenrose at Dorfji (Pischa) is also praised.

SCHOOLS AND GUIDES
Decent choice

There are several options. Reporters have praised friendly, English-speaking instructors at the main Swiss school – 'both my kids had a terrific time'. Top Secret now incorporates the former New Trend ski school and offers small groups (maximum of six). Swissfreeride is a new guiding company offering all-inclusive off-piste weeks.

FACILITIES FOR CHILDREN
Not ideal

Davos is a rather spread-out place in which to handle a family. The kids' ski school operates a special Disney-themed slope at Bolgen. We're told the nursery is 'well organised, but even the best instructors may slip into German'.

boarding

Davos is now part of the 'top snowboard resort' alliance. In conjunction with Val d'Isère, Ischgl and Madonna di Campiglio, the resort is working toward providing top-quality facilities for sideways sliders. The mountain has a lot to offer confident riders in terms of powder, tree runs, natural hits, cliffs and gullies. The established boarder mountain is the Jakobshorn with its 'monster-pipes', park and boardercross as well as night-riding facilities and funky Jatzhütte. The terrain is vast and will keep any boarder entertained for a long time. The Pischa has a freeride area with a large chunk of terrain left ungroomed and a park by the Mitteltäli lift. One reporter says, 'There are no problems with crowds. The powder is amazing, and there are endless kicker-building spots with loads of windlips and cliff drops.' There are wide, mellow slopes for beginners on Parsenn; however, watch out for the flats on the long runs down to the Schifer gondola. Top Secret (www.topsecretdavos.ch) is a specialist snowboard shop and school. There are several cheap hotels geared to snowboarders, notably the 180-bed Bolgenhof near the Jakobshorn, the Snowboardhotel Bolgenschanze and the Snowboarders Palace.

SKI SOLUTIONS.com

Stop surfing!

Call the human ski-holiday search engine

020 7471 7700

E-mail
sales@skisolutions.com

Get the cost of this book back when you book – details page 11.

ABTA C6711 ATOL Protected 4055

ACTIVITIES

Indoor Fitness centres, tennis, squash, swimming pools, sauna, solarium, massage, wellness centres, ice rink, cinema, casino, galleries, museums, libraries, badminton, golf-driving range

Outdoor Over 97km/ 60 miles of cleared paths, ice climbing, snowshoeing, tobogganing, ice rink, curling, sleigh rides, hang-gliding, paragliding

TOURIST OFFICE

t 415 2121
info@davos.ch
www.davos.ch

STAYING THERE

HOW TO GO
Hotels dominate the packages
Although most beds are in apartments, hotels dominate the UK market.
Hotels A dozen 4-stars and about 30 3-stars form the core. The tourist office runs a central booking service.
*****Flüela** (410 1717) The more atmospheric of the 5-star hotels, in central Dorf. Pool.
****Waldhuus** (417 9333) Convenient for langlaufers. Quiet, modern, tasteful. New pool and spa facility.
****Sunstar Park** (413 1414) At far end of Davos Platz. Pool, sauna, games room. Recommended by a couple of reporters. Spa facilities.
****Meierhof** (416 8285) Close to the Parsenn funicular. 'Large rooms and good food.' Pool, sauna.
***Davoserhof** (414 9020) Our favourite. Small, old, beautifully furnished, with excellent food; well placed in Platz.
***Panorama** (413 2373) In central Platz. Recommended by a reporter for 'excellent, good value' food. Piano bar.
***Hubli's Landhaus** (417 1010) 5km/ 3 miles out at Laret. Quiet country inn with sophisticated, expensive food. Highly recommended by a reporter.
Alte Post (414 9020) Traditional, cosy; in central Platz. Popular with boarders.
Ochsen (414 9020) Good-value dormitory accommodation.

EATING OUT
Wide choice, mostly in hotels
In a town this size, you need to know where to go – if you just hope to spot a suitable place to eat, you may starve. For a start, get the tourist office's pocket guidebook. The more ambitious restaurants are mostly in hotels. There are two good Chinese places – the lavish Zauberberg in the

Europe and the Goldener Drachen in the Bahnhof Terminus. Good-value places include the jolly Al Ponte (pizza and steak both approved of), the Carretta (good for home-made pasta), the small and cosy Gentiana (with an upstairs stübli), and the hotel Dischma's Röstizzeria. Excursions out of town are popular. The Höhenweg is open in the evenings, but you have to pay to ride the funicular. Schatzalp (also reached by a funicular), the Schneider and the Landhaus in Frauenkirch have been recommended.

APRES-SKI
Lots on offer, but quiet clientele
There are plenty of bars, discos and nightclubs, and a large casino in the hotel Europe. But we're not sure how some of them make a living – Davos guests tend to want the quiet life. At tea time, mega-calories are consumed at the Weber, and the Schneider might be worth a look. The Scala (hotel Europe) has a popular outside terrace. The liveliest place in town is the rustic little Chämi bar; popular with locals. The smart Ex-Bar attracts a mixed age group. Nightclubs tend to be sophisticated, expensive and lacking atmosphere during the week. The pick are the Cabanna, Cava Davos (both in the hotel Europe), Rotliechtli, and Paulaner's. Bolgenschanze and Bolgen-Plaza attract lots of boarders.

OFF THE SLOPES
Great, apart from the buildings
Looks aside, Davos has lots to offer the non-skier/rider. The towny resort has shops and other diversions, and transport along the valley and up on to the slopes is good – though the best of the mountain restaurants are well out of range. The sports facilities are excellent; Europe's biggest natural ice rink is supplemented by artificial rinks, both indoor and outdoor. Spectator events include speed skating as well as 'hugely popular' ice hockey. And there are lots of walks on the slopes as well as around the lake and along the valleys (special map available). There's a toboggan run on Rinerhorn, floodlit twice weekly, but the best in the area is the longer run on Madrisa, at Klosters. The Eau-là-là leisure centre incorporates pools and wellness facilities. A reader recommends the local museums and galleries. Day trips to St Moritz and Chur are possible.

One of the biggest verticals in the Alps with some snow-sure slopes and epic off-piste runs

RATINGS

The slopes

Fast lifts	★★★
Snow	★★★
Extent	★★
Expert	★★★★
Intermediate	★★★
Beginner	★★★
Convenience	★
Queues	★★
Mountain restaurants	★★★

The rest

Scenery	★★★★
Resort charm	★★
Off-slope	★★★★

NEWS

For 2008/09 the cable car to Brunni is being upgraded and will carry more passengers. The base station is also being moved from the centre of town to the nursery slope at Klostermatte behind the monastery. For 2007/08 a new table-service mountain restaurant opened at Stand and more snowmaking was installed.

+ Close to Zürich airport

+ Predominantly north-facing slopes keep their snow well

+ Some classic off-piste runs

– Fragmented slopes

– Town is spread out and it's a long walk or bus ride from town to lifts

– Limited piste area

The short transfer from Zürich airport and the large number of hotels and apartments makes Engelberg great for short breaks. It has one of the biggest verticals in the Alps, awesome off-piste and some good intermediate slopes.

THE RESORT

Engelberg was popular with Brits in the early 20th century, and its grand Victorian hotels, some recently renovated, have been joined by chalet-style buildings and concrete blocks. It is more of a town than a village, and it's a free shuttle-bus ride or long walk to the lifts from most hotels. There is one traffic-free cobbled street, and skiers on bicycles going to and from the lifts are a common sight. The resort was named after the 12th-century Benedictine monastery (Engelberg means the mountain of the angel) that dominates the town as you look down from the lifts.

THE MOUNTAINS

The main slopes rise almost 2000m/6,560ft above the town by three successive lifts: a gondola and two cable cars, the top one rising above glacial crevasses and rotating 360° on the way to Klein Titlis at 3030m/9,940ft. A second area of slopes, Brunni, is much smaller, largely intermediate and reached by a cable car from the other side of town. There's also a small kids'/nursery area behind the monastery, and an area just for walking and tobogganing, reached by a gondola up the valley.

Slopes The pistes in the main area are limited and fragmented by the glaciers and rugged terrain. There are two main sectors, both above the treeline: Titlis-Stand and Jochpass. Titlis-Stand is served by the two successive cable cars that are accessed from Trübsee at the top of the gondola out of town; there are three chairs and a drag here too. This area gives access to the two epic off-piste runs mentioned under 'Experts' below. From Trübsee, you can also head for Jochpass via a two-way chairlift to Alpstübli. At Jochpass the top is served by a fast six-pack, with another couple of chairs lower down. Brunni's slopes are sunnier and gently wooded, and served by a chair and a T-bar above the cable car.

Terrain parks The park is at Jochpass, with quarter-pipe, kickers and rails.

511

Titlis 3240m/10,630ft
Klein Titlis 3020m
Glacier
Jochstock 2565m
Fürenalp 1840m
2450m
Stand 2430m
Schonegg 2040m
Jochpass 2205m
TITLIS
Laub
Engstlenalp
Brunnihütte 1860m
Alpstübli
Trübsee 1800m
Ristis 1605m
Obertrübsee
BRUNNI
Klostermatte
Engelberg 1050m/3,440ft
Gerschnialp 1260m
Untertrübsee

KEY FACTS

Resort	1050m
	3,440ft
Slopes	1050-3020m
	3,440-9,910ft
Lifts	25
Pistes	82km
	51 miles
Blue	28%
Red	56%
Black	16%
Snowmaking	some

Phone numbers
From elsewhere in
Switzerland add the
prefix 041; from
abroad use the prefix
+41 41

TOURIST OFFICE

t 639 7777
welcome@
engelberg.ch
www.engelberg.ch

Snow reliability The high, north-facing slopes of Titlis and Jochpass keep their snow well and have a longer season than Brunni's sunnier slopes. The resort says 50% of the resort is snow-sure, including glacial runs and those with snowmaking.

Experts There is superb off-piste for experts who hire a guide. The classic Laub run is 1000m/3,280ft vertical down an immensely wide face with a consistent pitch and magnificent views of town. We enjoyed even more the 2000m/6,560ft vertical Galtiberg run, which starts over glaciers and trees among mountain streams and trees: we saw only three other people on it. You catch a bus back to town from the end of it. There's plenty more off-piste, too. There are few black pistes but lots of easily accessed off piste at the top of Titlis, and the itinerary route from there to Stand is seriously steep and usually mogulled.

Intermediates Most runs are steep reds and there are few easy cruises. The good snow on the reds at the top of the rotating cable car, along with the views, make it worth the trip to the top (catch the cable car down to avoid the itinerary mentioned above). The Jochpass area is often quieter than Titlis, with enjoyable red and blue runs, including long ones to town.

Beginners There's a good isolated beginner area, Gerschnialp, near the mid-station of the gondola, served by draglifts, and others at Trübsee and Untertrübsee. But you have to catch lifts up and down to use them and there are no ideal runs to progress to.

Snowboarding The beginner area is served by draglifts, so it's not ideal. But there is excellent freeriding if you hire a guide. Beware of the flat start to the runs down from Jochpass.

Cross-country There are 44km/27 miles in total with valley trails and loops at altitude. The 1.5km/1 mile World Cup route near the sports centre in town is floodlit two nights a week.

Queues Weekend queues can be long, especially for the gondola out of town. Sometimes the old funicular and cable car running parallel to the gondola operate to alleviate queues.

Mountain restaurants The Ritz (at the Gerschnialp beginner area and the bottom of the Laub run) and Jochpass are rustic table-service places.

Schools and guides As well as the Swiss ski and snowboard school there are two others, Prime/Boardlocal and

Active Snow Team. The local guiding outfit is Outventure (611 1441).

Facilities for children The ski school takes children from age three, and the kindergarten from two. Some hotels offer child care, and the tourist office has details of babysitters.

STAYING THERE

How to go There are many hotels and B&Bs and apartments. Chalet Espen (637 2220), which opened for 2007/08, is a catered chalet owned by a British couple ('very comfortable, friendly hosts, excellent food, a relatively short walk from the lift').

Hotels The 3-star Europe (639 7575) and Schweizerhof (637 1105) are centrally located (the latter with 'very comfortable rooms, pleasant public areas, tasty food'). Also 3-starred, the 'very grand' art nouveau Terrace (639 6666) is above the centre, reached by a free three-minute funicular trip. The recently renovated Alpenclub (637 1243) is a friendly, central guest house with popular restaurant.

Eating out There is a huge variety of restaurants – more than 50 – from traditional Swiss to Tex Mex (at the Yucatan), Chinese (Moonlight) and Indian (Chandra at the Terrace hotel). Try the Schweizerhaus for a Swiss/French gourmet blow out and the Alpenclub – 'great for pizza and traditional cheesy fare'. Once a month there is a dining trip to Titlis and there are also sleigh and fondue evenings.

Après-ski At the bottom of the gondola, the Chalet has a big terrace and a popular happy hour, while in the main square the Yucatan happy hour is 'really something'. The party at the Yucatan continues till late, and the CC bar and Eden are popular for dancing, along with the Spindle nightclub. Recent visitors 'enjoyed a trip up to the Terrace Hotel for a preprandial G&T – perfect for a relaxed drink'.

Off the slopes The 12th-century monastery and its cheese-making shop are worth a visit, and as Engelberg is a real town, there's quite a range of shops. It's worth taking a trip up the rotating cable car to the top for the views and a tour around the ice grotto. There are also many winter walking and snowshoeing trails, an igloo building at Trübsee (you can stay the night there), tubing and a good sports centre. Spa treatments are available at the Eienwäldli hotel.

Traditional resort in a spectacular setting – but slow lifts and dodgy natural snow-cover

COSTS

① ② ③ ④ ⑤ ⑥

RATINGS

The slopes

Fast lifts	****
Snow	**
Extent	***
Expert	**
Intermediate	****
Beginner	***
Convenience	**
Queues	**
Mountain restaurants	***

The rest

Scenery	*****
Resort charm	****
Off-slope	****

NEWS

On Kleine Scheidegg in 2007/08 the Honegg drag was replaced with a six-pack with covers, a new black run was built from First to Bort and the first part of a three-year project to increase snowmaking substantially was completed. For 2008/09 it is planned that 50% of the slopes in the Kleine Scheidegg/ Männlichen area will have snowmaking.

For 2009/10 there are plans to replace the Salzegg drag to Eigergletscher with a six-pack.

➕ Dramatically set in magnificent scenery, directly beneath the towering north face of the Eiger

➕ Lots of long, gentle runs, ideal for intermediates, with links to Wengen

➕ Pleasant old village with long mountaineering history

➕ Fair amount to do off the slopes, including splendid walks

➖ Main slopes accessed by a painfully slow, queue-prone gondola or by slow trains

➖ Few challenging pistes for experts

➖ Inconvenient for visiting Mürren

➖ Natural snow-cover unreliable (but snowmaking is at last being increased)

➖ Village gets little midwinter sun

For stunning views from the town and the slopes, there are few places to rival Grindelwald. The village is nowhere near as special as Mürren or Wengen, just over the hill, but staying here does give you direct access to Grindelwald's own First slopes. But you can spend ages queueing for, waiting for or sitting in the gondola or trains up into the slopes (and back down if snow is poor). (The gondola ride – the longest in Europe according to Grindelwald's literature – takes half an hour. The train to Kleine Scheidegg from Grindelwald takes about the same.) Grindelwald regulars accept all this as part of the scene.

THE RESORT

Grindelwald is set either side of a road along a narrow valley. Buildings are mainly traditional chalet style. Towering mountains rise steeply from the valley floor, which means that the resort and main slopes get very little sun in January.

Grindelwald can feel very jolly at times, such as during the ice-carving festival in January, when huge ice sculptures are on display along the main street. The village is livelier at night than the other Jungfrau resorts of Wengen and Mürren. There's live music in several bars and hotels, but it isn't a place for bopping until dawn.

The main lifts into the slopes shared with Wengen are at Grund, right at the bottom of the sloping village. Near the opposite end of the village, a gondola goes to the separate First area. Trains run from the centre to Grund or direct to Kleine Scheidegg, and buses link the lift stations – but these get congested at times and reporters say that they are too infrequent.

The most convenient place to stay for the slopes is at Grund. But this is out of the centre and rather charmless. There's a wide range of hotels in the heart of the village, handy enough for everything else, including the First area, at the foot of which are nursery slopes, ski school and kindergarten.

Trips to other resorts are not very easy, but you can drive to Adelboden. Getting to the tougher, higher slopes of Mürren is a lengthy business unless you go to Lauterbrunnen by car.

THE MOUNTAINS

The major area of slopes is shared with Wengen and offers a mix of wooded runs and open slopes higher up. The smaller First area is mainly open, though there are wooded runs to the village.

THE SLOPES
Broad and mainly gentle
From Grund, near the western end of town, you can get to **Männlichen** by an appallingly slow two-stage gondola or to **Kleine Scheidegg** by an equally slow cog railway. The slopes of the

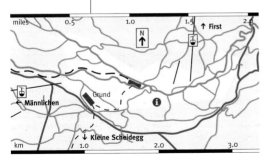

KEY FACTS

Resort	1035m
	3,400ft

Jungfrau region	
Slopes	945-2970m
	3,100-9,740ft
Lifts	44
Pistes	213km
	132 miles
Blue	35%
Red	45%
Black	15%
Snowmaking	85km
	53 miles

First-Männlichen-Kleine-Scheidegg	
Slopes	945-2485m
	3,100-8,150ft
Lifts	28
Pistes	160km
	99 miles
Snowmaking	75km
	47 miles

LIFT PASSES

Jungfrau Top Ski Region

Prices in SF

Age	1-day	6-day
under 16	29	148
16 to 19	46	236
20 to 61	57	295
over 62	51	266

Free under 6

Beginner points card

Notes
Covers Wengen, Mürren and Grindelwald, trains between them and Grindelwald ski-bus; day pass price is for First-Kleine Scheidegg-Männlichen area only

Alternative passes
Grindelwald and Wengen only; Mürren only; non-skier pass

UK PACKAGES

Alpine Answers, Crystal, Elegant Resorts, Independent Ski Links, Inghams, Interhome, Kuoni, Made to Measure, Momentum, Mountain Tracks, Powder Byrne, Ski Freshtracks, Switzerland Travel Centre, Thomson, White Roc

separate south-facing **First** area are reached by a long, slow gondola starting a bus ride east of the centre.

From all over the slopes there are superb views, not only of the Eiger but also of the Wetterhorn and other peaks. Piste marking is poor; several reporters found the Männlichen slopes, in particular, confusing ('marking is non-existent'). The piste map is clear, but huge.

TERRAIN PARKS
First things first
There is a terrain park on First with rails, boxes and jumps; plus a separate super-pipe.

SNOW RELIABILITY
Improved snowmaking may help
Grindelwald's low altitude means that natural snow is often in short supply or in poor condition. First is sunny, and so even less snow-sure than the main area. Last season was good for snow but 2007 was very poor, and one reporter said that she didn't ski at all on her long weekend ('just a few bare runs open'); others found key runs closed and had to download at the end of the day ('virtually no snow below 1400m'). We have also had reports of 'patchy' piste grooming. However, the resort's much-needed three-year project to increase snowmaking is under way; they tell us that by 2008/09, 50% of the slopes in the Kleine Scheidegg-Männlichen area will be covered by snowmaking. We look forward to receiving reports on the effectiveness of this.

FOR EXPERTS
They are trying
The area is quite limited for experts, but there is some fine off-piste if the snow is good. Heli-trips with mountain guides are organised. The black run/downhill route on First beneath the gondola back to town is quite tough, especially when the snow has suffered from the sun. A new black was built last season from First to join this.

FOR INTERMEDIATES
Ideal intermediate terrain
In good snow, First makes a splendid intermediate playground, though the general lack of trees makes the area less friendly than the larger Kleine Scheidegg-Männlichen area. The runs to the valley are great fun. Nearly all the runs from Kleine Scheidegg are

long blues or gentle reds. On the Männlichen there's a choice of gentle runs down to the mid-station of the gondola – and in good snow, down to the bottom. For tougher pistes, head for the top of the Lauberhorn lift and the runs to Kleine Scheidegg, or to Wixi (following the World Cup downhill course). The north-facing run from Eigergletscher to Salzegg often has the best snow late in the season.

FOR BEGINNERS
Depends where you go
The Bodmi nursery slope at the bottom of First is scenic but not particularly convenient, according to a recent reporter who says, 'The chore of getting to and from it with small children was too much.' It can also suffer from the sun and its low altitude – a recent reporter said Grindelwald instructors used it despite it being icy, full of craters and spoiled by fast skiers and tobogganers racing through. A section of the Oberjoch blue run at First is a designated slow speed zone. Kleine Scheidegg has a better, higher beginner area and splendid, long runs to progress to, served by the railway.

FOR CROSS-COUNTRY
Good but shady
There are 17km/10 miles of prepared tracks. Almost all of this is on the valley floor, so it's shady in midwinter and may have poor snow later on.

QUEUES
Can be dreadful
We still receive mixed reports on queues. Waiting times for the gondola and train at Grund can be very bad in high season, especially at weekends – partly because children up to 15 can ski free on Saturday if a parent buys a day pass. Some reporters have told of half-hour waits for the gondola, which then takes a further half-hour to get to the top – a 2007 reporter experienced not only this but 'big queues to download at the end of the day', too, when the lower runs were closed.

MOUNTAIN RESTAURANTS
Wide choice
See the Wengen chapter for options around Kleine Scheidegg and down towards Wengen. Brandegg, on the railway, is recommended for 'wonderful' apple fritters and its sunny terrace; Berghaus Bort does 'very good Alpler macaroni'. The table-service

SCHOOLS

Grindelwald Sports
t 854 1290
Buri Sport
t 853 3353
Snowsports Kleine Scheidegg
t 855 1545
Privat
t 853 0473

Classes (Sports prices) 5 (4hr) days SF395
Private lessons
SF75 for 1hr for 1 or 2 persons

CHILDREN

Kinderhort Sunshine
t 854 8080
Ages from 1mnth to 8yr; 8.30-5pm
Kinderhort Murmeli
t 077 414 9108
9.30-4.30; ages 6mnth to 7yr
Snowli Kinderclub
t 854 1290
From age 3; 9.30-4pm
Felix Ski Paradies
t 853 1288
From age 3;
10pm-3pm

Ski schools
Take children from age 3 or 4 (5 half days SF180)

boarding

Intermediates will enjoy the area most – the beginners' slopes can be bare, while experts will hanker for Mürren's steep, off-piste slopes. First is the main boarders' mountain, not only because of the terrain-park and big pipe but also because of the open freeride terrain accessed via the top lifts. There are quite a few drags.

restaurant at the Berggasthaus at the top of the Männlichen has splendid views, and a 2007 reporter says that 'the fillet of beef on toast was a highlight' and that the self-service section does good 'home-made hamburgers'. Other reader recommendations are the Jägerstubli, off the Rennstrecke piste, and the Berghaus Aspen ('huge portions'), above Grund. The Spycher has a cosy indoor bar plus deckchairs and an ice-bar, which also serves sandwiches. At First, Café Genepi, at the bottom of the Oberjoch chair, is 'a must' for Flammenkuchen (thin pizza) and a good place to begin your après-ski, says a recent visitor.

SCHOOLS AND GUIDES
Mixed views
Recent reports declare the main school, Grindelwald Sports, 'very good'; spoken English is normally excellent. But one reporter had a 'wasted' first day, because abilities were not assessed before the class. However, 'the teachers (three in three days!) were excellent'. The Privat school offers off-piste guiding.

FACILITIES FOR CHILDREN
Good choice
The First mountain restaurant runs a day nursery, which is a neat idea, and the Kinderhort Sunshine is a nursery at the top of Männlichen.

STAYING THERE

HOW TO GO
Limited range of packages
The hotels UK tour operators offer are mainly at the upper end of the market.
Hotels There's a 5-star, seven 4-stars and plenty of more modest places.
*****Grand Regina (854 8600) Big and imposing; right next to the station. Fifty rooms were refurbished in 2007. Nightly music in the piano bar. A recent reporter found it 'expensive but friendly, with good food, pool and amazing spa'. Another praised its 'excellent food and superb service'.
****Belvedere (854 5757) 100 years old, family-run, close to the station. 'Wonderful' pool. Recommended by a recent visitor on his fifth stay.
****Schweizerhof (854 5858) Chalet at west end of the centre, close to the station. Pool.
****Spinne (854 8888) Central. A

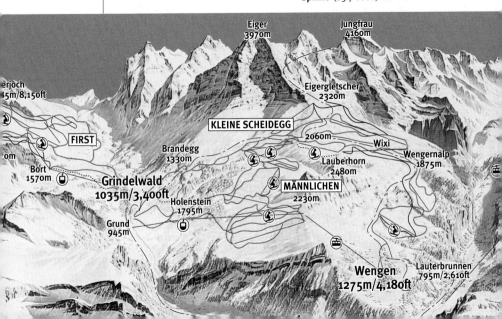

516

↑ Kleine Scheidegg with the north face of the Eiger towering above it

GRINDELWALD TOURISMUS

GETTING THERE

Air Zürich 195km/ 121 miles (3hr); Bern 70km/43 miles (1½hr)

Rail Station in resort

ACTIVITIES

Indoor Sports centre (pool, sauna, steam, fitness), ice rink, curling, museum, cinema

Outdoor 80km/ 50 miles of cleared paths, ice rink, tobogganing, snowshoeing, climbing, tubing, glacier tours, sleigh rides

Phone numbers From elsewhere in Switzerland add 033. From abroad use the prefix +41 33.

TOURIST OFFICE

t 854 1212
touristcenter@
grindelwald.ch
www.grindelwald.com

reporter 'cannot praise it enough: friendly, superb food, good rooms'.
***Hirschen (854 8484) Family-run; by nursery slopes. Good food.
***Derby (854 5461) Popular, modern, next to station, with 'first-class' service, good food and great views.
***Eigerblick (854 1020) A bit away from the station but 'great service, including free taxi'. Huge bedrooms.
*Wetterhorn (853 1218) Cosy, simple chalet way beyond the village, with great views of the glacier.
Apartments Readers have recommended those in the Hirschen and Eiger hotels.

EATING OUT
Hotel based

There's a wide choice of good hotel restaurants. Among the more traditional places are: Bistro-Bar Memory in the Eiger hotel; Schmitte in the Schweizerhof; Challi-Stübli in the Kreuz ('good meal and atmosphere'); and the Alte Post. The Kirchbühl and Oberland are good for vegetarians. Hotel Spinne has an Italian option and – for a special romantic meal – the candlelit Rôtisserie. The C&M Cafe und Mehr is 'well priced and friendly'.

Onkle Tom's Hütte has been recommended for pizza. The Latino does Italian home cooking.

APRES-SKI
Getting livelier

Tipirama at Kleine Scheidegg is a fun place immediately after skiing ('vibrant and welcoming'), sometimes with DJs and live bands. For 'unforgettable' speciality coffees try the Rancher bar, says a recent reporter. The Holzer bar is also suggested as a good drinking spot on the way down to Grund. In town, the terrace of the C&M Café und Mehr is good for coffee and cake. A handful of bars aim to keep going late. The Espresso bar in the Spinne hotel seems to be the liveliest and the Hotel Eiger has a couple of choices. From there, people head for the Mascelero club.

OFF THE SLOPES
Plenty to do, easy to get around

There are many cleared paths with magnificent views, especially around First – and there's a special (though expensive) pedestrian bus/lift pass. Many of the mountain huts are accessible to pedestrians. A trip to Jungfraujoch is spectacular (see below), and excursions by train are easy to Interlaken. There are 70km/ 43 miles of toboggan runs, including the world's longest (15km/9 miles) – but it's a two-and-a-half-hour uphill walk from the top of the gondola on First. There's a cinema, ice hockey and curling to watch and an excellent sports centre with pool. Helicopter flights from Männlichen are recommended.

STAYING UP THE MOUNTAIN
Several possibilities

See the Wengen chapter for details of rooms at Kleine Scheidegg. The Berghaus Bort (835 1762), at the gondola station in the middle of the First area, is an attractive alternative.

THE JOURNEY TO THE TOP OF EUROPE

From Kleine Scheidegg you can take a train through the Eiger to the highest railway station in Europe – Jungfraujoch at 3450m/11,320ft. The journey is a bit tedious – you're in a tunnel except when you stop to look out of two galleries carved into the sheer north face of the Eiger – magnificent views over to Männlichen, and then over the glacier. At the top is a big restaurant complex. There's an 'ice palace' carved out of the glacier and a viewing tower with fabulous views of the Aletsch glacier (a UNESCO World Heritage Site).

The cost for 2007/08 was SF52 with a Jungfrau lift pass for three days or more.

Ski the extensive slopes of Davos from a traditional village base –
with Davos traffic at last banished to a bypass

COSTS

① ② ③ ④ ⑤ ⑥

RATINGS

The slopes
Fast lifts	★★★
Snow	★★★★
Extent	★★★★★
Expert	★★★★
Intermediate	★★★★★
Beginner	★★★
Convenience	★★
Queues	★★
Mountain restaurants	★★★

The rest
Scenery	★★★★
Resort charm	★★★★
Off-slope	★★★★

NEWS

For 2007/08 a two-seat chair replaced the Zügenhüttli draglift on Madrisa, and the cross-country trails were made free to use.

Snowmaking was increased across all five sectors in the region.

ALAN SHEPHERD

Halfway down one of the long, easy runs to Schifer ↓

➕ Splendid, long intermediate runs to the village from the Parsenn

➕ Lots of accessible off-piste terrain

➕ Some cute mountain restaurants

➕ Pleasant traditional village, now bypassed by the valley traffic

➕ Very extensive slopes, shared with Davos, but ...

➖ The slopes are spread over five widely separated areas

➖ Preponderance of T-bars is a problem for some visitors

➖ Queue-prone cable car into the main Parsenn area

In a word association game, 'Klosters' might trigger 'Prince of Wales'. The resort has even named its queue-prone cable car after him. Don't be put off: Klosters is not particularly exclusive, and it does have a lot going for it. The relaxed, chalet-style village has always been an attractive alternative to staying in towny Davos, with which it shares its slopes; more so since 2005, when a bypass road removed the intrusive Davos and Vereina tunnel traffic from the village. It is far from traffic-free, but pedestrians no longer go in fear of their lives.

THE RESORT

Klosters is a comfortable, quiet village with a much more appealing Alpine flavour than Davos. Klosters Platz is the main focus – a collection of upmarket, traditional-style hotels around the railway station, at the foot of the steep, wooded slopes of Gotschna. Traffic bound for Davos and the Vereina rail tunnel, once an acute problem, now takes a bypass. The village spreads along the valley road, fading into the countryside; then you come to the even quieter village of Klosters Dorf, at the base of the gondola to Madrisa. The local bus service is good; but timetable information for Davos services is not easily found, according to one visitor.

THE MOUNTAINS

Most of the runs are on open slopes above steeper woodland.

Slopes A cable car from the railway station in Platz takes you to the Gotschnagrat end of the Parsenn area shared with Davos, and a gondola from Dorf takes you up to the scenic Madrisa area. There's also a little slope at Selfranga (floodlit some evenings), a suburb of Platz.

Terrain parks The Madrisa area has a boardercross course, and there are more options on the other mountains.

Snow reliability It's usually good higher up. The home runs are quite low, but are now equipped with snowmaking.

Experts The lift-served off-piste possibilities are the main appeal of the area– see Davos.

Intermediates There are excellent cruising runs in all five ski areas. Check out our Davos chapter for details.

Beginners There is a slope between Dorf and Platz, plus Selfranga; but the slopes of Madrisa are more appealing.

Snowboarding Local slopes are good, but more boarders stay in Davos.

Cross-country There are 35km/22 miles of trails and lots more up at Davos; a Nordic ski school offers lessons. Trails are now free to use.

Queues Queues for the Gotschna cable car can be a problem at weekends and peak times. A double chair has

517

KEY FACTS

Resort	1190m
	3,900ft
Slopes	810-2845m
	2,660-9,330ft
Lifts	58
Pistes	305km
	190 miles
Blue	20%
Red	44%
Black	36%
Snowmaking	50km
	30 miles

UK PACKAGES

Alpine Answers, Crystal Finest, Descent International, Flexiski, Inghams, Kuoni, Made to Measure, Momentum, Mountain Tracks, Oxford Ski Co, Powder Byrne, Ski Expectations, Ski Freshtracks, Ski Independence, Ski Safari, Ski Solutions, Ski Weekend, Snow Finders, Switzerland Travel Centre, White Roc

Phone numbers
From elsewhere in Switzerland add 081; from abroad use the prefix +41 81

TOURIST OFFICE

t 410 2020
info@klosters.ch
www.klosters.ch

---

replaced the Zügenhüttli draglift on the local Madrisa slopes.

Mountain restaurants There are a number of atmospheric huts in the woods above the village – see Davos chapter. The main restaurant on Madrisa is adequate, but a better option is to take the black run to the valley for lunch at the woody Erika at Schlappin – 'delicious local food'.

Schools and guides There is a choice. Saas is well regarded for good, English-speaking instructors and 'fun' private lessons, though one group got two instructors during their week. Adventure-Skiing is praised this year for private guiding.

Facilities for children The ski schools offer 'excellent' classes for children, and the Madrisa Kids' Land takes two to six year olds.

STAYING THERE

How to go There is a wide choice of packages offered by UK tour operators.

Hotels There are some particularly attractive hotels. For most people, central Platz is the best location. Here, the smart Chesa Grischuna (422 2222) combines traditional atmosphere with modern comfort. The readers' favourite is the 'wonderful' Alpina (410 2424) – 'friendly and helpful staff'. Excellent spa facilities. The 2-star Bündnerhof (422 1450), 400m/1,300ft from the train/lift station is good value. Next door, the very cosy old Wynegg (422 1340) is a perennial British favourite. In Dorf, the Sunstar Albeina (423 2100) is convenient for Madrisa and cheaper than the other 4-stars, has a good spa

and is 'very comfortable, friendly', with 'excellent food'. The Sport (423 3030) is 'pleasant with good facilities', and there's also the Sport-Lodge (422 1256) in Platz.

Apartments Apartments are available through local agencies.

Eating out Good restaurants abound, but a reporter comments that there are few cheap and cheerful places. Top of the range is the Walserhof, with two Michelin stars – 'one of the best meals we've had', says a 2008 visitor. Al Berto's serves 'wonderful' pizza, and the Alpina is recommended. The Casanna at Platz serves 'excellent steaks', and the Chesa Grischuna is recommended for 'fabulous venison' and good wines at moderate prices. Fellini's pizzeria is 'child-friendly'.

Après-ski In the village, the Chesa Grischuna is a focus from teatime onwards, with its live music. Gaudy's at the foot of the slopes is a popular stop after skiing 'if you're happy to drink in a tent', as is the lively bar at the 4-star Alpina and the warmly panelled Wynegg. The Rossli bar is the place to watch sport on TV. The It's Bar is new (opposite hotel Rustico). The Casa Antica is a small disco that livens up on Saturday night.

Off the slopes Klosters is an attractive base for walking (there's a special map available) and cross-country skiing – hiking to Schifer is 'a nice adventure'. Tobogganing is popular – there is an exceptional 8.5km/5 mile run from Madrisa to Saas. There is a leisure centre with an ice rink, and some hotel pools are open. Train outings can include the old town of Chur.

Pleasant, unremarkable villages – but with high, wide, sunny slopes that are slowly attracting more international attention

+ Extensive, varied slopes ideal for intermediates, shared with Flims

+ Impressive lift system with few queues most of the time

− Sunny orientation can cause icy or slushy pistes and bare lower runs

− Long walks or bus rides from some lodgings

− Quiet in the evenings

Laax, marketed in the past and in the summer as Flims, is a slumbering giant – in terms of piste quantity, one of Switzerland's biggest resorts – that has been waking up for the past decade. We've had a minor flood of enthusiastic reports this year, so perhaps it is at last finding its proper place on the UK market.

THE RESORT

The village of Laax – now called Laax Dorf – is a quiet holiday resort with pleasant suburbs spreading around a lake. Just outside it is a big, busy lift base/hotel/parking complex, formerly Murschetg but now known as Laax. The rebranding of the whole resort as Laax begins to make sense when you learn that a new 1,000-bed apartment/hotel development is under way here.

The slopes spread across to the second major lift base of Flims Dorf. This is the original resort village; it doesn't add up to much (shopping is limited) but is more appealing now that through-traffic uses a new bypass tunnel. Flims Waldhaus is a leafy suburb with no lifts, but it has smart hotels (which run courtesy buses). The free public ski-buses are 'infrequent'.

A further base is Falera – a quiet though much-expanded rustic village at the foot of its own fast chairlift.

THE MOUNTAINS

The villages share extensive, varied slopes beneath high, exposed peaks, with a small glacier. There are some treelined runs. Road trips are possible to Lenzerheide, Klosters and Arosa.

The resort piste map shows a growing number of ungroomed 'freeride routes'; apparently they are avalanche-protected and patrolled.

Slopes There are big gondolas into the slopes from both Flims Dorf and Laax (alongside a cable car of exceptional length). Above mid-mountain, there is a complex web of lifts and runs. A six-pack serves the main Flims slopes at Mutta Rodunda. The glacier offers

519

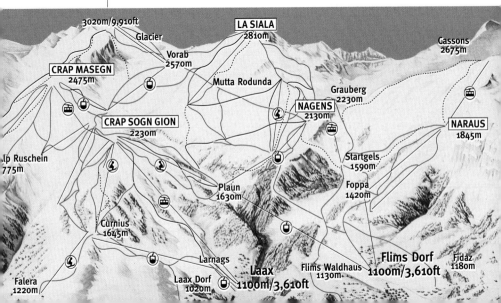

3020m/9,910ft
Glacier
Vorab 2570m
CRAP MASEGN 2475m
LA SIALA 2810m
Cassons 2675m
Mutta Rodunda
Grauberg 2230m
NAGENS 2130m
NARAUS 1845m
CRAP SOGN GION 2230m
lp Ruschein 775m
Startgels 1590m
Plaun 1630m
Foppa 1420m
Curnius 1645m
Larnags
Falera 1220m
Laax Dorf 1020m
Laax 1100m/3,610ft
Flims Waldhaus 1130m
Flims Dorf 1100m/3,610ft
Fidaz 1180m

↑ It's a huge, sunny area, mostly open

WENDY-JANE KING

NEWS

For 2008/09 the first phase of the huge Rocksresort complex is due to open at Laax.

KEY FACTS

Resort	1100m
	3,610ft
Altitude	1100-3020m
	3,610-9,910ft
Lifts	27
Pistes	220km
	137 miles
Blue	29%
Red	32%
Black	39%
Snowmaking	25km
	16 miles

UK PACKAGES

Alpine Answers, Crystal Finest, Erna Low, Made to Measure, McNab Snowsports, Ski Expectations, Snow Finders, Switzerland Travel Centre
Flims Alpine Answers, Crystal Finest, Interhome, Made to Measure, Momentum, Powder Byrne, Ski Freshtracks, Ski Safari, Ski Weekend, Skitracer, Switzerland Travel Centre, White Roc

Phone numbers
From elsewhere in Switzerland add the prefix 081; from abroad use the prefix +41 81

TOURIST OFFICE

For **Flims, Laax and Falera**
t 927 7777
info@
flimslaaxfalera.ch
www.laax.com

limited vertical, but also accesses a superb black run (and a new 'freeride' alternative) away from the lifts to Alp Ruschein – 1250m/4,100ft vertical.
Terrain parks The 'very impressive' terrain park at Crap Sogn Gion is claimed to be Europe's best. There are three areas plus, they say, Europe's largest pipe. Regular high-profile competitions are held here. The glacier sometimes has a half-pipe.
Snow reliability Upper runs are fairly snow-sure, but those back to Flims can suffer from sun. The runs from Cassons and the glacier are prone to closure. Snowmaking is still limited, despite increases. Grooming is good.
Experts The black pistes present few challenges, but the 'freeride routes' add a lot, and there is abundant off-piste terrain too. Timing your runs can be crucial, to avoid rock-hard moguls.
Intermediates This is a superb area for all intermediates. Reporters are often surprised by the extent and length of the slopes. The bowl below La Siala is huge and gentle. For the more confident, there are plenty of reds and some easy blacks. The sheltered Grauberg valley is a favourite – long and fast. The long black Sattel run from the glacier is challenging only at the top. The men's Downhill piste from Crap Sogn Gion to Larnags is excellent.
Beginners There are nursery lifts up the mountain at Crap Sogn Gion and Nagens. The Foppa and Curnius areas have good, easy runs to move on to.
Snowboarding This is a snowboard hot-spot. Apart from the terrain park, there's good freeriding to be had. Novices may find the number of flat/uphill stretches of piste tricky.
Cross-country There are 60km/37 miles of trails scattered around.
Queues Few problems, even in peak season. There can be short delays getting out of the villages at weekends and there may be queues for the isolated chair at Alp Ruschein. High winds can close the upper lifts.

Mountain restaurants About one-third of the 17 restaurants are described on the piste map. The Alpenrose (Startgels) is a firm favourite ('glorious views', 'top-notch grills'). There are some stylish modern table-service places at altitude – Das Elephant and Capalari. Tegia Curnius still does 'good food' and Segneshütte has a 'pleasant' terrace. The Vorab is 'the best self-service'. Lower down are the smartly rustic Tegia Larnags ('best schnitzel') and cosy Runcahöhe.
Schools and guides Rave reviews this year for kids' classes – 'outstanding'.
Facilities for children Children aged three and over can be looked after at one of three newly improved Kinderlands. There's a Kids Village in the ski school. Nannies are available.

STAYING THERE

How to go Only a handful of UK tour operators feature Laax or Flims.
Apartments The tourist office has a long list of available apartments.
Hotels At Laax lift-base the high-tech Riders Palace (927 9700) is a trendy place to stay. Laax Dorf offers the charming little Posta Veglia (921 4466). In Waldhaus the Adula (928 2828) has 'great spa facilities' and 'surprisingly good' food. The award-winning Park Hotel (928 4848) is popular with families: 'superb'; 'lovely pool'. In Flims Dorf the Vorab (911 1861), the Cresta (911 3535) ('fantastic pool') and the Arena (920 9393) get the nod.
Eating out In Laax Dorf the Posta Veglia does excellent food in a lovely old stube, and in a plainer room behind. In Flims, reporters recommend the Adula and Cavi Gilli (old farmhouse near the church) for fine dining, the Vorab, the Veneziana ('excellent pizzas and service'), Little China (Park hotel), the Central ('good, hearty meals') and the 'charming' Da Nus.
Après-ski There are busy bars at both main lift bases at close of play – the Iglu ('a good atmosphere') and the Legna are popular. Later on, the villages are pretty quiet. In Flims Dorf, the 'cosy' Segnes wine bar and the Living Room, with log fire and 'delicious' homemade cakes, are suggested. Casa Veglia, in Laax Dorf, has live bands.
Off the slopes There's an enormous sports centre on the edge of Flims, with ice rink, and 60km/37 miles of marked walks. Shopping is limited.

The dinky, car-free mountain village where the British invented downhill ski racing; stupendous views from one epic run

COSTS

① ② ③ ④ ⑤ ⑥

RATINGS

The slopes

Fast lifts	****
Snow	***
Extent	*
Expert	***
Intermediate	***
Beginner	**
Convenience	***
Queues	***
Mountain restaurants	**

The rest

Scenery	*****
Charm	*****
Off-slope	***

NEWS

For 2007/08 a free disco on the open-air ice rink took place on certain evenings. In good weather there was also an open-air cinema with woollen blankets provided.

There are plans to replace the chairlift from Winteregg with a high-speed quad, but not until 2009/10.

miles   0.5
↑ down to Lauterbrunnen
Allmendhubel
ℹ
Schilthorn ←
N ↑
↓ down to Stechelberg
km   0.5   1.

WENGEN-MÜRREN-
LAUTERBRUNNENTAL AG

Mürren is set on a sunny shelf high above the valley floor and with spectacular views ➔

➕ Tiny, charming, traditional village, with 'traffic-free' snowy paths

➕ Stupendous scenery, best enjoyed descending from the Schilthorn

➕ Good sports centre

➕ Good snow high up, even when the rest of the region is suffering

➖ Extent of local pistes very limited, no matter what your level of expertise

➖ Lower slopes can be in poor condition

➖ Quiet, limited nightlife

Mürren is one of our favourite resorts. There may be other mountain villages that are equally pretty, but none of them enjoys views like those from Mürren across the deep valley to the rock faces and glaciers of the Eiger, Mönch and Jungfrau: simply breathtaking. Then there's the Schilthorn run – 1300m/4,270ft vertical with an unrivalled combination of varied terrain and glorious views.

But our visits are normally one-day affairs; holidaymakers, we concede, are likely to want to explore the extensive intermediate slopes of Wengen and Grindelwald, across the valley. And that takes time.

It was in Mürren that the British more or less invented modern skiing. Sir Arnold Lunn organised the first ever slalom race here in 1922. Some 12 years earlier his father, Sir Henry, had persuaded the locals to open the railway in winter so that he could bring the first winter package tour here. Sir Arnold's son Peter has been a regular visitor since he first skied here in November 1916.

THE RESORT

Mürren is set on a shelf high above the valley floor, across from Wengen, and can be reached only by cable car from Stechelberg (via Gimmelwald) or from Lauterbrunnen (via Grütschalp where you change to catch a train). You can't fail to be struck by Mürren's beauty and tranquillity. Paths and narrow lanes weave between little wooden chalets and a handful of bigger hotel buildings – all normally blanketed by snow.

A two-stage cable car takes you up to the high slopes of Birg and the Schilthorn. Nearby lifts go to the main lower slopes, and a funicular halfway along the village accesses others.

Mürren's traffic-free status is being somewhat eroded; there are now a few delivery trucks. But it still isn't plagued by electric carts and taxis in the way that many other traditional 'traffic-free' resorts are.

It's not the place to go for nightlife, shopping or showing off your latest gear to admiring hordes. It is the place to go if you want tranquillity and stunning views. The village is so small that location is not a concern. Nothing is more than a few minutes' walk.

KEY FACTS

Resort	1650m
	5,410ft

Jungfrau region

Altitude	945-2970m
	3,100-9,740ft
Lifts	44
Pistes	213km
	132 miles
Blue	25%
Red	61%
Black	14%
Snowmaking	85km
	53 miles

Mürren-Schilthorn only

Slopes	1650-2970m
	5,410-9,740ft
Lifts	15
Pistes	53km
	33 miles
Snowmaking	10km
	6 miles

THE MOUNTAINS

Mürren's slopes aren't extensive (53km/33 miles in total). But it has something for everyone, including a vertical of some 1300m/4,270ft. And those happy to take the time to cross the valley to Wengen-Grindelwald will find plenty of options.

THE SLOPES
Small but interesting

There are three connected areas around the village, reaching no higher than 2145m/7,040ft. The biggest is **Schiltgrat**, served by a fast quad chair behind the cable car station. A funicular goes from the middle of the village to the nursery slope at **Allmendhubel** – from where a run and a fast double take you to the slightly higher **Maulerhubel**. Runs go down from here to Winteregg, on the railway.

Much more interesting are the higher slopes reached by cable car to **Birg**. Below Birg, the Engetal area has the Riggli quad, serving short, shady slopes including a black mogul run. Two chairlifts below this serve some snow-sure intermediate slopes. The final stage of the cable car takes you up to the Schilthorn and its revolving restaurant, made famous by the James Bond film *On Her Majesty's Secret Service*. In good snow you can ski down to Lauterbrunnen – almost 16km/10 miles and 2175m/7,140ft. The Inferno race (see separate box) takes place over this course, snow permitting. Below Winteregg, it's all boring paths.

TERRAIN PARKS
Affirmative

There is a terrain park on the lower slopes of Schiltgrat.

SNOW RELIABILITY
Good on the upper slopes

The Jungfrau region does not have a good snow record – but Mürren always has the best snow in the area. When Wengen-Grindelwald (and Mürren's lower slopes) have problems, the Schilthorn and Engetal often have packed powder snow because of their height and orientation – north-east to east. The runs from below Engetal to Allmendhubel and parts of the lower slopes have snowmaking.

FOR EXPERTS
One wonderful piste

The run from the top of the Schilthorn starts with a steep but not terrifying slope, in the past generally mogulled but now more often groomed. It flattens into a schuss to Engetal, below Birg. Then there's a wonderful, wide run with stunning views over the valley to the Eiger, Mönch and Jungfrau. Since the chairlifts were built here, you can play on these upper runs for as long as you like before resuming your descent. Below the lifts you hit the Kanonenrohr (gun barrel). This is a very narrow shelf with solid rock on one side and a steep drop on the other – protected by nets. After an open slope and scrappy zig-zag path, you arrive at the 'hog's back' and can descend towards the village on either side of Allmendhubel.

From Schiltgrat a short, serious mogul run – the Kandahar – descends towards the village, but experts are more likely to be interested in the off-piste runs into the Blumental – from here (the north-facing Blumenlucke) and from Birg (the sunnier Tschingelchrachen) – or the more adventurous runs from the Schilthorn.

FOR INTERMEDIATES
Limited, but Wengen nearby

Keen piste-bashers will want to make a few trips to the long cruising runs of Wengen-Grindelwald. The best easy cruising run in Mürren is the north-facing blue down to Winteregg. The reds on the other low slopes can get mogulled, and snow conditions can be poor. The runs served by the Riggli chair to Birg normally have good snow, and you can choose your gradient.

Competent, confident intermediates should consider tackling the Schilthorn run if snow conditions are good.

FOR BEGINNERS
Not ideal, but adequate

The nursery slopes at Allmendhubel, at the top of the funicular, are on the steep side. And there are not many easy runs to graduate to – though the blue down the Winteregg chair is easy, and a couple of blues are served by the long Gimmeln drag and the less tiring Schiltgrat chair.

FOR CROSS-COUNTRY
Forget it

There's a 12km/7 mile loop along the valley, between Stechelberg and

LIFT PASSES

Jungfrau Top Ski Region

Prices in SF

Age	1-day	6-day
under 16	29	148
16 to 19	46	236
20 to 61	57	295
over 62	51	266

Free under 6
Beginner points card

Notes
Covers Wengen, Mürren and Grindelwald, trains between them and Grindelwald ski-bus; day pass price is for Mürren-Schilthorn area only

Alternative passes
Grindelwald and Wengen only; Mürren only; non-skier pass

SCHOOLS

Swiss
t 855 1247

Classes
5 half-days SF170
Private lessons
SF130 for 2hr for 1-2 persons

Like many Swiss resorts, Mürren has a traditional image, but it is trying to move with the times and offer a more snowboard-friendly attitude – and the major lifts are cable cars and chairlifts. The terrain above Mürren is suitable mainly for good freeriders – it's steep, with a lot of off-piste. Intermediates will find the area tough and limited; nearby Wengen is ideal, and much better for beginners.

Lauterbrunnen. But snow is unreliable at valley height.

QUEUES
Generally not a problem
Mürren doesn't get as crowded as Wengen and Grindelwald, except on sunny Sundays. There can be queues for the cable cars to Birg and Schilthorn – usually when snow shortages bring in people from lower resorts. The top stage has only one cabin, so capacity is limited. And a visitor last year was not impressed with the lift staff's attitude when under pressure.

MOUNTAIN RESTAURANTS
Nothing outstanding
Piz Gloria revolves once an hour, displaying a fabulous 360° panorama of peaks and lakes. We don't like the ambience here, but a 2008 reporter had 'four different meals there – all

were amazingly tasty and good value'. Another reporter says, 'It is incredible value for money just for the view (and cheaper than Méribel).' The Schilthornhütte, by the Engetal chairlifts, is small and rustic, and has 'good food and friendly service', says a recent reporter. Lower down, the rustic Suppenalp in the Blumental is quietly set and gets no sun in January; but comments about it are good: 'cosy with excellent food', 'friendly service' and 'fantastic goulash soup and macaroni with apple sauce'. As you might expect, Sonnenberg is sunnier, and readers have enjoyed 'marvellous rösti', 'excellent value vegetarian quiche' and speciality coffees. Gimmeln is self-service with a large terrace, famous for its apple cake. Winteregg does 'superb rösti' and 'the best burger east of the Rockies'. Both have little playgrounds for kids.

Mürren

523

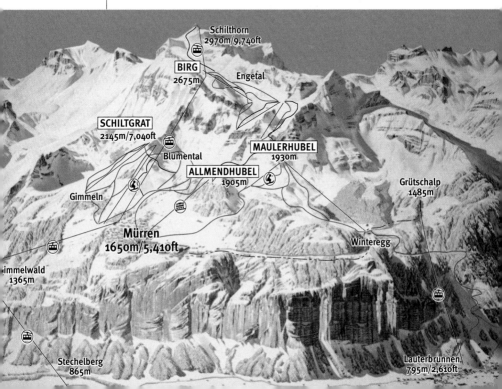

CHILDREN

Kinderhort
t 856 8686
Ages 18mnth to 5yr;
9.30-12noon;
1.30-4pm

Ski school
Takes age 5 and over
(5 2hr days SF170)

GETTING THERE

Air Zürich 195km/
121 miles (3½hr);
Bern 70km/43 miles
(1½hr)

Rail Lauterbrunnen;
transfer by mountain
railway and tram

UK PACKAGES

*Inghams, Kuoni, Made
to Measure, Ski
Freshtracks, Ski Line,
Ski Solutions,
Switzerland Travel
Centre*
Lauterbrunnen *Ski
Miquel*

ACTIVITIES

Indoor Alpine Sports
Centre: swimming
pool, sauna, solarium,
steam bath, massage,
fitness room, tennis,
gymnasium, squash,
library, museum

Outdoor Ice rink,
curling, tobogganing,
12km/7 miles cleared
paths, snowshoeing

Phone numbers
From elsewhere in
Switzerland add the
prefix 033; from
abroad use the prefix
+41 33

TOURIST OFFICE

t 856 8686
info@muerren.ch
www.wengen-
muerren.ch

SCHOOLS AND GUIDES
No recent reports
We lack recent reports. But the school
has a long tradition of teaching Brits;
a bad report we received in 2006 may
just be a glitch.

FACILITIES FOR CHILDREN
Adequate
There is a nursery slope with a rope
tow. The Children's Paradise nursery
takes children from 18 months and the
ski school takes children from the age
of five.

STAYING THERE

HOW TO GO
Mainly hotels, packaged or not
A handful of operators offer packages
to Mürren.
Hotels There are fewer than a dozen
hotels, ranging widely in style.
****Alpin Palace (856 9999) Victorian
pile near the station.
****Eiger (856 5454) Plain-looking
'chalet' blocks next to the station;
widely recommended; good blend of
efficiency and charm; good food; pool.
***Alpenruh (856 8800) Attractively
renovated chalet next to the cable car.
'Cuisine is second to none,' says a
2007 reporter. Sauna.
***Edelweiss (856 5600) Block-like
but friendly; praised by a recent visitor
('good wholesome food and excellent
views').
***Jungfrau (855 6464) Perfectly
placed for families, in front of the
baby slope and close to the funicular.
**Alpenblick (855 1327) Simple, small,
modern chalet near the station.
Apartments There are plenty of chalets
and apartments in the village for
independent travellers to rent.

EATING OUT
Mainly in hotels
The main alternative to hotels is the

rustic Stägerstübli – a bar as well as a
restaurant. The locals eat in the little
diner at the back. The food at the
Eiger hotel is good, and the Bellevue
and Alpenruh have both received good
reports too.

APRES-SKI
Not devoid of life
The tiny Stägerstübli is cosy, and the
place to meet locals. The Alpin
Palace's Ballon bar is an attempt at a
trendy cocktail bar; it also has a
weekend disco, the Inferno. The
Bliemlichäller disco in the Blumental
hotel caters for kids, the Tächi disco in
the Eiger for a more mixed crowd.

OFF THE SLOPES
Tranquillity but not much else
There isn't a lot to amuse people who
don't hit the slopes apart from the
scenery and a very good sports centre
with an outdoor ice rink. There are
12km/7 miles of prepared winter
walking trails, which a 2008 visitor
thoroughly enjoyed. Excursions to Bern
and Interlaken are easy, and you can
readily return to the village to meet
non-skiers for lunch. The only problem
with meeting non-skiers at the top of
the cable car is the expense of it.

STAYING DOWN THE VALLEY
A cheaper option
Lauterbrunnen is a good budget base,
with a resort atmosphere and access
to both Wengen (until late) and
Mürren. We've happily stayed at the
3-star Schützen (855 3026) and 2-star
Oberland (855 1241); rooms at the
3-star Silberhorn (856 2210) have been
renovated and it is highly
recommended by a regular visitor ('flat
screen TVs, great five course dinners'.
For more of a pub atmosphere, he
recommends the bar in the 'popular'
Horner hotel but it 'only has a telly
and plastic dart board'.

THE INFERNO RACE

*Every January 1,800 amateurs compete in Mürren's spectacular Inferno race.
Conditions permitting, and they usually don't, the race goes from the top of the
Schilthorn right down to Lauterbrunnen – a vertical drop of 2175m/7,140ft and
a distance of almost 16km/10 miles, including a short climb at Maulerhubel.
The racers start individually at 12-second intervals; the fastest finish the course
in around 15 minutes, but anything under half an hour is very respectable. The
race was started by Sir Arnold Lunn in 1928, when he and his friends climbed
up to spend the night in a mountain hut and then raced down in the morning.
For many years the race was organised by the British-run Kandahar Club, and
there is still a strong British presence among the competitors.*

Charming, car-free old village set amid spectacular scenery and snow-sure but rather less captivating slopes

COSTS

①②③④⑤⑥

RATINGS

The slopes
Fast lifts	****
Snow	*****
Extent	**
Expert	**
Intermediate	****
Beginner	*****
Convenience	***
Queues	***
Mountain restaurants	**

The rest
Scenery	****
Charm	*****
Off-slope	****

NEWS

For 2008/09 more snowmaking is planned.

For 2007/08 half-hourly buses were introduced from Visp, to meet demand from users of the new Lötschberg rail tunnel link.

An electric road-train carrying up to 56 passengers was introduced as an alternative to the village taxis.

Also, the limit on free children's lift passes was raised to age nine.

➕ Spectacular setting amid high peaks and glaciers

➕ Traditional, 'traffic-free' village

➕ Most of the runs are at exceptionally high altitude and are snow-sure

➕ Good off-slope facilities – even a mountain for non-skiing activities

➖ Disappointingly small area of slopes, with mainly easy runs

➖ Still lots of T-bar draglifts

➖ Not much to amuse experts –glacier limits off-piste exploration

➖ Shady and cold in midwinter

➖ Bad weather can shut the slopes

Saas-Fee is one of our favourite places – a sort of miniature Zermatt without the conspicuous consumption. And it's not just looks that attract us: good snow is guaranteed, even late in the season. The altitude you spend your day at – between 2500m and 3500m (8,200ft and 11,480ft) – is unrivalled in the Alps.

But we tend to drop in here for a couple of days at a time, so the limited extent of the slopes never becomes a problem; for a week's holiday, it would. Top to bottom there is an impressive 1800m/5,910ft vertical – but there aren't many alternative ways down. Keen, mileage-hungry intermediates should look elsewhere, as should experts (except those prepared to go touring). For the rest, it's a question of priorities and expectations. Over to you.

THE RESORT

Like nearby Zermatt, Saas-Fee is a high-altitude mountain village centred on narrow streets lined by attractive old chalets and free of cars (there are car parks at the resort entrance) but not free of electric taxis and delivery vehicles that one 2008 visitor judges extremely dangerous. In other respects, the two resorts are a long way apart in style.

There are some very smart hotels (plus many more modest ones) and plenty of good eating and drinking places. But there's little of the glamour and greed that, for some, spoil Zermatt. Saas-Fee still feels like a village, with its cow sheds more obviously still containing cows. The village may be chilly in January, but when the spring sun is beating down, it is a beautiful place just to stroll around and relax in.

Depending on where you're staying and which way you want to go up the mountain, you may do more marching through the village than strolling, though. It's a long walk from one end to the other. Three major lifts start from the southern end of the village, at the foot of the slopes, and lots of the hotels and apartments (particularly cheaper ones) are 1km/0.5 miles or

more away. The biggest lift, though – the Alpin Express gondola – starts from a more central location. Your hotel may run a courtesy taxi; regular taxis are not cheap – but there are little public buses and a new electric road-train. You can store kit near the lifts, which helps.

The village centre has the school and guides office, the church and a few more shops than elsewhere, but it doesn't add up to much. On a sunny day, though, the restaurant terraces by the nursery slopes at the south end of the village are a magnet, with stunning views up to the ring of 4000m/13,000ft peaks – sitting here, you can begin to

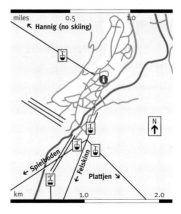

SWITZERLAND

526

KEY FACTS	
Resort	1800m
	5,910ft
Slopes	1800-3500m
	5,910-11,480ft
Lifts	22
Pistes	100km
	62 miles
Blue	25%
Red	50%
Black	25%
Snowmaking	8km
	5 miles

see why the village is called 'The Pearl of the Alps'.

The worthwhile slopes of Saas-Almagell and Saas-Grund are not far away, and you can buy a lift pass that covers all three resorts and linking buses. Day trips by car/train to Zermatt are also possible and a day there is covered by the six-day lift pass.

THE MOUNTAINS

The area is a strange mixture of powerful modern lifts and a lot of old-fashioned T-bars (there are only two chairlifts). Blame the glaciers, on which it's tricky to build chairlifts. Readers have complained about the walks and climbs involved in getting from one lift to another. Take it easy when climbing out of the top lift station: some people feel faint because of the thin air.

The upper slopes are largely gentle, while the lower mountain, below the glacier, is steeper and rockier, needing good snow-cover. There is very little shelter in bad weather: during and after heavy snowfalls you may find yourself limited to the nursery area.

Saas-Fee is one of the leading resorts for mountaineering and ski

touring, and the extended Haute Route from Chamonix via Zermatt ends here.

THE SLOPES
A glacier runs through it
There are two routes up to the main **Felskinn** area. The 30-person Alpin Express gondola, starting across the river from the main village, takes you to Felskinn via a mid-station at Morenia. The alternative is a short drag across the nursery slope at the south end of the village, and then the recently upgraded Felskinn cable car. From Felskinn, the Metro Alpin underground funicular hurtles up to **Allalin**. From below here, two draglifts access the high point of the area.

Also from the south end of the village, a gondola leaves for Spielboden. This is met by a cable car that takes you up to **Längfluh**.

Between Felskinn and Längfluh is an off-limits glacier area. A very long draglift from Längfluh takes you to a point where you can get down to the Felskinn area. These two sectors are served mainly by draglifts, and you can get down to the village from both.

Another gondola from the south end of the village goes up to Saas-Fee's smallest area, **Plattjen**.

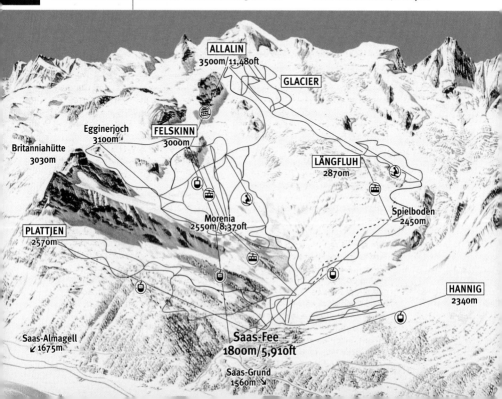

Saas-Fee

Prices in SF

Age	1-day	6-day
under 16	32	171
17 to 18	54	274
19 to 64	64	322
over 65	58	290

Free under 10

Beginner pass for village lifts only

Notes
Covers lifts in Saas-Fee only; single and return tickets available on most main lifts; also afternoon passes and family reductions

Alternative passes
Whole valley pass; separate passes for each of the other Saastal ski areas (Saas-Grund, Saas-Almagell, Saas-Balen); non-skier single fares

Alpine Answers, Alpine Life, Crystal, Crystal Finest, Erna Low, Esprit, Independent Ski Links, Inghams, Interactive Resorts, Interhome, Kuoni, Made to Measure, Momentum, Ski Activity, Ski Expectations, Ski Freshtracks, Ski Independence, Ski Line, Ski Solutions, Ski Total, Skitracer, Snow Finders, Switzerland Travel Centre, Thomson

boarding

Saas-Fee has backed snowboarding from its inception and provides year-round riding at more affordable prices than neighbouring Zermatt. The terrain suits intermediates and beginners best; there's little to satisfy experts and the glacier limits freeriding. The main access lifts are gondolas, cable cars and a funicular, but nearly all the rest are T-bars. The high altitude and the glacier mean the resort is a favourite for early-season and summer riding (the British Olympic half-pipe team uses Saas-Fee for off-season training). Carvers will find wide, well-groomed pistes to shred down. Half-pipe enthusiasts will love the perfect pipe next to the good terrain park at Morenia. The Popcorn bar and shop is the favourite spot for après-snowboard beers.

TERRAIN PARKS
Well developed
The 42 Crew (www.42crew.ch) are renowned for building great parks and maintaining them all year round. While the slopes may not provide the biggest challenge for advanced riders, the big Morenia park has a plethora of kickers, rails and boxes, and a truly world-class half-pipe that will challenge anyone on a board. There was a focus on females for 2007/08, with a Roxy kicker line. Shapers apparently rearrange the boxes and rails each month and have put a fun tree-trunk obstacle in place. Beginners can also check out the snow skate park in Stafelwald, near the nursery slopes. You'll find plenty of entry level jumps and rails here. In summer, a park is built on the glacier and you will often see pro riders honing their skills at the 'Laid Back' summer camp (www.laidback.ch).

SNOW RELIABILITY
Good at the highest altitudes
Most of Saas-Fee's slopes face north and many are above 2500m/8,200ft, making this one of the most reliable resorts for snow in the Alps. The glacier is open most of the year. There has been substantial investment in snow-guns, and more is planned for 2008/09; but reports say they aren't used enough. Grooming has been criticised too.

FOR EXPERTS
Not a lot to keep your interest
There is not much steep stuff, except on the bottom half of the mountain where the snow is less likely to be good (a short black run from Felskinn is the high-altitude exception). The slopes around the top of Längfluh often provide good powder, and there are usually moguls above Spielboden. The blacks and the trees on Plattjen

are worth exploring. The glacier puts limits on the local off-piste even with a guide – crevasse danger is extreme. But there are extensive touring possibilities.

FOR INTERMEDIATES
Great for gentle cruising
Saas-Fee is ideal for early intermediates and those not looking for much of a challenge. For long cruises, head for Allalin. The top of the mountain, down as far as Längfluh in one direction and as far as Morenia in the other, is ideal, with usually excellent snow. Gradients range from gentle blues to slightly steeper reds that can build up smallish bumps. For more of a challenge, head across to Längfluh.

The 1800m/5,910ft vertical descents from the top to the village are great tests of stamina – or, if you choose, an enjoyable long cruise with plenty of view stops. The lower runs have steepish, tricky sections and can have poor snow, especially if it isn't cold enough to make artificial snow – timid intermediates might prefer to take a lift down from mid-mountain.

Plattjen has a variety of runs, all of them fine for ambitious intermediates, and often under-used.

FOR BEGINNERS
A great place to start
There's a good, large, out-of-the-way nursery area at the edge of the village, as snow-sure as any you will find. Those ready to progress can head for the gentle blues on Felskinn just above Morenia – it's best to return by the Alpin Express. There are also gentle blues right at the top of the mountain, from where you can head down without difficulty to Längfluh. Again, use the lifts to return to base. A useful beginners' pass covers all the short village lifts.

Saas-Fee

527

Interactive resort shortlist builder at **www.wtss.co.uk**

↑ Like most glaciers, this one is of gentle gradient

WENDY-JANE KING

SCHOOLS

Swiss
t 957 2348
Eskimos
t 957 4904

Classes
5 3hr days SF188
Private lessons
SF70 for 1hr

FOR CROSS-COUNTRY
Good local trail and lots nearby
There is one short (6km/4 mile) pleasant trail at the edge of the village. It snakes up through the woods, providing about 150m/490ft of climb and nice views. There's more (26km/16 miles) down in the Saas valley.

QUEUES
Gradual improvement?
There are signs that Saas-Fee is at last getting on top of its queuing problems. The Felskinn cable car, which regularly produced long queues, has been upgraded and Morenia now has a six-pack at mid-mountain. Even so, there may be irritating queues up at Längfluh and for the draglifts at the top of the mountain. Crowded pistes can be a problem below Morenia at the end of the day, and when bad weather closes lifts higher up.

MOUNTAIN RESTAURANTS
Disappointing
The restaurants at the main lift stations are functional; reporters like the 'giant' Morenia for good value and a 'wide choice' – but it can get crowded. At least the table-service place at Allalin gives changing views – see separate box.

Editors' choice If you're up for a trek (about 15 minutes each way) the Britannia-hütte (957 2288) is special, not because of the food, which is understandably simple, but because of the setting: it's a real climbing refuge, with atmosphere and great views.

Worth knowing about The best places are slightly off the beaten track: the Berghaus Plattjen (just down from Plattjen) and the cosy Gletschergrotte, halfway down from Spielboden (watch for the arrow and sign on the left of the piste).

SCHOOLS AND GUIDES
Mixed reactions
It's a choice between the Swiss school and Eskimos. Reports of the Swiss school vary, but a 2008 visitor noted 'the instructors really seemed to go out of their way to help their students; even offered help when I looked a little intimidated on a steep piste.' Eskimos gets rave reviews; 'well-organised' and 'patient instructors'.

WORLD'S HIGHEST REVOLVING LUNCH?
If you fancy 360° views during lunch, head up to the world's highest revolving restaurant at Allalin, where you can get a different vista with starters, mains and pud. Only the bit of floor with the tables on it revolves; the stairs stay put (along with the windows – watch your gloves). The other two revolving cafes in the Alps are also in Switzerland – at Mürren and Leysin – and we rate the views there better. But it's an amusing novelty that most visitors enjoy, and lunch is OK too. To reserve a table next to the windows phone 957 1771.

CHILDREN

Kindergarten Ferien-Kinderparadies
t 957 4057
Ages 18mnth to 6yr;
9am-5pm, Mon to Fri;
SF76 per day

Swiss
t 957 2348
From age 4; 9.45 to
3.30 (half skiing, half
activities)

Ski school
From age 4 (SF36 for
90-minute lesson); full
junior ski school from
age 5 (5 days SF188)

GETTING THERE

Air Sion 70km/
43 miles (1hr);
Geneva 234km/
145 miles (3½hr);
Zürich 246km/
153 miles (4hr);
Milan 250km/
155 miles (3hr)

Rail Brig (38km/
24 miles); regular
buses from station

ACTIVITIES

Indoor Bielen leisure
centre (swimming, hot
tub, steam bath,
whirlpool, solarium,
sauna, aerobics,
massage, tennis,
badminton, gym,
bodyforming,
aquafitness),
museums

Outdoor 30km/
19 miles of cleared
paths, horse carriage
rides, ice rink
(skating, curling, snow
bowling),
tobogganing, ice
climbing,
snowshoeing

Phone numbers
From elsewhere in
Switzerland add the
prefix 027; from
abroad use the prefix
+41 27

TOURIST OFFICE

t 958 1858
to@saas-fee.ch
www.saas-fee.ch

FACILITIES FOR CHILDREN
Good reports
The Swiss school takes children from four years old. Reports are mixed: a 2007 visitor voted them a 'great success' for his seven-year-old – with small groups even at half-term; but one child was 'so frustrated' by being put in much too low a group for her. Eskimos is highly praised: one child's instructor 'could not do enough for the group, taking them out for activities in his own time'. The kids' fun park proved a 'great introduction' for one toddler. Several hotels have an in-house kindergarten.

STAYING THERE

HOW TO GO
Check the location
Quite a few UK tour operators sell holidays to Saas-Fee. But there are surprisingly few chalet holidays.
Hotels There are over 50.
****Schweizerhof (958 7575) Stylish, in quiet position above the centre. 'Fantastic food, friendly, excellent kindergarten, wonderful service.' Pool. Extended leisure facilities due for 2008/09.
****Beau-Site (958 1560) Central position. Good food. Pool. Recommended by a reporter.
***Bristol (958 1212) 'A quiet, quality hotel; beside the nursery slopes,' says a 2008 visitor. Highly recommended.
***Christiania (957 3166) Good value, central hotel, approved by readers in the past.
***Alphubel (958 6363) At the wrong end of town. Family-friendly, with a recommended nursery.
***Waldesruh (958 6464) Recommended for its location close to the Alpin Express.
***Astoria (958 5500) Very handy for the Alpin Express. Whirlpool and sauna.
***Jägerhof (957 1310) At foot of slopes. 'Service simply phenomenal.'
***Europa (958 9600) Near the Hannig gondola. Recommended in 2007 for 'exemplary' food. Wellness facilities.
**Belmont (958 1640) The most appealing of the hotels looking directly on to the nursery slopes.
Fletschhorn (957 2131) Not part of the Swiss star rating system, but distinctly upmarket, elegant chalet in the woods. Original art and individual rooms, a trek from the village and lifts, but fabulous food.

Hohnegg (957 2268) Small rustic alternative to the Fletschhorn, in a similarly remote spot.
Apartments Most apartments featured by UK operators are a long way from the slopes. A 2008 reporter recommends the 'great and convenient' Perla apartments, near the main gondola.

EATING OUT
Good variety
Gastronomes will want to head for the acclaimed and expensive Fletschhorn – 'the best meal I've ever had', says a reporter. We like the woody Bodmen, which has great food from a varied menu. We have also enjoyed meals at the hotel Ferienart's Mandarin (Thai restaurant). Don Ciccio's is 'child-friendly' and does 'great pizzas and veal'. Boccalino is also good for pizzas. The rustic Alp-Hitta is worth a try. The Ferme, Arvu Stuba, Zur Mühle, Gorge, Feeloch and the Sport-Hotel's Rôtisserie have all been recommended.

APRES-SKI
Excellent and varied
Late afternoon, Nesti's Ski-Bar, Zur Mühle, the Black Bull (with outdoor seating only) and the little snow-bars near the lifts are all pretty lively, especially if the sun's shining. Later on, Nesti's and the Alpen-Pub keep going till 1am. Popcorn is a long-time favourite for many visitors. The Metro-Bar is said to feel like a 19th-century mine shaft. Why-Not is the place for a Guinness and the Happy bar's happy hours are popular. Poison is the place to drink shots and party the night away, while the Metropol Hotel – with American diner, Night-Life disco and other bars – 'livens up late'.

OFF THE SLOPES
A mountain for pedestrians
The whole of the Hannig mountain is dedicated to walking, paragliding and tobogganing ('terrific'). The splendid Bielen leisure centre boasts a 25m/82ft pool, indoor tennis courts and a sun bed area. The museums are interesting – kids can make bread at the bakery one. The Feeblitz toboggan ride beside the Alpin Express is popular. If you like ice caves, don't miss the world's largest.

Ignore the stuffy 5-star hotels: you don't need to be rolling in it to enjoy this panoramic high-altitude playground

➕ Wonderful panoramic scenery
➕ Off-slope activities second to none
➕ Extensive, mainly intermediate slopes
➕ High, and fairly snow-sure
➕ Good mountain restaurants, some with magnificent views

➖ A sizeable town, with little traditional Alpine character and some hideous block buildings
➖ Several unlinked mountains, and inadequate valley bus service
➖ Runs on home mountain all fairly easy and most lacking variety
➖ Expensive

St Moritz is Switzerland's most famous 'exclusive' winter resort: glitzy, expensive, fashionable and, above all, the place to be seen – a place for an all-round winter holiday, with an unrivalled array of wacky diversions such as polo, golf and cricket on snow, and countless festivals. It has long been popular with upper-crust Brits, who stay in the top hotels in order to go sledging. Well, OK: in order to descend the world-famous Cresta Run. But like all such self-consciously smart resorts, it makes a perfectly good destination for anyone.

The town of St Moritz is undeniably an eyesore. But you may find, as we do, that you can ignore the scar, and appreciate the beauty of St Moritz's spectacular setting regardless. This is one of those areas where our progress on the mountain is regularly interrupted by the need to stand and gaze.

THE RESORT

St Moritz has two distinct parts. Dorf is the fashionable main part, on a steep hillside above the lake. It has two main streets – lined with boutiques selling Rolex watches, Cartier jewellery and Hermes scarves – a few side lanes and a small main square. A funicular takes you from Dorf to the slopes of Corviglia, also reached by cable car from Dorf's other half, the spa resort of St Moritz Bad, down beside the lake. Everything in Bad is less prestigious. Many of the buildings are block-like, and spoil otherwise superb views. There are no lifts from town into the second major area of slopes, Corvatsch – a bus ride away.

In winter the lake is used for eccentric activities including horse and greyhound racing, show jumping, polo, 'ice golf' and even cricket. It also makes a superb setting for walking and cross-country skiing, which is very big in the area; the Engadine Ski Marathon is held every March – over 12,000 racers take part. The town's clientele is typified by the results of a Cresta Run race we saw on one of our visits. In the top 30 were three lords, a count, an archduke and a baronet; the race was won by a local Swiss guy.

For our money Bad is the better base, with the advantage that you can ski back to it from Corvatsch as well as from Corviglia. Celerina, down the valley and with a lift towards Corviglia, is the obvious alternative, and an attractively rustic one (see end of this

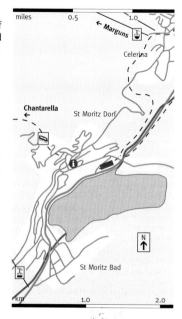

KEY FACTS

Resort	1770m
	5,810ft
Slopes	1730-3305m
	5,680-10,840ft
Lifts	58
Pistes	350km
	217 miles
Blue	20%
Red	70%
Black	10%
Snowmaking	70km
	43 miles

For Corviglia only

Slopes	1730-3055m
	5,680-10,020ft
Lifts	23
Pistes	158km
	98 miles

LIFT PASSES

Upper Engadine

Prices in SF

Age	1-day	6-day
under 13	24	118
13 to 17	48	232
Over 18	71	346

Free under 6
Senior no deals
Beginner no deals

Notes
Covers all lifts in Corviglia, Corvatsch, Diavolezza-Lagalb and Zuoz, and includes the Engadine bus services and certain stretches of the Rhätische Bahn railway

Alternative passes
Half-day and day passes for individual areas within Upper Engadine

chapter). But there are other options – 'chocolate-box-pretty' Sils Maria, for example, has immediate access to the Corvatsch slopes via Furtschellas.

There are good rail links from Zürich, but it's quicker to drive to the resort. A car is handy, too: the valley bus service (needed for access to Corvatsch) is free with the lift pass but extremely crowded at peak times. And a car greatly speeds up visits to the outlying mountains. Trips are possible to Davos and other resorts.

THE MOUNTAINS

There are lots of long, wide, well-groomed runs with varied terrain – practically all on open slopes above the trees. The 350km/217 miles of pistes are in three separate areas, covered on three gigantic piste maps; our maps show only the two main areas close to St Moritz. Piste signing is unhelpful: pistes are numbered on the map, but not on the ground. If the lift system irritates you, the local heli-skiing outfits will drop you at the top of the lifts. It's that kind of place.

THE SLOPES
Big but broken up

From St Moritz Dorf a two-stage railway goes up to **Corviglia**, a lift junction at the eastern end of a sunny and rather monotonous area of slopes facing east and south over the main valley. The peak of Piz Nair, reached from here by cable car, separates these slopes from the less sunny and more varied ones in the wide bowl above **Marguns** – and gives fabulous views across the valley to Piz Bernina. From Corviglia you can (snow permitting) head down easy paths to Dorf and Bad; you'll probably pass through Salastrains – just above Dorf, with nursery slopes, restaurants and two hotels. There is a red run from Marguns to Celerina.

From Surlej, a few miles from St Moritz, a two-stage cable car takes you to the north-facing slopes of **Corvatsch**, which reach glacial heights. From the mid-station at Murtèl you have a choice of reds to Stüvetta Giand'Alva and Alp Margun. From the latter you can work your way to **Furtschellas**, also reached by cable car from Sils Maria. If you're lucky with the snow, you can end the day with the splendid Hahnensee run, from the northern limit of the Corvatsch lift system at Giand'Alva down to St Moritz Bad – a black-classified run that is of red difficulty for 95% of its 6km/ 4 mile length. It often opens around noon, when the snow softens. It's a five-minute walk from the end of the run to the cable car to Corviglia.

The third area consists of two peaks on opposite sides of the road to the Bernina pass to Italy, about 20km/12 miles away (a 50-minute bus ride) – Diavolezza and Lagalb, which should be properly linked from the 2008/09 season (see 'News').

Diavolezza (2980m/9,780ft) has excellent north-facing pistes of 900m/2,950ft vertical, down under its big 125-person cable car.

Lagalb (2960m/9,710ft) is a smaller area with quite challenging slopes – west-facing, 850m/2,790ft vertical –

Interactive resort shortlist builder at **www.wtss.co.uk**

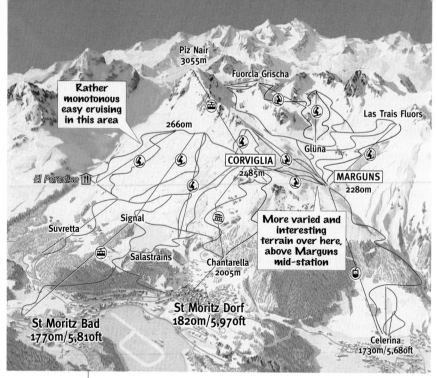

Rather monotonous easy cruising in this area

Piz Nair
3055m

Fuorcla Grischa

Las Trais Fluors

2660m

Glüna

El Paradiso

CORVIGLIA
2485m

MARGUNS
2280m

More varied and interesting terrain over here, above Marguns mid-station

Suvretta

Signal

Salastrains

Chantarella
2005m

St Moritz Dorf
1820m/5,970ft

St Moritz Bad
1770m/5,810ft

Celerina
1730m/5,680ft

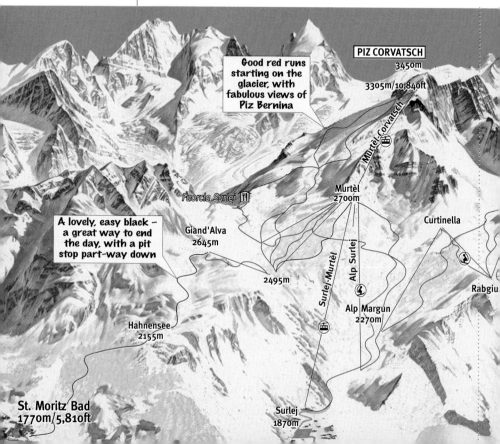

PIZ CORVATSCH
3450m

Good red runs starting on the glacier, with fabulous views of Piz Bernina

3305m/10,840ft

Mürtèl-Corvatsch

Fuorcla Surlej

Mürtèl
2700m

Curtinella

A lovely, easy black – a great way to end the day, with a pit stop part-way down

Giand'Alva
2645m

2495m

Surlej-Mürtèl

Alp Surlej

Rabgiu

Hahnensee
2155m

Alp Margun
2270m

St. Moritz Bad
1770m/5,810ft

Surlej
1870m

The terrain in St Moritz is boarder-friendly and there's a special boarder's booklet with a lot of good information. Freeride tours are available through the ski schools and the best freeride terrain is on Diavolezza and Corvatsch, but there are several draglifts on Corvatsch. Apart from those, most of St Moritz's lifts are chairs, gondolas, cable cars and trains; beginners will enjoy the rolling blue runs, and intermediates will relish the red runs. The great thing for freeriders is that most people tend to stay on-piste in this resort, leaving terrain untracked for days after the last snowfall. There's a very good terrain park on Corviglia that is open late for great sunset sessions. Playground in Paradise is a specialist board shop.

served by an 80-person cable car. It's worth noting that from mid-March the Lagalb cable car runs until 5pm and the Diavolezza one until 5.30. We thought a final sunny run from 2900m/ 9,510ft a great way to end the day.

TERRAIN PARKS
Three-year-old playground
The Mellow park on Corviglia is only three years old and is a welcome addition for freestylers in the area. Access is easier from Celerina than from St Moritz itself. The park was actually designed with female pro

skiers and snowboarders and advanced riders in mind and is home to some of the biggest contests for females. There are three lines, with the hardest comprising a big 12m/39ft table jump, plus a brilliant 400m long easy line. There are straight, kinked and rainbow rails and boxes of all sizes, and the park always has a great relaxed atmosphere to learn in. New for 2007/08 were a wall-ride and mini quarter-pipe. The team has worked hard to bring the total of different obstacles up to an impressive 30. And the park is covered by snowmaking.

SNOW RELIABILITY
Improved by good snowmaking
This corner of the Alps has a rather dry climate, but the altitude means that any precipitation is likely to be snowy. The top runs at Corvatsch are glacial and require good snow depths to be safe – a recent reporter discovered them closed on a February visit. There is snowmaking in every sector, and piste grooming is excellent.

FOR EXPERTS
Dispersed challenges
If you're looking for challenges, you're liable to find St Moritz disappointing on-piste. The few serious black runs are scattered about in different sectors, and few are genuine blacks; those at Lagalb and Diavolezza are the most challenging, and include one of the few sizeable mogul-fields – the Minor run down the Lagalb cable car (though it's seriously steep only at the start). But there is good off-piste terrain, and it doesn't get tracked out. There is an excellent north-facing slope immediately above Marguns, for example. Experts often head for the tough off-piste runs on Piz Nair or the Corvatsch summit. More serious expeditions can be undertaken – such as the Roseg valley from Corvatsch.
Out at Diavolezza, a very popular

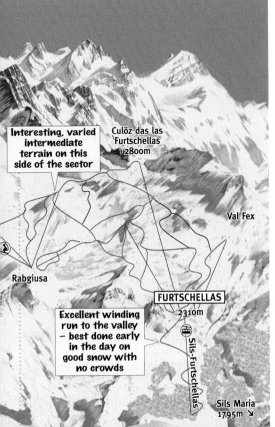

Culöz das las Furtschellas 2800m

Interesting, varied intermediate terrain on this side of the sector

Val Fex

Rabgiusa

FURTSCHELLAS 2310m

Excellent winding run to the valley – best done early in the day on good snow with no crowds

Sils-Furtschellas

Sils Maria 1795m

including descents to the two valley stations – particularly the Furtschellas one; do these in the morning, and return to St Moritz Bad via the lovely Hahnensee run – an easy black. Use the low-altitude way back to the Corvatsch sector from Furtschellas, to avoid a lot of tedious skating. The runs from the Corvatsch top station are genuinely red in parts, with fabulous views of Piz Bernina.

Diavolezza is mostly intermediate stuff, too. There is an easy open slope at the top, served by a fast quad, and a splendid long intermediate run back down under the lift. The link to Lagalb, despite the new lift and pistes (see 'News'), will still require use of parts of a black run, but it is of red gradient. Lagalb has more challenging pistes – basically two good reds and a genuine black.

FOR BEGINNERS
Not ideal

Beginners start up at Salastrains or Corviglia, or slightly out of town at Suvretta. Celerina has good, broad nursery slopes at village level and a child-friendly lift. Ironically, in a resort full of easy red runs, progression from the nursery slopes to longer runs is rather awkward – there are few blue runs without a difficult section.

FOR CROSS-COUNTRY
Excellent

The Engadine is one of the premier regions in the Alps for cross-country, with 180km/112 miles of trails, including floodlit loops, amid splendid scenery and with fairly reliable snow. A reporter recommends the lessons at the Langlauf Centre near the Hotel Kempinski. For cross-country, the best bases are outside St Moritz – Sils or Silvaplana, suggests one reporter.

QUEUES
Not much of a problem

St Moritz has invested heavily in new lifts, especially on Corviglia and Marguns, where there are fast chairs everywhere. The area as a whole has a lot of modest-sized cable cars – both for getting up the mountain from the resort and for access to peaks from mid-mountain. Queues can result, but reporters have had good experiences lately and comment that many St Moritz visitors are late risers and don't ski much after lunch, leaving the slopes quiet early and late in the day.

↑ Yup, St Moritz is more like a town than a village. And it's not pretty, though the surrounding scenery is stunning
ST MORITZ TOURIST BOARD

534

UK PACKAGES

Alpine Answers, Alpine Weekends, Club Med, Crystal, Crystal Finest, Elegant Resorts, Flexiski, Independent Ski Links, Inghams, Interhome, Jeffersons, Kuoni, Made to Measure, Momentum, Oxford Ski Co, Scott Dunn, Ski Freshtracks, Ski Independence, Ski Line, Ski Safari, Ski Solutions, Skitracer, Switzerland Travel Centre

and spectacular off-piste glacier route goes off the back beneath Piz Bernina to Morteratsch. It is not difficult, but requires a bit of energy and nerve. After a gentle climb, you skirt the glacier on a narrow ledge, with crevasses waiting to gobble you up on the right. At the end of the initial 30-minute slog, a welcoming ice bar greets you. After that, it's downhill over the glacier, with splendid views. On the front of the mountain, the Gletscher chair accesses an excellent shady run down Val d'Arlas. And across at Lagalb, a route goes steeply off the back of the mountain down towards La Rosa in Val Laguné.

There are a couple of firms offering heli-drops on Fuorcla Chamuotsch, for runs back to the Engadine valley down Val Suvretta or Valletta dal Guglia.

FOR INTERMEDIATES
Good but flattering

St Moritz is great for intermediates. Most pistes on Corviglia are very well groomed, easyish reds that could well have been classified blue – ideal cruising terrain, or monotonous, depending on your requirements. The Marguns bowl is more interesting, including some easy blacks and the pleasant Val Schattain run away from the lifts. The Corvatsch-Furtschellas area is altogether more varied, interesting and challenging, as well as higher and wider. There are excellent red runs in both parts of the area,

GETTING THERE

Air Zürich 200km/
124 miles (3hr);
Upper Engadine
airport 5km/3 miles

Rail Mainline station
in resort

SCHOOLS

Swiss
t 830 0101

Suvretta
t 836 6161

Privat
t 852 1885

Classes
(Swiss prices)
6 half days SF230

Private lessons
SF340 for one day

CHILDREN

Salastrains
t 830 0101
Run by Swiss school

Schweizerhof hotel
t 837 0707
From age 3;
9.30-6pm; Mon-Sat;
SF45 per day for non-
residents

**Palazzino – in
Badrutt's Palace Hotel**
t 837 1000
Ages 3 to 12; 9.30am
to 6pm; SF50 per day
for non-residents

**Kempi Kids Club – in
Kempinski Hotel**
t 838 3838

Ski school
Ages from 5; pick-up
service and all-day
care available

SMART LODGINGS

Check out our feature
chapters at the front
of the book.

MOUNTAIN RESTAURANTS
Some special places

Mountain restaurants are plentiful, and include some of the most glamorous in Europe. Prices can be high, but standards can be disappointing. We had the worst rösti in a skiing lifetime at the otherwise attractive Chamanna. The piste maps have helpful pictures and descriptions of the restaurants.

Editors' choice El Paradiso (833 4002), secluded at the extreme southern end of Corviglia, has it all: breathtaking views, a tastefully renovated, slightly trendy interior, great service and top-notch food. Fuorcla Surlej (842 6303), though we doubt they'll take a reservation), on the Fuorcla run from the Corvatsch glacier, is a good-weather option: a refuge serving basic food very slowly, but with a view from the ramshackle terrace that is among our top three in the world.

Worth knowing about On Corviglia, the top lift station houses several restaurants run under the umbrella title of Mathis Food Affairs, including the famous Marmite. The Salastrains continues to serve 'magnificent' food. The Chasellas is also recommended, particularly for strudel. Lej de la Pêsch, behind Piz Nair, is a cosy spot, better for a snowy day than a sunny one. On the Corvatsch side, a good place for a stormy day is the rustic Alpetta, near Alp Margun – 'nice food, lovely atmosphere and a great bar' (table service inside). On the other hand Hahnensee, on the lift-free run of the same name to Bad, is a splendid place to pause in the sun on the way home.

SCHOOLS AND GUIDES
Internal competition

There are two main schools, the St Moritz and the Suvretta (see 'Hotels'). A reporter received 'excellent' instruction from the latter. The St Moritz Experience runs heli-trips, and some hotels have their own instructors for private lessons.

FACILITIES FOR CHILDREN
Choose a hotel with a nursery

Children wanting lessons have a choice of schools. Reports suggest that classes with the Swiss school can have mixed ability levels, with better kids getting bored. There's a kindergarten and children's restaurant at Salastrains and some hotel nurseries are open to non-residents. Club Med has its usual good facilities.

STAYING THERE

HOW TO GO
Several packaged options

Packages are available. There is a Club Med. The tourist office can provide a list of apartments.

Hotels Over half the hotels are 4-stars and 5-stars – the highest concentration in Switzerland. We are persuaded by a reader to list one of the 5-stars, and we include another for its news value; the others – the staid but revamped Kulm, the Gothic Badrutt's Palace and the newish Kempinski – leave us cold.

*****Suvretta House (818 363636) The 5-star for skiers, in a secluded location with its own branch of the lift system. 'Splendid views, magnificent fitness centre and pool – difficult to fault, except that jackets and ties must be worn after 6pm.' Rules us out, then.

*****Carlton (836 7000) Re-opened in all-suite form last season. The fact that its website has a Russian version may be all you need to know.

****Crystal (836 2626) Big 4-star in Dorf, close to the Corviglia lift.

****Bären (830 8400) Heartily recommended in 2008. 'More welcoming than the glitzier places, top-notch staff and very good food.'

****Schweizerhof (837 0707) 'Relaxed' hotel in central Dorf, five minutes from the Corviglia lift, with 'excellent food and very helpful staff'. Après-ski hub.

****Monopol (837 0404) Good value (for St Moritz); in centre of Dorf. Repeatedly approved by readers: 'lovely food, delightful staff', says a 2007 visitor. Good new spa facilities.

***Laudinella (836 0000) Our Bad favourite: refreshing, innovative place with austere decor; you can dine enjoyably in any of five different restaurants in the hotel. 'Disappointing' fitness facilities, though, says a reporter.

***Nolda (833 0575) One of the few chalet-style buildings, close to the cable car in Bad.

EATING OUT
Mostly chic and expensive

It's easy to spend £50 a head eating out in St Moritz – without wine – but you can eat more cheaply. We liked the excellent Italian food at the down-to-earth Cascade in Dorf and the three smooth, expensive restaurants in the Chesa Veglia (an ancient farmhouse outpost of Badrutt's hotel) – 'excellent

ACTIVITIES

Indoor Swimming pool, sauna, solarium, golf range, tennis, squash, fitness centre, health spa, casino, cinema, museums, library

Outdoor Ice skating, curling, sightseeing flights, horse carriage rides, tobogganing, paragliding, hang-gliding, bobsleigh rides, Cresta Run, 180km/112 miles cleared paths, horse riding, snow kiting

Phone numbers
From elsewhere in Switzerland add the prefix 081; from abroad use the prefix +41 81

TOURIST OFFICES

St Moritz
t 837 3333
stmoritz
@estm.ch
www.stmoritz.ch

Celerina
t 830 0011
celerina@estm.ch
www.celerina.ch

food, service and ambience but expensive', confirms a 2008 reporter. The two top restaurants are out of town: Jöhri's Talvo at Champfèr and Bumanns Chesa Pirani in La Punt; both occupy fine old houses and are world-class for quality and price. We also liked the rustic Landhotel Meierei, by the lake.

An evening up at Muottas Muragl, between Celerina and Pontresina, offers spectacular views, a splendid sunset and an unpretentious dinner.

APRES-SKI
Caters for all ages
There's a big variety of après-skiing age groups here. The fur coat count is high – people come to St Moritz to be seen. At tea time, head for Hanselmann's – 'fabulous tea and strudels' but 'the place is a bit dull'.

Bobby's Pub attracts a young crowd, as does the loud music of the Stübli, one of three bars in the Schweizerhof ('excellent cocktails'): the others are the Mulibar, with a country and western theme and live music, and the chic Piano Bar. The Enoteca is said to be the place to sample 'wonderful wines'. The Cresta, at the Steffani, is popular with the British, while the Cava below it is louder, livelier and younger. A 2007 reporter's group enjoyed 'clubbing' at the Diamond's bar and disco.

The two most popular discos are Vivai (expensive) at the Steffani, and King's at Badrutt's Palace (even more expensive; jackets and ties required). And if they don't part you from enough of your cash, try the casino.

OFF THE SLOPES
Excellent variety of pastimes
Even if you lack the bravado for the Cresta Run, there is lots to do – a recent visitor found the only problem with the resort is there is 'too much to do'. In midwinter the snow-covered

lake provides a playground for bizarre events, but in March the lake starts to thaw. There's an annual 'gourmet festival', with chefs from all over the world. The Engadin museum is said to be 'very interesting'. And the shopping is simply 'incredible'.

There is extensive well-marked walking trails which a 2008 reporter loved (a map is available).

Some hotels run special activities, such as a curling week. Other options are hang-gliding and indoor tennis. Several reporters rave about the views from the Bernina Express train to Italy, with 'amazing bends and scenery'. And a 2008 reporter highly recommends a trip (90 minutes on the train) to Scual for the 'fabulous spa with lots of great facilities; buy the combi pass covering the train, bus and spa entrance'. There's a public pool in Pontresina.

STAYING UP THE MOUNTAIN
Excellent possibilities
Next door to each other at Salastrains are two chalet-style hotels, the 3-star Salastrains (833 3867), with 60 comfy beds, and the slightly simpler and much smaller Chesa Chantarella (833 3355). Great views, and no queues.

Celerina 1730m/5,680ft

At the bottom end of the Cresta Run, Celerina is unpretentious and villagey, if quiet, with good access to Corviglia. It is sizeable, with a lot of second homes, many owned by Italians (the upper part is known as Piccolo Milano). There are some appealing small hotels (reporters like Chesa Rosatsch, 837 0101) and a couple of bigger 4-stars. The Inn Lodge (834 4795) is new, with rooms and dormitories for the budget-conscious. The food at the Chesa Rosatsch attracts non-resident diners and is recommended.

THE CRESTA RUN

No trip to St Moritz is really complete without a visit to the Cresta Run. It's the last bastion of Britishness (until recently, payment had to be made in sterling) and male chauvinism (women who want to do the run need an invitation from a club member).

Any adult male can pay around £200 for five rides (helmet and lunch at the Kulm hotel included). You lie on a toboggan (aptly called a 'skeleton') and hurtle head-first down a sheet ice gully from St Moritz to Celerina. Watch out for Shuttlecock corner – that's where most of the accidents happen and the ambulances ply their trade.

Europe's best-kept secret: five charming unspoiled villages beneath high, snow-sure slopes with spectacular scenery

COSTS

① ② ③ ④ ⑤ ⑥

RATINGS

The slopes

Fast lifts	**
Snow	****
Extent	**
Expert	****
Intermediate	***
Beginner	***
Convenience	**
Queues	****
Mountain restaurants	**

The rest

Scenery	****
Charm	*****
Off-slope	*

NEWS

There are plans to build a gondola from the centre of Grimentz into the Zinal ski area and build a new easier slope back – the current date set is for the 2010/11 season. There are also plans to build Grimentz's first 4-star hotel and a spa with thermal baths. Building should start in 2010 but the opening will not be before 2013.

Zinal's first snowmaking was installed two seasons ago; they now have 82 snow-guns and plan to open for the 2008/09 season on 8 November (weekends only until 13 December).

+ Charming unspoiled villages
+ Four contrasting ski areas with good uncrowded intermediate cruising
+ Excellent extensive off-piste
+ Reliable snow-cover

− Resorts might be too quiet for some; few shops, no nightlife
− Each area has very limited pistes
− To make the most of all the areas you really need a car

Val d'Anniviers is one of Europe's rare 'undiscovered gems'. If you like ancient, quiet, totally unspoiled mountain villages with small varied ski areas attached, get to Val d'Anniviers now. The slopes are limited in extent for keen piste-bashers, but they are delightfully uncrowded and have a good snow record. And there is fabulous off-piste to explore with a guide.

When you turn off the Rhône valley road at Sierre and head up the Val d'Anniviers (opposite Crans-Montana) you head into a time-warp. It is incredible that the ski resorts in this valley can have remained so amazingly unspoiled when they are so close to big-name resorts such as Verbier, Crans-Montana and Zermatt. The villages all have lots of old wooden houses and barns, narrow paths and lanes and few shops except ski shops and those catering for locals' needs.

The handful of reader reports we have all enthuse about its charming, old-world atmosphere and most beg us not to publicise it for fear that it will be ruined by an influx of Brits.

Well, we've agonised hard. But we think we ought to let you into the secret. Our advice is to get there quickly before it has time to catch up

with the 21st century. There are signs of that, with a lot of (tasteful and low-rise) new building going on – mainly aimed at providing apartments and chalets for sale as second homes. And more (small) UK tour operators are beginning to move in.

There are four main areas of slopes, only two of which are linked (and then only in one direction, by a long black/itinerary run – but that is due to change by 2010, see 'News'). And if you plan to explore them all, it's best to have a car as the bus links are not great.

Nearly all the slopes are above the treeline and there's a lot of skiing above 2400m/7,870ft, which usually means good snow conditions. None of the areas is huge in terms of piste mileage (we skied all Zinal's pistes in an afternoon, St Luc-Chandolin's in a

537

Val d'Anniviers is charmingly unspoiled; this is the ice rink in Grimentz →

day, and Grimentz's in a day). But there is some very good off-piste (especially in Grimentz).

ST LUC / CHANDOLIN

1650m/5,410ft / 2000m/6,560ft
These are the sunniest of the main ski resort villages and share the biggest ski area. St Luc also has the attraction of a fabulous hotel.
A funicular goes up from the edge of St Luc and a high-speed chair from the edge of Chandolin. Both are served by free ski-buses. The 75km/47 miles of slopes face south and west so get a lot of sun, and it was classic spring skiing on our visit in March – hard in the morning, softening up by noon. Apart from the one fast quad from Chandolin, there is only one other chair – the other 11 lifts are all drags.

The pistes suit beginners and intermediates best; there are no black runs though there are three short itinéraires and a gnarly freeride area where competitions are held. Most of the reds and blues have a fairly similar pitch whatever the colour – best for those who like easy cruising in the sun. We loved the long red run from the high point of Bella Tola at

3000m/9,840ft away from all the lifts down to the Tipi bar in the valley, where you catch the navette back to town or the funicular – a great way to end the day. There's a good beginner area near the top of the St Luc funicular. Two good mountain restaurants are the tiny Cabane de Illhorn above Chandolin and the Cabane Bella Tola above St Luc – both with terraces with stunning views.

Both Chandolin and St Luc are fairly spread out. But St Luc has a charming compact centre with a small outdoor après-ski bar. The delightful, well-run, friendly 4-star hotel Bella Tola (475 1444) is just a few strides from here and loved by reporters. We managed to get in for one night only, but loved it too – built in 1859, it has been beautifully renovated by its current owners with a fine spa, great sunny terrace and excellent restaurant (and a jazz band was playing in the bar before dinner on our visit).

ZINAL 1670m/5,480ft

This small village near the head of the valley has a small area of slopes with stunning views over to a series of high peaks including the Matterhorn.
A cable car takes you up to Sorebois at 2440m/8,010ft, the hub of the small ski area. Most of the slopes face north or east and keep their snow well. It is popular with families and there's a good beginner area near the top of the cable car.

The runs are mainly short (some only 200m/660ft or 300m/980ft vertical) but include some good reds – our favourites were those from Combe Durand at the edge of the ski area and served by a draglift (there's a designated freeride area served by this drag too).

The two short black runs in the main ski area are really of red steepness, but the long black run back to town can be tricky and many people ride the cable car back down. There's also a long black run/itinéraire (Piste du Chamois) leading to Grimentz, which reporters rave about ('fabulous, lots of fresh tracks', 'one of the best runs in the Alps') – try it soon before it becomes an easier piste (see 'News'). And there's great off-piste in bowls between the pistes in the main ski area. Zinal has a handful of hotels, including the central, modern 3-star Europe (475 4404).

Combe Durand

Corne de Sorebois
2895m

2440m

ZINAL

288om

Zinal
167om/5,48oft

Mottec

GRIMENTZ

2130m

Grimentz
157om/5,15oft

Roc d'Orzival
2855m

St-Jean

lla Tola
000m

2770m

Tignousa
218om

St-Luc
165om/5,41oft

Vissoie

Mt Major
2375m

2470m

ST LUC-CHANDOLIN

lhorn
600m

VERCORIN

Chandolin
2000m/6,56oft

Vercorin
134om/4,4ooft

Chalais

To
Geneva
→

Sierre
56om/1,84oft

Phone numbers
From elsewhere in Switzerland add the prefix 0848 (for Coeur du Valais) and 027 (for everywhere else); from abroad use the prefix +41 and omit the initial '0'

TOURIST OFFICES

Val d'Anniviers
www.sierre-anniviers.ch

Grimentz
t 475 1493
grimentz@sierre-anniviers.ch
www.grimentz.ch

St Luc
t 475 1412
saint-luc@sierre-anniviers.ch
www.saint-luc.ch

Vercorin
t 455 5855
vercorin@sierre-anniviers.ch
www.vercorin.ch

Zinal
t 475 1370
zinal@sierre-anniviers.ch
www.zinal.ch

Chandolin
t 475 1838
chandolin@sierre-anniviers.ch
www.chandolin.ch

Coeur du Valais
www.coeurduvalais.ch

GRIMENTZ 1570m/5,150ft

Grimentz has a richly deserved reputation for its extensive off-piste terrain. And it has a small area of varied pistes above its very cute old village centre.

A gondola from the centre of the village takes you up to Bendolla at 2130m/6,990ft, where there's a good roped off beginner area.

Above this are two main sectors. On the right as you look up are easy blue and red runs. On the left are steeper and quieter runs including two blacks, one of which goes from the top to almost the bottom of the mountain (1300m/4,270ft vertical) and is interestingly varied.

But the real attraction for experts is the extensive off-piste. We did a great run with a guide off the back of Roc d'Orzival: a huge, ski-anywhere bowl that goes on for hundreds of turns before dropping into an area of widely spaced trees and a long run-out – we saw no one else for almost 1250m/4,100ft vertical. And there are plenty more off-piste options.

The International ski school has been 'highly recommended' by a reporter and his three beginner children who have used it for the past two seasons. The functional main restaurant near the top of the gondola is mainly self-service, with a small table-service section that serves good food. And we've had good reports of the rustic Etable du Marais – 'really good food'. As the lifts close, Chez Florioz on the piste just above the village is the place for après-ski.

The village is spread out on quite a steep slope and a lot of new building is going on. But the centre is charming – lots of tiny old barns and narrow paths. It's best to stay near the centre, close to the gondola. We stayed almost opposite it at the 3-star Alpina (476 1616) which is comfortable. The 2-star Moiry (475 1144) has been recommended by a reporter.

For 2008/09 UK tour operator Mountain Heaven is moving in. It has a catered chalet right on the slopes with an outdoor hot tub, indoor sauna and stunning views from the huge lounge. It also has self-catered chalet-apartments right by the old village. Grimentz Location is based in the village and has a large selection of apartments and chalets both to rent and for sale.

Claire Fontaine (a crêperie) and the Arlequin (a pizzeria) were praised by a 2008 reporter for family eating at reasonable prices.

VERCORIN 1340m/4,400ft

The smallest area of slopes and not as easy to get to from the other resorts.

The pretty village of Vercorin, perched on a shelf overlooking the Rhône valley, is reached by a winding road or by a cable car from just outside Sierre. The slopes suit intermediates best.

SIERRE 560m/1840ft

Not a ski resort but the hub of the Coeur du Valais region of which the Val d'Anniviers is a part.

This small town is known as the 'city of sunshine' and is the centre of the Valais vineyards; there's a wine-growing marked walk and a museum.

Verbier

Big, chalet-style resort that attracts powder hounds from all over the world – and big-spending night owls from Geneva

NEWS

For 2007/08 an eight-person gondola replaced the old one from La Tzoumaz on the back of Savoleyres. There are plans to replace the gondola on the Verbier side of Savoleyres, starting from a new base at the top of the nursery slopes at Les Esserts for 2009/10. A piste will be created down to the base from Le Carrefour; so Savoleyres' slopes will be fully connected to Verbier's main slopes in both directions.

The hotel Garbo will close for 2008/09 to be renovated and updated from a 2-star to a 3-star. It will reopen for 2009/10.

More snowmaking was installed for last season in the La Chaux and Savoleyres-La Tzoumaz areas.

➕ Extensive, challenging slopes with a lot of off-piste and long bump runs

➕ Upper slopes offer a real high-mountain feel plus great views

➕ Pleasant, animated village in a sunny, panoramic setting

➕ Lively, varied nightlife

➕ Much improved lift system, piste grooming and signposting, but...

➖ Piste map and signposting need further improvement

➖ Some overcrowded pistes and areas

➖ The 4 Valleys network is much less wonderful than it looks on paper

➖ Sunny lower slopes will always be a problem, even with snowmaking

➖ Some long walks/rides to lifts

➖ Off-piste is tracked out quickly

For experts prepared to hire a guide to explore off-piste, Verbier is one of the world's cult resorts. For vibrant nightlife, too, it is difficult to beat. With its claimed 410km/255 miles of pistes, Verbier also seems at first sight to rank alongside the French mega-networks that are so compelling for keen piste skiers. But if the Three Valleys and Paradiski are what floats your boat, you may be sorely disappointed by the 4 Valleys network, which is an inconveniently sprawling affair, with lots of tedious links to get from one end to the other. Verbier's local pistes leave a lot to be desired, too: by comparison with the slopes of somewhere like Courchevel, they are confined and crowded.

To look on the bright side, we're happy to recognise that Verbier has recently made great strides in tackling other issues that have in the past spoilt the place for the average visitor. Even its atrocious on-mountain signposting has been replaced – and linked to its piste map – but further improvement is needed.

THE RESORT

Verbier is an amorphous sprawl of chalet-style buildings in an impressive setting on a wide, sunny balcony facing spectacular peaks. It's a fashionable, informal, very lively place that teems with cosmopolitan visitors. Most are younger than visitors to other big Swiss resorts.

Most of the shops and hotels (but not chalets) are set around the Place Centrale and along the sloping streets stretching both down the hill and up it to the main lift station at Médran 500m/1,640ft away. Much of the nightlife is here, too. These central areas get unpleasantly packed with cars at busy times, especially weekends. More chalets and apartments are built each year, with many newer properties inconveniently situated along the road to the lift base for the secondary Savoleyres area, about 1.5km/1 mile from Médran.

The Médran lift station is a walkable distance from the Place Centrale, so staying near there has attractions, and it is sufficiently distant

from nightlife to avoid late-night noise. If nightlife is not a priority, staying somewhere near the upper (north-east) fringes of the village may mean that you can almost ski to your door – and there is a piste linking the upper nursery slopes to the one in the middle of the village. But most people just get used to using the free buses, which run efficiently on several routes until 8pm. Some areas have quite an infrequent service.

Verbier is at one end of a long, strung-out series of interconnected slopes, optimistically branded the 4

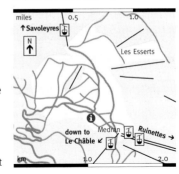

↑ The top of Mont-Fort in the distance, seen from the top of the hike to the Stairway to Heaven off-piste run

SNOWPIX.COM / CHRIS GILL

Valleys and linking Verbier to Nendaz, Veysonnaz, Thyon and other resorts. These other resorts have their own pros and cons. All are appreciably cheaper places to stay than Verbier, and some are more sensible bases for those who plan to stick to pistes rather than venture off-piste – the Veysonnaz-Thyon sector, in particular, is much more intermediate-friendly than Verbier. As bases for exploration of the whole 4 Valleys, only Siviez is much of an advance on Verbier. They are much less lively in the evening. You can also stay down in the valley village of Le Châble, which has a gondola up to Verbier and on into the slopes. Across the valley, Bruson is more attractive as a place to visit for a day than to stay in. For more on these alternatives, see end of the chapter.

Chamonix and Champéry are within reach by car. But a car can be a bit of a nuisance in Verbier itself. Parking is tightly controlled; your chalet or hotel may not have enough space for all guests' cars, which means a hike from the free parking at the sports centre or paying for garage space.

THE MOUNTAINS

Essentially this is high-mountain terrain. There are wooded slopes directly above the village, but the runs here are basically just a way home at the end of the day. There is more sheltered skiing in other sectors – particularly above Veysonnaz. The piste signposting has recently been improved and linked better to the piste map. And the map now has the runs named (but in ludicrously small type which is virtually impossible to read) in the Verbier and Bruson areas, but not in the rest of the 4 Valleys. And we saw no piste names on the mountain – though the man from the tourist office we were skiing with said that he had seen some (but he couldn't find any to show us). Come on, Téléverbier, get your act together – much bigger type on the piste map and markers on the pistes with their names on please!

THE SLOPES
Very spread out

Savoleyres is the smaller area, reached by a gondola from the north-west end of the village. This area is underrated and generally underused, and plans to encourage its use by building a new access gondola from the central nursery slopes for 2009/10 are to be welcomed (see 'News'). It has open, sunny slopes on the front side, and long, pleasantly wooded, shadier runs on the back. You can take a catwalk across from Savoleyres to the foot of Verbier's main slopes. These are served by lifts from Médran, at the opposite end of the village.

Two gondolas rise to **Les Ruinettes** and then a gondola and chairlift continue on to **Les Attelas**. From Les Attelas a small cable car goes up to Mont-Gelé, for steep off-piste runs only. Heading down instead, you can go back westwards to Les Ruinettes, south to La Chaux or north to Lac des Vaux. From Lac des Vaux chairs go to Les Attelas and to Chassoure, the top of a wide, steep and shady off-piste mogul field leading down to **Tortin**, with a gondola back.

The link between Les Ruinettes and La Chaux has been greatly improved by the chondola installed three years ago. The local La Chaux slopes are served by an additional slow chairlift and are the departure point of a jumbo cable car up to **Col des Gentianes** and the glacier area (there's a lovely, often quiet, red run back down to La Chaux which has been improved recently). A second, much smaller cable car goes up from Gentianes to the **Mont-Fort** glacier, the high point of the 4 Valleys. From the top, there's only a long, very steep black run back down. Or you can head down from Gentianes on another off-piste route to Tortin; the whole north-facing run from the top to Tortin is

Verbier's new signs: a great improvement on the ones we have struggled with for years →

WENDY-JANE KING

KEY FACTS

Resort	1500m
	4,920ft

4 Valleys area	
Slopes	1500-3330m
	4,920-10,930ft
Lifts	89
Pistes	410km
	255 miles
Blue	33%
Red	41%
Black	26%
Snowmaking	50km
	31 miles

Verbier, Bruson and Tzoumaz/Savoleyres sectors only (covered by Verbier pass)

Slopes	1500-3025m
	4,920-9,920ft
Lifts	40
Pistes	150km
	93 miles
Blue	33%
Red	33%
Black	34%
Snowmaking	20km
	12 miles

LIFT PASSES

4 Valleys/Mont-Fort

Prices in SF

Age	1-day	6-day
under 14	32	166
14 to 19	51	265
20 to 64	64	331
over 65	51	265
Free under 6; over 77		
Beginner no deals		

Notes
Covers all lifts and ski-buses in Verbier, Mont-Fort, Bruson, La Tzoumaz, Nendaz, Veysonnaz and Thyon; part-day passes; family reductions

Alternative passes
Verbier only; La Tzoumaz/Savoleyres only; Bruson only

almost 1300m/4,270ft vertical. A cable car returns to Col des Gentianes.

Below Tortin is the gateway to the rest of the 4 Valleys, **Siviez**, where one 'ridiculously outdated' chair goes off into the long, thin **Nendaz** sector (described later in this chapter) and a fast quad heads for the **Thyon-Veysonnaz** sector, via a couple of lifts and a lot of catwalks.

Allow plenty of time to get to and from these remote corners – the taxi-rides home are expensive.

The slopes of **Bruson** are described briefly at the end of this chapter.

TERRAIN PARKS
Expert and beginner options

The 1936 Neipark, Verbier's main freestyle area, is at La Chaux. The park has four separate lines they call soft, medium, hard and rail. These are made up of kickers, gap jumps, step-ups and hips. The rails are varied with boxes and rails of all types and a skate-style pyramid, which is the outstanding feature and gives the park its identity. There is a chill-out zone with deckchairs and DJs. New last season was a permanent BBQ, great for avoiding crowded restaurants. A day terrain park pass and freestyle coaching (check www.snowschool.ch) are both available. Note that helmets

are mandatory. A second smaller park in Savoleyres is more geared to beginner freestylers and a boardercross is situated in Le Taillay.

SNOW RELIABILITY
Improved snowmaking

The slopes of the Mont-Fort glacier always have good snow. The runs to Tortin are normally snow-sure, too. But nearly all of this is steep, and much of it is formally off-piste. Most of Verbier's main local slopes face south or west and are below 2500m/8,200ft – so they can be in poor condition at times. There is snowmaking on the main run down all the way from Attelas to Médran and to La Chaux. The nursery slopes and some of Savoleyres-La Tzoumaz are covered. At Veysonnaz-Thyon snowmaking was increased to cover 80% of the area a couple of seasons ago. We were very impressed with its use on the runs down to Mayens-de-L'Ours and to Veysonnaz. Piste grooming is good throughout the 4 Valleys, particularly at La Chaux.

FOR EXPERTS
The main attraction

Verbier has some superb tough slopes, many of them off-piste and needing a guide – see separate feature panel.

boarding

Verbier has become synonymous with extreme snowboarding and is generally seen as a freeriders' resort, with powder, cliffs, natural hits and trees all easily accessible. There is no wonder this is the best resort on the Freeride world tour (see www.freerideworldtour.com). For years the Bec des Rosses has been home to the most high-profile events of the sort on the calendar. There is a lot of steep and challenging terrain to be explored with a guide, but the pistes and itinéraires will provide most riders with plenty to think about. The main area is serviced by chairlifts and gondolas with no drags, and there is a good terrain park at La Chaux, which improves every year. Beginners should stick to the lower blue runs and the Savoleyres area, but there are several draglifts there. Advanced riders can find heli-boarding offers at www.lafantastique.com.

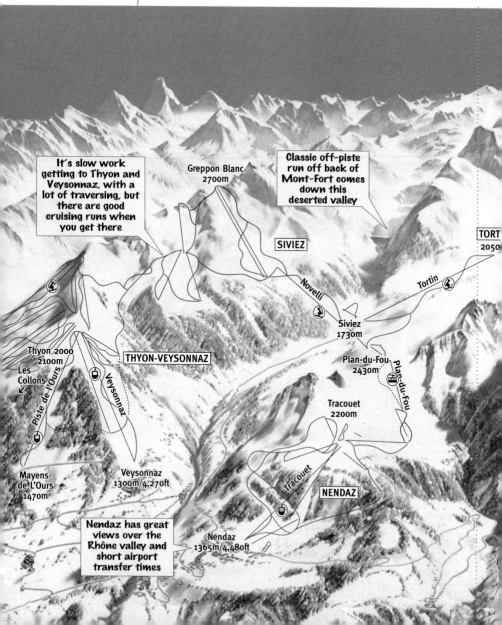

There are few conventional black pistes; most of the runs that might have this designation are now defined as itinéraires – which means they are 'marked, not maintained and not controlled'. But they are closed if unsafe or if snow-cover is insufficient. We'd like to see them given official black piste status, so you know clearly where you stand. The blacks that do exist are mostly indistinguishable from nearby reds. The front face of Mont-Fort is an exception: a long mogul field, with a choice of gradient from seriously steep to intimidatingly steep. The World Cup run (Piste de l'Ours) at Veysonnaz is a steepish, often icy ('sometimes quite dangerous' says a 2008 reporter) red, ideal for really speeding down when in good nick. The two itinéraires to Tortin are both excellent in their different ways. The one from Chassoure starts with a rocky traverse at the top ('Why can't they spend the summer making this a proper track?' asks a regular visitor)

It's slow work getting to Thyon and Veysonnaz, with a lot of traversing, but there are good cruising runs when you get there

Greppon Blanc 2700m

Classic off-piste run off back of Mont-Fort comes down this deserted valley

SIVIEZ

TORT 2050

Novelli

Tortin

Siviez 1730m

Thyon 2000 2100m
Les Collons

THYON-VEYSONNAZ

Plan-du-Fou 2430m

Plan-du-Fou

Piste de l'Ours

Veysonnaz

Tracouet 2200m

Mayens-de-L'Ours 1470m

Veysonnaz 1300m/4,270ft

Tracouet

NENDAZ

Nendaz has great views over the Rhône valley and short airport transfer times

Nendaz 1365m/4,48oft

and is then normally one huge, steep, wide mogul field. The north-facing itinéraire from Gentianes is longer, less steep, but feels much more of an adventure (keep left for quieter and shallower slopes and better snow).

FOR INTERMEDIATES
Hit Savoleyres – or Veysonnaz
Many mileage-hungry intermediates find Verbier disappointing. The intermediate slopes in the main area are concentrated between Les Attelas

and the village, above and below Les Ruinettes, plus the little bowl at Lac des Vaux and the sunny slopes at La Chaux. This is all excellent and varied intermediate territory, but there isn't much of it – to put it in perspective, this whole area is no bigger than the tiny slopes of Alpbach – and it is used by the bulk of the visitors staying in one of Switzerland's largest resorts. So it is often very crowded, especially the otherwise wonderful sweeping red from Les Attelas to Les Ruinettes (but

MONT-FORT
3330m/10,930ft

The top and bottom dotted lines here are the Gentianes and Tortin itinéraires, skied by most good skiers but technically off-piste. Outrageous – they should be official black pistes

Lovely red run, much improved by recent removal of rocks; often quiet

Col des Gentianes
2950m

Mont-Gelé
3025m

3 Jumbo

La Chaux
2260m

Col des Gentianes

Chassoure
2740m

Mont-Gelé

LES ATTELAS

Chaux Express

TORTIN
2050m

Chassoure

L. des Vaux I

2730m

Attelas

Funispace

Lac des Vaux
2545m

Col des Mines
2320m

LES RUINETTES

2200m

Bruson

Restaurant
de Clambin

Le Châble

Our favourite run in Verbier: the Vallon d'Arby itinéraire

The best (along with La Chaux) and quietest intermediate slopes

Vallon d'Arby

Medran I & II

Verbier
1500m/4,920ft

SAVOLEYRES

Taillay

Savoleyres

Savoleyres
2355m

Savoleyres

La Tzoumaz

Savoleyres

La Tzoumaz
1500m/4,920ft

Verbier has some of the best, most extensive and most varied off-piste in the world, and major freeride competitions are held there every year. Here, we pick out just a few of the off-piste runs on offer. See 'For experts' for the status of itinéraires. For the other runs here you should hire a guide.

The Col de Mines and Vallon d'Arby itinéraires, accessible from Lac des Vaux, are relatively easy (and usually less crowded and skied out than the better-known Tortin and Gentianes itinéraires) – the former is a long, open slope back to Verbier and the latter a very beautiful run in a steep-sided valley down to La Tzoumaz and the Savoleyres lifts. Further afield, the long Eteygeon itinéraire from Greppon Blanc above Siviez is 'heavenly and way better than Vallon d'Arby' says a reporter who lives locally; it ends up on the road and you catch a bus back to Les Masses (see end of chapter).

Stairway to Heaven is usually quiet (we were the only people on it when we did it last March) and its snow is kept in good condition by the lack of crowds and its shady orientation. It starts a short ski, pole and steep climb from Col des Gentianes. Then you drop over the ridge into a deserted valley, and it's a long, relatively easy ski down to Tortin, pretty much parallel to the Gentianes itinéraire.

The Mt-Gelé cable car offers some of the most amazing terrain accessible anywhere by lift, with long runs down to Siviez on steep but open slopes, before a scenic traverse and schuss along the valley. Or go down the opposite side of the mountain through the steep rock face towards Lac de Vaux (not a route for the faint hearted). The many couloirs accessible from Attelas can also be fantastic. There are serious adventures to be had off the back of Mont-Fort – we went last March and loved it (except for the long walk out past Lac de Cleuson); it's a vast bowl and we found fresh powder even though it hadn't snowed for days and there were lots of people dotted around; you end up at Siviez.

SCHOOLS

Swiss
t 775 3363 / 3369

Fantastique
t 771 4141

Adrenaline
t 771 7459

Altitude
t 771 6006

New Generation
t 771 1181 /
+33 479 010318

European Snowsport
t 771 6222

Powder Extreme
t 020 8123 9483 (UK)

Warren Smith Ski Academy
t 01525 374757 (UK)

Classes
(Swiss prices)
5 2½hr days SF240

Private lessons
From SF155 for 2hr
for 1 or 2 people

GUIDES

Bureau des guides
t 775 3363

Olivier Roduit
t 771 5317

this is quieter now there's the chondola from La Chaux to Les Ruinettes). There is excellent easy blue-run skiing at La Chaux (including a 'slow skiing' piste, though this doesn't seem to be policed). Getting back from La Chaux to Les Ruinettes is now a lot easier as you can ride the chondola instead of taking a red run.

Intermediates should exploit the under-used Savoleyres area. This has good intermediate pistes, usually better snow and far fewer people (especially on Sundays). It is also a good hill for mixed abilities, with variations of many runs. There is a blue run linking this sector to Médran but the way down to that link from the top of Savoleyres is not easy.

The Veysonnaz-Thyon and Nendaz sectors are worth exploring (those not willing to take on the itinéraires can ride down to Tortin, and down from Plan du Fou to get to Nendaz). Some of the reds here might be blacks elsewhere – the one at Combatzeline is consistently steep.

FOR BEGINNERS
OK but not ideal
There are sunny nursery slopes close to the middle of the village and at Les Esserts, at the top of it. These are fine provided they have snow (they have a lot of snowmaking, which helps). For progression, there are easy blues at La Chaux (you can ride the chondola back

to Les Ruinettes) and the back side of Savoleyres (from where you can ride the gondola down). Siviez has a really gentle, wide blue.

FOR CROSS-COUNTRY
Surprisingly little on offer
There's a 4km/2.5 mile loop in Verbier, 6km/4 miles at Les Ruinettes-La Chaux and 12km/7 miles down the valley in Champsec and Lourtier.

QUEUES
Not the problem they were
Queues have been greatly eased by recent investment in powerful new lifts. The cable car from Tortin to Col des Gentianes and the Mont-Fort cable car above it can still generate queues. Some queues at the main village lift station at Médran can arise if Sunday visitors fill the gondola down at Le Châble, but the crowds shift quickly.

Queues can occur for outdated double chairs and inadequate draglifts in the outlying 4 Valleys resorts.

Savoleyres is generally queue-free.

MOUNTAIN RESTAURANTS
Could do better
There are not enough huts, which means overcrowding in high season and queues unless you book ahead for table service – a 2008 visitor found 25-minute queues for self-service in early March and was surprised to 'queue once for food and once for

drinks'. But the standard of food and service is improving.

Editors' choice In the main area, the rustic Restaurant de Clambin (771 2524), on the off-piste run on the southern fringe of the area, is a classic cosy old chalet. It is used to be Chez Dany but is now under new management; still about the best, and gets packed – booking needed.

Worth knowing about For a choice of good spots, Savoleyres is the place to go. The rustic Marmotte does superb rösti, but the Namasté is 'the best restaurant on the mountain' (booking essential). The Sonalon, on the fringe of the village, is 'excellent, with great views', but reached off-piste, as is the nearby Marlenaz ('what a great find, hearty and well recommended').

The self-service at the top of Savoleyres has 'good value' Italian and traditional dishes. The Poste hotel by the Tzoumaz chair takes some beating for value and lack of crowds.

Back in the main sector, the restaurants at Les Ruinettes – table service upstairs – have big terraces with splendid views. The Olympique at Les Attelas is a good table-service restaurant. The Powder Spirit Bar

(formerly the Attelas) does light meals. Au Mayen has 'interesting seafood choices'. Everyone loves the Cabane Mont-Fort – a proper mountain refuge off the run to La Chaux from Col des Gentianes – get there early or book a table. Chalet Carlsberg has a good position at La Combe and impressed us with fast and efficient service. Le Carrefour by the road near the top of the nursery slopes is 'very, very good' says a reporter who lives locally in winter; further afield, he recommends Les Chottes beneath Greppon Blanc ('not cheap but excellent food') and La Cambeuse at Les Collons.

SCHOOLS AND GUIDES
Good reports
There's no shortage of schools to choose between. We were very impressed with our mountain guide from Adrenaline last season and it has had good reviews for its private lessons. Altitude was started by top British instructors in 2001 and a 2008 reporter found it 'excellent for children. English instructors guaranteed and only two in their class.' The Swiss school has received a good report for private snowboard lessons. A recent

The Lac des Vaux bowl has a couple of nice intermediate pistes ↓

CHILDREN

Schtroumpfs
t 771 6585
Ages 3mnth to 4yr;
8.30 to 5.30

Kids Club
t 775 3363
From age 3;
8.30-5pm; 6 days
SF495 including lunch

Ski school
Takes children aged 4 to 12 (5 half days SF225)

GETTING THERE

Air Geneva
170km/106 miles
(2hr)

Rail Le Châble (7km/ 4 miles); regular buses to resort or gondola

reporter praised his Swiss instructor with European Snowsport. British instructor Warren Smith runs his Ski Academy here. Powder Extreme specialises in off-piste. We have skied with both Warren Smith and Powder Extreme and thought them both good. New Generation (see Courchevel chapter for glowing comments on them) have opened their first Swiss branch in the resort.

FACILITIES FOR CHILDREN
Wide range of options
The Swiss school's facilities in the resort are good. The possibility of leaving very young babies at the Schtroumpfs nursery is valuable. A 2008 visitor recommends the nanny services provided by Chalet Services Verbier. There are considerable reductions on the lift pass price for families on production of passports.

STAYING THERE

HOW TO GO
Plenty of options
Given the size of the place there are surprisingly few apartments and B&Bs available, though those on a budget have inexpensive B&B options in Le Châble. Hotels are expensive for their gradings. If you take a sleeping bag, you can bed down at the sports centre for about £10 a night – and that includes the use of the pool.
Chalets Verbier is the chalet-party capital of Switzerland. Lots of companies have properties here. Ski Verbier repeatedly gets good reports from readers and has an extensive and impressive portfolio at the top of the market, including the superb Septième Ciel. Descent has the splendid Goodwood and Virgin The Lodge.
Hotels There is a 5-star, five 4-stars, 10 3-stars and a few simpler places.
*****Chalet d'Adrien (771 6200) Relais

& Chateaux. A beautifully furnished low-rise 29-room chalet, with top-notch cooking. In a peaceful setting next to the Savoleyres lift, with great views. Neat spa/gym/pool.
****Nevaï (771 6121) Modern, minimalist, trendy, next to Farm Club (and in same ownership).
****Montpelier (771 6131) Very comfortable, but out of town (free courtesy bus). Pool.
****Vanessa (775 2800) Central, with spacious apartments as well as rooms; 'great food', says a reporter.
***Rotonde (771 6525) Much cheaper; well positioned between centre and Médran; some budget rooms.
***Poste (771 6681) Midway between centre and Médran; pool. Some rooms small. 'Friendly staff and great food.'
***Farinet (771 6626) Central, British-owned, with a focal après-ski bar.
***Au Vieux Valais (775 3520) Charming old chalet with friendly service at entrance to resort. We stayed there in 2008 and enjoyed it.
Apartments Ski Verbier has some nice looking self-catered places.

EATING OUT
Plenty of choice
There is a wide range of restaurants; many are listed in a free pocket guide, which would be much more useful if it gave some clues about price.
Now that the Rosalp has been sold, the 5-star Chalet d'Adrien is one of the best gourmet places in town. We had an excellent meal in the Nevaï hotel. King's (under the same ownership) is another of our favourites – innovative food in a stylish, club-like setting. We've also had good meals in the stylish Millénium. The traditional, small Ecurie does 'excellent steaks'.
For Swiss specialities, try the Relais des Neiges, the Caveau, Au Mignon, Au Vieux Verbier by the Médran lifts or Esserts by the nursery slopes. The

ever-popular Fer à Cheval does reasonably priced pizza and other simple dishes. Or try downstairs in the Pub Mont-Fort for 'top British gastropub food at reasonable prices'. The 'hanging meat' has to be tried at Al Capone's, out near the Savoleyres gondola – also known for its pizzas; we had excellent pizzas at Borsalino, near the centre of town. Harold's Snack internet cafe is a 'reasonable burger joint', and a 2007 visitor recommends Chez Martin for pasta.

You can be ferried by snowmobile up to Chez Dany or the Marmotte for a meal, followed by a torchlit descent.

APRES-SKI
Throbbing but expensive
It starts with a 4pm visit to the Powder Spirit Bar and its new DJ ('the liveliest place on the mountain') and moves to either the tents of 1936 or the Chalet Carlsberg (with a pay-as-you-soak hot tub) – both on the slopes – or the Offshore Cafe at Médran, for people-watching, milk shakes and cakes. The Big Ben pub is 'great and lively on a sunny afternoon'. Au Mignon at the bottom of the golf course has a popular sun deck.

Then if you're young, loud and British, it's on to the Pub Mont-Fort – there's a widescreen TV for live sport. The Nelson and Fer à Cheval are popular with locals. The Farinet has won awards for its après-ski and regularly rocks to live bands ('beer, band and bop were great'). Or you can sip sophisticated cocktails in its lounge bar next door.

After dinner the Pub Mont-Fort is again popular (the shots bar in the

cellar is worth a visit). Crok No Name is a cool bar with good live bands or a DJ. King's is a quiet candlelit cellar bar with 60s decor – 'hip crowd, good music'. New Club is a sophisticated piano bar, with comfortable seating and a more discerning clientele. The Farm Club is seriously expensive – on Friday and Saturday packed with rich Swiss paying SF220 for bottles of spirits. You'll find us having a quiet nightcap in the basement Bar'Jo, across the road.

The Casbah, in the basement of the Farinet hotel, is a nightclub with a North African theme.

OFF THE SLOPES
No great attraction
Verbier has an excellent sports centre (with pool, saunas and hot tubs), some nice walks and a big Alpine museum, but otherwise not much to offer if you don't want to hit the slopes. Montreux is an enjoyable train excursion from Le Châble, and Martigny is worth a visit for the Roman remains and art gallery. The spa complex at Lavey-les-Bains has been highly recommended by a reporter. Various mountain restaurants are accessible to pedestrians. A walker's pass (SF42) covers most of the local lifts. Swiss Mountain Spirit offer dog sledding trips. There's floodlit tubing etc at Les Esserts at the weekends.

Nendaz 1365m/4,480ft

Nendaz is a big resort with over 17,000 beds, but is little known in Britain. Although it appears to be centrally set in the 4 Valleys, getting

Ski Verbier
The Verbier Specialists

020 7401 1101   www.skiverbier.com

to and from the other sectors is a slow business unless you drive/take a bus to Siviez ('To get into the Verbier skiing takes a decent skier about 50 minutes to an hour,' said a reporter). In other respects it has attractions, relatively low prices among them. Airport transfers are quick, especially from Sion (20 minutes away).

THE RESORT

Nendaz itself is a large place with great views of the Rhône valley. Most of the resort is modern but built in traditional chalet style, and the original old village of Haute-Nendaz is still there, with its narrow streets, old houses and barns, and baroque chapel dating from 1499.

THE MOUNTAIN

Nendaz has its own area of slopes and a link to rest of the 4 Valleys via Siviez.

Slopes There's a 12-person gondola straight to the top of the local north-facing slopes at Tracouet. Here there are good, snow-sure nursery slopes plus blue and red intermediate runs.

Intermediates and better can head off down the back of Tracouet to a cable car that takes you to Plan du Fou at 2430m/7,970ft (but this area has no snowmaking and the runs can be closed – as they were on our March 2008 visit). From there you can go down to Siviez, on to a couple of sunny, steeper runs and the links to Verbier one way and Veysonnaz-Thyon the other. To return to Nendaz you have to negotiate an itinéraire from Plan du Fou (or you can take the cable car down), followed by a black run.

When poor snow closes the runs mentioned above, you need to drive or catch the regular bus between Nendaz and Siviez.

Terrain parks The beginner and advanced terrain parks have kickers, slides and a box.

Snow reliability Nendaz sits on a north-facing shelf so its local slopes don't get the sun that affects Verbier. The main run back to town has snowmaking, as does another blue. But see above for the link with Plan du Fou.

Experts Access to the tough stuff is a bit slower from here than from Verbier.

Intermediates The local slopes are quite varied, but not very extensive.

Beginners There are good nursery slopes at Tracouet.

Snowboarding The terrain is fine but there are quite a few draglifts.

Cross-country There are 12km/7.5 miles of cross-country tracks.

Queues There may be queues during peak periods, especially for some old lifts either side of Plan du Fou.

Mountain restaurants The Cabane de Balavaux under the Prarion chair is rustic; views on its food are mixed.

Schools and guides There are four ski schools plus mountain guides.

Facilities for children The schools have a nursery area at Tracouet and there's a resort kindergarten (Le P'tit Bec).

STAYING THERE

How to go UK chalet company Ted Bentley has three chalets; all have outdoor hot tubs. We loved the chalets Merri (great views over the Rhône valley) and Alice (modern and sleek) especially.

Indoor Sports centre (swimming pools, ice rink, curling, squash, sauna, solarium, steam bath, hot tub), cinema, museums, galleries

Outdoor 25km/ 16 miles of cleared walking paths, hang-gliding, paragliding, snowshoeing, horse riding, dog sledding, tobogganing, ice climbing, airboarding

Alpine Answers, Alpine Weekends, Belvedere Chalets, Bramble Ski, Chalet Group, Chalet World Ski, Crystal, Crystal Finest, Descent International, Elegant Resorts, Erna Low, First Choice, Flexiski, Independent Ski Links, Inghams, Interactive Resorts, Interhome, Jeffersons, Kaluma, Made to Measure, Momentum, Mountain Beds, Mountain Tracks, Oxford Ski Co, Peak Ski, Powder White, Ski Activity, Ski Expectations, Ski Freedom, Ski Freshtracks, Ski Independence, Ski Line, Ski Solutions, Ski Total, Ski Verbier, Ski Weekend, Skiweekends.com, Ski with Julia, Skitracer, Skiworld, Snowrks, Supertravel, White Roc **Nendaz** Alpine Answers, Crystal, Interhome, Lagrange, Ski Independence, Ted Bentley **Siviez** Interhome **Les Collons** Ardmore

Hotels There are four small hotels. The 3-star Mont-Fort (288 2616) is 150m from the lifts.

Apartments There is no shortage of apartments and chalets to rent.

Eating out The Mont Rouge hotel restaurant is said to be 'the best in town, but not cheap'. La Cabane is 'very atmospheric, serves fondue, raclette etc'; Au Petit Valais and La Raccard also do local mountain food. Chez Edith, out of town on the way to Siviez is recommended by a local.

Après-ski The Cantina gets packed (outside and in) when the lifts close and is popular with ski instructors, the Malabar is 'a funky wine bar'. Later on 'head for the Canadian, which has a disco and opens till 4am or the T'Chin T'Chin piano bar for a quieter time'. A 17-year-old recommended the Cactus Saloon as one of the livelier spots.

Off the slopes Nendaz has 100km/ 62 miles of walks, an ice rink, fitness centre, climbing wall, squash courts.

Siviez 1730m/5,680ft

Siviez is a small huddle of buildings in an isolated spot, where the slopes of Verbier, Nendaz and Veysonnaz-Thyon meet. One of these buildings is the 3-star hotel de Siviez (288 1623). It is an ideal base from which to explore the whole 4 Valleys lift network, and the fast quad to Combatzeline has made this easier. The long and gentle blue run through the sheltered valley from Tortin is ideal beginner territory. Being set a little way down the valley from Tortin, at the foot of the steep itinerary runs from Chassoure and Mont-Fort, means it is also an excellent base for doing the tough skiing of Verbier – you can end the day with a descent of 1600m/5,250ft vertical from Mont-Fort; no noise in the evenings; perfect.

Veysonnaz 1300m/4,270ft

Veysonnaz is a small, quiet, family resort, sunny in the afternoon, at the foot of an excellent, long red slope from the ridge above Thyon. A second excellent (though often icy) red regularly used for international races descends to the isolated lift base of Mayens de l'Ours.

The resort is spread widely across and down the hillside, with wide views across the Rhone valley. The original attractive old village, complete with

church, is two hairpin bends below Veysonnaz Station, the lift base and the main focus of the place for the visitor. This has the essential facilities – half a dozen bars and cafes, four restaurants, a disco or two and a 'good' wellness centre with swimming pool and spa facilities. There are adequate shops.

Accommodation is mainly in apartments – substantial chalet-style buildings dotted along the road across the hillside from the lift base. There are plenty of smaller chalets, too. Of the two three-star hotels, the 'very comfortable' Chalet Royal (208 5644) is reportedly preferable to the Magrappé, which is the focus of noisy après-ski. There are some B&Bs.

Taking a car means you can drive to Siviez for quick access to the Verbier or Nendaz slopes, and the resort is only 15km/9 miles from the old town of Sion, which is at the heart of the Coeur du Valais region of which Veysonnaz is a part and which is well worth exploring. The link up to Thyon has been improved – it is now an eight-seat gondola – but after that progress towards Verbier is a slow business. There is, of course, a branch of the Swiss ski school, and its literature is in English as well as French and German.

There is a 5km/3 miles cross-country trail along the mountainside, with panoramic views.

Thyon 2000 2100m/6,890ft

Thyon 2000 – also part of the Coeur du Valais region – is a functional, purpose-built collection of plain, medium-rise apartment blocks just above the treeline at the hub of the Thyon-Veysonnaz sector of the 4 Valleys. It has the basics of resort life – supermarket, newsagent, a couple of bar-restaurants, an indoor pool, a disco. A free shuttle-bus runs to Les Collons. There's a fair-sized terrain park with snowmaking – reputedly one of Switzerland's first – and boardercross, 'good' children's snow-garden and a kindergarten as well as a ski school. The slopes are ideal for families and beginners, with two nursery lifts close to the accommodation. The lift network shared with Les Collons and Les Masses is elderly and slow – mainly draglifts, with three chairlifts at key points. There is extensive snowmaking.

↑ Nendaz is quite a large resort with splendid views
NENDAZ TOURISME

Weekly news updates and resort links at www.wtss.co.uk

Phone numbers
From elsewhere in Switzerland add the prefix 027; from abroad use the prefix +41 27

TOURIST OFFICES

Verbier
t 775 3888
info@verbier.ch
www.verbier.ch

Nendaz
t 289 5589
info@nendaz.ch
www.nendaz.ch

Siviez
www.siviez-nendaz.ch

Veysonnaz
t 207 1053
tourism
@veysonnaz.ch
www.veysonnaz.ch

**Thyon 2000 /
Les Collons**
t 281 2727
thyon-region
@coeurduvalais.ch
www.thyon-region.ch

Le Châble and Bruson
bagnestourisme
@verbier.ch

Les Collons 1800m/5,910ft

Some 300m/980ft below Thyon, at the foot of a broad, east-facing slope, Les Collons is a couple of strings of chalet-style buildings spread along two roads following the hillside, 50m/160ft vertical apart; a lot of building has been going on here recently. Most accommodation is in apartments, but there are also a couple of modest hotels – including the 3-star Cambuse (281 1883) just below one of the lift bases. There's a wider range of bars, restaurants and other diversions than in Thyon. There is a 1km/0.5 mile toboggan run through the woods above the village. Prepared walking trails add up to a modest 7km/4 miles. Three draglifts go up towards Thyon from the upper level of the resort, and a chairlift from the lower level takes you above Thyon. There's 6km/4 miles of cross-country. A free shuttle-bus runs to Thyon.

Les Masses 1515m/4,970ft

Half-a-dozen hairpins down the mountainside from Les Collons, Les Masses is no more than a hamlet at the base of the double chairlifts that form the southern limit of the Thyon-Veysonnaz slopes. The home run is a red. Accommodation is in apartments. There is a grocery and a restaurant.

Le Châble 820m/2,690ft

Le Châble is a busy roadside village in the valley, at the bottom of the hairpin road up to Verbier. It is linked to Verbier by a queue-free gondola that goes on (without changing cabins) to Les Ruinettes, which means access to the slopes can be just as quick as from Verbier. Le Châble is on the rail network, and is also convenient for drivers who want to visit other resorts in the Valais or further afield. And it is handy for Bruson. There are several modest hotels, of which the 2-star Giétroz (776 1184) is the pick. The Tzana restaurant has been praised by a 2008 reporter for 'good meat, well presented, very good wines'.

Bruson 1000m/3,280ft

Bruson is a small village on a shelf just above Le Châble, and reached by a short free bus ride. Its lifts are covered by the Verbier pass. From the village a slow chair goes up over gentle east-facing slopes dotted with chalets to Bruson les Forêts (1600m/5,250ft).

The open slopes above Bruson les Forêts are served by a quad chair up to the ridge, on the far side of which is a short draglift serving a tight little bowl. In addition to the intermediate pistes served by these lifts there are large areas of underused off-piste terrain, notably through woods on the front side accessed by the drag on the back. The off-piste down the back towards Orsières is good; you return by train. For years there have been plans to develop Bruson – building lifts from Le Châble and Orsières, and extending the lift network. A proposed new Intrawest village here has been held up at the planning stages. For now, it remains a great place to escape Verbier crowds: 'worth going for a day out – we had excellent powder', says a 2008 visitor.

Traditional year-round resort with local low-altitude slopes and a much needed but far-flung glacier

COSTS

① ② ③ ④ ⑤ ⑥

RATINGS

The slopes

Fast lifts	★★★
Snow	★★
Extent	★★★
Expert	★★
Intermediate	★★★
Beginner	★★★★
Convenience	★★
Queues	★★★
Mountain restaurants	★★★

The rest

Scenery	★★★
Resort charm	★★★★
Off-slope	★★★★

NEWS

A new 5-star hotel, Chalet Royalp, with 63 rooms, spa and pool is due to open in December 2008.

➕ Pleasant, relaxing year-round resort

➕ Fairly extensive intermediate slopes linked to Les Diablerets

➕ Good nursery slopes

➕ Quite close to Geneva airport

➕ Good range of off-slope diversions

➖ Unreliable snow-cover

➖ Overcrowded mountain restaurants

➖ Short runs on the upper slopes

➖ Getting up the mountain can be a bit of a trial

➖ Not much to amuse experts

With its mountain railway and gentle low-altitude slopes, Villars is the kind of place that has been overshadowed by modern mega-resorts. But for a relaxing and varied family holiday the attractions are clear – and the link with Les Diablerets and its glacier, known as Glacier 3000, adds to the appeal.

THE RESORT

Villars sits on a sunny shelf, looking across the Rhône valley to the Portes du Soleil. A busy high street lined with a variety of shops gives it the air of a pleasant small town; all around are chalet-style buildings, with just a few block-like hotels.

You can travel to the centre of Villars on a picturesque cog train from Bex in the valley that goes on (slowly) up to the slopes around Bretaye. A gondola at the other end of town is the main lift; stay nearby if you can, since ski-buses can be 'infrequent' and crowded. The linked sector of Les Chaux also has lodgings at Gryon or Alpes des Chaux – less convenient if the access draglift is closed.

You can get a whole area pass covering Les Diablerets and Glacier 3000, plus Leysin and Les Mosses, both of which are easy jaunts by rail or road. Getting to the glacier is a long, slow business though – buses from Les Diablerets are infrequent. Outings to Verbier are easily possible.

553

Bretaye ↗
SNOWPIX.COM / CHRIS GILL

KEY FACTS

Resort	1300m
	4,270ft

Villars, Gryon and Les Diablerets, but excluding Glacier 3000

Slopes	1115-2120m
	3,660-6,960ft
Lifts	35
Pistes	100km
	62 miles
Blue	40%
Red	50%
Black	10%
Snowmaking	10km
	6 miles

Phone numbers
From elsewhere in Switzerland add the prefix 024; from abroad use the prefix +41 24

TOURIST OFFICE

t 495 3232
information@villars.ch
www.villars.ch

THE MOUNTAINS

There's a good mix of open and wooded slopes throughout the area. Most reporters agree that the piste map and marking are poor.

Slopes The cog train goes up to the col of Bretaye, which has intermediate slopes on either side, with a maximum vertical of 300m/980ft to the col and much longer runs back to the village. To the east, open slopes (often spoilt by sun) go to La Rasse and the link to the Les Chaux sector. The gondola from town takes you to Roc d'Orsay, from where you can head for Bretaye or back to Villars. A long, slow, two-way chairlift links to Les Diablerets. The slopes on the glacier are limited, but there is a splendid run down the Combe d'Audon back to the valley (reclassified black this year).

Terrain parks There are parks at Les Chaux and Chaux Ronde, and a half-pipe at Les Diablerets.

Snow reliability Low altitude and sunny slopes mean snow reliability isn't good – though a modest snowfall produces good conditions on such gentle, grassy terrain. More snowmaking is badly needed.

Experts The main interest for experts is off-piste. Heli-skiing is available.

Intermediates The local slopes and Les Diablerets offer a good variety and add up to a fair amount of terrain. Chamossaire has some quieter reds.

Beginners Beginners will enjoy the village nursery slopes and riding the train to Bretaye. There are gentle runs here, too, but it's also very crowded.

Snowboarding There are quite a few draglifts, including some on the link with Les Diablerets.

Cross-country The trails up the valley past La Rasse are long and pretty, and there are more in the depression beyond Bretaye (44km/27 miles in all).

Queues Queues appear for the lifts at Bretaye mainly at weekends and peak periods, and the buses and train can get overcrowded.

Mountain restaurants They are often oversubscribed – most notably the Col de Soud. But the Golf is 'still excellent'. The Lac des Chavonnes is popular and worth the walk from Bretaye. The restaurant at the top of the Roc d'Orsay is also 'very good'.

Schools and guides A recent visitor praised 'excellent, friendly and conscientious' instructors from the Swiss school. The Villars ski school

has also had good reports in the past.

Facilities for children Both ski schools run children's classes, but group sizes were considered too large by one parent. There is also a non-ski nursery for children up to six.

STAYING THERE

How to go Several tour operators offer packages here. We have had glowing reports on the Club Med. If you fancy sleeping in a hi-tech tent out in the wilds, go to www.whitepod.com.

Hotels The new 5-star Chalet Royalp (495 9090) near the railway, with pool and spa facilities, is due to open for 2008/09. It will also have a couple of restaurants and a bar. The Golf (496 3838) is popular, with 'spacious rooms' and 'excellent restaurant'. The Eurotel Victoria (495 3131) lacks style but is near the gondola. The Bristol (496 3636) is not, but is comfortable and recommended. All are 4-star. The 3-star Alpe Fleurie (496 3070) near the railway station is 'spacious and comfortable'.

Eating out Many restaurants are hotel-based. Apart from these, the Sporting is recommended for pizza, the Vieux-Villars for local specialities and the Rôtisserie des Alpes for 'great service'.

Après-ski Charlie's, the Sporting and the Mini-Pub are the main bars. The Bowling bar is a fun alternative; and El Gringo's is a nightclub.

Off the slopes Paragliding is available, plus tennis, skating, snowshoeing, swimming, 'excellent' walks, and trips on the train – to Lausanne, say.

UK PACKAGES

Alpine Answers, Alpine Weekends, Club Med, Crystal, Crystal Finest, Independent Ski Links, Inghams, Kuoni, Lagrange, Made to Measure, Momentum, Ski Expectations, Ski Independence, Ski Line, Ski Solutions, Ski Weekend, Skitracer, Switzerland Travel Centre, Thomson

A charming old village amid stunning scenery, where life revolves around the mountain railway; the slopes, somehow, are secondary

COSTS

① ② ③ ④ ⑤ ⑥

RATINGS

The slopes

Fast lifts	****
Snow	**
Extent	***
Expert	**
Intermediate	****
Beginner	***
Convenience	***
Queues	***
Mountain restaurants	****

The rest

Scenery	*****
Charm	*****
Off-slope	****

NEWS

For 2007/08 the Honegg draglift (on the Grindelwald side of Kleine Scheidegg) was replaced by a six-pack with covers. And the first phase of substantial new snowmaking for the upper part of the mountain on both sides of Kleine Scheidegg began with the construction of a new artificial lake. For 2008/09 it is planned to cover 50% of the slopes in the Kleine Scheidegg-Männlichen area with snowmaking. For 2009/10 they plan to replace the Salzegg drag to Eigergletscher with a six-pack.

+ Some of the most spectacular scenery in the Alps

+ Tiny, traditional, nearly traffic-free Alpine village

+ Lots of long, gentle runs, ideal for intermediates

+ Nursery slopes in heart of village

+ Calm, unhurried atmosphere

+ Good resort for families and groups that include non-skiers – easy to get around on mountain railways

– Limited terrain for experts and adventurous intermediates

– Natural snow unreliable (but snow-making is at last being increased)

– Trains to slopes are slow – and there are quite a few drags and slow chairs

– Getting to Grindelwald's First area can take hours

– Subdued in the evening, with little variety of nightlife

Given the charm of the village, the friendliness of the locals and the drama of the scenery, it's easy to see why many people love Wengen – including large numbers of Brits who have been going for decades. It's great for a relaxing time, for those who don't take their skiing too seriously, for families and for mixed groups of intermediates and non-skiers.

But keen piste-bashers should beware of the drawbacks: slow lifts (the only ways up from the village are a slow, infrequent cog railway or a queue-prone cable car), poor natural snow reliability and a lack of challenging pistes are the key factors. If you're used to the modern village ambience and snow-sure networks of slopes of the Trois Vallées resorts or Val d'Isère, you'll find Wengen a huge contrast. Come here for the relaxed ambience, not for piste-bashing.

THE RESORT

Wengen is set on a shelf high above the Lauterbrunnen valley, opposite Mürren, and reached only by a cog railway, which carries on up the mountain as the main lift. It was a farming community long before skiing arrived; it is still tiny, but dominated by sizeable hotels, mostly of Victorian origin. So it is not exactly chocolate-box pretty, but it is charming and relaxed, and almost traffic-free. The only vehicles are electric hotel taxi-trucks and a few ordinary, engine-driven taxis. (Why, we wonder?)

The short main street is the hub of the village. Lined with chalet-style shops and hotels, it also has the ice rink and village nursery slopes right next to it. The nursery slopes double as the venue for floodlit ski jumping and parallel slalom races.

The views across the valley are stunning. They get even better higher up, when the famous trio of peaks comes fully into view – the Mönch (Monk) protecting the Jungfrau (Maiden) from the Eiger (Ogre).

The main way up the mountain is to use the regular, usually punctual trains from the southern end of the street to Kleine Scheidegg (about a half-hour journey), where the slopes of Wengen meet those of Grindelwald. The cable car is a much quicker way to the Grindelwald slopes, and starts conveniently close to the main street.

Wengen is small, so location isn't as crucial as in many other resorts. The main street is ideally placed for the station. There are hotels on the home piste, convenient for the slopes. Those who don't fancy a steepish morning climb should avoid places down the hill below the station.

You can get to Mürren by taking the train to Lauterbrunnen, then a cable car and train to Winteregg (where you get a chairlift up and ski down to the village) or to Mürren itself, where you have to walk though the village to the other lifts. Alternatively you can take a bus to Stechelberg and then a cable car up. The Jungfrau lift pass covers all of this. Outings further afield aren't really worth the effort.

KEY FACTS

Resort	1275m
	4,180ft
Jungfrau region	
Slopes	945-2970m
	3,100-9,740ft
Lifts	44
Pistes	213km
	132 miles
Blue	25%
Red	61%
Black	14%
Snowmaking	85km
	53 miles
First-Männlichen-Kleine-Scheidegg only	
Slopes	945-2485m
	3,100-8,150ft
Lifts	28
Pistes	160km
	99 miles
Snowmaking	75km
	47 miles

THE MOUNTAINS

Although Wengen is famous for the fearsome Lauberhorn Downhill course – the longest and one of the toughest on the World Cup circuit – its slopes are best suited to early intermediates. Most of the Downhill course is now open to the public and the steepest section (the Hundschopf jump) can be avoided by an alternative red route. Most of Wengen's runs are gentle blues and reds, ideal for cruising.

THE SLOPES
Picturesque playground
Most of the slopes are on the Grindelwald side of the mountain. From the railway station at Kleine Scheidegg you can head straight down to Grindelwald or work your way across the mountain with the help of a couple of lifts to the top of the Männlichen. This area is served by one drag and several chairlifts, and can be reached directly from Wengen by the cable car. There are a few runs back down towards Wengen from the top of the Lauberhorn, but there's really only one below Wengernalp.

TERRAIN PARKS
Try the Bumps
There was a park by the Bumps draglift below Wengernalp last season and we are told it is very likely to be there for 2008/09. Otherwise, the nearest parks are at First and Mürren – each a fair trek.

SNOW RELIABILITY
Improved snowmaking may help
Most slopes are below 2000m/6,560ft, and at Grindelwald they go down to less than 1000m/3,280ft. Very few slopes face north, and the long blue run back to the village suffers from sun and lack of altitude. So good natural snow is far from certain. Views on the snowmaking continue to improve ('very impressed – the main piste to Wengen was kept open', 'a white road in a sea of green'). We hope the increased snowmaking plan higher up (see 'News') will make a difference. A 2008 visitor found: 'piste maintenance awful'.

FOR EXPERTS
Few challenges
Wengen is quite limited for experts. The only genuine black runs in the area are parts of the Lauberhorn World

Cup Downhill and a couple of pistes from Eigergletscher towards Wixi including Oh God (which used to be off-piste). There are some decent off-piste runs such as White Hare from under the north face of the Eiger and more adventurous runs from the Jungfraujoch late in the season (see the Grindelwald chapter for more about going to the Jungfraujoch).

For more serious challenges it's well worth going to nearby Mürren, around an hour away.

Heli-trips with mountain guides are organised if there are enough takers.

FOR INTERMEDIATES
Wonderful if the snow is good
Wengen and Grindelwald share superb intermediate slopes. Nearly all are long blue or gentle red runs – see the Grindelwald chapter. The run back to Wengen is a relaxing end to the day, as long as it's not too crowded.

For tougher pistes, head for the top of the Lauberhorn lift and then the runs to Kleine Scheidegg, or to Wixi (following the start of the Downhill course). You could also try the north-facing run from Eigergletscher to Salzegg, which often has the best snow late in the season.

FOR BEGINNERS
Not ideal
There's a nursery slope in the centre of the village – convenient and gentle, but the snow is unreliable. There's a beginners' area at Wengernalp and another on the Grindelwald side of Kleine Scheidegg, but to get back to Wengen you either have to take the train or tackle the run down, which can be tricky, with some flat sections. There are plenty of good, long, gentle runs to progress to above Grindelwald.

FOR CROSS-COUNTRY
There is none
There's no cross-country in Wengen itself. There are 12km/7 miles of tracks down in the Lauterbrunnen valley, where the snow is unreliable.

QUEUES
Village crowds, better higher up
Both the train and the cable car can be crowded at peak periods. It is best to avoid travelling up at the same time as the ski school. Queues up the mountain have been alleviated a lot in the last few years by the installation of fast chairs, and recent reporters

Jungfrau Top Ski Region

Prices in SF

Age	1-day	6-day
under 16	29	148
16 to 19	46	236
20 to 61	57	295
over 62	51	266

Free under 6

Beginner points card

Notes
Covers Wengen, Mürren and Grindelwald, trains between them and Grindelwald ski-bus; day pass price is for First-Kleine Scheidegg-Männlichen area only

Alternative passes
Grindelwald and Wengen only; Mürren only; non-skier pass

boarding

Wengen is not a bad place for gentle boarding – the nursery area is not ideal, but beginners have plenty of slopes to progress to, with lots of long blue and red runs served by the train and chairlifts. Getting from Kleine Scheidegg to Männlichen means an unavoidable draglift, though. And the slope back to Wengen is narrow and almost flat in places, so you may have to scoot. For the steepest slopes and best freeriding, experts will want to head for Mürren.

have experienced few problems in midweek. But weekend invasions can increase the crowds, especially on the Grindelwald side and especially on a Saturday, when children up to 15 can ski free if a parent buys a day pass.

MOUNTAIN RESTAURANTS
Plenty of variety
Editors' choice The Jungfrau hotel at Wengernalp (855 1622) – where the rösti is excellent and the views of the Jungfrau from the sunny terrace are superb – is expensive but worth it; you need to book. 'The best lunch of the week', says a 2008 visitor. You also get magnificent views from the narrow outside balcony of Wengen's highest restaurant Eigergletscher – get there early to grab a table. 'A fresh half pineapple with curry filling is by far the most interesting dish,' says a recent reporter.

Worth knowing about The station buffet at Kleine Scheidegg gets repeated rave reviews, so it's not surprising it also gets packed – the

rösti and sausage are popular ('The best food we had on the mountain,' says a visitor). A 2007 reporter recommends the nearby Bellvue hotel for 'good food and excellent service'. The Grindelwaldblick is a worthwhile trudge uphill from Kleine Scheidegg, for 'a tasty and good value lunch with generous portions and attentive service' and views of the Eiger.

The Allmend, near the top of the Innerwengen chair and the train stop, is a 'great place to meet towards the end of the day' with 'friendly service' and wonderful views of the valley from the terrace. Reports on Mary's Cafe (situated at the end of the World Cup runs) are mixed: 'Very comfy, with open fires, but disappointed with the food.' For restaurants on the slopes towards Grindelwald, see that chapter.

SCHOOLS AND GUIDES
Healthy competition
Reports on the Swiss school are generally good. One recent visitor found the lessons 'excellent, well

Wengen

557

SCHOOLS

Swiss
t 855 2022

Privat
t 855 5005

Classes
(Swiss prices)
6 3hr days SF260

Private lessons
SF140 for 2hr

CHILDREN

Playhouse
t 855 2760
From 18mnth;
9am-5pm; Sun-Fri

Kinderhort Sunshine
t 854 8080
Ages from 1mnth to
8yr; 8.30-5pm

Babysitters
List available from
tourist office

Ski school
The Swiss school
takes ages 4 up
(6 3hr days SF260)

WENGEN-MÜRREN-
LAUTERBRUNNENTAL AG / SWISS-
IMAGE.CH

The ice rink is right in
the centre of the
village, near the
nursery slopes ↓

organised and friendly with the school prepared to change people from one class to another'. Another 'had private lessons with the Privat school and would recommend it'. Guides are available for heli-trips and off-piste.

FACILITIES FOR CHILDREN
Conveniently placed
It is an attractive and reassuring village for families. The nursery slope is in the centre. The Playhouse takes children from 18 months and the Sunshine from one month. There is a list of babysitters available at the tourist office. A recent reporter praised the children's ski school classes – 'The best so far by a mile. My four year old really enjoyed all the activities.'

The train gives easy access to higher slopes.

STAYING THERE

HOW TO GO
Wide range of hotels
Most accommodation is in hotels. There is only a handful of catered chalets (none especially luxurious). Self-catering apartments are few, too.
Hotels There are about two dozen hotels, mostly 4-star and 3-star, with a handful of simpler places.
****Beausite Park (856 5161) Reputedly the best in town. Good pool, steam and massage. But poorly situated at top of nursery slopes – a schlep up from the main street.
****Wengener Hof (856 6969) No prizes for style or convenience, but recommended for peace, helpful staff and spacious, spotless rooms with good views.
****Sunstar (856 5200) Family-friendly, modern hotel on main street

right opposite the cable car. Comfortable rooms, some with good valley views; lounge has a log fire. Live music most evenings. Pool with views. Recommended by reporters.
****Silberhorn (856 5131) Comfortable, modern and central (opposite station). Frequently praised by reporters.
****Caprice (856 0606) Small, smartly furnished chalet-style hotel just above the railway. Sauna and steam room. 'Comfortable and friendly'; 'fabulous views, excellent food'. Kindergarten.
***Belvédère (856 6868) Some way out, but we have good reports of buffet-style meals ('good for families'), spacious rooms and grand art nouveau public rooms. Endorsed by a 2008 reporter ('excellent').
***Alpenrose (855 3216) Long-standing British favourite; eight minutes' climb to the station, which rules it out for us. Small, simple rooms, but good views; 'first-class' food; friendly staff.
***Falken (856 5121) Further up the hill. Another British favourite, 'the staff were extremely hospitable, the service first class and the live jazz pianist had the place rocking'.
Apartments The hotel Bernerhof's decent Résidence apartments are well positioned just off the main street, and the hotel facilities are available for guests to use.

EATING OUT
Mainly hotel-based
Most restaurants are in hotels. They offer good food and service. The Eiger has a traditional restaurant and a stube with Swiss and French cuisine. The Bernerhof has good-value traditional dishes. The little hotel

There's a very strong British presence in Wengen. Many Brits have been returning for years to the same rooms in the same hotels in the same week, and treat the resort as a sort of second home. There is an English church with weekly services, and a British-run ski club, the DHO (Downhill Only) – so named when the Brits who colonised the resort persuaded the locals to keep the summer railway running up the mountain in winter, so that they would no longer have to climb up in order to ski down again. That greatly amused the locals, who until then had regarded skiing in winter as a way to get around on snow rather than a pastime to be done for fun. The DHO is still going strong and organises regular events throughout the season.

GETTING THERE

Air Zürich 195km/ 121 miles (3½hr); Bern 70km/43 miles (1½hr)

Rail Station in resort

ACTIVITIES

Indoor Swimming pools (in hotels), sauna, solarium, whirlpool, massage (in hotels), art gallery, museum

Outdoor Ice rink, curling, 50km/ 31 miles of cleared paths, tobogganing, snowshoeing, hang-gliding, helicopter flights

UK PACKAGES

Alpine Answers, Club Med, Crystal, Independent Ski Links, Inghams, Kuoni, Made to Measure, Ski Freshtracks, Ski Line, Ski Solutions, Switzerland Travel Centre, Thomson

Phone numbers
From elsewhere in Switzerland add the prefix 033; from abroad use the prefix +41 33

TOURIST OFFICE

t 855 1414
info@wengen.ch
www.wengen-muerren.ch

Hirschen has good steaks. There's no shortage of fondues in the village, and several bars do casual food. Da Sina does 'succulent and ample sirloin steaks' and is recommended by a couple of recent visitors. Cafe Gruebi has been recommended for 'the most wonderful cakes'. The Jungfrau at Wengernalp has an excellent restaurant – but you have to get back on skis or on a toboggan.

APRES-SKI
It depends on what you want
People's reactions to the après-ski scene in Wengen vary widely, according to their expectations and their appetites.

If you're used to raving in Kitzbühel or Les Deux-Alpes, you'll rate Wengen dead, especially for young people. If you've heard it's dead, you may be pleasantly surprised to find that there is a handful of bars that do good business both early and late in the evening. But it is only a handful of small places. The bar at the Bumps section of the home run is a popular final-run stop-off. A reporter enjoyed the 'fun' Start Bar on the Lauberhorn – but it's a long ski down afterwards. And the tiny, 'always welcoming' Eiger Bar is popular at the end of the day. The small, traditional Tanne is 'relaxed, friendly, and cocktails and champagne are popular' – but it can get 'crowded and smoky'. The Crystal, almost opposite, is lively, but it 'is smokey and lacked atmosphere' says a 2008 visitor. The 'animated' Sina's, a little way out by Club Med, has big screen TV, a live DJ and special evenings such as karaoke and quiz nights. The Caprice bar has been recommended, as has Rock's with 'its three plasma screens showing Sky Sports' – and 'it is the only no smoking bar in Wengen' says a 2008 reporter. There are discos and live music in some hotels

(including Tiffany's – 'full of under-18s' – in the Silberhorn). The cinema often shows English-language films.

OFF THE SLOPES
Good for a relaxing time
With its unbeatable scenery and pedestrian-friendly trains and cable car (there's a special, though expensive, pass for pedestrians), Wengen is a superb resort for those who want a completely relaxing holiday. It's easy for mixed parties of skiers and non-skiers to meet up for lunch on the mountain, but rides on the lifts can be time-consuming. There are some lovely walks, and ice skating and curling are popular with reporters. Several hotels have health spas. Excursions to Interlaken and Bern are possible by train, as is the trip up to the Jungfraujoch (see the Grindelwald chapter). Helicopter flights from Männlichen have been recommended.

STAYING UP THE MOUNTAIN
Great views
You can stay at two points up the mountain reached by the railway: the expensive Jungfrau hotel (855 1622) at Wengernalp – with fabulous views – and at Kleine Scheidegg, where there are rooms in the big Scheidegg Hotels (855 1212) and dormitory space above the Grindelwaldblick restaurant (855 1374) and the station buffet.

STAYING DOWN THE VALLEY
The budget option
Staying down in Lauterbrunnen will halve your accommodation costs and give faster access to Mürren, at the price of a much longer journey time to Kleine Scheidegg when you want to ski Wengen or Grindelwald. The trains run until 11.30pm and are included in your lift pass. See the Mürren chapter for hotel recommendations.

Wengen

559

Interactive resort shortlist builder at **www.wtss.co.uk**

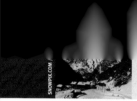

A magical combination of nearly everything you could want from a ski resort, both on and off the slopes

COSTS

① ② ③ ④ ⑤ ⑥

RATINGS

The slopes
Fast lifts	*****
Snow	****
Extent	****
Expert	*****
Intermediate	****
Beginner	*
Convenience	*
Queues	***
Mountain restaurants	*****

The rest
Scenery	*****
Charm	*****
Off-slope	****

NEWS

For 2008/09 a new beginner area is planned at Leisee, just above Sunnegga, with a lift linking the two. More snowmaking is planned too.

For 2007/08 the old Hohtälli-Stockhorn and Gornergrat-Hohtälli cable cars were removed. A new red piste (which is really of blue gradient and boringly narrow and straight) now goes from just below Hohtälli to Gifthittli and a T-bar was added from above Triftji to Stockhorn. A fast quad with heated seats replaced the double chair from Findeln to Sunnegga, with an extension from Findeln to Breithorn (above Riffelalp). It can be ridden both ways. The steepest part of the Kelle run at Breitboden was reclassified black and a red variant added.

➕ Wonderful, high and extensive slopes in four varied areas

➕ Spectacular high mountain scenery, dominated by the Matterhorn

➕ Charming, if rather sprawling, old mountain village, largely traffic-free

➕ Reliable snow at altitude

➕ World's best mountain restaurants

➕ Extensive helicopter operation

➕ Nightlife to suit most tastes

➕ Smart shops

➕ Linked to Cervinia in Italy

➖ Main lifts may be a long walk, or a crowded bus or taxi ride from home

➖ Beginners should go elsewhere

➖ One of Europe's priciest lift passes

➖ Some restaurants and hotels very expensive – so choose carefully

➖ Slow train up to Gornergrat annoys some people, but can be avoided

➖ Some lift queues at peak periods

➖ Annoying electric taxis detract from the car-free village ambience

➖ Walking can be treacherous on uncleared hard snow or ice

You must try Zermatt before you die. Few places can match its combination of excellent advanced and intermediate slopes, reliable snow, magnificent scenery, Alpine charm and mountain restaurants with superb food and stunning views.

Zermatt has its drawbacks – see the long list above. But for us, and for virtually all our reporters, these pale into insignificance compared with its attractions (especially as recent investment has ensured the mountains are better connected). It comes close to matching perfectly our notion of the ideal winter resort and is one of our favourites – one of us regularly takes his holiday here.

THE RESORT

Zermatt started life as a traditional mountain village, developed as a mountaineering centre in the 19th century, then became a winter resort. Summer is as big as winter here.

The car-free village is reached by rail or taxi from Täsch, where cars have to be left for a fee (they can be left for free at more distant Visp, from where you can also get a train). The village is a mixture of chocolate-box chalets and modern buildings, most in traditional style. It sprawls along both sides of a river, mountains rising steeply on each side. The main street runs away from the station, and is lined with luxury hotels, restaurants and shops. The oldest, most charming part of the village has narrow lanes and old wooden buildings with slate roofs; many of these are raised above ground level and supported at each corner on piles of stones.

But the village doesn't have the relaxed, rustic feel of other car-free resorts, such as Wengen and Saas-Fee. Zermatt is big business, and it shows. The clientele is more overtly part of

the jet set, and the electric taxis ferrying people around are more intrusive and aggressive. Most restaurants and hotels are owned by a handful of families. Many of the workers are brought in from outside the area – probably one of the reasons for the increased friendliness and improved service recently.

The resort attracts an older age group than you get in rival resorts with comparable slopes, such as Val d'Isère or St Anton, and there's not as much of the youthful vitality that you get in those resorts.

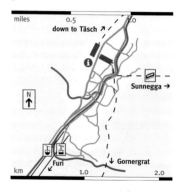

↑ Lovely red runs down to Furgg are served by a high-speed chair. This photo is taken from Schwarzsee
WENDY-JANE KING

is no problem. There's a smart newish station and underground car park with 2,000 spaces (SF11 a day), and you can wheel luggage trolleys from the car park onto and off the trains. You are met at Zermatt by electric and horse-drawn taxis and hotel shuttles.

THE MOUNTAINS

Practically all of the slopes are above the treeline – the runs served by the Sunnegga funicular are the main exception. A single piste map (in a handy quick-folding size) covers both Cervinia's and Zermatt's slopes fairly clearly. A recommended ski safari route (of either 10,000m/32,800ft or 12,000m/39,400ft vertical in a day) is now clearly listed on one edge of the map, not marked across it as it was on the 2006/07 version.

The yellow runs shown in each sector, and all those on the Stockhorn, are now called 'itineraires' on the piste map. In 2006/07 they were defined as 'freeride pistes'; neither term was explained on either year's map – ridiculous. Before 2006/07, they were described as 'ski runs' and at least defined as protected (from avalanches we presume – and we still believe them to be), marked but not prepared or checked. On our March 2008 visit we spotted one sign on a yellow run saying it wasn't patrolled.

But we have been impressed by recent service improvements: polite and helpful lift staff; big boards at the bottom of each sector indicating which lifts and pistes are open in all sectors; useful announcements in several languages (including English) on the train and some cable cars; and free tissues at most lift stations.

THE SLOPES
Beautiful and varied
Zermatt's piste map divides the slopes into several sectors and markets some as 'paradises'. We think this is bizarre, so here we drop 'paradises' and divide the slopes into four main sectors.

The **Rothorn** sector is reached by an underground funicular to Sunnegga starting by the river, not far from the centre. A 'chondola' (chair/gondola hybrid) goes from there to Blauherd, where a cable car goes up to Rothorn.

From the top of this area you can make your way – via south-facing slopes served by snowmaking – to Gant in the valley between Sunnegga

The cog railway to Gornergrat starts from near the main station. The Sunnegga underground funicular towards Rothorn is a few minutes' walk away, but the gondola to the Glacier and Schwarzsee areas (and the link to Cervinia) is at the opposite end of the long village. Walking from the station to the Glacier lifts can take 15 to 20 minutes. And be warned: walking anywhere (especially in ski boots) can be unpleasant because of the treacherous icy paths and the electric taxis and solar-powered buses darting around. The free buses get very crowded and cannot handle demand at peak times: 'We waited 30 minutes for one and lost valuable skiing time,' says a 2008 visitor. By contrast, the electric taxis are 'a godsend', according to another (from SF5 each if you share).

Staying near the lifts to Furi is more convenient for the slopes now that there's a gondola connection from Furi to Riffelberg. But being near the Gornergrat and Sunnegga railways, near the station end of the main street, is more convenient for most shops, bars and restaurants (and the other two ways up to the slopes). Some accommodation is up the steep hill across the river in Winkelmatten – you can ski back to it from all areas, and it has its own reliable bus service. Getting up to the village from Täsch

and the second main area, **Gornergrat**. A 125-person cable car links Gant to Hohtälli, on a ridge above Gornergrat. A gondola makes the link back from Gant to Sunnegga. The new fast quad from Sunnegga to Breitboden (via Findeln) can be ridden both ways and offers an alternative route between the Sunnegga and Gornergrat sectors. But note that the only run to Findeln from Breitboden is a tricky 'itineraire'. Gornergrat can be reached directly from Zermatt by cog railway trains that

leave every 24 minutes and take 30 or 40 minutes to get to the top – arrive at the station early to get a seat on the right-hand side and enjoy the fabulous views. It can be a long journey if you have to stand.

From Gornergrat there's a piste to Schweigmatten, just below Furi, where the newish gondola ('excellent, quiet') takes you up to Furi or back up to Riffelberg on the Gornergrat sector. From Furi, a cable car to Trockener Steg and then the spectacular Klein

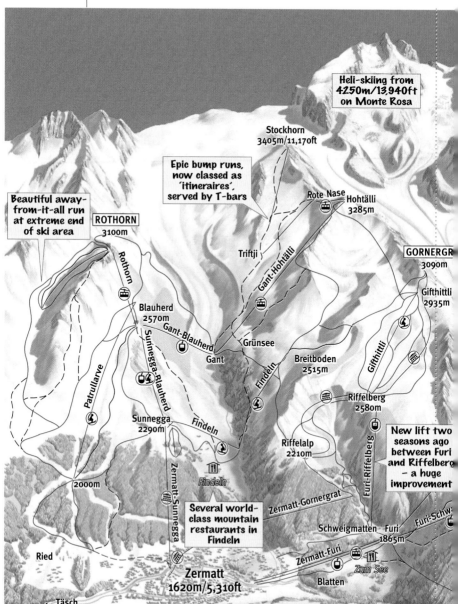

Heli-skiing from
4250m/13,940ft
on Monte Rosa

Stockhorn
3405m/11,17oft

Epic bump runs,
now classed as
'itineraires',
served by T-bars

Rote Nase   Hohtälli
             3285m

Beautiful away-
from-it-all run
at extreme end
of ski area

ROTHORN
3100m

Triftji

GORNERGR
3090m

Gifthittli
2935m

Rothorn

Blauherd
2570m

Gant-Blauherd

Grünsee

Gant-Hohtälli

Gifthittli

Patrullarve

Sunnegga-Blauherd

Gant

Findeln

Breitboden
2515m

Riffelberg
2580m

2000m

Sunnegga
2290m

Findeln

Riffelalp
2210m

Furi-Riffelberg

New lift two
seasons ago
between Furi
and Riffelberg
– a huge
improvement

Zermatt-Sunnegga

Findeln

Several world-
class mountain
restaurants in
Findeln

Zermatt-Gornergrat

Ried

Schweigmatten Furi
               1865m

Furi-Schw

Zermatt-Furi

Zum See

Zermatt
1620m/5,310ft

Blatten

← Täsch

Zmutt

Matterhorn cable car take you to the top of the third and highest **Glacier** sector. This area links to Cervinia – make sure you have an appropriate pass, and take your passport.

From Furgg, towards the bottom of the Glacier sector, a stop-start gondola goes up to the top of the small but worthwhile **Schwarzsee** area (also reached by gondola from Furi). There are plans for a new gondola directly to Trockener Steg from Schwarzsee, but not until 2009/10.

There are pistes back to the village from all sectors – though some of them can be closed or tricky due to poor snow conditions. They can be hazardous at the end of the day due to crowds and speeding skiers – particularly the black from Furgg.

TERRAIN PARKS
One of Switzerland's best
Gravity Park situated next to the Furggsattel six-seat chair is one of Switzerland's best winter parks. It

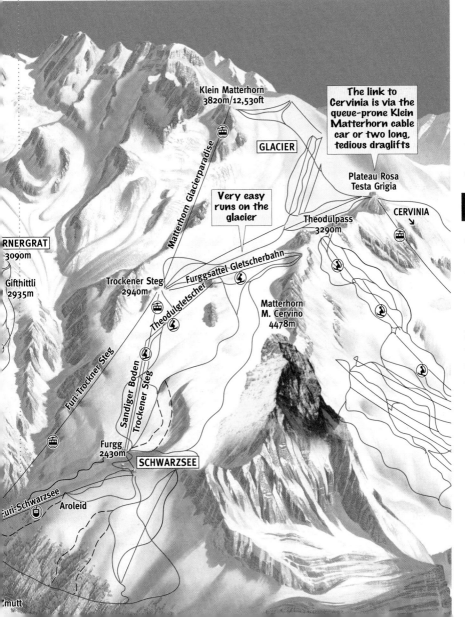

Klein Matterhorn
3820m/12,530ft

The link to Cervinia is via the queue-prone Klein Matterhorn cable car or two long, tedious draglifts

GLACIER

Matterhorn Glacierparadise

Plateau Rosa
Testa Grigia

CERVINIA

Very easy runs on the glacier

Theodulpass
3290m

RNERGRAT
3090m

Furggsattel Gletscherbahn

Gifthittli
2935m

Trockener Steg
2940m

Theodulgletscher

Matterhorn
M. Cervino
4478m

Furi-Trockner Steg

Sandiger Boden
Trockener Steg

Furgg
2430m

SCHWARZSEE

uri-Schwarzsee   Aroleid

mutt

KEY FACTS

Resort	1620m
	5,310ft

Zermatt only	
Slopes	1620-3820m
	5,310-12,530ft
Lifts	34
Pistes	200km
	124 miles
Blue	25%
Red	59%
Black	16%
Snowmaking	61km
	38 miles

Zermatt-Cervinia-Valtournenche combined	
Slopes	1525-3820m
	5,000-12,530ft
Lifts	58
Pistes	350km
	217 miles
Blue	22%
Red	60%
Black	18%
Snowmaking	114km
	71 miles

moves up to Plateau Rosa for slightly more elevation in the summer. This means the parks are open 365 days a year. There is a nicely integrated 120m/390ft-long super-pipe that sits next to an array of kickers, rails, a quarter-pipe, a wall ride and a new mail box and tree jib. The park is set up nicely so that you can choose either a kicker or rail line, and try several hits in a row. It is a short park, so you'll be doing a lot of laps (on a fast chair) during the day. Check www. matterhornparadise.ch for details.

SNOW RELIABILITY
Generally good
Zermatt has rocky terrain and a relatively dry climate. But it also has some of the highest slopes in Europe, and quite a lot of snowmaking. Three of the four sectors go up to over 3000m/9,840ft, and the Glacier area has summer skiing. There are loads of runs above 2500m/8,200ft, many of which are north-facing, guaranteeing decent snow except in freak years.

Snowmaking machines serve some of the pistes, on all four areas, from above 3000m/9,840ft right down to resort level. Coverage is gradually

increased each season – the runs to resort level were extremely well maintained during our March 2008 visit. Piste grooming is excellent.

FOR EXPERTS
Head off-piste
There is some great off-piste – see below – but few challenging pistes. The handful of black runs marked on the piste map are not worthy of their classification; the one with the steepest pitches (Blauherd-Patrullarve) is also very wide. That's one of the consequences of making their toughest regularly skied runs 'itineraires' (see under 'The Mountains' earlier in this chapter).

FOR INTERMEDIATES
Mile after mile of beautiful runs
Zermatt is ideal for adventurous intermediates. Many of the blue and red runs tend to be at the difficult end of their classification. There are very beautiful reds down lift-free valleys from both Gornergrat (Kelle) and Hohtälli (White Hare) to Breitboden – we love these first thing in the morning, before anyone else is on them. The steepest part of Kelle has

OFF-PISTE RUNS FROM THE ACCESSIBLE TO THE EPIC

Zermatt offers a wide variety of off-piste runs for all abilities, from off-piste beginner to expert. And if the runs reached from the lift system aren't enough, heli-skiing is available (and popular).

The 'itineraires' (see 'The Mountains' earlier in this chapter) marked in yellow on the piste map (and by broken black lines on our map) open up a lot of ungroomed terrain. If you love long mogul pitches, those between Stockhorn and Triftji, are the stuff of dreams. From the top of the Stockhorn there's a steep run (usually with big moguls) back down. Or you can carry on down further to the older Triftji T-bar that goes up to Rote Nase and serves a wide, long face that can be another vast mogul field. Being north-facing and high, the snow in the whole Stockhorn-Triftji area keeps in good condition long after a new snowfall. The 'itineraires' carry on down from the Triftji T-bar to Gant, but snow quality can deteriorate on this lower part. And be warned: this whole area does not normally open until February (sometimes not until March, because of insufficient snow). There are two wonderful 'itineraires' from Rothorn, with spectacular views. But they need good snow-cover to be really enjoyable. At Schwarzsee there are a couple of steep north-facing gullies through the woods.

Away from the marked runs, there are marvellous off-piste possibilities from the top lifts in each sector, but they are dangerous, because of rocky and glacial terrain; guidance is essential. Stockhorn is a great starting point; descending towards Gant, one special run goes down 'the lost valley'; going in the other direction, there is an excellent descent to the Gornergletscher, ending at Furi (but see below for a warning about the end of the glacier). In the Schwarzsee sector there are many good slopes, including 'innru waldieni', right underneath the Matterhorn, reached from the Hörnli T-bar.

Zermatt is the Alps' biggest heli-skiing centre; at times the helipad has choppers taking off every few minutes. The classic run is from over 4250m/13,940ft on Monte Rosa and descends over 2300m/7,550ft vertical through wonderful glacier scenery to Furi; it is not steep, but getting off the end of the glacier can be tricky and involve walking along narrow rocky paths above long drops or side-stepping down steep slopes, depending on the amount of snow around (we've encountered both). And there are lots of ski touring opportunities, too, including some among stunning glacial scenery.

LIFT PASSES

Zermatt

Prices in SF

Age	1-day	6-day
under 16	35	173
16 to 19	60	294
20 to 64	70	346
over 65	63	311

Free under 9

Beginner no deals

Notes

Covers all lifts on the Swiss side of the border; half-day passes and single-ascent tickets on some lifts also available

Alternative passes

International pass for Zermatt and Cervinia; International-Aosta for Zermatt and Cervinia plus 2 days in Val d'Aosta; Peak Pass for pedestrians

been reclassified black, but an easier red variant now bypasses it. From Breitboden you can go on down to Gant, or to Riffelalp on a run that includes a narrow wooded path with a sheer cliff and magnificent views to the right. The 5km/3 mile Kumme run, from Rothorn itself to the bottom of the Patrullarve chair, also gets away from the lift system ('beautifully remote', confirms a 2008 reporter) and has an interesting mix of straight-running and mogul pitches (but it gets a lot of sun and lacks snowmaking).

In the Glacier sector the reds served by the fast quad chair from Furgg are gloriously set at the foot of the Matterhorn. The Furggsattel chair from Trockener Steg serves more pistes with stunning views, notably the 1100m/3,610ft Matterhorn piste – a red that is more blue in gradient for most of its considerable length. It is classified red because of a short, steep pitch near the end, which a lot of less confident intermediates struggle on. It is often closed though, due to a lack of snowmaking.

For timid intermediates, the best runs are the blues from Blauherd on Rothorn, and above Riffelberg on

Gornergrat, and the runs between Klein Matterhorn and Trockener Steg. Of these, the Riffelberg area often has the best combination of good snow and easy cruising, and is popular with the schools. Blauherd gets afternoon sun, but the snowmaking means that heavy, slushy snow near the bottom is more likely than bare patches.

In the Glacier sector most of the runs, though marked red on the piste map, are very flat and represent the easiest slopes Zermatt has to offer, as well as the best snow. The problem here is the possibility of bad weather because of the height – high winds, extreme cold and poor visibility can make life very unpleasant (and if you are skiing into a headwind, downhill progress can be very slow).

Even an early intermediate can make the trip to Cervinia, crossing at Theodulpass rather than taking the more challenging Ventina run from Testa Grigia/Plateau Rosa.

Beware the run from Furgg to Furi at the end of the day, because it can be chopped up, mogulled in places and very crowded (the only reason it is classified black that we can see, because it isn't very steep); several

Interactive resort shortlist builder at **www.wtss.co.uk**

SCHOOLS

Swiss	t 966 2466
Stoked	t 967 7020
Summit	t 967 0001
European Snowsport	t 967 6787
Almrausch	t 967 0808
AER	t 967 7067
Prato Borni	t 967 5115

Classes (Swiss prices)
5 days (10am to 3.30 with lunch break) SF335

Private lessons
SF170 for 2hr for 1 or 2 people

boarding

Boarders in soft boots have one big advantage over skiers in Zermatt – they have much more comfortable walks to and from the lift stations! Even so, there aren't many snowboarders around. The slopes are best for experienced freeriders and there's a world-class terrain park above Trockener Steg on the glacier. There is, however, an excellent little beginner area at Blauherd, complete with moving carpet lift, which we've seen many beginner snowboarders having lessons on. The main lifts are boarder-friendly: train, funicular, gondolas, cable cars and fast chairs, and there aren't too many flat bits. Stoked is a specialist school.

2008 reporters have recommended avoiding it. A much more relaxed alternative is to use the beautifully scenic Weisse Perle run from Schwarzsee (the Stafelalp variant is even more scenic but has a short uphill section). Or you can ride the gondola from Schwarzsee.

FOR BEGINNERS
Learn elsewhere
There are many much better resorts for beginners. The best snow-sure nursery slope area here is at Blauherd – but even this can get very busy. The new beginner area at Leisee (see 'News') might make things better. But there are no long easy runs to progress to, except for those above Trockener Steg, which can be bitterly cold and windy.

FOR EVERYONE
Impressive cable car and grotto
If the weather is good, the Klein Matterhorn cable car is an experience not to be missed. There are stupendous views from the left side down to the glacier and its crevasses, as the car swings steeply into its hole, blasted out of the mountain at the top. When you arrive, you walk through a long tunnel, to emerge on top of the world for the highest piste in Europe. Remember to walk slowly: the air is thin and some people have altitude problems. There's a viewing platform, and substantial development is planned here, including a restaurant and shop. The ice grotto cut into the glacier is well worth a visit, with 'incredible ice carvings'.

FOR CROSS-COUNTRY
Fairly limited
There's a 4km/2.5 mile loop at Furi, 3km/2 miles of trails near the bottom of the gondola to the Glacier area and another 12km/7 miles from Täsch to Randa (don't count on good snow). There are also 'ski walking trails', best tackled as part of an organised group.

QUEUES
Main problems being solved
Zermatt has improved its lift system hugely in recent years, eliminating major bottlenecks. Our 2008 reporters are generally positive, though a few problems remain. Both the lifts out of Gant are still prone to queues at times: 'We waited for two or three cars to come and go before we could squeeze in,' says one 2008 visitor; the gondola can be a slow ride too (though you might be compensated by seeing herds of chamois on the slopes below – one of their favourite hang-outs). The high-speed quad from Furgg gets busy; it stopped frequently during our visit this year, resulting in long delays. And the Riffelberg-Gifthittli chair has short queues at busy periods. The Klein Matterhorn cable car has queues much of the time (up to an hour mid-morning; quieter in the afternoon). You may find there's only standing room on the Gornergrat train, which can be tiring and uncomfortable – you may prefer to wait for the next one. One thing we love about Zermatt is getting the 8am train with the lifties and restaurant staff. It arrives at the top just as they drop the rope to open the pistes, and you have the slopes to yourselves for an hour or two.

Now that the onward cable car to Gornergrat from Hohtälli has been removed, the top section of piste from there can get dangerously busy ('awful crowds on a narrow red that was bumped by mid-morning').

SCHOOLS AND GUIDES
Competition paying off
The main Swiss school has allegedly improved, but we'd like more reports please. Stoked snowboard school is generally well regarded by reporters. It is made up of talented young instructors, some of whom are British and all of whom speak good English. Group sizes are said to be small. A 2008 reader arranged a private lesson

CHILDREN

Kinderparadies
t 967 7252
Ages from 3mnth

Kinderclub Pumuckel
(Hotel Ginabelle)
t 966 5000
Ages from 30mnth

Snowflakes (Stoked)
t 967 7020
Ages from 4; 9am-12 noon

Schweizerhof Hotel
t 966 0000
Ages from 2 to 8;
9am-5pm; Mon-Sat

Snowli Village (Swiss)
t 966 2466
Ages 4 to 5: SF425 for 5 days

Private babysitters
List at tourist office

Ski school
From age 6; 5 full days incl. lunch SF378 (Swiss prices)

for four intermediates – 'pretty good at about £35 each; the instructor was great.' There are two other schools staffed mainly by Brits – Summit and European Snowsport. The wife of a 2007 reporter had 'very successful' private lessons with Summit and found them 'well organised', while beginners in another group 'progressed rapidly'.

FACILITIES FOR CHILDREN
Good hotel nurseries
The Ginabelle hotel has the Kinderclub Pumuckel. The Schweizerhof hotel is due to have a new Nico Kids' Club for two to eight year olds for 2008/09. The Kinderparadies, 200m/660ft from the station, takes children from three months and is reportedly popular with local families. Stoked runs Snowflakes for children aged at least four years old at Trockener Steg, and a kindergarten for kids from three years at Schwarzsee. There's a snow garden at Riffelberg. The tourist office has a list of babysitters.

STAYING THERE

HOW TO GO
A wide choice, packaged or not
Chalets Several operators have places here; many of the most comfortable are in apartment blocks. Reporters have praised Total Ski's operation here. VIP and Scott Dunn have some luxury chalets.
Hotels There are over 100 hotels, mostly comfortable and traditional-style 3-stars and 4-stars, but taking in the whole range. Inghams features a large selection (and has chalets and apartments too).
*****Mont Cervin (966 8888) Biggest in town. Elegantly traditional. Good pool and fitness centre. Also manages the luxury Petit Cervin (formerly the Nicoletta), which opened for 2007/08.
*****Zermatterhof (966 6600) Traditional 'grand hotel' style with piano bar and pool.
*****Riffelalp Resort (966 0555) Up the mountain, pool, spa, own evening trains. Service and location both highly recommended. 'Not at all stuffy or formal.'

THE WORLD'S BEST MOUNTAIN RESTAURANTS

Even reporters who don't normally stop long for lunch usually succumb to temptation here. The choice of restaurants is enormous, the food usually excellent, the small hut-based places very atmospheric (some with spectacular views), the table service friendly (if over-worked). It is impossible to list here all those worth a visit. It is best to book; check prices are within your budget first!

Down at Findeln below Sunnegga are several attractive, expensive, rustic restaurants. Chez Vrony (967 2552) is very popular and one of our favourites. We've had wonderful spicy fish soup, wild mushroom risotto, salmon pasta, great desserts, and views – but be prepared for slow service (a 2008 reporter complains of an hour and a half wait). We've also enjoyed Adler's (967 1058; 'friendly, efficient service; excellent spit-roasted chickens and seafood' and the Findlerhof (967 2588), aka Franz & Heidy's. Reporters praise Paradies (967 3451; 'friendly service') and Enzian (967 6404).

The simple hut at Tuftern has great views from the terrace, sells good Heida wine from the highest vineyard in Europe and does a basic menu of home-made soup, cheese and cold sausage, and tasty apple cake; you can also watch deer feeding here at the end of the afternoon. Othmar's Skihütte (967 1761), below the Patrullarve chair, has a 'good selection of fish and seafood'.

The restaurants at Fluhalp (967 2597, often with live music on the terrace) and Grünsee (967 2553) have beautiful, isolated situations, and the large terraces at Sunnegga (967 3046) and Rothorn (967 2675) have great views. The Kulmhotel (966 6400), at 3100m/10,170ft at Gornergrat, has both self- and table-service restaurants (we had two good table-service meals on our 2008 visit, with excellent food and good service). At Riffelalp, the Alphitta (967 2114) has several cosy rustic rooms for bad-weather days (no credit cards) and the Chämi-Hütte lower down is cute and cosy.

Up above Trockener Steg, Gandegghütte (607 8868) has stunning views of the glacier. The hotel at Schwarzsee (967 2263) is right at the foot of the Matterhorn, with staggering views and endless variations of rösti. Down the hill from here Stafelalp (967 3062) is charmingly situated, peaceful and simple ('great, good value food'). At Furi, the Restaurant Furri (966 2777) is 'welcoming', has large sun terraces and a cosy interior but gets very crowded. On the way back to the village, Zum See (967 2045) is a charming old hut with a reputation of being Zermatt's best ('fabulous tuna carpaccio') – we've eaten well there too, but some reporters were disappointed with the slow service.

↑ The cog railway from Zermatt to Gornergrat takes 30 or 40 minutes; but you get stunning views of the Matterhorn on the way up
WENDY-JANE KING

*****Omnia** (966 7171) Modern, minimalist, central, reached by a lift in a rock, smart fitness centre.
****Coeur des Alpes** (966 4080) At Klein Matterhorn end of town. Smart, modern; relaxed, friendly feel. Pool and fitness facilities visible through glass lobby floor. No restaurant. Being extended for 2008/09.
****Alex** (966 7070) Close to station. Repeatedly praised ('amazing hospitality'). Pool. Dancing.
****Ambassador** (966 2611) Peaceful position near Gornergrat station. Large pool; sauna. Comfortable but 'a bit faded'; 'good food'.
****Monte Rosa** (966 0333) Well-modernised original Zermatt hotel undergoing further refurbishment for 2008/09, near southern end of town; full of climbing mementos.
****Ginabelle** (966 5000) Smart pair of chalets not far from Sunnegga lift; own ski nursery as well as day care.
****Sonne** (966 2066) In quiet setting; 'superb' wellness centre.
****Julen** (966 7600) Charming, modern-rustic chalet over the river.
****Walliserhof** (966 6555) Central 'friendly' hotel. Good rooms. Spa.
****Metropol** (966 3566) 'Couldn't have been more friendly and helpful.' 'Great' wellness centre. Pool.
***Butterfly** (966 4166) Near the station. 'Very comfortable, friendly and good five-course meals.'
***Atlanta** (966 3535) No frills, but 'clean, warm, friendly and serves wholesome food'; close to centre, with Matterhorn views from some rooms.
***Matterhorn Blick** (967 2017) Next to the church. 'Extremely welcoming; returning guests treated as friends',

says a 2008 reader on a fourth visit.
Alpina (967 1050) Modest but very friendly, and close to centre.
Dufour (966 2400) B&B, fairly central. 'Only a 2-star but deserves much more, wonderful roomy bedrooms, great views.'
*Bahnhof** (967 2406) Right by Gornergrat station. Cheapest place to stay in town (SF108 a night for twin room with shower, SF35 a night for a dormitory bed; communal kitchen).
Apartments There is a lot of apartment accommodation. We have enjoyed staying in the hotel Ambassador apartments (966 2611) several times (with free use of all its facilities such as a pool and a sauna). Ski Solutions has a decent selection; www.zermattapartmentrentals.com and the Vanessa complex (966 3510) have been recommended by reporters. The tourist office website has apartments.

EATING OUT
Huge choice at all price levels
There are over 100 restaurants to choose from: top-quality haute cuisine, through traditional Swiss food, Chinese, Japanese and Thai to egg and chips. There is even a McDonald's.

We have enjoyed several dinners over the years at the Pipe (tiny with interesting dishes with Asian/West Indian influence; also endorsed by reporters) and the Schwyzer Stübli (local specialities and live Swiss music and dancing). And in 2008 we had good value Mexican and Swiss dishes at the Weisshorn (friendly, fast service) and decent Thai food at Rua Thai (in the basement of the hotel Abana Real and with decor based on a nautical theme). Fuji in the same building is a good Japanese. The Schäferstube (Hotel Julen) has been recommended for gourmet meals and a 2007 reporter enjoyed the buffet at the Mirabeau hotel – 'fantastic home-made duck pie – expensive but flawless'. A 2008 visitor recommends Nelly's Grotta for 'great food at reasonable prices'.

Readers also recommend Da Mario, Casa Rustica, the Swiss Chalet, the Derby, the Avenstube, the Old Spaghetti Factory (hotel Post – 'always great food'), the Stockhorn Grill ('meat grilled to perfection'), the Walliserhof ('good value set menu') and the Walliserkanne. Du Pont has good-value pasta and rösti; Grampi's, Broken, Roma and Postli do good pizzas.

APRES-SKI
Lively and varied

There's a good mix of sophisticated and informal fun, though it helps if you have deep pockets. On the way back from the Glacier or Schwarzsee sectors there are lots of restaurants below Furi. Hennu Stall blasts out loud music in a very un-Zermatt-like fashion but attracts huge crowds – live bands play most days. For a quieter time, try a cake or tart at Zum See. On the way back from Rothorn, Othmar's Skihütte has great views and organises dinners and tobogganing home, and the Olympia Stübli often has live music (and good food worth walking back up for in the evening, says a 2007 reporter). The new Snowboat bar (by the Sunnegga funicular) is a small, modern place, with a terrace and lounge bar. Good for a quiet drink.

Promenading the main street checking out expensive shoes and watches is a popular early-evening activity. The Papperla Pub is 'great day and night' (it has a nightclub downstairs too – 'still heaving at 3.30am', say reporters). Elsie's bar is wood-panelled and atmospheric, and gets packed with an older crowd both early and late. A 2008 visitor preferred the 'comfy sofas, service and pool table' at the hotel Alex. The Vernissage is our favourite bar for a quiet evening drink. It is unusual, stylish and modern, with the projection room for the cinema built into the upstairs bar and displays of art elsewhere. Heimberg was designed by the same guy and has a good cocktail bar downstairs and a restaurant above.

Later on, the hotel Post complex has something for everyone, from a quiet, comfortable bar (Papa Caesar's) to a lively disco (Broken), live music (Pink) and various restaurants. The T-Bar draws a young crowd for dancing and live bands. At Grampi's, 'watch out for the Elton John impersonator – very entertaining'. Z'alt Hischi (in an old house, popular with the locals) and the Little Bar (crowded if there are ten people in) are good for a quiet drink. The Hexen Bar is cosy, too. The Hotel Pollux has 'a general party ambience'.

OFF THE SLOPES
Considerable attractions

Zermatt is an attractive place to spend time. As well as expensive jewellery and clothes shops, there are interesting places selling food, wine, books and art. It is easy (but expensive) for pedestrians to get around on the lifts and meet others for lunch (purchase the Peaks Pass), and there are some nice walks – a special map is available. The Ice Grotto at Klein Matterhorn and the Matterhorn Museum in town are worth seeing. You can take a helicopter trip around the Matterhorn. There is a cinema, and free village guided tours. For an icy experience, visit (or stay at) the Igloo above Riffelberg.

STAYING UP THE MOUNTAIN
Comfortable seclusion

There are several hotels at altitude, of which the pick is the Riffelalp Resort at the first stop on the Gornergrat railway (see 'Hotels') – but the evening train service is a bit limited. At the top of the railway, at 3100m/10,170ft, is the Kulmhotel Gornergrat (966 6400) – an austere building but smart and modern inside with good-value rooms in which you can stay just a night or two if you wish.

STAYING DOWN THE VALLEY
Attractive for drivers

In Täsch, where visitors must leave their cars, there are five 3-star hotels costing less than half the price of the equivalent in Zermatt. Täscherhof (966 6262) – 'fine, ... and with a reasonably ...' – and the Walliser ... very good opti... recommende... very quiet ... 13-minute ... trains e... the da... 12.3... ho... t...

Most people who give it a try find America is pretty seductive, despite the relatively small sizes of its ski areas. What got the US started in the UK market was its (generally) reliable snow, and that remains a key factor. Others are the relatively deserted pistes, the quality of accommodation, the excellent, varied resort restaurants, the high standards of service and courtesy, and the immaculate piste grooming. Depending on the resort, you may also be struck by the cute Wild West ambience and the superb quality of the snow. Of course, US skiing does have some distinct disadvantages, too. Read on.

We have organised our American chapters in regional sections – California, Colorado, Utah, Rest of the West and New England.

Most American resorts receive serious amounts of snow – typically in the region of 6m to 12m (or 250 to 500 inches, as they measure it there) in a season. It tends to arrive in more frequent falls than in Europe, so your chances of hitting fresh snow are appreciably higher. (On a 10-day trip to the States, we expect to get fresh snow; on a 10-day trip to the Alps, it's a bonus.) And most resorts have serious snowmaking facilities that are used well – laying down a base of snow early in the season, rather than patching up shortages later. There are wide differences in quantity and quality of snowfall, both between individual resorts and between regions – check out our regional introductions.

The classification of pistes (or trails, to use the local term) is different from that in Europe. Red runs don't exist. The colours used are combined with shapes. Green circles correspond fairly closely to greens in France and easy blues in the rest of Europe. American blue squares correspond to blues and easy reds in Europe; the tougher ones are sometimes labelled as double-squares, or as blue-black squares. Then there are black diamond runs, which is where things get interesting. Single diamonds correspond fairly closely to European blacks and really tough reds. But then there are multiple diamonds. Double-diamond runs are seriously steep – usually steeper than the steepest pistes in the Alps. A few resorts have wildly steep 'extreme' double-diamonds, or triple-diamonds.

SNOWPIX.COM / CHRIS GILL

← Superb snow, trees all around, non-spectacular scenery, no crowds: the general American formula. Here in Aspen, the lack of crowds is taken to extremes

Many Europeans have the idea that American resorts don't have off-piste terrain, but this seriously misrepresents the position. The black slopes in many American resorts include wild and challenging terrain; add to this frequent dumps of powder, and what you've got

is very much like going off-piste in an Alpine resort, – with the important advantage that it is patrolled and avalanche-controlled, so you don't need to hire a guide. We rate this as one of the great attractions of US resorts. It's true that resorts practically always have a boundary, and that venturing beyond it into the 'backcountry' may be controlled, discouraged or forbidden.

The most obvious drawback to the US is that many resorts have slopes that are very modest in extent compared with major Alpine areas. But usually there are other resorts nearby – so if you are prepared to travel a bit, you won't get bored. Roads are good and car hire is cheap (watch out for extra insurance charges, though). But if snow is expected, you will need snow chains (you'll have to buy them – we've yet to find a US rental company that will provide them) or a 4WD. It's also true that in many resorts the mountains are slightly monotonous, with countless similar trails cut through the forest. You don't usually get the spectacular mountain scenery and the distinctive high-mountain runs of the Alps. But the forest runs do offer good visibility in bad weather.

Piste grooming is taken very seriously – most American resorts set standards that only the best Alpine resorts seem to be able to match. Every morning you can expect to step out on to perfect 'corduroy' pistes. But this doesn't mean that there aren't moguls – far from it. It's just that you get moguls where the resort says you can expect moguls, not everywhere.

The slopes of most American resorts are blissfully free of crowds – a key advantage that becomes more important every year as the pistes of Europe become ever more congested. If you want to ski quickly and safely with less fear of collisions, you're better off going to the States.

Ski schools offer consistently high standards, but work in a way that seems strange to Europeans – and disappointing to many. Your group will often have different instructors from day to day. Your classmates will vary too – people don't sign up for a week, but only for a day or two as they feel the need. This is no doubt partly because lessons are expensive – £60 a day in Vail last season, for example. But at least you don't have to join ski school to get to know the mountain: most resorts offer free guided tours of the area, once or twice a day; and many have 'mountain hosts' on hand to help you find your way. Piste maps are freely available at lift stations, and signposting is generally exemplary.

Child care, similarly, is impressive but expensive.

Lift passes are expensive too, if you just walk up to the ticket booth and pay the advertised rate. But in many resorts you can save huge amounts by buying in advance through tour operators or websites. Lifts are generally efficient, and queues are orderly and short, partly because spare seats are religiously filled with the aid of cheerful, conscientious attendants. But first-time visitors are surprised that many chairlifts in the States do not have safety bars; even on a chair that has one, you will find Americans curiously reluctant to use it, and eager to raise it as soon as the top station is in view. They worry about being trapped, not falling off. Weird.

The lifts close irritatingly early – often at 3pm or 3.30. That may explain another drawback of America – the dearth of decent mountain restaurants. The norm is a monster self-service refuelling station – designed to minimise time off the slopes. Small restaurants with table service and decent food are rare.

US resort towns vary widely in style and convenience, from cute restored mining towns miles from the lifts to purpose-built monstrosities. Two important things the resorts have in common are good-value, spacious accommodation and restaurants that are reliably good, reasonably priced and varied in cuisine. Young people should be aware that the rigorously enforced legal age for drinking alcohol is 21; even if you are older, carry evidence of age, especially if you look younger than you are.

Crossing the pond is never going to be cheap, but the basic cost is lower than you might think: you can get February packages to California for under £600; with the £ at around $2, eating out is not expensive; and it's not difficult to find rooms with kitchenettes where you do your own catering.

In the end, your reaction to skiing and snowboarding in America may depend on your reaction to America. If repeated cheerful exhortations to have a nice day wind you up – or if you like to ride chairlifts in silence – perhaps you'd better stick to the Alps.

California/Nevada

California? It means surfing, beaches, wine, Hollywood, Disneyland and San Francisco cable cars. Nevada means gambling. But this region also has the highest mountains in continental USA and some of America's biggest winter resorts, usually reliable for snow from November to May. What's more, winter holidays here are less expensive than you might expect.

Most visitors head for the Lake Tahoe area. Spectacularly set high in the Sierra Nevada 322km/200 miles east of San Francisco, Lake Tahoe is ringed by skiable mountains containing 14 downhill and 7 cross-country centres – the highest concentration of winter sports resorts in the USA. Then, a long way south (more often reached from LA), there is Mammoth.

Each of the three major 'destination' resorts – Heavenly and Squaw Valley in the Lake Tahoe area and Mammoth further south – is covered in its own chapter immediately after this page.

The other main Lake Tahoe resorts (shown on our map) each have an entry in the resort directory at the back of the book. Many are well worth visiting for a day or two, especially the four second-division resorts – Alpine Meadows, Kirkwood, Northstar and Sierra-at-Tahoe. We also enjoyed Sugar Bowl and Mount Rose. You could visit them all by car (best to have a 4WD) from a single base, but a two-centre holiday with some time at the north end of the lake and some at the south would be better. A lift pass covering various resorts around the lake and another valid at seven northern resorts are both available through tour operators (also see www.skilaketahoe. co.uk and www.gotahoenorth.com).

Californian resorts often have the deepest snowfall in North America, which Rockies powder connoisseurs are inclined to brand as wet 'Sierra Cement'. The snow can be heavy – our most recent visit was spoiled by rain. But most people find the snow just fine, especially in comparison with what you would expect in the Alps.

Resorts can get crowded with weekend visitors, but midweek the slopes are normally quiet.

In the past our main reservation has been the character of the resorts themselves; they don't have the traditional mountain-town ambience that we look for in the States.

But things are changing. At Heavenly a gondola now goes up from a newish car-free plaza in South Lake Tahoe called Heavenly Village. Squaw Valley and Northstar both have attractive new base villages. And a pedestrian village opened a few years ago in Mammoth – linked to the slopes by gondola.

Heavenly

It's unique: fabulous lake and 'desert' views from interestingly varied slopes above a tacky lakeside casino town

COSTS

① ② ③ ④ ⑤ ⑥

RATINGS

The slopes

Fast lifts	★★★
Snow	★★★★
Extent	★★★
Expert	★★★
Intermediate	★★★★
Beginner	★★★★
Convenience	★
Queues	★★★★
Mountain restaurants	★

The rest

Scenery	★★★★
Resort charm	★
Off-slope	★★

KEY FACTS

Resort	1900m
	6,230ft
Slopes	2000-3060m
	6,570-10,040ft
Lifts	30
Pistes	4,800 acres
Green	20%
Blue	45%
Black	35%
Snowmaking	70%

There are great views of Lake Tahoe from the slopes as well as the gondola; but it's a pity there's no ski run down ↓

➕ Spectacular setting, with amazing views of Lake Tahoe and Nevada

➕ Fair-sized mountain that offers a sensation of travelling around

➕ Large areas of widely spaced trees, largely on intermediate slopes – fabulous in fresh powder

➕ Some serious challenges for experts

➕ Numerous other worthwhile resorts within an hour's drive

➕ A unique nightlife scene

➕ Good snow record plus impressive snowmaking facilities

➖ South Lake Tahoe, where you stay, is a bizarre and messy place spreading along a busy highway

➖ No trail back to Heavenly Village at the base of the gondola

➖ Gondola vulnerable to wind closure

➖ If the tree skiing is not good, or if you are not up to it, you are mainly confined to easy groomed blues and mogulled blacks

➖ If natural snow is poor, most of the challenging terrain may be closed

➖ Very little traditional après-ski

A resort called Heavenly invites an obvious question: just how close to heaven does it take you? Physically, close enough: with a top height of 3060m/10,040ft and vertical of 1060m/3,470ft, it's the highest and biggest of the resorts set around Lake Tahoe. Metaphorically, it's not quite so close. In particular, anyone who (like us) is drawn to Heavenly partly by its exceptionally scenic setting is likely to be dismayed by the appearance and atmosphere of South Lake Tahoe.

The official line is that the place has been transformed into something like a European ski resort by the gondola between downtown and the mountain and by the pedestrianised Heavenly Village around its base. We don't buy that. It's great to have a gondola from downtown and the 'village' is quite smart (though quiet and small). But the general feel of South Lake Tahoe isn't much affected.

THE RESORT

Heavenly is on California's border with Nevada, at the south end of Lake Tahoe. Other resorts around the lake are easily visited from a base here.

Heavenly's base-town – South Lake Tahoe – is primarily a summer resort.

In this respect it is unusual, but not unique. What really sets it apart is that its economy is driven by gambling. The Stateline area at its centre is dominated by a handful of high-rise hotel-casinos located just inches on the Nevada side of the line. These brash but comfortable hotels offer good-value accommodation (subsidised by the gambling), swanky restaurants and big-name entertainers, as well as roulette wheels, craps and card games – and endless slot machines into which people feed bucketloads of quarters. It's bizarre to walk through the gambling areas in ski gear, carrying skis or board.

The casinos are a conspicuous part of the amazing lake views from the lower slopes (though not from above mid-mountain). They look like a classic American downtown area, which you'd expect to be full of shops and bars. But they are actually just a cluster of high-rise blocks bisected by the seriously busy US Highway 50. The rest of the town spreads for miles

For 2007/08 the slow Olympic chair on the Nevada side was upgraded to a high-speed quad. Four new trails were put in in the vicinity, plus one gladed run. For 2008/09 two new gladed runs are planned for Skiway Glades, plus a new trail in Powderbowl Woods. The Skyline Trail will also be redirected and remodelled to make it less flat. This is all part of Heavenly's Master Plan, a 10-year course of development.

Buildings on the opposite side of Highway 50 to the gondola have been demolished, to make way for a $420 million complex to be known as the Chateau, featuring a condominium hotel, outdoor pool, restaurants, shops and pedestrian walkways. It will include a bridge over the highway. Completion is expected for December 2009.

A much-needed new mountain restaurant (Powderbowl Lodge, with indoor seating for 425 people) is planned for 2009/10. There are also plans for the North Bowl lift above Boulder Lodge and the Galaxy lift, both on the Nevada side, to be replaced by fast quads, but no dates are fixed for these.

along this pedestrian-hostile road – dozens of low-rise hotels and motels (some quite shabby), stores, wedding chapels and so on. The general effect is less dire than it might be, thanks to the camouflage of tall trees.

Heavenly Village, built a few years ago right next to the base of the gondola, is an improvement, providing a downtown après-ski focus (basically just one bar) and pedestrianised area that the resort has lacked. But this could have been done much better (eg the ice rink has a huge generator/ chiller next to it). Despite this, and the fact there are no trails leading down to it, it is the obvious place to stay.

Some of the casino-hotels are within five minutes' walk of the gondola, making these an attractive choice even for those not keen on the gambling and entertainment, but others are enough of a hike away to justify using the shuttle-buses. And much of the cheaper accommodation is literally miles away. If that's where you're staying, you may prefer to access the mountain from the original lift base, California Lodge, up a heavily wooded slope 2km/1 mile out of South Lake Tahoe. That way, you'll be able to ski down at the end of the day instead of riding the gondola down.

Like the town, the slopes spread across the border into Nevada – and there are two other lift bases there, which can easily be reached by road. There are 'adequate' free shuttle-bus services to the three out-of-town bases. A car is still handy to explore the other resorts around Lake Tahoe (although buses, some of which are free, are available) and to get to many of the best restaurants, but parking can be expensive (maybe $20 a day).

There's a useful TV programme at 7.30am, Another Heavenly Morning, which covers weather and snow conditions. You can visit Squaw Valley by coach and return by boat across the lake. A reader recommends buying discount lift tickets from Don Cheepos.

THE MOUNTAIN

Practically all of Heavenly's slopes are cut through forest, but in many areas the forest is not dense and there is excellent tree skiing. The trail map gives a good indication of the density of trees, and the grading of nearby trails gives a good idea of steepness. As always in America, this 'off-piste' terrain is avalanche controlled. But it's 'patrolled' only by hollering; since collision with a tree may render you unconscious, don't ski the trees alone. The mountain is complicated, and getting from A to B requires more careful navigation than is usual on American mountains (eg it's not obvious from the piste map that it's much better to take the Comet rather than the Dipper chair back from Nevada to the California side).

THE SLOPES
Interestingly complex
The gondola between Heavenly Village and the mountain was a great improvement. But it can be closed far too often if it's windy (as several reporters have found). Quite a few of the links between different sectors involve flat tracks. Readers particularly mention Ridge Run, Roundabout and Skyline Trail – so the remodelling of Skyline (see 'News') is welcome.

There is a clear division between the California side of the mountain (above South Lake Tahoe) and the Nevada side (above Boulder and Stagecoach Lodges). Near the Nevada border you can see beautiful views over Lake Tahoe in one direction and the arid Nevada 'desert' in the other.

On the California side there are four fast chairs on the upper mountain. The steep lower slopes are served by the Aerial Tramway (a cable car) and Gunbarrel fast chair.

On the Nevada side, above East Peak Lodge, is an excellent intermediate area, served by two fast quad chairs, with a downhill extension

Heavenly's varied terrain makes a perfect natural playground for advanced freeriders. Intermediates will have fun too, as there are plenty of gentle powder runs, served mainly by chairs. And there are good areas for beginners. Heavenly has several terrain parks and the South Shore Soldiers spring freestyle camps (www.southshoresoldiers.com). The Block is pro rider Marc Frank Montoya's hotel in South Lake Tahoe. Each room is designed by a snowboard-associated brand and is the place for boarders to stay in the area (www.blockattahoe.com).

served by the Galaxy chair. From the fast Dipper chair back up, you can access the open terrain of Milky Way Bowl, leading to the seriously steep gladed runs of Mott and Killebrew canyons, served by the Mott Canyon chair. Below East Peak Lodge are runs down to Nevada's two bases, only the Stagecoach having a fast chair back up – it's successive slow chairs and then the fast Olympic quad from Boulder.

TERRAIN PARKS
Great facilities for all abilities

Heavenly has something for everyone. The Groove Park, between Groove and Patsy's chairlifts below the top of the lifts up from California Lodge, has beginner features such as small jumps and boxes for novice park riders. Intermediates should head to Powderbowl Park on the Powderbowl run; this is a great progression area with good size jumps and basic rails. High Roller Park, near the top of the Canyon chair, services expert riders; there are big kicker lines, and all sorts of jibs including an awesome pyramid jib box feature and three-level box; new for 2007/08 was a big metal water pipe feature and big step-up jump. Below this, at the top of the

Powderbowl chairlift, is a beast of a super-pipe with 7m/23ft walls. The Cascade boardercross can be found to the side of the Tamarack chair. High Roller Nightlife, served by the World Cup lift at the California base, is open Thursday to Saturday, 5pm-9pm.

SNOW RELIABILITY
No worries for intermediates

Heavenly was one of the first resorts to invest heavily in snowmaking. The system now covers around 70% of the trails and ensures that most sections are open most of the time. But good natural snow is needed for Mott and Killebrew Canyons to be enjoyable (or even open). Heavenly averages an impressive 360 inches per year.

FOR EXPERTS
Some specific challenges

The black runs under the California base lifts – including the Face and Gunbarrel (often used for mogul competitions) – are seriously steep and challenging. Lots of people were struggling on the top-to-bottom icy bumps on our last few visits. Ellie's, at the top of the mountain, may offer continuous moguls too, but was groomed and a great fast cruise when

Heavenly

577

SCHOOLS

Heavenly
t 775 586 7000

Classes
3-day (3 x 2¾hr)
learn-to-ski package
(includes equipment
and pass) $340

Private lessons
$350 for 3hr

CHILDREN

Day Care Center
t 775 586 7000
Ages 6wk to 6yr;
8.30-4pm; $120
including lunch; book
ahead

Ski school
For ages 4 to 13
(snowboarding 7 to
13); full day
(including 5hr of
teaching, equipment,
pass and lunch) $165

UK PACKAGES

All America Holidays,
Alpine Answers,
AmeriCan Ski, American
Ski Classics, Crystal,
Crystal Finest,
Directski.com, Erna
Low, Independent Ski
Links, Ski Activity, Ski
Dream, Ski
Independence, Ski Line,
Ski McNeill, Ski Safari,
Ski Solutions, Skitracer,
Skiworld, Trailfinders,
United Vacations,
White Mountains

we were last there. There's some really steep stuff on the Nevada side. Milky Way Bowl provides a gentle single-diamond introduction to the emphatically double-diamond terrain beyond it. The extremely steep, densely wooded Mott and Killebrew canyons have roped gateways; be warned, these are genuine double-black-diamond tree runs. The Mott Canyon chair is slow, but you may welcome the rest it affords.

Elsewhere, especially on the California side from the Sky chair, there are excellent ungroomed slopes with widely spaced trees – tremendous fun when conditions are right. Some wooded slopes are identified on the trail map, but you are not confined to those. Two new gladed trails are planned in this area for 2008/09.

FOR INTERMEDIATES
Lots to do
Heavenly is excellent for intermediates. The California side offers a progression from the relaxed cruising of the long Ridge Run, starting right at the top of the mountain, to more challenging blues dropping off the ridge towards Sky Deck. Confident intermediates will want to spend time on the Nevada side, where there is more variety of terrain, some longer runs down to the lift bases and more carving space. There are some great top-to-bottom cruises down to Stagecoach Lodge (served by a fast chair) and Boulder Lodge (served by successive very slow chairs and then the fast Olympic quad). And adventurous intermediates will enjoy exploring the tree runs from the fast Sky chair on the California side (see 'For experts').

FOR BEGINNERS
An excellent place to learn
There's an excellent beginner area at the top of the gondola and others at the California base lodge and Boulder Lodge in Nevada. On the California side there are gentle green runs to progress to at the top of the cable car.

FOR CROSS-COUNTRY
A separate world
You can try Adventure Peak at the top of the gondola. But the serious stuff is elsewhere around the lake – notably at the Spooner Lake Cross Country Area: over 80km/50 miles of prepared trails.

QUEUES
Gondola a problem
The gondola can have morning queues ('but we didn't queue for more than 10 minutes', says a 2008 reporter); you might prefer to take the shuttle to the much quieter Stagecoach Lodge base. There are also queues to ride the gondola down at the end of the day. Ignore the signs telling you to set off ridiculously early to catch the gondola; it keeps going until after 4pm and our advice is to stay out till whenever you like, then have a beer at the bar near the top until the queue disappears. A 2008 reporter suggests it's more fun and relaxing to get the bus back from one of the other bases. Sadly, too often the gondola seems to close because of wind, and then you have to catch a bus to another base to get up the mountain. Recent reporters have experienced few other problems.

MOUNTAIN RESTAURANTS
Even refuelling is problematic
We have long considered the on-mountain catering grossly inadequate, especially in bad weather. We used to like the table-service Lake View Lodge at the top of the cable car from California Lodge, but even that served mediocre food on our most recent visit. East Peak Lodge was fairly recently renovated and the menu widened, but most of the seating is outside. The other options consist of outdoor decks serving BBQs and pizzas (hugely unenjoyable in a blizzard, as we can testify) and grossly overcrowded cafeterias, 'I recommend starving, unless you're happy with crowds and stodge' and 'resoundingly awful with almost nowhere to sit indoors', say two recent reporters.

SCHOOLS AND GUIDES
Mixed reports
A past reporter joined the school for two days and was delighted to find only two in her class. However, another skier, looking for advanced tuition, found the attitude of the organisers 'terrible, really patronising'. A 2007 reporter tried the school's Mountain Adventure session ($75 for four hours) and found it 'well worth it to gain some local knowledge'.

FACILITIES FOR CHILDREN
Comprehensive
We lack recent feedback, but a past reporter praised the facilities.

↑ Fire+Ice at the foot of the gondola is the après-ski focus; note the usual US warning about fires being hot
SNOWPIX.COM / CHRIS GILL

GETTING THERE

Air San Francisco 274km/170 miles (3½hr); Reno 89km/55 miles (1¼hr); South Lake Tahoe, 15min

ACTIVITIES

Indoor Casinos, spas, art galleries, multiplex cinema, museums

Outdoor Lake cruises, snowmobiling, sleigh rides, dog sledding, hot springs, fishing, ice skating, snowshoeing, factory outlet shops

Phone numbers
Different area codes are used on the two sides of the stateline; for this chapter, therefore, the area code is included with each number

From distant parts of the US, add the prefix 1. From abroad, add the prefix +1

TOURIST OFFICE

t 775 586 7000
info@vailresorts.com
www.skiheavenly.com

STAYING THERE

HOW TO GO
Hotel or motel?
Accommodation in the South Lake Tahoe area is abundant and ranges from the huge casinos to small motels.
Chalets UK tour operators run some good catered chalets.
Hotels Of the main casino hotels, Harrah's (775 588 6611) and Harveys (775 588 2411) are the closest to the gondola. Rooms booked on the spot are expensive; packages are cheaper. The Block (530 544 2936) is a snowboarders' hotel – see 'Boarding'.
****Embassy Suites** (530 544 5400) Luxury suites close to the gondola. Huge breakfast spread and après cocktails included.
Rodeway Inn (530 541 7150) 'Basic. Seven minutes' walk to the gondola.'
Station House Inn (530 542 1101) Consistently recommended: 'Full cooked breakfast at no extra charge.'
Tahoe Chalet Inn (530 544 3311) Clean, friendly, near casinos. Back rooms (away from highway) preferable.
Timber Cove Lodge (530 541 6722) Bland but well run, with lake views from some rooms.
Lakeland Inn (530 544 1685) Recommended by a 2008 reporter as 'very comfortable'.
Apartments Plenty of choice. We've had a rave report about The Ridge Tahoe condos near Stagecoach Lodge.

EATING OUT
Good value
The casino hotels' all-you-can-eat buffets offer fantastic value and variety ('from pizza to Chinese to roast beef' at Montbleu); they have 'gourmet' restaurants too – some with superb views (try the Forest Buffet on the 18th floor at Harrah's and 19 on the 19th at Harveys). The sprawling resort area offers a huge variety. Reporters'

suggestions include Applebee's ('still the best value meals'), Hunan Garden ('best Chinese buffet ever'), Cecil's ('excellent and reasonable'), Fresh Ketch at Tahoe Keys Marina ('fresh fish and harbour views'), Zephyr Cove Resort ('excellent, reasonable'), the Brewery ('good food and beer'), Taj Mahal ('decent Indian'), Coyote Grill ('Mexican fast-food'), Freshies ('fish tacos are out of this world') and Riva Grill ('smart and pricey marina bar/grill'). For breakfast, try the Blue Angel or join locals at the Driftwood Cafe.

APRES-SKI
Getting better
Things have looked up in the last few years for 4pm drinking: there's now an Austrian-style igloo bar near the top of the gondola and Fire+Ice at the foot of it (with an outdoor seating area with fires and heaters). Both get busy. McP's is a locals' hangout directly across from the gondola. It will still operate for 2008/09 but is due to be razed to the ground as part of the demolition mentioned in 'News'. Whiskey Dicks, on the main highway, is a 'cool' bar with live music. Later on, the casinos on the Nevada side of the stateline have shows with top-name entertainers. And you can dance and dine your way across the lake on a paddle steamer.

OFF THE SLOPES
Luck be a lady
If you enjoy gambling you're in the right place. If you want to get away from the bright lights, try a boat trip on Lake Tahoe, snowmobiling or a hot-air balloon ride. Pedestrians can use the cable car or the gondola to share the lake views and at Adventure Peak, at the top of the gondola, you can go tubing, snow biking, tobogganing and snowshoeing, and try the Heavenly Flyer, a zip-line installed for 2007/08.

Mammoth Mountain

A big, sprawling mountain above a car-oriented, sprawling but pleasantly woody resort, a six-hour drive from Los Angeles

COSTS

① ② ③ ④ ⑤ ⑥

RATINGS

The slopes
Fast lifts	****
Snow	****
Extent	***
Expert	****
Intermediate	****
Beginner	****
Convenience	**
Queues	****
Mountain restaurants	*

The rest
Scenery	***
Resort charm	**
Off-slope	*

NEWS

For 2007/08 the 38-year-old Chair 9 was replaced with a six-pack, the Cloud Nine Express, and a new condo hotel, the Westin Monache Resort, opened in The Village.

Mammoth's airport is being extended and modernised and it is expected that commercial flights from Los Angeles to Mammoth will be re-introduced in December 2008.

580

➕ One of North America's bigger ski hills, with something for everyone

➕ Good mix of open Alpine-style bowls and classic American wooded slopes

➕ Impressive snowfall record

➕ Uncrowded slopes most of the time

➕ Mightily impressive terrain parks

➕ Good views, including more Alpine drama than usual in the US

➖ Mammoth Lakes is a rather straggling place with no focus, where life revolves around cars

➖ Most accommodation is miles from the slopes – though development is taking place at the lift bases

➖ Weekend crowds in high season

➖ Trail map and signing still poor

➖ Wind can be a problem

Mammoth may not be mammoth in Alpine terms – from end to end, it measures less than one-third of the size of Val d'Isère/Tignes, in area it's more like one-sixth – but it is big enough to amuse many people for a week. It can be a superb mountain for anyone who is happy in deep snow, but is equally suited to families and mixed-ability groups looking for groomed runs.

The main thing we dislike about it is the sprawling nature of the town itself, Mammoth Lakes where most people stay. Six years ago, Intrawest, owner of Whistler and now of various key plots of land here, started building the new pedestrian Village on the edge of Mammoth Lakes and connected by a gondola to one of the main lift bases. If your lodgings are at The Village, no doubt its restaurants and boutiques will attract your custom. But it doesn't have much impact on the resort as a whole. You can't ski down to The Village, so most visitors based elsewhere (ie the majority) ignore it.

THE RESORT

The mountain is set above Mammoth Lakes, a small year-round resort town that spreads over a wide area of woodland. The place is entirely geared to driving, with no discernible centre – hotels, restaurants and little shopping centres are scattered along the four-lane highway called Main Street and Old Mammoth Road, which crosses it.

The buildings are generally timber-clad in traditional style – even McDonald's has been tastefully designed – and are set among trees, so although it may be short on village ambience, the place has a pleasant enough appearance – particularly when under snow.

The town meets the mountain at two lift bases, both a mile or two from most of the hotels and condos.

The major base is Canyon Lodge, with a big day lodge and four chairlifts; there are hotels, condos and individual homes in the area below the lodge. Not far from here is Intrawest's pedestrian development,

The Village, which is linked to Canyon Lodge by a gondola.

The minor base, with a single six-pack, is Eagle Lodge (previously Little Eagle – also known as Juniper Springs, which strictly is the name of the condos built at the base).

A road runs along the north fringe of the mountain past an anonymous chairlift base to two other major base areas: The Mill Cafe, with two fast chairs, and Main Lodge, a mini-resort with three fast access lifts and a big day lodge. You can stay here, in the Mammoth Mountain Inn; but who wants to be based four miles from the 50+ restaurants in Mammoth Lakes? Not us.

Shuttle-buses run on several colour-coded routes serving the lift bases (though they are reported to be erratic in the mornings). Night buses run via The Village until midnight. A car is useful.

The Mammoth lift pass also covers June, a small mountain half an hour's drive north, chiefly attractive for its astonishingly people-free slopes. See

↑ Mammoth offers a good mix of open bowls and treelined trails

MAMMOTH MOUNTAIN SKI AREA

feature box, later in this chapter.

The drive up from Los Angeles takes six hours (more in poor conditions); but it is not without interest. You pass through the Santa Monica mountains close to Beverly Hills, then the San Gabriel mountains and Mojave Desert (with the world's biggest jet-plane parking lot) before reaching the Sierra Nevada range.

KEY FACTS

Resort	2425m
	7,950ft

Mammoth only	
Slopes	2425-3370m
	7,950-11,050ft
Lifts	29
Pistes	3,500 acres
Green	25%
Blue	40%
Black	35%
Snowmaking	
	700 acres

June Mountain only	
Slopes	2290-3075m
	7,510-10,090ft
Lifts	7
Pistes	500 acres
Green	35%
Blue	45%
Black	20%
Snowmaking	none

THE MOUNTAIN

The 29 lifts access an impressive area, suitable for all abilities. The highest runs are open, the lower ones more sheltered by trees.

Finding your way around is not easy at first. Many of the chairlifts now have names (the traditional practice was to give them numbers), but the trails are still ill defined: the map shows trails by means of isolated symbols, not continuous lines, and signposting of runs on the mountain is sporadic. On the lower part of the mountain this is mainly an inconvenience. But higher up there are real dangers in poor visibility. The map uses six classifications, including green/black and blue/black – a good idea, but somewhat pointless when you often end up on the wrong trail.

THE SLOPES
Interesting variety

From **Main Lodge** the two-stage Panorama gondola goes via McCoy Station right to the top. The views are great, with Nevada to the north-east and the jagged Minarets to the west. There are countless ways down the front of the mountain, which range from steep to very steep – or vertical if the wind has created a cornice, as it often does. Or you can go off the back, down to **Outpost 14**, whence Chair 14 or Chair 13 bring you back to lower points on the ridge. The third option is to follow the ridge, which eventually brings you down to the Main Lodge area. This route brings you past an easy area served by a double chair, and a very easy area served by the Discovery fast quad.

McCoy Station can also be reached using the Stump Alley fast chair from **The Mill Cafe**, on the road up from town. The fast Gold Rush quad, also from The Mill Cafe, takes you into the more heavily wooded eastern half of the area. This has long, gentle runs served by lifts up from **Canyon Lodge** and **Eagle Lodge** and seriously steep stuff as well as some intermediate terrain on the subsidiary peak known as Lincoln, served by lifts 25 and 22.

TERRAIN PARKS
Among the best

There are three award-winning parks. Main Park, situated above Main Lodge, is massive. Everything here is up to pro standard. Kickers in the Boneyard Bonanza range from 18m to 24m (60ft to 80ft) long and border the famous super-duper pipe (183m/600ft long, with 7m/23ft walls) that looms over the car park and is cut daily. There's also a super-pipe here. A warm-up mini park on Woolly's run, called Disco at Main, will heat up the muscles with small low-to-the-snow rails and boxes.

For intermediate to advanced

boarding

Mammoth has encouraged snowboarding since its early days. A huge amount has been spent on the terrain parks, and this tends to overshadow just how good the mountain's natural terrain really is. Almost entirely serviced by fast chairs and gondolas, this is a snowboarder's heaven. There are bowls, chutes, tree runs and cliffs dotted around the mountain, and you will be hard-pressed not to find something to your liking. Take the Panorama gondola and drop into the back bowls for plenty of powder runs. There are heaps of not-so-steep and wide runs for beginners on the lower parts of the resort. The terrain parks are about the best you will find. Wave Rave snowboard shop has a huge selection of gear.

LIFT PASSES

Mammoth Mountain

Prices in US$

Age	1-day	6-day
under 13	40	198
13 to 18	59	296
19 to 64	79	395
over 65	40	198

Free under 7, over 80

Beginner fixed price pass for four lifts only

Notes
Covers all lifts at Mammoth and June Mountains. Afternoon pass available

Alternative pass
June Mountain only

riders, South Park by the Roller Coaster fast chair is a real playground. Two tree-lined itineraries force you to choose between rails or kickers. These flowing lines allow you to hit six or seven obstacles in a row – perfect. There's also a boardercross here.

What used to be the Family Fun Park by Canyon Lodge has now relocated to Chair 7 and is dubbed the Wonderland Park. It has a fun mini-pipe, various micro-scale rails, boxes and mini-jumps, and has a great atmosphere to learn in. The parks can get very crowded on the weekends – try neighbouring June mountain's parks for a quiet and brilliantly underrated alternative. See http://unbound. mammothmountain.com for details on Mammoth's parks and events.

SNOW RELIABILITY
A long season
Mammoth has an impressive snow record – an annual average of 385 inches, which puts it ahead of major Colorado resorts and about on a par with Jackson Hole. It is appreciably higher than other Californian resorts, and has an ever-expanding array of snow-guns, so it enjoys a long season. The mountain faces roughly north; the relatively low and slightly sunny slopes down to Eagle Lodge are affected by warm weather before others. Strong winds are not uncommon on the upper mountain and the snow quality can be affected by these. This is not always a bad thing – the 'wind-compacted powder' can be 'just like spring snow'.

FOR EXPERTS
Some very challenging terrain
The steep bowls that run the width of the mountain top provide wonderful opportunities for experts. There are one or two single-diamond slopes, but most are emphatically double-diamond affairs requiring a lot of bottle.

There is lots of challenging terrain lower down, too; Chair 5, Chair 22 (the top of which is higher than the very top of Heavenly) and Broadway are often open in bad weather when the top is firmly shut, and their more sheltered slopes may in any case have the best snow. There are plenty of good slopes over the back towards Outpost 14, too. Many of the steeper trails are short by Alpine standards (typically under 400m/1,300ft vertical), but despite this we've enjoyed some great powder days here.

FOR INTERMEDIATES
Lots of great cruising
Although there are exceptions, most of the lower mountain, below the treeline, is intermediate cruising territory. What's more, Mammoth's piste maintenance is generally good, and many slopes that might become mogulled are kept easily skiable: 'very flattering', says one visitor.

As you might hope, the six-point trail difficulty scale – which we haven't tried to replicate on our own small trail map – is a good guide to what you'll find on the mountain.

Some of the mountain's longest runs, blue-blacks served by the Cloud Nine Express and Chair 25, are ideal for good intermediates. There are also

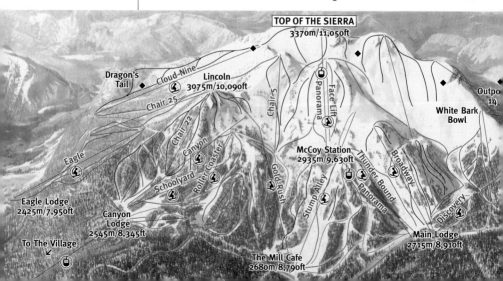

UK PACKAGES
All America Holidays, AmeriCan Ski, American Ski Classics, Independent Ski Links, Ski Activity, Ski Dream, Ski Independence, Ski Line, Ski Safari, Ski Solutions, Skitracer, Skiworld, Virgin Snow, White Mountains

SCHOOLS
Mammoth Mountain
934 2571

Classes
1 day (9.30-3.15)
$109
Private lessons
$150 for 1hr

CHILDREN
Small World
t 934 2571
Ages newborn to 8yr;
8.30-4.30

Ski school
Takes ages 4 to 12 at a cost of $135 all day (9am-3.15)

---

some excellent, fairly steep, woodland trails down to The Mill Cafe. Most of the long runs above Eagle Lodge, and some of the shorter ones above Canyon Lodge, are easy cruises. There is a variety of terrain, including lots of gentle stuff, at the western extremity of the slopes (the right hand side of the trail map), both on the front side and on the back side.

FOR BEGINNERS
Excellent
Chair 7 and the Schoolyard Express chair at Canyon Lodge and Discovery Chair at Main Lodge serve quiet, gentle green runs – perfect for progressing to from the nursery slopes. Excellent instruction, top-notch grooming and snow quality usually make progress speedy ('My eight-year-old son was skiing blue-black runs by the end of the week').

FOR CROSS-COUNTRY
Very popular
Two specialist centres, Tamarack and Sierra Meadows (ungroomed), provide lessons and tours. There are 30km/ 19 miles of trails at Tamarack, and lots of scenic ungroomed tracks, including some through the pretty Lakes Basin area: 70km/43 miles of trails in all.

QUEUES
Normally quiet slopes
During the week the lifts and slopes are usually very quiet, with few queues: 'empty', 'deserted', say reporters. One found only 5-10 minute waits at most in the busiest areas. But even the efficient lift system can struggle when 15,000 visitors arrive from LA on fine peak-season weekends. That's the time to try the wonderfully uncrowded June Mountain, half an hour away.

MOUNTAIN RESTAURANTS
Not a lot of choice
The only real mountain restaurants are at mid-mountain McCoy Station. This offers 'a good choice' of roasts, Italian, Asian and other dishes – but does get 'very busy'. The Parallax table-service restaurant next door does satisfying food with a calm atmosphere and a splendid view from its picture windows. New for 2007/08 was the Top of the Sierra Cafe, serving sandwiches and salads at Panorama Lookout. The other on-mountain possibility in good weather is the primitive outdoor BBQ at Outpost 14, on the back of the hill.

Most people eat at the lift bases. Talons at Eagle Lodge has its fans. The Mill Cafe is 'pleasant' but the 'choice of food was limited'. The Mountainside Grill at the Mammoth Mountain Inn has been recommended. Canyon Lodge offers Mexican, Italian, Asian and more. The Broadway Marketplace is in the Main Lodge.

SCHOOLS AND GUIDES
Excellent reports
Reporters are favourably impressed by the school, which apparently contains several Scottish instructors. One visitor wrote of 'very sympathetic' instructors and small classes. You can encounter the general American problem that you usually get a different instructor every day. There are some special 'camps' for experts, and for women.

FACILITIES FOR CHILDREN
Family favourite
Mammoth is keen to attract families. There is a dedicated Family Center at the Mountain Center at the base of The Village gondola, for organising lift passes and lessons etc in one go. The Woollywood school, based in the Panorama gondola station, works closely with the Small World child care centre. We've had glowing reports; one

---

JUNE MOUNTAIN: THE WORLD'S QUIETEST SLOPES?

June Mountain, a scenic half-hour drive from Mammoth, is in the same ownership and covered by the lift pass. It makes a pleasant haven if Mammoth is busy. When Mammoth isn't busy, June is quite simply deserted; on a March weekday we skied run after run without seeing another person.

A double chair goes up from the car park at 2290m/7,510ft over black slopes (often short of snow) to a lodge, June Meadows Chalet. A quad chair serves a gentle blue-run hill, and a double chair goes over very gentle green runs to a quad serving short but genuinely black slopes on June Mountain itself (3100m/ 10,170ft). There are two jib-parks and a super-pipe.

↑ The Village is a classic Intrawest development and linked to the slopes by a gondola

584

GETTING THERE
Air Los Angeles 494km/307 miles (5hr); Reno 270km/168 miles (3hr)

ACTIVITIES
Indoor Fitness centres, museum, art galleries, cinema, concerts

Outdoor Snowshoeing, dog sledding, snowmobiling

Phone numbers
From distant parts of the US, add the prefix 1 760; from abroad, add the prefix +1 760

TOURIST OFFICE
t 934 2571
800mammoth@
mammoth-mtn.com
www.mammoth
mountain.com

reporter rated the facilities as 'second to none'. Canyon Kids (at Canyon Lodge) has been recommended too.

STAYING THERE
HOW TO GO
Good value packages
A good choice of hotels (none very luxurious or expensive) and condos. The condos tend to be out of town, near the lifts or on the road to them.
★★★Mammoth Mountain Inn (934 2581) Way out of town at Main Lodge. 'Spacious and comfortable, perfect for access to the slopes but isolated.'
★★★Alpenhof Lodge (934 6330) Comfortable and friendly, in central location. Shuttle-bus stop and plenty of restaurants nearby.
Westin Monache Resort (934 0400) New for 2007/08. Condo hotel with restaurant, hot tubs and pool, next to the gondola in The Village.
Quality Inn (934 5114) Good main street hotel with a big hot tub.
Austria Hof Lodge (934 2764) Ski-in/ski-out location near Canyon Lodge, recommended by a reporter, despite modest-sized rooms.
Sierra Nevada Rodeway Inn (934 2515) Central, good value, 'great spa'.
Holiday Inn (924 1234) Central location, large, comfortable rooms and 'great restaurant'. Pool.
Apartments The Juniper Springs Lodge is near lifts and town. Close to the Canyon Lodge base-station, the 1849 Condos are spacious and well equipped. The Mammoth Ski and Racquet Club, a 10-minute walk from the same lifts, is very comfortable. There is an 'excellent' supermarket in the Minaret Mall, with good discounts.

EATING OUT
Outstanding choice
Reporters are impressed by the 50+ restaurants, varying widely in style,

cost and location. Start with a copy of the local menu guide. One reporting couple had a great time dining in a different restaurant every day for a fortnight. Meshing their findings with other reports, we offer the following guidance: Slocums Grill – very good meal in wood-panelled room; Angel's – popular, good-value diner; Nevados – best in town, excellent modern cooking; Chart House – excellent seafood, varied meat dishes; Alpenrose – intimate chalet-style place with good food; Berger's – 'excellent giant burgers'.

Also recommended are Shogun for Japanese, Giovanni's for Italian and Gomez's for Mexican food. One visitor says that the meal he had at the Lakefront in the Tamarack Lodge up at Twin Lakes was 'the best ever in a ski resort'. We've had excellent dinners at Skadi and Whiskey Creek, too. The Breakfast Club does a 'good value, tasty breakfast'. LuLu and the Side Door cafe are appealing eateries in The Village. Snowcat dinners up at the Parallax restaurant are also possible.

APRES-SKI
Lively at weekends
The liveliest immediate après-ski spot is the Yodler, at Main Lodge – a chalet transported from Switzerland, so they say. Tusks, also at Main Lodge, is apparently great for viewing the high jinks in the terrain parks. Later on, things revolve around a handful of bars, which come to life at weekends. The Clocktower Cellar is reported to be 'best in town – lively, friendly, good music, great choice of beers'. Whiskey Creek is the liveliest (and stays open latest); it has live bands at weekends. Slocums is popular with locals and 'ideal for an after-dinner drink'. Grumpy's is a sports bar. One reporter enjoyed the venues in The Village. He says you shouldn't miss Hawaiian-style Lakanuki's with its 'bikini tree'. A new Irish pub, the Auld Dubliner, has opened there too.

OFF THE SLOPES
Mainly sightseeing
There are various things to be done outdoors, including skating. You can go sightseeing by car (preferably 4WD). The town of Bishop, 40 minutes' drive south, makes an amusing day out. Factory-outlet shopping is recommended for bargains. Mono Lake is reported to be 'well worth a visit'.

Squaw Valley

The most compelling base in the Tahoe area – great terrain for novices and experts, above an attractive purpose-built village

SNOWPIX.COM / CHRIS GILL

Squaw's largely ungroomed terrain is great for experts and adventurous intermediates ↓

- ➕ Lots of challenging runs and ungroomed terrain
- ➕ Impressive snow record
- ➕ Superb beginner slopes
- ➕ Convenient, pleasant, purpose-built village at the base

- ➖ Not for mile-hungry intermediates
- ➖ Lifts prone to closure by wind
- ➖ Adventurous skiers need guidance to really exploit the area
- ➖ Limited range of village amenities

When Intrawest built a neat little pedestrian resort at the base, Squaw became an attractive 'destination' resort. It can't rival Heavenly for nightlife or for quantity of groomed runs, but it's now our favourite base in the Tahoe area.

THE RESORT

The car-free 'Village at Squaw Valley' was built a few years ago at the base of the main lifts by Intrawest, of Whistler/Arc 1950 fame. For a built-from-scratch development it is very successful, although still very small and limited in what it offers.

The self-contained, luxurious, conference-oriented Resort at Squaw Creek hotel is linked into one end of the lift network by its own chairlift.

Squaw is the major resort at the north end of Lake Tahoe, about an hour's drive from South Lake Tahoe and Heavenly. There are daily shuttle-buses, and you can go by boat.

THE MOUNTAINS

Squaw offers a lot of terrain by US standards on six linked peaks. The peaks and high bowls are treeless, but much of the terrain is lightly wooded.

Squaw has no trails marked on its mountain map (just lifts that are coloured green, blue or black) and few signs or other aids to route-finding on the ground. In some sectors, adventurous but not truly expert skiers could find themselves in real difficulty; to get the most out of the mountain, it's best to have a guide.

Slopes There are several distinct sectors. Two impressively powerful lifts leave the village – a gondola and a big cable car. They rise 600m/1,970ft to the twin stations of Gold Coast and High Camp (linked by the Pulse gondola). Above them is a gentle area of beginner slopes, and beyond that the three highest peaks of the area. Each has lifts of modest vertical – much the biggest is on Squaw Peak's Headwall six-pack: 535m/1,750ft.

From High Camp you can descend into a steep-sided valley from which the Silverado chair is the return. Gates 7 and 8 give the easiest runs down,

Two peaks are accessed directly from the village. The fast quad to KT-22 gives quick access to lots of steep routes. Snow King is a good intermediate hill, unjustly neglected because of its slow lift access.

Squaw's cable car runs in the evenings to serve the floodlit slopes (including a 5km/3 mile run to the base area), and terrain parks and the dining facilities at High Camp.

Terrain parks There are four parks. Belmont is mid-level and gives riders an opportunity to progress. Central Park is great for intermediate and advanced riders; there were new log jibs and a water tank feature in 2007/08, plus a new in-ground super-pipe. Mainline Park opens for peak season and has the biggest hits plus another super-pipe when snow

conditions allow. The Papoose Park is designed for freestyle novices.

Snow reliability An impressive 460 inches on average, plus snowmaking.

Experts The possibilities for experts on KT-22, Squaw Peak and Granite Chief – plus the Silverado valley – are huge, with lots of steep chutes and big mogul fields; many extreme skiing and boarding movies are made here. But at first it is very difficult to identify routes that are safe – you'll get the most of the area if you go with a guide/instructor. See www.squallywood thebook.com to buy a useful guide to steep, technical lines in Squaw.

Intermediates Blue-run skiers have a choice of some lovely cruises in the Emigrant and Snow King sectors and a three-mile top-to-bottom run. But there is not much more groomed cruising, so keen piste-bashers will find the area limited. There is, however, lots of steep blue and easy black terrain in which to develop deep-snow or mogul skills – particularly around the Siberia, Solitude and Granite Chief lifts.

Beginners The Papoose nursery area has a gentle slope served by a double chairlift – a special beginner lift pass is available. There's a superb choice of easy runs to progress to at altitude.

Snowboarding This is one of the most snowboarder friendly resorts in California. The higher areas are full of steep and deep gullies, cliff drops, kicker building spots and tree runs. And the three terrain parks are great.

Cross-country There are 18km/11 miles of groomed trails at Squaw Creek.

Queues Fast lifts now serve each sector, but there are still several old

chairs, notably around Emigrant.

Mountain restaurants The mid-mountain facilities are not inspiring, except in terms of views.

Schools and guides The school runs Ski with a Pro adult group lessons hourly. There are specialist workshops.

Facilities for children Squaw Kids takes children from three years. There is a children's on-slope play area at the Papoose base area too.

STAYING THERE

How to go The new village has widened the choice of accommodation.

Hotels The PlumpJack Inn (583 1576) is our favourite – comfortable, stylish, central. The Resort at Squaw Creek (583 6300) offers luxury rooms, an outdoor pool and hot tubs.

Apartments The Village has well-appointed ski-in/ski-out condos.

Eating out The PlumpJack Inn has an excellent restaurant; the Balboa Cafe, run by the same people, also has an impressive menu. More routine places include the Auld Dubliner pub, Fireside (pizza/pasta), Mamasake (sushi), ZenBu (tapas). Dining up the mountain is possible at Alexander's.

Après-ski The Olympic House has several venues. In the Village, the places above mostly function as bars, too: Auld Dubliner is the liveliest. A new wine bar, Uncorked at Squaw Valley, has opened, with live music on Thursdays and wine tastings.

Off the slopes High Camp has an ice rink and other activities. The Trilogy Spa offers a range of body-pampering treatments. Or you can take a paddle steamer cruise across Lake Tahoe.

SQUAW PEAK
2710m/8,900ft

EMIGRANT
2650m/8,700ft

GRANITE CHIEF
2760m/9,050ft

KT-22
2500m/8,200ft

Headwall

Shirley Lake

Gold Coast

High Camp
2500m/8,200ft

SNOW KING
2300m/7,550ft

KT-22 Express

Squaw One

Gold Coast

High Camp

Far East Express

Arrows mark the general direction and classification of runs, which are shown only as coloured lifts on the resort map.

Squaw Valley
1890m/6,200ft

Colorado

Colorado is the most popular American destination for UK visitors. And justifiably so: it has the most alluring combination of attractive resorts, slopes to suit all abilities and excellent, reliable snow – dry enough to justify its 'champagne powder' label. It also has direct scheduled BA flights to Denver (though no longer charter flights).

Colorado has amazingly dry snow. Even when the snow melts and refreezes, the moisture seems to be magically whisked away, leaving it in soft powdery condition. Even in times of snow shortage, the artificial snow is of a quality you'll rarely find in Europe. And like most North American rivals, Colorado resorts generally have excellent, steep, ungroomed terrain that has enormous appeal to the adventurous because you don't need guidance to ski it safely.

The resorts vary enormously. If you want cute restored buildings from the mining boom days of the late 1800s, try the dinky old towns of Telluride or Crested Butte or the much bigger Aspen. Others major on convenience – such as Aspen's modern satellite,

Snowmass. Some resorts deliberately pitch themselves upmarket, with lots of glitzy, expensive hotels – such as Vail and Beaver Creek – while others are much more down to earth – such as Winter Park and Breckenridge.

There is a cluster of resorts west of Denver that can be combined in a holiday tour by car. You could visit these while staying in cheaper lodging in a valley town such as Frisco.

It's important to be aware that many Colorado resorts are extremely high. As a result, lowlanders going there directly are at risk of altitude sickness, which can put you out of action for days. We now routinely plan our tours starting in one of the lower resorts – or spend a night or two in Denver to get acclimatised.

As elsewhere in the US, the trees go almost to the top in Aspen ↓

587

Aspen

Don't be put off by the ritzy image – with a fun, historic town and quiet, extensive slopes, this is America's best resort

- ➕ Notably uncrowded slopes
- ➕ Attractive, characterful old mining town, with lots of smart shops
- ➕ Great range of restaurants
- ➕ Excellent Snowmass just up the road
- ➕ Extensive slopes to suit every standard, but ...

- ➖ Slopes split over three separate mountains (four if you count Snowmass), though there's efficient, free transport
- ➖ Expensive, and tending to become more so as cheap places gradually close down

Another tour of Colorado in 2008 has confirmed that Aspen remains our favourite American resort. Despite the relentless drift of the place even further upmarket, we love the town, and we love the extensive and varied skiing. We admit that this affection for the skiing depends heavily on the presence of Aspen Highlands, a little way down the valley, and even more on the presence of Snowmass, considerably further down the valley (and therefore covered in a separate chapter). So most days you have to ride a bus, and the place scores only ★★ for convenience. That doesn't put us off, and doesn't seem to worry readers who report on the place – so it shouldn't deter you, either.

Don't be put off by the film star image. Yes, many rich and famous guests jet in here, and for connoisseurs of cosmetic surgery the bars of Aspen's top hotels can be fascinating places. But most celebs keep a low profile; and, like all other 'glamorous' ski resorts, Aspen is actually filled by ordinary holidaymakers.

THE RESORT

In 1892 Aspen was a booming silver-mining town, with 12,000 inhabitants, six newspapers and an opera house. But the town's fortunes took a nosedive when the silver price plummeted in 1893, and by the 1930s the population had shrunk to 700 or so, and the handsome Victorian buildings had fallen into disrepair. Development of the skiing started on a small scale in the late 1930s. The first lift was opened shortly after the Second World War, and Aspen hasn't looked back.

Now, the historic centre – with a typical American grid of streets – has been beautifully renovated to form the core of the most fashionable ski town in the Rockies. There's a huge variety of bars, restaurants, shops and art galleries – some amazingly upmarket. Spreading out from this centre, you'll find a mixture of developments, ranging from the homes of the super-rich through surprisingly modest hotels and motels to the mobile homes for the workers. Though the town is busy with traffic, it moves slowly, and pedestrians effectively have priority in much of the central area.

Aspen is very unusual in being a cute town with a major lift close to the centre: the Silver Queen gondola straight to the top of Aspen Mountain is only yards from some of the top hotels, and the streets running away from the lift base are lined by the restaurants and shops that make Aspen what it is. Downtown Aspen is quite compact by American resort standards, but it spreads far enough to make the free ski-bus a necessity for many visitors staying less centrally.

The other mountains are out of town, served by efficient buses from a station near the gondola base – 'They work really well between Snowmass and Aspen Mountain, but with other areas you need to check the timetables carefully,' says a 2008 reporter. A couple of miles out of town, Aspen Highlands now has some limited accommodation; 19km/12 miles away, Snowmass is a proper resort with great attractions as a base for families in particular, and it gets its own chapter.

↑ Sundeck (Aspen Mountain) has good restaurants, and a great view of Highland Bowl

THE MOUNTAINS

Most of the slopes are in the trees. All the mountains have regular, free guided tours, given by excellent amateur ambassadors. The ratio of acres to visitor beds is high, and the slopes are usually blissfully uncrowded. Lift passes are discounted heavily for pre-purchase or through tour operators – check your options well in advance. Signposting could be better where runs merge. A recent reporter found piste classification 'inconsistent' between mountains.

THE SLOPES
Widely dispersed
Each of the three local mountains is worth a visit – though novices should note that Aspen Mountain has no green runs. Much the most extensive mountain in the area is at Snowmass – see separate chapter.

Once you are up the gondola, a series of chairs serves the ridges of **Aspen Mountain**. In general, there are long cruising blue runs along the valley floors and short, steep blacks down from the ridges.

Buttermilk is the smallest, lowest and least challenging mountain, served by a fast quad from the fairly primitive main base lodge. The runs fan out from the top in three directions – back to the base, or down to the slow Tiehack chair, or down to the fast quad at West Buttermilk.

Aspen Highlands consists essentially of a single ridge served by three fast quad chairs, with easy and intermediate slopes along the ridge itself and steep black runs on the flanks – very steep ones at the top. And beyond the lift network is Highland Bowl, where gates give access to a splendid open bowl of entirely double-black gradient. The views from the upper part of Highlands are the best that Aspen has to offer – the famous Maroon Bells that appear on countless postcards.

Plum TV channel offers slope information.

TERRAIN PARKS
Some of the world's best
Aspen has a different kind of terrain park on each of its hills. Advanced riders should head to Buttermilk's huge X-Park, home of the Winter X Games until 2010 and designed by renowned shaping experts at Snow Park Technologies. The park stretches over 3km/2 miles and is said to be the

Aspen

589

GET THE BEST OF THE SNOW, ON- AND OFF-PISTE

Aspen offers special experiences for small numbers of skiers or riders.

Fresh Tracks *The first eight skiers to sign up each day get to ride the gondola up Aspen Mountain at 8am the next morning and get first tracks on perfect corduroy or fresh powder. Free! But take your time over the descent: if you get back to the base before the normal lift opening time, you'll have to wait, like everyone else.*

Powder Tours *Spend the day finding untracked snow in 1,500 acres of backcountry beyond Aspen Mountain, with a 10-passenger heated snowcat as your personal lift. You're likely to squeeze in about 10 runs in all. You break for lunch at an old mountain cabin. Full day last year $295.*

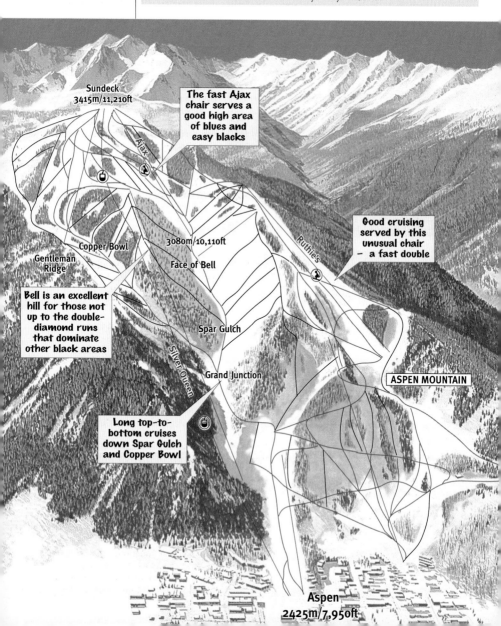

Sundeck
3415m/11,210ft

The fast Ajax chair serves a good high area of blues and easy blacks

Ajax

Copper Bowl

Gentleman Ridge

3080m/10,110ft

Face of Bell

Ruthie's

Good cruising served by this unusual chair – a fast double

Bell is an excellent hill for those not up to the double-diamond runs that dominate other black areas

Spar Gulch

Silver Queen

Grand Junction

ASPEN MOUNTAIN

Long top-to-bottom cruises down Spar Gulch and Copper Bowl

Aspen
2425m/7,950ft

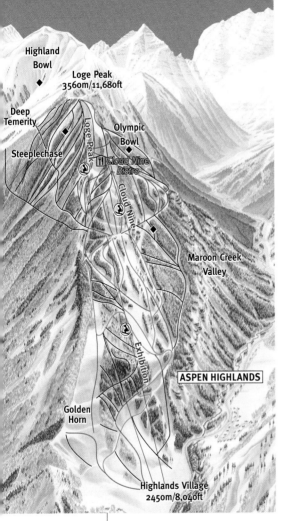

longest in the world. Hit the 170m/550ft long X-games pipe or the mini panda pipe. The slope-style course includes a log rail area, big kicker sections, hip jump and box. There is also a separate rail park, with new features popping up every year.

SNOW RELIABILITY
Rarely a problem
Aspen's mountains get an annual average of 300 inches of snow – not in the front rank, but not far behind. In addition, all areas have substantial snowmaking. Immaculate grooming adds to the quality of the pistes.

FOR EXPERTS
Buttermilk is the only soft stuff
There's plenty to choose from – all the mountains except Buttermilk offer lots of challenges.

Aspen Mountain has a formidable array of double-black-diamond runs. From the top of the gondola, Walsh's, Hyrup's and Kristi are on a lightly wooded slope and link up with Gentleman's Ridge and Jackpot to form the longest black run on the mountain. A series of steep glades drops down from Gentleman's Ridge. The central Bell ridge has less extreme single diamonds on both its flanks, including some delightful lightly wooded areas (as shown in the photo on the final page of the chapter). On the opposite side of Spar Gulch is another row of double-blacks, collectively called the Dumps, because mining waste was dumped here.

At Highlands there are challenging runs from top to bottom of the mountain. Consider joining a guided group as an introduction to the best of them. Highland Bowl, beyond the top lift, is superb in the right conditions: a big open bowl with pitches from a serious 38° to a terrifying 48°. There are free snowcat rides from the top of the lifts to the first access gate of Highland Bowl, but if these are not operating, it's a 20-minute hike. All the further gates require further hiking.

Left of the bowl, the Steeplechase area consists of a number of parallel natural avalanche chutes, and their elevation means the snow stays light and dry. The Deep Temerity lift (vertical 520m/1,700ft), built three years ago, added a useful amount of skiable vertical to these runs and to Highland Bowl. The Olympic Bowl area on the

Aspen Mountain	
Slopes	2425-3415m
	7,950-11,210ft
Lifts	8
Pistes	673 acres
Green	0%
Blue	48%
Black	52%
Snowmaking	
	210 acres

Aspen Highlands	
Slopes	2450-3560m
	8,040-11,680ft
Lifts	5
Pistes	1,010 acres
Green	18%
Blue	30%
Black	52%
Snowmaking	
	110 acres

Buttermilk	
Slopes	2400-3015m
	7,870-9,900ft
Lifts	9
Pistes	470 acres
Green	35%
Blue	39%
Black	26%
Snowmaking	
	108 acres

Total with Snowmass	
Slopes	2400-3815m
	7,870-12,510ft
Lifts	46
Pistes	5,285 acres
Green	10%
Blue	45%
Black	45%
Snowmaking	
	658 acres

SCHOOLS

Aspen
t 925 1227

Classes
Full day (5hr) $140,
incl. tax

Private lessons
$444 for 3hr for up to
5 people

boarding

There is a huge amount of terrain to explore, which will satisfy all levels of boarder – especially when you include Snowmass (see separate chapter) – and lots of excellent terrain on Aspen Mountain and Highlands. For more mellow carving runs and gentle freeriding head to Buttermilk, the least testing of the mountains – but also home to the most serious terrain park. There are countless good runs, cliff drops and tree lines. The hills are free of draglifts, with few flat sections.

opposite flank of the mountain has great views of the Maroon Bells and some serious moguls. Thunderbowl chair from the base serves a nice varied area that's often underused.

FOR INTERMEDIATES
Grooming to die for

Most intermediate runs on Highlands are concentrated above the mid-mountain Merry-Go-Round restaurant, many served by the Cloud Nine fast quad chair. But there are good slopes higher up and lower down – don't miss the vast, neglected expanses of Golden Horn, on the eastern limit of the area.

Aspen Mountain has its fair share of intermediate slopes, but they tend to be tougher than on the other mountains. Copper Bowl and Spar Gulch, running between the ridges, are great cruises early in the morning but can get crowded later. Upper Aspen Mountain, at the top of the gondola, has a dense network of well-groomed blues. The unusual Ruthie's chair – a fast double, apparently installed to rekindle the romance that quads have destroyed – serves more cruising runs.

The Main Buttermilk runs offer good, easy slopes to practise on, and can be extraordinarily quiet. And good intermediates should be able to handle the relatively easy black runs – when groomed, these are a real blast on carving skis. Buttermilk is also a great place for early experiments off-piste.

FOR BEGINNERS
Can be a great place to learn

Buttermilk is a great mountain for beginners. West Buttermilk has beautifully groomed, gentle, often deserted runs, served by a quad. The easiest slopes of all, though, are at the base of the Main Buttermilk sector – on Panda Hill. Despite its macho image, Highlands boasts the highest concentration of green runs in Aspen, served by the fast Exhibition chair.

FOR CROSS-COUNTRY
Backcountry bonanza

There are 60km/37 miles of groomed trails between Aspen and Snowmass in the Roaring Fork valley – the most extensive maintained cross-country system in the US. And the Ashcroft Ski Touring Center maintains around 35km/22 miles of trails around Ashcroft, a mining ghost town. The Pine Creek Cookhouse (925 1044) does excellent food and is accessible only by ski, snowshoe or horse-drawn sleigh. Aspen is at one end of the famous Tenth Mountain Division Trail, heading 370km/230 miles north-east almost to Vail, with 12 huts for overnight stops.

QUEUES
Few problems

There are rarely major queues on any of the mountains. At Aspen Mountain, the gondola can have delays at peak times; although this lift has been upgraded, it seems the changes are directed at improving comfort and views, not capacity. The alternative Shadow Mountain chair is 'old and slow', with a short uphill walk to reach it. Aspen Highlands is almost always queue-free, even at peak times. The two lifts out of Main Buttermilk sometimes get congested.

MOUNTAIN RESTAURANTS
Good by American standards

There aren't many good spots, but they are worth seeking out.
Editors' choice At Highlands, Cloud Nine bistro (544 3063) is the nearest thing in the States to a cosy Alpine hut, with excellent food – thanks to an Austrian chef. Not wildly expensive, either – $26 for soup and dish of the day last season.
Worth knowing about On Aspen Mountain the Sundeck self-service has been highly rated and gives great views across to Highland Bowl. And there's a recommended table-service area, Benedict's. Bonnie's self-service has also been approved by readers.

CHILDREN

Nanny Cub Care
t 923 1227
Nanny service for
ages 8wk to 3yr

Snow Cubs
t 923 1227
Ages 2½ to 3½

Big Burn Bears
t 923 0570
Ages 3 to 4

Grizzlies
t 923 1227
Ages 5 and 6

Powder Pandas
t 923 1227
Ages 3 to 4

All-day non-skiing nurseries
Several

Ski school
Ages 7 to 12, $92 per day (5¼hr, lunch included)

Aspen has a classic American grid street plan ↓

On Buttermilk the mountaintop Cliffhouse is known for its 'Mongolian Barbecue' stir-fry bar and great views of Pyramid Peak and the Maroon Creek valley.

SCHOOLS AND GUIDES
Simply the best?

There's a wide variety of specialised instruction – mountain exploration groups, off-piste tours, adrenalin sessions, women's groups, and so on. Past reports have praised the small group lessons and beginner classes, though one reader was unimpressed: 'Not enough mileage covered and I didn't get my video analysis as promised.' The Ski Doctor (Aspen Club and Spa) is an indoor simulator used in combination with some lessons. Lessons are said to be cheaper during Buttermilk's X-Games week (end of January).

FACILITIES FOR CHILDREN
Choice of nurseries

Child care arrangements usually receive excellent reviews, and parents are said to regularly request the same instructor for their children. Young children are bussed to and from Buttermilk's very impressive Fort Frog. The Kids' Trail Map is a great idea. But Snowmass has clear advantages for young families.

STAYING THERE

HOW TO GO
Accommodation for all pockets

There's a mixture of hotels, inns, B&Bs, lodges and condos.
Chalets Several UK tour operators have chalets here – some very luxurious.
Hotels There are places for all budgets. Most smaller hotels provide a good après-ski cheese and wine buffet.
*****St Regis Aspen** (920 3300) Opulent city-type hotel, near gondola. With a fancy spa facility.
*****Hyatt Grand Aspen** (920 3204) A newish grand place, near the gondola.
*****Little Nell** (920 4600) Stylish, modern hotel right by the gondola, with popular bar. Fireplaces in every room, outdoor pool, hot tub, sauna.
*****Jerome** (920 1000) Step back a century: Victorian authenticity combined with modern-day luxury. Several blocks from the gondola.
****Lenado** (925 6246) Smart modern B&B place with open-fire lounge, individually designed rooms.
***Aspen** (925 3441) Central, 'moderate' place, 10 minutes from lifts; comfortable, pool, hot tubs.
***Boomerang Lodge** (925 3416) Seven blocks from the centre and being fully renovated for 2008/09. Retaining its Lloyd-Wright inspired

Beautifully spaced trees on Face of Bell, Aspen Mountain →

SNOWPIX.COM / CHRIS GILL

UK PACKAGES

All America Holidays, Alpine Answers, AmeriCan Ski, American Ski Classics, Crystal, Crystal Finest, Directski.com, Erna Low, Independent Ski Links, Kuoni, Momentum, Neilson, Oxford Ski Co, Ski Activity, Ski Dream, Ski Expectations, Ski Freshtracks, Ski Independence, Ski Line, Ski McNeill, Ski Safari, Ski Solutions, Skitracer, Skiworld, Supertravel, Trailfinders, United Vacations, Virgin Snow, White Mountains

GETTING THERE

Air Aspen 5km/3 miles; Eagle 113km/ 70 miles (1½hr); Denver 355km/ 220 miles (4hr)

Rail Glenwood Springs (63km/39 miles)

ACTIVITIES

Indoor Club and Spa (sauna, swimming, weights, aerobics, steam, hot tubs); Recreation Center (pool, ice rink), galleries, cinemas, theatre

Outdoor Snowshoeing, sleigh rides, snowmobiles, hot-air ballooning

Phone numbers
From distant parts of the US, add the prefix 1 970; from abroad, add the prefix +1 970

TOURIST OFFICE

t 925 1220
intlres@skiaspen.com
www.aspensnowmass.
com

architecture, but with a contemporary lodge style. Pool and hot tub.
***Molly Gibson Lodge** (925 3434) Various room styles, all 'great value'. Pool, hot tub, bar.
***Aspen Mountain Lodge** (925 7650) Small, friendly lodge in a quiet location.
Mountain Chalet (925 7797) Cosy lodge five minutes from gondola. Pool, sauna and fitness room.
Apartments The standards here are high, even in US terms. Many of the smarter developments have their own free shuttle-buses. The Gant and Aspen Square are 'particularly good'.

EATING OUT
Dining dilemma
As you'd expect, there are excellent upmarket places, but also plenty of cheaper options – and an easy way to economise in many smarter places is to eat at the bar. Some giveaway magazines include menu guides.

On our 2008 visit we had excellent modern American cuisine at Elevation, and more classic steak-and-seafood stuff at Jimmy's. D19 was strongly recommended for Italian-American dishes. Two places riding the shared-platter wave are Social and DishAspen.

Piñons serves innovative American food. Syzygy is a suave upstairs place with live jazz from 10pm. Pacifica Seafood Brasserie is top-notch. The basement Steak Pit is a long-established and reliable favourite, with 'good choice, great food and service'. The Hostaria and Campo de Fiori are good Italians. Cache Cache does good value Provençal. Little Annie's is popular with reporters – 'good meals, huge portions'.

Cheaper recommendations include: Bentley's (main courses $8 upwards), Boogie's (family-friendly diner with

'good food and service'), Paradise Bakery ('great ice cream and muffins'), Mezzaluna, Hickory House and New York Pizzas ('excellent').

APRES-SKI
Lots of options
As the lifts shut, a few bars at the bases get busy – notably Iguana's at Highlands, the Ajax Tavern in Aspen. The Bar at the Little Nell is a great place for gazing at face-lifts.

Many of the restaurants are also bars – Jimmy's (spectacular stock of tequila) and Mezzaluna, for example. The J-bar of the Jerome hotel still has a traditional feel. For pool there's Aspen Billiards adjoining the fashionable Cigar Bar, with its comfortable sofas. The Popcorn Wagon is the place for munchies after the bars close. You can get a week's membership of the famous members-only Caribou club.

New venues for late-night dancing and drinking include, the Fly Lounge – designed to look like the interior of an aeroplane; the Regal Watering Hole, with nightly DJs, and Club Chelsea.

OFF THE SLOPES
Silver service
Aspen has lots to offer, especially if your credit card is in good shape. There are literally dozens of art galleries, as well as the predictable clothes and jewellery shops. There are plenty of shops selling affordable stuff – though a 2008 visitor found them 'disappointing'. Glenwood Springs is 'well worth a visit'. The best mountain restaurants are awkward for pedestrians to get to. The Aspen Recreation Center at Highlands has a huge swimming complex and an indoor ice rink. Hot-air ballooning is also recommended.

Beaver Creek

Exclusive and very pricey modern resort with quiet, varied slopes.
Good for a pampered stay or a day trip from Vail

COSTS

① ② ③ ④ ⑤ ⑥

RATINGS

The slopes

Fast lifts	*****
Snow	*****
Extent	**
Expert	****
Intermediate	****
Beginner	*****
Convenience	****
Queues	*****
Mountain restaurants	**

The rest

Scenery	***
Resort charm	**
Off-slope	***

NEWS

For 2008/09 a new children's ski school will open at the top of the Buckaroo Express gondola. A 210-room hotel, Westin Riverfront Resort, is due to open in Avon, and the Osprey (formerly Inn at Beaver Creek) is expected to reopen following a major revamp.

LIFT PASSES

See Vail chapter

UK PACKAGES

All America Holidays, Alpine Answers, AmeriCan Ski, American Ski Classics, Crystal Finest, Elegant Resorts, Kuoni, Ski Activity, Ski Dream, Ski Independence, Ski Line, Ski Safari, Ski Wild, Skitracer, Skiworld, Supertravel, Trailfinders, United Vacations

VAIL RESORTS, INC / JACK AFFLECK

The village is squeezed into a narrow valley ➔

- ➕ Blissfully quiet slopes, on weekdays at least
- ➕ Mountain has it all, from superb novice runs to daunting moguls
- ➕ Fast chairlifts all over the place
- ➕ Compact, traffic-free village centre with a smartly modern feel but ...

- ➖ Not much going on at night
- ➖ Lacks any Wild West or genuine US town atmosphere
- ➖ Very expensive
- ➖ Disappointing mountain restaurants

'Not exactly roughing it' is the strangely coy slogan of Vail's kid sister resort, discreetly underlining its status as about the smoothest resort in the US. We don't find the exclusive resort village particularly appealing, but the mountain is something else – we wouldn't dream of visiting Vail without spending a day or two here. A pity that it's impossible to get a decent lunch on the hill.

THE RESORT

Beaver Creek, 16km/10 miles to the west of Vail, was developed in the 1980s. It is unashamedly exclusive, with a choice of top-quality hotels and condos right by the slopes. It centres on a small, smart, modern pedestrian area with escalators to the slopes, upmarket shops, an open-air ice rink and heated pavements. The choice of bars and restaurants is limited.

The lift system spreads across the mountains to Bachelor Gulch, basically a Ritz-Carlton hotel, and to Arrowhead, a slope-side hamlet with luxury condos, less pricey than Beaver Creek.

At valley level by the town of Avon there are free car parks for day visitors (parking up in the resort is expensive and limited). There's an adequate free shuttle to the village. Or you can get on the hill directly by riding a fast chair from Beaver Creek Landing up to Bachelor Gulch. A gondola links the Riverfront area of Avon to this chair.

Resorts within day-trip range by road include Vail, Breckenridge and Keystone (covered by the lift pass) and Copper Mountain.

THE MOUNTAINS

All the slopes are below the treeline, though there are some more open areas. Free mountain tours are held every day at 10am.
Slopes The slopes immediately above Beaver Creek divide into two sectors, each accessed by a fast quad chair – one centred on Spruce Saddle, the other Bachelor Gulch mountain (which

links to Arrowhead). Between these are Grouse Mountain and Larkspur Bowl, again with fast quads. Off to the left is another varied sector served, unusually, by two slow chairs.
Terrain parks Park 101 is a small beginners' park, Zoom Room has intermediate-level features and Moonshine has big jumps and rails, best suited to advanced riders. There's a 110m/350ft long half-pipe, off Barrel Stave. Parkology is a park and pipe programme designed to offer tuition mainly to kids.
Snow reliability An impressive annual snow record (average 310 inches) plus extensive snowmaking means you can relax. Grouse Mountain can suffer from thin cover (some call it Gravel Mountain). Grooming is excellent.
Experts There is plenty of satisfying single-diamond and seriously steep double-diamond terrain. In the Birds of Prey and Grouse Mountain areas most runs are long, steep and mogulled from top to bottom (but watch the grooming map – when one of these is groomed it makes a great fast cruise,

595

KEY FACTS

Resort	2470m
	8,100ft
Slopes	2255-3485m
	7,400-11,440ft
Lifts	17
Pistes	1805 acres
Green	19%
Blue	43%
Black	38%
Snowmaking	
	605 acres

Central reservations
phone number
496 4500

Phone numbers
From distant parts of
the US, add the prefix
1 970; from abroad,
add the prefix +1 970

TOURIST OFFICE

t 845 2500
bcinfo@vailresorts.
com
beavercreek.snow.
com

COLORADO

596

especially the Birds of Prey downhill race-course). There are great steep glades on Grouse and in the newest area at Stone Creek Chutes.

Intermediates There are marvellous long, quiet, cruising blues almost everywhere you look, including top-to-bottom runs with a vertical of 1000m/3,28oft. The Larkspur and Strawberry Park chairs serve further cruising runs – and lead to yet more ideal terrain, served by the Bachelor Gulch and Arrowhead fast chairs.

Beginners There are excellent nursery slopes at resort level – served by a short new gondola – and more at altitude. And there are plenty of easy longer runs to progress to.

Snowboarding Good riders will love the excellent gladed runs and perfect carving slopes. The resort is great for beginners, too, with special teaching methods and equipment that they claim will help you learn quicker.

Cross-country There's a splendid, mountain-top network of tracks at McCoy Park (over 32km/20 miles), reached via the Strawberry Park lift.

Queues Weekdays are pretty much queue-free, but improving lift access from the valley seems to be attracting more weekend visitors. A 2008 visitor had 'a 10-minute wait' at the main Centennial chair. The Cinch chair has also been mentioned.

Mountain restaurants The new Spago at Bachelor Gulch is the best bet for table service – 'lovely terrace; great salads and upmarket main courses'. Saddle at mid-mountain is the main place – a food court in an airy log

building; but one reporter found it 'incredibly busy'. Red Tail Camp is basic; decent barbecues.

Schools and guides We've had very good reports over the years.

Facilities for children Small World Play School looks after non-skiing kids from two months to six years from 8.30 to 4.30. The area at the top of the new Buckaroo gondola has been developed especially for children – a new school, the Ranch, is due to open there for 2008/09. There are splendid adventure trails and play areas.

STAYING THERE

How to go There's a reasonable choice of packages.

Hotels Lots of upmarket places, such as the Ritz-Carlton, The Charter and Park Hyatt. The Osprey (formerly Inn at Beaver Creek) is being renovated for 2008/09 (see 'News').

Apartments A wide choice of condos.

Eating out SaddleRidge is luxurious and packed with photos and Wild West artefacts. Toscanini, the Golden Eagle Inn, Dusty Boot, and Beaver Creek Chophouse have been recommended. Spago offers fine dining at Bachelor Gulch. You can take a sleigh ride to dine at a swanky log cabin on the slopes.

Après-ski Try the Coyote Cafe, Whiskey Elk and McCoy's (live bands).

Off the slopes There are smart boutiques and galleries, an impressive ice rink, bonfire evenings, hot-air balloon rides, dog sledding, and shows and concerts.

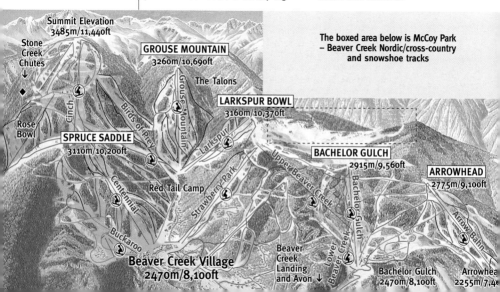

Summit Elevation
3485m/11,440ft

Stone Creek Chutes

GROUSE MOUNTAIN
3260m/10,690ft

The Talons

LARKSPUR BOWL
3160m/10,370ft

Rose Bowl

Cinch

Birds of Prey

Grouse Mountain

Larkspur

SPRUCE SADDLE
3110m/10,200ft

Red Tail Camp

Strawberry Park

Centennial

Upper Beaver Creek

BACHELOR GULCH
2915m/9,560ft

ARROWHEAD
2775m/9,100ft

Bachelor Gulch

Arrow Bahn

Buckaroo

Beaver Creek Village
2470m/8,100ft

Beaver Creek Landing and Avon ↓

Lower Beaver Creek

Bachelor Gulch
2470m/8,100ft

Arrowhea
2255m/7,4

The boxed area below is McCoy Park – Beaver Creek Nordic/cross-country and snowshoe tracks

Breckenridge

*A sprawling resort with a cute 'Wild West' core, beneath a wide,
varied mountain; increasing amounts of slope-side accommodation*

➕ Local mountains have something for all abilities – good for mixed groups

➕ Cute Victorian Main Street, with mainly sympathetic new buildings

➕ Plenty of lively bars and restaurants

➕ Shared lift pass with four other worthwhile resorts nearby

➕ Efficient lifts mean few queues

➕ Some slope-side accommodation

➕ One of the nearest major resorts to Denver; so a short transfer, but ...

➖ At 2925m/9,600ft the village is one of the highest you will encounter, with a risk of altitude sickness if you go there directly from the UK

➖ Prone to high winds, affecting particularly the high, exposed advanced slopes

➖ Intermediate terrain not very extensive, and few long runs

➖ Lack of good, central hotels

➖ Main Street is a thoroughfare – always busy with traffic

A visit last season confirmed that we like the town of Breckenridge a lot – and the slopes too, up to a point. Its drawbacks are non-trivial, though. Some of the expert slopes are exceptionally high (accessed by America's highest lift), and we've found them closed several times. Like many readers, one of us has been affected by altitude sickness here, and now always spends time in a lower resort before hitting Breckenridge; a night or two in Denver is an alternative way to cut the risk. Intermediates more interested in mileage than challenges should plan to explore other resorts (covered by the lift pass) by car or bus.

THE RESORT

Breckenridge was founded in 1859 and became a booming gold-mining town. The old clapboard buildings lining much of Main Street and the streets nearby have been well renovated. Small shopping malls and other buildings have been added in similar style. The town centre is lively in the evening – particularly at weekends – with lots of people strolling around the shops on their way to or from 100-plus restaurants and bars. Christmas lights and decorations remain throughout the season, giving the town a festive air. This is enhanced by a number of festivals such as Ullr Fest – honouring the Norse God of Winter – and snow sculpture championships.

Hotels and condominiums are spread over a wide, wooded area and are linked by regular, free shuttle-buses (less frequent in the evening – worth staying centrally if you plan to spend much time in Main Street). There are a couple of supermarkets; one is just behind Main Street, but the other is not in the centre and a long walk if you don't have a car. Although there is a lot of slope-side accommodation – more than any other

Colorado resort, it is claimed – there is also a fair amount that's inconveniently distant from Main Street and the lift base-stations. The new developments taking shape at the bases of Peaks 7 and 8 will increase the ski-in/ski-out options.

Breckenridge is in the same ownership as Vail, Beaver Creek and Keystone. A multi-day lift ticket covers

↑ Open upper slopes, with dense forest lower down

VAIL RESORTS, INC

KEY FACTS

Resort	2925m
	9,600ft
Slopes	2925-3915m
	9,600-12,840ft
Lifts	30
Pistes	2,358 acres
Green	14%
Blue	31%
Black	55%
Snowmaking	
	565 acres

all four resorts plus Arapahoe Basin. All of these resorts plus Copper Mountain are linked by regular buses (free except for the trips to Vail or Beaver Creek).

THE MOUNTAINS

The slopes are mainly cut through the forest. There is quite a lot of steeper skiing above the treeline; this is prone to closure by high winds.

Signposting is very clear and reporters recommend the free two-hour mountain tours, at 10am daily from the base of Peaks 8 and 9.

THE SLOPES
Small but fragmented

There are four sectors, linked by lift and piste. Two fast chairlifts go from one end of the town up to **Peak 9**, one accessing mainly green runs on the lower half of the hill, the other mainly blues higher up. From there you can get to **Peak 10**, which has blue and black runs served by one fast quad.

The **Peak 8** area – tough stuff at the top, easier lower down – can be reached by a fast quad from Peak 9. The base lifts of Peak 8 at the Bergenhof can also be reached by the slow Snowflake lift from the suburbs, or by gondola from the fringes of town – where there's ample parking. The long green runs back to town are perfectly satisfactory. The six-pack serving the lower slopes of **Peak 7** can now be accessed from the gondola's new mid-station.

The higher open slopes on Peaks 7 and 8 are accessed by a T-bar – a rarity in these parts – reachable from either base, and by the Imperial fast quad at the top of the Peak 8 lift network. The resort claims a top height of 3960m/13,000ft, but that involves a hike of 45m/150ft vertical at the very top.

TERRAIN PARKS
Something for everyone

Breckenridge continues to develop its freestyle facilities. There are now six parks, including four half-pipes. The

boarding

Breckenridge is pretty much ideal for all standards of boarder and hosts several major US snowboarding events. Beginners have ideal nursery slopes and greens to progress to. Intermediates have great cruising runs, all served by chairs. The powder bowls at the top of Peaks 7 and 8 make great riding and can be accessed via the Imperial quad, so avoiding the awkward T-bar (though it is still an important lift – see 'For experts'). Boarders of all levels will enjoy the choice of excellent terrain parks and half-pipes (see 'Terrain parks'). Nearby, newly expanded Arapahoe Basin is another area for hardcore boarding in steep bowls and chutes.

LIFT PASSES

Summit

Prices in US$

Age	1-day	6-day
under 13		258
13 to 64		498
over 65		438

Free under 5
Beginner included in price of lessons

Notes
Covers Breckenridge, Keystone and Arapahoe Basin, plus 3 days (on a 6-day pass) at Vail and Beaver Creek; prices are high-season rates paid in the resort; reduced prices are available if you book in advance and to international visitors who pre-book through a UK tour operator (it is not necessary to buy a complete holiday package to obtain these prices)

main focus is Peak 8, with three progressive areas. Freeway is one of the best in the US, featuring a series of big jumps, obstacles and enormous championship half-pipe – 'massive, steep, well kept and awesome'. Just above it, the Park Lane green run is now an intermediate-level park, with snowmaking. And Trygves has gentle jumps and an introductory pipe for beginners. There are three parks on Peak 9: Eldorado is small, with a half-pipe, Country Boy has medium-sized features and there is another medium park by the Beaver Run chair.

SNOW RELIABILITY
Excellent

With its high altitude, Breckenridge boasts an excellent natural snow record – annual average 300 inches. That is supplemented by substantial snowmaking (used mainly early in the season to form a good base). There are a lot of east- and north-east-facing slopes, which hold snow well. High winds can be more of a problem on exposed upper lifts and runs. Grooming is excellent.

FOR EXPERTS
Lots of short but tough runs

A remarkable 55% of the runs are classified black – that's a higher proportion than famous 'macho' resorts such as Jackson Hole, Taos and Snowbird. And a good proportion are classified as 'expert' (double-diamond) or 'extreme' terrain. But most runs are short – most of the key lifts offer

verticals of around 300m/990ft.

Peak 8 is at the core of the tough skiing. The lightly wooded slopes served by Chair 6 are a good place to start – picturesque and not too steep. Below, steeper runs lead further down to the junction with Peak 9. Above, the Imperial quad accesses the double-diamond Imperial Bowl, and the 'extreme' Lake Chutes and Snow White areas. Or you can move to the front face of Peak 8, where the T-bar serves single-diamond runs, the double-diamond Horseshoe and Contest bowls, and a traverse/hike to the steep upper slopes of Peak 7. On the lower, wooded part of Peak 8 is another worthwhile area of single diamonds.

Peak 9's wooded North Slope under Chair E is excellent – shady, sheltered and steep – we've had great runs down Devil's Crotch, Hades and Inferno.

Peak 10 has blue-black runs down the central ridge, but more challenging stuff on both flanks. To skier's left is a lovely, lightly wooded area called The Burn.

FOR INTERMEDIATES
Nice cruising, limited extent

Breckenridge has some good blue cruising runs for all intermediates. But dedicated piste-bashers are likely to find the runs short and limited in variety. Peak 9 has the easiest slopes. It is nearly all gentle, wide, blue runs at the top and almost flat, wide, green runs at the bottom. And the ski patrol

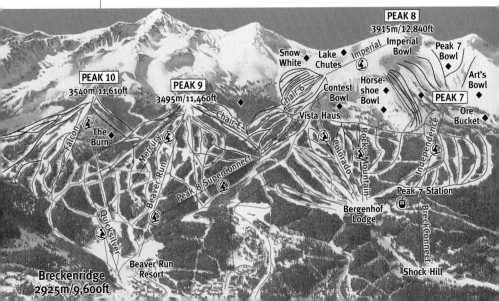

SCHOOLS

Breckenridge
t 453 3272

Classes
Half day (2½hr) $80
Private lessons
$425 for 3hr for up to
6 people

CHILDREN

**Children's Center,
Peak 8 and 9**
t +1 888 576 2754
All-day care from 8am
to 4.30 for children
from age 2mnth –
reservation
recommended

Ski school
For ages 3 to 12, 9.45
to 3.30 daily ($130
for full day)

GETTING THERE

Air Denver 167km/
104 miles (2½hr)

UK PACKAGES

All America Holidays,
Alpine Answers,
AmeriCan Ski, American
Ski Classics, Chalet
World Ski, Crystal,
Crystal Finest,
Directski.com, Erna
Low, Independent Ski
Links, Inghams,
Interactive Resorts, Ski
Activity, Ski Dream, Ski
Expectations, Ski
Freshtracks, Ski
Independence, Ski Line,
Ski McNeill, Ski Safari,
Ski Solutions, Ski Wild,
Skitracer, Skiworld,
Supertravel, Thomson,
Trailfinders, United
Vacations, Virgin Snow,
White Mountains

is supposed to enforce slow-speed skiing in narrow and crowded areas.

Peak 10 has a number of more challenging runs classified blue-black, such as Crystal and Centennial, which make for good fast cruising. Peaks 7 and 8 both have a choice of blues on trails cut close together in the trees. Adventurous intermediates will also like to try some of the high bowl runs and more gentle gladed runs such as Ore Bucket glades on the fringe of Peak 7 and the runs beneath Chair 6 on Peak 8. For a groomed black try Pika beside the T-bar, says a reporter.

FOR BEGINNERS
Excellent

The bottom of Peak 9 has a big, virtually flat area and some good, gentle nursery slopes. There's then a good choice of green runs to move on to. Beginners can try Peak 8 too, with another selection of green runs and a choice of trails back to town. There is a special beginner package available (see 'Schools and guides').

FOR CROSS-COUNTRY
Specialist centre in woods

There are 50km/31 miles of groomed trails in total. Breckenridge's Nordic Center is prettily set in the woods between the town and Peak 8 (served by the shuttle-bus). It has 30km/19 miles of trails and 20km/12 miles of snowshoeing trails. A further 20km/12 miles of cross-country trails are located at the golf course.

QUEUES
Not normally a problem

Breckenridge's gondola and nine fast chairlifts make light work of peak-time crowds. There are few problems outside exceptional times, such as President's Day weekend. But we have received reports of queues for some of the main Peak 8 lifts and the double Chair 6 at weekends – 'ten minutes', says a January 2008 visitor. The Snowflake double chair, giving access to Peak 8 for thousands of condo-dwellers, gets 'lengthy queues at peak times'.

MOUNTAIN RESTAURANTS
Slow progress

A grim day last season left us planning to reduce Breckenridge to a ✱ rating; we've put that on hold, pending reports on Sevens, due to open at the new Peak 7 base lodge in December

2008 – a table-service restaurant serving Mediterranean-style food. Of the self-service places above base level, Peak 9 restaurant is the 'best of a mediocre bunch': 'pretty good and reasonably priced', with 'friendly staff'. Both Tenmile Station, where Peak 9 meets 10, and the dreary Vista Haus on Peak 8 are food-court operations. But they get nightmarishly busy at weekends.

SCHOOLS AND GUIDES
Excellent reports

The school gets good reviews. Reporters have praised small classes doing what the class, not the instructor, wants ('you can buy three days of lessons and take them whenever you want', 'friendly, first-class instruction'). The good-value beginner package which includes lessons, equipment rental and lift pass is also highly recommended. Special clinics include women's, telemark and powder. The school's Big Mountain Experience offers guided instruction around Imperial Bowl. There is also a Burton Learn to Ride programme.

FACILITIES FOR CHILDREN
Excellent facilities

Past reports on the children's school and nursery have been full of praise for excellent instruction and positive attitudes, combined with lots of fun.

STAYING THERE

HOW TO GO
Lots of choice

A lot of tour operators feature Breckenridge.
Chalets Several tour operators have very comfortable chalets.
Hotels There's a noticeable lack of good places close to Main Street.
****Great Divide Lodge (453 5500) Vast rooms, a short walk to the slopes and a bearable walk to Main Street, but dreary. Pool, tub, sauna.
****Lodge at Breckenridge (453 9300) Stylish luxury spa resort set out of town among 32 acres, with great views. Private shuttle-bus. Pool, tub, steam, sauna and massage.
****Beaver Run (453 6000) Huge, slope-side resort complex with 520 spacious rooms. Pool, hot tubs.
****Barn on the River (800 795 2975) B&B on Main St. Hot tub.
***Little Mountain Lodge (453 1969) Luxury B&B near ice rink.

↑ Main Street is far from traffic-free, but despite that it's a very pleasant place to wander around in the evening, with lots of cheerful shops and bars in old or old-style buildings

VAIL RESORTS, INC

ACTIVITIES

Indoor Spas, theatre, museum, ice skating, recreation centre (pool, tubs, gym, tennis, climbing wall) on the outskirts of town – accessible by bus

Outdoor Horse-drawn sleigh rides, dog sledding, fishing, snowmobiles, snowshoeing, ice skating, hot-air balloon rides

Phone numbers
From distant parts of the US, add the prefix 1 970; from abroad, add the prefix +1 970

TOURIST OFFICE

t 453 5000
breckinfo@vail resorts.com
www.breckenridge.snow.com

***Village** (547 5725) Central 'Good value with spacious rooms.'
Apartments There is a huge choice of condominiums, many set conveniently off the aptly named Four O'Clock run. Main Street Station (near the Quicksilver lift) and Mountain Thunder Lodge (near the gondola and the supermarket) have been recommended at the luxury end. The Blue Sky condos also opened here in December 2007 and the new Crystal Peak Lodge is due at Peak 7 for 2008/09. There are lots of houses to rent, too.

EATING OUT
Over 100 restaurants
There's a very wide range of eating places, from typical American food to fine dining. At peak times they get busy and mostly don't take bookings. The Breckenridge Dining Guide lists the full menu of most places.

Our 2008 visit confirmed the attractions of the Hearthstone (modern American cuisine in a beautiful 120-year-old house) and introduced us to the nearby but much more stylish Cellar (multi-course small-plate menus – the current fad in Colorado resorts – best enjoyed in the ground-floor wine bar). Another newcomer, Relish, was strongly recommended to us. For no-nonsense grills-and-fries in a pub ambience, we've enjoyed both the Brewery (famous for its mega 'appetisers', such as buffalo wings, and splendid beers) and the Kenosha steakhouse.

Other reader recommendations include: the sophisticated food at Cafe Alpine ('excellent'), Whale's Tail ('great seafood and fish'), Wasabi (sushi), Downstairs at Eric's (classic American), Michael's (extensive Italian menu), Rasta Pasta (pasta with a Jamaican twist). Extreme Pizza serves 'great pizza' at 'tables made from beautiful Arbor snowboards', and Spencer's (out

at Beaver Run resort) is 'excellent both in quality and value'. The Blue Moose does the usual killer breakfasts; Cool River Cafe has some healthier options.

APRES-SKI
The best in the area
There's not much tea-time animation at the lift bases but the Park Avenue Pub, just off Main Street, and the Brewery were lively on our recent visits. Later on we've enjoyed the Gold Pan saloon (reputedly the oldest bar west of the Mississippi). Reader recommendations for the evenings include the Liquid Lounge, Fatty's sports-bar and Sherpa & Yetti's. Cecilia's serves good cocktails; Burke and Riley's is an Irish bar; Downstairs at Eric's is a disco sports-bar.

OFF THE SLOPES
Pleasant enough
Breckenridge is a pleasant place to wander around, with plenty of souvenir and gift shops. Silverthorne (about 30 minutes away) has excellent bargain factory outlet stores. A visit to Buffalo Bill's grave and museum has also been recommended.

STAYING DOWN THE VALLEY
Good for exploring the area
Staying in Frisco makes sense for those touring around or on a tight budget. It's a small town with decent bars and restaurants. There are cheap motels, a couple of small hotels and some B&Bs. Hotel Frisco (668 5009) is 'comfortable and convenient', says a recent visitor whose dining recommendations include the Backcountry Brewery, Tuscato ('good northern Italian food'), Blue Spruce Inn ('best food in town, in an old low-ceilinged cabin'), Farrellys steakhouse ('generous portions'), and Sampling (same stable as the Cellar in Breckenridge).

Copper Mountain

Great terrain with reliable snow for all ability levels, above a born-again but small and quiet Intrawest resort

COSTS

① ② ③ ④ ⑤ ⑥

RATINGS

The slopes

Fast lifts	**
Snow	****
Extent	**
Expert	****
Intermediate	****
Beginner	****
Convenience	****
Queues	****
Mountain restaurants	*

The rest

Scenery	***
Resort charm	**
Off-slope	*

NEWS

For 2008/09 a new freestyle training facility, Camp Woodward, is due to open. The indoor centre will provide teaching and training aids for improving park and pipe skills.

For 2007/08 the double-black-diamond Free Fall Glade opened above East Village.

+ Convenient purpose-built resort, transformed by owners Intrawest (of Whistler fame)

+ Fair-sized mountain, with good runs for all abilities

+ Good value by Colorado standards

+ Few queues on weekdays, but ...

− Can be long lift queues at weekends

− Black-diamond bowls at the top offer only limited vertical

− Risk of altitude sickness when coming from sea level

− Village still rather limited

− Poor mountain restaurants

Copper's slopes are some of Colorado's best, and the modern, purpose-built village has become quite a pleasant small resort. Great for an outing from another resort, or as a base if the budget is tight.

THE RESORT

Rather like the French resorts of the 1960s, Copper Mountain was originally high on convenience, low on charm. More recently, Intrawest has done a typically thorough job with the modern Village at Copper. The group of wood-and-stone-clad condo buildings with shops, restaurants and car-free walkways and squares, forms the heart of the resort – set just off the I-70 freeway from Denver. Within the limits of its small size, it works well.

There are two other bases: East Village at the foot of Copper's steeper terrain and Union Creek at the foot of the easiest runs and beginner area. Each of these is smaller and even quieter than the Village but has accommodation and restaurants. A free shuttle-bus runs between them. Keystone, Breckenridge and Arapahoe Basin are all nearby, and Vail and Winter Park a bit further.

THE MOUNTAIN

The area is medium-sized by American standards, and has great runs for all ability levels, with an attractive mix of wooded, gladed and open slopes.

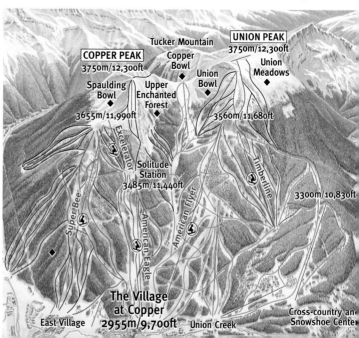

Tucker Mountain

COPPER PEAK
3750m/12,300ft

Copper Bowl

UNION PEAK
3750m/12,300ft

Union Meadows

Spaulding Bowl
◆

Upper Enchanted Forest
◆

Union Bowl
◆

3655m/11,990ft

3560m/11,680ft

Excelerator

Solitude Station
3485m/11,440ft

Timberline

3300m/10,830ft

Super Bee

American Flyer

American Eagle

The Village at Copper
2955m/9,700ft

East Village

Union Creek

Cross-country and Snowshoe Center

East Village is smaller and quieter than the main Village at Copper →

KEY FACTS

Resort	2955m
	9,700ft
Slopes	2960-3750m
	9,710-12,310ft
Lifts	22
Pistes	2,433 acres
Green	21%
Blue	25%
Black	54%
Snowmaking	
	380 acres

UK PACKAGES

All America Holidays, Alpine Answers, AmeriCan Ski, American Ski Classics, Crystal, Erna Low, Independent Ski Links, Ski Activity, Ski Dream, Ski Independence, Ski Safari, Skitracer, Skiworld, Supertravel, Thomson, United Vacations

Central reservations
Call 968 2882; toll-free number (from within the US)
1 888 219 1406

Phone numbers
From distant parts of the US, add the prefix 1 970; from abroad, add the prefix +1 970

TOURIST OFFICE

t 968 2318
contactcenter@
coppercolorado.com
www.coppercolorado.
com

Guided tours are available daily at 10.30 and 1.30.

Slopes The area divides into slopes below Copper Peak and below Union Peak, with fast quads towards each from the main base area. Between the two is Union Bowl. In general, as you look at the mountain the easiest runs are on the right and it gets progressively steeper the further left you go. On the back of the hill are the high Spaulding and Copper Bowls – open slopes, in contrast to the wooded lower runs.

Terrain parks The main Catalyst park has areas for all abilities, plus a super-pipe (there's a second super-pipe at the base area). There's the Kidz park and mini pipe (open to learning adults too), and freestyle zones on the High Point trail. A jib park is available early season, at the top of the American Eagle.

Snow reliability Height and extensive snowmaking give Copper an early opening date and excellent reliability. Snowfall averages 280 inches a year.

Experts There is a lot of good expert terrain. Spaulding and Copper bowls offer gradients ranging from moderate to seriously steep, but with limited vertical. Don't tackle Union Meadows on your own. The wooded bump runs lower down the left side of the main mountain are much longer. The new double-diamond Free Fall Glade isn't notably steep, just a bit tight in places.

Intermediates There are runs to suit everyone, from top-to-bottom greens on the right of the map through similarly long blues to challenging (usually bumpy) black runs.

Beginners The nursery slopes at Union Creek are excellent, and there are plenty of very easy green runs to graduate to.

Snowboarding There are great slopes for all abilities, plus the terrain parks.

Cross-country There are 24km/15 miles of trails through the White River forest.

Queues Few problems on weekdays, but crowds from Denver cause weekend queues at the main base and the Timberline lift, in particular. The Storm King rope tow can get busy at peak times. You can buy a Beeline Advantage pass to jump most queues.

Mountain restaurants Solitude Station is a dreary food court. The T-Rex Grill has only outside seating. Better options at the base – JJ's Rocky Mountain Tavern does 'great salads'.

Schools and guides The school offers a wide variety of courses and has a fine reputation, especially for children. 'Friendly, responsive instructors; very small groups', says a 2008 visitor.

Facilities for children The Belly Button child care facility takes children from two months old and ski school takes children from age three.

STAYING THERE

How to go A number of tour operators offer packages to Copper.

Hotels and condos There are no hotels but some condos are splendidly luxurious, with outdoor hot tubs.

Eating out The CB Grille is praised for the best food in town ('Colorado with Mediterranean flair'). Pizza Carlo, Endo's and JJ's Rocky Mountain Tavern ('excellent bison stew') are popular. The Imperial Palace, and Salsa Mountain Cantina have also been mentioned. The Incline Bar & Grill does southwestern dishes. Sleigh rides take people out to Western-style dinners in tents.

Après-ski There are some lively bars as the lifts close. Endo's Adrenaline Cafe and JJ's Rocky Mountain Tavern (with live music) are popular. Zizzo's Ski Bar is a new nightclub.

Off the slopes There's a good sports club with a huge pool, snow tubing, snowmobiling ('an absolute blast'), ice skating on the lake and regular events (fire jugglers, street entertainers, fireworks etc).

603

Interactive resort shortlist builder at **www.wtss.co.uk**

Keystone

A satisfying mountain with plenty of comfortable lodgings spread rather too widely around the valley at the base

604

- ➕ Good mountain with something for everyone
- ➕ Huge night-skiing operation
- ➕ Other nearby resorts on lift pass
- ➕ Plenty of good condominiums

- ➖ Scattered resort, with few conveniently placed lodgings
- ➖ No village atmosphere except in small River Run development
- ➖ Risk of altitude sickness for visitors coming straight from sea level

Keystone's slopes are quite extensive and varied, but there isn't a proper village at the foot of them. Condos are scattered over a wide area, and the nearest thing to a 'village' is the limited River Run development. We prefer to stay elsewhere and make day trips to Keystone's slopes.

THE RESORT

Keystone is a sprawling resort of condominiums spread around a partly wooded valley floor. It has no clear centre and is divided into seven 'neighborhoods'. Some are little more than groups of condos, while others have shops, restaurants and bars (though no supermarkets or liquor stores – they are on the main highway).

River Run, at the base of the main access gondola, is the nearest thing to a conventional ski resort village, with condo buildings, a short main street, a square and a few restaurants, bars and shops. A second lift base area half a mile to the west, Mountain House, is much less of a village. Another mile west is Lakeside Village, which is not a village at all but a hotel and condo complex, weirdly lacking animation, beside a lake – a huge natural ice rink.

Free, efficient buses link all the component parts. A regular visitor warns against late-season visits: 'From 1 April the resort pretty much closes down except for the main lifts.'

THE MOUNTAINS

By US standards Keystone offers extensive slopes both in the forest and above it. The resort is owned by Vail Resorts, and the lift pass covers Vail, Beaver Creek and Breckenridge as well as Arapahoe Basin (described at the end of this chapter). Copper Mountain is also nearby.

Slopes Three wooded mountains form Keystone's local slopes. Lifts depart from Mountain House and River Run to

the peak above the resort, Dercum Mountain. Its front face has Keystone's biggest network of lifts and runs. From the top you can drop over the back down to lifts up the next hill, North Peak. Or you can ride the Outpost gondola directly to the shoulder of North Peak. Beyond North Peak is the third peak, The Outback. It's a simple network, and finding your way around is no problem.

Keystone has the biggest floodlit skiing operation in the US, covering Dercum Mountain top to bottom up to 9pm on certain nights of the week.

Terrain parks The A-51 terrain park is huge, with features for all levels including a super-pipe; it has its own chairlift and is floodlit several nights a week.

Snow reliability Keystone doesn't get as much snow as its neighbours (average 230 inches), but shortage is rarely a problem. It has one of the world's biggest snowmaking systems.

Experts There is a lot of steep ungroomed terrain, but many of the lower runs in the forest are indistinct glade runs requiring guidance to be tackled safely, while the open higher ones are accessed by hiking (from all three peaks) or snowcat ($81 for four hours with guides from Dercum; $5 for a ride but no guide on Outback). There are also straightforward bump runs to be done on North Peak. You should have a day at the newly expanded Arapahoe Basin too.

Intermediates Keystone has lots to offer. The front face of Dercum Mountain itself is a network of beautifully groomed blue and green runs through the trees. The Outback

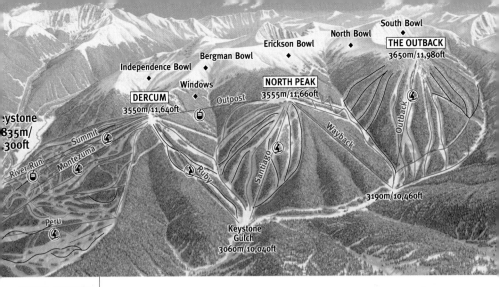

Map labels: South Bowl, North Bowl, Erickson Bowl, THE OUTBACK 3650m/11,980ft, Bergman Bowl, Independence Bowl, Windows, NORTH PEAK 3555m/11,660ft, Outpost, DERCUM 3550m/11,640ft, Outback, ystone 835m/ 300ft, Summit, Wayback, River Run, Montezuma, Ruby, Santiago, Peru, 3190m/10,460ft, Keystone Gulch 3060m/10,040ft

Keystone

605

Interactive resort shortlist builder at www.wtss.co.uk

KEY FACTS

Resort	2835m
	9,300ft
Slopes	2835-3650m
	9,300-11,980ft
Lifts	19
Pistes	3,148 acres
Green	19%
Blue	32%
Black	49%
Snowmaking	
	600+ acres

UK PACKAGES

All America Holidays, Alpine Answers, AmeriCan Ski, American Ski Classics, Crystal, Erna Low, Independent Ski Links, Ski Activity, Ski Dream, Ski Independence, Ski Safari, Skitracer, United Vacations

Central reservations phone number
Call 496 4500; toll free number (from within the US) 1 877 753 9786

Phone numbers
From distant parts of the US, add the prefix 1 970; from abroad, add the prefix +1 970

TOURIST OFFICE

t 496 2316
keystoneinfo@
vailresorts.com
www.keystone.snow.
com

and North Peak also have easy cruising and some steeper blues. Some of the blacks are groomed, and are tremendous fun early in the day.
Beginners There are good nursery slopes at the top and bottom of Dercum Mountain, and excellent long green runs to progress to.
Snowboarding Keystone is ideal for beginners and intermediates, with mainly chairlifts and gondolas, good beginner areas and cruising runs. Expert riders will love The Outback.
Cross-country There are 16km/10 miles of groomed trails and 56km/35 miles of unprepared trails.
Queues Reporters unanimously praise quiet slopes and few queues after the morning peak – the new River Run gondola should improve any delays there too (see 'News'). Dercum's front face can get congested at peak times where runs 'funnel' into each other.
Mountain restaurants The table-service Alpenglow Stube (North Peak) is a delightfully cosseting place (you are given slippers to replace ski boots) and one of our favourites in the US: the fixed-price lunch is a bargain at $30. The Timber Ridge Food Court next door is 'an attractive, decent option'. The alternatives are much less appealing.
Schools and guides As well as the normal lessons, there are bumps, race and various other advanced classes. Reporters praise very small groups and 'good' private lessons.
Facilities for children Excellent, with programmes tailored to specific age groups, dedicated children's teaching areas and organised kids' nights out.

STAYING THERE

How to go Regular shuttles operate from Denver airport.
Hotels There isn't a great choice but they're all of a high standard.
Apartments This is condo city, with thousands to choose from including some large and luxurious ones.
Eating out Disappointing: there isn't the range of mid-market restaurants that you get in most US resorts. You can dine on the mountain.
Après-ski The Summit House has live music and caters for night skiing customers too. But this is not the resort for late-night revellers.
Off the slopes There are plenty of activities, including spa centre, ice-skating, tubing and indoor tennis.
Staying down the valley You can cut costs and visit several resorts by staying in Dillon, 10km/6 miles away.

Arapahoe Basin
3285m/10,780ft

This small but exceptionally high area, on the lift pass and a short free bus-ride away, makes a great day out (there are no lodgings), especially since it virtually doubled in size last season. Pick your day, though: a weekday (for empty slopes) in good weather (top half of the mountain is above the treeline) after a snowfall (the steeps need it). A handful of slow chairs serve the 690m/2,270ft vertical front face, and one the new 335m/ 1,100ft vertical Montezuma bowl. Both offer varied slopes including serious double-diamond blacks.

Snowmass

Aspen's modern satellite – with impressively varied and extensive slopes, and a smart new Base Village taking shape

COSTS

① ② ③ ④ ⑤ ⑥

RATINGS

The slopes

Fast lifts	★★★
Snow	★★★★★
Extent	★★★★
Expert	★★★★★
Intermediate	★★★★★
Beginner	★★★★★
Convenience	★★★★
Queues	★★★★
Mountain restaurants	★★★

The rest

Scenery	★★★★
Resort charm	★★
Off-slope	★★★

NEWS

For 2008/09 a fast quad will replace the Sheer Bliss double chair. A table-service restaurant is to open up at Sam's Knob. At the Base Village, five new restaurants and a dozen shops are planned to open.

606

➕ Big, varied mountain with a vertical of 1340m/4,400ft – the biggest in the US

➕ Aspen's three mountains also accessible by free bus

➕ Uncrowded slopes

➕ Lots of slope-side lodgings

➖ Limited shopping and nightlife, though things are improving as the new Base Village takes shape

➖ Diversions of Aspen town are a bus ride away

The slopes of Snowmass are a key part of the attraction of nearby Aspen as a destination. As a base, Snowmass has obvious appeal for families wanting great green runs on their doorstep; its appeal is starting to broaden as more shops and restaurants open at the new Base Village – but don't expect miracles.

THE RESORT

Snowmass is a modern, purpose-built resort with most of its lodgings in low-rise buildings set alongside the gentle home slope. Within these buildings is Snowmass Village Mall, with a small cluster of shops and restaurants; but the centre of gravity is moving down the hill to where the new Base Village is taking shape – worth bearing in mind when choosing lodgings. Even with this development, Snowmass is likely to remain a quiet base.

Aspen is 19km/12 miles away, its Highlands and Buttermilk mountains slightly less. Efficient free bus services link the resorts and mountains. The service to Aspen town runs to 2am (small charge after 4.30pm).

THE MOUNTAIN

Snowmass is big by US standards: almost 8km/5 miles across and has the biggest vertical in the US. Most of the slopes are in the forest; higher ones are open or only lightly wooded.
Slopes Chairlifts and a gondola from the base go to the two extremes of Elk Camp and Sam's Knob. Links higher up go to the two sectors in the middle, High Alpine and Big Burn. A new fast quad is set to improve access here for 2008/09. There is also fast access from Two Creeks – nearer Aspen, and with free slope-side parking.
Terrain parks The main Snowmass park (formerly Pipeline) was moved and improved this year, with better access and more features. There's still

---

ELK CAMP 3450m/11,320ft

HIGH ALPINE 3590m
Hanging Valley

The Cirque 3815m/12,510ft

BIG BURN 3610m/11,830ft

SAM'S KNOB 3240m/10,630ft

Elk Camp

Cafe Suzanne

Sheer Bliss

Big Burn

Sam's Knob

Ullrhof 3005m

Coney Glade

Alpine Springs

Gondola

Village

Two Creeks

Two Creeks 2470m/8,100ft

Snowmass 2565m/8,420ft

↑ The new Base Village is fast developing

SNOWPIX.COM / CHRIS GILL

KEY FACTS

Resort	2565m
	8,420ft

Snowmass only	
Slopes	2470-3815m
	8,100-12,510ft
Lifts	24
Pistes	3,132 acres
Green	6%
Blue	50%
Black	44%
Snowmaking	
	230 acres

See Aspen chapter for statistics on other mountains – star rating for extent includes them all

UK PACKAGES

All America Holidays, Alpine Answers, AmeriCan Ski, American Ski Classics, Crystal, Ski Dream, Ski Independence, Ski Safari, White Mountains

Phone numbers
From distant parts of the US, add the prefix 1 970; from abroad, add the prefix +1 970

TOURIST OFFICE

t 925 1220
intlres@
skiaspen.com
www.aspen
snowmass.com

a rail park, super-pipe, quarter-pipe and kicker line. There are separate beginners' and kids' parks.

Snow reliability With 300 inches a year plus snowmaking, it's good.

Experts There's great terrain, although the steep runs tend to be short. Consider joining a guided group as an introduction. Our favourite area is around the Hanging Valley Wall and Glades – beautiful scenery and steep wooded slopes. The other seriously steep area is the Cirque, reached by draglift to the area's highest point. From here, the Headwall is not terrifyingly steep, but there are also narrow, often rocky, chutes – Gowdy's is one of the steepest. The runs funnel into a pretty, lightly wooded valley.

Intermediates Excellent – the best mountain in the Aspen area. All four sectors have lots to offer. Highlights include: the top slopes on Big Burn – a huge, varied, lightly wooded area, including the Powerline Glades for the adventurous; long, top-to-bottom cruises from Elk Camp and High Alpine; regularly groomed single-black runs from Sam's Knob. Long Shot is a glorious, ungroomed, 5km/3 mile run, lost in the forest, and well worth the short hike from the top of Elk Camp.

Beginners In the heart of the resort is a broad, gentle beginners' run. An even easier slope is the wide Assay Hill, at the bottom of Elk Camp. There's also a new beginner area served by three lifts, at the top of the Elk Camp gondola. From Sam's Knob there are long, gentle cruises back to the resort.

Snowboarding A great mountain, whatever your boarding style.

Cross-country Excellent trails between here and Aspen – see Aspen chapter.

Queues Any problems can usually be avoided. Some long, slow chairs can be cold in midwinter, and a February 2008 reader noted short queues for

the Cirque draglift. The home slope gets very crowded.

Mountain restaurants There are refuelling stops at several key points, but also some places worth seeking out. Gwyn's High Alpine is an elegant table-service restaurant serving above-average food. Sam's Knob gets a new table-service restaurant for 2008/09. Cafe Suzanne on Elk Camp has a distinctly French flavour.

Schools and guides Recent reports are mixed. A 2008 reporter enjoyed 'good' mogul classes, but another complains one of her party had 'three different instructors in one day; her confidence was completely destroyed'.

Facilities for children The Treehouse adventure centre at Base Village is a very impressive facility. There are special family skiing zones.

STAYING THERE

How to go Most accommodation is self-catering.

Hotels The focal hotel is the huge Silvertree (923 3520) – next to the home slope and the Mall – with excellent top-floor Brothers' Grille restaurant and pools.

Apartments Tamarack Townhouses, Terrace House, Top of the Village and Crestwood Condos are popular.

Eating out The choice is adequate. As well as the excellent Brothers' Grille, Big Hoss Grill is 'good value', Il Poggio is an 'excellent' Italian and there are Tex-Mex, Provençal and 'pan-Asian' choices. Artisan and Butch's Lobster Bar are recommended.

Après-ski The Cirque next to the home slope has live bands but closes at 6pm. The new places opening at the Base Village will include one or two bars with terrace.

Off the slopes There's tubing on Assay Hill, snowshoe trails, snowcat rides and dog sledding.

Snowmass

607

Interactive resort shortlist builder at **www.wtss.co.uk**

Steamboat

The home of Champagne Powder™, with a convenient slope-side base and a working cattle town a 10-minute bus ride away

COSTS

① ② ③ ④ ⑤ ⑥

RATINGS

The slopes

Fast lifts	★★★
Snow	★★★★
Extent	★★★
Expert	★★★
Intermediate	★★★★
Beginner	★★★★★
Convenience	★★★
Queues	★★★★
Mountain restaurants	★★★

The rest

Scenery	★★★
Resort charm	★★
Off-slope	★★

NEWS

Base area Developments are under way, with Ski Time Square and the Thunderhead Lodge and Condos being demolished during summer 2008. Reconstruction is set to begin in spring 2009, with upmarket ski-in/ski-out lodging, new restaurants and shops and pedestrian walkways. The replacement of the on-mountain signage will continue, and the snowmaking system will be upgraded.

For 2007/08, the Christie Express six-pack replaced three chairs in the Headwall beginner area at the base. Work was also done on the slopes here to make it even better for beginners, and the five moving carpets were lengthened. The Preview chairlift in the beginner area was upgraded to a longer three-seater, and the snowmaking was improved.

608

- Excellent easy runs
- Famed for its gladed terrain
- Good snow record
- Table-service mountain restaurants
- Plenty of high-quality slope-side lodgings at reasonable rates
- Town has some Western character

- Town is a drive from the slopes
- Modern base 'village' is sprawling and being redeveloped
- Not enough runs to amuse keen intermediates for a week unless you're prepared to try glades
- Not a huge amount of challenging terrain – some of it is a hike away

Steamboat's mountain may not match some of its competitors for extent, but it's one of the best for powder fun among the trees. The lift-base village is currently no beauty and part of it will have been demolished before the 2008/09 season. But it's best to stay there, and plan on just the occasional foray to the unremarkable 'cattle town' of Steamboat Springs. The resort was recently taken over by Intrawest (of Whistler fame) and is changing rapidly. We'll wait till the reconstruction is complete before making another visit.

THE RESORT

The resort village is a 10-minute bus ride from the old town of Steamboat Springs. Near the gondola there are a few shop- and restaurant-lined multi-level squares, some of which are receiving a much needed revamp over the next few years. Some lodgings are up the sides of the piste, but the resort also sprawls across the valley.

The old town can be a bit of a disappointment. It may be a working cattle town, but the Wild West isn't much in evidence. The wide main street is lined with bars, hotels and shops in a mixture of styles, from old wooden buildings to concrete plazas. The free bus service is said by reporters to be good.

The newly expanded local airport allows more flights and has improved accessibility to the resort.

THE MOUNTAINS

Steamboat's slopes are prettily set among trees, with extensive views over rolling hills and the wide Yampa valley. The place is relatively isolated, but you could combine it with resorts west of Denver, from Winter Park to Vail. We've had complaints about signposting in the past, so we welcome the installation of a new signage system. Maybe they should put up more signs about the danger of tree wells (unstable hollows that form

around the bases of trees when low branches prevent snow from filling in and creating snowpack around the trunk). Two people died in separate incidents last season by suffocating after falling into tree wells and being covered in snow while skiing intermediate blue trails in the Morningside Park area.

Slopes The gondola from the base rises to the low peak of Thunderhead. Beyond it are lifts to Storm Peak and Sunshine Peak – the latter offering a broad area of blue runs served by a fast quad. On the back of the hill is the Morningside Park area, with a slow chair back up to the high-point of Mt Werner, also accessing some of the top runs on the front side. Below these is an area served by the Pony Express fast chair. There are free daily mountain tours at 10.30, or you can ski with 1964 Olympic medallist Billy Kidd (now Steamboat's Director of Skiing) at 1pm when he's in town.

Terrain parks There are four. The 12-acre Mavericks park includes rails, jumps, a quarter-pipe and a super-pipe. Beehive is a special park for kids. Rabbit Ears is for beginners and Sunbeam for intermediates.

Snow reliability The term Champagne Powder™ was invented here, so it's no surprise to find that, despite a relatively low altitude, Steamboat has an excellent snow record. With a 10-year annual average of 335 inches, it's not far behind the Colorado leader,

Winter Park. There is snowmaking from top to bottom, too.

Experts The main attraction is the challenging terrain in the glades. A great area is on Sunshine Peak below the Sundown chair. Morningside Park and the Pony Express area also have excellent gladed runs. Three steep chutes are easily accessed via the lift back from Morningside, and a short hike gets you to the tree runs of Christmas Tree Bowl. For bumps, try the runs off Four Points or the Sundown Express. Many runs are of limited vertical; try Valley View for a longer black run to the base. You can also go snowcat skiing nearby (see www.steamboatpowdercats.com).

Intermediates Much of the mountain is ideal, with long cruising blue runs. Morningside Park is a great area for easy black as well as blue slopes – and 'lovely ungroomed terrain in the trees' (but see the warning about tree wells above). The Sunshine area is very gentle. Some of the black runs are regularly groomed, and 'much enjoyed' by reporters. Keen intermediates will find the mountain limited in extent, but given fresh powder it offers a great introduction to tree skiing.

Beginners There's a big nursery area,

the Headwall, at the base of the mountain, which had a total revamp last season to make it easier for beginners (see 'News'). The new Christie Peak chairlift has a mid-station so beginners can use it too. Lots of easy trails offer good progression – some of the blues are quieter and more relaxing than the greens, which include many cat tracks with steep drops at the side. The Sunshine area is particularly suited to families skiing together.

Snowboarding There's a good learning area (see above), gentle slopes to progress to and you can get around using chairlifts and the gondola. For experienced riders, riding the glades in fresh powder is unbeatable.

Steamboat

609

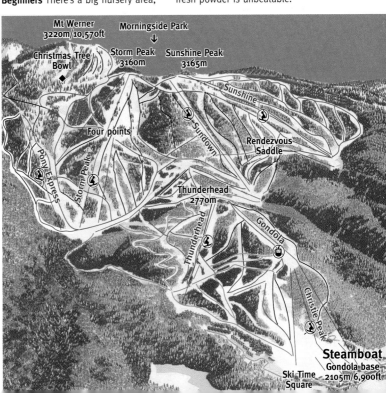

Steamboat
Gondola base
2105m/6,900ft

UK PACKAGES

All America Holidays, Alpine Answers, American Ski Classics, Crystal, Crystal Finest, Erna Low, Independent Ski Links, Interactive Resorts, Ski Activity, Ski Dream, Ski Independence, Ski Line, Ski Safari, Skitracer, Skiworld, Supertravel, Thomson, United Vacations, Virgin Snow

Central reservations phone number
879 0740

Phone numbers
Calling long-distance, add the prefix 1 970; from abroad, add the prefix +1 970

TOURIST OFFICE

t 879 6111
info@steamboat.com
www.steamboat.com

STEAMBOAT SKI & RESORT CORPORATION / LARRY PIERCE
Almost all the ski area is rolling and gentle, good for relaxed intermediate cruising
↓

Cross-country A free shuttle takes you to 16km/10 miles of groomed tracks at the Touring Center and there is a total of 160km/100 miles of trails in the area.

Queues Queues form for the gondola first thing, but they move quickly (and can be avoided by using chairs instead). But we now get few other complaints: 'Even on a busy holiday weekend queues were not a problem,' said a recent reporter.

Mountain restaurants There are food courts and table-service restaurants at Thunderhead and Rendezvous Saddle – better than the American fast-food norm, though peak-time crowds can be a problem. A recent reporter comments, 'One downside is the lack of restaurants/huts on the Pony Express/Storm Peak side of the mountain – none except for the very small Four Points Hut.'

Schools and guides Reports are very positive: 'very good in every respect', writes one visitor.

Facilities for children Arrangements are exceptional, winning awards from American magazines; there's even evening entertainment. Kids under 12 ski free with a parent or a grandparent buying a pass for at least five days. There's a similar deal for equipment rental.

STAYING THERE

How to go A fair number of UK tour operators feature Steamboat.

Chalets There are some catered chalets run by UK tour operators.

Hotels There are smart hotels at the base, including the Steamboat Grand (871 5050), and ones with more character in town. Recommendations by reporters include the downtown Rabbit Ears Motel (879 1150) and the slope-side Ptarmigan Inn (879 1730) ('friendly, comfortable and convenient').

Apartments There are countless condos, many with good pool/hot tub facilities, all on a free bus route. There are plenty of good places at the lift base. Antlers offers the best luxury ski-in/ski-out accommodation; Eagleridge and Canyon Creek are pretty luxurious, too. Timber Run, Ski Inn and the Rockies all offer good value. A recent reporter recommends the 'extremely comfortable' Bronze Tree condos.

Eating out There are over 70 bars and restaurants. Pick up a dining guide booklet to check out the menus, or visit www.steamboat-dining.com. You can dine in three restaurants up the mountain. Reader recommendations at the base area include the Tugboat Grill and Pub ('great food, good service and lively atmosphere'), Cafe Diva, the Ore House (steaks), La Montaña (Tex-Mex). The Tugboat is in the demolition area (see 'News'), but may still be operating next season. However, the popular Butcher Shop, which has been in Ski Time Square for 35 years, has closed. In downtown Steamboat Springs there is quite a wide range of options. Try Antares or Mahogany Ridge for Asian fusion cuisine, Old West Steakhouse, or the Cottonwood Grill for its 'fabulously tasty Pacific Rim cuisine', and Cugino's for Italian. Reporters also recommend the 8th Street Steakhouse with its communal barbecue ('great fun, good food'). For a budget meal, head for the Double Z (pronounced 'Zee', of course) or Johnny B Goods diner for burgers.

Après-ski The base lodge area is livelier than the old town in the evening. At close of play the big Slopeside Grill is popular. The Bear River Bar has a comedy club, and the Tugboat has live music and dancing. The Old Town Pub in the town is 'great for beer and a game of pool'. There's a nightlife trail map – presumably for the ultimate bar crawl.

Off the slopes Getting to Thunderhead restaurant complex is easy for pedestrians. Visiting town is, too. The Strawberry Park Hot Springs are 'a great experience – lovely and relaxing'. Snowmobiling, ice climbing, tubing, hot-air balloons, sleigh rides and dog sledding are also possible.

Telluride

Cute old town, smart new Mountain Village, slopes to suit all.
What more could you want? More terrain, that's all

COSTS

① ② ③ ④ ⑤ ⑥

RATINGS

The slopes

Fast lifts	★★★★
Snow	★★★★
Extent	★★
Expert	★★★★
Intermediate	★★★
Beginner	★★★★★
Convenience	★★★★
Queues	★★★★★
Mountain restaurants	★

The rest

Scenery	★★★★
Resort charm	★★★★
Off-slope	★★

NEWS

For 2008/09 Revelation Bowl – 50 acres of expert terrain behind Gold Hill Ridge – will be served by a new quad chairlift.

For 2007/08 Black Iron Bowl opened at the top of Prospect Bowl, offering eight hike-to runs. The Meadows beginner area was expanded.

+ Charming restored Victorian mining town with a Wild West atmosphere
+ Slopes for all, including experts
+ Dramatic, craggy mountain scenery – unusual for Colorado

− Isolated location
− Despite expansion, still small
− Mountain Village a little quiet
− Limited mountain restaurants

We love the old town of Telluride and always enjoy its scenic, varied slopes; but despite recent expansion (see 'News'), their limited extent makes the place difficult to recommend for a holiday except in combination with another resort – which means travelling some distance.

THE RESORT

Telluride is an isolated resort in south-west Colorado. It first boomed when gold was found – and Butch Cassidy robbed his first bank here. The town's old red-brick and timber buildings give it great Wild West charm. Shops and restaurants have gone upmarket since its 'hippy' days some years ago and a lot of celebrities have plush holiday homes here now. But Telluride is still friendly and small-scale. On the slopes, Mountain Village is a smart development of condos and hotels. A gondola links the two until midnight.

THE MOUNTAINS

There is something for everyone here, including 400 acres of newly-opened advanced and expert terrain.

Slopes Slow chairs and a gondola from the old town access steep wooded slopes above it and the main beyond – with easy runs down to Mountain Village. There are also steep open slopes at the very top.

Terrain parks There are three parks. The advanced Hoot Brown park has a super-pipe and all the features you could dream of. Next to it, Butterfly is for intermediates. And there's a beginner park off the Ute Park lift.

Snow reliability With an average of 309 inches of snow a year and some snowmaking, reliability is good, but there have been some slow starts; it gets a different weather pattern from that of the resorts further north.

Experts The double-black bump runs down from Giuseppe's towards town are classic tests, and there are steep gladed runs from all along the ridge

611

KEY FACTS

Resort	2665m
	8,750ft
Slopes	2665-3735m
	8,750-12,260ft
Lifts	17
Pistes	1,700 acres
Green	24%
Blue	38%
Black	38%
Snowmaking	
	204 acres

Palmyra Peak

Gold Hill 3735m/12,26oft

Revelation Bowl ↓

Giuseppe's

3650m

Gold Hill ↳4

Black Iron Bowl

Hike-to

3600m/ 11,81oft

Prospect Bowl ↳2

Ute Park

Palmyra 5

3280m

3315m

Station St Sophia 3210m

Village ↳4

Sunshine ↳o

Mountain Village 2910m/9,540ft

Telluride 2665m/ 8,75oft

Coonskin Base 2660m/8,73oft

Big Billie's 2790m/9,160ft

↑ Great views from Giuseppe's snackery

TELLURIDE SKI RESORT

Central reservations
Toll-free number (from within the US)
1 800 778 8581

Phone numbers
From distant parts of the US, add the prefix 1 970; from abroad, add the prefix +1 970

t 728 6900
info@
tellurideskiresort.com
www.tellurideskiresort.com

between Giuseppe's and Gold Hill. The fast Gold Hill lift accesses some truly challenging terrain, including the new Revelation Bowl off the back side (see 'News') – with wide open steeps, narrow chutes and gnarly wooded trails. There is also hike-to backcountry terrain in Prospect Bowl and newly opened Black Iron Bowl. Helitrax runs a heli-skiing operation.
Intermediates There are ideal blue cruising runs with great views from the top down to Mountain Village (including the aptly named See Forever). The Prospect Bowl lift accesses some great intermediate terrain, with dozens of rolling pitches through the trees – a very relaxing and pretty area. More challenging are some of the bumpy double-blues from the Apex and Palmyra chairs. Some of the blacks above the town get groomed – worth catching if you can. The blue Telluride Trail back to town is a narrow catwalk ('treacherous'). But the area is small, and keen piste-bashers could get bored after a couple of days.
Beginners There are ideal runs below Mountain Village, and splendid long greens served by the Sunshine chair.
Snowboarding The lift system means it is easy to get about, and the huge terrain park offers plenty of scope.
Cross-country The beauty of the area makes it splendid for cross-country – both in the valley and at altitude, with 30km/19 miles in total.
Queues These are rarely a problem.
Mountain restaurants Gorrono Ranch is the main on-mountain restaurant, with a bar and terrace, live music and a BBQ. There are a couple of snack shacks higher up, with great views.
Schools and guides As well as lessons, the school offers backcountry guiding.

Facilities for children The Mountain Village Activity Center has a nursery and ski lessons can start at age three.

Telluride is tricky to get to from the UK, involving two or three flights or a long 540km/335 mile drive from Denver.
How to go Packages fly into nearby Montrose or the tiny Telluride airport (prone to closure by the weather).
Hotels In town, hotel Columbia is luxurious, as is the plush yet friendly Camel's Garden Hotel and Spa. The New Sheridan is actually old – a Main Street US classic, and comfortable, too. In Mountain Village, the Peaks Resort was refurbished for 2007/08, with luxury condos. Its award-winning Golden Door Spa was also revamped. The Blue Mesa Lodge and the Inn at Lost Creek have been recommended.
Apartments There are plenty of luxurious-looking condos.
Eating out The Cosmopolitan in the hotel Columbia is renowned as the best in town. Other sophisticated options include the Marmotte. Flora Dora is reasonably priced and has a 'friendly atmosphere'. Honga's Lotus Petal has Asian dishes, cocktails and a huge tea menu. Allred's, at the top of the gondola has spectacular views and is open for gourmet dining in the evenings. In Mountain Village try 9545 at the Inn at Lost Creek. The restaurant at the Peaks Resort has re-opened. Poacher's Pub and the Piazza are recommended for more relaxed dining.
Après-ski There's a lively bar-based après-ski scene in town. The New Sheridan has a lovely old bar dating from 1895. The Last Dollar has been recommended by locals. The Fly Me to the Moon Saloon has live music and stays open late. There's a swanky candlelit lounge called the Noir Bar attached to the Blue Point Grill. The historic Sheridan Opera House has concerts and the Nugget shows the latest cinema releases. Mountain Village is quieter. Try Poacher's Pub or Skier's Union.
Off the slopes There's quite a lot to do, such as dog sledding, horse riding, snowshoeing, ice skating, snowmobiling and glider rides. Thrill Hill has floodlit tubing, sledding and snow biking. There's a 'beautiful' walk to Bear Creek.

Vail

A vast, swanky resort with some very swanky hotels at the foot of one of the biggest (but also busiest) ski areas in the States

COSTS

① ② ③ ④ ⑤ ⑥

RATINGS

The slopes

Fast lifts	*****
Snow	*****
Extent	****
Expert	****
Intermediate	*****
Beginner	***
Convenience	***
Queues	**
Mountain restaurants	**

The rest

Scenery	***
Resort charm	***
Off-slope	***

NEWS

For 2008/09 the Manor Vail Resort at Golden Peak is due to be fully renovated, with the addition of 17 luxury condos.

For 2007/08 two fast quads replaced the old Sourdough and Highline chairs below Two Elk, on the front face. The Arrabelle at Vail Square – a 5-star hotel, spa, restaurant and retail complex – opened at Lionshead.

The Golden Peak Children's Center was improved, and the Little Eagle beginner lift was upgraded to a triple chair.

➕ One of the biggest areas in the US – great for confident intermediates, especially

➕ The Back Bowls are big areas of treeless terrain – unusual in the US

➕ Fabulous area of ungroomed, wooded slopes at Blue Sky Basin

➕ Largely traffic-free resort centres, very pleasant in parts – but ...

➖ Resort is a vast sprawl; and a lot of redevelopment is going on

➖ Slopes can be crowded by American standards, with serious lift queues

➖ Inadequate mountain restaurants

➖ Blue Sky Basin and the Back Bowls may not be open in early season; warm weather can close the Bowls

➖ Expensive

We always enjoy skiing Vail; it's a big mountain with a decent vertical, and Blue Sky Basin adds hugely to its attractions. But it is far from being our favourite American mountain. In an American resort you expect the runs to be pretty much crowd-free – and in any resort, these days, you expect 20-minute lift queues to be a thing of the past. In these respects, Vail disappoints.

When the budget runs to a swanky billet in Vail Village, we're happy enough with the resort, too: there is no denying it is a pleasant enough place to wander around in the evening. But we're not enthusiastic about its pseudo-Tirolean style, and the rest of the huge resort – almost four miles long – is much less appealing. In the end, we reckon Vail can't compete with more distinctively American resorts based on old mining or cowboy towns.

THE RESORT

Standing in the centre of Vail Village, surrounded by chalets and bierkellers, you could be forgiven for thinking you were in the Tirol – which is what Vail's founder, Pete Seibert, intended back in the 1950s. But Vail Village is now just part of an enormous resort, mostly built in anonymous modern style, stretching along the I-70 freeway running west from Denver.

The vast village benefits from a free and efficient bus service which makes choice of location less than crucial. But the most convenient – and expensive – places to stay are in mock-Tirolean Vail Village, near the Vista Bahn fast chair, or in functional Lionshead, near the gondola – an improving area now that the smart Arrabelle at Vail Square complex has opened. The downside of all the rebuilding work that is going on though, is that some parts still resemble a building site. There is a lot of accommodation further out – the cheapest tends to be on the far side of the I-70.

Beaver Creek, 16km/10 miles away, is covered by the lift pass and is easily reached by bus. A short drive over Vail Pass gets you to Breckenridge (also served by bus from Vail three times a week) and Keystone – both owned by Vail Resorts and covered by the lift pass. Copper Mountain is also nearby.

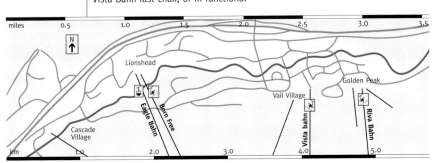

miles	0.5	1.0	1.5	2.0	2.5	3.0	3.5

Lionshead

Golden Peak

Vail Village

Eagle Bahn

Born Free

Vista bahn

Riva Bahn

Cascade Village

km	1.0	2.0	3.0	4.0	5.0

↑ No longer quite America's biggest ski area, but still an impressively wide area of slopes

VAIL RESORTS INC / KEN REDDING

KEY FACTS

Resort	2500m
	8,200ft
Slopes	2475-3525m
	8,120-11,570ft
Lifts	32
Pistes	5,289 acres
Green	18%
Blue	29%
Black	53%
Snowmaking	
	390 acres

THE MOUNTAINS

Vail has one of the biggest areas of slopes in the US (only recently overtaken by Big Sky/Moonlight Basin). You get a real sense of travelling around the mountain – something missing in many smaller American resorts. Some of the runs (especially blacks) are overclassified and we've had mixed reports on trail signposting. There are free three-hour mountain tours at 9.15 every day and tours of Blue Sky Basin starting at 10.30.

THE SLOPES
Something for everyone

The slopes above **Vail** can be accessed via three main lifts. From right next to Vail Village, the Vista Bahn fast chair goes up to the major mid-mountain focal point, Mid-Vail; from Lionshead, the Eagle Bahn gondola goes up to the Eagle's Nest complex; and from the Golden Peak base area just to the east of Vail Village, the Riva Bahn fast chair goes up towards the Two Elk area.

The front face of the mountain is largely north-facing, with well-groomed trails cut through the trees. At altitude the mountainside divides into three bowls – Mid-Vail in the centre, with Game Creek to the south-west and Northeast Bowl to the, er, north-east. Lifts reach the ridge at three points, all giving access to the **Back Bowls** (mostly ungroomed and treeless) and through them to the **Blue Sky Basin** area – mostly ungroomed and

wooded, with a 'backcountry' feel that the rest of Vail lacks.

The slopes have yellow-jacketed patrollers who stop people speeding recklessly. You can test equipment at the Vail Sports Demo Center.

TERRAIN PARKS
Four to fly between

There are four parks, all named with an aviation theme. The Flight School park is used by the ski school and is aimed at novices. It is adjacent to the big pro park, has its own entrance and is accessible by the Riva Bahn fast chair. The Sky Way park off the Wildwood Express lift out of Mid-Vail is also aimed at beginners. Intermediates should head up the Eagle Bahn gondola or Born Free chair from Lionshead to the Aviator park. Medium-sized kickers and rails will prepare you to step up to the Fly Zone on Golden Peak. This park and super-pipe – again served by the Riva Bahn fast chair – are home to various high-profile events and are often in the top ten in terrain park lists and polls. There are over 40 features, including a huge triple-jump line, a quarter-pipe, and a unique log rail park – all built in nice fluid lines. The pipe boasts 5m/18ft walls, and it is 130m/425ft long.

SNOW RELIABILITY
Excellent, except in the Bowls

As well as an exceptional natural snow record (average 348 inches), Vail has

Interactive resort shortlist builder at www.wtss.co.uk

LIFT PASSES

Colorado

Prices in US$

Age	1-day	6-day
under 13		285
13 to 64		445
over 65		395
Free under 5		
Beginner included in price of lessons		

Notes

Covers all Vail, Beaver Creek, Breckenridge and Keystone resorts, plus Arapahoe Basin; prices quoted are advance-purchase prices; further reductions for international visitors who pre-book through a UK tour operator (it is not necessary to buy a complete holiday package to obtain these prices)

extensive snowmaking, normally needed only in early season. Both the Back Bowls and Blue Sky Basin usually open later in the season than the front mountain. Blue Sky is largely north-facing (and wooded) and keeps its snow well, but the Bowls are sunny, and in warm weather snow can deteriorate to the point where they are closed or a traverse is kept open to allow access to Blue Sky Basin. Grooming is excellent.

FOR EXPERTS
Transformed by Blue Sky Basin

Vail's Back Bowls are vast areas, served by four chairlifts and a short draglift. You can go virtually anywhere you like in the half-dozen identifiable bowls, trying the gradient and terrain of your choice. There are interesting, lightly wooded areas, as well as the open slopes that dominate the area. Some 87% of the runs in the Back Bowls are classified black but are not

particularly steep, and they have disappointed some of our expert reporters. The snow can deteriorate rapidly in warm, sunny weather.

Blue Sky Basin has much better snow than the Back Bowls and some great adventure runs in the trees – some widely spaced, some very tight, some on relatively gentle terrain, some quite steep. All the runs funnel into the same run-out so you can't get lost.

On the front face there are some genuinely steep double-black-diamond runs, which usually have great snow; they are often mogulled but sometimes groomed to make wonderful fast cruising. The fast new Highline lift on the extreme east of the area serves three. Prima Cornice, served by the Northwoods Express, is one of the steepest runs on the front side of the hill.

If the snow is good, try the back-country Minturn Mile – you leave the ski area through a gate in the Game

boarding

The terrain is about as big as it comes in America. Beginners will enjoy the front side's gentle groomed pistes, ideal for honing skills and serviced by fast chairlifts. Beware of flat areas, however, especially at the top of the Wildwood and Northwoods lifts. The back bowls will keep most riders busy for days when the snow is right. Blue Sky Basin is definitely worth checking out, with its acres of natural trails, gladed trees and cornices. There are four terrain parks too. The Vail Sports Demo Center at the top of the Mountaintop chair, will help if you have any issues with your board, or want to demo the latest gear. There are plenty of specialist shops in town, as well as good snowboard school facilities, with adult-specific courses.

Two Elk Lodge
3420m/11,220ft

Sourdough

Patrol
Headquarters
3430m/11,250ft

Wildwood
3345m/10,9...

**The major
bottleneck that
gives Vail its
reputation for
serious queues**

Northeast Bowl

Northwoods

Mountaintop

Wildwood

Highline

Mid-Vail
3095m/10,150ft

Avanti

**Vail's most
challenging terrain,
now served by two
fast lifts**

Riva Bahn

Vista Bahn

FRONT SIDE

Golden Peak

Vail Village
2500m/8,200ft

Lionshead
2475m/8,120f

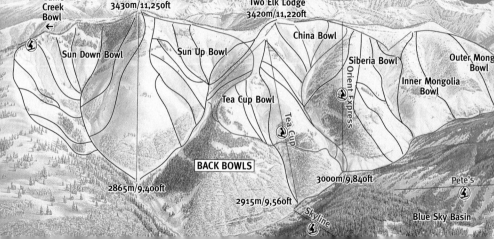

Game
Creek
Bowl
←

Patrol Headquarters
3430m/11,250ft

Two Elk Lodge
3420m/11,220ft

China Bowl

Sun Down Bowl

Sun Up Bowl

Siberia Bowl

Outer Mong
Bowl

Orient Express

Inner Mongolia
Bowl

Tea Cup Bowl

Tea Cup

BACK BOWLS

2865m/9,400ft

3000m/9,840ft

Pete's

2915m/9,56ft

Skyline

Blue Sky Basin

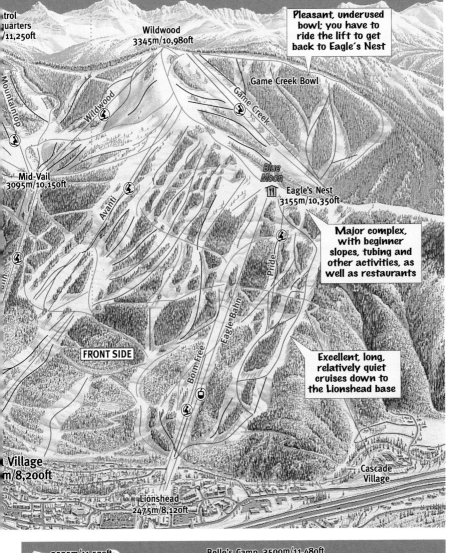

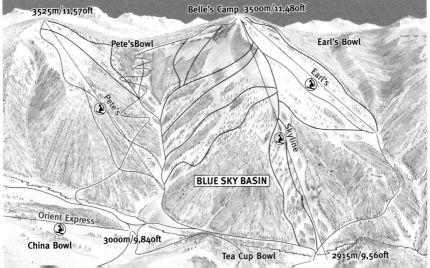

Interactive resort shortlist builder at www.wtss.co.uk

CHILDREN

Small World Play School
t 754 3285
Ages 2mnth to 6yr;
8am to 4.30; $105
per day; reservations
recommended

Ski school
Ages 3 to 12 at
Golden Peak and
Lionshead (full day
including lift pass and
lunch from US$130);
teens $153 per day

Creek area to descend a powder bowl and finish on a path by a river – ending up at the atmospheric Saloon. Go with a local guide.

FOR INTERMEDIATES
Ideal territory
The majority of Vail's front face is great intermediate territory, with easy cruising runs. Above Lionshead, especially, there are excellent long, relatively quiet blues – Born Free and Simba both go from top to bottom. Game Creek Bowl, nearby, is excellent, too. Avanti, underneath the chair of the same name, is a nice cruiser.

As well as tackling some of the easier front-face blacks, intermediates will find plenty of interest in the Back Bowls. Some of the runs are groomed and several are classified blue, including Silk Road, which loops around the eastern edge, with wonderful views. Some of the unpisted slopes make the ideal introduction to powder skiing. Confident intermediates will also enjoy Blue Sky Basin's clearly marked blue runs and trying the easier ungroomed runs there.

FOR BEGINNERS
Good but can be crowded
There are fine nursery slopes at resort level and at altitude, and easy longer runs to progress to. But they can be rather crowded.

FOR CROSS-COUNTRY
Some of the best
Vail's cross-country areas (17km/ 11 miles) are at the foot of Golden Peak and at the Nordic Center on the golf course. There are also 10km/6 miles of snowshoe trails.

QUEUES
Can be bad
Vail has some of the longest lift lines we've hit in the US, especially at weekends because of the influx from nearby Denver. Most of our reporters experience some lines. Mid-Vail is a bottleneck that is difficult to avoid; 20-minute waits are common. At peak times it's possible to queue for 45 minutes here. The Northwoods chairs is another notable hot-spot, say reporters and the Eagle Bahn gondola can have 'queues of up to 20 minutes virtually all day'. But other recent reporters have been luckier ('occasional' queues and 'only 10 minutes maximum wait at the

bottom'). One visitor was more upset by the unreliability of some lifts: 'We were stuck on the Game Creek chair twice for up to 30 minutes at –28°C.'

MOUNTAIN RESTAURANTS
Surprisingly poor (and pricey)
Vail's mountain restaurants are disappointing for such a big, upscale resort. The major self-service restaurants can be unpleasantly crowded from 11am to 2pm.
Editors' choice The table-service Blue Moon (754 4530) at Eagle's Nest, which was remodelled a couple of years ago, is one bright spot: an airy room doing excellent food at not exorbitant prices.
Worth knowing about There are self-service places at several major lift junctions. Two Elk is a huge, airy place that visitors have found satisfactory, despite crowds. Go to Wildwood Smokehouse for BBQs, and to Buffalo's for 'sandwich and soup combos'.

SCHOOLS AND GUIDES
Among the best in the world
The Vail-Beaver Creek school generates many glowing reports: 'excellent'; 'the best ski lesson I've ever had'. Class sizes are usually small: 'never more than four in the group lesson', says a 2007 reporter. You can sign up for lessons on the mountain.

FACILITIES FOR CHILDREN
Excellent
The comprehensive arrangements for small children look excellent, and we've had good reports on the school. The children's centre at Golden Peak has been improved and there are splendid areas with adventure trails and themed play zones. There's even a special kids' cafe area at Mid Vail. Family Night theatre and dinner events are held at Adventure Ridge.

STAYING THERE

HOW TO GO
Package or independent
There's a big choice of packages to Vail. It's easy to organise your own visit, with regular airport shuttles.
Chalets Several UK tour operators offer catered chalets. Many are out of the centre at East Vail or West Vail or across the busy I-70 freeway.
Hotels Vail has a fair choice of hotels, though nearly all are expensive. Check online for the best deals.

↑ Bavaria? The Tirol? Colorado: the Lodge at Vail

VAIL RESORTS, INC

SCHOOLS

Vail
t 754 4300

Classes
Full day (9.45-3.30)
$125

Private lessons
$665 for 1 day

GETTING THERE

Air Eagle 56km/ 35 miles (1hr); Denver 193km/ 120 miles (2½hr)

ACTIVITIES

Indoor Athletic clubs and spas, massage, ski museum

Outdoor Ice skating, fishing, tubing, snowmobiling, snowshoe excursions, bungee trampolining, tobogganing, dog sledding, horse riding

Central reservations phone number
t 496 4500

Phone numbers
From distant parts of the US, add the prefix 1 970; from abroad, add the prefix +1 970

TOURIST OFFICE

t 496 4500
vailinfo@vailresorts.com
vail.snow.com

*****Vail Cascade** A resort within a resort – lots of facilities and a chairlift right outside.
*****Sonnenalp** Very stylish, welcoming, central Bavarian-style place. Large spa and splendid piano bar-lounge.
*****Lodge at Vail** Right by the Vista Bahn. Some standard rooms small. Huge buffet breakfast. Outdoor pool. Recommended by a reporter.
****Marriot Mountain Resort** Also owned by Vail Resorts, near the Eagle Bahn gondola. Impressive spa facilities.
****Manor Vail Resort** At Golden Peak. Suites with sitting area, fireplace, kitchen and terrace. Hot tub and pool. Due to be fully refurbished for 2008/09 (see 'News').
****Plaza Hotel and Club** Newly opened in December 2007. Good position in Vail Village; smart rooms and suites. Pool, spa and fitness centre.
***Evergreen Lodge** Between village and Lionshead. Outdoor pool, sauna and hot tub. Sports bar. 'Excellent, value for money and spacious rooms', says a 2007 reporter.
Apartments The Racquet Club at East Vail has lots of amenities. Mountain Haus has high-quality condos in the centre of town. And the Pitkin Creek has been recommended.

EATING OUT
Endless choice
Whatever kind of food you want, Vail has it – but most of it is expensive.
Fine-dining options include the Wildflower in the Lodge, the Tour (modern French) and Ludwig's, in the Sonnenalp. For Alpine ambience try the Alpenrose II and Pepi's in the hotel Gramshammer. Centre V is a new French-inspired restaurant, cosy bar and outdoor terrace at the Arrabelle at Vail Square.

For more moderate prices, we've found Blu's 'contemporary American' food satisfactory; Billy's Island Grill does steaks; and Campo de Fiori is an excellent Italian. Bart & Yeti's is good for local ales and no-frills, hearty American food. Reader recommendations include Lancelot at Vail Village for steaks and seafood, Bagali's Italian Kitchen for pizza, May Palace (Chinese) and Nozawa (Asian) in West Vail, Sapphire (seafood), Montauk (seafood), the Bistro at the Racquet Club, Los Amigos ('decent Mexican fare', 'very family-friendly'), Russell's, Vendetta's, Pazzo's ('great pizzas and very good value') and Sweet Basil at Vail Village ('delicious food; good atmosphere'). The Chophouse is new at Lionshead, serving seafood and steaks.

APRES-SKI
Fairly lively
Lionshead is said to be quiet in the evenings; but Garfinkel's has a DJ, sun deck and happy hour. The Red Lion in the village centre is 'cheap and fun' with live music, big-screen TVs and huge portions of food. The George models itself on an English-style pub. Pepi's is also popular and Los Amigos is lively at four o'clock. The Tap Room in the Vista Bahn building is a relaxed woody bar.
You can have a good night out at Adventure Ridge at the top of the gondola. As well as bars and restaurants, there's lots to do on the snow – though a reporter reckons the tubing hill is no match for Keystone's.

OFF THE SLOPES
A lot to do
Getting around on the free bus is easy, and there are lots of activities to try. The factory outlets at Silverthorne (over Vail Pass) are a must if you can't resist a bargain.

Interactive resort shortlist builder at **www.wtss.co.uk**

Winter Park

A radical alternative to the run of Colorado resorts, for those more interested in snow and space than in après-ski amusements

620

➕ The best snowfall record of all Colorado's major resorts

➕ Superb beginner terrain and lots of groomed cruises

➕ Lots for experts, at least when conditions are right

➕ Quiet on weekdays

➕ Leading resort for teaching people with disabilities to ski and ride

➕ Largely free of inflated prices and ski-resort glitz

➖ 'Village' at the lift base is still very limited – dead in the evening

➖ Town is a bus ride away

➖ And it has little appeal, lacking the usual shops and restaurants

➖ Trails tend to be either easy cruises or stiff mogul fields

➖ Some tough terrain liable to closure by bad weather

➖ Can get crowded at weekends

Winter Park's ski area – developed for the recreation of the citizens of nearby Denver, and still owned by the city – is world class. Now there is the prospect of a world-class resort at the base, too: Intrawest (developers of resorts such as Whistler) is in the first phase of a massive expansion plan. The place looks set to be a construction site for a few years, but the end product should be good.

For the present, there's only a small, very quiet 'village' at the base and most lodging, shops and restaurants are a bus ride away. If that doesn't matter to you, Winter Park is well worth considering. Some of our reporters rate it their favourite Colorado resort, partly because it makes a refreshing change from the ski resort norm.

THE RESORT

Winter Park started life in the 19th century: when the Rio Grande railway was built, workers climbed the slopes to ski down. One of the resort's mountains, Mary Jane, is named after a legendary 'lady of pleasure', who is said to have received the land as payment for her favours.

The railway still plays an important part – at the station right at the foot of the slopes trains deposit Denverites on weekends; there's apparently quite a party on the homebound leg.

Most accommodation is a shuttle-bus ride away in spacious condos scattered around either side of US highway 40, the road through the town of Winter Park. Drive into the town at night, and the neon lights make it seem like a real ski resort town – but in the cold light of day it's clear that the place doesn't amount to much. It even lacks a proper supermarket – the nearest is a drive or bus ride away at Fraser.

More recently, stylish lodgings have been developed at or near the foot of the slopes, including a car-free mini-

resort known as The Village at Winter Park Resort. But as yet it's very small, without many shops, bars or restaurants. Confusingly, an area between the mountain and the town is known as Old Town. Shuttle-buses run between the town and the lift base, and the hotels and condos also provide shuttles. A car simplifies getting around; day trips to Denver or other resorts such as Copper Mountain, Breckenridge and Keystone are possible, if you're keen.

The approach road is distinctly Alpine, crossing the Continental Divide at Berthoud Pass (3450m/11,320ft). Don't plan on driving over in the dark. The resort is much lower, but high enough for a risk of altitude sickness.

THE MOUNTAINS

Winter Park's ski area is big by US standards, with a mix of terrain that suits all abilities – when it's all open. There are guided tours twice daily, and a Fresh Tracks breakfast at 8am on Saturdays enabling you to get up the mountain before the crowds. Route finding can be tricky in places.

↑ The familiar Colorado recipe – densely wooded slopes with open slopes above

INTRAWEST/ WINTER PARK / GREGG ADAMS

LIFT PASSES

Winter Park Resort

Prices in US$

Age	1-day	6-day
under 13	45	216
13 to 64	86	384
65 to 69	72	
over 70	35	

Free under 6
Beginner included in price of lessons

Notes
Multi-day prices quoted are advance-purchase prices; one-day prices are regular season window rates; special deals for disabled skiers

UK PACKAGES

All America Holidays, Alpine Answers, AmeriCan Ski, American Ski Classics, Crystal, Directski.com, Erna Low, Independent Ski Links, Inghams, Interactive Resorts, Ski Dream, Ski Independence, Ski McNeill, Ski Safari, Ski Solutions, Skitracer, Skiworld, Supertravel, Thomson, United Vacations, Virgin Snow, White Mountains

THE SLOPES
Interestingly divided
There are five distinct, but well-linked, sectors. From the main base, a fast quad takes you to the peak of the original **Winter Park** mountain. From there, you can descend in all directions. Runs lead back towards the main base and over to the **Vasquez Ridge** area on the far right, served by the Pioneer fast quad.

You can also descend to the base of **Mary Jane** mountain, where four chairs up the front face serve tough runs; other chairs serve easier terrain on the flanks. From here you can head for the **Parsenn Bowl** on the new Panoramic Express chair (see 'News') for intermediate terrain above and in the trees. This chair may be less prone to closure by wind than the old double, but it is far from immune. From Parsenn, conditions permitting, you can skate or walk for up to half an hour to access the advanced and extreme slopes of **Vasquez Cirque**. You can now return to Parsenn Bowl using the Eagle Wind chair, saving a long run-out to the Pioneer lift.

TERRAIN PARKS
Four levels for all standards
The flagship Rail Yard park, with 30 features including big jumps, new wall ride, a host of variously shaped rails and a super-pipe, is enough to challenge most experts. It runs down much of the front of Winter Park mountain for 1280m/ 4,200ft. Halfway

down it crosses a bridge so that those on the Cranmer Cutoff green run can cross the park safely. At the bottom are the huge features of Dark Territory, open to pass holders only (you need to pay $20, sign a waiver and watch a safety video to get one). For those who prefer smaller hits, there are two parks for intermediates nearby: Dog Patch and Dog Patch East. There's also a beginner-intermediate park, Kendrick, on the Jack Kendrick green run, plus a Starter park for beginners under Prospector Express. Check them out at www.rlyrd.com.

SNOW RELIABILITY
Among Colorado's best
Winter Park's position, close to the Continental Divide, gives it an average yearly snowfall of over 350 inches – the highest of any major Colorado resort. Snowmaking covers a lot of Winter Park mountain's runs.

FOR EXPERTS
Some hair-raising challenges
Mary Jane has some of the steepest mogul fields, chutes and hair-raising challenges in the US. On the front side is a row of long black mogul fields that are quite steep enough for most of us. There are some good genuine blacks on Winter Park mountain, too. Some of the best terrain is open only when there is good snow and/or weather – so it's especially unreliable early in the season. The fearsome chutes of Mary Jane's back side – all

boarding
There is some great advanced and extreme boarding terrain and a high probability of fresh powder to ride. The four levels of park (see 'Terrain parks') make Winter Park even more attractive to all levels of freestyler. The resort is also an ideal beginner and intermediate boarder area, with excellent terrain for learning. A good school provides classes for all levels, including learning to jump and ride rails.

steep, narrow and bordered by rocks – need a lot of snow and are accessed by a control gate. Parsenn Bowl, served by the new Panoramic six-pack, has superb blue/black gladed runs and black-diamond gladed runs on the back side down to the Eagle Wind chair. Vasquez Cirque, the least reliably open area, has excellent ungroomed expert terrain but not much vertical before you hit the forest.

FOR INTERMEDIATES
Choose your challenge
From pretty much wherever you are on Winter Park mountain and Vasquez Ridge you can choose a run to suit your ability. Most blue runs are well groomed every night, giving you perfect early morning cruising on the famous Colorado 'corduroy' pistes. Black runs, however, tend not to be groomed, and huge moguls form. If bumps are for you, try Mary Jane's front side. If you're learning to love them, the blue/black Sleeper enables you to dip in and out.

Parsenn Bowl has grand views and several gentle cruising pistes as well as more challenging ungroomed terrain. New blue and blue-black runs and glades opened here for 2007/08, offering a nice range of gradients. It's also an ideal place to try powder for the first time. But when it's actually snowing you are better off riding lower lifts, sticking to the powdery edges of treelined runs for better visibility.

The blue-black Hughes is a great thrash home at close of play.

FOR BEGINNERS
About the best we've seen
Discovery Park is a 25-acre dedicated area for beginners, reached by a high-speed quad and served by two more chairs and a tow. As well as a nursery area and longer green runs, it has an adventure trail through trees. And the Sorensen learning zone at the base area is good too. There are lots of long green runs from Mary Jane and Winter Park, but some are perilously close to being flat.

FOR CROSS-COUNTRY
Lots of it
There are several different areas nearby (none actually in the resort) with generally excellent snow, totalling

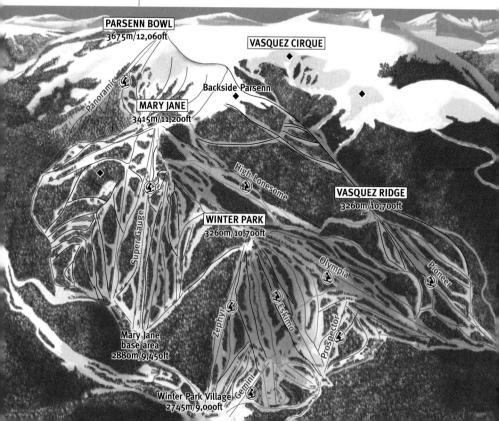

SCHOOLS

Winter Park
t 1 800 729 7907

National Sports Center for the Disabled
t 726 1540
Special programme for disabled skiers and snowboarders

Classes (Winter Park prices)
Half day (2½hr) $69

Private lessons
$339 for 3hr for 1 to 3 people

CHILDREN

Wee Willies
t 1 800 420 8093
Ages 2mnth to 6yr;
$95 per day; 8am to 4pm

Ski school
Takes ages 3 to 17
($115 per day including lift ticket and lunch)

GETTING THERE

Air Denver 137km/
85 miles (1½hr)

Rail Denver, Sat and Sun only; journey time 2¼hr

ACTIVITIES

Indoor Fitness clubs, hot tubs, museum

Outdoor Dog sledding, ice rink, snowshoeing, sleigh rides, snowmobiling, snowcat tours, hot springs

Central reservations
toll-free number (from within the US)
1 800 979 0332

Phone numbers
From distant parts of the US, add the prefix 1 970; from abroad, add the prefix +1 970

TOURIST OFFICE

t 726 5514
wpinfo@skiwinterpark.com
www.skiwinterpark.com

over 200km/125 miles of groomed trails, as well as backcountry tours.

QUEUES
Weekend crowds at the base
During the week the mountain is generally quiet. However, the Zephyr Express can get busy at peak times. The new Panoramic Express seems to have alleviated any queues to reach the Parsenn Bowl. At weekends the Denver crowds arrive and big queues form at the base when the train gets in (though they move quickly) – 'get up the mountain before 9am to avoid them', says a reporter.

MOUNTAIN RESTAURANTS
Some good facilities
The highlight is the Lodge at Sunspot, at the top of Winter Park mountain. This wood and glass building has a welcoming bar with a roaring log fire and table- and self-service sections – but it gets very busy. Lunch Rock Cafe at the top of Mary Jane does quick snacks and has a deli counter, and there is a newly expanded self-service at Snoasis, by the beginner area. Otherwise, it's down to the bases. The Club Car at the base of Mary Jane offers table service and 'a good atmosphere and more varied menu' than the American norm.

SCHOOLS AND GUIDES
Very good reports
A recent reporter with a school party said, 'I would like to stress how good, helpful and flexible the ski school is.' 'Three people in our group had lessons, and the improvement in all was quite startling to see,' said another visitor. As well as standard classes there are ideas such as Family Private (for different abilities together) and themed lessons such as bumps and women-only clinics.

FACILITIES FOR CHILDREN
Some of the best
The Children's Center at Winter Park base area houses day-care facilities and is the meeting point for children's classes, which have their own areas.

STAYING THERE

HOW TO GO
Fair choice
Several UK operators offer Winter Park.
Chalets A few are available.
Hotels There are a couple of hotel/

condo complexes with restaurants and pools near, but not in, the new Village.
***Iron Horse Resort 'Wonderful; ski-in/ski-out, great restaurant,' says a 2007 reporter.
***Winter Park Mountain Lodge
Inconveniently positioned across the valley from the lifts; incorporates a micro-brewery; gets mixed reports.
Apartments There are a lot of comfortable condos, including the slope-side Zephyr Mountain Lodge ('fantastic, spacious, comfy, good views') and Beaver Village condos, a five-minute shuttle-bus ride ('very high standard, but the last shuttle leaves the mountain at 5.15pm').

EATING OUT
A real weakness
There isn't the range of places you get in more established 'destination' resorts. 'Fine dining' isn't really an option unless you drive 8 miles out to Devil's Thumb Ranch. Get hold of the giveaway Grand County menu guide. In town, reporters are keen on the long-established Deno's – seafood, steaks etc (also a popular après-ski bar). In the Cooper Creek Square area the New Hong Kong serves 'excellent' Chinese food. Readers have also recommended Carlos and Maria's for Tex-Mex, Hernando's for pizza/pasta and Untamed for steaks/Tex-Mex. Gasthaus Eichler does German-influenced food, at slightly higher prices. Try the Crooked Creek Saloon, a drive away at Fraser, for atmosphere and typical American food.

APRES-SKI
If you know where to go ...
At close of play, there's action at the main lift base at the Derailer Bar ('the best and cheapest' says a reporter) and Doc's Roadhouse, and at the Club Car at the base of Mary Jane – but reporters are disappointed at how early they close. Later on, Randi's Grill and Pub can be lively and the Winter Park Pub attracts the younger crowd. Freestyle's and Buckets ('the liveliest in town') are funky sports-bars.

OFF THE SLOPES
Mainly the great outdoors
Most diversions involve getting about on snow in different ways. Several reporters are enthusiastic about the floodlit tubing at Fraser. The famous Silverthorne factory outlet stores are 90 minutes away.

'The Greatest Snow on Earth' is Utah's marketing slogan. And it's true that some Utah resorts do get huge amounts of snow – usually light, dry powder – and if you like the steep and deep, you should at some point make the pilgrimage here. Don't be put off by thinking its a 'dry' Mormon state – we've never found getting a beer or a bottle of wine a problem. But boarders beware: two of its top resorts don't allow snowboarding.

The biggest dumps fall at Alta (which bans boarding) and Snowbird. Their average of 500 inches of snow a year (twice as much as some Colorado resorts) has made them the powder capitals of the world. Park City, 45 minutes' drive away, is the main 'destination' resort of the area, and a

sensible holiday base; upmarket Deer Valley (which bans boarding) is next door; and The Canyons is only a short drive away. Although only a few miles from Snowbird/Alta as the crow flies, these resorts get 'only' 300 to 350 inches of snow. There are separate chapters on these five resorts. We spent a week in Park City in 2008, and it virtually never stopped snowing. Every day we had fresh, knee-high powder and we never made it to Alta or Snowbird: there was no need because the snow on the three local mountains was awesome.

Other Utah resorts worth visiting include Brighton and Solitude. They get similar amounts of snow, but it gets tracked out less quickly because the resorts attract far fewer experts. The main claim to fame of Sundance is that it's owned by Robert Redford; it gets 320 inches of snow a year. It was unknown Snowbasin (400 inches), well to the north, that hosted the Olympic downhill events in 2002. Powder Mountain (500 inches), a bit further north, is aptly named. There is more about these resorts in the resort directory at the end of the book.

Utah is the Mormon state, which means that sale and consumption of alcohol is tightly controlled. But we've never found getting a drink a problem. Provided you're over 21 and can prove it, neither should you. If you are eating, getting alcohol with your meal is no problem. But at bars and clubs more dedicated to drinking (ie don't feature food but do serve spirits or beer stronger than 3.2% alcohol) membership of some kind is required. This may involve one of your party handing over $4 or more – one member can introduce numerous 'guests'. A membership lasts three weeks. Places with tavern licences serve 3.2% beer and don't operate as clubs – but you do still need to be 21.

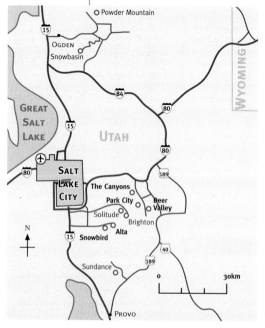

O Powder Mountain

15

OGDEN
Snowbasin O

84

80

WYOMING

GREAT
SALT
LAKE

15

UTAH

80

N

SALT
LAKE
CITY

15

189

The Canyons O
Park City O   O Deer
           O O Valley
Solitude O O
        O O Brighton
Snowbird   Alta

40

189

Sundance O

PROVO

0   30km

Alta

Cult powder resort linked to Snowbird but with less brutal architecture and a friendlier, old-fashioned feel

COSTS

① ② ③ ④ ⑤ ⑥

RATINGS

The slopes

Fast lifts	**★★★**
Snow	**★★★★★**
Extent	**★★★**
Expert	**★★★★★**
Intermediate	**★★★**
Beginner	**★★★**
Convenience	**★★★★**
Queues	**★★★**
Mountain restaurants	**★★**

The rest

Scenery	**★★★**
Resort charm	**★★**
Off-slope	**★**

KEY FACTS

Resort	2600m
	8,530ft

For Alta and Snowbird combined area see Snowbird

For Alta only

Slopes	2600-3200m
	8,530-10,500ft
Lifts	11
Pistes	2,200 acres
Green	25%
Blue	40%
Black	35%
Snowmaking	
	50 acres

NEWS

In 2007/08 Alta followed many European resorts by introducing a hands-free lift pass system – the Alta Card. Snowbird has stuck with the old barcode system, so joint passes issued in Alta have both systems on them.

ALTA SKI AREA

Lunchtime eating options include places at the base area; as is normal in the US, there's nothing spectacular →

- ➕ Phenomenal snow and steep terrain mean cult status among experts (there's great beginner terrain, too)
- ➕ Linked to Snowbird, making it one of the largest ski areas in the US
- ➕ Ski-almost-to-the-door convenience

- ➖ 'Resort' is no more than a scattering of lodges – not much après-ski atmosphere, and few off-slope diversions
- ➖ Limited groomed runs for intermediates

Alta and Snowbird are the powder capitals of the world (the snow here is as plentiful, frequent and light as it comes), and their combined area is one of the biggest in the US. Strangely, many locals we meet are still either Alta or Snowbird devotees (the ski areas were separate until 2001/02) and never ski the other area. Madness (unless you're a boarder, in which case Snowbird is your only option – boarding is banned in Alta). On balance, we'd choose to stay in Alta – it has a friendlier feel and less brutal architecture.

THE RESORT

Alta sits at the craggy head of Little Cottonwood Canyon, 2km/1 mile beyond Snowbird and less than an hour's drive from downtown Salt Lake City. Both the resort and the approach road are prone to avalanches and closure: visitors can be confined indoors for safety. Where once there was a bustling and bawdy mining town, there is now just a strung-out handful of lodges and parking areas. Life revolves around the two separate lift base areas – Albion and Wildcat – linked by a bi-directional rope tow along the flat valley floor. There are about a dozen places to stay.

THE MOUNTAINS

Alta's slopes are lightly wooded, with some treeless slopes. Check out the Snowbird chapter for the linked slopes. Unlike most US resorts, Alta's trail map does not differentiate between single- and double-black-diamond trails – a bad idea we think.
Slopes The dominant feature of Alta's terrain is the steep end of a ridge that separates the area's two basins. To the left, above Albion Base, the slopes stretch away over easy green terrain towards the blue and black runs from Point Supreme and from the top of the Sugarloaf quad (also the access lift for Snowbird). To the right, above Wildcat Base, is a more concentrated bowl with blue runs down the middle and blacks either side, served by the fast

two-stage Collins chair. The two sectors are linked at altitude, and by a flat rope tow along the valley floor.
Terrain parks There isn't one.
Snow reliability The quantity and quality of the snow and the northerly orientation put Alta in the top rank.
Experts Even before the Snowbird link Alta had cult status among local experts, who flocked to the high ridges after a fresh snowfall. There are dozens of steep slopes and chutes.
Intermediates Adventurous intermediates who are happy to try ungroomed slopes and learn to love

UK PACKAGES

All America Holidays,
AmeriCan Ski, Ski
Dream, Skitracer

Phone numbers
From distant parts of
the US, add the prefix
1 801; from abroad,
add the prefix +1 801

TOURIST OFFICE

t 359 1078
info@alta.com
www.alta.com

powder should like Alta, too. There are good blue bowls in both Alta and Snowbird and not-so-tough blacks to progress to. But if it is miles of perfectly groomed piste you are after, there are plenty of better resorts.

Beginners Timid intermediates and beginners will be very happy on the gentle lower slopes of the Albion side. But it's hard to recommend such a narrowly focused resort to beginners.

Snowboarding Boarding is banned (but guided snowcat boarding is available in nearby Grizzly Gulch).

Cross-country There's a 5km/3 mile groomed track.

Queues The slopes are normally uncrowded, but the fast Collins lift is said to be increasing numbers on the Wildcat side, with 'everybody skiing top to bottom, making it impossible to load at the mid-station'.

Mountain restaurants There's one in each sector of the slopes, offering mainly fast food. Alf's on the Albion side has 'fast service' and serves 'great chilli in bread bowls'. The 'nice, light and airy' Watson Shelter on the Wildcat side has self-service and table-service sections. Several lodges at the base do lunch.

Schools and guides The ski school specialises in powder lessons – though there are regular classes, too.

Facilities for children Day care for

children from two months is available at the Children's Center at Albion Base.

STAYING THERE

How to go None of the hotels is luxurious in US terms but most get booked up by repeat visitors; unusually for the US, most operate half-board deals, with dinner included.

Hotels The venerable Alta Lodge (742 3500) has comfortable rooms and an atmospheric bar, and has developed a cult following in the US by serving a limited dinner menu at shared tables, in two sittings, instead of enlarging its dining room. Ingenious. Rustler Lodge (742 2200) is more luxurious, with a big outdoor pool, but impersonal. The comfortable, modern and conveniently located Goldminer's Daughter (742 2300) and the basic Peruvian Lodge (742 3000) are cheaper. The Snowpine Lodge (742 2000) has a sauna and is 'convenient, comfortable and friendly' but rather 'old-fashioned'.

Eating out It is possible, but eating in is the routine.

Après-ski This rarely goes beyond a few drinks in one of the hotel bars. The Goldminer's Daughter has the main après-ski bar, with pool table etc.

Off the slopes Few options other than snowshoeing, a sightseeing trip to Salt Lake City, or the spa at Snowbird.

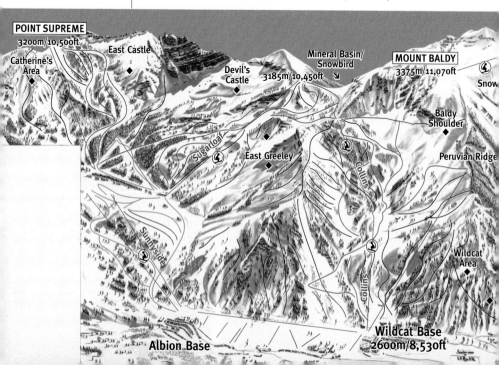

POINT SUPREME
3200m/10,500ft

East Castle

Catherine's
Area

Devil's
Castle   3185m/10,450ft

Mineral Basin/
Snowbird

MOUNT BALDY
3375m/11,070ft

Snow

Baldy
Shoulder

Sugarloaf

East Greeley

Peruvian Ridge

Collins

Sunnyside

Wildcat
Area

Collins

Wildcat Base
2600m/8,530ft

Albion Base

The Canyons

The fourth biggest ski area in the US and still growing, with a small resort developing at the base of the slopes on the edge of Park City

COSTS

① ② ③ ④ ⑤ ⑥

RATINGS

The slopes

Fast lifts	★★★
Snow	★★★★
Extent	★★★
Experts	★★★★
Intermediate	★★★★
Beginner	★★
Convenience	★★★★
Queues	★★★★
Mountain restaurants	★★★

The rest

Scenery	★★★
Resort charm	★★
Off-slope	★★

KEY FACTS

Resort	2075m
	6,800ft
Slopes	2075-3045m
	6,800-9,990ft
Lifts	17
Pistes	3,700 acres
Green	10%
Blue	44%
Black	46%
Snowmaking	
	215 acres

+ Relatively extensive area of slopes for all abilities

+ Modern lift system with few queues

+ Convenient (but soulless) purpose-built resort developing at the base

+ Very easy access to Park City and Deer Valley ski areas

− Snow on the many south-facing slopes affected by sun

− Many runs are short

− Few green runs suitable for those progressing from nursery slopes

− Resort village limited for après-ski, dining and off-slope diversions

The Canyons has the potential to become the most extensive ski area in the US (and already claims it is the fourth biggest). It has eight linked mountains, and anyone having a holiday in Park City should plan to spend some time here. Whether it makes sense to stay in the village at the base is another question.

THE RESORT

The Canyons has been transformed over the past decade or so. The area of the slopes has been doubled, and a car-free village at the base now has a few shops, some restaurants and some bars as well as accommodation (although there is still quite a lot of building going on).

Staying at the base is convenient, but the village isn't a very appealing place to spend time – it lacks character and soul – and we would much rather stay in the centre of Park City. Regular shuttle-buses run to the car park below the village from which you get a cabriolet lift up to the village (beware: this lift shuts at 5.30pm; after that you need to catch a resort bus down).

THE MOUNTAINS

The Canyons gets its name from the valleys between the eight mountains that make up the ski area.

Slopes Red Pine Lodge, at the heart of the slopes, is reached by an eight-seat gondola from the village. From here you can move in either direction across a series of ridges and valleys. Runs come off both sides of each ridge and generally face north or south. Most runs finish on the valley floors, with some long, quite flat run-outs, which make the areas feel somehow poorly linked with quite short runs. The core of the lift system either side of Red Pine Lodge consists of fast quads, but the left-hand third of the trail map has no fast lifts. If you return to the resort from the Sun Lodge area, you need to take the Towin rope tow, which some reporters

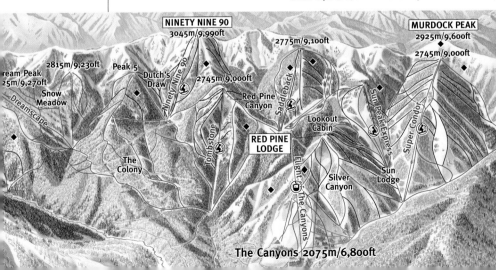

The Canyons 2075m/6,800ft

↑ The base area is developing but still soulless; we find it difficult to warm to it or the slopes

SNOWPIX.COM / CHRIS GILL

Weekly news updates and resort links at www.wtss.co.uk

NEWS

For 2008/09 a new fixed-grip quad is due to be built from the base of the Tombstone lift towards the Dream area, mainly to access housing. The grooming fleet will be increased by 25% and snowmaking will be increased by 20%.

For 2007/08 glading took place in Phantasm Woods near the new Dreamcatcher quad.

UK PACKAGES

AmeriCan Ski, Ski Dream, Ski Safari, Skitracer, Skiworld, United Vacations

Central reservations
Call 1 866 604 4171 (toll-free from within the US)
Phone numbers
From distant parts of the US, add the prefix 1 435; from abroad, add the prefix +1 435

TOURIST OFFICE

t 649 5400
info@thecanyons.com
www.thecanyons.com

find awkward: 'hard to grab the handles, impossible to put behind thighs, and you still have to walk uphill at the top'. Free daily mountain tours start at 10.30, and there's a First Tracks programme where former Olympic medallists guide you around the slopes before they officially open.

Terrain parks There are six natural half-pipes (marked on the trail map). The main terrain park is on Upper and Lower Respect trails, served by the Sun Peak chair, and includes a super-pipe, jumps and rails. The beginners' Progression park is just above here.

Snow reliability Snow here is not the best in Utah. It gets as much on average as Park City (350 inches) and more than Deer Valley. But the south-facing slopes suffer in late-season sun.

Experts There is steep terrain all over the mountain. We particularly liked the north-facing runs off Ninety Nine 90, with steep double-black-diamond runs plunging down through the trees. We had a great time here on our 2008 visit with fresh tracks everywhere after fresh snow. A short hike from the top accesses some fine powder descents even days after a snowfall. There is also lots of double-diamond terrain on Murdock Peak (a 20-minute hike from the Super Condor lift). Runs off the Peak 5 chair are more sheltered.

Intermediates There are groomed blue runs for intermediates on all the main sectors except Ninety Nine 90. Some are quite short, but you can switch from valley to valley for added interest. From the Super Condor and Tombstone fast chairs there are excellent double-blue-square runs. The Dreamscape area can be blissfully quiet, and is great for experiments off-piste to play in powder. Getting back from here you ski through The Colony

– a development of huge £5 million homes for the super-rich.

Beginners There are good areas with magic carpets up at Red Pine Lodge. But the run you progress to is rather short and gets very busy. Better to learn elsewhere.

Snowboarding Except for the flat run-outs from many runs, it's a great area, with lots of natural hits. Canis Lupis is a mile-long, natural half-pipe with high banked walls and numerous obstacles – like riding a bobsleigh course.

Cross-country There are prepared trails on the Park City golf course (20km/12 miles) and the Homestead Resort course (18km/11 miles).

Queues The gondola can be busy at peak times. And a recent reporter complained of queues for the key Tombstone fast chair.

Mountain restaurants The Red Pine Lodge is a large, attractive building with a busy, but 'efficient' cafeteria, a table-service restaurant and big deck. Reporters found the Sun Lodge and small Dreamscape Grill 'much quieter and more relaxing'. The Lookout Cabin has wonderful views, and we've had excellent table-service food there.

Schools and guides As well as group and 'good' private lessons, there are special clinics. Children's classes are for ages 4 to 14.

Facilities for children There's day care in the Grand Summit Hotel for children from six weeks to six years.

STAYING THERE

How to go Accommodation at the resort village is still fairly limited.

Hotels The luxurious Grand Summit and the Silverado Lodge both have a pool and hot tub.

Apartments The Sundial Lodge condos are in the resort village, with a rooftop hot tub and plunge pool.

Eating out The Cabin restaurant, in the Grand Summit, serves eclectic US cuisine; Smokie's in the village is more casual. There is a Viking yurt for 'gourmet' dining after a snowcat sleigh ride, and the Red Pine Lodge does a Western BBQ on Saturdays with a C&W band and dancing.

Après-ski The Cabin Lounge in the Grand Summit has live entertainment, and Smokie's is good for après-ski.

Off the slopes There's snowshoeing, dog sledding, hot-air ballooning, a factory outlet mall and Salt Lake City and Park City nearby.

Deer Valley

Top of the Ivy League of US ski resorts: it promises, and delivers, the best ski and gastronomic experience – we love it

COSTS

① ② ③ ④ ⑤ ⑥

RATINGS

The slopes

Fast lifts	★★★★
Snow	★★★★
Extent	★★
Expert	★★★
Intermediate	★★★★
Beginner	★★★★
Convenience	★★★★
Queues	★★★★
Mountain restaurants	★★★★

The rest

Scenery	★★★
Resort charm	★★★
Off-slope	★★

NEWS

For 2008/09 Cushing's Cabin at the top of Flagstaff Mountain is due to be replaced with a new cabin that will seat 40-45 guests. And Empire Canyon Lodge will be revamped to create more seating upstairs. The snowmaking from the base to the top of Carpenter and Silver Lake Express lifts is due to be improved. The piste grooming fleet will be upgraded again.

For 2007/08, a new fast quad, the Lady Morgan Express, was built in the Empire Canyon area. And a new 200-acre area, including a 65-acre gladed sector and nine new runs (ranging from beginner to expert) were added there.

Eleven fast quads whisk you efficiently throughout the ski area →

- ➕ Immaculate piste grooming, good snow record and lots of snow-guns
- ➕ Good tree skiing
- ➕ Brilliant free black-diamond tours
- ➕ Many fast lifts and no queues
- ➕ Good mid-mountain restaurants (and accommodation)
- ➕ Next to Park City and The Canyons

- ➖ Relatively expensive
- ➖ Small area of slopes
- ➖ Mostly short runs of less than 400m/1,310ft vertical
- ➖ Quiet at night – though Park City is right next door

Deer Valley prides itself on pampering its guests, with valets to unload your skis, gourmet dining, immaculately groomed slopes, limited numbers on the mountain – and no snowboarding. But it also has some excellent slopes, with interesting terrain for all abilities, including plenty of ungroomed stuff.

The slopes of Deer Valley and Park City are separated by nothing more than a fence, but it seems likely to be permanent, given Deer Valley's ethos. Any skier visiting the area should try both; for most people, Park City is the obvious base – but there are some seductive hotels here at mid-mountain Silver Lake.

THE RESORT

Just a mile from the end of Park City's Main Street, Deer Valley is overtly upmarket – famed for the care and attention lavished on both slopes and guests. But it remains unpretentious.

There is no village as such. The lodgings – luxurious chalets and swanky hotels – are scattered around.

THE MOUNTAINS

The slopes are varied and interesting. Deer Valley's reputation for immaculate grooming is justified ('the best I have ever seen', says a recent reporter) but there is also a lot of exciting tree skiing – and some steep bump runs, too. There are free mountain tours for

different standards. We went on two three-hour black-diamond tours in 2008, and they were both brilliant, taking us through fresh powder in the trees that we would never have found on our own. The leader of one was an airline pilot five days a week and a guide at Deer Valley for two (not a bad life!). Reporters praise these tours, too. There's a First Tracks tour at 8am.

Slopes There are fast quads everywhere. Two alternative ones take you up to Bald Eagle Mountain, just beyond which is the mid-mountain focus of Silver Lake Lodge. You can ski from here to the isolated Little Baldy Peak, served by a gondola and a quad chairlift, with mainly easy runs to serve property developments there. But the main skiing is on three linked peaks beyond Silver Lake Lodge – Bald Mountain, Flagstaff Mountain and Empire Canyon – all served by fast quads (nine in total). The top of Empire is just a few metres from the runs of the Park City ski area.

Terrain parks The TNT (Tricks 'n' Turns) park on Empire Canyon offers rails, jumps and boxes.

Snow reliability As you'd expect in Utah, snow reliability is excellent, and there's plenty of snowmaking too.

Experts Despite the image of pampered luxury there is excellent expert terrain on all three main mountains, including fabulous glades,

KEY FACTS

Resort	2195m
	7,200ft
Slopes	2000-2915m
	6,570-9,570ft
Lifts	22
Pistes	2,026 acres
Green	24%
Blue	43%
Black	33%
Snowmaking	
	560+ acres

UK PACKAGES

AmeriCan Ski, Ski Dream, Ski Independence, Ski Safari, Skitracer

Central reservations Call 645 6538.

Phone numbers From distant parts of the US, add 1 435; from abroad, add the prefix +1 435

TOURIST OFFICE

t 649 1000
skierservices@
deervalley.com
www.deervalley.com

bumps, chutes and bowls. And the snow doesn't get skied out quickly. The Ski Utah Interconnect Tour to Alta starts here (see the Park City chapter).
Intermediates There are lots of superbly groomed blue runs.
Beginners There are nursery slopes at Silver Lake Lodge as well as the base, and gentle green runs to progress to.
Snowboarding Boarding is banned.
Cross-country There are prepared trails on the Park City and Homestead Resort golf courses and lots of scope for backcountry trips.
Queues Waiting in lift lines is not something that Deer Valley wants its guests to experience, so it limits the number of lift tickets sold.
Mountain restaurants The best in Utah. There are attractive wood-and-glass self-service places at both Silver Lake (delicious lamb stew and turkey chilli on our 2008 visit) and the base lodge. The grill restaurant at Empire Canyon Lodge is consistently recommended, and the tiny Deer Crest Gondola grill on Little Baldy Peak is 'great for burgers and views'. For a bit of a treat, try the Stein Eriksen Lodge (including an excellent, good value, all-you-can-eat buffet), the Goldener Hirsch or the Royal Street Café table-service restaurant at Silver Lake Lodge.
Schools and guides The ski school is doubtless excellent, and booking is essential. Telemark lessons are

available. The Mahre Training Center (run by Olympian brothers Steve and Phil) is based here.
Facilities for children The Children's Center gives parents complimentary pagers. It accepts children aged between 2 months and 12 years.

STAYING THERE

How to go A car is useful for visiting other nearby Utah resorts, though Deer Valley, Park City and The Canyons are all linked by efficient shuttle-buses.
Hotels The Stein Eriksen Lodge and the Goldener Hirsch are two of the plushest hotels in any ski resort.
Apartments There are many luxury apartments and houses to rent.
Eating out Of the gourmet restaurants, the Mariposa is the best. The all-you-can-eat Seafood Buffet (it's not just seafood) is also recommended, 'despite its high cost'. We really enjoyed a 'Fireside Dining' evening at the Empire Canyon Lodge: four courses, each one served at a different fireplace. It's held three nights a week.
Après-ski The Lounge of the Snow Park Lodge at the base area is the main après-ski venue, with live music. Then there's Main Street in Park City.
Off the slopes Park City has lots of shops, galleries etc. Salt Lake City has concerts, sights and shopping. Balloon rides and snowmobiling are popular.

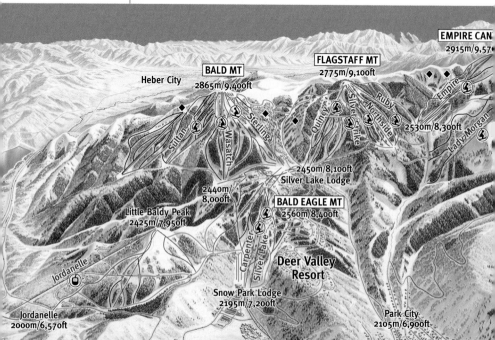

Park City

Stay near the cute and lively old Main Street and visit the three local mountains plus some further afield for a varied holiday

NEWS

For 2008/09 the Ski Team double is due to be replaced with a new fast Crescent quad. It will go from the base to the top of King Con Ridge and should relieve pressure on the Pay Day lift at the base area.

For 2007/08 a new gladed area – Motherlode Meadows – was made between the Motherlode and Thaynes chairs, and a new blue run was created off McConkey's chair to give less confident intermediates an alternative way down McConkey's Bowl.

Park City is a large sprawling place but with three good ski areas locally; that's Park City Mountain Resort on the right and Deer Valley in the distance →

- ➕ Entertaining, historic Main Street, convenient for slopes
- ➕ Lots of bars and restaurants make nonsense of Utah's Mormon image
- ➕ Easy to visit other resorts – Deer Valley and The Canyons (covered by area pass) are effectively suburbs

- ➖ Away from Main Street, town is an enormous sprawl and lacks charm
- ➖ Most lodgings involve driving or bussing to Main Street and slopes
- ➖ Runs tend to be rather short
- ➖ Snowfall record comes nowhere near that of Alta, Snowbird et al

Park City has clear attractions, particularly if you ignore its sprawling suburbs and stay near the centre to make the most of the lively bars and restaurants in Main Street. And it's an excellent base for touring other resorts – notably next-door Deer Valley and The Canyons, both covered by the Three Resort Pass.

Deer Valley is separated from Park City's slopes by a fence between two pistes, and by separate ownership with different objectives. They could be linked by removing the fence – but it stays in place. To European eyes, all very strange. The Canyons is only a little further away, and reached by free buses.

Then there are the famously powdery resorts of Snowbird and Alta, less than an hour away by car or bus. Even the Olympic downhill slopes of Snowbasin are within easy reach by car (and by special privately run buses).

THE RESORT

Park City is about 45 minutes by road from Salt Lake City. It was born with the discovery of silver in 1872. By the turn of the century the town boasted a population of 10,000, a red-light area, a Chinese quarter and 27 saloons.

Careful restoration has left the town with a splendid historic centrepiece in Main Street, now lined by a colourful selection of art galleries, boutiques, bars and restaurants, many quite smart. New buildings have been tastefully designed to blend in smoothly. But away from the centre (where most of the lodging is) the resort is an amorphous sprawl and still expanding. Traffic congestion can be bad, especially at weekends.

The slow Town chairlift (no safety bars) goes up to the slopes from Main Street, but the main lifts are on the fringes at Resort Base; there are lodgings out there.

Deer Valley, The Canyons and Park City are linked by free shuttle-buses, which also go around town and run until fairly late. 'Get a map,' says a recent reporter, 'as they are on a loop system and can be confusing at first.' We found it a pain waiting for buses

KEY FACTS

Resort	2105m
	6,900ft
Slopes	2105-3050m
	6,900-10,000ft
Lifts	15
Pistes	3,300 acres
Green	17%
Blue	50%
Black	33%
Snowmaking	
	475 acres

on our 2008 visit (especially if we wanted to go back to the hotel to drop our skis and boots off and then go straight back to Main Street to visit the shops or bars). A car is useful (especially for visiting other ski areas as well as the three local ones).

If you're not hiring a car, pick a location that's handy for Main Street and the Town chair or the free bus.

THE MOUNTAIN

Park City Mountain Resort consists mostly of blue and black trails cut through the trees on the flanks of rounded mountain ridges, with easier runs running along the ridges and the valleys between. The more interesting terrain is in the lightly wooded bowls and ridges at the top.

THE SLOPES
Bowls above the woods
Two fast chairlifts (one new for

2008/09) whisk you up from Resort Base, and others beyond those take you up to Summit House, the main mountain restaurant. Most of the easy and intermediate runs lie between Summit House and the base area, and are spread along the sides of a series of interconnecting ridges. Virtually all the steep terrain is above Summit House in a series of ungroomed bowls, and accessed by the McConkey's six-pack and the old Jupiter double chair.

Reporters have enjoyed the 'excellent' free mountain history tours of the slopes – looking at the area's silver mining heritage – that take place at 11am every day. A long floodlit intermediate run and a beginner run are open until 7.30pm. A map of groomed trails is available every day.

TERRAIN PARKS
Among the best in the world
There are four terrain parks here to suit all levels. The vast number of kickers, rails and pipes are maintained daily, and rank among the best in the world. Jonesy's park, located under the Bonanza lift, features a slew of pro-standard jumps and rails for advanced riders only. The Pick 'N' Shovel park, accessible via the Three Kings lift, is the beginner park and features six jumps and 20 rails and fun boxes. The King's Crown park, on the northern slope overlooking the resort, is of intermediate standard with kickers, newly renovated rails and butter boxes. New in 2007/08 were a quarter-transfer feature and Ball Tap, which is a giant bowling ball shaped jib. The Eagle super-pipe that was used for the 2002 Winter Olympics is consistently one of the finest-shaped pipes in the world. And the Pay Day jib park, along the Pay Day run, opens until 7.30pm with a host of lit rails and boxes.

SNOW RELIABILITY
Not quite the greatest on Earth
Utah is famous for the quality and quantity of its snow. Park City's record doesn't match those of Snowbird and Alta, but an annual average of 350 inches is still impressive, and ahead of most Colorado figures. Snowmaking covers about 15% of the terrain.

FOR EXPERTS
Lots of variety
There is a lot of excellent advanced and expert terrain at the top of the lift system. It is all marked as double

LIFT PASSES

Park City

Prices in US$

Age	1-day	6-day
under 13	50	264
13 to 64	79	438
over 65	50	264

Free under 7

Beginner no deals

Notes

Covers all lifts in Park City Mountain Resort, with ski-bus; 6-day prices are advance-purchase prices; additional discounts if purchased in advance with lodging

Alternative passes

Three Resort International Pass covering Park City, The Canyons and Deer Valley available through selected tour operators (around $395 for 6 days)

boarding

It was not until 1996, when Park City won its Olympic bid, that the resort lifted its ban on snowboarding. Since then it has steamrollered ahead to attract the snowboarding community by building some of the best terrain parks in the world. And Park City has some great ungroomed terrain as well: the higher bowls offer treelined powder runs and great kicker-building spots. Beginners will have no trouble on the lower slopes, all serviced by fast chairlifts. But beware: at weekends and peak season it can get very crowded, especially in the terrain parks. In addition one reporter said that the intermediate freeride clinics advertised on the official website 'weren't actually available'.

diamond on the trail map, but there are many runs that deserve only a single-diamond rating – so don't be put off. The prettily wooded McConkey's Bowl, served by a six-pack and offering a range of open pitches and gladed terrain, 'has a mountain feel and is always quiet', says a 2008 visitor. We've had some great runs here on each of our visits. The slow, old Jupiter lift accesses the highest bowls, which include some serious terrain – with narrow couloirs, cliffs and cornices – as well as easier wide-open slopes. We had some more enjoyable runs though fresh snow in lightly wooded terrain by heading right at the top of the lift, then skiing down before hiking became necessary. But if you are prepared to hike, you can find fresh powder most of the time – turn left for West Face, Pioneer Ridge and

Puma Bowl, right for Scott's Bowl and the vast expanse of Pinecone Ridge, stretching literally for miles down the side of Thaynes Canyon.

Lower down, the side of Summit House ridge, serviced by the Thaynes and Motherlode chairs, has some little-used black runs, plus a few satisfying trails in the trees. There's a zone of steep runs towards town from further round the ridge. And don't miss Blueslip Bowl near Summit House – so called because in the past when it was out of bounds, ski company employees caught skiing it were fired, and given their notice on a blue slip.

Good skiers (no snowboarders, due to some long flat run-outs) should not miss the Utah Interconnect – see feature panel. Park City Powder Cats offers snowcat skiing and Wasatch Powderbird Guides heli-skiing.

Park City

633

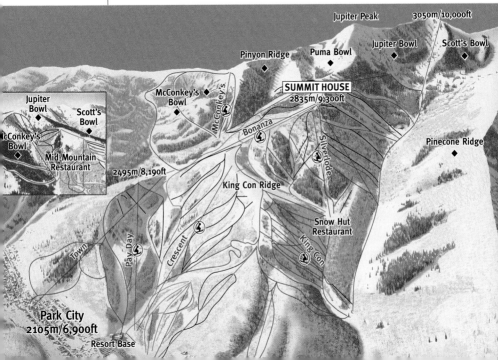

SCHOOLS

Park City
t 1 800 227 2754

Classes
1 3hr day $75
Private lessons
$125 for 1hr

CHILDREN

Signature 3
(run by ski school)
t 1 800 227 2754
Ages 3 to 5;
$155 per day,
includes ski tuition,
lunch (max class size
is 3)
Guardian Angel
t 783 2662
Babysitting service

Ski school
The school offers
classes for ages 6 to
14, 9am-3pm, $199
per day including
lunch (max class size
is 5)

UK PACKAGES

All America Holidays,
Alpine Answers,
AmeriCan Ski, American
Ski Classics, Crystal,
Crystal Finest,
Independent Ski Links,
Momentum, Ski
Activity, Ski Dream, Ski
Independence, Ski Line,
Ski Safari, Ski
Solutions, Skitracer,
Skiworld, United
Vacations, Virgin Snow

FOR INTERMEDIATES
OK for a day or two

There are blue runs served by all the main lifts, apart from Jupiter (the blue Jupiter Access is worth a go though, even if you don't ride the chair, for the sight of people coming down the chutes). The areas around the King Con high-speed quad and Silverlode high-speed six-pack have a dense network of great (but fairly short) cruising runs. There are also more difficult trails close by, for those looking for a challenge.

But there are few long, fast cruising runs – most trails are around 1 to 2km/0.5 to 1 mile, and many have long, flat run-outs. The Pioneer and McConkey's chairlifts are off the main drag and serve some very pleasant, often quiet runs. The runs under the Town lift have great views of the town.

FOR BEGINNERS
A good chance for fast progress

Novices start on short lifts and a beginners' area near the base lodge. Classes graduate up the hill quite quickly, and there's a good, gentle and wide 'easiest way down' – the three-and-a-half-mile Home Run – clearly marked all the way from Summit House. It's easy enough for most to manage after only a few lessons. The Town chair can be ridden down.

FOR CROSS-COUNTRY
Some trails; lots of backcountry

There are prepared trails on both the Park City golf course (20km/12 miles), next to the downhill area, and the Homestead Resort course (18km/11 miles), just out of town. There is lots of scope for backcountry trips.

QUEUES
Peak period crowds

It can get pretty crowded (on some trails as well as the lifts) at weekends and in high season. The Pay Day lift from Resort Base had big queues for much of the time on both days we visited in 2008. But the new fast quad (see 'News') should ease this problem. With a pass for five days or more, the Fast Track system means you can jump the queues on five main lifts.

MOUNTAIN RESTAURANTS
Standard self-service stuff

The Mid-Mountain Lodge is a picturesque 19th-century mine building which was heaved up the mountain to its present location near the bottom of Pioneer chair. The food is standard self-service fare ('lovely clam chowder') but most reporters have preferred it to the alternatives; but note that Vince Donile, who has run it for the last 20 years, has retired and that the resort will operate it from 2008/09. The Summit House is cafe-style – serving chilli, pizza, soup and 'good hot chocolate'. The Snow Hut, a 'cosier' log building that usually has an outdoor grill gets good reviews from reporters. 5-Way Cafe is a coffee house in a yurt (tent) halfway down the Bonanza chairlift. There are more options down at Resort Base ('a delicious salad bar and top-quality fresh fish', said a recent reporter).

SCHOOLS AND GUIDES
Good reports

A recent reporter's husband had a good private lesson – 'the instructor tried to take him to as much of the scarce powder as possible'. We continue to receive positive reports of snowboard lessons: 'tuition the best I've had, but over $120 an hour for private lessons', says a 2008 visitor. 'Excellent', said the daughter of a recent reporter, who was given a detailed record of her achievements in a small two-day class and was riding blue runs by the end.

THE UTAH INTERCONNECT

Good skiers prepared to do some hiking should consider this excellent guided backcountry tour that runs four days a week from Deer Valley to Snowbird. (Three days a week it runs from Snowbird, but only as far as Solitude.) When we did it (a few years back, starting from Park City) we got fresh tracks in knee-deep powder practically all day. After a warm-up run to weed out weak skiers, we went up the top chair, through a 'closed' gate in the area boundary and skied down a deserted, prettily wooded valley to Solitude. After taking the lifts to the top of Solitude we did a short traverse/walk, then down more virgin powder towards Brighton. After more powder runs and lunch back in Solitude, it was up the lifts and a 30-minute hike up the Highway to Heaven to north-facing, treelined slopes and a great little gully down into Alta. How much of Alta and Snowbird you get to ski depends on how much time is left. The price ($250) includes two guides, lunch, lift tickets and transport home.

FACILITIES FOR CHILDREN
Well organised
There are a number of licensed carers. The ski school takes children from age three and a half. Book in advance.

STAYING THERE

HOW TO GO
Packaged independence
We prefer to stay near Main Street and its bars and restaurants, but most accommodation is in the sprawling suburbs. These, such as Kimball Junction, are convenient and cheap (but soulless) if you have a car and want to try different resorts daily.
Hotels There's a wide variety, from typical chains to individual little B&Bs.
*****Park City (200 2000) Swanky all-suite place on outskirts, better placed for golf than skiing. Pool, sauna.
***Park City Peaks (649 5000) Decent rooms, 'service and prices of meals good', indoor-outdoor pool and 'fab hot tub', but out of town. We stayed here in 2008 and thought it adequate.
***Yarrow (649 7000) Adequate, charmless base, a 15-minute walk from Main Street. Pool, hot tub. 'The service is good, staff friendly and helpful.'
Silver King (649 5500) De luxe hotel/condo complex at base of the slopes, with indoor-outdoor pool.
Washington School Inn (649 3800) 'Absolutely excellent' historic inn with 'fantastic service', say reporters. In a great location near Main Street.
Best Western Landmark Inn (649 7300) At Kimball Junction. Pool.
Chateau Apres Lodge (649 9372) Near the slopes: comfortable, faded, cheap.
Apartments There's a big range. The Townlift studios near Main Street and Park Avenue condos are both modern and comfortable, and the latter has a pool and hot tubs. Silver Cliff Village is adjacent to the slopes and has spacious units and access to the facilities of the Silver King Hotel. Blue Church Lodge is a well-converted

19th-century Mormon church with luxury condos and rooms.

EATING OUT
Lots of choice
There are over 100 restaurants. Our favourites are Wahso (Asian fusion), 350 Main (new American) and Riverhorse – in a grand, high-ceilinged first-floor room with live music. Zoom is the old Union Pacific train depot, now a trendy restaurant owned by Robert Redford (we've had mixed reports – from 'our best meal' to 'mediocre and overpriced'). Chez Betty is small with 'excellent food' – expensive though. Other reporter recommendations include Fuego Bistro & Pizzeria, Cisero's and Grappa (Italian), Chimayo ('south-western-with-a-twist'), Bangkok Thai, Wasatch Brew Pub ('good steaks', 'best value'), Squatters (a micro brewery, out of town a bit; 'good atmosphere'), Bandit's Grill ('good value'), the 'excellent' Eating Establishment, No Name Saloon ('brill buffalo burgers') and Butcher's Chop House ('great prime rib and steaks'). There are lots of Tex-Mex places: Zona Rosa and El Chubasco have been praised. See Deer Valley for other options.

APRÈS-SKI
Better than you might think
As the slopes close, Legends is the place to head for at Resort Base. Pig Pen in the ice skating plaza was recommended by a reporter. The Bad Ass Coffee Shop in town is highly rated. The Wasatch Brew Pub makes its own ale. JB Mulligans, O'Shuck's and No Name Saloon are lively, and there's usually live music and dancing at weekends. For clubs, try Harry O's and Cisero's.

OFF THE SLOPES
Some things of interest
There's a factory outlet mall at Kimball Junction. Backcountry snowmobiling, balloon flights and trips to Nevada for gambling are popular. You can learn to ski jump or try the Olympic bob track at the Olympic Park down the road. There's Robert Redford's Sundance Film Festival in January and a 10-day Winterfest celebration of the 2002 Olympics in February. There are lots of shops and galleries. Salt Lake City is easily reached and has some good concerts, shopping and Mormon heritage sites.

Snowbird

A powder-pig paradise linked to neighbouring Alta; with big concrete and glass base buildings that remind us of Flaine

COSTS

① ② ③ ④ ⑤ ⑥

RATINGS

The slopes
Fast lifts	★★★
Snow	★★★★★
Extent	★★★
Expert	★★★★★
Intermediate	★★★
Beginner	★★
Convenience	★★★★★
Queues	★★★
Mountain restaurants	★

The rest
Scenery	★★★
Resort charm	★
Off-slope	★

NEWS

For 2007/08 part of Chip's Run (a blue that runs from top to bottom of the mountain) was remodelled to make it more intermediate-friendly, and more snowmaking was installed so that this run now has top-to-bottom coverage. Work began on a 5-star condominium development – it is scheduled for completion for 2010/11.

636

UK PACKAGES

All America Holidays, Alpine Answers, AmeriCan Ski, American Ski Classics, Ski Activity, Ski Dream, Ski Independence, Ski Safari, Skitracer, Skiworld, United Vacations

---

- ➕ Quantity and quality of powder snow unrivalled
- ➕ Link to Alta makes one of the largest ski areas in the US
- ➕ Fabulous ungroomed slopes, with steep and not-so-steep options
- ➕ Slopes-at-the-door convenience

- ➖ Limited groomed runs for intermediates
- ➖ Tiny, claustrophobic resort 'village'
- ➖ Stark concrete Bauhaus architecture
- ➖ Mainly slow chairlifts
- ➖ Very quiet at night

There can be few places where nature has combined the steep with the deep better than at Snowbird and next-door Alta. The two resorts' combined area is one of the top powder-pig paradises in the world. So it is a shame that Snowbird's concrete, purpose-built 'base village' is so lacking in charm and ski resort ambience. Boarders are banned from Alta's slopes and therefore cannot take advantage of the link.

THE RESORT

Snowbird lies 40km/25 miles from Salt Lake City in Little Cottonwood Canyon – just before Alta. The setting is rugged and rather Alpine – and both the resort and (particularly) the approach road are prone to avalanches and closure: visitors are sometimes confined indoors for safety. The resort buildings are mainly block-like – but they provide ski-in/ski-out lodging.

The resort area and the slopes are spread along the road on the south side of the narrow canyon. The focal Snowbird Center (lift base/shops/restaurants) is towards the eastern, up-canyon end. All lodgings are within walking distance. There are shuttle-buses, with a service to Alta.

THE MOUNTAINS

Snowbird's link with Alta forms one of the largest ski areas in the US.
Slopes The north-facing slopes rear up from the edge of the resort. Six access lifts are ranged along the valley floor, the main ones being the 125-person cable car (the Aerial Tram) to Hidden Peak, the Peruvian Express quad and the Gadzoom fast quad. To the west, in Gad Valley, there are runs ranging from very tough to nice and easy. Mineral Basin, on the back of Hidden Peak, offers 500 acres of terrain for all abilities, but can be badly affected by sun. One of the two fast quads there forms the link with Alta. There are free mountain tours at 9am and 10.30 each

day – 'it was quite adventurous, taking some of us down double-black-diamond territory at one point', says a 2008 visitor. The nursery slopes are floodlit three evenings a week.
Terrain parks There is one for all levels, containing rails, hits and a box, plus a 100m/330ft super-pipe.
Snow reliability Snowbird and Alta average 500 inches of snowfall a year – twice as much as some Colorado resorts and around 50% more than the nearby Park City area. There's snowmaking in busy areas.
Experts The trail map is liberally sprinkled with double-black diamonds, and some of the gullies off the Cirque ridge – Silver Fox and Great Scott, for example – are exceptionally steep and frequently neck-deep in powder. Lower down lurk the bump runs, including Mach Schnell – a great run straight down the fall line through trees. There is wonderful ski-anywhere terrain in the bowl beneath the high Little Cloud chair, and the Gad 2 lift opens up attractive tree runs. Fantastic go-anywhere terrain under the High Baldy traverse is controlled by gates. Mineral Basin has more expert terrain. Backcountry tours and heli- and cat-skiing are offered.
Intermediates The winding Chip's Run on the Cirque ridge provides the only comfortable route down from the top. For adventurous intermediates wanting to try powder skiing, the bowl below the Little Cloud lift is a must. There are some challenging runs through the trees off the Gad 2 lift and some nice

↑ Mineral Basin has some enjoyable intermediate cruises and a lift (the one on the right) linking with Alta

SNOWPIX.COM / CHRIS GILL

long cruises in Mineral Basin. But the groomed runs don't add up to a lot.

Beginners There is a nursery slope next to Cliff Lodge and the Mountain Learning area part-way up the hill. But progression to longer runs is not easy. Beginners should learn elsewhere.

Snowboarding Competent freeriders will have a wild time in Snowbird's powder (though a recent reporter complains of 'flat sticky spots where you have to walk'). Alta bans boarders.

Cross-country No prepared trails.

Queues The big problem has always been the cable car, with queues of up to an hour at times. But the Peruvian Express chair provides an alternative way to the top (via Mineral Basin and then the Mineral Basin Express chair) and seems to have made a big difference, say recent reporters.

Mountain restaurants It's the Mid-Gad Lodge self-service cafeteria or back to one of the bases. The table-service Forklift and Rendezvous have been recommended by reporters.

Schools and guides The school offers a range of lessons and clinics – such as women-only and Big Mountain. A recent visitor was 'highly impressed' with her private lessons.

Facilities for children Camp Snowbird takes children aged six and under. The 'kids ski free' programme allows children (six and under) to ski for free with an adult ($15 a day for the Tram).

STAYING THERE

How to go A few UK tour operators feature Snowbird.

Hotels There are several lodges and smaller condo blocks. Cliff Lodge is a huge concrete hotel with renovated rooms, but is generally depressing; the rooftop pool and spa facilities cost $20 a day extra. The Lodge at Snowbird was recently renovated. Reporters tell of 'friendly but amateurish staff' in both places.

Eating out Cliff Lodge and Snowbird Center are the focal points. The 'fine dining' Aerie in the Cliff Lodge gets mixed reviews. Readers recommend the Steak Pit in Snowbird Center.

Après-ski Après-ski is a bit muted. The Tram Club and El Chanate Cantina are lively as the slopes close. But a recent visitor had a problem getting a drink at all, and another complained that many places close early.

Off the slopes Apart from spas in the various lodges, there's ice skating, ice climbing, snowshoeing, snowmobiling.

Snowbird

637

Rest of the West

This section contains detailed chapters on just two resorts – Jackson Hole and Big Sky. Below are notes on these and various other resorts in different parts of the great Rocky Mountain chain that stretches from Montana and Idaho down through Wyoming and Colorado to New Mexico.

Sun Valley, Idaho, was America's first purpose-built resort, developed in the 1930s by the president of the Union Pacific Railway. It quickly became popular with the Hollywood movie set and has managed to retain its stylish image and ambience; it has one of our favourite luxury hotels.

Also in Idaho is America's newest purpose-built resort – **Tamarack**, at McCall (two hours north of Boise). The resort opened in December 2004 and now has seven lifts, including three fast quads, serving 1,100 skiable acres and 855m/2,800ft vertical. Tamarack gets more snow than Sun Valley (300+ inches on average), and it still gets a lot of sun. An American reader reports: 'Tamarack skis like a mountain that has been open 20 years or more. Great top-to-bottom fall line cruising with bowls and glades at the top of the lifts.' There is a super-pipe and two terrain parks. A Village Plaza is being built, with cafes, shops, galleries and condos (completion scheduled for 2009). Current lodging options include hotel rooms, condos and chalets. A Fairmont hotel is on its way.

Jackson Hole in Wyoming is a resort with an impressive snow record and equally impressive steep slopes. Jackson is the nearest there is to a town with a genuine Wild West cowboy atmosphere. A 90-minute drive (or slower excursion buses) from Jackson over the Teton pass brings you to **Grand Targhee**, which gets even

more snow. The slopes are usually blissfully empty, and much easier than at Jackson. The main Fred's Mountain offers 1,500 acres and 610m/2,000ft vertical accessed from a central fast quad. One-third of smaller Peaked Mountain is accessed by a fast quad, while the rest – over 1,000 acres – is used for guided snowcat skiing.

About four hours north of Jackson, just inside Montana, is **Big Sky** (not to be confused with Big Mountain, away to the north), with the biggest ski area and one of the biggest verticals in the US (1280m/4,200ft). We visited in 2006, and were very impressed – particularly by the lack of crowds. From Big Sky you might visit **Bridger Bowl**, a 90-minute drive away. It boasts broad, steep, lightly wooded slopes that offer wonderful powder descents after a fresh snowfall.

A long way south of all these resorts, **Taos** in New Mexico is the most southerly major resort in America, and because of its isolation it is largely unknown on the international market. Until last March, snowboarding was banned but it is now allowed. There's a small chalet-style base village with a handful of lodges; the adobe town of Taos, home to many famous artists and writers over the years, is 29km/18 miles down the road. There's some good terrain for all standards but the ski area is best known for steep, challenging terrain, some of which you have to hike to.

This is Moonlight Basin, whose slopes are linked to Big Sky to form the biggest ski area in the US ➜

Big Sky

Now America's biggest linked ski area, with extraordinarily quiet slopes; unappealing modern resort village, though

COSTS

① ② ③ ④ ⑤ ⑥

RATINGS

The slopes
Fast lifts	★★★
Snow	★★★★★
Extent	★★★★
Expert	★★★★
Intermediate	★★★★
Beginner	★★★★★
Convenience	★★★★
Queues	★★★★★
Mountain restaurants	★

The rest
Scenery	★★★
Resort charm	★
Off-slope	★★

NEWS

For 2008/09 access to the Swift Current area is due to be improved.

For 2007/08 Big Sky installed a triple chairlift to serve runs on Lone Mountain's south face, including the recently opened Dakota Territory.

The Village Center building opened at the base.

Flights to Bozeman from within the US have improved, including new direct connections from Denver. This will reduce travelling time from the UK as well.

The gondola is to be replaced by a chondola, but this is unlikely for 2008/09.

➕ Ski area (shared with neighbouring Moonlight Basin) is slightly bigger than Vail, with the bonus of a big vertical by US standards

➕ By far the quietest slopes you will find in a major resort, anywhere

➕ Excellent snow record

➕ Wide range of runs for all abilities, including great expert terrain

➕ Some comfortable slope-side accommodation, but ...

➖ Many condos are spread widely away from the lift base

➖ Base area lacks charm, though things are improving, slowly

➖ Resort amenities are limited, with little choice of nightlife

➖ Tiny top lift accessing the most testing terrain is prone to queues

➖ Remote location

Big Sky is renowned for its powder, steeps and big vertical. Since the resort buried the hatchet with next-door Moonlight Basin and agreed a joint lift pass, the two of them have been able to boast the biggest linked ski area in the US. They should also be boasting the world's least crowded slopes – we and our reporters have been astonished by the lack of people. Between them, Big Sky and Moonlight get an average of around 2,500 people a day on their slopes. So that's about two acres each.

We have no idea how they make this arrangement work financially. We're happy to take advantage of it while it lasts – and to put up with staying in the seriously flawed resort village. But if ambling around in the evening soaking up the mountain village atmosphere is part of your holiday, forget it.

THE RESORT

Big Sky has been purpose-built at the foot of the slopes on Lone Mountain and Andesite Mountain. The main focus of development is Mountain Village, at the lift base, with three hotels, a handful of bars and restaurants, a variety of shops and some slope-side condos.

But purpose-designed it was not. Mountain Village is a hotchpotch of buildings in different styles set vaguely around a traffic-free central plaza and bordered by car parks and service roads. The French-style underground Mountain Mall has shops and access to many of the bars and restaurants and some of the lodging.

Happily, over the next decade a new pedestrian village will take shape at the base. As a start, the Village Center building opened last season – with lodgings, restaurants and shops. It is stylish, convenient and has created more of a village focus. Some outlying condos and chalets are served by lifts to the slopes, others by free buses.

The resort is set amid the wide open spaces of Montana, one hour from the airport town of Bozeman. Bridger Bowl ski area is an easy day trip by car.

THE MOUNTAINS

Taking Big Sky and Moonlight Basin's slopes together, they cover a big area (5,512 acres) spread over two linked mountains, with long runs for all abilities. There is a gondola and five fast quad chairs, but many of the chairs are still old triples and doubles. There are free mountain tours at both Big Sky and Moonlight. It is cheapest to buy tickets just for the area you are staying in and to buy a Big Sky-Moonlight Interconnect ticket (substantially more expensive) only for days you intend to ski both areas.

THE SLOPES
Deserted terrain for all abilities
Lone Mountain provides the resort's poster shot, with some seriously steep, open upper slopes. From Mountain Village a gondola and a

parallel fast quad go to mid-mountain. From there you can get to the Lone Peak chair, which takes you up to the Lone Peak Tram – two 15-person gondola cabins, operated as if they were a cable car. This leads to the top and fabulous 360° views. The new Dakota triple chairlift serves Lone's south face and its steep bowls and glades. But 2008 reporters on January and March trips found the area prone to closure due to avalanche risk. Lone Mountain's lower slopes are wooded and varied, as are those of **Andesite Mountain**, which has less vertical, but three of the fast lifts, including one from Mountain Village. From various points on Lone Mountain you can head down to the **Moonlight Basin** slopes, which start with a slow chair

from Moonlight Lodge. Runs from the top of that lead to the Six Shooter fast chair which, together with the slow Lone Tree quad near the top, serves nearly all Moonlight's wooded, largely easy intermediate terrain. The Headwaters lift at the top serves expert-only runs.

TERRAIN PARKS
Choose from three
Ambush on Andesite is an advanced park, with big jumps, rails, boxes, slides and half-pipe, served by the Ramcharger fast quad. Lone Mountain has a park and half-pipe by the Swift Current lift and a beginner park by the Pony chair. The Zero Gravity park at Moonlight has boxes, rails, berms and small hits.

KEY FACTS

Resort	2285m
	7,500ft
Slopes	2070-3400m
	6,800-11,150ft
Lifts	21
Pistes	3,812 acres
Green	14%
Blue	26%
Black	60%
Snowmaking	
	350 acres

Note: Big Sky and Moonlight Basin areas combined have 5,812 acres of slopes

LIFT PASSES

Big Sky

Prices in US$

Age	1-day	6-day
under 18	55	330
18 to 69	75	420
over 70	65	390

Free under 11

Beginner first half-day lesson includes lift pass, then costs $25 to continue for the rest of the day

Notes
Covers the lifts in Big Sky; a day pass for Moonlight is $51 for adults

Andesite has great cruising runs, although the vertical isn't huge

ANDESITE
2680m/8,800ft

Southern Comfort

Ramcharger

Thunder Wolf

2070m/6,800ft
Lone Moose Meadows

Mountain Village
2285m/
7,500ft

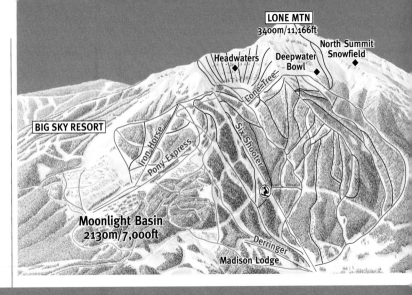

LONE MTN
3400m/11,166ft

North Summit
Snowfield

Headwaters
Deepwater
Bowl

Lone Tree

BIG SKY RESORT

Six Shooter

Iron Horse

Pony Express

Moonlight Basin
2130m/7,000ft

Derringer

Madison Lodge

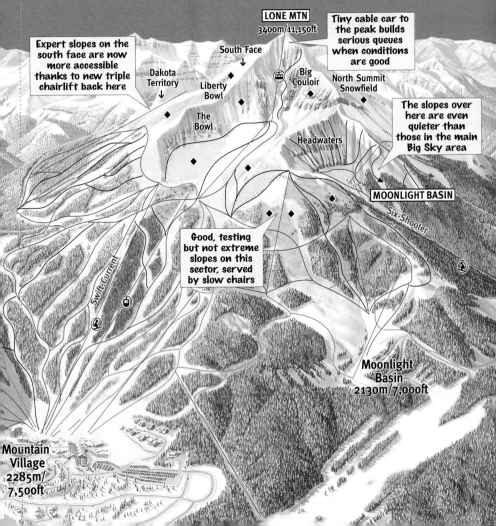

LONE MTN
3400m/11,150ft

Tiny cable car to
the peak builds
serious queues
when conditions
are good

South Face

Dakota
Territory

Liberty
Bowl

Big
Couloir

North Summit
Snowfield

Expert slopes on the
south face are now
more accessible
thanks to new triple
chairlift back here

The Bowl

Headwaters

The slopes over
here are even
quieter than
those in the main
Big Sky area

MOONLIGHT BASIN

Six-Shooter

Good, testing
but not extreme
slopes on this
sector, served
by slow chairs

Swift Current

Moonlight
Basin
2130m/7,000ft

Mountain
Village
2285m/
7,500ft

↑ The new base village is starting to take shape; the tall building is the Summit, this side of it is Snowcrest Lodge and on the left is the new Village Center

TANYA BOOTH

SCHOOLS

Big Sky
t 995 5743

Classes
Half day (2½hr) $64
Private lessons
$235 for 2 hr for 1 to 2 persons

SNOW RELIABILITY
No worries here
Snowfall averages 400+ inches – more than most resorts in Colorado. Grooming is good, too.

FOR EXPERTS
Enough to keep you amused
All of the terrain accessed from the Tram is single- or double-black diamond. The steepest runs are the Big Couloir on the Big Sky side and the North Summit Snowfield on the Moonlight side. For both, you are required to have a partner to ski with, an avalanche transceiver and a shovel. We'd recommend a guide, too. There are easier ways down, though – Liberty Bowl is easiest (stay left for the best snow that the prevailing wind blows in). Marx and Lenin are a little steeper. The Dakota Territory has opened up 212 acres of black-diamond glades, chutes and high bowls, to skier's right of Liberty Bowl – served by a new triple chairlift. Lower down, the Lone Peak Triple, Challenger and Shedhorn chairs also serve good steep terrain. There are some excellent gladed runs, especially on Andesite. In the Moonlight sector the Headwaters is the biggest challenge – but it gets windblown and you may have to pick your way through rocks at the top. The further you hike to skier's left the steeper the couloirs. There are some good gladed runs lower down.

FOR INTERMEDIATES
Great deserted cruising
The bulk of the terrain on both mountains is of intermediate difficulty (including lots of easy blacks). The main complaint we have is that they don't seem to groom any blacks – which means that you can't hurtle down them taking advantage of the lack of people. But there is lots of excellent blue run cruising served by fast chairs and with few others on the runs – Ramcharger and Thunder Wolf on Andesite, Swift Current on Lone Mountain and Six Shooter in the Moonlight sector. Several wide, gentle bowls offer a good introduction to off-piste. And there are some good easy glade runs such as Singlejack on Moonlight and The Congo on Andesite. In general the groomed blues in Moonlight are easier than those in Big Sky, especially the ones served by the Lone Tree chair. Adventurous intermediates could try Liberty Bowl from the top of the Tram; but be prepared for a rocky, windswept traverse between wooden barriers at the top to access the run.

FOR BEGINNERS
Ideal – lots of lovely greens
Go to Big Sky rather than Moonlight. There's a good, recently improved nursery area at the base of the Explorer chair and gondola. There are long, deserted greens to progress to from those lifts and on Andesite ('Sacajewa and Deep South would give timid skiers a real sense of adventure and achievement').

FOR CROSS-COUNTRY
Head for the Ranch
There are 65km/40 miles of trails at Lone Mountain Ranch, and more at West Yellowstone.

QUEUES
Only for the Tram
The tiny Tram still attracts queues on powder days and in peak season. Queues are rare otherwise. But there are still a lot of slow lifts. We hear the gondola has become unreliable – and it has to serve at least another season before replacement.

boarding

The terrain has lots of variety, with few flats. Experts will enjoy the steeps and the glades, freeriders the good terrain parks, and novices the easy cruising runs served by chairlifts. We have a 2008 report of 'excellent' instruction.

CHILDREN

Lone Peak Playhouse
t 995 5847
Ages 6mnth to 8yr;
8.30 to 4.30;
from $80 per day; or
from $127 per day
incl ski school

Ski school
Ages 7 to 14; 9.30 to
3pm; $135 per day

GETTING THERE

Air Bozeman 93km/
58 miles (1hr)

UK PACKAGES

AmeriCan Ski, Ski
Dream, Ski
Independence, Ski
Safari

ACTIVITIES

Indoor Solace Spa
(massage, beauty
treatments), fitness
centres in hotels

Outdoor Snowmobiles,
snowshoeing, sleigh
rides, horse riding, fly
fishing, visiting
Yellowstone National
Park

Central reservations
Call 995 5000; toll-
free number (from
within the US) 1 800
548 4486

Phone numbers
From distant parts of
the US, add the prefix
1 406; from abroad,
add the prefix +1 406

TOURIST OFFICE

Big Sky
t 995 5000
info@bigskyresort.
com
www.bigskyresort.com
Moonlight Basin
t 993 6000
resort@
moonlightbasin.com
www.moonlightbasin.
com

MOUNTAIN RESTAURANTS
Back to base for lunch?
Big Sky's one option is the Pinnacle on Andesite. There's a table-service area, offering the 'standard burgers, stews and grills'; a large terrace and live music at weekends – but little space for drinks-only customers. In Moonlight there's the Headwaters Grill at Madison. Otherwise, it's back to base – the Carabiner Lounge does 'very good homemade soups'.

SCHOOLS AND GUIDES
Good reputation
The Big Sky school has a good reputation and small groups. A 2008 reporter praises beginner snowboard classes: 'friendly, excellent tuition'.

FACILITIES FOR CHILDREN
Usual high US standard
Lone Peak Playhouse in the slope-side Snowcrest Lodge takes children from age six months to eight years and will take them to and from ski school ('perfection', says a reporter). It also operates on Thursday evening, and babysitters are available with 48 hours' notice. Children 10 years and under ski free. There's a Kids' Club in the Huntley Lodge and snow garden at the base. Moonlight has its own care programme and a kids' centre.

STAYING THERE

HOW TO GO
Prepare for a long journey
Only North American specialist tour operators offer Big Sky.
Hotels There's not much choice at the mountain.
***Summit (995 5000) Best in town; central, slope-side, good rooms, outdoor hot pool with mountain views.
***Huntley Lodge (995 5000) Big Sky's original hotel; central, part of Mountain Mall, outdoor pool, hot tubs, sauna. 'Enormous breakfasts.'
***Rainbow Ranch (995 4132) Five miles south of Big Sky. Luxury riverside rooms and cabins. Recommended.
Apartments The good-value Stillwater condos have been recommended, along with Arrowhead, Beaverhead, Snowcrest Lodge, Big Horn and, way out of town, Powder Ridge Cabins.

EATING OUT
A fair choice for a small place
Recommendations include: Huntley Dining Room (smart restaurant, 'huge bowls of pasta'); The Peaks in the Summit for lots of choice; The Cabin (fish and steaks); Bambu (Asian fusion); M.R. Hummers (ribs, prawns, popular with locals); Chet's (giant burgers, sandwiches). Whiskey Jack's is back in town for burgers, beers, 'good Tex-Mex' and 'friendly staff'. Down in the valley Buck's T-4 is popular with carnivores and has 'a phenomenal wine list'. They'll fetch you from your condo. Rainbow Ranch, also in the valley, has been highly recommended for 'fine dining'. Moonlight dinners and live music are available at a backcountry lodge.

APRES-SKI
Limited but entertaining
There are a few places to try; most with regular live music. Chet's bar is 'entertaining', and also has pool. The Carabiner in the Summit and Whiskey Jack's are popular. The Black Bear can be lively, and the basement Alpine Lodge is popular with locals.

OFF THE SLOPES
Mainly the great outdoors
There's snowmobiling, snowshoeing, sleigh rides, a floodlit tubing hill, visiting Yellowstone National Park (highly recommended by a 2008 reporter), treatments at the Solace Spa; the Huntley Lodge pool etc is open to all for a fee.

Moonlight Basin
2135m/7,000ft
There's not much at Moonlight base except a few condos and cabins and the impressive Moonlight Lodge – spacious and log-built, with high ceilings and beams. The bar in the Lodge is lively as the slopes close, and the Timbers restaurant there gets good reviews. But when we visited a couple of years back we were disappointed by the spa, and our nearby condo was poorly maintained. Maybe the Cowboy Heaven Cabins spread up the hillside are better. We had an enjoyable dinner a drive away at what is now the Headwaters Grill, at Madison.

Jackson Hole

Touristy 'Wild West' town, big, exciting slopes and a rapidly changing base village; in some eyes, the best the US has to offer

COSTS

① ② ③ ④ ⑤ ⑥

RATINGS

The slopes
Fast lifts	✭✭✭
Snow	✭✭✭✭
Extent	✭✭✭
Expert	✭✭✭✭✭
Intermediate	✭✭
Beginner	✭✭✭
Convenience	✭✭✭
Queues	✭✭✭
Mountain restaurants	✭

The rest
Scenery	✭✭✭
Resort charm	✭✭✭
Off-slope	✭✭✭

NEWS

The new Tram (a cable car) that will access the top of Rendezvous from the village is due to open in December 2008; it replaces the ancient former Tram and has over double the hourly capacity. The temporary double chairlift, East Ridge, installed to access the summit while the cable car was under construction, will stay in place for one season as back-up.

Three restaurants, Couloir, Bridger and the Headwall Deli, opened at the top of the Bridger gondola last season.

644

- + Some real expert-only terrain and one of the US's biggest verticals
- + Jackson town has an entertaining Wild West ambience
- + Unspoiled, remote location
- + Excellent snow record and even more snow (and quiet slopes) 90 minutes away at Grand Targhee
- + Some unique off-slope diversions
- + The town is only 15 minutes from the airport, but ...

- − The town is also 15 minutes from the slopes – though the lift-base Teton Village is an increasingly attractive alternative
- − Intermediates wanting groomed cruises will find the area very limited, especially in fresh snow
- − Low altitude and sunny orientation mean snow can deteriorate quickly
- − Getting there from the UK involves at least one stop and plane change

With its wooden sidewalks, country-music saloons and pool halls, tiny Jackson is a determinedly Western town, designed to amuse summer visitors to Yellowstone – great fun, if you like that kind of thing.

For those who like steep slopes smothered in deep powder or plastered with big bumps, Jackson Hole is ideal. Like many American mountains, Jackson has steeps that you can't find in Europe except by going off-piste with a guide. What marks it out is the sheer quantity of this terrain, and the almost Alpine vertical. Of course, there is also skiing for those afraid of steep terrain, but intermediates wanting to build up confidence should look elsewhere.

With a double-capacity cable car (see 'News'), four smooth, upmarket hotels at the base and now a table-service restaurant on the mountain, Jackson Hole has changed rapidly in the last few years. Many locals will tell you the place is losing its soul, going soft, selling out. Maturing nicely, we'd say.

THE RESORT

The town of Jackson sits at the south-eastern edge of Jackson Hole – a high, flat valley surrounded by mountain ranges, in north-west Wyoming. Jackson gets many more visitors in summer than in winter, thanks to the nearby national parks. To entertain summer tourists the town strives to maintain its Wild West flavour, with traditional-style wooden buildings and sidewalks, and a couple of 'cowboy' saloons. It has lots of clothing and souvenir shops, as well as upmarket galleries appealing to second-home owners. In winter it's half-empty and accommodation prices come down. Visitors are generally full of praise for the friendly and helpful locals and say the free town bus is 'very efficient'.

The slopes, a 15-minute drive or $3 bus-ride north-east, rise abruptly from the flat valley floor. At the lift base is Teton Village, which has expanded over the last few years to become a much more attractive base, with an increased choice of bars, restaurants and hotels – some of these notably upscale. We are told the expansion is starting to attract a wider range of visitors to the slopes, including more families. Homes to rent are spread over quite an area.

A popular excursion by car or daily bus is over the Teton pass to the smaller resort of Grand Targhee, which gets even more snow (and keeps it better, with gentler, shadier slopes). See the Rest of the West introduction.

THE MOUNTAINS

Most of the slopes are below the treeline, but one of the attractions of the place is that most of the forest is not dense. Trail classifications are accurate: our own small map does not distinguish black from double-black-diamond runs, but the distinction matters – 'expert only' tends to mean just that. There are complimentary tours daily.

triple, from which you can traverse over to the Apres Vous area.

Snow King is a separate area right by Jackson town. There's a good choice of short, steep slopes. Locals use it at lunch time and in the evenings (it's partly floodlit).

TERRAIN PARKS
On Apres Vous
There's a terrain park by the Apres Vous chair, with jumps and rails, music and a 137m/450ft long super-pipe. Dick's Ditch is a natural pipe and there's a mini park for novices. But you really come to Jackson for the steeps and deeps of the freeriding.

SNOW RELIABILITY
Steep lower slopes can suffer
The claimed average of 460 inches of snow is much more than most Colorado resorts claim. But the base elevation is relatively low for the Rockies, and the slopes are quite sunny – they basically face south-east. You may find the steep lower slopes, like the Hobacks, in poor shape, or even shut. Locals claim that you can expect powder roughly half the time, but even after a fall the Hobacks deteriorate quickly. Don't assume early-season conditions will be good.

FOR EXPERTS
Best for the brave
For the good skier or boarder who wants challenges without the expense of hiring a guide to go off-piste, Jackson is one of the world's best

THE SLOPES
One big mountain, one small
The main lifts out of Teton Village for 2008/09 will be the Bridger gondola and (if everything goes to plan) the new Tram. The Tram will take you straight up a 1260m/4,130ft vertical to the summit of **Rendezvous** mountain – an exceptional vertical for the US. It can be incredibly cold and windy at the top of the Tram, even when it's warm and calm below.

To the right looking up is **Apres Vous** mountain, with half the vertical and mostly much gentler runs, reached from the village by the short Teewinot and the longer Apres Vous fast quad.

Between these two peaks, the Bridger gondola goes up over a broad mountainside split by gullies, and gives speedy access to the Thunder and Sublette quad chairs, serving some of the steepest terrain on Rendezvous, and the Casper Bowl

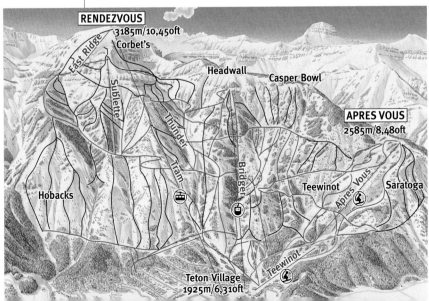

RENDEZVOUS
3185m/10,450ft
Corbet's
East Ridge
Sublette
Headwall
Casper Bowl
Thunder
Tram
APRES VOUS
2585m/8,480ft
Bridger
Hobacks
Teewinot
Apres Vous
Saratoga
Teewinot
Teton Village
1925m/6,310ft

KEY FACTS

Resort	1925m
	6,310ft

Jackson Hole

Slopes	1925-3185m
	6,310-10,450ft
Lifts	12
Pistes	2,500 acres
Green	10%
Blue	40%
Black	50%
Snowmaking	
	160 acres

Grand Targhee

Slopes	2440-3050m
	8,000-10,000ft
Lifts	5
Pistes	2,000 acres

(plus 1,000 acres served by snowcat)

Green	5%
Blue	77%
Black	18%
Snowmaking	none

LIFT PASSES

Jackson Hole

Prices in US$

Age	1-day	6-day
under 15	39	213
15 to 21	63	349
22 to 64	77	426
over 65	39	213

Free under 6 (Eagle's Rest and Teewinot lifts only)

Beginner ticket for Eagle's Rest and Teewinot lifts ($10)

Notes Covers all lifts in Jackson Hole; half-day ticket available

Alternative passes Grand Targhee; Snow King Mountain

boarding

Jackson Hole is a cult resort for expert snowboarders, as for skiers. It's not bad for novices, either, with the beginner slopes served by a high-speed quad chair. But intermediates not wishing to venture off the groomed runs will find the resort limited. Two terrain-parks and a super-pipe provide the freestyle thrills. There are some good snowboard shops, including the Hole-in-the-Wall at Teton Village.

resorts. Rendezvous mountain offers virtually nothing but black slopes. The routes down the main Rendezvous Bowl are not particularly fearsome; but some of the alternatives are. Go down the East Ridge at least once to stare over the edge of the notorious Corbet's Couloir. It's the jump in that's special; the slope you land on is a mere 50°, they say.

Below Rendezvous Bowl, the wooded flanks of Cheyenne Bowl offer serious challenges, at the extreme end of the single-black-diamond spectrum. If instead you take the ridge run that skirts this bowl to the right, you get to the Hobacks – a huge area of open and lightly wooded slopes, gentler than those higher up, but still black.

Corbet's aside, most of the steepest slopes are more easily reached from the slightly lower quad chairs. From Sublette, you have direct access to the short but seriously steep Alta chutes, and to the less severe Laramie Bowl beside them. Or you can track over to Tensleep Bowl – pausing to inspect Corbet's from below – and on to the less extreme (and less chute-like) Expert Chutes, and the single-black Cirque and Headwall areas. Casper Bowl often has good powder and the Crags is an area of bowls, chutes and glades (it's a good half-hour hike to reach it) – both are accessed through gates only. Thunder chair serves more steep, narrow, north-facing chutes.

Again, the lower part of the mountain here offers lightly wooded single-black-diamond slopes.

The gondola serves terrain not without interest for experts. In particular, Moran Woods is a splendid, under-utilised area. Even Apres Vous has a – usually very quiet – area of serious single blacks in Saratoga bowl, where the snow gets skied out much less quickly than on Rendezvous.

The gates into the backcountry access over 3,000 acres of amazing terrain, which should be explored only with guidance. You can stay out overnight at a backcountry yurt. There are some helicopter operations.

FOR INTERMEDIATES
Exciting for some
There are great cruising runs on the front face of Apres Vous, and top-to-bottom quite gentle blues from the gondola. But they don't add up to a great deal of mileage, and you shouldn't consider Jackson unless you want to tackle the blacks. It's then important to get guidance on steepness and snow conditions. The steepest single blacks are steep, intimidating when mogulled and fearsome when hard. The daily grooming map is worth consulting.

FOR BEGINNERS
Fine, up to a point
There are good broad, gentle beginner slopes. The progression to the blue Werner run off the Apres Vous chair is gradual enough and the mid-mountain blues on the Casper Bowl chair are reached via the chairs from the beginner area. But few other runs will help build confidence.

FOR CROSS-COUNTRY
Lots of possibilities
The Spring Creek Nordic Center has some good beginner terrain and moonlight tours. The Nordic Center at Teton has 20km/12 miles of trails and organises trips into the National Parks.

QUEUES
What queues?
The old cable car was famous for its queues. But its capacity was trivial, and the capacity of the Bridger gondola was increased to compensate for its loss; let's hope the new cable car will be able to cope with the demands of experts doing laps of the full vertical. 2008 reporters had no complaints, except for one who found queues of 'no more than 10 minutes' at Bridger on powder days. But the Teewinot chair, which serves the beginner area, is now said to generate queues at peak periods – is this another sign of the resort's changing character, we wonder?

↑ Teton Village has expanded a lot in the last few years, and there is now some very smart accommodation, including the Four Seasons Resort (on the left in this picture)

SNOWPIX.COM / CHRIS GILL

GETTING THERE

Air Jackson 19km/ 12 miles (½hr)

SCHOOLS

Jackson Hole
t 1 800 450 0477

Classes
Full day (5½hr) $100
Private lessons
Half day (3hr) $340

CHILDREN

Kids' Ranch
t 1 800 450 0477
Wranglers: ages 6mnth to 3yr;
8.30-4.30; $130 per day
Rough Riders: ages 3 to 6; 9am-3.15; includes skiing; $130 per day
Little Rippers: ages 5-6; 9am-3.15; includes boarding; $195 per day

Ski school
Explorers: ages 7 to 14; 9.00-3.30; $130 per day

MOUNTAIN RESTAURANTS
New choices at top of Bridger
We've always complained about Jackson's on-mountain eateries. So we can't wait to sample the places at the smart new development at the top of the Bridger gondola that opened last season. We've had good reports of the 'fine dining' at the table-service Couloir ('excellent elk pasta'). The self-service Rendezvous has separate areas serving soups and salads, Asian dishes, grills etc. Both have great views of the Headwall and outdoor decks as well as indoor seating. And there's a simpler Headwall Pizza and Deli option. The restaurant at the base of the Casper chairlift does a good range of self-service food. There are simple snack bars at four other points on the mountain.

One 2008 visitor liked to lunch off the slopes in the Four Seasons hotel where it's all you can eat for $20.

SCHOOLS AND GUIDES
Learn to tackle the steeps
As well as the usual lessons, there are also special types on certain dates. A 2008 visitor had impressive coaching in the four-day Steep and Deep Camp (pre-booking required) – 'carefully matched to ability, good value, maximum five in each group'. His wife had 'consistently excellent instruction' in the normal ski school lessons.

Backcountry guides can be hired – Rendezvous Ski Tours is 'highly recommended' by a reporter who enjoyed exploring the backcountry from Teton Pass and elsewhere.

FACILITIES FOR CHILDREN
Just fine
The area may not seem to be one ideally suited to children, but there are enough easy runs and the 'Kids' Ranch' facilities are good. There are classes catering for ages 3 to 17.

STAYING THERE

HOW TO GO
In town or by the mountain
Teton Village is convenient, while Jackson has the cowboy atmosphere – but bear in mind that some of the town hotels are far from central.
Hotels Because winter is low season, prices are low.
TETON VILLAGE
*****Four Seasons Resort (732 5000) Stylish luxury, with art on the walls, superb skier services, health club, an exceptional outdoor pool, perfect position just above the base.
****Teton Mountain Lodge & Spa (734 7111) Very comfortable. Good indoor and outdoor pool and fitness centre. 'Decent dinner.'
****Snake River Lodge & Spa (732 6000) Smartly welcoming and comfortable, with fine spa facilities.
****Terra (739 4000) Opened last season. Smart, boutique 'eco' hotel, with rooftop pool and hot tub. Spa.
***Alpenhof (733 3242) Tirolean-style, with varied rooms ('small by American standards'). Good food, lively bar. Pool, sauna, hot tub.
*Hostel x (733 3415) Basic, good value. Recommended by a reporter.
JACKSON TOWN
****Wort (733 2190) Comfortable, central, above the lively Silver Dollar Bar. Hot tub.
****Rusty Parrot Lodge (733 2000) Stylish place with a rustic feel. Hot tub. 'Superb' restaurant/breakfasts.
***Painted Porch Inn (733 1981) Gorgeous B&B full of antiques.
***Lodge at Jackson Hole (739 9703) Western-style place on outskirts. Comfortable mini-suite rooms, and free breakfast. Pool, sauna, hot tubs. Shuttle to the slopes. 'Good value.'
***Parkway Inn (733 3143) 'Friendly and helpful owners, convenient, with free transport to Teton Village.'

ACTIVITIES

Indoor Fitness centres, swimming, tennis, library, concerts, wildlife art and other museums

Outdoor Snowmobiles, snowshoeing, sleigh rides, dog sledding, hot springs, snow kite boarding

UK PACKAGES

All America Holidays, Alpine Answers, AmeriCan Ski, American Ski Classics, Crystal, Independent Ski Links, Inghams, Momentum, Ski Activity, Ski Dream, Ski Freshtracks, Ski Independence, Ski Line, Ski Safari, Ski Solutions, Skitracer, Skiworld, Supertravel, Trailfinders, United Vacations

Phone numbers
From distant parts of the US, add the prefix 1 307; from abroad, add the prefix +1 307

TOURIST OFFICES

Jackson Hole
t 733 2292
info@jacksonhole.com
www.jacksonhole.com

**Forty Niner Inn and Suites (733 7550) Central, good value. Recently recommended.
**Trapper Inn (733 2648) Friendly, good value, fairly central. Hot tubs.
BETWEEN THE TWO
*****Amangani Resort (734 7333) Hedonistic luxury in isolated position way above the valley.
****Spring Creek Ranch (733 8833) Exclusive retreat; cross-country on hand. Hot tub.
Apartments There is lots of choice at Teton Village but surprisingly little in and around Jackson town. The Love Ridge and Snow King condos in town have been recommended.

EATING OUT
A wide range of options
Jackson offers a range of excellent dining options. To check out menus, get hold of the local dining guide.

Most of the best bets at Teton Village are in the hotels. One reporter enjoyed 'scallops to die for' at the Alpenhof Bistro. The Vertical (Inn at Jackson Hole) is excellent, with a short, eclectic menu and a long wine list. It's rivalled by the Cascade Grillhouse and Spirits (Teton Mountain Lodge). Options at the Four Seasons include the Peak – a 'good value' casual place. The lively Mangy Moose does steaks and seafood.

In Jackson town there is more choice. The cool art deco Cadillac Grille serves 'well-prepared fish dishes'. The Blue Lion is small and casually stylish, 'excellent, and busy with locals'. The 'saloons' (see 'Après-ski') do hearty meals and good steaks. The Rusty Parrot Lodge has been recommended 'for a treat'. Thai Me Up has 'attentive service and good food', Bon Appe Thai does 'fantastic (and hot) authentic curries', the cute log cabin Sweetwater serves 'Greek-inspired' food, and Stone Table does 'awesome' South American dishes as well as tapas. The Snake River brew-pub – not to be confused with the 'outstanding' but expensive Snake River Grill – serves 'award winning beers and excellent pasta'. The Old Yellowstone Garage has 'superb Italian food in an elegant setting' and Rendezvous Bistro is popular with reporters and locals ('tasty meals, excellent service'). We're told that you won't get a beer at Bubba's BBQ but they serve 'great ribs' and 'fantastic food, despite the rustic surroundings'.

The Merry Piglets is 'a terrible name but a great Mexican restaurant'.

Out of town, The Grill at Amangani has 'a supremely stylish setting, stunning food and prices lower than expected'. Calico is a much more modest spot – a large Italian place, popular with locals.

APRES-SKI
Amusing saloons
For immediate après-ski at Teton Village, the Mangy Moose is a big, happy, noisy place, often with live music ('a cool hangout', says a snowboarder). For a quieter time head for The Bar at the Alpenhof.

In Jackson there are two famous 'saloons'. The Million Dollar Cowboy Bar features saddles as bar stools and a stuffed grizzly bear, and is usually the liveliest place in town, with live music and dancing some nights. The Silver Dollar around the corner is less tacky and more subdued; there may be ragtime playing as you count the 2032 silver dollars inlaid into the counter. The Rancher is a huge pool-hall. The Shady Lady saloon sometimes has live music. The Virginian saloon is much quieter and a locals' hang-out: 'If you like beer, guns and ammo, you'll be in good company,' says one. For a night out of town, join the locals at the Stagecoach Inn at Wilson, especially Sundays for 'a real western and blue grass swing night with music from a band that has not missed a night since 1969'.

OFF THE SLOPES
'Great' outdoor diversions
Yellowstone National Park is 100km/ 62 miles to the north. You can tour the park by snowcat or snowmobile with a guide; numbers are now restricted to reduce pollution. Some visitors really enjoy the park; we were distinctly underwhelmed (largely because of the noise and fumes from the snowmobiles and driving everywhere in convoy). The National Elk Refuge, with the largest elk herd in the US, is next to Jackson and across the road from the National Museum of Wildlife Art. Reporters recommend both. In town there are some 40 galleries and museums and a 'good range' of shops, including a number of outlets for Western arts and crafts. Joining the Jackson Hole Ski Club ($30) has been recommended – good discounts in shops, restaurants, lodgings etc.

New England

You go to Utah for the deepest snow, to Colorado for the lightest powder and swankiest resorts, to California for big mountains and low prices. You go to New England for ... well, for what? Extreme cold? Rock-hard artificial snow? Mountains too limited to be of interest beyond New Jersey? Yes and no: all of these preconceptions have some basis, but they don't give the full picture.

Yes, it can be cold: one of our reporters recorded −27°C, with wind chill producing a perceived −73°C. Early in the season, people routinely wear face masks to prevent frostbite. It can also be warm – another reporter had a whole week of rain that washed away the early-season snow. The thing about New England weather is that it varies – rather like ours. The locals' favourite saying is: 'If you don't like the weather, wait two minutes.'

New England doesn't usually get much super-light powder or deep snow to play in. But the resorts have big snowmaking installations, designed to ensure a long season and to help the slopes to 'recover' after a thaw or a spell of rain. They were the pioneers of snowmaking technology; and 'farming' snow, as they put it, is an art form and a way of life – provided the weather is cold enough. Many of the resorts get impressive amounts of natural snow too – in some seasons.

The mountains are not huge in terms of trail mileage (the largest,

Killington, is the smallest American resort to get its own chapter in these pages). But several have verticals of over 800m/2,620ft (on a par with Colorado resorts such as Keystone), and most have over 600m/1,970ft (matching Breckenridge), and are worth considering for a short stay, or even for a week if you like familiar runs. For more novelty, a two- or three-centre trip is the obvious solution. Most resorts suit snowboarders well, often having more than one terrain park.

You won't lack challenge – most of the double-black-diamond runs are seriously steep. And you won't lack space: most Americans visit over weekends, which means deserted slopes on weekdays – except at peak holiday periods. It also means the resorts are keen to attract long-stay visitors, so UK package prices are low.

But the big weekend and day-trip trade also means few New England resorts have developed atmospheric resort villages – just a few condos and a hotel, maybe, with places to stay further out geared to car drivers.

New England is easy to get to from Britain – a flight to Boston, then perhaps a three- or four-hour drive to your resort. And there are some pretty towns to visit, with their clapboard houses and big churches. You might also like to consider spending a day or two in Boston – one of America's most charming cities. And you could have a shopping spree at the factory outlet stores that abound in New England.

We cover two of the most popular resorts on the UK market in the chapters that follow – a long chapter on **Killington**, a short one on **Stowe**. But there are many other small areas, too, shown on the map and covered in our directory at the back of the book. Consider renting a car and visiting several resorts.

649

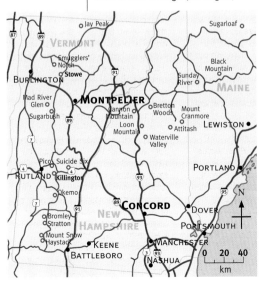

Killington

New England's leading resort, in most respects; good slopes,
great après-ski, no real village – for the moment, at least

COSTS

① ② ③ ④ ⑤ ⑥

RATINGS

The slopes
Fast lifts	**
Snow	***
Extent	**
Expert	***
Intermediate	***
Beginner	****
Convenience	*
Queues	****
Mountain restaurants	*

The rest
Scenery	***
Resort charm	*
Off-slope	*

NEWS

Killington's new owners continue to invest, but plans for a new base 'village' are on hold.

For 2008/09 a fast quad is due to replace the Skye Peak fixed-grip quad out of Bear Mountain base.

For 2007/08 the Killington Grand hotel was renovated. A Burton Learn to Ride and new kids' programmes were also introduced.

KEY FACTS

Resort	670m
	2,200ft
Slopes	355-1285m
	1,170-4,220ft
Lifts	32
Pistes	1,215 acres
Green	26%
Blue	34%
Black	40%
Snowmaking	92 km
	57 miles

650

+ The biggest mountain in the east, matching some Colorado resorts

+ Lively après-ski, with lots of bar-restaurants offering happy hours and late-night action

+ Excellent nursery slopes

+ Comprehensive and very effective snowmaking

+ Good child care, although it's not a notably child-oriented resort

− No resort village yet: restaurants, hotels and condos are widely spread, mostly along the five-mile access road – a car is needed

− Crowds on weekends

− New England weather – highly changeable, and can be very cold

− The trail network is complex

− Terminally tedious for anyone who is not a skier or boarder

It's difficult to ignore Killington. It claims to have the largest mountain, largest number of quad chairs, largest grooming fleet and longest season in the eastern US, and the biggest snowmaking installation in the world. (It tries to be the first resort in the US to open, in October, but often shuts again shortly afterwards.) It also claims to have America's longest lift and longest trail (a winding 16km/10 miles) and New England's steepest mogul slope (Outer Limits – average gradient 46%). These things may matter if your choice of destination is limited to those in the eastern US. In the general scheme of things, they count for very little. Killington is a minor resort, chiefly of interest if you find yourself within driving distance at a time when conditions look good.

THE RESORT

Killington is an extraordinary resort, especially to European eyes. Most of its hotels and restaurants are spread along a five-mile approach road. The nearest thing you'll find to a focus is the occasional set of traffic lights with a cluster of shops, though there is a concentration of buildings along a two-and-a-half mile stretch of the road. The resort caters mainly for weekend visitors who drive in from the east-coast cities. The car is king; but there's also a good 'but infrequent' free day-time shuttle-bus service around the base areas and lodgings. Beyond this it costs $2.

There are lodgings around the lift base, and the resort's new owners are keen to revive plans for something like a village there – but the project appears to be on hold once again. Staying near the start of the access road leaves you well placed for the gondola station on the main highway leading past the resort, and for outings to Pico, a separate little mountain in the same ownership, perhaps one day to be linked to Ramshead.

THE MOUNTAINS

Runs spread over a series of wooded peaks, all quite close together but giving the resort a basis for claiming to cover six mountains – or seven if you count Pico. An impressive number of runs and lifts are crammed into a modest area. To some extent the terrain on each sector suits a different ability level. But there are also areas where a mixed ability group would be happy, and there are easy runs from top to bottom of each peak.

Some runs of all levels are left to form bumps; there is half-and-half grooming on selected trails; and terrain features – ridges etc – are created. There are also gladed forest areas, not patrolled, where you pick your own line. They come in blue and single- and double-black-diamond grades. We found them great fun.

The result of all this is a complex network of runs. Signposting hasn't been adequate in the past, but concentrated efforts to improve matters have paid off.

There are free guided tours given by 'knowledgeable, enthusiastic and entertaining' 'ambassadors'.

boarding

A cool resort like Killington has to take boarding seriously, and it does. There are terrain features scattered around the area, with lots of interest for all levels, and parts of the mountain have been reshaped to cut out some of the unpleasant flats on green runs. There are excellent beginner slopes, and plenty of friendly (ie slow-loading) high-speed chairlifts – and the Killington school now offers the Burton Learn to Ride programme; instruction just for first-time boarders. Several big-name board events are held here, and the terrain parks just get bigger and better.

THE SLOPES
Complicated

The Killington Base area has chairs radiating to three of the six peaks – **Snowdon**, **Killington** (the high-point of the area) and **Skye** – the last also accessible by a gondola starting beside US Highway 4 or by a new fast quad from Bear (see 'News'). Novices and families head for the other main base area, which has two parts: Snowshed, at the foot of the main beginner slope, served by several parallel chairs; and Ramshead, just across the road up to Killington Base, where there's a Family Center at the foot of the entirely gentle **Ramshead** mountain.

The two remaining peaks are behind Skye Peak; they can be reached by trails from Killington and Skye, but each also has a lift base accessible by road. **Bear Mountain** is the experts' hill, served by two quad chairs from its mid-mountain base area. The sixth 'peak', **Sunrise**, is a slight blip on the mountainside, with a short triple chair up from the Sunrise Village condos.

TERRAIN PARKS
Lots of possibilities

There's a good choice, plus one at Pico. Bear mountain is home to the main freestyle area, with separate sections along the Wildfire, Bear Trap and Dreammaker trails. Features include a super-pipe, new large jumps, tabletops and an urban-style rail park. There's also a boardercross course with berms and rollers. All suit advanced riders best. Timberline on Ramshead has a quarter-pipe and is better suited to intermediates, as is Reason (early season park) on Killington Peak. Easy Street is a beginner mini park, and kids have their own park and pipe classes. The Snow Action Park at Snowshed offers kids the chance to jib and skate into the evenings.

SNOW RELIABILITY
Good if it's cold

Killington has a good snowfall record (average 250 inches) and a huge snowmaking system that seems to receive regular upgrades. But even that is no good if temperatures are

651

Killington

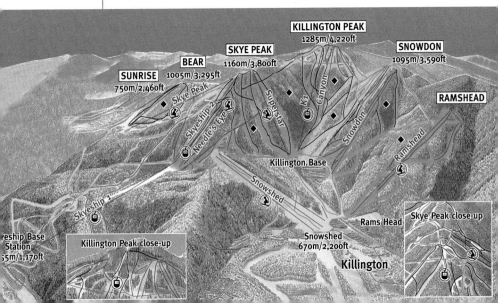

SCHOOLS
Killington
t 1 800 923 9444
Learn to ski clinics
(including lift pass,
equipment and use of
Discovery Center)
1 2hr lesson $99

Classes
One 2hr group lesson
$52
Private lessons
$104 for 1hr

CHILDREN
t 1 800 923 9444
**Friendly Penguin Day
Care**
Ages 12wk to 6yr;
$100 a day
First Tracks
Ages 2 to 3;
8.30-4.00; $130 a
day; includes skiing
MiniStars/Lowriders
Ages 4 to 6;
8.30-3.00; $130 a
day; includes skiing

Ski school
'Superstars' for ages
6 to 12 and
'Snowzone' for ages
13 to 18 ($130 for a
full day incl. lift pass
and lunch)

UK PACKAGES
All America Holidays,
American Ski Classics,
Crystal, Directski.com,
Independent Ski Links,
Inghams, Ski Dream,
Ski Independence, Ski
Line, Ski McNeill, Ski
Safari, Ski Solutions,
Skitracer, Thomson,
Trailfinders, Virgin
Snow

GETTING THERE
Air Boston 251km/
156 miles (2½hr)

too high to operate it. Bad weather can ruin a holiday even in mid-season – and conditions can change rapidly; reporters have experienced everything from 'frostbite warnings to pouring rain' in the same trip. Grooming has been reported to be poor, but the resort has bought additional machines, which should help.

FOR EXPERTS
Some challenges
The main areas that experts head for are Killington Peak, where there is a handful of genuine double-diamond fall-line runs under the two chairlifts, and Bear mountain – though one reporter did not find them very challenging. Most of the slopes here are single blacks, but Outer Limits, under the main quad chair, is a double diamond, claimed to be 'the steepest mogul slope in the east'. We suspect there are steeper runs at Stowe and Smugglers' Notch, in fact. There are two or three worthwhile blacks on Snowdon and Skye, too. The designated glades on Skye, Snowdon and Bear are also worth seeking out.

FOR INTERMEDIATES
Limited extent
There are lots of easy cruising blue and green runs all over the slopes, except on Bear mountain, where the single blacks present a little more of a challenge for intermediates. Snowdon is a splendid area for those who like to vary their diet, although a reporter favoured the trails on Skye. There's a blue-classified gladed area on Ramshead. One reporter enjoyed an outing to Pico but complained that the blue run down was more difficult than some blacks.

FOR BEGINNERS
Splendid
The facilities for complete beginners are excellent. The Snowshed home slope is really one vast nursery slope served by three chairlifts and a very slow draglift. Ramshead also has excellent gentle slopes. The school runs separate Learn to Ski and Ride programmes just for first-time skiers and boarders.

FOR CROSS-COUNTRY
Two main options
Extensive loops are available at two specialist 'resorts' – Mountain Meadows, down on US Highway 4, and Mountain Top Ski Touring, just a short drive away at Chittenden.

QUEUES
Weekend crowds
Killington gets a lot of weekend and holiday business, but at other times the slopes and lifts are likely to be quiet. One holiday visitor found long lines for the Ramshead chair, the K1 gondola and the Bear Mountain chair. The new fast quad from Bear Mountain to Skye Peak planned for 2008/09 (see 'News') should make moving between those two sectors much smoother – the ride time will now be just five minutes instead of the previous thirteen minutes. Overcrowded slopes are more of a problem than lift queues – the approaches to Bear lift base have been mentioned.

MOUNTAIN RESTAURANTS
Bearable base lodges
The Killington Peak Lodge is the only real mountain restaurant; we lack reports, but we've received mixed reviews in the past. There's a warming hut at Northbrook station on Skye Peak where you can get soups, and areas are provided if you wish to bring your own food. Most people use the base lodges; those at Bear, Ramshead and Snowshed have all been improved, and reporters comment on 'freshly cooked food'. The restaurant at the Snowshed Lodge offers a family menu. But the K-1 lodge is said to be the liveliest of the bunch.

SCHOOLS AND GUIDES
Improving your strengths
The philosophy of the Killington school is to build on your strengths, and it seems to work for most people. Beginners start and finish their day in a dedicated building with easy chairs, coffee, videos and help with fitting equipment. Speciality clinics include mogul weekends and park classes.

FACILITIES FOR CHILDREN
Fine in practice
There is a Family Center at the Ramshead base, which takes kids from 12 weeks and will introduce them to skiing from age two years. Classes are small – now guaranteed groups of three or five. The Adventure Center at the Snowshed base offers most snow-related sports you can think of, as well as indoor amusements and a family dining area at the lodge.

↑ At these altitudes, the trees go right to the top

ACTIVITIES

Indoor Killington Grand Resort Hotel has massage, fitness centre, outdoor pool, hot tub, sauna; theatre, cinemas, bowling, at Rutland; climbing wall at Snowshed base

Outdoor Ice rink, snowshoeing, dog sledding, snowmobile tours, sleigh rides

Central reservations phone number
Call 1 800 621 6867 (toll-free from within the US)

Phone numbers
From distant parts of the US, add the prefix 1 802; from abroad, add the prefix +1 802

TOURIST OFFICE

t 422 3333
info@killington.com
www.killington.com

STAYING THERE

HOW TO GO
Wide choices
There is a wide choice of places to stay. As well as hotels and condos, there are a few chalets.
Hotels There are a few places near the lifts, but most are a drive or bus ride away, down Killington Road or on US4.
****Grand Resort** (422 6888) Swanky resort-owned place at Snowshed, with outdoor pool, spa and health club. Refurbished for 2007/08.
***Cortina Inn** (773 3333) 20 minutes away on US4, near Pico. Pool. Recommended, but 'poor soundproofing'.
***Inn of the Six Mountains** (228 4676) Couple of miles down Killington Road; 'spacious rooms, good pool'.
North Star Lodge (422 2296) Well down Killington Road. Good value. Pool and shuttle-bus to the slopes.

EATING OUT
You name it
There are all sorts of restaurants spread along the Killington Road, from simple pizza or pasta through to 'fine dining' places. Many of the places in the Après-ski section serve food – be aware, though, that most bars do not allow children. The local menu guide is helpful. Choices, the 'excellent' Grist Mill, Hemingway's, Charity's and the Cortina Inn have been recommended. Peppinos is the place for Italian choices and Wally's (formerly Ppeppers) is a family-friendly diner, with 'good burgers' and desserts.

APRES-SKI
The beast of the east
Killington has a well-deserved reputation for a vibrant après-ski scene; many of its short-stay visitors are clearly intent on making the most of their few days (or nights) here.

There are bars at the base lodges – the Long Trail at Snowshed has been revamped and has a good range of beers – but keen après-skiers head down Killington Road to one of the lively places scattered along its 8km/5 mile length. From 3pm it's cheap drinks and free munchies, then in the early evening it's serious dining time, and later on the real action starts (and admission charges kick in).

The train-themed Casey's Caboose and Charity's – another lively bar, with an interior apparently lifted from a late-19th-century Parisian brothel – are well-established. The popular Wobbly Barn is a famous live-music place that still claims to be one of the leading après-ski venues in the US. The Pickel Barrel caters for a younger crowd, with theme nights. The Outback complex has something for everyone, from pizzas and free massages to disco and live bands.

OFF THE SLOPES
Rent a car
If there is a less amusing resort in which to spend time off the slopes, we have yet to find it. Make sure you have a car, as well as a supply of good books. Factory outlet shopping at Manchester is recommended (a 45-minute drive).

Interactive resort shortlist builder at **www.wtss.co.uk**

Stowe

Classic, charming Vermont town, some miles from its small but serious – and improving – area of slopes on Mount Mansfield

COSTS

① ② ③ ④ ⑤ ⑥

RATINGS

The slopes
Fast lifts	★★★
Snow	★★★
Extent	★
Expert	★★★
Intermediate	★★★★
Beginner	★★★★
Convenience	★
Queues	★★★★
Mountain restaurants	★★

The rest
Scenery	★★★
Resort charm	★★★★
Off-slope	★

KEY FACTS

Resort	475m
	1,560ft
Slopes	390-1135m
	1,280-3,720ft
Lifts	13
Pistes	485 acres
Green	16%
Blue	59%
Black	25%
Snowmaking	90%

654

- ➕ Cute tourist town in classic New England style
- ➕ Some good slopes for all abilities, including serious challenges
- ➕ Few queues
- ➕ Excellent cross-country trails
- ➕ Great children's facilities

- ➖ Slopes a bus ride from town
- ➖ Slopes limited in extent
- ➖ New England weather – highly changeable, and can be very cold
- ➖ Slow chairlifts in main sector
- ➖ Weekend queues
- ➖ Lacks après-ski animation

Stowe is one of New England's cutest little towns, its main street lined with dinky clapboard shops and restaurants. Its mountain, 10km/6 miles away, is another New England classic: something for everyone, but not much of it. This season, an upscale hotel will offer an alternative base, right by the gondola.

THE RESORT

Stowe is a picture-postcard New England town – and a popular spot for tourists year-round, with bijou shops and more 3- and 4-diamond hotels and restaurants than any other place in New England except Boston. The slopes of Mount Mansfield, Vermont's snow-capped (though mainly wooded) highest peak, are a 15-minute drive away and much of the accommodation is along the road out to it – though you can now stay at the swanky new Stowe Mountain Lodge, right by the lifts. There's a good day-time shuttle-bus service, but a car is useful.

THE MOUNTAINS

There are two main sectors, linked by lift. Free daily mountain tours.
Slopes The main Mansfield sector, served by a trio of chairlifts from Mansfield base lodge, is dominated by the famous Front Four – a row of double-black-diamond runs. But there is plenty of easier stuff, too. An eight-seat gondola serves a second part of this sector. Spruce Peak has the main nursery area at the bottom. A fast quad heads up to mid-mountain, and another serves the upper slopes. There is a backcountry link with Smugglers' Notch from the top of this sector. A

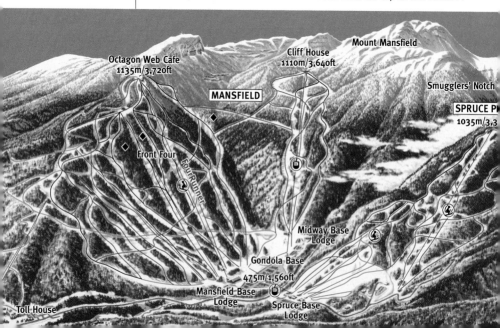

↑ Some of the trails are seriously narrow, in classic New England style

STOWE MOUNTAIN RESORT

NEWS

For 2008/09 the long-awaited Stowe Mountain Lodge luxury hotel complex and Spruce Camp day lodge (skier services building) are due to open at Spruce Peak – beside the gondola. Both buildings incorporate new restaurants and shops.

UK PACKAGES

All America Holidays, American Ski Classics, Crystal, Crystal Finest, Independent Ski Links, Ski Activity, Ski Dream, Ski Independence, Ski Line, Ski Safari, Skitracer, Virgin Snow

Central reservations phone number
Call 1 800 253 4754 (toll-free from within the US)

Phone numbers
From distant parts of the US, add the prefix 1 802; from abroad, add the prefix +1 802

TOURIST OFFICE

t 253 3000
info@stowe.com
www.stowe.com

gondola links the bases of Spruce Peak and Mt Mansfield. Night-skiing is offered on Saturdays.

Terrain parks Stowe has three terrain parks and a super-pipe: one is for beginners, the others (now located on Spruce Peak) are best suited to advanced users. There's also a separate early/late season rail park.

Snow reliability This is helped by snowmaking on practically all the blue (and some black) runs of the main sectors, and on all of Spruce Peak – keeping the slopes 'in great shape', says a recent visitor. Grooming is reported to be 'excellent'.

Experts The 'scarily narrow' and seriously steep Front Four and their variants on the top half of the main sector present a real challenge (if they are open); there are others nearby. There are various gladed areas.

Intermediates The usual New England reservation applies: the terrain is limited in extent; there's also a severe shortage of ordinary black runs (as opposed to double-diamonds). The gondola link between the sectors means you can get around easily.

Beginners The nursery slopes at Spruce Peak are excellent. There are also splendid long green runs to progress to in the main sector, down to Toll House base.

Snowboarding Stowe attracts many snowboarders. Beginners learn on special customised boards at the Burton Method Center on Spruce Peak. There's a dedicated resort website: www.stowked.com.

Cross-country There are excellent centres scattered around (including one at the musically famous Trapp Family Lodge) – 150km/93 miles of groomed and 100km/62 miles of backcountry trails form the largest network in the eastern US.

Queues The area is largely queue-free mid-week, but we've had reports of long queues at weekends – the Four

Runner quad has been mentioned. Improvements at Spruce Peak should have reduced congestion there.

Mountain restaurants The Cliff House, at the top of the gondola, has good views, table service and an improved menu; it is Vermont's highest restaurant, not surprisingly. Next best is Midway Cafe near the base of the gondola, with a BBQ deck and table service inside.

Schools and guides We lack recent reports. You can try out the latest equipment, with instruction, at the Stowe Toys Demo Centre. Semi-private lessons are available (maximum of three in a group).

Facilities for children Facilities are excellent; the nursery takes children from age three months to three years.

STAYING THERE

How to go There are hotels in and around Stowe itself and along the road to the slopes, some with Austrian or Scandinavian names and styles.

Hotels The luxury Stowe Mountain Lodge is new at Spruce base; pool and wellness centre. Readers have recommended 1066 Ye Olde England Inne (despite the appalling name), the Stowehof Inn, Green Mountain Inn and the 'pleasant' Stowe Inn. The Golden Eagle has also been praised; pool and hot tub. The smart Inn at the Mountain, at Toll House, offers slope-side accommodation.

Apartments There is a reasonable range of condos available for rent.

Eating out There are restaurants of every kind. The Whip in the Green Mountain Inn, Gracie's, the Shed (basic pub food) and Trattoria La Festa have all been recommended. Solstice is new at the Stowe Mountain Lodge.

Après-ski Rather muted, but there's a choice. The Matterhorn, Shed and Rusty Nail (live music, dancing) on the access road are popular. The Hourglass Barr at Stowe Mountain Lodge will serve rare wines, cocktails and beers when it opens. There's a good cinema.

Off the slopes Stowe is a pleasant town in which to spend time off the slopes – at least if you like shopping. The Vermont Ski Museum is 'worth a visit'. A trip to the Burlington shopping mall and a tour (with samples) of Ben & Jerry's ice cream factory just down the road have also been recommended. There is snowmobiling and dog sledding.

Stowe

655

Interactive resort shortlist builder at www.wtss.co.uk

More British skiers and snowboarders go to Canada than to the USA. In many ways it combines the best that the US has to offer – good service, a warm welcome, relatively quiet slopes, good lift systems with lots of fast lifts, frequent dumps of snow, great grooming and a high standard of accommodation – with more spectacular scenery and lower prices. It also has the advantage that you can get direct flights to its main airports without having to change planes and go through customs part-way through your journey. There are charter flights as well as direct Air Canada, British Airways and Zoom flights.

If Canada – well, western Canada at least – has one central attraction, it is snow. In an average year, you can expect much better snow than in the Alps – not only good conditions on the pistes, but frequent fresh falls to provide the powder you dream of. And, as in the States, there is lots of steep terrain within resort boundaries, which is therefore avalanche protected and safely skiable without guidance. If you really want untracked powder and are feeling flush, there is nothing to beat western Canada's amazing heli-skiing and snowcat skiing operations – see the Heli-skiing feature at the front of the book. The east is different: expect snow and extremes of weather, much like in New England. The main attraction of Québec for us is the French culture and unique ambience, plus the advantage of a shorter flight time. In both east and west, lifts close much earlier than in Europe – as early as 3pm in some cases.

A holiday in Canada can be reasonably cheap. Package prices start at around £500 for a week in Banff (no meals included). Eating and drinking still tend to be cheaper than in the US or the Alps, despite exchange rate changes in the last couple of years.

Another attraction is the Canadians. They share the American service culture but have a sincerity in putting it into practice that our reporters appreciate. In the west you'll also find spectacular scenery quite unlike what you generally find in the US. You may also see an impressive range of wildlife, especially in the Rockies and the interior of British Columbia.

Note that the legal age for buying and consuming alcohol is 18 in Alberta and Québec, 19 in British Columbia, and the law is strictly enforced; carrying your passport as evidence of age is a good idea even if you are well over the required age.

Ski Canada for less
with Canadian Affair

Toronto & Montreal
from
£129
prices one way inc tax

Calgary & Vancouver
from
£149
prices one way inc tax

Ski Tremblant
from
£429
Inc rtn flts & 6nts 3★ Hotel (room only)

Ski Banff
from
£599
Inc rtn flts & 7nts 3★ Hotel (room only)

London **0207 616 9911**
Glasgow **0141 223 7526**
www.canadianaffair.com

CANADIAN *Affair*

Prices based on departures from Gatwick in January 09. subject to availbaility and terms and conditions. Flights also available from Manchester and Glasgow - see online for details.

Western Canada

For international visitors to Canada, the main draw is the west. It has fabulous scenery, good snow and a wonderful sense of the great outdoors. The big names of Whistler, Banff and Lake Louise capture most of the British market, but there are lots of good smaller resorts that more Brits are now starting to explore. You can have a great trip by renting a car and combining two or more of these, perhaps with a couple of days on virgin powder served by helicopters or snowcats as well.

The three big resorts mentioned above and six of the smaller ones get their own write-ups in this section.

Whistler is plenty big enough to amuse you for a whole holiday. Most visitors to Banff or Lake Louise, a half-hour drive apart, will spend time at both (and could also fit in day trips to Kicking Horse and Panorama).

But none of the others have enough terrain to keep a keen piste-basher amused for a week or ten days without skiing the same runs several times. So we'd suggest that, if you want variety, you combine two or more on one holiday. Even if you don't want to drive, it is easy to combine, say, Sun Peaks with Whistler, Big White or Silver Star (and the latter two with each other) using regular buses between them.

Places that don't get a full chapter that you might also consider for a longer tour include Jasper (which you can reach via the spectacular Icefields Parkway drive from Lake Louise), Revelstoke (an exciting new resort that opened last season and by 2008/09 will have the biggest vertical in North America: 1715m/5,620ft), Apex, Red Mountain and Kimberley – these all have entries in the resort directory.

A few seasons ago we spent two weeks driving from Whistler to Banff, calling in at lots of smaller resorts on the way. It was a fantastic trip and for eight days in the middle it did not stop snowing. The skiing was spectacular – day after day of dry, light powder. And the variety of slopes and resorts made for interesting contrasts throughout the trip.

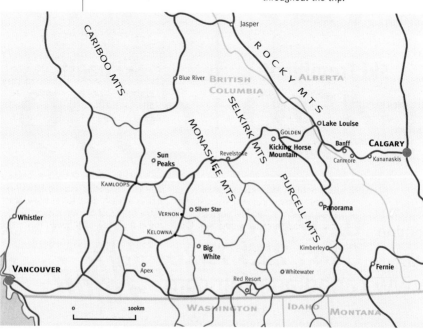

A major summer resort amid spectacular National Park scenery, with varied ski areas a bus ride from town – including Lake Louise

COSTS

① ② ③ ④ ⑤ ⑥

RATINGS

The slopes

Fast lifts	★★★★
Snow	★★★★
Extent	★★★★
Expert	★★★★
Intermediate	★★★★
Beginner	★★★
Convenience	★
Queues	★★★★
Mountain restaurants	★★★

The rest

Scenery	★★★★
Resort charm	★★★
Off-slope	★★★★★

NEWS

At Sunshine, new for 2007/08 was SlopeTracker: you wear an armband with GPS technology that records your speed, number of runs and number of calories burnt. The resort tells us they'll be using a different company but hope to offer a similar facility in 2008/09. The grooming fleet was improved too.

At Mt Norquay, new mobile snow-guns have been added to groomed runs.

➕ Spectacular high-mountain scenery – quite unlike the Colorado Rockies

➕ Excellent snow and long season at Sunshine Village, the big local area

➕ Lots of touristy shops

➕ Good-value lodging because winter is the area's low season

➖ Three separate ski areas all a bus ride out of town (up to 45 minutes)

➖ Most lifts/runs are of limited vertical – 200/400m (660/1300ft) is typical

➖ Can be very cold (−30°C or less and feel colder when riding lifts)

➖ Banff lacks ski resort atmosphere – though it's not an unattractive town

Huge numbers of British skiers and boarders go to Banff. Price has been a key factor in putting it on the map. Package costs have crept up, but most visitors are still delighted with what they find, and are keen to go back for more of Banff's distinctive combination of majestic scenery and excellent snow – plus the standard Canadian assets of people who are friendly and welcoming, and low prices for meals and other on-the-spot expenses.

We're not wild about the town of Banff, and we're distinctly unkeen on the daily commuting, even with a hire car – so our preferred strategy for a visit here is to stay a few nights in town, a couple at Sunshine Village, a couple at Lake Louise and a day trip to Kicking Horse (see separate chapters for the last two).

THE RESORT

Banff is a big summer resort that happens to have some nearby ski areas. Norquay is a small area of slopes overlooking the town. Sunshine Village, reached by a long access gondola from a base station 20 minutes' drive from Banff, is a much bigger mountain; despite the name, it's not a village (it has just one hotel at mid-mountain) – nor is it notably sunny. Most visitors buy a three-area pass that also covers Lake Louise, 45 minutes' drive away – covered by a separate chapter.

Banff is spectacularly set, with a few towering peaks on its outskirts. It has grown substantially over the years, but it still consists basically of a long main street and a small network of side roads built in grid fashion, lined with clothing and souvenir shops (aimed mainly at summer visitors) and a few ski shops. The buildings are low-rise and some are wood-clad. The town is pleasant enough, but it lacks genuine charm; it's essentially a modern tourist town, and there isn't much history in evidence.

Some of the lodgings (even on the main Banff Avenue) are quite a way from downtown. A car can be helpful here, especially in cold weather. But

taxis are 'plentiful and cheap'.

Unless you stay mid-mountain at Sunshine Village (see 'Staying up the mountain'), getting to the slopes means a drive or a bus-ride. Frequent buses (free with a Tri-area lift pass) tour all the main hotels, picking up guests as they go – 'efficient and easy' says a 2008 visitor.

Buses are also arranged to the more distant major resorts of Panorama and Kicking Horse (see separate chapters) and the smaller (and closer) resort of Nakiska, and day trips for heli-skiing and boarding are offered locally. Banff Airporter does transfers to and from Calgary airport.

THE MOUNTAINS

The Sunshine Village slopes are set on the Continental Divide – the watershed between the Pacific and the Atlantic – and as a result get a lot of snow. Most of the slopes above the village are above the treeline. Although there is a

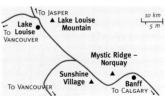

↑ Sunshine Village at the top of the gondola is the hub of the ski area, with lifts fanning out in all directions
SNOWPIX.COM / CHRIS GILL

KEY FACTS

Resort	1380m
	4,530ft

Norquay, Sunshine and Lake Louise, covered by the Tri-area pass

Slopes	1630-2730m
	5,350-8,950ft
Lifts	27
Pistes	7,748 acres
Green	23%
Blue	39%
Black	38%
Snowmaking	
	1,900 acres

Norquay only
Slopes	1630-2135m
	5,350-7,000ft
Lifts	5
Pistes	190 acres
Green	20%
Blue	36%
Black	44%
Snowmaking	85%

Sunshine only
Slopes	1660-2730m
	5,440-8,950ft
Lifts	12
Pistes	3,358 acres
Green	20%
Blue	55%
Black	25%
Snowmaking	none

wooded sector served by the second section of the gondola, and some lightly wooded slopes higher up, in bad weather you're better off at Lake Louise. The season goes on until May.

Norquay is much smaller. But it's worth a visit, especially in bad weather or as a first-day warm-up – it has a small area of quiet, wooded slopes. And you'll want to visit Lake Louise as well, of course (see our separate chapter).

There are good, free mountain tours led by friendly volunteer hosts.

THE SLOPES
Lots of variety

The main slopes of **Sunshine Village** are not visible from the base station: you ride a gondola to Sunshine Village itself, with a mid-station at the base of Goat's Eye Mountain.

Goat's Eye is served by a fast quad rising 580m/1,900ft – much the most serious lift on the mountain. Although there are some blue runs, this is basically a black mountain, with some genuine double diamonds at the extremities (including the 'backcountry' Wild West area).

Further up at Sunshine Village, lifts

fan out in all directions, with short runs back from Mount Standish and longer ones from Lookout Mountain. Lookout is right on the Continental Divide. From the top here experts can pass through a gate and hike up to more extreme terrain.

Many people ride the gondola down at the end of the day. But the 2.5km/1.5 mile green run to the bottom is a pretty cruise. If you go down while the lifts are running, you can take the Jackrabbit chair to cut out a flat section, but the run gets crowded and is much more enjoyable if you delay your descent a bit. The Canyon trail is a fun alternative for more advanced skiers and riders. Though the lower part is marked black, it's not steep – just a bit narrow and twisty in places.

The slopes at **Norquay** are served by a row of five parallel lifts and have floodlit trails on Friday nights.

TERRAIN PARKS
Park – and ride ...

At Sunshine, the Rogers terrain park on Lookout Mountain has 21 main features. These include medium to large 15m/50ft kickers and a host of

boarding

Boarders will feel at home in Banff, and there is some excellent freeriding terrain. 'There are so many natural ledges, jumps and tree gaps to play with that the terrain park seems almost unnecessary!' said a reporter. Delirium Dive, Silver City and Wild West are controlled off-piste playgrounds. A transceiver, probe, shovel and companion are required in all three. Not for the faint hearted, they are steep and deep. But Sunshine also has some flat areas to beware of, where scooting or walking is required (such as the green run to the base), and the blue traverse on Goat's Eye is tedious. A trip to Lake Louise's Powder Bowls is a must for freeriders. There are specialist snowboard shops in Banff: Rude Boys, Rude Girls and Unlimited Skate & Snow.

LIFT PASSES

Tri-area lift pass

Prices in C$

Age	1-day	6-day
under 13	26	228
13 to 17	55	432
18 to 64	78	485
over 65	63	432

Free under 6

Beginner lift, lesson and rental package

Notes

Day pass is for Sunshine only; 3-day-plus pass covers all lifts and transport between Banff, Lake Louise, Norquay and Sunshine Village; prices include tax

rails and boxes, including a whale tail box, banked C box and whopping 12m/40ft hand rail – 'great fun', said a recent reporter. The opening of Grizzly section of the terrain park added four acres of new features in 2007/08, its 'pièce de resistance' being a 7m/24ft long by 1.2m/4ft high box, painted by local artists. There is also a big and more advanced park at Norquay, which is designed by Jeff Paterson, head park designer for Triple Crown events. Gap jumps, tabletops, rails and boxes litter the park, which also boasts a good-sized half-pipe. On Friday nights from January to March the park is lit for night sessions. There is a special reduced pass for avid freestylers, which covers just the park. Then there's the Lake Louise park to try as well, of course.

SNOW RELIABILITY
Excellent

Sunshine Village claims '100% natural snow', a neat reversal of the usual snowmaking hype. In a poor snow season, some black runs can remain rocky (especially those on Goat's Eye), but the blues are usually fine. 'Three times the snow' is another Sunshine

slogan – a cryptic reference to the fact that the average snowfall here is 360 to 400 inches (depending on which figures you believe) – as good as anything in Colorado – compared with a modest 140 inches at Lake Louise and 120 inches on Norquay. But we're told the Sunshine figures relate to Lookout, and that Goat's Eye gets less. At Norquay there is snowmaking on all green and blue pistes. So all in all, lack of snow is unlikely to be a problem in a normal season, and late-season snow on Sunshine is usually good (we've had great April snow there on recent visits).

FOR EXPERTS
Pure pleasure

Sunshine has plenty of open runs of genuine black steepness above the treeline on Lookout, but Goat's Eye is much more compelling. It has a great area of expert double-black-diamond trails and chutes, both above and below the treeline ('beautiful, quiet, a real adventure'). The slopes are rocky and need good cover, and the top can be windswept. But a contented reporter says that the double-diamond runs at skier's left hold their snow

Interactive resort shortlist builder at **www.wtss.co.uk**

better than the rest of the mountain.

There are short, not-too-steep black runs on Mount Standish. One more challenging novelty here is a pitch known as the Waterfall run – because you do actually ski down over a snow-covered frozen fall. But a lot of snow is needed to cover the waterfall and prevent it reverting to ice. Also try the Shoulder on Lookout Mountain; it is sheltered, tends to accumulate powder and has been deserted whenever we've been there; access involves a long traverse that can be tricky and is poorly marked.

A popular backcountry route follows the back of the Wawa ridge, through a river valley ('great fun – tight turns in the trees of the river bed'); a guide is essential, of course.

Real experts will want to get to grips with Delirium Dive and Silver City on Lookout Mountain's north face and the Wild West area on Goat's Eye (with some narrow chutes and rock bands). For all three you must have a companion, an avalanche transceiver and a shovel – and a guide is recommended. ('Book in advance' and 'rent your transceiver and shovel in Banff – you can't at Sunshine', advise disappointed reporters.) We tried Delirium in a group with the ski patrol, who provided equipment, and the scariest part was the walk in, along a narrow, icy path with a sheer drop (protected by a flimsy-looking net).

Norquay's two main lifts give only 400m/1,310ft vertical, but both serve black slopes, and the North American chair accesses a couple of serious double-diamond runs.

Lake Louise has good steep terrain as well (see separate chapter).

Heli-skiing is available from bases outside the National Park in British Columbia – roughly two hours' drive.

Goat's Eye has some great steep terrain – single- and double-black-diamond runs and an extreme zone. But it's very rocky and windswept and needs a lot of snow to be enjoyable

GOAT'S EYE
2600m/8,530ft

Goat's Eye

Wild West
◆◆

1660m/5,440ft

2020m/6,630ft

Wolverine

Gondola

If it's snowing hard, visibility is usually best on the easy runs in the trees around here and on the long run down to the bottom of the gondola

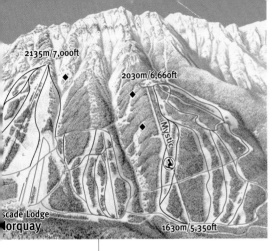

2135m/7,000ft

2030m/6,66oft

Mystic

scade Lodge
lorquay

1630m/5,350ft

FOR INTERMEDIATES
Ideal runs

Half the runs on Sunshine are classified as intermediate. Wherever you look there are blues and greens – some of the greens as enjoyable (and pretty much as steep) as the blues. We particularly liked the World Cup Downhill run, from the top of Lookout to the Village. All three chairs on Mount Standish are excellent for building confidence, provided you choose a sensible route down. The slow Wawa chair gives access to the Wawa Bowl and Tincan Alley ('great first blues'). This area also offers some shelter from bad weather. There's a delightful wooded area under the second stage of the gondola served by Jackrabbit and Wolverine chairs. The blue runs down Goat's Eye are good cruises too, some of them with space to indulge in fast carving.

The Mystic Express quad at Norquay serves a handful of quite challenging tree-lined blues and a couple of sometimes groomed blacks.

You'll want to visit Lake Louise as well, of course (see separate chapter).

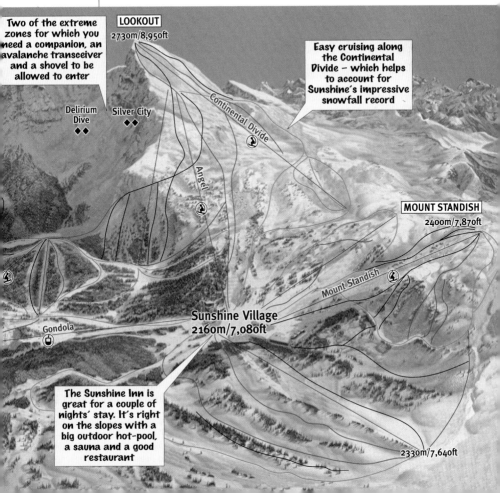

Two of the extreme zones for which you need a companion, an avalanche transceiver and a shovel to be allowed to enter

LOOKOUT
2730m/8,95oft

Easy cruising along the Continental Divide – which helps to account for Sunshine's impressive snowfall record

Delirium Dive ◆◆

Silver City ◆◆

Continental Divide

Angel

MOUNT STANDISH
2400m/7,87oft

Mount Standish

Sunshine Village
216om/7,08oft

Gondola

The Sunshine Inn is great for a couple of nights' stay. It's right on the slopes with a big outdoor hot-pool, a sauna and a good restaurant

2330m/7,64oft

SCHOOLS

Ski Big 3
t 760 7731

Banff-Norquay
t 760 7716

Sunshine Village
t 762 6560

Classes (Big 3 prices)
3 days guided tuition
of the three areas
C$269 incl. tax

Private lessons
Half day (3hr) C$377,
incl. tax, for up to 5
people

CHILDREN

Tiny Tigers (Sunshine)
t 762 6560
Ages 19mnth to 6yr;
8.30-4.30

Kid's Place (Norquay)
t 760 7709
Ages 19mnth to 6yr;
9am to 4pm

Childcare Connection
t 760 4443
Childminding in guest
accommodation

Ski school
Takes ages 6 to 12 (3
days C$293, incl. tax
and lunch)

FOR BEGINNERS
Pretty good terrain

Sunshine has a good area at the Village, served by a moving carpet. And there are great, long green runs to progress to – notably Meadow Park. Norquay has a good small nursery area with a moving carpet and gentle greens served by the Cascade chair. And Lake Louise has good beginner terrain (see separate chapter).

Banff is not the ideal destination for a mixed party of beginners and more experienced friends (who are likely to want to travel around more).

FOR CROSS-COUNTRY
High in quality and quantity

It's a good area for cross-country. There are trails near Banff, around the Bow River, and on the Banff Springs golf course. But the best area is around Lake Louise. Altogether, there are around 80km/50 miles of groomed trails within Banff National Park.

QUEUES
Sunshine can get busy

Half the visitors come for the day from cities such as Calgary – so the slopes are fairly quiet during the week. But Sunshine can get busy at weekends and public holidays; we've had reports of queues of up to 30 minutes for the gondola at Christmas and Easter, and there were big queues for Goat's Eye on our last visit (early April) – though they moved quickly and there are effective singles line so you can jump the queue if in a hurry. On busy weekends, we're told the trick is to arrive at the gondola by 9am.

MOUNTAIN RESTAURANTS
Quite good

The Sunshine Mountain Lodge has the best food – table service in the Chimney Corner Lounge ('good food, service and great views'). The Day Lodge offers three different styles of food on three floors (table service in the top-floor Lookout Bistro, with great views). Mixed reports of the food. Mad Trapper's Saloon is a jolly Western-style place in Old Sunshine Lodge, serving good beer, but we have reports of poor food and service.

At the base of Norquay, the big, stylish, timber-framed Cascade Lodge is excellent – it has great views and a table-service restaurant upstairs as well as a self-service cafeteria.

SCHOOLS AND GUIDES
Some great ideas

Each mountain has its own school. But recognising that visitors wanting lessons won't want to be confined to just one mountain, the resorts have organised an excellent Club Ski and Club Snowboard Program – three-day courses starting on Sundays and Thursdays that take you to Sunshine, Norquay and Lake Louise on different days, offering a mixture of guiding and instruction, a fun race, a group photo and an après-ski event. Nearly all reporters rave about it: 'absolutely brilliant', 'a great way to meet other people', 'learnt more in three days than I did in the whole week last year'. But a 2008 visitor had mixed experiences: 'our advanced group had a perfect balance of skills training and guidance, but the rest of our party had an instructor who spoke little and gave virtually no specific skills training'. All abilities are catered for, including beginners. A 2008 reporter did five days of the Performance Clinic at Sunshine and found the instructors 'excellent: they picked up your mistakes and encouraged you; they also videoed you; my class size was never more than four'.

FACILITIES FOR CHILDREN
Excellent

One reporter who used the facilities at Sunshine, Norquay and Lake Louise said: 'I'd recommend all three.' The school is praised: an 11-year-old experienced 'kind and friendly instructors', while his mum approved of the 'enthusiastic and motivational' tuition – but she also points out that 'enrolment can be chaotic and afternoon classes were less about learning, more about fun'.

STAYING THERE

HOW TO GO
Superb-value packages

A huge amount of accommodation is on offer; as well as hotels and self-catering, there are catered chalets.
Hotels Summer is peak season here, with lower prices in winter (though they have crept up in recent years).
*****Fairmont Banff Springs (762 2211) A late-19th-century, castle-style property, well outside town (with no shuttle-bus – you have to use taxis). It's virtually a town within itself – 2,000 beds, over 40 shops, several

GETTING THERE

Air Calgary 122km/
76 miles (1½hr)

UK PACKAGES

*All America Holidays,
Airtours, Alpine
Answers, AmeriCan Ski,
American Ski Classics,
Canadian Powder
Tours, Crystal, Crystal
Finest, Directski.com,
Elegant Resorts,
Frontier, Independent
Ski Links, Inghams,
Kuoni, Neilson, Ski
Activity, Ski Dream, Ski
Independence, Ski Line,
Ski McNeill, Ski Safari,
Ski Solutions, Skitracer,
Skiworld, Solo's,
Supertravel, Thomson,
Trailfinders, United
Vacations, Virgin Snow,
White Mountains*
Sunshine Village *Ski
Dream*

ACTIVITIES

Indoor Film theatre,
museums, galleries,
swimming pools (one
with water slides),
gym, squash,
racquetball, weight
training, bowling, hot
tub, sauna, climbing
wall

Outdoor Swimming in
hot springs, ice rink,
sleigh rides, dog
sledding,
snowmobiles, curling,
ice walks, ice fishing,
helicopter tours,
snowshoeing

Phone numbers
From distant parts of
Canada, add the
prefix 1 403; from
abroad, add the prefix
+1 403

TOURIST OFFICE

Banff
t 277 7669
info@SkiBig3.com
www.SkiBig3.com
www.skibanff.com

restaurants and bars, a nightclub and
a superb spa (which costs extra).
★★★★Rimrock (762 3356) Spectacularly
set, out of town, with great views and
a smart health club. Luxurious.
★★★★Banff Park Lodge (762 4433)
Best-quality, central hotel, with hot
tub, steam room and indoor pool.
★★★★Banff Caribou Lodge (762 5887)
On the main street, slightly out of
town. Wood-clad, individually designed
rooms, sauna and hot tub, new spa,
'excellent' restaurant and bar.
Repeatedly recommended by reporters.
★★★★Banff International (762 5666)
'Central, saving walking in the
evenings. Excellent, can't fault it.'
★★★Juniper (762 2281) At foot of
Norquay and reachable on skis.
Comfortable, good views, hot tub.
'Outstanding service and food.'
★★★High Country Inn (762 2236)
'Great: big rooms, pool, hot tub and
sauna, easy walk to centre.'
★★Homestead Inn (762 4471) Central,
cheap, good-sized rooms, approved of
by two recent reporters.
Apartments Don't expect luxury – but
there are some decent options. The
Banff Rocky Mountain Resort is set in
the woods on the edge of town, with
indoor pool and hot tubs. Families
have recommended the Douglas Fir
resort ('kids loved the water-slides') –
though it's 'a bit out of town'.

EATING OUT
Lots of choice

Banff boasts over 100 restaurants,
from McDonald's to fine dining in the
Banff Springs hotel.

We've enjoyed the designer-cool
Saltlik – good game, steak and fish.
Reader recommendations include Earl's
(burgers and ethnic dishes, popular,
lively), Magpie & Stump ('excellent',
but busy Mexican, with Wild West
decor, 'serves beer in jam jars'),
Coyotes ('good fresh fish'), Caramba in
the Ptarmigan Inn (Mediterranean,
'well worth the money'), the Keg
('fabulous steaks', 'great ribs'), Wild
Bill's ('the biggest and best burgers in
town', dancing and live entertainment),
Bumpers ('big slabs of rib', 'best
steaks'), the Old Spaghetti Factory
('great for families'), Tony Roma's
('rack of ribs to die for', 'fantastic
value'), Tommy's Neighbourhood Pub
('very informal and good food'),
Giorgios ('good and unpretentious'),
the Bison ('good food and
atmosphere') with live music. Evelyn's

and Jump Start ('cosy and full of
locals, not tourists') are cafes.

APRES-SKI
Livens up later on

Tea time après-ski is limited because
the town is a drive from the slopes.
But Mad Trapper's Saloon at the top of
the Sunshine gondola is popular
during the close-of-play happy hour
(with endless free peanuts). They also
do evenings with tobogganing, a
buffet, live music and dancing,
followed by a gondola ride down. In
town later, the two main live music
venues are the Rose & Crown and Wild
Bill's – country and western music with
line dancing. The St James's Gate Irish
pub has 'splendid Guinness'. Melissa's
and Saltlik are popular. The Elk and
Oarsman nightclub has 'a good
atmosphere'. Hoodoo Lounge attracts
a young lively crowd; Aurora is for
more serious clubbing.

OFF THE SLOPES
Lots to do

There's wildlife to see, lovely walks
(including ice canyon walks – Johnson
Canyon is recommended), and you can
go snowshoeing, dog sledding, skating
and snowmobiling. There are
sightseeing tours and several
museums. Some reporters have been
disappointed by the natural hot
springs. Others have enjoyed evenings
in Calgary watching the ice hockey.

STAYING UP THE MOUNTAIN
Worth considering

The newly renovated Sunshine
Mountain Lodge (277 7669) – used to
be called Sunshine Inn – makes a very
welcoming, comfortable base at
Sunshine Village. Luggage is delivered
while you ski. Rooms vary in size. Big
outdoor hot-pool. Sauna. Good
restaurant. Guests can get on the
slopes half an hour before the public.

It's not big by Euro-resort standards, but it's certainly white. There are few places to match it for learning to ski powder

COSTS

① ② ③ ④ ⑤ ⑥

RATINGS

The slopes

Fast lifts	★★★
Snow	★★★★★
Extent	★★★
Expert	★★★
Intermediate	★★★★
Beginner	★★★★
Convenience	★★★★
Queues	★★★★★
Mountain restaurants	★

The rest

Scenery	★★★
Resort charm	★★
Off-slope	★★

KEY FACTS

Resort	1755m
	5,760ft
Slopes	1510-2320m
	4,950-7,610ft
Lifts	16
Pistes	2,765 acres
Green	18%
Blue	54%
Black	28%
Snowmaking	
	In terrain park

666

➕ Great for learning to ski powder

➕ Slopes quiet except at weekends and holidays

➕ Convenient, purpose-built village with high-quality, good-value condos

➕ Very friendly staff; good for families

➖ Visibility can be poor, especially on the upper mountain, because of snow, cloud or freezing fog

➖ Few off-slope diversions – and isolated without a car

➖ Limited après-ski

'It's the snow' says the Big White slogan. And as slogans go, it's spot on. If you want a good chance of skiing powder on reasonably easy slopes, put Big White high on the shortlist. If you want a suntan (or lively après-ski, or extensive steep bowls and chutes), look elsewhere; but if you are an intermediate looking to learn to ski powder or try gladed skiing for the first time, there can be few better places. Consider combining it with another BC resort such as Sun Peaks or Silver Star for variety.

THE RESORT

Big White is a rapidly growing, purpose-built resort less than an hour from Kelowna airport. The village is rather piecemeal but attractive in wood and stone, with a family-friendly traffic-free centre; and much accommodation is ski-in/ski-out and in smart modern condos, some very luxurious. Reporters remark on the large number of 'friendly and happy' Aussie workers that the resort recruits for the season. Silver Star resort (see separate chapter) is under the same ownership; there are weekly day trips by bus, and twice-a-week transfers make a two-centre holiday easy.

THE MOUNTAINS

Much of the terrain is heavily wooded. But the trees thin out towards the summits, leading to almost open slopes in the bowls at the top. There's at least one green option from the top of each lift but the one from Gem Lake is narrow and can be tricky and busy. In general, the easiest slopes are on the right as you look at the mountain (including some very easy glade skiing) and get steeper the further left you go.

Slopes Fast chairs run from points below village level to above mid-mountain, serving the main area of wooded beginner and intermediate

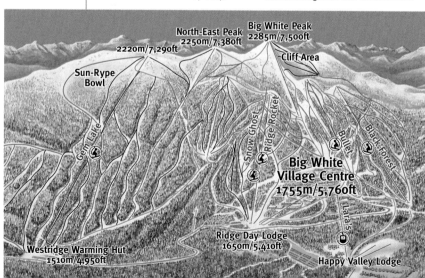

Kelowna airport (56km/35 miles away) is being improved so that it will be able to take bigger planes (including transatlantic flights). Work is expected to be complete by autumn 2008.

Work has also started on building the new 4-star Chateau Blanc hotel and casino, but it won't be ready until the 2009/10 season.

runs above and beside the village. Slower lifts – a T-bar and four chairs – serve the higher slopes. Quite some way across the mountainside is the Gem Lake fast chair, serving a range of long top-to-bottom runs; with its 710m/2,330ft vertical, this lift is in a different league from the others. 'Snow hosts' (highly praised by reporters) run twice-daily guided ski tours.

Terrain parks Served by a double chair and by Big White's first snowmaking, the excellent Telus park includes a half-pipe, super-pipe, boardercross, rails and hits for all levels. It is floodlit Thursday to Saturday evenings – and is highly praised by reporters.

Snow reliability Big White has a reputation for great powder; average snowfall is about 300 inches, which is similar to many Colorado resorts. At the top of the mountain the trees usually stay white all winter and are known as snow ghosts; they make visibility tricky in a white-out but are great fun to ski between on clear days. One reporter points out that most slopes face south-west to south-east and the snow can suffer in periods of sunshine; but on both our visits, it has snowed practically non-

stop and we hardly saw the sun.

Experts The Cliff Area at the top right of the ski area is of serious double-black-diamond pitch; the runs are short, but you can ski them repeatedly using the Cliff chair. The area was closed in January last season after an avalanche; but it reopened in mid-March and we are told it will be 'fully operational' for 2009. The Sun-Rype bowl at the opposite edge of the ski area is more forgiving. There are some long blacks off the Gem Lake chair and several shorter ones off the Powder and Falcon chairs. There are glades to explore and bump runs too.

Intermediates The resort is excellent for cruisers and families, with long blues and greens all over the hill. Good intermediates will enjoy the easier blacks and some of the gladed runs too. In general the runs get steeper from right to left as you look at the mountain. There is marvellous easy skiing among the trees in the Black Forest area (which we loved when it was snowing) and among the snow ghosts (see above), which we loved when it was clear. Some of the blues off the Gem Lake chair are quite steep, narrow and challenging.

Interactive resort shortlist builder at **www.wtss.co.uk**

UK PACKAGES

*All America Holidays,
Alpine Answers,
AmeriCan Ski, American
Ski Classics, Frontier,
Independent Ski Links,
Ski Dream, Ski
Independence, Ski Line,
Ski Safari, Skiworld,
Snowebb*

Central reservations
Call 765 8888; toll-
free (within Canada)
1 800 663 1772
Phone numbers
From distant parts of
Canada, add the
prefix 1 250; from
abroad, add +1 250

TOURIST OFFICES

Big White
t 765 3101
bigwhite@bigwhite.
com
www.bigwhite.com

Beginners There's a good dedicated
nursery area in the village and lots of
long easy runs to progress to.
Snowboarding There's some excellent
beginner and freeriding terrain with
boarder-friendly chairlifts and few flat
areas to worry about.
Cross-country 25km/16 miles of trails.
Queues Queues are rare.
Mountain restaurants There aren't any
– it's back to the bottom for lunch.
School and guides We receive rave
reviews from reporters for both adult
and children's lessons – and for the
free mountain tours.
Facilities for children The excellent
Kids' Centre takes children from 18
months. Evening activities are
organised too.

STAYING THERE

How to go There's an increasing range
of packages to Big White including
Canada specialist Frontier Ski and
North America specialists AmeriCan Ski
and Ski Independence.
Hotels The White Crystal Inn receives
better reviews from reporters than the
Inn at Big White.
Apartments Condo standards are high.
We stayed at Stonebridge and loved it
– big rooms, central, well furnished,
private hot tub on the balcony. A
recent reporter recommends the
Towering Pines ('superb, huge lounge,

well equipped, private hot tub,
convenient for slopes and centre').
Eating out We had good meals in the
Copper Kettle in the White Crystal Inn
and the Kettle Valley Steakhouse at
Happy Valley ('superb food, amazing
choice of wines', says a recent visitor).
Reporters also recommend Snowshoe
Sam's ('imaginative food'), and Swiss
Bear in the Chateau Big White.
Après-ski The atmospheric Snowshoe
Sam's has a DJ and live entertainment;
try its trademark alcoholic gunbarrel
coffee. Raakel's in the Hofbrauhaus
has live music and dancing. The Snow
Ghost Lounge in the White Crystal Inn
has 'live music some nights and
impressive malt whiskies'.
Off the slopes Happy Valley has ice
skating, snowmobiling, tubing, dog
sledding, sleigh rides and
snowshoeing. There are two spas.

Fernie

Lots of snow and lots of steeps – best explored with a guide; a choice of convenient base lodging or a drive from Fernie town

COSTS

①②③④⑤⑥

RATINGS

The slopes

Fast lifts	★★
Snow	★★★★★
Extent	★★★
Expert	★★★★★
Intermediate	★★
Beginner	★★★★
Convenience	★★★★
Queues	★★★★
Mountain restaurants	★

The rest

Scenery	★★★
Resort charm	★★
Off-slope	★★

NEWS

For 2007/08 snowmaking was improved around Timber Bowl and a children's dining room built at the ski school.

The notoriously poor signposting was apparently revamped last season to 'make the mountain easier to navigate for newcomers'. But this year's reports suggest little improvement.

➕ Good snow record, with less chance of rain than at Whistler (and less chance of Arctic temperatures than at resorts up in the Rockies)

➕ Great terrain for those who like it steep and deep; good for confident intermediates too

➕ Snowcat operations nearby

➕ Some good on-slope accommodation available, but ...

➖ Mountain resort is very limited

➖ Access to many excellent runs is a slow business, involving slow lift rides and long traverses

➖ After a dump it can take time to make the bowls safe

➖ Limited groomed cruising

➖ Awful trail map and on-mountain signposting

➖ No proper mountain restaurants

Fernie has long had cult status among Alberta and British Columbia skiers. It now attracts quite a few British visitors, and the reports we get are almost all positive. Like us, reporters are impressed by the adventurous nature of the skiing – it's mostly steep and ungroomed, with a lot of lightly wooded slopes (not common in Europe). Curiously, it's now quite a good resort for novices, too – it's the broad band of people in between who need to look elsewhere.

The resort village is convenient but small and nothing special. Fernie town, a couple of miles away, has few of the usual tourist trappings, but makes an amusing change from the resort norm.

THE RESORT

Fernie Alpine Resort is set a little way up the mountainside from the flat Elk Valley floor and a couple of miles from the little town of Fernie. It has grown from very little in the past few years, but there's still not much there except convenient lodging and a few restaurants, bars and small shops. It is quiet at night.

The town of Fernie is named after William Fernie – a prospector who discovered coal here and triggered a boom in the early 1900s. Much of the town was destroyed by fire in 1908, but some buildings survived. It is primarily a town for locals, not tourists. There are some lively bars, decent places to eat and good outdoor shops. It is down to earth rather than charming, and reporters' reactions to it vary: 'I liked the way it felt like real Canada and enjoyed staying in a town with some history,' said one. 'The flip side of being a real

Classic Fernie: Cedar Bowl, which contains no lifts apart from a short drag at the bottom to bring you back to the main lifts
➔

We have been complaining for years about the dreadful piste map and inadequate on-mountain signposting. A repeat visit in 2007 showed us that nothing had changed. For 2008 there were apparently new larger maps and signs at base level, but readers' reports make it clear that route finding is still a serious challenge. Finding some of the black runs is almost impossible without a guide, and you can easily end up in tight trees on slopes of triple-diamond steepness – as we did on an earlier visit. In 2007, on one day we skied with an instructor and on another with Kathy Murray, who runs the Steep and Deep camps (see 'Schools and guides'). They took us to runs that are marked on the map but that we'd never have found. Accessing them normally entails long traverses through the trees; there might be a sign at the start (often high up in a tree), but once you set off, there are no further clues about where to go or when to start heading down. Locals don't use the piste map, and when asked about it and the signposting, they just shrug their shoulders or laugh. If you want to explore the best of Fernie's steep terrain, join a Steep and Deep camp or take a guide.

town is having a real highway run through it,' said another. Most stress the friendliness of the locals, though not that of seasonal 'immigrant' workers.

There are buses between the town and the mountain, which run at half-hourly intervals at peak times and cost C$3 one way (they are free in the evenings and run every half an hour until 2am). Each hotel has specific pick-up times, although we have a report that the service is unreliable, and a recent visitor found the information on routes 'inadequate'.

Outings to Kimberley are possible; a coach does the trip every Tuesday – the drive takes about 90 minutes.

THE MOUNTAINS

Fernie's 2,500 acres pack in a lot of variety, from superb green terrain at the bottom to ungroomed chutes (that will be satisfyingly steep to anyone but the extreme specialist) and huge numbers of steep runs in the trees. Quite a few runs have the quality of going directly down the fall line.

THE SLOPES
Bowl after bowl
What you see when you arrive at the lift base is a trio of impressive mogul slopes towering above you. These excellent black runs exemplify one of the weaknesses of Fernie's lift system: to get to them you must ride lifts way off to the left or right, and then make long traverses – a slow business. The slow Deer chair approaches the foot of these slopes, but goes no further. It's there to serve the main green-run slow-skiing zone.

On the right, **Lizard Bowl** is a broad snowfield reached by the slow Elk quad then the fast Great Bear quad.

Above this is the short Face Lift, a dreadful rope tow that rarely runs. The Face Lift is the best way into **Cedar Bowl** and to Snake Ridge beyond it, but you can still traverse into the lower parts of both Lizard and Cedar Bowls when the Face Lift isn't working. The Haul Back T-bar brings you out of Cedar. There is a mini-bowl between Lizard and Cedar, served by the Boomerang chair.

Off to the left, the Timber Bowl fast quad chair gives access to **Siberia Bowl** and the lower part of **Timber Bowl**. But for access to the higher slopes and to **Currie Bowl** you must take the White Pass quad. A long traverse from the top gets you to the steeper slopes on the flanks of Currie (our favourite area). From there you have to go right to the bottom (unless you head over into Lizard Bowl) and it takes quite a while to get back up for another go.

There are free tours in groups of different abilities, but only on blue and green runs. For the steeper, deeper stuff you need to pay (see 'Schools and guides') – we strongly recommend you do so early in your stay, to help you find your way around and get the most out of your holiday (see the 'Why you need a guide' feature). A reporter recommends chatting to the locals: 'If you are a good skier, they will be delighted to show you the best runs.'

TERRAIN PARKS
Demise of the park?
Fernie no longer builds a traditional park. Instead, there is a patrolled rail park beside the Great Bear Express – you'll need a special pass ($5 per day) and to sign a waiver to use it. There are rails and boxes of various sizes, for all levels.

KEY FACTS	
Resort	1065m
	3,490ft
Slopes	1065-1925m
	3,490-6,320ft
Lifts	10
Pistes	2,504 acres
Green	30%
Blue	40%
Black	30%
Snowmaking	
	125 acres

boarding

Fernie is a fine place for good boarders (and there are a lot of local experts here). Lots of natural gullies, hits and endless off-piste opportunities – including some adrenalin-pumping tree runs and knee-deep powder bowls – will keep freeriders of all abilities grinning from ear to ear. But there's a lot of traversing involved to get to many of the best runs – hard work in fresh snow and bumpy later. The main board shops, Board Stiff and Edge of the World, are in downtown Fernie, the latter with an indoor skate park to use while your board gets tuned. It's not a brilliant place for freestylers – the terrain park has gone; replaced by a smaller rail park – for which you'll need a special pass (see 'Terrain parks'). And faint-hearted intermediates should stay away. A 2008 visitor recommends the website far.treeride.com for 'detailed descriptions and blogs on conditions, from a local Fernie resident'.

LIFT PASSES

Fernie

Prices in C$

Age	1-day	6-day
under 13	26	156
13 to 17	56	336
18 to 64	78	468
over 65	64	384

Free under 6

Beginner rental, pass and tuition deals

Notes
Prices include taxes; half-day pass available

SNOW RELIABILITY
A key part of the appeal

Fernie has an excellent snow record – with an average of 350 inches per year, better than practically all of Colorado. But the altitude is modest: rain is not unknown, and in warmer weather the lower slopes can suffer. Too much snow can be a problem, with the high bowls prone to closure – we've had reports of them being shut all week. Snowmaking has been increased and now covers most of the base area. Piste grooming has also been increased; we were impressed with it on our 2007 visit and so are most reporters.

FOR EXPERTS
Wonderful – but get a guide

The combination of heavy snowfalls and abundant steep terrain with the shelter of trees makes this a superb mountain for good skiers, so long as you know where you are going. To get the most out of the terrain we strongly recommend getting guidance early in your holiday (see feature panel).

There are about a dozen identifiable faces offering genuine black or double-black slopes, each of them with several alternative ways down. Pay attention to the diamonds: the singles are usually pretty tough, and the doubles are serious. Even where the trail map shows trees to be sparse, expect them to be close together, and where there aren't any, expect alder bushes unless there's lots of snow. There are a couple of areas where you can do laps fairly efficiently, but mostly you have to put up with the long traverse-descent-runout-lift-lift cycle on each lap (see 'The slopes').

There are backcountry routes you can take with guidance (some include an overnight camp) and snowcat operations in other nearby mountains – see feature panel. A regular reporter especially enjoyed exploring Fish Bowl, a short hike outside the resort boundary from Cedar Bowl.

Fernie

671

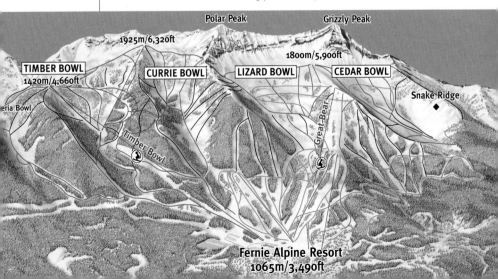

Fernie Alpine Resort
1065m/3,490ft

Good skiers who relish off-piste should consider treating themselves to some cat skiing (where you ride snowcats instead of lifts); there are several operations in this area. Island Lake Lodge (423 3700) does three- or four-day all-inclusive packages in a cosy chalet 10km/6 miles from Fernie, amid 7,000 acres of spectacular bowls and ridges. It has 36 beds and four cats. In a day you might do eight powder runs averaging 500m/1,640ft vertical, taking in all kinds of terrain from gentle open slopes to some very Alpine adventures. You can do single days on a standby basis; we managed this once and loved it, but our second attempt failed. One visitor picked up a late-season bargain with Powder Cowboy (422 8754). It has two cats accessing 6,000 acres, 60km/37 miles from Fernie. 'Absolutely superb; best day's skiing we have ever had.' Fernie Wilderness Adventures (423 6704) has three cats, and reports have been positive.

FOR INTERMEDIATES
Getting better
When we first visited, years ago, only the green and blue runs on the lower mountain were groomed. But on our 2007 visit a few runs from the top were also groomed, including some great blue cruisers down Lizard Bowl – easily reached using the fast quad. But it doesn't add up to much, and if you are not happy to try some of the easier ungroomed terrain in the bowls and glades, we'd recommend you go elsewhere. For the adventurous willing to give the powder a go, though, Fernie should be on your shortlist.

FOR BEGINNERS
Surprisingly, pretty good
There's a good nursery area served by two lifts (a moving carpet and a drag), and the lower mountain served by the Deer and Elk chairs has lots of wide, smooth trails to gain confidence on. But the green runs from the top of the mountain are usually cat-tracks, which nonetheless have tough parts to them.

FOR CROSS-COUNTRY
Some possibilities
There are 10km/6 miles of trails marked out in the forest adjacent to the resort. In the Fernie area as a whole there are around 50km/31 miles of tracks (including some on the fairways of the Fernie golf course).

QUEUES
Not usually a problem
Queues are generally rare unless there are weekend crowds from Calgary or heavy snow keeps part of the mountain closed. But a January 2008 visitor experienced 'lengthy' morning queues for the first lifts during the week, and busier slopes than is normally reported. People also complain about the slow chairlifts, and about breakdowns on one or two.

MOUNTAIN RESTAURANTS
One small sit-down place
Lost Boys Cafe is a small place with good views at the top of the Timber Express chairlift. It has a basic, limited menu and gets mixed reviews – but 'the chilli is lovely – huge portions', says a 2008 visitor. Bear's Den at the top of the Elk chair is an open-air fast-food kiosk. Most people head back to base for lunch. The ancient Day Lodge is a no-frills place serving salads and burgers ('friendly with good service'), Snow Creek is handy for the nursery slopes, has 'comfy sofas by an open fire' and does 'great nachos and wraps'. Kelsey's is popular for burgers, soups and the like. On Sundays you can try the brunch at the Lizard Creek ('you won't eat for the rest of the day').

SCHOOLS AND GUIDES
Highly praised
Reporters praise the school, which seems to achieve rapid progress – no doubt partly because groups are often very small. But we've received a mixed report of private instruction this year: 'Our friends had two lessons, with different instructors; the first one was excellent, the second was poor.'

There are several programmes to help you get the best out of the mountain. The Steep and Deep camps have had good feedback; it is a two-day programme (C$289) where you get technique tips while exploring steep terrain – a great way to get to know the mountain. There is also a Mountain Guide programme (C$129 a day) where you are guided around the groomed and ungroomed runs but not given any coaching. 'First Tracks' (C$169) gets you up the mountain at 8am for two hours – a recent reporter was delighted with this: 'He took us to an untracked bowl and invited us to rip it up!'

SCHOOLS
Fernie
t 423 4655

Classes
Half day (2hr) C$89
(incl. taxes)

Private lessons
C$235 (incl. taxes) for
2hr for up to 5 people

CHILDREN

Telus Resort Kids
t 423 2430
Age 19mnth to 6yr;
8.30 to 4.30

Ski school
For ages 5 to 12
(C$113 per day, incl.
taxes and lunch)

GETTING THERE

Air Calgary 322km/200
miles (3½hr)

ACTIVITIES

Indoor Museum,
galleries, Aquatic
Centre, bowling,
fitness centre, ice
skating, cinema,
curling

Outdoor Sleigh rides,
snowmobiling, dog
sledding, snowshoe
excursions, walking

UK PACKAGES

All America Holidays,
Alpine Answers,
AmeriCan Ski, American
Ski Classics, Canadian
Powder Tours, Chalet
Group, Crystal, Frontier,
Independent Ski Links,
Inghams, Interactive
Resorts, Kuoni, Neilson,
Ski Activity, Ski Dream,
Ski Freshtracks, Ski
Independence, Ski
Safari, Skitracer,
Skiworld, Snoworks,
Virgin Snow

**Central reservations
phone number**
Call 1 877 333 2339
(toll-free from within
Canada)

Phone numbers
From distant parts of
Canada, add the
prefix 1 250; from
abroad, add the prefix
+1 250

TOURIST OFFICE

t 423 4655
info@skifernie.com
www.skifernie.com

FACILITIES FOR CHILDREN
Good day care centre
There's a day care centre in the
Cornerstone Lodge. A 2008 reporter's
son was 'very happy' there – 'the staff
were friendly and efficient'. There are
also 'Kids' Activity Nights' for children
aged six to 12. And there's a
Wilderness Adventure Park where kids
ski past cut-outs of bears and wolves.

STAYING THERE

HOW TO GO
More packages
Fernie is increasingly easy to find in
tour operator brochures.
Chalets Some UK tour operators run
chalets. Beavertail Lodge at the resort
is run along chalet lines and has
received several rave reviews: 'The
best chalet I have ever stayed in; food
equal to a Michelin-starred restaurant.'
Canadian Powder Tours has a chalet in
town and includes in the price guiding
by the owners: 'Food excellent. I am a
novice off-piste but had a brilliant
time.'
Hotels and condos There's a wide
choice, some impressively comfortable.
AT THE RESORT
****Lizard Creek Lodge** Best ski-in/
ski-out condo hotel – 'excellent and
beautifully decorated', says a 2008
visitor. Spa, outdoor pool and hot tub.
****Snow Creek Lodge** Similar to the
Lizard Creek Lodge. 'Fantastic and
extremely convenient.'
***Wolf's Den Mountain Lodge** 'Simple
but comfortable', say reporters. Indoor
hot tub, small gym. At base of slope.
Cornerstone Lodge Condo hotel – 'very
clean, modern and well equipped'.
Griz Inn Sport Hotel Condo hotel with
good facilities. Pool.
Timberline Lodges Very comfortable
condos a shuttle-ride from the lifts.
Alpine Lodge B&B praised by a
reporter – 'welcoming and convenient'.
IN OR TOWARDS TOWN
****Best Western Fernie Mountain
Lodge** Next to golf course near town.
Recommended by reporters. Pool, hot
tub, fitness room. But a 30-minute bus
ride to the slopes.

EATING OUT
Steadily improving
At the base, there isn't a huge choice.
The restaurant of Lizard Creek Lodge
gets mixed reports in 2008: 'excellent
Alberta tenderloin and lobster', but
'food variable', says another reporter.

Gabriella's does cheap and cheerful
Italian, and lots of readers have
enjoyed it. Kelsey's (part of a chain)
serves standard, reliable steaks,
burgers, soups etc.
  In the town of Fernie, there are
quite a few options, which may be a
key factor in deciding where to stay.
Reporter recommendations include the
expensive Old Elevator (a converted
grain store; 'excellent service; the
salmon and elk were delicious'),
Jamochas (a coffee house that does
meals), Curry Bowl (various Asian
styles; 'great meal'), Mojo Rising
(Cajun food) in the Royal hotel, Rip'n
Richard's Eatery (south-western food
and a lively atmosphere), the Corner
Pocket in the Grand Central Hotel
('excellent bison'), Yamagoya ('great
sushi') and Sawai Thai ('out of town a
bit but the best value around; very
popular'). El Guapo, in the Edge of the
World board shop, does 'fresh, tasty,
very cheap' Mexican.

APRES-SKI
Have a beer
During the week, the resort bars are
pretty quiet later on. In town, the bars
of the Royal hotel are popular with
locals. Other recommendations are the
Park Place Lodge Pub ('service, prices
and atmosphere were excellent') and
the bar in the Grand Central hotel
('live music and a good crowd'). The
resort offers BBQs at the mid-
mountain Bear's Den on Fridays, with
a torchlit descent to follow.

OFF THE SLOPES
Get out and about
There is a walking tour of historic
Fernie and visits to the Art Station (old
railroad station). You could take in an
ice hockey game. There's a pool at the
Aquatic Centre and a bowling alley in
town. But the main diversion is the
great outdoors.

Interactive resort shortlist builder at **www.wtss.co.uk**

One of Canada's newest resorts: only a few lifts, but great powder at the top, and a fledgling village at the base

COSTS

① ② ③ ④ ⑤ ⑥

RATINGS

The slopes

Fast lifts	**
Snow	****
Extent	***
Expert	****
Intermediate	***
Beginner	***
Convenience	****
Queues	*****
Mountain restaurants	**

The rest

Scenery	***
Resort charm	**
Off-slope	*

➕ Great terrain for experts and some for adventurous intermediates

➕ Big vertical served by a fast lift

➕ Splendid mountain-top restaurant

➖ Resort village still in early stages

➖ Gondola has no mid-station, so you may have to ski crud lower down

➖ Few groomed intermediate runs

In 2000/01 Whitetooth, a tiny locals' hill with lifts only on the lower slopes, was transformed by a new gondola rising 1150m/3,770ft to access high, powder-filled bowls. In 2002 came a new quad chairlift serving more high slopes. Now, with a choice of lodgings forming a small mountain village at the lift base, Kicking Horse is a proper little resort. If you can't arrange to include a stay here in your plans, it makes a good day trip from Banff or Lake Louise.

THE RESORT

Eight miles from the logging town of Golden, Kicking Horse is planned for completion around 2015. The first phase of a resort village at the lift base now has several lodges, a few restaurants and bars, a ski shop and a general store. Daily buses run from Banff and Lake Louise – C$75 including a lift pass. Golden is a spread-out place beside the transcontinental highway. It has no real charm or centre; we prefer to stay at the mountain, though we don't dispute the view of a recent visitor that there is 'more fun' to be had in the bars of Golden.

THE MOUNTAINS

The lower two-thirds of the hill are wooded, with trails cut in the usual style. The upper third is a mix of open and lightly wooded slopes, with scores of ways down for experts through the bowls, chutes and trees. More terrain served by a new lift is planned, but not until 2010/11.

Slopes The eight-seat gondola to Eagle's Eye takes you to the top in one stage of 1150m/3,770ft vertical. It serves two bowls and CPR Ridge, which separates them. If you want to stay high, you can repeat-ride the slow chair to the slightly higher peak of Blue Heaven. But most of the high slopes lead you below this chair, and with no mid-station on the gondola you have to make the full descent – and the snow conditions on the lower slopes may be poor. Two chairlifts from near the base serve the lower runs that formed the original ski area. There are free mountain tours.

Terrain park There's a small park on the lower slopes.

Snow reliability An average of 275 inches of snow a year is not enough to put the resort in the top flight, but it's not far off. The top slopes usually have light, dry powder but the lower ones may have crud and thin cover.

Experts It's advanced skiers and riders who will get the most out of the area. From CPR Ridge, drop off to skier's

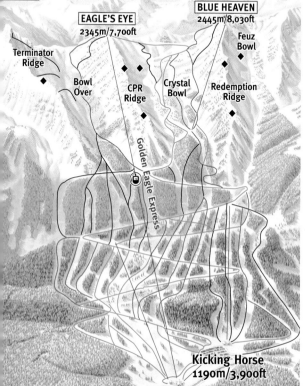

EAGLE'S EYE
2345m/7,700ft

BLUE HEAVEN
2445m/8,030ft

Feuz Bowl

Terminator Ridge

Bowl Over

CPR Ridge

Crystal Bowl

Redemption Ridge

Golden Eagle Express

Kicking Horse
1190m/3,900ft

↑ The Blue Heaven bowl, pictured on our first visit before the chairlift was put in

SNOWPIX.COM / CHRIS GILL

NEWS

For 2007/08 a new blue trail was built from the top of CPR Ridge to Bowl Over, and an ice rink opened at the base.

KEY FACTS

Resort	1190m
	3,900ft
Slopes	1190-2445m
	3,900-8,030ft
Lifts	5
Pistes	2,750 acres
Green	20%
Blue	20%
Black	60%
Snowmaking	Some

UK PACKAGES

All America Holidays, Alpine Answers, AmeriCan Ski, Bramble Ski, Canadian Powder Tours, Crystal, Frontier, Independent Ski Links, Inghams, Kuoni, Neilson, Ski Dream, Ski Freshtracks, Ski Independence, Ski Safari, Skitracer, Skiworld, Snowebb

Central reservations
Call 439 5424
Phone numbers
From distant parts of Canada, add the prefix 1 250; from abroad, add the prefix +1 250

TOURIST OFFICE

t 439 5424
guestservices@kicking horseresort.com
www.kickinghorse resort.com

right through trees or to skier's left through chutes – there are endless options. You can also hike to Terminator Ridge (often closed due to avalanche danger). The chair to Blue Heaven opens up easier ski-anywhere terrain back into Crystal Bowl and access to the wide Feuz Bowl via steep treeless chutes. The lower half of the mountain has short black runs cut through the woods, some with big moguls. There is heli-skiing nearby.

Intermediates Adventurous intermediates will have a fine time learning to play in the powder from Blue Heaven down to Crystal Bowl. Most of it is open, but you can head off into trees if you want to. There is very little groomed cruising, though there is a top-to-bottom 10km/6 mile winding green run. Timid intermediates should go elsewhere.

Beginners We can't imagine why a UK-based beginner would come here, but the beginner slopes are fine.

Snowboarding Freeriders will love this powder paradise.

Cross-country 25km/16 miles of loops plus skating trails at Dawn Mountain; a 5km/3 mile loop on the golf course.

Queues We had our first reports of serious queues for the gondola in 2008: one reporter had a 50-minute wait on a Sunday and another found queues after each run. We have always walked straight on during our visits.

Mountain restaurants The Eagle's Eye at the top of the gondola is Canada's best mountain restaurant – excellent food and service in stylish log-cabin surroundings with splendid views. The Heaven's Door yurt (tent) in Crystal Bowl serves snacks.

Schools and guides Two reporters booked group lessons, and each was the only pupil: 'excellent' was the verdict from both. Another joined a free mountain tour and again was the only one. Yet another took an

avalanche safety course that 'was worth every penny; truly memorable'.

Facilities for children The school teaches children from the age of three.

STAYING THERE

How to go There are smart, quite large condo-style lodges on the slopes and three more captivating places (each with about 10 rooms) a short walk away – described below.

Hotels The log-built Vagabond Lodge features a fabulous first-floor living room, comfortable, traditional-style rooms, a steam room and an outdoor hot tub. Copper Horse Lodge has spacious but more austere rooms in modern styles; outdoor hot tub. Our favourite is Highland Lodge – rooms warmly done out with hardwood furniture from India, a welcoming sitting room and a cosy, woody bar; outdoor hot tubs; 'gourmet breakfast'.

Apartments The Whispering Pines town homes were 'the most luxurious ski lodgings we've had', said a reporter. The 'luxurious' Selkirk apartments are recommended by a 2008 reporter.

Eating out Eagle's Eye at the top of the gondola opens at weekends ('a wonderful evening to remember'). The bar in Highland Lodge does 'well-priced' modern Canadian cooking with a Scottish flavour. Corks in Copper Horse Lodge does excellent 'mountain bistro dining'. Kuma is a sushi bar. Extreme Peaks is a big restaurant in Glacier Lodge. In Golden, Kicking Horse Grill and the out-of-town Cedar House are highly rated.

Après-ski The liveliest place as the lifts close is reportedly The Local Hero with its deck, blazing outdoor fireplace and music. In Golden the Mad Trapper and Golden Taps are lively bars.

Off the slopes There is snowmobiling, snowshoeing, dog sledding, tubing and a new outdoor ice rink.

Kicking Horse

675

Interactive resort shortlist builder at **www.wtss.co.uk**

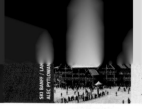

Stunning views and the biggest ski area in the Banff region, with some good places to stay but no real village

RATINGS

The slopes

Fast lifts	★★★
Snow	★★★
Extent	★★★★
Expert	★★★★
Intermediate	★★★★
Beginner	★★★
Convenience	★
Queues	★★★★
Mountain restaurants	★★

The rest

Scenery	★★★★★
Resort charm	★★★
Off-slope	★★★★

NEWS

For 2007/08 snowmaking was improved and various improvements were made to the lodges and Kokanee Kabin. There are longer-term plans to build a new mountain restaurant close to the top of the Grizzly Express gondola.

676

+ Spectacular high-mountain scenery
+ Relatively large ski area
+ Snowy slopes of Sunshine Village within reach (see Banff chapter)
+ Lots of wildlife around the valley
+ Good value for money

− 'Village' is just a few hotels and shops, fairly quiet in the evening
− Local slopes a short drive from the 'village', Banff areas further
− Snowfall modest by local standards
− Can be very cold and the chairlifts have no covers

If you care more for scenery than for après-ski action, Lake Louise is worth considering for a holiday. We've seen a few spectacular mountain views, and the view from the Fairmont Chateau Lake Louise hotel of the Victoria Glacier across the frozen Lake Louise is as spectacular as they come: simply stunning.

Even if you prefer the more animated base of Banff, you'll want to make expeditions to Lake Louise during your holiday. It can't compete with Sunshine Village for quantity of snow, but it's a big and interesting mountain. And from the slopes you get a distant version of that stunning view.

THE RESORT

Although it's a small place, Lake Louise is a resort of parts. First, there's the lake itself, in a spectacular setting beneath the Victoria Glacier. Tom Wilson, who discovered it in 1882, declared, 'As God is my judge, I never in all my exploration have seen such a matchless scene.' Neither have we. And it can be appreciated from many of the rooms of the vast Fairmont Chateau Lake Louise hotel on the shore. Then there's Lake Louise 'village' – a collection of a few hotels, condos, petrol station, liquor store and shops, a couple of miles away on a road junction. Finally, a mile or two across the valley, there's the lift base station. A car helps, especially in cold weather. Buses run every half hour to the Lake Louise ski area, but a lot less frequently to the Banff areas, Sunshine and Norquay. Bus trips to the more distant resorts of Panorama and Kicking Horse and to the small resorts of Nakiska and Fortress are all possible, as are heli-skiing day trips. Banff Airporter do transfers from and to Calgary airport.

THE MOUNTAINS

The Lake Louise ski area is big by North American standards, with a mixture of high, open slopes, low trails cut through forest and gladed slopes between the two. But to us it doesn't feel as big as they try to make out; if you stick to the groomed trails, a good intermediate could ski it all in a day or two. Reporters are usually full of praise for the free guided tours at 10am and 1.15pm. There has been some criticism of inconsistent piste grading and lots about cold lifts with no covers.

THE SLOPES
A wide variety

From the base area you have a choice of a fast quad to mid-mountain, followed by a six-pack to the top centre of the **Front Side** (also called the South Face), or the gondola direct to a slightly lower point on the right side of the Front Side. From both, as elsewhere, there's a choice of green, blue or black runs (good for a group of mixed abilities who want to keep meeting up). In poor visibility, the gondola is a better option, as the treeline goes almost to the top there. Or you can stay on the lower part of the mountain using the chairs. From mid-mountain on the left, the long Summit draglift takes you to the high point of the area – where there are stunning views of peaks and glaciers,

Top of the World
West Bowl
2635m/8,650ft
Powder Bowls and Larch
Powder Bowls and Larch
2500m/8,200ft
Eagle Ridge
Powder Bowls and Larch
238om/7,810ft
Whitehorn Lodge 2055m
2090m
LAKE LOUISE FRONT SIDE
Temple Lodge 2015m
LARCH
Glacier
Grizzly
Whiskeyjack Lodge 1645m/5,400ft
Lodge of the Ten Peaks

KEY FACTS

Resort	1645m
	5,400ft

Sunshine, Norquay and Lake Louise, covered by the Tri-area pass

Slopes	1630-2730m
	5,350-8,950ft
Lifts	27
Pistes	7,748 acres
Green	23%
Blue	39%
Black	38%
Snowmaking	
	1,900 acres

Lake Louise only

Slopes	1645-2635m
	5,400-8,650ft
Lifts	9
Pistes	4,200 acres
Green	25%
Blue	45%
Black	30%
Snowmaking	40%

including Canada's Matterhorn lookalike, Mount Assiniboine.

From here or the top chair you can go over the ridge and into the almost treeless **Powder Bowls** – open, predominantly north-facing and mainly steep. From the top of the gondola, the Ptarmigan area is more wooded.

From low down in the bowls you can take the Paradise lift back to the top again or continue lower to the separate **Larch** area, served by a fast quad chair. With a lift-served vertical of 375m/1,230ft it's not huge, but it has pretty wooded runs of all grades. From the bottom you can return to the top of the main mountain via the Ptarmigan chair or take a long green path back to the main base area. Grooming is 'good'.

TERRAIN PARKS
No more jumps

The Telus park under the Glacier lift was completely changed for 2007/08. Man-made jumps were scrapped (a decision that caused much local disapproval). On the upside there has been a significant amount of investment in boosting rail and box features. Small rollers are still present to give novices a chance to experience a bit of air-time. The speedy Glacier lift takes riders up to the top of the park.

SNOW RELIABILITY
Usually OK

Lake Louise gets around 140 inches a year on the Front Side, which by the standards of western Canada is not a lot, and nowhere near as much as Sunshine Village down the road (see

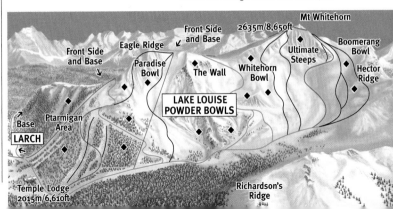

Mt Whitehorn
2635m/8,650ft
Front Side and Base
Eagle Ridge
Front Side and Base
Paradise Bowl
The Wall
Whitehorn Bowl
Ultimate Steeps
Boomerang Bowl
Hector Ridge
LAKE LOUISE POWDER BOWLS
Base
Ptarmigan Area
LARCH
Temple Lodge 2015m/6,610ft
Richardson's Ridge

LIFT PASSES

Tri-area lift pass

Prices in C$

Age	1-day	6-day
under 13	25	228
13 to 17	53	432
18 to 64	76	485
over 65	61	432

Free under 6

Beginner lift, lesson and rental package

Notes

Day pass is for Lake Louise only; 3-day-plus pass covers all lifts and transport between Banff, Lake Louise, Norquay and Sunshine Village; prices include tax

SCHOOLS

Ski Big 3
t 760 7731
Lake Louise
t 522 1333

Classes (Big 3 prices)
3 days guided tuition of the three areas
C$269 incl. tax
Private lessons
Half day (3hr) C$377, incl. tax, for up to 5 people

CHILDREN

Telus Play Station & Daycare
t 522 3555
Ages 18 days to 6yr;
8.30 to 4.30

Ski school
Takes ages 5 to 12 (3 days C$267, incl. tax and lunch)

boarding

Lake Louise is a great mountain for freeriders, with all the challenging terrain in the bowls and glades. The two sides of the mountain mean there is ample space at this sometimes very crowded resort. Get up early and head to the Powder Bowls first thing for some epic fun. Ask a local or hire a guide to get the best out of the bowls, as there is often great terrain only a short hike away. Beginners will have fun on the Front Side's blue and green runs. But there's a T-bar at the base area and beware of the vicious Summit button lift (top left looking at the trail map). Also avoid the long, flat green run through the woods from Larch back to base. For those less into freeriding there are three terrain parks to suit all levels. The terrain park no longer has man-made jumps, and is now strictly a rail and jib area.

the Banff chapter). But it is usually enough, and there is snowmaking on 40% of the pistes. The north-facing Powder Bowls and Larch hold the snow pretty well.

FOR EXPERTS
Widespread pleasure
There are plenty of steep slopes. On the Front Side, as well as a score of marked black-diamond trails in and above the trees, there is the alluring West Bowl, reached from the Summit drag – a wide, open expanse of snow outside the area boundary. Because this is National Park territory, you can in theory go anywhere. But outside the boundaries there are no patrols and, of course, no avalanche control. A guide is essential. 'You get a real feel of being in the middle of nowhere. The return through thick woods is great fun,' says a reporter.

Inside the boundaries, going over to the Powder Bowls opens up countless black mogul/powder runs. From the Summit drag, you can drop into The Ultimate Steeps (if it is open), directly behind the peak. The runs here gave our fearless Aussie editor what she called 'some of the most exciting in-bounds skiing in North America' – a row of extreme chutes, almost 1km/0.5 miles long. You can also access lots of much tamer, wide, open Powder Bowl slopes that take you right away from all signs of lifts.

The Top of the World six-pack takes you to the very popular Paradise Bowl/Eagle Ridge/Quadra Ridge area, also served by its own triple chair on the back side – there are endless variants here, ranging from the comfortably steep single diamonds to very challenging double diamonds. The seriously steep slope served by the Ptarmigan quad chair has great gladed terrain and is a good place to beat the

crowds and find good snow. The Larch area has some steep double-diamond stuff in the trees, and open snowfields at the top for those with the energy to hike up ('needs good snow-cover though', says a reporter). Heli-skiing is available outside the National Park.

FOR INTERMEDIATES
Some good cruising
Almost half the runs are classified as intermediate. But from the top of the Front Side the blue runs down are little more than paths in places, and there are very few blues or greens in the Powder Bowls. Once you get part-way down the Front Side the blues are much more interesting. And when groomed, the Men's and Ladies' Downhill black runs are great fast cruises on the lower half of the mountain. Juniper is a wonderful cruising run in the same area. Meadowlark is a beautiful treelined run to the base area – to find it from the Grizzly Express gondola, first follow Eagle Meadows. The Larch area has some short but ideal intermediate runs – and reporters have enjoyed the natural lumps and bumps of the aptly named blue, Rock Garden ('never had so much fun; really away from it all'). The adventurous should also try the blue Boomerang run – which starts with a short side-step up from the top of the Summit drag – and some of the ungroomed Powder Bowls terrain.

FOR BEGINNERS
Excellent terrain
Louise has a good nursery area near the base that has attracted praise, served by a short T-bar that has not. You progress to the gentle, wide Wiwaxy, Pinecone Way and the slightly more difficult Deer Run or Eagle Meadows (all designated 'slow skiing zones'). There are even green slow-

↑ The ski area base on the left and the frozen Lake Louise itself in the distance

SNOWPIX.COM / CHRIS GILL

skiing zones round the Powder Bowls and in the Larch area – worth trying for the views, though some do contain slightly steep pitches ('our beginner was very nervous trying the Saddleback Bowl'). A past reporter lost confidence by tackling these, and found that people still skied fast in the slow areas and that they were quite crowded.

FOR CROSS-COUNTRY
High in quality and quantity
It's a very good area for cross-country, with around 80km/50 miles of groomed trails in the National Park – plenty of scenic stops needed. There are 14km/9 miles of excellent trails in the local area and on Lake Louise itself. And Emerald Lake Lodge 40km/25 miles away has some lovely trails and has been recommended as a place to stay for a peaceful time.

QUEUES
Not unknown
Half of the area's visitors come for the day from nearby cities, such as Calgary, so there can be queues at weekends and public holidays – 10 minutes, says a recent visitor – especially for the slow chairs on the back of the mountain.

MOUNTAIN RESTAURANTS
Good base facilities
There's not much choice up the mountain. Temple Lodge, near the bottom of Larch and the Ptarmigan chair, is built in rustic style with a big terrace, but can get crowded. Its restaurant, Sawyer's Nook, is the only table-service option on the mountain, and it continues to receive praise from reporters; reserve a table. Whitehorn Lodge, at mid-mountain on the Front Side, is a cafeteria with fine views across to Lake Louise from its balcony.

Most people eat at the base, where there are big-scale facilities. The Lodge of the Ten Peaks is a hugely impressive, spacious, airy, modern, log-built affair with various eating, drinking and lounging options, including the Great Bear Room self-service. The neighbouring Whiskeyjack building has another self-service. The Kokanee Kabin enlarged its BBQ area and installed a fire pit last season.

SCHOOLS AND GUIDES
Generally good reports
We get good reports. 'The best teaching we've encountered' is how a reporter described his 'bumps' lesson at Lake Louise. Another reporter enjoyed the lessons, but said she could not get afternoon-only classes. And her five-year-old daughter did not like being put in classes with eight to ten year olds. See the Banff chapter for details on the excellent three-day, three-mountain Club Ski and Club Snowboard Program.

FACILITIES FOR CHILDREN
Varying reports
We lack recent reports, but past reporters have been full of praise; it's best to book day care in advance. The Minute Maid Wilderness Adventure Park is a children's discovery and learning area situated at the bottom of the gondola.

STAYING THERE

HOW TO GO
Good value accommodation
How to go You might like to consider a two-centre holiday, combining Lake Louise with, say, Banff or Kicking Horse. There are plenty of packages to Lake Louise, including those offered by Canada specialist Frontier Ski and North America specialists AmeriCan Ski and Ski Independence.

↑ The Lodge of the Ten Peaks is one of the smartest base lodges in Canada
LAKE LOUISE / JOHNEVELYPHOTO. COM

ACTIVITIES

Indoor Mainly hotel-based pools, saunas and hot tubs, bowling, cinema, museums

Outdoor Ice rinks, walking, swimming in hot springs, sleigh rides, dog sledding, snowshoeing

Phone numbers
From distant parts of Canada, add the prefix 1 403; from abroad, add the prefix +1 403

TOURIST OFFICE

t 522 3555
info@skilouise.com
www.skilouise.com
www.SkiBig3.com

Hotels Summer is the peak season here. Prices are much lower in winter.
*****Fairmont Chateau Lake Louise (522 3511) Grand monster with 500 rooms and seven restaurants in a fantastic setting with stunning glacier views over frozen Lake Louise; shops, pool, hot tub, sauna.
****Post (522 3989) Small, relaxed, comfortable Relais & Châteaux place in the village, with excellent restaurant (huge wine list), pool, hot tub, steam room. Avoid rooms on railway side.
***Lake Louise Inn (522 3791) Cheaper option in the village, with pool, hot tub and sauna. 'Comfortable rooms'; 'good food'; 'staff helpful'.
***Deer Lodge (522 3991) Charming old hotel next to the Chateau, but a 2008 visitor was 'very disappointed' and thought it 'not well organised or run'. Roof-top hot tub.
Apartments Some are available but local shopping is limited. The Baker Creek Chalets (522 3761) were highly recommended by reporters on their honeymoon ('really romantic').

EATING OUT
Limited choice
The Post hotel's restaurant has repeatedly impressed us with its ambitious food and excellent service.

The Fairview Dining Room at the Chateau is also top-notch. The Station restaurant is in an atmospheric old station building ('interesting menu, reasonable prices and attentive but relaxed service').

APRÈS-SKI
Lively at teatime, quiet later
There are several options at the bottom of the slopes. The Lodge of the Ten Peaks has lovely surroundings, an open fire and a relaxed atmosphere. The Kokanee Kabin has live music on spring weekend afternoons, outdoor fire and terrace. The Powderkeg was refurbished a couple of seasons ago. On Fridays there's live music and dancing and a buffet dinner at the mid-mountain Whitehorn Lodge. You ski or ride there as the lifts close, and the evening ends with a torchlit descent. It is hugely popular with British visitors.

Later on, things are fairly quiet. But the Glacier Saloon, in Chateau Lake Louise, with traditional Wild West decor, often has live music until late. Explorer's Lounge, in the Lake Louise Inn, has entertainment.

OFF THE SLOPES
Beautiful scenery
Lake Louise makes a lovely, peaceful place to stay for someone who does not intend to hit the slopes. The lake itself makes a stunning setting for walks, snowshoeing, cross-country skiing and ice skating. You can go on ice canyon walks, sleigh rides, dog sledding, snowmobiling, sightseeing tours and visits to the natural hot springs. For a more lively day or for shopping you can visit Banff.

Lake Louise is near one end of the Columbia Icefields Parkway, a three-hour drive to Jasper through National Parks, amid stunningly beautiful scenery of high peaks and glaciers – one of the world's most beautiful drives.

STAYING UP THE MOUNTAIN
Try ski touring
Skoki Lodge (522 3555) is 11km/ 7 miles on skis from Temple Lodge. Built in the 1930s, the lodge and cabins and allegedly has 'gourmet food'. Reports welcome.

A purpose-built Intrawest resort with an unusual mountain – not many lifts, but a sizeable area and an impressive vertical

COSTS

① ② ③ ④ ⑤ ⑥

RATINGS

The slopes

Fast lifts	★★★
Snow	★★★
Extent	★★
Expert	★★★★
Intermediate	★★★
Beginner	★★★★
Convenience	★★★★
Queues	★★★★★
Mountain restaurants	★

The rest

Scenery	★★★
Resort charm	★★
Off-slope	★

NEWS

For 2007/08 the Hay Fever World Cup black run was widened. Grooming equipment was updated, and dog sledding tours were introduced.

+ Car-free village with some slope-side lodgings, plus a lower part

+ Fair-sized ski area with big vertical

+ Runs are usually deserted

– Not many easy cruising runs

– Snowfall record not impressive by high local standards

– Quiet, even lifeless village

Panorama's vertical of 1220m/4,000ft is one of the biggest in North America, and it has some excellent terrain for experts and adventurous intermediates. It's good for beginners, too. But timid intermediates may find themselves confined to the rather limited lower mountain.

THE RESORT

Panorama is a small, quiet, purpose-built resort above the lakeside town of Invermere in eastern British Columbia, about two hours' scenic drive south-west of Banff. Accommodation is concentrated mainly in two car-free areas. There are attractive lodges with a hot-pool complex and a skating rink at the foot of the main slopes; with ski-in/ski-out convenience, this is the best place to stay. But a lot of lodging is in a 'lower village' that lacks character or life. This is linked to the 'upper village' and the slopes by a bucket lift that runs until 10pm. The resort runs day trips to Lake Louise and Kicking Horse (given a demand).

THE MOUNTAINS

The slopes basically follow three ridges, joined at top and bottom. Almost all of the terrain is wooded. The trail map is twice the size it needs to be, but is clear. Helpful handwritten boards at the lifts show trail conditions. Free tours of the mountain are available twice daily. Night skiing is offered Thursday to Saturday.

Slopes From the upper village, a fast quad goes over gentle slopes to mid-mountain, and above it another fast quad serves both intermediate and expert slopes. Then a slow quad takes you to the summit. From here there are long blue and black runs down various ridges and two expert bowls.

Terrain parks There are two: the main Showzone park on the Powder trail is 1km/0.5 mile long, with tabletops, spines, rails and fun boxes. There's a medium-sized park and half-pipe near the Toby lift.

Snow reliability Annual snowfall is low by local standards (188 inches – about half the Fernie figure). But 40% of trails are covered by snowmaking, and grooming is 'excellent'.

Experts There are genuine black runs scattered all over the mountain, and some expert-only areas. At the very top of the mountain and accessed through a gate is the Extreme Dream Zone – seriously steep trails with cliffs and tight trees. Off the back of the summit is the Taynton Bowl area. We loved this – open areas, lightly and more densely forested areas, very few people, best snow on the hill. It is marked double black diamond, but it really isn't worryingly steep. And the vertical of 1220m/4,000ft is one of the greatest in North America. But doing laps is a rather slow business – a long

681

KEY FACTS

Resort	1160m
	3,800ft
Slopes	1160-2380m
	3,800-7,810ft
Lifts	9
Pistes	2,847 acres
Green	20%
Blue	55%
Black	25%
Snowmaking	40%

UK PACKAGES

AmeriCan Ski, Ardmore, Frontier, Inghams, Ski Dream, Ski Independence, Ski Safari, Snoworks

Central reservations
Call 342 6941

Phone numbers
From distant parts of Canada, add the prefix 1 250; from abroad, add +1 250

TOURIST OFFICE

t 342 6941
paninfo@intrawest.com
www.skipanorama.com

PANORAMA MOUNTAIN VILLAGE

Taynton Bowl – great expert terrain, but doing laps is a rather slow business ↓

blue cruise run-out, then three lifts (one slow). There's local heli-skiing, too (see 'Intermediates').

Intermediates For adventurous intermediates the terrain is excellent – there are easy blacks all over the mountain, some of them regularly groomed. The black View of 1000 Peaks has fabulous views but can be a bit tricky in parts. Both this and the blue run from the top are long for North America (up to 3.5km/2 miles). Sun Bowl is a good introduction to a powder bowl and Millennium (black running into blue) is a great roller coaster. But the less confident may find all this uncomfortably challenging. The blues in the centre of the area are gentler but they don't add up to a lot. RK Heli-Skiing is based in the village and specialises in one-day sessions for first-time heli-skiers.

Beginners There are a couple of nursery lifts and a moving carpet serving a quiet and gentle nursery area. There are good, longer runs to progress to on the Mile 1 fast quad.

Snowboarding There is good steep terrain and tree runs for expert freeriders. The main lifts are all chairs, and beginners have several good long green runs to practise on.

Cross-country There are 10km/6 miles of trails starting at the Nordic Centre.

Queues We get no reports of queues, but the Sunbird triple chair is said to be prone to breakdowns.

Mountain restaurants Reserve a table at Elkhorn Cabin, a tiny, charming old mountain hut (complete with roaring log fire) that many European resorts would be proud of. They serve a C$17 two-course lunch – go for the delicious Quebec Meat Pie followed by Maple Syrup ice cream. The Ski Tip Lodge at the base is OK, but gets busy. The clubhouse at the Nordic Centre is quieter – 'good soups'.

Schools and guides We have mainly had glowing reports of the ski school.

'Excellent boarding lessons on each of our three visits,' says a repeat visitor. 'Progressed quickly' and 'massive leap in skiing' are typical comments. There's an Extreme Makeover clinic.

Facilities for children Wee Wascals is the child care centre, taking children from 18 months to five years. The school runs Snowbirds for three to four year olds, and the Adventure Club for kids from 5 to 14. Kids' themed nights are arranged some evenings. Evening babysitters are also available.

STAYING THERE

How to go The better places are the newer ones in the upper village.

Hotels Earl Grey Lodge is a smart, central, six-bedroom, log-built place.

Apartments Panorama Springs is right on the slopes with a big outdoor hot-pool and sauna facility. We stayed at the 1000 Peaks Summit recently and thought it very comfortable and spacious. The 1000 Peaks Lodge is similar. The grocery store is inadequate, so stock up in Invermere.

Eating out Options are limited but improving. Earl Grey Lodge has established itself at the top of the market with excellent fixed menus. The Wildfire Grill, Chopper's Landing ('excellent menu and a relaxed, friendly atmosphere') and the Great Hall (pasta and pizza) are recommended by reporters. The ski school organises BBQs at the Elkhorn Cabin (see 'Mountain restaurants'), followed by a torchlit descent. There's a horse-drawn wagon ride followed by chilli around a campfire. A bus goes once a night to and from restaurants in Invermere. Recent reporters recommend Angus McToogle's, Portabellas and Strands there.

Après-ski This revolves around the Crazy Horse Saloon in the Pine Inn, which has live music, and the Jackpine pub in the Horsethief Lodge. Ski Tip Lodge is popular as the lifts close. The Earl Grey Lodge has 'upmarket après-ski cocktails/sushi'.

Off the slopes The hot-pool facility – with thermal baths, a swimming pool, slides and a sauna – is excellent, but it gets rather taken over by kids. There are new dog sledding tours, snowmobiling, ice fishing, snowshoeing and skating. The Wolf Education Centre and Bavin Glassworks ('quirky handmade glass jewellery') are worth visiting.

SILVER STAR KL
PHOTOGRAPHY

Tiny, car-free, purpose-built village designed to resemble a Victorian-era mining town, with slopes for all standards

➕ Atmospheric purpose-built village
➕ Very family-friendly
➕ Some good runs for all abilities
➕ Excellent cross-country skiing

➖ Tiny village with little choice of bars and restaurants; very quiet at night
➖ Limited choice of accommodation
➖ Ski area not huge

This quiet, family-friendly resort has a tiny traffic-free centre resembling a 19th-century mining town. There are slopes to suit everyone, and it's easy to combine a stay here with one at Big White, which has the same owners.

THE RESORT

Silver Star is a small, recently built resort right on the slopes and with a compact, car-free centre of brightly painted Victorian-style buildings with wooden sidewalks and pseudo gas lights. It's a bit Disneyesque but works surprisingly well. Big (also brightly coloured) chalets are dotted in the trees. Big White resort (see separate chapter) is under the same ownership; there are weekly day trips by bus, and the twice-a-week transfers make a two-centre holiday easy.

THE MOUNTAINS

The mountain has trees going right to the top and three main linked faces. Free daily tours are offered at 9.30 and 1.15.

Slopes The mainly south-facing Vance Creek slopes around the village have largely easy intermediate slopes served by a six-pack, which starts below the main village. From there you can reach the Silver Woods area of north-east-facing, mainly intermediate slopes and glades, served by a high-speed quad. The top of the Vance

683

Champagne powder awaits at the friendly picturesque boutique resort of Silver Star. It's not surprising those who ski here call it "My Mountain" and with one visit you will too! Frontier Ski are specialists in Canada and offer holidays at Silver Star Mountain Resort.

NEWS

For 2007/08 a new Pipe Magician tool improved the sculpting of the half-pipe, and a new quad chair replaced the old Silver Queen chair (mainly used for accessing some accommodation).

Kelowna airport (one hour away) is being improved so that it will be able to take bigger planes (including transatlantic flights). Work is expected to be complete by autumn 2008.

KEY FACTS

Resort	1610m
	5,280ft
Slopes	1155-1915m
	3,790-6,280ft
Lifts	12
Pistes	3,065 acres
Green	20%
Blue	50%
Black	30%
Snowmaking	none

UK PACKAGES

All America Holidays, AmeriCan Ski, American Ski Classics, Frontier, Ski Dream, Ski Independence, Ski Line, Ski Safari, Skiworld, Snowebb

Central reservations Call 558 6083; toll-free (within Canada) 1 800 663 4431
Phone numbers From distant parts of Canada, add the prefix 1 250; from abroad, add +1 250

TOURIST OFFICE

t 542 0224
star@skisilverstar.com
www.skisilverstar.com

Creek area links to the Putnam Creek face on the back side, which has lots of steep black and double-black trails, mostly with big moguls, served by a fast quad. But you can stick to easier alternatives too. There are lots of flattish areas, including the link with the back side.

Terrain parks The Telus park on the Vance Creek side is aimed at beginner and intermediate park users and has tabletops, hips, fun boxes, rails, wall rides and a half-pipe. There's a separate Aerial Training Site with big air jumps.

Snow reliability Silver Star gets an average of 276 inches a year, not enough to put it in the top flight but it's not far off.

Experts Putnam Creek has a dense network of single- and double-black-diamond runs plunging through the trees, many of them mogul runs. The runs to the left as you ride up the chair are north-facing and keep their snow well. There are some short blacks on the Vance Creek side, too.

Intermediates Vance Creek has mainly easy cruising runs. Silver Woods has lovely runs cut through the trees and easy blue gladed runs amid the trees themselves. Putnam Creek also has excellent blue cruising – we especially liked Gypsy Queen and Sunny Ridge. Good intermediates will appreciate the two black runs they groom daily (look on the boards for which they are).

Beginners There's a nursery area by the village with a moving carpet and long easy green runs to move on to.

Snowboarding There's a T-bar at the top of the Putnam side, but the other lifts are all chairs. Several flattish areas make life difficult though.

Cross-country Cross-country is big; they claim 'The Best Nordic Skiing in

North America', and several national teams are training here in the run-up to the 2010 Winter Olympics. There are over 100km/62 miles of trails.

Queues None of our reporters mention any queues.

Mountain restaurants There's a small atmospheric hut near the top of the Powder Gulch chair on Putnam Creek, serving simple hot food.

School and guides The ski school has a good reputation. A 2008 reporter said, 'The instructors were fantastic with our three-year-old having his first lessons; adult lessons were also very good, often with only two in a group.'

Facilities for children Star Kids takes children aged five and under. 'Our children loved it,' said a 2008 reporter.

STAYING THERE

How to go It is mainly specialist North American operators who come here, such as Frontier Ski, AmeriCan Ski and Ski Independence.

Hotels Silver Star Club Resort has three separate properties including the Vance Creek right in the village centre.

Apartments The ski-in/ski-out Snowbird Lodge in the village centre is the best in town, with private hot tubs. There are lots of other options, including renting houses.

Eating out A 2008 reporter praises the Bulldog Grand Cafe ('great food and very child-friendly') and Long John's Pub in the Lord Aberdeen Hotel with mining theme decor.

Après-ski It's very quiet. But the Club Saloon and the Den Bistro and Bar may be lively and have live entertainment.

Off the slopes There's a pretty natural ice rink on a lake, a nearby tubing hill and horse-drawn sleigh rides.

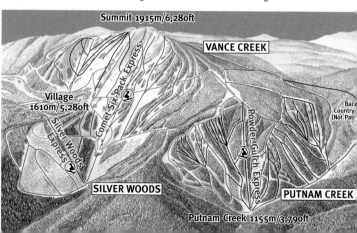

Attractive, car-free village at the foot of three linked mountains with varied slopes including some unusual easy groomed gladed runs

COSTS

① ② ③ ④ ⑤ ⑥

RATINGS

The slopes

Fast lifts	★★★
Snow	★★★★
Extent	★★★
Expert	★★★
Intermediate	★★★★
Beginner	★★★★
Convenience	★★★★
Queues	★★★★★
Mountain restaurants	★

The rest

Scenery	★★★
Resort charm	★★★
Off-slope	★★

NEWS

For 2007/08 new features were added to the terrain parks for beginners and intermediates. The Delta Residences, a 41-suite hotel, opened in the heart of the village, together with a larger grocery and a liquor store inside.

For 2008/09 snowmaking is to be increased, and a new machine will result in improved grooming of the cross-country tracks.

➕ Some great terrain for all standards

➕ Excellent glades

➕ Slopes very quiet during the week

➕ Attractive, traffic-free, slope-side village – with some smart shops

➕ Good for families

➖ Village may be too small and quiet for some tastes

➖ Snow on some of the lower steep terrain can suffer from the sun

➖ It's the second largest ski area in BC, but not big by Alpine standards

Sun Peaks has sprung from the drawing board since the mid-1990s. It now has an almost complete small village and a fair amount of varied terrain. Former Olympic Giant Slalom champion Nancy Greene and husband Al Raine, who were instrumental in developing Whistler, have made Sun Peaks their home and live in the Cahilty Lodge. Nancy is Director of Skiing and skis with guests daily. We suggest combining it with, say, Whistler, Silver Star or Big White on a two- or three-centre trip. There are regular inter-resort transfers.

THE RESORT

Until 1993 Sun Peaks was known as Tod Mountain, a local hill for the residents of nearby Kamloops. Since then the ski area has been expanded, and a small, attractive resort village with low-rise pastel-coloured buildings with a vaguely Tirolean feeling to them developed. The traffic-free main street is lined with accommodation, restaurants and shops, including a smart art gallery, a great chocolate shop and a few coffee bars. It's a pleasant place to stroll around and very family-friendly.

THE MOUNTAINS

With almost 3,700 acres of skiable terrain, Sun Peaks is the second biggest ski area in British Columbia (Whistler is the biggest). There are free guided tours twice a day (9.15 and 1pm) and at 1pm you can ski for free with former Olympic champion and Canada's Female Athlete of the 20th Century Nancy Greene when she's in town (don't miss it – she is great fun!). At the top of all main lifts there is a board with the grooming conditions of the pistes in that area.

Slopes There are three distinct sectors, each served by a high-speed quad.

One goes from the centre of the village to mid-mountain on Sun Peaks' original ski hill, Mt Tod. This has mainly black runs, but there are easier blues and greens. A tiny snowcat

offers day-long backcountry skiing here, but runs are very short (100-130m/330-430ft vertical), and lots of slopes had been tracked by snowmobilers when we did it. Many of Mt Tod's steepest runs are served only by the slow Burfield quad (there's a mid-station that allows you to ski the top runs only) – and these runs are

KEY FACTS	
Resort	1255m
	4,120ft
Slopes	1200-2080m
	3,930-6,820ft
Lifts	12
Pistes	3,678 acres
Green	10%
Blue	58%
Black	32%
Snowmaking	
	40 acres

'even quieter than the rest', says a recent reporter.

Also reached from the village centre, the Sundance area has mainly blue and green cruising runs. Both Sundance and Tod have some great gladed areas to play in (12 of them marked on the trail map).

Mt Morrisey is reached by a long green run from the top of Sundance and has a delightful network of easy blue runs with trees left uncut in the trails, effectively making them groomed glade runs that even early intermediates can try.

Terrain parks There are three levels of park on Sundance – advanced with rails, jumps, jibs and fun boxes, plus intermediate and beginner areas that were expanded for 2007/08 with extra features. But there is no half-pipe.

Snow reliability Sun Peaks gets an average snowfall of 220 inches a year: not in the top league but better than some. The snow can suffer on the lower part of Mt Tod's south-facing slopes, especially later in the season.

Experts Mt Tod has most of the steep terrain, though some of the blacks on Mt Morrisey (such as Static Cling) are long mogul runs, too. You can ski lots of good steep and gladed runs without descending to the bottom of Mt Tod by riding the Burfield quad from its mid-station, and the Crystal and Elevation chairs. You could also

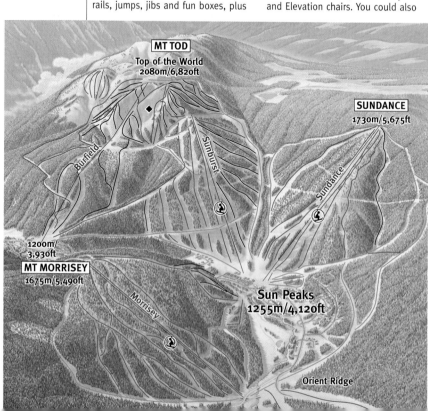

MT TOD
Top of the World
2080m/6,820ft

SUNDANCE
1730m/5,675ft

Burfield

Sunburst

Sundance

1200m/
3,930ft
MT MORRISEY
1675m/5,490ft

Morrisey

Sun Peaks
1255m/4,120ft

Orient Ridge

↑ The small village has been prettily developed and is largely traffic-free and very family-friendly

SUN PEAKS RESORT

UK PACKAGES

All America Holidays, AmeriCan Ski, American Ski Classics, Cold Comforts Lodging, Erna Low, Frontier, Ski Dream, Ski Independence, Ski Line, Ski Safari, Skitracer, Skiworld, Snowebb

Phone numbers
From distant parts of Canada, add the prefix 1 250; from abroad, add the prefix +1 250

TOURIST OFFICE

t 578 5474
info@sunpeaksresort.
com
www.sunpeaksresort.
com

try the backcountry snowcat operation.
Intermediates This is great terrain for early intermediates, with the easy and charming groomed glades of Mt Morrisey, lovely swooping blues on Sundance and the long 5 Mile run from Mt Tod. More adventurous intermediates can also tackle the easier glades (such as Cahilty) and blacks (such as Peek-A-Boo).
Beginners There are nursery slopes right in the village centre, with long easy greens to progress to.
Snowboarding Boarders can explore the whole mountain. But beware the flat greens to and from Mt Morrisey.
Cross-country 40km/25 miles of trails.
Queues Weekdays are usually very quiet; it's only at peak weekends that you might find short queues (of about six or seven minutes, suggests a recent reporter).
Mountain restaurants The Sunburst Lodge is the only option but has 'well-priced fare with a good choice', says a recent reporter; its cinnamon buns are highly recommended. The Umbrella Cafe at the Morrisey base serves hot soup and sandwiches and 'has the best toilets on the mountain'. And it's easy to return to a village restaurant for lunch.
Schools and guides A recent visitor chose private lessons and 'found the instruction second to none and worth every cent'. Another reporter had a 'fantastic instructor' and was the only person in a group lesson. Her kids 'were happy', too, but her husband found that his lesson (with five others) was 'more like a guided tour'.

Facilities for children The playschool takes kids from age 18 months and the ski school kids from three years.

STAYING THERE

How to go There's a lot of self-catering accommodation as well as hotels.
Hotels Nancy Greene's Cahilty Lodge is a friendly and comfortable ski-in/ski-out base and you get the chance to ski with her and husband Al Raine (former Canadian ski team coach): 'It was great fun skiing with Nancy and Al; good rooms – a very welcoming hotel,' says a reporter. The ski-in/ski-out Delta Sun Peaks Resort (outdoor pool and hot tub) in the village centre is 'luxurious with lovely rooms' and 'really good food'. We've enjoyed staying at both.
Eating out For a small resort, there's a good choice of restaurants, including Thai, Italian and, of course, North American. Macker's Bistro is popular, and we had great Thai-style sea bass there. Powder Hounds (good steaks), Steak House ('good honest steaks'), Servus (more sophisticated food) and Mantles in the Delta Sun Peaks ('excellent quality dining').
Après-ski Bottoms, Masa's and Macker's are the main après-ski bars. At weekends MackDaddy's nightclub in The Delta can get lively. There are fondue evenings with torchlit descents and winter bonfires.
Off the slopes You can choose from skating, tubing, tobogganing, snowmobiling, dog sledding, snowshoeing and sleigh rides.

North America's biggest mountain, with terrain to suit every standard and a big, purpose-built, largely car-free village

COSTS

① ② ③ ④ ⑤ ⑥

RATINGS

The slopes

Fast lifts	★★★★
Snow	★★★★
Extent	★★★★
Expert	★★★★★
Intermediate	★★★★★
Beginner	★★★
Convenience	★★★★
Queues	★★
Mountain restaurants	★★

The rest

Scenery	★★★
Resort charm	★★★
Off-slope	★★

NEWS

Whistler's two mountains will at last be connected at mid-mountain for 2008/09: the 28-person Peak to Peak gondola will run between Whistler's Roundhouse Lodge and the Rendezvous Lodge on Blackcomb. The lift will span 4.4km/2.7 miles with a capacity of over 2,000 people per hour in each direction.

For 2007/08 the gondola up Whistler Mountain from the base area was upgraded and a new hotel, Nita Lake Lodge, opened at Creekside.

688

➕ North America's biggest, both in area and vertical (1610m/5,280ft)

➕ Good slopes for most abilities, with an unrivalled combination of high open bowls and woodland trails

➕ Good snow record

➕ Almost Alpine scenery

➕ Attractive modern village at the foot of the slopes, with car-free central areas and lively après-ski

➕ Good range of restaurants (but long waits where you can't book)

➖ Proximity to Pacific Ocean means a lot of cloudy weather, and rain at resort level is not unusual

➖ Two separate mountains till now – but with a gondola connection due to open in December 2008

➖ Lift queues and crowded runs can be a problem – a really serious one at weekends

➖ Mountain restaurants are mostly functional (and overcrowded)

➖ Resort restaurants oversubscribed

Whistler is unlike any other resort in North America. In some respects – the scale, the scenery, the crowds – it is more like an Alpine resort. But it follows the North American pattern in offering excellent snow and a lot of woodland runs, as well as the high bowls and glaciers that evoke the Alps.

All things considered, the mountain is about the best that North America has to offer, and for us a visit here is always a highlight of the season (except for the crowds). But we'll admit that we are generally lucky with the weather, and haven't had to put up with much rain at resort level – a real hazard.

Whistler will host many events during the 2010 Winter Olympics. In preparation, the resort has made huge investments in infrastructure and base area facilities; but it is the project to connect its two mountains with a record-breaking gondola for 2008/09 that is making the current headlines (see 'News').

THE RESORT

Whistler Village sits at the foot of its two mountains, Whistler and Blackcomb, a scenic 113km/70 mile drive from Vancouver on Canada's west coast. Whistler started as a locals' ski area in 1966 at what is now the revamped Whistler Creek (aka Creekside). Whistler Village, a 10-minute bus ride away, developed in the late 1970s. More development spread around the base of Blackcomb Mountain in the 1980s; this area, a 10-minute walk from central Whistler, is now known simply as Upper Village.

The village centres are all traffic-free. The architecture is varied and, for a purpose-built resort, quite tasteful – but it is all a bit urban, with lots of blocks approaching 10 storeys high. There are also lots of chalet-style apartments on the hillsides.

Whistler Village has most of the bars, restaurants and shops, and two gondolas (one to each mountain). A pedestrian bridge over an access road

links the main centre to newer Whistler North, further from the lifts, making a huge car-free area of streets lined with shops, condos and restaurants. Upper Village is much smaller and quieter.

Creekside has been revamped and expanded and it will play an important role in the Olympics, with many of the Alpine events finishing above here.

There is a free bus between central Whistler and Upper Village, but it can be just as quick to walk. Some lodging is a long way from the centre and means taking (inexpensive) buses or taxis. Some hotels have free buses, which will pick you up as well as take you to restaurants and nightlife.

The most convenient place to stay is Whistler Village, as you can access either mountain by gondola (though some reporters find the central area around Village Square noisy in the early hours). Creekside is quieter, and the new Peak to Peak gondola will make it convenient for Blackcomb Mountain as well as for Whistler.

↑ Whistler's high bowls have easy groomed trails as well as lots of fabulous go-anywhere terrain for experts

TOM COOK

KEY FACTS

Resort	675m
	2,210ft
Altitude	650-2285m
	2,140-7,490ft
Lifts	38
Pistes	8,171 acres
Green	18%
Blue	55%
Black	27%
Snowmaking	
	565 acres

THE MOUNTAINS

Whistler and Blackcomb together form the biggest area of slopes, with the longest runs, in North America.

Many reporters enthuse about the mountain host service and the 'go slow' patrol – some find the latter 'over zealous', but crowded slopes, especially on the runs home, mean they're often needed; we approve.

But reporters also comment on the early closing times for lifts (3pm until end-January, 3.30 in February and 4pm thereafter). Grooming 'could be better', and some blues and greens 'get mogulled quickly', says a 2008 visitor.

THE SLOPES
The best in North America

Whistler Mountain is accessed from Whistler Village by a two-stage, 10-person gondola that rises over 1100m/3,610ft to Roundhouse Lodge at mid-mountain. Or you can use two fast quads – if they are running (see 'Queues'); they don't go as high, but they avoid queues for the gondola.

Runs down through the trees fan out from the gondola: cruises to the Emerald and Big Red chairs and longer runs to the gondola mid-station.

From Roundhouse you can see the jewel in Whistler's crown – magnificent above-the-treeline bowls, served by the fast Peak and Harmony quads. The bowl beyond Harmony is now served by the Symphony fast quad. The bowls

are mostly go-anywhere terrain for experts, but there are groomed trails, so anyone can appreciate the views. Roundhouse is also where you catch the new Peak to Peak gondola to transfer to Blackcomb Mountain.

A six-seat gondola from Creekside also accesses Whistler Mountain.

Access to **Blackcomb** from Whistler Village is by an eight-seat gondola, followed by a fast quad. From the base of Blackcomb you take two consecutive fast quads up to the main Rendezvous restaurant. From there you can go left for great cruising terrain and the Glacier Express quad up to the Horstman Glacier area, or right for steeper slopes, the terrain park or the 7th Heaven chair. The 1610m/5,280ft vertical from the top of 7th Heaven to the base is the biggest in North America. Or you can go into the glacier

Interactive resort shortlist builder at www.wtss.co.uk

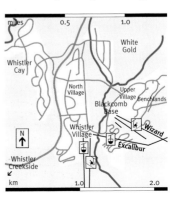

area. A T-bar from the Horstman Glacier brings you (with a short hike) to the Blackcomb Glacier in the next valley – away from all lifts. Rendezvous is also where you catch the new Peak to Peak gondola to Whistler Mountain.

Fresh Tracks is a deal that allows you to ride up Whistler Mountain (at extra cost) from 7.15, have a buffet breakfast and get to the slopes as they open – very popular with many reporters. Free guided tours of each mountain are offered at 11.30.

TERRAIN PARKS
World class for all abilities

'The best parks I've come across,' said a recent reporter. There's a good rating system based on size (S, M, L, XL). Novices should begin in the Terrain Garden in Blackcomb. It features small rails and rollers to get a feel for airtime and improve your control. For the S-M line hit the Habitat park by the Emerald chair on Whistler Mountain. Initiate yourself on a host of rails, boxes, medium kickers and a

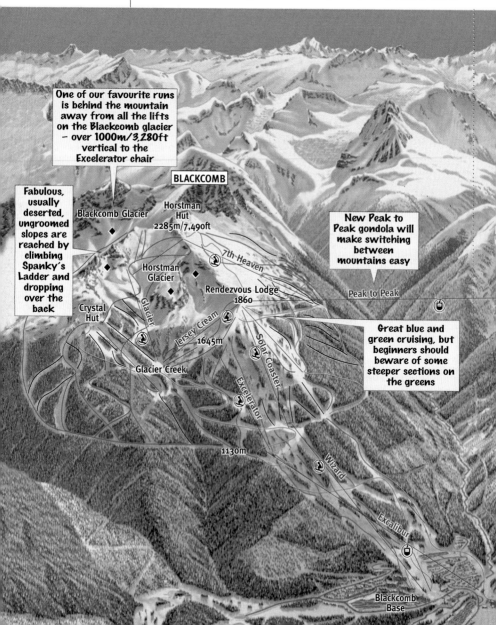

One of our favourite runs is behind the mountain away from all the lifts on the Blackcomb glacier – over 1000m/3,280ft vertical to the Excelerator chair

Fabulous, usually deserted, ungroomed slopes are reached by climbing Spanky's Ladder and dropping over the back

BLACKCOMB

Blackcomb Glacier

Horstman Hut 2285m/7,490ft

7th Heaven

Horstman Glacier

Rendezvous Lodge 1860

New Peak to Peak gondola will make switching between mountains easy

Peak to Peak

Crystal Hut

Glacier

Jersey Cream 1645m

Solar Coaster

Great blue and green cruising, but beginners should beware of some steeper sections on the greens

Glacier Creek

Excelerator

1130m

Wizard

Excalibur

Blackcomb Base

hip. The M-L Nintendo park is huge, but is usually the busiest and is by the Catskinner chairlift on Blackcomb. Step-up jumps, hips, tabletops, rails, boxes: this park will suit most intermediate to advanced riders. Pros and very confident freestylers should hit the Highest Level Park (this was moved to the Jersey Cream chair in the 2007/08 season because of construction work on the new Peak to Peak gondola); the fact that you need to sign a waiver, wear a helmet and buy a special pass indicates the size of the obstacles here. The super-pipe in Blackcomb is over 137m/450ft long with 5m/16.5ft high walls, and it is shaped daily. From Thursday to Saturday in the evening the super-pipe and a mini jib park are open near the Magic Chair on Blackcomb; the same pass will get you into both. There is also a boardercross track visible from the Solar Coaster Chair next to the super-pipe ('lots of fast, flowing corners; excellently groomed').

Symphony Express lift (new in 2006) makes the Flute Bowl area much more accessible – with blue runs and easy glades as well as expert terrain

The classic high bowls that first gave Whistler cult status among expert skiers in the 1980s and 1990s

Rhapsody Bowl

Piccolo

Flute Bowl

Symphony

Symphony Bowl

WHISTLER MOUNTAIN
2180m/7,160ft

Glacier Bowl

The Peak

Whistler Bowl

West Bowl

Bagel Bowl

Roundhouse Lodge 1850m

Harmony

Emerald

1595m

The 1500m/ 4,920ft vertical Peak-to-Creek runs are excellent in good snow

1425m

Big Red

Whistler Village

Garbanzo

Take the gondola from 7.15am for uncrowded fresh tracks skiing and a buffet breakfast

Raven's Nest 1300m

Creekside

1005m

Fitzsimmons

These runs are to be the 2010 Winter Olympic downhill and Super G courses

Creekside 650m/2,140ft

Whistler Village 675m/2,210ft

LIFT PASSES

Whistler/Blackcomb

Prices in C$

Age	1-day	6-day
under 13	47	240
13 to 18	75	394
19 to 64	86	464
over 65	75	394

Free under 7
Beginner lift, lesson and rental deal

Notes
Covers Whistler and Blackcomb mountains; prices include sales tax

SNOW RELIABILITY
Excellent at altitude
Snow conditions at the top are usually excellent – the place gets an average of over 400 inches of snow a year (that's way more than Colorado resorts). But because the resort is low and close to the Pacific, the bottom slopes can have poor snow – leading people to 'download' from the mid-stations, especially in late season.

FOR EXPERTS
Few can rival it
Whistler Mountain's bowls are enough to keep experts happy for weeks. Each has endless variations, with chutes and gullies of varied steepness and width. The biggest challenges are around Flute, Glacier, Whistler and West Bowls, with runs such as The Cirque and Doom & Gloom – though you can literally go anywhere in these high, wide areas. The Symphony quad (new two seasons ago) makes Flute Bowl, on the area boundary, much more accessible.

Blackcomb's slopes are not as extensive as Whistler's, but some are more challenging. From the top of the 7th Heaven lift, traverse to Xhiggy's Meadow for sunny bowl runs. If you're feeling brave, go in the opposite direction and drop into the extremely steep chutes down towards Glacier

Creek, including the infamous 41° Couloir Extreme (which can have moguls the size of elephants at the top), Secret Bowl and the very steep Pakalolo couloir (you can slide a long way there if you fall, as one of our group did last season). Our favourite runs are the also serious, but less frequented, steep bowls reached by a short hike up Spanky's Ladder, after taking the Glacier Express lift. You emerge after the hike at the top of a huge deserted area with several ways down; best to have a guide.

Both mountains have challenging trails through trees. The Peak to Creek area offers another 400 acres below Whistler's West Bowl to Creekside, and there are new gladed runs on Blackcomb near 7th Heaven and below Chick Pea on Whistler.

If all this isn't enough, there's also out-of-bounds backcountry guiding, cat-skiing and local heli-skiing available by the day. A 2007 reporter used Coast Range and praised them for 'top-quality guides and superb skiing', and two 2008 reporters tried the heli-skiing and found it 'expensive but a great experience'. We'd recommend the two-day Extremely Canadian clinic (see 'Schools and guides') for getting the most out of the in-bounds steep terrain.

boarding

Whistler has world-class terrain parks as well as epic terrain for freeriders: bowls with great powder and awesome steeps, steep gullies, tree runs, and shedloads of natural hits, wind lips and cliffs. Get up early if you fancy cutting first tracks, however. There are mellow groomed runs ideal for beginners, too, and the lifts are generally snowboard-friendly; there are T-bars on the glacier, but they're not vicious and any discomfort is worth it for the powder. The resort is fast gaining as big a reputation for its summer snowboarding facilities and camps on the glacier as for its winter snowboarding. The resort's specialist school will teach riders how to ride piste, pipe, park and powder according to your level. Specialist snowboard shops include Showcase and Katmandu Boards.

FOR INTERMEDIATES
Ideal and extensive terrain

Both mountains are an intermediate's paradise. In good weather, good intermediates will enjoy the easier slopes in the high bowls.

One of our favourite intermediate runs is down the Blackcomb Glacier, from the top of the mountain to the bottom of the Excelerator chair over 1000m/3,280ft below. This 5km/3 mile run, away from all lifts, starts with a two-minute walk up from the top of the Showcase T-bar. Don't be put off by the sign that says 'Experts only'. You drop over the ridge into a wide bowl; traverse the slope to get to gentler gradients – descend too soon and you'll get a shock in the very steep double-diamond Blowhole.

You are guaranteed good snow on the Horstman Glacier too, and typically gentle runs. The blue runs served by the 7th Heaven chair are 'heavenly on a sunny day', as a reporter put it. Lower down there are lots of perfect cruising runs through the trees – ideal when the weather is bad.

On Whistler Mountain, the ridges and bowls served by the Harmony and Symphony quads have lots to offer – not only groomers but excellent terrain for experiments off-piste. The Saddle run from the top of the Harmony Express lift is a favourite with many of our reporters, though it can get busy. The blue Highway 86 path, which skirts West Bowl from the top of the Peak chair, has beautiful views over a steep valley and across to the rather phallic Black Tusk mountain. The green Burnt Stew Trail also has great views.

Lower down the mountain there is a vast choice of groomed blue runs, with a series of efficient fast chairs to bring you back up to the top of the gondola. It's a cruiser's paradise – especially the aptly named Ego Bowl. A great long run is the fabulous Dave Murray Downhill all the way from mid-mountain to the finish at Creekside. Although it will be the Olympic men's downhill course and is classed black, it's a wonderful fast and varied cruise when it has been groomed. There is also the blue Peak to Creek run to try if it has been groomed (check first).

FOR BEGINNERS
OK if the sun shines

Whistler has excellent nursery slopes by the mid-station of the gondola, as does Blackcomb at the base area. Both have facilities higher up too.

The map has a guide to easy runs, and slow zones are marked. On Whistler, after progressing from the nursery slopes, there are some gentle first runs from the top of the gondola. Their downside is other people speeding past. You can return by various chairs or continue to the base area on greens.

On Blackcomb, Green Line runs from the top of the mountain to the bottom. The top part is particularly gentle, with some steeper pitches lower down.

In general, greens can be trickier than in many North American resorts – steeper, busier and on the lower mountain in less good condition. 'Our tentative beginner found it hard to move around with confidence because of the varying steepness of green runs,' says a reporter.

Another serious reservation is the weather. Beginners don't get a lot out of heavy snowfalls, and might be put off by rain.

FOR CROSS-COUNTRY
Picturesque but low

There are over 32km/20 miles of cross-country tracks around Lost Lake, starting by the river, on the path between Whistler and Blackcomb. But it is low altitude here, so conditions

SCHOOLS

Whistler and Blackcomb
t 904 8134

Classes
3 days Ski Esprit
C$362 (incl. taxes)
Private lessons
Half day (3hr) from
C$349

GUIDES

Whistler Guides
t 904 8134

can be unreliable. There's a specialist school, Cross-Country Connection (905 0071) offering lessons, tours and rental. Keen cross-country merchants can catch the train to better areas.

QUEUES
An ever-increasing problem
Whistler has become a victim of its own success. Even with 17 fast lifts – more than any other resort in North America – the mountains are queue-prone, especially at weekends when people pour in from Vancouver ('horrendous'). There are displays of waiting times at different lifts, which readers generally find useful, but queues are 'unpredictable – some days Whistler was very busy, other days quiet and Blackcomb busy for no apparent reason'.

Some reporters have signed up with the ski school just to get lift priority. Others have visited Vancouver at the weekend to avoid the crowds.

The routes out of Whistler Village in the morning can be busy (we had a report this season of a queue of more than 200 metres for the gondola to Blackcomb). Creekside is less of a problem. Some of the chairs higher up also produce long queues: the Harmony quad, especially, is no longer up to the job (even the singles line can take ages), and the Emerald chair often has queues. And we had a report of a 45-minute wait for the Peak chair on a Sunday in early January. We have several reports of lift closures – a March 2007 visitor noted the Peak Chair open 'only once during eleven days', and a 2008 visitor said, 'On powder days, it wouldn't open until 11.30.' Another reader found the Fitzsimmons and Garbanzo quads 'rarely open', despite queues for the gondola. Visiting outside peak season may not help – we found some lifts, including the gondola to Blackcomb, were kept closed during a visit in early December. Crowds on the slopes, especially the runs home, can be annoying, too.

MOUNTAIN RESTAURANTS
Overcrowded
The main restaurants sell decent, good-value food but are charmless self-service stops with long queues. They're huge, but not huge enough. 'Seat-seekers' are employed to find you space, but success is not guaranteed. You may have to resort to

eating at about 11am, or just surviving on breakfast.

Blackcomb has the Rendezvous, mainly a big (850-seat) self-service place but also home to Christine's, a table-service restaurant that is the best on either mountain. Glacier Creek Lodge, at the bottom of the Glacier Express, is a better self-service place. But even this (1,496 seats) gets incredibly crowded. Whistler has the massive (1,740-seat) Roundhouse Lodge; Steep's Grill is its unremarkable table-service refuge.

Reporters generally prefer the smaller places – but they're still packed unless you time it right, and may be closed early and late season. On Blackcomb, Crystal Hut (great waffles) and Horstman Hut are tiny, with great views.

On Whistler, Raven's Nest, at the top of the Creekside gondola, is a small and friendly deli/cafe. The Chic Pea near the top of the Garbanzo chairlift was a 2008 reporter's favourite: 'great Naan bread sandwiches and Chick Pea stew'. Harmony Hut, at the top of the Harmony chair, specialises in stews and cider. You can, of course, descend to the base – the table-service Dusty's at Whistler Creek has been recommended. We're told that behind the Grind cafe is 'a good place to get a quick breakfast'.

SCHOOLS AND GUIDES
A great formula
Ski Esprit and Ride Guides programmes run for three or four days and combine instruction with showing you around the mountains – with the same instructor daily. Many of our reporters have joined these groups (usually small), and all reports are glowing: 'big improvement in confidence and skill' and 'highly recommended' are typical. A 2007 reporter comments on 'small, personalised and attentive' instruction at the Whistler school. There are various specialist clinics and snowboard classes (a 2008 reporter recommends the Supergroup classes for good skiers, with a maximum of three in a group).

Extremely Canadian specialises in guiding and coaching adventurous advanced intermediates upwards in Whistler's steep and deep terrain. A lot of its coaches compete in freeride and skier-cross competitions. We have

GETTING THERE

Air Vancouver
115km/71 miles (2hr)

CHILDREN

Whistler Kids
t 1 866 218 9690
Ages 3mnth to 4yr;
from 8am; non-skiing;
C$108 per day (incl.
taxes)

Ski school
Offers Adventure
Camps for ages 3 to
12 and Teen Ski
programmes for ages
13 to 18 (C$488 incl.
taxes for 4 days)

There's a great
mixture of open bowls
and trails cut through
the trees ↓

been with them several times and they
really are great. And reporters have
said, 'I would never have found some
of the runs we were taken on; I'd
certainly book them again' and 'They
really push you'. They run two-day
clinics three times a week.

Backcountry day trips or overnight
touring are available with the Whistler
Alpine Guides Bureau, and one 2008
visitor had a great day with Whistler
Heli-skiing: 'expensive though'.

FACILITIES FOR CHILDREN
Impressive

Blackcomb's base area has a slow-
moving magic chair to get children
part-way up the mountain. Whistler's
gondola mid-station has a splendid
kids-only area. A reporter found the
staff 'friendly, and instilled confidence'.
Classes are said to be 'very flexible'.

The Children's Adventure Park on
Blackcomb features a Magic Castle,
terrain features and 'colourful
characters'. One reporter was
enthusiastic about 'climb and dine',
where children can spend a few fun
hours at the Great Wall climbing centre
(see 'Off the slopes'), including a meal,
while parents go out to eat.

STAYING THERE

HOW TO GO
High-quality packages

A lot of British tour operators go to
Whistler and some run catered chalets.
Hotels There is a wide range, including
a lot of top-end places.
*****Fairmont Chateau Whistler (938
8000) Well run, luxurious, at the foot
of Blackcomb. Consistently
recommended by reporters. Excellent
spa with pools and tubs. The Gold
floor is expensive and cosseting.
*****Westin Resort & Spa (905 5000)
Luxury all-suite hotel at the foot of
Whistler mountain next to the lifts,
with pools and hot tubs.
*****Four Seasons (935 3400) Luxury
hotel five minutes from Blackcomb
base, but with ski valet service at the
base. Unremarkable public areas but
good food. Good fitness/spa facilities.
*****Pan Pacific Mountainside (905
2999) Luxury, all-suite, at Whistler
Village base. Pool/sauna/hot tub.
Recommended by a 2008 reporter.
****Crystal Lodge (932 2221)
'Comfortable, friendly, convenient'; in
Whistler Village. Pool/sauna/hot tub.
****Sundial Boutique (932 2321)

Interactive resort shortlist builder at **www.wtss.co.uk**

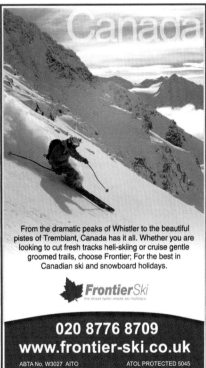

From the dramatic peaks of Whistler to the beautiful
pistes of Tremblant, Canada has it all. Whether you are
looking to cut fresh tracks heli-skiing or cruise gentle
groomed trails, choose Frontier; For the best in
Canadian ski and snowboard holidays.

FrontierSki
the finest tailor-made ski holidays

020 8776 8709
www.frontier-ski.co.uk

ABTA No. W3027 AITO   ATOL PROTECTED 5045

UK PACKAGES

All America Holidays, Alpine Answers, AmeriCan Ski, American Ski Classics, Chalet World Ski, Cold Comforts Lodging, Crystal, Crystal Finest, Directski.com, Elegant Resorts, Erna Low, Frontier, Independent Ski Links, Inghams, Interactive Resorts, Kaluma, Kuoni, Mark Warner, Momentum, Neilson, Oxford Ski Co, Scott Dunn, Ski Activity, Ski Dream, Ski Expectations, Ski Freshtracks, Ski Independence, Ski Line, Ski McNeill, Ski Miquel, Ski Safari, Ski Solutions, Ski Wild, Skitracer, Skiworld, Solo's, Supertravel, Thomson, Trailfinders, United Vacations, Virgin Snow, White Mountains

ACTIVITIES

Indoor Sports arena (ice rink, pool, hot tubs), museum, art galleries, tennis, spa and health clubs, library, cinemas, climbing wall

Outdoor Flightseeing, snowshoeing, snowmobiling, sno-limo (chauffeur-driven motorised sled), walking, fishing, dog sledding, sleigh rides, bungee jumping, ice climbing, treetrek, ziplining

Phone numbers From distant parts of Canada, add the prefix 1 604; from abroad, add the prefix +1 604

TOURIST OFFICE

t 904 8134
wbres@intrawest.com
www.whistler-blackcomb.com
www.mywhistler.com

One and two bedroom suites. 'Great for groups and families, excellent location in Whistler Village.' Hot tubs.
***Lost Lake Lodge (932 2882) 'Excellent' place: studios and suites, out by the golf course. Pool/hot tub.
***Glacier Lodge (932 2882) In Upper Village. 'Big rooms, quiet area, recommended.' Pool/hot tub.
***Tantalus Resort Lodge (932 4146) In Whistler Village. 'Fine.' Shuttle service to lifts.
***Whistler Village Inn & Suites (932 4004) 'Great location, good sized rooms and enough breakfast to keep you going all morning.'
Apartments There are plenty of spacious, comfortable condominiums in both chalet and hotel-style blocks.

EATING OUT
Good but crowded

Reporters are enthusiastic about the range, quality and value of places to eat, but find that Whistler doesn't have enough restaurant seats to meet demand. You have to book well ahead, even to eat in bars; but a lot of places won't take bookings for small groups so you have to queue 'or eat early (before 7.30pm)'. There's a dining guide booklet, but it's not comprehensive and it doesn't give prices, so it's of limited use.

At the top of the market, Il Caminetto di Umberto in Whistler Village has classy Italian cuisine ('excellent food, worth the price'). The Rimrock Cafe at Whistler Creek serves 'outstanding seafood and game' and Araxi (Pacific) is repeatedly praised ('superb', 'excellent service').

Good mid-market Whistler Village places include the Keg ('great value' steak and seafood, 'efficient service'), Teppan (Japanese), Mongolie (Asian) and Kypriaki Norte ('excellent duck'). Reporters also suggest the Bocca (Italian: 'excellent home-made pasta', 'inexpensive'), the Bearfoot Bistro (European, 'the best gourmet restaurant, with a stellar wine list', 'bar is out of this world') and Sushi Village ('impressive quality for quite a simple place', 'worth waiting for; go for the frozen sake margaritas' but 'not the best fish dinner ever'). A 2007 visitor rates 21 Steps and suggests you may get a table here when everywhere else is busy.

In Village North the good-value Brewhouse (steaks, burgers, beef ribs, 'exceptionally tasty steak sandwich')

has good microbrews and a lively atmosphere, Caramba has 'good Mediterranean food at reasonable prices'. Hy's Steakhouse has 'melt in your mouth' steaks. Sushi-Ya and Quattro (Italian) are good.

In Upper Village, options are limited. Thai One On is 'excellent' with 'friendly but patchy service'; Monk's Grill has 'good steaks and service'.

There are plenty of budget places, including the après-ski bars below. The Old Spaghetti Factory in Whistler Village has been recommended for pasta. Morgan's at Creekside (organic specialities) has blues music.

APRES-SKI
Something for most tastes

Whistler is very lively. Popular at Whistler are the Longhorn ('lively, good music and local beer'), with a terrace, the Brewhouse ('excellent atmosphere', 'serve their own really tasty stout'), the Garibaldi Lift Company ('the tables are full by 3pm'), Dubh Linn Gate Irish pub (live music) and Tapley's ('popular with locals'). Merlin's is the focus at Blackcomb base (with live music on Fridays and the 'tastiest burgers') though readers also recommend the Monk's Grill. Dusty's is the place at Creekside – good beer, loud music.

Later on, Buffalo Bill's is lively and loud, and the Amsterdam Cafe is 'a favourite'. Tommy Africa's, Maxx Fish, the Savage Beagle, Garfinkel's and Moe Joe's are the main clubs. Try the Mallard bar in Chateau Whistler and the Crystal Lounge for a quieter time.

OFF THE SLOPES
Not ideal

Whistler is a long way to go if you don't intend to hit the slopes. Meadow Park Sports Centre has a full range of fitness facilities. There are also several luxurious spas. Reporters have recommended walks around the lake and the Great Wall Underground climbing centre. There's an eight-screen cinema in Whistler Village. And Ziptrek Ecotours offers 'adrenaline tours' on ziplines and suspension bridges through the forest between Whistler and Blackcomb mountains. You can also do ATV/ snowmobile trips and dog sledding. Excursions to Squamish (famous for its eagles) are easy, as are day trips to Vancouver. The Fire and Ice show on Sundays is recommended.

STONEHAM / JEAN VAUDREUIL

For us the main attraction of skiing or riding in eastern Canada is the French culture and language that are predominant in the province of Québec. It really feels like a different country from the rest of Canada – as, indeed, many of its residents want it to become. It is relatively easy to get to – only a six-hour flight from the UK, compared with a 10-hour flight for western Canada.

Tremblant is the main destination resort and is one of the cutest purpose-built resorts we've seen (though it is now in danger of being spoiled by expansion). The other main base is Québec city, which dates from 1608 and is full of atmosphere and Canadian history. Slopes of the main resorts are small, both in extent and in vertical drop, and the weather can be perishingly cold in early and midwinter (one reporter experienced -42°C in February). But at least this means that the extensive snowmaking systems, common to all the resorts, can be effective for a long season. Be prepared for variable snow conditions, and don't go expecting light, dry powder – if that's what you want, head west.

There are lots of ski and snowboard areas in Ontario – Canada's most populated province – but most of them are tiny and cater just for locals. For people heading on holiday for a week or more, eastern Canada really means the province of Québec. The province and its capital, Québec city, are heavily dominated by the French culture and language. Notices, menus, trail maps and so on are usually printed in both French and English. Many ski area workers are bilingual or just French-speaking. And French cuisine abounds. The Frenchness of it is one of the big attractions for us.

The weather is very variable. Hence the snow, though pretty much guaranteed by snowmaking, can vary enormously in quality. When we were there one April, we were slush skiing in Tremblant one day and rattling along on a rock-hard surface in Mont-Ste-Anne the next. One reporter who visited Mont-Ste-Anne, Stoneham and Le Massif in late January experienced mild temperatures and several perfect blue-sky days. Another who visited Tremblant in February experienced a day when it was -42°C.

The main destination resort is **Tremblant** (covered in the next chapter), about 90 minutes' drive from Montreal. The other main place to stay for easy access to several ski areas is **Québec city**. Old Québec, at the city's heart, is North America's only walled city and is a World Heritage site. Within the city walls are narrow, winding streets and 17th- and 18th-

century houses. It is situated right on the banks of the St Lawrence river. In January/February there is a famous two-week carnival, with an ice castle, snow sculptures, dog-sled and canoe races, parades and balls. But most of the winter is low season, with good-value rooms available in big hotels.

There are several ski areas close to Québec city. The biggest and most varied is **Mont-Ste-Anne**, 30 minutes from Québec and with accommodation of its own. It extends to only 450 acres – easily skied in a day by a good skier. A gondola takes you to the top, and slopes lead down the front (south) and back (north) sides. The views over the ice floes of the St Lawrence river are spectacular.

Stoneham is the closest resort to Québec city, around 20 minutes away. It also has its own small village with accommodation and an impressive base lodge. It is a small area, with 325 acres of terrain spread across three linked peaks. But it is very sheltered in a sunny setting protected from wind. It suits families well, with mainly intermediate and beginner terrain.

Le Massif is around an hour away from Québec city and is a cult area with locals. It is in a UNESCO World Biosphere Reserve and is just metres from the St Lawrence river. The views of the ice floes are stunning, and you feel you are heading straight down into them when you are on the pretty, treelined trails. The area of slopes, though small, has the largest vertical in the east – 770m/2,530ft.

INTRAWEST

Cute, purpose-built, traffic-free village with a real French Canadian feel, at the foot of a very small area of slopes

COSTS

① ② ③ ④ ⑤ ⑥

RATINGS

The slopes

Fast lifts	★★★★
Snow	★★★★
Extent	★
Expert	★★
Intermediate	★★★
Beginner	★★★★
Convenience	★★★★
Queues	★★★
Mountain restaurants	★★

The rest

Scenery	★★★
Resort charm	★★★★
Off-slope	★★★

KEY FACTS

Resort	265m
	870ft
Slopes	230-875m
	750-2,870ft
Lifts	13
Pistes	631 acres
Green	17%
Blue	33%
Black	50%
Snowmaking	75%

698

➕ Charming, purpose-built core village

➕ Good snow reliability with extensive artificial backup

➕ Some good runs for all abilities

➖ Very limited area for piste-bashers

➖ Can be perishingly cold in midwinter

➖ Weekend queues and overcrowding

➖ Recent reports of poor service

Tremblant is eastern Canada's main destination resort and attracts quite a lot of Brits. But for keen piste-bashers the limited slopes don't really match the appeal of the cute and lively little core village, built in traditional style and with typical thoroughness by Intrawest.

THE RESORT

Tremblant has been transformed from a locals' hill to being eastern Canada's leading destination ski resort. Intrawest (which also owns Whistler and several other North American resorts) developed a purpose-built village in the style of old Québec. Buildings in vibrant colours line narrow, cobbled, traffic-free streets and squares, and it has a very French feel to it. Recent expansion on the edge is not so cute. There's a regular, free ski-bus and a local town service for C$1.75. We have 2008 reports of poor service ('not up to usual North American standards', said two separate reporters) and extreme cold (-42°C in February, said one reporter).

THE MOUNTAINS

In its small area, Tremblant has a good variety of pleasantly wooded terrain.
Slopes A heated gondola takes you to the top, from where there are good views over the village and a 14km/9 mile lake on the so-called South Side – and over National Park wilderness on the North Side (which is really north-east facing and gets the morning sun). A high-speed quad brings you back and there are two other chairs to play on. The slow Edge lift accesses another summit, serving mainly expert terrain. On the South Side (really south-west facing and so good for the afternoon sun) you can go right back to town on blue or green runs, or use two high-speed quads to explore the top and bottom halves. The Versant Soleil area is more directly south-facing and has mainly black and tree runs with one top-to-bottom blue. Free mountain tours go twice daily.

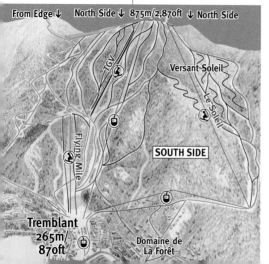

From Edge ↓   North Side ↓ 875m/2,870ft ↓ North Side

TGV

Versant-Soleil

Le Soleil

SOUTH SIDE

Flying Mile

Tremblant
265m/
870ft

Domaine de
La Forêt

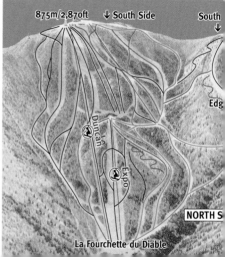

875m/2,870ft   ↓ South Side   South ↓

Edg

Duncan

Expo

NORTH S

La Fourchette du Diable

Terrain parks The excellent 18-acre Advanced terrain park and a Progression park for beginners are on the South Side, just above the village. On the North Side there's a third park for intermediates plus a super-pipe. The school offers freestyle classes. Helmets are compulsory.

Snow reliability Canada's east coast doesn't get as much snow as western Canada does, but around 75% of the trails are covered by snowmaking. Grooming is excellent.

Experts Half the runs are classified black, but we found many of them did not deserve their grading. There are steep, top-to-bottom bump runs on the North Side and great gladed tree runs off the Edge lift. The Versant Soleil area has more black runs and some tough runs in the trees. However, the gladed runs really need decent snow, preferably fresh, to be much fun.

Intermediates Both North and South Sides have good cruising, and we found the North Side less crowded. There are blue-classified runs in the trees as well as on groomed trails.

Beginners The 2-acre beginner area is excellent, and there are long, easy, top-to-bottom greens to progress to.

Snowboarding The slopes are good for beginners, but better boarders can't count on fresh natural snow to play in. A specialist shop, Adrénaline, runs a Burton learn-to-ride programme. And there are good terrain parks.

Cross-country There are around 65km/40 miles of trails, some at the top of the mountain, with great views.

Queues At weekends there can be queues, but they tend to move quickly. We found crowds on the main run back to the village more of a problem.

Mountain restaurants The main Grand Manitou restaurant has good views and decent food, but can get crowded. Many people go back to town.

Schools and guides Past reporters praised the school: 'good instructors and both children made progress'. However, a 2008 visitor found that the two ski instructors their daughter had were 'not up to the usual North American standard'.

Facilities for children The Kids Club offers day care from ages one to six years. There's a children's adventure area on the Nansen trail.

STAYING THERE

How to go There's no shortage of packages from the UK.

Hotels and condos The luxurious Fairmont Tremblant ('one of the best hotels I have ever stayed in') and the condos in the Place St Bernard, the Tour des Voyagers and the Chouette have been recommended by readers.

Eating out Try the Forge, Ya'ooo Pizza Bar, Shack, Casey's, Spag & Co, Windigo, Plus Minus (but it's 'very expensive' says a 2008 visitor) and the Loup Garou at the Fairmont. Fat Mardi's (steaks and seafood) has a kids' menu.

Après-ski Octobar Rock is popular with British visitors, the Forge is good as the slopes close, and the Shack brews its own beer, as does La Diable in the Residence Inn.

Off the slopes The Aquaclub La Source pool complex resembles a lake set in a forest, but reporters complain it's expensive (C$14.85 for three hours). For adults only, the 'excellent' Spa Scandinavie offers sauna, steam room, outdoor hot tubs and waterfalls. You can also go hiking, ice climbing, horse riding, ice skating, curling, snowshoeing, tubing, snowmobiling, dog sledding and on sleigh rides. You can visit Montreal (highly recommended by reporters), and you can take a helicopter charter with a scenic stop on top of a mountain.

These days it's dangerous to generalise about Spanish resorts – which is why we don't provide the lists of ➕ and ➖ points that we do for other second-division countries. There are now some well-equipped Pyrenean resorts with fine, snow-sure slopes that compare favourably with mid-sized places in the Alps. Two resorts are certainly not downmarket – Sierra Nevada and Baqueira-Beret (see next chapter) are both frequented by Spanish royalty. Winter sports are becoming more popular with the prosperous Spanish themselves, and as a result many of the smaller resorts are continually improving.

UK PACKAGES

Sierra Nevada *Crystal, Independent Ski Links, Thomson*
Formigal *Crystal, Neilson, White Roc*

700

The general ambience of Spanish resorts is attractive – with eating, posing and partying taken seriously.

Sierra Nevada (2100m/6,890ft) is in the extreme south of Spain, near Granada (a must-see, and much quieter than in summer), with views to the Atlas mountains in Morocco.

The hub of the resort is Pradollano, a stylish modern development with shops and a few restaurants and bars set around traffic-free open spaces.

Most of the accommodation is in older, less smart buildings set along a road winding up the steep hillside. A two-stage chairlift also goes up the hillside, with red runs back down to the main lift stations at Pradollano.

From Pradollano a new eight-person gondola and parallel 14-person one go up to Borreguiles, at the heart of the 87km/54 miles of slopes. Here there are excellent nursery slopes, and lifts going up to the broad upper slopes beneath the peak of Veleta, where there is also a terrain park. There are three identifiable sectors, well linked, with a good range of intermediate and easy runs. There is not a lot for experts.

Queues can develop at Pradollano (though the new gondola should help) and higher up there are quite a lot of slow old lifts that cause queues at peak times. The chair up the village slope gets the biggest queues of all. Most chairs have singles lines, though. The home run can get crowded.

Sierra Nevada can have good snow years when the Alps has bad, and vice versa. Most slopes face north-west, but some get the afternoon sun. And when the wind blows, as it does, the slopes close; there are no trees.

There is a group of worthwhile resorts in the western Pyrenees, between Pau and Huesca.

Formigal now claims to be the largest ski area in the Spanish Pyrenees (137km/85 miles of runs), having expanded this year. It is a favourite with experts for its 38 black runs (10 new) – though many of them could be red. New developments include four freeride areas, heli- and snowcat skiing and boarding, a second terrain park and revamped restaurants. The village, of solidly built apartment blocks, is on the east side of the Tena valley, while all the slopes are on the west side, spreading over a series of side-valleys with north- and south-facing treeless slopes served by 22 lifts. So ski-in/ski-out this is not. The whole thing is really set up for motorists, who can park at one of four lift bases. Sextas, the first and the nearest to the village, has a smart day lodge and eight-seat chair.

Although the top station is only 2250m/7,380ft, Formigal has a justified reputation for wind. If it gets too bad you can slip down to **Panticosa**, about 10km/6 miles away and under the same ownership. It has also seen some modernisation, and the 34km/21 miles of runs offer something for everybody in a more sheltered environment. Thermal baths and two 4-star hotels opened this year.

Candanchu and nearby **Astún**, with almost 80km/50 miles of pistes between them, are popular on the Spanish market. They offer a wide range of lodging set in some of the Pyrenees' most stunning scenery. Both resorts have some tough runs.

The other main group of Spanish resorts is just east of Andorra. The 53km/33 miles of runs at **La Molina** are linked to those of **Masella**, over the mountain, via a gondola and six-pack. The whole area, called Alp 2500 offers 121km/75 miles of slopes.

TOURIST OFFICES

Sierra Nevada
www.cetursa.es
Formigal and Panticosa
www.aramon.co.uk
www.formigal.com
Candanchu/Astún
www.astun.com
La Molina
www.lamolina.com

Baqueira-Beret

Spain's leading winter resort, with high, extensive, north-facing slopes; for Spanish animation, though, stay down the valley

COSTS

① ② ③ ④ ⑤ ⑥

RATINGS

The slopes

Fast lifts	**
Snow	***
Extent	**
Expert	***
Intermediate	****
Beginner	**
Convenience	***
Queues	****
Mountain restaurants	**

The rest

Scenery	***
Resort charm	**
Off-slope	*

UK PACKAGES

Crystal Finest, Inghams, Ski Miquel

The Bonaigua sector has excellent intermediate slopes ↓

+ Compact modern resort
+ Reasonable snow reliability
+ Some good off-piste potential
+ Lots of good intermediate slopes
+ Friendly, helpful locals

− Drab blocks dominate the main village, which lacks atmosphere
− Resort is not cleverly laid out, and traffic intrudes
− Still lots of old, slow lifts

Baqueira is in a different league from other resorts in the Spanish Pyrenees – a smart, family-oriented resort with a wide area of slopes that gives a real feeling of travel. It attracts an almost entirely Spanish clientele (which regularly includes their royal family), so don't count on English being spoken.

THE RESORT

Baqueira was purpose-built in the 1960s and has its fair share of drab, high-rise blocks; these are clustered below the road that runs through to the high pass of Port de la Bonaigua, while the main lift base is just above it. But up the steep hill from the main base are some newer, smaller-scale stone-clad developments. At the very top is an alternative chairlift into the slopes. The most convenient base is close to the main lifts, but the village is small enough for location not to be too much of an issue. There is a lot of accommodation spread down the valley, and big car parks with road-train shuttles up to the lift base.

THE MOUNTAINS

There is an extensive area of long, mainly intermediate runs, practically all of them on open, treeless slopes and facing roughly west.

Slopes The slopes are split into three distinct but well-connected areas – Baqueira, Beret and Bonaigua. From the base station at Baqueira, a fast quad, which you ride with skis off, and a parallel gondola take you up to the nursery slopes at 1800m/5,910ft. Fast chairs go on up to Cap de Baqueira. From here there is a wide variety of long runs, served by chairs and drags – including a long black down to Orri. From several points you can descend into the Bonaigua sector, leading over to the summit of the Bonaigua pass. Beyond the pass is an expanding area of slopes descending to the east of the pass and served by a fast quad.

From the opposite extremity of the Baqueira sector at Orri a triple chair takes you off to the Beret sector, where a series of more-or-less parallel chairs serve mainly blue and red runs. A fast quad from Beret accesses a fourth sector at Blanhiblar, with red and blue pistes and an itinerary. All main lift bases are accessible by road.

Terrain parks There's a terrain park with half-pipe in the Bonaigua area.

Snow reliability Most of the slopes are above 1800m/5,910ft and there is extensive snowmaking (recently upgraded), but afternoon sun is a problem in spring. We've had mixed reports of the grooming.

Experts Experts will find few on-piste challenges, but there are extensive off-piste opportunities all over the area. And there are four ungroomed itinerary

BONAIGUA 1.900

ISO LA PEULLA

KEY FACTS

Resort	1500m
	4,920ft
Slopes	1500-2510m
	4,920-8,230ft
Lifts	33
Pistes	104km
	65 miles
Green	7%
Blue	51%
Red	34%
Black	8%
Snowmaking	
	549 guns

Phone numbers
From abroad use the prefix +34

TOURIST OFFICE

t 973 639010
viajes@baqueira.es
www.baqueira.es

runs including the steep and narrow Escornacrabes, from the top of Cap de Baqueira. Cheap heli-lifts are available.

Intermediates It's excellent, with lots of good long runs such as the 4km/2 mile blue from Tuc deth Dossau and some classic reds such as Muntanyó down to Port de la Bonaigua and Mirador above town. Less daring intermediates will enjoy the Beret and Bonaigua areas best.

Beginners There are good, improved nursery runs above Baqueira. Some of the longer blues can be a bit tough. Beret has an excellent nursery slope and gentler blues.

Snowboarding The main nursery slopes are served by a draglift and moving carpets. Experienced freeriders have plenty of chair-served off-piste.

Cross-country There are 7km/4 miles of trails between Orri and Beret.

Queues Weekdays are quiet and the gondola seems to have dealt with weekend queues. The Blanhiblar sector is always quiet.

Mountain restaurants All run by the lift company, the huts are said to be 'lacking in number and variety, and very smoky'. The self-service places at Beret, and the table-service place at 1800m have been recommended. You can also get table service at Cap del Port (at the Bonaigua pass), at Baqueira 2200 and at Beret.

Schools and guides A reporter 'highly recommends' the Baqueira British Ski School (four British instructors) – which offers a cheaper rate for guiding only.

Facilities for children The kindergarten takes very young children, but lack of spoken English is a problem. Ski school classes start from age four and there are snow gardens in each sector.

STAYING THERE

How to go There is a reasonable choice of hotels and apartments locally. Ski Miquel has a chalet.

Hotels The 4-star Montarto (973 639001) is recommended, and the 5-star Rafael La Pleta (973 645550), just above the village has 'spacious rooms, wonderful service'. The Parador (973 640801) down the valley in Arties and the 2-star Husa Vielha (973 640275) in Vielha, 15km/9 miles away, have been recommended.

Eating out The more interesting restaurants are down the valley in Salardu, Arties and Vielha. Reporters have enjoyed the local tapas bars.

Après-ski There are pubs and discos down the valley. Pacha, in the main village, gets going late.

Off the slopes Pool and spa facilities are available in some hotels. Vielha has a sports centre and ice rink.

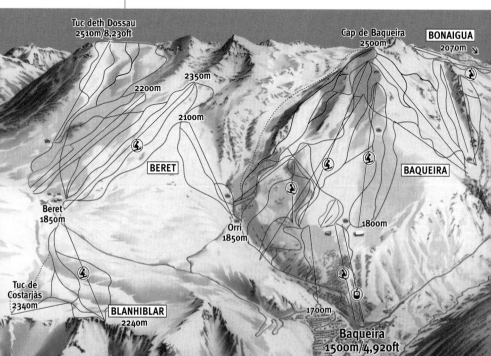

Finland

COSTS

① ② ③ ④ ⑤ ⑥

NEWS

Ylläs installed a gondola for 2007/08. The new lift runs from the Sport Resort Ylläs base and forms part of a major expansion project here, with shops, restaurants and apartments; the first phase opened last season. A new competition slope runs alongside the gondola. In the Ylläs-Ski sector, a new fast quad, 11 more runs, a restaurant and two terrain parks opened, as did the first phase of a new development of shops, bars and restaurants. A new beginner tow is planned for 2008/09.

At Ruka a new pedestrian village at the foot of the slopes is being built, with the first phase due to open for 2009/10. For 2008/09 an ice rink and a new kids' slope with moving carpet are planned.

In Levi for 2007/08 a new eight-seat gondola and a six-pack were opened. For 2008/09 the new Sokos hotel and several new restaurants are due to open.

In Pyhä new apartments and a mountain restaurant opened for 2007/08.

➕ Peace, quiet and Lapp charm
➕ Ideal terrain for cross-country and gentle downhilling
➕ Reliable late snow
➕ Good for families and beginners

➖ Can be bitterly cold (and dark all day in early season)
➖ Small ski areas lacking challenge
➖ Mainly dull hotels and food
➖ Quite expensive

For skiers with no appetite for the hustle and hassle of Alpine resorts in high season – perhaps especially for families – escape to the white silence of Lapland can be an attractive alternative. Finland has the lion's share of Lapland and we are getting many more reports on it than we used to. The resorts are rapidly developing both their ski areas and facilities – see 'News'. Of the resorts covered here, only Ruka and Iso-Syöte are south of the Arctic Circle.

The Arctic landscape of flat and gently rolling forest punctuated by many lakes and the occasional treeless hill is a paradise for cross-country skiing. Weather permitting, it also offers good beginner and intermediate downhilling, albeit on a small scale.

The resorts usually open a few runs in late November. For two months in midwinter the sun does not rise – at least, not at ground level. Most areas have floodlit runs. The mountains do not open fully until mid-February, when a normal skiing day is possible and Finnish schools have holidays that usually coincide with ours – a busy time. Finland comes into its own at the end of the season, with friendlier temperatures and long daylight hours. Understandably, Easter is extremely popular, and the slopes are crowded. Conditions are usually hard-packed powder or fresh snow from the start of the season to the end (early May).

The temperature can be extremely variable, yo-yoing between zero and minus 30°C several times in a week. Fine days are the coldest, but the best for skiing: it may be 10 to 15 degrees warmer on the slopes than at valley level. 'Mild' days of cloud and wind are worse, and face masks are sold.

The staple Finnish lift is the T-bar. Ruka has some chairs, Levi has two gondolas and Ylläs one. Pistes are wide and well maintained, with good nursery slopes. The Finns are great boarders and consider their terrain parks far superior to those in the Alps; super-pipes are increasingly common.

None of the areas has significant vertical by alpine standards, and in some cases it is seriously limited.

There is no need for mountain restaurants – you are never far from the base, with its self-service restaurants. The ski areas also have shelters or 'kotas' – log-built teepees with an open fire and a smoke hole – where you can eat a snack.

Ski school is good, with English widely spoken. All ski areas have indoor playrooms for small children, but they may be closed at weekends.

Excursions are common – husky-sledding, snowmobile safaris, a reindeer sleigh ride and tea with the Lapp drivers in their tent. 'The whole experience is wonderful,' says a typically enthusiastic participant.

Hotels are self-contained resorts, large and practical rather than stylish, typically with a shop, a cafe, a bar with dance floor, and a pool and sauna with outdoor cooling-off area. Hotel supper is typically served no later than seven, sometimes followed by a children's disco or dancing to a live band. Finns usually prefer to stay in cabins, and tour operators offer the compromise of staying in a cabin but taking half-board at a nearby hotel.

Cabins vary, but are mostly well equipped, with a sauna and drying cupboard as standard.

The main resorts are Levi and Ylläs, respectively 17km/10 miles north and 50km/31 miles west of Kittilä, which has direct charter flights from Britain.

Ylläs mountain has two gateways, both 4km/2 miles from the mountain. The minor one is Ylläsjärvi near the Sport Resort Ylläs base, the major one Äkäslompolo near the Ylläs-Ski base. Development is taking place at both bases (see 'News'). Cross-country skiing makes sense of a resort such as Äkäslompolo, which has 330km/205 miles of trails, transforming it from awkward sprawl to doorstep ski resort of limitless scope. From the lift base trails fan out around the mountain, across the frozen lake and away through the endless forest.

Ylläs is the largest downhill ski area, with 463m/1,520ft vertical. Lifts and pistes on two broad flanks of the mountain give plenty of scope for novices. Second- and third-week skiers will rapidly conquer the benign black runs. Ylläs has a welcoming mountain-top restaurant ('excellent and with stunning views' says a 2008 visitor).

Reporters in 2008 thought the Äkäs cabins at Äkäslompolo 'excellent' but the 'buffet-style' meals at the Äkäs hotel (016 553000) 'very average', and they recommended the restaurants Julie's ('pizzas and Lapp dishes') and Poros ('more upmarket', 'very good').

Levi is a purpose-built village of hotels and cabins at the foot of its slopes: 44 runs served by 27 lifts, including 22 red and 3 black slopes. It claims Finland's biggest terrain park and 230km/143 miles of cross-country trails. Its biggest hotel, Levitunturi (016 646301), was highly rated by a recent reporter, with 'excellent' facilities – pool, tennis, and a children's centre. The Levilheto apartments (403 120200) are 'great, all mod cons and we loved having our own sauna', says a 2008 visitor. Of the 30 or so restaurants, readers recommend the Steak House, Myllyn Aijä, Arran and the White Reindeer; and of the bars, Crazy Reindeer (karaoke) and Panimo microbrewery.

Ruka lies 80km/50 miles south of the Arctic Circle, close to Kuusamo airport and the Russian border, in a region known for abundant and enduring snow. The ski area, on two sides of a single low hill (Ruka East

and Ruka West), has a mixture of open and forest terrain, 19 lifts (including one six-pack and four other chairs), and 20km/12 miles of pistes, most covered by floodlighting and snowmaking. There are runs of all colours, but none is steep and the vertical is a very modest 200m/660ft. There are, of course, terrain parks.

A reporter was very happy with the ski school, despite having to join a class below his standard.

The cross-country scope is vast: they advertise 500km/310 miles, of which 50km/31 miles are floodlit.

The atmosphere at the resort and on the slopes is upbeat – with live music in the Monomesta bar and sun terraces outside the Piste, very popular in spring. Hotels include the Rantasipi Rukahovi (08 85910), only 50m/160ft from the slopes, and the Royal Ruka (08 868 6000), the resort's flagship property. The best accommodation is in cabins. Most of it requires use of the ski-bus. Good restaurants include Riipinen, Vanha Karhu, and Kalakeidas – an intimate little place doing 'a range of traditional Finnish food'. There's lots to do off the slopes.

Pyhä, 150km/93 miles north-east of Rovaniemi, has seven lifts (including two chairs) and 10 runs on land that is mainly National Park. The vertical is only 280m/920ft and there is no steep terrain, but it has good off-piste. The best powder runs are on both sides of a long T-bar on the north slope. There's 140km/87 miles of cross-country. The Hotel Pyhätunturi (016 856111) is at mid-mountain.

Iso-Syöte, 150km/93 miles south of the Arctic Circle and 140km/87 miles from Oulu airport, is Finland's southernmost fell region – but it receives the most snow in the country. Catering mainly for families, it suits beginners and intermediates since, of its 12 pistes (covering 20km/12 miles), there are only two black runs. However, there is a freeride area among the trees. The runs are short, with the longest 1200m/3940ft and a maximum vertical of less than 200m/660 feet. Seven runs are floodlit at night. There's a terrain park, a snow tubing area, a tobogganing hill and 120km/75 miles of cross-country trails. Accommodation is mainly hotels and cabins, including the Iso-Syöte hotel (0201 476400) at the top of the slopes (pool, sauna).

UK PACKAGES

Ylläs Crystal, First Choice, Inghams, Inntravel, Kuoni, Neilson
Levi Crystal, Crystal Finest, First Choice, Inghams, Kuoni, Neilson
Ruka Crystal, Inghams, Thomson
Pyhä Crystal
Iso-Syöte Crystal, Thomson

Phone numbers
From abroad use the prefix +358 and omit the initial '0' of the phone number

TOURIST OFFICES

Levi
www.levi.fi
Ylläs
www.yllas.fi
Ruka
www.ruka.fi
Pyhä
www.pyha.fi
Iso-Syöte
www.isosyote.fi

➕ One of the best places in Europe for serious cross-country skiing

➕ The home of telemark – plenty of opportunities to learn and practise

➕ Freedom from the glitz and ill-mannered lift queues of the Alps

➕ Impressive snowboard parks

➕ Usually reliable snow conditions throughout a long season

➖ Very limited downhill areas

➖ Very basic mountain restaurants

➖ Booze is prohibitively taxed

➖ Scenery more Pennine than Alpine

➖ Après-ski that is either deadly dull or irritatingly rowdy

➖ Short daylight hours in midwinter

➖ Highly changeable weather

➖ Limited off-slope activities

Norway and its resorts are very different from the Alps, or indeed the Rockies. Some people find the place very much to their taste. For downhillers who dislike the usual ski-resort trappings and prefer a simpler approach to winter holidays, it could be just the place. For families with young children, in particular, it might make sense; you'll have no trouble finding junk food to please the kids – the mountain restaurants serve little else.

Speaking for ourselves, any one of the first three ➖ points we've listed above would probably be enough to put us off. Combine these in a single destination – then add in the other non-trivial negative points – and you can count us out.

There is a traditional friendship between Norway and Britain, and English is widely spoken.

For the Norwegians and Swedes, skiing is a weekend rather than a special holiday activity, and not an occasion for extravagance. So at lunchtime they tend to haul sandwiches out of their backpacks as we might while walking the Pennine Way, and in the evening they cook in their apartments. Don't expect a tempting choice of restaurants.

The Norwegians have a problem with alcohol. Walk into an après-ski bar at 5pm on a Saturday and you may find young men already inebriated – not merry, but incoherent. And this is despite – or, some say, because of – prohibitively high taxes on booze. Restaurant prices for wine are ludicrous, and shop prices may be irrelevant – Hemsedal has no liquor store. Our one attempt at self-catering there was an unusually sober affair as a result. Other prices are generally not high by Alpine standards.

Cross-country skiing comes as naturally to Norwegians as walking; and even if you're not very keen, the fact that cross-country is normal, and not a wimp's alternative to 'real' skiing, gives Norway a special appeal. Here, cross-country is both a way of getting about the valleys and a way of exploring the hills. What distinguishes Norway for the keen cross-country skier is the network of long trails across the gentle uplands, with refuges along the way where backpackers can pause for refreshment or stay overnight.

More and more Norwegians are taking to telemarking, and snowboarding is very popular – local youths fill the impressive terrain parks at weekends.

For downhill skiing, the country isn't nearly so attractive. Despite the fact that it is able to hold downhill races, Norway's Alpine areas are of limited appeal. The most rewarding resort is **Hemsedal**, covered in the next chapter.

UK PACKAGES

Lillehammer Directski.com, Ski McNeill
Geilo Headwater, Inntravel, Neilson
Beitostølen Neilson
Voss Ardmore, Inghams

Phone numbers
From abroad use the prefix +47

TOURIST OFFICES

Tryvann
www.tryvann.no
Lillehammer
www.lillehammerturist.no
Geilo
www.geilo.no
Beitostølen
www.beitostolen.com
Oppdal
www.oppdal.com
Trysil
www.trysil.com
Voss
www.skiinfo.no/voss/

Just 20 minutes from the centre of Oslo on an extension of the underground system is **Tryvann** (150m/490ft), a small area popular with the locals. The train arrives near the top station (525m/1720ft) on Holmenkollen. The main slopes – with a vertical of 380m/1,250ft – are served by two drags and two chairs, one of them fast. Two drags serve a separate nursery slope. There's a good terrain park, half-pipe and boardercross. The whole area has snowmaking. The slopes are floodlit most evenings – and are busier then than in the day. A new day lodge opened this year.

The site of the 1994 Olympics, the little lakeside town of **Lillehammer**, is not actually a downhill resort at all. The slalom events were held 15km/9 miles north at Hafjell (230m/750ft). This is a worthwhile little area with a vertical of 830m/2,720ft, 12 lifts (including an eight-person gondola) and 33km/21 miles of pistes. The downhill and super-G races went to Kvitfjell, about 35km/22 miles further north, developed for the purpose. It's steeper but smaller – 18km/11 miles of pistes. Children can enjoy a new snow garden and family area.

Norway's other widely known resort is **Geilo** (800m/2,620ft). This is a small, quiet, unspoiled community on the railway line from Bergen to Oslo. It provides all the basics of a resort – a handful of cafes and shops around the railway station, a dozen hotels more widely spread around the wide valley, children's facilities and a sports centre.

Geilo is a superb cross-country resort. As the Bergen-Oslo railway runs through the town it is possible to go for long tours and return by train.

Geilo is very limited for downhillers, but it does claim to have Scandinavia's only super-pipe. The 32km/20 miles of piste are spread over two small hills – one, Geilolia, a bus ride away from Geilo, with a good, informal hotel, a restaurant at its foot and a pizzeria on the mountain. This area has a six-pack link to the family beginners' zone. None of the runs is really difficult. The terrain parks there and at Fugleleiken have been upgraded recently.

Clearly the best hotel, and one of the attractions of staying in Geilo, is the Dr Holms (call central reservations on 320 95940) – smartly white-painted outside, beautifully furnished and spacious inside, with spa facilities and bar/cafe. This is the centre for après-ski, but prices are steep. The resort is quiet at the end of the day, but the main hotels provide entertainment.

On the edge of the beautiful Jotunheimen National Park, about 225km/140 miles north-west of Oslo, lies the small resort of **Beitostølen** (750m/2,460ft). The 18 slopes are best suited to beginners and early intermediates. Confident intermediates and experts will find more of a challenge at the Alpine Centre, 6km/4 miles away, where they will find blacks, moguls and off-piste. There's a good terrain park and 150km/93 miles of cross-country.

A long way north of the other resorts is **Oppdal** (550m/1,800ft), with more pistes than any of its rivals (55km/34 miles). The total vertical is 790m/2,590ft, but this is misleading – most runs are short. A chairlift and blue run were added recently.

There are slightly more extensive slopes at **Trysil** (460m/1,510ft), off to the east, on the border with Sweden, and the runs are longer (up to 4km/2 miles and 685m/2,250ft vertical). Well suited to families, it has a fast lift to the nursery area and gentle runs to progress to. A six-pack with heated seats replaced several old draglifts, and there's a good children's area. The 'long blue runs' and the ski school have been recommended. The runs here are all around the conical Trysilfjellet, some way from Trysil itself – though there are some lodgings at the hill. A connecting lift serves accommodation at Fageråsen and there's now a shuttle-bus service at Høyfjellssenter. Nightlife is 'fun and lively' – the Låven and Ski-pub'n are popular hangouts.

In complete contrast to all of these resorts is **Voss** (50m/160ft), a sizeable lakeside town quite close to the sea, which is 'child friendly and has high standards of accommodation'. Fleischer's hotel (520500) is reportedly 'comfortable'. A cable car links the town to the slopes on Hangur and Slettafjell, with a total of 40km/25 miles of 'well groomed' pistes and 'no queues'. There's a fast quad from Bavallan and new children's area at the base there. The ski school is praised as 'very accommodating' with 'excellent', small classes. And there are 11km/7 miles of cross-country trails. There are plenty of excursion possibilities, in particular the spectacular Flåm railway.

The best place for Alpine skiing in Norway (though we prefer the Alps) with the slopes an awkward distance from Hemsedal village

COSTS

① ② ③ ④ ⑤ ⑥

RATINGS

The slopes

Fast lifts	**
Snow	****
Extent	*
Expert	**
Intermediate	****
Beginner	***
Convenience	**
Queues	****
Mountain restaurants	*

The rest

Scenery	**
Resort charm	**
Off-slope	*

NEWS

A new day lodge and skier services centre, including apartments, restaurants, bars and shops, is due to open for 2008/09.

The children's area continues to grow; it is now claimed as Norway's largest and includes seven runs and eight lifts. Even more features are due for 2008/09.

Snowmaking was increased this year and more floodlights added for night skiing. The Fjellet and Hollvin restaurants were revamped and have new menus.

KEY FACTS

Resort	650m
	2,130ft
Slopes	670-1450m
	2,200-4,760ft
Lifts	22
Pistes	43km
	27 miles
Green	41%
Blue	25%
Red	18%
Black	16%
Snowmaking	26km
	16 miles

➕ Impressive snow reliability because of northerly location

➕ Increasing amounts of convenient slope-side accommodation

➕ Extensive cross-country trails compared to the Alps

➕ Some quite challenging slopes, and hills with a slightly Alpine feel

➕ Excellent children's nursery slopes

➖ Not much of a village

➖ Limited slopes

➖ Exposed upper mountain prone to closure because of bad weather

➖ Weekend queues

➖ Limited on-mountain dining

➖ No liquor store for miles

➖ Après-ski limited during the week and rowdy at weekends

Hemsedal's craggy terrain is reminiscent of a small-but-serious Alpine resort. Most people not resident in Scandinavia would be better advised to go for the real thing, but if you like the sound of Norway, Hemsedal is the place for downhill skiing. Go after the February school holidays, if possible.

THE RESORT

Hemsedal is both an unspoiled valley and a village, also referred to as Trøym and Sentrum ('Centre'), which is little more than a couple of apartment/hotel buildings, a few shops, a garage, a bank and a couple of cashpoints that are usually empty by evening. Note the absence of a liquor store. There has been talk of a lift from Trøym to the slopes, but for now the lift base is a mile or two away, across the valley.

There are self-catering apartments and houses beside the slopes (more seem to open each year) in the Skarsnuten area, which is linked to the main network by its own lift and red piste – and in a pleasantly woody separate cluster a walkable distance down the hill from the lifts.

A ski-bus links these points and others, but has been criticised by one reporter as 'busy and irregular'. The place is geared to weekenders arriving by car or coach.

THE MOUNTAINS

Hemsedal's slopes pack a lot of variety into a small space. They are shaded in midwinter, and can be very cold.

Slopes With four fast chairs to play on, you can pack a lot of runs into the day. And there's night skiing until 9pm, Tuesdays to Fridays. The lift pass also covers smaller Solheisen, up the valley. For a small supplement you can ski at Geilo, an hour away.

Terrain parks There are three terrain parks ('absolutely fantastic'). The main one has sections for advanced and expert jibbers, a half- and two quarter-pipes plus a big jump, rails and boxes. The beginner park also has a half- and quarter-pipe, improved jumps, rails and tabletops.

Snow reliability The combination of latitude, altitude and orientation makes for impressive snow reliability. The snowmaking was increased along two more runs this year.

Experts There is quite a bit to amuse experts – several black pistes of 450m/1,480ft vertical served by a fast eight-seat chair (or the adjacent 'very steep and very bumpy' T-bar) from the base (a couple left as a mogul slope) – and wide areas of gentler off-piste terrain served by drags above the treeline.

Intermediates Mileage-hungry piste-bashers will find Hemsedal's runs very limited. There are quite a few red and blue runs to play on, but the difference in difficulty is slight.

Beginners There's a gentle nursery area for absolute beginners. And there are splendid long green runs – but they get a lot of traffic, some of it irresponsibly fast. Some long blues and reds also suit near-beginners.

Snowboarding There is plenty of freeriding terrain, and some pistes are suitable for carving. The parks are popular and there's a boardercross.

Cross-country By Alpine standards there is lots to do – 130km/81 miles of

Schools and guides We lack recent reports; past feedback has been good.
Facilities for children The facilities at the lift base are good, with day care for children over three months. But a reporter complains that 'you can't book in advance and parents are expected to check on their children hourly and provide snacks and meals'. The kids' nursery slopes keep growing (now Norway's largest). Classes are available for four year olds.

STAYING THERE

How to go Most of the accommodation is in apartments, varying widely in convenience. Catered chalets are available through certain UK operators.
Hotels The best hotel is the refurbished Skogstad (320 55000) in central Hemsedal – comfortable, but its bar and nightclub may be noisy at weekends. Other hotels along the valley are used by UK tour operators. The hotel Skarsnuten (320 61700), on the mountain, is stylishly modern.
Apartments The Alpin apartments, a walk from the lift base, are satisfactory if you don't fill all the beds. The adjacent Tinden ones are quite smart.
Eating out The Oxen restaurant and bar and Peppe's pizza are recommended.
Après-ski It's minimal in the week, rowdy at weekends and holidays.
Off the slopes Diversions include dog sledding, tobogganing, activity centre (with bowling) and snowmobiling.

↑ By Norwegian ski resort standards, the scenery is dramatic
HEMSEDAL TOURIST OFFICE

prepared trails in the valley and forest and (later in the season) 80km/ 50 miles at altitude. There is a special trail map. Most of the trails are a few miles down the valley at the Gravset centre and 12km/7 miles of them are floodlit.
Queues Hemsedal is only a three-hour drive from Oslo, the capital. Good weekend weather fills the car parks, leading to queues for the main access lifts. But during the week it is quiet. The upper lifts are very exposed, and are easily closed by bad weather, producing crowds lower down.
Mountain restaurants The one functional self-service mountain restaurant is basic, but was revamped this year to include a new sun terrace and menu. There are also two or three kiosks with benches.

COSTS

① ② ③ ④ ⑤ ⑥

NEWS

For 2007/08 in the Sälen area a new eight-seat chair replaced a quad, a new blue run was built and more snowmaking was installed.

In Vemdalen, new lodging was built at all the bases. And for 2008/09 a new six-pack will open at Klövsjö.

➕ Snow-sure from December to May

➕ Unspoiled, beautiful landscape

➕ Uncrowded pistes and lifts

➕ Vibrant (but regimented) après-ski

➕ Excellent cross-country and good range of off-slope activities

➖ Limited challenging downhill terrain

➖ Small areas by Alpine standards

➖ Lacks the dramatic peaks and vistas of the Alps

➖ Short days during the early season

Sweden's landscape of forests and lakes and miles of unspoiled wilderness is entirely different from the Alps' grandeur and traffic-choked roads. Standards of accommodation, food and service are good, and the people are welcoming, lively and friendly. There are plenty of off-slope activities, but most of the downhill areas are limited in size and challenge. Sweden appeals most to those who want an all-round winter holiday in a different environment and culture.

Holidaying in Sweden is a completely different experience from a holiday in the Alps. The language is generally incomprehensible to us and, although virtually everyone speaks good English, the menus and signs are often written only in Swedish. The food is delightful, especially if you like fish and venison. And resorts are very family-friendly. It is significantly cheaper than neighbouring Norway, but reporters still complain that alcohol and traditional Swedish restaurants are very expensive.

One myth about Swedish skiing is that it is dark. It is true that the days are very short in December and early January. But from early February the lifts generally work from 9am to 4.30 and by March it is light until 8.30pm. Most resorts have some floodlit pistes.

On the downside, downhill slopes are limited in both challenge and extent and the lift systems dominated by T-bars. But there is lots of cross-country and backcountry skiing. Après-ski is taken very seriously – with live bands from mid- to late-afternoon. But it stops suddenly, dinner is served and then the nightlife starts. There is plenty to do off the slopes: snowmobile safaris, ice fishing, dog sled rides, ice climbing, and saunas galore. You can also visit a local Sami village.

The main resort is **Åre** (see separate chapter). **Sälen** is Scandinavia's largest winter sports area – and is made up of four separate sets of slopes totalling 144km/89 miles of piste. Most slopes

are very gentle, suiting beginners and early or timid intermediates best. Lindvallen and Högfjället are vaguely linked by a lift and a long cross-country slog, and Tandålen and Hundfjället by lift. There's also a bus service between them.

Vemdalen has three main areas of slopes linked by buses with a total of 45km/28 miles of pistes. A joint lift pass serves them all, there are no queues and T-bars dominate. Björnrike is great for families, beginners and early intermediates, with nine lifts and mainly gentle pistes. There is a hotel right on the slopes, built in modern style. Vemdalsskalet has more advanced intermediate terrain, with nine lifts and a terrain park. The Högfjällshotell at the base is large, dates from 1936 and prides itself on its après-ski with live entertainment. Klövsjö/Storhogna has 12 lifts, mainly easy green runs but three blacks and a hotel and apartments at the base.

Riksgränsen, above the Arctic Circle, is an area of jagged mountain peaks and narrow fjords. The season starts in mid-February and ends in June – when you can ski under the midnight sun. There are only six lifts and 21km/13 miles of piste. But there is some good off-piste and heli-skiing.

Björkliden, also above the Arctic Circle, is famous for its subterranean skiing inside Scandinavia's largest cave system. You need to go with a guide.

Ramundberget is a small, quiet, ski-in/ski-out family resort. It gets lots of snow and has 22km/14 miles of mainly easy or intermediate pistes.

UK PACKAGES

Vemdalen Neilson

TOURIST OFFICES

www.visit-sweden.com

Sälen
www.skistar.com

Vemdalen (Björnrike, Vemdalsskalet)
www.skistar.com

Riksgränsen
www.riksgransen.nu

Björkliden
www.bjorkliden.com

Ramundberget
www.ramundberget.se

Sweden's best slopes, strung out along a frozen lake above a small but charming town and with lots of non-skiing activities

COSTS

① ② ③ ④ ⑤ ⑥

RATINGS

The slopes
Fast lifts	**
Snow	***
Extent	**
Expert	**
Intermediate	****
Beginner	****
Convenience	***
Queues	****
Mountain restaurants	***

The rest
Scenery	***
Resort charm	***
Off-slope	***

NEWS

For 2007/08 the children's areas at Duved and Björnen were expanded, and a lift pass was introduced for those who only want to use the Björnen area. The budget Åre Torg hotel (51590) opened, with prices per person from 24 euros a night for 2008/09.

710

➕ Cute little town centre

➕ Good snow reliability

➕ Good for intermediates and novices

➕ Extensive cross-country trails

➕ Excellent children's facilities

➕ Lively après-ski scene

➕ Lots of off-slope diversions

➖ Lots of T-bars

➖ Exposed upper mountain prone to closure because of bad weather

➖ High winds detrimental to snow conditions

➖ Few expert challenges

➖ High season and weekend queues

Åre has the biggest area of linked slopes in Sweden and some of its most challenging terrain. But it suits beginners, intermediates and families best. It has a dinky little town centre and a long area of slopes set along a frozen lake.

THE RESORT

Åre is a small town made up of old, pretty, coloured wooden buildings and some larger modern additions. When we were there the main square had a roaring open fire to warm up by. As well as accommodation in town, there is lots spread out along the valley, with a concentration in the Duved area. All the slopes and lodging are set on the shore of a huge, long lake, frozen in the winter months.

THE MOUNTAINS

The terrain is mainly beginner and intermediate tree-lined slopes, with a couple of windswept bowls above.
Slopes There are two main areas (linked by an efficient shuttle-bus). The largest is accessed by a funicular from the centre of town or by a six-pack or cable car a short climb above it. This takes you to the hub of a

network of runs and (mainly) T-bars that stretches for 10km/6 miles from end to end. The cable car is often shut because it goes above the treeline to the top of the slopes (known as the 'high zone'), which often suffers from howling gales. A gondola also accesses the high zone from a different point. You can get back on-piste right into the town square. A separate area of slopes is above Duved and served by a high-speed chair. There are several floodlit slopes, open different nights.
Terrain parks There's a boardercross course, a half-pipe and a big terrain park, plus two parks for novices.
Snow reliability Snow reliability is good from November to May. But high winds can blow fresh snow away. They also mean that artificial snow is often made wet so that it doesn't blow away and it compacts to a hard, icy surface.
Experts Experts will find Åre's slopes limited, especially if the high zone is closed. If it is open, there is a lot of

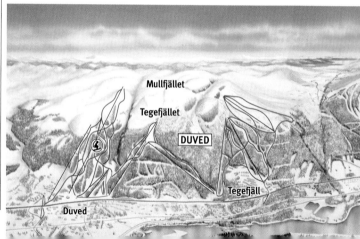

off-piste available and guides to take you there, including an 8km/5 mile run over the back, accessed by a snowmobile tow (which costs extra). The piste map shows 10 avalanche zones to be wary of. On the main lower area the steepest (and iciest when we were there) pistes are in the Olympia area. There are also steep black and red runs back to town.

Intermediates The slopes are ideal for most intermediates, with pretty blue runs through the trees. Because they tend to be more sheltered, the blue runs also often have the best snow. You can get a real sense of travelling from hill to hill on the main area. The snowmobile tow to the top services some gentle off piste, and there are great views and a cafe at the top.

Beginners There are good facilities, both on the main area and at Duved.

Snowboarding There's good varied terrain for boarders. But there are a lot of draglifts (31 out of a total of 40).

Cross-country There's an amazing 400km/250 miles of prepared cross-country trails and three times as much unprepared. Some trails are floodlit.

Queues In high season there can be ('orderly and polite') queues for some lifts, especially in the central area immediately above Åre.

Mountain restaurants There are some good ones. Our favourite was the rustic Buustamons Fjällgärd, in the woods near Ullådalsområdet.

Schools and guides The ski school has a good reputation and a reporter was impressed with his private lesson.

Facilities for children There are special children's areas, and kids under eight year old get free lift passes if wearing helmets. There's a kindergarten that takes children from the age of two.

STAYING THERE

How to go Neilson is the only UK tour operator to offer packages to Åre.

Hotels The best central hotel is the charming old Diplomat Åregården. The renovated slope-side Tott has good spa facilities and views, and 'friendly and efficient staff'. The Holiday Club by the lake and the Renen in Duved are popular with families.

Apartments There are plenty of cabins and apartments; reporters have recommended the ones at Åre Fjällby, near the chondola.

Eating out The Bistro at Åre Fjällby and Werséns in town are good.

Après-ski Après-ski is lively. The Fjällgården on the slopes, the Tott and the Åregården are packed from 3pm and have live bands. Later on, the Country Club and Bygget also have live bands and there are plenty of bars for a quiet drink – including the Black Sheep at Åre Fjällby, which is decorated like a British pub.

Off the slopes Lots to do, including dog or reindeer sled rides, skating, ice fishing, tobogganing, ice driving, ice climbing and snowmobiling. There's also the longest zipline in Europe.

Åre

711

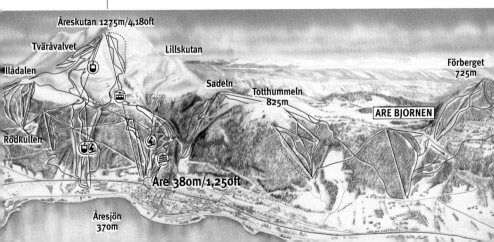

Bulgaria has traditionally attracted beginners and early intermediates looking for a jolly time on a tight budget. Standards have been low. But Bansko's arrival on the scene has raised the bar for Bulgarian resorts (see separate chapter).

A reporter who went to Borovets over New Year 2007 summed up his stay vividly: 'Skis: old and well used. Ski school: easily arranged, no shortage of English speakers. Hotels: modern, clean, over-heated. Staff: mostly operating scams to relieve you of cash. Food: in the hotel and resort restaurants, good standard stuff; on the mountain, rubbish. Bars: all a bit quiet. Bulgarians: mainly miserable. Conclusion: you get what you pay for – and next time we will be paying a lot more to get a lot more.'

Pamporovo is strictly for beginners and very unadventurous intermediates, with mostly easy runs. Others will find the limited area of short runs inadequate, despite recent expansion.

Work has started on building links to the slopes of nearby Mechi Chal in an ambitious project known as 'Perelik', which would result in a linked area of some 80km/50 miles of pistes, but it won't be finished until 2009/10 at the earliest.

The slopes are pretty and sheltered, with pistes starting at a high point of 1925m/6,320ft and cutting through pine forest. The ski schools are repeatedly praised – instructors are patient, enthusiastic and speak good English, and class sizes are usually quite small. The main hotels are in a purpose-built village in an attractively wooded setting slightly away from the slopes – there is a shuttle-bus. The 5-star hotel Pamporovo gets the best reports, but the food is reportedly

'very poor'. There is a handful of lively bars and discos.

Borovets has more to offer intermediates with 58km/36 miles of slopes. The resort is a collection of large, modern hotels in a beautiful wooded setting, with bars, restaurants and shops housed within them. There is a small selection of quirkier bars, shops and eating places.

A long gondola rises over 1000m/ 3,280ft to reach both the small, high, easy slopes of Markoudjika and the longer, steepish Yastrebets pistes. The runs are best for good intermediates. There are no challenges for experts and the resort is not ideal for novices; nursery slopes are crowded, and the step from the Markoudjika blue runs to testing reds is a big one.

Our reporter met disastrously long queues for the gondola and other lifts, partly explained by other lift closures.

Grooming is erratic. The gondola is said to be prone to closure by wind.

Instructors are generally praised by reporters, but classes can be large. There is night skiing and 35km/ 22 miles of cross-country.

Most reporters stay at the Rila or the Samokov hotels – both huge but with 'good, clean rooms'. The Lion was recommended in 2007. There are lively bars catering well to an '18-30' type crowd – Buzz is said to be the best. Tour operator reps organise pub crawls, folklore evenings etc. Excursions to the Rila monastery or Sofia by coach are interesting.

Small area of beginner and intermediate slopes served by a modern lift system above a rapidly growing resort town and base

- Bulgaria's best mountain
- Lots of fast lifts on the mountain
- Picturesque town at the base
- Smart new or renovated hotels
- Low prices
- Friendly, helpful locals
- Cheap and very cheerful traditional restaurants all over the town

- Long gondola-ride up to the main lift base – and long queues at the morning peak
- Limited slopes by Alpine standards
- Long airport transfers; poor roads
- Few off-slope diversions
- Lots of building going on and half-finished buildings around

Bansko completed its first season in full operation in 2004/05 and has shown what eastern Europe can offer the skiing world, given proper investment – more than £20 million spent on smart lifts, snowmaking and hands-free passes. Readers are impressed with the small ski area. But the bed-base is expanding rapidly (many apartments have been sold to Brits), the access gondola cannot cope with peak morning demand, and the base area resembles a building site.

THE RESORT

Bansko, set on a flat valley floor circled by spectacular peaks, looks like a giant goods yard on the outskirts – more of an industrial town than a tourist destination. But around the central square the town has a quiet and charming heart, with architecture straight out of Disney's *Beauty And The Beast*. There are few outward signs of commercial tourism here except for hotels, which nestle between homes, shops, restaurants and churches. But a new hub is developing rapidly near the gondola base. 'It looked like a building site with many unfinished apartments and hotels; pavements were hazardous to walk on,' says a 2008 visitor. It's a fair walk from the centre and 'a shuttle-bus would be a good idea'.

Although euros are accepted at the airport, the local currency – the Lev – is standard in the resort.

THE MOUNTAINS

Until 2003/04, the draglifts and pistes in the Pirin National Park were accessible only by army jeeps and minibuses up a tortuous 12km/7 mile road. Now an eight-seater gondola ferries skiers to Bunderishka. There is a blue piste back to the town, with snowmaking and floodlighting.

Slopes From Bunderishka two successive fast quad chairs take you up mainly north-facing slopes to the high point of the area. From there you can ski down reds or blues to Shiligarnika, or a red followed by a black (called Alberto Tomba, after the famous Italian racer who opened the revamped ski area) to Bunderishka. There are also a few slopes near the mid-station of the gondola – a new quad and draglift were built here for 2007/08 (see 'News'). A 2008 visitor found the slopes quiet and 'well groomed' but was disappointed to find

NEWS

For 2007/08 a fast quad replaced the draglift below the mid-station. The two runs here now have snowmaking and a new draglift accesses the beginner slopes in this area. Snowmaking has increased and it is claimed that 80% of pistes are now covered. Neither the ring road being built to ease traffic congestion nor a planned new shopping centre at the base of the gondola, including a restaurant and casino, will be ready for the coming season.

TOURIST OFFICE

www.banskoski.com

some pistes not open, including the Alberto Tomba black. There is also a chair marked on the piste map going up a mountain to the right of Bunderishka and a long red run back down. This has not worked for several years so is not shown on our map.

Terrain parks There's a half-pipe and a terrain park near the top.

Snow reliability A claimed 80% of the pistes are covered by snowmaking. This – together with good grooming (by Bulgarian standards) and north-facing slopes – means more reliable snow than the Bulgarian norm.

Experts There are no challenging pistes – the one black ought to be red. But there is some good tree skiing and a reporter enjoyed some good off-piste with a ski instructor.

Intermediates Good medium-to-difficult reds come straight down the face from the top, and varied blues go round to skier's right. All in all, there are four or five ways down the 900m/2,950ft vertical of the main area.

Beginners The nursery slopes near the top of the gondola are good, with little through traffic. There are blue runs served by draglifts at the top of

the mountain and the long ski road down to town is gentle and easy.

Snowboarding Varied, but limited. A recent visitor 'had great fun' in his second week on a snowboard.

Queues One reporter complains of waiting 'hours' for the gondola – clearly a problem at peak times. A 2008 visitor 'gave up early in the week and drove to the top of the gondola'; then he discovered the gondola opened well before its advertised time and beat the queues that way.

Mountain restaurants A fair sprinkling, including some modern ones with outdoor bars (but not enough seating). The char-grills they serve are 'delicious and cheap'. The Platoto near the top is our reporters' favourite.

Schools and guides The main Ulen school gets good reports, but one visitor said her children could 'wander freely out of lessons' and were grouped with much younger children. A recent reporter was 'very impressed' with the small Pirin 2000 school – 'very good and flexible tuition'.

Facilities for children There's a kindergarten.

STAYING THERE

How to go Several UK operators feature Bansko including the specialist Balkan Holidays.

Hotels There are newish hotels around the gondola station, including the swanky but traditional-style 5-star Kempinski Grand Arena, with 'excellent facilities', the more modern Perun and the 'spacious' Lion. Refurbished places include the 'excellent' Pirin, near the town square and the 'wonderful' Strazhite, near the gondola. All these have pools and some spa/fitness facilities. Most central hotels run a shuttle-bus service to the gondola.

Eating out Reporters enthuse about the town's scores of mehanas (traditional inns) with roaring fires, real Bulgarian food and good wine.

Après-ski There are lively bars at the gondola base and new ones keep opening. The Lion pub, B4 and Amigos are popular with reporters, as is the bowling alley at the hotel Strazhite. The nightclub Amnesia is 'good' on some nights, 'empty' on others.

Off the slopes Excursions to the Rila monastery and trips across the border into Greece are possible. The spa at the Grand Arena got a rave review and there's an ice rink.

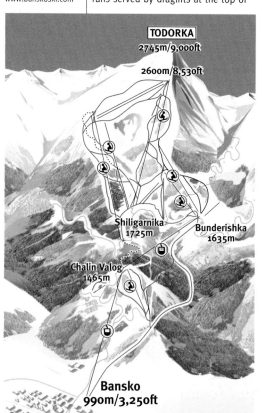

TODORKA
2745m/9,000ft

2600m/8,530ft

Shiligarnika
1725m

Bunderishka
1635m

Chalin Valog
1465m

Bansko
990m/3,250ft

COSTS

① ② ③ ④ ⑤ ⑥

- ➕ Cheap packages, and extremely low prices on the spot
- ➕ Interesting excursions and friendly local people
- ➕ Good tuition, keen instructors

- ➖ Primitive facilities – especially mountain restaurants and toilets
- ➖ Uninspiring food
- ➖ Very limited slopes – of no interest to anyone other than novices

Romania sells mainly on price. On-the-spot prices, in particular, are very low. Provided you don't have unreasonably high expectations, you'll probably come back from Poiana Brasov content. It allows complete beginners to try a ski holiday at the absolute minimum cost, and to have a jolly time in the evenings without adding substantially to that cost.

Plans to open a new airport near Brasov might encourage more visitors, but we haven't had any reader reports for years – if you go, please send us your views.

UK PACKAGES

Poiana Brasov *Airtours, Balkan Holidays, Inghams, Neilson, Ski Balkantours, Thomson, Transylvania Live*

Phone numbers
From abroad use the prefix +40 and omit the initial '0' of the phone number

TOURIST OFFICE

www.poiana-brasov.com

Romania's main resort – and now the only one featuring regularly in UK package programmes – is **Poiana Brasov** (1030m/3,380ft). It is a short drive above the city of Brasov in the Carpathian mountains, about 120km/ 75 miles (on alarmingly rough, slow roads) north-west of the capital and arrival airport, Bucharest. A new airport is apparently being built near Brasov that will cut transfer time.

Poiana Brasov is purpose-built, but not designed for convenience: the hotels are scattered about a pretty, wooded plateau, served by regular buses and cheap taxis. The place has the air of a spacious holiday camp, but with some serious-sized hotels – some right by the lifts.

The slopes are extremely limited – approximately 14km/9 miles of pistes in total. They consist of decent intermediate treelined runs of about 750m/2,460ft vertical, roughly following the line of the main cable car and gondola (recently upgraded), plus an open nursery area at the top. There are also some nursery lifts at

village level, which are used when snow permits. Night skiing is also available. The resort gets weekend crowds from Brasov and Bucharest, and queues can result, but during the week there are few problems.

A key part of the resort's appeal is the friendly and effective teaching.

Hotel standards are higher than you might expect. The linked Bradul (0268 407330) and Sport (0268 407330) hotels are handy for the lower nursery slopes and for one of the cable cars, and look smart after refurbishment. Guests in both have use of the Sport's sauna/hot tub/fitness room. The resort has a five-star hotel, the Heraldic Club.

Après-ski revolves around the hotel bars and nightclubs – plus outings to rustic barns for barbies with gypsy music, and to the bars and restaurants of Brasov. With cheap beer and very cheap spirits on tap, things can be quite lively. Off-slope facilities are limited; there is a good-sized pool, and bowling. An excursion to nearby Bran Castle (Count Dracula's home) is also popular.

715

COSTS

①②③④⑤⑥

➕ Good value for money

➕ Beautiful scenery

➕ Good beginners' slopes and lessons

➖ Limited, easy slopes on the whole

➖ Mainly slow, antiquated lifts

➖ Uninspiring food, but improving

Slovenia offers good value for money 'on the sunny side of the Alps'. The main resorts are popular with economy-minded British and Dutch visitors and with visitors from neighbouring Italy and Austria, giving quite a cosmopolitan feel.

Slovenia is a small country bordering Italy to the west and Austria to the north. The first state to break away from Yugoslavia, Slovenia managed to escape the turmoil that engulfed the Balkans. There is a positive feel to the resorts and a warm and hospitable welcome. Prices are low.

The main resorts are within two-and-a-half hours' bus ride of the capital, Ljubljana. The ski areas are small, but have improving lift systems and few queues. Ski schools are high quality and cheap, reputedly with good English. Hotel star ratings tend to be a trifle generous, but standards of service and hygiene are high.

In addition to the resorts covered here, a couple are in our directory at the back of the book – notably Kanin.

Kranjska Gora (810m/2,660ft) is the best-known resort, a pretty village not far from the borders with Austria and Italy and dominated by the majestic Julian Alps. The Lek, Kompas and Larix hotels – with pools – are the best for slope-side convenience. There are 30km/19 miles of mainly intermediate slopes, rising up to 1570m/5,150ft. Challenges are largely confined to the World Cup slalom run. Snow reliability is not good, despite snowmaking. The lifts are rather antiquated (mostly T-bars), but queues are rare, except on local holidays. A terrain park is

planned for 2008/09. There are 40km/25 miles of cross-country.

Vogel (1535m/5,040ft), in the beautiful **Bohinj** basin, has the best slopes and conditions in the area. The 18km/11 miles of slopes are reached by a cable car up from the valley. There's a collection of small hotels and restaurants at the base. Pistes of varying difficulty run from the high point at 1800m/5,910ft back into a central bowl with a small beginner area. When conditions permit, there is a long red run to the bottom cable car station. Two new quads were installed for 2007/08. For a change of scene, **Kobla**, with 23km/14 miles of wooded runs, is a short bus ride away. There are 13km/8 miles of cross-country.

Bled, with its beautiful lake and fairly lively nightlife, is an attractive base. Its local slopes are very limited, but free buses run to Vogel (20km/12 miles) and Kobla (a bit nearer).

Slovenia's second city, **Maribor** (265m/870ft), in the north-east, is 6km/4 miles from its local slopes – the biggest ski area in the country, with 40km/25 miles of runs, 21 lifts and 36km/22 miles of cross-country. A new six-pack and run are planned for 2008/09. The area lift pass also covers Kranjska Gora. There are several atmospheric old inns serving good, Hungarian-influenced food.

UK PACKAGES

Kranjska Gora *Balkan Holidays, Crystal, Directski.com, First Choice, Inghams, Just Slovenia, Mountain Tracks, Neilson, Ski McNeill, Thomson* **Bohinj** *Balkan Holidays, Crystal, Directski.com, Ski McNeill, Thomson* **Bled** *Balkan Holidays, Crystal, Directski.com, First Choice, Ski McNeill, Thomson, Waymark*

TOURIST OFFICES

www.slovenia.info

Kranjska Gora
www.kranjska-gora.si

Vogel (Bohinj)
www.vogel.si

Kobla (Bohinj)
www.bohinj.si/kobla

Bled
www.bled.si

Maribor
www.maribor-pohorje.si

- Easy to get to from northern Britain
- It is possible to experience perfect snow and stirring skiing
- Decent, cheap accommodation and good-value packages
- Mid-week it's rarely crowded
- Extensive ski-touring possibilities
- Lots to do off the slopes

- Weather is extremely changeable and sometimes vicious
- Snowfall is erratic, to say the least, and pistes can be closed through lack of snow
- Slopes limited; runs mainly short
- Queueing can be a problem
- Little ski resort ambience and few memorable mountain restaurants

Conditions in Scotland are unpredictable, to say the least. If you live nearby and can go at short notice when things look good, the several ski areas are a tremendous asset. But booking a holiday here as a replacement for your usual week in the Alps is just too risky.

For novices who are really keen to learn, Scotland could make sense, especially if you live nearby. You can book instruction via one of the excellent outdoor centres, many of which also provide accommodation and a wide range of other activities. The ski schools at the resorts themselves are also very good.

Most of the slopes in most of the areas suit intermediates best. But all apart from The Lecht offer one or two tough or very tough slopes.

Snowboarding is popular and most of the resorts have some special terrain features, but maintaining these facilities in good nick is problematic. The natural terrain is good for free-riding when the conditions are right.

Cairngorm is the best-known resort,

FURTHER INFORMATION

The VisitScotland organisation runs an excellent website at:
ski.visitscotland.com

t 0845 22 55 121
info@visitscotland.com

with 12 lifts and 37km/23 miles of runs. Aviemore is the main centre (with a shuttle-bus to the slopes), but you can stay in other villages in the Spey valley. The slopes are accessed by a funicular from the main car park up to Ptarmigan at 1100m/3,610ft.

Nevis Range is the highest Scottish resort and has 11 lifts in addition to the long six-seat gondola accessing the slopes and 35km/22 miles of runs on the north-facing slopes of Aonach Mor. There are many B&Bs and hotels in and around Fort William, 10 minutes away by shuttle.

Glenshee boasts 21 lifts and 40km/25 miles of runs, spread out over three minor parallel valleys and some natural quarter-pipes. Glenshee remains primarily a venue for day-trippers, though there are hotels, hostels and B&Bs in the area.

Glencoe's more limited slopes (seven lifts, 20km/12 miles of runs) lie just east of moody Glen Coe itself. You have to ride a double chairlift and a button lift to get to the main slopes, including the nursery area. The isolated Kings House Hotel is 2km/1 mile away.

The Lecht is largely a novices' area, with 13 lifts and 20km/12 miles of runs on the gentle slopes beside a high pass, with a series of parallel lifts and runs above the car parks. With a maximum vertical of only 200m/660ft, runs are short. There's extensive snowmaking, a terrain park, and a day lodge at the base. The village of Tomintoul is 10km/6 miles away.

INVERNESS

The Lecht

Cairngorm

ABERDEEN

Glenshee

Nevis Range

Glencoe

DUNDEE

PERTH

STIRLING

GLASGOW

EDINBURGH

KEY FACTS	
Niseko	
Vertical	920m
	3,020ft
Lifts	38
Pistes	48km
	30 miles
Green	30%
Blue	40%
Black	30%
Rusutsu	
Vertical	595m
	1,950ft
Lifts	19
Green	30%
Blue	40%
Black	30%
Furano	
Vertical	955m
	3,130ft
Lifts	10
Pistes	32km
	20 miles
Green	40%
Blue	40%
Black	20%

+ Reliable deep powder snow in Hokkaido resorts, lift-served

+ Exotic atmosphere, fabulous food

+ Polite and gracious locals

+ Inexpensive alcoholic drinks

+ Night skiing is the norm, allowing a long ski day if you want one

− The language barrier

− It's a long way – around 6,000 miles and you have to change planes

− Lack of off-slope diversions

− Snowfall can go on for weeks in Hokkaido resorts

Although it is roughly the same size as the British Isles, Japan has hundreds of ski resorts. Several UK tour operators feature Japanese resorts, going to places on the northern island of Hokkaido that have developed something like cult status with keen skiers and riders from Australia, in particular. The reason? Snow – huge and reliable falls of powder snow.

In these remote parts of Japan, hardly anything is written in English and no English-language media are available (except websites). Going independently sounds like hard work; but presumably going with a tour operator is not.

You fly in to Sapporo (about two hours by bus from Rusutsu and a bit longer to Niseko or Furano), via Tokyo or Osaka. As you are travelling such a great distance you might want to combine your skiing with a stay in Tokyo or (preferably) Kyoto.

Niseko is made up of three areas of slopes – Grand Hirafu (Hirafu and Hanazono), Annupuri and Higashiyama – with a total of 38 lifts covered by a single pass. The three are linked, but not as efficiently as you might wish. There are modern lifts, but also some old single chairs on upper slopes.

The most popular and most easily accessible area, Grand Hirafu, is open from 8.30am to 9.00pm, thanks to what is one of the world's largest – and most heavily used – night skiing operations.

Niseko has a well-deserved reputation for powder snow, which falls almost constantly from December to the end of February. Skiing waist-deep powder is an everyday occurrence. Clearly, this will suit some holiday skiers and not others. Niseko does offer groomed runs, but you can get those closer to home, and get a tan while you ski them. The snow does stop sometimes, and when it does the powder gets tracked out quickly. But it's usually not too long before another snowstorm marches in across the Sea of Japan from Siberia, and the powder returns. The terrain is not steep, disappointing some experts.

The lack of sun has not proved a deterrent to Australians, who now come in their thousands. For them, guaranteed powder and reasonable

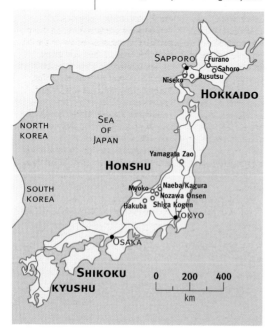

← There are lots of resorts on the main island of Honshu; only the better-known ones are shown on our map. But the best snow is on Hokkaido

↑ No, the skiing doesn't take place on the volcano; the 500-room hotel Prince is at the foot of Niseko's Higashiyama slopes

TRAVELPLAN AUSTRALIA

costs are an unbeatable combination. For UK-based travellers, the cost is higher: between around £1,000 and £1,900 for a week.

There are several modern ski-in/ski-out hotels (but little else) at the bases. Or you can stay in the atmospheric little town of Hirafu where there are now some impressive modern apartments alongside traditional pensions and lodges, raising accommodation standards well above the norm for the simple country town. The lift bases are well serviced by shuttle-buses.

While there isn't a lot to do outside of ski, eat and drink in Hirafu, the Australian influx means that the little town makes up for its lack of sophistication with a vibrant nightlife and plenty of variety in the way of bars, restaurants and tiny underground-style clubs. There are now a few very upmarket restaurants in town and several chic bars. And an igloo-style Ice Bar is dug out of a snowdrift each year, complete with icicles on the roof and a real bar selling all manner of cocktails.

Rusutsu is about an hour from Niseko, and makes a viable day trip; or you could combine the two in a two-centre holiday. The slopes, over three interlinked mountains, are more limited, but offer slightly more challenge. And for 2007/08 they installed a double chairlift direct from the Rusutsu Tower hotel to the slopes, and have opened up more tree skiing between the pistes. The snow here can

be as good as in Niseko (though it doesn't fall in quite the same quantity), and it doesn't get tracked out so quickly. There's also a good terrain park and half-pipe.

The pivotal, self-contained Rusutsu Resort Hotel complex offers a wide choice of good restaurants plus all sorts of other facilities – bars, shopping mall, swimming, wave pool, spas and a new thermal baths area.

One of the main alternatives to these two on Hokkaido is **Furano** – one of the most famous resorts within Japan, capable of hosting World Cup events and offering a tad more vertical than Niseko, at 955m/3,130ft over two linked sectors. It is five to six hours from Niseko and Rusutsu, so not within day-trip range. This is a resort where you can either stick to the relatively easy trails or join a guided group to explore off-piste, including the lift-served but ungroomed Asahidake mountain (over an hour away). You can stay either at the base or in the town, a bus ride away.

The largest ski area in Japan is on the main island of Honshu: **Shiga Kogen**, comprising 21 interlinked resorts and a huge diversity of terrain covered by one lift ticket. It was the site of several major events in the 1998 Winter Olympics.

Hakuba is also handy to reach by train if you find yourself in Tokyo and don't have time for the trip to Hokkaido. It is a group of 10 resorts accessing more than 200 runs amid the rugged peaks of Japan's 'Alps'.

Introduction

719

Interactive resort shortlist builder at www.wtss.co.uk

THE ONSEN EXPERIENCE

Onsen are complexes of hot baths to soak in, showers and communal volcanic thermal pools; they are a key part of Japanese culture and a major part of après-ski. All onsen are basically set up in the same way: men and women shower and bathe in their separate areas. Then, if they wish, they can congregate to soak and have a drink in a communal thermal pool, which more often than not will be outside and surrounded by snow.

- ➕ Offers skiing and boarding during the European summer
- ➕ Some of the resorts offer upmarket slope-side accommodation
- ➕ Snowcat skiing offered in a couple of resorts

- ➖ It's a long way from Britain
- ➖ Mountains rather low and slopes rather limited by Alpine standards
- ➖ Day lift passes are very expensive – up to £40 per day

Even more than New Zealand, Australia offers resorts that are basically of local interest, but that can amuse people with other reasons to travel there – escaping a European summer to catch up with those long-lost relatives, say.

The major resorts are concentrated in the populous south-east corner of the country, between Sydney and Melbourne, with the largest in New South Wales (NSW) – in the National Park centred on Australia's highest mountain, Mt Kosciusko (2230m/7,320ft), about six hours' drive south of Sydney. It costs A$27 a day just to enter the Kosciusko National Park. Skiing has been going on here since the early 1900s – as it has in the next-door state of Victoria.

The season generally runs from early June to mid-October. In the last few years there have been major dumps in early July or even June, but August and September remain the most reliable months.

Thredbo, established in 1957, is a sophisticated, upmarket Alpine-style village in NSW. It hosted the only World Cup race event held in Australia, thanks to a vertical of 670m/2,200ft.

Thredbo is rather like a small French purpose-built resort – user-friendly, and mostly made up of modern apartments, many new luxury ski-in/ski-out chalets, and lodges run by clubs. There are many upmarket chalets for rent, too. Originally Thredbo had an Austrian flavour but this has now given way to lively, modern, casual-elegant bars and restaurants, increasing numbers of very smart architect-designed apartments and a pedestrian mall with good shopping and sculptures. It's a steep place, with some stiff climbs. Road access is easy.

The slopes, prettily wooded with gum trees, rise up across the valley from the village, served by a regular shuttle-bus through the resort. Snowmaking has been doubled in the last two seasons and now covers the most problematic lower slopes. When the big falls arrive conditions can be as good as anywhere, but it's rarely cold enough for powder to last for more than a few hours. The runs are many and varied. The dozen lifts include three fast quad chairs, and the trails include Australia's highest (2035m/6,680ft) and longest (6km/4 miles). While the blacks are not steep – except for Funnelweb, named after Australia's most poisonous spider – on the higher lifts there are off-piste variants, including a beautiful guided backcountry tour to Dead Horse Gap, with transport back to the resort provided. There are now three distinct terrain parks and the slopes are also dotted with natural terrain features.

There is an attractive pedestrian mall with good shopping and some high-class restaurants both on and off the mountain. There is also an impressive sports training complex open to the public, with an Olympic-size pool. The 700m/2,300ft public bobsleigh track is popular.

On the other side of the mountain range is the large **Perisher Blue** resort complex, with a pass covering 50 lifts and six base stations – more than anywhere else in Australia – but a vertical of less than 400m/1,310ft. Next year the resort will add an eight-seat chairlift to help serve Mt Perisher. The main area is Perisher/Smiggins, where lifts and runs – practically all easy or intermediate – range over three lightly wooded sectors. The resort is reachable by road, or by the Skitube, a rack railway that tunnels up from Bullocks Flat and goes on to the second area, **Blue Cow/Guthega**, where the slopes offer more challenges.

Perisher Blue is doing its best to catch up with Thredbo by upgrading hotels and building more facilities. The resort is very spread out and has no central focus except for one cavernous base facility full of shops and eateries, and while a sophisticated pedestrian village has been widely talked about, the project has stalled. Perisher has more ski-in/ski-out accommodation than Thredbo, although it does appeal more to the masses, with its shopping-mall-style village centre filled with every manner of shop, bar and fast food restaurant. Its main advantage over Thredbo is its snow, thanks to its position further within the mountain ranges and its higher altitude. For this reason it is one of the few resorts offering a first tracks program, as it is actually worth rising early here after a big snowfall. There is a super-sized terrain park at Blue Cow.

Many on a budget stay in the lakeside town of Jindabyne, a half-hour drive from both Thredbo and Perisher, with a lively youth-oriented nightlife scene. There are also some upmarket chalets on the road up to Thredbo.

From Perisher, a snowcat can take you on an 8km/5 mile ride to the isolated chalets of Australia's highest resort, **Charlotte Pass** (1760m/5,770ft), with five lifts but only 200m/66oft vertical and 50 hectares of terrain – the entire ski field can be seen from most of the lodges. People visit the Pass more for its charm and Alpine beauty than for the skiing although it is popular with families and beginners. The major hotel is the historic and turreted Kosciusko Chalet, a good spot for romantic weekends. Mt Kosciusko is easily reached on cross-country skis.

If you want to learn to ski among the gum trees at the lowest price, **Selwyn Snowfields** is the place. Its lift ticket prices are more than 25% below the other ski fields. Selwyn has 12 lifts across 45 hectares, of which 80% is beginner or intermediate, plus snow tubing and tobogganing, and is about an hour from Cooma, near Jindabyne.

In Victoria, resorts are not as high as in NSW but many have good snow. **Mount Hotham** has a justified reputation for good snow and bills itself 'the powder capital of Australia'. Some of Australia's most exclusive hotels are being built here in a bid to turn Hotham into a year-round destination. It is an eight-hour drive from Sydney, and a four-hour drive

from Melbourne. (The airport 20 minutes' drive from Hotham does not currently have commercial flights.) Hotham's 13 lifts serve a complete range of runs, with plenty of variety, and free cat skiing on the more powdery slopes. The longest run is 2.5km/1.5 miles, and there is more consistently steep terrain here than anywhere else in Australia. The resort has introduced snow kiting lessons, as well as dog sledding and snowshoe tours. The village is built along the top of a ridge, with the slopes below it. The focus is Mount Hotham Central, with apartments, shops, a few good restaurants and the new White Mountain Spa. Hotham Heights Chalets is a nest of upscale architect-designed multi-storey buildings. You can also stay 15 minutes' drive away at Dinner Plain – stunning architect-designed chalets set prettily among gum trees. There are also a number of restaurants and bars here, and cross-country trails.

A six-minute A$99 return helicopter ride (Hotham Heli Link) takes you to another resort nearby (and covered by the same lift pass), **Falls Creek**. Falls Creek is the most Alpine of Australia's resorts, completely snow-bound in winter (there are snowcats from the car park). There are 18 lifts, though the area is smaller than Mount Hotham's and the runs are mostly intermediate. There are extensive terrain park features. Falls Creek also has a lavish spa to rival Mt Hotham's, and is always adding to the number of funky architect-designed lodges. For some, the big attraction at Falls Creek is being able to access Australia's steepest skiing on the adjacent **Mt McKay** – 365m/1,200ft vertical of true black-diamond terrain. Guided snowcat rides ($A69) are worth the trip.

The other Victorian resort of note is the isolated peak of **Mt Buller**. Only a two-hour drive from Melbourne, this place is a magnet for old money, which has financed a proper sophisticated resort village with a luxury hotel, a pampering spa, Australia's highest cinema complex and even a university campus. Draped around the mountain are 25 lifts – the largest network in Victoria. There are fees to enter and to park overnight.

Mt Buffalo is worth visiting mainly to stay in the historic Mt Buffalo Chalet, with its dramatic views over the craggy Victorian Alps. The Chalet is done up in true 1930s style.

Interactive resort shortlist builder at **www.wtss.co.uk**

- For Europeans, more interesting than summer skiing on glaciers
- Huge areas of off-piste terrain accessible by helicopter
- Some spectacular scenery, as seen in *The Lord of the Rings* movies

- Limited on-mountain restaurants – though these are being upgraded
- Half-hour-plus drives from accommodation up to the ski areas
- Highly changeable weather
- No trees

The number of keen Kiwi skiers and boarders kicking around the Alps gives a clue that there must be some decent slopes back home – and indeed there are. The networks of lifts and runs are rather limited. But the heli-skiing around the Mt Cook region on the South Island is definitely worth writing home about. For Europeans already spending a lot to travel to New Zealand, the extra cost of a day or two's heli-drops around the Methven area is well worthwhile.

There are resorts on both North Island and South Island. The main concentration on South Island is around the scenic lakeside resort of Queenstown – see next chapter.

As in the northern hemisphere, the season doesn't really get under way until midwinter – mid or late June; it runs until some time in October. Mount Hutt aims to open first, in mid-May, and disputes the longest-season title with Whakapapa, generally open until mid-November and again in December for Christmas skiing.

Skiing at almost every New Zealand ski resort involves at least a half-hour drive from a nearby town – usually below the snowline – to the ski field itself. Coach transfers from the hotels and towns to the ski fields are generally well organised. The ski field will have a base lodge, usually with a restaurant and a cafeteria, equipment rental and one or two shops, as well as the main lifts. The only on-snow accommodation is in smart apartments at Cardrona on the South Island, and some private lodges at the base of Whakapapa on the North Island.

In what follows, we describe the most prominent resorts (apart from Queenstown and its mountains), but there are other possibilities.

Any of the major resorts is worth a day or two of your time if you're in the area and the conditions are right. But if your credit card is also in good condition, don't miss the heli-skiing; even if you're no expert off-piste, with powder skis it's a doddle, and tremendously satisfying.

Methven Heliski or Wilderness Heliski (03 302 8108) offer the longest and most spectacular runs. Both are operated by the same company, Alpine Guides (based at Mt Cook), but fly to different regions. The cost for about five runs averaging 1000m/3,280ft vertical each is NZ$850. There are several other companies operating on South Island. Harris Mountains Heli-ski (03 442 6722), operating out of Queenstown and Wanaka, caters mainly for the large Japanese market, and the three-run days (NZ$775) are generally very easy skiing, with long waits between lifts. Alpine Heli-ski (03 441 2300), based in Queenstown, was started by a breakaway group from the major Queenstown operation, Southern Lakes Heliski (03 442 6222). Alpine's prices start at NZ$729 for three runs; Southern offers two-, four-, six- and eight-run packages ranging from NZ$675 to NZ$1035, or NZ$1399 to $NZ1490 for a private charter. Both Alpine and Southern are more amenable than Harris Mountains to exciting skiing. Try to leave the arrangements loose, to cope with the changeable weather.

An alternative adventure is to fly by plane to ski down the Tasman Glacier. For two gentle 10km/6 mile schusses down the length of the glacier the cost is high – about NZ$750 for the day. The main draw is the immense grandeur of the place, along with the flights over stunning blue ice floes. If you're a good skier, you will find the Clarke Glacier eight-run day out of Queenstown with Southern Lakes

Whakapapa/Turoa

Altitude	1630-2300m
	5,350-7,550ft
Lifts	23
Pistes	1050 hectares
	2,590 acres
Blue	25%
Red	50%
Black	25%
Snowmaking	some

Mount Hutt

Altitude	1405-2085m
	4,610-6,840ft
Lifts	9
Pistes	365 hectares
	900 acres
Green	25%
Blue	50%
Black	25%
Snowmaking	
	42 hectares
	104 acres

Treble Cone

Altitude	1200-1960m
	3,940-6,430ft
Lifts	5
Pistes	550 hectares
	1,360 acres
Green	10%
Blue	45%
Black	45%
Snowmaking	
	50 hectares
	124 acres

Cardrona

Altitude	1670-1895m
	5,480-6,220ft
Lifts	7
Pistes	320 hectares
	791 acres
Green	25%
Blue	55%
Black	20%
Snowmaking	none

Snow Park

Altitude	1530m
	5,020ft
Lifts	1
Snowmaking	100%

Heliski more satisfying, though priced at NZ$995. There is an extensive range of ski touring on offer through Alpine Guides (03 302 8108) as well, from NZ$1695 for two people for three days in the Arrowsmith Ranges.

Snowboarding is very popular in New Zealand, and most of the major resorts have special terrain parks.

New Zealand's biggest resorts are on the slopes of the active volcano Mt Ruapehu, which has occasionally erupted in recent years, leaving the slopes black with volcanic ash. Mt Ruapehu is within four hours' drive of both Auckland and Wellington.

The two ski fields, Whakapapa (pronounced Fukapapa) and Turoa, are in the same ownership and are in the middle of a NZ$30 million upgrade. Both fields offer exciting skiing and wide open slopes on a larger scale than found on the South Island.

Whakapapa, New Zealand's largest ski field with 550 hectares of terrain and 43 runs, is located on the north-facing slopes. It offers a vertical of 670m/2,200ft served by 16 lifts including three fast lifts. Next to the base lodge is an extensive and self-contained beginners' area, Happy Valley, with half-a-dozen rope tows, a chairlift and snowmaking that allows this particular section to open early in the season. The resort's lifts and runs range across craggy terrain made especially interesting because of the twists, turns and drops of the solidified lava on which it sits. The ski field is in fact divided by an ancient lava flow, and the terrain features

many cliffs and unexpected breaks along with wide open cruisers and challenging off-piste. There is also a mix of deep gullies, superb natural half-pipes for snowboarders and narrow chutes. There are six mountain restaurants including New Zealand's highest cafe at 2020m/6,630ft.

Accommodation is mostly 6km/ 4 miles away at Whakapapa village, and the best middle-of-the-road property is a motel named the Skotel. There is on-snow accommodation at the base. A complete anomaly in this area of rustic lodges is the Chateau, a hotel in the grand style of the 1920s, with high ceilings, sweeping drapes over picture windows and marble floors. It has undergone major renovations and extensions in recent years and is highly recommended.

Worth knowing about is the hike to Mt Ruapehu's fizzing Crater Lake. Ask a ski patroller for directions or, better, talk them into taking you on a guided trip. This involves about a half-hour (500m/1,640ft) hike up from the top of the highest T-bar, and then a long traverse across a large flat tundra-like area. A few lefts and rights and you are staring into the mouth of a volcano. Awesome views and neighbouring volcanos give this area an other-worldly feel.

Turoa has an impressive 720m/2,360ft vertical – the biggest in Australasia, over 500 hectares of terrain and plenty of backcountry. The longest run is 4km/2.5 miles. Along with a snazzy new cafe and base lodge, a new six-seater chairlift

Interactive resort shortlist builder at **www.wtss.co.uk**

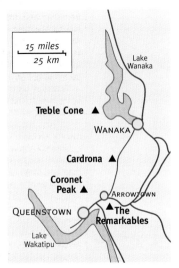

Phone numbers

From abroad use the prefix +64 and omit the initial '0' of the phone number

TOURIST OFFICES

Whakapapa
t 07 892 3738
info@mtruapehu.com
www.mtruapehu.com

Mount Hutt
t 03 302 8811
service@mthutt.co.nz
www.nzski.com

Treble Cone
t 03 443 7443
info@treblecone.com
www.treblecone.co.nz

Cardrona
t 03 443 7341
info@cardrona.com
www.cardrona.com

Snow Park
t 03 443 9991
info@snowparknz.com
www.snowparknz.com

Waiorau Snow Farm
t 03 443 0300
info@snowfarmnz.com
www.snowfarmnz.com

UK PACKAGES

Wanaka *American Ski*

debuted in 2007 opening up far more advanced terrain. There's plenty of off-piste scope away from the gentle intermediate runs, plus the chance to ski on the Mangaehuehu Glacier. Accommodation is 20 minutes away in the funky and lively town of Ohakune.

The South Island has 15 ski areas, including five club fields. **Mt Hutt**, an hour west of Christchurch in the northern part of the island, has a 670m/2,200ft vertical and some of the country's most impressive, consistently steep, wide-open terrain – all within view of the Pacific Ocean. On a clear day you can even see the sandy beaches in the distance beyond the patchwork Canterbury plains – in fact it often snows on the beaches here. The lift system is half the size of Whakapapa's but recently it was totally upgraded and rearranged. The main area is an open bowl with gentle terrain in the centre and the steeper terrain up higher, ringing the ski field.

Mt Hutt has an impressive modern base lodge, including a spacious, welcoming cafe and brasserie with a glorious outdoor terrace, plus a well-stocked rental shop.

Mt Hutt Heliskiing operated by the Alpine Guides team (03 302 8401) offers three runs in the Mt Hutt backcountry for NZ$465, or one 800m/2,620ft vertical on a peak just behind Mt Hutt for NZ$155, with extra runs for NZ$90. The helicopter departs from the heli-pad right in the car park – just book in at the heli-hut or take the NZ$79 per person one-way heli-taxi to the ski field.

There is no accommodation on-mountain – most people stay in the little town of **Methven**, where there are several comfortable up-market B&Bs as well as motels. The very British South Island capital of Christchurch, 90 minutes away, is also an option.

About six hours' drive south of Christchurch is the quiet lakeside town of Wanaka, which is also 90 minutes from Queenstown, and there are two resorts accessible from here.

Treble Cone, 20km/12 miles from Wanaka, has more advanced slopes than any other NZ ski area, plus the advantage of a better lift system. In area, the ski field comes second only to the North Island fields. Three new runs were added in 2006. There are backcountry ski tours, the only ones out of a resort in NZ, offering powder runs in Treble's back bowls. Back on

the ski field, there are two well-maintained intermediate trails, one 3.5km/2 miles, the other 2km/1.2 miles. Both on the main flank and off to the side in Saddle Basin there are long natural half-pipes which are great fun when snow is good, as well as smooth, wide runs for cruising. Treble Cone is reached by a long and winding dirt track that adds to the excitement, although the new owners are planning a gondola from the valley for the 2009 season. The ski field offers stunning views across Lake Wanaka, with snow-capped Alpine-style peaks in the distance. There's a good cafe at the lift base with an enormous sun deck.

Cardrona, 34km/21 miles from Wanaka, is famous for its dry snow and is popular with families due to its superior child care and teaching facilities. The terrain is noted for its well-groomed, flattering cruisers. But there are some serious if short chutes, and the middle basin, Arcadia, has hosted the New Zealand Extreme Skiing Championships. The total vertical is a modest 390m/1,280ft. Millions have been poured into the resort by its family owners over the past few years, resulting in a large base area focused around an odd clock tower. Cardrona is unique in that it has a 1.2km/0.75 mile long terrain park – the largest in the southern hemisphere, with four half-pipes and three tabletop jumps – plus a park for intermediates/beginners.

There's a bar and brasserie-style restaurant, a new ski-in/ski-out noodle bar with sun deck overlooking the nursery slopes, large rental facility and a licensed child care centre, plus 15 modern apartments at the base. Learners are looked after well, with three moving carpets.

Snow Park – a dedicated terrain park across the valley from Cardrona – is really making waves and attracting the cream of international freeriders. Two super-pipes, a quarter-pipe, big kickers and more than 40 rails, hits and jumps across a 60-hectare field are served by one fast quad. A proper restaurant, the Woolshed, and bar have now been built, along with budget and luxury accommodation.

Nearby, at 1500m/4,920ft, is New Zealand's only cross-country ski area, the **Waiorau Snow Farm**, a beautiful place with 55km/34 miles of what the owners claim are the best-prepared trails in the world.

Queenstown

A lively lakeside year-round resort, famous for its adrenalin-rush activities and well placed for a range of South Island resorts

RATINGS

The slopes

Fast lifts	**
Snow	**
Extent	*
Experts	***
Intermediates	***
Beginners	***
Convenience	*
Queues	***
Mountain restaurants	*

The rest

Scenery	****
Resort charm	**
Off-slope	*****

➕ For Europeans, more interesting than summer skiing on glaciers

➕ Huge heli-skiing areas

➕ Lots to do off the slopes, especially for adrenalin junkies

➕ Lively town, with good restaurants

➕ Grand views locally, and the spectacular 'fjord' country nearby

➖ Slopes (in two separate areas locally) are a drive from town

➖ Limited lift-served slopes

➖ Highly changeable weather

➖ No trees, so skiing in bad weather is virtually impossible

If you want a single destination in New Zealand – as opposed to visiting a few different mountains on your travels – Queenstown is probably it, especially if you can cope with the cost of a few heli-drops. Although the resorts of North Island are impressive, the Southern Alps are, in the end, more compelling – and their resorts are free of volcanic interruptions.

From Queenstown you have a choice of the two local ski areas – Coronet Peak and The Remarkables – plus the option of an outing to Cardrona and Treble Cone, perhaps with a few nights in the up and coming lakeside town of Wanaka. You can fly to Queenstown from Sydney, Brisbane and Melbourne.

THE RESORT

Queenstown is a winter-and-summer resort on the shore of Lake Wakatipu. (There is a map of the area in the chapter on New Zealand.) Although the setting is splendid, with views to the peaks of the aptly named Remarkables range beyond the lake, the town itself is no great beauty – it has grown up to meet tourists' needs, and has a very commercial feel; it is now a hotbed of property development.

In recent years much effort has been put into smartening up the town, with such additions as the classy Steamer Wharf, many new lakeside luxury apartments and swanky hotels. The town has a lively, relaxed feel, and makes a satisfactory base, with more than 160 licensed bars and cafes, some good restaurants, and lots of touristy clothes shops. No fewer than 173 activity operators offer every kind of adventure activity, from bungee jumping, jet boating, river surfing to horse trekking.

There are four lift-served mountains – all small by Alpine standards – that you can get to from Queenstown. The two described here – Coronet Peak and The Remarkables – are close by (about a 30-minute drive). The others – Treble Cone and Cardrona – are at least 90 minutes away, near Wanaka –

a much quieter town in another beautiful lakeside setting. See the New Zealand introduction.

THE MOUNTAINS

At each base area you'll find a mini-resort – a ski school, a ski rental shop, a functional self-service restaurant, but no accommodation except at Cardrona.

All the areas have something for all abilities of skier or boarder, with off-piste opportunities as well as prepared and patrolled trails. They use the American green/blue/black convention for run classification. New last season were the Burton Learn To Ride systems at both The Remarkables and Coronet Peak, designed to turn beginners into life-time riders.

THE SLOPES
Not the height of convenience
The Remarkables, true to their name, are a dramatic range of craggy peaks visible across the lake from some parts of Queenstown. The slopes are tucked in a bowl right behind the largest visible peak, a 45-minute drive from town that can now be done in brand new custom-made skier shuttle buses. This resort is fine for families and beginners (though there is limited extreme skiing for experts). Children under 10 ski for free. It's a good place

NEWS

The biggest news of the 2008 season at The Remarkables was The Stash, a new 1km/0.5 mile long terrain park that uses the area's natural lines, rock walls and cliff drops. Built by the Burton team, the signature trail is only the third of its kind in the world and a first in this hemisphere.

Coronet Peak installed another 141 snow-guns just before the 2008 season, bringing the total to 203 and virtually guaranteeing skiing from its opening date in June. And a big new day lodge opened at the base, with a brasserie, cafe, bar and coffee area, and a deck more than triple the size of the original.

Resort	310m
	1,020ft

The Remarkables	
Slopes	1580-1945m
	5,180-6,380ft
Lifts	5
Pistes	220 hectares
	545 acres
Green	30%
Blue	40%
Black	30%
Snowmaking	
	25 acres

Coronet Peak	
Slopes	1230-1650m
	4,040-5,410ft
Lifts	6
Pistes	280 hectares
	690 acres
Green	25%
Blue	45%
Black	30%
Snowmaking	
	203 guns

boarding

Boarding is popular in New Zealand, and although the two mountains close to Queenstown don't seem to have quite such a hold on the boarding market as Cardrona (see New Zealand introduction), they have everything you need, including equipment and tuition. You needn't go anywhere near a draglift, and there are no flats to worry about except on the lowest green at The Remarkables and a few lower dips to watch in the Rocky Gully area of Coronet.

for taking it easy and enjoying the restaurant's sun deck (which overlooks the beginner areas), but there is also a strong emphasis on its exceptional terrain parks.

Two chairs go up from the base, a fast quad serving easy runs and the Sugar Bowl chair, which accesses mainly long, easy runs plus a couple of black chutes. The terrain parks have transformed the resort and attracted a whole new market of jibbers. The Shadow Basin chair leads to steeper terrain, including three hike-accessed, expert-only chutes that drop down to Lake Alta, and the Homeward Run – a broad, fairly gentle, unprepared slope down to the resort access road, where a shuttle-truck takes you back to the base.

Coronet Peak, about 25 minutes' drive from Queenstown, is a far more satisfying resort, especially for intermediates and above. There is a big new day lodge at the base – see 'News'. There is some seriously steep terrain in the back bowls for experts. Again, there are three main chairlifts, including a fast quad that accesses practically all the runs, and new in the 2005 season was a six-seater that

opened up more terrain and improved the resort dramatically. A novice trail was added a few seasons ago to appeal to beginner skiers and boarders, and the main trail down the face of the mountain is 1.8km/1.1 miles long. The main mountainside is a pleasantly varied intermediate slope, full of highly enjoyable rolling terrain that snowboarders adore, though it steepens near the bottom. A fourth lift, a T-bar, serves another intermediate area to one side. There are also drags intended specially for beginners. Two seasons ago the beginners' area was enlarged and separated from the main slopes. There's night skiing at weekends.

TERRAIN PARKS
The Remarkables rules
Coronet Peak has two half-pipes but The Remarkables is now the big competitor in the park market with its spectacular mountain-top super-pipe, the trendy new 1km/0.5 mile long Stash natural terrain area designed by Burton (see 'News'), plus two enormous 30m/100ft wide terrain parks, one for beginners and the other for intermediates/advanced.

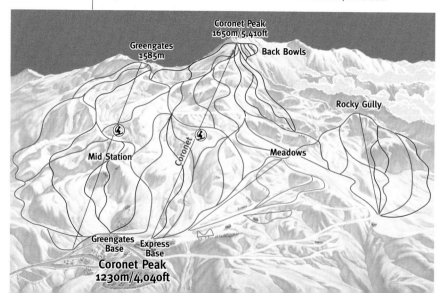

Coronet Peak
1230m/4,040ft

SNOW RELIABILITY
Good overall, but unpredictable

The New Zealand weather is highly variable, so it's difficult to be confident about snow conditions – though the mountains certainly get oodles of snow. The South Island resorts are at the same sort of latitude as the Alps, but are much more influenced by the ocean; fortunately, their ocean is a lot colder than ours. Coronet tends to receive sleet and/or rain even when it's snowing in The Remarkables. But Coronet Peak now has snowmaking on practically all its intermediate terrain (see 'News').

FOR EXPERTS
Challenges exist

Both areas have quite a choice of genuinely black slopes. Coronet's Back Bowls is a seriously steep experts-only area, and there are other black slopes scattered around the mountain. The main enjoyment comes from venturing off-piste all over the place. The Remarkables' Shadow Basin chair serves some excellent (if short) slopes. And The Remarkables' hike-up expert chutes are truly world-class.

FOR INTERMEDIATES
Fine, within limits

There's some very enjoyable intermediate skiing in both areas – appreciably more at Coronet, where there are also easy blacks to go on to.

FOR BEGINNERS
Excellent

There are gentle slopes at both areas, served by rope tows, and longer green runs served by chairs. And many other diversions if you decide it's a drag.

FOR CROSS-COUNTRY
Limited

There is a short loop around a lake in the middle of The Remarkables area, but the only serious cross-country area is the large mountain-top Waiorau Snow Farm, near Cardrona (see New Zealand intro).

QUEUES
It depends

Coronet and The Remarkables can suffer a little from high-season crowds – there are certainly enough beds locally to lead to queues at peak times. But these aren't normally a major worry.

MOUNTAIN RESTAURANTS
Er, what mountain restaurants?

In such small areas, restaurants above base level don't really make sense. Both areas have a simple cafeteria at the base, and Coronet now has a fancy restaurant too. The Remarkables cafeteria has a big sunny deck and is regularly visited by the local parrots (keas).

SCHOOLS AND GUIDES
All the usual classes

The schools are well organised, with a wide range of options, including 'guaranteed' beginner classes.

FACILITIES FOR CHILDREN
Look good

Child care looked okay to us. At both resorts there are nurseries and clubs for children aged from two to five years old. There's also a wide range of kids' activities on offer each day. The Queenstown nursery can take younger children all day.

UK PACKAGES
AmeriCan Ski, Kuoni,
Ski Dream

Phone numbers
From abroad use the
prefix +64 and omit
the initial '0' of the
phone number

TOURIST OFFICE
The Remarkables and
Coronet Peak
t 03 442 4640
snowcentre@nzski.
com
www.nzski.com

STAYING THERE

HOW TO GO
Sheer luxury?
There are lots of big luxury hotels – all either new or refurbished – built to meet the big summer demand.
Hotels Some hotels are quite some way from central Queenstown – inconvenient for après-ski unless there's a shuttle-bus. In town they range from the very simple to the glossily pretentious Millennium (03 441 8888), the new 19-room-only Queenstown Park Boutique Hotel, the five-star Sofitel (03 450 0045) and the exquisite Spire (03 441 0004) – a chic spot. Also new last year were the luxury Commonage Villas on a hill overlooking Queenstown, as well as the Alta apartments and The Rees Apartment Hotel right on the lake. Two of the best and most reasonable places to stay are the Heritage Hotel (03 442 4988) or the Mercure Grand Hotel St Moritz (03 442 4990).

EATING OUT
Lots of choice
We're told there are now over 160 bars and restaurants – a quite astonishing figure. Restaurants include Chinese, Italian, Malaysian, Japanese – you name it, Queenstown has it. The Boardwalk in the Steamer Wharf complex overlooking the lake is the place to go for seafood, especially the Wai. Breakfast at Joe's Garage is a must. A dining experience with a difference is the Bath House, located in a 1911 Victorian bath house right on the lake shore. Solero Vino has delicious Mediterranean food and a rustic bar. The Halo restaurant is one of the most recent additions to town and serves up delicious organic meals with vegan options. Opposite Halo is the new Destination Organic, which sells organic fruit and veg. The Bunker does excellent local cuisine such as Bluff oysters and lamb. Gantley's, in a historic home a little way out of town, is a classic restaurant with the most expensive wine list in the area. At the other end of the scale, pizza-lovers crowd into The Cow, a cosy barn-like place where you sit on logs around a fire waiting for tables. Lone Star offers satisfying American-style food.

APRES-SKI
Lively little town
Queenstown has a good range of bars and clubs that stay open late, with disco or live music. The best upmarket bars are Bardeaux, Barmuda and Dux de Lux, an excellent brew-pub in a stone cottage. Winnebagos is very lively and has a roof that slides back to the night sky to allow the hot and sweaty dance floor a blast of fresh air and even fresh snow. There's a small upmarket casino in the plush Steamer Wharf, and Skycity Casino in the mall. The Steamer Wharf also contains Minus Five, an ice bar, and The Boiler Room for 80s music. There's duty-free shopping in the mall opposite.

OFF THE SLOPES
Scare yourself silly
There are lots of scary things to do – see the feature box below. To the west is the spectacularly scenic 'fjord country', and you can go on independent or guided walks. The sightseeing flights by plane or helicopter are to be preferred to the slow bus ride – weather permitting. The Skyline gondola rises 400m/1,310ft above Queenstown for a great view; try a spin down the public go-cart track, too. Cruise the lake on an historic steamship or go wine tasting. Arrowtown is interesting for a quick visit – it's a cute, touristy old mining town where you can kit yourself out to go panning for gold. The Winter Festival, in early July, is an annual 'action-packed week of mayhem'.

GET THAT ADRENALIN RUSH

The streets of Queenstown are lined by no fewer than 173 activity operators offering various artificial thrills. We've sampled just a few.

AJ Hackett's bungee jump at Kawarau Bridge is where this crazy activity got off the ground, as it were. The Shotover Jet Boat experience is less demanding – whizzing along the rocky river in a boat that can get along in very shallow water, passing very close to cliffs and trees. Fly By Wire involves swinging through a canyon on a cable propelled by a fan engine on your rear. The whitewater rafting takes you over some exciting rapids. One route even passes through a tunnel excavated in the gold-mining days.

+ Varied terrain and excellent off-piste

+ Favourable exchange rate means cheap local prices

− Remote and inaccessible, even from Buenos Aires

− Very little English spoken

Argentina's two main resorts are of sharply contrasting character and a long way apart physically as well. Go to San Carlos de Bariloche for the cultural experience and the intermediate piste skiing, and go to Las Leñas for the best and most extensive off-piste terrain in the southern hemisphere. We combined Las Leñas with Chilean resorts on our visit – something we'd recommend.

KEY FACTS

Las Leñas

Slopes	2240-3430m
	7,350-11,250ft
Lifts	13
Pistes	27
Green	8%
Blue	23%
Red/Black	69%

Bariloche

Slopes	1030-3630m
	3,380-11,910ft
Lifts	40
Pistes	103km
	64 miles
Green	15%
Blue	75%
Red/Black	10%

UK PACKAGES

Las Leñas *Scott Dunn Latin America, Ski All America*
San Carlos de Bariloche (Gran Catedral) *Kuoni, Scott Dunn Latin America, Ski All America*

TOURIST OFFICES

Las Leñas
www.laslenas.com
Bariloche
www.bariloche.com
Cerro Castor
www.cerrocastor.com

Argentina lies on the eastern, rain-shadowed side of the Andes, a recipe for dry, light powder at high altitudes throughout a season that lasts from June to October.

The premier resort is **Las Leñas**, built by Frenchmen in the 1980s when pyramid architecture ruled. It dominates a white wilderness, miles from civilisation; the nearest major airport is Mendoza 400km/250 miles away (Malargue is much nearer but has few scheduled flights).

But be warned: gales and blizzards can close most of the resort down for days, especially during late July and early August. Mid-August to mid-September is the best time to visit.

A dozen lifts serve a few groomed slopes, and freestylers can rip it up in the terrain park and half-pipe. But the real attraction is for experts: an antiquated double chair called El Marte opens up 270° of ski-anywhere off-piste terrain (plus a couple of pistes) – from gentle slopes suiting powder novices to couloirs and cliffs for the brave. But before you are allowed to venture into the great off-piste, you have to stop at a mountain-top hut where a local asks you to enter your name and passport number, and sign a document in Spanish releasing the resort from all responsibility for you. He then sticks a coloured tag, valid for a week, on your clothing, which allows you to venture where you like.

But venture not without a guide. We saw snowboarders precariously perched on top of 100m/330ft cliffs and skiers riding under dodgy-looking cornices. The place is vast and you need to know where you are going. Our recommendation would be to book a week with the Whistler-based

ski school Extremely Canadian, which specialises in steep and deep terrain and runs trips to Las Leñas every year (see www.extremelycanadian.com). We went with them and had a great time. There's good snowcat-skiing too.

The smartest hotel is the 5-star Pisces, with pool, hot tub, sauna and gym. Escorpio is a 4-star option. There are a few bars and clubs and a casino.

San Carlos de Bariloche has almost nothing in common with Las Leñas, except that it is Argentina's only other international winter sports option. Founded in 1903 by Swiss and German immigrants, it is a substantial resort town with a cheerful lifestyle, and is still influenced by the Swiss-German culture. The smart Llao Llao Resort and Spa, on a bluff above the lake, has a pool, sauna and fitness centre. The Edelweiss offers top-quality facilities in the town centre.

The slopes are at Gran Catedral, 20 minutes by shuttle-bus. They are well below the treeline, and good-quality snow cannot be guaranteed. The runs, which are cut through the forest, face east as protection from the prevailing westerlies and suit intermediates best, though there is some good off-piste. There's a terrain park and half-pipe. It's best to avoid August, which is the Argentinian society choice and therefore prone to long queues.

Cerro Castor, the most southerly city in the world, is a remote outpost just 195m/64oft above sea level. The Beagle Strait off Tierra del Fuego is famously windy, but winter is the calmest period and conditions are often surprisingly good. It has a small ski area with 19 runs but a vertical drop of 770m/2,53oft. The British team trained here in the run-up to the Turin Winter Olympics.

- ✚ One of the most varied options for the European summer
- ✚ The Andes are spectacular
- ✚ Good snow records
- ✚ Good local food and wine

- ➖ It's a long way from Britain
- ➖ By Alpine standards, the ski areas are small and resorts lack character
- ➖ Little English spoken outside hotels
- ➖ Nightlife is limited

If you want to carry on skiing or boarding in our summer, Chile is a good choice. It's a long way to go (it took us 36 hours from leaving home to arriving at our first hotel on our visit) and the ski areas are small; but if you combine visits to at least two resorts with, say, a tour of Chile's wine areas or a visit to the Atacama desert, it can make a varied and compelling holiday.

KEY FACTS

Valle Nevado/La Parva/El Colorado

Slopes	2430-3670m
	7.970-12,040ft
Lifts	43
Pistes	113km
	70 miles
Green	14%
Blue	30%
Red	42%
Black	14%

Portillo

Slopes	2560-3320m
	8,400-10,890ft
Lifts	13
Pistes	1200 acres
Green	10%
Blue	35%
Red	35%
Black	20%

Termas de Chillán

Slopes	1600-2700m
	5,250-8,860ft
Lifts	11
Pistes	46km
	29 miles
Green	22%
Blue	41%
Red	31%
Black	6%

Lying in the path of the prevailing winds off the Pacific, the Chilean Andes are ideally located to catch all the snow that's going, resulting in truly dramatic falls in good years. In such a long narrow country, conditions vary considerably from north to south. In general, the season starts in mid-June and finishes in early October (mid-July to mid-September is the best time to visit). The ski areas are small in comparison with big Alpine resorts (a keen piste-basher could ski all the pistes in an area in a day) but there's a lot of off-piste available. Adventurous skiers and boarders should sign on for the well-run heli-ski operations, both for the spectacular flights over 5000m/16,400ft peaks and the remote powder fields. We'd recommend visiting two or three ski areas as you are travelling so far.

Valle Nevado (just 60km/37 miles from Santiago), La Parva and El Colorado form the biggest area of linked pistes and are known as the Tres Valles (Chile's equivalent of the Three Valleys). **La Parva** is condoville for the capital's elite, a collection of apartments occupied mostly at weekends, while **El Colorado** offers a scattering of accommodation around a shabby base station. Both are linked to **Valle Nevado**, a high-rise, wood-clad tourist development in the mode of Les Arcs, not surprisingly as it was designed by the Chilean architect Eduardo Stern after he'd worked in France and on the Les Arcs project. The best hotel is called Valle Nevado and has the best restaurant, the Fourchette d'Or which serves delicious international food and excellent breakfasts. Puerta del Sol is the mid-

market option (with Swiss and Italian restaurants) and 3 Puntas (with a buffet restaurant) the budget choice. All three offer half-board packages and you can generally eat dinner at a restaurant in a different hotel if you like. There is a small communal outdoor pool, a few shops, hotel bars and a nightclub.

Valle Nevado is ski-in/ski-out and has a network of well-groomed, mainly intermediate pistes served by 11 lifts including the Andes Express (South America's only high-speed chair).

Portillo, 164km/102 miles from Santiago, consists of little more than the startlingly bright yellow Hotel Portillo, set beside the potholed main road from Chile to Argentina. It was built in the 1940s and owned and run by the Chilean government until they sold it to two Americans in 1962. It is now run by Henry Purcell (the nephew of one of the Americans) and his son Michael (aka Miguel). Service is impeccable, with 550 staff (mostly long-serving – the head waiter has been there over 40 years) serving a maximum of 450 guests. The traditional public rooms are handsomely furnished with polished wood and leather. And there's a huge outdoor hot pool to relax in after coming off the slopes.

The hotel and a lake in front of it stand between two unconnected areas. Turn right for the El Plateau double chair to Tio Bob's, the only mountain restaurant. Then drop into the rocky jaws of Garganta, the challenging black run back to base, or sweep down the friendly blue. The Laguna quad chair, on the other side of the hotel, accesses the Juncalillo piste, the

Valle Nevado is part of Chile's equivalent of the Three Valleys, the biggest ski area in South America →

DAVE WATTS

UK PACKAGES

Parva *Scott Dunn Latin America*
Valle Nevado *AmeriCan Ski, Crystal, Crystal Finest, Kuoni, Momentum, Scott Dunn Latin America, Ski All America, Ski Safari*
Portillo *AmeriCan Ski, Crystal, Crystal Finest, Kuoni, Momentum, Scott Dunn Latin America, Ski All America, Ski Dream, Ski Safari*
Pucón *Snoworks*
Termas de Chillán *Momentum, Scott Dunn Latin America, Ski All America, Ski Safari*

TOURIST OFFICES

Valle Nevado
www.vallenevado.com
Portillo
www.skiportillo.com
Termas de Chillán
www.skichillan.cl

longest in the resort. But to stick to the groomers – and there are few of them (you could ski them all in a couple of hours) – is to miss the point. Portillo has radical terrain on both sides of the mountain, but the first challenge is the unique Va et Vient slingshot lifts. Skiers ride on linked buttons, four or five abreast, blasting upwards at high speed to a treacherously steep landing point. From the top of Roca Jack, the longest of the four slingshots, a high traverse, leads to a series of chutes. When the lake is frozen, skiers can take the steep powder slopes down to the shore and skate back to the hotel. To get the most out of the area you need a guide (and you need to be prepared to hike from the top of the lifts). Good off-piste skiers should consider going on former World Freeskiing Champion, Chris Davenport's, Ski with the Superstars week here – see www.steepskiing.com.

Termas de Chillán is Chile's leading ski and spa resort, in a forested setting and with a small network of lifts under twin volcanoes, which provide the thermal water and mud for the spa. You can ski all day and then enjoy a relaxing soak and a spa treatment to get rid of the aches and pains. It is around 80km/50 miles from the railway station at Chillán, a small town four hours by train to the south of Santiago (or you can fly to Concepción 195km/121 miles away).

There are three contrasting hotels. The ski-in/ski-out 5-star Gran is the biggest and best and is home to the main spa, two restaurants, a casino and a conference centre. The nearby 3-star, Pirigallo has a thermal pool and a spa, a restaurant, a pub and a games room. The cosier, chalet-style

Pirimahuida is 10 minutes drive down the valley in Las Trancas. And there are slope-side apartments, a shop and a rustic Club Haus restaurant.

The top of the El Tata T-bar at 2700m/8,860ft is the starting point for the wonderful, away-from-all-the-lifts top-to-bottom of the mountain Golf Alto run – at 13km/8 miles long and with a vertical drop of 1100m/3,610 feet it is South America's longest piste. It is rolling, undulating and interestingly varied with some narrow sections and some where you need to schuss to get up the incline beyond. As well as 33 largely intermediate pistes (which we skied in three hours or so), there is off-piste (best in September, when there is spring snow normally). For freestylers, there's a terrain park with half- and quarter-pipes, jumps and a fun box. As well as downhill skiing there is cross-country, snowmobiling and dog sledding.

Like Termas de Chillán, **Pucón**, on the eastern shore of Lake Villarrica, was developed as a summer resort. The present lift system was installed between 1988 and 1990 and serves limited terrain for all standards. The climb up to the crater, which requires skins and crampons, takes between two and four hours from the top of the lifts, but it's worth it for the awesome close-up of molten lava. The Gran Hotel Pucón, built in 1934 on the lake shore, is the best place to stay.

Cerro Mirador is Chile's most southerly snow-zone, located 8km/5 miles outside Punta Arenas in the Magellanes National Reserve. It has wooded runs and dramatic views over the Magellan Straits. But it is tiny, with just 11 pistes accessed by a double chair and a T-bar. There is no on-mountain accommodation.

Introduction

731

Interactive resort shortlist builder at **www.wtss.co.uk**

REFERENCE SECTION

A classified listing of the names, numbers and addresses you are likely to need.

Tour operator directory 732

Most people still prefer the convenience of a package holiday, which is what most of the companies listed are set up to provide. But note that we've also included some operators that offer accommodation without travel arrangements.

732

Tour operator directory

Weekly news updates and resort links at www.wtss.co.uk

TOUR OPERATOR DIRECTORY

This is a list of all the UK-based companies we know of that offer ski holidays – mainly but not exclusively package holidays including travel as well as accommodation.

360 Sun and Ski
Family holidays in Les Carroz, French Alps
Tel 0870 068 3180

Action Outdoor Holidays
All-inclusive holidays in the French Alps
Tel 0845 890 0362

Airtours
Mainstream operator
Tel 0871 664 7661

Albus Travel
St Anton specialist
Tel 01449 711952

All America Holidays
US, Canadian and S American holidays
Tel 0844 770 0752

Alpine Action
Chalets in Les Trois Vallées
Tel 01273 466535

Alpine Answers
Tailor-made holidays
Tel 020 7801 1080

Alpine Club
Chalets in St-Martin-de-Belleville
Tel +33 (0)630 226215

Alpine Life
Apartment in Saas-Fee
Tel 0780 198 2645

Alpine Ski and Golf Company
Catered chalet in Les Houches
Tel 07791 147106

Alpine Weekends
Weekends in the Alps
Tel 020 8944 9762

Alps Accommodation
Accommodation in Samoëns and Les Carroz
Tel +33 (0)6 88 65 50 70

Alpsholiday
Apartments in Serre-Chevalier
Tel +33 (0)492 204426

Altitude Holidays
Catered chalet and in-resort services in Le Grand Massif
Tel 0870 870 7669

AmeriCan Ski
North America specialist plus undiscovered gems in France
Tel 01892 511894

American Ski Classics
Holidays in major North American resorts
Tel 0870 242 0623

Aravis Alpine Retreat
Renovated Alpine farmhouse in St Jean-de-Sixt (La Clusaz) for bespoke groups by arrangement
Tel 020 8748 6057

Ardmore Educational Travel Ltd
Group and school trips
Tel 01344 883888

Balkan Holidays
Holidays in Bulgaria, Slovenia, Romania and Serbia
Tel 0845 130 1114

Barrelli Ski
Chalets in Champagny, Chamonix and Les Houches
Tel 0117 940 1500

Belvedere Chalets
Specialist luxury chalet operator in Méribel and Verbier
Tel 01264 738 257

Bigfoot Travel
Variety of holidays in the Chamonix Valley
Tel 0870 300 5874

BoardnLodge.com Ltd
Catered and self-catered holidays in Europe
Tel 020 3239 8181

Borderline
Specialist in Barèges
Tel +33 (0)562 926895

Bramble Ski
Chalets in Verbier and
Kicking Horse
Tel 0871 218 0988

**Canadian Powder Tours
Chalet Holidays**
Chalet holidays in Western
Canada
Tel +1 250 423 3019

Chalet Bezière
Chalet in Samoëns
Tel +33 (0)450 905181

Chalet Chocolat
Chalet in Morzine
Tel 01872 580814

The Chalet Company
Catered chalets in Morzine
Tel 0871 717 4208 /
+33 (0)450 79 68 40

Chalet Entre Deux Eaux
Chalet in Morzine
Tel +33 (0)450 37 47 55

Chalet Espen
Chalet in Engelberg
Tel +41 (0)41 637 2220

The Chalet Group
Chalet accommodation in
Europe and Canada

Chalet Gueret
Luxury chalet near Morzine
Tel 01884 255437

Chalet Kiana
Chalet in Les Contamines
Tel 00 33 450 915518

Chalet Number One
Chalet in Ste-Foy
Tel 0115 924 0428 /
+33 (0)479 064755

Chalet Snowboard
Snowboard holidays in
Morzine
Tel 020 8133 4180

Chalet World Ski
Chalets in big-name resorts
Tel 01743 231199

Challenge Activ
Chalets and apartments in
Morzine
Tel 0871 717 4113 /
+33 (0)450 790307

Chamonix.uk.com
Apartment holidays in central
Chamonix
Tel 01224 641559

Chamonix Backcountry
Backcountry skiing in the
Chamonix Valley
Tel 01274 530313

**Le Chardon Mountain Lodges
Val d'Isère**
Upmarket chalets in Val
d'Isère
Tel 0845 092 0350

Chez Michelle
Self-catering apartment in
Samoëns
Tel 01372 456463

Chill Chalet
Accommodation in Paradiski
Tel 07931 967861

Classic Ski Limited
Holidays for 'mature' skiers/
beginners
Tel 01590 623400

Club Europe Schools Skiing
Schools trips to Europe
Tel 0800 496 4996

Club Med
All-inclusive holidays in 'ski
villages'
Tel 0845 3676767

Cold Comforts Lodging
Whistler specialist
Tel 020 7993 8544

Collineige
Chamonix valley specialist
Tel 01483 579242

Connick Ski
Chalet in Châtel
Tel 00 33 450 732212

Contiki Holidays
Coach-travel holidays for
18-35s
Tel 020 8290 6422

Cooltip Mountain Holidays
Chalets in Méribel
Tel 01964 563563

Crystal
Major mainstream operator
Tel 0871 231 2256

Crystal Finest
Ski holidays to Europe and
North America
Tel 0871 971 0364

Descent International
Luxury chalets in France and
Switzerland
Tel 020 7384 3854

Directski.com
Holidays in Europe and North
America
Tel 0800 587 0945

Elegant Resorts
Luxury ski holidays
Tel 01244 897333

Elevation Holidays
Holidays in the Austrian Alps
Tel 0845 644 3578

Equity Ski
All-in holidays
Tel 01273 622111

Erna Low
Hotel and self-catering
holidays in the Alps and
North America
Tel 0845 863 0525

Esprit Ski
Families specialist in Europe
Tel 01252 618300

The Family Ski Company
Family holidays in France
Tel 01684 540333

Ferme de Montagne
Luxury chalet hotel in Les
Gets
Tel 00 33 450 753679

Finlays
Catered chalets in Val
d'Isère, Courchevel and
Paradiski; short breaks in
France and Switzerland
Tel 01573 226611

**First Choice Holidays and
Flights**
Major mainstream operator
Tel 0871 664 0130

Flexiski
Weekends and corporate
events in Europe
Tel 020 8939 0861

Friendship Travel
Holidays for singles 25 to 60
Tel 0871 200 2035

Frontier Ski
Holidays in Canada and
Alaska
Tel 020 8776 8709

Haig Ski
Chalet with guiding near
Morzine
Tel +33 (0)450 811947

Hannibals
Holidays in Serre-Chevalier
Tel 01233 813105

Headwater Holidays
Cross-country skiing holidays
Tel 01606 720033

High Mountain Holidays
Holidays in Chamonix
Tel 01993 775540

Holiday in Alps
Chalets and apartments in
the French Alps
Tel 01327 828239

Hucksters
Lodges in the French Alps
Tel 01208 821100

Huski
Chalet holidays in Chamonix
Tel 08000 971 760

Independent Ski Links
Accommodation, packages
and tailor-made holidays in
Europe and N America
Tel 01964 533905

Inghams
Major mainstream operator
Tel 020 8780 4433

Inntravel
Cross-country skiing holidays
Tel 01653 617906

Inspired to Ski
Holidays with tuition in
France
Tel 0845 890 0390

Interactive Resorts
Catered chalets worldwide
Tel 020 3080 0202

Interhome
Apartments and chalets in
Europe
Tel 020 8780 6633

Interski
Group holidays with tuition
in Italy
Tel 01623 456333

Italian Safaris
Italian ski specialists and
multi-resort safaris
Tel +39 347 348 5757 /
07930 902590

James Orr Heli-ski
Heli-skiing packages in
Canada
Tel 01799 516964

**Jeffersons Private Jet
Holidays**
Luxury holidays by private jet
Tel 020 8746 2496

Just Skiing
Courmayeur specialist plus
other Italian resorts
Tel 01202 479988

Just Slovenia
Accommodation in Slovenia
Tel 01373 814230

> >> **Peak Ski Verbier**
>
> >> Catered Chalets >> High Resort
> >> Great Locations >> Skiing above
> >> Experienced Staff 2,300m
>
> > **01442 832 629** > **www.peak-ski.co.uk**

Kaluma Ski
Holidays in the Alps
Tel 0870 442 8044

Karibuni
Short-break chalet holidays
in La Clusaz
Tel 01202 661865

Kuoni
Worldwide trips
Tel 01306 747000

Lagrange Holidays
Ski holidays in Europe
Tel 020 7371 6111

The Last Resort
Catered chalet and self-
catered apartments in the
Aravis ski region
Tel 0800 652 3977

Le Ski
Chalets in Courchevel, Val
d'Isère and La Tania
Tel 01484 548996

Made to Measure Ski
Wide variety of tailor-made
holidays
Tel 01243 533333

Mark Warner
Chalet hotel holidays in big-
name resorts
Tel 0871 703 3881

McNab Snowsports
Snowboarding holidays
worldwide
Tel 0141 416 3828

Meriski
Chalet specialist in Méribel
Tel 01285 648510

MGS Ski Limited
Hotel and apartments in Val
Cenis
Tel 01603 742842

Momentum Ski
Tailor-made and ski weekend
specialists
Tel 020 7371 9111

Mountain Action
Chalet in St-Martin-de-
Belleville
Tel 0871 717 4213

Mountain Beds
Tailor-made holidays, mainly
in Verbier
Tel 020 7924 2650

A Mountain Chalet
Chalet in La Rosière
Tel +33 (0)479 065738

Mountain Heaven
Self-catered accommodation
in France and Switzerland
Tel 0151 625 1921

Mountainsun Ltd
Chalets in Europe
Tel 07941 196517

Mountain Tracks
Off-piste courses, hut to hut
ski touring and avalanche
awareness programmes
Tel 020 8877 5773

Neilson
Major mainstream operator
Tel 0870 333 3347

Nick Ski
Catered chalet in La Tania
Tel 00 33 673 436769

Optimum Ski
Chalet in Villaroger, part of
Les Arcs ski area
Tel 0131 208 1154

The Oxford Ski Company
Chalets and hotels in Europe
and North America
Tel 0870 787 1785

Peak Leisure
Chalet in Ste-Foy
Tel 0870 760 5610

Peak Retreats
Holidays to traditional French
Alps resorts
Tel 0844 576 0123

Peak Ski
Chalets in Verbier
Tel 01442 832629

PGL Ski
Specialist in school group
holidays and holidays for
teenagers
Tel 0870 162 6622

Powder Byrne
Small programme of luxury
hotel holidays in Europe
Tel 020 8246 5300

**Powder Skiing in North
America Limited**
Heli-skiing holidays in
Canada
Tel 020 7736 8191

Powder White
Chalets in big-name resorts
Tel 020 8877 8888

Première Neige
Catered and self-catered
holidays in Ste-Foy
Tel 0870 383 1000

Purple Ski
Chalet holidays in Méribel
Tel 01885 488799

Pyrenees Ski Experience
Catered chalet and self-
catered holidays in the
Pyrenees
Tel 00 33 468 041879

Ramblers Holidays
Mostly cross-country holidays
Tel 01707 331133

Reach4theAlps
Holidays in the French Alps
Tel 0845 680 1947

Richmond Holidays
Christian holidays
Tel 020 3004 2661

Ride&Slide
Chalets in Morzine
Tel +33 450 388 962

Rocketski.com
All-in holidays online
Tel 01273 810777

Rude Chalets
Holidays in Morzine, Avoriaz
and Chamonix
Tel 0870 068 7030

Scott Dunn Latin America
Tailor-made holidays to
South America
Tel 020 8682 5030

Scott Dunn Ski
Luxury chalet and hotel
holidays
Tel 020 8682 5050

Silver Ski
Chalet holidays in France
Tel 01622 735544

Simon Butler Skiing
Holidays with ski instruction
in Megève
Tel 0870 873 0001

Ski 2
Specialists in Champoluc
(Monterosa) and San
Cassiano (Sella Ronda)
Tel 01962 713330

Ski Activity
Holidays in big-name resorts
Tel 01738 840888

Ski Addiction
Chalets and hotels in the
Portes du Soleil
Tel 01580 819354

Ski Adventures
Chalet holidays in Paradiski
Tel 00 33 385 546515

Ski à la Carte
Luxury chalets in Alpe-d'Huez
Tel 020 8542 5559

Skialot
Chalet in Châtel
Tel 0780 156 9264

Ski Alpage
Chalet in St-Martin-de-
Belleville
Tel +33 (0)4 79 08 92 28

Ski Amis
Catered chalet and self-
catered holidays in the
French Alps
Tel 020 7692 0850

Ski Balkantours
Holidays in eastern Europe
Tel 028 9024 6795

Ski Basics
Chalets in Méribel
Tel 01225 444143

Ski Beat
Chalets in the French Alps
Tel 01243 780405

Ski Blanc
Chalet holidays in Méribel
Tel 020 8502 9082

SkiBound
Schools division of First
Choice
Tel 01273 244500

Skibug
Catered chalets in La Plagne
Tel 0208 886 0271

Ski Chamois
Holidays in Morzine
Tel 01302 369006

Ski Collection
French self-catering 4-star
apartment specialist
Tel 0844 576 0175

Ski Cuisine
Chalets in Méribel
Tel 01702 589543

Ski-Dazzle
Chalet holidays in Les Trois
Vallées
Tel 00 33 479 001725

Ski Deep
Chalets in La Tania and Le
Praz
Tel 01483 722706 /
        +33 (0)479 081905

Ski Dream
Major operator to worldwide
destinations, specialising in
North America
Tel 0845 277 3333

Ski Etoile
Chalets, hotels and
apartments in Montgenèvre
Tel 01952 253252

Ski Expectations
Chalets and hotels in Europe,
the USA and Canada
Tel 01799 531888

Ski Famille
Family holidays in Les Gets
and Morzine
Tel 0845 644 3764

Ski France
Packaged and tailor-made
holidays and accommodation
in France
Tel 0870 787 3402

Skifrance4less
Self-catered apartments/
chalets in the French Alps
Tel 01724 290660

Ski Freedom
Chalets in Verbier, Champéry
and Zinal
Tel +41 (0)788 810978

Ski Freshtracks
Holidays for Ski Club of GB
members
Tel 0845 458 0784 /
        020 8410 2022

Ski Hame
Catered chalets in Méribel
and La Tania
Tel 01875 320157

Ski High Days
Holidays for groups to Italy
and France
Tel 0117 955 1814

Ski Hillwood
Austrian and French family
holidays
Tel 01923 290700

Ski Hiver
Chalets in Peisey (Paradiski)
Tel 01329 847788

Skiholidayextras.com
Accommodation in France
plus cheap deals on lift
passes etc
Tel 0870 787 3402

Ski-in.co.uk
Apartment in Serre-Chevalier
Tel 01630 672540

Ski Independence
USA, Canada, Japan, France,
Switzerland and Austria
Tel 0845 310 3030

Skiing Austria
Accommodation in Austria
Tel 020 8123 7817

Ski La Cote
Catered chalet holidays in
the Portes du Soleil
Tel 01482 668357

Ski Leisure Direction
Resorts in the French Alps,
but also the Pyrenees and
Italy
Tel 0844 576 5504

Ski Line
Chalet holidays in Europe
and North America
Tel 020 8313 3999

Ski Link
Courchevel specialist
Tel 0871 218 0174

Ski Magic
Chalet holidays in La Tania
Tel 0151 677 2317

Ski McNeill
Packages to top US and
European resorts plus tailor-
made flexible trips to Europe
Tel 028 9066 6699

Ski Miquel Holidays
Small but eclectic
programme
Tel 01457 821200

Ski-Monterosa Ltd
Monterosa (Alagna)
specialist
Tel 0151 353 2317

Ski Morgins Holidays
Chalet holidays in Morgins
Tel 01568 770681

Ski Morzine
Accommodation in Morzine
Tel 01932 837639

Skiology.co.uk
Chalet in Les Carroz
Tel 0780 907 5649

Ski Olympic
Chalet holidays in France
Tel 01302 328820

Ski Peak
Specialist in Vaujany
Tel 01428 608070

SkiPlan Travel Service
Schools programme
Tel 0870 241 4499

Ski Power
Chalets in La Tania and
Courchevel 1650
Tel 01737 306029

Ski Rosie
Luxury catered chalet in
Morgins and self-catered
apartments in Châtel
Tel 01480 211808

Ski Safari
Canada/US tailor-made
specialist, but also
Switzerland, Austria, Chile
and Japan
Tel 01273 224060

Ski Soleil
Chalet and apartments in La
Plagne
Tel 020 3239 3454

Ski Solutions
Tailor-made holidays
Tel 020 7471 7777

Ski Supreme
Holidays to France
Tel 0845 194 7541

Skitopia
Hotels and chalets in the
French Alps
Tel 0844 412 9919

Ski Total
Chalet holidays in Europe
Tel 01252 618333

Skitracer.com
Holidays in Europe, Canada
and America
Tel 020 8600 1668

Ski-Val
Catered chalets in France
and Austria
Tel 01822 611200

Tour operator directory

Interactive resort shortlist builder at **www.wtss.co.uk**

Ski Verbier
Specialists in Verbier
Tel 020 7401 1101

Ski Weekend
Weekend and ten-day holidays
Tel 01392 878353

Skiweekends.com
Three- and six-day holidays to the Three Valleys and the Chamonix Valley
Tel 0870 442 3400

Ski Wild
Holidays in Europe and North America; specialise in Austria
Tel 0870 746 9668

Ski with Julia
Hotels and catered chalets in Verbier
Tel 01386 584478

Skiworld
European and North American programme
Tel 0870 241 6723

Ski Yogi
Hotels and catered chalets in Italy
Tel 01799 531886

Sloping Off
Schools holidays
Tel 01273 648200

Snowbizz
Family ski specialist in Puy-St-Vincent
Tel 01778 341455

Snowcoach
Holidays to Austria and France
Tel 01727 866177

SnowCrazy
Chalets in La Rosière and La Plagne
Tel 01342 302910

Snowebb
Catered chalets in Big White, Sun Peaks and Silver Star
Tel 020 8123 5861 / +1 250 765 9058

Snow Finders
Holidays to Europe and N America
Tel 01858 466888

Snowfocus
Chalet in Châtel
Tel 01392 479555 / +33 (0)450 732863

Snowlife
Catered chalet in La Clusaz
Tel 01534 863630

Snowline
Catered chalets in France with child care
Tel 0844 557 3118

Snoworks
Holidays with ski courses
Tel 08701 225549

Snowscape
Flexible trips to Austria
Tel 08453 708570

Snowstar Holidays
Tignes specialist in catered chalets
Tel 020 8133 8411

SnowTrex
Accommodation in Europe
Tel 0870 626 0020

SnowYourWay.com
Valfréjus (Maurienne) with transport provided
Tel 0870 760 6448

Snowy Pockets
Chalet and apartment holidays in Arosa
Tel 01707 251696

Solo's
Singles' holidays, ages 25 to 69
Tel 0844 815 0005

La Source
Chalet and other accommodation in Villard-Reculas (Alpe-d'Huez)
Tel 01707 655988

Stanford Skiing
Megève specialist
Tel 01603 477471

St Anton Ski Company
Hotels and chalets in St Anton
Tel 020 7632 1414

Sugar Mountain
Chalet in Morzine
Tel +33 (0)672 619 936

Supertravel
Upmarket European and N American holidays
Tel 020 7962 9933

Susie Ward Alpine Holidays
Upmarket accommodation in Châtel
Tel +33 (0)675 819196

Switzerland Travel Centre
Specialists in Swiss resorts
Tel 020 7420 4900

Ted Bentley Chalet Holidays
Luxury chalets in Nendaz
Tel 01934 820854

TheWhiteChalet.com
Chalet in Argentière
Tel 01274 530 313

Thomson Ski
Major mainstream operator
Tel 0871 971 0578

Trail Alpine
Chalet in Morzine
Tel 0870 750 6560

Trailfinders
North American programme
Tel 0845 050 5900

Transylvania Live
Holidays in Romania
Tel 0808 101 6781

UCPA
All-inclusive budget trips to France
Tel +33 (0)892 680 599

United Vacations Ski USA & Canada
US and Canada programme
Tel 0844 4990033

Val d'Isère A La Carte
Specialists in Val d'Isère hotels and self-catering holidays
Tel 01481 236800

Vanilla Ski
Chalet in Seez (near La Rosière and Les Arcs)
Tel 01932 860696

VIP
Chalets in Val d'Isère, Méribel and Zermatt
Tel 0844 557 3119

Virgin Snow
Holidays to America and Canada
Tel 0844 557 3962

Waymark (Exodus)
Cross-country skiing holidays
Tel 0845 863 9600

White Mountains
Ski holidays in North America
Tel 0871 222 6006

White Roc
Weekends and tailor-made hotel holidays; luxury chalets/apartments with hotel services
Tel 020 7792 1188

YSE
Chalet holidays in Val d'Isère
Tel 0845 122 1414

SKI BUSINESS DIRECTORY

This is a list of companies and organisations providing goods and services you might find helpful in organising a holiday, grouped under a dozen headings. Tour operators are listed separately, in the previous section, starting on page 732.

AIRLINES

Air Canada
Tel 0871 220 1111

Air France
Tel 0870 142 4343

Air New Zealand
Tel 0800 028 4149

Air Southwest
Tel 0870 043 4553

Alitalia
Tel 08714 241424

American Airlines
Tel 020 7365 0777

Austrian Airlines
Tel 0870 124 2625

Bmibaby
Tel 0871 224 0224

British Airways
Tel 0844 493 0787

Continental Airlines
Tel 0845 607 6760

Delta Airlines
Tel 0845 600 0950

EasyJet
Tel 0871 244 2366

Flybe
Tel 0871 700 2000

Jet2.com
Tel 0871 226 1737

KLM
Tel 08705 074074

Lufthansa
Tel 0871 945 9747

Qantas
Tel 0845 774 7767

Ryanair
Tel 0871 246 0000

Swiss International Air Lines
Tel 0845 601 0956

Thomsonfly
Tel 0871 231 4869

United Airlines
Tel 0845 844 4777

Virgin Atlantic Airways
Tel 08705 747 747

Zoom Airlines
Tel 0870 240 0055

AIRPORTS

Aberdeen
Tel 0870 040 0006

Belfast
Tel 028 9448 4848

Birmingham
Tel 08707 335511

Bournemouth
Tel 01202 364000

Bristol
Tel 0871 334 4444

Cardiff
Tel 01446 711111

Coventry
Tel 024 7630 8600

Doncaster
Tel 08708 332210

Dublin
Tel 0353 1 814 1111

Durham Tees Valley
Tel 08712 242426

Edinburgh
Tel 0870 040 0007

Exeter
Tel 01392 367433

Glasgow
Tel 0870 040 0008

Leeds Bradford
Tel 0113 250 9696

London Gatwick
Tel 0870 000 2468

London Heathrow
Tel 0870 000 0123

London Luton
Tel 01582 405100

London Stansted
Tel 0870 000 0303

Manchester
Tel 08712 710 711

Newcastle
Tel 0871 882 1121

Nottingham East Midlands
Tel 0871 919 9000

Southampton Airport
Tel 0870 040 0009

AIRPORT TRANSFERS

Airport Transfer Service
Switzerland, France and Austria to most resorts
Tel +33 (0)450 536397

AlpineCab
Chambéry, Geneva, Lyon and Grenoble to lots of resorts
Tel +33 (0)450 731938

Alp-Line
Six airports, including Turin and Geneva to Swiss, French and Italian resorts
Tel +33 (0)450 743842

Arlberg Shuttle
Weekend coach service from Friedrichshafen to St Anton and Lech
Tel +43 (0)664 5187040

Bensbus.co.uk
Grenoble to Les Deux-Alpes and Alpe-d'Huez

ChamVan
Geneva to Chamonix
Tel +33 (0)632 240394

Cool Bus
Geneva, Grenoble, Chambéry, Lyon to Tarentaise and Three Valleys
Tel +33 (0)632 192 962

Flytransfer
Tel 07775 578919

Geneva Airport Transfers
Portes du Soleil and Mont Blanc resorts
Tel +33 (0)619 423752

Graubunden Express
From Friedrichshafen to 12 resorts in eastern Switzerland
Tel +49 (0)7541 398615

Holiday Shuttle
Salzburg to Saalbach-Hinterglemm and Zell am See
Tel +43 (0)699 8155 8969

Mountain Drop-Offs
Geneva Airport to Chamonix valley, Megève, Les Contamines, St-Gervais, Courmayeur and Zermatt.
Tel 0871 575 4810

Mountain Express
Three Valleys from Geneva, Grenoble, Chambéry and Lyon
Tel +33 (0)619 172600

MT Bus
Bergamo or Milan to Bormio, Livigno and rest of Valtellina region

Skihoppa.com
Over 40 airports to lots of Alpine resorts; heli-transfers available
Tel 0871 855 0350

SnowTransfers
Private transfers mainly to Mont Blanc region, Courmayeur and Verbier
Tel 01539 445706

Terravision
Verona, Bergamo and Venice to the Dolomites
Tel +39 331 781 4916

Threevalleetransfers
Key airports and Moûtiers (Eurostar) to Méribel and Courchevel
Tel 01782 644420

Whitetracks
Shared helicopter transfers to Swiss and French resorts
Tel 0779 664 0841 / +33 (0)686 123417

BREAKDOWN INSURANCE

AA Five Star Europe
Tel 0800 085 7253

Autohome
Tel 0800 371 280

Direct Line Rescue
Tel 0845 246 8702

Europ Assistance
Tel 0844 338 5533

Green Flag Motoring Assistance
Tel 0845 246 1557

Interactive resort shortlist builder at **www.wtss.co.uk**

Mondial Assistance UK
Tel 020 8681 2525

RAC Travel Services
Tel 0800 015 6000

CAR HIRE

Alamo Rent A Car
Tel 0870 400 4562

Avis Rent A Car
Tel 0844 581 0147

Budget Car and Van Rental
Tel 0353 9066 27711

Europcar UK
Tel 0845 758 5375

Hertz UK Ltd
Tel 08708 448844

Holiday Autos International Ltd
Tel 0871 472 5229

Suncars
Tel 0870 902 8021

CAR WINTER EQUIPMENT

Brindley Chains Ltd
Pewag snowchains
Tel 01925 825555

GT Towing Ltd
Ski boxes and snowchains
Tel 01707 262526

Latchmere Motor Spares
Snowchains, roof bars, ski clamps, boxes
Tel 020 7228 3907

Motor Traveller / Carbox
Thule racks and boxes; Milz snowchains
Tel 01753 833442

The Roof Box Company
Roof boxes and ski carriers
Tel 01539 621884

RUD Chains Ltd
Snowchains
Tel 01227 276611

Skidrive.co.uk
Thule roof systems, Karrite boxes, Skandibox, Konig snowchains
Tel 01223 750800

Snowchains Ltd
Thule ski boxes, roof bars and ski racks; Weissenfels snowchains
Tel 01732 884408

Thule Ltd
Boxes, bars and carriers
Tel 01275 340404

CROSS-CHANNEL TRAVEL

Brittany Ferries
Portsmouth–Caen
Tel 0870 9076 103

Eurotunnel
Folkestone–Calais/Coquelles via the Channel Tunnel
Tel 0870 750 6824

LD Line
Portsmouth-Le Havre
Tel 0870 420 1267

Norfolkline
Dover–Dunkerque
Tel 0844 847 5007

P&O Ferries
Dover–Calais; Hull-Rotterdam; Hull-Zeebrugge
Tel 08716 645645

SeaFrance
Dover–Calais
Tel 0871 423 7119

SpeedFerries
Dover-Boulogne
Tel 0871 222 7456

Stena Line
Harwich–Hook of Holland
Tel 08705 707070

DRY SKI SLOPES

SOUTH-WEST ENGLAND

Avon Ski and Action Centre
Lyncombe Drive, Churchill, North Somerset
Tel 01934 852335

Dorset Snowsport Centre
Warmwell, Dorchester, Dorset
Tel 01305 853245

Exeter and District Ski Club
Clifton Hill Sports Ground, Belmont Road, Exeter
Tel 01392 211422

John Nike Leisuresport Plymouth
Plymouth Ski Centre, Alpine Park, Marsh Mills, Plymouth
Tel 01752 600220

Snowtrax
Matchams Lane, Hurn, Christchurch, Dorset
Tel 01202 499155

Torquay Alpine Ski Club
Barton Hall, Kingskerswell Road, Torquay, Devon
Tel 01803 313350

Yeovil Alpine Village
Addlewell Lane, Nine Springs, Yeovil, Somerset
Tel 01935 421702

SOUTH-EAST ENGLAND

Alpine Snowsports Aldershot
Gallwey Road, Aldershot, Hampshire
Tel 01252 325889

Bowles Outdoor Centre
Sandhill Lane, Eridge Green, Tunbridge Wells, Kent
Tel 01892 665665

Bromley Ski Centre
Sandy Lane, St Paul's Cray, Orpington, Kent
Tel 01689 876812

Calshot Activities Centre
Calshot Spit, Fawley, Southampton
Tel 023 8089 2077

Christ's College Ski Club
Larch Avenue, Guildford, Surrey
Tel 01483 504988

Folkestone Sports Centre Ski Slope
Radnor Park Avenue, Folkestone, Kent
Tel 01303 850333

John Nike Leisuresport Bracknell
Bracknell Ski Centre, Amen Corner, Bracknell, Berkshire
Tel 01344 789000

John Nike Leisuresport Chatham
Chatham Ski and Snowboard Centre, Alpine Park, Capstone Road, Gillingham, Kent
Tel 01634 827979

Knockhatch Ski and Snowboard Centre
Hailsham Bypass, Hailsham
Tel 01323 442051

Sandown Ski Centre
More Lane, Esher, Surrey
Tel 01372 467132

Southampton Alpine Centre
The Sports Centre, Bassett,
Southampton
Tel 023 8079 0970

MIDDLE ENGLAND

The Ackers
Golden Hillock Road, Small
Heath, Birmingham
Tel 0121 772 5111

Bassingbourn Snowsports Centre
Royston, Hertfordshire
Tel 0845 072 8293

Gloucester Ski and Snowboard Centre
Matson Lane, Robinswood
Hill, Gloucester
Tel 01452 874842

John Nike Leisuresport Swadlincote
Swadlincote Ski Centre, Hill
Street, Swadlincote,
Derbyshire
Tel 01283 217200

Kidsgrove Ski Centre
Bathpool Park, Kidsgrove,
Stoke-on-Trent
Tel 01782 784908

Stoke Ski Centre
Festival Park, Stoke-on-Trent
Tel 01782 204159

Tallington Ski and Snowboard Centre
Tallington Lakes Leisure
Park, Barholm Road,
Tallington, Stamford,
Lincolnshire
Tel 01778 347000

Tamworth Snowdome
Leisure Island, River Drive,
Tamworth, Staffordshire
Tel 08705 000011

Telford Snowboard and Ski Centre
Court Street, Madeley,
Telford, Shropshire
Tel 01952 586862

Xscape Milton Keynes
602 Marlborough Gate,
Central Milton Keynes
Tel 0871 200 3220

EASTERN ENGLAND

Brentwood Park Ski and Snowboard Centre
Warley Gap, Little Warley,
Brentwood, Essex
Tel 01277 211994

Gosling Ski Centre
Stanborough Road, Welwyn
Garden City, Hertfordshire
Tel 01707 331056

Norfolk Ski Club
Whitlingham Lane, Trowse,
Norwich, Norfolk
Tel 01603 662781

Snow Centre
St Albans Hill, Hemel
Hempstead, Herts
Tel 01442 241321

Suffolk Ski Centre
Bourne Hill, Wherstead,
Ipswich
Tel 01473 602347

NORTHERN ENGLAND

Alston Training and Adventure Centre
High Plains Lodge, Alston,
Cumbria
Tel 01434 381886

Chill Factor
Trafford Way, Trafford Quays,
Manchester
Tel 0161 749 2222

Halifax Ski and Snowboard Centre
Sportsman Inn and Leisure,
Bradford Old Road, Halifax
Tel 01422 340760

Kendal Ski Club
Canal Head North, Kendal,
Cumbria
Tel 0845 6345 173

Pendle Ski Club
Clitheroe Road, Sabden,
Clitheroe, Lancs
Tel 01200 425222

Runcorn Ski and Snowboard Centre
Town Park, Palace Fields,
Runcorn, Cheshire
Tel 01928 701965

Sheffield Ski Village
Vale Road, Parkwood
Springs, Sheffield
Tel 0114 276 9459

Ski Rossendale
Haslingden Old Road,
Rawtenstall, Rossendale,
Lancashire
Tel 01706 226457

Whickham Thorns Outdoor Centre
Market Lane, Dunston
Tel 0191 433 5767

Xscape Castleford
Colorado Way,
Glasshoughton, Castleford,
West Yorkshire
Tel 0871 200 3221

WALES

Cardiff Ski & Snowboard Centre
198 Fairwater Rd, Cardiff
Tel 029 2056 1793

Dan-yr-Ogof Ski Slopes
Glyn Tawe, Abercraf, West
Glamorgan
Tel 01639 730284

John Nike Leisuresport Llandudno
Wyddfyd Road, Great Orme,
Llandudno
Tel 01492 874707

Plas y Brenin
Capel Curig, Conwy
Tel 01690 720214

Pontypool Ski Centre
Pontypool Leisure Park,
Pontypool, Gwent
Tel 01495 756955

Ski Pembrey
Pembrey Country Park,
Pembrey, Llanelli, Dyfed
Tel 01554 834443

SCOTLAND

Alford Ski Centre
Greystone Road, Alford,
Aberdeenshire
Tel 01975 563024

Ancrum Outdoor Education Resource Centre
10 Ancrum Road, Dundee,
Tayside
Tel 01382 435911

Bearsden Ski & Board
Stockiemuir Road, Bearsden,
Glasgow
Tel 0141 943 1500

Firpark Ski Centre
Tillicoultry, Clackmannanshire
Tel 01259 751772

Glasgow Ski & Snowboard Centre
Bellahouston Park,
16 Dumbreck Road, Glasgow
Tel 0141 427 4991

Ski business directory

739

Interactive resort shortlist builder at **www.wtss.co.uk**

Glenmore Lodge
Scottish National Sports Centre, Aviemore, Inverness-shire
Tel 01479 861256

Loch Insh Watersports and Ski Centre
Kincraig, Kingussie, Invernesshire
Tel 01540 651272

Midlothian Snowsports Centre
Hillend, Near Edinburgh, Midlothian
Tel 0131 445 4433

Polmonthill Ski Centre
Polmont Farm, Polmont, Falkirk
Tel 01324 503835

Xscape Braehead
Kings Inch Road, Braehead, Renfrew
Tel 0871 200 3222

NORTHERN IRELAND

Craigavon Golf Ski Centre
Turmoyra Lane, Silverwood, Lurgan, Co Craigavon
Tel 028 3832 6606

EVENT MANAGEMENT COMPANIES

The Corporate Ski Company
Tel 020 8542 8555

Flexiski
Tel 020 8939 0861

Momentum Ski
Tel 020 7371 9111

Ski 2
Tel 01962 713330

Ski Line
Tel 020 8313 3999

Ski Verbier
Tel 020 7401 1101

INSURANCE COMPANIES

Atlas Insurance
Tel 0870 811 1700

Best Ski Insurance
Tel 0870 458 2985

CGNU
Tel 01603 622200

Direct Line Travel Insurance
Tel 0845 246 8704

Direct Travel Insurance
Tel 0845 605 2700

Gosure.com
Tel 0845 222 0020

P J Hayman & Company
Tel 0845 230 0631

Preferential
Tel 0871 221 4008

Primary Insurance Group
Tel 0870 220 0634

Skicoverdirect.co.uk

Ski-insurance.co.uk
Tel 0870 755 6101

Snowcard Insurance Services
Tel 01327 262805

Sportscover Direct
Tel 0845 120 6400

Travelcover.co.uk
Tel 0845 450 0610

Travelinsuranceplus.co.uk
Tel 029 2066 8686 / 029 2078 3010

Worldwide Travel Insurance Services
Tel 0870 112 8100

Read all about the new pace-setting **Black Diamond** policy, designed by skiers, on **page 36**.

NATIONAL TOURIST OFFICES

Andorran Embassy
Tel 020 8874 4806

Argentine Embassy
Tel 0800 555 0016

Australia Tourism
Tel 020 7887 5871

Austrian National Tourist Office
Tel 0845 101 1818

Canadian Tourism Commission
Tel 0870 380 0070

Chile – Consulate General
Tel 020 7580 6392

Czech Tourism
Tel 020 7631 0427

Finnish Tourist Board
Tel 020 8600 7282

French Government Tourist Office
Tel 09068 244123

German National Tourist Office
Tel 020 7317 0908

Italian State Tourist Office
Tel 020 7408 1254

Japan National Tourist Organisation
Tel 020 7398 5678

Norwegian Tourist Board
Tel 020 7591 5500

Polish Tourist Office
Tel 08700 675010

Romanian Tourist Office
Tel 020 7224 3692

Scottish Tourist Board
Tel 0845 225 5121

Slovak Embassy
Tel 020 7313 6470

Slovenian Embassy
Tel 020 7222 5400

Spanish Tourist Office
Tel 020 7486 8077

Swedish Travel and Tourism Council
Tel 020 7108 6168

Switzerland Tourism
Tel 00800 100 200 30

Tourism New Zealand
Tel 020 7930 8422

Turkish Tourist Board
Tel 020 78397778

Visit USA Association
Tel 0870 777 2213

RAILWAYS

Deutsche Bahn AG
Tel 08718 80 80 66

Eurostar
Tel 08705 186 186

Rail Europe
Tel 08448 484064

Swiss Federal Railways
Tel 00800 100 200 30
(Switzerland Tourism)

RETAILERS

SOUTH-WEST ENGLAND

Devon Ski Centre
Oak Place, Newton Abbot, Devon
Tel 01626 351278

Mission Adventure
1 Bank Lane, Brixham, Devon
Tel 0870 1430 689

Skate and Ski
104 High Street, Staple Hill, Bristol
Tel 0117 970 1356

Snow & Rock
Units 1-3 Shield Retail Centre, Link Road, Filton, Bristol
Tel 0117 914 3000

Snow Togs
6 St Michaels Road, Bournemouth, Dorset
Tel 01202 557690

Snowtrax
Matchams Lane, Hurn, Christchurch, Dorset
Tel 01202 499155

Team Ski
37 High East Street, Dorchester, Dorset
Tel 01305 268035

Westsports
Market House, Marlborough Rd, Old Town, Swindon, Wiltshire
Tel 01793 532588

SOUTH-EAST ENGLAND

Alpine Room
71-73 Main Road, Danbury, Essex
Tel 01245 223563

Captains Cabin Sevenoaks
113-115 St John's Hill,
Sevenoaks, Kent
Tel 01732 464463

Edge2Edge
Unit 10, Oakwood Industrial
Park, Gatwick Road, Crawley,
West Sussex
Tel 01293 649300

Finches Ski and Sports
25-29 Perry Vale, Forest Hill,
London
Tel 020 8699 6768

John Pollock
157 High Road, Loughton,
Essex
Tel 020 8508 6626

John Pollock
67 High Street, Barnet
Tel 020 8440 3994

Mountain High
41 Reading Road,
Pangbourne, Berkshire
Tel 0118 984 1851

Ski Bartlett
1-2 Rosslyn Parade,
Uxbridge Road, Hillingdon,
Middlesex
Tel 020 8848 0040

Snow & Rock
188 Kensington High Street,
London
Tel 020 7937 0872

Snow & Rock
4 Mercer Street, Covent
Garden, London
Tel 020 7420 1444

Snow & Rock
4 Grays Inn Road, Holborn,
London
Tel 020 7831 6900

Snow & Rock
99 Fordwater Road, Chertsey,
Surrey
Tel 01932 566886

Snow & Rock
The Boardwalk, Port Solent,
Portsmouth, Hampshire
Tel 023 9220 5388

Snow & Rock
Sporting Club, 38-42 King's
Road, London
Tel 020 7589 5418

Snow & Rock
Unit 1 Davidson Way, Rom
Valley Way, Romford, Essex
Tel 01708 436400

Snow & Rock
47-51 William Street, London
Tel 020 7256 3940

Snow & Rock
54-55 Market Street,
Brighton, East Sussex
Tel 01273 827660

Snow Togs
431 Millbrook Road,
Southampton, Hampshire
Tel 023 8077 3925

MIDDLE ENGLAND

Active Outdoor & Ski
Active Clothing Ltd,
77 Castle Quay, Banbury,
Oxfordshire
Tel 01295 273700

Beans
86 Sheep Street, Bicester,
Oxfordshire
Tel 01869 246451

BestBuys
Nene Court, 27-31 The
Embankment,
Wellingborough,
Northamptonshire
Tel 01933 272699

Lockwoods Ski Shop
125-129 Rugby Road,
Leamington Spa,
Warwickshire
Tel 01926 339388

Mountain High
Tower Court, Hornes Lane,
Princes Risborough,
Buckinghamshire
Tel 01844 274260

Snow & Rock
14 Priory Queensway,
Birmingham
Tel 0121 236 8280

Two Seasons
Unit 3-4, Fletcher Gate,
Nottingham
Tel 0115 950 1333

Two Seasons
229-231 Wellingborough
Road, Northampton,
Northamptonshire
Tel 01604 627377

Two Seasons
15 Pump Street, Worcester
Tel 01905 731144

Two Seasons
64 Lower Precinct, Coventry
Tel 024 7663 0020

Two Seasons
32-34 Mill Lane, Solihull
Tel 0121 705 5544

Two Seasons
26 Bakers Lane, Lichfield,
Staffordshire
Tel 01543 411422

Two Seasons
Regents Court, Livery Street,
Leamington Spa,
Warwickshire
Tel 01926 888169

Two Seasons
43-47 High Street, Leicester
Tel 0116 262 5855

Two Seasons
Level 1, North Mall, The
Westfield Centre, Derby
Tel 01332 343284

EASTERN ENGLAND

Snow & Rock
Norman House, 97-99
London Road, St Albans,
Hertfordshire
Tel 01422 235305

SnowFit
2 Cucumber Lane, Brundall,
Norwich
Tel 01603 716655

Two Seasons
34 Chesterton Road,
Cambridge
Tel 01223 356207

Two Seasons
16 Westgate, Peterborough
Tel 01773 312184

Where to shop!
www.johnpollock.co.uk

Barnet 020 8440 3994   Loughton 020 8508 6626

741

Ski business directory

Interactive resort shortlist builder at www.wtss.co.uk

SNOW + ROCK

Birmingham	**0121 236 8280**
Brighton	**01273 827660**
Bristol	**0117 914 3000**
Chertsey - Surrey	**01932 566886**
Covent Garden	**020 7420 1444**
Gateshead	**0191 493 3680**
Holborn	**020 7831 6900**
Kensington	**020 7937 0872**
King's Road	**020 7589 5418**
Manchester	**0161 448 4444**
Manchester Chill Factor[e]	**0161 746 1010**
Monument	**020 7256 3940**
Portsmouth	**023 9220 5388**
Romford	**01708 436400**
Sheffield	**0114 275 17700**
St Albans	**01422 235305**
Wirral	**0151 328 5500**
Snow+Rock Direct	**0845 100 1000**

Ski business directory

742

Weekly news updates and resort links at www.wtss.co.uk

NORTHERN ENGLAND

Freetime Climb + Ski
1-2 Market Street, Carlisle,
Cumbria
Tel 01228 598210

Glide & Slide
5/7 Station Road, Otley,
West Yorkshire
Tel 01943 461136

**Severn Sports Mountain
Adventures Ltd**
80 Town Street, Armley,
Leeds, West Yorkshire
Tel 0113 279 1618

**Severn Sports Mountain
Adventures Ltd**
5-7 Church Lane, Crossgates,
Leeds, West Yorkshire
Tel 0113 264 3847

Snow & Rock
Sheffield Ski Centre, Vale
Road, Parkwood Springs,
Sheffield
Tel 0114 275 1700

Snow & Rock
Princess Parkway, Princess
Park, Didsbury, Manchester
Tel 0161 448 4444

Snow & Rock
Chill Factor⁶, Unit 6, Trafford
Way, Trafford Quays,
Manchester
Tel 0161 746 1010

Snow & Rock
Metro Park West, Gibside
Way, Gateshead,
Tyne And Wear
Tel 0191 493 3680

Snow & Rock
Unit 1 Eastham Point, New
Chester Road, Eastham,
Wirral
Tel 0151 328 5500

SCOTLAND

Craigdon Mountain Sports
Advertising House, Burghmuir
Circle, Inverurie, Highland
Tel 01467 624900

NORTHERN IRELAND

Macski
140 Lisburn Road, Belfast
Tel 028 9066 5525

REPUBLIC OF IRELAND

The Great Outdoors
Chatham Street, Dublin 2,
Ireland
Tel 00 353 1679 4293

SKI/BOARDING ORGANISATIONS

**British Association of
Snowsport Instructors
(BASI)**
Tel 01479 861717

**British Ski Club for the
Disabled**
Tel 01582 793518

Disability Snowsport UK
Tel 01479 861272

Ski Club of Great Britain
Tel 020 8410 2000

**Snowboard Club UK
(SCUK)**
Tel 01273 620877

Snowsport England
Tel 0121 501 2314

SnowsportGB
Tel 0131 445 7676

Snowsport Scotland
Tel 0131 445 4151

Snowsport Wales
Tel 029 2056 1904

SKI EMPLOYMENT ORGANISATIONS

Bunac / Gap Canada
Tel 020 7251 3472

Free Radicals
Tel 07968 183848 /
+33 (0)643 152659

Just Jobs 4 Students
Tel 020 7000 9994

Natives
Tel 08700 463377

Seasonal-Jobs.com
Tel 0203 006 2608

Season Workers
Tel 0845 643 9338

Skiconnection.co.uk

SKI TRAVEL AGENTS

Alpine Answers
Tel 020 8871 4656

Catered Ski Chalets
Tel 020 3080 0202

Chaletfinder.co.uk
Tel 01453 766094

Ifyouski.com
Tel 020 7471 7733

Iglu.com
Tel 020 8542 6658

Independent Ski Links)
Tel 01964 533905

I Need Snow
Tel 020 8123 7817

Kwik Ski
Tel 0800 655 6805

Ski-direct.co.uk
Tel 08700 171935

Ski Expectations
Tel 01799 531888

Ski Line
Tel 020 8313 3999

Ski McNeill
Tel 0870 600 1359

Ski Solutions
Tel 020 7471 7700

Skitracer
Tel 0870 420 5782

Ski Travel Centre
Tel 0141 649 9696

Snow Finders
Tel 01858 466888

Snow Hounds
Tel 01243 788487

Snow-Line
Tel 0871 222 6000

WorldSki
Tel 0870 428 8706

Want to get other views?

Our website has an active forum, where readers swap experiences and views on resorts and other stuff. The WTSS editors join in, when they have time, so it's a good way to get their views.

Find out more at:

www.wtss.co.uk

RESORT DIRECTORY / INDEX

This is an index to the resort chapters in the book; you'll find page references for about 400 resorts that are described in those chapters. But you'll also find brief descriptions here of another 700 resorts, most of them smaller than those we've covered in full.

Key

⊥ *Lifts*
⊥ *Pistes*
⊨ *UK tour operators*

49 Degrees North USA
Inland area with best snow in Washington State, including 120-acre bowl reserved for powder weekends.
1195m; slopes 1195–1760m
⊥5 ⊥ *780 acres*

Abetone Italy
Resort in the exposed Appennines, less than two hours from Florence and Pisa.
1390m; slopes 1390–1900m
⊥25 ⊥ *50km*

Abtenau Austria
Sizeable village in Dachstein-West region near Salzburg, on large plain ideal for cross-country.
710m; slopes 710–1260m
⊥6 ⊥ *10km*

Achenkirch Austria
Unspoiled, low-altitude Tirolean village close to Niederau and Alpbach. Beautiful setting overlooking a lake.
930m; slopes 930–1800m
⊥7 ⊥ *25km;* ⊨ *Ramblers*

Adelboden 493

Les Aillons-Margériaz France
Traditional village near Chambéry.
1000m; slopes 1000–1900m
⊥20 ⊥ *40km*

Alagna 452
Small resort on the western fringe of Monterosa Ski area.

Alba 481
Trentino village with a small, quiet area.

Alberschwende 134

Albiez-Montrond France
Authentic old French village in Maurienne valley with panoramic views. Own easy slopes; close to other areas.
1500m; slopes 1500–2200m
⊥13 ⊥ *67 hectares*
⊨ *Lagrange*

Alleghe Italy
Dolomite village near Cortina in a pretty lakeside setting close to numerous areas.
980m; ⊥24 ⊥ *80km*
⊨ *Interhome*

Les Allues 325
Rustic village on the road up to Méribel.

Alpbach 126

Alpe-d'Huez 245

Alpe-du-Grand-Serre France
Tiny resort near Alpe-d'Huez and Les Deux-Alpes. Good for bad-weather days.
1370m; slopes 1370–2185m
⊥19 ⊥ *55km*

Alpendorf Austria
Outpost of St Johann im Pongau, at one end of an extensive three-valley lift network linking via Wagrain to Flachau – all part of the Salzburger Sportwelt area. Good cruising, intermediate runs. New gondola for 2007/08.
850m; slopes 800–2185m
⊥64 ⊥ *200km*

Alpenglow USA
Alaskan ski resort.
762m; slopes 2500–3900m
⊥4 ⊥ *320 acres*

Alpine Meadows USA
Squaw Valley's neighbour has similar, lightly wooded terrain, with runs of all classifications and an impressive snow record, but a modest total vertical. The slopes are lightly wooded, with broad open runs between glades. The base sits in a broad bowl, with excellent beginner slopes. The resort boundary is open – expeditions require guidance. There is no resort in the European sense of the word, but there's lots of lodgings close by in lakeside Tahoe City.
2085m; slopes 2085–2635m
⊥13 ⊥ *2400 acres*

Alps Resort South Korea
Korea's most northerly, snow-reliable resort, about five hours from Seoul. ⊥5

Alta 625

Alta Badia 463

Altenmarkt Austria
Unspoiled village, well placed just off the Salzburg-Villach autobahn for numerous resorts including snow-sure Obertauern and those in the Salzburger Sportwelt.
855m; slopes 855–2130m
⊥23 ⊥ *150km;* ⊨ *Interhome*

Alto Campoo Spain
Barren, desolate place near Santander, with undistinguished slopes, but magnificent wilderness views.
1650m; slopes 1650–2130m ⊥13

Alt St Johann Switzerland
Old cross-country village with Alpine slopes connecting into Unterwasser area near Liechtenstein.
900m; slopes 900–2260m
⊥19 ⊥ *60km*

Alyeska USA
Alaskan area 60km/37 miles from Anchorage, with luxury hotel.
75m; slopes 75–1200m
⊥9 ⊥ *785 acres*
⊨ *All America Holidays, Frontier*

Aminona 502
Purpose-built resort in the Crans-Montana network.

Andalo 481
Trentino village not far from Madonna.

Andelsbuch 134

Andermatt 495

Andorra la Vella 108

Angel Fire USA
Intermediate area near Taos, New Mexico. Height usually ensures good snow.
2620m; slopes 2620–3255m
⊥5 ⊥ *455 acres*

Les Angles France
Attractive resort with one of the best ski areas in the Pyrenees. Pretty, treelined, mostly easy skiing.
1600m; slopes 1600–2400m
⊥18 ⊥ *40km*
⊨ *Lagrange, Pyrenees Ski Experience, Ski Collection, Ski France, Skiholidayextras*

Ankogel 120

Annaberg-Lungötz Austria
Peaceful village in a pretty setting, sharing a sizeable area with Gosau. Close to Filzmoos.
775m; slopes 775–1620m
⊥33 ⊥ *65km;* ⊨ *Lagrange*

Annupuri 718
One of the three interlinked ski areas of Niseko.

Anthony Lakes USA
Ski resort in Oregon, 300 miles E of Portland.
slopes 2165–2435m
⊥2 ⊥ *23 trails*

Anzère 497

Aosta Italy
Historic valley town with 18-minute gondola ride up to mountain resort of Pila. Aosta is a real working town with people in suits rather than skiwear. It has good-value accommodation, a lot more bars and restaurants than

Pila, and a lovely traffic-free centre. Other resorts in the Aosta valley are within day-trip distance and are covered by the lift pass.
1800m; slopes 1550–2750m
⊥14 ⊥ *70km*

Apex Canada
Small, friendly, rather isolated resort, well worth stopping off here for a night or two on a tour of western BC resorts. Modern, purpose-built slope-side base with some accommodation and a few bars and restaurants. The slopes suit confident intermediates upwards best. There are some steep, narrow double-black-diamond runs in the trees, wonderful single-diamond Wildside glades, great cruising blues which adventurous intermediates will love but more timid ones might freeze on. There are also excellent beginner slopes and runs to progress to. There's an ice-skating trail through the woods, floodlit at night.
1575m; slopes 1575–2180m
⊥4 ⊥ *1112 acres*
⊨ *AmeriCan Ski, Frontier, Ski Dream, Ski Safari, Snowebb*

Aprica Italy
Ugly, straggling village between Lake Como and the Brenta Dolomites, with bland slopes and limited facilities.
1180m; slopes 1180–2310m
⊥24 ⊥ *40km*
⊨ *Equity, Rocketski*

Arabba 463

Aragnouet-Piau France
Purpose-built mid-mountain satellite of St-Lary, best suited to families, beginners and early intermediates.
1850m; slopes 1420–2500m
⊥18 ⊥ *80km*

Arapahoe Basin 604
Small, exceptionally high day-skiing area near Keystone.

Araucarias Chile
Exotic area in central Chile, around and below a mildly active volcano in the Conguillio National Park.
1500m; ⊥4 ⊥ *350 hectares*

Arcalis 108

Les Arcs 255

Ardent 264
Quiet hamlet with quick access to Avoriaz.

Bethel USA
Pleasant, historic town very close to Sunday River, Maine. Attractive alternative to staying in the slope-side resort.

Le Bettex 315
Small base above St-Gervais, with links to Megève.

Bettmeralp Switzerland
Central village of the sizeable Aletsch area near Brig, high above the Rhône valley, amid spectacular glacial scenery. Reached by cable cars from the valley.
1955m; slopes 1900–2870m
⛟ 35 ⛷ 99km

Beuil-les-Launes France
Alpes-Maritimes resort closest to Nice. Medieval village which shares area with Valberg.
1450m; slopes 1400–2100m
⛟ 26 ⛷ 90km

Bezau 134
Village in the Bregenzerwald region.

Biberwier 236
Little village in the Zugspitz Arena.

Bichlbach 236
Little village in the Zugspitz Arena.

Bielmonte Italy
Popular with day trippers from Milan. Worthwhile on a bad-weather day.
1200m; slopes 1200–1620m
⛟ 13 ⛷ 20km

Big Mountain USA
See Whitefish – name changed in 2007.
✉ AmeriCan Ski, Ski All America, Ski Dream

Big Powderhorn USA
Area with the most 'resort' facilities in south Lake Superior region – and the highest lift capacity too. The area suffers from winds.
370m; slopes 370–560m
⛟ 10 ⛷ 250 acres

Big Sky 639

Big White 666

Bischofshofen Austria
Working town and mountain resort near St Johann im Pongau, with very limited local runs and the main slopes starting nearby at Muhlbach (Hochkönig area).
545m; slopes 545–1000m
⛟ 1 ⛷ 2km

Bivio Switzerland
Quiet village near St Moritz and Savognin, with easy slopes opened up by a few lifts.
1770m; slopes 1780–2560m
⛟ 4 ⛷ 40km

Bizau Austria
Area in the Bregenzerwald region north-west of Lech.
680m; slopes 680–1700m
⛟ 6 ⛷ 24km

Björkliden 709

Björnrike 709

Black Mountain USA
New Hampshire area with lodging in nearby Jackson.
⛟ 4 ⛷ 143 acres

Blatten Switzerland
Mountainside hamlet above Naters, beside the Rhône near Brig. Small but tall Belalp ski area, with larger Aletsch area nearby. Recently installed six-pack.
1320m; slopes 1320–3100m
⛟ 9 ⛷ 60km

Bled 716

Blue Cow 720

Blue Mountain Canada
Largest area in Ontario, with glorious views of Lake Huron. High-capacity lift system and 100% snowmaking.
230m; slopes 230–450m
⛟ 15 ⛷ 275 acres

Blue River Canada
Base of world-famous Mike Wiegele heli-ski operation in Cariboo and Monashee mountains.

Bluewood USA
Particularly remote area even by American north-west standards. Worth a visit if you're in Walla Walla.
1355m; slopes 1355–1725m
⛟ 3 ⛷ 530 acres

Bogus Basin USA
Sizeable area overlooking Idaho's attractive, interesting capital, Boise. Limited accommodation at the base.
1760m; slopes 1760–2310m
⛟ 8 ⛷ 2600 acres

Bohinj 716

Bois-d'Amont France
One of four resorts that make up Les Rousses area in Jura region on the Franco-Suisse border.
1050m; slopes 1120–1680m
⛟ 40 ⛷ 40km
✉ Lagrange

Boi Taull Spain
A typical Pyrenean resort set high above the Boi Valley, close to the stunning Aigues Tortes National Park. Good intermediate terrain. Recently installed fast quad.
slopes 2020–2750m
⛟ 15 ⛷ 44km

Bolognola Italy
Tiny area in Macerata region near the Adriatic Riviera.
1070m; slopes 1070–1845m
⛟ 7 ⛷ 5km

Bolton Valley USA
Resort near Stowe with mostly intermediate slopes.
465m; slopes 465–960m
⛟ 6 ⛷ 155 acres

Bonneval-sur-Arc France
Unspoiled, remote old village in the Haute Maurienne valley with many of its slopes at high altitude. Pass to neighbouring Val d'Isère is closed in winter.
1800m; slopes 1800–3000m
⛟ 11 ⛷ 25km

Bons 298
Rustic, unspoiled old hamlet linked to Les Deux-Alpes.

Boreal USA
Closest area to north Lake Tahoe town, Truckee. Limited slopes, best for novices.
2195m; slopes 2195–2375m
⛟ 9 ⛷ 380 acres

Bormio 428

Borovets 712

Bosco Chiesanuova Italy
Weekend day trippers' place near Verona. A long drive from any other resort.
1105m; slopes 1105–1805m
⛟ 18 ⛷ 20km

Bosco Gurin Switzerland
Highest ski area in Ticino. The only German speaking village in the Italian canton.
1500m; slopes 1500–2400m
⛟ 6 ⛷ 30km

Les Bottières 383

La Bourboule France
Spa and cross-country village with the Alpine slopes of Le Mont-Dore nearby. Spectacular extinct-volcano scenery.
850m; slopes 1050–1850m
⛟ 41 ⛷ 80km
✉ Lagrange

Bourg-d'Oisans France
Pleasant valley town on main Grenoble-Briançon road. Cheap base for visits to Alpe-d'Huez and Les Deux-Alpes.

Bourg-St-Maurice 255
French valley town with a funicular to Les Arcs.

Bovec Slovenia
Town near the small area of Kanin on the Italian border.
✉ BoardnLodge

Boyne Highlands USA
Area with impressive, high-capacity lift system for weekend Detroit crowds. Fierce winds off Lake Michigan a major drawback.
225m; slopes 225–390m
⛟ 10 ⛷ 240 acres

Boyne Mountain USA
Resort popular with weekend Detroit crowds. Not as windy as sister resort Boyne Highlands.
190m; slopes 190–340m
⛟ 12 ⛷ 115 acres

Bozel France
Small town that, in good snow conditions, you can ski down to off-piste from Courchevel and catch a bus back. Also near access road for Champagny-en-Vanoise (which has a gondola up to the La Plagne ski area).
860m

Bramans France
Old cross-country village near Modane. Well placed for touring numerous nearby resorts such as Val Cenis and Valloire.
1230m
⛟ 1 ⛷ 3km

Bramberg Austria
Village near Pass Thurn (Kitzbühel area). Shares odd area with Neukirchen – the only valley lift is in Neukirchen.
820m; slopes 820–900m ⛟ 2

Brand Austria
Family resort with small, low area. Linked to Burserburg ski area since 2007/08 via a high altitude cable car across a dividing valley.
1050m; slopes 1050–1920m
⛟ 13 ⛷ 50km
✉ Ski Wild

Les Brasses France
Collective name for six traditional hamlets with some of the closest slopes to Geneva, but best known for cross-country.
900m; slopes 900–1600m
⛟ 14 ⛷ 50km

Braunwald Switzerland
Sunny but limited area near Zurich, a funicular ride above Linthal. Newish combi-mix lift.
1300m; slopes 1300–1905m
⛟ 8 ⛷ 32km

Breckenridge 597

Bregenzerwald 134

Brentonico Italy
Little resort just off Verona-Trento motorway.
1160m; slopes 1160–1520m ⛟ 16

Bressanone Italy
Valley town 20 minutes by free ski-bus from the lift base of Plose.
565m

La Bresse France
Largest resort in the northerly Vosges mountains near Strasbourg. Three separate downhill areas (with a lot of snowmaking), but also extensive ski de fond and lots of other activities.
900m; slopes 900–1350m
⛟ 26 ⛷ 62km

Briançon 369
Part of the Grand Serre Chevalier region, but with own ski area.

Brian Head USA
Utah area south of Salt Lake City, too far from Park City for a day trip.
2925m; slopes 2925–3445m
🚡 10 ⛷ 500 acres

Brides-les-Bains 325
Quiet spa town in valley below Méribel.

Bridger Bowl 638

Brigels-Andiast Switzerland
In the same valley as Laax/Flims. Access from two sunny villages. Mostly red runs.
1300m; slopes 1100–2415m
🚡 7 ⛷ 75km

Brighton USA
Brighton is linked with Solitude in the valley next to Alta and Snowbird. Total acreage is half that of Alta/Snowbird, but is fair by general US standards. This valley attracts fewer people so the powder doesn't get tracked out in hours, as it does over the hill. Brighton has four fast chairs, including one serving the resort's maximum vertical of 530m/1,740ft on Clayton Peak. This and the slightly lower Mt Millicent are almost all expert terrain, but other lifts serve a wide spectrum of runs. The resorts' boundaries are open, and there are excellent backcountry adventures to be had. There are four terrain parks. Accommodation is in the slope-side Brighton Lodge and some cabins.
2670m; slopes 2665–3200m
🚡 15 ⛷ 2250 acres
🚠 AmeriCan Ski

Brixen 205
Grossraum village that shares slopes with Söll and Ellmau.

Brodie Mountain USA
Largest Massachusetts area. 100% snowmaking and mostly easy slopes.
440m; slopes 440–820m
🚡 6 ⛷ 250 acres

Bromley USA
New York City weekend retreat, reputedly the warmest place to ski in chilly Vermont.
595m; slopes 595–1000m
🚡 9 ⛷ 300 acres

Bromont Canada
Purpose-built resort an hour east of Montreal, with one of the best small areas in eastern Canada, popular for its night skiing.
slopes 405–575m
🚡 6 ⛷ 135 acres
🚠 AmeriCan Ski

Bruck am Grossglockner
Austria
Low beginners' resort, but could suit intermediates looking for a small, quiet base from which to visit nearby Zell am See.
760m

Brundage Mountain USA
Remote, uncrowded Idaho area with glorious views across the lake towards Hell's Canyon. Mostly intermediate slopes. Also has a snowcat operation.
1760m; slopes 1760–2320m
🚡 5 ⛷ 1300 acres

Bruneck Italy
Town with gondola link into the Plan de Corones/Kronplatz area. Italian name is Brunico.

Brunico Italy
Town with gondola link into the Plan de Corones/Kronplatz area. German name is Bruneck.

Bruson 541
Relaxing respite from Verbier's crowds.

Les Bugnenets–Savagnieres
Switzerland
Very small area in the Jura mountains, north of Neuchatel. Short runs served by drag lifts. Valid with the Valais Ski Card.
slopes 1090–1440m
🚡 7 ⛷ 30km

Bukovel Ukraine
Ukraine's second highest resort. Major expansion scheme planned for 278km of pistes and 35 lifts by 2008/09.
slopes 900–1370m
🚡 14 ⛷ 50km

Burke Mountain USA
Uncrowded, isolated family resort in Vermont with mostly intermediate slopes. Great views from the top.
385m; slopes 385–995m
🚡 4 ⛷ 130 acres

Bürserberg Austria
Undistinguished valley town linked to Brand since 2007/08, via a high altitude cable car across a dividing valley.
900m; slopes 1035–1850m
🚡 13 ⛷ 50km

Cairngorm 717

Caldirola Italy
Genoese weekend day-tripper spot in a remote region off the motorway to Turin.
1010m; slopes 1010–1460m
🚡 3 ⛷ 5km

Cambre-d'Aze France
Quiet ski area in the Pyrenees with few British visitors. Good beginner and intermediate terrain. Forms part of the Neiges Catalan (10 resorts on one pass).
1640m; slopes 1640–2400m
🚡 17 ⛷ 35km
🚠 Pyrenees Ski Experience

Camigliatello Italy
Tiny area on the foot of the Italian 'boot' near Cosenza. Weekend/day-trip spot.
1270m; slopes 1270–1750m
🚡 4 ⛷ 6km

Campitello 481
Linked to the Sella Ronda, with quick connections to the interesting Arabba section.

Campitello Matese Italy
The only slopes near Naples. Surprisingly large area when snowcover is complete. Weekend crowds.
1440m; slopes 1440–2100m
🚡 8 ⛷ 40km

Campo di Giove Italy
Highest slopes in L'Aquila region east of Rome.
1070m
🚡 6 ⛷ 23km

Campodolcino Italy
Valley town with new funicular up to the fringe of Madesimo's slopes.
1070m; slopes 1545–2880m
🚡 6 ⛷ 8km

Campo Felice Italy
Easiest resort to reach from Rome, off Aquila motorway. One of the better lift systems in the vicinity.
1410m; slopes 1520–2065m
🚡 14 ⛷ 40km

Campo Imperatore Italy
One of the best of many little areas east of Rome in L'Aquila region.
1980m
🚡 8 ⛷ 20km

Canazei 481
Sizeable and lively rustic village in the Sella Ronda's most heavily wooded section of mountain.

Candanchu/Astún 700

Canillo 115
Small, quiet village linked to Soldeu.

Canmore Canada
Old frontier town on the way to Nakiska/Fortress, well placed for touring the region and an attractive alternative to staying in Banff.

Cannon Mountain USA
One of several small New Hampshire resorts scattered along the Interstate 93 highway; a ski area and nothing more. High, steep mountain by eastern standards.
605m; slopes 605–1260m
🚡 9 ⛷ 165 acres

The Canyons 627

Cardrona 722

Les Carroz-d'Arâches 304
An attractive, spacious village on the road up to Flaine.

Caspoggio Italy
Attractive, unspoiled village north-east of Lake Como, with easy slopes (and more at nearby Chiesa).
1100m; slopes 1100–2155m
🚡 8 ⛷ 22km

Castelrotto Italy
Picturesque village west of Sella Ronda circuit with small sunny Alpine area and good cross-country trails.
1060m

Castel S Angelo Italy
Tiny area in Macerata region near Adriatic Riviera.
805m
🚡 4 ⛷ 2km

Castle Mountain Canada
Remote resort south of Calgary. Good proportion of intermediate and advanced terrain. New area on Haig Ridge planned to provide more beginner and intermediate terrain, says a 2006 visitor.
1410m; slopes 1410–2270m
🚡 5 ⛷ 250 acres

Cauterets 423

Cavalese 481
Unspoiled medieval town in Val di Fiemme.

Caviahue Argentina
Mountain village at the foot of the Copahue Volcano, 357km/222 miles from Neuquén City.
1645m; slopes 1645–2045m
🚡 8 ⛷ 37km

The Cedars Lebanon
The largest of Lebanon's ski areas, 130km/80 miles inland from Beirut. Good, open slopes with a surprisingly long season. New hotel and gondola planned for 2008/09.
slopes 2100–2870m 🚡 6

Ceillac France
Tight cluster of rustic old buildings near Serre-Chevalier. Not far from the highest village in Europe, St-Veran.
1600m; slopes 1600–2450m
🚡 7 ⛷ 25km

Celerina 530
Quiet village with links to St Moritz's slopes.

Cerkno Slovenia
Modern, family resort 50km/31 miles from Ljubljana. Lifts include three fast chairs.
900m
🚡 8 ⛷ 18km

Cerler Spain
Very limited, purpose-built resort with a compact ski area similar to that of nearby Andorra's Arinsal.
1500m; slopes 1500–2630m
🚡 18 ⛷ 61km

Le Cernix France
Hamlet near Megève where Les Saisies' slopes link to those of Crest-Voland. Uncrowded retreat.
1250m; slopes 1150–1950m
🚡 45 ⛷ 80km

Cerrato Lago Italy
Very limited area near the coastal town of La Spezia.
1270m; slopes 1270–1890m
🚡 5 ⛷ 3km

Cerro Bayo Argentina
Limited area amid stunning scenery 10km/6 miles from La Angostura, and 90km/56 miles from San Carlos de Bariloche.
slopes 1050–1780m
🚡 12 🚠 200 hectares
🏂 Snoworks

Cerro Castor 729
Cerro Catedral (Bariloche) 729
Cerro Mirador 730
Cervinia 430
Cesana Torinese 336
Little Italian village in the Milky Way.

Le Châble 541
Small village below Verbier.

Chacaltaya Bolivia
Highest lift-served ski area in the world and the only ski area in Bolivia. Reached by four-wheel drive vehicle from La Paz 30km/19 miles away. Only open in summer (too cold in winter).
5190m; slopes 5220–5420m
🚡 1 🚠 2km

Chaillol France
Cross-country base on the edge of the beautiful Ecrins National Park, near Gap. Small Alpine area, lots of snowmakers.
1600m; slopes 1450–2000m
🚡 10

Chamois Italy
Small area above Buisson, a few miles down the road from Valtournenche (near Cervinia) – worth a look on bad-weather days.
1815m; slopes 1815–2270m
🚡 9 🚠 20km

Chamonix 268
Champagny-en-Vanoise 348
Charming village linking to the La Plagne network.

Champéry 500
Champex-Lac Switzerland
Lakeside hamlet tucked away in the trees above Orsières. A nice quiet, unspoiled base from which to visit Verbier's area.
1470m; slopes 1470–2220m
🚡 4 🚠 25km

Champfér 530
Village just outside St Moritz on the way to the Corvatsch lifts.

Champoluc 452
Unspoiled village at one end of the Monterosa Ski area.

Champorcher Italy
Small village south of Aosta valley with tall but narrow ski area, mostly red runs on open slopes, with one black through the trees to the lift base at Chardonney.
1430m; slopes 1430–2500m
🚡 5 🚠 21km

Champoussin 500
Quiet mountainside village in the Champéry area.

Chamrousse France
Functional family resort near Grenoble, with good, sheltered slopes. Chairlifts and a cable car from three bases (1650, 1700 and 1750) serve largely beginner and intermediate slopes.
1650m; slopes 1400–2255m
🚡 24 🚠 92km
🏂 Crystal, Erna Low, Lagrange, Ski Collection, Ski France, Skiholidayextras.com, Thomson

Chandolin 537
Chantemerle 369
One of the main valley villages making up the big resort of Serre-Chevalier.

Chapa Verde Chile
60km/37 miles north-east of Rancagua and 145km/90 miles from Santiago.
1200m; slopes 1200–2500m
🚡 4 🚠 1200 hectares

Chapelco Argentina
Small ski area with full infrastructure of services 19km/12 miles from sizeable town of San Martin de Los Andes. Accommodation in hotels 11km/7 miles from the slopes.
slopes 1250–1980m
🚡 10 🚠 140 hectares
🏂 Snoworks

La Chapelle-d'Abondance 278
Unspoiled village 5km/3 miles down the valley from Châtel.

Charlotte Pass 720
Château d'Oex Switzerland
Pleasant little valley town that is the main French-speaking component of the shared lift-pass area around Gstaad. Local slopes are pleasant and undemanding but low (La Braye, at the top, is at only 1650m/5,400ft), and not connected to any of the Gstaad sectors – though the local railway makes moving around to other resorts painless. This is where Alpine hot-air ballooning first took off, and it's still a local speciality.
960m; slopes 890–3000m
🚡 63 🚠 250km
🏂 Ardmore

Châtel 278
Le Chatelard France
Small resort in remote Parc des Bauges between Lake Annecy and Chambéry.

Chiesa Italy
Attractive beginners' resort with a fairly high plateau of easy runs above the resort.
1000m; slopes 1700–2335m
🚡 16 🚠 50km

Le Chinaillon France
Modern, chalet-style village at base of lifts above Le Grand-Bornand.
1300m; slopes 1000–2100m
🚡 37 🚠 90km

Chiomonte Italy
Tiny resort on the main road east of Bardonecchia and Sauze d'Oulx. A good half-day trip from either.
745m; slopes 745–2210m
🚡 6 🚠 10km

Chsea Algeria
Largest of Algeria's skiable areas, 135km/84 miles south-east of coastal town of Alger in the Djur Djur mountains.
1860m; slopes 1860–2510m 🚡 2

Chur–Brambruesch Switzerland
Chur's local ski area a cable car and gondola ride from the town.
595m; slopes 1170–2200m
🚡 6 🚠 25km

Churwalden Switzerland
Hamlet on fringe of Lenzerheide-Valbella area, linked via a slow chair. Four short local runs served by a quad and steep drag.
1230m; slopes 1230–2865m
🚡 40 🚠 155km

Claviere 336
Small Italian village linked to Montgenèvre (in France).

La Clusaz 283
Les Coches 348
Small, purpose-built ski area, linked to the La Plagne ski area.

Cogne Italy
One of Aosta valley's larger villages. Small area worth a short visit from nearby Pila.
1530m; slopes 1530–2245m
🚡 5 🚠 8km

Colfosco 463
Sprawling village next to Corvara at the junction of the Alta Badia and the Sella Ronda circuit.

Colle di Tenda Italy
Dour, modern resort that shares a good area with much nicer Limone. Not far from Nice.
1400m; slopes 1120–2040m
🚡 33 🚠 80km

Colle Isarco Italy
Brenner Pass area – and the bargain-shopping town of Vipiteno is nearby.
1095m; slopes 1095–2720m
🚡 5 🚠 15km

Collio Italy
Tiny area of short runs in a remote spot between lakes Garda and d'Iseo.
840m; slopes 840–1715m 🚡 14

Les Collons 541
A collection of chalets below Thyon 2000 in the Verbier area.

Combelouvière France
Quiet hamlet tucked away in the trees at the foot of Valmorel's slopes, linked by easy pistes and a series of draglifts.
1250m
🏂 Lagrange

Combloux 315
Quiet, unspoiled alternative to linked Megève.

Les Contamines 285
Copper Mountain 602
Le Corbier 383
Corno alle Scale Italy
Small resort in the Emilia Romagna region of the Apennines.
1355m; slopes 1355–1945m
🚡 9 🚠 36km

Coronet Peak 725
Closest area to Queenstown (20 minutes).

Corrençon-en-Vercors France
Charming, rustic village at foot of Villard-de-Lans ski area. Good cross-country, too.
1160m; slopes 1160–2170m
🚡 25 🚠 130km

Cortina d'Ampezzo 436
Corvara 463
Lively village with lots of facilities at the junction of the Alta Badia and the Sella Ronda circuit.

Courchevel 287
Courmayeur 441
Cranmore USA
Area in New Hampshire with attractive town/resort of North Conway. Easy skiing. Good for families.
150m; slopes 150–515m
🚡 9 🚠 190 acres

Crans-Montana 502
Crested Butte USA
Crested Butte has one of the cutest old Wild West towns in Colorado, and the steep, gnarly terrain enjoys cult status among experts. It's a small area, but it packs in an astonishing mixture of perfect beginner slopes, easy cruising runs and expert terrain. Snowfall is modest by Colorado standards, but for those who like steep, ungroomed terrain, if the snow is good, it's idyllic. You can stay there or at the mountain, a couple of miles away, with its modern resort 'village'.
2860m; slopes 2775–3620m
🚡 16 🚠 1165 acres
🏂 AmeriCan Ski, American Ski Classics, Crystal, Ski Dream, Ski Safari, United Vacations

Crest-Voland France
Attractive, unspoiled traditional village near Megève and Le Grand Bornand with wonderfully uncrowded intermediate slopes linked to Les Saises and beyond to Praz sur Arly, as part of the new Espace Diamant region.
1035m; slopes 1230–2070m
⛷ 84 ⛷ 175km

Crissolo Italy
Small, remote day-tripper area, south-west of Turin. Part of the Monviso ski area.
1320m; slopes 1745–2340m
⛷ 4 ⛷ 20km

La Croix-Fry **283**
Couple of hotels on the pass close to La Clusaz.

Les Crosets **500**
Isolated mini-resort above Champéry, on the Portes du Soleil circuit.

Crystal Mountain USA
Area in glorious Mt Rainier National Park, near Seattle. Good, varied area given good snow/weather, but it's often wet. Lively at weekends. New fast quad for 2007/08.
1340m; slopes 1340–2135m
⛷ 9 ⛷ 2300 acres

Cuchara Valley USA
Quiet little family resort in southern Colorado, some way from any other ski area.
2800m; slopes 2800–3285m
⛷ 4 ⛷ 250 acres

Cutigliano Italy
Sizeable village near Abetone in the Appennines. Less than two hours from Florence and Pisa.
1125m; slopes 1125–1850m
⛷ 9 ⛷ 13km

Cypress Mountain Canada
Vancouver's most challenging area, 20 minutes from the city and with 40% for experts. Good snowfall record but rain is a problem.
920m; slopes 910–1445m ⛷ 5

Daemyeong Vivaldi Resort
South Korea
One of the less ugly Korean resorts, 75km/47 miles from Seoul. ⛷ 10

La Daille **403**
Ugly apartment complex at the entrance to Val d'Isère, with lifts into the Bellevarde slopes.

Daisen Japan
Western Honshu's main area, four hours from Osaka.
800m; slopes 740–1120m ⛷ 21

Damüls **134**
Scattered but attractive village in Bregenzerwald area close to the German and Swiss borders.

Davos **504**

Deer Mountain USA
South Dakota area close to 'Old West' town Deadwood and Mount Rushmore.
1825m; slopes 1825–2085m
⛷ 4 ⛷ 370 acres

Deer Valley **629**

Les Deux-Alpes **298**

Les Diablerets Switzerland
Unspoiled but spread-out village towered over by the Diablerets massif, with two areas of local slopes, plus Glacier 3000. A high-speed quad followed by a slow chair lead up to the red runs of the Meilleret area and the link to Villars. A gondola in the centre of town takes you to Isenau, a mix of blues and reds served by draglifts. From Isenau there's a red run down to Col du Pillon and the cable car to and from the glacier. On Glacier 3000, you'll find blue runs above 3000m/9,840ft, stunning views and the long, black Combe d'Audon – a wonderful, usually quiet, run away from all the lifts with sheer cliffs rising up on both sides. Snow reliability away from the glacier is not great – especially on sunny Isenau.
1150m; slopes 1115–3000m
⛷ 46 ⛷ 125km
📧 Alpine Answers, Crystal, Independent Ski Links, Interhome, Lagrange, Momentum, Solo's, Switzerland Travel Centre

Diamond Peak USA
Quiet, pleasant, intermediate area on Lake Tahoe, with lodging in Incline Village five minutes' drive away. Its narrow area consists of a long ridge served by one fast chair; there are great lake views from the run along the ridge and from the terrace of Snowflake Lodge. There are black runs off the ridge, but nothing seriously steep.
2040m; slopes 2040–2600m
⛷ 6 ⛷ 655 acres

Dienten **146**
Quiet village at the heart of the Hochkönig area.

Dinner Plain Australia
Attractive resort best known for cross-country skiing. Shuttle to Mt Hotham for Alpine runs. Four hours from Melbourne.
1520m; slopes 1490–1520m

Discovery Ski Area USA
Pleasant area miles from anywhere except Butte, Montana, with largely intermediate slopes but double-black runs on the back of the mountain – and the chance of seriously good snow. Usually deserted. Fairmont Hot Springs (two

huge thermal pools) are nearby. There are plans to extend the ski area on south-eastern side, including a new connecting road from Philipsburg.
1975m; slopes 1975–2485m
⛷ 6 ⛷ 614 acres

Disentis Switzerland
Unspoiled old village in a pretty setting on the Glacier Express rail route near Andermatt. Scenic area with long runs. Cable car upgraded for 2007/08.
1135m; slopes 1150–2830m
⛷ 9 ⛷ 60km
📧 Interhome, Switzerland Travel Centre

Dobbiaco Italy
Small resort in the South Tyrol. Toblach is its German name.
1250m; slopes 1250–1610m
⛷ 5 ⛷ 15km
📧 Headwater, Ramblers, Waymark

Dodge Ridge USA
Novice/leisurely intermediate area north of Yosemite. The pass from Reno is closed in winter, preventing crowds.
2010m; slopes 2010–2500m
⛷ 12 ⛷ 815 acres

Dolonne **441**
Quiet suburb of Courmayeur.

Donnersbachwald Austria
Small area in the Dachstein-Tauern region
950m; slopes 950–1990m
⛷ 4 ⛷ 25km

Donner Ski Ranch USA
One of California's first ski resorts, still family owned and operated.
2140m; slopes 2140–2370m
⛷ 6 ⛷ 460 acres

Dorfgastein **128**
Quieter, friendlier alternative to Bad Gastein.

Dundret Sweden
Lapland area 100km/62 miles north of the Arctic Circle with floodlit slopes open through winter when the sun barely rises.
slopes 475–825m
⛷ 7 ⛷ 15km

Durango Mountain ResortUSA
This is not a resort you would cross the Atlantic to visit – it's a small area even by US standards, and won't amuse most non-beginners for more than a day or two. Directly above the resort is a steepish slope with a slow double chair off to the right serving gentle green runs. All link to the shady mountainside that forms the main part of the area, served by a row of three chairs with a vertical of not much over 350m/1,150ft. Snowcat skiing is said to operate from the top. The heart of the resort is Purgatory Village, a modern,

purpose-built affair. Evening options in the 'village' are extremely limited. The city of Durango has a historic district and is worth a look.
2680m; slopes 2680–3300m
⛷ 11 ⛷ 1200 acres
📧 AmeriCan Ski

Eaglecrest USA
Close to famous Yukon gold rush town Skagway. Family resort famous for its ski school.
365m; slopes 365–790m
⛷ 3 ⛷ 640 acres

Eben im Pongau Austria
Part of Salzburger Sportwelt Amadé area that includes nearby St Johann, Wagrain, Flachau and Zauchensee. Village spoiled by the autobahn passing through it.
855m; slopes 855–2185m
⛷ 100 ⛷ 350km

Ehrwald **236**
Friendly, relaxed, pretty village with several nicely varied areas, notably the Zugspitz glacier. Poor bus services, so a car is desirable.

El Colorado/Farellones **730**
Area connected to the Valle Nevado ski area.

Eldora Mountain USA
Day-visitor resort with varied terrain (including plenty of steep stuff) close to Denver Boulder (45 minutes by regular scheduled bus). All forest trails, but with some good glade areas. Crowded at weekends, and all the chairs are slow.
2795m; slopes 2805–3230m
⛷ 12 ⛷ 680 acres

Elk Meadows USA
Area south of Salt Lake City, more than a day trip from Park City.
2775m; slopes 2745–3170m
⛷ 6 ⛷ 1400 acres

Ellmau **137**

Elm Switzerland
One hour from Zürich, at the head of a quiet, isolated valley. Good choice of runs including a long black to the valley.
1000m; slopes 1000–2105m
⛷ 6 ⛷ 40km

Encamp **108**

Enego Italy
Limited weekend day-trippers' area near Vicenza and Trento.
1300m; slopes 1300–1445m
⛷ 7 ⛷ 30km

Engelberg **511**

Entrèves **441**
Hotels at the base of the lift up to Courmayeur's slopes.

Escaldes Andorra
Central valley town, effectively part of Andorra la Vella.

Etna Italy
Scenic, uncrowded, short-season area on the volcano's flank, 20 minutes from Nickolossi.
1800m; slopes 1800–2350m
⛷ *5km*

Evolène Switzerland
Charming rustic village with own little area in unspoiled, attractive setting south of Sion. Area lift pass gives access to the 4 Valleys.
1370m; slopes 1405–2680m
⛡ *7 ⛷ 42km*

Faak am See Austria
Limited area, one of five overlooking town of Villach.
560m; slopes 560–800m
⛡ *1 ⛷ 2km*

Fai della Paganella 481
Trentino village that shares its slopes with Andalo.

Fairmont Hot Springs Canada
Major luxury spa complex ideal for a relaxing holiday with some gentle skiing thrown in.
⛡ *2 ⛷ 60 acres*

Faistenau Austria
Cross-country area close to Salzburg and St Wolfgang. Limited Alpine slopes.
785m; slopes 785–1000m
⛡ *5 ⛷ 3km*

Falcade 481
Trentino village south of the Sella Ronda.

Falera 519
Small village with access to ski area shared by Flims and Laax.

Le Falgoux France
One of the most beautiful old villages in France, set in the very scenic Volcano National Park. Several ski areas nearby.
930m; slopes 930–1350m

Falkertsee Austria
Base area rather than a village, with bleak, open slopes in contrast to nearby Bad Kleinkirchheim.
1690m; slopes 1690–2385m
⛡ *5 ⛷ 15km*

Falls Creek 720

La Feclaz France
One of several little resorts in the remote Parc des Bauges. Popular cross-country ski base.
1165m

Fernie 669

Fieberbrunn Austria
Atmospheric and friendly Tirolean village, sprawling along the valley road for 2km/1 mile, but mostly set back from the road and railway. Its small but attractive area of wooded slopes is a bus ride away. One sector consists mainly of blue runs, the other mainly of easy reds, all mostly below the treeline. Across a valley are separate

lifts going up to the high point of 2020m/6,630ft on Hochhörndl. The addition of a big gondola extended the slopes down to a new valley station and so opened up an off-piste area. The resort is boarder-friendly, hosting major competitions in its terrain park. Accommodation in the village is in hotels, and there is also accommodation at the lift station.
800m; slopes 835–2020m
⛡ *11 ⛷ 35m*
🚠 *First Choice, Snowscape, Thomson*

Fiesch Switzerland
Traditional Rhône valley resort close to Brig, with a lift up to Fiescheralp (2220m/7,280ft) at one end of the beautiful Aletsch area extending across the mountainside via Bettmeralp to Riederalp.
1050m; slopes 1900–2900m
⛡ *36 ⛷ 100km*

Fiescheralp Switzerland
Mountain outpost of Fiesch, down in the Rhône valley. At one end of the beautiful Aletsch area.
2220m; slopes 1900–2870m
⛡ *36 ⛷ 99km*

Filzmoos Austria
Charming, unspoiled, friendly village with leisurely slopes that are ideal for novices. Good snow record for its height. 'Quiet pistes', 'superb piste preparation' and 'splendid nursery slopes', say reporters.
1055m; slopes 1055–1645m
⛡ *12 ⛷ 32km*
🚠 *Inghams, Interhome*

Finkenberg 140
Village between Mayrhofen and Hintertux, linked to the first but not the second.

Fiss Austria
Nicely compact, quiet, traditional village sharing an extensive, sunny area with bigger Serfaus.
1435m; slopes 1200–2700m
⛡ *42 ⛷ 160km*
🚠 *Ardmore, Interhome*

Flachau Austria
Quiet, spacious village in a pretty setting at one end of an extensive three-valley lift network linking via Wagrain to Alpendorf. Flachauwinkl, up the valley, is at the centre of another similarly extensive and impressive lift system. All these resorts are covered by the Salzburger Sportwelt area.
925m; slopes 800–2185m
⛡ *64 ⛷ 200km*
🚠 *Interhome, Made to Measure*

Flachauwinkl Austria
Tiny ski station beside Tauern autobahn, at the centre of an extensive three-valley lift network linking Kleinarl to Zauchensee. Flachau, down the valley, is at one end of a similarly extensive lift system. All these resorts are covered by the Salzburger Sportwelt ski pass that our figures relate to.
930m; slopes 800–2185m
⛡ *64 ⛷ 200km*

Flaine 304

Flims 519
Long-established resort sharing a huge area with Laax.

Flumet France
Surprisingly large traditional village, the main place from which to ski the sizeable Val d'Arly ski area, now linked through to Les Saisies/ Crest Voland. Close to better-known Megève.
1000m; slopes 1000–2070m
⛡ *84 ⛷ 175km*

Flumserberg Switzerland
Collective name for the villages sharing a varied area an hour south-east of Zürich. Part of the wider Heidiland region. Mostly red and black runs, served by good network of fast lifts.
425m; slopes 1220–2220m
⛡ *16 ⛷ 65km*

Folgaria 481
Largest of several resorts east of Trento. Old lift system.

Folgarida 481
Small Trentino village, with links to Madonna di Campiglio.

Foncine-le-Haut France
Major cross-country village in the Jura Mountains with extensive trails.
🚠 *Lagrange*

Fonni Gennaragentu Italy
Sardinia's only 'ski area' – and it's tiny.
⛡ *1 ⛷ 5km*

Font-Romeu 423

Foppolo Italy
Relatively unattractive but user-friendly village, a short transfer from Bergamo.
1510m; slopes 1610–2160m
⛡ *9 ⛷ 47km*

Forca Canapine Italy
Limited area near the Adriatic and Ascoli Piceno. Popular with weekend day-trippers.
1450m; slopes 1450–1690m
⛡ *11 ⛷ 20km*

Formazza Italy
Cross-country base with some downhill slopes.
1280m; slopes 1275–1755m
⛷ *8km*

Formigal 700

Formigueres France
Small downhill and cross-country area in the Neiges Catalanes. There are 110km cross-country trails.
slopes 1700–2350m
⛡ *8 ⛷ 19km*
🚠 *Chalet Group, Pyrenees Ski Experience*

Le Fornet 403
Rustic old hamlet 3km/2 miles up the valley from Val d'Isère, with cable car up to the Col de l'Iseran slopes.

Forstau Austria
Secluded hamlet above Radstadt–Schladming road. Very limited area with old lifts, but nice and quiet.
930m; slopes 930–1885m
⛡ *7 ⛷ 14km*

La Foux-d'Allos France
Purpose-built resort that shares a good intermediate area with Pra-Loup.
1800m; slopes 1800–2600m
⛡ *52 ⛷ 190km*

Frabosa Soprana Italy
One of numerous little areas south of Turin, well placed for combining winter sports with Riviera sightseeing.
850m; slopes 860–1740m
⛡ *7 ⛷ 40km*

Frisco 597
Small town down the valley from Breckenridge.

Frontignano Italy
Best lift system in the Macerata region, near the Adriatic Riviera.
1340m; slopes 1340–2000m
⛡ *8 ⛷ 10km*

Fucine 481

Fügen Austria
Unspoiled Zillertal village with road up to satellite Hochfügen – part of fair-sized Ski Optimal area, along with Kaltenbach.
550m
🚠 *Interhome, Lagrange, Ski Wild*

Fulpmes 223

Furano 718

Fusch Austria
Cheaper, quiet place to stay when visiting Zell am See. Across a golf course from Kaprun and Schuttdorf.
805m; slopes 805–1050m

Fuschl am See Austria
Attractive, unspoiled, lakeside village close to St Wolfgang and Salzburg, 30 minutes from its slopes. Best suited to part-time skiers who want to sightsee as well.
670m

Gåla Norway
Base for downhill and cross-country skiing, an hour's drive north of Lillehammer.
930m; slopes 830–1150m
⛡ *7 ⛷ 20km* 🚠 *Inntravel*

Gallio Italy
One of several low resorts near Vicenza and Trento. Popular with weekend day-trippers.
1100m; slopes 1100–1550m
⛷ 11 🚡 50km

Galtür 153
Charming village near Ischgl.

Gambarie d'Aspromonte Italy
Italy's second most southerly ski area (after Mt Etna). On the 'toe' of the Italian 'boot' near Reggio di Calabria.
1310m; slopes 1310–1650m ⛷ 3

Gantschier Austria
No slopes of its own but particularly well placed for visiting all the Montafon areas.
700m

Gargellen 181
Quiet village tucked up a side valley in the Montafon area.

Garmisch-Partenkirchen
Germany
Twin, classic old-fashioned winter sports resorts – unspoiled, traditional Partenkirchen is much the prettier. The ski areas are a bus ride away, and offer limited challenge for experts and adventurous intermediates (though the long Kandahar black downhill course is excellent). There are good beginners' areas.
720m; slopes 720–2830m
⛷ 38 🚡 71km
🚐 *Momentum, SnowTrex*

Gaschurn 181
Village in the Montafon area.

Gaustablikk Norway
Small snow-sure Alpine area on Mt Gausta in southern Norway with plenty of cross-country. 🚡 15km

Gavarnie France
Traditional village and fair-sized ski area, with the longest green run in the Pyrenees. Grand views of the Cirque de Gavarnie.
1400m; slopes 1850–2400m
⛷ 11 🚡 45km

Geilo 705

Gérardmer France
Sizeable lakeside resort in the northerly Vosges mountains near Strasbourg, with plenty of amenities. Limited downhill slopes nearby include one of almost 4km/2.5 miles. Extensive ski de fond trails in the area.
665m; slopes 750–1150m
⛷ 20 🚡 40km
🚐 *Lagrange*

Gerlitzen 120

Gerlos 176
Inexpensive but fairly snow-sure resort east of the Zillertal, and linked to Zell and Königsleiten.

Gerlosplatte Austria
Inexpensive but fairly snow-sure area above the village of Krimml, linked to Königsleiten, Gerlos and Zell am Ziller to form a fair-sized intermediate area. 'Good runs, if unchallenging' was the verdict of one 2006 visitor.

Les Gets 311

La Giettaz 315
Tiny village between La Clusaz and Megève.

Gitschtal/Weissbriach Austria
One of many little areas near Hermagor in eastern Austria, close to Italian border.
690m; slopes 690–1400m
⛷ 4 🚡 5km

Glaris Switzerland
Hamlet base station for the uncrowded Rinerhorn section of the Davos slopes.
1455m; slopes 1455–2490m
⛷ 5 🚡 30km

Glencoe 717

Glenshee 717

Going 137
Tiny, attractively rustic village with small local ski area near Ellmau and linked to the huge SkiWelt area.

Goldegg Austria
Year-round resort famous for its lakeside castle. Limited slopes but Wagrain (Salzburger Sportwelt) and Grossarl (Gastein valley) are nearby.
825m; slopes 825–1250m
⛷ 4 🚡 12km

Golden Canada
Small logging town, the place to stay when visiting Kicking Horse resort 15 minutes away. Also the launch pad for Purcell heli-skiing.

Golte Slovenia
Ski area in the East Karavante mountains, above Mozirje. Gondola to the slopes from Zekovec village. Mostly advanced runs.
⛷ 7 🚡 18km

Gore Mountain USA
One of the better areas in New York State. Near Lake Placid, sufficiently far north to avoid worst weekend crowds. Intermediate terrain.
455m; slopes 455–1095m
⛷ 9 🚡 290 acres

Göriach Austria
Hamlet with trail connecting into one of the longest, most snow-sure cross-country networks in Europe.
1250m

Gortipohl Austria
Traditional village in pretty Montafontal.
920m; slopes 900–2395m
⛷ 62 🚡 209km

Gosau Austria
Family-friendly resort, with straggling village. Plenty of pretty, if low, runs. Fast lifts mean queues are rare. Snow-sure Obertauern and Schladming are within reach.
755m; slopes 755–1800m
⛷ 37 🚡 80km

Göstling Austria
One of Austria's easternmost resorts, between Salzburg and Vienna. A traditional village in wooded setting.
530m; slopes 530–1880m
⛷ 12 🚡 19km

Götzens Austria
Valley village base for Axamer Lizum slopes.
870m ⛷ 1

Gourette-Eaux-Bonnes France
Most snow-sure resort in the French Pyrenees. Very popular with local families, so best avoided at weekends. Recently revamped lifts and slopes.
1400m; slopes 1400–2400m
⛷ 15 🚡 30km

Grächen Switzerland
Charming chalet-village reached by tricky access road off the approach to Zermatt. A small area of open slopes, mainly above the trees and of red-run difficulty, reached by two gondolas – one to Hannigalp (2115m/6,940ft), the main focus of activity with a very impressive children's nursery area. The village has almost a score of hotels, mostly 3-star; most of the accommodation is in chalets and apartments. The sports centre offers tennis and badminton, as well as a natural ice-rink.
1615m; slopes 1615–2865m
⛷ 13 🚡 40km
🚐 *Interhome*

Le Grand-Bornand France
Covered by the Aravis lift pass, and much smaller and even more charming than La Clusaz. The slopes can be accessed from either the outskirts of the village or from the satellite village of Le Chinaillon. There are worthwhile shady black runs on Le Lachat, and on the lower peak of La Floria. There are plenty of good cruising blue and red intermediate runs, and also good beginner slopes. There are extensive cross-country trails in the Vallée du Bouchet and towards Le Chinaillon.
1000m; slopes 1000–2100m
⛷ 37 🚡 90km
🚐 *AmeriCan Ski, Erna Low, Karibuni, Lagrange, Last Resort, Peak Retreats, Ski France, Skiholidayextras.com, Thomson*

Grand Hirafu 718
One of the three interlinked ski areas of Niseko.

Grand Targhee 638
🚐 *AmeriCan Ski, Ski Safari*

Les Granges 255
Hamlet at the mid-station of the funicular up from Bourg.

Grangesises Italy
Small satellite of Sestriere, with lifts up to the main slopes.

Granite Peak USA
One of the oldest areas in the Great Lakes region, and now one of the largest. New base village. Good selection of black runs on the upper mountain.
⛷ 7 🚡 400 acres

Grau Roig 113
Mini-resort between Pas de la Casa and Soldeu.

La Grave 313

Great Divide USA
Area near Helena, Montana, best for experts. Mostly bowls; plus near-extreme Rawhide Gulch.
1765m; slopes 1765–2195m
⛷ 6 🚡 720 acres

Gresse-en-Vercors France
Resort south of Grenoble. Sheltered slopes worth noting for bad-weather days.
1250m; slopes 1600–1750m
⛷ 13 🚡 18km
🚐 *Interhome*

Gressoney-la-Trinité 452
Villages in the Monterosa Ski area.

Gressoney-St-Jean 452
Village in the Monterosa Ski area.

Grimentz 537

Grindelwald 513

Grossarl 128
Secluded village linked to Dorfgastein in the Gastein valley.

Grossglockner area 120

Grosskirchheim Austria
Very limited area near Heiligenblut.
1025m; slopes 1025–1400m

Grouse Mountain Canada
The Vancouver area with the largest lift capacity. Superb city views from mostly easy slopes; night skiing.
880m; slopes 880–1245m
⛷ 11 🚡 120 acres
🚐 *AmeriCan Ski, Ski Dream*

Grünau Austria
Spacious riverside village in a lovely lake-filled part of eastern Austria. Nicely varied area, but very low.
525m; slopes 600–1600m
⛷ 14 🚡 40km

Gryon 553
Village below Villars.

Gstaad Switzerland
Despite its exclusive reputation, Gstaad is an attractive, traditional village where anyone could have a relaxing holiday. There are

four sectors, covered by a single, confusing map. The largest sector is above Saanenmöser and Schönried, reached by train. Snow-cover can be unreliable except on the Glacier des Diablerets, 15km/9 miles away. Few runs challenge experts. Black runs rarely exceed red or even blue difficulty. There is off-piste potential. Given good snow, this is a superb area for intermediates, with long, easy descents in the major area. The nursery slopes at Wispile are adequate, and there are plenty of runs to progress to. Time lost on buses or trains is more of a problem than queues.
1050m; slopes 950–3000m
⛷ 62 ⛷ 250km
🚌 *Alpine Answers, Interhome, Made to Measure, Momentum, Oxford Ski Co, Ski Weekend, Switzerland Travel Centre, White Roc*

Gunstock USA
One of the New Hampshire resorts closest to Boston, popular with families. Primarily easy slopes. Gorgeous Lake Winnisquam views.
275m; slopes 275–700m
⛷ 8 ⛷ 220 acres

Guthega 720

Guzet France
A charming cluster of chalets set among a pine forest at Guzet 1400. Three main sectors offer slopes for all levels.
1400m; slopes 1100–2100m
⛷ 14 ⛷ 40km

Hafjell Norway
Main ski area for Lillehammer.
⛷ 12 ⛷ 33km

Haider Alm Italy
Area in the Val Venosta in the South Tyrol close to Nauders.

Haideralm Italy
Small area in Val Venosta, close to Austrian border. Malda Haider is its Italian name.
⛷ 5 ⛷ 20km

Hakuba Happo One 718
European-style resort four hours from Tokyo.

Harper Mountain Canada
Small, family-friendly resort in Kamloops, British Colombia.
1100m; slopes 1100–1525m
⛷ 3 ⛷ 400 acres

Harrachov Czech Republic
Closest resort to Prague, with enough terrain to justify a day trip. No beginner area.
650m; slopes 650–1020m
⛷ 4 ⛷ 8 runs

Hasliberg Switzerland
Four rustic hamlets on a sunny plateau overlooking Meiringen and Lake Brienz. Two of them are the bottom stations of a varied intermediate area.
1050m

Haukelifjell Norway

Haus 198
Village next to Schladming.

Haystack USA
Minor satellite of Mount Snow, in Vermont, but with a bit more steep skiing.
580m; slopes 580–1095m
⛷ 26 ⛷ 540 acres

Heavenly 575

Hebalm Austria
One of many small areas in Austria's easternmost ski region near Slovenian border. No major resorts in vicinity.
1350m; slopes 1350–1400m
⛷ 6 ⛷ 11km

Heiligenblut 120

Heiterwang 236

Hemlock Resort Canada
Area 55 miles east of Vancouver towards Sun Peaks. Mostly intermediate terrain and with snowfall of 600 inches a year. Lodging is available at the base area.
1000m; slopes 1000–1375m
⛷ 4 ⛷ 350 acres

Hemsedal 707

Heremence Switzerland
Quiet, traditional village in unspoiled attractive setting south of Sion. Verbier's slopes are accessed a few minutes' drive away at Les Masses.
1250m

Hermagor Austria
Main village base for the Nassfeld ski area in Carinthia.
600m; slopes 610–2000m
⛷ 30 ⛷ 100km

Higashiyama 718
One of the three interlinked ski areas of Niseko.

Hintermoos 146
Village in the Hochkönig area.

Hintersee Austria
Easy slopes very close to Salzburg. Several long top-to-bottom runs and lifts means the size of the area is greatly reduced if the snowline is high.
745m; slopes 750–1470m
⛷ 9 ⛷ 40km

Hinterstoder Austria
A very quiet valley village – neat but not overtly charming – spread along the road up the dead-end Stodertal in Upper Austria. The local Höss slopes are pleasantly wooded, less densely at the top, with splendid views. It's a small area, but has a worthwhile vertical of 1250m/4,100ft, and 450m/1,475ft above mid-mountain. A gondola from the

main street goes up to the flat-bottomed bowl of Huttererböden (1400m/4,600ft), where there are very gentle but limited nursery slopes and lifts up to higher points. Most of the mountain is of easy red steepness. The run to the valley is a pleasant red with one or two tricky bits where it takes a quick plunge; it has effective snowmaking.
600m; slopes 600–1860m
⛷ 10 ⛷ 35km

Hinterthal 146
Village in the Hochkönig area.

Hintertux/Tux valley 140

Hippach 176
Hamlet near a crowd-free lift into Mayrhofen's main area.

Hittisau 134

Hochfügen Austria
High-altitude ski-station outpost of Fügen, part of Ski Optimal area linked with Kaltenbach. Best suited to intermediates.
1500m; slopes 560–2500m
⛷ 35 ⛷ 155km

Hochgurgl 184
Quiet village with connection to Obergurgl's slopes.

Hochkönig 146

Hochpillberg Austria
Peaceful, virtually traffic-free hamlet with fabulous views towards Innsbruck and an antique chairlift into varied terrain above Schwaz with good vertical of 1000m/3,280ft. Wonderfully safe for children; all accommodation within two minutes of lift.
1300m; slopes 1300–2100m
⛷ 5 ⛷ 14km

Hochsölden 202
Satellite above Sölden.

Hoch-Ybrig Switzerland
Purpose-built complex only 64km/40 miles south-east of Zürich, with facilities for families.
1050m; slopes 1050–1830m
⛷ 10 ⛷ 40km

Hohuanshan Taiwan
Limited ski area with short season in high, wild, inaccessible Miitaku mountains. Also known as Mt Hehuan.
3275m ⛷ 1

Holiday Valley USA
Family resort in New York State, an hour's drive south-east of Buffalo.
slopes 485–685m
⛷ 12 ⛷ 270 acres

Hollersbach Austria
Hamlet near Mittersill, over Pass Thurn from Kitzbühel, which has a gondola up to the Resterhöhe above Pass Thurn.
805m; slopes 805–1000m
⛷ 2 ⛷ 5km

Homewood USA
Uncrowded area near Tahoe City with the most sheltered slopes in the vicinity. All the slopes are served by slow chairlifts, and the views are as much of an attraction as the slopes. Set right on the western shore of the lake, so access is quick and easy. The notably quiet slopes include plenty of short black pitches as well as cruisers.
1900m; slopes 1900–2400m
⛷ 7 ⛷ 1260 acres

Hoodoo Ski Bowl USA
Typical Oregon area with sizeable but short runs. Snow record isn't as good as its competitors near Portland.
1420m; slopes 1420–1740m
⛷ 5 ⛷ 800 acres

Hopfgarten 205
Small chalet village with lift link into the Ski Welt area.

Horseshoe Resort Canada
Toronto region resort with high-capacity lift system and 100% snowmaking. The second mountain – The Heights – is open to members only.
310m; slopes 310–405m
⛷ 7 ⛷ 60 acres

Hospental 495
Small village connected to Andermatt by road and rail.

Les Houches 268
Varied, tree-lined area at the entrance to the Chamonix valley.

Hovden Norway
Big, modern luxury lakeside hotel in wilderness midway between Oslo and Bergen. Cross-country venue with some Alpine slopes.
820m; slopes 820–1175m
⛷ 5 ⛷ 14km

La Hoya Argentina
Small uncrowded resort 15km/9 miles from the small town of Esquel.
slopes 1350–2150m
⛷ 9 ⛷ 22km

Huez 245
Charming old hamlet on the road up to Alpe-d'Huez.

Hunter Mountain USA
Popular New Yorkers' area so it gets very crowded at weekends.
485m; slopes 485–975m
⛷ 14 ⛷ 230 acres
🚌 *Ski Dream*

Hüttschlag Austria
Hamlet in a dead-end valley with lifts into the Gastein area at nearby Grossarl.
1020m; slopes 1020–1220m ⛷ 1

Hyundai Sungwoo Resort
South Korea
Modern high-rise resort,
140km/87 miles from Seoul.
Host to the 2009 World
Snowboard Championships.
Own English-language web
site at www.hdsungwoo.co.kr.
🛒 9

Idre Fjäll Sweden
Collective name for four areas
490km/305 miles north-west
of Stockholm.
slopes 590–890m
🛒 30 ⛷ 28km

Igls 149

Iizuna Japan
Tiny area 2.5 hours from
Tokyo.
slopes 1080–1480m 🛒 7

Incline Village USA
Large village on northern
edge of Lake Tahoe – it is a
reasonable stop-off if you are
touring.

Indianhead USA
South Lake Superior area with
the most snowfall in the
region. Winds are a problem.
395m; slopes 395–585m
🛒 12 ⛷ 195 acres

Inneralpbach 126
Small satellite of Alpbach.

Innerarosa 498
The prettiest part of Arosa.

Innichen Italy
Small resort in South Tyrol.
San Candido is its Italian
name.
1175m; slopes 1175–1580m
🛒 4 ⛷ 15km

Innsbruck 149

Interlaken Switzerland
Lakeside summer resort near
Wengen, Grindelwald and
Mürren. ✉ *Kuoni*

Ischgl 153

**Ishiuchi Maruyama-Gala-
Yuzawa Kogen** Japan
Three resorts with a shared
lift pass 90 minutes from
Tokyo by bullet train and
offering the largest ski area in
the central Honshu region.
255m; slopes 255–920m 🛒 52

Isola 2000 France
A small, high, purpose-built
family resort, a long way
south but Nice airport is only
90km/55 miles away. The
compact slopes are linked in
a horseshoe shape around the
resort and most runs are
above the treeline. Isola often
has snow when other French
resorts lack it, but at other
times it misses out. There are
excellent nursery slopes in the
heart of the resort.
Accommodation is largely self-
catering, much of it slope-
side. The après-ski scene is
muted, but trips to the Riviera
and Monte Carlo are easy.
2000m; slopes 1840–2610m
🛒 24 ⛷ 120km

✉ *Crystal, Erna Low,
Lagrange, Ski Collection, Ski
France, Ski Leisure Direction,
Ski Solutions, Skiholidayextras.
com*

Iso Syöte 703

Itter 205
Next to Söll.

Jackson USA
Classic New England village,
and a major cross-country
base. A lovely place from
which to ski New Hampshire's
Alpine areas.
✉ *Virgin Snow, White
Mountains*

Jackson Hole 644

Jasná Slovakia
Largest area in the Low Tatras
mountains, linked to Chopok,
which has an additional 11
lifts covering 11 km/7 miles.
slopes 1240–2005m
🛒 14 ⛷ 21km

Jasper Canada
Set in the middle of Jasper
National Park, this low-key,
low-rise little town appeals
more to those keen on
scenery and wildlife (and
cross-country skiing) rather
than piste miles. A visit could
be combined with a stay in
Whistler, Banff or Lake Louise.
Snowfall is modest by North
American standards and there
is lots of steep terrain that
needs good snow to be fun.
Keen piste-bashers will cover
all the groomed runs in half a
day. There are excellent
nursery slopes. There are
300km/186 miles of cross-
country trails. Most
accommodation is out of town
or on the outskirts and the
local slopes are a 30-minute
drive. A 2007 visitor enthuses:
'Great skiing, no queues
anywhere and a lot of fun in
the gladed bowl.'
1065m; slopes 1065–2610m
🛒 9 ⛷ 1675 acres
✉ *All America Holidays,
AmeriCan Ski, Crystal, Elegant
Resorts, Frontier, Inghams,
Kuoni, Ski Dream, Ski
Independence, Ski Safari,
Skiworld, Trailfinders, Virgin
Snow*

Jay Peak USA
In northern Vermont, near the
Canadian border. Crowded at
weekends but quiet in the
week. Vermont's only cable
car takes you to the summit
and to views of four US states
plus Canada. The only fast
chair goes almost as high. It
gets a lot of snow (350 inches
on average) and has some
good runs for advanced skiers
and good intermediates –
notably 100+ acres of glades.
There's good beginner terrain,

and there are blue cruisers,
too, but they don't add up to
a lot. There is slope-side
accommodation, mainly in
condos.
550m; slopes 550–1205m
🛒 8 ⛷ 385 acres

Jochberg 160
Straggling village, 8km/5 miles
from Kitzbühel.

La Joue-du-Loup France
Slightly stylish little purpose-
built ski-in/ski-out family
resort a few km north-west of
Gap. Shares a fair-sized
intermediate area with
Superdévoluy.
1500m; slopes 1500–2510m
🛒 32 ⛷ 100km
✉ *Lagrange, Ski Collection*

Jouvenceaux 458
Less boisterous base from
which to ski Sauze d'Oulx's
terrain.

Jukkasjärvi Sweden
Centuries-old cross-country
resort with unique ice hotel
rebuilt every December.

June Mountain USA
Small area a half-hour drive
from Mammoth and in same
ownership. Empty slopes
except on peak weekends.
2300m; slopes 2300–3090m
🛒 8 ⛷ 500 acres

Juns 140
Small village between
Lanersbach and Hintertux.

Kals am Grossglockner
Austria
Village in a remote valley
north of Lienz.
1325m; slopes 1325–2305m
🛒 7 ⛷ 28km

Kaltenbach Austria
One of the larger, quieter
Zillertal areas, with plenty of
high-altitude slopes, mostly
above the treeline.
560m; slopes 560–2500m
🛒 35 ⛷ 155km

Kananaskis Canada
Small area near Calgary, nicely
set in woods, with slopes at
Nakiska and Fortress
Mountain.
slopes 1525–2465m
🛒 12 ⛷ 605 acres
✉ *Frontier*

Kandersteg Switzerland
Good cross-country base set
amid beautiful scenery near
Interlaken. Easy, but limited,
slopes. Popular with families.
1175m; slopes 1175–1900m
🛒 7 ⛷ 14km
✉ *Headwater, Inghams,
Inntravel, Kuoni, Switzerland
Travel Centre*

Kanin Slovenia
Small area near Bovec,
17km/11 miles from the Italian
border, with plans to link with
Sella Nevea. The slopes are
Slovenia's highest. A visitor
was impressed with the
quality of the area and

particularly enjoyed its
'massive' area of off-piste.
There are plans for a lift link
to the slopes of nearby Sella
Nevea in the next few years.
980m; slopes 1600–2300m
🛒 6 ⛷ 15km

Kappl 153
Small village down the valley
from Ischgl.

Kaprun 231
Village near Zell am See with
local slopes and convenient
access to Kitzsteinhorn glacier.

Les Karellis France
Resort with slopes that are
more scenic, challenging and
snow-sure than those of
better-known Valloire, nearby.
Six-pack has improved access.
'Great little place for a day
out,' says a reporter.
1600m; slopes 1600–2550m
🛒 17 ⛷ 60km

Kastelruth Italy
German name for Castelrotto.
✉ *Inntravel*

Kasurila Finland
Siilinjärvi ski area popular
with boarders. 🛒 5

Katschberg 120
✉ *Ardmore, Neilson*

Keystone 604

Kicking Horse 674

Killington 650

Kimberley Canada
This mining town turned twee
mock Austro-Bavarian/English
Tudor resort enjoys a beautiful
setting 2 hours from Banff.
The terrain offers a mix of
blue and black runs (plus the
occasional green) and a
vertical of 750m/2,460ft. In
addition to the lifts up the
front there are two other slow
chairs. The mainly forested
runs are spread over three
rather featureless hills. There
are only a few short double-
diamonds, but classification
tends to understate difficulty,
and many of the single
diamonds are quite
challenging. It has a
reputation for good powder,
although it doesn't get huge
amounts by the standards of
this region.
1230m; slopes 1230–1980m
🛒 5 ⛷ 1800 acres
✉ *AmeriCan Ski, Frontier,
Inghams, Ski Dream, Ski Safari*

Kirchberg 160
Lively town close to Kitzbühel.

Kirchdorf Austria
Attractive village a bus ride
from St Johann in Tirol.
640m
✉ *Snowcoach, Thomson*

Kirkwood USA
Kirkwood is renowned for its
powder, and has a lot to offer
experts and confident
intermediates, but it's limited
for intermediates who are not

happy to tackle black runs. It makes a great outing from South Lake Tahoe, though heavy snowfall may close the high-level passes to get there. Deep snow is often the attraction, often reportedly better than Heavenly.
2375m; slopes 2375–2985m
⛷ 12 🚡 2300 acres

Kitzbühel 160

Kleinarl Austria
Secluded traditional village up a pretty side valley from Wagrain, at one end of a three-valley lift network linking it via Flachauwinkl to Zauchensee – all part of the Salzburger Sportwelt ski pass area that our figures relate to.
1015m; slopes 800–2185m
⛷ 59 🚡 200km
📬 *Interhome*

Klippitztörl Austria
One of many little areas in Austria's easternmost ski region near Slovenian border. 'Great little area with pretty treelined runs,' says a 2007 visitor.
1550m; slopes 1460–1820m
⛷ 6 🚡 25km

Klösterle Austria
Valley village at the base of the Sonnenkopf ski area a few km west of the Arlberg pass – and covered by the Arlberg ski pass.
1100m; slopes 1100–2300m
⛷ 10 🚡 39km

Klosters 517

Kobla 716

Kolsass-Weer Austria
Pair of Inn-side villages with low, inconvenient and limited slopes.
555m; slopes 555–1010m
⛷ 3 🚡 14km

Königsleiten 176
Quiet, high resort sharing fairly snow-sure area with Gerlos, now also linked to Zell im Zillertal to form the fair-sized Zillertal Arena area.

Kopaonik Serbia
Modern, sympathetically designed family resort in a pretty setting.
1770m; slopes 1110–2015m
⛷ 23 🚡 60km
📬 *Balkan Holidays, BoardnLodge, Crystal, Thomson*

Koralpe Austria
Largest and steepest of many gentle little areas in Austria's easternmost ski region near the Slovenian border.
1550m; slopes 1550–2050m
⛷ 10 🚡 25km

Kössen Austria
Village near St Johann in Tirol with low, scattered and limited local slopes.
600m; slopes 600–1700m
⛷ 9 🚡 25km

Kötschach-Mauthen Austria
One of many little areas near Hermagor in eastern Austria, close to the Italian border.
710m; slopes 710–1300m
⛷ 4 🚡 7km

Kranjska Gora 716

Krimml Austria
Sunny area, high enough to have good snow usually. Shares regional pass with Wildkogel resorts (Neukirchen).
1075m; slopes 1640–2040m
⛷ 9 🚡 33km

Krispl-Gaissau Austria
Easy slopes very close to Salzburg. Several long top-to-bottom lifts mean the size of the area is greatly reduced if the snow line is high.
925m; slopes 750–1570m
⛷ 11 🚡 40km

Kronplatz Italy
Distinctive ski area in South Tyrol, with amazingly efficient lifts from Brunico and San Vigilio di Marebbe. Plan de Corones is its Italian name.
1200m; slopes 1200–2275m
⛷ 32 🚡 103km
📬 *Momentum, Neilson*

Krvavec Slovenia
Slopes spread across Kalska mountain. Lifts include a gondola.
1450m; slopes 1450–1970m
⛷ 10 🚡 35km

Kühtai 149

Kusatsu Kokusai Japan
Attractive spa village with hot springs, three hours from Tokyo.
slopes 1250–2170m ⛷ 13

Laax 519

Le Lac Blanc France
Mini-resort with recently installed first six-pack in the northerly Vosges mountains near Strasbourg. Extensive ski de fond trails.
830m; slopes 830–1235m
⛷ 9 🚡 14km

Laces Italy
Village in the Val Venosta in the South Tyrol covered by the Ortler Skiarena pass.

Lachtal Austria
Second largest ski resort in the Styrian region NE of Salzburg.
1600m; slopes 1600–2100m
⛷ 8 🚡 29km

Ladis Austria
Smaller alternative to Serfaus and Fiss, with lifts that connect into the same varied ski area.
1200m; slopes 1200–2540m
⛷ 42 🚡 160km
📬 *Ardmore*

Lagunillas Chile
83km/52 miles south-east of Santiago. 🚡 494 acres

Le Laisinant 403
Tiny hamlet a short bus ride up the valley from Val d'Isère, with a chairlift up to the Solaise and Le Fornet slopes.

Lake Louise 676

Lake Tahoe USA
Collection of 14 ski areas spectacularly set on California-Nevada border – Heavenly and Squaw Valley best known in Britain.
📬 *AmeriCan Ski, Independent Ski Links, Ski Activity, Skiworld, Supertravel, Virgin Snow*

Lamoura France
One of four villages that makes up the Les Rousses area in the Jura.
1120m; slopes 1120–1680m
⛷ 40 🚡 40km
📬 *Headwater*

Landeck-Zams Austria
Small ski area in the Tirol region
816m; slopes 816–2210m
⛷ 7 🚡 22km

Lanersbach 140
Attractive village near Hintertux.

Lans-en-Vercors France
Village close to Villard-de-Lans and 30km/19 miles from Grenoble. Highest slopes in the region; few snowmakers.
1020m; slopes 1400–1805m
⛷ 16 🚡 24km

Lanslebourg France
One of the villages that makes up Val Cenis.

Lanslevillard France
One of the villages that makes up Val Cenis.

Laturns-Gapfohl Austria
900m; slopes 900–1785m
⛷ 6 🚡 27km

Lauchernalp-Lötschental Switzerland
Small but tall slopes reached by cable car from Wiler in the secluded, picturesque dead-end Lötschental, north of Rhône valley. Glacier runs above 3000m.
1420m; slopes 1420–2700m
⛷ 7 🚡 33km

Lauterbrunnen 521
Valley town with rail connection up to Mürren.

Le Lavancher 268
Quiet village between Chamonix and Argentière.

Lavarone 481
One of several areas east of Trento.

Leadville USA
Old mining town full of historic buildings. Own easy area (Ski Cooper) plus snowcat operation. Picturesque inexpensive base for visiting Copper Mountain, Vail and Beaver Creek.

Lech 167

The Lecht 717

Lélex France
Family resort with pretty wooded slopes between Dijon and Geneva.
900m; slopes 900–1680m
⛷ 29 🚡 50km

Las Leñas 729

Lenggries-Brauneck Germany
Bavarian resort south of Munich.
680m; slopes 700–1700m
⛷ 21 🚡 34km

Lenk 493
Traditional village that shares a sizeable area of easy, pretty terrain with Adelboden and has its own separate slopes at Betelberg. A bus and cable car from Rothenbach connect with a fast chair towards Adelboden or there's a six-pack from Buhlberg (above Lenk).

Lenzerheide Switzerland
The senior partner with Valbella in an extensive area of intermediate slopes in a pretty setting around a lake, at a decent altitude. The slopes are on the two sides of the valley. The east-facing, morning-sun slopes are mainly fairly gentle. The west-facing slopes have more character, both in skiing and visual terms, including a run on the back of the dramatic peak of the Rothorn. There is considerable off-piste potential.
1470m; slopes 1230–2865m
⛷ 28 🚡 155km
📬 *Alpine Answers, Crystal Finest, Interhome, Made to Measure, Switzerland Travel Centre*

Leogang 191
Quiet village with link to Saalbach-Hinterglemm.

Lermoos 236
Focal resort of the Zugspitze area: a pleasant little village with a small area of shady intermediate slopes. New six-pack for 2006/07.

Lessach Austria
Hamlet with trail connecting into one of longest, most snow-sure cross-country networks in Europe.
1210m ⛷ 1

Leukerbad   Switzerland
Major spa resort of Roman origin, spectacularly set beneath towering cliffs, which are scaled by a cable car up to high-altitude cross-country trails. The downhill slopes are on the opposite side of the valley, mainly above the treeline, served by draglifts and of red gradient, though there are a couple of blacks including a World Cup downhill course, which descends from the high, open slopes into the woods. There is also a slightly separate wooded sector served by a couple of chairlifts. A new six-pack is due to replace three draglifts for 2008/09.
1410m; slopes 1410–2700m
⛷ 13 ⛸ 50km
🚡 *Kuoni, Made to Measure, Switzerland Travel Centre*

Leutasch   Austria
Traditional cross-country village with limited slopes but a pleasant day trip from nearby Seefeld or Innsbruck.
1130m; slopes 1130–1605m
⛷ 3 ⛸ 6km
🚡 *Headwater, Inntravel*

Levi   **703**

Leysin   Switzerland
This is a spread-out village, climbing up a wooded hillside. The lifts are to the east of the village and take you to a pretty mix of mainly red and blue runs. Itineraries from the top of Chaux de Mont provide the best options for experts, along with a heli-operation. There are nursery slopes at village level. The revolving Kuklos restaurant at La Berneuse has stunning views.
1250m; slopes 1300–2200m
⛷ 14 ⛸ 60km
🚡 *Crystal, Mountain Tracks, Switzerland Travel Centre*

Lienz   Austria
Pleasant town in pretty surroundings.
675m; slopes 730–2290m
⛷ 17 ⛸ 41km

Lillehammer   **705**

Limone   Italy
Pleasant old town not far from Turin, with a pretty area, but far from snow-sure.
1010m; slopes 1030–2050m
⛷ 25 ⛸ 80km

Lincoln   USA
Sprawling New Hampshire town from which to visit Loon mountain.
🚡 *White Mountains*

Lindvallen-Högfjället   Sweden
Two of the mountains that make up the four unlinked ski areas of Sälen.
800m; slopes 590–890m
⛷ 46 ⛸ 85km

Le Lioran   France
Auvergne village near Aurillac with a purpose-built satellite above. Spectacular volcanic scenery.
1160m; slopes 1160–1850m
⛷ 24 ⛸ 60km
🚡 *Lagrange*

Livigno   **446**

Lizzola   Italy
Small base development in remote region north of Bergamo. Several other little areas nearby.
1250m; slopes 1250–2070m
⛷ 9 ⛸ 30km

Loch Lomond   Canada
Steep, narrow, challenging slopes near Thunder Bay on the shores of Lake Superior. Candy Mountain is nearby.
215m; slopes 215–440m
⛷ 3 ⛸ 90 acres

Lofer   Austria
Quiet, traditional village in a pretty setting north of Saalbach with a small area of its own, and Waidring's relatively snow-sure Steinplatte nearby.
640m; slopes 640–1745m
⛷ 14 ⛸ 46km
🚡 *Ski Line, Ski Wild, Snowscape*

Longchamp   **414**
Purpose-built resort that shares slopes with Valmorel.

Loon Mountain   USA
Small, smart, modern resort just outside Lincoln, New Hampshire. Mostly intermediate runs.
290m; slopes 290–910m
⛷ 10 ⛸ 275 acres
🚡 *Directski.com, Ski McNeill, Virgin Snow*

Lost Trail   USA
Remote Montana area, open only Thursday to Sunday and holidays. Mostly intermediate slopes.
2005m; slopes 2005–2370m
⛷ 6 ⛸ 800 acres

Loveland   USA
Exceptionally high and snowy slopes right next to highway I70, just east of the Continental Divide, easily reached from other Colorado resorts, especially Keystone.
3230m; slopes 3230–3870m
⛷ 9 ⛸ 1365 acres

Luchon   France
Sizeable village with plenty of amenities, with gondola (eight minutes) to its ski area at purpose-built Superbagnères.
630m; slopes 1440–2260m
⛷ 16 ⛸ 35km
🚡 *Lagrange, Ski Leisure Direction*

Lurisia   Italy
Sizeable spa resort, a good base for visits to surrounding little ski areas and to Nice.
750m; slopes 800–1800m
⛷ 8 ⛸ 35km

Lutsen Mountains   USA
Largest ski area in between Vermont and Colorado, with panoramic views of Lake Superior. Four small linked hills with 95% snowmaking offer surprisingly good and extensive terrain, with something for everyone. Moose Mountain has the biggest vertical (250m/820ft), with cruisers or bumps top to bottom, great views of the lake, and backcountry glade runs. Small slope-side village. Good cross-country and snowshoeing nearby.
80m; slopes 80–335m
⛷ 9 ⛸ 1000 acres

Luz-Ardiden   France
Spa village below its ski area. Cauterets and Barèges nearby.
710m; slopes 1730–2450m
⛷ 15 ⛸ 60km

Macugnaga   Italy
A pair of quiet, pretty villages dramatically set at the head of a remote valley, over the mountains from Zermatt and Saas-Fee. Lifts run up to the foot of the Belvedere glacier. A chairlift rises very slowly from the village to Burky, in the middle of the small, woody area of gentle runs. There is an excellent nursery slope beside the village and a two-stage cable car going over sunny slopes to the Swiss border. There are good, varied red runs down the 1100m/3,610ft vertical of the top cable car. In the right conditions, off-piste possibilities from the cable car are considerable.
1325m; slopes 1325–2800m
⛷ 12 ⛸ 38km

Madesimo   Italy
Remote valley village, a mix of traditional buildings and piecemeal modern development, north of Bergamo, great for a weekend. From mid-mountain there are pleasant runs to the village, or you can cut across to the open slopes above Motta, equipped with fast quads. The top of the gondola serves the famous Canalone, a long, sweeping, easy black, but classed as off-piste. There is also an off-piste route to Fracisico.
1545m; slopes 1545–2880m
⛷ 12 ⛸ 60km
🚡 *Inghams, Italian Safaris*

Madonna di Campiglio   **450**

Mad River Glen   USA
Cult resort, co-operatively owned, with some tough ungroomed terrain, a few well-groomed intermediate trails and antique lifts. Snowboarding is banned.
485m; slopes 485–1110m
⛷ 4 ⛸ 115 acres

La Magdelaine   Italy
Close to Cervinia, and good on bad-weather days.
1645m; slopes 1645–1870m
⛷ 4 ⛸ 4km

Maishofen   Austria
Cheaper place to stay when visiting equidistant Saalbach and Zell am See.
765m

Malbun   Liechtenstein
Quaint user-friendly little family resort, 16km/10 miles from the capital, Vaduz. Limited slopes and short easy runs.
1600m; slopes 1595–2100m
⛷ 6 ⛸ 21km

Malcesine   Italy
Large summer resort on Lake Garda with a fair area of slopes, served by a revolving cable car.
1430m; slopes 1430–1830m
⛷ 8 ⛸ 12km

Malga Ciapela   Italy
Resort at the foot of the Marmolada glacier massif, with a link into the Sella Ronda. Cortina is nearby.
1445m; slopes 1445–3270m
⛷ 8 ⛸ 18km

Malga Haider   Italy
Small area in Val Venosta, close to Austrian border. Haideralm is its German name.
⛷ 5 ⛸ 20km

Mallnitz   **120**

Mammoth Mountain   **580**

Manigod   France
Small valley village, sharing quiet, wooded slopes with La Clusaz – over the Col de la Croix-Fry. 'Fantastic place to avoid the crowds,' says a visitor.
1100m ⛸ 132km

Marble Mountain   Canada
Tiny area in the Humber Valley on the island of Newfoundland, near the charming town of Corner Brook and Gros Morne National Park. Good snow record by east coast standards. Splendid base lodge, and some slope-side lodging. Blomidon Cat Skiing operates nearby.
85m; slopes 10–545m
⛷ 5 ⛸ 175 acres
🚡 *Frontier*

Les Marecottes   Switzerland
Small area near Martigny. Valid with the Valais Ski Card.
1100m; slopes 1775–2200m
⛷ 5 ⛸ 25km

Maria Alm   **146**
Charming village at one end of the Hochkönig area.

Mariapfarr Austria
Village at the heart of one of the longest, most snow-reliable cross-country networks in Europe. Sizeable Mauterndorf-St Michael Alpine area and Obertauern area are nearby.
1120m
⛷ 5 ⛷ *30km*

Mariazell Austria
Traditional Styria village with an impressive basilica. Limited slopes.
870m; slopes 870–1265m
⛷ 5 ⛷ *11km*

Maribor **716**

Marilleva **481**
Small Trentino resort linked with Madonna di Campiglio.

Le Markstein France
Long-standing small resort in the northerly Vosges mountains near Strasbourg, which has hosted World Cup slalom races. Extensive ski de fond trails.
slopes 770–1270m ⛷ 10

Masella Spain
Friendly Pyrenean village linked with slopes of La Molina to form the Alp 2500 area. Weekend crowds.
1600m; slopes 1600–2535m
⛷ 31 ⛷ *121km*

La Massana **108**

Les Masses **541**
A hamlet below Les Collons in Thyon sector of the Verbier ski area.

Le Massif **697**
✉ AmeriCan Ski, Frontier, Ski Dream, Ski Safari

Matrei in Osttirol Austria
Large market village south of Felbertauern tunnel. Mostly high slopes.
1000m; slopes 1000–2400m
⛷ 7 ⛷ *33km*

Maurienne Valley France
A great curving trench with over 20 winter resorts, ranging from pleasant old valley villages to convenience resorts purpose-built in the 1960s.

Mauterndorf Austria
Village near Obertauern with tremendous snow record.
1120m; slopes 1075–2360m
⛷ 10 ⛷ *35km*

Maverick Mountain USA
Montana resort with plenty of terrain accessed by few lifts. Cowboy Winter Games venue – rodeo one day, ski races the next.
2155m; slopes 2155–2800m
⛷ 2 ⛷ *500 acres*

Mayens de Riddes
Switzerland
Hamlet at the base of lifts on the back of Verbier's Savoleyres sector, more often referred to as La Tzoumaz.
1500m ✉ Interhome

Mayens-de-Sion Switzerland
Tranquil hamlet off the road up to Les Collons – part of the Verbier area. *1470m*

Mayrhofen **176**

Méaudre France
Small resort near Grenoble with good snowmaking to make up for its low altitude.
1000m; slopes 1000–1600m
⛷ 10 ⛷ *18km*

Megève **315**

Meiringen Switzerland
Varied terrain, a good outing from the nearby Jungfrau resorts or Interlaken. Particularly suitable for beginners. High-speed gondola to the slopes.
600m; slopes 600–2435m

Melchsee-Frutt Switzerland
Limited, but high and snow-sure bowl above a car-free village. Family-friendly.
1920m; slopes 1080–2255m
⛷ 11 ⛷ *32km*

Mellau **134**

Les Menuires **322**

Merano 2000 Italy
Small ski area just outside Merano, with main lift base at Falzeben above Avelengo/Hafling.
2000m; slopes 2000–2240m
⛷ 7 ⛷ *40km*

Méribel **325**

Métabief-Mont-d'Or France
Twin villages in the Jura region, not far from Geneva.
900m; slopes 880–1460m
⛷ 22 ⛷ *42km*

Methven **722**
Nearest town/accommodation to Mt Hutt.

Mieders **223**

Mijoux France
Pretty wooded slopes between Dijon and Geneva. Lélex nearby.
1000m; slopes 900–1680m
⛷ 29 ⛷ *50km*

Mission Ridge USA
Area in dry region that gets higher-quality snow than other Seattle resorts but less of it. Good intermediate slopes.
1390m; slopes 1390–2065m
⛷ 6 ⛷ *300 acres*

Misurina Italy
Tiny village near Cortina. A cheap alternative base.
1755m; slopes 1755–1900m
⛷ 4 ⛷ *13km*

Mittersill Austria
Valley-junction village south of Pass Thurn. A gondola runs from Hollersbach up to the Resterhöhe sector above Pass Thurn.
790m; slopes 1265–1895m
⛷ 15 ⛷ *25km*

Moena Italy
Large village between Cavalese and Sella Ronda resorts, ideally located for touring the Dolomites area.
1180m; slopes 1180–2515m
⛷ 24 ⛷ *35km*
✉ Interhome

La Molina **700**

Mölltal Glacier **120**

Molveno Italy
Lakeside village on edge of Dolomites, with a couple of lifts – but mostly used as a base to ski nearby Andalo.

Monarch USA
Wonderfully uncrowded area, a day trip from Crested Butte. Great powder. Good for all but experts.
3290m; slopes 3290–3645m
⛷ 5 ⛷ *800 acres*

Monesi Italy
Southernmost of the resorts south of Turin. Close to Monaco and Nice.
1310m; slopes 1310–2180m
⛷ 5 ⛷ *38km*

Le Monêtier **369**
Quiet little village with access to Serre-Chevalier's slopes.

La Mongie **423**

Montafon **181**

Montalbert **348**
Traditional village with direct access to the La Plagne network.

Mont Blanc Canada
Small locals' hill near Tremblant, with only 300m/980ft of vertical and no resemblance to the Franco-Italian item.
⛷ 7 ⛷ *36*

Montchavin **348**
Attractive village on the fringe of La Plagne.

Mont-de-Lans **298**
Low village near Les Deux-Alpes.

Le Mont-Dore France
Attractive traditional small town, the largest resort in the stunningly beautiful volcanic Auvergne region near Clermont-Ferrand.
1050m; slopes 1350–1850m
⛷ 18 ⛷ *42km*

Monte Bondone **481**
Trento's local hill.

Monte Campione Italy
Tiny purpose-built resort, spread thinly over four mountainsides. 80% snowmaking helps to offset the low altitude.
1100m; slopes 1200–2010m
⛷ 16 ⛷ *80km*

Monte Livata Italy
Closest resort to Rome, popular with weekenders.
1430m; slopes 1430–1750m
⛷ 8 ⛷ *8km*

Monte Piselli Italy
Tiny area with the highest slopes of the many little resorts east of Rome.
2100m; slopes 2100–2690m
⛷ 3 ⛷ *5km*

Monte Pora Italy
Tiny resort near Lake d'Iseo and Bergamo. Several other little areas nearby.
1350m; slopes 1350–1880m
⛷ 11 ⛷ *30km*

Monterosa Ski **452**

Mont Gabriel Canada
Montreal area with runs on four sides of the mountain, though the south-facing sides rarely open. Two short but renowned double-black-diamond bump runs. ⛷ 9

Montgenèvre **336**

Mont Glen Canada
Least crowded of the Montreal areas, so a good weekend choice.
680m; slopes 680–1035m
⛷ 4 ⛷ *110 acres*

Mont Grand Fonds Canada
Small area sufficiently far from Québec not to get overrun at weekends.
400m; slopes 400–735m ⛷ 4

Mont Habitant Canada
Very limited area in the Montreal region but with a good base lodge. ⛷ 3

Mont Olympia Canada
Small, two-mountain area near Montreal, one mostly novice terrain, the other best suited to experts. ⛷ 6

Mont Orford Canada
Cold, windswept lone peak (no resort), worth a trip from nearby Montreal on a fine day.
slopes 305–855m
⛷ 8 ⛷ *180 acres*

Mont-Ste-Anne **697**
✉ AmeriCan Ski, Frontier, Ski Dream, Ski Safari

Mont-St-Sauveur Canada
Perhaps the prettiest resort in Canada, popular with Montreal (60km/37 miles) day trippers and luxury condo owners.

Mont Sutton Canada
Varied area with some of the best glade skiing in eastern Canada, including some for novices. Quaint Sutton village nearby.
⛷ 9 ⛷ *175 acres*

Moonlight Basin **639**
Quiet area of slopes linked to Big Sky, Montana.

Morgins **500**
Chalet resort just on the Swiss side of the Portes du Soleil circuit.

Morillon France
Valley village with a gondola link up to its purpose-built satellite and the Flaine network.
700m ⛟ *Altitude, AmeriCan Ski, Chalet Group, Erna Low, Lagrange, Peak Retreats*

Morin Heights Canada
Area in the Montreal region with 100% snowmaking. Attractive base lodge. ⛟ 6

Morzine 340

Les Mosses Switzerland
Peaceful resort and area, best for a day trip from Villars or Les Diablerets. Mainly reds and blues served only by draglifts.
1500m; slopes 1500–2200m
⛟ *13* ⛟ *40km*

Mottaret 325
Purpose-built but reasonably attractive component of Méribel.

Mottarone Italy
Closest slopes to Lake Maggiore. No village – just a base area.
1200m; slopes 1200–1490m
⛟ *25km*

Les Moulins Switzerland
Village down the road from Château d'Oex with its own low area of slopes, part of the big Gstaad lift-pass area.
890m; slopes 890–3000m
⛟ *67* ⛟ *250km*

Mount Abram USA
Small, pretty, treelined area in Maine, renowned for its immaculately groomed easy runs.
295m; slopes 295–610m
⛟ *5* ⛟ *170 acres*

Mountain High USA
Best snowfall record and highest lift capacity in Los Angeles vicinity – plus 95% snowmaking. Mostly intermediate cruising.
2010m; slopes 2010–2500m
⛟ *12* ⛟ *220 acres*

Mount Ashland USA
Arty town in Oregon renowned for Shakespeare. Mountain includes glaciated bowl rimmed with steeps. Best for experts.
1935m; slopes 1935–2285m
⛟ *4* ⛟ *200 acres*

Mount Bachelor USA
Extinct volcano in Oregon offering deserted runs on every side served by many fast chairs. Gets a lot of rain. You have to stay in Bend, 40km/25 miles away.
1740m; slopes 1740–2765m
⛟ *13* ⛟ *3680 acres*
⛟ *AmeriCan Ski, Ski Dream*

Mount Baker USA
Almost on the coast near Seattle, yet one of the top resorts for snow (averages 600 inches a year). Plenty of challenging slopes. Known for spectacular avalanches.
1115m; slopes 1115–1540m
⛟ *9* ⛟ *1000 acres*

Mount Baldy Canada
Tiny area, but a worthwhile excursion from Big White. Gets ultra light snow – great glades/powder chutes. A lift and ten runs were added in 2006/07.
slopes 1705–2150m
⛟ *2* ⛟ *150 acres*

Mount Baldy USA
Some of the longest and steepest runs in California. Only an hour's drive from Los Angeles so a day trip is feasible, but 20% snowmaking and antiquated lifts are major drawbacks.
1980m; slopes 1980–2620m
⛟ *4* ⛟ *400 acres*

Mount Baw Baw Australia
Small but entertaining intermediate area in attractive woodland, with great views. Closest area to Melbourne (150km/93 miles).
1450m; slopes 1450–1560m
⛟ *7* ⛟ *35 hectares*

Mount Buffalo 720

Mount Buller 720

Mount Dobson New Zealand
Mostly intermediate slopes in a wide, treeless basin near Mt Cook, with good snow-cover. Accommodation in Fairlie, 40 minutes away.
1610m; slopes 1610–2010m
⛟ *3* ⛟ *990 acres*

Mount Falakro Greece
Area two hours' drive from Salonica in northern Greece; almost as big as Parnassos, uncrowded and with good views. Now with a fast quad
1720m
⛟ *8* ⛟ *22km*

Mount Hood Meadows USA
One of several sizeable areas amid magnificent Oregon scenery. Impressive snowfall record but snow tends to be wet, and weather damp.
1375m; slopes 1375–2535m
⛟ *12* ⛟ *2150 acres*
⛟ *Ski Dream*

Mount Hood Ski Bowl USA
Sizeable area set amid magnificent Oregon scenery. Weather can be damp.
1095m; slopes 1095–1540m
⛟ *9* ⛟ *960 acres*

Mount Hotham 720

Mount Hutt 722

Mount Lemmon USA
Southernmost area in North America, close to famous Old West town Tombstone, Arizona. Reasonable snowfall.
2500m; slopes 2500–2790m
⛟ *3* ⛟ *70 acres*

Mount McKay 720

Mount Pilio Greece
Pleasant slopes cut out of dense forest, only 15km/9 miles from the holiday resort of Portaria above town of Volos. 'Very small and disorganised,' says a reporter.
1500m ⛟ *3*

Mount Rose USA
Only 35km/22 miles from Reno. Relatively high, with good slopes of its own and well placed for trips to other Tahoe resorts.
2520m; slopes 2410–2955m
⛟ *6* ⛟ *1200 acres*

Mount Shasta Ski Park USA
Californian resort 300 miles N of San Francisco.
⛟ *4* ⛟ *425 acres*

Mount Snow USA
A one-peak resort, with a long row of lifts on the front face (two fast quads among them) serving easy and intermediate runs of just over 500m/1,640ft vertical. There's a separate area of black runs on the north face.
580m; slopes 580–1095m
⛟ *19* ⛟ *590 acres*

Mount Spokane USA
Little intermediate area outside Spokane (Washington State).
1160m; slopes 1160–1795m
⛟ *5* ⛟ *350 acres*

Mount St Louis / Moonstone Canada
Premier area in Toronto region, spread over three peaks. Very high-capacity lift system and 100% snowmaking.
⛟ *13* ⛟ *175*

Mount Sunapee USA
Area in New Hampshire closest to Boston; primarily intermediate terrain.
375m; slopes 375–835m
⛟ *10* ⛟ *230 acres*

Mount Vermio Greece
Oldest ski base in Greece. Two areas in central Macedonia 60km/37 miles from Thessaloniki. Barren but interesting slopes.
slopes 1420–2000m ⛟ *7*

Mount Washington Resort Canada
Scenic area on Vancouver Island with lodging in the base village. Impressive snowfall record but rain is a problem.
1110m; slopes 1110–1590m
⛟ *6* ⛟ *970 acres*
⛟ *Frontier*

Mount Washington Resort USA
Area formerly called Bretton Woods, with best snowfall record in New Hampshire, and one of several small resorts scattered along the Interstate 93 highway. Mostly easy slopes. Attractive base lodge, good views. Plans include a new pedestrian village.
480m; slopes 480–940m
⛟ *9* ⛟ *435 acres*
⛟ *Ski Dream*

Mount Waterman USA
Small Los Angeles area where children ski free. The lack of much snowmaking is a drawback.
2135m; slopes 2135–2440m
⛟ *3* ⛟ *210 acres*

Mühlbach 146
Village in the Hochkönig area.

Mühltal Austria
Small village halfway between Niederau and Auffach in the Wildschönau. No local skiing of its own.
780m; slopes 830–1900m
⛟ *29* ⛟ *42km*

Muhr Austria
Village by Katschberg tunnel well placed for visiting St Michael, Badkleinkirchheim, Flachau and Obertauern.
1110m

Muju Resort South Korea
Largest area in Korea and with a fair amount of lodging. Though it is the furthest resort from Seoul (four hours south) it is still overcrowded.
⛟ *14*

Mürren 521

Mutters 149

Myoko Suginohara Kokusai Japan
A series of small resorts two or three hours from Tokyo, which together make up an area of extensive slopes with longer, wider runs than normal for Japan. ⛟ *15*

Naeba Japan
Fashionable resort with lots of accommodation two hours north of Tokyo. Crowded slopes.
900m; slopes 900–1800m ⛟ *30*

Nakiska Canada
Small area of wooded runs between Banff and Calgary, with emphasis on downhill speed. Unreliable snow, but state-of-the-art snowmaking and pancake-flat grooming.
1524m; slopes 1525–2215m
⛟ *4* ⛟ *230 acres*

Nasserein 212
Quiet suburb of St Anton.

Nassfeld Ski Arena 120
⛟ *BoardnLodge, Interhome, Neilson, Ski Line, Ski Wild, Thomson*

Nauders/Reschenpass Austria
Spacious, traditionally Tirolean village tucked away only 3km/2 miles from the Swiss border and almost on the Italian one. Its slopes start 2km/1 mile outside the village (free shuttle-bus) and are mainly high and sunny intermediate runs spread over three areas. There is lots of snowmaking. The area is not ideal for experts, though there is a lot of off-piste terrain. It's not ideal for complete beginners either – the village nursery slopes are some way out. There are five cross-country trails amounting to 40km/25 miles in all.
1400m; slopes 1400–2850m
⛷ 25 ⛠ 115km

Nax Switzerland
Quiet, sunny village in a balcony setting overlooking the Rhône valley. Own little area and only a short drive from Veysonnaz. Handful of red and blue runs.
1300m ⛷ 6

Nendaz 541
A sizeable family resort linked in to the Verbier ski area.

Neukirchen Austria
Quiet, pretty beginners' resort with a fairly snow-sure plateau at the top of its mountain.
855m; slopes 855–2150m
⛷ 14 ⛠ 35km
🚠 Crystal

Neustift 223

Nevegal Italy
Weekend place near Belluno, south of Cortina.
1030m; slopes 1030–1650m
⛷ 14 ⛠ 30km

Nevis Range 717

Niederau 227

Niederdorf Italy
Cross-country village in South Tyrol. Villabassa is its Italian name.

Niseko 718

Nockberge Innerkrems Austria
Area just south of Katschberg tunnel.
1500m; slopes 1500–2300m
⛷ 10 ⛠ 33km

Nordseter Norway
Cluster of hotels in deep forest north of Lillehammer. Some Alpine facilities but best for cross-country.
850m; slopes 1000–1090m
⛷ 2 ⛠ 2km

Norefjell Norway
Norway's toughest run, a very steep 600m/1,970ft drop. 120km/75 miles north-west of Oslo.
185m; slopes 185–1185m
⛷ 10 ⛠ 23km

La Norma France
Traffic-free, purpose-built resort near Modane and Val Cenis. Readers report 'good atmosphere, no high-rise blocks, pistes mostly easy except red Crêtes' and 'uncrowded at half-term, good for kids, low prices for pass, school, rentals'.
1350m; slopes 1350–2750m
⛷ 18 ⛠ 65km
🚠 AmeriCan Ski, Erna Low, Interhome, Lagrange, Peak Retreats, Ski France, Ski Leisure Direction, Skiholidayextras

Norquay 659
Banff's quiet local hill.

North Conway USA
Attractive factory-outlet-shopping town in New Hampshire close to Attitash and Cranmore ski areas.
🚠 Virgin Snow, White Mountains

Northstar-at-Tahoe USA
Classic US-style mountain, with runs cut through dense forest and a pleasant new base village that is still growing. The whole area is very sheltered and good for bad-weather days. A gondola and a fast quad go up to a lodge at Big Springs, only 160m/520ft above the village. From this point three fast chairs radiate to serve a broad bowl with some short steep pitches at the top, with easier blue runs lower down and around the ridges. From the ridge you can access the Backside, a steeper bowl with a central fast quad chair serving a row of easy black runs and there are more black runs with a modest vertical of 390m/1,280ft on Lookout Mountain – where new trails are planned for 2008/09.
1930m; slopes 1930–2625m
⛷ 17 ⛠ 2655 acres
🚠 All America Holidays, American Ski Classics, Ski Dream, United Vacations

Nôtre-Dame-de-Bellecombe France
Pleasant 'very French' village spoiled by the busy road. Inexpensive base from which to visit Megève, though it has fair slopes of its own. Queues and slow lifts can be a problem now it is linked to Les Saises. Free bus to/from Crest Voland.
1150m; slopes 1035–2070m
⛷ 84 ⛠ 175km
🚠 AmeriCan Ski, Erna Low, Lagrange, Peak Retreats

Nova Levante 481
Trentino village close to Bozen/Bolzano.

Nozawa Onsen Japan
Spa village with good hot springs three hours from Tokyo. The runs are cut out of heavy vegetation.
500m; slopes 500–1650m ⛷ 21

Nub's Nob USA
One of the most sheltered Great Lakes ski areas (many suffer fierce winds). 100% snowmaking; weekend crowds from Detroit. Wooded slopes suitable for all abilities.
275m; slopes 275–405m
⛷ 8 ⛠ 245 acres

Oberau 227

Obereggen 481
Tiny resort close to Bozen/Bolzano.

Obergurgl 184

Oberjoch–Hindelang Germany
Small, low-altitude resort, particularly good for beginners.
850m; slopes 1140–1520m
⛷ 12 ⛠ 32km

Oberlech 167
Car- and crowd-free family resort alternative to Lech.

Oberndorf Austria
Quiet hamlet connected to St Johann's area.
700m
🚠 Lagrange

Oberperfuss 149

Obersaxen-Mundaun-Lumnezia Switzerland
Several quiet villages above Ilanz, in the Vorderrhein Valley, near Laax. Sizeable area of mainly red and blue runs on four linked mountains. The main lifts are fast chairs. Recommended by a reporter.
1300m; slopes 1200–2310m
⛷ 18 ⛠ 120km

Oberstaufen Germany
Three small areas: Steibis; Thulkirchdorf and Hochgrat. Within an hour of Friedrichshafen.
600m; slopes 860–1880m
⛷ 30 ⛠ 45km

Oberstdorf Germany
Attractive winter-sports town near the Austrian border with three small areas. Famous ski-jumping hill.
815m; slopes 800–2220m
⛷ 31 ⛠ 30km

Obertauern 189

Ochapowace Canada
Main area in Saskatchewan, east of Regina. It doesn't get a huge amount of snow but 75% snowmaking helps.
⛷ 4 ⛠ 100 acres

Ohau New Zealand
Some of NZ's steepest slopes, with great views of Lake Ohau 9km/6 miles away (where you stay). 320km/200 miles south of Christchurch.
1500m; slopes 1425–1825m
⛷ 3 ⛠ 310 acres

Okemo USA
Family-oriented resort with worthwhile and nicely varied intermediate area above the old Vermont town of Ludlow.
345m; slopes 345–1020m
⛷ 18 ⛠ 624 acres

Oppdal 705

Orcières-Merlette France
High, convenient family resort a few km north-east of Gap, Merlette being the ugly, purpose-built ski station above the village of Orcières (1450m/4,760ft). Snow-sure beginner area. Slopes have a good mix of difficulty spread over several mountain flanks, and have been recently expanded – a process that culminated with the opening of a cable car up to almost 3000m/9,840ft on Roche Brune.
1850m; slopes 1850–2725m
⛷ 29 ⛠ 85km
🚠 Lagrange, Ski Collection, Ski France, Skiholidayextras.com

Ordino 108

Orelle France
Village in the Maurienne with access by gondola to Val Thorens in the Trois Vallées. High, exposed slopes better suited to confident intermediates.

Oropa Italy
Little area just off the Aosta–Turin motorway. An easy change of scene from Courmayeur.
1180m; slopes 1200–2390m
⛠ 15km

Les Orres France
Friendly modern resort with great views and varied intermediate terrain, but the snow is unreliable, and it's a long transfer from Lyon.
1550m; slopes 1550–2720m
⛷ 23 ⛠ 62km
🚠 Lagrange, Ski Collection, Ski France, Skiholidayextras.com, UCPA

Orsières Switzerland
Traditional, winter resort near Martigny. Close to Grand St Bernard resorts, including Champex-Lac. Well-positioned base from which to visit Verbier and the Chamonix valley.
900m

Ortisei 470
Charming market town in Val Gardena with indirect links to the Sella Ronda circuit.

Oslo Norway
Capital city with cross-country ski trails in its parks. Alpine slopes and lifts in Nordmarka region, just north of city boundaries.
🚠 Headwater, Ski McNeill

Otre il Colle Italy
Smallest of many little resorts near Bergamo.
1100m; slopes 1100–2000m
⛷ 7 ⛷ 7km

Ötz Austria
Village at the entrance to the Ötz valley with an easy/intermediate ski area of its own and access to the Sölden, Kuhtai and Niederau areas.
820m; slopes 820–2200m
⛷ 10 ⛷ 25km

Oukaimeden Morocco
Slopes 75km/47 miles from Marrakech with a surprisingly long season.
2600m; slopes 2600–3260m
⛷ 7 ⛷ 15km

Ovindoli Italy
One of the smallest areas in L'Aquila region east of Rome, but it has higher slopes than most and one of the better lift systems.
1375m; slopes 1375–2220m
⛷ 9 ⛷ 10km

Ovronnaz Switzerland
Pretty village set on a sunny shelf above the Rhône valley, with a good pool complex. Limited area but Crans-Montana and Anzère are close.
1350m; slopes 1350–2080m
⛷ 8 ⛷ 30km

Owl's Head Canada
Steep mountain rising out of a lake, in a remote spot bordering Vermont, away from weekend crowds.
⛷ 7 ⛷ 90 acres

Oz-en-Oisans 245
Attractive old village with satellite at the lifts into Alpe-d'Huez.

Pajarito Mountain USA
Los Alamos area laid out by nuclear scientists. Atomic slopes too – steep, ungroomed. Open Fridays, weekends and holidays. Fun day out from Taos.
2685m; slopes 2685–3170m
⛷ 6 ⛷ 220 acres

Pal 111
Prettily wooded mountain linked with slopes of Arinsal.

Palandöken Turkey
Varied skiing area, transformed by three big hotels, overlooking the Anatolian city of Erzurum.
slopes 2150–3100m ⛷ 4

Pampeago 481
Trentino area convenient for a trip from Milan.

Pamporovo 712

Panarotta Italy
Smallest of the resorts east of Trento. It is at a higher altitude than nearby Andalo, so it is worth a day out from there.
1500m; slopes 1500–2000m
⛷ 6 ⛷ 7km

Panorama 681

Panticosa Spain
Charming old Pyrenees spa village near Formigal with sheltered but limited slopes.
1500m; slopes 1500–2220m
⛷ 15 ⛷ 34km
⛺ White Roc

Paradiski 346

Park City 631

Parnassos Greece
Biggest and best-organised area in Greece, 180km/112 miles from Athens and with surprisingly good slopes and lifts. 'The Mykonos of winter and very crowded at weekends,' says a reporter.
slopes 1600–2300m
⛷ 9 ⛷ 14km

Parpan Switzerland
Pretty village linked to the large intermediate area of Lenzerheide.
1510m; slopes 1230–2865m
⛷ 37 ⛷ 155km

Partenen 181
Traditional village in the Montafon.

La Parva 730
Area linked with Valle Nevado, 50km/31 miles east of Santiago.

Pas de la Casa 113

Passo Costalunga 481
Dense network of short lifts in Trentino.

Passo Lanciano Italy
Closest area to Adriatic. Weekend crowds from nearby Pescara when the snow is good.
1305m; slopes 1305–2000m
⛷ 13

Passo Rolle Italy
Small group of lifts either side of the road over a high pass just north of San Martino di Castrozza.

Passo San Pellegrino 481
Little ski area south of the Sella Ronda, in Trentino.

Passo Tonale 456

Pass Thurn 160
Road-side lift base for one of Kitzbühel's ski areas.

Pebble Creek USA
Small area on Utah-Jackson Hole route. Blend of open and wooded slopes.
1920m; slopes 1920–2530m
⛷ 3 ⛷ 600 acres

Pec Pod Snezku
Czech Republic
Collection of hamlets spread along the valley road leading to the main lifts and the very limited ski area.
770m; slopes 710–1190m
⛷ 10 ⛷ 9km

Peisey 255
Small village linked to Les Arcs.

Peisey-Vallandry 255
Group of villages linked to Les Arcs and the Paradiski area.

Pejo 481
Trentino resort near Madonna.

Penitentes Argentina
Inaugurated in 1979, 180km/112 miles from Mendoza. Accommodation at the base.
⛷ 10 ⛷ 300 hectares

Perelik Bulgaria
New development aiming to link Pamporovo with Mechi Chal. Construction of the first lodgings is planned for 2008, but it's not clear when the planned 12 lifts and 28km/17 miles of pistes will be open.

Perisher/Smiggins 720

Pescasseroli Italy
One of numerous areas east of Rome in L'Aquila region.
1250m; slopes 1250–1945m
⛷ 6 ⛷ 25km

Pescocostanzo Italy
One of numerous areas east of Rome in L'Aquila region.
1395m; slopes 1395–1900m
⛷ 4 ⛷ 25km

Pettneu Austria
Beginners' resort with an irregular bus link to nearby St Anton.
1250m; slopes 1230–2020m
⛷ 4 ⛷ 15km

Petzen Austria
One of many little areas in Austria's easternmost ski region near the Slovenian border.
600m; slopes 600–1700m
⛷ 5 ⛷ 16km

Peyragudes-Peyresourde
France
Small Pyrenean resort with its ski area starting high above.
1000m; slopes 1600–2400m
⛷ 15 ⛷ 37km
⛺ Lagrange, Ski France, Skiholidayextras.com

Pfelders Italy
Resort near Merano in the South Tyrol covered by the Ortler Skiarena pass.
⛷ 4 ⛷ 5km

Pfunds Austria
Picturesque valley village with no slopes but quick access to several resorts in Switzerland and Italy, as well as Austria.
970m

Phoenix Park South Korea
Golf complex with 12 trails in winter. Two hours (140km/87 miles) from Seoul.
slopes 650–1050m ⛷ 9

Piancavallo Italy
Uninspiring yet curiously trendy purpose-built village, an easy drive from Venice. 'Not for piste-bashers and experts but highly suitable for beginners and intermediates,' says a reporter.
1270m; slopes 1270–1830m
⛷ 17 ⛷ 45km

Piani delle Betulle Italy
One of several little areas near the east coast of Lake Como.
730m; slopes 730–1850m
⛷ 6 ⛷ 9km

Piani di Artavaggio Italy
Small base complex rather than a village. One of several little areas near Lake Como.
875m; slopes 875–1875m
⛷ 7 ⛷ 15km

Piani di Bobbio Italy
Largest of several tiny resorts above Lake Como.
770m; slopes 770–1855m
⛷ 10 ⛷ 20km

Piani di Erna Italy
Small base development – no village. One of several little areas above Lake Como.
600m; slopes 600–1635m
⛷ 5 ⛷ 9km

Piau-Engaly France
User-friendly St-Lary satellite in one of the best Pyrenean areas.
1850m; slopes 1700–2500m
⛷ 20 ⛷ 40km

Piazzatorre Italy
One of many little areas in the Bergamo region.
870m; slopes 870–2000m
⛷ 5 ⛷ 25km

Pichl 198
Hamlet outside Schladming, with lifts into two of the local areas.

Pico USA
Low-key little family area (no resort village) close to Killington.
605m; slopes 605–1215m
⛷ 2 ⛷ 160 acres

Piesendorf Austria
Cheaper, quiet place to stay when visiting Zell am See. Tucked behind Kaprun near Niedernsill.
780m
⛷ 3 ⛷ 3km

Pievepelago Italy
Much the smallest and most limited of the Appennine ski resorts. Less than 2 hours from Florence and Pisa.
1115m; slopes 1115–1410m
⛷ 7 ⛷ 8km

Pila Italy
Modern, car-free, purpose-built, ski-in, ski-out resort, linked by gondola to old Roman town of Aosta below. An interesting mix of well-groomed, snow-sure, mainly intermediate slopes, with stunning views from the top. For experts there are steep pistes and mogul fields at the top and some good off-piste, but not huge amounts. It's good for beginners, with a secluded nursery area and the slopes are generally uncrowded. Snow reliability is good. There are few queues, except at weekends and for

the gondola down to Aosta. Other resorts in the Aosta valley are within day-trip distance and are covered by the lift pass. A visitor says, 'If you like small and friendly with flattering pistes, Pila is for you.'
1550m; slopes 1550–2750m
🚠 14 ⛷ 70km
🚐 *Crystal, Independent Ski Links, Interhome, Interski, Thomson*

Pinzolo 481
Trentino resort near Madonna.

Pitztal Austria
Long valley with good glacier area at its head, accessed by underground funicular.
1250m; slopes 880–3440m
🚠 19 ⛷ 87km
🚐 *Interhome*

Pla-d'Adet France
Limited purpose-built complex at the foot of the St-Lary ski area (the original village is further down the mountain).
1680m; slopes 1420–2450m
🚠 32 ⛷ 80km
🚐 *Lagrange*

La Plagne 348

Plan de Corones Italy
Distinctive ski area in South Tyrol, with amazingly efficient lifts from Brunico and San Vigilio di Marebbe. Better known by its German name, Kronplatz.
1200m; slopes 1200–2275m
🚠 32 ⛷ 103km

Plan-Peisey 255
Small development with link to Les Arcs.

Plose Italy
Varied area close to Bressanone, with the longest run in the South Tyrol.
560m; slopes 1065–2500m
🚠 11 ⛷ 40km

Poiana Brasov 715

Pomerelle USA
Small area in Idaho on the Utah–Sun Valley route.
2430m; slopes 2430–2735m
🚠 3 ⛷ 300 acres

Pontechianale Italy
Highest, largest area in a remote region south-west of Turin. Day-tripper place.
1600m; slopes 1600–2760m
🚠 8 ⛷ 30km

Ponte di Legno 456
Attractive sheltered alternative to Passo Tonale.

Pontresina Switzerland
Small, sedate, sunny village with one main street, rather spoiled by the sanatorium-style architecture. All downhill skiing involves travel by car or bus, except the single long piste on Pontresina's own hill, Languard. It's cheaper to stay here than St Moritz.
1805m
🚠 56 ⛷ 350km
🚐 *Switzerland Travel Centre*

Port-Ainé Spain
Small but high intermediate area in the Spanish Pyrenees near Andorra. Lifts include a six-pack; eponymous 3-star hotel at base.
1975m; slopes 1650–2440m
🚠 8 ⛷ 44km

Port del Comte Spain
High resort in the forested region of Lleida, north-west of Barcelona. The slopes spread across three linked sectors: El Sucre, El Hostal and El Estivella.
slopes 1700–2400m
🚠 15 ⛷ 40km

Porté Puymorens France
Little-known Pyrenean area close to Pas de la Casa in Andorra. Plans to link the two are now moving forward with the opening in 2005 of the first lift on the French side of Pas de la Casa.
slopes 1600–2600m
🚠 13 ⛷ 45km
🚐 *Pyrenees Ski Experience*

Porter Heights New Zealand
Closest skiing to Christchurch (one hour). Open, sunny bowl offering mostly intermediate skiing – with back bowls for powder.
1340m; slopes 1340–1950m
🚠 5 ⛷ 200 acres

Portes du Soleil 358
Portillo 730
Powderhorn USA
Area in west Colorado perched on the world's highest flat-top mountain, Grand Mesa. Sensational views. Day trip from Aspen.
2490m; slopes 2490–2975m
🚠 4 ⛷ 300 acres

Powder King Canada
Remote resort in British Columbia, between Prince George and Dawson City. As its name suggests, it has great powder. Plenty of lodging.
880m; slopes 880–1520m
🚠 3 ⛷ 160 acres

Powder Mountain USA
Massive Utah area sprawled over six ridges, an hour and a quarter's drive from Salt Lake City. An ample 2,800 acres is lift served, a mix of mainly north-facing slopes with enough green, blue and black runs to satisfy all abilities. You access the rest by snowcat or snowmobile tow, buses and hiking. It is the abundance of intermediate freeride terrain that makes it special. You can also stay in Ogden, 32km/20 miles away.
2100m; slopes 2100–2740m
🚠 7 ⛷ 5500 acres

Pozza di Fassa 481
Pretty Trentino village with its own slopes.

Pragelato Italy
Inexpensive base, linked by cable car to Sestriere. Its own area is worth a try for half a day.
1535m; slopes 1535–2700m
🚠 6 ⛷ 50km
🚐 *Kuoni, Neilson, Scott Dunn, White Roc*

Prägraten am Grossvenediger
Austria
Traditional mountaineering/ski touring village in lovely setting south of Felbertauern tunnel. The Alpine ski slopes of Matrei are nearby.
1310m; slopes 1310–1490m
🚠 2 ⛷ 30km

Prali Italy
Tiny resort east of Sestriere – a worthwhile half-day trip.
1450m; slopes 1450–2500m
🚠 7 ⛷ 25km

Pralognan-la-Vanoise France
Unspoiled traditional village overlooked by spectacular peaks. Champagny (La Plagne) and Courchevel are close by.
1410m; slopes 1410–2355m
🚠 14 ⛷ 30km
🚐 *Erna Low, Lagrange, Ski France, Ski Independence, Skiholidayextras*

Pra-Loup France
Convenient, purpose-built family resort with an extensive, varied intermediate area linked to La Foux-d'Allos.
1500m; slopes 1500–2600m
🚠 32 ⛷ 83km
🚐 *Lagrange, Ski Collection, Ski France, Ski Leisure Direction, Skiholidayextras.com*

Prati di Tivo Italy
Weekend day-trip place east of Rome and near the town of Teramo. A sizeable resort by southern Italy standards.
1450m; slopes 1450–1800m
🚠 6 ⛷ 16km

Prato Nevoso Italy
Purpose-built resort with rather bland slopes. Part of Mondolé ski area with Artesina.
1500m; slopes 1500–1950m
🚠 25 ⛷ 90km
🚐 *Equity, Rocketski, Thomson*

Prato Selva Italy
Tiny base development (no village) east of Rome near Teramo. Weekend day-trip place.
1370m; slopes 1370–1800m
🚠 4 ⛷ 10km

Le Praz 287
Aka Courchevel 1300 – the lowest and most attractive of the Courchevel resorts.

Les Praz 268
Quiet hamlet 4km/2 miles from Chamonix.

Praz-de-Lys France
Little-known snow-pocket area near Lake Geneva that can have good snow when nearby resorts (eg La Clusaz) do not.
1500m; slopes 1200–2000m
🚠 23 ⛷ 60km
🚐 *Lagrange*

Praz-sur-Arly France
Traditional village in a pretty, wooded setting just down the road from Megève. Newly linked slopes to Notre Dame de Bellecombe and beyond to Crest Voland/Les Saises, to form the Espace Diamant.
1035m; slopes 1035–2070m
🚠 84 ⛷ 175km
🚐 *Lagrange, Ski France, Ski Leisure Direction, Skiholidayextras.com*

Le Pré 255
Hamlet with lifts up to Arc 2000.

Predazzo 481
Small, quiet place in Trentino near Sella Ronda resorts.

Premanon France
One of four resorts that make up Les Rousses area in Jura region.
1050m; slopes 1120–1680m
🚠 40 ⛷ *Lagrange*

La Presolana Italy
Large summer resort near Bergamo. Several other little areas nearby.
1250m; slopes 1250–1650m
🚠 6 ⛷ 15km

Pucón 730
Ski area on the side of the active Villarrica volcano in southern Chile, 800km/500 miles south of Santiago. Lodgings are at Pucón village, 30 minutes away from the slopes.

Puigmal France
Resort in the French Pyrenees with accommodation in nearby villages.
1830m; slopes 1830–2700m
🚠 12 ⛷ 34km
🚐 *Pyrenees Ski Experience*

Puy-St-Vincent 359
Pyhä 703
Pyrenees, French 423
Pyrenees 2000 France
Tiny resort built in a pleasing manner. Shares a pretty area of short runs with Font-Romeu. Impressive snowmaking.
2000m; slopes 1750–2250m
🚠 32 ⛷ 52km
🚐 *Pyrenees Ski Experience*

Québec City 697
🚐 *All America Holidays, AmeriCan Ski, Crystal, Kuoni, Ski Dream*

Queenstown 725

Radium Hot Springs   Canada
Summer resort offering an alternative to the purpose-built slope-side resort of Panorama.
slopes 975–2155m
⛷ 8 ⛰ 300 acres

Radstadt   Austria
Interesting, unspoiled medieval town near Schladming that has its own small area, with the Salzburger Sportwelt slopes accessed from nearby Zauchensee or Flachau.
855m; slopes 855–2185m
⛷ 100 ⛰ 350km

Ragged Mountain   USA
Family-owned ski area in New Hampshire.
⛷ 9 ⛰ 200 acres

Rainbow   New Zealand
Northernmost ski area on South Island. Wide, treeless area, best for beginners and intermediates. Accommodation at St Arnaud.
1440m; slopes 1440–1760m
⛷ 5 ⛰ 865 acres

Ramsau am Dachstein Austria
Charming village overlooked by the Dachstein glacier. Renowned for cross-country, it also has Alpine slopes locally, on the glacier and at Schladming.
1200m; slopes 1100–2700m
⛷ 18 ⛰ 30km

Ramundberget   709

Rauris   Austria
Small village in a quiet, dead-end valley south-east of Zell, about 25km/16 miles by road. Across the valley road from the village are nursery draglifts and a gondola accessing intermediate slopes with a vertical of 1250m/4,100ft. 'Well groomed slopes, few queues and a day or two's visit from Zell,' says a reporter.
950m; slopes 950–2200m
⛷ 8 ⛰ 30km
🚢 *Crystal, Neilson, Thomson*

Ravascletto   Italy
Resort in a pretty wooded setting near Austrian border, with most of its terrain high above on an open plateau.
920m; slopes 920–1735m
⛷ 12 ⛰ 40km

Reallon   France
Traditional-style village, with splendid views from above Lac de Serre-Ponçon.
1560m; slopes 1560–2115m
⛷ 6 ⛰ 20km

Red Lodge   USA
Picturesque Old West Montana town. Ideal for a combined trip with Big Sky or Jackson Hole.
1800m; slopes 2155–2860m
⛷ 8 ⛰ 1600 acres
🚢 *AmeriCan Ski*

Red Mountain Resort   Canada
Area renowned for its deep and deep powder, eight hours east of Vancouver, 3km/2 miles from Rossland, a sleepy old mining town. The main mountain is Granite, a conical peak with more or less separate faces of blue, black and double-black steepness. Next-door Red Mountain itself is half the size. There is an increasing amount of green and blue runs to warm up on, but it's the black and double-black stuff that dominates, and is the real attraction. The tough stuff is marked on the map but not on the mountain; and it's mostly in trees, with cliffs and gnarly narrow bits, so you need a guide.
1185m; slopes 1185–2075m
⛷ 6 ⛰ 1685 acres
🚢 *AmeriCan Ski, Frontier, Ski Dream, Ski Independence, Ski Safari*

Red River   USA
New Mexico western town – complete with stetsons and saloons – with intermediate slopes above.
2665m; slopes 2665–3155m
⛷ 7 ⛰ 290 acres

Reichenfels   Austria
One of many small areas in Austria's easternmost ski region near the Slovenian border.
810m; slopes 810–1400m

Reinwald   Italy
Resort near Merano in the South Tyrol covered by the Ortler Skiarena pass.

Reit im Winkl   Germany
Southern Bavarian resort, straddling the German–Austrian border. Winklmoos ski area is best suited to intermediates.
750m; slopes 750–1800m
⛷ 7 ⛰ 40km

The Remarkables   725
Three bleak basins 45 minutes from Queenstown.

Rencurel-les-Coulumes   France
One of seven little resorts just west of Grenoble. Unspoiled, inexpensive place to tour. Villard-de-Lans is the main resort.

Reschenpass   Austria
Area in the Tirol, but only just – it's right on the Swiss border, and it includes two small resorts in Italy – Schöneben and Haider Alm (this bit of Italy is German-speaking). Nauders is the main resort.
1520m
⛷ 7 ⛰ 28

Rettenberg   Germany
Small resort near Austrian border.
750m; slopes 820–1650m
⛷ 15 ⛰ 40km

Reutte   Austria
500-year-old market town with many traditional hotels, and rail links to nearby Lermoos.
855m; slopes 855–1900m
⛷ 9 ⛰ 19km

Revelstoke   Canada
Scenic new resort developed from a small existing hill in heli-skiing territory, Powder Springs, three hours from Kelowna or longer from Calgary. In 2008/09 Revelstoke will have North America's biggest vertical (1715m/5,620ft) and over 3,000 acres of terrain. The slopes offer a mix of fairly steep blues and blacks, served by four lifts. North Bowl has good expert terrain, soon to be served by a fast quad. There are 2,200 acres available for cat skiing and heli-skiing – both accessed directly from the resort centre. The average snowfall is an amazing 500 to 700 inches. A proper 'village' is taking shape at the base, with restaurants, shops and accommodation. The master plan provides for over 20 lifts and 10,000 acres – bigger than Whistler.
515m; slopes 515–2225m
⛷ 4 ⛰ 3032 acres
🚢 *Canadian Powder Tours, Crystal, Erna Low, Frontier, Mark Warner, Momentum, Powder Skiing in North America, Ski Dream, Ski Safari, Snowebb*

Rhêmes-Notre-Dame   Italy
Unspoiled village in the beautiful Rhêmes valley, south of Aosta. Courmayeur and La Thuile within reach.
⛷ 2 ⛰ 5km

Riederalp   Switzerland
Pretty, car-free village perched high above the Rhône valley. Access by cable car or gondola from the valley village of Mörel near Brig. A reader reports 'friendly locals, stunning views, no crowds, not much après'.
1900m; slopes 1900–2870m
⛷ 36 ⛰ 99km
🚢 *Made to Measure*

Rifensberg   134

Rigi-Kaltbad   Switzerland
Resort on a mountain rising out of Lake Lucerne, with superb all-round views, accessed by the world's first mountain railroad.
1440m; slopes 1195–1795m
⛷ 7 ⛰ 9km

Riihivuori   Finland
Small area with 'base' at the top of the mountain. 20km/12 miles south of the city of Jyväskylä. ⛷ 5

Riksgränsen   709

Riscone   Italy
Dolomite village sharing a pretty area with San Vigilio. Good snowmaking. Short easy runs.
1200m; slopes 1200–2275m
⛷ 35 ⛰ 40km

Risoul   361

Rittner Horn   Italy
Resort near Merano in the South Tyrol covered by the Ortler Skiarena pass.
⛷ 3 ⛰ 15km

Rivisondoli   Italy
Sizeable mountain retreat east of Rome, with one of the better lift systems in the vicinity.
1350m; slopes 1350–2050m
⛷ 7 ⛰ 16km

Roccaraso   Italy
Largest of the resorts east of Rome – at least when snow-cover is complete.
1280m; slopes 1280–2200m
⛷ 12 ⛰ 56km

Rohrmoos   198
Suburb of Schladming, with vast area of nursery slopes.

La Rosière   364

Rossland   Canada
Remote little town 5km/3 miles from cult powder paradise Red Mountain.

Rougemont   Switzerland
Cute rustic hamlet just over the French/German language border near Gstaad, with worthwhile local slopes and links to Gstaad's Eggli sector.
991m; slopes 890–3000m
⛷ 62 ⛰ 250km

Les Rousses   France
Group of four villages – Les Rousses, Premanon, Lamoura and Bois d'Amont – in the Jura mountains, 50km/31 miles from Geneva airport.
1120m; slopes 1120–1680m
⛷ 40 ⛰ 40km
🚢 *Lagrange*

Ruka   703

Russbach   Austria
Secluded village tucked up a side valley and linked into the Gosau-Annaberg-Lungotz area. The slopes are spread over a wide area.
815m; slopes 780–1620m
⛷ 33 ⛰ 65km

Rusutsu   718

Saalbach-Hinterglemm   191

Saalfelden   Austria
Town ideally placed for touring eastern Tirol. Extensive lift networks of Maria-Alm and Saalbach are nearby.
745m; slopes 745–1550m
⛷ 3 ⛰ 3km

Saanen Switzerland
Cheaper and more convenient alternative to staying in Gstaad – but much less going on.
slopes 950–3000m
⬆ 62 ⬆ 250km

Saanenmöser Switzerland
Small village with rail/road links to Gstaad. Scenic and quiet local slopes, with good mountain restaurants (Horneggli and Kübelialp are recent recommendations).
1270m; slopes 1270–3000m
⬆ 67 ⬆ 250km

Saas-Almagell Switzerland
Compact village up the valley from Saas-Grund, with good cross-country trails and walks, and a limited Alpine area.
1670m; slopes 1670–2400m
⬆ 8 ⬆ 12km

Saas-Fee 525

Saas-Grund Switzerland
Sprawling valley village below Saas-Fee, with a separate, small but high Alpine area.
1560m; slopes 1560–3200m
⬆ 7 ⬆ 35km

Saddleback USA
Small area between Maine's premier resorts. High slopes by local standards.
695m; slopes 695–1255m
⬆ 5 ⬆ 100 acres

Sahoro Japan
Ugly, purpose-built complex on snowy northern Hokkaido island, with a limited area.
610m; slopes 610–1030m
⬆ 8 ⬆ 15km
✉ Club Med

Les Saisies France
Traditional-style cross-country venue, surrounded by varied four-mountain Alpine slopes. Now part of Espace Diamant. Easy runs, but some lift queues at peak times.
1650m; slopes 1035–2070m
⬆ 84 ⬆ 175km
✉ AmeriCan Ski, Classic Ski, Erna Low, Lagrange, Peak Retreats, Ski Collection, Ski France, Ski Independence, Ski Leisure Direction, Skiholidayextras.com

Sälen 709

Salt Lake City USA
Underrated base from which to ski Utah. 30 minutes from Park City, Deer Valley, The Canyons, Snowbird, Alta, Snowbasin. Cheaper and livelier than the resorts.
✉ AmeriCan Ski

Salzburg-Stadt Austria
A single, long challenging run off the back of Salzburg's local mountain, accessed by a spectacular lift-ride from a suburb of Grodig.
425m

Samedan Switzerland
Valley town, just down the road from St Moritz. A run heads back to base from Corviglia-Marguns.
1720m; slopes 1740–2570m
⬆ 56 ⬆ 350km

Samnaun 153
Shares large ski area with Ischgl.

Samoëns 367

San Bernardino Switzerland
Pretty resort south of the road tunnel, close to Madesimo.
1625m; slopes 1600–2525m
⬆ 8 ⬆ 35km

San Candido Italy
Small resort in the South Tyrol. Innichen is its German name.
1175m; slopes 1175–1580m
⬆ 4 ⬆ 15km

San Carlos de Bariloche 729

San Cassiano 463
Quiet village linked via the Alta Badia to the Sella Ronda circuit.

Sandia Peak USA
The world's longest lift ride ascends from Albuquerque. Mostly gentle slopes; children ski free.
slopes 2645–3165m
⬆ 7 ⬆ 100 acres

San Grée di Viola Italy
Easternmost of resorts south of Turin, surprisingly close to the Italian Riviera.
1100m; slopes 1100–1800m
⬆ 30km

San Martin de los Andes Argentina
Sizeable town with accommodation, 19 km/12 miles from the Chapelco ski area.
✉ Scott Dunn Latin America

San Martino di Castrozza 481
Trentino village south of Val di Fassa.

Sansicario 458
Small, stylish resort in the Milky Way near Sauze d'Oulx.

San Simone Italy
Tiny development north of Bergamo, close to unappealing Foppolo area.
2000m; slopes 1105–2300m
⬆ 9 ⬆ 45km

Santa Caterina Italy
Pretty, user-friendly village near Bormio, with a snow-sure novice and intermediate area.
1740m; slopes 1740–2725m
⬆ 8 ⬆ 25km
✉ Airtours

Santa Cristina 470
Quiet village in Val Gardena on the periphery of the Sella Ronda circuit.

Santa Fe USA
Interesting area only 15 miles from beautiful Santa Fe town. A tree-filled bowl with a good variety of terrain crammed into its small area. Ideal stopover en route from Albuquerque airport to Taos.
3145m; slopes 3155–3680m
⬆ 7 ⬆ 550 acres

Santa Maria Maggiore Italy
Resort south of the Simplon Pass from the Rhône valley, and near Lake Maggiore.
820m; slopes 820–1890m
⬆ 5 ⬆ 10km

San Vigilio di Marebbe/ Kronplatz Italy
Pretty village in South Tyrol with lifts on two mountains, one being the quite impressive Plan de Corones.
1200m; slopes 1200–2275m
⬆ 32 ⬆ 103km
✉ Italian Safaris

San Vito di Cadore Italy
Sizeable, alternative place to stay to Cortina. Negligible local slopes, though.
1010m; slopes 1010–1380m
⬆ 9 ⬆ 12km

Sappada Italy
Isolated resort close to the Austrian border below Lienz.
1215m; slopes 1215–2050m
⬆ 17 ⬆ 21km

Sappee Finland
Resort within easy reach of Helsinki, popular with boarders and telemarkers. Lake views. ⬆ 7

Sarnano Italy
Main resort in the Macerata region near Adriatic Riviera. Valley village with ski slopes accessed by lift.
540m; slopes ⬆ 9 ⬆ 11km

Le Sauze France
Fine area near Barcelonnette, sadly remote from airports.
1400m; slopes 1400–2440m
⬆ 23 ⬆ 65km

Sauze d'Oulx 458

Savognin Switzerland
Pretty village with a good mid-sized area; a good base for the nearby resorts of St Moritz, Davos/Klosters and Laax.
1200m; slopes 1200–2715m
⬆ 10 ⬆ 80km
✉ Switzerland Travel Centre

Scheffau 205
Rustic village not far from Söll.

Schia Italy
Very limited area of short runs – the only ski area near Parma. No village.
1245m; slopes 1245–1415m
⬆ 7 ⬆ 15km

Schilpario Italy
One of many little areas near Bergamo.
1125m; slopes 1125–1635m
⬆ 5 ⬆ 15km

Schladming 198

Schnalstal Italy
Valley and high ski area, in the Dolomites near Merano. Val Senales is its Italian name.
3210m; slopes 2110–3210m
⬆ 12 ⬆ 35km

Schöneben Italy
Area in the Val Venosta in the South Tyrol, close to Austrian border and Nauders.
1520m
⬆ 7 ⬆ 28km

Schönried Switzerland
A cheaper and quieter resort alternative to staying in Gstaad.
1230m; slopes 890–3000m
⬆ 67 ⬆ 250km
✉ Interhome

Schoppernau 134
A scattered farming community, one of two main areas in Bregenzerwald north-west of Lech.

Schröcken 134
Bregenzerwald area village near Lech.

Schruns 181
Pleasant town at the heart of the Montafon region.

Schüttdorf 231
Ordinary dormitory satellite of Zell am See.

Schwarzach im Pongau Austria
Riverside village with rail links. There are limited slopes at Goldegg; Wagrain (Salzburger Sportwelt) and Grossarl (Gastein valley) are also nearby.
600m

Schwaz Austria
Valley town beside the Inn with a lift into varied terrain shared with the village of Pill and its mountain outpost, Hochpillberg.
540m; slopes 540–2030m
⬆ 6 ⬆ 10km

Schweitzer USA
Excellent family-friendly resort in northern Idaho, 85 miles from Spokane (Washington state) and 45 miles from Canada. Area of slopes on a par with places like Keystone and Steamboat. Lifts include two fast quads and a six pack. A reader who went there from Fernie preferred Schweitzer; he reports 'nice condo blocks at the base, terrain for all levels including black chutes and glades at the top, fresh tracks all day'.
1220m; slopes 1229–1950m
⬆ 10 ⬆ 2900 acres
✉ AmeriCan Ski

Schwemmalm Italy
Resort near Merano in the South Tyrol covered by the Ortler Skiarena pass.
⬆ 5 ⬆ 18km

Scopello Italy
Low area close to the Aosta valley, worth considering for a day trip in bad weather.
slopes 690–1700m
⛷6 ⛡ 35km

Scuol Switzerland
Year-round spa resort close to Austria and Italy, with an impressive range of terrain.
1250m; slopes 1250–2800m
⛷15 ⛡ 80km
✉ Switzerland Travel Centre

Searchmont Resort Canada
Ontario area with modern lift system and 95% snowmaking. Fine Lake Superior views.
275m; slopes 275–485m
⛷4 ⛡ 65 acres

Sedrun 495
Charming, unspoiled old village on the Glacier Express rail route close to Andermatt. Fine terrain amid glorious scenery; covered on Gotthard Oberalp lift pass.

Seefeld Austria
Traditional Tirolean style, upmarket resort, with a large, pedestrian-only centre. The slopes, on the outskirts, are served by a regular free shuttle-bus. Gschwandtkopf is a rounded hill of 300m/980ft vertical and intermediate runs on two main slopes. Rosshütte is more extensive, and has a terrain park and half-pipe. There is a cable car across to the separate peak of Härmelekopf. Seefeld's cross-country trails are some of the best in the Alps.
1200m; slopes 1200–2100m
⛷25 ⛡ 38km
✉ Crystal, Directski.com, Inghams, Interhome, Lagrange, Thomson

See im Paznaun 153
Small family-friendly area in the Paznaun Valley, near Ischgl.

Le Seignus-d'Allos France
Close to La Foux-d'Allos (which shares large area with Pra-Loup) and has own little area, too.
1400m; slopes 1400–2425m
⛷13 ⛡ 47km

Seis Italy
German name for Siusi.

Sella Nevea Italy
Limited but developing resort in a beautiful setting on the Slovenian border (there are plans to link to Kanin). Summer glacier nearby.
1140m; slopes 1190–1800m
⛷11 ⛡ 8km

Sella Ronda 463

Selva/Val Gardena 470

Selvino Italy
Closest resort to Bergamo.
960m; slopes 960–1400m
⛷9 ⛡ 20km

Selwyn Snowfields 720

Semmering Austria
Long-established winter sports resort set in pretty scenery, 100km/62 miles from Vienna, towards Graz. Mostly intermediate terrain.
1000m; slopes 1000–1340m
⛷5 ⛡ 14km

Les Sept-Laux France
Ugly, user-friendly family resort near Grenoble. Pretty slopes for all grades.
1350m; slopes 1350–2400m
⛷25 ⛡ 100km
✉ Lagrange, Mountain Heaven

Serfaus Austria
Charming traffic-free village (with underground people-mover to get you to the lifts) at the foot of a long, narrow, relatively snow-sure ski area, linked to Fiss. There are few challenging slopes for experts, but it is a good area for touring. Most of the area is ideal for intermediates and the nursery slopes are good. Most of the slopes are above the treeline, and with good snowmaking the area is fairly snow-sure, despite the sun. The 60km/37 miles of cross-country trails include very pretty loops at altitude. It's virtually unknown in the UK – a lack of English speakers may be a drawback.
1430m; slopes 1200–2750m
⛷53 ⛡ 185km
✉ Ardmore, Crystal, Crystal Finest, Inghams, Interhome

Serrada Italy
Very limited area near Trento.
slopes 1250–1605m ⛷5

Serre-Chevalier 369

Sesto Italy
Dolomite village off the Alta Val Pusteria, surrounded by pretty little areas. Sexten is its German name.
1310m; slopes 1130–2200m
⛷31 ⛡ 50km

Sestola Italy
Appennine village a short drive from Pisa and Florence with its pistes, some way above, almost completely equipped with snowmakers.
900m; slopes 1280–1975m
⛷23 ⛡ 50km

Sestriere 477

Seven Springs Mountain USA
Pennsylvania's largest resort.
slopes 220–2995m
⛷18 ⛡ 494 acres

Sexten Italy
Dolomite village off the Hochpustertal, surrounded by pretty little areas. Sesto is its Italian name.
1310m; slopes 1130–2200m
⛷31 ⛡ 50km

Shames Mountain Canada
Remote spot inland from coastal town of Prince Rupert and with impressive snowfall record. Deep powder.
670m; slopes 670–1195m
⛷3 ⛡ 183 acres

Shawnee Peak USA
Small area near Bethel and Sunday River renowned for its night skiing. Spectacular views. Mostly groomed cruising.
185m; slopes 185–580m
⛷5 ⛡ 225 acres

Shemshak Iran
Most popular of the three mountain resorts within easy reach of Tehran (60km/37 miles). 'Plenty of untracked lines and bumps; lifts get quite busy,' says a reporter.
3600m; slopes 2550–3050m
⛷7

Shiga Kogen 718
Largest area in Japan.

Showdown USA
Intermediate area in Montana cut out of forest north of Bozeman. 50km/30 miles to the nearest hotel.
2065m; slopes 2065–2490m
⛷4 ⛡ 640 acres

Sierra-at-Tahoe USA
A Colorado-style resort, with runs cut on densely wooded slopes. It claims an impressive average of 420 inches of snow. The slopes are spread over two flanks of Huckleberry Mountain, above the base lodge, and West Bowl, off to one side – 'As a boarder the whole mountain was excellent,' says one visitor. The fronts of both offer good intermediate cruising plus some genuine single-diamond blacks. The backside of Huckleberry has easier blue and green slopes. This is a natural day trip for those staying in South Lake Tahoe.
2210m; slopes 2025–2700m
⛷10 ⛡ 2000 acres

Sierra Nevada 700

Sierra Summit USA
Sierra Nevada area accessible only from the west. 100% snowmaking.
2160m; slopes 2160–2645m
⛷8 ⛡ 250 acres

Sierre 537
Not a ski reosrt but the hub of the Coeur du Valais region of which the Val d'Anniviers is a part.

Silbertal 181
Low secluded village in the Montafon area.

Sillian Austria
A gondola and two fast quads serve this varied area in Austria's Hochpustertal region.
1100m
⛷6 ⛡ 45km

Sils Maria 530
Pretty lakeside village, linked to the St Moritz Corvatsch slopes.

Silvaplana 530
Pretty lakeside village near St Moritz.

Silver Mountain USA
Northern Idaho area near delightful resort town of Coeur d'Alene. Best for experts, but plenty for intermediates too.
1215m; slopes 1215–1915m
⛷6 ⛡ 1500 acres

Silver Star 683

Silverthorne USA
Factory outlet town on main road close to Keystone and Breckenridge. Good budget base for skiing those resorts plus Vail and Beaver Creek.
✉ AmeriCan Ski

Silverton USA
Expert-only area in southern Colorado that used to be heli-ski country. Served by one lift. Avalanche transceiver, shovel and probe compulsory.
3170m; slopes 3170–3750m ⛷1

Sinaia Romania
Dreary main-road town with a modest, open area of slopes. Recent investment in new lifts, included a gondola for 2007/08.
795m; slopes 795–2030m
⛷10 ⛡ 20km

Sipapu USA
Great little New Mexico area, with mostly treelined runs. Snow unreliable, but 70% snowmaking. Nice day out from Taos when conditions are good.
slopes 2500–2765m
⛷4 ⛡ 70 acres

Siusi 470
Village west of the Sella Ronda circuit; Seis in German.

Siviez 541
A quieter and cheaper base for Verbier's Four Valleys circuit.

Sixt-Fer-a-Cheval 304
Traditional village near Samoëns.

Sjusjøen Norway
Cluster of hotels in deep forest close to Lillehammer. Some Alpine facilities but better for cross-country.
885m; slopes 1000–1090m
⛷2 ⛡ 2km
✉ Inntravel, Waymark

Ski Apache USA
Apache-owned area south of Albuquerque noted for groomed steeps. Panoramic views. Nearest lodging in charming Ruidoso.
2925m; slopes 2925–3505m
⛷11 ⛡ 750 acres

Ski Cooper USA
Small area close to historic
Old West town of Leadville.
Good ski/sightseeing day out
from nearby Vail, Beaver Creek
and Copper Mountain.
slopes 3200–3565m ⛷ 4

Ski Windham USA
Two hours from New York City
and second only to Hunter for
weekend crowds. Decent
slopes by eastern standards.
485m; slopes 485–940m
⛷ 7 ⛷ 230 acres

Smokovec Slovakia
Spa town with small modern
centre near Poprad, with three
small areas known collectively
as High Tatras. Funicular
railway and snowmaking
facilities.
1480m; slopes 1000–1500m
⛷ 8 ⛷ 4km

Smugglers' Notch USA
Family oriented resort with
sympathetic instructors,
comprehensive child care,
child-friendly layout and long,
quiet, easy runs. There are
varied and satisfying slopes,
spread over three hills, with a
worthwhile vertical of
800m/2,610ft. It's a great area
for beginners, but mileage-
hungry intermediates should
go elsewhere. Snowboarding
is encouraged, and there are
three impressive terrain parks
and an Olympic-size super-
pipe.
315m; slopes 315–1110m
⛷ 8 ⛷ 1000 acres
✈ Ski Dream

Snowbasin USA
Underrated hill, usually with
very good snow. No base
village, but a worthwhile day
out from Park City. The crowd-
free slopes cover a lot of
pleasantly varied terrain. This
is a great mountain for
experts – the Grizzly Downhill
course drops 885m/2,900ft
and is already claimed to be a
modern classic. Between the
race course and the area
boundary is a splendid area
of off-piste wooded glades
and gullies. Middle Bowl is
great terrain for the
adventurous, with a complex
network of blues and blacks.
You have to stay in the town
of Ogden on the Salt Lake
plain in the backwater of
Huntsville.
1965m; slopes 1965–2865m
⛷ 12 ⛷ 2820 acres

Snowbird 636

Snowbowl (Arizona) USA
One of America's oldest areas,
near Flagstaff, Arizona, atop
an extinct volcano and with
stunning desert views. Good
snowfall record.
2805m; slopes 2805–3505m
⛷ 5 ⛷ 135 acres

Snowbowl (Montana) USA
Montana area renowned for
powder, outside lively town of
Missoula. Intermediate pistes
plus 700 acres of extreme
slopes. Grizzly Chute is the
ultimate challenge.
1520m; slopes 1520–2315m
⛷ 4 ⛷ 1400 acres

Snowmass 606

Snow Park 722

Snow Summit USA
San Bernardino National
Forest ski area near Palm
Springs. Lovely lake views.
100% snowmaking. High-
capacity lift system for
weekend crowds.
2135m; slopes 2135–2500m
⛷ 12 ⛷ 230 acres

Snow Valley USA
Area quite near Palm Springs.
Fine desert views. High-
capacity lift system copes with
weekend crowds better than
nearby Big Bear.
2040m; slopes 2040–2390m
⛷ 11 ⛷ 230 acres

Sochi Russia

Solda Italy
Small resort in South Tyrol.
1905m; slopes 1905–2625m
⛷ 10 ⛷ 40km

Sölden 202

Soldeu 115

Soldier Mountain USA
Family resort in Central Idaho;
backcountry snowcat tours.
slopes 1770–2195m
⛷ 4 ⛷ 670 acres

Solitude USA
Smart, car-free mini-village
linked with Brighton in the
valley next to Alta and
Snowbird. Most (not all) of
the slopes are easy or
intermediate, including a wide
area served by the one fast
quad. When open, the top lift
accesses lots of steeps in
Honeycomb Canyon, on the
back of the hill, with a short
quad to bring you back to the
front face. Headwall Forest
and Eagle Ridge also have
good blacks. The resorts'
boundaries are open, and
there are excellent
backcountry adventures to be
had. Two fast quads are due
to replace old chairs out of
the resort for 2008/09.
2490m; slopes 2435–3200m
⛷ 14 ⛷ 2250 acres
✈ AmeriCan Ski, Ski Safari

Söll 205

Solvista USA
Child-oriented resort close to
Winter Park. Low snowfall
record for Colorado.
2490m; slopes 2490–2795m
⛷ 5 ⛷ 250 acres

Sommand France
Purpose-built base that shares
area with Praz-de-Lys.
1420m; slopes 1200–1800m
⛷ 22 ⛷ 50km

Sonnenkopf Austria
Ski area above Klösterle a few
km west of the Arlberg pass –
and covered by the Arlberg ski
pass. 'Uncrowded, gentle
runs, interesting off-piste,'
says a reporter
slopes 1100–2300m
⛷ 9 ⛷ 30km

Sorenberg Switzerland
Popular weekend retreat
between Berne and Lucerne,
with a high proportion of
steep, low runs.
1165m; slopes 1165–2350m
⛷ 18 ⛷ 50km

South Lake Tahoe USA
Tacky base for skiing
Heavenly, with cheap lodging,
traffic and gambling.

South Tyrol Italy

Spindleruv Mlyn Czech Republic
Largest Giant Mountains
region resort but with few
facilities serving several little
low areas.
715m; slopes 750–1310m
⛷ 16 ⛷ 25km

Spital am Pyhrn Austria
Small village near Hinterstoder
in Upper Austria, a bus ride
from its limited intermediate
slopes at Wurzeralm. From the
valley station a 3km/2 mile
funicular goes up to a mid-
mountain col with several
restaurants and nursery
slopes. Lifts and runs go off
from here in several directions
over pleasantly wooded
intermediate terrain; the blues
are tough, so transition from
the nursery slopes is not easy.
On the flat Teichlboden there
are cross-country loops. The
local lift pass also covers the
slopes at Hinterstoder, a short
drive away.
650m; slopes 810–1870m
⛷ 8 ⛷ 14km

Spittal an der Drau Austria
Historic Carinthian town with
a limited area starting a lift-
ride above it. A good day trip
from Bad Kleinkirchheim or
from Slovenia.
555m; slopes 1650–2140m
⛷ 12 ⛷ 27km

Spitzingsee Germany
Beautiful small lake (and
village) an hour from Munich.
⛷ 18 ⛷ 25km

Splugen Reinwald Switzerland
Small intermediate area south
of Chur.
1455m; slopes 1455–2215m
⛷ 7 ⛷ 30km

Sportgastein 128
Remote, high ski area at the
top of the Badgastein valley.

Squaw Valley 585

Stafal 452
Tiny, isolated village, with
good access to the Monterosa
Ski area.

St Andra Austria
Valley-junction village ideally
placed for one of the longest,
most snow-sure cross-country
networks in Europe. Close to
the Tauern pass and to St
Michael.
1045m

St Anton 212

Starhill Resort South Korea
Purpose-built resort formerly
called Cheonmasan, 30km/19
miles north-east of Seoul. ⛷ 8

Stari Vrh Slovenia
About 30 minutes from
Ljubljana airport. A reader
who lives there says: 'Runs
range from a never-groomed
black and three interesting
reds to a winding blue
virtually from top to bottom.'
Recently installed heated six-
pack.
slopes 580–1200m
⛷ 5 ⛷ 12km

St Cergue Switzerland
Limited resort in the Jura
mountains, less than an hour
from Geneva and good for
families with young children.
1045m; slopes 1045–1700m
⛷ 7 ⛷ 20km

St Christoph 212
Small village on Arlberg pass
above St Anton.

St-Colomban-des-Villards 383

Steamboat 608

Ste-Foy-Tarentaise 379

Steinach Austria
Pleasant village in picturesque
surroundings, just off the
autobahn near the Brenner
Pass. An easy outing from
Innsbruck.
1050m; slopes 1050–2205m
⛷ 6 ⛷ 15km

Stevens Pass USA
A day trip from Seattle, and
accommodation 60km/37
miles away in Bavarian-style
town Leavenworth. Low
snowfall and no snow-guns.
Mostly intermediate slopes,
1235m; slopes 1235–1785m
⛷ 14 ⛷ 1125 acres

St-François-Longchamp 414
Sunny, gentle slopes linked to
Valmorel.

St Gallenkirch 181
Small village in the Montafon
valley.

St-Gervais 315
Small town sharing its ski
area with Megève.

St Jakob in Defereggen
Austria

Unspoiled traditional village in a pretty, sunny valley close to Lienz and Heiligenblut, and with a good proportion of high-altitude slopes.
1400m; slopes 1400–2520m
⛚ 9 ⛷ 34km

St Jakob in Haus
Austria

Snowy village with its own slopes. Fieberbrunn, Waidring and St Johann are nearby.
855m; slopes 855–1500m
⛚ 8 ⛷ 16km

St-Jean-d'Arves
383

St Jean d'Aulps
France

Small village in Portes du Soleil area, not part of main circuit but with its own interesting slopes consisting of two small areas – Domaine Chèvrerie and Domaine Grande Terche.

St-Jean-de-Sixt
France

Traditional hamlet, a cheap base for La Clusaz and Le Grand-Bornand (3km/2 miles to both).
960m
⛺ Karibuni, Last Resort

St-Jean-Montclar
France

Small village at the foot of thickly forested slopes. Good day out from nearby Pra-Loup.
1300m; slopes 1300–2500m
⛚ 18 ⛷ 50km
⛺ Lagrange

St Johann im Pongau
Austria

Bustling, lively working town with its own small area. An extensive three-valley lift network starts 4km/2 miles away at Alpendorf, linking via Wagrain to Flachau – all part of the Salzburger Sportwelt ski pass area.
650m; slopes 800–2285m
⛚ 64 ⛷ 200km

St Johann in Tirol
Austria

An attractive place for beginners and leisurely part-timers – keen piste-bashers will ski all the local slopes in a day and need to go on to explore nearby resorts covered by the Kitzbüheler Alpenskipass as well. There is nothing here to challenge an expert. The main access lift is a 10-minute walk from the centre. It gets more snow than neighbouring Kitzbühel and the SkiWelt, and also has substantial snowmaking. Given good snow, St Johann is one of the best cross-country resorts in Austria – trails total 275km/171 miles.
650m; slopes 670–1700m
⛚ 17 ⛷ 60km
⛺ Crystal, Directski.com, Equity, Inghams, Ski Line, Ski McNeill, Ski Wild, Snowscape, Thomson

St Lary Espiaube
423

St-Lary-Soulan
423

St Leonhard in Pitztal
Austria

Village beneath a fine glacier in the Oetz area, accessed by underground funicular.
1250m; slopes 1735–3440m
⛚ 12 ⛷ 40km

St Luc
537

St Margarethen
Austria

Valley village near Styria/Carinthia border, sharing slopes with higher Katschberg.
1065m; slopes 1075–2210m
⛚ 14 ⛷ 70km

St Martin bei Lofer
Austria

Traditional cross-country village in a lovely setting beneath the impressive Loferer Steinberge massif. Alpine slopes at Lofer.
635m

St-Martin-de-Belleville
381

St Martin in Tennengebirge
Austria

Highest village in the Dachstein-West region near Salzburg. It has limited slopes of its own but nearby Annaberg has an interesting area.
1000m; slopes 1000–1350m
⛚ 5 ⛷ 4km

St-Maurice-sur-Moselle
France

One of several areas near Strasbourg. No snowmakers.
550m; slopes 900–1250m
⛚ 8 ⛷ 24km

St Michael im Lungau
Austria

Quiet, unspoiled village in the Tauern pass snowpocket with an uncrowded but disjointed intermediate area. Close to Obertauern and Wagrain.
1075m; slopes 1075–2360m
⛚ 25 ⛷ 105km
⛺ Ardmore

St Moritz
530

St-Nicolas-de-Véroce
315

Small hamlet in the Megève network.

St-Nicolas-la-Chapelle
France

Small village close to larger Flumet, in the Val d'Arly.
1000m; slopes 1000–1600m
⛚ 10 ⛷ 40km

St-Nizier-du-Moucherotte
France

Unspoiled, inexpensive resort just west of Grenoble with no lifts of its own. Villard-de-Lans is the main resort.

Stoneham
697

⛺ AmeriCan Ski, Frontier, Ski Dream, Ski Safari

Stoos
Switzerland

Small, unspoiled village an hour from Zürich. Overcrowded at weekends. Magnificent views of Lake Lucerne.
1300m; slopes 570–1920m ⛚ 9

Storlien
Sweden

Small family resort amid magnificent wilderness scenery. One hour from Trondheim, 30 mins from Åre.
600m; slopes 600–790m
⛚ 7 ⛷ 16km

Stowe
654

St-Pierre-de-Chartreuse
France

Locals' weekend place near Grenoble. Unreliable snow.
900m; slopes 900–1800m
⛚ 14 ⛷ 35km

Stratton
USA

Something like the classic Alpine arrangement of a village at the foot of the lifts: a smart, modern development with a car-free shopping street. The slopes are mostly easy and intermediate, with some blacks and some short double-black pitches, spread widely around the flanks of a single peak, served by modern lifts. Stratton calls itself the 'snowboarding capital of the east', with no fewer than five terrain parks. The Suntanner Park has a super-pipe.
570m; slopes 570–1180m
⛚ 14 ⛷ 660 acres

Strobl
Austria

Close to St Wolfgang in a beautiful lakeside setting. There are slopes at nearby St Gilgen and Postalm.
545m; slopes 545–1510m
⛚ 8 ⛷ 12km

St-Sorlin-d'Arves
383

St Stephan
Switzerland

Unspoiled old farming village at the foot of the largest sector of slopes in the area around Gstaad. Upgraded chairlift for 2006/07.
995m; slopes 950–3000m
⛚ 67 ⛷ 250km

Stubai valley
223

Stuben
212

Small, unspoiled village linked to St Anton.

St Veit im Pongau
Austria

Spa resort with limited slopes at Goldegg; Wagrain (Salzburger Sportwelt) and Grossarl (Gastein valley) are nearby. *765m*

St-Veran
France

Said to be the highest 'real' village in Europe, and full of charm. Close to Serre-Chevalier and the Milky Way. Snow-reliable cross-country skiing.
2040m; slopes 2040–2800m
⛚ 15 ⛷ 30km

St Wolfgang
Austria

Charming lakeside resort near Salzburg, some way from any slopes, best for a relaxing winter holiday with one or two days on the slopes.
540m; slopes 665–1350m
⛚ 9 ⛷ 17km
⛺ Crystal, Inghams, Thomson

Sugar Bowl
USA

Exposed area north of Lake Tahoe. The first Sierra Nevada area to be developed, next to the railway from the Bay area to Truckee (and so away from the lake); but with five fast quads, there is nothing antique about it now. Sugar Bowl claims a huge average snowfall of 500 inches a year. We were impressed by the varied terrain, including lots of genuine black and double-diamond runs from the higher lifts as well as good cruising; the single-black Silver Belt is rated by an experienced American reader as his favourite run in the US. There is lodging at the base in The Inn, and a small development of condos is under way at the Mt Judah base, near the smart day lodge.
2100m; slopes 2100–2555m
⛚ 8 ⛷ 1500 acres

Sugarbush
USA

Fast-developing resort, midway between Killington and Stowe, and one of the physically larger ski areas in the east. Its runs spread over broad mountainsides rather than being cut close together. The main sector is an extensive bowl below Lincoln Peak, with lifts up to six points on the rim; a long up-and-over chairlift accesses the Mt Ellen area – smaller, but with more altitude and more vertical (795m/2,600ft). The easy runs are confined to the lower slopes; higher up, the direct runs are seriously steep. Most accommodation is in the historic village of Waitsfield, but a village is developing at the base.
480m; slopes 450–1245m
⛚ 16 ⛷ 508 acres
⛺ Ski Safari

Sugarloaf
USA

Maine resort that has a much better-developed village at the base than most small New England resorts. The mountain is fair-sized by local standards, but a keen piste-basher could ski it out in a day or two. With 860m/2,820ft it claims the biggest continuous vertical in New England, and there is something for everybody, with genuine steeps up around and above the treeline and gentle terrain lower down in the woods. The resort has a super-pipe and a terrain park.
430m; slopes 405–1290m
⛚ 15 ⛷ 1410 acres
⛺ American Ski Classics, Ski Dream

Sulden
Italy

Small resort in South Tyrol. Solda is its Italian name.
1905m; slopes 1905–2625m
⛚ 10 ⛷ 40km

Summit at Snoqualmie USA
Four areas – Summit East, Summit Central, Summit West and Alpental – with interlinked lifts. Damp weather and wet snow are major drawbacks.
slopes 915–1645m
🚡 24 ⛷ *2000 acres*

Sun Alpina Japan
Collective name for three ski areas four hours away from Tokyo. 🚡 21

Sundance USA
Robert Redford-owned, tastefully designed family resort set amid trees in snow-sure Utah. It's a small, narrow mountain but the vertical is respectable, the setting beneath Mt Timpanogos is spectacular and there is terrain to suit all abilities. The lower mountain is easy-intermediate, served by a quad chair, the upper part steeper: one triple chair serves purely black slopes, the other blue and black trails. There are 17km/11 miles of cross-country trails, of varying difficulty, in a separate area just beyond the downhill slopes.
1860m; slopes 1860–2515m
🚡 4 ⛷ *450 acres*
📧 *All America Holidays, AmeriCan Ski, Ski Dream, Ski Safari*

Sunday River USA
One of the more attractive resorts in the East, four hours from Boston, best for intermediate cruisers. Condos cluster at the three main lift bases at the eastern end of the mountain. The slopes spread across eight peaks, each basically served by one lift, with links from one to the next. But it's a small area. The western sector has far fewer lifts and runs than the eastern end, where most of the beds, as well as most of the beds, are concentrated. Only four of the chairs are fast quads but queues are not a problem – midweek, the resort is very quiet. Cross-country is big around here. Sunday River was one of the pioneers of snowmaking, and over 90% of its trails are served by it.
245m; slopes 245–955m
🚡 18 ⛷ *667 acres*
📧 *American Ski Classics, Ardmore, Ski Dream, Ski Independence, Ski Safari*

Sunlight Mountain Resort USA
Quiet, small area 10 miles south of Glenwood Springs. Varied terrain with some serious glades. A reader who included it in a tour of Colorado thought it 'well worth a visit for the day'.
2405m; slopes 2405–3015m
🚡 3 ⛷ *470 acres*

Sun Peaks 685
Sunrise Park USA
Arizona's largest area, operated by Apaches. Slopes are spread over three mountains; best for novices and leisurely intermediates.
2805m; slopes 2805–3500m
🚡 12 ⛷ *800 acres*

Sunshine Village 659
One-hotel mountain station in Banff's ski area.

Sun Valley USA
Built in the 1930s, Sun Valley was the US's first luxury purpose-built winter resort and soon became popular with the stars. For a peaceful, relaxing time, it's hard to beat. For skiing and boarding alone, there are better resorts. The slopes of Bald Mountain (known locally as Baldy) are accessed from luxurious base lodge complexes at River Run and Warm Springs. The separate Dollar Mountain has good beginner slopes. The resort has an erratic natural snow record, but snowmaking covers over 70% of the runs. There are a few tough slopes for experts, but most of the terrain is ideal for intermediates, with lots of runs at a consistent pitch. For years snowboarding wasn't allowed; but it is now and there's even a super-pipe. The mountain restaurants and base lodges are way ahead of most US on-slope facilities. There are 40km/25 miles of good cross-country. The town retains its old-world charm and has atmospheric bars, restaurants and shops. Shuttle-buses link the slopes to most accommodation.
1750m; slopes 1750–2790m
🚡 19 ⛷ *2,054 acres*
📧 *AmeriCan Ski, Ski Dream, Ski Safari*

Suomu Finland
A lodge (no village) right on the Arctic Circle with a few slopes but mostly a ski-touring place.
140m; slopes 140–410m 🚡 3

Superbagnères France
Little more than a particularly French-dominated Club Med; best for a low-cost, low-effort family trip to the Pyrenees. Said to have good off-piste if the snow is good.
1880m; slopes 1440–2260m
🚡 16 ⛷ *35km*
📧 *Lagrange*

Super-Besse France
Purpose-built resort amid spectacular extinct-volcano scenery. Shares area with the spa town of Mont-Dore. Limited village.
1350m; slopes 1300–1850m
🚡 22 ⛷ *43km*
📧 *Lagrange*

Superdévoluy France
Purpose-built but friendly family resort in a remote spot near Gap, with huge tower blocks plus traditional chalets. Sizeable intermediate area shared with La Joue-du-Loup. A first-time visitor who had a 'fantastic' half-term holiday reports 'skiing for all levels, queues not too bad, lots of reasonably priced restaurants, good food shops'.
1450m; slopes 1450–2450m
🚡 23 ⛷ *100km*
📧 *Crystal, Erna Low, Lagrange, Thomson*

Super Espot Spain
Small area on the eastern edge of the Aigues Tortes National Park, close to the valley town of Sort.
slopes 1500–2500m
🚡 8 ⛷ *28km*

Supermolina Spain
Dreary, purpose-built satellite of Pyrenean resort of La Molina, with a reasonable sized area of its own and linked to the slopes of Masella to form an area called Alp 2500.
1700m; slopes 1600–2535m
🚡 31 ⛷ *121km*

Les Sybelles 383
Tahko Finland
Largest resort in southern Finland. Plenty of intermediate slopes in an attractive, wooded, frozen-lake setting.
🚡 9

Tahoe City USA
Small lakeside accommodation base for visiting nearby Alpine Meadows and Squaw Valley.

Talisman Mountain Resort
Canada
One of the best areas in the Toronto region, but with a relatively low lift capacity. 100% snowmaking.
235m; slopes 235–420m 🚡 8

Tamarack 638
📧 *Ski Dream*

Tamsweg Austria
Large cross-country village with rail links in snowy region close to Tauern Pass and St Michael.
1025m

La Tania 388
Taos USA
Set high above an arid New Mexico valley, Taos Ski Valley is the most southerly of North America's major ski areas. It offers some good expert terrain but snowboarders are banned. There are numerous long steep runs through the trees, and many of the best runs require a hike from the top lifts. And there's enough to keep intermediates happy for a few days too. Beginners have their own dedicated

area. Snowfall averages over 300 inches but because it is so far south, snow can be bad here when it's good elsewhere (and vice versa). At the foot of the slopes there are a handful of hotels and condos. Down the valley the traditional adobe town of Taos, with its art and craft galleries and shops, makes an alternative base.
2805m; slopes 2805–3600m
🚡 12 ⛷ *1294 acres*
📧 *AmeriCan Ski, Ski Dream*

Tärnaby-Hemavan Sweden
Twin resorts in north Sweden, offering downhill, cross-country and heli-skiing. Own airport.
slopes 465–1135m
🚡 13 ⛷ *44km*

El Tarter 115
Relatively quiet, convenient alternative to Soldeu.

Tarvisio Italy
Interesting, animated old town bordering Austria and Slovenia. A major cross-country base with fairly limited Alpine slopes.
750m; slopes 750–1860m
🚡 12 ⛷ *15km*
📧 *Ardmore*

Täsch 560
The final road base on the way to car-free Zermatt.

Tauplitz Austria
Traditional village at the foot of an interestingly varied area north of Schladming. Readers have found 'wonderful snow, plenty of good off-piste, friendly locals', and 'varied runs, good lift system, few queues, spectacular scenery'.
900m; slopes 900–2000m
🚡 18 ⛷ *40km*

Telluride 611
Temù Italy
Sheltered hamlet near Passo Tonale. Worth a visit in bad weather.
1155m; slopes 1155–1955m
🚡 4 ⛷ *5km*

Tengendai Japan
Tiny area three hours by train and bus from Tokyo. One of Japan's best snow records, including occasional powder.
920m; slopes 920–1820m 🚡 4

Termas de Chillán 730
Termignon France
Traditional rustic village 6km/4 miles down the Maurienne valley from Lanslebourg and the slopes of Val Cenis, to which a link is planned. The local slopes are limited and served by slow lifts, but have the advantage of being extremely quiet.
1300m; slopes 1300–2500m
🚡 6 ⛷ *35km*
📧 *Lagrange, Peak Retreats*

Terminillo Italy
Purpose-built resort 100km/62 miles from Rome with a worthwhile area when its lower runs have snow cover.
1500m; slopes 1500–2210m
⛷ 15 🚡 40km

Thollon-les-Mémises France
Attractive base for a relaxed holiday. Own little area and close to Portes du Soleil.
1000m; slopes 1600–2000m
⛷ 19 🚡 50km
🚠 Lagrange

Thredbo 720

Three Valleys 392

La Thuile 479

Thyon 2000 541
Mid-mountain resort above Veysonnaz in the Verbier ski area.

Tignes 394

Timberline (Palmer Snowfield) USA
East of Portland, Oregon, and the only lift-served summer skiing in the US: winter snow is maintained by spreading vast amounts of salt to harden it.
slopes 1830–2600m
⛷ 6 🚡 2500 acres

Toblach Italy
Small resort in South Tyrol. Dobbiaco is its Italian name.
1250m; slopes 1250–1610m
⛷ 5 🚡 15km

Togari Japan
One of several areas close to the 1998 Olympic site, Nagano, 2.5 hours from Tokyo.
slopes 400–1050m ⛷ 9

Torgnon Italy
Small village off the road up to Cervinia, good for bad-weather days. Some good cross-country loops.
1500m; slopes 1500–1965m
⛷ 7 🚡 6km

Torgon Switzerland
Old village in a pretty wooded setting, with a connection to the Portes du Soleil. Still some steep draglifts.
1150m; slopes 975–2275m
⛷ 209 🚡 650km
🚠 Interhome

Le Tour 268
Charming, unspoiled hamlet at the head of the Chamonix valley.

La Toussuire 383

Trafoi Italy
Quiet, traditional village in the Val Venosta in the South Tyrol covered by the Ortler Skiarena pass.
1570m; slopes 1570–2550m
⛷ 4 🚡 10km

Treble Cone 722

Tremblant 698

Trentino 481

Trois Vallées 392
The French name for the Three Valleys.

Troodos Cyprus
Ski area on Mt Olympus, a 70-minute drive from Nicosia. Pretty, wooded slopes and fine views.
slopes 1730–1950m
⛷ 4 🚡 5km

Tröpolach Austria
Small village at base of access gondola for Nassfeld ski area.
610m; slopes 610–2195m
⛷ 30 🚡 100km

Trysil 705

Tryvann 705

Tschagguns 181
Village in the Montafon valley.

Tsugaike Kogen Japan
Sizeable resort four hours from Tokyo, three hours from Osaka. Helicopter service to the top station.
800m; slopes 800–1700m ⛷ 26

Tulfes Austria
Hamlet on mountain shelf close to Innsbruck, with small main area above the trees and long runs back to base.
920m; slopes 920–2305m
⛷ 7 🚡 20km

Turoa 722

Turracherhöhe Austria
Tiny, unspoiled resort on a mountain shelf, with varied intermediate slopes above and below it. A good outing from Bad Kleinkirchheim.
1765m; slopes 1400–2200m
⛷ 11 🚡 30km
🚠 Ardmore

Tyax Mountain Lake Resort Canada
Heli-skiing operation in the Chilcotin mountains – transfers from Whistler or Vancouver.

La Tzoumaz Switzerland
Hamlet at the base of lifts on the back of Verbier's Savoleyres sector, sometimes referred to as Mayens de Riddes.
1500m

Uludag Turkey
Surprisingly suave, laid-back, well-equipped, purpose-built resort near Bursa, south of Istanbul.
1750m; slopes 1750–2322m
⛷ 14 🚡 15km

Unken Austria
Traditional village hidden in a side valley. Closest slopes to Salzburg.
565m; slopes 1000–1500m
⛷ 4 🚡 8km

Untergurgl 184
Valley-floor alternative to staying in Hochgurgl or Obergurgl.

Unternberg Austria
Riverside village with trail connecting into one of the longest, most snow-sure cross-country networks in Europe. St Margarethen downhill slopes close by.
1030m

Unterwasser-Toggenburg Switzerland
Old but not especially attractive resort 90 minutes from Zürich. Fabulous lake and mountain views. The more challenging half of the Toggenburg area shared with Wildhaus.
910m; slopes 900–2260m
⛷ 19 🚡 60km

Uttendorf-Weiss-See Austria
Astute alternative to crowded Kaprun when the snowline is high.
805m; slopes 1485–2600m
⛷ 9 🚡 18km

Vail 613

Valbella Switzerland
Convenient but ordinary village sharing large intermediate Lenzerheide area.
1540m; slopes 1230–2865m
⛷ 37 🚡 155km

Valberg France
Large Alpes-Maritimes resort (bigger than better-known Isola 2000) close to Nice.
1650m; slopes 1430–2100m
⛷ 26 🚡 90km

Val Cenis France
Two quiet villages – Lanslebourg and Lanslevillard – in a high and remote part of the Maurienne valley. Lifts go from base stations in and between the two villages – the main one a gondola starting near Lanslevillard. Above mid-mountain is a good range of open runs. Below mid-mountain all the runs are prettily wooded. Most of the runs are north-facing, and there is snowmaking on the home runs. There is ample off-piste and a few bump runs for experts, and cruises of up to 1400m/4,590ft vertical for intermediates. Lanslevillard has excellent nursery slopes, and there are extensive cross-country trails at Bessans.
1400m; slopes 1400–2800m
⛷ 20 🚡 80km
🚠 AmeriCan Ski, Crystal, Erna Low, Lagrange, MGS, Peak Retreats, Ski Collection, Ski France, Ski Leisure Direction, Skiholidayextras.com, Snowcoach, Thomson

Val d'Anniviers 537

Val di Fassa 481
Valley area of Campitello and Canazei – part of the Sella Ronda circuit.

Val d'Illiez Switzerland
Peaceful, unspoiled village a few minutes below Champoussin. Open-air thermal baths. Good views of impressive Dents du Midi.
950m
⛷ 209 🚡 650km

Val d'Isère 403

Val Ferret Switzerland
Old climbing village near Martigny, with spectacular views. Own tiny area.
1600m
⛷ 3 🚡 20km

Valfréjus France
Small and unusual modern resort on a narrow, shady shelf in the Maurienne valley – built in the woods, with the slopes higher up above the treeline. The focus is Plateau d'Arrondaz, with steep, open slopes above, offering genuine bumpy blacks with excellent snow (snowmaking on the lower runs is urgently required, though). There's a natural terrain park, and good off-piste is available above the main plateau. The nursery slopes are at mid-mountain and village levels.
1550m; slopes 1550–2740m
⛷ 13 🚡 65km
🚠 AmeriCan Ski, Erna Low, Lagrange, Peak Retreats, Ski France, Skiholidayextras, SnowYourWay.com

Val Gardena 470
Valley area of Selva, Ortisei and Santa Cristina – part of the Sella Ronda circuit.

Vallandry 255
Family-friendly satellite of Les Arcs. For package holidays see Peisey-Vallandry.

Valle Nevado 730

Valloire France
Friendly, bustling old mountain village free of through-traffic in winter and sharing with Valmeinier the most extensive slopes in the Maurienne region, spreading over three sectors. The Sétaz sector generally has the best snow and the toughest slopes. The broad, open, west-facing slopes of Crey du Quart offer a choice of routes to link to the Valmeinier valley. Snow on most of the slopes is affected by the sun, but there is a lot of snowmaking. The gondolas can have queues in the morning peak. Experts will find the area limited: the area from Crey du Quart down into the Valmeinier valley has some decent off-piste if the snow is good. The vast majority of the slopes are ideal for intermediates. There are nursery slopes at village level and up the mountain.
1430m; slopes 1430–2595m

34 150km
AmeriCan Ski, Crystal, Erna Low, Lagrange, Peak Retreats, Ski France, Ski Independence, Ski Leisure Direction, Skifrance4less, Skiholidayextras.com

Vallorcine 268
Quiet village on road between Chamonix and Switzerland.
Erna Low, Peak Retreats

Vallter 2000 Spain
Small resort on the far eastern fringes of the Pyrenees, close to the Costa Brava.
slopes 1960–2535m
10 420 acres

Valmeinier France
Quiet, old mountain village with a modern purpose-built satellite where most people stay. Shares with Valloire the most extensive slopes in the Maurienne region, spreading widely over three mostly sunny sectors. New quad installed towards Valloire for 2007/08.
1500-1800m; slopes 1430–2595m
33 150km
Crystal, Erna Low, Lagrange, Peak Retreats, Ski Collection, Ski France, Ski Independence, Ski Leisure Direction, Skifrance4less, Skiholidayextras.com, Snowcoach

Valmorel 414

Val Senales Italy
Valley near Merano in South Tyrol.
3210m; slopes 2110–3210m
12 35km

Val Thorens 416

Valtournenche 430
Cheaper alternative to Cervinia.

Vandans 181
Sizeable working village in the Montafon area.

Vars 361
Large, convenient purpose-built resort linked to Risoul.

Vasilitsa Greece
Resort in northern Greece, in the Pindos range, offering 'very good intermediate skiing', according to reports.
1780m 8

Vaujany 245
Tiny village in the heart of the Alpe-d'Huez ski area.

Vegas Resort USA
Area formerly known as Lee Canyon, cut from forest only 50 minutes' drive from Las Vegas. Height and snowmaking gives fairly reliable snow. Night skiing.
2590m; slopes 2590–2840m
3 200 acres

Velka–Raca Slovakia
Small resort near Oscadnica, with a modern lift system, including a 'chondola'.
630m; slopes 630–1050m
6 14km

Vemdalen 709

Vemdalsskalet 709

Venosc France
Captivating tiny village of cobbled streets, ancient church and craft shops with fast gondola to Les Deux-Alpes.
Peak Retreats

Vent Austria
High, remote Oztal village known mainly as a touring base, with just enough lift-served skiing to warrant a day trip from nearby Obergurgl.
1900m; slopes 1900–2680m
4 15km

Ventron France
Small village near La Bresse in the northerly Vosges mountains near Strasbourg, with more ski de fond than downhill terrain.
630m; slopes 900–1110m
8 15km

Verbier 541

Vercorin 537

Verditz Austria
One of several small, mostly mountain-top areas overlooking the town of Villach.
675m; slopes 675–2165m
5 17km

Vex Switzerland
Major village in unspoiled, attractive setting south of Sion. Verbier slopes accessed nearby at Mayens-de-l'Ours.
900m

Veysonnaz 541
Little, old village within Verbier's Four Valleys network.

Vichères–Liddes Switzerland
Limited area near to Martigny. Part of the Grand St Bernard region, including Val Ferret and Champex-Lac. Valid with the Valais ski Card.
1350m; slopes 1350–2270m
4 15km

Vic-sur-Cère France
Charming village with fine architecture, beneath Super-Lioran ski area. Beautiful extinct-volcano scenery.
680m; slopes 1250–1850m
24 60km
Lagrange

Viehhofen Austria
Cheaper place to stay when visiting Saalbach. It is 3km/2 miles from the Schönleiten gondola, and there is a run back to the village from the Asitz section.
860m 1

Vigla-Pisoderi Greece
The longest run in Greece (over 2km), in an unspoiled setting 18km/11 miles from the town of Florina in the north.
1600m 5

Vigo di Fassa 481
Best base for the Fassa valley.

La Villa 463
Quiet Sella Ronda village.

Villabassa Italy
Cross-country village in South Tyrol. Niederdorf is its German name.

Villach-Dobratsch Austria
One of several small, mostly mountain-top areas overlooking the town of Villach.
900m; slopes 980–2165m
8 15km

Villar-d'Arêne France
Tiny area on main road between La Grave and Serre-Chevalier. Empty, immaculately groomed, short easy runs, plus a couple of hotels.
1650m

Villard-de-Lans France
Unspoiled, lively, traditional village west of Grenoble. Snow-sure, thanks to snowmaking.
1050m; slopes 1160–2170m
29 130km
AmeriCan Ski

Villard-Reculas 245
Rustic village on periphery of Alpe-d'Huez ski area.

Villaroger 255
Rustic hamlet with direct links up to Arc 2000.

Villars 553

Villeneuve 369
One of the main valley villages making up the big resort of Serre-Chevalier.

Vipiteno Italy
Bargain-shopping town close to Brenner Pass.
960m; slopes 960–2100m
12 25km

Virgen Austria
Traditional village in a beautiful valley south of the Felbertauern tunnel. Slopes at Matrei.
1200m

Vitosha Bulgaria
Limited area of slopes and a few widely scattered hotels, 22km/14 miles from Sofia, leading to crowds at weekends. The slopes are north-facing and have a decent snow record.
1810m; slopes 1515–2290m
12 29km

Vogel 716

Vorderlanersbach 140
Village with access to Mayrhofen's ski area.

Voss 705

Vuokatti Finland
Small mountain in a remarkable setting, surrounded on three sides by lots of little lakes. Good activity base. 8

Wagrain Austria
A towny little resort at the centre of a lift system that is typical of many in Salzburgerland – spreading widely across several low, partly wooded ridges. Flachau and Alpendorf/St Johann are at its extremities, and all these resorts are covered by Salzburger Sportwelt lift pass that our figures relate to. It's pleasant without being notably charming, and though it's a compact place the main lift bases are still a good walk apart. The slopes – wooded at the bottom, open higher up – are practically all easy/intermediate stuff, but cover a huge area almost 15km/9 miles across. The lift system is impressive, with a lot of fast chairs and gondolas, including a new six-pack for 2007/08. Despite the altitude, most of the upper slopes are fairly open. Some get too much sun for comfort, and snow reliability is not a strong point.
850m; slopes 850–2190m
64 200km

Waidring Austria
Quiet valley village north of Kitzbühel, with nursery slopes on the doorstep and a powerful gondola (with big car parks) on the outskirts going up to Steinplatte – an area of mainly gentle open slopes which is also accessible from Germany. Impressive lift system with two six-packs and four quads, but still prone to weekend queues. Slopes face north, and there is extensive snowmaking.
780m; slopes 1230–1860m
8 25km
Thomson

Waiorau Snow Farm 722

Wald im Pinzgau Austria
Cross-country village surrounded by Alpine areas – Gerlos, Krimml and Neukirchen – and with Pass Thurn also nearby.
885m
55 155km

Wanaka 722

Warth 134
Bregenzerwald area village near Lech.

Waterville Valley USA
Compact New Hampshire area with runs dropping either side of a broad, gentle ridge rising 615m/2,020ft above the lift base. A couple of short but genuine double-black-diamond mogul fields, but most of the slopes are intermediate. The village is a Disneyesque affair a couple of miles away down on the flat valley bottom.
600m; slopes 600–1215m

⛷ 12 🎿 255 acres

Watles Italy
Village in the Val Venosta in the South Tyrol covered by the Ortler Skiarena pass.
⛷ 3 🎿 18km

Weinebene Austria
One of many gentle little areas in Austria's easternmost ski region near the Slovenian border. No major resorts in the vicinity.
1560m; slopes 1560–1835m
⛷ 5 🎿 12km

Weissbach bei Lofer Austria
Traditional resort between Lofer and Saalfelden. It has no slopes of its own, but it's well placed for touring the Tirol. Kitzbühel, Saalbach, St Johann and Zell am See are nearby.
665m

Weissensee Naggeralm
Austria
Little area in eastern Austria and the location of Europe's largest frozen lake, which is used for all kinds of ice sports, including ice-golf.
930m; slopes 930–1400m
⛷ 5 🎿 6km

Weisspriach Austria
Hamlet on snowy pass near Obertauern that shares its area with Mauterndorf and St Michael.
1115m; slopes 1115–2050m
⛷ 5 🎿 30km

Wengen 555

Wentworth Canada
Long-established Nova Scotia area with largest accessible acreage in the Maritime Provinces. Harsh climate ensures good snow-cover despite low altitude.
55m; slopes 55–300m
⛷ 6 🎿 150 acres

Werfen Austria
Traditional village spoiled by the Tauern autobahn, which runs between it and the slopes. Good touring to the Dachstein West region.
620m

Werfenweng Austria
Hamlet with the advantage over the main village of Werfen of being away from the autobahn and close to the slopes. Best for novices.
1000m; slopes 1000–1835m
⛷ 10 🎿 25km 🚡 Thomson

Westendorf 225

Whakapapa 722

Whistler 688

Whitecap Mountains Resort
USA
Largest, snowiest area in Wisconsin, close enough to Lake Superior and Minneapolis to ensure winds and weekend crowds.
435m; slopes 435–555m
⛷ 7 🎿 500 acres

Whiteface Mountain USA
Varied area in New York State 15km/10 miles from attractive lakeside resort of Lake Placid. 93% snowmaking ensures good snowcover. Plenty to do off the slopes.
365m; slopes 365–1345m
⛷ 10 🎿 211 acres
🚡 Ski Dream

Whitefish Mountain Resort
USA
Formerly known as Big Mountain, and set close to the Canadian border and to Montana's Glacier National Park. This place has revamped its image, and at least one of our reporters (who now makes an annual pilgrimage) rates it as simply the best. Lots of redevelopment is taking place, both on and off the slopes. Its 3,000 acres embrace a wide range of slopes that are not only impressively snowy but also blissfully devoid of people. There's easy cruising in dense forest around the base area, and steeper stuff higher up on 'gladed' slopes. There are two 'excellent' terrain parks. There is accommodation at the base and you can also stay in the small town of Whitefish, a few miles away.
1370m; slopes 1370–2135m
⛷ 12 🎿 3000 acres
🚡 Ski Dream, Ski Safari

White Pass Village USA
Closest area to Mt St Helens. Remote and uncrowded during the week, with a good snowfall record. Some genuinely expert terrain, as well as intermediate cruising.
1370m; slopes 1370–1825m
⛷ 5 🎿 635 acres

Whitewater Canada
Renowned for powder (40% off-piste), food ('Excellent day lodge,' says a 2006 reporter) and weekend party atmosphere. Accommodation in the historic town of Nelson or a great day out from nearby Red Resort.
1640m; slopes 1640–2040m ⛷ 3
🚡 Frontier, Ski Dream

Wildcat Mountain USA
New Hampshire area infamous for bad weather, but one of the best areas on a nice day. Lodging in nearby Jackson and North Conway.
slopes 600–1250m
⛷ 4 🎿 225 acres

Wildhaus Switzerland
Undeveloped farming community in stunning scenery near Liechtenstein; popular with families and serious snowboarders. Shares its slopes with Unterwasser.
1050m; slopes 900–2260m
⛷ 19 🎿 60km

Wildschönau 227

Willamette Pass USA
US speed skiing training base in national forest near beautiful Crater Lake, Oregon. Small but varied slopes popular with weekenders.
1560m; slopes 1560–2035m
⛷ 7 🎿 550 acres

Williams USA
Tiny area above the main place to stay for the Grand Canyon.
slopes 2010–2270m
⛷ 2 🎿 50 acres

Windischgarsten Austria
Large working village in Upper Austria with cross-country trails around and downhill slopes at nearby Hinterstoder and Spital am Pyrhn.
600m

Winter Park 620

Wolf Creek USA
Remote area on a pass of the same name, with 'the most snow in Colorado' – 465 inches a year. One-third of the terrain is standard American trails through the trees; two-thirds is 'wilderness', served by a single lift. Great stop en route between Taos and Telluride. Stay in Pagosa Springs or South Fork.
3140m; slopes 3140–3630m
⛷ 6 🎿 1600 acres
🚡 AmeriCan Ski

Wolf Mountain USA
Utah cross-country area close to Salt Lake City. Powder Mountain and Snowbasin are nearby Alpine areas.
⛷ 3 🎿 100 acres

Xonrupt France
Cross-country venue only 3km/2 miles from nearest Alpine slopes at Gérardmer.
715m
🚡 Lagrange

Yangji Pine Resort
South Korea
Modern resort an hour (60km/37 miles) south of Seoul, with runs cut out of dense forest. Gets very crowded. ⛷ 6

Ylläs 703

Yong Pyong Resort
South Korea
The first of South Korea's dozen recently developed resorts, also known as Dragon Valley. 200km/125 miles east of Seoul, close to the east coast. Self-contained purpose-built resort village is centred on 200-room Dragon Valley Hotel. Modern lifts serve a small, mainly wooded slope area, with snowmaking on all its runs. English web site at www.yongpyong.co.kr.
750m; slopes 750–1460m
⛷ 15 🎿 20km

Zakopane Poland
An interesting old town 100km/62 miles south of Kraków on the Slovakian border. Mostly intermediate slopes, branded as 14 small and fragmented sectors. Recently reported to have renovated its 70-year-old cable car.
830m; slopes 1000–1960m
⛷ 20 🎿 10km
🚡 Interhome

Zao Japan
Big area with unpredictable weather, 4 hours from Tokyo by train. Known for 'chouoh' – pines frozen into weird shapes. Hot springs.
780m; slopes 780–1660m ⛷ 42

Zauchensee Austria
Purpose-built resort isolated at the head of its valley, at one end of big three-valley lift network linking it via Flachauwinkl to Kleinarl – all part of the Salzburger Sportwelt ski pass area that our figures relate to. A reader reports 'attractive, compact village, shops limited to ski kit, no nightlife, dining only in hotels, relatively easy family-friendly skiing'.
855m; slopes 800–2185m
⛷ 64 🎿 200km
🚡 Ski Hillwood

Zell am See 231

Zell im Zillertal 176
Sprawling valley town with slopes on two mountains.

Zermatt 560

Zillertal Austria
Valley of ten ski resorts, of which the most well known is Mayrhofen.

Zinal 537

Zug 167
Tiny village with Lech's toughest skiing on its doorstep.

Zugspitz Arena 236

Zürs 167
High, smart but soulless village on road to Lech.

Zweisimmen Switzerland
Limited but inexpensive base for slopes around Gstaad, with its own delightful little easy area too.
965m; slopes 950–3000m
⛷ 67 🎿 250km